WEST'S LAW SCHOOL ADVISORY BOARD

DEVELOPING JUDGMENT ABOUT PRACTICING LAW

Second Edition

■ ■ ■

By

David McGowan

Lyle L. Jones Professor of Competition and Innovation Law
University of San Diego School of Law

AMERICAN CASEBOOK SERIES®

WEST®

Mat #41446633

610 Opperman Drive
St. Paul, MN 55123
1–800–313–9378

Printed in the United States of America

ISBN: 978–0–314–28791–5

This book is for Miranda and Benjamin

PREFACE

The economic contraction that began in 2008 reduced demand for many types of legal services. Since that time fewer and fewer students have applied to law school. As of 2013 we have seen double-digit reduction in the applicant pool for three years running. Bar organizations are studying the structure of legal education with an eye to reform, and the drop in demand both for seats in schools and for graduates of many schools suggest that schools themselves need to take action. Everyone talks about closing the gap between school and practice,[1] but concrete steps likely to achieve this goal are hard to come by.

Developing legal judgment is one such step and is the purpose this book seeks to advance. Good judgment is what shrewd clients value most and training students to exercise judgment is a necessary element of any reform program. This book is the result of my conviction, grounded in both teaching and practicing this subject that professional responsibility is an excellent field for such training and quite possibly the best field. For example, this book stresses that in any given situation practicing lawyers almost always face two types of possible errors: They may be too aggressive, violating disciplinary rules and possibly incurring civil or criminal liability, or they may be too passive and risk-averse, thus failing to do legally permissible things that could benefit a client. This latter error is less often stressed in law school, and its consequences are harder to see, but it is important. Excessive passivity may lead to dissatisfied clients, reputational harm, and professional mediocrity or failure. Excessive aggression may make clients happy in the near term but lead to greater long-term harm for both lawyers and clients. Exercising judgment is how lawyers find ways to practice both safely and effectively, thus minimizing the sum of the expected costs of these errors.

Two familiar problems plague all professional responsibility courses. First, students often are forced to take the class and many do so unwillingly. Second, students go into many different areas of practice that present different issues; problems common in one area are almost totally foreign to others. M&A lawyers will not have to worry about the *Strickland* standard for effectiveness; public defenders will not have to worry about Sarbanes-Oxley reporting requirements.

---

[1] Myself included. *See Making law school more useful*, available at http://papers.ssrn.com/sol3/papers.cfm?abstract_id=2181793 (posted November 28, 2012).

Two less familiar problems also plague the course but get less attention. The first of these is that PR casebooks are commonly edited to focus more on the rules than on practical problems in which the rules play a part but are far from the whole. The most common symptom of this problem is that cases are edited so heavily that the stories they tell get lost. This problem is important because it is the stories students remember and it is the stories that describe the situations in which lawyers bump into the law.

This book aims to solve or at least ameliorate these problems by focusing on judgment as the central concept in legal ethics.[2] Practicing lawyers exercise judgment to assess situations with an eye to solving their client's problems. This book aims to teach students as much as can be taught about how to do the same thing regarding problems they will face as lawyers. Its goals are to teach students to spot trouble coming, avoid it if possible, and get out of it with minimal harm, if necessary.

Why judgment? It is one of the few things all lawyers need to exercise, it is the thing practicing lawyers and shrewd clients value most highly, and while it does not ignore rules it goes beyond them to take into account things like reputation and competition, which dominate the day-to-day concerns of many lawyers.

Conventional wisdom in practice holds that judgment is the most important thing a lawyer can have. That is true. Conventional wisdom in law schools holds that it cannot be taught. That is only partly true. Law school cannot teach students how to exercise good judgment in the many situations they will encounter in practice—sufficient conditions for good judgment are beyond our grasp. But necessary conditions are not, and they are a central theme of this book.

To exercise judgment in practice students must be able to identify the situation they are in, distinguish it from others, and analyze it three ways: dynamically, interactively, and probabilistically. Missing any of these aspects of a situation leaves lawyers open to being blindsided by forces or risks they have not seen and therefore have not taken into account. This book also identifies practical concerns—such as competition, reputation, and reliance interests—that shape lawyers' lives and practices.

Knowing the law is an essential element of judgment, of course, and this book introduces students to the full range of laws that will apply to them in their work. The doctrinal foundation is comprised of the ABA

[2] The book cannot make a required course optional but it aims to take some of the sting out of the requirement by presenting (in addition to the disciplinary rules) lots of practical information students can use to help identify a wide variety of situations and assess risks they present.

Model Rules and agency law principles often reflected in those rules and the *Restatement (Third) of the Law Governing Lawyers.* To counteract the common law school problem of teaching the law of nowhere, the text also teaches California variations on the ABA rules and some California specifics regarding related doctrines, such as work product.

Cases bring rules to life, and this book selects cases and case studies that tell stories students will remember. Often any number of cases can illustrate a legal rule; this book favors cases involving relatively junior lawyers and cases illustrating common practice pressures, such as conflicts between a lawyer's desire to look good to a judge and the lawyer's duty to a (possibly erratic) client. Concepts such as doubling down, the ethics ostrich, loss aversion, and Mark Twain Ethics ("It's easier to stay out, than to get out") help students bridge the gap between doctrine and practice.

This book does not teach moral philosophy. It has no ideological axe to grind. Nor is it a memorization book with multiple-choice problems to check students' memories. The book aims to be pragmatic, which is to say it takes the view that there are better and worse choices from a practical point of view regardless of one's view on more theoretical views on morality or social justice.

Occasionally the book offers advice from the author's experience practicing this subject for 20 years and teaching it for ten. These passages are clearly marked: The Six Rules of Survival and notes such as "There May Be Places to Get Justice In This World: This Is Not One of Them," are examples. Otherwise the book offers examples of lawyers who got into trouble or avoided it, leaving to students the question whether a given branch of law is good or bad.

The book does contain some economics translated into English. Markets for legal services are changing and changing fast. The author both participates in some of those markets and analyzes the rest from an economic point of view. Students need to know why these changes are occurring if they are to be prepared to navigate the changes we see now and those that are sure to come soon. No text can give each student a personal roadmap, but this one identifies the most important forces and explains how they work.

The author welcomes complaints, criticisms, corrections, or suggestions from teachers and students alike. I may be reached at dmcgowan@sandiego.edu. Thanks for reading.

ACKNOWLEDGMENTS

I taught these materials for eight years in draft form, and I am grateful to my students over that time; their questions, criticisms, and suggestions have improved the materials tremendously. I owe even larger debts to my teachers. Robert Post showed me that rigorous analysis can be realistic, in every sense of the word, and led me to teaching as a career. He epitomizes good judgment. Paul Mishkin displayed and hopefully imparted intellectual discipline and an insistence on rigorous analysis; I hope this text some day approaches his work on Hart & Wechsler. Steve Bundy's class first interested me in these topics 22 years ago and his example still guides me; he is a careful and generous analyst and a consummate academic citizen.

Thanks to the inimitable Steve Lubet for his thoughts on judicial ethics. Thanks as well to Deborah DeMott, Bill Henderson, David Luban, the Hon. Jed Rakoff, John Yoo, the California State Bar and the ethics committees of the Los Angeles and San Diego County Bar Associations for permission to reprint excerpts of their work.

When I taught a course on judgment and decision making a few years ago, Paul Brest generously allowed me to use the draft form of materials (coauthored with Linda Krieger) since published as *Problem Solving, Decision Making, and Professional Judgment* (Oxford 2010). The materials and the book are superb, and they clarified my thinking about many topics in this book. My thanks to the authors.

My work and friends at Durie Tangri LLP help keep these materials current and relevant. It is a privilege to practice with such talented and generous people.

Miranda McGowan gently suggested that I actually turn these materials into a book rather than just talk about doing so; Benjamin McGowan kept me focused on the important question: Daddy, why are you writing a book? Words cannot express my thanks to both.

SUMMARY OF CONTENTS

TABLE OF CONTENTS

TABLE OF CASES

The principal cases are in bold type.

Cases

DEVELOPING JUDGMENT ABOUT PRACTICING LAW

Second Edition

CHAPTER 1

WHAT THIS COURSE IS ABOUT

■ ■ ■

Here is a story that seems to have nothing to do with legal ethics. The point is that it has everything to do with legal ethics.

In 1973 two psychologists named Darley and Batson conducted an experiment. Student participants were taken into a room, asked to prepare a talk on one of two topics, and then asked to give the talk in a nearby building. As each student went from one building to the other he passed a man sitting slumped in a doorway. The man (who was part of the experiment) moaned, coughed and asked for help.

The psychologists varied time pressure—some students were told they were late for the talk, others were told it was time to go over and give the talk, and others were told they had time to spare. 63% of the students who were told they had time to spare stopped to help the man; 45% of the students who were on time stopped to help the man. Only 10% of the students who were late stopped.

The psychologists also varied the subjects of the talks. Half of the students had been told to prepare a talk on the Biblical parable of the good Samaritan (who, of course, stops to aid an injured man). The other half was told to prepare a talk on job opportunities for students in their field of study.

All the students were seminarians.

Seminarians bound to give a talk on helping the injured were no more likely to stop and help the man than students who were told to prepare a talk on jobs seminarians were qualified to do. Some students actually stepped over the ailing man to get to their talk on the Samaritan.

Ergo what? Context matters. The situations people find themselves in are a much stronger influence than you might think. Stronger, in fact, than more abstract notions of whether someone is a good or bad person. You might well think yourself a moral person who would never do a callous or bad thing. The seminarians probably thought that, too.

The purpose of this book is to teach you the law that applies to you as a lawyer and to invite you to learn how to exercise judgment in situations you may face as a lawyer. Both the concept of judgment and the concept of a situation are important to your career.

Judgment is the most important thing you can have as a lawyer. The highest praise clients give lawyers, and lawyers give each other, is to say that a lawyer has good judgment. No client would choose a lawyer with bad judgment; no lawyer with bad judgment is safe from herself. Judgment is not exercised abstractly, however. It is exercised in contexts, which this book refers to as situations. The key point about situations is that they involve different persons with different interests whose actions affect each other.

Exercising judgment in situations is necessary to achieving three practical things important to your career: How to spot trouble coming, avoid it if possible, and get out of it if necessary. This book and this class are designed to help you achieve these goals. They do so by inviting you to begin developing judgment about decisions you will have to make as a lawyer. "Develop" is the right word. You cannot learn judgment as a black-letter formula. You must develop it as a facility that, when exercised in a particular situation, helps you make wise choices.

This text presents the legal rules governing lawyers, cases and problems that bring those rules to life, and examples of both good and bad judgments. These materials invite you to begin working on developing judgment about your own actions as a lawyer. Only you can do that, however. You must make the choice.

A. *The Role of Judgment in Law*

Judgment is the ability to evaluate all aspects of a situation and choose the course of action most likely to achieve a given goal. Often the goal is to solve a problem. That is true of problems you must solve for yourself as well as problems you must solve for your clients. We will define these terms more precisely in a moment. But first it is useful to identify three important elements of this conception of judgment: it is ***interactive, dynamic***, and ***probabilistic***.

"Interactive" means that judgment requires more than thinking about what you want. Exercising good judgment requires that you identify all the parties affected by a decision and think through what their interests are and what they want to achieve. What they think they can achieve may depend on what they think you will do, so you must understand how they view you and what they think you are likely to do. Thinking through these points is the only way you can choose the decision that is best for you (or your client) given what you expect the other parties to do in response to your choice and in response to each other's choices.

"Dynamic" means you cannot stop the analysis after just one step. You must think ahead. If you do *X* and other parties do *Y* and *Z*, what will you do then? What will they do in response to what you do? You must be able to extend such analysis as far as is useful.

"Probabilistic" means that exercising judgment requires dealing with uncertainty. You will rarely know for sure what other people's incentives are, what they are likely to do, or what the consequences of some choice will be. You must make wise decisions nonetheless. In part you must decide how much uncertainty to live with. Should you try to reduce uncertainty by acquiring more information? How much information is worth how much effort? Is there some irreducible level of uncertainty you cannot escape? Different people have different tolerances for uncertainty. You will need to learn your own tolerances and adjust your practice accordingly. If you deal poorly with uncertainty it is a good idea to practice in areas where you don't have to deal with it too much.

Getting started: Analyzing situations

The first step to exercising judgment about your practice is to recognize the situation you are in. If you assess the situation correctly you will have identified the persons and interests relevant to your choices. If you do not assess it correctly you risk being surprised by forces you did not see but which can frustrate your chosen course of action. Some basic definitions will help us get started.

(1) A situation is an intersection of interests relative to a problem or problems.[1]

That is good, you might say, but what is a problem?

(2) A problem is a difference between the way things are and the way at least one person in a situation wants them to be.[2]

Note that as defined here a problem may be entirely personal ("I have a problem with my weight") but a situation is always social. You may *have* a problem but you are always *in* a situation. This definition implies a definition of problem solving:

(3) Problems are solved by moving a state of affairs closer to the way you want things to be.[3]

---

[1] Professor Karl Llewellyn referred to the need for judges to have a "situation sense" about cases, by which he meant a sense of the interests of each party to a given situation: whose interests count, how strong are they, how do they affect each other, how do they affect each party's expectation of what the others will do, how do those expectations affect behavior, how a given action or decision is likely to affect this complex web of interacting interests, and how those affects relate to the purposes the law wishes to advance. Karl N. Llewellyn, THE COMMON LAW TRADITION: DECIDING APPEALS 121–22 (1960). This is a good working definition of judgment.

[2] Gerald P. Lopez, *Lay Lawyering*, 32 UCLA. L. REV 1, 2 (1984); Allen A. Newell & Herbert A. Simon, HUMAN PROBLEM SOLVING (1972).

[3] *Id.*

The notion of movement implies that there is a space in which movement occurs:

(4) Strategy space is the set of choices available to solve a problem.

Your strategy space is determined in large part by the movement you need to get closer to the state of affairs you would like to see and by how that movement affects others in the situation.

(5) Strategy spaces are interdependent: The options you have depend in part on the options others have, and their options depend in part on you. You must choose your actions given what they are likely to do, and what they are likely to do depends in part on what they think you are likely to do.

These definitions are a bit abstract, so let's think about them in terms of a concrete example. Here is a story in which a young lawyer had to exercise judgment in extremely difficult circumstances:

When Silence Isn't Golden

Dennis is a junior lawyer. He worked for Douglas, a family lawyer with his own small practice. They both represented Inez, who wanted an order granting her custody of her children pending resolution of another case and requiring her former husband, Felipe, to stay away from her.

Inez lived in Connecticut. Felipe lived in New Jersey, where he had custody of the children. Inez and Felipe were then litigating custody issues before Judge Peterson in New Jersey. He had just held a trial on custody issues but had not yet ruled.

Douglas filed in Connecticut an ex parte motion for the order Inez wanted. (Ex parte means it was filed on short notice and Felipe was not represented at the hearing.) The motion was assigned to the Hon. Jon Alander.

At the hearing Judge Alander asked Douglas why the New Jersey court couldn't deal with the issue. Douglas replied that Dennis had talked to Inez's New Jersey lawyer, Veronica, who advised Dennis not to file the motion in New Jersey. Douglas said Veronica gave several reasons "none of which I think are flattering to the judiciary there."

Douglas lied. Veronica did tell Dennis it was a bad idea to file a motion for interim custody but she said if Inez could not wait for Judge Peterson's ruling then she, Veronica, would file such a motion in New Jersey. She did not disparage Judge Peterson or the New Jersey bench.

Sitting there in court, Dennis knew Douglas lied, and lied about a conversation Dennis had, to boot.

Suppose you are Dennis. What do you do?

Because the first step in analysis is to understand the situation, which in turn is an intersection of interests, we need to decide who has an interest. (In game theory terms we must identify the relevant players.) The basic rule is easy:

(6) Anyone likely to be affected by the problem or a possible solution to it is part of the situation.

In Dennis's case at first glance the players might appear to be: (1) Inez, who wants (2) Douglas and (3) Dennis to obtain an order from (4) Judge Alander that she have custody of her (5) children and that (6) Felipe not have custody and have limited visitation rights. But this list is too short because it does not account for everyone likely to be affected by the order Inez desires. Her case is already pending in New Jersey and an order from a Connecticut judge might conflict with what the New Jersey judge planned to do. That means we have to add (7) Judge Peterson in New Jersey. And Douglas tried to obtain the order in part by making statements about what (8) Veronica said.

How do these 8 players affect each other? Because there are two court proceedings, we can think of this situation as having two structures—one in Connecticut and one in New Jersey. Differences between these structures provide the answer to what Dennis should do. What are the salient differences? Most importantly, Felipe's interests are at issue in Connecticut but he is not present or represented there. Felipe has appeared in and has a lawyer in the New Jersey proceeding.

That Felipe has a lawyer and has appeared in New Jersey automatically makes that forum more appealing to Judge Alander in Connecticut. Why? Judges are used to hearing from each side. If one side misstates an important fact or omits it, the judge can count on the other side to point it out. That is not true when only one party is before the court. *Ex parte* proceedings therefore risk treating the absent party unfairly, and judges know that.

The significance of this difference is increased by the second difference: Judge Peterson in New Jersey is familiar with the case because he just held a trial in it. Judge Alander is not familiar with the case and he knows he is not familiar with it. Consider the situation from his point of view: He would like to make the correct decision but he does not know the case and there is no one in court to defend Felipe's interests.

In sum, Judge Alander is faced with making a quick decision based on a one-sided presentation of unfamiliar facts. In contrast, Judge Peterson has just presided over a custody hearing in which Felipe was represented. He is in every way better suited to rule on Inez's motion. Looking at the case from Judge Alander's point of view, his problem is that an important decision must be made but he knows he is not in the best position to make it. He will want to know why Judge Peterson shouldn't decide the issue.

For all these reasons, if they are thinking strategically Dennis and Douglas should know from the outset that Judge Alander will want to know why he should grant their request when another judge is in a much better position to make a good decision. He is very likely to ask them why he should not defer the matter to Judge Peterson. Probably that is why Dennis was talking on the phone to Veronica—to find out where things stood in New Jersey. But Veronica didn't give Douglas and Dennis a reason why Judge Alander should rule. To the contrary, she said she was willing to submit the motion to Judge Peterson if Inez insisted. If Douglas told Judge Alander that, however, Judge Alander would almost certainly deny the motion and tell Inez to go to Judge Peterson in New Jersey. So instead Douglas lied and implied that Veronica had disparaged the New Jersey courts, which in this case means Judge Peterson.

But Douglas and Dennis should also know that Veronica's reputation is important to her. If her local judges heard she was disparaging them her reputation would suffer and her practice would suffer with it. She therefore would not be happy to learn that Douglas falsely stated that she had disparaged her local bench, and in particular Judge Peterson (who, after all, still had Inez's case under submission). So when Douglas lied he must either not have thought about Veronica's reaction or must have thought she would never find out.

That was a risky bet. Judge Alander might have called Veronica to learn directly about the New Jersey case, for example. As it turned out Judge Alander called Judge Peterson, who agreed to hold a hearing three days later. That meant Veronica wound up litigating the issue. She received a transcript of the hearing before Judge Alander. The transcript included Douglas's misstatement that she advised against filing in New Jersey and said uncomplimentary things about the New Jersey court—i.e., about Judge Peterson, who at that point was hearing the motion.

Both Veronica's self-interest in her own reputation and Inez's interest in a favorable ruling from Judge Peterson converged at this point: The lie could not go unchallenged. Veronica wrote Judge Alander a letter telling him Douglas lied in the hearing. Judge Alander convened a hearing on that charge. The result was a public reprimand for both Douglas, who lied, and also for Dennis, the junior associate, who sat silently by.[4]

What should Dennis have done? Thinking interactively in this case means recognizing that Judge Alander would want Judge Peterson to weigh in on Inez's motion and that Veronica was therefore likely to participate in the ultimate resolution of Inez's request. That meant Veronica would find out what Douglas said. Thinking dynamically means recognizing that for personal and professional reasons she would object to Douglas's misrepresentation. That means realizing—in the instant Douglas lied—that he was unlikely to get away with it.

So far the analysis might seem to be about Douglas alone. But recall that: (i) Douglas's representation was about a conversation Dennis had; (ii) it was an *ex parte* proceeding, so Judge Alander had to rely more heavily than usual on Douglas and Dennis to present *all* the facts; (iii) Judge Alander would be very unhappy to learn; (iv) as he was likely to learn; that (v) Dennis sat by silently and let Judge Alander be misled about a conversation Dennis had. For all these reasons, Dennis should have recognized that Douglas's lie would be exposed and it was in Dennis's own self interest to do something about the lie. That is one answer to our question: Dennis should not just have sat there; he should have done something.

But what can a young lawyer do when his boss lies about him in court? To get the answer Dennis would have to exercise judgment about a new situation, in which he has a new goal: Help Inez without getting sanctioned personally. Try to put yourself in his position: What options come to your mind?

When thinking about your answer, bear in mind two considerations that drive this story: ***reliance*** and ***reputation***. They are tremendously important factors in legal ethics. You will see them play an important role again and again in this book, and they will play an important role in your career.

Regarding reliance, there is a world of difference between a situation in which a party sees you as an advocate taking positions and making a case and a situation in which a party relies on you to tell the truth. It mattered a lot that Inez's motion was *ex parte* so that Felipe had no one there to present his side of the story. In that circumstance the court must rely on the lawyers present to a much greater extent than usual. It follows that the court would expect fuller disclosure of facts than otherwise would be the case, and the relevant rules in fact require such disclosure. When reliance is at stake, sanctions for disappointing the reliance interest are, too.

---

[4] The basis for this action was Connecticut's Rule of Professional Conduct 3.3(d). It was the same as the Model Rule, which we will study in chapter 16.

Reputation is your most important asset as a lawyer. It attracts clients, helps persuade judges and other lawyers, and in general determines your social status in the profession. It also may create conflicts with clients or with co-counsel, as happened in this case. One lesson of the case is that lawyers guard their reputations jealously, as you will guard your reputation when you begin practice. If you disparage another lawyer's reputation you had better have an absolutely solid basis for doing so, and probably a good reason for doing so as well. If you do not, as Douglas did not, your own reputation will suffer as a consequence.

A final point about this story: Dennis got in trouble because his boss put him in an impossible situation. Some students think they will learn the professional ropes after school, when they start working in the real world. That may be true in many cases, but remember: Your first boss could be like Douglas. He or she may be as likely to get you in trouble as to teach you how to stay out of it. Ultimately you are responsible for your own career and your own safety.

Perception, Categorization, and Judgment

Your goal, in this course and in your career, is to move from your current status as a fairly inexperienced analyst of legal situations to become an expert in such analysis. To do that it helps to think about what exactly you are doing when you size up a situation. Most obviously, you are observing things and drawing conclusions about them and their relationship to each other. You make decisions based on your perceptions, and perceptions are therefore a good place to start in thinking about judgment.

How does perception work? The psychologist Jerome Bruner famously wrote: "perception involves an act of categorization."[5] At the most basic level, to perceive something is to identify it as one type of thing and, by implication, as not something else. The shaggy beast with a wagging tale and floppy ears is a "dog" and not a "cat."

"Dog," "cat," and the like are categories. They are defined by sets of necessary and sufficient conditions. Where do these conditions come from and how do they get organized? It is possible that some categories are essentially hard-wired but the ones relevant to your practice are learned and created by experience; in fact you may think of categories as distilled experience. The conditions that constitute a category may be very precise ("speeding") or relatively loose ("nice" boss; "good" teacher). How do you categorize people or things and how much precision is necessary? The answer is that it depends on what you are trying to do when you categorize. "Categories form in response to what you are up to, talking about, thinking about."[6] A dog is also a mammal and if you care particularly about

[5] Jerome S. Bruner, *On Perceptual Readiness*, 64 PSYCH. REV. 123 (1957). For an updated treatment, *see* Anthony G. Amsterdam & Jerome Bruner, MINDING THE LAW (2000).

[6] Amsterdam & Bruner, *supra* note 5, at 42.

mammals but not dogs you will apply that category to the shaggy beast. Any old bulbous plant might be a mushroom if your purpose is to tell the gardener what to get rid of; more discrete categories are needed if you are cooking dinner.

This point implies, as Bruner and Anthony Amsterdam put it, that categories are made, not found. That they are made implies that they perform functions that serve certain purposes. For example, categorizing economizes on thinking. We don't have to wonder about the characteristics of each particular shaggy beast we encounter. We identify the salient characteristics of dogs and presume that the shaggy beast has them and will behave accordingly. Categorizing also helps us communicate with each other. When I refer to a dog you have a rough idea of what I am talking about; if I refer to a flying dog you know I am talking fiction. Shared categories are a large part of what constitutes a culture, including any of the many legal cultures you may enter on leaving school.

Equally importantly, and perhaps more importantly for purposes of this course, categories help predict the behavior or properties of a person or thing and thereby guide your own actions toward that person or thing. If you categorize the mushroom on your plate as poisonous you will not eat it but if you categorize it as nonpoisonous you may. You may think of the predictions generated by the category as a script describing what the things in the category will do and what will happen if you deal with them one way or another.[7]

The predictive function of categories helps explain what it means for a characteristic of a person or thing to be salient. A salient characteristic is one that is relevant to predicting the attributes or behavior of a thing or a person you are interested in given your purposes. These concepts generate a way of checking your categorization decisions. Let's call it the "fit" test: If the behavior or results you observe are consistent with what you expected when you made the category choice, then your category choice fits the thing you have categorized. If the behavior or results are not consistent with your expectations, then your category does not fit the thing you have categorized. You have made a mistake and, if you want better results in the future, you need to re-think your choice.

Checking the fit of your categorization decisions is an important part of judgment. Fit checking updates your category choices based on new observations and therefore is one aspect of dynamic thinking. If what you thought was an edible mushroom makes you sick, you need to update your category choice or get sicker.

---

[7] Amsterdam and Bruner refer to scripts as containing "familiar characters taking appropriate actions in typical settings. They play out *recurrent* situations in our lives, and we don't so much create them as assimilate them from the people with whom we live." *Id.* at 45. They contrast scripts with narratives, which in their model arise when a script is thrown off track.

More practically for purposes of this course, the fit test generates "red flags," which are things that should warn you about danger. Suppose you are Dennis in the story we just examined. If you have little experience in the law you might have classified Douglas as simply a lawyer, or perhaps "solo practitioner" or "small-firm lawyer." When you hear him in court you will refine your category to include the modifier "liar." If you are smart and want to do well in your career, you will treat people in the category of "lying lawyers" very differently from lawyers in general. And people in the category of "lawyers who lie about my conduct" are people to avoid if you possibly can. (Even if you can't that category choice will lead you to take steps to protect yourself; we'll cover some of those later.)

To sum up, judgment depends largely on perception and perception involves categorization. Categorization in turn requires you to (i) identify what it is that you are doing—what your purpose is; (ii) observe people and things with that purpose in mind; (iii) identify characteristics salient to that purpose (meaning characteristics that will predict properties or behavior relevant to that purpose); (iv) based on this conception of salience as prediction, choose a category for the person or thing in question; and (v) check your choice of category against further observation to determine whether the behavior predicted by that choice fits the behavior your observe. If it does, that fact will reinforce your initial choice. If it does not, that fact calls for revisiting your decision.

You may think of this process as a recursive flow chart, like this:

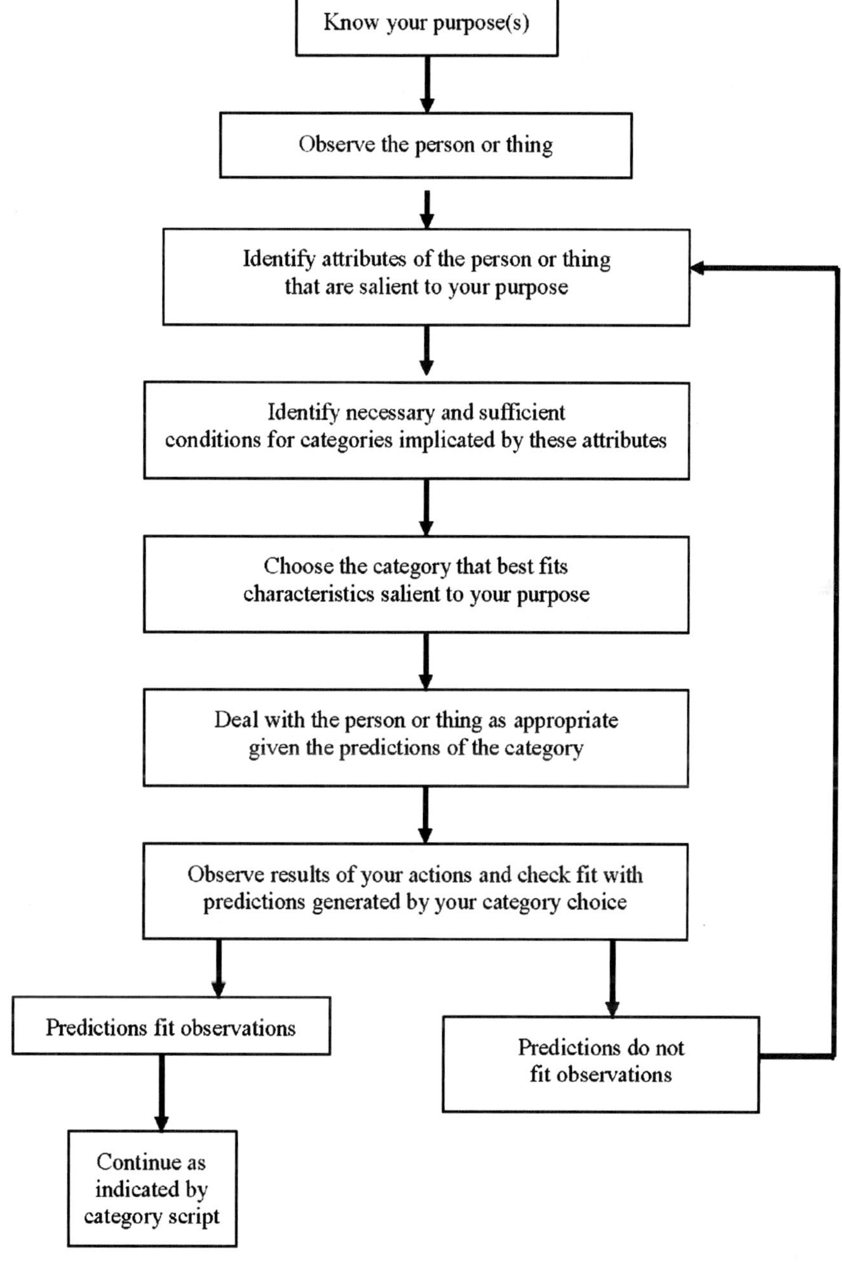

This chart might make categorization seem scientific and mechanistic. It's important to remember that it's not. The process is subject to all the foibles of perception and inference you are familiar with and some you may not be. And categorizing compounds these problems because once you place a person or thing in a category you tend to notice things that confirm that choice and disregard things that do not. That is one reason why anomalies—poor fit between your choice and future observations—are so important and need close attention.

This brief overview of categorization may seem a bit abstract but it is very important to your understanding of legal culture and your ability to protect yourself from risk. Legal doctrines are themselves categories and a large part of what you learn in law school is how they are formed and intersect. Categories you will learn in this course include such things as "fiduciary"—which is you—duty of confidentiality, attorney-client privilege, malpractice, and so on.

More specifically, the flow chart above tells you three very important things. First, you cannot categorize things properly unless you know what you are doing—what your purpose is. Knowing where you stand is necessary to knowing where others stand in relation to you.

Second, you must know what categories are out there and how to recognize them. What is an "unethical boss," or a "loose cannon" employee, or a "risky client" and how do you know them? Unfortunately, such decisions are so nuanced they cannot be taught very well in school. You learn them through experience. The stories of lawyers who have had trouble may give you insight to what categories are out there, however, and how to tell them apart. The cases (stories) in this book have been selected for that purpose as much as for the doctrinal points the cases make.

Third, you must understand the predictions your category choices imply so you can perceive deviations from those predictions. Deviations are red flags warning you that your category choice may be off—that you may have misperceived the situation you are in. And if you have misperceived your situation you are at risk. The risk may or may not be severe, and may or may not pan out, but misperception limits and may eliminate your ability to do anything about it.

It is important to make two final points about the concept of fit and your perceptions. We tend to notice things that seem unusual and out of place rather than things that seem ordinary. What we think of as ordinary depends on the behavior we see repeated in particular environments. Once you become accustomed to seeing bathing suits at the beach and ties in courtrooms you don't notice them very much, but you would notice and remember a person wearing a tie at the beach or a bathing suit in court.

You can think of your expectations for particular contexts as a template for proper and improper behavior, a template forged from routine day-to-day behavior you see in those contexts. Law offices have a wide variety of templates. What is aggressive, borderline behavior in one office may well be the usual state of affairs in another.

Like it or not, over time you will become accustomed to the templates at work in your office and to some degree you will internalize them. It is therefore important to figure out what those templates are and perform a different kind of fit test—a test for fit between your workplace and your own temperament and moral beliefs. If these fit well with the prototypical behaviors in your office you will feel relatively comfortable and probably do well, as judged by the standards of the office. If your temperament or moral code fit poorly with your workplace, you will probably do poorly in the office and be unhappy. It is at least disruptive and possibly poisonous to internalize behavior you find repugnant or frightening.

Thus a final rule of perception and inference: Know yourself, know your office, find a good fit.

B. *Where Laws Governing Lawyers Come From*

In any given representation, there are five sources of potential trouble for a lawyer. In order from most general to most particular, they are: (1) general legal rules; (2) rules creating duties to your client; (3) rules creating duties to non-clients; (4) rules of professional conduct (disciplinary rules); and (5) rules governing practice before particular government institutions.

(1) *General Legal Rules*

Being a lawyer does not mean being above the law. Lawyers are subject to the same rules as everyone else and then some. If you allow a client to use your law firm to launder drug money you will be subject to discipline under the rules of professional conduct but you will also go to jail under ordinary principles of criminal law. Lawyers who run offices are subject to the same laws as other proprietors: They may not harass employees, make false statements to lenders, or the like.

There are some particular rules governing the business aspects of law, such as that lawyers keep client funds separate from their own and that they not draw down on client retainers until they have earned the money. And there are some interesting questions, such as whether courts will enforce agreements prohibiting a lawyer from competing against a firm if she leaves it and whether the general rule that a client may fire a lawyer at any time means that in-house attorneys do not get the protection of the employment laws. The main point, however, is that lawyers do all sorts of things in the practice of law and, in doing those things, they are for the most part subject to the general legal rules that everyone else has to obey, too.

(2) *Your Client*

The client is the person you represent and the main person to whom you owe duties. This text is built around the most important of those duties—the duty of loyalty, the duty of care, and the duty of confidentiality. In a nutshell, the duty of loyalty requires you to place your client's interests ahead of your own, within the bounds of the law. The duty of care requires that you perform your work competently. The duty of confidentiality requires that you not disclose to others or use for your own benefit (or to the client's detriment) confidential information you learn while representing a client. (It is related to, but distinct from, the attorney-client privilege.)

In general, the purpose of duties running from lawyers to clients is to vindicate the trust and confidence clients are presumed to place in lawyers. These duties vindicate that trust and confidence by allowing clients harmed by a breach of these duties to sue for damages or other relief such as disgorgement of fees.

Lawyer-client relationships are both complementary and adversarial. They are complementary in the sense that the duties of loyalty and care tell the lawyer to look after the client's interests, which is what the client wants too. Lawyers who want to stay in business must develop a good reputation, which gives them additional incentives to make the client happy. At the same time, the client is also the person who pays the lawyer so the lawyer can pay rent and student loans. All else being equal, the client would like to pay as little as possible and the lawyer would like to make as much as possible. Sometimes lawyers and clients disagree on what should be done, or on whether a lawyer breached a duty. Disagreements can lead to fee disputes or litigation.

Sometimes clients wish to obey the law and they consult lawyers to find out what the law is so they can obey it. That is not always the case. Some clients either actually want to break the law or are indifferent to whether they do so. These clients may see a lawyer as a form of protection ("the lawyer said it was OK. . . . . . ") or even as a scapegoat to blame if they get caught breaking the law ("I left all that detail stuff to the lawyer. . . . . "). About the only thing one can say about all clients is that they have some problem they want solved and they look to lawyers to help solve it.

(3) *Related Parties*

Related parties are persons your client deals with and whom you encounter while representing your client. The purposes of related-party rules are similar to the purpose of lawyer-client rules. In some cases the rules help advance the purposes of representation by allowing third parties to sue lawyers for breach of duties to a client, as when a beneficiary is allowed to sue a lawyer who negligently drafts a will. In some cases the rules vindicate the interests of non-clients who reasonably rely on representations by lawyers. In rarer cases, the law may create a duty running from a lawyer to people to whom the client owes a duty, as the trustee of a trust might owe. The legal rules vary with the facts of particular cases, but you can owe duties to persons you do not actually represent as clients, and those duties can lead to liability or professional discipline.

(4) *Rules of Professional Conduct*

The rules of professional conduct are the formal rules adopted by states to regulate lawyers. Many of the most important rules are based on the duties of loyalty, care, and confidentiality. They differ from those duties, however, because violation of the rules creates a basis for administrative discipline of lawyers, such as a reprimand, suspension from practice, or disbarment. The rules are relevant to private causes of action in some cases, and to judicial decisions of an administrative nature, such as disqualification of counsel with a conflict of interest, but violation of the rules does not entail such results.

(5) *Government Institutions*

Often lawyers deal with government institutions such as courts or administrative agencies. Courts have inherent power to sanction lawyers in some cases, and express power (such as under Federal Rule of Civil Procedure 11) in others. Some agencies, such as the Securities and Exchange Commission and the Patent and Trademark Office, claim the right to discipline lawyers or take other action based on acts by lawyers that affect the agency's work. Lawyers can be fined or prevented from practicing before the agency in the future, which can in some cases destroy the lawyer's business.

C. *Six Rules of Survival*

The best way to avoid trouble in the real world is to follow these rules of thumb:

1. Never create a duty you don't want to create
2. Always be prepared to walk away
3. Assume everything you do or say will become publicly known
4. Never mistake the client's problem for your own
5. Never do as a lawyer anything you find repugnant as a person
6. If you mess up, fess up

The first rule stems from a basic fact. When lawyers get into trouble it is generally because they have violated a duty they have assumed themselves.[8] Lawyers assume duties either by agreeing to do so, as when they agree to represent a client, or by doing things that induce non clients reasonably to rely on the lawyer to have acted competently or to maintain confidential information. Duties are the benchmarks against which your

[8] Lawyers have some duties simply because they are lawyers (duties to report misconduct by other lawyers, for example, discussed in Part 13.A.), but these are less commonly the source of trouble than duties lawyers assume by their actions.

conduct is measured. If you are unwilling or unable to comply with the obligations of a duty, don't assume it.

The second rule has two aspects: (a) Always be prepared to quit a firm or fire a client; (b) always be prepared to be fired by a firm or by a client. Either way, the bottom line is that you will be better able to handle the situations you encounter in practice if you are prepared to walk away from a situation in which the only alternative is to violate the law.

This rule may mean more than is evident at first glance. Many lawyers get in trouble because they feel economic or social pressure to do things they know they should not do. Modern legal practice is highly competitive. Some lawyers compete by taking aggressive positions in litigation or negotiation, or by assuming business as well as legal responsibilities in transactions. Competition is ethical but it can drive competitors too far. At some point "aggressive" lawyering bleeds into unlawful lawyering, and it is often hard to distinguish between the two. In general, the less able you are to leave a job or a client the more leverage the job or the client has in situations in which you might be asked to do something your instinct tells you is wrong.

You should take the third rule literally. With modern technology anyone who is really determined to prove a fact can pretty much do so. The only real question is whether they care enough to spend the time and money needed to do it. No document ever really disappears, much less an e-mail. Invoke this rule anytime you hear anyone say "they'll never find out" or "how could they know?" The answer is easy: they could take your deposition. And then you have to decide between admitting the fact in question or committing perjury.

The fourth rule is a reminder that you have to keep a cool head. Lawyers who get too wrapped up in a case and view it as a personal contest are more likely to do the wrong thing than lawyers who keep their perspective. There is an old maxim (supposedly originating with Thurman Arnold, a well-known antitrust lawyer), which goes like this: At some point in your career you will face a situation in which either you or your client will go to jail; make sure it is your client. Put differently, you represent your client in dealing with your client's problem. The trick is to remember that it is your client's problem, not yours.

The fifth rule is basic common sense. You have to sleep at night. You have to be able to tell your spouse, partner, or children what you do for a living without being ashamed. Different people will have different tolerances for different things. Most people manage to find stories to tell themselves about why what they do is all right. The point is not to let the pressures of work push you outside the bounds of your tolerances, whatever they may be. In 30 or 40 years your career will be over and you will look back and ask yourself what you've done. Spend your career crafting an answer to that question that you will be able to live with.

The last rule is a practical one. Everyone makes mistakes. At some point in your career, you will, too. When you do (*when* you do), admit it, try to make it right, and move on. Do not try to weasel out of it or cover it up. You will only make things worse.

This point can be seen in a lesson we see re-learned repeatedly in Washington D.C. In the words of Richard Nixon, *it's the cover-up that kills you.* Nothing is more common than for a lawyer to take some action they shouldn't, or fail to take some action they should, and to say to themselves that they will break a rule just this once, in this one exceptional case, and then go back to following the law. Nobody will know, they say to themselves; everybody cuts corners at one time or another. (We will study this problem as an aspect of the psychological phenomenon known as loss aversion.) The problem is that almost invariably the first infraction is followed by a situation in which the lawyer has to admit wrongdoing or lie. The first lie requires another, and so on, until the original infraction, which might have been fairly minor, has borne a monster.

Lastly, a note on the text

The materials that follow include two types of questions. Case questions follow most of the cases. These questions are designed to help you make sure you understood the case and what it stands for. The questions do have answers (they are not law school imponderables), and the answers are in the cases. If you cannot answer the case questions, you have not understood the case. You should go back and read it again.

The text also poses "problems." These are more open-ended questions. They are designed to see if you are able to apply to new circumstances the lessons you have learned from the ABA Model Rules, the Restatement of the Law Governing Lawyers, and the cases. Sometimes they are designed to make you think about what kind of lawyer you want to be—whether you are the type of person who thrives on risk or prefers to avoid it, whether you would be willing to mislead a client for their own benefit, and so on. Because the problems are designed to make you think, they do not have certain answers, or at least not as certain as the case questions.

In several places the text summarizes the requirements of various rules of professional conduct. These summaries are designed to introduce the subjects addressed by the materials that follow; they are not substitutes for careful reading of the rules themselves.

All the cases have been edited. Citations are generally omitted unless the cited reference is significant. Because omission of citations is the default, the text generally does not signal the omission.

CHAPTER 2

DUTIES LAWYERS OWE CLIENTS

■ ■ ■

Generalizing about lawyers is risky because lawyers do many different things. They advise clients, negotiate for them, argue for them in courts and agencies, lobby for them in legislatures, and so on. A public interest lawyer trying to preserve a poor person's government benefit and a business lawyer negotiating a billion-dollar merger are both lawyers, but that shows only that the word "lawyer" tells you little about what someone does.

Clients differ, too. The corporate executive who deals with lawyers every day and who may know more about the law than a junior associate is not the same sort of client as a criminal defendant with no previous experience with lawyers. It makes no sense to pretend these clients are equivalent.

Lawyers therefore live and practice in many different worlds. This class surveys some of those worlds and tries to give you a sense of how the same rule can mean different things in different contexts. We will begin, however, with an overview of three obligations all lawyers owe all clients: the duty of loyalty, the duty of care, and the duty of confidentiality.

Within the bounds of the law, the duty of loyalty requires the lawyer to put the client's interests ahead of the lawyer's own interests and to do nothing to harm the client. The duty of care requires the lawyer to act reasonably and live up to the standard of care of a reasonable lawyer doing similar work in similar circumstances. The duty of confidentiality requires the lawyer not to use client confidences for the lawyer's benefit or to the client's detriment, unless the information has become generally known, and not to disclose client information unless required by law to do so.

A. THE DUTY OF LOYALTY

Restatement of the Law Governing Lawyers ("Restatement") § 16(3)

All lawyers are fiduciaries, which is to say they owe clients fiduciary duties. What are those?

> A fiduciary duty is the duty of an agent to treat his principal with the utmost candor, rectitude, care, loyalty, and good faith—in fact to treat the principal as well as the agent would treat himself. The common law imposes that duty when the disparity between the parties in knowledge or power relevant to the performance of an undertaking is so vast that it is a reasonable inference that had the parties in advance negotiated expressly over the issue they would have agreed that the agent owed the principal the high duty that we have described, because otherwise the principal would be placing himself at the agent's mercy. An example is the relation between a guardian and his minor ward, or a lawyer and his client. The ward, the client, is in no position to supervise or control the actions of his principal on his behalf; he must take those actions on trust; the fiduciary principle is designed to prevent that trust from being misplaced.

Burdett v. Miller, 957 F.2d 1375 (7th Cir. 1992) (Posner, J.)

Fiduciary duties are related to agency law. Agency is one type of fiduciary relationship, and most lawyers are agents of their clients. Agency law is the foundation for many rules specifically addressed to lawyers.[1] As the *Restatement (Third) of Agency,* § 1.01 defines it,

> Agency is the fiduciary relationship that arises when one person (a "principal") manifests assent to another person (an "agent") that the agent shall act on the principal's behalf and subject to the principal's control, and the agent manifests assent or otherwise consents so to act.

---

[1] For a general survey of the relationship between agency and the practice of law, *see* Deborah A. DeMott, *The Lawyer As Agent*, 67 FORD. L. REV. 301 (1998). Professor DeMott summarizes the relationship this way:

> The law of agency provides the foundational structure for many of the legal consequences that follow from the relationship between a lawyer and a client, as well as the relationship between an individual lawyer and a law firm. Definitional precision in the law aside, the lawyer-client relationship is a commonsensical illustration of agency. A lawyer acts on behalf of the client, representing the client, with consequences that bind the client. Lawyers act as clients' agents in transactional settings as well as in litigation. Moreover, a lawyer who is a member of a law firm acts as an agent of the firm in firm-related activity, as does an associate employed by a law firm and in-house counsel for a client organization. It is unsurprising, then, that the legal consequences of these relationships parallel the legal consequences of agency generally, even when they are not identical. In any agency relationship, for example, the agent's loyalty to the interests of the principal is a dominant concern, as is the loyalty of a lawyer to the client.
>
> Despite its foundational significance, the law of agency does not by itself capture all of the legal consequences of relationships between lawyers and clients and between lawyers and others to whom the lawyer owes duties. In this context, agency is roughly comparable to the structural steel members that support a building and define its size and basic shape but do not govern how the building functions and looks. Lawyers are agents, but lawyers perform functions that distinguish them from most other agents. That a lawyer is an agent is sometimes irrelevant to the legal consequences of what the lawyer has done or has failed to do, making an unswerving focus on agency misleading. It is not surprising, then, that courts on occasion differentiate among agency's consequences, rather than according agency a monolithic or inexorable set of consequences.

The fiduciary principle requires that agents place the principal's interests above their own. *Restatement (Third) of Agency*, § 8.01, states the "General Fiduciary Principle" of Agency:

> An agent has a fiduciary duty to act loyally for the principal's benefit in all matters connected with the agency relationship.

Fiduciary duties may be summarized under the general rubric of the duty of loyalty. *Owen v. Pringle,* 621 So.2d 668, 671 (Miss. 1993). This general duty implies several things. Agents may not: acquire a material benefit from a third party in connection with the agent's actions as an agent (§ 8.02); take a position adverse to the principal, or on behalf of a party adverse to the principal, regarding a matter related to the scope of the agency (§ 8.03); while an agent, compete with the principal or assist the principal's competitors (though an agent may prepare to compete with the principal during this time and compete with the principal, subject to certain restrictions, after the agency is over) (§ 8.04); use the principal's property, or either use or communicate the principal's confidential information for the benefit of the agent or a third party (§ 8.05); or engage in "conduct that is likely to damage the principal's enterprise" (§ 8.10). Fiduciaries also must segregate the principal's property from their own and keep and render an account of money or property received or paid by the agent for the principal (§ 8.12).

Fiduciary duties are fundamental to practicing law. You must master them. In many respects they are intuitive but in others they are not. For example, you may be sued in tort for violating a fiduciary obligation even if you do a good job for your client (i.e., you satisfy the applicable standard of care). In some cases, fiduciary violations can lead to the forfeiture of your fee.

Perhaps most importantly, in the real world you must sometimes make fast decisions in complex situations that present many ethical problems. If you remember your fiduciary basics you have a much better chance of doing the right thing than if you don't, even if you forget the details of particular disciplinary rules.

The duty of loyalty is often said to expire at the end of a representation, in contrast to the duty of confidentiality, which survives termination. Opinions addressing conflicts of interest sometimes read that way. But some cases appear to extend aspects of the duty of loyalty beyond termination, most notably in the form of a conflict of interest rule effectively precluding lawyers from attacking their previous work regardless whether confidences might be at issue. *See, e.g. Brennan's Inc. v. Brennan's Rests. Inc.*, 590 F.2d 168 (5th Cir. 1979); *Knight v. Ferguson*, 149 Cal.App.4th 1207 (2007).

"I did the best I could . . . to lose."

Daniel Bibb had been a prosecutor for 21years. His office had prosecuted two men, Olmedo Hidalgo and David Lemus, for murder. Over time new evidence appeared suggesting Hidalgo and Lemus might be innocent. Bibb had not worked on the original case but was assigned to investigate it in light of the new evidence.

Bibb concluded the two men were not guilty. He recommended that the cases be dismissed but his superiors nevertheless ordered him to defend the convictions in court. He decided to help defense counsel. He tracked down defense witnesses and helped defense lawyers prepare their testimony. He advised defense lawyers on strategy and helped them understand the new evidence he uncovered. After six weeks of hearings his superiors agreed to drop charges against Hidalgo and to retry Lemus (who was later acquitted).

Bibb resigned from the district attorney's office a year later. The consensus of ethics experts is that Bibb violated his duty of loyalty. As Professor Stephen Gillers of NYU put it, "[h]e's entitled to his conscience, but his conscience does not entitle him to subvert his client's case, . . . [i]t entitles him to withdraw from the case, or quit if he can't."

B. THE DUTY OF CARE

Restatement §§ 16(2), 52(1)

The second major duty applicable to lawyers is the duty of care. The duty of care should remind you of tort law. It requires lawyers to act carefully in performing work for clients. Care is judged by the prevailing standards of professional competence in the relevant field of law and geographic region. The *Restatement (Third) of Agency* provides some particular manifestations of the duty of care. Agents must: comply with the express and implied terms of any contract with the principal (§ 8.07); act only within the scope of their actual authority, and comply with all lawful instructions from the principal regarding the agent's actions for the principal (§ 8.09); and inform the principal of all facts material to the agency relation and all facts the agent knows or has reason to know the principal would want to have (§ 8.11). Disciplinary rules governing lawyers, such as that you must inform a client of developments material to the representation, embody some of these principles.

The duty of care is not a fiduciary duty. The concept of loyalty corresponds with the notion of betrayal and faithlessness, while the concept of care corresponds with the notion of mistake or accident. When you see a duty of loyalty violation it is almost always because the lawyer acted out of self-interest rather than for the client's interest. When you see a duty of care violation it is often because a lawyer was foolish, lazy, overextended, or debilitated.

"I have a high volume practice—.I'm like an over eager little puppy dog. The client comes in. I want to help them."

Joseph Muto practiced immigration law. He focused on Chinese immigrants in New York City. He had over 450 matters pending at one point; at a disciplinary hearing he was unable to remember the names of four clients identified by disciplinary officials. He had no notes or calendar entries of meetings with these clients, nor any records of payment they made. Clients could not reach him, he did not give them business cards, he moved without informing them, and did not return calls placed to the only number he gave them, his home answering machine. He missed hearings and did not inform clients of the status of their matters.

Muto charged $150 to represent clients in deportation hearings. An immigration attorney called by disciplinary officials testified he charged $3,000 – $8,000 for such services and could not imagine that they could be provided for $100 – $200 per case.

Disciplinary officials portrayed Muto as receiving many cases from immigration service agencies, which performed much of the relevant paperwork (thus unlawfully practicing law). This relationship, they contended, explained why he "never met, spoke, or had meaningful contact with his clients." Muto denied knowing involvement with the agencies, but the panel hearing his disciplinary case did not accept the denial. One might conjecture a relationship between Muto's low fees and the agencies' involvement in his cases.

Muto was disbarred for neglecting his cases. He commented on an account of his case (Richard Abel: LAWYERS IN THE DOCK (2008)): "I admit that I got in over my head and never should have attempted a high volume low cost law practice. . . . My biggest mistake was that I took on more than I could handle in private practice. I never should have taken on so many cases. . . . "

C. THE DUTY OF CONFIDENTIALITY

Restatement §§ 59–60

Lawyers also owe clients a duty not to use or disclose confidential information the lawyer learns while representing the client. Some of this information—confidential communications between a client and a lawyer with regard to legal services—is also covered by the attorney-client privilege. That is a rule of evidence, however, which applies in proceedings where the rules of evidence apply. The duty to maintain client confidences is broader. It applies all the time, and it forbids lawyers from *using* client information for the lawyer's own benefit or to the client's detriment as well as from *disclosing* such information. Sometimes lawyers use information by disclosing it but you can use information without disclosing it, too, as would be the case if you bought or sold securities based on a client's material nonpublic information.

The duty of confidentiality created by agency law is qualified in an important way that the duty of confidentiality recognized by disciplinary rules is not. The *Restatement (Third) of Agency* § 8.05(2) states that an agent has a duty "not to use or communicate confidential information of the principal for the agent's own purposes or those of a third party." The comment to this section, however, states: "an agent's duty of confidentiality is not absolute. An agent may reveal otherwise privileged information to protect a superior interest of the agent or a third party. Thus, an agent may reveal to law-enforcement authorities that the principal is committing or is about to commit a crime. An agent's privilege to reveal such information also protects the agent's revelation to a private party who is being or will be harmed by the principal's illegal conduct."

Modern disciplinary rules provide narrower exceptions for disclosure by a lawyer. For example, Model Rule of Professional Conduct 1.6(b)(1)–(3) allows for disclosure only when a lawyer reasonably believes a client intends to commit an act reasonably certain to result in injury or death, or when the client is using or has used the lawyer's services to commit a crime or fraud that has harmed the financial interests of a third party. California's Rule 3–100 provides an even narrower exception to the rule against disclosure.

Attorneys who violate the duty of confidentiality generally do so either by acting carelessly or out of self-interest. It therefore would be logical to treat a lawyer's obligations regarding client confidences as simply one aspect of the duties of loyalty and care. Most lawyers treat it separately, however, as do disciplinary rules, so it is best to consider it on its own. The duties of loyalty and care may help you think about confidentiality, however: One thing a careful, loyal lawyer does is to keep client confidences and not use them to advance the lawyer's personal interests.

"There was nothing else that these lawyers could have done"

Dale Coventry and James Kunz worked for the Cook County public defender's office in Chicago. They represented Andrew Wilson, who was accused of murder. Wilson conveyed to them that he had killed a security guard in an unrelated crime. Another man, Alton Logan, was convicted of killing that guard. He was sentenced to life in prison.

Wilson was convicted and sentenced to death. Coventry and Kunz asked Wilson to give them permission to disclose his confession after his death. He agreed. The lawyers signed a notarized affidavit stating they had obtained through privileged sources information showing that Logan was not guilty. It was dated March 17, 1982.

Wilson died in November 2007. Logan was then represented by Harold Winston, who had heard Coventry and Kunz had information that might help Logan. Winston spoke to Kunz, who then revealed the secret. In January 2008 the affidavit was submitted to the court. Alton Logan was declared innocent in April 2009.

According to one Illinois legal ethics expert, Kunz and Coventry had no choice but to remain silent about Wilson's confession. That is a correct reading of the relevant rules.

Kunz has stated he would have revealed Wilson's statements had Logan been sentenced to death. "I would have been prepared to lose my license," says Kunz. "I wasn't going to let him be executed. It would have been an ethical lapse, but the execution I couldn't allow to happen."

The current version of Model Rule 1.6(b)(1) permits (but does not require) a lawyer to disclose information "to prevent reasonably certain death or substantial bodily harm." Before 2002, however, the rule allowed disclosure only to prevent the client from committing a criminal act likely to result in such harm.

Though agency principles such as fiduciary duties provide the basis for many disciplinary rules relevant to this course they do not provide the basis for all. For example, Model Rules of Professional Conduct 4.2 through 4.4 forbid lawyers from communicating with persons they know to be represented by counsel, detail the manner in which lawyers must deal with unrepresented persons, and require lawyers to respect the rights of third parties.

One important category of rules not grounded in agency law works from the premise that lawyers are officers of the court as well as agents for their clients. Model Rules 3.1–3.9 impose obligations on lawyers designed to make advocacy fair and efficient, possibly at the expense of the client's interest. Lawyers in firms are agents of their firms as well as of their clients, and relations among lawyers within a firm can influence a lawyer's behavior in important ways. Model Rules 5.1–5.3 deal with the responsibilities of supervising and subordinate lawyers, while Rules 5.4–5.7 deal with some economic aspects of practice. You need to be aware of such non-fiduciary rules as well as those that embody fiduciary principles.

D. AN OVERVIEW OF THE IMPLICATIONS OF LOYALTY, CARE, AND CONFIDENTIALITY

Several reasons justify making lawyers agents and fiduciaries for their clients. Agency law reduces the cost of contracting for legal services by supplying default rules governing relations between client and lawyer, as well as rules dealing with the lawyer's relationship with third parties on the client's behalf. Fiduciary rules protect the client from overreaching or opportunistic behavior by the lawyer. Different reasons are more prominent in some cases than others, however, and it is useful to begin this course by getting a sense of the issues to which these concepts apply.

Some of these reasons are utilitarian. For example, the law of agency generally imputes to the client the consequences of a lawyer's acts or omissions. Such imputation protects third parties whose interests a lawyer may affect and gives lawyers incentives to act carefully when representing clients. The first case below illustrates this type of reasoning.

In other cases, the risk is more that the lawyer will take advantage of the client than that the lawyer's mistakes will prejudice a third party. The second case below illustrates this type of reasoning. Notice in particular the distinction the court draws between competence—the malpractice claim—and the idea that a fiduciary may not take advantage of a principal.

This logic is clearest in cases where a plaintiff alleges a cause of action for breach of fiduciary duty but it is not limited to such cases. It also extends to cases where a plaintiff alleges some other tort but the defendant is a fiduciary. In such cases, the defendant's fiduciary obligations may alter the normal burdens of production or persuasion, making it easier for a plaintiff to prevail. The material following the second case illustrates this type of reasoning.

UNITED STATES V. 7108 WEST GRAND AVENUE

15 F.3d 632 (7th Cir.) *cert. denied sub nom. Flores v. United States*, 512 U.S. 1212 (1994)

EASTERBROOK, CIRCUIT JUDGE.

Claimants in this forfeiture proceeding pose the question whether their former attorney's gross negligence in representing their interests entitles them to another opportunity to litigate. The answer is No. Malpractice, gross or otherwise, may be a good reason to recover from the lawyer but does not justify prolonging litigation against the original adversary.

Feliberto Flores is in prison for federal drug offenses. See *United States v. Flores,* 5 F.3d 1070 (7th Cir.1993). The United States began forfeiture proceedings against three parcels of real property in his name, contending that they had been acquired with the proceeds of his drug business. Feliberto contends that he and his wife Isabellita retained Robert Habib to represent them in the forfeiture proceeding. Habib did not file a timely claim on Feliberto's behalf with respect to any of the three properties, and he filed a verified claim on Isabellita's behalf with respect to one parcel only. The United States filed a motion for default judgment concerning the property at 7108 West Grand Avenue (which is, by virtue of a Rule 54(b) judgment, the sole parcel in dispute on this appeal). Habib filed papers in opposition on behalf of Isabellita but did not contend that she has an ownership interest in the property. Feliberto is the sole record owner; Isabellita contends that an attorney other than Habib neglected to transfer a joint tenancy interest to her name. Habib did not request a stay under 21 U.S.C. § 881(i), which applies when a criminal proceeding is ongoing against a claimant. Neither Habib nor Isabellita appeared at the hearing on the motion for default judgment, which the district court granted. (Habib says that he had a conflicting engagement in another court, but this would be a reason to ask the court for a postponement, not to ignore the hearing.) Habib did not file a timely notice of appeal.

Represented by new counsel, Feliberto and Isabellita filed a motion under Fed.R.Civ.P. 60(b) for relief from the judgment. They blamed the lack of timely claims on Habib, and they contended that each had a good defense to the forfeiture action: Feliberto that he paid for the property with lottery winnings rather than drug money, Isabellita that she is an "innocent owner" under 21 U.S.C. § 881(a)(6). The district court denied this motion. . . .

Feliberto and Isabellita insist that Habib was grossly negligent—that his acts were worse than merely negligent but short of intentional misconduct. They characterize Habib's efforts in this way in an effort to avoid the principle that an attorney's errors and misconduct are attributed to his clients. The clients are principals, the attorney is an agent, and under the law of agency the principal is bound by his chosen agent's deeds. So much is clear for an attorney's wilful misconduct. . . . It is equally clear for negligent errors. . . . None of these cases involves gross negligence, which the appellants see as an opening.

Yet why should the label "gross" make a difference to the underlying principle: that the errors and misconduct of an agent redound to the detriment of the principal (and ultimately, through malpractice litigation, of the agent himself) rather than of the adversary in litigation? We know how to treat both ends of the continuum: negligence and wilful misconduct alike are attributed to the litigant. When the polar cases are treated identically, intermediate cases do not call for differentiation. Holding that negligence and wilful misconduct, but not gross negligence, may be the basis of a default judgment would make hay for standup comics. No lawyer would dream of arguing on behalf of a hospital that, although the hospital is liable in tort for staff physicians' negligence and intentional misconduct, it is not liable for their "gross negligence." The argument makes no more sense when presented on behalf of a lawyer or litigant. . . .

"Holding the client responsible for the lawyer's deeds ensures that both clients and lawyers take care to comply. If the lawyer's neglect protected the client from ill consequences, neglect would become all too common. It would be a free good—the neglect would protect the client, and because the client could not suffer the lawyer would not suffer either." *Tolliver v. Northrop Corp.,* 786 F.2d 316, 319 (7th Cir.1986). See also *United States v. Boyle,* 469 U.S. 241 (1985) (client may be penalized when lawyer files a tardy tax return). A distinction between ordinary and gross negligence would put an end to "mere" negligence in federal litigation but would create a land office business in gross negligence. . . .

It is unnecessary to ask the district court to determine where on the line from "mere" negligence to intentional misconduct attorney Habib's handling of this litigation falls, because the answer does not make any difference.

CASE QUESTIONS

1. What principle governs this case?
2. The court made an instrumental argument for holding Habib liable. What is it?
3. In terms of the duties discussed above, what duty was breached in this case?

The clients in *7108 West Grand Avenue* suffered because their lawyer had power to act for them but failed to act. Many cases reach this conclusion. As the Court of Appeals for the Eighth Circuit has said, "A litigant chooses counsel at his peril. Counsel's disregard of his professional responsibilities can lead to extinction of his client's claims." *Boogaerts v. Bank of Bradley*, 961 F.2d 765, 767 (8th Cir. 1992). This principle likely holds even if an uninsured lawyer deceives a client about the status of a matter, leading to judgment against the client. *Bakery Mach. & Fabrication, Inc. v. Traditional Baking, Inc.*, 570 F.3d 845, 848 (7th Cir. 2009)("Deception of a client becomes the liability of the client's attorney and not the client's opponent").

Federal Rule of Civil Procedure 60(b)(1) grants courts discretion to relieve "a party or its legal representative" from a judgment or order if the court finds "excusable neglect" contributed to entry of the judgment or order. *Pioneer Investment Services Co. v. Brunswick*, 507 U.S. 380, 397 (1993). (That case involved bankruptcy rules but the "excusable neglect" language is the same as in FRCP 60(b)(1)). The court found that whether neglect is excusable is an equitable issue, in which courts should take into account all relevant factors, including "the danger of prejudice to the debtor, the length of the delay and its potential impact on judicial proceedings, the reason for the delay, including whether it was within the reasonable control of the movant, and whether the movant acted in good faith." 507 U.S. at 395.

Thinking Dynamically and Interactively I

Who had a stake in the situation described in *7108 West Grand Avenue*? Who did Habib's actions affect and who would be affected by the court's ruling? Obvious parties include Feliberto and Isabellita, Habib, the prosecutor, the U.S. government, and the court itself. Try this exercise. Imagine each of these parties as connected to each other, as if they are each different points in a web. You might picture the web as something like this:

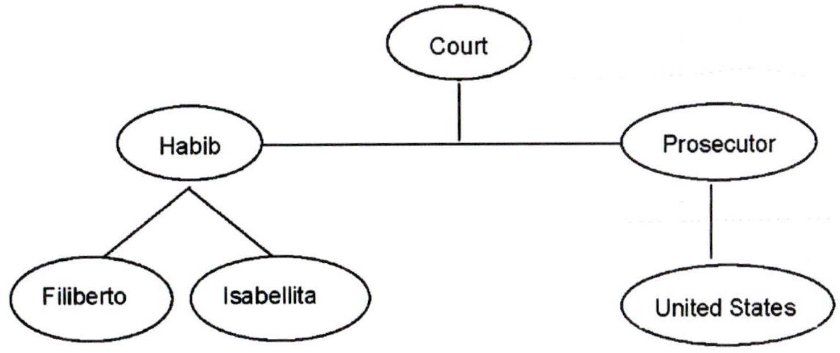

Think about these relationships from the point of view of each participant. They each will expect certain things from Habib. For example, Filiberto and Isabellita rely on Habib to represent them, while the prosecutor sees Habib as an adversary and as the representative of Filiberto's and Isabellita's interests.

Look at the court's perspective on this diagram. When the court sees Habib, it sees not only his clients but also the prosecutor and the United States. Whatever decision the court makes will ripple through this web of connections. If the court lets Habib off the hook his clients get a second chance to oppose forfeiture of the property. But because each player in this web is connected to each other player such a decision would affect the prosecutor and the United States, too. The prosecutor would have to spend time getting back up to speed on the case and trying it—time that could be spent on another matter if the court refuses to let Habib off the hook. The United States would have to pay for that time. And letting Habib off the hook would also mean putting the case back on the trial court's calendar, creating more work for the trial judge. Ruling for Isabellita, in other words, would impose costs on the other parties, including the party making the ruling.

If you were Habib, exercising judgment about this case would involve understanding how each player in the web sees you. You would have to think about the costs a ruling in your favor would impose on the government and the court. And what benefits would justify creating those costs? Filiberto and Isabellita might benefit, if they can keep their house. But in this situation there is a way Filiberto and Isabellita could get relief without creating costs for third parties: They could sue Habib. That option minimizes the costs of re-litigating the forfeiture action and places liability on the party who most deserves it. If you were Habib, you would need to work through all this analysis to understand what was likely to happen to you if you ignored the filing deadlines and the hearing.

Judgment requires putting yourself in the place of each person affected by an action and asking yourself how the action affects that person. Once you understand that, you understand the interactive aspect of judgment. You still need to think about the dynamic aspect of judgment, however. The cost analysis mentioned above is one part of dynamic thinking. The effect of precedent is another part.

What would happen if courts let lawyers off the hook in order to save clients from lawyers' mistakes? Judge Easterbrook suggests that lawyers would be more careless because they would face no serious consequences for their mistakes. If the court lets the client off the hook the client would have no damages (or at least low damages) and therefore probably would not sue the lawyer. If the lawyer knew he was unlikely to suffer consequences for making mistakes he would be less careful, which would lead to more mistakes, which would waste scarce court time, etc. (Later we will think dynamically in terms of how different parties would react to different actions.)

TANTE V. HERRING

453 S.E.2d 686 (1994)

HUNT, CHIEF JUSTICE.

We granted certiorari to the Court of Appeals in *Tante v. Herring,* 211 Ga.App. 322, 439 S.E.2d 5 (1993) to determine whether the Court of Appeals was correct in upholding Laura and Bobby Herring's claims against their former attorney, T. Edward Tante. We affirm in part and reverse in part.

The Herrings retained Tante to pursue a claim for social security disability benefits for Mrs. Herring before the Social Security Administration. During his representation of Mrs. Herring, Tante appeared with her at a hearing before an administrative law judge and wrote a letter brief on her behalf. Thereafter, the administrative law judge issued a favorable award to Mrs. Herring. Tante's subsequent request for attorney fees for his work in representing Mrs. Herring, which request had been approved by both the Herrings, was approved by the administrative law judge.

The issues underlying this appeal involve the Herrings' action against Tante for legal malpractice, breach of fiduciary duty and breach of contract, all pertaining to Tante's adulterous relationship with Mrs. Herring during the period in which he was pursuing the disability claim on her behalf. The Herrings allege that Tante caused physical and mental harm to Mrs. Herring by taking advantage of confidential information regarding her emotional and mental condition to convince her to have an affair with him. The Herrings also allege Tante violated rules and standards of the State Bar of Georgia, violated his fiduciary duty, and breached his contract with the Herrings. The trial court granted partial summary judgment to the Herrings on the question of Tante's liability and denied summary judgment to Tante. The Court of Appeals affirmed.

The Court of Appeals correctly pointed out that the elements of an action for legal malpractice consist of employment of an attorney; failure of the attorney to exercise ordinary care, skill and diligence; and damages proximately caused by that failure. This is simply a corollary of the traditional formula for the elements necessary to a cause of action in tort: duty, breach (failure to conform to the required standard) and damage proximately caused by the breach. It is axiomatic that the element of *breach* of duty in a legal malpractice case—the failure to exercise ordinary care, skill, and diligence—must relate directly to the *duty* of the attorney, that is, the duty to perform the task for which he was employed. Of course, in an action for legal malpractice, the plaintiff must file with the complaint an expert's affidavit setting forth at least one negligent act constituting the alleged breach of duty and the factual basis for each claim of negligence. Although the Herrings did attach an expert's affidavit to their complaint, the expert did not set forth a negligent act which would constitute the basis for a claim of legal malpractice.

There is no evidence that Tante's conduct of which the Herrings complain had any effect on his performance of legal services under his agreement with the Herrings. Indeed, Tante obtained for Mrs. Herring precisely the results for which he was retained, the recovery of social security disability benefits. Contrary to the holding of the Court of Appeals, a satisfactory result under an agreement for legal services by necessity precludes a claim for legal malpractice. Accordingly, the Court of Appeals erred in affirming the trial court's grant of summary judgment to the Herrings on their claim against Tante for legal malpractice.

However, we agree with the Court of Appeals that the Herrings have a claim against Tante for damages for breach of fiduciary duty. That claim is not one for professional malpractice based on negligence involving Tante's performance of legal services, and, therefore, no expert affidavit is required in support of it. The fiduciary duty in this context arises from the attorney-client relationship. Tante was a fiduciary with regard to the confidential information provided him by his client just as he would have been a fiduciary with regard to money or other property entrusted to him by a client.[2] Thus, the Herrings' claim is based on Tante's alleged misuse, to his own advantage, of confidential information in medical and psychological reports concerning Mrs. Herring obtained in and solely because of Tante's representation of her.[3]

Tante did not controvert the allegations that he took advantage of information contained in Mrs. Herring's confidential medical and psychological reports about her impaired emotional and mental condition, that Tante took advantage of that condition, convincing her to have an affair with him, resulting in physical and mental harm to the Herrings. The Court of Appeals correctly noted that, as a fiduciary with regard to infor-

---

[2] FN4. Whether and to what extent a lawyer has a fiduciary duty to a client depends on the facts in each case. Here, however, there is no question that the confidential information shared with Tante arose out of the attorney-client relationship and that Tante was a fiduciary with respect to that information.

[3] FN5. See Canon 4 of the Code of Professional Responsibility; Directory Rule 4–101(B)(3). This violation of the Code, does not, in and of itself, provide a private cause of action for damages. *Davis v. Findley,* 262 Ga. 612, 422 S.E.2d 859 (1992). Rather, the breach of fiduciary duty in this case, which, incidentally, constitutes a violation of the Code of Professional Responsibility, along with a claim of resulting damages, supports the claim for breach of fiduciary duty in this action. That claim does not depend on any violation of the Code of Professional Responsibility, and we do not here decide whether evidence of a violation of the disciplinary rules is relevant in a claim against a lawyer for legal malpractice or breach of fiduciary duty. Of course, the violation of the Code subjects Tante to disciplinary action. See, *Davis v. Findley,* supra; *In re: T. Edward Tante,* 264 Ga. 692, 453 S.E.2d 688, pending before this court.

mation shared with him by his client, Tante owed his client the utmost good faith and loyalty. By using information available to him solely because of the attorney client relationship to his advantage and to the Herrings' disadvantage, he breached that fiduciary duty. Accordingly, the Herrings may pursue their claim for damages resulting from that breach.

CASE QUESTIONS

1. What causes of action does the court mention? How do their elements differ?
2. Did Tante commit malpractice? Did he breach a contract with the Herrings?
3. Did Tante disclose any confidential information?
4. What is the relationship between the confidences Mrs. Herring confided to Tante and the cause of action in the case?
5. What is the point of the court's analogy between confidential information and money? What does it mean to say someone is a fiduciary with respect to information?
6. Did Tante breach any disciplinary rules? What is the relationship between those rules and the causes of action in the case?
7. In terms of the duties discussed above what duty was at issue in this case? (Hint: how did Tante's conduct differ from Habib's?)

Mapping Risk

Tante illustrates an important point about the rules that apply to you. You can think of *Tante* as involving three sets of rules—the duty of care, the duty of loyalty, and disciplinary rules. You may depict them using a Venn Diagram, like this:

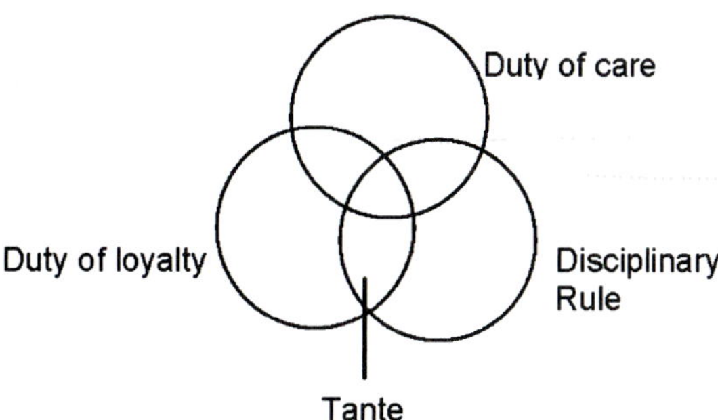

Tante breached the duty of loyalty and, the court tells us, a Georgia disciplinary rule, but he did not breach the duty of care. He did a good job but he is still potentially liable for betraying his client's trust. Under disciplinary rules different from Georgia's it would have been perfectly possible for Tante to have satisfied the duty of care and violated no rule of professional conduct but still be liable to Mrs. Herring.

Each rule you are subject to, and each duty you owe, creates distinct obligations. Often they will point in the some direction—acts breaching the duty of loyalty often violate disciplinary rules, too—but that is not always true. You cannot infer from the fact that you have complied with one rule, such as the duty of care, that you are safe under the others. You have to determine each rule to which you are subject and analyze its requirements separately.

Overlapping Causes of Action I

The duty of loyalty and the duty of care are distinct duties but the cases do not distinguish cleanly between them. In part that is because plaintiffs often allege the same facts as a basis for causes of action for breach of fiduciary duty and for malpractice. Liberal pleading rules suggest plaintiffs should be allowed to plead in the alternative, and many jurisdictions are not too picky about distinguishing which facts support which claim. As we will see, some courts have dealt with this practice by dismissing fiduciary duty claims that duplicate duty of care claims, though these courts have not explained in any detail the reasoning for this rule. For an overview of this situation, *see* Charles W. Wolfram, Charles W. Wolfram, *A Cautionary Tale: Fiduciary Breach As Legal Malpractice*, 34 HOFSTRA L. REV. 689, 699–701 (2006).

For now, it may be helpful to think of the core case of fiduciary duty in terms of the nature of the alleged breach and the nature off the remedy sought. In particular, the core fiduciary duty case is one in which the client-plaintiff alleges: (1) self-interested conduct by the lawyer either (a) at the expense of the client or (b) making use of the client's information or other resources to profit the lawyer; resulting in (2) a claim in which the client seeks either (a) damages for harm done or (b) disgorgement of the lawyer's profits. *Restatement* §§ 37, 49, 53, 60(2).

Note that this core case centers on the lawyer's self-serving conduct rather than an innocent mistake. Simple incompetence, as might well be the case in *7108 West Grand Avenue*, presents a clear duty of care violation. Examples of core fiduciary duty cases include intentional use of client information for personal gain, discussed in chapter 4.A.2, and unfair transactions with clients, discussed in chapter 11.F.

There are hard cases, however, where incompetence and disloyalty seem to go hand in glove. A plaintiff may allege that a lawyer performed incompetently because of a conflict of interest between two current clients, for example. The lawyer may have acted self-interestedly in accepting the representation that created the conflict, blurring the lines between these two duties.

Disciplinary rules such as Model Rules 1.7 and 1.9 forbid conflicts of interest. Such rules are based on the risk of harm to clients, however, not actual harm. *E.g. Restatement* § 121. It can be hard for a client to prove that a lawyer engaged in harmful misconduct and these rules provide clients with some peace of mind by forbidding representation where there is a risk of harm. A conflicted representation therefore may violate the duty of loyalty as reflected in the disciplinary rules even if it does not cause harm and thus does not support a civil cause of action for damages. Even then, however, there may be economic consequences for violating a rule: If a lawyer earns fees from a client while representing a conflicting interest the client may be entitled to disgorgement of fees (provided the conflict was severe enough) even if the client suffers no harm. *Restatement* § 37; *cf. Pringle v. La Chapelle*, 73 Cal.App.4th 1000, 1007 (1999) (denying disgorgement claim for non-prejudicial conflict). We will explore this and other problems of overlapping causes of action in more detail in chapter 7.

Why should you care? Differences in these causes of action might affect whether a client may bring a claim against you and, if so, what it might be worth. Depending on the jurisdiction, the fiduciary duty cause of action might be treated differently from a malpractice cause of action in several respects: the need for expert witnesses to establish liability, the need to show damages (and, relatedly, the standard of causation), the limitations period, and the availability of punitive damages.

Finally, courts in some jurisdictions have found a lawyer's fiduciary status relevant to the elements of causes of action that might at first glance seem unrelated to the practice of law. In general, the law presumes that (i) clients trust lawyers to know and do what is best for the client; (ii) lawyers are the smart, experienced parties in the lawyer-client relationship; (iii) these facts give lawyers power over clients; (iv) which power lawyers may misuse to harm clients; and (v) which power the law therefore must police in order to protect clients.

Barbara A. v. John G., 145 Cal.App.3d 369 (1983) illustrates this point. John G. represented Barbara A. in a family law matter. The two became romantically involved during the representation. Barbara later alleged that she had sex with John but only after he promised her that he could not possibly get her pregnant. He did get her pregnant, of course. It was a tubal pregnancy that required surgery that left Barbara sterile.

John later sued Barbara for $1,520 in unpaid fees.[4] She counterclaimed for fraud, battery, and infliction of emotional distress. Barbara argued that John's status as a fiduciary extended to their sexual relationship as well as his legal work. If so, he would bear the burden of showing that he had fully informed Barbara of all circumstances relevant to their sexual encounters and that she had freely consented after such disclosure.

The court did not accept the proposition that John's fiduciary status automatically extended to the parties' sexual relations. The court did leave open the possibility that Barbara could show that she trusted and relied on John to tell the truth, thus forming a "confidential relationship." John's status as her lawyer would be relevant to this factual inquiry but would not be decisive. Here is an excerpt from the opinion:

> "[F]iduciary" and "confidential" have been used synonymously to describe " '. . . any relation existing between parties to a transaction wherein one of the parties is in duty bound to act with the utmost good faith for the benefit of the other party. Such a relation ordinarily arises where a confidence is reposed by one person in the integrity of another, and in such a relation the party in whom the confidence is reposed, if he [or she] voluntarily accepts or assumes to accept the confidence, can take no advantage from his [or her] acts relating to the interest of the other party without the latter's knowledge or consent. . . . ' " Technically, a fiduciary relationship is a recognized legal relationship such as guardian and ward, trustee and beneficiary, principal and agent, or attorney and client (see Frankel, *Fiduciary Law* (1983) 71 Cal.L.Rev. 795), whereas a "confidential relationship" may be founded on a moral, social, domestic, or merely personal relationship as well as on a legal relationship. The essence of a fiduciary or confidential relationship is that the parties do not deal on equal terms, because the person in whom trust and confidence is reposed and who accepts that trust and confidence is in a superior position to exert unique influence over the dependent party.
>
> Our Supreme Court has stated that "[t]he relation between attorney and client is a fiduciary relation of the very highest character, and binds the attorney to most conscientious fidelity. . . . " Further, the court has admonished that "[a] member of the State Bar should not under any circumstances attempt to deceive another person, . . . " Numerous cases have applied these basic principles where an attorney in breaching the fiduciary obligation has gained financial advantage. We can find no valid reason to restrict these principles to actions involving financial claims of a client and not to apply them to

[4] It is often the case that clients raise malpractice or other breach of duty claims against lawyers only as counterclaims when a lawyer sue a former client for unpaid fees. Keep that in mind if you are ever tempted to sue a client for a fee.

actions in which the client alleges physical damage resulting from a violation of the attorney's fiduciary obligation.

Generally, the existence of a confidential relationship is a question of fact for the jury or the trial court. Where a legally recognized fiduciary relationship exists, however, the law infers a confidential relationship, i.e., it becomes a question of law for the court. If the fact finder determines that a confidential relationship exists or the court determines as a matter of law that a fiduciary relationship exists, it is presumed that the one in whom trust and confidence is reposed has exerted undue influence. Because a presumption is no longer independent evidence, the effect of the presumption of undue influence is to shift the burden of proof to the fiduciary. The undue influence in the case before us is, of course, relevant on the issue of consent in appellant's cause of action for battery and on the issue of justifiable reliance in her cause of action for misrepresentation.

Nevertheless, the unique facts in the case before us compel a more cautious approach in imposing on respondent, as *a matter of law*, the highest fiduciary standard in all his relations with appellant, social as well as legal. The existence of a confidential relationship between appellant and respondent is more properly a question of fact for the jury, or court, who can better assess whether the legal relationship was dominant or whether the parties functioned on a more equal basis in their personal relations. Thus, appellant would have the burden of proving the existence of a confidential relationship. If such a relationship were established, respondent would then have the burden of proving that consent was informed and freely given in the battery cause of action, or, in the alternative, that her reliance was unjustified in the misrepresentation cause of action. To hold otherwise would have a chilling and far-reaching effect on any personal relations between an attorney and his or her clients. The possibility of a factual determination of a confidential relationship should be a sufficient warning to monitor the profession in personal or social relations with clients.

Boundary Issues I: When Are You a Lawyer and When Are You Just an Ordinary Person?

When is a lawyer a lawyer and when is a lawyer just a person? May a lawyer represent a client during the day, wearing his "lawyer hat," as it were, and carry on a romance with the client in the evening? If you have a law degree is everything you do "lawyering"? Does the law always look at you as a lawyer, no matter what you are doing? If not, what distinguishes your role as a lawyer from your role as an ordinary person? How do you know what hat you are wearing? Whatever rule the law lays down to distinguish between these roles, what purpose should such a rule serve? What values should it embody and express?

Tante and *Barbara A* both involve lawyers who became romantically involved with clients they represented. You might think that situation would be fairly rare. It happened often enough, however, that we now have rules prohibiting such relationships unless they existed before the attorney began representing the client. Model Rule of Professional Conduct 1.8(j) provides that a lawyer "shall not have sexual relations with a client unless a consensual sexual relationship existed between them when the lawyer-client relationship commenced." California Rule of Professional Conduct 3–120 includes a more lenient provision, which forbids post-representation relationships only if the relationship causes the lawyer to perform legal services incompetently. Cal. R. Prof. C. 3–120(b)(3). (It also specifies that lawyers may not "Require or demand sexual relations with a client incident to or as a condition of any professional representation." *Id.* § 3–120(b)(1). Why do you suppose that situation is specifically mentioned?)

Lawyers and law students often giggle over these rules but they provide a useful perspective on how the law regulates lawyers. As comment 17 to Model Rule 1.8(j) puts it,

> The relationship between lawyer and client is a fiduciary one in which the lawyer occupies the highest position of trust and confidence. The relationship is almost always unequal; thus a sexual relationship between lawyer and client can involve unfair exploitation of the fiduciary role, in violation of the lawyer's basic ethical obligation not to use the trust of the client to the client's disadvantage.

In other words, when you do things with a client—even things that seem to have nothing to do with "lawyering"—the power you are presumed to have as a lawyer, and the trust you are presumed to hold, may affect your legal standing. If you do not represent the person in question, and you make sure no reasonable person could believe you do represent them, then you may act as an ordinary person. Your legal background may still come into play, as might happen if you entered into a contract and later had a dispute in which you argued that you did not understand its terms, but that is a collateral effect of your education not of duties you owe as a lawyer.

In reality the strength of this presumption varies depending on facts such as the client's sophistication and the complexity and novelty of particular matters. A chief executive who hires and fires lawyers all the time, and who may know areas of the law better than many lawyers, is not the same sort of client as Mrs. Herring. The law does not ignore that fact on issues where client sophistication is relevant. The presumption never goes away completely, however. If it is to be rebutted, it will be the lawyer's burden to rebut it.

That the presumption may vary does not mean the duties of care and loyalty are sometimes absent. They are always present. They may apply differently in different contexts (consent to waive a conflict might be easier to obtain from sophisticated than from unsophisticated clients, for example), but some duties apply equally to all clients (the duty to keep client confidences, for example) and neither the duty of loyalty nor the duty of care ever goes away.

Exercise: Framing Legal Ethics

An interesting aspect of *Barbara H* is the way fiduciary duties frame relationships between lawyers and clients. "Frame" here refers to a concept known as "framing," popularized through research by psychologists Amos Tversky and Daniel Kahneman. They defined a frame as "the decision makers conception of the acts, outcomes, and contingencies associated with a particular choice." Amos Tversky & Daniel Kahneman, *The Framing of Decisions and the Psychology of Choice*, 211 SCIENCE 453, 455 (1981).

Tversky and Kahneman's research showed that people respond differently to problems depending on how the problem is presented to them. To see their point, try this simple exercise.

Suppose there is an outbreak of some disease. Two programs are proposed to combat it. If program A is adopted, 200 people will be saved. If program B is adopted, there is a 1/3 chance that 600 people will be saved and a 2/3 chance that no one will be saved. Now suppose that someone proposes programs C and D. If program C is adopted, 400 people will die; if program D is adopted, there is a 1/3 chance that no one will die and a 2/3 chance that 600 people will die.

Choice One

Program A	Program B
200 Saved	1/3 Chance of 600 saved
	2/3 Chance of 0 saved

Choice Two

Program C	Program D
400 deaths	1/3 chance 0 deaths
	2/3 chance 600 deaths

For choice one, do you prefer program A or B? For choice two, do you prefer program C or D?

Tversky and Kahneman found that 72% of respondents favored program A, even though programs A and B are statistically equivalent. You might think that this result only shows that people do not like thinking about life and death in purely statistical terms, such as the "expected" number of lives saved or lost. But Tversky and Kahneman also found that respondents reversed preferences when it came to choice two: 78% of respondents preferred to gamble on program D rather than accept a sure loss of 400 lives. An aversion to statistical thinking does not explain the difference. Instead, people were more willing to take risks to avoid a choice when framed as a loss than they were when the choice was framed as a gain. (We will study loss aversion in more detail in chapter 3.)

What does this have to do with legal ethics? Recall that in *Barbara H* the court says "the essence of a fiduciary or confidential relationship is that the parties do not deal on equal terms, because the person in whom trust and confidence is reposed and who accepts that trust and confidence is in a superior position to exert unique influence over the dependent party." You can think of this as a frame that depicts clients as dependent people, who rely on and are thus vulnerable to lawyers, who in turn are sophisticated, powerful people who have power over clients.

Even if these features are not directly relevant in terms of the elements of a cause of action or defense, they may be very relevant to the way third parties such as judges, jurors, or disciplinary officials view causes of action or defenses. As you study the material in this course and move on into practice remember: You operate in the fiduciary frame.

The Main Points to Recall From Chapter 2 Are:

- All lawyers owe fiduciary duties to clients.
- Agency is one type of fiduciary relationship.
- Most lawyers are agents and are bound by agency law.
- The true fiduciary duty is the duty of loyalty. It requires lawyers to put the interests of their clients first—ahead of the lawyer's personal interests.
- The duty of care requires lawyers to act carefully as defined by the standards of practice for the relevant subject matter and geographic area.
- When lawyers fail to act carefully the law may hold the client responsible for the lawyer's misconduct, leaving the client to settle up with the lawyer.
- The duty of confidentiality requires lawyers not to use confidential client information for their own personal benefit or to the

likely detriment of the client, and not to disclose confidential information without the client's consent.

- Confidential client information is information relating to a representation that is not generally known.
- Lawyers may satisfy one duty, such as the duty of care, while breaching another, such as the duty of loyalty.
- Fiduciary duties create their own cause of action (breach of fiduciary duty) and may affect elements of other causes of action, such as misrepresentation (by creating a duty to disclose).
- The law presumes lawyers are the sophisticated, powerful half of lawyer-client relationships; fiduciary duties reflect this presumption.
- The strength of the presumption will vary according to context; lawyers may rebut this presumption with respect to certain aspects of certain matters, but the fiduciary duties never go away and may not vary with client sophistication.

CHAPTER 3

DIVISION OF AUTHORITY BETWEEN LAWYER AND CLIENT

▪ ▪ ▪

There are some things lawyers may do for clients on their own initiative, some things lawyers may do if the client authorizes them to, and some things only the client may do. The basic disciplinary rule on this topic is Model Rule 1.2(a). It creates a continuum between means and ends: The client decides on the ends of the representation while the lawyer decides on the means. (Although with respect to many means-related decisions clients may exert control if they want to; relatively few decisions are up to the lawyer even if a client objects.) Here is an illustration of the point with examples of some decisions that fall at either end of the continuum.

Authority	
Client	Lawyer
Ends:	**Means:**
Plead	Object to questions
Settle	Manner of questioning

As with continuums generally, this one has grey areas in the middle. The cases in this chapter explore this continuum and related topics. This chapter also explores the concept of authority, which is fundamental to all representation.

The basic points are that a client creates authority for a lawyer to act on his or her behalf by agreeing that the lawyer may do so (authority) or by representing to a third party that the lawyer may do so (apparent authority). Absent such agreement or representations, a lawyer has no power to act for or bind a client.

This chapter also illustrates two things that are very important to practice and often important to ethical issues: Reliance and reputation. People rely on lawyers to say and do things that bind clients. If a lawyer says or does something a client later repudiates the lawyer's reputation will be at stake and, if the lawyer acted carelessly, will be tarnished. The risk of harm to his or her reputation creates potential and sometimes very real conflicts between lawyers and clients.

A. AUTHORITY, APPARENT AUTHORITY, AND INHERENT AUTHORITY

Restatement §§ 14, 26–30

We will begin with some Agency terminology. The first important term is *power. Restatement (Second) of Agency* § 6 defines power as "an ability on the part of a person to produce a change in a given legal relation by doing or not doing a given act." Section seven of the *Restatement* relates power to "authority," which it defines as "the power of the agent to affect the legal relations of the principal by acts done in accordance with the principal's manifestations of consent to him." (The *Restatement Third* does not define power and authority separately, treating these terms in connection with authority, but that treatment is consistent with the old definitions.)

Authority is created by the principal's consent that the agent act on his or her behalf. Section 2.01 of the *Restatement (Third) of Agency* provides that "[a]n agent acts with actual authority when, at the time of taking action that has legal consequences for the principal, the agent reasonably believes, in accordance with the principal's manifestations to the agent, that the principal wishes the agent so to act."

Principals generally do not detail every single thing a lawyer is to do. For example, the principal might ask the lawyer to file a motion objecting to a subpoena. The request creates authority to file the motion on the principal's behalf and also creates a degree of authority to do things necessary to accomplish the act requested. For example, the request to file the motion implies authority to pay any fees that might be necessary to get it filed. The authority by implication is sometimes called *implied authority* but it is better to think of it as actual authority. The main point is that it is based on the client's consent.

How does an agent determine the scope of actual authority? Section 2.02 of the *Restatement (Third) of Agency* provides that actual authority extends to actions "designated or implied in the principal's manifestations to the agent and acts necessary or incidental to achieving the principal's objectives, as the agent reasonably understands the principal's manifestations and objectives when the agent determines how to act." The agent's understanding of the principal's expressions or intentions is reasonable if the agent knows what the principal meant or if the agent interprets the principal's expressions or intentions as a reasonable person would.

A second form of authority is also relevant to the lawyer-client relationship. It is called *apparent authority*. Section 2.02 of the *Restatement*

(Third) of Agency states "[a]pparent authority is the power held by an agent or other actor to affect a principal's legal relations with third parties when a third party reasonably believes the actor has authority to act on behalf of the principal and that belief is traceable to the principal's manifestations."

The two forms of authority are created in different ways. Authority is based on communications between the client and the lawyer, in which the client grants authority to the lawyer. Apparent authority is created by a principal's "manifestations" to third persons with whom the lawyer might deal. If the client tells the lawyer "you may settle the case for $10,000," the lawyer has authority to settle for that amount. If the client tells an opposing party, but not the lawyer, that "I gave my lawyer power to settle for $10,000," then the lawyer has apparent authority, but not authority, to settle for that amount.

The following diagram summarizes the difference between authority and apparent authority. The lawyer-client relationship is depicted vertically, with authority resting on the assent of the client or, in a relatively few cases, on the lawyer's position as a lawyer. The relationship between lawyers and third parties is depicted horizontally. Apparent authority is depicted diagonally, in the comparatively few cases in which a client manifests to a third party that the lawyer has authority to do something:

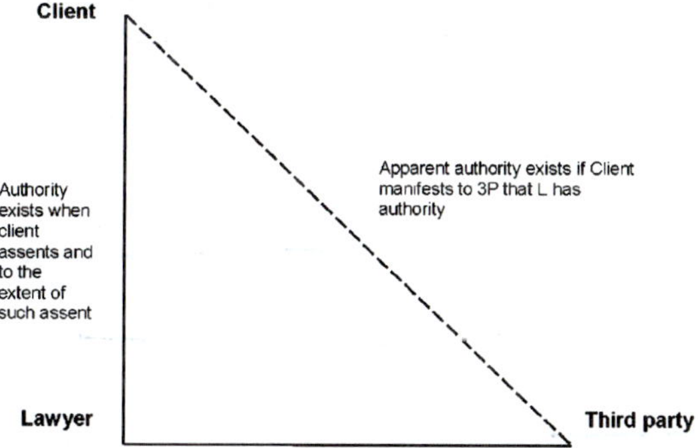

These general principles are sometimes hard to apply to lawyer-client relationships. As a matter of social convention, third parties often assume a lawyer has the power to bind a client to at least some things just because the lawyer is a lawyer. In the terms we used in the Introduction, the power to bind a client is part of the "script" most people have for how lawyers behave. That is true even if the client has neither given the lawyer authority nor created apparent authority by leading a third party to believe the lawyer has the power to act on the client's behalf. The materials in this section explore such problems.

B. CLIENT CALLS

Clients have the final say over the goals or purposes of the representation. These include such things as whether to accept a settlement or whether to plead guilty or not guilty. One implication of this rule, codified in Model Rule 1.8(g), is that where a lawyer represents several clients each one of them must consent to a settlement or a plea; the lawyer for the group may not participate in any settlement that purports to bind the group by majority consent or some means other than individual consent of each affected client. Consent to a group arrangement must be informed, and the group's lawyer must inform each member of the pleas or claims involved and who is (and by implication is not) participating.

Model Rule of Professional Conduct 1.2(a), 1.4, 1.8(g)
Restatement §§ 19–23
California Rules of Professional Conduct 3–500, 3–510

1. AUTHORITY TO SETTLE CIVIL MATTERS

IN RE GRIEVANCE PROCEEDING

171 F. Supp. 2d 81 (D. Conn. 2001)

UNDERHILL, DISTRICT JUDGE.

The Respondent was referred to the Grievance Committee of the United States District Court for the District of Connecticut by a judge of this Court. The referral concerned Respondent's use of a written fee agreement (the "Agreement"), dated November 20, 1996, in which the client: (1) delegated to Respondent complete discretion "with respect to any settlement offers;" (2) authorized counsel to reject settlement offers in counsel's sole discretion, "for any reason whatsoever;" and (3) waived any requirement that Respondent "communicate such settlement offer(s) to" the client. The Grievance Committee concluded that the Agreement violated the Rules of Professional Conduct (the "Rules"), but recommended that this grievance proceeding be dismissed without imposition of any disciplinary action.

The court agrees that the Agreement violated the Rules. Because imposing discipline on the Respondent would not serve the intended purposes of attorney discipline under the circumstances of this case, however, this grievance proceeding is dismissed. This decision will be made public, without use of Respondent's name, in order to improve understanding of and compliance with the Rules.

Background

This matter was referred to the Grievance Committee of the United States District Court for the District of Connecticut (the "Grievance Committee") in December 1998. After receiving a response from the Respondent, the Grievance Committee issued a recommendation dated September 23, 1999. The Grievance Committee concluded that Respondent's fee agreement violated the Rules,[1] but recommended that the grievance complaint be dismissed due to the unique circumstances of this case. Thereafter, this matter was transferred to the undersigned from the judge initially assigned to hear it.

On February 14, 2000, the court remanded the matter to the Grievance Committee for consideration of several questions. The Grievance Committee, after receiving a written submission from and taking testimony of the Respondent, issued a Supplemental Recommendation on July 17, 2000, again concluding that the Agreement violated the Rules, but again recommending that this grievance proceeding be dismissed without imposition of any disciplinary action. The Grievance Committee noted, among other things, that the Respondent had stopped using this form of fee agreement upon learning of the issuance of Connecticut Bar Association Informal Opinion 97–31, which withdrew earlier advice that a lawyer could agree with a client that the lawyer would have the right to reject a settlement satisfactory to the client, but which did not provide for a legal fee to the lawyer's satisfaction. In addition, the Grievance Committee relied on the fact that, despite the terms of the Agreement, Respondent had not kept settlement offers and decisions from the client; instead, Respondent actually did communicate a settlement offer to the client, who rejected it. . . . 

Analysis

Rule 1.2 of the Rules of Professional Conduct provides, in part, that: "A lawyer shall abide by a client's decision whether to accept an offer of settlement of a matter." The Comment to Rule 1.2 explains: "An agreement concerning the scope of representation must accord with the Rules of Professional Conduct and other law. Thus, the client may not be asked . . . to surrender . . . the right to settle litigation that the lawyer might wish to continue." Similarly, the Comment to Rule 1.4 provides: "A lawyer who receives from opposing counsel an offer of settlement in a civil controversy . . . should promptly inform the client of its substance unless prior discussions with the client have left it clear that the proposal will be

[1] FN1. The Recommendation noted that, "on its face, the Agreement is inconsistent with Rule 1.2(a), which requires a lawyer to 'abide by a client's decision whether to accept an offer of settlement of a matter;' and Rule 1.4 which requires the lawyer to keep a client 'reasonably informed about the status of a matter' and to 'explain a matter to the extent reasonably necessary to permit the client to make informed decisions regarding the representation.' Taken together, the Committee concluded that these Rules require that a client be informed of settlement offers and given the opportunity to accept or reject them." Recommendation at 2.

unacceptable. See Rule 1.2(a). Even when a client delegates authority to the lawyer, the client should be kept advised of the status of the matter."

In short, since adoption of the Rules in 1986, the complete surrender of settlement authority to a lawyer has been expressly prohibited in Connecticut. The fundamental principles that a client must be informed of a settlement proposal and that the decision to settle a case rests with the client alone, however, are much older than the Rules.

Respondent seeks dismissal of the grievance, arguing: (1) good faith reliance on Connecticut Bar Association Informal Ethics Opinion 85–19; and (2) Respondent's actions did not violate Rule 1.2 itself, but merely the Comment to Rule 1.2. Neither argument has merit.

Respondent's claimed reliance on the Connecticut Bar Association's Informal Opinion 85–19 was misplaced. Because Informal Opinion 85–19 was premised on the Code of Professional Responsibility, that opinion was called into doubt when the State of Connecticut adopted the Rules of Professional Conduct on October 1, 1986, more than ten years before the fee agreement at issue was executed. . .

Respondent also argues that there was no violation of Rule 1.2(a), but only of the Comment to Rule 1.2. The court disagrees. Implicit in Rule 1.2(a)'s requirement that a lawyer "shall abide by a client's decision whether to accept an offer of settlement" is both a requirement to communicate all settlement offers to the client and a requirement that the client be permitted to decide whether to accept or not to accept any such offer. Nor can a lawyer escape a violation of the Rules if the lawyer's conduct is expressly prohibited by the explanatory language in the Comments, but not expressly prohibited by the Rules themselves. "The Comment accompanying each Rule explains and illustrates the meaning and purpose of the Rule." Rules of Professional Conduct, Note on Scope. Even if the court were to accept Respondent's argument that the conduct at issue was expressly prohibited only by language in the Comment to Rule 1.2, which it does not, Respondent's acknowledgment that the Agreement violated the Comment is sufficient to violate Rule 1.2. . . .

Not every violation of the Rules requires the imposition of discipline. The Rules "presuppose that whether or not discipline should be imposed for a violation, and the severity of a sanction, depend on all the circumstances, such as the willfulness and seriousness of the violation, extenuating factors and whether there have been previous violations." Rules of Professional Conduct, Note on Scope. Under all of the circumstances, the court concludes that discipline is not warranted in this case.

The primary purpose of attorney disciplinary proceedings "is the protection of the court, the profession of the law and the public against offenses of attorneys which involve their character, integrity and professional standing." *Statewide Grievance Committee v. Shluger,* 230 Conn.

668, 681 (1994). Therefore, "[i]f a court disciplines an attorney, it does so not to mete out punishment to an offender, but [so] that the administration of justice may be safeguarded and the courts and the public protected from the misconduct or unfitness of those who are licensed to perform the important functions of the legal profession.". . . . American Bar Association Standards for Imposing Lawyer Sanctions, standard 1.1 (1991) . . .

Under the circumstances of this case, imposing discipline would not serve a legitimate purpose. First, although the Agreement violated the Rules, Respondent's conduct did not. The Respondent did not actually rely on rights purportedly granted by the Agreement when communicating with the client. Moreover, Respondent stopped including language violative of Rule 1.2(a) in new fee agreements before the referral to the Grievance Committee that initiated this proceeding, so this is not a situation involving recalcitrant counsel or counsel likely to violate the Rules in the future unless disciplined.

Second, the passage of time since Respondent's use of the Agreement renders any discipline to be imposed merely punitive; discipline would not now serve to protect the public. Nor is discipline now required to protect the administration of justice. Respondent has continued to practice law in this District since the referral in 1998 without using the offending language in fee agreements. Accordingly, disciplining Respondent years after an unrepeated and relatively minor violation of the Rules that did not actually harm the public would not serve the primary purposes of attorney disciplinary proceedings.

Conclusion

The Grievance Committee's Recommendation and Supplemental Recommendation in this matter (docs. 3, 7) are accepted. This grievance proceeding is dismissed. The clerk is instructed to close this file.

It is so ordered.

CASE QUESTIONS

1. Did the court hold the attorney did not violate the rule?
2. Why wasn't the attorney disciplined?
3. What does this case hold?
4. What is the "primary purpose" of disciplinary rules?

Not all disciplinary rules are worded like Model Rule 1.2. For example, California Rule of Professional Conduct 3–510 states that a lawyer "shall promptly communicate to the [lawyer's] client" all the terms and conditions of any offer in a criminal matter and any written settlement offer in a civil matter. California Business and Professions Code § 6103.5 is to the same effect. Minnesota Rule 1.2(a) states "[a] lawyer shall abide by a client's decision whether to accept an offer of settlement of a matter." In jurisdictions with such rules, must a lawyer convey an offer *from* a client as well as an offer *to* a client? *In re Panel File Number 99–5*, 607 N.W.2d 429 (Minn. 2000), says they must.

In addition, failures to communicate plea offers may raise constitutional issues under the standards the Supreme Court has developed to determine whether a lawyer has provided effective assistance, and thus has acted as the "counsel" to which the Court has held certain defendants have a Sixth Amendment right. (Note: this is *not* a civil malpractice standard.) *Missouri v. Frye*, 132 S.Ct. 1399 (2012), holds that, "as a general rule, defense counsel has the duty to communicate formal offers from the prosecution to accept a plea on terms and conditions that may be favorable to the accused."

PROBLEM 3–1

Why did the attorney include these provisions in the retainer? Why didn't he enforce them?

PROBLEM 3–2

Why can't a client delegate settlement authority to counsel? What is wrong with that?

Purposivism, Discipline and Discretion

The court in *In re Grievance Proceeding* declined to discipline the lawyer in question even though it found he had violated a disciplinary rule. Note 14 to the Preamble to the Model Rules of Professional Conduct (the first Scope note) says "The Rules of Professional Conduct are rules of reason. They should be interpreted with reference to the purposes of legal representation and the law itself."

In re Grievance Proceeding illustrates what this provision means. The lawyer's retainer agreement purported to give him the power to decide whether to accept a settlement offer. The court found that this provision was inconsistent with Model Rule 1.2(a)'s requirement that a lawyer "shall abide by a client's decision whether to settle a matter," a conclusion supported by a comment to Model Rule 1.4, which requires lawyers to keep clients reasonably informed. Model Rule 1.2(a) does not explicitly say "and you can't have the client delegate this power to you in the retainer agreement," but the court looked to the purpose of the rule in deciding whether the lawyer violated it. Because the purpose of the rule is to give clients power over settlements, the contractual provision delegating that power to the lawyer violated the rule.

In one sense this result seems paradoxical. The court effectively says the Rules are designed to preserve the client's autonomy and authority, which they do by penalizing lawyers who ask clients to exercise that autonomy and authority to delegate power to the lawyer. You may think of Model Rule 1.2(a) as a mandatory contract term that neither lawyers nor clients are free to alter.[2] This rule might make sense if one believed, as cases such as *Tante* and *Barbara A* suggest, that lawyers are powerful, sophisticated parties from whom clients must be protected. From that perspective, one can see how agency and fiduciary principles run through the disciplinary rules.

So why doesn't the court discipline the attorney? No harm, no foul. The attorney included the provision in the retainer but did not actually enforce it. He conveyed the settlement offer to the client, and abided by the client's rejection of it. (Note here that he violated the rule just by putting the term in the agreement.) When he learned that the applicable rules had changed, he changed his retainer agreement. His conduct adhered to the law even though his agreement didn't. In that case, the court found, no purpose would be served by disciplining him.

In re Grievance Proceeding is not the average case. You shouldn't count on getting a free pass if you violate a disciplinary rule. (That is especially true if the violation involves deception of any kind, or any financial misconduct; you get no breaks in such cases.) The case provides useful clues on how to think about disciplinary rules, however. When analyzing the rules, think about what purpose the rules are trying to accomplish, and how your conduct relates to that purpose. Purposive analysis is relevant to both the probability and magnitude (and thus the expected cost) of discipline.

Lawyers have adopted various tactics to try to regain some of the control Rule 1.2 denies them. Here are some examples.

[2] *Restatement* § 22(1) states that the decision "whether and on what terms to settle a claim" belongs to the client "except when the client has validly authorized the lawyer to make the particular decision." Section 22(3) states that a client may revoke authority granted to a lawyer, however, a provision that only makes sense if the client knows a decision has to be made.

Assigning Around?

Suppose you represent plaintiffs in civil rights suits in which a successful plaintiff may be entitled to attorney's fees. Suppose also that defendants often ask plaintiffs to agree to settlements in which the plaintiff waives his right to such fees. In a case where the complaint asks for a change in conduct or policy, for example, a government entity might agree to change the conduct or policy as part of a settlement but require that the plaintiff waive attorney's fees, which could be your principal or even only way of getting paid. Could you get around this problem by having your client assign to you his or her right to claim fees?

The court in *Pony v. County of Los Angeles*, 433 F.3d 1138 (9th Cir. 2006), said "no." Attorney Michael Mitchell agreed to represent Ms. Pony in bringing tort claims against the County of Los Angeles. He had her sign a retainer including such an assignment of her right to any statutory fee award. The county offered to settle for a lump sum, including fees. Mitchell wrote counsel for the county stating that the offer created a conflict of interest for him, in light of his statutory obligation not to delay the case in pursuit of personal gain. Cal. Bus & Prof. Code § 6128(b). The County left the offer open, Mitchell resigned, Pony accepted the offer, and the court dismissed the case.

Mitchell then filed motions aimed at collecting his fees, based on the assignment in the retainer agreement. The district court ruled that he had no standing to pursue a fee claim; the Ninth Circuit affirmed. The court held "Pony's putative assignment to Mitchell is invalid because the right to seek attorney's fees under 42 U.S.C. § 1988 is a substantive cause of action which cannot be transferred contractually."

A settlement refusal tax?

Would it violate Rule 1.2(a) for a lawyer to write a contingent fee contract that said the lawyer would cover litigation expenses unless the client unreasonably rejected a settlement offer, in which case the client would be liable for such expenses? How about a provision holding the client liable only for expenses incurred after rejecting the offer?

Washington State Bar Association Informal Opinion 2148 (2007) finds that both provisions would violate the rule. Reasoning that costly options are harder to exercise than free ones, the opinion holds that lawyers may not include a provision in a written contingent fee agreement requiring a client to pay costs advanced towards litigation if the client rejects a settlement offer that appears to counsel to be fair and reasonable under the circumstances.

In *Compton v. Kittleson*, 171 P.3d 172, 177 (Alaska 2007), the Alaska Supreme Court held unlawful a fee agreement in which the lawyer would represent the client on a contingent basis unless the client accepted a settlement offer that would generate a fee for the lawyer amounting to less than $175 per hour. In that event, the agreement provided, the client would owe the lawyer an amount reflecting that rate. The court held "Alaska law prohibits a fee agreement that uses a client's decision to settle as a trigger to convert contingent-fee representation into an obligation to pay hourly fees because a hybrid agreement of this kind impermissibly burdens the client's exclusive right to settle a case."

Anti gag-rule provisions?

The Los Angeles County Bar Association was asked to opine on the following scenario:

"In the present case the attorney, a retired physician, became an attorney for the purpose of creating a nonprofit organization to represent patients denied medical care or given inadequate care by managed health care organizations. Through his organization, the attorney hopes to improve the standards of care throughout the managed care industry by alerting regulators to violations and exposing fraudulent practices to consumers.

To that end, the attorney seeks to include a clause in the initial engagement agreement which provides that, under certain conditions, the client will not agree to a confidentiality clause in any settlement. The provision reads in pertinent part as follows:

> 3. GAG CLAUSE SETTLEMENTS RULED OUT
>
> [Attorney's firm] and I agree that acceptance of money in return for silence about wrong-doing is repugnant, immoral, and possibly illegal. Therefore, as a matter of policy and in return for the very advantageous fee structure herein, I agree that neither [Attorney's firm] nor its attorneys will be required to agree to any clause in any proffered settlement which requires that they refrain from disclosing, to regulatory agencies or consumer groups, information about any acts or policies of HMO which they reasonably believe may adversely affect public health or safety, represent consumer fraud, or violate any regulations or laws. I authorize [Attorney's firm] to make this limitation known in advance to opposing counsel.
>
> I realize and accept that this may result in loss of an otherwise beneficial settlement, and I have been given the opportunity to seek alternate counsel.
>
> If I nevertheless accept a settlement containing such a gag clause, as I have a right to do, and I cooperate in obtaining a judicial order binding [Attorney's firm] or its attorneys to it as well, then the waiver of fees outlined below will not occur, and I will pay [Attorney's firm], as the reasonable value of its services, its full fee for all the time spent on my case, plus reimbursement of its expenses, for which it will have a lien upon the settlement recovery.

Attorney claims that most of the attorney's clients are unable to obtain legal representation and typically must pay large medical bills. The clients cannot pay hourly fees and are often seeking only equitable remedies leaving little chance for a contingency fee. The attorney, therefore, is providing free or reduced fee legal services to clients who are otherwise unable to obtain representation on the condition that the client does not agree to keep the results of any settlement confidential."

Note that, unlike the first two provisions, this provision purports to serve the public interest in exposing unlawful conduct as well as private interests of the lawyer and client. L.A. County Bar Association Opinion 505 (2000) finds this tactic acceptable: "An attorney may ethically include in an engagement agreement terms that include a reduction of the attorney's fee as long as the client does not agree to keep any settlement confidential, provided the client retains the authority to settle the case without the lawyer's consent and without the imposition of any penalty that would constitute an unconscionable fee."

Can you distinguish between a penalty for agreeing to a gag clause and a fee reduction for not agreeing to one? Note the reference to unconscionable fees, which we will study in chapter 14.A.3.

Majority rule settlement

A related question can arise in "aggregate" litigation. Suppose you represent a large number of individual clients (not a class, but a large number of individuals), such as 100+ franchisees, in a particular matter. Each client has the same claims. May you ask them to sign a retainer in which they consent to any settlement approved by a majority of the clients?

No. Model Rule 1.8(g) provides that a lawyer representing more than one client in a related matter may not agree to an aggregate settlement "unless each client gives informed consent, in a writing signed by the client." The rule further requires that in obtaining such consent the lawyer disclose "the existence and nature of all the claims or pleas involved and of the participation of each person in the settlement." *The Tax Authority, Inc. v. Jackson Hewitt, Inc.*, 187 N.J. 4 (2006), illustrates the operation of this rule. Four plaintiffs formed a steering committee to evaluate the claims, and they recommended a settlement, approved by a (weighted) majority of the clients. 18 Clients refused to sign, and the defendant sued to enforce the settlement against them.[3] The court ruled that the advance consent to any settlement approved by a majority of clients violated New

[3] The retainer language provided: "[t]he Client agrees that the Matter may be resolved by settlement as to any portion or all of the Matter upon a vote of a weighted majority of the Client and all of the Co–Plaintiffs. Each Plaintiff shall have one vote for each funded RAL for the 2002 Tax Season. The Client will be eligible to vote only if current in all payments required under this agreement. . . . A quorum for such vote shall be sixty percent (60%) of the votes eligible to be cast."

Jersey's Rule 1.8(g), which is substantively the same as the Model Rule. According to the court: "Before a client may be bound by a settlement, he or she must have knowledge of the terms of the settlement and agree to them."

Clients can play that game, too

These three examples involve lawyers attempting to control settlement. But clients can use their approval power as leverage against lawyers, too. In *Dweck Law Firm, L.L.P. v. Mann*, 340 F.Supp. 2d 353 (S.D.N.Y. 2004), a firm represented a client with respect to gender-related claims against her employer. The firm received a flat fee plus a contingency interest in any recovery. The client ultimately decided not to pursue claims against her employer and instead "go on with her life." She nevertheless received a $1,350,000 settlement offer from her employer.

The client refused to execute a settlement agreement, allegedly because she wanted to deprive her lawyers of the fees the settlement would generate for them. The firm sued her for breach of the covenant of good faith and fair dealing implied in every contract (and thus in the retainer agreement). The district court denied the client's motion to dismiss the claim:

> Where a client refuses a settlement offer because she believes her claim is worth more, and that her attorney has not effectively advocated on her behalf, she is not acting in bad faith. The client would have an absolute right to terminate the attorney in such circumstances. Moreover, the terminated attorney likely could not prevail on a claim for breach of the covenant of good faith and fair dealing because the attorney would be unable to demonstrate that the client rejected the settlement in bad faith or in an effort to harm the attorney. If, on the other hand, the client believes the settlement offer is satisfactory, but refuses it because she does not want to forfeit any of the recovery to her attorney, her actions may constitute bad faith. Nonetheless, she would not lose her absolute right to terminate the attorney, and the termination itself would not give rise to a cause of action. However, the client's bad faith conduct during the course of the representation *may* be actionable. Allowing the attorney to protect himself in this way is not "incompatible" with the client's right to terminate the attorney-client relationship; a client may always terminate her attorney. However, the fact that a client has an absolute right to terminate her attorney at any time does not give her free reign to abuse the attorney, or act in bad faith in her dealings with the attorney, during the course of the representation.
>
> It will be the rare case, indeed, where an attorney may bring an action against a client as a result of the client's refusal to accept a proposed settlement. . . . [But here] Dweck claims that Mann *told*

Dweck she would accept the settlement proposals if Dweck substantially reduced or eliminated the fee. . . .

The court's opinion merely denied a motion to dismiss. The docket reveals, however, that the plaintiff law firm prevailed after a short bench trial.

Thinking Dynamically and Interactively II

You can think of an agreement that asks clients to give lawyers the power to reject settlements as an attempt to hedge the risk that lawyers and clients may disagree about whether to accept a settlement offer. The agreements, in other words, are written because lawyers are thinking dynamically and interactively—they are exercising sound judgment about a type of problem they are likely to face. The rule voiding such provisions is needed precisely because the lawyers who write disciplinary rules do exactly the same thing.

You can see this by thinking of litigation as a simplified game involving three players: a plaintiff, a plaintiff's lawyer, and a defendant. (The defendant has a lawyer, too, but I collapse them to simplify.) Suppose the plaintiff's lawyer thinks that if the case goes to trial there is a 30% chance of receiving a $10,000 award and a 70% chance of receiving a $250,000 reward. The expected value of going to trial would therefore be $178,000 (($10,000 x .3 = $3,000) + ($250,000 x .7 = $175,000)). The following table summarizes these results.

Probability	Result	Expected Value (P x R)
.3	$10,000	$3,000
.7	$250,000	$175,000
		$178,000

Suppose further that it will cost the lawyer $30,000 to prepare and try the case and that the lawyer gets 1/3 of any recovery as a fee. Suppose as well that the client is risk-averse and does not like the idea of getting only $6,667 (2/3 of $10,000) if the trial goes badly. Finally, suppose defense counsel has ascertained that the client is risk-averse (which she might do during the client's deposition, for example).

If the defendant agreed with the plaintiff's counsel's estimate of the likely result of a trial, the defendant might try to settle the case for less than $178,000, which is the expected cost to the defendant of a trial verdict. Obviously the defendant wants to settle as cheaply as possible. The defendant therefore might propose a settlement that would be much better for the plaintiff than the worst that the plaintiff could do, and also much better for the defendant than the worst the defendant could do.

Suppose the defendant offers $50,000. A risk-averse plaintiff might accept the award, even though the net result after fees, $33,334 ($50—($50/3)), was lower than the expected result from going to trial: $118,667 ($178—(178/3)). Notice that the lawyer's share of $50,000—$16,666—is not enough to cover the costs the lawyer incurs in going to trial. That means that if the lawyer incurs a significant fraction of those costs before settlement the case is a money-loser for the lawyer. That may be one reason why the term is in the agreement.

You can think of this situation in terms of the following diagram. The effect of the term granting counsel power to approve settlements is to take the choice away from the client, therefore rendering the "settle" option a nullity.

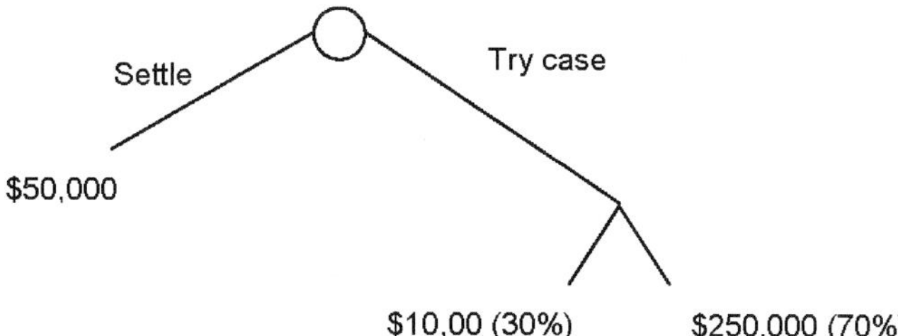

Notice the process by which counsel arrives at the conclusion that he needed to write the retainer agreement to eliminate the left-hand branch of this tree. Counsel (i) realized that the moves the defense might make would affect his relationship with the client, so that defense counsel had to be taken into account in drafting the retainer; (ii) realized that his client might be risk averse, and therefore have preferences that differed from his own; (iii) thought about how the defense might exploit this characteristic; (iv) thought ahead to the possibility of a settlement offer that the client would like but he would not; (v) realized that such an offer would be attractive to the defense, which might also recognize this vulnerability in the client relationship and try to take advantage of it; and (vi) wrote a term guarding against this risk. That is what dynamic and interactive thinking looks like.

Diversification, Risk Tolerances, and Client Conflicts

In the illustration above, the client is willing to accept a low settlement offer because the client is risk-averse. Implicit in the conflict the illustration describes is a difference between the client's risk-aversion and the lawyer's: the lawyer is willing to tolerate a greater risk of a low verdict than the client is willing to tolerate.

Not all lawyers will have greater tolerance for risk than all clients, in all cases, of course. Sometimes a lawyer might have reasons to prefer a sure but modest payout over a chance at a home run. Such situations would likely present loyalty problems, as might be the case if the lawyer favored a quick but cheap settlement to solve the lawyer's own cash-flow problems. But it is at least a plausible conjecture that, on average, lawyers may be less risk averse than clients. Why might this be the case?

One answer is that lawyers might be more diversified than clients with respect to the risk of litigation. If a lawyer has a number of cases that are not identical to each other, so that a weakness in one does not imply a weakness in all, the lawyer might be willing to take a risk on one particular case knowing there is a good chance that some of the other cases will provide enough of a payoff so the portfolio of cases as a whole generates an acceptable return. In contrast, the client in a particular case is likely to care only about that case. A complete loss would leave the client with nothing, while the lawyer could move on.

A rational lawyer will not pursue a case that has a negative expected value, of course, but a diversified lawyer might well be less concerned with risk in a specific case than the client in that case would be. This difference in risk tolerance could generate the conflict over settlements to which Model Rule 1.2 is relevant.

Diversification will appear in a different and more favorable light when we study the question of in-house counsel. (It is an important element in the California Supreme Court's decision in *General Dynamics Corp. v. Superior Court*, 7 Cal.4th 1164 (1994), discussed in chapter 9.) There the point is that diversification provides independence from client demands that un-diversified lawyers such as in-house attorneys do not enjoy. The point here is that independence can create problems as well as solve them.

Prospect Theory and Valuation

The diversification explanation above points to an important reason why lawyers and clients might value a case differently but it does not discuss the fundamentals of valuation. Indeed, to the extent it touches on the subject at all it assumes a particular way of valuing gains and losses, in which the nominal amount of a gain or loss is multiplied by the probability that it will be realized. That method is associated with neoclassical economics, and it has important virtues. Practicing lawyers commonly value cases that way. It does not fit with social science data regarding how people actually make decisions, however.

Prospect theory is an important aspect of modern cognitive psychology that takes these data into account. It also provides lawyers with useful insights that can help them deal with mistakes in their own judgments or those of their clients.

It is useful to explain the theory by comparing it to the presumptions employed by neoclassical economic analysis. That analysis presumes that people evaluate gains and losses in a particular way: (1) They evaluate the amount of a gain or loss by itself, not by reference to something else; (2) they value uncertain gains and losses by multiplying the nominal gain or loss by the probability that it will occur; and (3) the resulting expected gains and losses are evaluated in a linear fashion, which is to say that people value the marginal gain or loss at the same rate as the initial gain or loss (i.e., the $1,000th dollar counts for $1, just like the first dollar).

Prospect theory holds that each of these assumptions is wrong. In particular, it takes into account several observations from experiments in which people were asked to evaluate gains and losses: (1) They do so with respect to some reference point, rather than in purely nominal terms; (2) They weight losses more heavily than gains, and thus display "loss aversion"; and (3) they show diminishing sensitivity to the size of gains or losses (i.e., the $1,000th dollar counts less to them than the first). As a result, loss curves are convex and gain curves are concave, rather than being linear.

The following diagram, adapted from Paul Brest & Linda Krieger, PROBLEM SOLVING, DECISIONMAKING, AND PROFESSIONAL JUDGMENT (2010) (in turn adapted from Daniel Kahneman & Amost Tversky, *Prospect Theory: An Analysis of Decision under Risk*, 47 ECONOMETRICA 263, 279 (1979)), summarizes the theory:

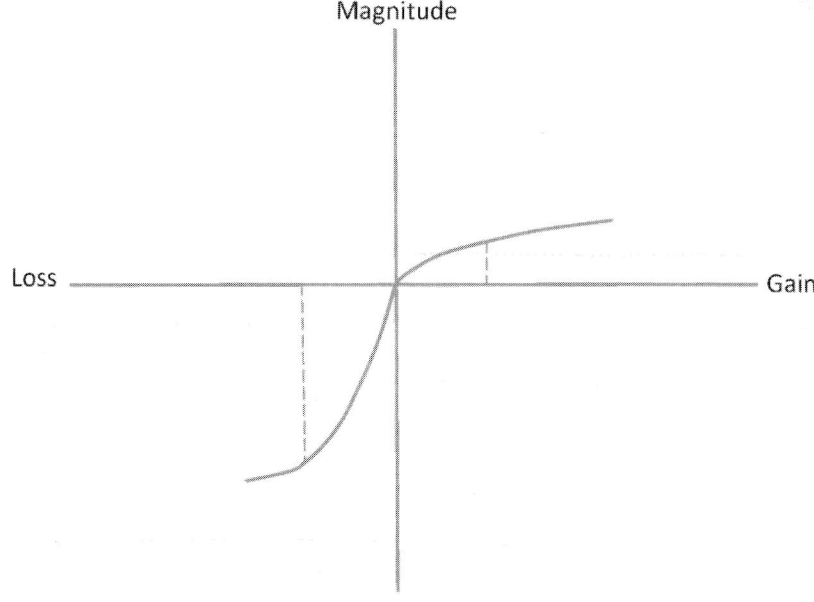

Note that in this diagram the curve is steepest as it intersects the origin on the graph, which is the reference point. This steepness reflects the fact that people are sensitive to departures from the reference point and do not simply think in terms of $500 gained or lost. Note also that the loss curve slopes more steeply than the gain curve, reflecting the fact that people feel losses more keenly than gains. And, finally, note that neither curve is linear; as the losses or gains mount, the curve begins to flatten out, reflecting the fact that people feel marginal losses and gains less keenly than initial departures from the reference point.

These tenets of prospect theory have important implications for practicing lawyers. For one thing, reference points are not given. They may vary from person to person, and they are sensitive to framing. Recall the exercise in chapter 2: it worked as it did because framing a policy as avoiding a loss tapped into the phenomenon of loss aversion. Put differently, if a lawyer understands loss aversion, she may frame problems for clients or jurors in order to take advantage of or defuse that phenomenon. In dealing with a client, for example, a lawyer might make a settlement offer seem like a loss by comparing it to higher numbers, or make it seem like a gain by comparing it to lower numbers.

More saliently for this course, a lawyer who understands loss aversion should watch for its effects in her own decision-making. Throughout this course we will see examples of lawyers "doubling down"—trying to avoid a bad result by taking a risk that leads to a worse result. Understanding the judgmental biases captured by prospect theory is therefore an important step in learning to protect yourself from yourself, as well as learning to help your clients.

For a nice application of these theories to legal problems, *see* Richard S. Painter, *Irrationality and Cognitive Bias At A Closing in Arthur Solmssen's* The Comfort Letter, 69 FORD. L. REV. 111 (2000).

2. APPARENT AUTHORITY

The *Restatement (Third) of Agency* § 2.03 defines a second type of authority, called apparent authority: "Apparent authority is the power held by an agent or other actor to affect a principal's legal relations with third parties when a third party reasonably believes the actor has authority to act on behalf of the principal and that belief is traceable to the principal's manifestations."

This definition is slightly less precise than the definitions used in the *Restatement (Second) of Agency*, which is quoted in the following case. The main point remains unchanged, however: Authority is created by communications from the principal (client) to the agent (lawyer). Apparent authority is created by representations from the principal (client) to a third party. *See also Restatement (Third) of the Law Governing Lawyers* § 27.

LOUIS FENNELL V. TLB KENT COMPANY

865 F.2d 498 (2d Cir. 1989)

MAHONEY, CIRCUIT JUDGE:

Plaintiff-appellant Louis Fennell commenced this action in the United States District Court for the Southern District of New York on January 7, 1985 against his employer, alleging wrongful discharge because of his race and age in violation of 42 U.S.C. § 1981 (1982). Fennell was represented by C. Vernon Mason and several of his associates, including Fred K. Brewington.

The case was on Judge Stanton's ready calendar on January 6, 1987. On January 16, 1987, however, Brewington and Eugene Frink, defendants' attorney, agreed to settle the case for $10,000 during a telephone conversation. The settlement was reported to the court by both attorneys in a telephone conference call on January 20, 1987. The district court issued an order of dismissal on the same day which provided that either party could apply to the court by letter to restore the case to the court's calendar within sixty days of the order. The settlement was conditioned upon Fennell signing a general release and a stipulation of discontinuance being filed with the court, which never occurred.

Fennell expressed his dissatisfaction with the settlement in a letter to the district court dated March 28, 1987. Fennell there contended that he had told Brewington on January 16, 1987 that he would not approve a $10,000 settlement, but he was willing to settle the case out of court "with the intentions of getting it out of the way and behind me." He also claimed that he had told Mason on January 20, 1987 that $10,000 was not a satisfactory settlement, and that he had tried several times in early February, 1987 to contact Mason's office by telephone about the case, but elicited no response. Fennell further stated that he had gone to Mason's office on February 20, 1987, at which time Mason informed him that the case has been settled for $10,000, whereupon Fennell reiterated his dissatisfaction with that settlement.

On February 27, 1987, Fennell wrote Mason expressing his dissatisfaction with the settlement agreement and indicating that he had "no further use of [Mason's] services." A copy of this letter was sent to the district court and received there on March 3, 1987. On March 20, 1987, Brewington wrote to the district court requesting that the "matter be restored to the calendar as the settlement which was authorized and accepted by our client is no longer acceptable to him," and that Mason and his associates be released by the court as counsel to Fennell.

Following a status conference on June 5, 1987, the district court held a hearing on June 16, 1987 to determine whether Fennell's case should be restored to the calendar. At the conclusion of the hearing, the district court dismissed the action and approved the settlement. This ruling was based upon a finding that Fennell's attorney had been clothed with "apparent authority" when he settled the case, and the court's expressed view that "[t]o allow a client to reject a settlement which has been agreed upon by his attorney with apparent authority is to open the door to a mild form of chaos."

On appeal, Fennell asserts that it was an abuse of discretion for the district court not to have vacated its order of dismissal pursuant to Fed.R.Civ.P. 60(b)(1). Appellees contend that since Fennell's attorney was clothed with apparent authority to settle the case, Fennell is bound by that settlement.

Discussion

A. *The Applicable Law.*

. . . . [T]wo circuits have ruled that where an action is based upon federal law, the authority of an attorney to settle that action is a federal question. . . . In the absence of weighty countervailing considerations, we are inclined to follow our sister circuits in deeming federal law applicable to the question before us. In any event, to the extent that deference might be accorded to New York precedents concerning what is at root a fairly general question of agency law, *see Greater Kansas City Laborers Pension Fund v. Paramount Indus.,* 829 F.2d 644, 646 (8th Cir.1987) (rules governing attorney's authority to settle case "the same as those which govern other principal-agent relationships"), the outcome would in our view be the same, as will hereinafter appear.

B. *The Merits.*

We turn now to the district court's determination that Fennell's attorney was clothed with apparent authority to settle the case, resulting in denial of the motion to vacate the prior order of dismissal.

We begin with the undisputed proposition that the decision to settle is the client's to make, not the attorney's. On the other hand, if an attorney has apparent authority to settle a case, and the opposing counsel has no reason to doubt that authority, the settlement will be upheld. *International Telemeter Corp. v. Teleprompter Corp.,* 592 F.2d 49, 55 (2d Cir.1979).

The district court made the following findings concerning the issue of apparent authority: 1) that Mason and his associates represented Fennell "in dealing with the other side," 2) that they were authorized to appear at conferences for him, 3) that Fennell knew that settlement was being discussed, 4) that Fennell did not tell his counsel not to continue discussing

settlement, 5) that Fennell would have accepted a higher settlement figure ($50,000–75,000), and 6) that Fennell did not tell defendants' counsel that the authority of plaintiff's counsel was limited in any way. The district court concluded that Fennell's counsel "had every appearance of being authorized to make a binding agreement with [defendants' counsel]." The district court then applied the common law principle that an agent clothed with apparent authority binds the principal as to actions taken within the scope of that authority, together with the principle favoring settlement agreements, to conclude that Fennell was bound by the settlement agreement.

Apparent authority is "the power to affect the legal relations of another person by transactions with third persons, professedly as agent for the other, arising from and in accordance with *the other's manifestations* to such third persons." Restatement (Second) of Agency § 8 (1958) (emphasis added). Further, in order to create apparent authority, the *principal must manifest to the third party* that he "consents to have the act done on his behalf by the person purporting to act for him." *Id.* § 27. Second Circuit case law supports the view that apparent authority is created only by the representations of the principal to the third party, and explicitly rejects the notion that an agent can create apparent authority by his own actions or representations.

In this case, taking the facts as the district court found them, Fennell made no manifestations to defendants' counsel that Mason and his associates were authorized to settle the case. Fennell's attorneys accordingly had no apparent authority to settle the case for $10,000 without Fennell's consent. The district court's findings that Mason and his associates represented Fennell, and that they were authorized to appear at conferences for him, do not prove otherwise. A client does not create apparent authority for his attorney to settle a case merely by retaining the attorney. *See United States v. Beebe,* 180 U.S. 343, 352 (1901).

Further, the court's findings that Fennell knew settlement was being discussed, did not ask his attorneys not to discuss settlement, would have accepted a higher settlement figure, and did not tell defendant's counsel that the authority of plaintiff's counsel was limited in any way, do not lead to a different outcome. These findings involve only discussions between Fennell and his attorneys or things that Fennell did *not* say to opposing counsel. None of these findings relates to positive actions or manifestations by Fennell to defendants' counsel that would reasonably lead that counsel to believe that Fennell's attorneys were clothed with apparent authority to agree to a definitive settlement of the litigation.

Finally, we note that the application of state law would not yield a contrary result. Since all parties are New York residents and the settlement negotiations occurred in New York, New York law would obviously be applicable. Defendants contend that *Hallock v. State,* 64 N.Y.2d 224,

474 (1984), would call for a decision in their favor if New York law were considered applicable. We disagree.

Hallock held that a stipulation of settlement made by counsel in open court may bind his clients even where it exceeds his actual authority, provided that there is apparent authority. In that case, however, an applicable court rule required that attorneys attending pretrial conferences have authority to enter into binding court settlements on behalf of their clients, a co-plaintiff attended the conference from which Hallock was absent because of illness, and more than two months passed before plaintiffs made any objection to the settlement. *Hallock* explicitly recognized that "without a grant of authority from the client, an attorney cannot compromise or settle a claim," 64 N.Y.2d at 230, and that:

> Essential to the creation of apparent authority are *words or conduct of the principal, communicated to a third party,* that give rise to the appearance and belief that the agent possesses authority to enter into a transaction. The agent cannot by his own acts imbue himself with apparent authority.

64 N.Y.2d at 231 (emphasis added).

We do not think the rule stated in *Hallock* would apply here, where a purported settlement agreement was reached in a telephone conference by counsel in which no party participated and Fennell made prompt objection to that agreement upon being advised as to its terms. *See Gordon v. Town of Esopus,* 486 N.Y.S.2d 420, 421 (3d Dep't) (*Hallock* "can and should be read" as limited to cases involving stipulations in open court), *leave to appeal denied,* 65 N.Y.2d 609 (1985). The generally applicable New York rule is that " '[a] party who relies on the authority of an attorney to compromise an action in his client's absence deals with such an attorney at his own peril.' "

We realize that the rule we announce here has the potential to burden, at least occasionally, district courts which must deal with constantly burgeoning calendars. A contrary rule, however, would have even more deleterious consequences. Clients should not be faced with a Hobson's choice of denying their counsel all authority to explore settlement or being bound by *any* settlement to which their counsel might agree, having resort only to an action against their counsel for malpractice. In any event, even if we were to consider such a rule advisable, the applicable precedents and settled principles of agency law would preclude its adoption.

CASE QUESTIONS

1. How are authority and apparent authority different?

2. What law (state or federal) did the court hold governs settlement authority in federal court?
3. How is apparent authority created?
4. What facts did the district court believe justified enforcing the settlement?
5. Why was the trial court finding of "every appearance" of authority not enough here?
6. How is the *Hallock* case different from this case?

Some courts disagree with *Fennell's* conclusion that federal law governs authority to settle cases in federal court based on federal claims. In *Makins v. District of Columbia*, 277 F.3d 544 (D.C. Cir. 2002), the parties disagreed on whether state or federal law should govern an alleged settlement of a claim under Title VII. The court relied upon prior circuit precedent, which "held that whether the parties have reached a settlement is a matter of local law." The court surveyed the relevant precedents and found "national disarray" on the question whether state or federal law governs issues such as the authority question in *Fennell*. *See also* Grace M. Giesel,*Enforcement of Settlement Contracts: The Problem of the Attorney Agent,* 12 GEO. J. LEGAL ETHICS 543, 563–80 (1999).

PROBLEM 3–3

Look at the language in Brewington's letter to the court (at the end of the fourth paragraph in the opinion). Why did Brewington write the letter that way? Whose interests did it serve?

Agency Cost I: The Importance of Reputational Capital and Conflicts Between Your Client and Your Reputation

You will have noticed from cases such as *Tante* and *Barbara A* that you don't stop being human when you become a lawyer. In economic terms, we can say that lawyers are as self-interested as anyone else, which is to say that lawyers try to get the things they want in the least costly way.

The self-interest of a lawyer can create a conflict between the lawyer's interests and the client's. To take a simple example, all else being equal a self-interested lawyer would rather be paid a high fee than a low one. Even a lawyer on a fixed salary, as government lawyer or in-house attorney might be, would rather work less than more (again, all else being equal) because the less a lawyer puts into the job (the cost of work) the greater the net benefit from the salary. Public interest lawyers may find it more satisfying to try to reform social institutions or practices than to work on specific (possibly mundane) individual problems, accepting a low wage in return for the chance to influence social policy.

Other types of divergence are less obvious but no less real. Lawyers may pursue work past the point of diminishing returns, for example, turning out beautiful but unnecessarily expensive briefs that may burnish the lawyer's reputation but cost more than is needed to get a job done.

Excessive risk-aversion also may cause the lawyer's interests to diverge from the client's. It is harder to see than slacking off or perfectionism but it may be as common or even more common. Risk-averse counsel may worry that they will be second-guessed if they fail to warn a client of something that later happens. They therefore might warn clients of, and spend money hedging against, improbable risks the client cannot assess directly. Such a lawyer might exaggerate even risks she knows are improbable, so when they do not materialize she can take credit for having guided the client safely through waters the client thinks are treacherous but which are actually calm. A less malevolent lawyer might exaggerate all risks simply to avoid being blamed for not having provided adequate warning.[4] In each case the lawyer's interest in looking good, or at least in not looking bad in hindsight, can cost the client unnecessary fees or cause the client to forgo lawful business opportunities. Either result is costly.

Agents who pursue their own interests rather than sticking strictly to the interest of the principal create costs for the principal. Such costs are referred to in general terms as agency costs.[5] Because such costs make agency relationships less efficient, the law tries to limit them. Fiduciary duties try to limit such costs by requiring agents to do what is best for the principal rather than themselves. Model Rule 1.2's requirement that the client control the goals of a representation is another example of a cost-reducing rule.

Laws cannot eliminate agency cost, however. Clients may not have the information they need to assess counsel's performance, so fiduciary violations may go undetected. Clients may rely so heavily on counsel for advice that the allocation of authority is more form than substance. There are, however, two other forces that combine with legal rules to limit agency costs: competition and reputation (which we saw play an important role in Dennis's trouble in the Introduction).

---

4 Donald C. Langevoort & Robert K. Rasmussen, *Skewing the Results: The Role of Lawyers in Transmitting Legal Rules*, 5 S. CAL. INTERDISC. L.J. 375 (2001).

5 *E.g.* John C. Coates IV, *Explaining Variation in Takeover Defenses: Blame the Lawyers*, 89 CAL. L. REV. 1301, 1309–10 (2001); George M. Cohen, *When Law and Economics Met Professional Responsibility*, 67 FORDHAM L. REV. 273, 283–88 (1998); Jonathan R. Macey and Geoffrey P. Miller, *An Economic Analysis of Conflict of Interest Regulation*, 82 IOWA L. REV. 965, 968 (1997).

Suppose for purposes of analysis that there are two types of lawyers: faithful agents and faithless agents. (In the real world, of course, there is a continuum of lawyers running from very faithful to relatively unfaithful; if disciplinary rules and competition work even moderately well, there should be relatively few totally faithless lawyers.) Competition among lawyers helps limit agency costs because, in a reasonably efficient market, lawyers who are faithful agents will be more attractive to clients and get more business than lawyers who are faithless agents. Faithless lawyers will face pressure to shape up or exit the market.

Reputation helps limit agency costs because it is the primary means by which competition occurs. Competition will not reward faithful lawyers and weed out unfaithful ones unless clients have a way of telling the two types of lawyers apart. In economic terms, this is an information problem. To make choices, clients need information about which lawyers are good and which are bad. Reputations provide clients such information by distilling information about a lawyer (let's call him *X*) from past clients, other lawyers who have worked with or against *X*, and judges or other officials who have seen *X* in action. Clients hire or decline to hire lawyers based on reputations. The aggregate of such choices drives competition among lawyers, which in turn constrains the degree of agency costs clients must bear.

Reputations are not perfect, of course. It is often very hard to tell whether a lawyer has done a bad job or just had a hopeless case. Suppose, for example, that a criminal defense lawyer decides to call a client to testify in her own defense and the client is then convicted. Is that an example of bad judgment on the lawyer's part, or was the client a bad witness, or was the case hopeless anyway because the prosecution's case was so strong? Who knows? You don't get definitive answers to such questions. Sometimes you are criticized or praised when you don't deserve to be. In the end, however, reputations and skill tend to correlate well enough to support reasonably competitive markets.

What does all this have to do with apparent authority? Although we cannot know for sure what happened between Fennell and Brewington, it is possible to read the case as an example of how important reputation is and how it may create tensions between a lawyer and client.

Recall that after Fennell fired the Mason firm Brewington wrote to the court and asked that the "matter be restored to the calendar as the settlement which was authorized and accepted by our client is no longer acceptable to him." Why did Brewington say that the client had authorized and accepted the settlement? That certainly did not help Fennell. It made it more likely that the court would enforce the settlement, which is not what Fennell wanted. It is of course possible that the letter simply told the truth, but Brewington did not have to say anything about Fennell in order to make this request. So why the disclosure? (Remember—if the court found that Brewington had authority it would not have to rely on apparent authority, so don't accept the letter at face value.)

On this reading, the letter helped protect Brewington's reputation. Suppose Brewington worried that the court would think he had erred by agreeing to a settlement he had no power to agree to. Brewington might worry that the judge would think he had bad judgment and would be less likely to trust him in similar situations in the future. He might worry that the judge would talk to other judges or to lawyers who would come to share this opinion, giving Brewington a bad reputation. By stating explicitly that Fennell had agreed to the settlement and was trying to back out, Brewington represents himself as the diligent and careful victim of a fickle client rather than as a negligent or perhaps dishonest attorney.

If the court accepts this explanation, Brewington's reputation with the court survives intact but at the expense of Fennell's interests. The situation thus presents a trade-off in terms of reputation. Is it better to have a bad reputation with the court and a good one with Fennell or vice versa? On this reading of the case, one might conclude Brewington opted to protect his reputation with the court and accept the risk that Fennell might bad-mouth him. Would that be rational? Probably. Brewington makes his living in court so his reputation among judges would be very important to him. He would be a repeat player before judges, whereas he might only have the one matter for Fennell. And how likely is it that a prospective client would track down Fennell, at least as compared to hearing about Brewington from a judge or from someone who had heard about Brewington from a judge?

Perhaps there is another, better explanation for the events related in the opinion. On this reading, however, Brewington's letter illustrates how much practicing lawyers value their reputations. This interpretation also is a good introduction to the forces that can set your self-interest against the interests of your clients. Much of this course, and much of your practice, will be an exercise in managing this tension.

Penumbras and Emanations: Inherent Agency Power

Authority and apparent authority are the most important sources of power for most lawyers. Historically, however, there was a third type of power, called "inherent agency power" or, sometimes, "inherent authority." Understanding this source of power requires you to distinguish two types of agents: general and special. According to the *Restatement (Second) of Agency* § 2, "[a] general agent is an agent authorized to conduct a series of transactions involving a continuity of service." Insurance agents and store clerks would be examples of general agents. "A special agent is an agent authorized to conduct a single transaction or a series of transactions not involving continuity of service." Most lawyers are special agents.

Section 8A of the *Restatement (Second) of Agency* defines "inherent agency power" as "a term used . . . to indicate the power of an agent which is derived not from authority, apparent authority or estoppel, but solely from the agency relation and exists for the protection of persons harmed by or dealing with a servant or other agent." The point of this "power" is to avoid harm to third parties by binding a principal to an agent's acts "regardless of the consent or manifestations of the principal." Grace M. Giesel, *Enforcement of Settlement Contracts: The Problem of the Attorney Agent*, 12 GEO. J. LEGAL ETHICS 543 (1999). In most cases courts will find inherent agency power only with respect to general agents, which means there will be relatively few cases in which the black-letter doctrine applies to lawyers. *Id.* at 562–63.[6]

The notion of inherent agency power has been elusive in practice, and the *Restatement (Third) of Agency* does away with it. Nevertheless, and notwithstanding the division of authority reflected in Model Rule 1.2, and the fact that most lawyers are special rather than general agents, you sometimes see the concept used in connection with the power of lawyers. You often see courts stretching to express something similar to inherent agency power to enforce what the court sees as a genuine settlement one party no longer wants.

PROBLEM 3–4

Suppose you represent a client in a breach of contract action. In preparation for an upcoming mandatory settlement conference, you ask your client what she would be willing to accept in settlement of her claim. She replies that she does not know how to value a case, or what a good settlement would be, so she has to trust your judgment. She reminds you that she expected to earn $50,000 on the contract, and that she has already paid you $10,000 in fees, and she states she would like to get at least that much, so she would be no worse off for hiring you than she would have been if the contract had been performed. Do you have authority to settle the case? For how much? Do you have apparent authority to settle the case?

---

[6] It is important to distinguish inherent agency power (or inherent authority) from the similar-sounding notion of "implied authority." Implied authority is a form of actually authority. It applies when the principal gives power to an agent that grant of power implies the power to do what is necessary to achieve the purposes of the grant. By contrast, inherent authority is relevant only when there is no actual authority. So instead of looking to the principal's grant of authority, a party relying on an inherent authority theory argues that authority inheres in some position held by an agent or in some set of contextual facts.

The following table summarizes the three types of authority discussed above.

Type of authority	Created by	Grants power to
Authority	Assent of client, manifested to lawyer	Alter client's legal rights and obligations within bounds of client assent
Implied authority (Still "Authority")	Implication from assent of client, manifested to lawyer	Do things necessary to carry out client instruction
Apparent authority	Manifestations by client to third party that lawyer has authority	Alter client's legal rights and obligations within bounds of manifestation

---

Performative Utterances and the Practice of Law

Growing up you may have heard the aphorism "sticks and stones may break your bones, but names can never hurt you." The notion behind the aphorism was that you could ignore name-calling because it was just words, not physical harm. That notion, of course, was ridiculous. Name-calling hurts, which is just one example of an aphorism that is both true and highly relevant to the practice of law: "Words are deeds." Ludwig Wittgenstein, CULTURE AND VALUE ¶ 46e (P. Winch trans. 1980).

Lawyers practice law with words. Depending on the context, a lawyer's words count as the acts of advocacy, negotiation, counseling, threatening, warning, examining, and so on. Just as the words "I offer" and "I accept" may form a contract, and thus place parties under obligations the law will enforce, a lawyer's words can create legal obligations for herself, her clients, and others.

As you know from your own experience, the meaning of language depends on the context in which language is used. Two people stand in front of a third person dressed in clerical clothing. They promise each other to have and to hold, for richer and for poorer, in sickness and in health, until death. Are they married? It depends. If they are on stage, they are not. Their language performs an action, but it is the action of putting on a play, not of getting married. If they are in a church or garden, maybe. But you do not know yet. What if both of them are men or both women? In some states they may be married but in others they will not be.

The general point is that meaning depends on context, and that is true when you practice law, too. But what is a context? What does it consist of and how do you tell one from another? How do you know what context you are in, and how do you change the context if you don't want to be in the one you are in?

The answer to these questions is complex, but it will invariably involve the intersection of three things: (i) the facts at hand; (ii) the legal rules pertaining to those facts; and (iii) social norms and expectations pertaining to the situation. In a sense this division is arbitrary, because what counts as "the facts" depends in part on the applicable laws and norms. For example, one important "fact" in most cases would be whether you dealt with a client or non-client but whether someone is a client is a legal conclusion that rests in part on social norms and expectations. Nevertheless, even though these three things interact, you can think of them as conceptually distinct for purposes of helping you identify the relevant aspects of a situation.

You may combine these points to distill a very important conclusion regarding judgment in the practice of law. Because (i) lawyers practice through words, which can be deeds; (ii) the meaning of words depends on the context in which they are used; (iii) contexts are created by the intersection of facts, rules, norms and expectations; therefore (iv) in order to exercise judgment about your own conduct you must be sensitive to the intersection you are in, and change it if you do not want to be there. For example, if you are in court in a jurisdiction following the approach adopted in the *Hallock* case, discussed in *Fennel*, those facts (that you are in court and that the court follows that rule) make your words highly performative in terms of binding your client. You are presumed to have authority to do so.

If you do not want to operate in this context you may and should change it. How? By disclaiming authority to bind the client. (In fact, if you do not actually have authority to bind the client the court suggests you are obligated to disclaim it.) Your disclaimer is a performative utterance—it performs the important task of letting everyone know where you stand, and therefore where they stand in relation to you—but the task the words perform is to change the context rather than to accomplish a result within a particular context.

BLANTON V. WOMANCARE INC.

38 Cal.3d 396 (1985)

GRODIN, JUSTICE.

Plaintiff Harriette Blanton appeals from a judgment upon an award entered for defendants in an arbitration proceeding arising out of the alleged malpractice of a medical student during an abortion performed in the clinic of defendant Womancare, Inc. Plaintiff contends the trial court erred in refusing to nullify the agreement providing for the dispute to be resolved through binding arbitration, because the stipulation to submit her claim to this procedure was made without her consent. Plaintiff's point is well taken. Accordingly, we reverse and remand to the trial court with instructions to set aside the arbitration agreement and subsequent award, and order a trial de novo.

On February 17, 1977, plaintiff allegedly suffered a perforated uterus during an abortion performed by a fourth-year medical student at the clinic of defendant Womancare. Plaintiff brought an action for malpractice against the clinic, the student, and the supervising physician. The case was set for trial on July 29, 1980.

Wesley Harris was employed by plaintiff as her attorney in the malpractice action. He prepared the necessary complaints, then requested that the trial be continued until April 6, 1981. His request was granted. Shortly thereafter, the trial was continued until July 30, 1981, again at Harris's behest. On July 28, 1981, two days before the case was finally to be tried, Harris requested an agreement from defendants that the case be submitted to arbitration.

An examination of Harris conducted by the trial judge reveals Harris discussed the possibility of arbitration with his client at some point before he approached defendants with his offer to arbitrate. Harris conceded, however, that his client would only consent to arbitration if her right to a trial de novo were preserved.[7] Nevertheless, when on July 28, 1981, Har-

[7] FN1. Harris testified as follows:

"Q. Did she tell you when you had the discussion and recommended arbitration that she objected to any arbitration?

"A. Yes. She indicated that she wanted a trial and I thought that it would be best to go to arbitration and to see what an arbitrator would award, and if she wasn't happy we could go to trial.

"Q. What did she say?

"A. She said, that's fine.

"Q. She said it's all right to go to arbitration?

"A. But not binding.

"Q. All right. Was that conversation before you signed the letter agreeing to binding arbitration on her behalf?

"A. There was no discussion about binding arbitration before I signed this letter. . . .

"Q. Did you discuss binding arbitration with her?

"A. Never, I never even knew there was binding arbitration until you mentioned it."

ris obtained a stipulation from defendants that the case be submitted to arbitration, the agreement contained the following provisions:

> "1. The captioned case will be taken off the trial calendar and submitted to *binding* arbitration.
>
> "2. Any award rendered to the plaintiff in arbitration shall be limited to a maximum of $15,000.
>
> "3. Daniel S. Belsky, attorney for defendant, Womancare, shall have the right to select the arbitrator pursuant to the following conditions:
>
> "(a) There shall be only one arbitrator.
>
> "(b) The arbitrator shall be an individual reasonably familiar with the law pertaining to medical malpractice.
>
> "(c) Mr. Belsky's right to choose the arbitrator shall be exclusive in the event he chooses an arbitrator whose practice consists primarily of defending medical malpractice actions.
>
> "(d) In the event Mr. Belsky chooses an arbitrator whose practice consists primarily of prosecuting medical malpractice actions, said individual shall also be approved by Mr. Wes Harris."[8] (Emphasis supplied.)

The stipulation was approved by the court, which issued an order to arbitrate . . . The order declared, "The arbitration and award shall be binding." Harris also sought, and obtained, a dismissal with prejudice of defendant's supervising physician from the lawsuit.

Plaintiff did not learn of this stipulation, nor of the dismissal of the supervising physician, for nearly three months. When apprised that her attorney had submitted her dispute to binding arbitration, she immediately objected, and fired Harris. She then hired new counsel, and through him moved to invalidate the stipulation to binding arbitration executed by Harris, as well as the stipulation to dismiss the supervising doctor from the lawsuit, on the ground she had never given her consent to either decision.

The physician withdrew his opposition to the motion to set aside the dismissal, and was reinstated as a party defendant. The trial court, however, affirmed the validity of the agreement for binding arbitration, apparently in the belief the agreement concerned a "procedural" matter within the scope of an attorney's unilateral discretion. After a continuance in the arbitration proceeding was granted to allow new counsel an

---

[8] Harris testified, and plaintiff argues, that the trial court gave the attorneys the limited option of going to trial or accepting binding arbitration. It was under the compulsion of this narrow choice, plaintiff contends, that Harris submitted to binding arbitration. While the record is not clear on the point, it appears that defendant's counsel indicated it would submit to arbitration only if it were binding; under these circumstances, the judge simply stated the choices available to the parties. Harris chose binding arbitration.

opportunity to prepare for the hearing, the proceeding was held and the arbitrator ruled for the defense. Plaintiff's new attorney filed a request for trial de novo, but was notified that since the arbitration was binding the request was "not acceptable." Thereafter, the award was entered as a judgment and plaintiff appealed.

I

The stipulation which the attorneys entered into in this case, since it provided that the award would be binding, was something of a hybrid. From a legal standpoint it could be viewed as an agreement for private arbitration, governed by the general arbitration statute, or as an agreement for judicial arbitration with advance waiver of the right to request a de novo trial... In either event, however, the legal effect of the agreement, if it be given effect, was to relinquish the rights of the parties to judicial trial, whether by court or jury, and to waive any right to judicial review except upon the extremely narrow grounds accorded to arbitration awards under the arbitration statute and the Judicial Arbitration Act alike.

Of course, such an agreement may often be in the best interests of a client. Here, however, the client did not consent to the agreement; she did nothing beyond retention of the attorney to suggest that he had authority to enter into such an agreement on her behalf; and she repudiated the agreement as soon as she learned of it. The question is whether she is nevertheless bound by her attorney's signature, purportedly on her behalf.

II

In our analysis of this question we distinguish at the outset between the rights which a client may have against his attorney for breach of a duty owed the client, and the right which an opposing party or the court may have to rely upon a stipulation or agreement which an attorney has made, purportedly on his client's behalf. The two categories are related, but not necessarily congruent, for a client may be bound by the actions of his attorney and at the same time have a legal claim against him on the ground that those actions were undertaken without or in excess of authority. Here, the question concerns the binding effect of the attorney's agreement.

As a general proposition the attorney-client relationship, insofar as it concerns the authority of the attorney to bind his client by agreement or stipulation, is governed by the principles of agency. Hence, "the client as principal is bound by the acts of the attorney-agent within the scope of his actual authority (express or implied) or his apparent or ostensible authority; or by unauthorized acts ratified by the client."

It is undisputed in this case that plaintiff's attorney, in signing the arbitration agreement, acted not only without his client's express authority but contrary to her express instructions. Consequently, though subject to the possibility of ratification which we consider later in this opinion, she is bound by the agreement only if the attorney had either implied actual authority or apparent authority to enter into the agreement on her behalf.

An attorney retained to represent a client in litigation is clothed with certain authority by reason of that relationship. "The attorney is authorized by virtue of his employment to bind the client in procedural matters arising during the course of the action. . . . 'In retaining counsel for the prosecution or defense of a suit, the right to do many acts in respect to the cause is embraced as ancillary, or incidental to the general authority conferred, and among these is included the authority to enter into stipulations and agreements in all matters of procedure during the progress of the trial. Stipulations thus made, so far as they are simply necessary or incidental to the management of the suit, and which affect only the procedure or remedy as distinguished from the cause of action itself, and the essential rights of the client, are binding on the client.' [Citation.]" (*Linsk v. Linsk* (1969) 70 Cal.2d 272, 276–277.)

The authority thus conferred upon an attorney is in part apparent authority—i.e., the authority to do that which attorneys are normally authorized to do in the course of litigation manifested by the client's act of hiring an attorney—and in part actual authority implied in law. Considerations of procedural efficiency require, for example, that in the course of a trial there be but one captain per ship. An attorney must be able to make such tactical decisions as whether to call a particular witness, and the court and opposing counsel must be able to rely upon the decisions he makes, even when the client voices opposition in open court. In such tactical matters, it may be said that the attorney's authority is implied in law, as a necessary incident to the function he is engaged to perform. . . .

An attorney is not authorized, however, merely by virtue of his retention in litigation, to "impair the client's substantial rights or the cause of action itself." (*Linsk v. Linsk,* supra, 70 Cal.2d at p. 276.) For example, "the law is well settled that an attorney must be specifically authorized to settle and compromise a claim, that merely on the basis of his employment he has no implied or ostensible authority to bind his client to a compromise settlement of pending litigation.". . . . Similarly, an attorney may not "stipulate to a matter which would eliminate an essential defense [citation]. He may not agree to the entry of a default judgment [citation], may not . . . stipulate that only nominal damages may be awarded [citation] and he cannot agree to an increase in the amount of the judgment against his client. [Citation.] Likewise, an attorney is without authority to waive findings so that no appeal can be made. . . . " (*Linsk v. Linsk,* supra, 70 Cal.2d at p. 278; see *Bowden v. Green* (1982) 128

Cal.App.3d 65, 73–74 [no authority to dismiss cross-complaint].) Such decisions differ from the routine and tactical decisions which have been called "procedural" both in the degree to which they affect the client's interest, and in the degree to which they involve matters of judgment which extend beyond technical competence so that any client would be expected to share in the making of them. . . .

It is, of course, accepted practice within the legal profession, and one that is commendable, for attorneys to rely upon representations made by other attorneys with respect to the scope of their authority. As in the case of any other agency, however, apparent authority is created, and its scope defined, by the acts of the principal in placing the agent in such a position that he appears to have the authority which he claims or exercises. If authority is lacking, then nothing the agent does or says can serve to create it. (See Seavey, Agency (1st ed. 1964) Definitions, § 8D, p. 13.). . . .

The agreement which plaintiff's attorney entered into, purportedly on his client's behalf, called for binding arbitration which, as we have explained, entails a waiver of all but minimal judicial review. It provided for unilateral selection of the arbitrator by the defendant's attorney, from among attorneys whose practice consists primarily in *defending* medical malpractice actions. And, it waived any right to recovery beyond $15,000. By any test, these are consequences which affected substantial rights of the client. Moreover, the agreement did not constitute a tactical maneuver in pending litigation; rather, it called for a *diversion* of the dispute from the judicial to the arbitral arena. It was a contract to arbitrate, such as might be entered into in the absence of any litigation at all.

"[A]bsent express authority, it is established that an attorney does not have implied plenary authority to enter into contracts on behalf of his client. [Citation.]" (*Wilson v. Eddy* (1969) 2 Cal.App.3d 613, 618.) And, that authority is not enlarged simply because the contract is entered into in conjunction with pending litigation. . .

Here, similarly, an attorney, merely by virtue of his employment as such, has no apparent authority to bind his client to an agreement for arbitration. We find no reason in logic, or policy, for holding his apparent authority in that respect is enlarged by reason of the fact that he has been retained to engage in litigation. When a client engages an attorney to litigate in a judicial forum, the client has a right to be consulted, and his consent obtained, before the dispute is shifted to another, and quite different, forum, particularly where the transfer entails the sort of substantial consequences present here. . .

Finally, while unauthorized acts of an attorney may be binding upon his client through ratification (*Fidelity & Casualty Co. of New York v. Abraham,* supra, 70 Cal.App.2d 776, 783), no ratification appears here. Immediately upon learning of the arbitration agreement plaintiff fired her attorney and engaged new counsel to set it aside. At that point defense counsel, knowing of plaintiff's objections and her attorney's lack of actual authority, could have allowed the case to proceed to trial but chose not to do so. Only after the trial judge refused to invalidate the agreement, and reaffirmed his order that the case proceed to arbitration, did plaintiff appear and participate in the arbitration hearing. . . . The judgment is reversed.

CASE QUESTIONS

1. Can this case be squared with *7108 West Grand Avenue*? How are they alike or different?
2. What standard did the court establish for limiting counsel's authority to agree to something on behalf of a client?
3. Under this case, would Harris have authority to consent to *non-binding* arbitration?
4. What are the terms of the arbitration? Do they favor one side or the other?

PROBLEM 3–5

After reading *Blanton*, how would you deal with an opposing attorney who proposed arbitration?

PROBLEM 3–6

Would defense counsel or Womancare, Inc. have a claim against Harris? *See* Restatement § 30(3).

PROBLEM 3–7

Suppose you are a new associate working for Ms. Blanton's counsel and, as trial approaches, you realize your firm is not prepared for trial. Your boss tells you not to worry about trial preparations because he is confident the case will go to arbitration, and there will be more time to prepare. What should you say? Do you have any obligations in this regard? To whom?

Suppose further that your boss returns from a meeting and informs you of the arbitration terms outlined above. He instructs you to prepare an agreement for counsel to sign memorializing those terms. May you or must you do so? Suppose you are aware of Ms. Blanton's instructions that she would participate only in non-binding arbitration. Would that fact affect your analysis? Suppose finally that Ms. Blanton must sign the agreement and your boss instructs you to send it to her with a cover letter asking her to sign. What should you do?

Where Does Trouble Come From? Doubling Down I

Blanton does not tell us why the arbitration agreement read as it did. It does provide the basis for a useful hypothetical exercise. (With respect to *Blanton*, we do not know for sure why counsel agreed to the terms and we do not want to second-guess counsel unfairly. There may be some fact not related in the opinion that makes his choice make sense. Because we do not know the answers to these questions in *Blanton*, we'll use generic names for the lawyer and client.)

Suppose a plaintiff, Ms. B, told the truth when she testified that she authorized her lawyer, Mr. H, to agree only to nonbinding arbitration and specifically told him that she would not consent to binding arbitration. If that were the case, why would Mr. H, agree to binding arbitration?

Perhaps Mr. H thought Ms. B would get a better result that way? The problem with this theory is that no facts suggest a reason why that might be and the terms of the arbitration agreement make the theory hard to accept. After all, the arbitration agreement capped Ms. B's possible damages at $15,000. Even if this cap might be considered sensible for some reason, why would her lawyer agree to binding arbitration before an arbitrator *selected by defense counsel*?

If this answer seems implausible, what other answers might explain the facts? Suppose you went to work for a small firm representing Ms. Blanton on a contingent fee basis, so that your firm would not get paid unless she won her case. Suppose further your boss decided the case was a loser. He therefore might want to avoid putting time and money into the case so he could cut his losses. Binding arbitration might allow him to avoid out-of-pocket costs such as hiring experts, taking depositions, and so on. It would also allow him to devote much less time to the case and spend more time on cases with better profit potential.

On these suppositions, your boss would have a conflict between his desire to make money (which he would use to pay you, don't forget) and his duties of care and loyalty to Ms. B. Even if your boss wanted to cut his losses, however, he would not want to do so in a way so obvious as to raise suspicions that he was serving his own interests at Ms. B's expense. An arbitration agreement that was one-sided against the client might do that. Perhaps a different hypothetical explanation might fit the facts better.

Consider the timing of the case as a whole. The injury occurred in 1977. The opinion does not say when the complaint was filed but it does say the case was initially set for trial on July 29, 1980. Ms. B's counsel requested that the trial be delayed until April 6, 1981. That request was granted. He then requested that the trial date be bumped back another three months, to July 30, 1981. That request was granted, too, so that at counsel's request the trial had been moved back a year from the original trial date, which itself would have been set for some considerable period after the complaint was filed, to allow time for discovery and motion practice.

Ms. B's lawyer requested arbitration on July 28, two days before trial. That he accepted such unfavorable terms—binding arbitration before a defense-selected arbitrator with a cap on damages—suggests that the defense had the power in negotiating the terms of arbitration. Why did the defense have the power? Perhaps it was because the defense case was so strong, though in that event why not just try the case and get it over with? (As noted above, one reason might be that arbitration would cost less, though one would have to include the risk of appeals over the award in calculating the expected cost.)

Another explanation, perhaps equally plausible, is that counsel chose to arbitrate because that would postpone the trial. Maybe he was not ready for trial. Arbitration would take some time to arrange and would require less preparation, providing breathing space to get ready. If this conjecture were correct, counsel would have violated Ms. B's instructions and sold out her interests (by agreeing to such unfavorable arbitration terms) to cover up his own fault in not being ready for trial.

Suppose for purposes of analysis that this conjecture is correct. You may think of this strategy as an example of "doubling down." That happens when an attorney realizes she has violated some rule or duty and then decides to violate another rule or duty in the hope that the second violation will cover up the first.

Doubling down violates Rule Six: If you mess up, fess up. Doubling down is never a good idea. It makes bad situations worse. Often, the first violation is relatively innocuous. Perhaps counsel was not prepared because he had a family emergency. Or, less sympathetically (but it happens), perhaps he had a drug or alcohol problem. Perhaps he had just taken on too much work and could not get it all done. None of these reasons would get a lawyer off the hook for being unprepared. On these facts, if he showed up on July 30 and admitted he was not ready to try the case the court might dismiss the case for lack of prosecution and Ms. B might sue him for malpractice. (As we will see, that can be a tough claim to prove. Ms. B would have to show that she had a good claim—i.e., that she would have won if counsel had been prepared.) Counsel would have to look to his malpractice insurer for solace.

Nevertheless, though none of these reasons would excuse counsel from liability to Ms. B if his negligence caused her harm, each of these reasons represents ordinary human frailty. They would not show plaintiff's counsel to be greedy, dishonest, or sneakily self-serving. Doubling down changes all that. When a lawyer tries to cover one violation with another he invariably shows himself to be unworthy of client trust. Often he shows himself to be dishonest. If this version of the story of Ms. B's case is correct, then honest thing for her lawyer to have done would have been to admit to Ms. B and to the court that he was unprepared, ask for yet another extension of the trial date, and take the consequences if he did not get it. (If he was not prepared, trying the case would not have been an acceptable option.)

Self-serving misconduct invites worse punishment than mere negligent conduct. An attorney who acts negligently may be civilly liable but she is less likely to be disciplined than an attorney who puts her own interests before her clients' interests. Thus Rule 6: If you mess up, fess up.

Doubling Down and Loss Aversion

As you will see throughout this course, doubling down is surprisingly common. Smart people make stupid choices that make bad results worse. Why is that?

No doubt there are many reasons, which vary case by case. But one common reason may be the tendency for people to feel losses more keenly than gains—loss aversion. Loss aversion might make some people unwilling to take risks that might lead to losses, a reaction we may call risk aversion. But loss aversion might also make people more willing to take risks to avoid losses they are otherwise certain to incur. Their aversion to losses might lead them to "double down" precisely because they feel the initial loss so keenly and (to borrow from a separate element of prospect theory) because they feel further losses less keenly than the initial losses.

Here is an example that illustrates this tendency, similar to the one you read in chapter 1. Suppose you are presented with two financial choices.

Choice A	Choice B
A sure gain of $240	A 25% chance of receiving $1,000, and a 75% chance of receiving $0

Choice C	Choice D
A sure loss of $750	A 75% chance to lose $1,000 and a 25% chance to lose $0

What are your choices? In experiments conducted by Daniel Kahneman and Amos Tversky, 84% of respondents chose A over B, and 87% of respondents chose D over C. They were, in other words, willing to take the big risk of losing $1,000 for a relatively slight chance of losing nothing. They were willing to double down.[9]

Doubling down is not some erratic, irrational response that only other people have. It might be the result of a very natural tendency that most people have—the tendency to feel losses very keenly and to be all too willing to take risks to avoid them. Thus a corollary to Rule Six: Beware the loss frame. If you work with people who are facing a serious loss they are more likely (which is not to say necessarily very likely) to do the wrong thing to try to avoid the loss. You may not be able to stop them, but you must be able to avoid being dragged down with them.

Client Ratification

The Court in *Blanton* mentioned that Ms. Blanton could have ratified Harris's acceptance of the arbitration but did not. The doctrine of ratification allows principals to accept the benefits of actions their agents have taken without authority or apparent authority. The flip side of accepting the benefits, of course, is that a principal who ratifies an act must also accept the costs of that act. According to the *Restatement (Third) of Agency* 4.01(2), ratification does not occur unless a principal manifests assent to the act or engages in "conduct that justifies a reasonable assumption that the person so consents." Ratification may also create an agency relationship after the fact, which might happen if A engaged in conduct benefiting B even though A was not B's agent. B could ratify the conduct, thus retroactively making A an agent for B.

Ratification focuses on the principal's intention. As comment a to this section of the *Restatement* puts it, "the sole requirement for ratification is a manifestation of assent or other conduct indicative of consent by the principal. To be effective as a ratification, the principal's assent need not be communicated to the agent or to third parties whose legal relations will be affected by the ratification." Ratification is subject to some common-sense constraints, such as the rule that ratification is not effective if the principal lacked knowledge of facts material to the transaction, unless the principal ratified knowing that he lacked such knowledge, as well as some constraints that might seem less intuitive, such as the "equal dignities" rule that ratification of an action required to be in writing must itself be written. *See* Cal. Civ. Code § 2310.

---

[9] Note that this combination of choices is inferior to the opposite choice. Combining A and D means a sure gain of $240 is added to a 75% chance of losing $1,000 and a 25% chance of losing nothing, which combine to produce a 75% chance of losing $760 (—$1,000 + $240) and a 25% chance of gaining $240. Combining B and C means a sure loss of $750 is offset by a 25% chance of gaining $250, producing a 75% chance of losing $750 and a 25% chance of gaining $250.

C. LAWYER CALLS

Disciplinary rules sometimes allocate authority, at least presumptively, to lawyers rather than clients. This allocation tends to occur on issues where lawyers are likely to have much greater expertise than clients or where the court has an interest in moving a case along efficiently. Not all allocations of authority have these characteristics, however, as the next case illustrates.

1. CRIMINAL MATTERS

Model Rules of Professional Conduct 1.2(c), 1.14
Restatement of the Law Governing Lawyers § 24

ARKO V. COLORADO

183 P.3d 555 (Colo. 2008)

JUSTICE BENDER delivered the Opinion of the Court.

This case arises from a domestic altercation between Johnnie Erick Arko and a woman he had been periodically dating. The victim told Arko over the phone that she thought they should see less of each other. Later that evening, Arko called the victim and said he was coming to her house with a pizza. The victim thought Arko had been drinking and told him not to come over. Arko arrived at her home anyway and entered without knocking or ringing the doorbell. After Arko surprised the victim by appearing in the living room, an argument began which resulted in a physical altercation.

Arko testified that the altercation lasted only a few minutes. He admitted to causing injury but denied attempting to kill the victim or to cause serious bodily injury. The victim testified that it was a much more violent incident that lasted for a half-hour. She testified that Arko choked her repeatedly and that she was unable to breathe or speak, that he pinned her to the floor with his knees on her shoulders while he strangled her, and that he hit her in the mouth with his fist. She also described a karate-style hold Arko used that she said felt like it would cause her head to snap. She testified that Arko repeatedly said she was going to die that night. . . .

Arko was tried on charges of attempted second-degree murder, second-degree burglary with intent to commit second-degree murder, and second-degree burglary with intent to commit third-degree assault. The jury acquitted him on the burglary charges, but a mistrial was declared when the jury was unable to reach a verdict on the attempted murder charge. This charge was retried to another jury. The jury was instructed on attempted second-degree murder and the lesser included offense of attempted reckless manslaughter. The jury found Arko guilty of attempted reckless manslaughter, and the trial court sentenced him to five years in the Department of Corrections, a sentence in the aggravated range.

Arko appealed his conviction to the court of appeals, claiming, among other things, that the trial court erroneously refused his trial counsel's request to instruct the jury on the lesser non-included offense of third-degree assault. He argued that the trial court was obligated to submit this instruction to the jury, even though he himself objected to the submission of this instruction. The court of appeals held that the trial court did not err because the decision whether to request a jury instruction on a lesser non-included offense implicates a defendant's fundamental rights and therefore belongs to the defendant. . . .

Some trial decisions implicate inherently personal rights which would call into question the fundamental fairness of the trial if made by anyone other than the defendant. Thus, a lawyer must abide by a client's decision regarding "a plea to be entered, whether to waive jury trial, and whether the client will testify." Colo. RPC 1.2(a). Indeed, these rights are so important to the integrity of the legal process that the decision to waive them may require a trial court to determine that the defendant has made a voluntary, knowing, and intelligent decision.

Other decisions are regarded as strategic or tactical in nature, and final authority to make such decisions is reserved to defense counsel. "Defense counsel stands as captain of the ship in ascertaining what evidence should be offered and what strategy should be employed in the defense of the case." *Steward v. People,* 179 Colo. 31, 34 (1972). Examples of such strategic decisions include "what witnesses to call (excepting the defendant), whether and how to conduct cross-examination, what jurors to accept or strike, and what trial motions to make." The attorney has the authority to make tactical decisions with which the client disagrees.

In this case, the court of appeals concluded that the decision whether to request a lesser non-included offense instruction implicates a defendant's fundamental rights because it is more like a decision to plead guilty than a tactical decision. . . The court reasoned that because the decision exposes the defendant, who may be convicted of both the greater offense and the lesser non-included offense, to additional culpability, the decision should rest solely with the defendant.

However, the decision whether a lesser offense instruction should be requested is distinguishable from the decision to plead guilty. When a defendant pleads guilty, he waives all rights attendant to a jury trial. . . . On the other hand, a defendant retains all of his trial rights when he requests that a jury consider a lesser offense instruction. He also retains the opportunity to advocate for outright acquittal. Thus, this decision is not analogous to the decision whether to plead guilty.

Because the defendant retains these fundamental trial rights, we conclude that the decision to request a lesser offense instruction is strategic and tactical in nature, and is therefore reserved for defense counsel. This tactical decision requires sophisticated training and skill which attorneys possess and defendants do not . . . The decision to submit lesser offense instructions "is often based on legal complexities only the most sophisticated client could comprehend, not unlike the tactical decisions involved regarding the assertion of technical defenses." *Van Alstine v. State,* 263 Ga. 1 (1993).

This conclusion finds support in the Colorado Rules of Professional Conduct. Rule 1.2(a)'s omission of the decision to request lesser offense instructions from the enumerated list of decisions reserved to the defendant suggests that this decision is in the realm of trial tactics, where the attorney has authority to decide. . . .

The commentary to the American Bar Association's Standards for Criminal Justice also supports the conclusion that the decision whether to request lesser offense instructions rests with defense counsel. The current third edition overrules the previous edition that allocated the decision to request lesser offense instructions to the defendant. The commentary to the third edition states only that defense counsel must confer with the defendant regarding lesser offense instructions: "It is also important in a jury trial for defense counsel to consult fully with the accused about any lesser included offenses the trial court may be willing to submit to the jury." *ABA Standards for Criminal Justice: Prosecution Function and Defense Function,* Standard 4–5.2, Commentary (3d ed.1993). . .

Recent cases analyzing the effect of this change have concluded that under the current ABA standards, the decision whether to request lesser offense instructions is for defense counsel. . . . Additionally, we note that several jurisdictions that give the defendant ultimate authority over the decision to seek lesser offense instructions rely at least in part on the second, outdated edition of the ABA standards. . . . The change in the third edition undermines such reliance.

Accordingly, we hold that the decision whether to request jury instructions on lesser offenses is a tactical decision that rests with defense counsel after consultation with the defendant. Therefore, the trial court erred in accepting the defendant's decision over the objection of defense counsel and refusing to give the lesser non-included offense instruction on third-degree assault. . . .

JUSTICE COATS dissents, JUSTICE EID joins in the dissent.

JUSTICE COATS, dissenting.

Because I agree with the court of appeals that the decision to request a lesser non-included offense instruction in this jurisdiction implicates a fundamental right, and therefore must remain with the defendant himself rather than his counsel, I respectfully dissent. More to the point, I believe the majority opinion simply fails to address the unique situation created by this jurisdiction's liberal (and highly unusual) procedure allowing criminal defendants to present juries with offenses neither charged by, nor even included within charges filed by, the prosecution. Although they may use the similar term "lesser offense," none of the majority's authorities-including both federal and state case law and ABA Standards-remotely contemplate an instruction on a "lesser non-included offense," and therefore none offer the slightest support for its conclusion. . . .

Unlike the case of a lesser included offense, which merges with the greater, and therefore can, at most, result in a conviction for a less serious form of the charged offense, the effect of injecting a lesser non-included offense into the jury's considerations is to subject the defendant to an additional conviction and harsher punishment than would otherwise be the case. . . . In fact, granting such a request amounts not merely to a defendant's consent to an added count but actually to adding another charge against him, without even the acquiescence, much less the aim, of the prosecuting authority. . . .

The Colorado Rules of Professional Conduct represent the only authority from this jurisdiction even peripherally relied on by the majority. Besides the fact that these rules purport to govern only attorney ethics, as distinguished from constitutional rights; and that Rule 1.2(a) represents a verbatim adoption of the model rule, whose drafters clearly never contemplated Colorado's broad allowance of defense requested non-included offense instructions; it seems particularly ironic for the majority to look to a body of rules prescribing an attorney's obligations to his client as support for counsel's authority to tactically subject his client to greater criminal liability than that sought by the state, without even the client's agreement.

Apart from its argument from authority (inapposite as its offered authorities may be), the majority seems merely to argue that a request by counsel for additional charges, unlike a guilty plea, does not actually admit additional crimes or deprive the defendant of his right to advocate for outright acquittal. While this may be an accurate statement, it is difficult to understand why the decision to *subject* a criminal defendant to harsher punishment should not also be personal to him, or why he should be forced even to risk, at the hands of his own counsel, greater criminal liability. It remains unclear to me that defense counsel should be permitted to deprive his client of the option to go for broke, rather than seeking a compromise verdict on even an included lesser offense; but I can see absolutely no justification for subjecting a criminal defendant, without his agreement, to greater criminal liability than that charged by the state.

I therefore respectfully dissent.

CASE QUESTIONS

1. What is a lesser non-included offense?
2. How does requesting an instruction on it it differ from a guilty plea?
3. What criteria did the court use to distinguish authority reserved to a lawyer from authority reserved to a client?

"Is This *1984,* or What?" Defending the Unabomber

Theodore Kaczynski, better known as the "Unabomber" was indicted for mailing bombs that killed three people and injured nine others. He maintained his actions were self-defense against the intrusion of modernity into Montana.

Kaczynski's lawyers were Quin Denvir, Judy Clarke, and Gary Sowards. They wanted to present the jury a defense based on Kaczynski's mental state. Kaczynski bitterly opposed any defense suggesting he was mentally deranged. He wrote his lawyers at one point "I categorically refuse to use a mental-status defense." His lawyers nevertheless suggested he agree to be interviewed by mental health specialists and file a notice required for the presentation of mental-state evidence; Kaczynski agreed, he said later, only because he thought his lawyers had in mind evidence from a psychologist who thought he was sane.

As trial approached Kaczynski learned that defense experts who interviewed him diagnosed him as a paranoid schizophrenic and that this information had been given to the government. When he learned this he wrote Denvir and Clarke:

> Did Gary [Sowards] give that info to the prosecutors with your knowledge and consent? If you all assume responsibility for revealing what is being revealed now, then this is the end between us. I will not work with you guys any more, because I can't trust you. . . .
>
> This case is developing in a direction that I certainly did not expect. I was lead [sic] to believe that this was not really a "mental health" kind of defense, but that you would try to show that my actions were a kind of "self defense." Gary [Sowards] gave me the impression that we would use only Dr. Kriegler, and would use her only to show I would not "do it again."

Thereafter Kaczynski wrote the trial judge complaining his lawyer had deceived him and explaining his objection to the presentation of any mental status defense:

> I do not believe that science has any business probing the workings of the human mind, and . . . my personal ideology and that of the mental-health professions are mutually antagonistic. . . . [I]t is humiliating to have one's mind probed by a person whose ideology and values are alien to one's own. . . . [Denvir, Clarke, and Sowards] calculatedly deceived me in order to get me to reveal my private thoughts, and then without warning they made accessible to the public the cold and heartless assessments of their experts. . . . To me this was a stunning blow . . . [and] the worst experience I ever underwent in my life. . . . I would rather die, or suffer prolonged physical torture, than have the 12.2b defense imposed on me in this way by my present attorneys.

Kaczynski wrote that his agreement to be examined and file the notice of intention to present such evidence was "meaningless because my attorneys misled me as to what that defense involved."

The judge interceded and brokered a compromise between Kaczynski and his lawyers in which the lawyers would withdraw the notice with respect to the penalty phase of the trial but not with respect to sentencing in the event Kaczynski was found guilty. The notice pertained only to expert testimony, however, not to fact testimony, although neither the judge nor Kaczynski seem to have appreciated this fact.

After a jury was chosen Denvir and Clarke read Kaczynski their opening statement, which referred to non-expert testimony about his mental condition. Kaczynski was horrified and again told the judge of his conflict with his lawyers. Two days later the judge ruled that the lawyers could present mental-state evidence even over Kaczynski's objection—it was their call, not his. The court told Kaczynski he had the right to represent himself, but Kaczynski said he was too tired to do so.

That night Kaczynski apparently attempted suicide.

Trial began the next day. Kaczynski changed his mind and decided to attempt to represent himself. Ms. Clarke conveyed his request to the court with great reluctance:

> Your Honor, if I may address the Court, Mr. Kaczynski had a request that we alert the Court to, on his behalf—it is his request that he be permitted to proceed in this case as his own counsel. This is a very difficult position for him. He believes that he has no choice but to go forward as his own lawyer. It is a very heartfelt reaction, I believe, to the presentation of a mental illness defense, a situation in which he simply cannot endure.

Ms. Clarke stressed that Kaczynski was not asking for delay and was prepared to proceed that morning.

The trial judge seemed to understand Kaczynski's request was driven by the judge's ruling that Kaczynski's lawyers controlled the presentation of mental status evidence: "In my opinion, the defendant would not be asking to represent himself if he was in control of the mental status defense. That's my opinion. . . . I believe that Mr. Kaczynski has expressed the interest of representing himself because I told him he doesn't control that defense."

Notwithstanding Kaczynski's statement that he was ready to proceed immediately with his own defense, the district court later ruled that he exercised his self-defense right for purposes of delay and therefore forfeited that right. Kaczynski's lawyers then negotiated an agreement under which Kaczynski pleaded guilty and the government agreed not to seek the death penalty. When Kaczynski challenged the plea on the ground that it had been coerced by his lawyers' deception, the Ninth Circuit affirmed his plea without deciding whether Kaczynski or his lawyers controlled the defense.[10]

The issue in Kaczynski turned on his assertion of his right to represent himself, in accordance with *Faretta v. California*, 422 U.S. 806 (1975). In *Indiana v. Edwards*, 554 U.S. 164 (2008), the Supreme Court qualified *Faretta*, ruling that a state may require a defendant to proceed to trial with counsel if the court finds the defendant is not competent to conduct his own defense but is competent to proceed with counsel. The Court's ruling is permissive; it does not require states to adopt such a rule.[11]

The Court reasoned in part that *Faretta* seeks to vindicate the dignity of the defendant by not forcing counsel upon him, and that the right does not "affirm the dignity" of a defendant "who lacks the mental capacity to conduct his defense without the assistance of counsel." It further reasoned that "proceedings must not only be fair, they must 'appear fair to all who observe them.' " (citation omitted). The Court did not elaborate on this principle.

PROBLEM 3–8

One way of looking at this case is that Mr. Kaczynski's lawyers lied to him and coerced him by threatening to pursue a course of conduct he ab-

[10] The American Bar Association Standards Relating to the Administration of Criminal Justice discuss the division of authority between lawyer and client in Standard 4–5.2.

[11] "The Constitution permits judges to take realistic account of the particular defendant's mental capacities by asking whether a defendant who seeks to conduct his own defense at trial is mentally competent to do so."

horred, and thereby saved his life. Suppose that is right. Did they do the right thing?

PROBLEM 3–9

Suppose you represent a client accused of selling drugs. He has no criminal history, so the prosecutor has offered to allow him to plea to a reduced charge, though still a felony. Your client tells you he is innocent of the charge, but he wants to accept the plea. He explains that it is a case of mistaken identity, and that his brother, who has two prior felony convictions, actually sold the drugs. He would rather plead guilty than expose his brother to the risk of a third strike. What are your duties? Would it affect your answer if the client had to answer questions from the court and explain that he was in fact guilty (an "allocution")?

No Matter Where You Go There You Are, I

Mr. Kaczynski's lawyers seem to have felt confident enough about what was right for him that they at least resisted his instructions regarding his defense. One appellate judge thought they flat-out lied to him. Regardless whether that is true, it is fair to infer that they felt comfortable exerting a great deal of influence over their client. Though they were agents, they took command of the case.

Would you do that? Could you do that? Are you confident enough in your own judgment that you would disregard your client's wishes if you thought those wishes were misguided or wrong? Would you feel better acting solely as an agent, or are you the type of person comfortable with venturing deeply into client space? Would you lie to your client to save his life? Could you live with yourself if you went by the book and then watched your client be convicted and executed?

Different people will answer these questions differently. The point is not that there is a right or wrong answer because in terms of your own peace of mind there isn't. There are answers you can live with and answers you can't. *United States v. Kaczynski* does suggest a useful lesson though. If you are not the type of person who could feel comfortable doing what the lawyers in the case actually did, following your client's wishes and (in all probability) seeing your client convicted and executed, then you may not want to put yourself in a position where you have to make such choices. There are plenty of other options.

The general point is this: However you manage your career, including your ethical choices, it will be you who manages it, not someone else. Knowing who you are and how you react to situations will help you find situations in which you are comfortable. And that will help you avoid making bad decisions simply because you are in a position you are not temperamentally well-equipped to handle.

Appointed Counsel and Client Control

The Sixth Amendment guarantees to criminal defendants indicted for felonies, or for misdemeanor offenses for which jail time might be imposed, the right to counsel at all critical stages of the prosecution. *Iowa v. Tovar*, 541 U.S. 77 (2004); *Gideon v. Wainwright*, 372 U.S. 335 (1963). If a jurisdiction allows initial appeals as a matter of right, the right to counsel extends to the initial appeal as well. *Douglas v. California*, 372 U.S. 353 (1963).

In *Kaczynski*, the trial judge ruled that counsel had the discretion to make an argument the defendant did not want made. What happens if counsel appointed to represent a criminal defendant does not want to make an argument the defendant wants made? This situation is more common than the one in *Kaczynski* and it can create conflicts for criminal lawyers. For example, suppose a client wants the lawyer to assert a factually ridiculous or legally frivolous claim. The client's demand could put the lawyer in a bind between her duty to the client, on the one hand, and disciplinary and court rules forbidding the assertion of frivolous claims, on the other.[12]

A client does not have a constitutional right to present frivolous arguments on appeal, and therefore has no right to have counsel present such arguments. *Smith v. Robbins*, 528 U.S. 259 (2000). But what if appellate counsel looks over the record and decides there are no issues worth appealing? What if they request to withdraw, or ask the court to dispose of the appeal without having them file a merits brief? What if counsel missed an issue? If counsel offered no argument at all then meritorious issues might never get briefed and courts might never have a chance to hear them. On the other hand, flogging away at obviously worthless arguments wastes everyone's time and might mean that meritorious claims get lost in the avalanche of useless verbiage.

The solution to this problem is generally known as an "Anders brief," after *Anders v. California*, 386 U.S. 738 (1967). Under the California procedure at issue in that case, a lawyer could file a summary letter stating he had read the record and found no meritorious issues. The court could then affirm the conviction after its own review of the record but without briefs and argument. In *Anders,* the Court held that this procedure violated the Constitution. It distinguished between an attorney's view that a

---

[12] Disciplinary rules such as Model Rule 3.1 forbid lawyers from asserting arguments for which there is no good-faith basis in fact, law, or an argument to modify or extend the law. (Criminal defense counsel may nevertheless put the government to its proof.)

record showed no meritorious issues and a record on which an appeal would be frivolous. It held a lawyer could request to withdraw if she concluded an appeal would be "wholly frivolous," wrote a brief stating that fact but also pointing to anything in the record that might arguably support an appeal, gave a copy of the brief to the client, and gave the client a chance to raise any points he wanted argued. The appellate court would then review this brief. If it found that any appeal on the record would be frivolous, it could grant the lawyer's request to withdraw and dismiss or dispose of the appeal. If it found any arguable points, however, the court would have to provide counsel to argue them.

In *Smith v. Robbins*, 528 U.S. 259 (2000), the Court held the Constitution permits but does not require the precise procedure the Court specified in *Anders*. After *Anders*, California modified its procedure for dealing with appeals counsel believe have no merit. As the *Robbins* Court described it, under *People v. Wende*, 25 Cal. 3d 436 (1979),

> counsel, upon concluding that an appeal would be frivolous, files a brief with the appellate court that summarizes the procedural and factual history of the case, with citations of the record. He also attests that he has reviewed the record, explained his evaluation of the case to his client, provided the client with a copy of the brief, and informed the client of his right to file a *pro se* supplemental brief. He further requests that the court independently examine the record for arguable issues. Unlike under the *Anders* procedure, counsel following *Wende* neither explicitly states that his review has led him to conclude that an appeal would be frivolous (although that is considered implicit, *see Wende*, 25 Cal.3d, at 441–442) nor requests leave to withdraw. Instead, he is silent on the merits of the case and expresses his availability to brief any issues on which the court might desire briefing.

What about non-frivolous arguments? In *Jones v. Barnes*, 463 U.S. 745 (1983), the Court held that the Constitution does not require appellate counsel to raise on appeal all nonfrivolous arguments a client instructs the lawyer to make. Writing for the Court, Chief Justice Burger said selectivity is a key to effective appellate advocacy and that "[f]or judges to second-guess reasonable professional judgments and impose on appointed counsel a duty to raise every 'colorable' claim suggested by a client would disserve the very goal of vigorous and effective advocacy that underlies *Anders*." Justice Brennan dissented. He wrote "I find myself in fundamental disagreement with the Court over what a right to "the assistance of counsel" means. The import of words like "assistance" and "counsel" seems inconsistent with a regime under which counsel appointed by the State to represent a criminal defendant can refuse to raise issues with arguable merit on appeal when his client, after hearing his assessment of the case and his advice, has directed him to raise them."

What about counsel retained by a client rather than appointed by a court? In his dissent in *Robbins*, Justice Souter suggested the market will fix any problems with the diligence of retained counsel:

> *Anders* addressed the problem as confronted by assigned counsel, though in theory it can be equally acute when counsel is retained. It is unlikely to show up in practice, however. Paying clients generally can fire a lawyer expressing unsatisfying conclusions and will often find a replacement with a keener eye for arguable issues or a duller nose for frivolous ones. As a practical matter, the States may find it too difficult or costly to prevent moneyed appellants from wasting their own resources, and those of the judicial system, by bringing frivolous appeals. This does not mean, however, that the States are obligated to subsidize such efforts by indigents.[13]

These topics provide perspective for a first look at a problem we will see again when we examine constitutional standards for the effective assistance of counsel. Why did the Court recognize a right to appointed counsel? What purpose does it serve? Two ideas establish a continuum for thinking about this question: client autonomy and the accuracy of criminal proceedings.

In *Jones*, Justice Brennan's dissent advanced a theory holding that the purpose of the right to counsel is to advance the autonomy of the defendant. As he put it, "the right to counsel is more than a right to have one's case presented competently and effectively. It is predicated on the view that the function of counsel under the Sixth Amendment is to protect the dignity and autonomy of a person on trial by *assisting* him in making choices that are his to make, not to make choices for him, although counsel may be better able to decide which tactics will be most effective for the defendant."

An alternative view of the right takes a more utilitarian approach. On this view the right exists to make sure criminal proceedings produce reliable results, defined as convicting the person who did it. In *Robbins*, for example, the Court held that a state procedure affords "adequate and effective" appellate review "so long as it reasonably ensures that an indigent's appeal will be resolved in a way that is related to the merit of that appeal." Justice Thomas's opinion specified the goal of providing appellate counsel to indigent defendants is "to ensure that those indigents whose appeals are not frivolous receive the counsel and merits brief required by *Douglas,* and also to enable the State to 'protect itself so that frivolous appeals are not subsidized and public moneys not needlessly spent.' "

---

[13] 528 U.S. at 294 n.2 (Souter, J., dissenting).

These two ideas are in obvious tension with each other, and that tension forms an important part of the context in which courts, legislatures, and disciplinary officials operate in creating the rules that govern criminal defense counsel.

2. CIVIL LITIGATION

Lawyers get to make some decisions even if a client disagrees. This is most often the case in litigation, where decisions may need to be made immediately, without the chance to consult with a client (clients are not always present in judicial proceedings) and which may affect third parties such as judges, opponents, and litigants in unrelated cases who are waiting for their matters to be heard. The more a particular question affects the efficiency of courts the more likely it is for lawyers to have the final say on that question. (A significant exception to this principle is the constitutional right of a criminal defendant to represent himself—the right Kaczynski tried to invoke.) Even on matters within a lawyer's discretion, however, to the extent possible a lawyer must keep a client informed about what is going on and should consult with a client to ascertain the client's wishes. *See Restatement (Third) of the Law Governing Lawyers* § 23, cmt d.

Applegate v. Dobrovir, Oakes & Gebhardt, 628 F.Supp. 378 (D. D.C. 1986), provides a good illustration of matters left to the lawyer's discretion in civil litigation. Applegate was a former Department of Defense employee who alleged he had been fired because he blew the whistle on government waste. After three and a half years of litigation, the case settled shortly before trial. Applegate then sued Dobrovir for malpractice, alleging in part that Dobrovir had failed to follow up on leads Applegate had provided and had failed to interview witnesses Applegate wanted interviewed.

The court rejected this claim as a matter of law: "To the extent that plaintiff claims defendants breached their professional duty by failing to introduce specific items of evidence at trial, his claim must fail. Questions of tactics are in the lawyer's discretion." 628 F.Supp. at 383.[14] The court quoted the Tenth Circuit's opinion in *Frank v. Bloom*, 634 F.2d 1245, 1256–57 (10th Cir. 1980), which said:

> The fact, . . . that the attorney in the heat of the trial disregards the direction of the client as to trial strategy or activity does not give the client a right of action against the attorney. After all, it is the duty of the attorney who is a professional to determine trial strategy. If the client had the last word on this, the client could be his or her own lawyer. Therefore, an attorney does not ordinarily violate his duty to the client by rejecting a client's suggested tactic.

---

[14] The court's reference to introducing evidence at trial appears to be an error; the case settled before trial.

Disciplinary Rules and the Efficient Conduct of Litigation

MODEL RULES OF PROFESSIONAL CONDUCT 3.1–3.4

Litigation differs from other matters in important ways. In non-litigation matters, such as negotiations for the sale of a business, the parties internalize a large portion of the total costs of lawyering. If the lawyer for one side is too aggressive and runs up costs needlessly the other side can walk away. Even the threat to do so may discipline wasteful posturing and curb work that produces fewer benefits than costs.

In contrast, litigators may impose significant costs on third parties such as opposing litigants, non-party witnesses, and the court system itself. There are no disciplinary measures that correspond to the private party's ability to walk away. You generally don't get to pick who sues you or whom they hire to represent them. In some cases the incentives are reversed. For example, one side in a lawsuit may try to bring the other side to the bargaining table by propounding broad discovery requests that would cost hundreds of thousands of dollars to satisfy.[15] Such tactics are a particular risk if one side has very few facts and therefore faces low costs of discovery compliance while the other side faces high costs. (Class action litigation often presents this cost structure.) Where litigation costs are asymmetric, they can become a bargaining tool in and of themselves.

Disciplinary rules make some attempt to limit the third-party effects of litigation. Model Rule 3.1 forbids lawyers from asserting frivolous claims. Model Rule 3.2 requires counsel to make reasonable efforts to expedite litigation. Model Rule 3.3 forbids lawyers from lying to tribunals or from introducing evidence the lawyer knows to be false. Lies and false evidence tend to undermine the degree to which litigation produces the results required by law and thus impedes the deterrent and compensatory goals of litigation, in addition to making it likely that some third party will incur the cost of an erroneous judgment. If lying and perjury became common enough, litigation might be discredited as a valid process of resolving disputes, leading people to take inefficient measures of self-defense or self-help. Similarly, Model Rule 3.4 forbids lawyers from obstructing access to evidence, falsifying evidence, making frivolous discovery requests, or asking third parties to refrain from giving evidence.

These rules are some help but they do not solve the problem completely. Concerned that cases be resolved on their merits, and knowing that they cannot know any given case as well as the counsel involved, courts often give counsel great discretion over the pace of litigation and

---

[15] As noted below, Model Rule 3.4(d) forbids frivolous discovery requests but asymmetric costs may be imposed by requests that do not violate this standard.

the scope of discovery. The flip side of this quite legitimate concern is that ethical rules and rules of court do not solve the problem of third party costs and asymmetric costs.

D. UNBUNDLING

Cal. Rules of Court 3.35–3.37; 5.70–5.71

Our final topic concerns a way of dividing authority between a lawyer and client by limiting the things the lawyer agrees to do. "Unbundling" refers to an agreement between a lawyer and client that the lawyer will provide some but not all services necessary to resolve the client's problem. The lawyer might merely coach the client to negotiate with another party, for example, or might prepare pre-trial motions for the client to file but assume no trial obligations. Unbundling has received increased attention in recent years as a way to provide some level of representation to people who cannot afford to have a lawyer handle all aspects of some matter.

Model Rule 1.2(c) allows lawyers to limit the scope of their representation of a client if the limitation is reasonable and the client gives informed consent to it. This provision provides conceptual approval for unbundling but it does not address more specific issues that unbundled representation may present. We survey some of those issues here and analyze them in connection with the substantive rules to which they pertain.

Suppose a lawyer agrees to help a client prepare pleadings or motion papers to be filed in court but does not want to enter an appearance in court. Does such work violate counsel's duty of candor to the tribunal under Model Rule 3.3? Or suppose a lawyer is dealing with an opposing party who is receiving limited assistance from another lawyer: Is that party represented by the other lawyer for purposes of Model Rule 4.2, forbidding a lawyer from contacting a represented party without consent of that party's lawyer? How does unbundling affect the duty of care? Does it make malpractice actions more likely? What happens between the lawyer and client if a lawyer appears in court for a limited purpose and the court later denies the lawyer's request to withdraw? Does a limitation on the scope of representation alter a lawyer's duties upon withdrawal?

Some jurisdictions have dealt with some of these issues by adopting special rules for unbundled representation. California's rules allow for two types of limited representation. Counsel may either appear in court for some but not all purposes, in which case counsel and client must notify the court and the opposing party of the limited representation agreement, or counsel may not appear at all, in which case no notice need be given. The rules specifically contemplate that non-appearing counsel could draft pleadings for a client. Cal. R. Court 3.37.

Other jurisdictions have adopted rules that would require disclosure of limited representation in litigation. Colorado Rule of Civil Procedure 11(b), for example, provides that "pleadings or papers filed by the pro se party that were prepared with the drafting assistance of the attorney" must include the attorney's contact information and bar registration number. The rule also provides that the lawyer's assistance in drafting a pleading or other paper filed with the court constitutes the lawyer's certification that the pleading or paper is (i) well grounded in fact, based upon a reasonable inquiry of the client by the lawyer;[16] (ii) supported by existing law or a good-faith argument for extension, modification, or reversal of existing law; and (3) is not filed for any improper purpose. Courts in other jurisdictions have found such "ghostwriting" to constitute professional misconduct. For a recent summary of the relevant law, *see In re Liu*, 664 F.3d 367 (2d Cir. 2011)(declining to impose discipline for failure to disclose ghostwriting of petitions for review).

Whatever is the case regarding notification of courts and opposing parties, lawyers who limit the scope of their representation must make sure the client understands (i) what the lawyer will do; (ii) what the lawyer won't do; and (iii) the practical implications of the limitation in point (ii). California's Committee on Professional Responsibility and Conduct advised lawyers who unbundle "to fully advise their clients on the limitations on the representation, including the matters the attorneys are *not handling*. Clients also should be advised of the possible adverse consequences of limited scope representation, and to consult with other counsel about legal matters their attorney is not handling." California State Bar Committee on Professional Responsibility and Conduct, *An Ethics Primer on Limited Scope Representation* (available at http://calbar.ca.gov/calbar/pdfs/ethics/COPRAC/COPRAC_02–0005_11–17–04.pdf).

Finally, it is important to remember that some unbundling arrangements might be impermissible either as a matter of disciplinary rules or as a matter of tort law. Model Rule 1.2(c) requires that the limitation be reasonable. Model Rule 1.1 and the duty of care require that the lawyer be able to provide competent service to the extent he or she undertakes to do so. It is conceivable that some proposed limitations might make competent representation impossible, in which case both disciplinary and tort rules should cause counsel to decline the arrangement.

---

16 The rule goes on to provide that counsel may rely upon the client's representations of fact "unless the attorney has reason to believe that such representations are false or materially insufficient, in which case the attorney shall make an independent reasonable inquiry into the facts."

The Main Points to Recall From Chapter 3 Are:

- Fiduciary duties and disciplinary rules give clients final authority over some things and lawyers final authority over others. In general clients control the ends of representation and lawyers control some of the means, subject in some cases to lawful client instructions.
- Where the law does not allocate authority the lawyer and client may do so either through implication from the facts of the job at hand or by agreement.
- Lawyers and clients may not by contract alter authority allocated by law; attempts to do so look suspicious and may violate Model Rule 1.2.
- The keys to understanding legal (mandatory) allocation of authority are the purposes and goals of representation and third-party costs.
- All else being equal, the more a decision affects the client's ultimate goal in the representation, such as settlement or a plea, the more likely it is that the decision is the client's to make.
- All else being equal, the more a decision affects the costs of litigation (especially third party costs) the more likely it is the lawyer's decision to make.
- Clients therefore have more control over non-litigation matters than litigation matters, because decisions outside litigation impose fewer non-avoidable costs on third parties.
- Lawyers may limit the scope of a representation, taking on responsibility only for some subset of issues or tasks, so long as the limitation is reasonable and the client gives informed consent. Limited representation may increase the risk of violating a Model Rule provision; some jurisdictions are adopting special rules pertaining to limited representation.

CHAPTER 4

THE DUTY OF CONFIDENTIALITY

■ ■ ■

As you saw in the chapter 2, lawyers owe clients duties of loyalty and care. The duty of loyalty requires lawyers to put their clients' interests ahead of their own, within the limits of the law. Putting your clients' interests first includes keeping their confidential information to yourself and not exploiting that information for your own benefit. Acting carefully means not negligently disclosing client information. This seemingly simple rule may be complex in operation, however. This chapter begins with some basic definitions and rules and then elaborates on them.

Confidential client information is a broad category. The *Restatement (Third) of the Law Governing Lawyers* § 59 provides that "confidential client information" includes all "information relating to the representation of a client, other than information that is generally known."

The duty of confidentiality extends to forbid both disclosure and use of such information. According to the *Restatement (Third) of Agency* § 8.05:

> An agent has a duty . . . (2) not to use or communicate confidential information of the principal for the agent's own purposes or those of a third party.

This basic prohibition appears in different places in the various laws governing lawyers. Looking only at the disciplinary rules therefore may provide a misleading picture of a lawyer's obligations. For example, Model Rule 1.6 does not address use of client information at all and Model Rule 1.8(b) provides only that a lawyer may not use information relating to representation of a client to the client's disadvantage. Similarly, Model Rule 1.9(c) provides that after representation terminates a lawyer may not use client information to the disadvantage of a client (unless the information has become generally known). The agency rule stated above goes further, however, extending to all cases where use benefits a lawyer even if it does not harm a client.[1]

---

[1] The *Restatement (Third) of the Law Governing Lawyers* 60(2) similarly provides that "a lawyer who uses confidential information of a client for the lawyer's pecuniary gain other than in the practice of law must account to the client for any profits made." Comment j to this section states a lawyer may use confidential client information to benefit another client (thus the "other than in the practice of law" language in Section 60(2)), so long as there is no reasonable risk that the use will harm the client the lawyer represented when obtaining the information. So if Law-

The prohibitions on use or disclosure overlap but they are not the same. You may *use* information without disclosing it. A lawyer might trade securities on the basis of client confidences, for example. In that case, the lawyer uses the information to make money but does not disclose it. The converse is generally not true: a lawyer who discloses client confidences generally does so to make use of them.

Some courts construe "use" of confidential information quite broadly, as did the California Supreme Court when it held that a former client stated a *prima facie* case of breach of fiduciary duty against a lawyer who opposed politically a development project he previously worked on for the client. The Court reasoned a factfinder might conclude that the lawyer used information learned during that representation in the sense that his opposition to the project "developed over the course of the representation, fueled by the confidential information he gleaned during it." *Oasis West Realty LLC v. Goldman*, 51 Cal. 4th 811 (2011). The Court held:

> It is well established that the duties of loyalty and confidentiality bar an attorney not only from using a former client's confidential information in the course of "making decisions when representing another client," but also from "taking the information significantly into account in framing a course of action" such as "deciding whether to make a personal investment"—even though, in the latter circumstance, no second client exists and no confidences are actually disclosed. (Rest.3d, Law Governing Lawyers, § 60, com. c(i), p. 464.)

Keeping this background in mind, the basic confidentiality rules are: (i) counsel may not disclose confidential information on their own initiative and may not use such information to harm the client or to benefit themselves outside the practice of law; (ii) counsel must disclose confidential information if required to do so by law; unless (iii) the confidential information is also privileged, in which case counsel must assert the privilege against disclosure unless the client instructs otherwise. This chapter analyzes the confidentiality obligation. The next chapter analyzes the attorney-client privilege.

A. THE DUTY DESCRIBED

Model Rule of Professional Conduct 1.6(a) forbids you from revealing information relating to representation unless the client gives informed

---

yer represents client *X* against chemical manufacturer *Z* and learns facts about *Z*'s manufacturing practices, Lawyer may use those facts in representing client *Y* in a similar suit against *Z*, so long as such use does not pose a threat to *X*'s interests. The exclusion in Section 60(2) for information used in the practice of law could be read to qualify the general agency rule, but no case has ruled on that question.

consent (expressly or by implication) or an exception applies. Rule 1.6(b) lists exceptions allowing disclosure to prevent reasonably certain death or substantial bodily harm, to prevent or rectify substantial financial harm caused by a client and in which your services were or are being used, to obtain advice about your obligations under the rules, to establish a claim or defense in a controversy with a client, to respond to allegations regarding your representation, to comply with a law or court order, or to detect and resolve conflicts when moving from one firm to another (so long as disclosure does not prejudice the client). These rules do not exhaust the duty of confidentiality, however, as the following materials illustrate.

Model Rule of Professional Conduct 1.6
Cal. Bus. & Prof'n Code § 6068(e);
Cal. R. Prof'n Conduct 3–100
Restatement §§ 59–67

1. THE DUTY OF CONFIDENTIALITY DISTINGUISHED FROM THE ATTORNEY–CLIENT PRIVILEGE

The duty of confidentiality is related to the attorney-client privilege in that both have to do with lawyers not disclosing information they learn while representing clients. The two are different in important ways, however.

The duty of confidentiality arises from the duties of loyalty and care that lawyers owe clients; the privilege is a rule of evidence. The obligations of care and loyalty apply to everything a lawyer does in connection with representing a client and the duty of confidentiality based in those obligations applies to information learned in any aspect of this work. The evidentiary privilege applies only where rules of evidence apply.

The confidentiality obligation applies to all information not generally known that an attorney learns in the course and scope of representing a client. The evidentiary privilege applies to confidential communications between a lawyer and client made for the purpose of obtaining legal advice. The confidentiality obligation is therefore broader than the evidentiary privilege: All privileged communications are confidential information but not all confidential information is privileged. A lawyer could learn confidential information through some means other than a confidential communication from a client. For example, the lawyer might learn such information from a third party related to the client, such as a sibling.

You can use a simple Venn diagram to help understand the relationship between confidential information and privileged communication. The subset of "privileged communications" represents confidential information received from a client under circumstances that satisfy the elements of the privilege (which we study in detail below). The set of "confidential information" includes both such privileged communications and confidential information counsel learns in circumstances that do not satisfy the elements of the privilege.

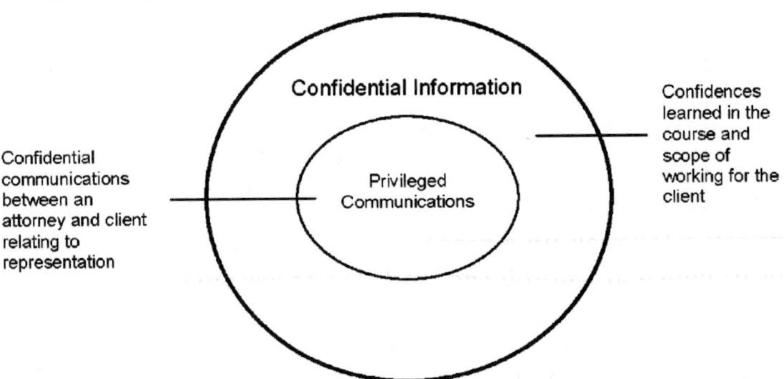

E.g., *Brennan's Inc. v. Brennan's Rests. Inc.*, 590 F.2d 168 (5th Cir. 1979) (lawyer could not act adversely to former client and attack his own prior work even though joint-client exception removed any privilege between the parties); *X Corp. v. Doe*, 805 F.Supp. 1298 (E.D. Va. 1992) (noting different standards for ruling on preliminary injunction to stop voluntary disclosure of client confidences compared to more lenient standard for crime-fraud exception to privilege).

Finally, confidentiality restricts voluntary use or disclosure while the privilege provides protection against compelled disclosure. It follows that if a court determines that the privilege does not protect some evidence from compelled production the duty of confidentiality does not protect it either. A lawyer who asserts but loses a privilege claim therefore may be compelled to give evidence even if the duty of confidentiality would prevent the lawyer from initiating such disclosure voluntarily. *E.g. Adams v. Franklin*, 924 A.2d 993 (D.C. 2007).

This table recaps the most fundamental differences between the duty of confidentiality and the attorney-client privilege. (*Note: this table does not include all relevant elements of either the duty or the privilege; those tables come later. This table just summarizes some basic points of difference between the two doctrines.*)

	Duty of Confidentiality	**Attorney-Client Privilege**
Covers	All information relating to representation and not generally known	Confidential communications between attorney and client relating to representation
Applies When	At all times	Rules of evidence apply
Effect	Forbids voluntary disclosure (but not disclosure requires by law)	Defense against disclosure tribunal could otherwise compel

QUESTIONS

Are the following examples (a) privileged, (b) confidential, (c) both, or (d) neither?

1. A client accused of a crime tells her lawyer she arrived in town on a 9:00 flight (which left her enough time to be at the scene of the crime when it was committed)

2. The lawyer in (1) met the client at the airport and observed she was wearing an orange jacket and blue hat (clothes seen by witnesses to the crime)

3. The lawyer visits the crime scene with an investigator and observes the investigator pick up a piece of evidence that had been overlooked and pocket it; police attending the visit do not see this

4. A client sends a lawyer a copy of a patent applications, which is available on the PTO website

5. In reviewing documents for a corporate client an attorney determines an officer of the corporation is guilty of bribery

6. A lawyer and client negotiate an agreement for the client to buy the business of a third party, who is present with her lawyer

2. USE OF CLIENT INFORMATION FOR PERSONAL BENEFIT

DAVID WELCH CO. V. ERSKINE & TULLEY

203 Cal.App.3d 884 (1988)

CHANNELL, ASSOCIATE JUSTICE.

Following a court trial, defendants Erskine & Tulley (E & T) and Michael Carroll appeal from a judgment entered against them and in favor of David Welch Co. (Welch). The trial court held that E & T, a law corporation, and Attorney Carroll had breached their fiduciary duty towards Welch, their former client, and had received a benefit of $350,000, which defendants were deemed to hold in constructive trust for Welch. Defendants were ordered to disgorge that benefit to Welch. Welch cross-appeals from that portion of the judgment providing that its recovery shall be only from those defendants, and only in the amount of $350,000.

This controversy arises from the fact that after E & T and Welch terminated their attorney-client relationship in December 1980, E & T gradually acquired the collection business activities formerly performed by Welch in behalf of several employee benefit trust funds. The basic issue in the trial court was whether, in doing so, the law firm or any of its attorneys breached a fiduciary duty towards their former client.

I. FACTS

Welch is a licensed collection agency which, over several years, developed a highly profitable specialty in collecting delinquent employer contributions owed to 35 or more employee benefit trust funds. From 1972 to 1980, E & T acted as counsel for Welch, with Attorney Carroll doing most of the work for them in the later years. Before undertaking the representation of Welch, neither E & T nor Carroll had experience in collection agency work for trust funds.

The evidence was in conflict as to how defendants acquired their knowledge for conducting this type of collection activity. Defendants presented evidence indicating that, from a legal standpoint, it was like any other collection work, and that no specialized knowledge or expertise was required. Welch presented evidence that the E & T attorneys were specially trained by the owner, David Welch, on these matters; they were entrusted with complete access to information about Welch's confidential and profitable business techniques; and they were introduced by Welch as its attorneys to the trustees of the various trust funds. All of the information so provided was intended by Welch to be confidential.

When collecting a debt, Welch had the trust fund assign legal title to it, with the trust fund retaining equitable title. If its own collection efforts proved unsuccessful, Welch had E & T file suit in Welch's name as assignee of the trust fund. Before turning a case over to its counsel, Welch would carry out its own collection efforts, investigate the financial status of the delinquent employer, and prepare a case file which included all of the background documents, suggestions for handling the matter, and a draft complaint ready for filing in court.

Because collecting for trust funds was so profitable, David Welch organized his business in a manner designed to preserve the confidentiality of its procedures. He separated the trust fund activity from his other collection activities, used only his most trusted employees, physically located the activity on a separate floor of his office, and took other steps to minimize dissemination of information and to protect against someone within his firm from breaking away and starting a competitive business.[2]

In late 1979, the collection agency was sold, and Welch was taken over by Philip W. Coyle. In 1980, Welch stopped referring collection matters to E & T. The parties thereafter agreed to terminate their relationship, effective after December 31, 1980. At approximately the same time,

[2] FN1. The trial court found that while acting as Welch's attorney, defendants gained their first exposure to the trust fund collection business; gained their first exposure to Welch's clients, including many trust fund administrators; gained access to Welch's fee schedules for trust fund clients; and generally obtained confidential information from Welch.

notices were sent by Coyle to Welch's trust fund clients indicating that Welch soon would be increasing its fees for those clients for the first time since 1968.

In mid–1981, the Sheet Metal Workers Trust severed its relationship with Welch, and transferred its collection business to E & T. At the time, Welch viewed this as an isolated incident. During 1982 and early 1983, several more trust funds did likewise. The evidence indicates that E & T did not solicit these particular clients, but instead responded to inquiries from each trust fund requesting a proposal. On the other hand, there was no evidence that E & T disclosed to Welch, its former client, that it was submitting these proposals, nor that E & T sought to secure Welch's consent to take over these accounts. In each instance, Welch learned it had lost its account from someone other than E & T, usually in the form of a letter from the trust fund announcing as a fait accompli that their business was being transferred to E & T.

By the time Welch filed its complaint against E & T in February 1983, the law firm had obtained the collection accounts of at least 10 of Welch's former trust fund clients, with annual billings approximating $156,715.

II. DISCUSSION

A. *Breach of Fiduciary Duty*

Defendants' first set of contentions relates to whether substantial evidence supports the trial court's findings that they breached their fiduciary duty towards Welch. With respect to a cause of action alleging breach of a fiduciary duty, the existence of the duty is a question of law. "The relation between attorney and client is a fiduciary relation of the very highest character, and binds the attorney to most conscientious fidelity—*uberrima fides*."[3] (*Cox v. Delmas* (1893) 99 Cal. 104, 123; *Barbara A. v. John G.* (1983) 145 Cal.App.3d 369, 383.) There is no dispute that a fiduciary duty did exist in this case. The issue is whether defendants breached that duty towards Welch, which is a question of fact. . . .

Defendants' initial contention concerning this issue is that the trial court erred in finding a breach of fiduciary duty based on alleged violations of rules 4–101 and 5–101 of the Rules of Professional Conduct (rules). Before trial, defendants had successfully moved for summary judgment as to the first cause of action, which had alleged that a violation of the rules, as a matter of law, provided a basis for civil liability. (See *Noble v. Sears, Roebuck & Co.* (1973) 33 Cal.App.3d 654, 658 [violation of rules does not render attorneys liable in damages].) Nevertheless, these rules, together with statutes and general principles relating to other fidu-

---

[3] FN2. *Uberrima fides* means "[t]he most abundant good faith; absolute and perfect candor or openness and honesty; the absence of any concealment of deception, however slight." (Black's Law Dict. (Rev. 4th ed. 1968) p. 1690.)

ciary relationships, all help define the duty component of the fiduciary duty which the attorney owes to his or her client. (*Day v. Rosenthal* (1985) 170 Cal.App.3d 1125, 1147.)

In their argument, defendants cite rules 4–101 and 5–101 and then proceed to argue why their conduct neither fits within one of those rules nor otherwise constitutes a breach of a fiduciary duty. Defendants repeatedly suggest that the trial court concluded that their "mere acceptance of legal work from plaintiff's former clients" constituted such a breach. But more than that is required to establish a breach, and more than that was proven.

For example, the trial court found that defendants "breached their ficuciary [*sic*] duty owed to plaintiff by accepting employment adverse to plaintiff without plaintiff's informed and written consent relating to a matter in reference to which defendants had obtained confidential information by reason of or in the course of their employment by plaintiff. . . ."

This finding was patterned after rule 4–101, a rule which on its face applies to former as well as present clients. The primary purpose of that rule is to protect the confidential relationship which exists between attorney and client. It has been said that an attorney may not "at any time use against his former client knowledge or information acquired by virtue of the previous relationship. . . . " (*Wutchumna Water Co. v. Bailey* (1932) 216 Cal. 564, 573–574. The actual use or misuse of confidential information is not determinative; it is the possibility of the breach of confidence which controls. (*Woods v. Superior Court* (1983) 149 Cal.App.3d 931, 934.) This duty to protect confidential information continues even after the formal relationship ends.

Although neither party is able to cite a case involving a fact pattern analogous to this one, rule 4–101 seems to apply literally to this case. The typical case falling within the rule arises in the context of legal representation of a client whose interests are adverse to another client or former client of the attorney. But "adverse" also connotes being "opposed to one's interest" or "unfavorable." The acquisition by an attorney of business clientele of a former client operates to the economic advantage of the attorney and unfavorably upon the former client. Concerning access to confidential information, David Welch testified as to his company's efforts to maintain the confidentiality of this portion of Welch's business, including its fees schedules, its methods of operation, and other information. Nevertheless, all of this information was shared with defendants. Finally, defendants accepted the new employment without first notifying or in any way seeking the informed consent of Welch before submitting its proposals to the various trust funds.

The trial court further found that "defendants breached their fiduciary duty owed to plaintiff by knowingly acquiring a pecuniary interest adverse to plaintiff without first obtaining plaintiff's informed written consent. . . . " This finding highlights what we consider to be a critical factor in finding a breach of duty in this case, namely, the fact that defendants, who previously had been privy to Welch's confidential information, in no way informed Welch that they were preparing proposals designed to undercut Welch's business relationships.

We agree with defendants that the various trust funds were free to send their business to any entity they chose, as absent a contract to that effect, they were under no continuing duty to continue business with Welch. Similarly, any law firm, *other than E & T,* was free to make proposals at the request of those trust funds in an effort to obtain their business, as E & T did in this case. But, due to the pre-existing attorney-client relationship during which defendants were in a position to and did obtain confidential information about Welch's business, *these defendants* had a higher duty, which was to refrain from acquiring any pecuniary interest involving collection work for these trust funds unless they first notified and obtained the informed consent of Welch to submit their business proposals. As they did not do so, the trial court properly found that they had breached their fiduciary duty towards Welch. . . .

CASE QUESTIONS

1. What confidential information is at stake in this case?
2. What result if the court had found Welch's collection techniques were in fact ordinary, well-known business practices?
3. Did Erskine & Tully disclose any confidential information?
4. Did the court find that the firm used such information?
5. After this opinion, is there any way Erskine & Tully could represent the trust funds? How?
6. What role did the rules of professional conduct play in this case?

PROBLEM 4–1

Does the result in this case affect the trust funds? How?

PROBLEM 4–2

Could Erskine & Tully have dealt with this problem in the retainer agreement? How?

Risk vs Harm I

Welch may be more complex than it first appears to be. Welch argued that he revealed confidential information to Erskine & Tully, which then used that information to compete against Welch and his successor, Coyle. This allegation is a straightforward claim of harm from improper use of confidential information. It fits comfortably within the terms of *Restatement* § 49, which provides that lawyers may be liable for breach of the duties recited in *Restatement* § 16(3) if the lawyer's fiduciary misconduct is (i) the cause of (ii) injury to the client.

The law firm defended on two grounds. The first was that the information was not confidential. The court found against it on this point. The second was that the trial court wrongly found it liable simply for accepting the trust fund's work, without an additional finding of harm. The court of appeal denied that this was the case ("more than that is required to establish a breach and more than that was found"). But the court of appeal did not discuss harm and seemed to believe the additional element required was the firm's failure to obtain Welsh's consent.

The disciplinary rules the court discussed related to conflicts of interest, and the risk of harm is generally sufficient to establish a conflict of interest. *Restatement* § 121 (a conflict of interest exists if there is a substantial risk that the lawyer's representation of the client would be materially and adversely effected by another interest). Harm need not be shown to establish a conflict. Indeed, as we study in chapter 11, one purpose of the conflicts rule is to prevent situations where a client may suspect he or she has been harmed but finds harm hard to prove; disqualifying lawyers from matters in which they have a conflict of interest serves that purpose.

It may be that both the trial court and court of appeal thought it obvious that Erskine & Tully's conduct harmed Welch by taking business from Coyle. If so, it is an unremarkable opinion. The opinion is not clear on this point, however, and it may be read as a caution against putting yourself in a position where a court disapproves of your conduct and thus skips over or presumes an element of a tort claim against you.

A final point is that the language of *Restatement* § 60(2), which deals with gain to the lawyer rather than harm to the client, applies only to the use of client information in work unrelated to the law. Lawyers may use confidential information learned while working for one client for the benefit of another even if the lawyer benefits from doing so as long as the use does not harm the first client. *Id.* cmt j.

Client Information as Client Property

Recall that the court in *Tante v. Herring* said "Tante was a fiduciary with regard to the confidential information provided him by his client just as he would have been a fiduciary with regard to money or other property entrusted to him by a client." The court's analogy between information and property is a useful way of thinking about the duty of confidentiality. Confidential information you obtain while working for a client belongs to the client. You may no more take that information and use it for your own benefit than you may take anything else belonging to a client.

This analogy can be hard to see because consumption of information is nonrivalrous. That means that when you take a client's information for your own benefit you do not take it away from the client, just as if you copied music on a file-sharing network both you and the original uploader would have copies. The problem is that by taking the information you may take away its commercial value. That is what happened in *Welch v. Erskine & Tully*. The court tells us that the client incurred costs in developing methods for the efficient recovery of debts. The client could only make money on this investment if it kept its practices confidential. If others could copy the practices they could undercut the client's prices and prevent the client from making a profit on the investment.

Not all client information will have commercial value. The fact of Mrs. Herring's fragile emotional condition did not have such value, for example (though on the facts of the case it appears that her information was valuable to Tante). You can think of such information as property that has emotional but not market value to a client, as might be the case with a keepsake from a relative.

Where Does Trouble Come From?
Doubling Down II

James O'Hagan was a partner in a prestigious Minneapolis law firm. His name is now synonymous with misuse of client confidences and securities fraud. *United States v. O'Hagan*, 521 U.S. 642 (1997), holds that a securities fraud indictment (for insider trading) may rest on an agent's use of a principal's information for the agent's own benefit if the agent does not first disclose his planned use to the principal. (Compare the holding in *Welch*, above.) Mr. O'Hagan traded on inside information his firm possessed regarding a client's planned takeover of another company.

Why did Mr. O'Hagan get in such trouble? He seems to have doubled down. Here are a few facts from the Minnesota Supreme Court opinion affirming O'Hagan's conviction on state-law charges.

> Between 1963 and 1989, O'Hagan practiced law with the firm of Dorsey & Whitney in Minneapolis, Minnesota. O'Hagan was a successful attorney, highly respected by clients and fellow attorneys. He became a senior partner in the firm and handled many major litigation matters, specializing in medical malpractice and securities cases. Although a partner, he enjoyed much independence and, to some extent, could be viewed as operating his own practice within the firm. During the period of 1986 to 1988, he was the number one or number two producer for the Dorsey firm, with annual billings in excess of $2 million. . . .
>
> Since 1970, O'Hagan had been the lead lawyer for the Mayo Clinic in medical malpractice litigation. Benjamin Hippe has been in the office of the general counsel for Mayo since 1962. O'Hagan and Hippe had worked closely together since 1970 and had developed a close professional relationship. O'Hagan represented Mayo in three lawsuits which are here relevant.
>
> In January 1987 a lawsuit was brought against Mayo on behalf of a child, represented by attorney John Carey. Carey testified that the parties settled for $270,000. According to Ben Hippe, however, O'Hagan told Hippe the case settled for $595,000. A check for the latter sum from Mayo, dated January 16, 1987, was deposited into an interest-bearing account, with O'Hagan as the sole signer on the account. Subsequently, a check was drawn for $270,000 for John Carey and his client. At O'Hagan's direction, the remaining $325,000 was distributed from the account on January 22, 1987, by three cashier's checks: $100,000 payable to Wayzata Bank and Trust Company; $100,000 payable to Investor's Savings Bank of Minneapolis; and $125,000 payable to Dakota County State Bank. It was later discovered these checks went to pay off loans on accounts belonging to O'Hagan. . . .

State v. O'Hagan, 474 N.W.2d 613, 615–17 (Minn.App. 1991).

One point to note here is that this sort of tampering with client funds is the third rail of professional ethics. We will study the rules in detail in chapter 14, but for now simply note that what happened to O'Hagan—jail and disbarment—is not out of line for such offenses. It is the rule (at least where the funds are stolen rather than "borrowed") rather than the exception. Even in cases where no money is actually stolen—such as where client funds are intermingled with lawyer funds, or where lawyers draw down on retainers before earning the money—severe discipline is the norm.

But to get back to Mr. O'Hagan, why was a high-powered, successful lawyer (with more than $2 million per year in billings, in 1980s dollars) using client money to pay off personal loans? Why did such a successful lawyer have such large loans to pay off? How could such a smart, skilled lawyer ever think he would get away with it? O'Hagan seems to have been a gambler. His favored form of gambling was the securities markets. He borrowed money to finance his speculation. We may presume his speculation produced net losses (why else would he have to tap client funds to pay the loans?).

At the point he lost so much money that he could not pay his debts O'Hagan had a choice. He could declare bankruptcy, in which case he would suffer whatever shame attends to such a filing in his relatively high-flying social circle. Perhaps more seriously, his practice might suffer if word got out to his clients that he was so enthralled with speculation that it had ruined him. If O'Hagan had declared bankruptcy, however, he might well have survived all right. His clients probably would not care too much about his personal finances and he might persuade them that he had just had an investment go South on him. That happens.

O'Hagan chose to double down instead. Perhaps he could not stand to admit to himself that he was not as shrewd a trader as he had thought he was. Perhaps he was irrationally optimistic. Perhaps he just loved the thrill of speculation and could not live without it. Whatever the reason, he chose to try to cover personal failure with illegal conduct. Once he tapped client funds to pay personal debts the only questions were when he would be caught and how badly he would be punished.[4]

---

[4] Securities and Exchange Commission v. Dean A. Goetz, Case No. 11CV1220-IEG-NLS (S.D. Cal. June 3, 2011), illustrates a variation of the breach of trust theory of insider trading applied to lawyers and, improbably, provides an even more remarkable example of such a breach than that offered by *O'Hagan*. The defendant in *Goetz* "traded based on material, nonpublic information regarding the impending merger and acquisition involving Advanced Medical Optics that he misappropriated from his daughter, a lawyer who, at the time, worked for the law firm representing Advanced Medical Optics in the transaction. Goetz and his daughter shared a relationship of trust and confidence. Unbeknownst to his daughter, Goetz misappropriated confidential deal information from her while she worked on the transaction at her parents' house over the holidays in December 2008. By trading on the material, nonpublic information he misappropriated, Goetz breached the duty of trust and confidence that he owed to his daughter." Without admitting or denying liability, Goetz settled charges against him in return for disgorgement of allegedly unlawful trading profits plus a penalty equal to the amount of those profits.

3. DISCLOSURE OF CLIENT INFORMATION FOR PERSONAL BENEFIT

Model Rules of Professional Conduct 1.6(a), 1.9(c)

WOOD'S CASE

137 N.H. 698 (1993)

THAYER, JUSTICE.

The Supreme Court Committee on Professional Conduct (committee) filed a petition seeking public censure, alleging that the respondent, Blair C. Wood, violated various Rules of Professional Conduct (Rules).

The committee's petition was not referred to a judicial referee because the parties stipulated to the material facts and exhibits. Wood practices law in Hanover and has lived in Lebanon for approximately twenty years. In June 1990, he met with representatives of Heritage Companies (Heritage) to discuss the possibility of developing a mall near exit 15 of Interstate 89 in Enfield. Wood had previously dealt with the Enfield site and had obtained town approvals for its commercial development. Heritage retained Wood because of his knowledge of Enfield planning issues and of the composition of the Enfield zoning and planning boards. Wood knew that Heritage had previously considered other sites but did not know that other sites were still under consideration.

In June and July 1990, Wood twice conferred with Heritage representatives by telephone and responded in writing to their request for a review of Enfield's zoning ordinance. He informed Heritage that his partner, Jay P. Cooper, would be responsible for developing a strategy to gain approvals for a mall in Enfield. Through July and August, Heritage's requests continued to focus on the Enfield property. Unknown to either Wood or Cooper, however, Heritage secured an option to purchase property in Lebanon. In early November, Heritage asked Cooper for advice on gaining approval of a mall on the McQuade site in Lebanon at exit 16 of Interstate 89. Cooper contacted the Lebanon city engineer and the planning board chairman regarding possible commercial and rezoning of the McQuade property, and responded to Heritage's request with a detailed memorandum on November 21, 1990.

At some point after November 21, Cooper discovered that the McQuade site for the mall in Lebanon abutted Wood's property. Cooper informed Wood that Heritage was exploring developing the mall on the McQuade property. Wood and his family opposed rezoning the McQuade property and building a mall there. Cooper notified Heritage of Wood's conflict and of the firm's decision to withdraw from further representation, and recommended replacement counsel.

Over the weekend of December 8–9, 1990, Heritage commissioned a survey of selected residents asking how they would react to the development of a large regional mall near exit 16 of Interstate 89, and possible rezoning of property in that area. Neither Heritage nor the McQuade site were identified in the survey. On December 10, 1990, a petition signed by thirty-two Lebanon residents was filed with the Lebanon City Council seeking to rezone a portion of the McQuade property, tax lot 55, from a rural zone to a commercial zone. The signatures were obtained by Heritage's new attorney.

Heritage's plans for developing a mall on the McQuade property involved rezoning 122 acres of undeveloped land to allow for general commercial use. The mall was to be located on two lots: one in Enfield, which Wood had explored, and the McQuade lot in Lebanon, which Cooper had explored. On December 11, 1990, Heritage's new attorney gave an interview to the *Valley News,* a Lebanon newspaper, about the proposed mall. The reporter also contacted Wood, who made statements that were published in an article on the proposed mall on December 12, 1990.

The newspaper article identified Heritage as the developer and described the size of the project. It noted that because of the scope of the proposed zoning change, "its fate is left to Lebanon voters, who will decide in a referendum in March." The article included favorable descriptions of the project from various residents, and then referred to Wood as an opponent of the project, stating the reasons for his opposition. On December 17, 1990, Heritage's attorney wrote to Wood indicating Heritage's concerns about Wood taking a public position adverse to Heritage.

Wood and his family wrote letters to the Lebanon City Council and attended public meetings to express their opposition to rezoning the McQuade site to allow commercial development, including the proposed mall. On December 22, 1990, another article on the proposed mall was published in the *Valley News.* This article contained references to Wood's letter to the city council and his arguments in opposition to the mall contained in the letter.

On January 3, 1991, the Lebanon Conservation Commission gave an advisory opinion to the city council and unanimously recommended rejecting the proposed zoning change. On January 7, 1991, the Lebanon Planning Board held a public meeting for the purpose of giving an advisory opinion to the city council. The board voted to recommend that the McQuade property not be rezoned. Wood attended these meetings and spoke in opposition at the January 7 meeting. On January 9, 1991, the Lebanon Zoning Map Change Committee determined that it did not have enough time to adequately evaluate the proposed zoning change. Without having filed an application for subdivision approval or site plan review,

Heritage withdrew its plans to develop the McQuade site on January 23, 1991.

The committee's petition for public censure alleged that Wood violated Rules 1.9(a), 1.9(b), 1.16(b), 1.16(d), and 8.4(a). . . .

This petition presents issues that are before this court for the first time, implicating an attorney's duty of loyalty to a client and an attorney's ability to pursue and express his or her personal beliefs.

[In an omitted portion of the opinion, the court rejected the committee's claim that Wood violated Rule 1.9(a). That rule prohibits a lawyer who has represented a client from later representing "another person" in the same or a substantially related matter if the "other person's" interests are materially adverse to the interests of the former client. The court held that " 'another person' in Rule 1.9(a) is synonymous with 'another client' and does not encompass a lawyer's *pro se* activities. Accordingly, we hold that the respondent did not violate the Rule. Our interpretation of Rule 1.9(a), however, does not relieve lawyers of the duty of loyalty to former clients, or abrogate the attorney-client privilege."]

Rule 1.9(b) provides:

> "A lawyer who has formerly represented a person in a matter shall not thereafter: . . . (b) use information relating to the representation to the disadvantage of the former client except as Rule 1.6 would permit with respect to a client or when the information has become generally known."

The committee alleges that Wood violated this rule through his interview with the *Valley News* reporter and the subsequent publication on December 12, 1990. Wood contends that his comments in the *Valley News* were directed to generally known information, and that the information was not used to Heritage's disadvantage. We agree with the committee but base our holding on different portions of the article. The article provided:

> "Blair Wood, a Hanover attorney who lives on Eastman Hill and who plans to mount 'a serious campaign to defeat the project,' cited a number of objections: a devastating effect on traffic on Eastman Hill Road; a tremendous amount of new lighting to the neighborhood; and damage to the area's wildlife habitat.
>
> . . . .
>
> Wood said that within the last year, after the developer had decided against a site near Exit 15, Heritage representatives came to his law firm—Stebbins Bradley Wood & Harvey—and asked the firm to represent them in their attempts to put a mall on the Exit 16 site. Wood, who didn't disclose the name of the developers, said his law firm didn't take the case because of his opposition to the project. Wood

said he thinks the developers want to bypass the efforts of a committee that will review the city's zoning map, because the committee might not agree with the developer's proposed zoning change and might not come up with any definite proposals by voting time in March.

Between now and March, Wood said, 'they've got a big selling job to do' to Lebanon residents.

'The burden will be on them to convince the people this is good for them.' He said the developers will promote the mall 'based on the mentality of more and bigger shopping, employment, and taxes' being paid to the city.

'To me it's a test of this community,' Wood continued. 'Do we want a community that's well planned? Pretty? Or are we what they think we are? Greedy? Materialistic?' "

The committee argues that Wood's reference to increased traffic and lighting, wildlife impacts, and that the developer would promote the mall on a theory of more taxes, employment and shopping, is information related to the representation because Cooper's November 21, 1990, memo to Heritage included references to these topics. We do not agree. Heritage retained Wood for his zoning expertise and because of his past success record. Wood, an experienced real estate attorney, did not need to refer to the specific proposal before the city in order to identify which disadvantages a developer would downplay, or which selling points would be emphasized when proposing the development of a regional mall. In our view, the references made to traffic and related impacts, and taxes and related benefits, are not related to Wood's representation of Heritage, but are commonly known effects of any large commercial development.

Nor are we persuaded that Wood was using information related to the representation when he opined that the developers would seek to bypass the city zoning map committee since a citizen's petition had already been filed to rezone the McQuade site. By filing the petition, which Wood learned of by checking with the Lebanon City Council, Heritage indicated that its strategy was to seek a referendum vote on rezoning only one tax lot, instead of seeking to rezone every lot in the rural zone by trying to amend the zoning map.

Although we find information related to the representation was not used to the disadvantage of the former client in the above comments, we hold that Wood's references to the fact that Heritage representatives explored another site and that the firm of Stebbins, Bradley, Wood & Harvey refused to represent Heritage because of his opposition to the project are related to the representation and were used to Heritage's disadvantage. We recognize that Wood did not name the developer who explored a site near exit 16 of Interstate 89, but note that the context in which Wood's statements were made certainly gives the impression that it was Heritage who explored the alternate site. In addition, we are troubled by Wood's misrepresentation of the facts. He told the reporter that the firm refused to represent Heritage, when, in fact, the firm represented Heritage on this project for several months. We also look disfavorably on Wood's use of his law firm's prestige to Heritage's disadvantage by Wood's implication that the firm would have nothing to do with advising Heritage on developing a mall in Lebanon. These facts had not become generally known at the time the article was published. We therefore hold that the respondent violated Rule 1.9(b). . . .

The finding that the respondent violated Rule 1.9(b) triggers a finding that he also violated Rule 8.4(a). The respondent is hereby publicly censured for his violation of these Rules.

CASE QUESTIONS

1. Did Wood's discussion of traffic, lighting, wildlife, employment, and taxes breach any duties? How did the court treat these remarks, and why?
2. How did Wood's statement that his firm refused to represent the developer relate to the language of Rule 1.9(b)? How did the court say it related?
3. What confidential information was used here? How was it used?

Client Information as Client Property II What Is Generally Known?

Wood illustrates the difference between confidential information and information that is generally known. General, generic advantages and disadvantages of development and the citizens' petition were generally known. Wood's discussion of that information therefore did not subject him to discipline. That the developer was considering an alternative site was not generally known, and Wood's reference to that fact led to his censure.

Restatement § 59 cmt d provides some guidance on distinguishing generally known information from confidential information: "Information contained in books or records in public libraries, public-record depositaries such as government offices, or in publicly accessible electronic-data storage is generally known if the particular information is obtainable through publicly available indexes and similar methods of access. Information is not generally known when a person interested in knowing the information could obtain it only by means of special knowledge or substantial difficulty or expense."

This comment may be understood as stating that information is generally known if a reasonably diligent person with ordinary knowledge in some field could obtain the information employing lawful means. An example may help make this standard clear.

Suppose a tire company develops a new process for treating rubber that makes tires last longer. The process (i) starts out as an experiment, (ii) is then perfected and employed at the company's plants, (iii) is then made the subject of a patent application filed with the Patent & Trademark Office, (iv) then becomes public after it has been pending for 18 months, and (v) is then embodied in an issued patent. During stages (i)–(iii) the process would constitute confidential client information (and, indeed, a trade secret). After the application becomes public, however, it would be available to anyone searching the PTO website for pending applications, a very common practice. It therefore would be generally known. *See also Jamaica Pub. Serv. Co. v. AIU Ins. Co.,* 92 N.Y.2d 631 (1998)(reversing order disqualifying firm that submitted an affidavit from a former employee of an opposing party concerning that party's corporate structure: "information regarding the interrelationship of AIG and its member companies was readily available in such public materials as trade periodicals and filings with State and Federal regulators. It was thus "generally known").

Some information learned while representing a client is never considered confidential client information in the first place. In the example above, suppose a lawyer working on the patent application learns everything there is to know about a particular doctrine of patent law. That information "is part of the general fund of information available to the lawyer" and is never the client's in the first place. *Restatement (Third) of the Law Governing Lawyers* § 59 cmt. e. The same could be said for general principles of economics or engineering a lawyer might learn to better represent a client but which do not pertain specifically to the client.

Knowledge of the law or legal institutions also is generally known. A lawyer learns a particular legal doctrine while working for one client may use that knowledge freely while working for others. The same is true of knowledge about the legal system, such as whether a particular jurisdiction is good for plaintiffs or defendants.

There is a dynamic element to this topic. Information may be confidential when a lawyer acquires it and become generally known thereafter. The Model Rules also differ according to when a lawyer wants to use information. Model Rule 1.9(c) allows lawyers to use information from a *former* client if that information has become generally known. The rule for current clients, Model Rule 1.8(b) does not distinguish between information that is generally known and any other information acquired in connection with the representation. It states "A lawyer shall not use information relating to representation of a client to the disadvantage of the client unless the client consents after consultation, except as permitted or required by Rule 1.6 or Rule 3.3."

The *Restatement* takes the position that defining confidential information to exclude generally known information is consistent with the absence of such an exclusion from Model Rule 1.8(b). Comment d to Section 59 states that use of even generally known information would violate the duty of loyalty principles underlying Model Rule 1.7, which forbids representation of a client where there is a conflict of interest between that client and a personal interest of a lawyer or one of the lawyer's other clients.

---

4. DISCLOSURE NOT FOR PERSONAL BENEFIT

The lawyers in the preceding section got something for themselves out of the use or disclosure of client information. Personal benefit is not required to show a breach of duty, however. Sometimes the violation can take the form of inadvertent or defensive disclosure. In reading the following material ask yourself whether the lawyers are as culpable as the lawyers in the preceding section. If you were representing them how would you try to use the differences to their advantage?

IN RE PRESSLY

160 Vt. 319 (1993)

PER CURIAM

Respondent Thomas Pressly appeals from a decision of the Professional Conduct Board recommending a public reprimand as discipline for his misconduct in violating Disciplinary Rule (DR) 4–101(B)(1) ("a lawyer shall not knowingly . . . [r]eveal a confidence or secret of his client"). DR 1–102(A)(1); A.O. 9, Rule 7A(4). We affirm and impose the recommended sanction.

In 1989, respondent, a member of the Vermont bar since 1975, represented complainant in connection with relief from abuse and divorce proceedings. Complainant informed respondent that her husband had a history of alcoholism, battering, and abuse. After a hearing at which she was represented by respondent, complainant was granted a temporary order requiring her husband to refrain from abusing her, and, by stipulation of the parties, temporary custody of the couple's two children with supervised visitation by the father. About a month later, respondent filed a divorce complaint on his client's behalf. The parties negotiated an agreement under which complainant would retain temporary custody of the children and her husband would be allowed unsupervised visitation. Complainant, on respondent's advice, reluctantly agreed to the visitation provision.

At that time, complainant told respondent that she was being harassed by her husband, that his alcoholism was a continuing problem, and that she wanted the children's visits with their father to be supervised. Respondent advised her, however, that there were insufficient legal grounds to require supervised visits. Complainant continued to press respondent to help her prevent her husband from continuing unsupervised visitation, but no motion was filed seeking supervised visitation.

Near the end of August 1989, complainant told respondent her suspicions, based on consultation with a counselor, that her nine-year-old daughter had been sexually abused by the father. According to the counselor, a "yellow flag" went up when she observed several symptoms of abuse. Complainant told respondent her suspicions, the basis for them, and her plan to arrange for a doctor's appointment for the daughter, which she thought might provide needed evidence against the father. She asked that respondent not discuss her suspicions or plans with her husband's lawyer.

In response to opposing counsel's question as to why the wife continued to request supervised visitation and whether sexual abuse was an issue in the case, respondent, notwithstanding his client's request, revealed to him the suspicions of sexual abuse. Respondent then asked the husband's lawyer not to communicate this information to the husband.[5] The next day, opposing counsel wrote respondent stating, "I mentioned to [my client] the representation [your client] had made to you about their daughter making statements to her counselor about sexual abuse. . . . [They] are totally unfounded and he views them to be a blatant attempt on the part of [your client] to manufacture evidence to keep him away from his children."

Complainant confronted her attorney about the disclosure, and was told by respondent that he provided the information in response to questions from opposing counsel. She discharged respondent and retained new counsel. After the disclosure, complainant perceived that her husband became increasingly uncooperative, which heightened her sense of fear and anxiety and created emotional distress. . . . .

[5] FN* Complainant's testimony indicated that she directed her attorney not to disclose anything about sexual abuse to the husband. No mention was made of the opposing counsel. Although respondent points out this distinction as being contrary to the findings, we fail to understand its significance. The only ethical way respondent could communicate about the case was through the husband's lawyer. DR 7–104(A)(1) (lawyer not to communicate directly with adverse party). Respondent could not reasonably expect husband's counsel to keep the wife's confidences unrevealed. Respondent acknowledged that if he had been given similar information by opposing counsel, he would have disclosed it to *his* client, notwithstanding a request not to do so.

Whatever mental state we ascribe to respondent's conduct, he should have known not to disclose his client's confidence. He testified before the panel that he knew the information was to be held in confidence, but felt that when pressured as to why his client wanted supervised visitation, informing opposing counsel was best. When asked whether he had thought of ending the conversation with counsel by stating that an attorney-client privilege precluded him from revealing anything further, he stated "If I say that, I think I'm letting the cat out of the bag also." He understood that he should not have revealed what his client had requested him to hold in confidence; therefore, his conduct satisfied the "knowingly" element of DR 1–102(A)(1).

"Knowingly" has two connotations, however. In addition to the knowledge respondent had that his conversations with his client were protected under the attorney-client privilege, the Board may consider in fashioning a remedy the degree and quality of the lawyer's knowledge in committing the violation; for example, whether respondent actually considered the repercussions of the violation to his client. That respondent did not actually understand the duty established by the Code is not the same as whether he committed the violation with knowledge of all probable consequences.

The Board gave respondent the benefit of the doubt on whether he knew that his disclosure to opposing counsel would cause his client anguish or jeopardize her case. If respondent did not actually know that his conduct would injure his client—his conduct being negligent because of his good intention (good faith) in making the disclosure—he still knew that his conduct violated a confidence. He nevertheless misunderstood his duty to disclose under the circumstances. If this is, for all practical purposes, negligence, we still fail to find error in the Board's determination that a public reprimand is the appropriate sanction.

Regardless of the Board's characterization of respondent's mental culpability, the Board's recommendation of reprimand is consistent with the prevailing standards for determining sanctions under such circumstances. The ABA Standards advise public reprimand, even though the attorney may have acted in good faith and was merely negligent. That is as far as the Board went in its recommendation of discipline.

The Board found that complainant suffered "emotional distress" as a result of the disclosure, which "heightened her level of fear and anxiety." Respondent complains that the Board did not sufficiently analyze the level of seriousness of the injury in light of the ABA Standard recommending at least a public reprimand when "injury or potential injury to a client" occurs. Further analysis, however, seems unnecessary in this case. As the Board discussed,

> Complainant was shocked by this news. She had relied upon respondent to protect the confidentiality of this information. She felt that Respondent had betrayed her trust.
>
> . . . .
>
> Respondent's conduct was injurious to his client to the extent that his actions caused her emotional distress. We do not find, however, that the disclosure had an adverse impact on the pending litigation although there was a potential for such injury.

That fairly sums up a finding of more than "little or no actual or potential injury," justifying more than a private admonition.

We adhere to the Board's recommendation. Respondent's infraction violated a core component of the attorney-client relationship, of which he, as an attorney in practice in this state for approximately sixteen years at the time of the infraction, should have been well aware. Respondent does not contend, nor does the record reflect, that his disclosure was intended or necessary to protect the child. His hope that opposing counsel would not disclose the information to the husband demonstrates naivete, rather than any intent to simply disregard his client's confidence. Consequently, we agree with the Board that a suspension would be too harsh. On the other hand, a private admonition would unduly depreciate the violation.

According to ABA Standard 1.2., it is "[o]nly in cases of minor misconduct, when there is little or no injury to a client, the public, the legal system, or the profession, and when there is little likelihood of repetition by the lawyer" that private discipline is appropriate. The Board found and we agree that respondent "will not make a similar error in the future," but complainant was obviously injured by the disclosure. Persons seek a lawyer's help not just for a favorable outcome or sage advice, but for the peace of mind that their interests are being taken into account and protected. Public reprimand is appropriate under the circumstances.

CASE QUESTIONS

1. Did Pressly act disloyaly?
2. What mental state does the court mention as warranting public reprimand?

PROBLEM 4–3

Pressly argued that he was in a box once opposing counsel asked if his client was claiming that her former husband was sexually abusing their child. He thought that citing the attorney-client privilege (actually, the duty of confidentiality) would "let the cat out of the bag." Isn't that right? In context, wouldn't you take such an answer as confirmation that your client was making such a claim?

Is there any way you could respond to such a question without letting the cat out of the bag? Remember, Model Rule 4.1 states that, in the course of representing a client, "a lawyer shall not knowingly (a) make a false statement of material fact or law to a third person." How could you obey that rule and still serve your client's interests in a situation like the one facing *Pressly*?

---

5. CONFIDENTIALITY WITH MULTIPLE CLIENTS

The basic rule of joint representation is that neither of two co-clients may assert privilege as against the other co-client with respect to communications pertaining to the joint representation. As noted above, however, the privilege and the duty are two different things. Privilege is a rule of evidence general asserted against compelled disclosure while confidentiality pertains to voluntary disclosure. It is therefore possible for you to be ethically prohibited from voluntarily disclosing unprivileged information. (If you were compelled to disclose by a court order then disclosure would be permitted by Rule 1.6(b)(6) and the disclosed information would be admissible.) Such situations are probably not common, because careful lawyers would make sure their confidentiality obligations matched the default privilege rule. Divergence is possible, however, as the following case illustrates. In reading it note that the New Jersey rules cited in the case are substantively similar to current Model Rule 1.6(b)(2)-(3) but that the resolution reached by the court in this case might not be available in states, such as California, that do not allow disclosure to avoid or rectify harm to financial interests.

Restatement § 75

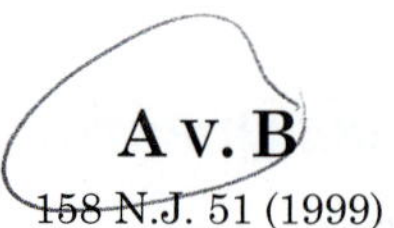

A v. B

158 N.J. 51 (1999)

POLLOCK, J.

This appeal presents the issue whether a law firm may disclose confidential information of one co-client to another co-client. Specifically, in this paternity action, the mother's former law firm, which contemporaneously represented the father and his wife in planning their estates, seeks to disclose to the wife the existence of the father's illegitimate child.

A law firm, Hill Wallack (described variously as "the law firm" or "the firm"), jointly represented the husband and wife in drafting wills in which they devised their respective estates to each other. The devises created the possibility that the other spouse's issue, whether legitimate or illegitimate, ultimately would acquire the decedent's property.

Unbeknown to Hill Wallack and the wife, the husband recently had fathered an illegitimate child. Before the execution of the wills, the child's mother retained Hill Wallack to institute this paternity action against the husband. Because of a clerical error, the firm's computer check did not reveal the conflict of interest inherent in its representation of the mother against the husband. On learning of the conflict, the firm withdrew from representation of the mother in the paternity action. Now, the firm wishes to disclose to the wife the fact that the husband has an illegitimate child. To prevent Hill Wallack from making that disclosure, the husband joined the firm as a third-party defendant in the paternity action. . . .

I.

Although the record is both informal and attenuated, the parties agree substantially on the relevant facts. Because the Family Part has sealed the record, we refer to the parties without identifying them by their proper names. So viewed, the record supports the following factual statement.

In October 1997, the husband and wife retained Hill Wallack, a firm of approximately sixty lawyers, to assist them with planning their estates. On the commencement of the joint representation, the husband and wife each signed a letter captioned "Waiver of Conflict of Interest." In explaining the possible conflicts of interest, the letter recited that the effect of a testamentary transfer by one spouse to the other would permit the transferee to dispose of the property as he or she desired. The firm's letter also explained that information provided by one spouse could become available to the other. Although the letter did not contain an express waiver of the confidentiality of any such information, each spouse consented to and waived any conflicts arising from the firm's joint representation.

Unfortunately, the clerk who opened the firm's estate planning file misspelled the clients' surname. The misspelled name was entered in the computer program that the firm uses to discover possible conflicts of interest. The firm then prepared reciprocal wills and related documents with the names of the husband and wife correctly spelled.

In January 1998, before the husband and wife executed the estate planning documents, the mother coincidentally retained Hill Wallack to  pursue a paternity claim against the husband. This time, when making its computer search for conflicts of interest, Hill Wallack spelled the husband's name correctly. Accordingly, the computer search did not reveal the existence of the firm's joint representation of the husband and wife. As a result, the estate planning department did not know that the family law department had instituted a paternity action for the mother. Similarly, the family law department did not know that the estate planning department was preparing estate plans for the husband and wife.

A lawyer from the firm's family law department wrote to the husband about the mother's paternity claim. The husband neither objected to the firm's representation of the mother nor alerted the firm to the conflict of interest. Instead, he retained Fox Rothschild to represent him in the paternity action. After initially denying paternity, he agreed to voluntary DNA testing, which revealed that he is the father. Negotiations over child support failed, and the mother instituted the present action.

After the mother filed the paternity action, the husband and wife executed their wills at the Hill Wallack office. The parties agree that in their wills, the husband and wife leave their respective residuary estates to each other. If the other spouse does not survive, the contingent beneficiaries are the testator's issue. The wife's will leaves her residuary estate to her husband, creating the possibility that her property ultimately may pass to his issue. . . . the term "issue" includes both legitimate and illegitimate children. When the wife executed her will, therefore, she did not know that the husband's illegitimate child ultimately may inherit her property.

The conflict of interest surfaced when Fox Rothschild, in response to Hill Wallack's request for disclosure of the husband's assets, informed the firm that it already possessed the requested information. Hill Wallack promptly informed the mother that it unknowingly was representing both the husband and the wife in an unrelated matter.

Hill Wallack immediately withdrew from representing the mother in the paternity action. It also instructed the estate planning department not to disclose any information about the husband's assets to the member of the firm who had been representing the mother. The firm then wrote to the husband stating that it believed it had an ethical obligation to disclose to the wife the existence, but not the identity, of his illegitimate child. Additionally, the firm stated that it was obligated to inform the wife "that her current estate plan may devise a portion of her assets through her spouse to that child." The firm suggested that the husband so inform his wife and stated that if he did not do so, it would. Because of the restraints imposed by the Appellate Division, however, the firm has not disclosed the information to the wife.

II.

This appeal concerns the conflict between two fundamental obligations of lawyers: the duty of confidentiality, Rules of Professional Conduct (RPC) 1.6(a), and the duty to inform clients of material facts, RPC 1.4(b). The conflict arises from a law firm's joint representation of two clients whose interests initially were, but no longer are, compatible.

Crucial to the attorney-client relationship is the attorney's obligation not to reveal confidential information learned in the course of representation. Thus, RPC 1.6(a) states that "[a] lawyer shall not reveal information relating to representation of a client unless the client consents after consultation, except for disclosures that are impliedly authorized in order to carry out the representation." Generally, "the principle of attorney-client confidentiality imposes a sacred trust on the attorney not to disclose the client's confidential communication." *State v. Land*, 73 N.J.24, 30 (1977).

A lawyer's obligation to communicate to one client all information needed to make an informed decision qualifies the firm's duty to maintain the confidentiality of a co-client's information. RPC 1.4(b), which reflects a lawyer's duty to keep clients informed, requires that "[a] lawyer shall explain a matter to the extent reasonably necessary to permit the client to make informed decisions regarding the representation." [citations omitted] In limited situations, moreover, an attorney is permitted or required to disclose confidential information. Hill Wallack argues that RPC 1.6 mandates, or at least permits, the firm to disclose to the wife the existence of the husband's illegitimate child. RPC 1.6(b) requires that a lawyer disclose "information relating to representation of a client" to the proper authorities if the lawyer "reasonably believes" that such disclosure is necessary to prevent the client "from committing a criminal, illegal or fraudulent act that the lawyer reasonably believes is likely to result in death or substantial bodily harm or substantial injury to the financial interest or property of another." RPC 1.6(b)(1). Despite Hill Wallack's claim that RPC 1.6(b) applies, the facts do not justify mandatory disclosure. The possible inheritance of the wife's estate by the husband's illegitimate child is too remote to constitute "substantial injury to the financial interest or property of another" within the meaning of RPC 1.6(b).

By comparison, in limited circumstances RPC 1.6(c) permits a lawyer to disclose a confidential communication. RPC 1.6(c) permits, but does not require, a lawyer to reveal confidential information to the extent the lawyer reasonably believes necessary "to rectify the consequences of a client's criminal, illegal or fraudulent act in furtherance of which the lawyer's services had been used." RPC 1.6(c)(1). Although RPC 1.6(c) does not define a "fraudulent act," the term takes on meaning from our construction of the word "fraud," found in the analogous "crime or fraud" exception to the attorney-client privilege. . . . When construing the "crime or fraud" exception to the attorney-client privilege, "our courts have generally given the term 'fraud' an expansive reading." *Fellerman v. Bradley*, 99 N.J. 493, 503–04 (1985).

We likewise construe broadly the term "fraudulent act" within the meaning of RPC 1.6(c). So construed, the husband's deliberate omission of the existence of his illegitimate child constitutes a fraud on his wife. When discussing their respective estates with the firm, the husband and wife reasonably could expect that each would disclose information material to the distribution of their estates, including the existence of children who are contingent residuary beneficiaries. The husband breached that duty. Under the reciprocal wills, the existence of the husband's illegitimate child could affect the distribution of the wife's estate, if she predeceased him. Additionally, the husband's child support payments and other financial responsibilities owed to the illegitimate child could deplete that part of his estate that otherwise would pass to his wife.

From another perspective, it would be "fundamentally unfair" for the husband to reap the "joint planning advantages of access to information and certainty of outcome," while denying those same advantages to his wife. Teresa S. Collett, *Disclosure, Discretion, or Deception: The Estate Planner's Ethical Dilemma from a Unilateral Confidence*, 28 Real Prop. Prob. Tr. J. 683, 743 (1994). In effect, the husband has used the law firm's services to defraud his wife in the preparation of her estate. . . .

Under RPC 1.6, the facts support disclosure to the wife. The law firm did not learn of the husband's illegitimate child in a confidential communication from him. Indeed, he concealed that information from both his wife and the firm. The law firm learned about the husband's child through its representation of the mother in her paternity action against the husband. Accordingly, the husband's expectation of nondisclosure of the information may be less than if he had communicated the information to the firm in confidence.

In addition, the husband and wife signed letters captioned "Waiver of Conflict of Interest." These letters acknowledge that information provided by one client could become available to the other. The letters, however, stop short of explicitly authorizing the firm to disclose one spouse's confidential information to the other. Even in the absence of any such explicit authorization, the spirit of the letters supports the firm's decision to disclose to the wife the existence of the husband's illegitimate child.

Neither our research nor that of counsel has revealed a dispositive judicial decision from this or any other jurisdiction on the issue of disclosure of confidential information about one client to a co-client. Persuasive secondary authority, however, supports the conclusion that the firm may disclose to the wife the existence of the husband's child. . . .

Because Hill Wallack wishes to make the disclosure, we need not reach the issue whether the lawyer's obligation to disclose is discretionary or mandatory. In conclusion, Hill Wallack may inform the wife of the existence of the husband's illegitimate child. . . .

CASE QUESTIONS

1. What duties conflicted to create Hill Wallack's problem?
2. The court found an exception to a rule solved this problem; what exception was it?
3. What would the result have been in a jurisdiction without that exception?
4. Did the possibility that the husband's illegitimate child would inherit the wife's property justify disclosure? What was the court's reasoning on that issue?

PROBLEM 4–4

How could the Hill, Wallack firm avoided this problem?

It's Easier to Stay Out Than to Get Out: I

As Mark Twain once said, "it is easier to stay out than to get out." In the context of legal ethics that means it is better to avoid a problem than to have to solve it. *A v. B* exemplifies the point. The spouses in that case signed documents called "Waiver of Conflict of Interest," which the court said warned each spouse that "information provided by one client could become available to the other" but which "stop[ped] short of explicitly authorizing the firm to disclose one spouse's confidential information to the other."

Though the court let the Hill Wallack firm off the hook in *A v. B*, the firm could have put itself in a better position by requiring, as a condition of the representation, that each spouse agree that the firm could share all confidences relevant to the representation with each client. (Comment l to *Restatement* section 60 states that "co-clients may understand from the circumstances those obligations on the part of the lawyer and their own obligations, or they may explicitly agree to share information.").

One client might try to revoke that authority—one can always try—but then the firm would have a sound argument that both the firm and the other client relied on the agreement in undertaking the representation. The equities would be all on the firm's side and a court would likely find the agreement an adequate defense to any *post hoc* claim that the firm violated a duty of confidentiality that one client tried to assert after waiving it up front.

6. ENTITY REPRESENTATION AND ENTITY CONSTITUENTS

Model Rule of Professional Conduct 1.13(f)–(g)

It is an important rule of legal ethics that when you represent an entity client, such as a corporation, partnership, or joint venture, you represent the entity as such. You do not represent the officers, directors, or other people who act on behalf of the entity (entity constituents). That means the people who hire you, tell you what to do, pay you, and can fire you, are not your clients unless both you and a particular constituent agree that you will represent the constituent as well as the entity. Subject to conflict of interest rules (which we study in chapter 11), Model Rule 1.13(g) permits such representation. Model Rule 1.13 also has "reporting up" and "reporting out" requirements and permissions, which are discussed in chapter 17(B).

This rule presents some confidentiality and privilege issues that are clear enough conceptually but which can be very hard to implement in practice. Company employees may assume that the company's lawyer (you) is their lawyer as well, at least with regard to their work-related conduct. And, as just noted, in some cases you may be their lawyer. But in some cases the interests of an employee will conflict with the interests of your entity client. You will still need to communicate with the employee to get information you need to represent the entity, but you need to be careful not to mislead the employee or create duties you don't want to create. Model Rule 1.13(f) makes this point explicit.

PEREZ V. KIRK & CARRIGAN

822 S.W.2d 261 (Tex.App. 1991)

DORSEY, JUSTICE.

Ruben Perez appeals a summary judgment rendered against him on his causes of action against the law firm of Kirk & Carrigan, and against Dana Kirk and Steve Carrigan individually (henceforth all three will be collectively referred to as "Kirk & Carrigan"). We reverse the summary judgment and remand this case for trial.

The present suit arises from a school bus accident on September 21, 1989, in Alton, Texas. Ruben Perez was employed by Valley Coca–Cola Bottling Company as a truck driver. On the morning of the accident, Perez attempted to stop his truck at a stop sign along his route, but the truck's brakes failed to stop the truck, which collided with the school bus. The loaded bus was knocked into a pond and 21 children died. Perez suffered injuries from the collision and was taken to a local hospital to be treated.

The day after the accident, Kirk & Carrigan, lawyers who had been hired to represent Valley Coca–Cola Bottling Company, visited Perez in the hospital for the purpose of taking his statement. Perez claims that the lawyers told him that they were his lawyers too and that anything he told them would be kept confidential.[6] With this understanding, Perez gave them a sworn statement concerning the accident. However, after taking Perez' statement, Kirk & Carrigan had no further contact with him. Instead, Kirk & Carrigan made arrangements for criminal defense attorney Joseph Connors to represent Perez. Connors was paid by National Union Fire Insurance Company which covered both Valley Coca–Cola and Perez for liability in connection with the accident.

Among other things, Perez generally stated that he had a previous accident while driving a Coke truck in 1987 for which he was given a citation, that he had a speeding violation in 1988, that he had not filled out a daily checklist to show that he had checked the brakes on the morning of the accident, that he had never before experienced problems with the brakes on his truck and that they were working just before the accident, that he tried to apply the brakes to stop the truck, but that the brakes for the trailer were not working at all to stop the truck (the truck had two sets of brakes: the ones for the cab worked; the ones for the trailer did not and the greater weight of the trailer had the effect of pushing the entire truck, even though the cab brakes were working), that Perez did not have enough time to apply the emergency brakes, and that there was nothing the managers or supervisors at Valley Coca–Cola could have done to prevent the accident.

Some time after Connors began representing Perez, Kirk & Carrigan, without telling either Perez or Connors, turned Perez' statement over to the Hidalgo County District Attorney's Office. Kirk & Carrigan contend that Perez' statement was provided in a good faith attempt to fully comply with a request of the district attorney's office and under threat of sub-

[6] FN1. The summary judgment affidavits offered by Perez show the following with regard to Kirk & Carrigan's representations to him at the time they took Perez' statement:

Ruben Perez—"Kirk told me that they were lawyers hired by Valley Coca Cola, that they were my lawyers too, and that whatever I told them would be kept confidential. I trusted what these lawyers told me and I answered their questions."

Israel Perez (Ruben's father)—"Before beginning the questions, Kirk told Ruben that they were his lawyers, that they were going to help him, and that what they, they lawyers, learned from Ruben would be kept a secret."

Joe Perez (Ruben's uncle)—"Before Ruben gave his statement to Kirk, Kirk told Ruben that they (the lawyers) represented Valley Coca Cola, that they were Ruben's lawyers too, and that they did not want anyone else to come in the room and to talk to Ruben. Kirk then told Ruben 'I know you are in pain, but we need to ask you these questions. Your mind would be fresh to tell us what happened. This will be kept confidential. We will get you a copy of it tomorrow. We will not give anyone a copy. It is between you and us.' Kirk and Carrigan did not say that they represented only Valley Coca Cola."

poena if they did not voluntarily comply. Partly on the basis of this statement, the district attorney was able to obtain a grand jury indictment of Perez for involuntary manslaughter for his actions in connection with the accident.[7]

Ruben Perez filed the present suit as a Plea in Intervention and Original Petition in a suit brought on behalf of the children injured in the accident against Valley Coca–Cola. Perez sued Kirk & Carrigan, along with Valley Coca–Cola, a number of other Coca–Cola entities, and National Union Fire Insurance Company. Perez asserted numerous causes of action against Kirk & Carrigan [including] breach of fiduciary duty [and] negligent and intentional infliction of emotional distress. . . . Perez complained generally by his petition that Kirk & Carrigan had caused him to suffer public humiliation and emotional distress by turning over his supposedly confidential statement to the district attorney. In addition to the turnover of this statement, Perez alleged generally that Kirk & Carrigan, Valley Coca–Cola, and National Union engaged in an overall plan to shift the blame for the accident away from them and onto Perez, by concealing information tending to show that Valley Coca–Cola's faulty maintenance of the brakes on the truck was the real cause of the accident.

Kirk & Carrigan moved for summary judgment on all of the claims made against them by Perez, on the grounds that no attorney-client or other fiduciary relationship existed, that even if a fiduciary relationship did exist no damages resulted from the asserted breach, that all of Perez' claims basically allege groundless prosecution and therefore constitute an invalid claim for malicious prosecution, that Perez was not a consumer under the DTPA, and that Perez failed to state a cause of action for conspiracy to violate the Texas Insurance Code.

After hearing the motion for summary judgment, the trial court rendered judgment that Perez take nothing on his claims against Kirk & Carrigan. When the trial court then severed these claims from others within the suit, it became a final summary judgment, from which Perez presently appeals.

By his sole point of error, Perez complains simply that the trial court erred in granting Kirk & Carrigan's motion for summary judgment. . . .

Breach of Fiduciary Duty

With regard to Perez' cause of action for breach of the fiduciary duty of good faith and fair dealing, Kirk and Carrigan contend that no attor-

---

[7] FN3. By his summary judgment affidavit offered in support of Perez, Joseph Connors stated that, in his professional opinion as a board certified criminal law specialist, if he had known that the statement had been provided and had been able to have Perez explain his lack of training or knowledge about the brake system to the grand jury, Perez would not have been indicted for manslaughter. Ruben Perez also stated in his affidavit that Valley Coca–Cola Bottling Company had not given him any instruction in brake inspection, maintenance, or use in an emergency situation.

ney-client relationship existed and no fiduciary duty arose, because Perez never sought legal advice from them.

An agreement to form an attorney-client relationship may be implied from the conduct of the parties. Moreover, the relationship does not depend upon the payment of a fee, but may exist as a result of rendering services gratuitously.[8]

In the present case, viewing the summary judgment evidence in the light most favorable to Perez, Kirk & Carrigan told him that, in addition to representing Valley Coca Cola, they were also Perez' lawyers and that they were going to help him. Perez did not challenge this assertion, and he cooperated with the lawyers in giving his statement to them, even though he did not offer, nor was he asked, to pay the lawyers' fees. We hold that this was sufficient to imply the creation of an attorney-client relationship at the time Perez gave his statement to Kirk & Carrigan.

The existence of this relationship encouraged Perez to trust Kirk & Carrigan and gave rise to a corresponding duty on the part of the attorneys not to violate this position of trust. Accordingly, the relation between attorney and client is highly fiduciary in nature, and their dealings with each other are subject to the same scrutiny as a transaction between trustee and beneficiary. Specifically, the relationship between attorney and client has been described as one of *uberrima fides,* which means, "most abundant good faith," requiring absolute and perfect candor, openness and honesty, and the absence of any concealment or deception. In addition, because of the openness and candor within this relationship, certain communications between attorney and client are privileged from disclosure in either civil or criminal proceedings under the provisions of Tex.R.Civ.Evid. 503 and Tex.R.Crim.Evid.503, respectively.[9]

There is evidence that Kirk & Carrigan represented to Perez that his statement would be kept confidential. Later, however, without telling either Perez or his subsequently-retained criminal defense attorney, Kirk & Carrigan voluntarily disclosed Perez' statement to the district attorney. Perez asserts in the present suit that this course of conduct amounted, among other things, to a breach of fiduciary duty.

[8] FN4. An attorney's fiduciary responsibilities may arise even during preliminary consultations regarding the attorney's possible retention if the attorney enters into discussion of the client's legal problems with a view toward undertaking representation. *See Nolan v. Foreman,* 665 F.2d 738, 739 n. 3 (5th Cir.1982).

[9] FN5. Disclosure of confidential communications by an attorney, whether privileged or not under the rules of evidence, is generally prohibited by the disciplinary rules governing attorneys' conduct in Texas. *See* Supreme Court of Texas, Rules Governing the State Bar of Texas art. X, § 9 (Disciplinary Rules of Professional Conduct) Rule 1.05. In addition, the general rule is that confidential information received during the course of any fiduciary relationship may not be used or disclosed to the detriment of the one from whom the information is obtained. *Numed, Inc. v. McNutt,* 724 S.W.2d 432, 434 (Tex.App.—Fort Worth 1987, no writ) (former employee is obligated not to use or divulge employer's trade secrets).

Kirk & Carrigan seek to avoid this claim of breach, on the ground that the attorney-client privilege did not apply to the present statement, because unnecessary third parties were present at the time it was given. *See* Tex.R.Civ.Evid. 503(a)(5); Tex.R.Crim.Evid. 503(a)(5). However, whether or not the Rule 503 attorney-client privilege extended to Perez' statement, Kirk & Carrigan initially obtained the statement from Perez on the understanding that it would be kept confidential. Thus, regardless of whether from an evidentiary standpoint the privilege attached, Kirk & Carrigan breached their fiduciary duty to Perez either by wrongfully disclosing a privileged statement or by wrongfully representing that an unprivileged statement would be kept confidential. Either characterization shows a clear lack of honesty toward, and a deception of, Perez by his own attorneys regarding the degree of confidentiality with which they intended to treat the statement. . . .

[I]n the present case, the attorneys were at least under a fiduciary duty not to misrepresent to Perez that his conversations with them were confidential. Kirk & Carrigan should not now be able to assert the lack of attorney-client privilege . . . to excuse the harm caused by their own misrepresentation to Perez. We hold that it was error for the trial court to grant summary judgment on the ground that Kirk & Carrigan did not owe or breach a fiduciary duty to Perez.

In addition, however, even assuming a breach of fiduciary duty, Kirk & Carrigan also contend that summary judgment may be sustained on the ground that Perez could show no damages resulting from the breach. Kirk & Carrigan contend that their dissemination of Perez' statement could not have caused him any damages in the way of emotional distress, because the statement merely revealed Perez' own version of what happened. We do not agree. Mental anguish consists of the emotional response of the plaintiff caused by the tortfeasor's conduct. It includes, among other things, the mental sensation of pain resulting from public humiliation.

Regardless of the fact that Perez himself made the present statement, he did not necessarily intend it to be a public response as Kirk & Carrigan contend, but only a private and confidential discussion with his attorneys. Perez alleged that the publicity caused by his indictment, resulting from the revelation of the statement to the district attorney in breach of that confidentiality, caused him to suffer emotional distress and mental anguish. We hold that Perez has made a valid claim for such damages. *Cf. Billings v. Atkinson,* 489 S.W.2d 858 (Tex.1973) (damages for mental suffering are appropriate for an invasion of privacy).

CASE QUESTIONS

1. What causes of action did Perez assert?
2. What evidence supported his claim that Kirk & Kerrigan represented him?
3. What breach did Perez allege?
4. What explanation did Kirk & Kerrigan offer for its conduct?
5. What was Kirk & Kerrigan's position regarding attorney-client privilege?
6. Did the presence or absence of privilege matter to Perez's cause of action?
7. Would it have mattered if the district attorney subpoenaed the statement?

Doing It Right: The Civil "Miranda" or "Upjohn" Warning

Perez turns on a disagreement between lawyers representing an entity (Valley Coca Cola Bottling) and an entity employee (Perez) regarding whom the lawyers represented. If Kirk & Kerrigan represented only the entity then it would owe no duties to Perez and could not be liable for breaching them. If it represented both the entity and Perez, however, the opposite is true.

The practical lesson cases like *Perez* teach is that entity counsel must know whom they do and do not represent and must make sure the entity constituents they deal with—directors, officers, and employees—know it, too. Prudent lawyers in situations like *Perez* therefore caution constituents before conducting interviews such as the one in that case. The precise language of such cautions varies (it is not like the archetypal *Miranda* warning you see on television) but a proper warning includes four core points. In conversational form they are:

1. I represent [entity] and I am here to talk to you about [subject matter].
2. I do not represent you personally.
3. Our conversation is privileged, but [entity] controls the privilege. That means [entity] may disclose to third parties what you tell me if entity management chooses to do so.
4. You are free to consult with your own lawyer if you wish to do so. [In some cases the entity will recommend and pay for counsel for its employees.]

Such warnings are often called *Upjohn* warnings, after *Upjohn Co. v. United States*, 449 U.S. 383, 386–396 (1981), which held that employee communications with entity counsel may be covered by the entity's privilege. The purpose of the warning is to let employees know what could happen to what they tell you. The warning therefore creates a tension you must manage deftly: The stronger and clearer the warning is, the less an employee may want to confide in you and the harder it may be for you to do your work. To avoid problems such as you see in *Perez*, however, it is wise to err on the side of clarity.

To limit the risk of incurring civil liability yourself, or limiting the entity's ability to cooperate with an investigation, it is useful to document both that the warning was given and what was said. One firm follows the practice of having attorneys read a prepared statement to entity constituents at the outset of such interviews; the statement is then appended to the firm's summary of the interview, which begins by reciting that the statement was read to the witness before questioning began.

Must They Ask or Must You Tell?

There was evidence in *Perez* that Kirk & Carrigan represented that it would keep Perez's statements confidential, the very thing it did not do. What if the lawyers make no specific representations to an entity constituent regarding their relationship to her? As Model Rule 1.13(f) makes clear, it is the lawyer's job to clarify the situation. Ambiguity is therefore construed against the lawyer. As the court said in *Schiffli Embroidery Workers Pension Fund v. Ryan, Beck & Co.*, 1994 WL 62124 (1994):

> When representing a corporation or legal fiction, contact with its fiduciaries or other constituents is not only inevitable, but it is essential to effective legal representation of the client. However, attorneys must tread carefully. Today, the constituent might be the source of vital information as a representative of the client. Tomorrow, however, that same constituent might be a defendant in a lawsuit by the client. The lawyer has the responsibility of preempting the formation of an attorney-client relationship with the constituent where such a relationship is not intended.

1994 WL 62124 at *4–5. *See also Home Care Indus., Inc. v. Murray,* 154 F. Supp. 2d 861 (D. N.J. 2001). This issue often arises when a former constituent becomes involved with litigation against the entity and moves to disqualify entity counsel on the ground that entity counsel formerly represented the constituent individually. Disqualification is discretionary, and some courts will consider the constituent's legal sophistication in ruling on such a motion. *See, e.g., Ferranti Int'l plc v. Clark,* 767 F.Supp. 670 (E.D.Pa.1991). The Rule itself does not change in such cases, however.

When do you know, or should you know, that an entity's interests are adverse to those of a constituent? You have to use your judgment to decide how likely it is that the constituent's conduct will or has harmed the entity, as by making the entity liable to a third party or by creating a conflict with other entity constituents.

7. DISCLOSURE AUTHORIZED BY IMPLICATION

Section 61 of the *Restatement* provides that "a lawyer may use or disclose confidential client information when the lawyer reasonably believes that doing so will advance the interests of the client in representation." The comments to this section state that it is a specific application of the general rule of authority stated in Section 21(3), which provides that a lawyer "may take any lawful measure within the scope of representation that is reasonably calculated to advance a client's objectives as defined by the client, consulting with the client as required by Section 20." Because this authority is implied as a default rule, a client has the power to instruct you not to use or disclose confidential information, even if the rule stated in Section 61 would otherwise allow use or disclosure.

Adams v. Franklin, 924 A.2d 993 (D.C. 2007) illustrates the principle of implied authorization in the context of the attorney-client privilege. (You will recall that the duty of confidentiality and the privilege are different rules with different scopes, but the reasoning in this case applies equally well to the duty of confidentiality.)

Adams accused the defendants of defrauding her into selling her property below the market price. They asserted the statute of limitations as a defense. "To support this defense, [defendants] note a demand letter, which is dated August 16, 1999, purportedly authored and sent by appellant's former attorney, Leonard Koenick, to many of the same parties in the present suit. In order to establish the authenticity and appellant's authorization of the demand letter, appellees sought to depose Mr. Koenick on" four topics, the fourth of which was "where Mr. Koenick learned of the information contained in the letter." The court rejected Koenick's assertion of privilege against disclosure:

> With respect to the fourth topic—where Mr. Koenick learned of the information—we similarly do not find protection by the attorney-client privilege. The attorney-client privilege protects only communications from a client to an attorney that are, at the time they are communicated, intended to be confidential. . . . [Assuming the client was the source of the relevant information], then it is reasonable to assume that such information was relayed to Mr. Koenick with the intent that it be used as the basis of the demand letter. As appellant knew and intended that the information be published, it cannot be said to have been "confidential" ab initio. In the event that the original communication was in fact intended to be "confidential," we find

> that whatever privilege may have protected its disclosure has since been waived by the transmission of the demand letter to third parties not covered by the attorney-client privilege. Because the discrete topics of appellees' questioning do not implicate any privileged communications, we find that Mr. Koenick must subject himself to the deposition and answer any question reasonably within the scope of the identified.

924 A.2d at 999–1000.

Use or disclosure authorized by implication can present tricky problems. When in doubt, the safer course is to get explicit client consent to the action you wish to take (so long as the client is competent to make such a decision; *cf.* Model Rule 1.14).

B. EXCEPTIONS TO THE DUTY

As noted above, Model Rule 1.6(b) permits disclosure necessary to prevent reasonably certain death or substantial bodily harm, to prevent or rectify serious financial harm caused by a client and in which your services were used, to secure advice about your own obligations under the rules, to establish a claim or defense in a dispute with a client, to respond to allegations concerning your representation, or to comply with the law or a court order. The materials in this section survey the exceptions pertaining to self-defense and the prevention of death or substantial bodily harm. The exception allowing disclosure to prevent or rectify substantial financial harm is relatively new and not well developed in the case law.

1. LAWYER SELF-DEFENSE

Model Rule 1.6, Cmt. 10

FIRST FEDERAL SAVINGS & LOAN ASSOCIATION OF PITTSBURGH V. OPPENHEIM, APPEL, DIXON & CO.

110 F.R.D. 557 (S.D.N.Y. 1986)

MICHAEL H. DOLINGER, UNITED STATES MAGISTRATE:

Three savings and loan associations and the City of Farmington, New Mexico commenced this action in 1985 to recover for losses incurred as a result of the financial collapse of Comark, a California-based government securities dealer. The plaintiffs were customers of Comark and seek to hold Comark's former auditor—Oppenheim, Appel, Dixon & Co. ("OAD")—responsible for their damages based on a variety of federal statutory and state common-law and statutory causes of action. In its turn OAD has impleaded the former general partners of Comark—which is now in bankruptcy proceedings in the Central District of California—together with the former general counsel of Comark, Daniel Harkins, Esq., and Comark's former outside counsel, John J. Giovannone and his firm, Memel, Jacobs, Pierno, Gersh & Ellsworth.

At present the Court faces a set of related motions by various of the parties concerning the proposed disclosure by Comark's former general counsel, Mr. Harkins, of information that is concededly within the scope of the attorney-client privilege. Mr. Harkins proposes to provide this information, in the form of documents and deposition testimony, on the theory that, as a named third-party defendant, he is entitled to use in his defense any helpful information even if it would otherwise be protected from disclosure by his client's privilege. None of the other parties nor Comark's bankruptcy trustee—who has appeared solely for purposes of these motions—disagrees with the general proposition that such a "self-defense" exception to the privilege has been recognized by the Second Circuit. Nonetheless they are in dispute as to the preliminary showing, if any, that must be made before a party-attorney may override the privilege, and as to the scope of the disclosure that may be made if the exception is established.

The announced intention of Mr. Harkins to make the disclosures in question initially triggered a motion for a protective order by third-party defendant E. Keith Owens, formerly a general partner of Comark. Mr. Owens has since conceded that he has no standing to invoke the privilege of Comark, *see CFTC v. Weintraub,* 471 U.S. 343 (1985) (trustee of corporation in bankruptcy holds the privilege), but he claims to be asserting a personal privilege on the theory that, as a general partner, he was personally liable for Comark's debts and accordingly Harkins was necessarily functioning as his attorney when representing Comark. Owens contends that the "self-defense" exception is limited to information that is "necessary" to the attorney's defense and furthermore that no disclosure may be permitted unless OAD, as the discovering party, establishes a *prima facie* case against Harkins on its claim that he aided and abetted a fraud by Comark.

The privilege of Comark has been asserted in this case by the bankruptcy trustee, Sam Jonas, who appeared in this action at the request of the Court. Initially, the trustee did not address the questions of the "self-defense" exception but has since urged that Harkins must demonstrate, on a document-by-document basis, the "necessity" for each item of information that he proposes to disclose.

Not surprisingly, OAD has argued that no initial showing by it or by Harkins is necessary before he may disclose otherwise privileged information. OAD also asserts that the disclosure may encompass all information that may be useful to Harkins and, necessarily, all related information—even if harmful to Harkins—so that waiver of the privilege will not result in unfairness to OAD. . . .

The "Self–Defense" Exception to the Attorney–Client Privilege

The principle has long been accepted that, in appropriate circumstances, an attorney may disregard the privilege of a current or former client, and disclose otherwise protected attorney-client communications. The definition of the appropriate circumstances has, however, been a matter of some dispute.

The most frequently invoked rule, which was principally a product of nineteenth-century American common law, permitted disclosure by the attorney if he was suing the client to collect a fee, *e.g., Mitchell v. Bromberger,* 2 Nev. 345, 349 (1866); *cf. Nakasian v. Incontrade, Inc.,* 409 F.Supp. 1220, 1224 (S.D.N.Y.1976); if he was being sued by the client for malpractice, *e.g., Nave v. Baird,* 12 Ind. 318, 319 (1859); or if his client challenged his competence or integrity even though the attorney was not a party to the lawsuit. *E.g., State v. Madigan,* 66 Minn. 10, 68 N.W. 179 (1896).[10]

In each of these circumstances, the factual dispute is, in effect, between the attorney and his client. To the extent that the client initiates the dispute, he can be said to have put in issue his communications with his attorney and thus waived his right to the protection of the privilege. [citations omitted] In the fee collection case, even though it is initiated by the attorney and thus not easily characterized as a waiver by the client, invasion of the privilege was justified, according to the courts, because it would be a "manifest injustice" to "permit [ ] a client to use the privilege to his attorney's disadvantage." In short, the traditional rule did not contemplate an exception to the privilege merely because it was in the attorney's pecuniary or legal interest to make the disclosure, such as when he was sued by someone other than the client.

This narrow rule was in general followed in the wording of Uniform Rule of Evidence 26(2)(c) and Federal Standard of Evidence 503(d)(3). Both permit disclosure only of a "communication relevant to an issue of breach of duty by the lawyer to his client or by the client to his lawyer." *See* 2 *Weinstein's Evidence, supra,* at 503–2. As Professor Weinstein notes: "[T]he exception is required by consideration of fairness and policy when questions arise out of dealings between attorney and client, as in cases of controversy over attorney's fees, claims of inadequacy of representation, or charges of professional misconduct." *Id.* at 503–7 (*citing, in-*

[10] FN5. The prototypical example of such a claim is the assertion by a convicted defendant that he was denied effective assistance of counsel. *See, e.g., United States ex rel. Richardson v. McMann,* 408 F.2d 48, 53–54 (2d Cir.1969), *vac. on other gds.,* 397 U.S. 759, 90 S.Ct. 1441, 25 L.Ed.2d 763 (1970).

ter alia, C. McCormick, *Evidence* § 95 (2d ed. 1972); Cal.Evid.Code § 958). As the examples suggest, the wording is apparently designed to limit the exception to instances in which the client and attorney are in conflict: "Standard 503(d)(3) codifies the generally accepted view that when the attorney and client become opponents in a subsequent controversy, the attorney may, to the extent necessary to defend his rights, reveal any communication or advice given." *Id.,* ¶¶ 503(d)(3)[01] at 503–72 to 73.

If the foregoing authority were deemed to govern the scope of the privilege and the exceptions to it in this case, it is at least doubtful that the proposed disclosure by Harkins would be tenable since his former client does not charge him with a breach of duty in the attorney-client relationship, or indeed in any other respect. Accordingly, to justify his proposed disclosure Harkins points to a different body of law, comprising principally a provision of the ABA's Code of Professional Responsibility—DR 4–101(C)(4)—and a Second Circuit decision interpreting that provision.

The Code provision states that, notwithstanding the general prohibition against disclosure by the attorney of the "confidences" and "secrets" of the client,[11] he may make disclosure of

> [c]onfidences or secrets necessary to establish or collect his fee or to defend himself or his employees or associates against an accusation of wrongful conduct.

DR 4–101(C)(4). Although the notes to this provision could be read as reflecting an intention to incorporate only the traditional rule that an attorney may reveal otherwise privileged information when sued by the client or charged by him with malfeasance or when the attorney sues for fees, *see* DR 4–101 Note 19, the wording of the provision itself is considerably broader. It appears to encompass disclosure when the attorney is being sued by someone other than the client or, indeed, when an "accusation" of misconduct has been levelled against the attorney, even if a suit has not been filed.

This broader view of DR 4–101 has been explicitly endorsed by the Second Circuit in *Meyerhofer v. Empire Fire & Marine Ins. Co.,* 497 F.2d 1190, 1194–96 (2d Cir.), *cert. denied,* 419 U.S. 998 (1974). The initial question, however, is whether *Meyerhofer* is controlling in this case.

Plaintiffs in *Meyerhofer* commenced a securities fraud class action against an insurance company, its officers and directors, an underwriter, certain selling shareholders, and the attorneys that had represented the insurance company in connection with a public offering. Apparently

---

[11] FN8. "Confidence" is defined as "information protected by the attorney-client privilege under applicable law," whereas "secret" is deemed to be "other information gained in the professional relationship that the client has requested be held inviolate or the disclosure of which would be embarrassing or would be likely to be detrimental to the client." DR 4–101(A).

shortly after the filing of the complaint, one of the defendant attorneys—Stuart Charles Goldberg, Esq.—approached plaintiffs' counsel and offered to demonstrate that he had not been involved in whatever fraud may have occurred. To substantiate his innocence he provided to plaintiffs' counsel a copy of an affidavit, with attachments, that he had previously prepared for and submitted to the Securities and Exchange Commission in connection with its investigation of the transaction. Apparently satisfied with this information, plaintiffs dropped Goldberg as a defendant. On this set of facts the district court dismissed the complaint without prejudice and enjoined plaintiff's attorneys and Goldberg "from acting as counsel or participating with counsel for plaintiffs in . . . any . . . action against Empire involving the transactions placed in issue in this lawsuit and from disclosing confidential information to others." In so ruling the Court relied upon "the broader obligations of Canons 4 and 9" of the Code of Professional Responsibility.

On appeal the Second Circuit reversed the dismissal and disqualification orders except insofar as they enjoined Goldberg "from acting as a party . . . in any action arising out of the facts herein alleged, or from disclosing material information except on discovery or at trial. . . . " In so holding, the Court observed that the suit had been based on disclosure by Empire and not Goldberg, who had communicated with plaintiffs' attorneys only after he was named as a defendant. According to the Court . . . a lawyer may reveal confidences or secrets necessary to defend himself against "an accusation of wrongful conduct." This is exactly what Goldberg had to face when, in their original complaint, plaintiffs named him as a defendant who wilfully violated the securities laws. . . . Under these circumstances Goldberg had the right to make an appropriate disclosure with respect to his role in the public offering. Concomitantly, he had the right to support his version of the facts with suitable evidence. The Court went on to conclude that the particular disclosure made by Goldberg—via the detailed affidavit and exhibits—was justifiable under the circumstances even though it not only dealt with his role in preparing the offering plan but also with the discovery by the underwriter's counsel of an intended non-disclosure in connection with another transaction. As explained by the Court, Goldberg "was clearly in a situation of some urgency. . . . ," he consulted with his own attorney before making the disclosure, and disclosure of the entire SEC submission was an effective way of demonstrating his innocence.

Meyerhofer does not directly control the present case. The Second Circuit did not purport to adjudicate an attorney-client privilege claim or an attempt by an attorney to overcome his client's assertion of the privilege. What was at issue was an alleged breach of the standards of ethical conduct defined by the Code of Professional Responsibility, and the pertinent provisions of the ABA's Code are not necessarily coterminous with the privilege.

The Code provision is, in one respect, broader than the commonly recognized privilege since it covers not merely information protected under the privilege—the so-called client "confidence"—but also any other information obtained by the attorney in the course of his "professional relationship that the client has requested be held inviolate or the disclosure of which would be embarrassing or would be likely to be detrimental to the client." DR 4–101(A) (defining "secret"). On the other hand, the Code appears to narrow the client's protection from that recognized in the common law insofar as it authorizes disclosure by the attorney whenever he is accused of wrongful conduct, and it is to be assumed that such a narrowing by the ABA does not automatically or necessarily result in a corresponding change in the rules of privilege recognized by the courts. [citations omitted].[12]

The ambiguous scope of *Meyerhofer* is also suggested by the fact that the Second Circuit affirmed the District Court's orders insofar as they barred Goldberg from disclosing any "material information" relating to facts in the case except in the course of discovery or at trial. This indicates that the precise contours of the attorney-client privilege in that case were still to be decided and would be dealt with by the District Court in a manner that permitted the client to articulate and assert whatever privilege claims it wished to interpose.

The cases that have followed *Meyerhofer* have not shed a great deal of light on the parameters of the exception to the attorney-client privilege, although all are consistent with a recognition of the exception in some form. Most of the cases have either involved solely questions of attorney disqualification . . . or limited their comments—whether dictum or holding—to the effect of an attack by a client on the conduct of his attorney. . . . Others have recognized the right of an attorney under the Code to disclose privileged information if charged with, or even investigated for, criminal misconduct. [citations committed] Finally, several courts have indicated that the attorney is entitled to disclose privileged information over an assertion of privilege when sued by someone other

[12] FN12. The relationship between the Code and the privilege is suggested by the Comment to Rule 1.6 of the Model Rules of Professional Conduct:

> The principle of confidentiality is given effect in two related bodies of law, the attorney-client privilege (which includes the work-product doctrine) in the law of evidence and the rule of confidentiality established in professional ethics. The attorney-client privilege applies in judicial and other proceedings in which a lawyer may be called as a witness or otherwise required to produce evidence concerning a client. The rule of client-lawyer confidentiality applies in situations other than those where evidence is sought from the lawyer through compulsion of law. The confidentiality rule applies not merely to matters communicated in confidence by the client but also to all information relating to the representation, whatever its source. A lawyer may not disclose such information except as authorized or required by the Rules of Professional Conduct or other law.
>
> See also Rhode, Why the ABA Bothers: A Functional Perspective on Professional Codes, 59 Texas L.Rev. 689, 709–10 (1981).

than the former client on an aider-and-abettor theory, provided that the information is necessary to the attorney's defense. . . .

Notwithstanding the distinctions that could be drawn between the *Meyerhofer* case and the present situation, there is good reason for recognizing a "self-defense" exception to the attorney-client privilege in appropriate circumstances. First, if an attorney is sued for alleged misconduct in representing a client, it is self-evident that he has a compelling interest in being able to defend himself. Second, that interest may well outweigh the interest of the client in maintaining the confidentiality of his communications, particularly if disclosure of those communications will not imperil the legal interests of the client. . . Third, such disclosure will serve the truth-finding function of the litigation process, and is thus consistent with the general principle of narrowly construing evidentiary privileges. . .

In sum, the exception for attorney self-defense is recognized and accepted by the courts, albeit with varying degrees of warmth. The key issue, then, involves what limitations—both procedural and substantive—must be placed on its invocation.

The most obvious potential abuse is that, in an otherwise *bona fide* suit against the client, the plaintiff may assert claims against the attorney for the sole purpose of forcing counsel to divulge confidential material in order to defend himself. To avoid this danger in the present case, third-party defendant Owens urges that OAD, the party that has asserted the aiding-and-abetting claim against the attorney, be required to establish a *prima facie* case against Harkins before disclosure by him is permitted.

I need not reach the question of whether any showing is required of OAD, although I note that it is Harkins, and not OAD, who is the immediate beneficiary of an order permitting disclosure. In any event, OAD's claim against Harkins is plainly legally sufficient—indeed, the District Court recently denied a motion to dismiss a similar claim asserted against Comark's outside counsel, the firm of Memel, Jacobs—and the evidentiary record made by OAD in support of its cross-motion to compel is sufficient to establish that the claim asserted against Harkins is not pretextual.[13]

[13] FN15. OAD proffers evidence that at least arguably supports a suspicion that Harkins assisted a fraud committed by Comark. The specific activities alleged include giving legal advice to Comark to assist it in delaying disclosure of the improper commingling of partnership and client assets, and providing misleading information to California state regulatory officials. Without characterizing the weight of the evidence, I find it sufficient to demonstrate that OAD's claims against Harkins pass muster under Fed.R.Civ.P. 11. *See, e.g., Nemeroff v. Abelson,* 620 F.2d 339, 350 (2d Cir.1980); *see also Eastway Const. Corp. v. City of New York,* 762 F.2d 243, 253–54 (2d Cir.1985). That should suffice for present purposes.

The second question is the proper scope of disclosure to be permitted under the exception. . . [14] Harkins was directed to submit to the Court for its *in camera* review all of the documents he proposes to disclose, together with an affidavit explaining the necessity for his proposed disclosures, both by deposition and by document production. The trustee, as the holder of the privilege, has responded to Harkins' showing on this point.

In reviewing the proposed disclosures, I have applied a standard of reasonable necessity, a somewhat opaque term derived from Rule 1.6 of the Model Rules of Professional Conduct. In effect, disclosure is authorized for those items that, as a practical matter, seem likely to provide significant assistance to Harkins' defense. In general terms, this standard permits Harkins to testify about all of his conversations with Comark officers or employees concerning the commingling problem since it will be necessary for Harkins to explain what he knew about the issue, what he did about it, what he advised his client to do about it, and what he did not do about it. Necessarily, the production of documents must be similar in scope.

A related issue is whether discovery should be ordered in addition to that which Harkins proposes to reveal in his defense. Specifically, OAD raises the question whether it should be provided all privileged documents—if any—that are potentially damaging to Harkins' defense and that are thus not being volunteered by him. Assuming hypothetically that Harkins chose to provide helpful documents while not disclosing any damaging ones, I conclude that fairness would require disclosure of all documents pertaining to the communications at issue, whether Harkins volunteered them or not. This is a logical and unavoidable extension of the long-settled rule that a client's disclosure of a portion of an attorney-client privileged document, or of some but not all privileged documents relating to a particular event, may constitute a waiver of the privilege. As described by Wigmore:

> [W]hen [the client's] conduct touches a certain point of disclosure, fairness requires that his privilege cease whether he intended that result or not. He cannot be allowed, after disclosing as much as he pleases, to withhold the remainder. . . .

8 Wigmore, *supra,* § 2327 at 636. In such a situation, at a minimum waiver will be found for so much of the withheld information "as will make the disclosure complete and not misleadingly one-sided."

These waiver decisions differ from this case because the initial disclosure here is being made by the attorney and not by the client. Nevertheless, the paramount concern must be fairness to the party against

[14] FN16. I note also that, as in *Meyerhofer,* the disclosure sought to be made by Harkins would of course not induce the filing of a suit against his client. Comark has been held liable for fraud in a related case and is not a party here. As for Owens, even assuming he were deemed a client of Harkins, he is already a third-party defendant in this action.

whom the information disclosed by the attorney is to be used—in this case OAD—and it necessarily follows from the initial decision to override the privilege to permit Harkins to disclose relevant favorable information, that he must also be compelled to disclose relevant unfavorable information.

In order to assure that the disclosure is not misleadingly one-sided, the Court directed Harkins to submit for *in camera* review all documents originally listed by him as privileged that he has not sought authorization to disclose under the "self defense" exception to the privilege. That submission has been made and the documents inspected for the purpose of identifying any that appear to relate to communications concerning the alleged fraud. . .

CASE QUESTIONS

1. When is the self-defense exception triggered?
2. What standard governs what may be disclosed?
3. What rule applies if an attorney proposes to disclose only part of the communications on a subject?
4. How does this case differ from *Meyerhofer*?

PROBLEM 4–5

Suppose you are an immigration lawyer. One day the FBI knocks on your office door and serves you with a search warrant. They search your office and confiscate most of your records. When you ask what is going on, an agent tells you the FBI is gathering information regarding persons who might be associated with the bombing of train stations in Madrid, Spain. Your name has come up because you represent a local Muslim charitable organization, whose director is on the government's terrorism watch list. You had no records regarding that organization, so none were seized.

You have not been indicted, nor have you received a "target letter" stating that you are the subject of a grand jury investigation. You are worried, however, that you might be arrested on a material witness warrant, as a person having information regarding terrorist activities. You have reason to believe such arrests occur suddenly, and without warning. May you disclose to the FBI confidential information regarding your representation of the charitable organization in order to clear yourself of suspicion?

Suppose that in the course of representing the charitable organization you have learned that it has violated several tax laws. Would this fact affect your decision?

Meet "Bones"

Sometimes disclosure can compound mistakes. Matter of Ponds, *D.C. Court of Appeals Board of Professional Responsibility, April 27, 2005, involved Ponds's representation of a criminal defendant accused of being a felon in possession of a handgun—a semi-automatic weapon whose serial numbers had been removed. The client previously was convicted of robbery, grand theft, assault with intent to disable, and carrying a deadly weapon. Ponds was paid $6,000 to defend him in the felony possession case.*

Ponds persuaded the court to let the client out on bail subject to certain conditions. The client violated those conditions and the court issued a warrant for his arrest. One evening, the client appears in Ponds's office with an associate (of the client) known to Ponds as "Bones." Bones remained in the reception area with Ponds's employees, both young women. Ponds and the client met in Ponds's office. The client demanded $5,000 from Ponds and stated he intended to flee the country with the money. Ponds urged the client to turn himself in and stand trial. The client rejected this advice; he said that if he did not get the money immediately "someone is going to get hurt."

Worried about injury to his employees, Ponds wrote the client a backdated check for $5,000. The client and Bones left. Ponds worried that if the client fled the country, the prosecutor would suspect Ponds of having colluded with him to do so. Ponds called the prosecutor and related these facts to him. Ponds stopped payment on the check the next day. When the client appeared at the bank to cash the check the bank manager called Ponds. Worried that the client would retaliate for the stop payment order, Ponds told the manager to call the police and called the prosecutor himself. The client was arrested at the bank. Ponds also disclosed these facts in a motion to be relieved as counsel.

The District of Columbia Bar found that Ponds's disclosures violated Rule 1.6. Though Ponds worried he might be suspected of being an accomplice, no accusation had been made against him. (Note that the client's communications would not have been privileged, being in furtherance of the crime of jumping bail.) He also could have rebutted any implication of conspiracy by stopping payment on the check, which would not have required disclosure of client confidences.

All states except California have some form of self-defense exception to the duty of confidentiality. Roger C. Crampton, *Proposed Legislation Concerning A Lawyer's Duty of Confidentiality*, 22 PEPP. L. REV. 1467, 1471

(1995). Dicta in one case, *Arden v. State Bar*, 52 Cal.2d 310, 320 (1959), suggested that "[w]henever the disclosure of a communication, otherwise privileged, becomes necessary to the protection of the attorney's own rights, he is released from those obligations of secrecy which the law places upon him," but the case involved a dispute between jointly represented parties who knew their confidences would not be protected as against each other, and the court cited no California authority for this proposition.

California's duty of confidentiality is codified in Business & Professions Code § 6068(e), which has no such exception. California Evidence Code § 958 provides such an exception to the attorney-client privilege, allowing the introduction of otherwise privileged communications pertaining to "an issue of breach, by the lawyer or by the client, of a duty arising out of the lawyer-client relationship."

The relationship between these statutes is not clear. On the one hand, the Evidence Code states a rule of evidence, not a substantive duty of confidentiality. On the other, it make little sense to amend the Evidence Code to allow the introduction of evidence a lawyer is duty-bound not to volunteer. The Evidence Code provision does not reference the Business & Professions Code, and vice versa. (For a scholarly summary of the general question of the relationship between the Evidence Code and Business & Professions Code, *see* Fred C. Zacharias, *Privilege and Confidentiality in California*, 28 U.C. DAVIS L. REV. 367 (1995)).

Brockway v. State Bar, 53 Cal.3d 51, 63–64, 278 Cal.Rptr. 836, 806 P.2d 308 (1991), stated the privilege exception narrowly:

> Evidence Code section 958 creates an exception to the privilege for communications "relevant to an issue of breach, by the lawyer[,] . . . of a duty arising out of the lawyer-client relationship." Contrary to what petitioner claims, the statute is not a general client-litigant exception allowing disclosure of any privileged communication simply because it is raised in litigation. Evidence Code section 958 only authorizes disclosure of relevant communications between a client . . . and an attorney charged with professional wrongdoing. . . .

Citing *Brockway*, the California State Bar Standing Committee on Professional Responsibility and Conduct opined that California law recognizes an exception to the duty of confidentiality where a lawyer must disclose confidential information to defend herself against charges of professional misconduct. COPRAC Formal Opinion No. 1997–151. *See* also *Pacific Tel. & Tel. Co. v. Fink,* 141 Cal.App.2d 332 (1956) (court denied motion to strike portions of attorney's affidavit under Evid. Code, § 958 or Bus. & Prof. Code, § 6068 (e) when such statements were offered in defense to allegations that attorney entered into stipulation without client's authorization).

Dicta in cases preceding *Brockway* could be read to imply that lawyers could disclose otherwise privileged communications when they were plaintiffs as well as defendants, as was the lawyer in *Brockway*. That might be the case if a lawyer sued a client to collect a fee, for example. *E.g. Carlson, Collins,*

Gordon & Bold v. Banducci, 257 Cal.App.2d 212, 227–228 (1967); *Glade v. Superior Court,* 76 Cal.App.3d 738, 746–747 (1978). The question was not squarely presented in these cases, however, because in each case the client alleged misconduct by the attorney, thus triggering a self-defense right regardless of the right to disclose in pursuit of the lawyer's own claim.

Some commentary presumes that the privilege exception extends to cases where lawyers are plaintiffs and also that it creates an implicit exception to the duty of confidentiality. The Los Angeles County Bar Association, for example, offered this summary:

> Evidence Code § 958 permits an attorney to disclose attorney-client communications in a dispute with a client or former client when the communication is "relevant to an issue of breach, by the lawyer or by the client, of a duty arising out of the lawyer-client relationship." As with sections 956 and 962, this self-defense exception is not recognized in section 6068(e). Nonetheless, it is clear that attorneys are allowed to make disclosures in aid of their defense to a client malpractice action, in support of a claim for unpaid legal fees against a client and in defense of client-initiated State Bar disciplinary complaints.

L.A. County Bar Ass'n Op. No. 519, February 26, 2007.

This opinion goes on to note that "less clear are the circumstances where a terminated lawyer-employee may make disclosures in aid of his or her wrongful termination claim against the employer-client based on an alleged public policy violation." *Id.* That statement is quite right, and the issue is discussed in connection with termination of in-house counsel in chapter 10.

Does it matter whether the charge against an attorney is made by (or whether the claim an attorney seeks to vindicate is made against) a client or by a third party? Recall that Evidence Code § 958 allows the introduction of communications pertaining to "an issue of breach, by the lawyer or by the client, of a duty arising out of the lawyer-client relationship." This language does not actually limit itself to actions by or against clients. As we see in chapter 8 in some circumstance a third party might raise "an issue of breach" by the lawyer. On the other hand, referring to breach "by the lawyer or by the client" certainly can be read as presuming that such evidence may be introduced only in lawyer-client conflicts, and this interpretation is consistent with the language of *Brockway* quoted above.

Solin v. O'Melveny & Myers, 89 Cal.App.4th 451 (2001), sheds some indirect light on this question. Solin was a lawyer who represented two individuals, Reich and Jossem, doing business through a corporate entity. He signed an agreement to represent them in connection with the entity's business for five years. In the course of his representation Solin learned facts implicating Reich and Jossem in criminal conduct. At the end of the five-year term, Solin was considering whether to renew his representation. He was worried that if he continued the representation he might risk indictment along with Reich and Jossem.

To leverage Solin into continuing his representation Reich and Jossem threatened to sue him for default on a loan that Solin believed was actually a fee payment. Solin decided to continue the representation but wanted to protect himself from future fee disputes. He consulted Alan Cohen, a criminal law expert with the firm of O'Melveny & Myers. Solin later sued Cohen and the firm alleging that they gave him incompetent advice about how best to structure his fee agreement. Cohen denied advising Solin regarding fees and claimed he had only advised Solin on substantive criminal law issues.

Reich, Jossem, and their entity then took steps to prevent Solin from disclosing at his deposition confidential information Solin had obtained while representing them. Solin argued that he did not need to disclose such information to prove his case but O'Melveny argued it needed to disclose such information (which Solin evidently had related to Cohen) in its defense. The trial court concluded O'Melveny could not defend itself without disclosing the information and dismissed Solin's case. The court of appeal affirmed, holding

> Pursuant to Evidence Code section 955, Solin would be duty-bound to object to any . . . evidence which revealed his Clients' Secrets. The trial court must exclude information subject to a claim of privilege (Evid.Code, § 916), and therefore must sustain the objection. Solin would benefit from the exclusion of evidence that could bolster O'Melveny's defense and its credibility. Thus, solely as a result of his disclosure of his Clients' confidences, Solin would obtain an unfair advantage in his lawsuit against O'Melveny. . . . It strikes us as fundamentally unfair for a client to sue a law firm for the advice obtained and then to seek to forbid the attorney who gave that advice from reciting verbatim, as nearly as memory permits, the words spoken by his accuser during the consultation.

89 Cal.App.4th at 463.

The absence of a self-defense exception with regard to third-party suits was an implicit basis for the decision in *McDermott, Will & Emery v. Superior Court*, 83 Cal.App.4th 378 (2000). Plaintiffs in that case brought a derivative action (one brought on behalf of and in the name of an entity such as a corporation, for harm done to the entity) against outside counsel to a corporation. The firm moved for judgment on the pleadings in part on the ground that it had no way to defend itself because Section 958 did not extend to allegations made by shareholders rather than the client—the entity itself acting through management. The court held that "in the absence of a waiver by the corporate client . . . such a derivative action against the corporation's outside counsel, necessarily brought in equity, cannot proceed." *Accord Reilly v. Greenwald & Hoffman, LLP*, 196 Cal.App.4th 891 (2011) (same result with respect to dissolved corporation).

Both *Solin* and *McDermott, Will & Emery* discuss the attorney-client privilege but the facts of the cases implicate the duty of confidentiality as well. For example, when Solin met with O'Melveny attorneys the rules of evidence did not apply at all. The duty of confidentiality governed whether he could disclose to his lawyers confidential information he obtained from his clients. Model Rule 1.6(b)(4) expressly allows disclosure for a lawyer "to secure legal advice about the lawyer's compliance with these Rules." Note, however, that Solin's disclosures to O'Melveny went beyond this very limited exception; California in any event has no counterpart to this provision of the Model Rules. Did Solin breach the duty of confidentiality by disclosing confidences to his own counsel? *Solin* seems to presume that an attorney may disclose to her own lawyer confidential information about her clients.

Thinking Dynamically and Interactively III
Ethical Rules and Strategic Behavior

Ethical rules create incentives. To appreciate fully the legal significance of such rules you must think not only about discipline but also about the incentives the rules create, and how those incentives relate to your matter.

Suppose you represent an investor or class of investors who believe they have been defrauded by a firm in a transaction in which the firm was represented by counsel. Suppose also that you have some good-faith basis to believe counsel knew of the fraud, or was reckless in not knowing about it, and that counsel did something to further the transaction and harm your client.

Can you see how the self-defense exception to the duty of confidentiality might help your client? If you name counsel in the suit, counsel will have the option of disclosing to you facts she otherwise could not disclose, as happened in *Meyerhofer*. Even if counsel were not liable, or paid only a relatively small amount, counsel could be a valuable source of discovery the client might otherwise be able to keep silent. In other words, the way you draft your complaint either creates or fails to create an option you might want the lawyer to have.

Assuming the lawyer is rational, and the evidence inculpates the client more than the lawyer, you might assume that the lawyer would consider exercising the option if he or she had it (thinking interactively) and therefore write the complaint in a way that triggers the option (thinking dynamically about what move now will help you when it is the other side's turn to move).

Even a lawyer named as a defendant does not have to disclose any facts informally, of course, and if the facts tended to inculpate rather than exculpate them they probably would not disclose unless and until forced to by discovery proceedings. Nevertheless, a rule that at first glance seems to relate only to counsel and the client also is relevant to the pleading choices of lawyers on the other side of such a case.

2. PHYSICAL AND ECONOMIC HARM

The Model Rules of Professional Conduct allow counsel to disclose confidential client information if disclosure is necessary "to prevent reasonably certain death or substantial bodily injury." M.R. 1.6(b)(1). The language of this provision is permissive—it allows but does not require disclosure. That places emphasis on counsel's judgment of the facts at hand. When is disclosure warranted, and when would it be better to keep silent? See what you think of the judgment exercised by the lawyer in the next case.

Bear in mind: the issue in the case is whether counsel was ineffective for purposes of the right to counsel guaranteed by the Constitution. The court interpreted the rule in that context rather than in the context of a proceeding to discipline the attorney.

MCCLURE V. THOMPSON

323 F.3d 1233 (9th Cir.), *cert. denied, sub nom. McClure v. Belleque*, 540 U.S. 1051 (2003)

FLETCHER, J.

Oregon state prisoner Robert A. McClure appeals the district court's denial of his 28 U.S.C. § 2254 habeas corpus petition challenging his jury trial conviction for three aggravated murders. McClure's original defense attorney, Christopher Mecca, placed an anonymous telephone call to law enforcement officials directing them to the locations of what turned out to be the bodies of two children whom McClure was ultimately convicted of killing. The district court rejected McClure's arguments that the disclosure constituted ineffective assistance of counsel, holding there was no breach of the duty of confidentiality and no actual conflict of interest. We affirm. . . .

On Tuesday, April 24, 1984, the body of Carol Jones was found in her home in Grants Pass, Oregon. She had been struck numerous times on the head, arms and hands with a blunt object. A gun cabinet in the home had been forced open and a .44 caliber revolver was missing. Two of Jones' children—Michael, age 14, and Tanya, age 10—were also missing. The fingerprints of Robert McClure, a friend of Jones, were found in the blood in the home. On Saturday, April 28, McClure was arrested in connection with the death of Carol Jones and the disappearance of the children.

That same day, McClure's mother contacted attorney Christopher Mecca and asked him to represent her son. As discussed in more detail below, sometime in the next three days, under circumstances described differently by McClure and Mecca, McClure revealed to Mecca the separate remote locations where the children could be found. On Tuesday, May 1, Mecca, armed with a map produced during his conversations with McClure, arranged for his secretary to place an anonymous phone call to a sheriff's department telephone number belonging to a law enforcement officer with whom Mecca had met earlier.

Later that day and the following day, sheriff's deputies located the children's bodies, which were in locations more than 60 miles apart. The children had each died from a single gunshot wound to the head. Mecca then withdrew from representation. On May 3, McClure was indicted for the murders of Carol Jones and her children. At trial, the prosecution produced extensive evidence that stemmed from the discovery of the children's bodies and introduced testimony regarding the anonymous phone call. McClure was found guilty of all three murders and was sentenced to three consecutive life sentences with 30–year minimums. . . .

The parties agree that Mecca and McClure met at the jail and spoke on the telephone on a number of occasions between April 28 and May 1. However, the substance of the conversations between McClure and Mecca are the subject of significant dispute.

Mecca recorded his account in notes that he wrote immediately after the children's bodies were discovered. Mecca also gave deposition testimony for McClure's state post conviction proceeding, submitted an affidavit prior to McClure's federal habeas proceeding, and gave testimony at the federal district court evidentiary hearing in the habeas proceeding.

In his notes, Mecca wrote that McClure had initially claimed that he was "being framed" for the murder, but that he was nervous about his fingerprints being in the house. He had asked Mecca to help him remove some other potential evidence, which Mecca declined to do. According to the notes, on the Sunday night after McClure's Saturday arrest, Mecca received a "frantic phone call" from McClure's sister, who was convinced that McClure had murdered Jones, but had reason to believe that the children were alive and perhaps "tied up or bound someplace." In response, Mecca set up a meeting with McClure, his sister and his mother at the jail, at which McClure's sister "directly confronted [McClure] and begged him to divulge information about the whereabouts of the kids." McClure and his sister discussed how McClure sometimes did "crazy things" when he was using drugs, but McClure strongly maintained his innocence as to Carol Jones' murder and the children's disappearance.

According to his notes, when Mecca next spoke with McClure on Monday, McClure was less adamant in his denial. Mecca described how, when they met on Monday afternoon, McClure began to tell him of his "sexual hallucinations and fantasies" involving young girls and about "other situations that happened in the past . . . involving things he would do while under the influence of drugs." "It was at that time," Mecca wrote, "when I realized in my own mind that he had committed the crime and the problem regarding the children intensified." Mecca wrote that he "was extremely agitated over the fact that these children might still be alive."

After a Monday night visit to the crime scene, Mecca returned to the jail to speak with McClure again, at which time he "peeled off most of the outer layers of McClure and realized that there was no doubt in my mind that he had . . . killed Carol Jones." McClure told Mecca he wanted to see a psychiatrist, then launched into "bizarre ramblings." "[E]ach time as I would try to leave," Mecca recalled in his notes, "[McClure] would spew out other information, bits about the children, and he would do it in the form of a fantasy." Mecca wrote that he "wanted to learn from him what happened to those children." He told McClure "that we all have hiding places, that we all know when we go hiking or driving or something, we all remember certain back roads and remote places," and that McClure "related to me . . . one place where a body might be" and then "described [where] the other body would be located." Mecca wrote that he "wasn't going to push him for anything more," but "when I tried to leave, he said, and he said it tentatively, 'would you like me to draw you a map and just give you an idea?' and I said 'Yes' and he did[.]" Mecca recorded that "at that time, I felt in my own mind the children were dead, but, of course, I wasn't sure."

Very late on Monday evening, McClure telephoned Mecca at home and said, "I know who did it." Mecca recorded in his notes that the next morning he went to meet with McClure, and asked him about this statement. McClure told Mecca that "Satan killed Carol." When Mecca asked, "What about the kids?" McClure replied, "Jesus saved the kids." Mecca wrote in his notes that this statement "hit me so abruptly, I immediately assumed that if Jesus saved the kids, that the kids are alive[.]" Mecca wrote that he "kind of felt that [McClure] was talking about a sexual thing, but, in any event, I wasn't sure."

Mecca's notes indicate that on Monday, before McClure made the "Jesus saved the kids" comment, and again on Tuesday, immediately after the meeting at which he made that comment, Mecca had conversations with fellow lawyers, seeking advice regarding "the dilemma that [he] faced." After the second of these conversations, which took place Tuesday morning, Mecca arranged for a noon meeting with the undersheriff and the prosecutor. At the meeting, he "mentioned to them that I may have information which would be of interest to the State" and attempted to negotiate a plea.

When the prosecutor responded that there would be no deal, Mecca recorded in his notes, "I had made up my mind then that I had to do the correct thing. The only option I had, as far as I was concerned, was to disclose the whereabouts of the body [sic]." (Recall that by the time Mecca wrote these notes, he had learned that the children were dead.) A law enforcement official testified in a federal court deposition that, after both the state bar association and the attorney general "recommended that it would be unwise for Mr. Mecca to provide us information," Mecca "indicated that, even though there might be sanctions, that he still was wanting to provide information that he had regarding the children." Mecca stated that when he spoke with McClure's sister and mother, they were adamant that he do whatever he could to locate the children, and that "[t]hey were still under the impression that one or both of the children were alive, or at least there was a chance they were alive."

Mecca then returned to the jail Tuesday afternoon and, according to his notes, "advised McClure that if there was any possibility that these children were alive, we were obligated to disclose that information in order to prevent, if possible, the occurrence of what could be [the elevation of] an assault to a murder, for instance. I further indicated that if he really requested psychiatric help, to help him deal with his problem, that this perhaps was the first step." "In any event," Mecca recorded in his notes, "he consented." "I arranged to have the information released anonymously to the Sheriff's Department with directions to the bodies." He noted that there was "no provable way to connect" McClure to the information, "but I think it's rather obvious from those in the know, who the information came from."

In the deposition conducted in conjunction with McClure's state habeas proceeding, Mecca gave a similar account of the events surrounding disclosure of the locations of the children. He emphasized that "it all happened relatively quickly" and that there was a public "hysteria about these kids, whether the kids were dead, whether the kids were alive." Mecca reiterated that much of the later conversations with McClure consisted of hypotheticals and fantasies—"like he was playing a game with me"—but that it was clear that McClure wanted to tell him where the children were. Mecca stated in his deposition that "the condition of the children [was] never discussed," but that the insistence by McClure's mother and sister that McClure wouldn't hurt the children put him "in this mode [of thinking] these kids might be alive someplace."

Mecca testified in his deposition that he thought that if the children were alive, it might relieve McClure of additional murder charges, but that the children were his main concern. When asked if he was "primarily concerned with the children's welfare or . . . with Mr. McClure's welfare" at the time he disclosed the location of the bodies, Mecca replied, "At that point I was concerned with the children's welfare." When asked if he explained to McClure that "if they were in fact dead, that revealing the location of the bodies would lead to evidence which could implicate Mr. McClure in their murders," Mecca answered: "No. I don't think I had the presence of mind to sit down and analyze every single detail and go over with him, 'Geez, you know, if they are really dead, why don't you tell me.' " However, he testified, "McClure knew I thought there [was] a chance those kids were alive."

Mecca testified in the deposition that the plan to place the anonymous telephone call was his, but that McClure knew that he planned to do it, and that, in his late-night call, McClure had made clear that he "absolutely" "wanted to disclose where those kids were." When asked, "Did he give you permission to reveal this information?" Mecca responded, "Oh, yes."

In a 1999 affidavit submitted in conjunction with McClure's federal habeas proceeding, Mecca gave an additional statement regarding McClure's consent: "Mr. McClure did not orally or expressly consent to the disclosure. I inferred consent from the circumstances, specifically, the fact that Mr. McClure called me at home on several occasions with the request that I see him at the jail, and the fact that he drew a map of the location of the bodies of the victim in his own handwriting and gave me the map.". . . . [Mecca also testified at an evidentiary hearing]: Mecca testified that McClure never expressly said that he consented to the disclosure, and that Mecca never asked for such consent. He confirmed his earlier testimony that he inferred consent, and added for the first time that this inference was based on McClure's nodding, saying "okay," and otherwise manifesting assent. He said this was what he had meant when he had written in his notes that McClure consented. Mecca also reiterated that he never told McClure of the legal risks involved in disclosing the children's locations. . . .

McClure disagreed with Mecca's account of the events leading up to the anonymous call. In testimony in both the state and federal district court proceedings, he repeatedly insisted that he did not give Mecca permission to disclose any information and that he was reassured that everything he told Mecca would remain confidential. He said Mecca pressured him into disclosing information by setting up the meeting with his sister and mother, and then disseminated that information to his detriment without his knowledge or consent.

McClure testified that Mecca never asked him directly if the children were alive or dead, but that the hypothetical conversations that they had were about where Mecca might find dead "bodies," not live "children." He said his disclosure of those locations was his way of admitting to having killed them. He testified that Mecca never told him that he intended to make an anonymous telephone call. . . .

McClure's single claim is that habeas relief is appropriate because he received ineffective assistance of counsel under the Sixth Amendment. He asserts three independent grounds on which ineffectiveness could be found. The first two are based on alleged breaches of Mecca's professional duty to maintain client confidentiality. McClure argues that this duty was breached both by a failure to obtain informed consent prior to the disclosure of confidential information and by a failure to inquire thoroughly before concluding that disclosure was necessary to prevent the deaths of the children. . . . .

The duty of an attorney to keep his or her client's confidences in all but a handful of carefully defined circumstances is so deeply ingrained in our legal system and so uniformly acknowledged as a critical component of reasonable representation by counsel that departure from this rule "make[s] out a deprivation of the Sixth Amendment right to counsel." [citation omitted] With this uncontested premise as our starting point, we. . . . look to see if Mecca's client "consent[ed] after consultation" or if Mecca "reasonably believe[d] [the revelation was] necessary to prevent the client from committing a criminal act that [Mecca] believe[d] [was] likely to result in imminent death or substantial bodily harm[.]" We conclude that the first of these exceptions does not apply to justify Mecca's behavior, but that the second does.

The state court made the following finding: "Trial counsel received petitioner's permission to anonymously disclose the whereabouts of the children to the authorities.". . . . [The court found McClure had not rebutted the finding under the applicable standard.] the client can provide valid consent only if there has been appropriate "consultation" with his or her attorney. . . . It is not enough, as the district court suggests, that McClure "did not dissuade Mecca from his intentions" to share the map with authorities. The onus is not on the client to perceive the legal risks himself and then to dissuade his attorney from a particular course of action. . . .

The State contends that, even if Mecca did not have informed consent, his revelation of client confidences did not amount to ineffective assistance of counsel because he reasonably believed that disclosing the location of the children was necessary in order to prevent further criminal acts. That is, Mecca reasonably believed that revealing the children's locations could have prevented the escalation of kidnapping to murder. This is not a traditional "prevention of further criminal acts" case, because all of the affirmative criminal acts performed by McClure had been completed at the time Mecca made his disclosure. Mecca was thus acting to prevent an earlier criminal act from being transformed by the passage of time into a more serious criminal offense. Nonetheless, we believe that where an attorney's or a client's omission to act could result in "imminent death or substantial bodily harm" constituting a separate and more severe crime from the one already committed, the exception to the duty of confidentiality may be triggered. ABA Model Rule 1.6(b)(1).

This exception, however, requires that an attorney reveal confidences only to the extent that he "reasonably believes necessary to prevent" those criminal acts and imminent harms . . . . . we must determine what basis the attorney had for believing that the precondition to disclosure was present, and how much investigation he or she must have undertaken before it was "reasonabl[e]" to "believ[e] [it] necessary" to make the disclosure to prevent the harm. The second step is to apply that standard to the facts surrounding Mecca's decision to disclose.

There is remarkably little case law addressing the first analytical step. Citing cases dealing with a separate confidentiality exception allowing attorneys to reveal intended perjury on the part of their clients, McClure argues that a lawyer must have a "firm factual basis" before adopting a belief of impending criminal conduct. [citations omitted] However, we are not persuaded that the perjury cases provide the proper standard. . . . we hold that the guiding rule for purposes of the exception for preventing criminal acts is objective reasonableness in light of the surrounding circumstances. Reasonableness of belief may be strongly connected to adequacy of investigation or sufficiency of inquiry in the face of uncertainty. . . .

McClure argues that any conclusion that Mecca had a reasonable belief is unsupported because Mecca himself indicated that he harbored doubts as to the children's state, and yet failed to inquire further. He points to evidence in the record that Mecca, at least at some stages of his representation of McClure, did not believe the children were alive—or that he, at the least, suspected that they were dead. It is indisputable that this evidence exists, and that most of this evidence is contained in statements by Mecca himself, whom the district court found "highly credible." Mecca's notes state that, after McClure drew the map, Mecca "felt in my own mind that the children were dead, but, of course, I wasn't sure." He testified in the district court evidentiary hearing that the conclusion he came to was that, "without telling me, [McClure had] told me he had killed three people." And he stated in this same testimony that, at the time he had his secretary place the anonymous call, he thought there was a "possibility," but not a "strong possibility," that the children were alive.

McClure argues that the statement Mecca says abruptly changed his mind about the status of the children—McClure's comment that "Jesus saved the kids"—was so vague and ambiguous that it was not a sufficient basis for a "reasonable belief" that disclosure was necessary. Despite Mecca's acknowledgment that this comment led him only to "assume" that McClure was saying the children were alive, Mecca never directly asked a question that could have confirmed or refuted that assumption. Mecca repeatedly testified that he never squarely asked about the condition of the children or whether McClure had killed them. Accordingly, McClure argues, any finding that Mecca believed the children were alive is not sufficient to establish effective assistance of counsel, because Mecca's failure to engage in a reasonable level of investigation and inquiry rendered that belief unreasonable.

Given the implicit factual findings of the state court, and the explicit factual findings of the district court, which are at least plausible in light of the record viewed in its entirety . . . we disagree. . . .

The district court made a number of specific findings regarding the factual basis for Mecca's belief that the children were alive. It found that only McClure knew the true facts and that he deliberately withheld them, leading Mecca to believe the children were alive. It found that McClure controlled the flow of information, and that when Mecca informed McClure that he had an obligation to disclose the children's whereabouts if there were a chance they were alive, McClure did not tell him they were dead. It specifically rejected McClure's assertion that Mecca in fact believed that the children were dead or that he lacked information that they were alive, noting that at the time there was no evidence, other than their disappearance and the passage of time, that they had been injured or killed.

The district court also made specific factual findings regarding the nature of Mecca's investigation and inquiry. It found that "Mecca attempted to discern whether the children were alive" and "that Mecca investigated to the best of his ability under extremely difficult circumstances." McClure argues that these findings are clearly erroneous, and that "arguments that Mr. McClure was manipulative and difficult are essentially irrelevant to the lawyer's obligations." But *Strickland* [*v. Washington*, 466 U.S. 668 (1984)] holds otherwise. The *Strickland* Court emphasized that "[t]he reasonableness of counsel's actions may be determined or substantially influenced by the defendant's own statements or actions." More specifically, it held that "what investigation decisions are reasonable depends critically" on the "information supplied by the defendant."

This is a close case, even after we give the required deference to the state and district courts. The choices made by McClure's counsel give us significant pause, and, were we deciding this case as an original matter, we might decide it differently. But we take as true the district court's specific factual findings as to what transpired—including what McClure said and did, and what actions Mecca took and why he took them—and we conclude that Mecca made the disclosure "reasonably believ[ing] [it was] necessary to prevent the client from committing a criminal act that [Mecca] believe[d] [was] likely to result in imminent death or substantial bodily harm[.]" ABA Model Rule 1.6(b)(1). Mecca therefore did not violate the duty of confidentiality in a manner that rendered his assistance constitutionally ineffective. . . .

[FERGUSON, CIRCUIT JUDGE, Dissenting]

McClure's attorney, Christopher Mecca, breached one of the most sacred obligations of the attorney-client relationship, the duty of confidentiality, and in turn violated McClure's Sixth Amendment right to counsel. Based on an utterly unreasonable interpretation of the events surrounding the disclosure at issue in this case, the majority finds that Mecca met an exception to the duty of confidentiality. As a result, the majority holds that it was reasonable for Mecca to believe that two missing children were alive but dying, when he disclosed their location to authorities, without McClure's consent, without asking McClure directly whether he had killed them, and without conducting any investigation to find out. . . .

Mecca based much of his belief that the children were alive on a comment that McClure made to him on Monday, that "Satan killed Carol," but "Jesus saved the kids." Specifically, Mecca wrote in his notes that these statements hit him so abruptly, he immediately assumed that it meant the children were alive. In the face of mounting evidence pointing to the fact that the children were most likely dead, this assumption was utterly unreasonable. As Mecca himself admits, it was a hope against all hope. By Tuesday, the date of the disclosure, a reasonable attorney would have understood the complete unlikelihood that McClure spared the children, particularly after viewing the map to the bodies that McClure drew for him.

While the above is sufficient to render Mecca's belief that the children were alive unreasonable, the way in which McClure conveyed to Mecca the location of the bodies, as well as the content of the map itself, would not lead a reasonable attorney to believe the children were alive. McClure had exhibited odd behavior throughout the days preceding the disclosure, placing numerous desperate calls to Mecca from the jail and asking Mecca to dispose of crime scene evidence. When McClure finally told Mecca where the children were, he did so obscurely: in the course of discussing "places he had been with the family[,]" McClure drew a rough map, never directly telling Mecca what he would find there. The map showed two locations, which were more than sixty miles apart from one another, in a deserted and wooded area. Receiving such information after the children had been missing for eight days, although surely disturbing, is insufficient to lead a reasonable attorney to believe the children were alive and that disclosure of that information was warranted, much less necessary. . . . .

I too sympathize with Mecca for being concerned with the welfare of the children, as do the majority, the District Court and the state court. It would scarcely be wrong to criticize him for, as the District Court stated, being "a human being." However, because at the time of the disclosure Mecca was playing a critical and unique role as McClure's defense attorney, I cannot sanction his behavior. It seems that the time has come for Mecca to take responsibility for the choice he made to breach his client's confidence and for a court, this court, to recognize that whether or not Mecca did the "right" thing does not diminish the fact that his doing so constituted an abdication of his professional duties and rendered his performance as McClure's defense attorney deficient under the Sixth Amendment.

The question in *McClure* was not whether Mecca's disclosure was right or wrong but whether it deprived McClure of the effective assistance of counsel guaranteed to criminal defendants under the Supreme Court's opinions in *Gideon v. Wainwright*, 372 U.S. 335 (1963), and *Strickland v. Washington*, 466 U.S. 668 (1984). As we will see in chapter 7, the latter case provides that counsel is ineffective only if a lawyer's acts fall outside a broad range of reasonable conduct and the deficiency was reasonably likely to affect the result of the case.

Professional norms such as ABA Rules are relevant to the first part of this test, and that is why the rule was discussed in *McClure*. Had the court found that Mecca violated the rule it might have found that the first part of the test was met. Such a finding would not subject Mecca to discipline, however. The disciplinary authority in his licensing jurisdiction would have to make its own determination on that question.

Note that the court held Mecca's disclosure was permissible even though the language of the rule referred to disclosure necessary to prevent a criminal act and even though McClure's acts had already been committed. The court reasoned McClure's liability for kidnapping might increase to liability for murder if the children died. *Cf.* New York City Bar Association Formal Opinion 2002–01 (disclosure of burial location was necessary because of lawyer's reasonable belief that children were still alive and could be rescued).

Don't Threaten the Judge

For an easier case in which disclosure was ethically permissible, see In the Matter of A Grand Jury Investigation, *453 Mass. 453 (2009). In that case, "Attorney John Doe was representing Michael Moe, a father, in a care and protection proceeding in the Juvenile Court. On November 8, 2007, two days after an adverse ruling by a Juvenile Court judge, Moe left six messages on Attorney Doe's answering machine between 1:08 A.M. and 1:24 A.M. Moe indicated that he knew where the judge lived and that she had two children. In the fourth message, a voice that Attorney Doe recognized as Moe's wife stated that she and Moe were going to 'raise some hell.' In the fifth message, Moe stated that 'some people need to be exterminated with prejudice.' Attorney Doe subsequently erased the messages from the answering machine.*

During the following week, Attorney Doe observed that Moe had become 'more and more angry,' and on November 13, 2007, he filed a motion to withdraw as Moe's counsel, which was subsequently allowed. Concerned for the safety of the judge and her family, he disclosed the substance of the messages to the judge.

On November 21, 2007, Attorney Doe was interviewed by a State trooper regarding the substance of the messages, but declined to sign a written statement." A criminal complaint was filed against Moe and Doe was summoned to the grand jury.

Doe moved to quash the ground jury subpoena on the ground that the relevant communications were privileged. (We will read that part of the opinion in chapter 5.) In connection with the privilege objection, the Supreme Court noted "[n]either party disputes that Attorney Doe could, consistent with rule 1.6, disclose the substance of Moe's messages. . . . While nothing in rule 1.6(b) required Attorney Doe to disclose Moe's communications to the judge or police, he had discretion to do so."

May You Disclose or Must You Disclose?

Under Model Rule 1.6 disclosure is only permissive, not mandatory. *In the Matter of William Goebel*, 703 N.E.2d 1045 (Ind. 1998), illustrates the point. Goebel was a partner in a law firm. He represented a client in a criminal matter. Another partner represented a client in a guardianship matter. That client's husband was a witness against Goebel's criminal client.

The criminal client appeared in Goebel's office one day and told Goebel he planned to find and kill the guardianship client's husband; he demanded the guardianship client's address. Goebel tried to dissuade the client, who persisted in his demands. Goebel then held up an envelope that had been returned because it was misaddressed, implying that he did not know where the guardianship client lived. The criminal client copied down the address and left. Goebel told no one about the encounter. Two days later the criminal client murdered the guardianship client's husband.

In later proceedings Goebel described the encounter as follows:

Respondent: . . . I think what the conversation was. Was he pressing me to find out the address and uh I ask [the partner] about it and she said every piece of mail that she had sent to the address given to her by [the guardianship client] had been returned and I believe I showed him an envelope to substantiate that I didn't know her address by showing him an envelope with whatever address it was.

Police: Did he write that address down?

Respondent: I think he did. Yes.

Police: And

Respondent: Pretty sure he did.

Police: All the information that he was trying to gather from you and other sources was for what purpose?

Respondent: To track down [the guardianship client's husband], it appeared.

Police: To do what?

Respondent: To get rid of him. I assume.

Police: To kill him?

Respondent: Yes. I think so.

Goebel was publicly reprimanded for disclosing to the criminal client the address of the guardianship client. He explicitly was not reprimanded for failing to disclose the criminal client's stated intention to kill the guardianship client's husband.

Disclosure may be mandatory, however, in cases to which Model Rule 4.1 applies. Rule 4.1(b) states that a lawyer shall not knowingly "fail to disclose a material fact to a third person" when disclosure "is necessary to avoid assisting a criminal or fraudulent act by a client" unless Rule 1.6 forbids disclosure. Note the operative verb "assisting," which is consistent with the exceptions in Rule 1.6(b)(2)–(3). Those exceptions allow disclosure to prevent, or rectify the effects of, a client's criminal or fraudulent act reasonably certain to harm, or which has harmed, the financial or property interests of a third party *and* "in furtherance of which the client has used or is using the lawyer's services." In other words, if a client is using or has used your services to engage in criminal or fraudulent conduct reasonably certain to cause (or having already caused) financial harm to a third party, and if disclosure of a material fact is necessary to avoid assisting such conduct, then you *must* disclose such facts.

It seems unlikely that lawyers often will assist clients in violent acts causing substantial injury or death. More common would be situations in which lawyers draft, for example, an opinion letter they later learn to be false but on which a third party might rely in connection with a transaction. In such a case the Model Rules would require disclosure so long as one of the exceptions to Rule 1.6 applied. If you ever confront such a situation in your own practice it would be important to read the actual rule adopted by the relevant jurisdiction. A state with narrower exceptions to the duty of confidentiality might not impose the duty derived from the intersection of Model Rules 4.1 and 1.6.

PROBLEM 4–6

Why do you suppose disclosure is generally permissive, even if a lawyer believes murder or mayhem is at hand? What purpose is served by permissive rather than mandatory disclosure?

No Matter Where You Go, There You Are II: The Dead Bodies Case

Mecca had discretion to disclose in *McClure* because it was not certain that Carol Jones's children were dead. Disclosure therefore might have averted their death and thus have fallen within the exception of Model Rule 1.6(b)(1). But what if Mecca knew they were dead? At that point, no exception would justify disclosure.

This was the problem in the famous "dead bodies case," which occurred in Lake Pleasant, New York, in 1973 and 1974. After an 11–day manhunt Robert Garrow was arrested and charged with murdering Philip Domblewski in the mountains of upstate New York. Garrow was also suspected of killing Alicia Hauck, 16, who had disappeared on her way home from school in Syracuse, New York, and Susan Petz, who had been missing since her boyfriend, Daniel Porter, had been found murdered at a campsite.

Frank Armani and Francis Belge were appointed to represent Garrow. They questioned him about Domblewski, Hauck, and Petz. Garrow eventually told his lawyers he had killed Porter, raped and killed Petz (leaving her body in an abandoned mine shaft) and had killed Hauck, whose body he left in a cemetery. To confirm the story the two lawyers went to the mine shaft. There they found Petz's body, which they photographed. The next day, Belge found Hauck's body in the cemetery. He also photographed it, moving her skull several feet to be nearer to her body.

Armani and Belge did not tell the police that the girls were dead. The girls' parents suspected Garrow, however, and Susan Petz's father came from Illinois to New York to plead with Armani to tell him whether his daughter was dead. Armani did not disclose Garrow's confidences. To add to the pressure on Armani, his daughter attended high school with Alicia Hauck's sisters, and Hauck's father worked in the courthouse where Armani frequently worked.

Armani and Belge tried but failed to negotiate a plea for Garrow, who then went to trial. Belge called Garrow to testify and Garrow admitted that he murdered Domblewski, Hauck, and Petz. Garrow was convicted of murder and sentenced to 35 years to life in prison. When it became clear that Armani and Belge had known about Susan and Alicia, the community turned against the lawyers. Their practices withered. Belge, who had moved Hauck's skull, was indicted but later cleared.

Several years later, Garrow escaped from prison. Officials found in his cell a list of people he planned to kill. Armani and Belge were on the list. Armani was informed of this; he also recalled that during trial his daughter, Dorina, had come to see him at the courthouse. Garrow greeted her though he had never met her, leading Armani to conclude Garrow had stalked his daughter. Armani later said: "I was on a death list [a]nd my family was threatened. Nothing goes before that . . . I felt that my primary duty to society and to my family was to get him recaptured and locked up to serve his sentence. He and I had parted company when he threatened my life." With Garrow on the loose, Armani divulged to police officers information Garrow had given him. The police found Garrow and killed him in a gunfight.

Many lawyers consider Armani and Belge heroes. The case pits the commands of the positive law in the form of the Rules of Professional Conduct against sympathy for the father of Susan Petz, whose body lay in the mine shaft while Armani looked her father in the eye and remained silent. It also pits that sympathy against Garrow's claim to rely on Armani and Belge to look after his interests, rather than to betray him to soothe their own consciences.[15]

However you choose to interpret the case, two things are clear. First, both then and now Armani and Belge would have been subject to discipline for disclosing Garrow's confidences. They did what the law required. Second, that fact may or may not answer any small-e ethical questions the case may raise in your mind. Ultimately, you have to live with yourself (which Armani has done quite well—as mentioned above, he is a hero to many), so you should think about whether you want to be in a position where you may have to look a father in the eye and tell him nothing about where his daughter's body lies.

There is a trend toward broadening disciplinary rule exceptions to confidentiality. In August, 2003, the ABA amended Model Rule 1.6 to allow disclosure of client misconduct in which lawyer's services were involved and which cause or threaten harm to the financial interests or

[15] For details of the case, *see* Lisa G. Lerman, Frank H. Armani, Thomas D. Morgan, and Monroe H. Freedman, *The Buried Bodies Case: Alive and Well After 30 years*, 2007 Prof. Lawyer 19.

property of another. There are very few cases involving lawyer disclosure of client financial misconduct, though *Meyerhofer* provides a good example of a case in which this exception might apply. Because the exception is limited to cases in which a client used a lawyer's services to engage in financial misconduct this exception probably will overlap significantly with the self-defense exception.

The possibility of disclosing client financial misconduct provides a window into how lawyers who think dynamically and interactively are likely to think about the costs and benefits of disclosure. For a discussion of this issue, *see* David McGowan, *Why Not Try the Carrot? A Modest Proposal to Grant Immunity to Lawyers Who Disclose Client Financial Misconduct*, 92 CAL. L. REV. 1825 (2004).

3. PROTECTING AN ENTITY CLIENT

As noted above, when you represent an entity client, such as a corporation, partnership, or joint venture, you represent the entity as such. You do not represent the officers, directors, or other people who act on behalf of the entity (entity constituents).

Under Model Rule 1.13, if you know a constituent is (i) breaching a duty to the entity or breaking the law in a way attributable to the entity; (ii) the conduct is related to your representation; and (iii) threatens substantial harm to the entity; then (iv) you must act in the best interests of the entity and not the constituent.

That includes taking the matter to entity officials with enough power to take action to protect the entity including, if warranted, the board (this is often referred to as "reporting up"). If these people do not do what is necessary to protect the entity, and so long as the conduct in question is a clear violation of the law, then, under Model Rule 1.13(c)(2), you may reveal confidences as reasonably necessary to protect the entity from harm, regardless whether an exception to Rule 1.6 applies (this option is often referred to as "reporting out"). This exception does not apply, however, to lawyers investigating an alleged violation of the law on behalf of an entity or defending an entity against charges of unlawful behavior. Some jurisdictions do not follow this rule, however, and do not distinguish between entity clients and individual clients when defining a lawyer's ability to disclose confidential information without client consent. *See* Cal. R. Prof. Conduct 3–600(B).

C. INTERROGATING THE "AMERICAN TALIBAN": A CASE STUDY IN THE STRATEGY OF JUDGMENT

Thinking dynamically and interactively can work retrospectively as well as prospectively. It can help you make sense of the past—why things happened as they did—and therefore help guide your future judgments. Here is an exercise in retrospective thinking that helps set the stage for a judgment about what to do.

Jesselyn Radack is an elite lawyer. A graduate of Brown University and the Yale Law School, in 2001 she worked for the Professional Responsibility Advisory Office (PRAO) of the United States Department of Justice. The PRAO advised Justice Department lawyers regarding their obligations under state disciplinary rules.

On December 7, 2001, Ms. Radack received a call from John DePue, a prosecutor in the Terrorism and Violent Crimes Section ("TVCS") of the Criminal Division of the Department of Justice. Mr. DePue told Ms. Radack that John Walker Lindh, later popularly known as the "American Taliban," had been captured in Afghanistan. FBI agents wanted to question him but his parents had already hired a lawyer, James Brosnahan, to represent him. Mr. DePue wanted to know whether the FBI agents could still question Lindh.

Ms. Radack said: "No." Her e-mail to Mr. DePue reads:

> The FBI wants to interview American Taliban member John Walker some time next week. The interview would occur in Afghanistan. Walker's father retained counsel for him. The FBI wants to question Walker about taking up arms against the U.S.
>
> I consulted with a Senior Legal Advisor here at PRAO and we don't think you can have the FBI agent question Walker. It would be a pre-indictment, custodial overt interview, which is not authorized by law.
>
> However, the FBI agent can say something to Walker to the effect of: "We understand that your father has retained counsel for you. Do you want this lawyer to represent you?" Given that Walker's parents think he was brainwashed, maybe he doesn't want a lawyer of their choosing. This option would be more risky, but I wanted to make you aware of it.
>
> Another possibility might be to do an undercover interview. However, the Circuits are not in agreement about whether such communications are authorized by law. If you want to explore this idea, which you indicated was not very likely, we would need additional factual information, such as where you think this case would eventually be brought, whether there is currently a grand jury investigation and, if so, where it is taking place, etc. If there is a grand jury, you could always ask the judge presiding over it to authorize the contact.

Mr. DePue wrote Ms. Radack back to say he had passed her advice on to other lawyers in the Department, whom he did not identify

Contrary to Ms. Radack's advice, the FBI interviewed Lindh on December 9 and 10, 2001. On February 4, 2002, Ms. Radack received an unscheduled, unsigned, and strongly negative evaluation of her work from her supervisor, Claudia Flynn. Ms. Flynn offered to let Ms. Radack resign without placing the evaluation in her official file. If Ms. Radack stayed with the PRAO, however, the review would become part of her record.

The review shocked Ms. Radack. It was the "first adverse assessment [she had received] in her long years of professional excellence." Ms. Radack rejected the review (and continues to do so) as a gross distortion of her performance. Ms. Radack came to view her review as part of an attempt to discredit her and punish her for giving unwanted advice regarding Lindh.

Lindh eventually retained Mr. Brosnahan to represent him and the defense sought discovery from the government. In part the defense wanted to know if the government had information that would support Lindh's motion to suppress statements he had made when he was interrogated in Afghanistan—the very interrogation that Ms. Radack had warned against.

The prosecutors assigned to the *Lindh* case double-checked to make sure they had all the relevant material. On March 7, 2002, one of the prosecutors, Randy Bellows, sent Ms. Radack an e-mail. He wrote that he had two of her e-mails regarding Lindh and he wanted to make sure there were no more. Ms. Radack had not known of the discovery request until Mr. Bellows called her—a circumstance that seems very odd given that she was a party to correspondence responsive to the request.

As Ms. Radack tells the story, she checked the file, but was "stunned" to find only three e-mails. Most of the relevant e-mails were missing from the file. The critical early message she sent conveying the substance of her analysis was not there. Ms. Radack thought the incompleteness of the file meant that something was very wrong. She consulted with Donald Mackay, a seasoned colleague in the PRAO, whose judgment she trusted. She reports that Mr. Mackay inspected the file and declared "this file has been purged."

With the assistance of the computer helpline at the Department Ms. Radack retrieved 14 e-mails from her computer. She gave them to Ms. Flynn who unhappily asked: "Why weren't those e-mails in the file?" Earlier, when Ms. Radack received Mr. Bellows's e-mail and told Ms. Flynn that he had only two of Ms. Radack's e-mails Ms. Flynn "whispered in a slow, deliberate tone 'I sent everything that was in the file.' "

On April 5, 2002, Ms. Radack left the Department for private practice. Earlier, on the day she discovered that the PRAO's Lindh file was incomplete, she had taken home copies of her e-mails regarding Lindh. She retained these after her resignation.

In June 2002, Ms. Radack heard on National Public Radio a story regarding Lindh, in which Department officials claimed the Department had never taken the position that Lindh was entitled to counsel during his interrogations in Afghanistan. The story shocked Ms. Radack. She interpreted the Department's statement as a flat-out lie because it contradicted her December 7 e-mail message to Mr. DePue, which Ms. Flynn, the head of the PRAO, and Ms. Goldfrank, Ms. Flynn's deputy, had reviewed and approved. Explaining her reaction, Ms. Radack said:

> I knew this statement was not true. It also indicated to me that the Justice Department must not have turned over <u>my</u> e-mails to the *Lindh* court . . . because I did not believe the Department would have the temerity to make public statements contradicted by its own court filings, even if those filings were *in camera*.

Suppose Ms. Radack comes to you asking whether she could or should leak her copies of her e-mails to a reporter covering the *Lindh* case, as a way of ensuring that the government complied with the court's discovery order. How would you analyze her situation? In particular, on the facts as stated, would you agree that lawyers in the Justice Department were deliberately suppressing her messages? How would you think about that question?

D. CONFIDENTIALITY AND CONFLICTS OF INTEREST

Restatement § 132

The duty to maintain client confidences applies until a client releases the lawyer from the duty or the information in question becomes generally known.[16] It therefore survives termination of representation. Conflict of interest rules are one way the duty is enforced after representation has ended. We study those rules in detail in chapter 11, but a brief survey here will help you understand the relationship.

Conflict of interest rules enforce the duty of confidentiality by preventing a lawyer from representing a client whose interests are adverse to the interests of one of the lawyer's former clients in the same matter as the lawyer represented the former client or in a matter substantially related to the previous representation. As the California Supreme Court said in *Flatt v. Superior Court*, 9 Cal.4th 275, 283 (1995), "where the potential conflict is one that arises from the *successive* representation of cli-

---

[16] Though, as noted above, if the information becomes generally known during the representation the general duty of loyalty would preclude a lawyer from using the information to the client's disadvantage.

ents with potentially adverse interests, the courts have recognized that the chief fiduciary value jeopardized is that of client *confidentiality*."

The conflict of interest rule is broader than the duty itself. It turns on whether matters are substantially related (which means whether in the usual sort of case a lawyer would have received confidential information material to a later representation) not whether a lawyer actually received confidential information. Thus, a lawyer could be disqualified from representation even if for some unusual reason the lawyer did not receive confidential information and therefore could not use or disclose such information.

The Main Points to Recall From Chapter 4 Are:

- The duty of confidentiality is different from (and broader than) the rule of evidence known as the attorney-client privilege.
- Lawyers may not disclose client confidences without the client's informed consent, unless a particular exception applies.
- Lawyers may not use information relating to a representation to the detriment of the client or the benefit of the lawyer outside the practice of law, unless the information is generally known.
- Lawyers are impliedly authorized to use or disclose client confidences as necessary to achieve the goals of representation.
- Implied authorization does not require client assent (that is why it is implied) but may be overridden by express client instructions.
- Lawyers may disclose confidences to prevent death or substantial bodily injury they reasonably believe would occur absent disclosure.
- Lawyers may disclose client confidences to "respond to allegations" against the lawyer in connection with the lawyer's work for a client.
- Unlike privilege, the duty of confidentiality is not a defense to compelled production.

The following chart summarizes the main points regarding the duty of confidentiality. We will add to it in the next two chapters so you may compare the duty with the attorney-client privilege and compare each of these doctrines with the work-product doctrine.

	Duty of Confidentiality
Covers	All information relating to representation not generally known
Applies When	At all times
Effect	Forbids voluntary disclosure (but not disclosure required by law) or use of information that harms clients, or outside the practice of law, that benefits lawyer
Controlled by	Client
Exceptions	Prevent death or serious bodily injury; prevent or rectify serious financial harm in which L's services have been used; self-defense (respond to allegation of representation-related misconduct); seek advice about compliance with rules; disclosure required by law

CHAPTER 5

ATTORNEY–CLIENT PRIVILEGE

■ ■ ■

Restatement (Third) of the Law Governing Lawyers §§ 68–72; 77; 86

This chapter explores the privilege of attorneys to refuse to provide as evidence communications between them and their clients that relate to legal advice. As noted in chapter 4 the privilege is a rule of evidence, not an affirmative duty. It precludes discovery or admission in evidence of communications that otherwise would be discoverable or admissible. In terms of the duty of confidentiality discussed in chapter 3, all privileged communications are confidential but not all confidential information is privileged.

Privilege law may vary among states and between state and federal law. Federal Rule of Evidence 501 provides that "[t]he common law--as interpreted by United States courts in the light of reason and experience--governs a claim of privilege unless" the Constitution, a statute, or a rule prescribed by the Supreme Court provides otherwise, except that "in a civil case, state law governs privilege regarding a claim or defense for which state law supplies the rule of decision." Federal courts thus have greater flexibility than some state courts in resolving privilege disputes. For example, in *Swidler & Berlin v. United States*, 524 U.S. 399, 411 (1998), the Supreme Court held that the privilege survives the client's death, following what the Court saw as the majority rule at common law. In contrast, in *HLC Properties, Ltd. v. Superior Court*, 35 Cal.4th 54 (2005), the California Supreme Court held that under California's evidence code a decedent's privilege expires when the decedent's personal representative is discharged. Similarly, federal courts may order a party claiming privilege to submit the relevant communication to the court for review *in camera* (by the court on its own, without disclosure to the party demanding for production), *United States v. Zolin,* 491 U.S. 554 (1989), while some states would not allow a court to order such disclosure (though a party facing an adverse privilege ruling might volunteer such disclosure to bolster its case). *Costco Wholesale Corp. v. Superior Court*, 47 Cal.4th 725, 738-739 (2009).

The following materials illustrate general privilege principles that commonly govern privilege issues. Because the relevant rules may vary, however, in resolving such issues in practice you must always determine which body of law provides the rule of decision.

A. ELEMENTS

Judge Wyzanski summarized the elements of the attorney-client privilege:

> The traditional elements of the attorney client privilege that identify communications that may be protected from disclosure in discovery are: (1) the asserted holder of the privilege is or sought to become a client; (2) the person to whom the communication was made (a) is a member of the bar of a court, or his or her subordinate, and (b) in connection with this communication is acting as a lawyer; (3) the communication relates to a fact of which the attorney was informed (a) by his client (b) without the presence of strangers (c) for the purpose of securing primarily either (i) an opinion of law or (ii) legal services or (iii) assistance in some legal proceeding, and (d) not for the purpose of committing a crime or tort; and (4) the privilege has been (a) claimed and (b) not waived by the client.

United States v. United Shoe Machinery Corp., 89 F.Supp. 357, 358–59 (D.Mass.1950). The material in this section explores these concepts.

1. COMMUNICATIONS, NOT FACTS

The attorney-client privilege protects some communications between an attorney and a client. The privilege does not extend to the facts communicated. As the United States Supreme Court wrote in *Upjohn Co. v. United States*, 449 U.S. 383, 395–396 (1981):

> [T]he protection of the privilege extends only to *communications* and not to facts. A fact is one thing and a communication concerning that fact is an entirely different thing. The client cannot be compelled to answer the question, 'what did you say or write to the attorney?' but may not refuse to disclose any relevant fact within his knowledge merely because he incorporated a statement of such fact into his communication to his attorney.

That means that a client might have to testify about facts he or she has discussed with a lawyer; the client could not be compelled to testify about the discussion, however. The facts themselves are not privileged; the communications of those facts are. This seemingly simple principle can be a bit slippery in practice. For example, is the client's identity privileged because it is known only through communications or is the fact of the relationship alone not privileged because it is treated as a fact?

LEFCOURT V. UNITED STATES

125 F.3d 79 (2d Cir. 1997)

WALKER, CIRCUIT JUDGE:

Plaintiff-appellant Gerald B. Lefcourt, P.C. ("Lefcourt" or "the law firm") appeals from the May 16, 1996 judgment entered in the United States District Court for the Southern District of New York (Robert P. Patterson, Jr., *District Judge*), granting the United States' motion for summary judgment and denying plaintiff's cross-motion for summary judgment in plaintiff's tax refund action. In so doing, the district court affirmed the imposition of a $25,000 penalty by the Internal Revenue Service ("IRS") on the ground that Lefcourt had intentionally failed to comply with certain reporting requirements set forth in 26 U.S.C. § 6050I and that the law firm had not established "reasonable cause" for doing so.

Lefcourt has advanced a number of reasons for failing to file the information required by § 6050I, all of which are animated by a concern for the sensitive relationship that exists between attorney and client. We recognize the importance of this privilege and the impulse of attorneys to defend it vigorously, as Lefcourt has done here. However, for the following reasons, we affirm the judgment of the district court.

BACKGROUND

Title 26, section 6050I, of the United States Code requires "[a]ny person . . . engaged in a trade or business" who "in the course of such trade or business, receives more than $10,000 in cash . . . " to report to the IRS the person from whom the cash was received, the amount of cash received, the date and nature of the transaction, and "such other information as the Secretary may prescribe." 26 U.S.C. § 6050I(a), (b). Form 8300 is the form used to report such a transaction.

During the summer of 1993, Lefcourt, a law firm specializing in criminal defense work, undertook the representation of a client facing federal drug and money laundering charges. The client paid Lefcourt over $10,000 in cash for legal services. On July 9, 1993, the law firm submitted a Form 8300 to the IRS, stating that it had received in excess of $10,000, and particularizing the date of the payment. The firm, however, deliberately omitted the payor's name. In doing so, Gerald Lefcourt, the law firm's name partner, attached to the Form 8300 an affidavit asserting that revealing the client-identifying information called for by § 6050I would prejudice the interests of a client whom the law firm was actively representing and that the confidentiality of the information was protected by the Fifth and Sixth Amendments of the Constitution and by the Lawyers' Code of Professional Responsibility.

On December 14, 1993, the IRS served the law firm with a Notice of Proposed Penalties under 26 U.S.C. § 6721(e), which allows for the imposition of a penalty where "intentional disregard" of § 6050I's reporting requirements is established. . . . on August 8, 1994 the IRS assessed the law firm a $25,000 penalty pursuant to § 6721.

In September of 1994, the law firm paid the full amount of the assessed penalty and, on that date, claimed a refund for the same amount. The following day, the IRS notified Lefcourt that no refund would be granted. On December 6, 1994, Lefcourt brought this refund action in the district court pursuant to 28 U.S.C. § 1346(a)(1). . . .

DISCUSSION

. . . . Lefcourt argued to the IRS and to the district court that under Second Circuit law the attorney-client privilege protects an attorney from disclosing the client-identifying information required under § 6050I in certain "special circumstances." The law firm contended that it did not submit the required information principally because it believed that a special circumstance might be found to exist where the completed Form 8300 would provide the government with evidence of its client's unexplained wealth—evidence that could incriminate the client in the same proceedings for which the client had retained the law firm. . . .

Our assessment of the reasonableness of the law firm's claimed "special circumstances" begins with *United States v. Goldberger & Dubin, P.C.,* 935 F.2d 501 (2d Cir.1991). In *Goldberger,* upon a law firm's refusal to file a completed Form 8300, the IRS issued a summons, subsequently enforced by the district court, directing the firm to produce its clients' names. On appeal, the attorneys argued that § 6050I's reporting requirements were unconstitutional and violative of the attorney-client privilege. We rejected both claims and affirmed the district court's order directing disclosure of the client-identifying information. . . .

As a general rule, a client's identity and fee information are not privileged.. Although the court in *Goldberger* did not elaborate on the meaning of the special circumstances exception to the rule, it offered some guidance as to what might and what might not constitute such a circumstance. Significant to this case, the court expressly rejected the essence of Lefcourt's claim when it stated that the "asserted possibility" that a client may be incriminated by disclosure does not constitute a special circumstance. *See* 935 F.2d at 505.

In so doing, the court cited *In re Grand Jury Subpoena Duces Tecum Served Upon Gerald L. Shargel,* 742 F.2d 61 (2d Cir.1984), which involved a defense attorney's appeal of a district court order denying a motion to quash a subpoena issued by a grand jury that sought to compel the attorney to produce records of money he had received from several clients who had been indicted for RICO violations. The government in *Shargel* admitted that the grand jury wanted the information as possible evidence that the defendants possessed unexplained wealth. *See id.* 742 F.2d at 62. Shargel argued that disclosure of the information would violate the attorney-client privilege by incriminating his clients in the RICO case. The court unequivocally rejected this "incrimination rationale" that Lefcourt now claims provided a reasonable basis for its own noncompliance:

> We have consistently held that client identity and fee information are, absent special circumstances, not privileged. This result follows from defining the privilege to encompass only those confidential communications necessary to obtain informed legal advice. This definition, which focuses upon facilitating the role of the lawyer as a professional advisor and advocate, is to be distinguished from the so-called "incrimination rationale," which focuses upon whether the materials sought may be used as evidence against the client. While the attorney-client privilege historically arose at the same time as the privilege against self-incrimination, it was early established that the privileges had distinct policies and that the "point of honor"—the attorney's reluctance to incriminate his client—was not a valid reason to invoke the attorney-client privilege.

Shargel, 742 F.2d at 62–63 (citations and footnote omitted). The court thus held that "information is not protected by the privilege even though the client may strongly fear the effects of disclosure, including incrimination." *Id.* 742 F.2d at 63.[1]

Goldberger and *Shargel,* read together, squarely reject the principal argument put forward by Lefcourt here: that possible or even likely client incrimination constitutes a special circumstance justifying nondisclosure.

Lefcourt attempts to avoid the force of *Goldberger* and *Shargel* by arguing that its case presents a unique twist on the incrimination rationale because the incrimination would have occurred in the very case for which the funds triggering the obligation to file a Form 8300 were expended as legal fees. . . .

The foregoing argument by Lefcourt has been characterized by courts as the "legal advice exception," which holds client-identifying information privileged "where there is a strong probability that disclosure would implicate the client in the very criminal activity for which legal advice was sought." *In re Grand Jury Subpoenas (Anderson),* 906 F.2d 1485, 1488 (10th Cir.1990). However, this exception (which has been described by another court as one of "questionable validity," *see Anderson,* 906 F.2d at 1488) has never once been accepted in this circuit. In fact, we all but categorically rejected it in *Vingelli v. United States,* 992 F.2d 449 (2d Cir.1993), a case not cited by Lefcourt, where we took pains to distinguish the legal advice exception from the confidential communications exception

1 FN4. Lefcourt suggests without citation that *Shargel* may be distinguished on the ground that it involved a grand jury subpoena and not an IRS proceeding. Brief of Appeal of Gerald B. Lefcourt, P.C. at 21 n. 11. Because the same rules of attorney-client privilege apply in either context—rules developed by federal courts "in the light of reason and experience," Fed.R.Evid. 501—there is no basis for this distinction.

that is recognized in this circuit. *Id.* 992 F.2d at 452–53 (citing *Shargel,* 742 F.2d at 62–63).

Thus the law is clear, and was so when Lefcourt refused to file its completed Form 8300: to the extent that the legal advice exception exists in any jurisdiction, it plainly is not recognized as a special circumstance in this circuit . . . . . In sum, we conclude that Lefcourt had no reasonable basis for failing to provide the information required by § 6050I under the facts presented here. . . . We therefore agree with the district court that Lefcourt has not established "reasonable cause" for its willful noncompliance with § 6050I.

Not all courts follow the rule employed in *Lefcourt.* For a different result in a case applying California law, *see Baird v. Koerner*, 279 F.2d 623 (9th Cir. 1960), citing *Ex parte McDonough*, 170 Cal. 230 (1915). In addition, California's Business & Professions Code § 6149 provides that a written fee agreement is both confidential and privileged. These examples from California law illustrate an important point: the content of the attorney-client privilege may vary among states and between any given state and federal law. A lawyer therefore has to know where her client might have to litigate in order to know whether a particular conversation or document would or would not be privileged.

Leaving aside the problem of conflicting versions of the privilege, the basic rule applied in *Lefcourt* is not limited to client names. For example, recall that in *Adams v. Franklin,* 924 A.2d 993 (D.C. 2007), the plaintiff accused the defendants of defrauding her into selling her property below the market price. The defendants asserted the statute of limitations as a defense. "To support this defense, [defendants] note a demand letter, which is dated August 16, 1999, purportedly authored and sent by appellant's former attorney, Leonard Koenick, to many of the same parties in the present suit. In order to establish the authenticity and appellant's authorization of the demand letter, appellees sought to depose Mr. Koenick on this subject matter. . . . Mr. Koenick appeared for the deposition, but was instructed by appellant's current attorney not to answer any questions due to attorney-client privilege." The trial court disagreed, and held that the information being sought from Mr. Koenick—"(1) whether the letter is authentic . . . ; (2) whether Mr. Koenick sent the letter or caused it to be sent; (3) whether Mr. Koenick represented plaintiff in August 1999; and (4) where Mr. Koenick learned of the information contained in the letter—is not protected by any privilege." The court of appeals affirmed, holding "topics (1) through (3) are not communications between Mr. Koenick and appellant, and are not entitled to the protection of any privilege."

By implication the fourth category would be privileged because to identify a set of information and then to identify the client as the source of that information would implicitly reveal the client's communications to the lawyer. Recall, however, the court also ruled the client communicated information to the lawyer with the intent that it be relayed to the other side. In that circumstance, once the information was in fact relayed the communication would not be treated as confidential.

Similarly, the district court in *East Maine Baptist Church v. Regions Bank,* 2007 WL 1445257 (E.D. Mo. 2007), held "[t]he production of conflict memoranda, new matter forms, and correspondence regarding conflicts is not protected by the attorney-client privilege or work product doctrine." At issue was a discovery request by defendants opposing a motion by Capes Sokol, a law firm seeking appointment as counsel for a class of plaintiffs. The defendant argued the motion should be denied because counsel had a conflict of interest. To support this claim, it sought from Capes Sokol several categories of documents. The court held the defendant "is entitled to documents regarding: (i) any initial inquiries regarding the potential of Capes Sokol's representation of the plaintiffs, (ii) any conflict checks related to the lawsuit, (iii) any fee arrangements related to the lawsuit, (iv) the engagement of Capes Sokol as attorneys for the plaintiffs, and (v) Capes Sokol's substitution as counsel for the plaintiffs in the lawsuit."

---

2. IN CONFIDENCE

Restatement of the Law Governing Lawyers § 79

MINNESOTA V. RHODES

627 N.W.2d 74 (Minn. 2001)

BLATZ, CHIEF JUSTICE.

This case comes before us on appeal from appellant Thomas Rhodes' conviction for the first- and second-degree murder of his wife and the postconviction court's subsequent denial of postconviction relief. Appellant argues that he received ineffective assistance of counsel at trial, that the district court erroneously admitted certain prejudicial evidence, and that the district court improperly denied appellant's request for a new trial based on newly discovered evidence. . . . We conclude that the district court did not err in admitting the disputed evidence, but remand for an evidentiary hearing on two of appellant's three postconviction ineffective assistance of counsel claims.

On the night of August 2, 1996, appellant and his wife Jane were vacationing with their two sons at the Northern Inn near Spicer, Minnesota. The inn is located at the southwest corner of Green Lake. Between approximately 11:15 and 11:30 p.m., the Rhodes left their sons in the inn room and drove the family jet boat onto the lake. Appellant told investigators that he drove the boat in a northerly direction from the dock by the inn, then stopped the boat and began watching the stars and "necking" with his wife. At some point, he and Jane allegedly saw a boat with no lights driving wildly to their south. To escape the boat and "take a spin" before heading back, appellant drove further north at about 40 miles per hour.

As he was driving, appellant glanced to the left and saw Jane get up from her seat. She appeared to be looking for something, which appellant believed to be an earring. A clip-on earring was later found in the boat. Continuing north on the lake, appellant looked back again and "saw [Jane's] leg or her tennis shoes go over" the edge of the boat. It is undisputed that Jane was not wearing a life jacket and was not a good swimmer.

In a police interview 2 weeks after the drowning, authorities asked appellant what he did when Jane fell in the water. Appellant responded:

> I went to grab for the throttle and—and missed it the first time. And then I pulled it back, started to turn, and then accelerated and went right back to where I thought—thought she was, and I couldn't see her. I stood up on the—the—the deck. And she's not by any means a good swimmer, so I got in the water to see if I could rescue her, and I couldn't find her. . . .

The state also sought to prove motive. The state first introduced evidence of an alleged extramarital affair in order to show that the Rhodes' marriage was unstable. Kathy Mason admitted to having a nonsexual relationship with appellant from approximately January to July of 1995, or about 1 year before Jane's death. Mason testified that she and appellant met once a week or three times a month and that she and appellant once went to a motel, where they hugged and kissed, talked, played cards, and drank champagne. Mason claimed that appellant ended the relationship in mid 1995 because he wanted to work on his marriage.

In addition, attorney C. Andrew Johnson testified that he met with appellant and Jane in May 1995 about a possible divorce, and that he calculated the amount of child support each spouse would have to pay the other if only one had custody of the children. Johnson testified that he told the Rhodes that appellant would have to pay $650 or $742 in child support out of his $2400 net monthly income. After this meeting, the Rhodes never again met with Johnson about a divorce. . . . appellant claims that the district court erroneously allowed Johnson to violate the attorney-client privilege by testifying about the meeting in which Johnson, appellant, and Jane discussed the financial aspects of divorce. The attorney-client privilege does not apply to confidences given in the presence of third parties. *See Kobluk v. Univ. of Minn.*, 574 N.W.2d 436, 443 (Minn.1998) (noting that disclosure to a third party may waive the confidentiality element of the attorney-client privilege). Although appellant argues that he and his wife were joint clients, Johnson testified and the district court determined that appellant alone was the client. Because Jane was a nonclient third party, her presence prevented the attorney-client privilege from attaching. . . .

CASE QUESTIONS

1. Why weren't the communications at issue in *Rhodes* protected by a marital privilege?
2. Would the attorney-client privilege have applied if Mr. Rhodes met with Mr. Johnson and then related the substance of that conversation to Mrs. Rhodes?

---

3. BETWEEN AN ATTORNEY AND A CLIENT

UNITED STATES V. KOVEL

296 F.2d 918 (2d Cir. 1961)

FRIENDLY, CIRCUIT JUDGE.

This appeal from a sentence for criminal contempt for refusing to answer a question asked in the course of an inquiry by a grand jury raises an important issue as to the application of the attorney-client privilege to a non-lawyer employed by a law firm. . . .

Kovel is a former Internal Revenue agent having accounting skills. Since 1943 he has been employed by Kamerman & Kamerman, a law firm specializing in tax law. A grand jury in the Southern District of New York was investigating alleged Federal income tax violations by Hopps, a client of the law firm; Kovel was subpoenaed to appear on September 6, 1961, a few days before the date, September 8, when the Government feared the statute of limitations might run. The law firm advised the Assistant United States Attorney that since Kovel was an employee under the direct supervision of the partners, Kovel could not disclose any communications by the client of the result of any work done for the client, unless the latter consented; the Assistant answered that the attorney-client privilege did not apply to one who was not an attorney.

The record reveals nothing as to what occurred on September 6. On September 7, the grand jury appeared before Judge Cashin. The Assistant United States Attorney informed the judge that Kovel had refused to answer 'several questions * * * on the grounds of attorney-client privilege'; he proffered 'respectable authority * * * that an accountant, even if he is retained or employed by a firm of attorneys, cannot take the privilege.' The judge answered 'You don't have to give me any authority on that.' A court reporter testified that Kovel, after an initial claim of privilege had admitted receiving a statement of Hopps' assets and liabilities, but that, when asked 'what was the purpose of your receiving that,' had declined to answer on the ground of privilege 'Because the communication was received with a purpose, as stated by the client'; later questions and answers indicated the communication was a letter addressed to Kovel. After verifying that Kovel was not a lawyer, the judge directed him to answer, saying 'You have no privilege as such.' The reporter then read another question Kovel had refused to answer, 'Did you ever discuss with Mr. Hopps or give Mr. Hopps any information with regard to treatment for capital gains purposes of the Atlantic Beverage Corporation sale by him?' The judge again directed Kovel to answer, reaffirming 'There is no privilege—you are entitled to no privilege, as I understand the law.' Kovel asked whether he might say something; the judge instructed him to answer, saying 'I'm not going to listen.' Kovel also declined to tell what Hopps had said concerning a transaction underlying a bad debt deduction in Hopps' 1954 return, and whether Hopps had told him that a certain transfer of securities 'had no effect whatsoever' and was just a form of accommodation; the judge gave similar directions after the reporter had read each question and refusal to answer. Then the grand jury, the Assistant and Kovel returned to the grand jury room.

Later on September 7, they and Kovel's employer, Jerome Kamerman, now acting as his counsel, appeared again before Judge Cashin. The Assistant told the judge that Kovel had 'refused to answer some of the questions which you had directed him to answer.' A reporter reread so much of the transcript heretofore summarized as contained the first two refusals. The judge offered Kovel another opportunity to answer, reiterating the view, 'There is no privilege to this man at all.' Counsel . . . sought an adjournment until co-counsel could appear; the judge put the matter over until the next morning.

On the morning of September 8, the same dramatic personae, plus the added counsel, attended in open court. Counsel reiterated that an employee 'who sits with the client of the law firm * * * occupies the same status * * * as a clerk or stenographer or any other lawyer * * * '; The judge was equally clear that the privilege was never 'extended beyond the attorney.' . . . The court held him in contempt, sentenced him to a year's imprisonment, ordered immediate commitment and denied bail. Later in the day, the grand jury having indicted, Kovel was released until September 12, at which time, without opposition from the Government, I granted bail pending determination of this appeal.

Here the parties continue to take generally the same positions as below—Kovel, that his status as an employee of a law firm automatically made all communications to him from clients privileged; the Government, that under no circumstances could there be privilege with respect to communications to an accountant. The New York County Lawyers' Association as amicus curiae has filed a brief generally supporting appellant's position.

I.

Decision under what circumstances, if any, the attorney-client privilege may include a communication to a nonlawyer by the lawyer's client is the resultant of two conflicting forces. One is the general teaching that 'The investigation of truth and the enforcement of testimonial duty demand the restriction, not the expansion, of these privileges,' 8 Wigmore, Evidence (McNaughton Rev. 1961), § 2192, p. 73. The other is the more particular lesson 'That as, by reason of the complexity and difficulty of our law, litigation can only be properly conducted by professional men, it is absolutely necessary that a man * * * should have recourse to the assistance of professional lawyers, and * * * it is equally necessary * * * that he should be able to place unrestricted and unbounded confidence in the professional agent, and that the communications he so makes to him should be kept secret * * *,' Jessel, M.R. in Anderson v. Bank, 2 Ch.D. 644, 649 (1876). Nothing in the policy of the privilege suggests that attorneys, simply by placing accountants, scientists or investigators on their payrolls and maintaining them in their offices, should be able to invest all communications by clients to such persons with a privilege the law has not seen fit to extend when the latter are operating under their own steam. On the other hand, in contrast to the Tudor times when the privilege was first recognized, see 8 Wigmore, Evidence, § 2290, the complexities of modern existence prevent attorneys from effectively handling clients' affairs without the help of others; few lawyers could now practice without the assistance of secretaries, file clerks, telephone operators, messengers, clerks not yet admitted to the bar, and aides of other sorts. 'The assistance of these agents being indispensable to his work and the communications of the client being often necessarily committed to them by the attorney or by the client himself, the privilege must include all the persons who act as the attorney's agents.' 8 Wigmore, Evidence, § 2301; Annot., 53 A.L.R. 369 (1928).

Indeed, the Government does not here dispute that the privilege covers communications to non-lawyer employees with 'a menial or ministerial responsibility that involves relating communications to an attorney.' We cannot regard the privilege as confined to 'menial or ministerial' employees. Thus, we can see no significant difference between a case where

the attorney sends a client speaking a foreign language to an interpreter to make a literal translation of the client's story; a second where the attorney, himself having some little knowledge of the foreign tongue, has a more knowledgeable non-lawyer employee in the room to help out; a third where someone to perform that same function has been brought along by the client; and a fourth where the attorney, ignorant of the foreign language, sends the client to a non-lawyer proficient in it, with instructions to interview the client on the attorney's behalf and then render his own summary of the situation, perhaps drawing on his own knowledge in the process, so that the attorney can give the client proper legal advice . . . . . We find no valid policy reason for a different result in the fourth case, and we do not read Wigmore as thinking there is. Laymen consulting lawyers should not be expected to anticipate niceties perceptible only to judges—and not even to all of them.

This analogy of the client speaking a foreign language is by no means irrelevant to the appeal at hand. Accounting concepts are a foreign language to some lawyers in almost all cases, and to almost all lawyers in some cases. Hence the presence of an accountant, whether hired by the lawyer or by the client, while the client is relating a complicated tax story to the lawyer, ought not destroy the privilege, any more than would that of the linguist in the second or third variations of the foreign language theme discussed above; the presence of the accountant is necessary, or at least highly useful, for the effective consultation between the client and the lawyer which the privilege is designed to permit. By the same token, if the lawyer has directed the client, either in the specific case or generally, to tell his story in the first instance to an accountant engaged by the lawyer, who is then to interpret it so that the lawyer may better give legal advice, communications by the client reasonably related to that purpose ought fall within the privilege; there can be no more virtue in requiring the lawyer to sit by while the client pursues these possibly tedious preliminary conversations with the accountant than in insisting on the lawyer's physical presence while the client dictates a statement to the lawyer's secretary or in interviewed by a clerk not yet admitted to practice. What is vital to the privilege is that the communication be made in confidence for the purpose of obtaining legal advice from the lawyer. If what is sought is not legal advice but only accounting service . . . or if the advice sought is the accountant's rather than the lawyer's, no privilege exists. . . .

We recognize this draws what may seem to some a rather arbitrary line between a case where the client communicates first to his own accountant (no privilege as to such communications, even though he later consults his lawyer on the same matter, *Gariepy v. United States*, 189 F.2d 459, 463 (6 Cir. 1951)),[2] and others, where the client in the first in-

[2] FN4. We do not deal in this opinion with the question under what circumstances, if any, such communications could be deemed privileged on the basis that they were being made to the

stance consults a lawyer who retains an accountant as a listening post, or consults the lawyer with his own accountant present. But that is the inevitable consequence of having to reconcile the absence of a privilege for accountants and the effective operation of the privilege of client and lawyer under conditions where the lawyer needs outside help. We realize also that the line we have drawn will not be so easy to apply as the simpler positions urged on us by the parties-the district judges will scarcely be able to leave the decision of such cases to computers; but the distinction has to be made if the privilege is neither to be unduly expanded nor to become a trap. . . .

The application of these principles here is more difficult than it ought be in future cases, because the extreme positions taken both by appellant and by the Government, the latter's being shared by the judge, resulted in a record that does not tell us how Hopps came to be communicating with Kovel rather than with Kamerman. The Government says the burden of establishing the privilege was on Kovel and, since he did not prove all the facts essential to it even on our view, the sentence must stand. Kovel rejoins that the Government always has the burden of showing a criminal defendant's guilt and, since the proof does not negate the possible existence of a privilege, the sentence must fall.

We follow the Government's argument at least to this extent; If we were here dealing with a trial at which a claim of privilege like Kovel's had been overruled and the witness had answered, we should not reverse, since the burden is on the objector to show that the relation giving rise to the privilege existed. On the other hand, appellant is right that, in a prosecution for criminal contempt, the ultimate burden of persuasion on the issue of privilege remains the Government's [citations omitted]; e.g., if Kamerman had testified he had told Hopps preliminarily to discuss with Kovel the transactions Kovel declined to disclose, and the Government challenged this testimony, it would have had the burden of convincing the judge on the facts.

The burden that the Government's proof did shift to Kovel was that of going forward with evidence supporting the claim of privilege. Kovel did not discharge that burden, on our view of the law; he claims he was relieved of any need of doing so since the course of the proceedings had made it apparent that no evidence he could have submitted would have influenced the district judge and the law does not require the ritual performance of a useless act. . . . However, the needs of the appellate court also must be considered; in order to preserve Kovel's position on appeal counsel should have proffered the necessary evidence and, if the judge

---

accountant as the client's agent for the purpose of subsequent communication by the accountant to the lawyer; communications by the client's agent to the attorney are privileged, 8 Wigmore, Evidence, § 2317–1. *See Lalance & Grosjean Mfg. Co. v. Haberman Mfg. Co.*, 87 F. 563 (C.C.S.D.N.Y., 1898).

would not receive it, should have made an offer of proof. . . . Without this we are left in the dark whether a remand will serve any purpose. . . . However, the uncertainty as to the applicable legal principle, the fixed view of the judge, and the haste with which the proceedings were here conducted because of the prospective running of the statute of limitations, extenuate although they do not altogether excuse the failure of Kovel's counsel to make a proper offer of proof; and a remand for determination of a few simple facts by the judge will not be burdensome. With petitioner's liberty at stake, we believe that the proper course, 28 U.S.C. § 2106. . .

The judgment is vacated and the cause remanded for further proceedings consistent with this opinion.

CASE QUESTIONS

1. What standard did the court announce for determining whether the privilege applies here?
2. What analogy did the court draw to show why the privilege must extend to some non-lawyers?
3. What facts should the district judge establish on remand?

PROBLEM 5–1

Which of the following situations (if any) are within the rule of *Kovel*?

1. A criminal defense attorney hires a chemist to determine whether his client's white, powdery substance is cocaine; the chemist tests the substance and attorney and chemist discuss the chemist's findings.
2. An antitrust attorney hires an economist to determine whether her client has market power in a given market; the economist interviews several executives and delivers a report to the attorney.
3. A business attorney hires a software developer to help trace the origins of software code in a certain program; the developer discusses the program with the client's developers and reports back to the attorney.
4. The attorney in (3) instructs the retained developer to show the client's own programmers how to implement the attorney's recommendations for avoiding copyright infringement; the retained developer instructs the programmers.

5. A partnership that owns office buildings hires a property management company (which is a separate entity) to run the buildings. In litigation over the condition of the buildings, counsel for the partnership (not the management company) interviews employees of the property management company.

6. In an insurance coverage dispute, counsel for the owner of the lease on the World Trade Centers interviews employees of an insurance broker that obtained the policies on the buildings.

PROBLEM 5–2

Consider the situation of two people after *Kovel.* The first person, *X* has a legal problem having to do with his finances. He goes first to his accountant, talks over the problem, and then to his lawyer. The second, *Y*, goes first to his lawyer, who then brings in an accountant to listen to *Y* and report back. What is the privilege situation of the conversations *X* and *Y* had with the accountants? Does this result make sense?

4. RELATING TO LEGAL ADVICE

Judge Wyzanski's recitation of the elements of the privilege included a requirement that a communication be "for the purpose of securing primarily" legal assistance. This requirement is commonly stated as requiring that the primary purpose of a communication be to obtain such assistance, or that legal advice predominate other aspects of a communication, such as business advice. In practice, such distinctions may be hard to draw.

NEUDER V. BATTELLE PACIFIC NORTHWEST NATIONAL LABORATORY

194 F.R.D. 289 (D. D.C. 2000)

URBINA, DISTRICT JUDGE.

This matter comes before the court upon the parties' separate motions to reconsider discovery decisions rendered by the Honorable Alan Kay, United States Magistrate Judge.

Stanley Neuder was employed [by Battelle Pacific Northwest National Laboratory's ("Battelle's")] as a Senior Scientist and Engineer for nearly nine years before his employment was terminated. Mr. Neuder alleges that Battelle wrongfully terminated him and engaged in discriminatory and retaliatory conduct on the basis of his age and disability. Mr. Neuder further alleges that Battelle interfered with his ERISA benefits and retaliated against him for taking sick leave . . . Battelle responds by asserting that Mr. Neuder was terminated because he failed to comply with Battelle's policies, specifically by: (1) failing to complete time sheets on a daily basis, (2) excessively using sick leave and (3) failing to complete an ethics training course.

By Battelle's account, the decision to terminate the plaintiff was made by its Personnel Action Review Committee ("PARC"). The events that led to Mr. Neuder's termination are as follows. First, in November 1997, William Farris, the plaintiff's immediate supervisor, issued the plaintiff a written warning concerning alleged recurrent performance-related shortcomings. Second, Mr. Farris conferred with a Human Resources Manager, Ms. Lamberson, to devise a plan for taking appropriate action against Mr. Neuder. Third, Mr. Farris and Ms. Lamberson requested that the PARC convene to address what personnel actions, if any, should be taken against Mr. Neuder.

On June 5, 1998, Battelle convened the first PARC meeting. David Maestas, Battelle's Senior Attorney, attended this meeting. Indeed, David Maestas was a member of the PARC committee according to its bylaws. After meeting, the PARC committee decided to obtain an Independent Medical Examination ("the IME") and to suspend the plaintiff. Once Battelle received the IME, it convened a second PARC meeting on June 26, 1998. Mr. Maestas again attended, as did other members of the PARC committee. At the second meeting, the PARC decided to terminate the plaintiff's employment. The plaintiff, accordingly, was terminated by decision of the PARC effective June 30, 1998. . . .

[T]he attorney-client privilege "applies only to communications made to an attorney in his capacity as legal advisor." *Marten v. Yellow Freight System, Inc.*, 1998 WL 13244, *7 (D.Kan. Jan. 6, 1998). Where business and legal advice are intertwined, the legal advice must predominate for the communication to be protected. . . . Relatedly, "communications by a corporation with its attorney, who at the time is acting solely in his capacity as a business advisor, would not be privileged." [citation omitted] In other words, "when the legal advice is merely incidental to business advice, the privilege does not apply."

Faced with a situation where a party potentially used in-house counsel to cloak otherwise unprivileged business advice, the magistrate judge applied well-settled principles of law. . . . The magistrate judge correctly cautioned the parties that "a corporate client should not be allowed to conceal a fact by disclosing it to the corporate attorney." Indeed, the mere fact that in-house counsel is present at a meeting does not shield otherwise unprivileged communications from disclosure.

Moreover, the magistrate judge correctly determined that the analysis in *Marten v. Yellow Freight* pertains to the facts of this case. *Marten* provides:

> [T]he mere attendance of an attorney at a meeting does not render everything done or said at that meeting privileged. For communications at such meetings to be privileged, they must have related to the acquisition or rendition of professional legal services. The mere fact that clients were at a meeting with counsel in which legal advice was being requested and/or received does not mean that everything said at the meeting is privileged. *The party seeking to assert the privilege must show that the particular communication was part of a request for advice or part of the advice,* and that the communication was intended to be and was kept confidential. To be privileged, the communication must relate to the business or transaction for which the attorney has been retained or consulted. [citation omitted]

Based on the foregoing, the court turns to consider Battelle's objections, which are premised upon its assertion that communications made during the PARC meetings are privileged because Mr. Maestas was acting as a legal advisor.

Battelle argues that the primary purpose of the PARC meetings was to render legal advice. . . . the magistrate judge found that the PARC's primary purpose was to render a business decision and, accordingly, that Mr. Maestas' presence did not make all documents generated and distributed in connection with the PARC privileged. In *Marten,* where a similar personnel action was contemplated by a similar personnel review committee, this one called the Employee Review Committee (ERC), the court found that the primary function of the ERC was to determine appropriate employment action to take against an employee. The *Marten* court held that "[w]hen a committee inquires about the legal implications of a proposed decision to terminate an employee, the business purpose of the decision predominates over the legal issues discussed." *Marten* reasoned that when a meeting is required in order to determine the legal implications of an employment action, legal advice sought or received is incidental to considerations of what is most prudent for the successful operation of the business. The court, accordingly, held that the business purpose of the ERC decision to terminate the *Marten* plaintiff predominated over the legal issues.

In this case, the magistrate judge determined that the PARC committee's primary function was to terminate Mr. Neuder. As in *Marten,* although legal review was one purpose for the meeting, it was merely incidental to the primary business function. The record in this case similarly supports the conclusion that the PARC served predominantly a business purpose-terminating the plaintiff. First, Battelle's Disciplinary Policy provides that the PARC is called to review and concur in termination decisions and to approve proposed terminations. Second, the Memorandum Order references the depositions of Mr. William Farris and Ms. Marilyn Merryman in support of the conclusion that the PARC functioned primarily in a business capacity. These depositions reveal that the PARC functioned to terminate Mr. Neuder. And finally, the termination letter sent to the plaintiff ("the Farris letter") reflects that the PARC terminated the plaintiff. . . .

It happens to be that in *Marten,* the in-house attorney was a voting member of the ERC committee. The court remarked that "[m]ere membership on a committee does not of itself necessitate a finding that counsel was not acting as an attorney." The court added, "[m]embership on a committee which decides if an employee should be terminated, however, may lead to an inference that the attorney, at least in part, was acting in a non-legal capacity. When an attorney is a voting member, the indication is even stronger."

This court concurs in the magistrate judge's determination that Mr. Maestas's non-voting status is not a significant, distinguishing factor that would make *Marten* inapposite to this case. Rather, the record contains other affirmative indicators that Mr. Maestas was acting in a non-legal capacity as a PARC member. It is notable, for example, that Battelle's Disciplinary Policy requires an attorney to sit on the PARC committee. Moreover, the attorney serves as the chairperson of the PARC committee in the event that a proposed termination involves a Human Resources staff member.

The court, accordingly, agrees that Mr. Maestas' self-serving declaration does not suffice to establish that he was acting in a legal capacity as a PARC member. . . . . "When an attorney serves in a non-legal capacity . . . his advice is privileged upon a clear showing that he gave it in a professional legal capacity." In order to determine whether the attorney was acting in a professional legal capacity, the magistrate judge closely examined the facts of the specific communication and determined:

> the documents listed in Defendant's privilege log contain statements of facts that were provided to the PARC in order to make a personnel decision as to Plaintiff. There is nothing in the record to suggest that the documents were given to Mr. Maestas for the express or sole purpose of receiving legal advice and not in his capacity as a participant in the PARC. . . . Similarly, there is nothing in the privilege log or in the documents themselves to suggest that these documents were provided to Maestas to form the basis of a legal opinion.

Based on a review of the magistrate judge's memorandum order, including factual findings and review of the law, the court is convinced that [certain documents] are privileged. Moreover, the magistrate judge correctly held that the remaining documents . . . are not privileged. The court found some documents privileged because "[i]t is clear from their contents that Mr. Maestas was sent these documents in order to provide legal advice and that he provided that advice in a professional legal capacity." As to others it held "[t]he fact that the documents reflect communications resulting from the PARC meetings is not alone sufficient to give rise to an attorney-client privilege. The magistrate judge has already determined that the discussions and deliberations of the PARC meetings are not privileged because the PARC's primary function was to make a business decision, not to obtain legal advice . . . the communications do not reflect that Mr. Maestas provided legal advice in a professional capacity."

CASE QUESTIONS

1. What test governs cases where communications with a lawyer mix business and legal questions together?
2. Does a lawyer's presence at a meeting privilege facts discussed at the meeting?
3. What did the magistrate find was the PARC's primary function relative to this case?
4. Was it significant that Maesta was a non-voting member of the PARC?

The *Neuder* court asked in part whether Maestas acted in a legal capacity as a PARC member. That may not be the most helpful way to ask the question. If Maestas had been acting as a lawyer that would make it more likely that any given communication would be privileged but it would not entail that everything said in a PARC meeting was privileged. And even with the court's finding that Maestas acted in a business capacity generally on the committee it still found that some of his work was legal advice. To the extent possible, privilege questions are better answered by focusing on particular communications than on general capacities.

If a communication between a lawyer and a client relates to the representation, however, the entire communication will be privileged even though some things communicated, such as facts the client provides the lawyer, might be discovered from the client directly. For example, suppose a client informs its lawyer of its employment practices and asks the lawyer for an opinion letter pertaining to those practices. Such a letter likely would recite those practices as a foundation for its opinion. But even though the client could be asked directly about those practices the entire opinion letter, including its recitation of facts, is privileged because the letter is a communication from the lawyer to the client through which legal advice is provided and because the client could not be forced to disclose communications to the lawyer, even though the client could be forced to testify directly about facts communicated. *Costco Wholesale Corp. v. Superior Court*, 47 Cal.4th 725 (2009) (" because the privilege protects the *transmission* of information, if the communication is privileged, it does not become unprivileged simply because it contains material that could be discovered by some other means"). *Costco* holds that the primary purpose test discussed above (which it calls the "dominant purpose" test) is used to determine whether a communication was made within an attorney-client relationship, as opposed to a business relationship. If so, the whole communication is privileged, including the transmission of public documents. 47 Cal. 4th at 734. If not, no part of the communication is privileged

PROBLEM 5–3

Suppose you are outside counsel to Battelle. Suppose further that your client contact tells you the reason for putting a lawyer on the PARC is to cloak employment deliberations in privilege. Your client contact asks you to revise Battelle's practices and procedures in light of this opinion so as to maximize the chance that courts will reach a different result in future cases. What suggestions would you make? Would it be ethical to make them?

PROBLEM 5–4

Suppose you start work at a firm representing a drug company. Soon you notice that the drug company routinely copies your firm on its test results, and always has a lawyer present for meetings where the health risks of drugs might be discussed. In litigation regarding the health effects of the company's drugs, you notice that the firm asserts the attorney-client privilege against the production of documents showing test results and with regard to statements at such meetings. When you ask your partner about this, she says there is always litigation risk when health issues come up, so it is appropriate to have a lawyer involved in any communications regarding such issues. Is the firm's conduct ethical? Do you have any obligations to do anything about it?

What About Threats?

Recall that Moe, the client in In the Matter of A Grand Jury Investigation, *453 Mass. 453 (2009), left Doe, his lawyer, voice mail messages threatening the judge. Were those communications privileged? Could threats against the judge be made for the purpose of obtaining legal services?*

The Court said: "Yes." It reasoned "Moe's communications were made in furtherance of the rendition of legal services and thus protected by the at-

torney-client privilege. The Commonwealth's argument to the contrary essentially raises an issue of germaneness. . . .

Scholars, commentators, and courts have formulated a number of tests for determining the germaneness of a client's communication. However, none of these formulations appears to give clients breathing room to express frustration and dissatisfaction with the legal system and its participants. The expression of such sentiments is a not uncommon incident of the attorney-client relationship, particularly in an adversarial context, and may serve as a springboard for further discussion regarding a client's legal options.

If a lawyer suspects that the client intends to act on an expressed intent to commit a crime, the lawyer may attempt to dissuade the client from such action, and failing that, may make a limited disclosure to protect the likely targets. Requiring the privilege to yield for purposes of a criminal prosecution would not only hamper attorney-client discourse, but also would discourage lawyers from exercising their discretion to make such disclosures, as occurred here, and thereby frustrate the beneficial public purpose underpinning the discretionary disclosure provision of rule 1.6.

Furthermore, any test to ascertain the germaneness of an ostensibly threatening communication on a case-by-case basis would make the privilege's applicability uncertain, rendering the privilege 'little better than no privilege.' [citations omitted] Warning clients that communications deemed irrelevant to the matter for which they have retained counsel will not be protected may not only discourage clients from disclosing germane information, but also may disincline clients to share their intentions to engage in criminal behavior. In the latter circumstance, a lawyer's ability to aid in the administration of justice by dissuading a client from engaging in such behavior is impaired.. . . . The lawyer also may never receive the very information necessary for him or her to determine whether to make a limited disclosure to prevent the harm contemplated by the client."

Advising or Conspiring? Two Cases

Ford Motor Company was sued on the theory that its Bronco II SUV designs were defective. The company's general counsel, Henry R. Nolte, Jr., drafted a report on the Bronco II and presented it to a committee advising Ford's CEO. The plaintiff sought discovery of the minutes of the meeting. Finding that the minutes "disclose only factual material, contain no legal discussion, were not created in anticipation of litigation . . . , and contain no communication to counsel which was intended to be kept confidential," the trial court ordered that the minutes be produced. The court later stated that the minutes were "business records" that memorialized "essentially business and safety decisions."

In re Ford Motor Company, 110 F.3d 954 (3d Cir. 1997), the court reversed. It held that

* * *

"Our review of the final minutes, the draft minutes, the report Nolte summarized at the meeting, and relevant affidavits, leads us to conclude that the communications in the meeting were made for the purpose of securing legal advice. Ford clearly had concerns about the Bronco II; this is not surprising given that the product was in the early stages of its development. Nolte examined the legal implications of some of those concerns and proposed a particular course of action, contained in his report to the Policy and Strategy Committee, to address them. The Policy and Strategy Committee meeting itself was called in part to discuss Nolte's proposal. The discussion at the meeting, then, was intended to secure Nolte's legal advice.

The district court initially ruled that the minutes "disclose only factual material, contain no legal discussion, were not created in anticipation of litigation . . . , and contain no communication to counsel which was intended to be kept confidential." The court later stated that the minutes were "business records" that memorialized "essentially business and safety decisions." We disagree with the district court's conclusions as to the nature of the documents. The documents do not contain merely factual material nor do they detail mere business decisions; in that respect, the district court clearly erred in describing these documents. Certainly, the ultimate decision reached by the Policy and Strategy Committee could be characterized as a business decision, but the Committee reached that decision only after examining the legal implications of doing so. Even if the decision was driven, as the district court seemed to assume, principally by profit and loss, economics, marketing, public relations, or the like, it was also infused with legal concerns, and was reached only after securing legal advice. At all events, disclosure of the documents would reveal that legal advice. We thus hold that the minutes of the 1982 meeting are protected from discovery by the attorney-client privilege."

* * *

A second issue related to the work product doctrine, which is the subject of chapter 6. On this issue the court reversed the district court's order that Ford produce

* * *

"a series of agendas, one with handwritten notations, for a meeting in 1988, and one document pertaining to a 1989 meeting on which handwritten notes refer to the 1988 agendas. By 1988, numerous lawsuits similar to that brought by [the plaintiff] were pending, alleging faulty design of the Bronco II. As part of its defense strategy, Ford retained an outside technical consultant, Failure Analysis Associates (FAA), to assist in the defense of those lawsuits. FAA, in turn, relied in part on the help of in-house technical assistants to Ford. Ernest Grush, one of these technical assistants, prepared the agendas for the 1988 meeting. The meeting was called to explain the technical aspects of the Bronco II litigation defense strategy, and Ford attorneys were present. Grush has declared that the handwritten notes on the document pertaining to the 1989 meeting are his, and that they refer to the 1988 meeting. . . .

[O]ur in camera review leads us to conclude that the agendas for the 1988 meeting and the handwritten notes on the document pertaining to the 1989 meeting are protected from discovery by the work product doctrine. . . . [T]he agendas disclose material prepared as part of Ford's legal strategy for defending the type of case [the plaintiff] brought here. The agendas outline the results of studies conducted as to the safety of the Bronco II and, in so doing, highlight important aspects of those studies. Those studies were found by the district court to be protected by the work product doctrine because they would be used in defending anticipated lawsuits. Ford persuasively contends that experts acting on behalf of Kelly and working backwards from the agendas could determine the methodology of the studies. Ford's attorneys and their agents called for the studies, and Ford credibly demonstrates that if Kelly learns the methodology of the studies, then she has effectively learned of the issues of most concern to Ford's litigation defense team. Moreover, the agendas themselves were for meetings at which the experts would, inter alia, explain the technical aspects of Ford's legal defense strategy by referring to those studies. We are satisfied, in view of the foregoing, that these agendas, core work product, were prepared in anticipation of litigation.

That the agendas do not necessarily include legal advice is, as a matter of law, irrelevant provided, as we note above, they were prepared in anticipation of litigation. Moreover, it is of no import, again as a matter of law, that the meetings for which the agendas were prepared were not legal department meetings. Thus, the district court clearly erred (a function in part of legal error) in concluding that the agendas were not prepared in anticipation of litigation. In this case, the context in which the agendas were discussed does not change the reasons for their preparation."[3]

---

[3] In a portion of the opinion not reproduced here the Third Circuit held in *In re Ford Motor Co.* that a party may appeal immediately an order to produce documents as to which the party asserts privilege or work product protection. This portion of the opinion was overruled in *Mohawk Indus., Inc. v. Carpenter*, 130 S.Ct. 599, 606–07 (2009), in which the Court held "postjudgment appeals generally suffice to protect the rights of litigants and assure the vitality

* * *

Compare these rulings to *Burton v. R.J. Reynolds Tobacco Co., Inc.*, 170 F.R.D. 481 (D. Kan. 1997). The plaintiffs sued R.J. Reynolds tobacco ("RJR") on product liability theories.

Over a period of years, RJR involved its lawyers in every aspect of its research into the health effects of cigarettes. Lawyers participated in deciding what studies to conduct, in reviewing the results of such studies, in deciding which new product should be developed, and how the development process should be structured to minimize the risk of future liability, and so on. Lawyers also attended conferences on smoking and health held by universities, government agencies, and others outside the company; they reported back on such meetings. They also attended meetings with scientists and lawyers from other tobacco companies to exchange information and ideas regarding smoking and health, and health-related litigation in particular.

The plaintiffs in *Burton* moved to compel production of 33 documents from the Council for Tobacco Research ("CTR"). RJR claimed the documents were protected by the privilege and the work product doctrine. The court rejected this claim: "RJR seems to believe and argues that when an attorney is somehow referenced within a document or generates a document, attorney-client privilege or work product immunity must protect disclosure of the subject document. Such is simply not the law." The court held

* * *

"Information is not privileged simply because it comes from an attorney. The mere fact that one is an attorney does not render everything he does for or with the client privileged. Minutes of meetings attended by attorneys are not automatically privileged and business documents sent to attorneys are not automatically protected. When raised as to documents pre-existing, given by the client to the attorney to aid in legal representation, the privilege protects only material that would have been privileged in the hands of the client.

Some courts have been influenced by whether the work being performed at the time of the communication required the services of an attorney or could be performed equally well by a non-lawyer. The fact that the client chose to channel the work through an attorney rather than perform the work with non-legal personnel does not provide the basis for a

---

of the attorney-client privilege. Appellate courts can remedy the improper disclosure of privileged material in the same way they remedy a host of other erroneous evidentiary rulings: by vacating an adverse judgment and remanding for a new trial in which the protected material and its fruits are excluded from evidence."

claim of privilege. When an attorney is merely acting as a conduit for information, the privilege does not apply." *Id.*

* * *

The court's treatment of five research-related documents is representative of its general approach:

* * *

"RJR claims that the documents at Tabs 10–15 are protected by the attorney-client privilege. The correspondence is devoid of legal advice or any suggestion of such advice. The documents reflect no communications from the client. Each document relates to an active or proposed study being conducted by a third party concerning the effects of tobacco. The activities reported and the communications in the documents are those which could have been performed by company personnel, a scientist, or any non-lawyer knowledgeable in the subject matter. The activities and the advice given are that of a business and not a legal nature. The reported activities are not tied to pending litigation and make no reference to legal issues. They contain no legal strategy. The subject matter is scientific data. The studies are ongoing scientific studies related to tobacco and health issues generally. The documents do not contain communications protected by the attorney-client privilege, notwithstanding that they were prepared by attorneys and contain communications to the clients. The correspondence is of a procedural nature and reports either the activities of third parties or the status of a study and the third party's request for funding of its study. A party may not cloak a document with a privilege by simply having business, scientific or public relations matters handled by attorneys, whether in-house or outside counsel."

Boundary Issues
What Are You Selling? Part I

Burton can be read as holding that Liggett used its attorneys as a conduit for research on smoking and health in the hope that, by passing through the hands of an attorney, the research would be cloaked in privilege. To switch metaphors for a moment, the attorneys were not so much providing legal advice as a shield; they were acting as a shield by placing themselves between Liggett and anyone who wanted Liggett's information, such as plaintiffs' lawyers or legislative reformers.

To the extent this is true, one could characterize the *Burton* court as concluding (or at least suspecting) that Liggett's counsel was selling secrecy, not legal services. There is in fact a respectable line of academic criticism of the attorney-client privilege that says the privilege harms society (by making it harder to get the truth) and serves mainly to benefit lawyers, by giving them a comparative advantage over other professionals who do not get the benefit of privilege, such as accountants, bankers, or tobacco researchers. *E.g.* Daniel R. Fischel, *Lawyers and Confidentiality*, 65 U.CHI. L. REV. 1 (1998).

This line of analysis implies that lawyers may do well for themselves by getting in between their clients and someone who would like to hurt their clients. Selling secrecy rather than legal advice might make financial sense. It has its risks, however. As *Burton* demonstrates, the more a judge (or other authority) believes you are trading on the accoutrements of legal practice rather than providing "real" legal services, the less likely you are to be treated as a lawyer. If you are not treated as a lawyer, you should consider what you will be treated as, a question closely related to what your client is doing and how it appears to others. The line between "lawyer" and "tobacco shill" or "securities tout" or "co-conspirator" might be finer than you think. As a general matter, as the ratio of lawyering to shielding goes down, the risk of being treated as part of your client's business goes up.

This point is related to another, more general, point concerning decisions you will make in practice: There are almost always two types of errors you can make. You can be too cautious, as by not asserting privilege with respect to communications that might in fact be privileged and therefore not subject to discovery, or too aggressive, as by asserting privilege over material to which the privilege does not extend. Being too cautious might harm your client by virtue of releasing information the client might be entitled to withhold. Being too aggressive might harm your client, or perhaps harm you, by suggesting to a tribunal that you are playing games with the privilege and are willing to take unsupportable positions. Such a belief might make the tribunal more skeptical even of very solid arguments you might make. Because privilege calls tend to be made by lawyers rather than clients, excessive assertions of privilege might harm your reputation in addition to creating skepticism that might make your client's case less likely to prevail.

MATTER OF MICHAEL FELDBERG

862 F.2d 622 (7th Cir. 1988)

EASTERBROOK, CIRCUIT JUDGE.

A grand jury investigating agents who signed amateur athletes to undisclosed contracts issued a subpoena to World Sports and Entertainment in March 1987. The subpoena called for all contracts between World Sports and college football players. World Sports, as a corporation, had no privilege to resist disclosure. See *Braswell v. United States,* 487 U.S. 99

(1988). Norby Walters, the president of World Sports, engaged Michael Feldberg, a partner of Shea & Gould, to represent both of them. Feldberg came into possession of 51 contracts (just how is the principal issue today) and turned them over to the grand jury on behalf of World Sports. All of these contracts were dated after the expiration of the athletes' collegiate eligibility. The grand jury was not satisfied; after it made a further request, Feldberg produced another seven contracts. Six of these pertained to athletes who held themselves out as eligible to participate in the fall 1987 college football season. The contracts had been post-dated to make it appear that they had been signed after the players' college careers ended; the disclosures revealed that World Sports made a practice of surreptitiously contracting with "amateur" athletes. Such contracts terminated the players' amateur status and made them ineligible to compete; the contracts also exposed the players' colleges to the risk that contests in which they participated would be forfeited. The post-dating came to light only because these contracts had been produced in advance of the date they bore. After receiving the post-dated contracts, the grand jury indicted World Sports and Walters for mail fraud. One of the players involved, Cris Carter (now a wide receiver with the Philadelphia Eagles), has pleaded guilty to mail fraud and obstruction of justice. Sports Illustrated 113 (Sept. 26, 1988).

I

The grand jury wants to know why it did not receive the second set of contracts in response to the subpoena. The prosecutor believes that there may have been obstruction of justice. Although the United States Attorney does not suspect Feldberg of wrongdoing, the grand jury summoned him to testify about how he obtained the initial batch of contracts. Feldberg is the obvious source of information, because Walters, if summoned, doubtless would invoke his privilege against self-incrimination. . . .

The subpoena put Feldberg in an uncomfortable position, because he had served World Sports in two capacities. He was on the one hand its agent, a delivery boy in connection with the documents; he was simultaneously the firm's attorney and undoubtedly had supplied legal advice to Walters and World Sports with respect to their obligations under the March 1987 subpoena. File clerks may be required to testify about their search for documents, but lawyers ordinarily may not be required to testify about facts they learned in confidence in the course of rendering legal advice.

Feldberg answered many questions but asserted the attorney-client privilege in response to the ones of greatest interest to the grand jury—such as who searched the files, and how. The prosecutor asked the district court to compel Feldberg to answer. Walters and World Sports intervened to protect their interests. The district court instructed Feldberg to answer; Walters and World Sports immediately filed this appeal. . . .

The district court . . . ordered Feldberg to answer all of the questions on the basis of an argument the prosecutor had not made: that there is a distinction "between communications relating to the act of production on one hand and communications relating to the general subject matter of the grand jury investigation on the other. The pending questions which Feldberg has refused to answer appear to be of the former type, and they should be answered." In this court the prosecutor not only reasserts the two arguments that did not persuade the district court but also defends the ground that court advanced for its decision. . . .

III

Although the prospect of establishing obstruction of justice prevents the case from being moot and provides a potential basis for overcoming a claim of privilege, it does not supply a basis for affirming the decision, because the district court never subjected the prosecutor's claims to the test. The court's order rests on a different ground, a distinction between Feldberg's role as substitute for the corporate records custodian and his role as lawyer. Walters and World Sports contend that no such distinction is tenable. To the contrary, a distinction of this kind is essential if the privilege is to be limited to those disclosures related to legal advice. A business that gets marketing advice from a lawyer does not acquire a privilege in the bargain; so too a business that obtains the services of a records custodian from a member of the bar.

The attorney-client privilege has not been codified. But statements of that privilege from every perspective recognize a limitation to legal topics. Wigmore's treatise, which we quoted favorably in *Radiant Burners, Inc. v. American Gas Ass'n,* 320 F.2d 314, 319 (7th Cir.1963), says that the privilege applies "[w]here legal advice of any kind is sought from a professional legal adviser in his capacity as such, *the communications relating to that purpose*" (8 Evidence § 2292, internal numbering omitted, emphasis added). The Supreme Court's proposal in 1972, which treated the privilege as an exception to the rule of access and therefore one of limited scope, stated things this way: "A client has a privilege to refuse to disclose and to prevent any other person from disclosing confidential communications *made for the purpose of facilitating the rendition of professional legal services to the client*". Proposed Fed.R.Evid. 503(b), 56 F.R.D. at 236 (emphasis added). The American Law Institute's *Restatement of the Law Governing Lawyers* (Tent. Draft No. 1, 1988), which contains perhaps the broadest privilege ever proposed in the United States, has similar language. A communication is privileged under the ALI's treatment if made for "the purpose of obtaining or providing legal assistance for the client", § 118(4), which the *Restatement* further defines as a communication that "relates to legal advice or other legal assistance that a lawyer is to render to a client", § 122(1). The comment adds: "the person consulted must be functioning in the professional capacity of a lawyer".

Most corporate records custodians are not lawyers. Answers to questions such as "where did you look for the documents?" will not reveal legal advice; recognizing the grand jury's right to ask such questions will not dissuade persons from obtaining legal advice. A grand jury may compel a corporate records custodian to testify about the nature of his search and the adequacy of the disclosure, *In re Grand Jury Proceedings (John Doe Co.)*, 838 F.2d 624, 626 (1st Cir.1988). Such an inquiry may be essential to determine whether the grand jury has received the documents to which it is entitled. If the inquiry itself is legitimate, the addressee of the subpoena cannot put the subject off limits by having counsel turn over the documents. After all, the attorney-client privilege covers "only those disclosures necessary to obtain informed legal advice." *Fisher v. United States,* 425 U.S. 391, 403 (1976). Since questions about the adequacy of the search do not entail legal advice, the topic is not off limits just because an attorney plays a role.

The privilege is not good in itself. The legal system needs information to decide cases correctly. See *United States v. Nixon,* 418 U.S. 683, 708–13 (1974). When the privilege shelters important knowledge, accuracy declines. Litigants may use secrecy to cover up machinations, to get around the law instead of complying with it. Secrecy is useful to the extent it facilitates the candor necessary to obtain legal advice. The privilege extends no further. Courts protect adverse information in the hands of counsel because counsel needs both favorable and adverse news to devise a strategy. It is not possible to separate adverse from favorable information in advance; a client, knowing this, would find disclosures of all sorts more costly if there were no privilege. See also *Upjohn Co. v. United States,* 449 U.S. 383 (1981).

There is no need for a privilege to cover information exchanged in the course of document searches, which are mostly mechanical yet which entail great risks of dishonest claims of complete compliance. Dropping a cone of silence over the process of searching for documents would do more harm than good. It is easy for a firm such as World Sports to hire an attorney to render advice on all legal matters while hiring a clerk to look through the records. The categories would merge if the clerk should find a questionable document, leading the firm to inquire of the lawyer whether the document fell within the scope of the subpoena (and whether, if it did, it had to be produced). Perhaps some of the conversations in this case were of that character, and if so they are privileged. But a corporation may be required to disclose its books and documents to a grand jury, e.g., *Consolidated Rendering Co. v. Vermont,* 207 U.S. 541, 554 (1908), and may not throw the veil of privilege over the details of how files were searched, and by whom, through the expedient of involving a lawyer in the process. We suppose that a grand jury could refuse to accept documents from the hand of a lawyer, could insist that the corporation's own records custodian or its principal officer, as in *Braswell* and *Brown v.*

United States, 276 U.S. 134 (1928), produce them personally. If the grand jury did so, no attorney-client privilege would attach to questions about the mechanics (who, how, when, where) of the search. If we were to recognize a privilege with the scope Walters and World Sports assert, that would simply lead prosecutors to disdain the proffered cooperation of counsel. That would complicate life for both grand jury and target (surely World Sports thought responding through counsel was in its own interests), without affording any confidentiality to the process of the search.

The distinction between the mechanical and advisory portions of Feldberg's role shows that the district court was right to compel answers to several but not all of the questions. . . .

IV

Our analysis implies the need for a remand, so that the district judge may refine his directions about which questions must be answered and explore the crime/fraud exception. The prosecutor submits that further investigation is unnecessary because any disclosures were made to Feldberg for the purpose of relaying the documents to the grand jury. Information imparted to counsel without any expectation of confidentiality is not privileged. World Sports knew that Feldberg would disclose what he received, so, the prosecutor concludes, the clients could not have anticipated confidence.

This line of argument confuses expectations about the *documents* with expectations about the *communications.* Rare is the case in which attorney-client conversations do not lead to some public disclosure. The criminal defense lawyer gathers information and formulates strategy in preparation for a trial; since the trial is public, does it follow that the antecedent communications are unprivileged? A lawyer writes a brief to be filed with the court; does it follow that the drafts of the brief are available to the adversary? A corporation prepares and publishes an internal report about "questionable payments" abroad; we know from *Upjohn Co.* that it does not follow that the government has access to the interviews underlying the published report. An accountant prepares worksheets underlying a tax return; we may infer from *United States v. Arthur Young & Co.,* 465 U.S. 805 (1984), that if there were an accountant-client privilege (there isn't) its domain would include these worksheets. None of the prosecutor's arguments suggests that Feldberg, Walters, and World Sports anticipated (or should have anticipated) the disclosure of their conversations. . . .

Boundary Issues
What Are You Selling? Part II

In the Introduction you learned the importance of categorization as an aspect of perception. Categories classify people and things in relation to an observer's purpose, and the classification both predicts the behavior or attributes of the thing classified and suggests to the observer the appropriate way to deal with the person or thing in order to achieve the purpose to which the classification relates.

"Lawyer" is a category, and often observers will perceive your actions to be the practice of law just because you are a lawyer. But *Feldberg* reinforces the point that not everything a lawyer does amounts to the practice of law. Sometimes an observer, especially a sophisticated person such as a judge, will classify a lawyer as an ordinary person for some purpose. The gathering of documents at issue in *Feldberg* is a good example, and one you should pay particular attention to: Junior lawyers are often tasked with rounding up documents (though this work is being outsourced to non-lawyer technology specialists more and more frequently).

Some aspects of document collection require legal judgment. Interpreting the scope of a subpoena and the scope of applicable privileges are examples here. Other aspects, such as actually finding the documents and collecting them, do not. Neither the attorney-client privilege nor the work-product doctrine is likely to protect from discovery information relevant to the document-gathering function.

Lawyers who try to cloak unprivileged tasks in privilege by performing such tasks themselves are likely to receive the same treatment you see in *Feldberg*. There is more at stake here than might appear at first glance. If you assume that your discussions with your client are privileged just because you are a lawyer, rather than because the discussion pertains to legal advice, you might say things you otherwise would not say, and be called on to testify about those things later on. That might not change substantive law very much—you cannot help a client break the law even when you are acting as a lawyer—but it might lead to some embarrassing testimony on your part, especially if you did not point out to the client that a conversation would not be privileged and the client assumed that it would be.

The point is to know what you are doing when you are doing it. Much of what you do will constitute the practice of law, but some of it will not. The difference is important, and it is up to you to know the difference.

I'm Only Your Lawyer When You're Not Trying to Kill People

Feldberg distinguishes communications for the purpose of obtaining legal services and communications for some other purpose. How do the relevant rules work if a lawyer represents a client in one matter and has a discussion related to a different matter (or to acts that would lead to a different matter). Consider the reasoning of the court in *State v. Branham*, 952 So.2d 618 (Fla.App. 2007).

Michael Branham was indicted for murdering his wife, Janette. The government gave notice that it had information concerning Branham from a lawyer named W. James Kelly. Kelly told the government that in conversation with Kelly a week before Janette's death Branham had threatened to kill Janette. Branham filed a motion seeking a declaration that this conversation was privileged. The trial court granted the motion but the court of appeals reversed.

"At the hearing on the State's motion, Kelly testified that several months before the death of the victim, the Branhams began having marital problems and discussed filing for divorce. Because Kelly was a friend to both of the Branhams, Kelly made it clear to them that he would not represent either of them in the divorce proceedings. However, Kelly agreed to act as a "go-between" for the Branhams in their efforts to resolve their differences.

Sometime during the week prior to the victim's death, Kelly went to the defendant's house on a social visit. Kelly testified that he and the defendant were discussing the Branhams' marital problems and that "some of [the discussion] was just shooting the breeze, some of it was just talk." During the conversation, the defendant inquired if Kelly was his attorney and Kelly responded "Sure." Immediately thereafter the defendant stated that he was going to kill his wife. According to Kelly, the defendant's threat occurred "right in the middle of the conversation." The defendant subsequently repeated the threat several more times during their conversation. Kelly's response to the defendant each time he made the threat was "You're crazy. I don't even want to hear it" and "Don't talk like that." When Kelly was asked whether he gave the defendant advice or counsel, Kelly testified:

> I don't think he was asking me. I don't know what his intentions were. I just know what I replied to him was certainly not in the context of a criminal lawyer. As far as I know, the issue of what he was telling me, I didn't think that had anything to do with anything going on. I mean, it just came whistling out of the clear blue.

Kelly also testified that the defendant never requested Kelly's assistance to plan, commit, or get away with a crime.

When asked if he was "talking to [the defendant] as his attorney with regard [ ] to the divorce," Kelly said "No." When asked if he was "talking to [the defendant] strictly as a friend," Kelly said "Yes." Kelly further testified that he warned the victim concerning the threats made by the defendant. There was no testimony before the trial court indicating that in the conversation between the defendant and Kelly, the defendant either sought or received any legal advice concerning any matter. . . .

[T]he evidence before the trial court unequivocally established that in the conversation with Kelly at the defendant's home, the defendant never asked for any legal advice and Kelly never gave any legal advice. The defendant did not "consult" Kelly "with the purpose of obtaining legal services," and Kelly did not "render[ ] legal services" to the defendant. § 90.502(1)(b).[4] The defendant's statements to Kelly that the defendant intended to kill his wife were not "made in [connection with] the rendition of legal services to" the defendant. § 90.502(2). In ruling that the statements made by the defendant to Kelly were subject to the lawyer-client privilege, the trial court failed to apply the clear-and clearly applicable-provisions of sections 90.502(1)(b) and 90.502(2).

There is no legal basis for the trial court's conclusion that because Kelly told the defendant that Kelly was the defendant's attorney, the defendant was entitled to rely on the lawyer-client privilege. The lawyer-client privilege is not established by incantation. Nor does the privilege come into existence simply because a party believes that it exists.

Kelly was the defendant's attorney in a then-pending negligence case, and Kelly had previously represented the defendant in other civil matters. But the existence of the lawyer-client relationship between Kelly and the defendant with respect to the negligence case and the other matters did not establish a lawyer-client relationship with respect to the matters discussed in the course of the conversation at issue here. That conversation was totally unrelated to any lawyer-client relationship between Kelly and the defendant."

B. ENTITIES AND PRIVILEGE

The cases in this section are premised on an important rule: When you represent an entity, such as a corporation, partnership, or LLC, you represent the entity itself, *as* an entity. MR 1.13. You do not represent the individuals who work for or are otherwise involved in the entity, such as officers, directors, shareholders, or creditors. We will call these people "constituents" of the entity.

---

[4] [Ed's note] Statutory references in this paragraph are to Florida's codification of the privilege.

Entities are legal fictions, of course—they can only act through real human beings. The upshot of this rule, therefore, is that when you represent an entity, the person who hires you, has the power to fire you, pays you, and instructs you on what to do, is *not* your client. He or she does so as a constituent of the entity and on behalf of the entity. In the cases in this section, this rule means that the entity itself holds the attorney-client privilege. Constituents who communicate on behalf of the entity do not hold the privilege, even though it is their communications that are or are not protected. This may seem like an abstract point of law of interest only to corporate lawyers. Most people who want to engage in a continuous endeavor choose an entity form, however, so you will probably encounter this rule in whatever field you choose to practice in.

Restatement of the Law Governing Lawyers § 73

TEKNI–PLEX, INC. V. MEYNER AND LANDIS

89 N.Y.2d 123 (1996)

KAYE, CHIEF JUDGE.

Tekni–Plex, Inc., incorporated under the laws of Delaware in 1967, manufactured and packaged products for the pharmaceutical and other industries. For nearly 20 years, from 1967 to 1986, Tekni–Plex had 18 shareholders and was managed by a five-member Board of Directors. Appellant Tom Y.C. Tang was both a director and a shareholder of the company. In 1986, Tang became the sole shareholder of Tekni–Plex. From that time until the corporation's sale in 1994, Tang was also the president, chief executive officer and sole director of Tekni–Plex.

Appellant Meyner and Landis (M & L), a New Jersey law firm, was first retained as Tekni–Plex counsel in 1971. During the ensuing 23 years, M & L represented Tekni–Plex on various legal matters, including environmental compliance. As the record indicates, M & L in the mid–1980's assisted Tekni–Plex in securing an environmental permit for the operation of a laminator machine at its Somerville, New Jersey, plant. Similarly, the law firm apparently assisted the company in an investigation by the New Jersey Department of Environmental Protection into Tekni–Plex's compliance with environmental laws. Additionally, during this period M & L represented Tang individually on several personal matters.

In March 1994, Tang and Tekni–Plex entered into an Agreement and Plan of Merger (the Merger Agreement) with TP Acquisition Company (Acquisition), whereby Tang sold the company to Acquisition for $43 million. M & L represented both Tekni–Plex and Tang personally. The two instant lawsuits grow out of that transaction.

Acquisition was a shell corporation created by the purchasers solely for the acquisition of Tekni–Plex. Under the Merger Agreement, Tekni–Plex merged into Acquisition, with Acquisition the surviving corporation, and Tekni–Plex ceased its separate existence. Tekni–Plex conveyed to Acquisition all of its tangible and intangible assets, rights and liabilities. Acquisition in return paid Tang the purchase price "in complete liquidation of Tekni–Plex," and all of Tang's shares in Tekni–Plex—the only shares outstanding—were canceled.

The Merger Agreement contained representations and warranties by Tang concerning environmental matters, including that Tekni–Plex was in full compliance with all applicable environmental laws and possessed all requisite environmental permits. It further provided for indemnification of Acquisition by Tang for any losses incurred by Acquisition as the result of misrepresentation or breach of warranty by either Tang or Tekni–Plex. Acquisition, in turn, agreed to indemnify Tang and Tekni–Plex for any similar losses suffered by them.

Following the transaction, Acquisition changed its name to "Tekni–Plex, Inc." (new Tekni–Plex). In June 1994, new Tekni–Plex commenced an arbitration against Tang, alleging breach of representations and warranties contained in the Merger Agreement regarding the former Tekni–Plex's (old Tekni–Plex) compliance with environmental laws.

Among other things, new Tekni–Plex claimed that Tang falsely represented that a laminator machine at the Somerville facility did not emit volatile organic compounds (VOCs). New management, however, allegedly learned that the machine did indeed emit VOCs into the air. New Tekni–Plex further claimed that the permit for the laminator machine had been obtained on the false premise that it did not emit VOCs and that VOC emissions were therefore not authorized. New Tekni–Plex also contended that Tang and old Tekni–Plex had taken steps to conceal from Acquisition the emission of VOCs at the Somerville facility.

Tang retained M & L to represent him in the arbitration. New Tekni–Plex moved to disqualify the law firm from representing Tang, but the arbitrator concluded that he lacked authority to rule on the motion. New Tekni–Plex then moved by order to show cause in Supreme Court for an order disqualifying M & L. By separate order to show cause in Supreme Court, new Tekni–Plex moved for an order against M & L (1) enjoining the law firm from representing Tang in any action against new Tekni–Plex, (2) enjoining M & L from disclosing to Tang any information obtained from old Tekni–Plex, and (3) ordering M & L to return to new Tekni–Plex all of the files in the law firm's possession concerning its prior legal representation of old Tekni–Plex. Tang and M & L each cross-moved for orders dismissing the complaints on the ground that there was another action pending in New Jersey.[5]

Supreme Court concluded that New York was the proper forum for resolution of the disqualification issue and that the arbitrator's conclusion that he did not have authority to decide the issue was proper. The court held that M & L should be disqualified from representing Tang in the arbitration. It further enjoined M & L from representing Tang in the arbitration, enjoined M & L from disclosing to Tang any information obtained from old Tekni–Plex, and directed M & L to return to new Tekni–Plex all of the files in M & L's possession concerning its prior representation of old Tekni–Plex. Finally, the court denied both cross motions to dismiss. The Appellate Division affirmed.

We agree with the courts below that, in the circumstances presented, M & L should be disqualified from representing Tang in the arbitration. As for confidential communications between old Tekni–Plex and M & L generated during the law firm's prior representation of the corporation on environmental compliance matters, authority to assert the attorney-client privilege passed to the corporation's successor management. Moreover, because the record fails to establish that M & L also represented Tang individually on these matters, the exception to the privilege for co-clients who subsequently become adversaries in litigation is inapplicable. Thus, the Appellate Division correctly concluded that M & L should be enjoined from disclosing the substance of these communications to Tang and directed the law firm to return the files relating to this representation to new Tekni–Plex.

New Tekni–Plex, however, does not control the attorney-client privilege with regard to discrete communications made by either old Tekni–Plex or Tang individually to M & L concerning the acquisition—a time when old Tekni–Plex and Tang were joined in an adversarial relationship to Acquisition. Consequently, new Tekni–Plex cannot assert the privilege in order to prevent M & L from disclosing the contents of such communications to Tang. Nor is new Tekni–Plex entitled to the law firm's confidential communications concerning its representation of old Tekni–Plex with regard to the acquisition.

B. The Applicable Ethics Principles

Attorneys owe fiduciary duties of both confidentiality and loyalty to their clients (*see, Solow v. W.R. Grace & Co.,* 83 N.Y.2d 303, 306). The Code of Professional Responsibility thus imposes a continuing obligation

[5] FN1. Tang had commenced an action against new Tekni–Plex in New Jersey Superior Court seeking a declaration that (1) the arbitrator had authority to decide the disqualification issue, or (2) he had a right to be represented by M & L in the arbitration, and (3) as sole shareholder and director of old Tekni–Plex, he owned and controlled the attorney-client privilege attaching to communications between M & L and old Tekni–Plex. The New Jersey court indicated that it would not rule on this application until the motions pending in New York were resolved.

on attorneys to protect their clients' confidences and secrets. Even after representation has concluded, a lawyer may not reveal information confided by a former client, or use such information to the disadvantage of the former client or the advantage of a third party. . . .

In accordance with these duties, the Code precludes attorneys from representing interests adverse to a former client on matters substantially related to the prior representation. . . . Under [this rule] a party seeking disqualification of its adversary's lawyer must prove: (1) the existence of a prior attorney-client relationship between the moving party and opposing counsel, (2) that the matters involved in both representations are substantially related, and (3) that the interests of the present client and former client are materially adverse. Satisfaction of these three criteria by the moving party gives rise to an irrebuttable presumption of disqualification.

This rule of disqualification fully protects a client's secrets and confidences by preventing even the possibility that they will subsequently be used against the client in related litigation. This prophylactic measure thus frees clients from apprehension that information imparted in confidence might later be used to their detriment, which, in turn, "fosters the open dialogue between lawyer and client that is deemed essential to effective representation" . . . .

C. Disqualification of Counsel

New Tekni–Plex, as the party seeking M & L's disqualification, thus has the burden of satisfying the three-pronged test for disqualification by establishing that (1) it assumed the role of M & L's "former client," (2) the matters involved in both representations are substantially related, and (3) the interests of M & L's present client Tang are materially adverse to the interests of the former client. We next consider each of these elements.

1. Is New Tekni–Plex a "Former Client" of M & L? It is undisputed that M & L represented old Tekni–Plex for over 20 years on a variety of legal matters. As counsel to the corporation, the law firm's duties of confidentiality and loyalty ran to old Tekni–Plex on these matters. Concomitantly, the attorney-client privilege attached to any confidential communications that took place between M & L and Tekni–Plex corporate actors in the course of this representation (*see, Commodity Futures Trading Commn. v. Weintraub,* 471 U.S. 343, 348). The power to assert or waive the privilege, moreover, belonged to the management of old Tekni–Plex, to be exercised by its officers and directors (*see, id.,* at 349; *see also,* Business Corporation Law § 701).

Appellants (Tang and M & L) argue that the purchase of old Tekni–Plex by Acquisition did not transfer the corporation's attorney-client relationship to the newly formed entity. According to appellants, the transaction effected nothing more than a transfer of assets, with old Tekni–Plex expiring upon the merger, there being no "former client" still in existence. In support of this contention, appellants point out that, under the Merger Agreement, Acquisition was designated the surviving corporation, old Tekni–Plex explicitly ceased to exist and all of the outstanding shares of stock in old Tekni–Plex were liquidated. They further note that, for tax purposes, the transaction was deemed a sale of assets.

When ownership of a corporation changes hands, whether the attorney-client relationship transfers as well to the new owners turns on the practical consequences rather than the formalities of the particular transaction. In *Commodity Futures Trading Commn. v. Weintraub*, 471 U.S. 343, *supra*, the Supreme Court held that power to exercise the attorney-client privilege of an insolvent corporation passed to the bankruptcy trustee, who assumed managerial responsibility for operating the debtor company's business. . .

Weintraub establishes that, where efforts are made to run the pre-existing business entity and manage its affairs, successor management stands in the shoes of prior management and controls the attorney-client privilege with respect to matters concerning the company's operations. It follows that, under such circumstances, the prior attorney-client relationship continues with the newly formed entity. By contrast, the mere transfer of assets with no attempt to continue the pre-existing operation generally does not transfer the attorney-client relationship.. . . .

Here, appellants emphasize that old Tekni–Plex merged into Acquisition and ceased to exist as a separate legal entity. That Acquisition, rather than old Tekni–Plex, was designated the surviving corporation, however, is not dispositive. Acquisition was a mere shell corporation, created solely for the purpose of acquiring old Tekni–Plex. Following the merger, the business of old Tekni–Plex remained unchanged, with the same products, clients, suppliers and non-managerial personnel. Indeed, under the Merger Agreement, new Tekni–Plex possessed all of the rights, privileges, liabilities and obligations of old Tekni–Plex, in addition to its assets. Certainly, new Tekni–Plex is entitled to access to any relevant pre-merger legal advice rendered to old Tekni–Plex that it might need to defend against these liabilities or pursue any of these rights.

As a practical matter, then, old Tekni–Plex did not die. To the contrary, the business operations of old Tekni–Plex continued under the new managers. Consequently, control of the attorney-client privilege with respect to any confidential communications between M & L and corporate actors of old Tekni–Plex concerning these operations passed to the management of new Tekni–Plex. An attorney-client relationship between M & L and new Tekni–Plex necessarily exists.

Thus, the first of the three prongs for disqualification is established: new Tekni–Plex is a "former client" of M & L.

2. Is There a Substantial Relationship Between the Current and Former Representations? M & L previously assisted old Tekni–Plex on at least two matters that are substantially related to its current representation of Tang in the arbitration. First, the record indicates that M & L represented old Tekni–Plex during negotiation of the Merger Agreement. That Agreement contains representations and warranties that are the subject of the arbitration.

Second, the record evidences that M & L counseled old Tekni–Plex concerning environmental compliance and assisted the company in obtaining the permit for the laminator machine at the Somerville facility. The alleged misrepresentations made by old Tekni–Plex and Tang relate to that permit and the corporation's compliance with environmental laws.

There is thus a substantial relationship between the current and former representations.

3. Are the Interests of M & L's Present Client Materially Adverse to the Interests of Its Former Client? The arbitration claims pit Acquisition's interest as purchaser against Tang's interest as the selling shareholder. Furthermore, the Merger Agreement provides that Tang is responsible for indemnifying Acquisition for any misrepresentation or breach of warranty made by either Tang *or old Tekni–Plex.* Plainly the parties contemplated a unity of interest between old Tekni–Plex and Tang should a dispute arise between the buyer and seller regarding the representations and warranties. Thus, to the extent the arbitration relates to the merger negotiations—as opposed to corporate operations—Tang and old Tekni–Plex remain on the same side of the table. The interest of M & L's former client old Tekni–Plex is aligned with the interest of the law firm's present client Tang—both in opposition to the buyer. . . .

The dispute here, however . . . goes beyond the merger negotiations. It also involves issues relating to the law firm's longstanding representation of the acquired corporation on matters arising out of the company's business operations—namely, M & L's separate representation of old Tekni–Plex prior to the merger on environmental compliance matters. Any environmental violations will negatively affect not only the purchasers but also the business interests of the merged corporation. In this regard, the interests of M & L's current client Tang are adverse to the interests that new Tekni–Plex assumed from old Tekni–Plex.

Indeed, M & L's earlier representation of old Tekni–Plex provided the firm with access to confidential information conveyed by old Tekni–Plex concerning the very environmental compliance matters at issue in the arbitration. M & L's duty of confidentiality with respect to these communications passed to new Tekni–Plex; yet its current representation of Tang creates the potential for the law firm to use these confidences against new Tekni–Plex in the arbitration.

Under the circumstances, the appearance of impropriety is manifest and the potential conflict of interest apparent. M & L should therefore be disqualified from representing Tang in the arbitration.

D. Confidential Communications

As a final matter, we must determine whether M & L was properly enjoined from revealing to Tang any confidential communications obtained from old Tekni–Plex and whether new Tekni–Plex owns the confidences created during the law firm's prior representation of old Tekni–Plex. For analytical purposes, the attorney-client communications must be separated into two categories: general business communications and those relating to the merger negotiations.

1. General Business Communications. As explained above, the management of new Tekni–Plex continues the business operations of the pre-merger entity. Control of the attorney-client privilege with regard to confidential communications arising out of those operations—including any pre-merger communications between old Tekni–Plex and M & L relating to the company's environmental compliance—thus passed to the management of new Tekni–Plex. As a result, new Tekni–Plex now has the authority to assert the attorney-client privilege to preclude M & L from disclosing the contents of these confidential communications to Tang. Likewise, ownership of the law firm's files regarding its pre-merger representation of old Tekni–Plex on environmental compliance matters passed to the management of new Tekni–Plex. This conclusion comports with new Tekni–Plex's right to invoke the pre-merger attorney-client relationship should it have to prosecute or defend against third-party suits involving the assets, rights or liabilities that it assumed from old Tekni–Plex.

Appellants urge that because Tang and old Tekni–Plex were co-clients of M & L, none of the communications made by corporate actors to the law firm are confidential from Tang. Generally, where the same lawyer jointly represents two clients with respect to the same matter, the clients have no expectation that their confidences concerning the joint matter will remain secret from each other, and those confidential communications are not within the privilege in subsequent adverse proceedings between the co-clients (*see,* Wolfram, Modern Legal Ethics § 6.4.8, at 274–275). While M & L jointly represented Tang and old Tekni–Plex during the acquisition, with respect to the environmental compliance matters the record before us establishes only M & L's representation of the corporation.

We note that some courts have held that, in the case of a close corporation, corporate representation may be individual representation as well. Here, the record indicates that at least some of M & L's representation of old Tekni–Plex on the environmental matters at issue took place before Tang became the corporation's sole shareholder and manager. Whether corporate counsel also functioned as Tang's individual attorney on the environmental matters involved factual questions not addressed by the trial court or Appellate Division. In this particular case there is an insufficient record from which we can conclude that M & L jointly represented the corporation and Tang individually on matters other than the merger.[6]

2. Communications Relating to the Merger Negotiations. As to the other category of attorney-client communications between old Tekni–Plex and M & L—those relating to the merger transaction—new Tekni–Plex did not succeed to old Tekni–Plex's right to control the attorney-client privilege. New Tekni–Plex's misrepresentation and breach of warranty claims do not derive from the rights it inherited from old Tekni–Plex but from the rights retained by the buyer, Acquisition, with respect to the transaction. Under the Merger Agreement, moreover, the rights of old Tekni–Plex with regard to disputes arising from the merger transaction remain independent from—and, indeed, adverse to—the rights of the buyer. During this dispute stemming from the merger transaction, then, new Tekni–Plex cannot both pursue the rights of the buyer (Acquisition) and simultaneously assume the attorney-client rights that the buyer's adversary (old Tekni–Plex) retained regarding the transaction. . . .

In light of the facts of this particular transaction and the structure of the underlying agreement, new Tekni–Plex is without authority to assert the attorney-client privilege to preclude M & L from revealing to Tang the contents of communications conveyed by old Tekni–Plex concerning the merger transaction. Similarly, new Tekni–Plex does not control M & L's files relating to its prior representation of old Tekni–Plex during the acquisition. Of course, nothing in our decision today prevents new Tekni–Plex from obtaining through the normal course of discovery any non-confidential documents, or confidential documents for which the privilege has been waived, to which it is entitled.

Accordingly, the order of the Appellate Division, insofar as appealed from, should be modified, without costs, in accordance with the opinion herein, and, as so modified, affirmed.

Client Information as Client Property III

Tekni–Plex is a complex case but it can be made simpler by thinking of attorney-client communications as information in which the client has a property right. A client owns the rights in communications with her lawyer. When the client is an entity you can think of the rights in those

---

[6] FN2. We underscore that we resolve only those attorney-client issues that are presented by the merger dispute before us. In any other matter Tang is of course not foreclosed from making the requisite showing of joint representation or alternative basis for access to attorney-client communications.

communications as one of the entity's assets, like its equipment, leases, accounts receivable, and so on.

When one entity buys another the buyer typically gets all the assets of the seller. That is true regardless whether the form of the transaction is a true merger (in which the acquired company ceases to exist) or of an asset acquisition (in which the acquired company continues to exist formally, but sells all its assets to the buyer). So when the substance of a transaction is that an entity is sold, the privileges the entity holds pass from seller to buyer and the buyer (generally the new managers of the entity) obtain the right to assert or waive the privilege. If the substance of the transaction is not a sale of an entity, however, but only the sale of some assets, such as a lease, or equipment, or receivables, the privilege rights will not change hands. That is one reason the Court held the buyer did not receive control over communications regarding the merger itself. Those related to the sale not the operations of the business being sold and therefore could not be considered an asset the buyer had any reasonable expectation of receiving in the transaction.

Donald Oswall, a former Tekni–Plex employee, sued the company for breach of a contract signed by Mr. Tang on behalf of the company. The company served a deposition subpoena on Mr. Tang. He stated he would appear so long as Edwin Landis, of Meyner and Landis, could represent him at the deposition. The company objected on the ground that Landis owed duties to the company. In *Oswall v. Tekni–Plex, Inc.*, 299 N.J.Super. 658, 691 A.2d 889 (1997), the court affirmed an order disqualifying Landis from representing Mr. Tang after it became clear that Mr. Tang's interests at the deposition were adverse to the company's interests.

In *Goodrich v. Goodrich*, 158 N.H. 130, 960 A.2d 1275 (2008), the New Hampshire Supreme Court endorsed what it called a "practical consequences" analysis to determine whether an entity's new owners control the entity's attorney-client privilege. This analysis distinguishes between the transfer of assets alone and the transfer of rights and liabilities to which pre-transfer legal advice might be relevant:

> courts usually examine whether the corporate transaction was a pure asset sale or effectuated a transfer of the establishing corporation's business operations, rights and liabilities. . . . A pure asset sale transfers only ownership over property, not control of the establishing corporation itself, and, accordingly, does not transfer the attorney-client privilege. . . . If, however, an entity acquires control of the establishing corporation's business operations, rights and liabilities, it is generally accepted that it also acquires authority over the attorney-client privilege. . . . Transfer of the privilege allows the

acquiring entity to pursue pre-existing rights or defend against pre-existing liabilities

Goodrich involved a family-owned company that provided surveying and engineering services and also managed a building. As a result of a dispute among shareholders (and family members), Morgan Goodrich transferred the stock in the company to his sons. Under their management the company managed the building but provided no engineering or surveying services. Once they had the stock the sons moved to disqualify Clauson, the lawyer representing their father in their dispute, on the ground that Clauson previously had represented the company.

The trial court denied the motion on the ground that the sons had not shown that the company's business was the same under their management as it had been under their father's, or that the company retained rights or liabilities incurred under their father's management. The Supreme Court reversed. It held that the privilege presumptively transfers with control of an entity and that any party arguing otherwise bears the burden of rebutting that presumption.

IN RE GRAND JURY SUBPOENA

274 F.3d 563 (1st Cir. 2001)

SELYA, CIRCUIT JUDGE.

This appeal requires us to traverse largely unexplored terrain concerning the operation of the attorney-client and work product privileges. The underlying controversy arises out of a subpoena duces tecum issued by a federal grand jury to a corporation, seeking records pertaining to the affairs of a subsidiary. Although the corporation and the subsidiary waived all claims of privilege, the subsidiary's former attorney and two of its former officers intervened and moved to quash the subpoena. They claimed that the subsidiary had entered into a longstanding joint defense agreement with the former officers and contended that the subpoenaed materials were privileged (and, thus, not amenable to disclosure). The district court eschewed an evidentiary hearing and denied the motion to quash, but stayed production of the documents pending appeal.

We affirm the district court's order. We hold that an individual privilege may exist in these circumstances only to the extent that communications made in a corporate officer's personal capacity are separable from those made in his corporate capacity. Because the intervenors do not allege that any of the subpoenaed documents are solely privileged to them but rest instead on the theory that all the documents are jointly privileged, their claim, as a matter of law, does not survive the subsidiary's waiver. The joint defense agreement does not demand a different result:

privileges are created, and their contours defined, by operation of law, and private agreements cannot enlarge their scope. Moreover, this particular joint defense agreement is unenforceable. . . .

I. BACKGROUND

On March 26, 2001, Oldco—a Massachusetts corporation in the business of processing, packaging, and distributing food products—entered into a plea agreement with the United States Attorney for the District of Massachusetts. Under the agreement's terms, Oldco pled guilty to charges of conspiracy to defraud the Internal Revenue Service and agreed to cooperate with the government's ongoing investigation of certain present and former officers, employees, and customers. As part of this cooperation, Oldco expressly waived applicable attorney-client and work product privileges. Soon thereafter, a federal grand jury issued a subpoena duces tecum to Oldco's parent corporation, Newparent, Inc., demanding the production of documents relating to its "rebate program"—a program under which, according to the government, Oldco would charge certain complicit customers more than the going rate for its products, but would then refund the difference by payments made directly to principals of these customers.

At the time the subpoena was served, Oldco was a wholly-owned subsidiary of Newparent. Its records were in the possession of Newparent's counsel, a law firm that we shall call Smith & Jones. Newparent had acquired Oldco in June of 1998, but the grand jury investigation focused on conduct that occurred prior to the acquisition date. During that earlier period, Oldco had operated as a closely held corporation, owned by a number of members of a single family; one family member (Richard Roe) served as its board chairman and chief executive officer, and another (Morris Moe) served on the board and as executive vice-president for sales and marketing. A. Nameless Lawyer was Oldco's principal outside counsel. These three individuals—Roe, Moe, and Lawyer—intervened in the proceedings and filed a motion to quash the subpoena.

The factual premise for the motion to quash is derived largely from Lawyer's affidavit. He states that while representing Oldco he also represented Roe and Moe in various individual matters. Moreover, he claims to have conducted this simultaneous representation of corporate and individual clients under a longstanding joint defense agreement. According to Lawyer, this agreement, although never committed to writing, provided that communications among the three clients were jointly privileged and could not be released without unanimous consent. Despite the absence of any reference to this agreement in the corporate records—there was no resolution or other vote of the board of directors authorizing Oldco to participate in such an arrangement—the intervenors assert that Roe, as chief executive officer, had the authority to commit the corporation to it.

Pertinently, Lawyer claims to have represented Oldco and its officers in connection with the grand jury investigation from and after October 1997 (when the grand jury served Oldco with an earlier subpoena requesting the production of certain customer records). He says that the oral joint defense agreement applies to this multiple-party representation and that he told the government that he represented Oldco and "all of its executives."

There is, to be sure, a written joint defense agreement entered into by and between Lawyer, as counsel for Roe/Moe, and Smith & Jones, as counsel for Newparent/Oldco. However, that agreement was not executed until the fall of 1999 (by which time Lawyer was no longer representing Oldco). There is no evidence in the voluminous record (apart from Lawyer's affidavit) that any joint defense agreement existed before that time. Moreover, the intervenors neglected to mention the existence of an oral joint defense agreement when Newparent acquired Oldco and likewise failed to incorporate any reference to such a pact into the subsequent written agreement.

Notwithstanding these discrepancies, the intervenors solemnly maintain that the oral joint defense agreement existed from 1990 forward; that its terms apply to the grand jury investigation; and that it gives them a joint privilege—they mention both attorney-client and work product privileges—in the Oldco documents currently in the hands of Smith & Jones. But they do not identify any particular documents as privileged, nor do they specify the reasons why certain communications should be considered privileged. Thus, like soothsayers scrutinizing the entrails of a goat, we are left to scour the record for indications of what these documents might be and what they might contain. As best we can tell, some of the documents comprise transcripts of interviews with Oldco employees (including Roe and Moe); others comprise Lawyer's written summaries of Oldco's internal investigation into the rebate program.

Not surprisingly, the government and Oldco both filed oppositions to the intervenors' motion to quash. In response, the intervenors sought leave to present immunized evidence with respect to the privilege claims. They also filed a formal offer of proof and requested an evidentiary hearing. The district court denied the motion to quash at a non-evidentiary hearing held on July 2, 2001, thereby implicitly denying the intervenors' other requests. This expedited appeal ensued. . . .

III. THE MERITS

This appeal presents a smorgasbord of legal issues, but we must forgo the temptation to sample them all. Instead, we masticate only those issues that are necessary to a principled resolution of the matter.

We begin by discussing the ramifications of Roe's and Moe's claim that they were individual clients of Lawyer with respect to the grand jury investigation. We conclude that although such individual representation might have occurred in theory, no individual privilege exists as to documents in which Oldco also has a privilege. Because no independently enforceable privilege is alleged here, the corporation's waiver is effective for all communications covered by the subpoena, notwithstanding the existence *vel non* of the oral joint defense agreement. In all events, the intervenors failed adequately to inform the district court of the particular communications to which their claims of privilege allegedly attached. In the pages that follow, we proceed to discuss these issues one by one.

A. *Privilege Claims.*

Because the attorney-client and work product privileges differ, we treat them separately.

1. *Individual Attorney–Client Privilege Claims. . . .*

Roe and Moe can mount a claim of attorney-client privilege only if, and to the extent that, Lawyer represented them individually. If the only attorney-client privilege at stake is that of their corporate employer, then Oldco's waiver defeats the claim of privilege. After all, the law is settled that a corporation's attorney-client privilege may be waived by current management. *See CFTC v. Weintraub,* 471 U.S. 343, 349 (1985) ("[W]hen control of a corporation passes to new management, the authority to assert and waive the corporation's attorney client privilege passes as well.").

It is often difficult to determine whether a corporate officer or employee may claim an attorney-client privilege in communications with corporate counsel. The default assumption is that the attorney only represents the corporate entity, not the individuals within the corporate sphere, and it is the individuals' burden to dispel that presumption. *See United States v. Bay State Ambul. & Hosp. Rental Serv., Inc.,* 874 F.2d 20, 28 (1st Cir.1989). This makes perfect sense because an employee has a duty to assist his employer's counsel in the investigation and defense of matters pertaining to the employer's business. *See United States v. Sawyer,* 878 F.Supp. 295, 296 (D.Mass.1995).

To determine when this presumption bursts, several courts have adopted the test explicated in *In re Bevill, Bresler & Schulman Asset Mgmt. Corp.,* 805 F.2d 120 (3d Cir.1986). That test enumerates five benchmarks that corporate employees seeking to assert a personal claim of attorney-client privilege must meet:

> First, they must show they approached [counsel] for the purpose of seeking legal advice. Second, they must demonstrate that when they approached [counsel] they made it clear that they were seeking legal advice in their individual rather than in their representative capacities. Third, they must demonstrate that the [counsel] saw fit to communicate with them in their individual capacities, knowing that a possible conflict could arise. Fourth, they must prove that their con-

> versations with [counsel] were confidential. And fifth, they must show that the substance of their conversations with [counsel] did not concern matters within the company or the general affairs of the company.

Id. at 123.

We think that *Bevill*'s general framework is sound. Of course, the first four elements of its test are most relevant when an attorney disputes a corporate officer's claim of individual privilege. Here, however, Lawyer's affidavit makes it clear that he represented both Roe and Moe in their personal capacities. Thus, even though the intervenors' brief does not specifically address the *Bevill* factors, we assume for argument's sake that the first four prongs of the test are satisfied.

With respect to the final prong, the government claims that all of Roe's and Moe's communications were within the orbit of Oldco's general affairs, and therefore could not be individually privileged. In the government's view, *Bevill* precludes a finding of individual representation with respect to matters—such as the grand jury investigation into the rebate program—that involve the corporation. We do not read *Bevill* so grudgingly. As the Tenth Circuit explained:

> The fifth prong of *In Matter of Bevill,* properly interpreted, only precludes an officer from asserting an individual attorney client privilege when the communication concerns the *corporation's* rights and responsibilities. However, if the communication between a corporate officer and corporate counsel specifically focuses upon the *individual officer's* personal rights and liabilities, then the fifth prong of *In Matter of Bevill* can be satisfied even though the general subject matter of the conversation pertains to matters within the general affairs of the company.

Grand Jury Proceedings, 156 F.3d at 1041. We adopt this interpretation and conclude that, theoretically, Lawyer could have represented Roe and Moe individually with respect to the grand jury investigation. Still, this attorney-client relationship would extend only to those communications which involved Roe's and Moe's individual rights and responsibilities arising out of their actions as officers of the corporation.

2. *The Corporation's Right to Waive the Attorney–Client Privilege.* Having concluded that there are potentially some communications protected by the attorney-client privilege, we next consider the effect of Oldco's waiver of that privilege. The major difficulty—there are others, but we need not discuss them here—is that the individuals' allegedly protected communications with Lawyer do not appear to be distinguishable from discussions between the same parties in their capacities as corporate officers and corporate counsel, respectively, anent matters of corporate concern. The intervenors propose that such "dual" communications be

treated as jointly privileged such that the consent of all parties would be required to waive the privilege. But they fail to cite authority supporting this position, and we ultimately decline to accept it: permitting a joint privilege of this type would unduly broaden the attorney-client privilege by allowing parties outside a given attorney-client relationship to prevent disclosure of statements made by the client.

The reference to an alleged joint defense agreement does little to advance the intervenors' argument on this point. "The joint defense privilege protects communications between an individual and an attorney for another when the communications are 'part of an ongoing and joint effort to set up a common defense strategy.' " *Bay State Ambul.,* 874 F.2d at 28 (citation omitted). Because the privilege sometimes may apply outside the context of actual litigation, what the parties call a "joint defense" privilege is more aptly termed the "common interest" rule. *See United States v. Schwimmer,* 892 F.2d 237, 243 (2d Cir.1989). Even when that rule applies, however, a party always remains free to disclose his own communications. *See In re Grand Jury Subpoena Duces Tecum,* 112 F.3d 910, 922 (8th Cir.1997). Thus, the existence of a joint defense agreement does not increase the number of parties whose consent is needed to waive the attorney-client privilege; it merely prevents disclosure of a communication made in the course of preparing a joint defense by the third party to whom it was made.

In the clamor over the existence *vel non* of a joint defense agreement, the parties tend to overlook case law dealing directly with the circumstances under which statements made in a joint conference remain privileged. Although these cases do not speak with one voice, they inform our resolution of the issue. They establish that joint communications with a single attorney are privileged with respect to the outside world because clients must be entitled to the full benefit of joint representation undiluted by fear of waiving the attorney-client privilege. Nevertheless, the privilege does not apply in subsequent litigation between the joint clients; in that sort of situation, one client's interest in the privilege is counterbalanced by the other's interest in being able to waive it.

The instance of a criminal investigation in which one former co-client is willing to aid in the prosecution of the other lies in the wasteland between these two doctrinal strands, and courts have split on whether the target of the prosecution may block disclosure in this context. *See McCormick on Evidence,* § 91 at 365 n.13 (John W. Strong ed., 5th ed. 1999) ("Whether the privilege is effective where one joint client is prosecuted and the other is willing to testify as to the joint consultations is a question which has divided the courts."); *see also Conn. v. Cascone,* 195 Conn. 183 (1985) (collecting cases on both sides of the issue).

Although the instant case arises as a motion to quash a subpoena, rather than as an attempt to block a former co-client's testimony, the issue of privilege is entirely congruent. But there is another difference here—a significant one that cuts against the intervenors. In this iteration, the former co-clients were not independent actors, but, rather, corporate officers who owed a fiduciary duty to the corporation. Faced with an analogous assertion of privilege by corporate managers, the Fifth Circuit has held that the managers' interest must yield to the shareholders' interest in disclosure of the privileged materials. *Garner* v. *Wolfinbarger,* 430 F.2d 1093, 1101–04 (5th Cir.1970). Taking a similar tack, we hold that a corporation may unilaterally waive the attorney-client privilege with respect to any communications made by a corporate officer in his corporate capacity, notwithstanding the existence of an individual attorney-client relationship between him and the corporation's counsel.

The line we draw parallels the holding of *Bevill,* 805 F.2d at 124 (rejecting the contention that "because [corporate officers'] personal legal problems were inextricably intertwined with those of the corporation, disclosure of discussions of corporate matters would eviscerate their personal privileges"). In this regard, we think it significant that the fifth prong of the *Bevill* test is stated in the negative: communications may be individually privileged only when they "*[do] not* concern matters within the company or the general affairs of the company," rather than when they *do* concern an individual's rights. *Id.* at 123 (emphasis supplied).

On this view, it follows that Roe or Moe may only assert an individual privilege to the extent that communications regarding individual acts and liabilities are segregable from discussions about the corporation. When one bears in mind that a corporation is an incorporeal entity and must necessarily communicate with counsel through individuals, the necessity for such a rule becomes readily apparent. Holding otherwise would open the door to a claim of jointly held privilege in virtually every corporate communication with counsel.

Here, neither Roe nor Moe have even attempted to make any showing of segregability. On the contrary, their main argument in the district court and on appeal appears to be that the documents at issue do not lend themselves to separation into individual and corporate categories. The intervenors' brief is replete with references to "joint privilege," but contains no allegation that any particular communication related solely to the representation of Roe or Moe. Given the absence of such an allegation and the allocation of the burden of proof (which, on this issue, rests with the intervenors), we perceive no error in the district court's explicit finding that "all communications in this case are corporate communications." That dooms the intervenors' claim of attorney-client privilege, *see Grand Jury Proceedings,* 156 F.3d at 1042 (rejecting claim of individual privilege when "appellant has not produced for [the court's] review the particular documents at issue nor has he otherwise adequately demonstrated in the record that any of the documents ordered produced were limited to the topic of his *individual* legal rights and responsibilities"), and renders moot the question of whether Roe and Moe also possessed an attorney-client privilege in these documents. . . .

IV. CONCLUSION

We need go no further. We hold that the intervenors' claims of privilege fail because the oral joint defense agreement on which they rely cannot defeat Oldco's express waiver of privilege, and, alternatively, because the intervenors failed without justification to produce a privilege log (thereby waiving the underlying attorney-client and work product privileges). Similarly, the district court did not err either in refusing to convene an evidentiary hearing or in ruling simultaneously on the motion to quash and the motion for immunity. Accordingly, the order refusing to nullify the grand jury subpoena is unimpugnable.

Affirmed.

Under *Newparent*, even if entity counsel forms a personal attorney-client relationship with an entity constituent, the entity controls privilege regarding the constituent's work-related communications to entity counsel. This rule is probably best considered an exception to the normal joint client arrangement, in which neither client has a privilege against the other with respect to the subject matter of their joint representation but in which each client controls his or her communications.

The rule applied in *Newparent*, which originates with *In re Bevill, Bresler & Schulman Asset Mgmt. Corp.*, 805 F.2d 120 (3d Cir.1986), is the majority rule. *See United States v. Graf*, 610 F.3d 1148 (9th Cir. 2010). At least one jurisdiction does not follow it, however. *See United States v. Walters*, 913 F.2d 388 (7th Cir. 1990) (corporate officers were personally represented by counsel they contacted regarding legality of contracts they caused college athletes to enter into with their agency).

PROBLEM 5–5

Suppose you represent a client who is considering investing in a company. If the company takes off, the client will make a lot of money, but the client is not sure how competent or even honest the company's managers are. Do the principles discussed in the last two cases suggest anything you might do in negotiations with the company to give your client some comfort regarding the integrity or competence of management?

PROBLEM 5–6

Suppose you are investigating allegations of wrongdoing within a corporation. In the course of your investigation, you have to interview dozens of employees, from line workers to top management. What should you tell them about the attorney-client privilege?

C. INTRA–FIRM COMMUNICATIONS AND PRIVILEGE

Suppose you work for a firm with several lawyers, including one who advises other lawyers in the firm on ethics and liability-related issues. Suppose a question comes up regarding whether you (and therefore the firm) breached a duty to a client. If you discuss the issue with your in-house ethics lawyer, is that discussion privileged?

Many cases hold that a firm may not withhold from a current client at least some privileged or work product information produced during the firm's investigation of its conduct regarding that client's matter.[7] The cases do not provide a clear rule defining the scope of information the client may discover. In part that is because they rest on varying mixtures of two arguments. One is that a firm's fiduciary obligation to a client entails a duty to inform the client of material developments and this duty vitiates the privilege.[8] The firm owes this obligation so long as it continues representation. The second rationale is that the lawyer's misconduct creates a conflict between the firm and the client. The basic reasoning here is that the firm must disclose to the client enough information for the client to decide whether to fire the firm.[9]

The *Restatement (Third) of the Law Governing Lawyers* § 90 cmt c, holds that lawyers must disclose work product material if the client chooses to waive work product protection. Courts compelling production of privileged information have compelled production of work product information as well.[10] *Accord* Cal. Code Civ. P. § 2018.080("In an action between an attorney and a client or a former client of the attorney, no work

---

[7] *E.g., In re SonicBlue, Inc.*, 2008 WL 170562 (Bankr.N.D.Cal.2008); *Burns v. Hale and Dorr LLP,* 242 F.R.D. 170 (D.Mass.2007); *Thelen Reid & Priest LLP v. Marland,* 2007 WL 578989 (N.D.Cal. 2007); *Koen Book Distributors v. Powell, Trachtman, Logan, Carrle, Bowman & Lombardo P.C.,* 212 F.R.D. 283 (E.D.Pa.2003); *Bank Brussells Lambert v. Credit Lyonnais (Suisse),* 220 F.Supp.2d 283, 286 (S.D.N.Y.2002); *In re Sunrise Securities Litig.*, 130 F.R.D. 560 (E.D.Pa.199089). The *Restatement (Third) of the Law Governing Lawyers* § 46(2) cmt. c is to the contrary, but this provision predates most of the cases on this topic.

[8] *Burns*, 242 F.R.D. at 173 ("Because the firm owed a fiduciary duty to Alexis Burns as the trust beneficiary, there is no policy reason why H & D should be allowed to withhold disclosure of information relevant to her claim."); *Bank Brussells*, 220 F. Supp. 2d at 286 ("while [Rogers & Wells] was still in the employ of CLS, it was still obligated to maintain a fiduciary duty to CLS, even in performing its internal conflict review.")

[9] *SonicBlue, supra* note 5 at *8–9; *In re Sunrise Sec. Litig., supra* note 4, at 595; *Thelen, Reid & Priest, supra* note 5 at *7–8. *See also Versuslaw Inc. v. Stoel Rives*, 127 Wash.App. 309, 111 P.3d 866 (2005) (remanding privilege claims to special master to determine whether firm's interests conflicted with fiduciary obligations to client). As noted above, one should presume that firing the client will not discharge this obligation.

[10] *Thelen, supra* note 5 at *8; *Koen Books, supra* note 5 at 286 ("does not apply where a client, as opposed to some other party, seeks discovery of the lawyer's mental impressions. It cannot shield a lawyer's papers from discovery in a conflict of interest context anymore than can the attorney-client privilege").

product privilege under this chapter exists if the work product is relevant to an issue of breach by the attorney of a duty to the client arising out of the attorney-client relationship.")

Two recent cases depart from these rulings. *Hunter, MacClean, Exley & Dunn v. St. Simons Waterfront, LLC.*, 317 Ga.App. 1 (firm's conflict arising from malpractice or similar issue should not be imputed to firm counsel "[s]o long as counsel in this position has had "no involvement in the outside representation at issue and the firm is clearly established as the client before the infirm communication occurs, firm counsel should be treated as the functional equivalent of corporate in house counsel"); *Garvy v. Seyfarth Shaw LLP*, 966 NE2d 523, 536 (¶ 35) (Ill. App. 2012).

D. EXCEPTIONS TO THE PRIVILEGE

This section surveys the main exceptions to the privilege, which does not extend to communications by which a client furthers a crime or fraud or to communications between joint clients. Courts agree that the person or entity claiming the privilege has the burden of showing the elements discussed above. There is less agreement on the burden necessary to establish at least the crime-fraud exception, as the following materials show.

1. COMMUNICATIONS FURTHERING CRIME OR FRAUD

Restatement (Third) of the Law Governing Lawyers § 82

The *Restatement* states the basic exception to the privilege for communications furthering a crime or fraud: Where the purpose or consequence of a consultation is to commit a crime or fraud, communications in connection with that consultation are not privileged. It does not matter whether the lawyer knows of the fraud or is an innocent pawn of the client.

Often this exception operates in a straightforward manner. For example, Monica Lewinsky, the White House intern who had a brief sexual relationship with President Clinton, received a subpoena in connection with a civil suit against the president. She retained Francis D. Carter to help her respond. At her direction he drafted a declaration, which she signed under penalty of perjury. It falsely stated that she had no sexual relationship with President Clinton.

An independent counsel investigating President Clinton's conduct then issued a subpoena to Carter requesting documents and testimony relating to his representation of Lewinsky. Carter objected on privilege grounds. The independent counsel argued that the privilege did not apply because Ms. Lewinsky used the representation to commit perjury. Even though there was no suggestion that Carter knew this, the court of appeals found that the crime/fraud exception applied. *In re Sealed Case*, 162 F.3d 670 (D.C.Cir.1998).

The exception can raise more difficult questions, however. Consider the following cases:

IN RE SEALED CASE

107 F.3d 46 (D.C. Cir. 1997)

RANDOLPH CIRCUIT JUDGE:

This appeal arises out of ongoing grand jury proceedings. The grand jury is investigating violations of federal election laws. The record is sealed. The appellant is a corporation, which we shall call the "Company." The Company refused to produce two subpoenaed documents, for which it was held in contempt. One of the documents is a memorandum from a Company vice president to the president, with a copy to the Company's general counsel. The memorandum reflects a conversation between the vice president and the Company's general counsel about campaign finance laws. The Company withheld it on the basis of the attorney-client privilege. The other document is a memorandum written by the general counsel, apparently at the request of outside counsel. The Company withheld it on the basis of the attorney-client privilege and work product immunity.

The district court examined both documents *in camera* (*see United States v. Zolin,* 491 U.S. 554 (1989)), and, without deciding whether they were covered by the privilege or the work product doctrine, ordered the Company to turn them over. The court found that the crime-fraud exception applied because of these circumstances. In late June 1994, the Company's political action committee contributed the maximum amount permitted by law to a former candidate for federal office who was seeking to retire his campaign debt. The vice president wrote his memorandum and had his discussion with the general counsel in early August 1994. Later in the same month, the vice president called two individuals who did business with the Company and asked them to contribute to the former candidate. The individuals and their wives made the contributions. After several weeks had passed, the vice president authorized checks to be drawn from his department's budget to reimburse these individuals not only for the amount of their contributions, but also to make up for the additional taxes they would incur from reporting the reimbursement as income. The vice president's solicitation may have been permissible but, according to the government, this use of corporate funds was illegal.

The other subpoenaed document—the general counsel's memorandum to the file—was written more than a year later. It mentions dates in November 1995, and according to the Company's appellate counsel, recites actions the Company took to correct the vice president's use of corporate funds to reimburse the donors.

In addition to appealing from the order to produce the documents and the contempt citation, the Company appeals the district court's order compelling the vice president to testify in the grand jury about a late August 1994 meeting between him, the Company's president, and its general counsel. The participants at the meeting discussed certain facts and the general counsel gave legal advice about federal election laws. In the grand jury, the vice president—who had been granted immunity—invoked the attorney-client privilege on behalf of the Company. Again, the district court ruled that the crime-fraud exception applied and ordered him to testify about the late August 1994 meeting. The vice president then signed an affidavit stating that he would honor the court's directive. The court stayed its order pending the outcome of the Company's appeal.[11]

I

We will take up first the vice president's early August 1994 memorandum and his meeting in late August 1994 with the president and general counsel. Both the memorandum and the meeting, as the Company sees it, are covered by the attorney-client privilege. Since the district court has yet to pass on this question, we will assume the Company is correct. The "privilege of a witness," Fed.R.Evid. 501 tells us, is "governed by the principles of the common law as they may be interpreted by the courts of the United States in the light of reason and experience." Those principles recognize the importance of maintaining the confidentiality of attorney-client communications in order to promote the rendering of legal services. . . .

The relationship between client and counsel may, however, be abused. And so the attorney-client privilege is subject to what is known as the crime-fraud exception. Two conditions must be met. First, the client must have made or received the otherwise privileged communication with the intent to further an unlawful or fraudulent act.[12] Second, the client must have carried out the crime or fraud. In other words, the exception does not apply even though, at one time, the client had bad intentions.

---

[11] FN1. An order compelling testimony is not generally appealable unless the witness refuses to comply and is held in contempt. But under *Perlman v. United States,* 247 U.S. 7, 38 S.Ct. 417, 62 L.Ed. 950 (1918), the Company, as holder of the privilege, may appeal so long as the witness swears he will give the testimony. *See In re Sealed Case,* 754 F.2d 395, 399 (D.C.Cir.1985) (*Sealed Case II*).

[12] FN2. In nearly all cases, a client's innocence will bar application of the crime-fraud exception. We say "nearly all" because there may be rare cases—this is not one of them—in which the attorney's fraudulent or criminal intent defeats a claim of privilege even if the client is innocent. *See, e.g., Moody v. IRS,* 654 F.2d 795, 800–01 (D.C.Cir.1981); *In re Impounded Case (Law Firm),* 879 F.2d 1211, 1213–14 (3d Cir.1989).

Otherwise "it would penalize a client for doing what the privilege is designed to encourage—consulting a lawyer for the purpose of achieving law compliance." *See* Restatement of the Law Governing Lawyers § 142 cmt. c, at 461 (Proposed Final Draft No. 1, 1996).[13]

The privilege is the client's, and it is the client's fraudulent or criminal intent that matters. A third party's bad intent cannot remove the protection of the privilege. For example, a stenographer hired to record a meeting between an attorney and a client might intend to use his notes to commit some kind of crime—say extortion—but the contents of the meeting would not therefore cease to be privileged. Otherwise, existence of the attorney-client privilege would be unpredictable and the interest of "full and frank communication" between client and counsel would be undermined. *See Upjohn Co.,* 449 U.S. at 389.[14]

As the party seeking to overcome the privilege, the government had the burden of showing that the crime-fraud exception applied to the memorandum and the meeting. What was the nature of that burden? Here we encounter some confusion. This court and others have described the required showing in terms of establishing a "prima facie" case. *See, e.g., Sealed Case II,* 754 F.2d at 399. The formulation can be traced to the Supreme Court's opinion in *Clark v. United States,* 289 U.S. 1, 14 (1933). The problem is, as the Supreme Court mentioned in *Zolin,* 491 U.S. at 563 n. 7, that "prima facie" evokes the concept, familiar in civil litigation, of shifting the burden from one party to another. Yet it is altogether clear where the burden in these cases lies—on the party invoking the crime-fraud exception. In terms of the level of proof, is a "prima facie showing" a preponderance of the evidence, clear and convincing evidence, or something else?

Our opinion in *Sealed Case II* contains this answer: "The government satisfies its burden of proof if it offers evidence that if believed by the trier of fact would establish the elements of an ongoing or imminent crime or fraud." 754 F.2d at 399. We appended a footnote to this statement explaining that although the Second Circuit had "framed the test in terms of probable cause to believe that a crime or fraud had been committed and that the communications were in furtherance thereof" (*see In re John Doe*

[13] FN3. To this the Restatement drafters added: "By the same token, lawyers might be discouraged from giving full and candid advice to clients about legally questionable courses of action." *Id.* This seems to us rather doubtful. Why would a lawyer put his client—and himself—at such risk? Fully advising the client may prevent possibly unlawful action. On the other hand, if the lawyer gives less than "full and candid" advice, the client may rely on it, wind up violating the law and thus lose the privilege anyway. A lawyer representing such a client would have reason to be concerned about his own personal civil and criminal liability. Rather than discouraging full advice, that prospect plus the danger to the client provides a strong incentive for the lawyer to advise the client clearly and firmly.

[14] FN5. At least one district court seems to have said that anyone's use of a communication to further a crime or fraud defeats the attorney-client privilege, regardless of the innocence of the attorney and the client. *See Duttle v. Bandler & Kass,* 127 F.R.D. 46, 53, 55–56 (S.D.N.Y.1989). We think this is incorrect.

Corp., 675 F.2d 482, 491 & n. 7 (2d Cir.1982)), there was "little practical difference" between that standard and the one just quoted from *Sealed Case II.* We confess some difficulty in understanding why the differences between the two formulations were considered slight, but there is no reason to dwell on the matter.[15] It is apparent here that the government failed to make the sort of probable cause showing the Second Circuit would demand, or the showing *Sealed Case II* contemplated.

The critical consideration is that the government's presentation had to be aimed at the intent and action of the client. It was not enough for the government to show that the vice president committed a crime after he wrote his memorandum and attended the late August meeting with Company counsel. The holder of the privilege is the client and, in this case, the client was the Company, not the vice president. Unless the government made some showing that the Company intended to further and did commit a crime, the government could not invoke the crime-fraud exception to the privilege.

As to the late August meeting, the government's evidence reveals that the participants discussed campaign finance laws. That is not enough. One cannot reasonably infer from the meeting that the Company was consulting its general counsel with the intention of committing a crime, or even that the vice president was then doing so. Companies operating in today's complex legal and regulatory environments routinely seek legal advice about how to handle all sorts of matters, ranging from their political activities to their employment practices to transactions that may have antitrust consequences. There is nothing necessarily suspicious about the officers of this corporation getting such advice. True enough, within weeks of the meeting about campaign finance law, the vice president violated that law. But the government had to demonstrate that the Company sought the legal advice with the intent to further its illegal conduct. Showing temporal proximity between the communication and a crime is not enough.

Moreover, from the material before the district court, there was no way of knowing or even guessing whether the vice president was on a frolic of his own, against the advice of Company counsel, when he reimbursed the donors with corporate funds. The government suggested at oral argument that even if he was, the Company still could be held criminally liable. There are circumstances under which corporations are responsible for the crimes of their agents. . . . But neither in this court nor in the

[15] FN6. *Zolin* left the standard of proof question for another day. The Supreme Court decided only that the crime-fraud exception need not be established entirely with independent evidence; that courts may review allegedly privileged materials *in camera* in order to determine whether the crime-fraud exception applies, 491 U.S. at 565–70, 109 S.Ct. at 2627–30; and that before "engaging in *in camera* review . . . , the judge should require a showing of a factual basis adequate to support a good faith belief by a reasonable person that *in camera* review of the materials may reveal evidence to establish the claim that the crime-fraud exception applies," *id.* at 572, 109 S.Ct. at 2631 (internal quotation marks and citation omitted).

district court did the government offer anything in terms of evidence or law to support the idea that the Company bore criminal responsibility for the acts of this officer. *Cf. Egan v. United States,* 137 F.2d 369, 378–80 (8th Cir.1943). The government therefore did not sustain its burden. In so holding, we express no view on the Company's ultimate criminal liability. The law of corporate criminality is not well developed in this circuit. Given the government's complete failure to address the subject, this is not the case to develop it.

Many of the same points can be made about the vice president's memorandum. Like the district court, we have examined this document, which the Company submitted *in camera* and *ex parte.* From the memorandum and the other information the government presented, all that can be discerned is that the Company's vice president and its general counsel discussed federal election laws in early August 1994, perhaps at the suggestion of the Company's president. The memorandum reflected that discussion. Again, given the need for corporations and their officers to seek legal advice about activities like political contributions, there is nothing suspect about this discussion. And the fact that the vice president broke the law weeks later does not, without more, demonstrate the validity of the government's assumption that the Company intended or probably intended to further that crime. . . .

The district court decided this case by assuming that the meeting and the memoranda fell under either the attorney-client privilege or the work product doctrine and then finding that the crime-fraud exception applied. Since we disagree with the district court's conclusions regarding the crime-fraud exception, we reverse and remand the case.

So Ordered.

CASE QUESTIONS

1. Whose intention counts for purposes of the crime-fraud exception?
2. Where the client is an entity, how is that intention to be established?
3. What constitutes a *prima facie* showing for purposes of the exception?

(The facts of this case are related in Section A(4), above.)

MATTER OF MICHAEL FELDBERG

862 F.2d 622 (7th Cir. 1988)

II

We start with the question whether there is reason to believe that a crime occurred. At the time the district court ruled, the grand jury had not decided whether to indict Walters and World Sports for substantive offenses. Learning how the search had been conducted might have helped the grand jury decide whether to continue its investigation in the hope that there might be more documents where the second set came from. After the district judge's decision, the grand jury returned an indictment. The prosecutor is not entitled to use the grand jury after the return of an indictment to obtain discovery in the criminal case. So unless there is some prospect of demonstrating obstruction of justice, there is no need for Feldberg's testimony, and the case is moot.

Although the district judge gave the back of his hand to the prosecutor's suggestion of fraud or obstruction of justice, it is not so easy to dismiss the possibility. World Sports was a small outfit. Although Walters had some aides, he held the firm's principal documents. Walters apparently kept the contracts in his office. Disclosing 51 innocent-seeming contracts, while retaining six highly suspicious ones, is not a common result of random errors, and the compact nature of World Sports' files makes it doubtful that one box was overlooked during a trudge through a mile-long warehouse. Cf. *In re Grand Jury Subpoenas,* 773 F.2d 204, 206–07 (8th Cir.1985) (omission of two out of 800 relevant documents does not raise suspicion of obstruction of justice). The missing documents reflected the active business of the corporation, so it should have turned to them first (and probably had them ready to hand). The subpoena unquestionably called for these contracts; a misunderstanding (or mistaken legal advice), though conceivable, is not likely. There may of course be an innocent explanation for the problem. Perhaps the folder of current contracts had been misplaced; perhaps a messenger mislaid them. We need not try to figure out whether an innocent explanation is more likely than a culpable one. "To drive the privilege away, there must be 'something to give colour to the charge;' there must be '*prima facie* evidence that it has some foundation in fact.' When that evidence is supplied, the seal of secrecy is broken." *Clark v. United States,* 289 U.S. 1, 15, 53 S.Ct. 465, 469, 77 L.Ed. 993 (1933) (citations omitted). The charge of obstruction has a foundation in fact; the circumstances give color to the charge.

The language "*prima facie* evidence" has suggested to some courts enough to support a verdict in favor of the person making the claim. *E.g., In re International Systems & Controls Corp.,* 693 F.2d 1235, 1242 (5th Cir.1982); *In re Sealed Case,* 676 F.2d 793, 814–15 & n. 88 (D.C.Cir.1982). We are not among them, see *In re Special September 1978 Grand Jury (II),* 640 F.2d 49 (7th Cir.1980), nor are most of the other courts of appeals, e.g., *In re Grand Jury Subpoena*, 731 F.2d 1032, 1039 (2d Cir.1984); *In re Antitrust Grand Jury (Advance Publications, Inc.)*, 805 F.2d 155, 165–66 (6th Cir.1986). The question here is not whether the evidence supports a verdict but whether it calls for inquiry. Courts often use "*prima facie* evidence" to refer to enough to require explanation rather than evidence that by itself satisfies a more-likely-than-not standard. One need only think of litigation about claims of racial or age discrimination, in which most of those who satisfy the lax standards of a *prima facie* case go on to lose on the merits. Here, as in the law of discrimination, a *prima facie* case must be defined with regard to its function: to require the adverse party, the one with superior access to the evidence and in the best position to explain things, to come forward with that explanation. If the court finds the explanation satisfactory, the privilege remains. . . . .

CASE QUESTIONS

1. What constitutes a *prima facie* showing for purposes of the exception?
2. *Feldberg* involves both an individual, Walters, and a corporation, *World Sports*. Do you suppose the *Feldberg* court would take the same approach to the role of the entity as did the court in *In re Sealed Case*? How might the courts differ?

Show What?

The *prima facie* case language traces back to *Clark v. United States*, 289 U.S. 1, 15 (1933), where the Court said, in dicta, "there must be 'something to give colour to the charge'; there must be 'prima facie evidence that it has some foundation in fact.' . . . When that evidence is supplied, the seal of secrecy is broken."[16]

In re Sealed Case and *Feldberg* agree that a party asserting the crime-fraud exception must make a *prima facie* showing that the communication it wants disclosed was made in furtherance of a crime or fraud. They define that showing differently. *Sealed Case* offers two definitions. One, adopted by the D.C. Circuit, requires enough evidence to "establish the elements of an ongoing or imminent crime or fraud." The other, adopted by the Second Circuit, requires evidence sufficient to establish "probable cause to believe that a crime or fraud had been committed and that the communications were in furtherance thereof." As Judge Randolph points out, the two are hardly equivalent. The Seventh Circuit in

[16] The British spelling is because the Court quoted from *O'Rourke v. Darbishire* [1920] A.C. 581, 604.

Feldberg offered a third phrase: evidence sufficient "to require explanation rather than evidence that by itself satisfies a more-likely-than-not standard."

The Ninth Circuit follows none of these approaches. In *In re Napster, Inc. Copyright Litigation*, 479 F.3d 1078 (9th Cir. 2007), the court held that "in a civil case the burden of proof that must be carried by a party seeking outright disclosure of attorney-client communications under the crime-fraud exception should be preponderance of the evidence." The court also held, as *Feldberg* implies, that "in civil cases where outright disclosure is requested the party seeking to preserve the privilege has the right to introduce countervailing evidence."

The Ninth Circuit employs a different standard when the crime-fraud exception is asserted in grand jury proceedings: "The standard in our circuit for grand jury cases is 'reasonable cause to believe' that the attorney's services were 'utilized . . . in furtherance of the ongoing unlawful scheme.' " [citations omitted] We have explained our "reasonable cause to believe" standard as follows: "Reasonable cause is more than suspicion but less than a preponderance of evidence."

By this point in your law school career you no doubt have noticed that the burden of proof often decides who wins. Usually, this means that whoever has to prove things that are hard to prove will lose. In this context it also means that whether the crime-fraud exception applies may depend on where you litigate the issue. The doctrine has one name, but many different applications.

---

2. JOINT CLIENTS

Restatement of the Law Governing Lawyers § 75

Lawyers sometimes represent two clients jointly. A lawyer may represent both spouses in drafting a will for example, as happened in *A v. B* in chapter 4, or may represent a company and one or more executives in the company. In such a case the lawyer may share with one client communications from another joint client. Such sharing does not waive the privilege as against third parties, and either joint client may assert the privilege against disclosure sought by a third party. In contrast, if the joint clients wind up in litigation against each other neither client may assert the privilege against the other. *E.g.* Cal. Evid. Code § 962. Each co-client may waive privilege with respect to his or her own communications with counsel, but no co-client may waive privilege with respect to another client's communications. *Restatement* § 75 cmt e.

The joint client exception is clear enough with regard to communications made when the clients' interests are aligned. But what if the clients' interests diverge? *In re Teleglobe Communications Corp.*, 493 F.3d 345 (3d Cir. 2007), describes the basic rule:

"The Restatement's conflicts rules provide that when a joint attorney sees the co-clients' interests diverging to an unacceptable degree, the proper course is to end the joint representation. *Restatement (Third) of the Law Governing Lawyers* § 121 cmts. e(1)–(2). As the Court of Appeals for the D.C. Circuit noted in *Eureka Inv. Corp. v. Chicago Title Ins. Co.*, 743 F.2d 932 (D.C. Cir. 1984) (*per curiam*), courts are presented with a difficult problem when a joint attorney fails to do that and instead continues representing both clients when their interests become adverse. *Id.* at 937–38. In this situation, the black-letter law is that when an attorney (improperly) represents two clients whose interests are adverse, the communications are privileged against each other notwithstanding the lawyer's misconduct. *Id.; see also* 8 J. WIGMORE, EVIDENCE § 2312 (McNaughton rev. ed. 1961).

The context of the *Eureka* case was the joint representation of an insured and insurer. Over the course of the litigation, the parties began to disagree. The insured, a developer trying to effect a condo conversion, wanted to settle in order to get its conversion plans back on track. The title insurer, on the other hand, wanted to continue opposing liability and would not agree to within-policy-limits settlement terms. Having decided that the insurer's refusal to settle was tortious, the insured entered into a unilateral settlement with its adversaries and promptly sued the insurer for indemnification and consequential damages. The trouble was that the insured continued to use the joint attorneys throughout the process, relying on their advice in deciding to enter into a unilateral settlement and to sue the insurer. Thus, upon filing its action, the insurer sought discovery of the insured's communications with the joint attorneys in the hope that those communications would support the affirmative defense of noncooperation. The insurer argued that because those communications were generated during the attorneys' joint representation of the parties on the claim against the insured, they were discoverable in an action between the joint clients.

The Court rejected the insurer's argument, holding instead that "[t]he policy behind [the co-client privilege]—to encourage openness and cooperation between joint clients—does not apply to matters known at the time of communication not to be in the common interest of the attorney's two clients." *Eureka*, 743 F.2d at 937. It emphasized that both the insured and the joint attorneys thought that they had begun a separate, individual representation of the insured on the insurance bad-faith claim that was distinct from the underlying liability action, calling these understandings "crucial." *Id.* Noting the attorneys' potential ethical violations, the Court concluded that they were of no moment: "[C]ounsel's failure to avoid a conflict of interest should not deprive the client of the privilege. The privilege, being the client's, should not be defeated solely because the attorney's conduct was ethically questionable." *Id.* at 938. Though not yet explicitly adopted by the Delaware courts, the *Eureka* principle is widely accepted. *See Restatement (Third) of the Law Governing Lawyers* § 60 cmt. *l.*; RICE 4:33."

The joint client arrangement should be distinguished from a somewhat less common arrangement in which one lawyer represents two clients concurrently on related matters but where the clients do not seek to coordinate their representation through the lawyer. *Roush v. Seagate Tech., LLC,* 150 Cal. App. 4th 210, 223 (Cal. App. 2007)(clients not jointly represented with respect to employment claims against common employer where clients asserted different theories and success of one case did not turn on success of the other, though clients would be witnesses in each other's cases). If a lawyer represents clients concurrently but not jointly then the two clients may assert privilege against each other. In addition, if *X* and *Y* are concurrent but not joint clients of lawyer *Z*, then a third party, such as the former employer of *X* and *Y*, may learn what *X* knows about *Y* without necessarily facing the risk of disqualification for intruding into the attorney client relationship between *Y* and *Z*. *See also Sky Valley Ltd P 'ship v. ATX Sky Valley, Ltd.,* 150 F.R.D. 648, 653 (N.D. Cal. 1993)(purpose of joint client privilege as against third parties is to facilitate communication; purposes of joint client exception to privilege are "(1) to prevent unjustifiable inequality in access to information necessary to resolve fairly disputes that arise between parties who were in the past joint clients-when the disputes relate to matters that were involved in the joint representation and (2) to discourage abuses of fiduciary obligations and to encourage parties to honor any legal duties they had to share information related to common interests").

---

3. THE FIDUCIARY EXCEPTION

Some courts will allow the beneficiaries of a fiduciary relation, such as the beneficiaries of a trust, to discover the contents of communications between the fiduciary, such as a trustee, so long as the communications pertain to the performance of the fiduciary's obligations. *United States v. Jicarilla Apache Nation,* 131 S. Ct. 2313 (2011), describes the outlines of the doctrine.

English courts first developed the fiduciary exception as a principle of trust law in the 19th century. The rule was that when a trustee obtained legal advice to guide the administration of the trust, and not for the trustee's own defense in litigation, the beneficiaries were entitled to the production of documents related to that advice. The courts reasoned that the normal attorney-client privilege did not apply in this situation because the legal advice was sought for the beneficiaries' benefit and was obtained at the beneficiaries' expense by using trust funds to pay the attorney's fees.

The fiduciary exception quickly became an established feature of English common law, see, *e.g., In re Mason,* 22 Ch. D. 609 (1883), but it did not appear in this country until the following century. American courts seem first to have expressed skepticism. *See In re Prudence–Bonds Corp.,* 76 F.Supp. 643, 647 (E.D.N.Y.1948) (declining to apply the fiduciary exception to the trustee of a bondholding corporation because of the "important right of such a corporate trustee . . . to seek legal advice and nevertheless act in accordance with its own judgment"). By the 1970's, however, American courts began to adopt the English common-law rule. *See* Garner v. Wolfinbarger, 430 F.2d 1093, 1103–1104 (C.A.5 1970) (allowing shareholders, upon a showing of "good cause," to discover legal advice given to corporate management).[17]

The leading American case on the fiduciary exception is *Riggs Nat. Bank of Washington, D.C. v. Zimmer,* 355 A.2d 709 (Del.Ch.1976). In that case, the beneficiaries of a trust estate sought to compel the trustees to reimburse the estate for alleged breaches of trust. The beneficiaries moved to compel the trustees to produce a legal memorandum related to the administration of the trust that the trustees withheld on the basis of attorney-client privilege. The Delaware Chancery Court, observing that "American case law is practically nonexistent on the duty of a trustee in this context," looked to the English cases. Applying the common-law fiduciary exception, the court held that the memorandum was discoverable. It identified two reasons for applying the exception.

First, the court explained, the trustees had obtained the legal advice as "mere representative[s]" of the beneficiaries because the trustees had a fiduciary obligation to act in the beneficiaries' interest when administering the trust. For that reason, the beneficiaries were the "real clients" of the attorney who had advised the trustee on trust-related matters, and

[17][3] Today, "[c]ourts differ on whether the [attorney-client] privilege is available for communications between the trustee and counsel regarding the administration of the trust." A. Newman, G. Bogert & G. Bogert, Law of Trusts and Trustees § 962, p. 68 (3d ed.2010) (hereinafter Bogert). Some state courts have altogether rejected the notion that the attorney-client privilege is subject to a fiduciary exception. See, *e.g., Huie v. DeShazo,* 922 S.W.2d 920, 924 (Tex.1996) ("The attorney-client privilege serves the same important purpose in the trustee-attorney relationship as it does in other attorney-client relationships"); *Wells Fargo Bank v. Superior Ct.,* 22 Cal.4th 201, 208–209, 91 Cal.Rptr.2d 716, 990 P.2d 591, 595 (2000) ("[T]he attorney for the trustee of a trust is not, by virtue of this relationship, also the attorney for the beneficiaries of the trust" (internal quotation marks omitted)). Neither party before this Court disputes the existence of a common-law fiduciary exception, however, so in deciding this case we assume such an exception exists.

therefore the attorney-client privilege properly belonged to the beneficiaries rather than the trustees. The court based its "real client" determination on several factors: (1) when the advice was sought, no adversarial proceedings between the trustees and beneficiaries had been pending, and therefore there was no reason for the trustees to seek legal advice in a personal rather than a fiduciary capacity; (2) the court saw no indication that the memorandum was intended for any purpose other than to benefit the trust; and (3) the law firm had been paid out of trust assets. That the advice was obtained at the beneficiaries' expense was not only a "significant factor" entitling the beneficiaries to see the document but also "a strong indication of precisely who the real clients were." The court distinguished between "legal advice procured at the trustee's *own* expense and for his *own* protection," which would remain privileged, "and the situation where the trust itself is assessed for obtaining opinions of counsel where interests of the beneficiaries are presently at stake." In the latter case, the fiduciary exception applied, and the trustees could not withhold those attorney-client communications from the beneficiaries.

Second, the court concluded that the trustees' fiduciary duty to furnish trust-related information to the beneficiaries outweighed their interest in the attorney-client privilege. "The policy of preserving the full disclosure necessary in the trustee-beneficiary relationship," the court explained, "is here ultimately more important than the protection of the trustees' confidence in the attorney for the trust." Because more information helped the beneficiaries to police the trustees' management of the trust, disclosure was, in the court's judgment, "a weightier public policy than the preservation of confidential attorney-client communications." The Federal Courts of Appeals apply the fiduciary exception based on the same two criteria.

As the Court states in its footnote, modern authorities regarding the fiduciary exception are somewhat mixed. ERISA plan administration is a common context in which the doctrine is applied, however. *Stephan v. Unum Life Ins. Co. of America*, 697 F.3d 917 (9th Cir. 2012), summarizes the current state of the law in that field.

E. WAIVER

A party may waive privilege either intentionally or through a lack of care. Accidental disclosure not resulting in waiver creates risks for lawyers receiving the information, as shown in our first case. Intentional disclosure presents no such issues but does pose the question of how far waiver should extend. The second case explores that issue.

1. INADVERTENT DISCLOSURE

Restatement §§ 78–80
Model Rule of Professional Conduct 4.4(b)

Privileged communications are sometimes disclosed by accident, often by an attorney or the attorney's staff. Inadvertent disclosure brings two principles into conflict. The first is that the privilege belongs to the client and only the client can waive it; traditionally waiver requires an intentional act. The second is that the lawyer is the client's agent and the client is bound by the agent's actions. Often lawyers intend to do one thing—such as produce a box of documents—but do not intend to do another—such as produce a small group of privileged documents in the box. The question then is what level of intention matters and whether it should be imputed to the client.

Courts have adopted three basic approaches to this problem. As described by the California court of appeal in *State Compensation Insurance Fund v. WPS, Inc.*, 70 Cal.App.4th 644, 652 n.2 (1999) (citations omitted):

> "Courts faced with the issue of whether intent is necessary to effectuate a waiver of the attorney-client privilege by inadvertent disclosure have approached the problem in one of three ways. Some courts have followed a 'strict responsibility' approach, viewing the client's intent as irrelevant. Other courts have used a balancing approach. Under the balancing approach, several objective factors may be considered in rendering a decision. A third group of courts has focused specifically upon whether the client intended to waive the privilege. Regardless of the approach used, the final determination of whether an assertion of the attorney-client privilege will be upheld in an inadvertent disclosure context depends upon whether the client either expressly or impliedly waived the privilege.

Whether inadvertent disclosure waives a party's privilege matters for both the disclosing party and the party receiving the disclosure. If disclosure amounts to waiver a party receiving the information may study and use it without penalty. If the disclosure does not amount to waiver, however, then a lawyer who receives it may be disqualified from further involvement in the case if the lawyer studies the information. The next case provides an example of this remedy. (It deals with work-product protection but the principle applies to the privilege as well.) If a client studies the information then simply disqualifying a lawyer may not be enough; sanctions against the client may be required. For these reasons, it is very important that the recipient of such information deal with it properly.

RICO V. MITSUBISHI MOTORS CORP.

42 Cal.4th 807 (2007)

Here we consider what action is required of an attorney who receives privileged documents through inadvertence and whether the remedy of disqualification is appropriate. We conclude that, under the authority of *State Comp. Ins. Fund v. WPS, Inc.* (1999) 70 Cal. App. 4th 644 *(State Fund)*, an attorney in these circumstances may not read a document any more closely than is necessary to ascertain that it is privileged. Once it becomes apparent that the content is privileged, counsel must immediately notify opposing counsel and try to resolve the situation. We affirm the disqualification order under the circumstances presented here.

FACTUAL BACKGROUND

Two Mitsubishi corporations(collectively Mitsubishi or defendants), and the California Department of Transportation (Caltrans), were sued by various plaintiffs after a Mitsubishi Montero rolled over while being driven on a freeway. Subsequently, Mitsubishi representatives met with their lawyers, James Yukevich and Alexander Calfo, and two designated defense experts to discuss their litigation strategy and vulnerabilities. Mitsubishi's case manager, Jerome Rowley, also attended the meeting. Rowley and Yukevich had worked together over a few years. Yukevich asked Rowley to take notes at the meeting and indicated specific areas to be summarized. The trial court later found that Rowley, who had typed the notes on Yukevich's computer, had acted as Yukevich's paralegal. At the end of the six-hour session, Rowley returned the computer and never saw a printed version of the notes. Yukevich printed only one copy of the notes, which he later edited and annotated. Yukevich never intentionally showed the notes to anyone, and the court determined that the sole purpose of the document was to help Yukevich defend the case.

The notes are written in a dialogue style and summarize conversations among Yukevich, Calfo, and the experts. They are dated, but not labeled as "confidential" or "work product." The printed copy of these compiled and annotated notes is the document at issue here.[18] Less than two weeks after the strategy session, Yukevich deposed plaintiffs' expert witness, Anthony Sances, at the offices of plaintiffs' counsel, Raymond Johnson. Yukevich, court reporter Karen Kay, and Caltrans counsel Darin Flagg were told that Johnson and Sances would be late for the deposition.

After waiting in the conference room for some time, Yukevich went to the restroom, leaving his briefcase, computer, and case file in the room. The printed document from the strategy session was in the case file.

[18] FN2. Because the document was confidential, the court ordered it sealed along with relevant portions of the reporter's transcript where the contents of the document were discussed. The document has remained sealed since that time.

While Yukevich was away, Johnson and Sances arrived. Johnson asked Kay and Flagg to leave the conference room. Kay and Flagg's departure left only the plaintiffs' representatives and counsel in the conference room. Yukevich returned to find Kay and Flagg standing outside. Yukevich waited approximately 5 minutes, then knocked and asked to retrieve his briefcase, computer, and file. After a brief delay, he was allowed to do so.

Somehow, Johnson acquired Yukevich's notes. Johnson maintained that they were accidentally given to him by the court reporter. Yukevich insisted that they were taken from his file while only Johnson and plaintiffs' team were in the conference room. As a result, Mitsubishi moved to disqualify plaintiffs' attorneys and experts. The trial court ordered an evidentiary hearing to determine how Johnson obtained the document. . . .

The court ultimately concluded that the defense had failed to establish that Johnson had taken the notes from Yukevich's file. It thus ruled that Johnson came into the document's possession through inadvertence. The court found the 12–page document was dated, but not otherwise labeled. It contained notations by Yukevich. Johnson admitted that he knew within a minute or two that the document related to the defendants' case. He knew that Yukevich did not intend to produce it and that it would be a "powerful impeachment document." Nevertheless, Johnson made a copy of the document. He scrutinized and made his own notes on it. He gave copies to his cocounsel and his experts, all of whom studied the document. Johnson specifically discussed the contents of the document with each of his experts.

A week after he acquired Yukevich's notes, Johnson used them during the deposition of defense expert Geoffrey Germane. The notes purportedly indicate that the defense experts made statements at the strategy session that were inconsistent with their deposition testimony. Johnson used the document while questioning Germane, asking about Germane's participation in the strategy session.

Defense Counsel Calfo defended the Germane deposition. Yukevich did not attend. Calfo had never seen the document and was not given a copy during the deposition. When he asked about the document's source, Johnson vaguely replied that, "It was put in Dr. Sances' file." Calfo repeatedly objected to the "whole line of inquiry with respect to an unknown document." He specifically said that, "I don't even know where this exhibit came from." Only after the deposition did Johnson give a copy of the document to Calfo, who contacted Yukevich. When Yukevich realized that Johnson had his only copy of the strategy session notes and had used it at the deposition, he and Calfo wrote to Johnson demanding the return of all duplicates. The letter was faxed the day after Germane's deposition. The next day, defendants moved to disqualify plaintiffs' legal team and their experts on the ground that they had become privy to and had used Yukevich's work product. As a result, they complained, Johnson's unethical use of the notes and his revelation of them to cocounsel and their experts irremediably prejudiced defendants.

The trial court concluded that the notes were absolutely privileged by the work product rule.[19] The court also held that Johnson had acted unethically by examining the document more closely than was necessary to determine that its contents were confidential, by failing to notify Yukevich that he had a copy of the document, and by surreptitiously using it to gain maximum adversarial value from it. The court determined that Johnson's violation of the work product rule had prejudiced the defense and "the bell cannot be 'unrung' by use of in limine orders." Accordingly, the court ordered plaintiffs' attorneys and experts disqualified.[20] Plaintiffs appealed the disqualification order. The Court of Appeal affirmed.

DISCUSSION

Attorney Work Product

Plaintiffs contend that the Court of Appeal erred by holding that the entire document was protected as attorney work product. We reject that contention. . . . the codified work product doctrine absolutely protects from discovery writings that contain an "attorney's impressions, conclusions, opinions, or legal research or theories." (§ 2018.030, subd. (a); see *Wellpoint Health Networks, Inc. v. Superior Court* (1997) 59 Cal.App.4th 110, 120.) The protection extends to an attorney's written notes about a witness's statements [citations omitted]. When a witness's statement and the attorney's impressions are inextricably intertwined, the work product doctrine provides that absolute protection is afforded to all of the attorney's notes.

Plaintiffs urge that the document is not work product because it reflects the statements of declared experts. They are incorrect. The document is not a transcript of the August 28, 2002 strategy session, nor is it a verbatim record of the experts' own statements. It contains Rowley's summaries of points from the strategy session, made at Yukevich's direction. Yukevich also edited the document in order to add his own thoughts

[19] FN4. The trial court also held that the document fell under the attorney-client privilege. The Court of Appeal held to the contrary. That issue is not before us and we express no view thereon.

[20] FN5. The court continued the case to provide the plaintiffs an opportunity to retain new counsel. The court noted that it did not appear that the plaintiffs were made privy to the document's contents, so disqualification would be an effective remedy, because there was no issue about the plaintiffs providing new counsel with the information. The court also imposed a gag order on all who attended the hearing on the motion to disqualify, specifically instructing plaintiffs' counsel and experts to keep the contents of the document confidential and not reveal any information about the document to plaintiffs and their new attorneys.

and comments, further inextricably intertwining his personal impressions with the summary. . . .

Ethical Duty Owed Upon Receipt Of Attorney Work Product

Because the document is work product we consider what ethical duty Johnson owed once he received it. Plaintiffs rely on *Aerojet–General Corp. v. Transport Indemnity Insurance* (1993) 18 Cal.App.4th 996 (*Aerojet*), to argue that because the document was inadvertently received, Johnson was duty bound to use the nonprivileged portions of it to his clients' advantage. This argument fails. *Aerojet* is distinguishable because there are no "unprivileged portions" of the document.

A review of *Aerojet* demonstrates that it does not assist plaintiffs. Aerojet's insurance brokers had sent a package of materials to Aerojet's risk manager. The risk manager sent them on to Aerojet's attorney, DeVries. Among these documents was a memo from an attorney at an opposing law firm. It was never ascertained how opposing counsel's memo found its way into the package of documents. The memo revealed the existence of a witness whom DeVries ultimately deposed. When opposing counsel learned that DeVries had received the memo and thus discovered the witness, counsel sought sanctions.

The trial court imposed monetary sanctions under section 128.5, subdivision (a). The Court of Appeal reversed the sanctions order. The *Aerojet* court first noted that DeVries was free of any wrongdoing in his initial receipt of the document. The court also observed that the existence and identification of the witness was not privileged. "Nor can 'the identity and location of persons having knowledge of relevant facts' be concealed under the attorney work product rule. . . . [Citations.]" Defendants claimed no prejudice to their case as a result of the witness' disclosure. Indeed, they prevailed at trial. Because counsel was blameless in his acquisition of the document *and because* the information complained of was not privileged, DeVries was free to use it. Plaintiffs' reliance on *Aerojet* founders on the facts that distinguish it. Here, Yukevich's notes were absolutely protected by the work product rule. Thus, Johnson's reliance on *Aeorjet* is unavailing, particularly in light of the clear standard set out in *State Fund, supra,* 70 Cal.App.4th 644.

In *State Fund*, the plaintiff sent defendant's attorney (Telanoff) three boxes of documents that were identical to the documents provided during discovery. Inadvertently, plaintiff also sent 273 pages of forms entitled, "Civil Litigation Claims Summary," marked as "ATTORNEY–CLIENT COMMUNICATION/ATTORNEY WORK PRODUCT," and with the warning, "DO NOT CIRCULATE OR DUPLICATE." In addition, "[t]he word 'CONFIDENTIAL' [was] repeatedly printed around the perimeter of the first page of the form." When counsel discovered the mistake and demanded return of the documents, Telanoff refused. The trial court, relying on American Bar Association (ABA) Formal Ethics Opinion No. 92–368 (Nov. 10, 1992), imposed monetary sanctions. . . .

The Court of Appeal disagreed that the ABA opinion should regulate Telanoff's conduct. The court noted that the ABA Model Rules on which the opinion was based "do not establish ethical standards in California, as they have not been adopted in California and have no legal force of their own. [Citations.]" Likewise, the court held that an "ABA formal opinion does not establish an obligatory standard of conduct imposed on California lawyers." Thus, under the circumstances "Telanoff should not have been sanctioned for engaging in conduct which has been condemned by an ABA formal opinion, but which has not been condemned by any decision, statute or Rule of Professional Conduct applicable in this state."

The *State Fund* court went on to articulate the standard to be applied prospectively: "When a lawyer who receives materials that obviously appear to be subject to an attorney-client privilege or otherwise clearly appear to be confidential and privileged and where it is reasonably apparent that the materials were provided or made available through inadvertence, the lawyer receiving such materials should refrain from examining the materials any more than is essential to ascertain if the materials are privileged, and shall immediately notify the sender that he or she possesses material that appears to be privileged. The parties may then proceed to resolve the situation by agreement or may resort to the court for guidance with the benefit of protective orders and other judicial intervention as may be justified." To ensure that its decision was clear in setting forth the applicable standard in these cases, the court explicitly stated that it "declared the standard governing the conduct of California lawyers" in such instances.

The existing *State Fund* rule is a fair and reasonable approach.[21] The rule supports the work product doctrine (§ 2018.030), and is consistent with the state's policy to "[p]reserve the rights of attorneys to prepare cases for trial with that degree of privacy necessary to encourage them to prepare their cases thoroughly and to investigate not only the favorable but the unfavorable aspects of those cases" and to "[p]revent attorneys from taking undue advantage of their adversary's industry and efforts." (§ 2018.020, subds. (a), (b).). . . .

Finally, we note that "[a]n attorney has an obligation not only to protect his client's interests but also to respect the legitimate interests of fellow members of the bar, the judiciary, and the administration of justice."

[21] FN9. We also reject plaintiffs' contention that *State Fund*, *supra*, 70 Cal.App.4th 644, only applies to materials protected by the attorney-client privilege. The Court of Appeal held that there was no distinction "between the attorney-client privilege and the work product privilege in this context [because] . . . [t]he *State Fund* standard applies to documents that are plainly privileged and confidential, regardless of whether they are privileged under the attorney-client privilege, the work product privilege, or any other similar doctrine that would preclude discovery based on the confidential nature of the document." We agree.

(*Kirsch v. Duryea* (1978) 21 Cal.3d 303, 309.) The *State Fund* rule holds attorneys to a reasonable standard of professional conduct when confidential or privileged materials are inadvertently disclosed.

Here, it is true that Yukevich's notes were not so clearly flagged as confidential as were the forms in *State Fund*. But, as the Court of Appeal observed, "[T]he absence of prominent notations of confidentiality does not make them any less privileged." The *State Fund* rule is an objective standard. In applying the rule, courts must consider whether reasonably competent counsel, knowing the circumstances of the litigation, would have concluded the materials were privileged, how much review was reasonably necessary to draw that conclusion, and when counsel's examination should have ended.

The standard was properly and easily applied here. Johnson admitted that after a minute or two of review he realized the notes related to the case and that Yukevich did not intend to reveal them. Johnson's own admissions and subsequent conduct clearly demonstrate that he violated the *State Fund* rule. We note, however, that such admissions are not required for the application of the objective standard in evaluating an attorney's conduct.

Disqualification Of Counsel And Experts

The court properly applied the *State Fund* rule and determined that Johnson violated it. The next question is whether disqualification was the proper remedy. We review the court's disqualification order for abuse of discretion. (*People ex rel. Dept. of Corporations v. SpeeDee Oil Change Systems, Inc.* (1999) 20 Cal.4th 1135, 1143.) The *State Fund* court held that " '[m]ere exposure' " to an adversary's confidences is insufficient, standing alone, to warrant an attorney's disqualification. The court counseled against a draconian rule that " '[could] nullify a party's right to representation by chosen counsel any time inadvertence or devious design put an adversary's confidences in an attorney's mailbox.' " However, the court, did not "rule out the possibility that in an appropriate case, disqualification might be justified if an attorney inadvertently receives confidential materials and fails to conduct himself or herself in the manner specified above, assuming other factors compel disqualification."

After reviewing the document, Johnson made copies and disseminated them to plaintiffs' experts and other attorneys. In affirming the disqualification order, the Court of Appeal stated, "The trial court settled on disqualification as the proper remedy because of the unmitigable damage caused by Johnson's dissemination and use of the document." Thus, "the record shows that Johnson not only failed to conduct himself as required under *State Fund,* but also acted unethically in making full use of the confidential document." The Court of Appeal properly concluded that such use of the document undermined the defense experts' opinions and placed defendants at a great disadvantage. Without disqualification of plaintiffs' counsel and their experts, the damage caused by Johnson's use and dissemination of the notes was irreversible. Under the circumstances presented in this case, the trial court did not abuse its discretion by ordering disqualification for violation of the *State Fund* rule.

Plaintiffs attempt to justify Johnson's use of the document by accusing the defense experts of giving false testimony during their depositions. Plaintiffs allege that the statements attributed to the experts in the document contradicted their deposition statements and that the experts lied about the technical evidence involved in the case. As an initial matter, we are not persuaded that any of the defense experts ever actually adopted as their own the statements attributed to them. The document is not a verbatim transcript of the strategy session, but Rowley's summary of points that Yukevich directed him to note. Yukevich then edited the document, adding his own thoughts and comments. As the trial court observed, the document was an interpretation and summary of what others thought the experts were saying.

Moreover, we agree with the Court of Appeal that, "when a writing is protected under the absolute attorney work product privilege, courts do not invade upon the attorney's thought processes by evaluating the content of the writing. Once [it is apparent] that the writing contains an attorney's impressions, conclusions, opinions, legal research or theories, the reading stops and the contents of the document for all practical purposes are off limits. In the same way, once the court determines that the writing is absolutely privileged, the inquiry ends. Courts do not make exceptions based on the content of the writing." Thus, "regardless of its potential impeachment value, Yukevich's personal notes should never have been subject to opposing counsel's scrutiny and use."

We also reject plaintiffs' argument that the crime or fraud exception should apply to privileged work product in this civil proceeding. Under the work product doctrine "[a] writing that reflects an attorney's impressions, conclusions, opinions, or legal research or theories *is not discoverable under any circumstances.* (§ 2018.030, subd. (a) italics added.) With respect to such a writing, the Legislature intended that the crime or fraud exception only apply "in any official investigation by a law enforcement agency or proceeding or action brought by a public prosecutor . . . if the services of the lawyer were sought or obtained to enable or aid anyone to commit . . . a crime or fraud." (§ 2018.050.) By its own terms, the crime or fraud exception does not apply here. . . .

For a case drawing an analogy to a state adoption of Model Rule 4.4, and holding that an attorney who receives documents from an anonymous source "must promptly notify opposing counsel, or risk being in violation of his or her ethical duties and/or being disqualified as counsel," *see Merits Incentives, LLC v. Eighth Judicial Dist. Court of State, ex rel. County of Clark*, 262 P.3d 720, 725 (Nev. 2011). The court held "[n]otification must adequately put opposing counsel on notice that the documents were not received in the normal course of discovery and describe, with particularity, the facts and circumstances that explain how the documents or evidence came into counsel's or his or her client's possession."

Even when a lawyer satisfies his or her ethical obligations, trial courts may retain discretion to disqualify the lawyer. (Note here that the Model Rule, unlike the holding in *Rico*, does not require that a recipient lawyer stop reading material as soon as he or she recognizes that the material may be privileged.) To guide the exercise of that discretion the *Merits Incentives* court adopted a non-exhaustive list of factors articulated in *In re Meador,* 968 S.W.2d 346 (Tex.1998). Those factors include:

1) [W]hether the attorney knew or should have known that the material was privileged;

2) the promptness with which the attorney notifies the opposing side that he or she has received its privileged information;

3) the extent to which the attorney reviews and digests the privileged information;

4) the significance of the privileged information; i.e., the extent to which its disclosure may prejudice the movant's claim or defense, and the extent to which return of the documents will mitigate that prejudice;

5) the extent to which movant may be at fault for the unauthorized disclosure; [and]

6) the extent to which the nonmovant will suffer prejudice from the disqualification of his or her attorney.

Inadvertent Disclosure and the Federal Rules of Evidence

Federal Rule of Evidence 502 deals with inadvertent disclosure in several ways. First, by providing that waiver extends to the subject matter of a communication only if fairness requires Section 502(a) makes clear that even when it is found inadvertent waiver does not extend beyond the communication disclosed. Second, as to the waiver question itself Section 502(b) provides that inadvertent disclosure in a federal proceeding or to a federal agency does not waive privilege in either federal or state proceedings if (i) the disclosure was unintentional; (ii) the disclosing party took reasonable steps to guard against disclosure; and (iii) the disclosing party promptly took reasonable steps to rectify the error.

Section 502(c) deals with state-federal issues and adopts the principle of applying the rule most protective of privilege. It provides that an inadvertent disclosure in a state proceeding, as to which a state court has not entered an order concerning waiver, does not waive privilege for federal purposes if either rule 502 or state law would not find waiver. This provision does not affect treatment of the disclosed communication in later state proceedings.

Section 502(d) provides that a federal court may order that inadvertent disclosure "connected with the litigation" pending in federal court is not waiver in either a federal or a state proceeding. Section 502(e) provides that parties to a federal proceeding may agree among themselves on the effects of disclosure in a federal proceeding, but this agreement binds only the parties to it unless a court embodies the agreement in an order. These provisions are meant to reduce the cost of discovery by reducing the risk that failure to catch a privileged document will waive privilege.

Metadata and Inadvertent Disclosure

Metadata refers to information about a document that is contained in the digital file for the document but is not part of the text of the document. In a Microsoft Word document, for example, the file properties menu lists who drafted the document and when, and when it was revised. Comments also may count as metadata, at least if they are not meant to be shared. In some cases lawyers have been embarrassed by publicly disclosing documents without deleting comments that revealed information they did not want to disclose.

Metadata present two issues for lawyers. The first concerns the duty of confidentiality. If a document contains metadata the client wants kept confidential (which should be the presumption for anything the client has not authorized you to disclose), the duty of confidentiality requires the lawyer to "scrub" such data (render it unreadable by third parties) before distributing the document. *Cf* COPRAC Opinion 2007–174 (Finding obligation to provide clients with electronic versions of client information, subject to obligation to strip documents of metadata containing information pertaining to other clients).

What if a lawyer fails to scrub a document you receive? ABA Formal Opinion 06–442 finds no prohibition in the Model Rules on using inadvertently produced metadata. The opinion believes Rule 4.4(b) forecloses such a conclusion. Maryland (2007–09) reaches the same conclusion.

Pointing the other way, the New York County Lawyers' Association Op. 738 (3/24/08) finds that New York law prohibits receiving lawyers from searching for metadata: "Using the metadata is unethical if the recipient's intent is to investigate opposing counsel's work product or client confidences or secrets or if the recipient is likely to find opposing counsel's work product or client confidences or secrets by searching the metadata. Without a prior understanding to the contrary, there is a presumption that disclosure of metadata is inadvertent and would be unethical to view." The Alabama (2007–02), Arizona (07–03), and Florida (06–2) bars reach the same conclusion. The District of Columbia bar (Opinion 341, 2007) has opined that receiving counsel should not review metadata before checking with sending counsel to determine whether such data contain client confidences.

---

2. DELIBERATE DISCLOSURE

IN RE VON BULOW

828 F.2d 94 (2d Cir. 1987)

CARDAMONE, CIRCUIT JUDGE:

Petitioner Claus von Bulow seeks a writ of mandamus directing the United States District Court for the Southern District of New York (Walker, J.) to vacate its discovery order of February 12, 1987, 114 F.R.D. 71, granting plaintiff the right to discover certain conversations between petitioner and his attorneys. Because the discovery order raises significant issues of first impression, mandamus is an appropriate remedy. Hence, the petition is granted.

FACTS

On July 6, 1981 petitioner was indicted by a Newport County, Rhode Island, grand jury on two counts of assault with intent to murder for allegedly injecting his wife Martha von Bulow with insulin causing her to lapse into an irreversible coma. After a widely publicized jury trial, von Bulow was convicted on both counts on March 16, 1982. In April 1982 petitioner retained Harvard law professor Alan M. Dershowitz to represent him on appeal. In May 1982 von Bulow was sentenced to 30–years imprisonment, but granted bail pending appeal. On April 27, 1984 the Rhode Island Supreme Court reversed both convictions, State v. von Bulow, 475 A.2d 995 (R.I.), cert. denied, 469 U.S. 875 (1984), and upon retrial, he was acquitted on June 10, 1985.

Shortly after the acquittal, petitioner's wife, by her next friends, Alexander Auersperg and Annie Laurie Auersperg–Kneissal, Martha von Bulow's children from a prior marriage (plaintiff), commenced this civil action in federal court against petitioner alleging common law assault, negligence, fraud, and RICO violations. These claims arose out of the same facts and circumstances as the Rhode Island criminal prosecution.

In May 1986 Random House published a book entitled Reversal of Fortune—Inside the von Bulow Case, authored by attorney Dershowitz, which chronicles the events surrounding the first criminal trial, the successful appeal, and von Bulow's ultimate acquittal. After obtaining an advance copy of the book, plaintiff's counsel notified petitioner on April 23, 1986 that it would view publication as a waiver of the attorney-client privilege. Von Bulow's counsel responded that no waiver had occurred and that, accordingly, he would not act to stop the book's publication. After the book was released, von Bulow and attorney Dershowitz appeared on several television and radio shows to promote it.

Plaintiff then moved to compel discovery of certain discussions between petitioner and his attorneys based on the alleged waiver of the attorney-client privilege with respect to those communications related in the book. In order to avoid piecemeal rulings on each communication, counsel stipulated in July 1986 as to those controversial subjects appearing in Reversal of Fortune. On February 12, 1987 the United States District Court for the Southern District of New York (Walker, J.) found a waiver of the attorney-client privilege and ordered von Bulow and his attorneys to comply with discovery requested by plaintiff. *Von Bulow By Auersperg v. von Bulow*, 114 F.R.D. 71 (S.D.N.Y.1987).

Von Bulow now petitions this Court for a writ of mandamus directing the district court to vacate its discovery order. Because the relief sought is an extraordinary writ, we consider whether mandamus is an appropriate remedy and, if so, whether it should issue in this case.

DISCUSSION

II The Propriety of the Discovery Order

The district court made several relevant rulings, holding initially that the petitioner waived his attorney-client privilege by acquiescing in and encouraging the publication of Reversal of Fortune. It then examined the scope of that waiver. In so doing, the district judge found that the waiver extended to (1) the contents of the published conversations, (2) all communications between petitioner and attorney Dershowitz relating to the published conversations, and (3) all communications between petitioner and any defense counsel relating to the published conversations. We examine each of these rulings.

A. The Waiver of the Attorney–Client Privilege

By allowing publication of confidential communications in his attorney's book Reversal of Fortune, petitioner was held to have waived his attorney-client privilege. In reaching that conclusion, the district court considered the following facts. First, petitioner knew of, consented to, and actually encouraged attorney Dershowitz's plans to write a book providing an "insider look" into his case. Second, petitioner was warned before publication that such an act might trigger a waiver and, yet, took no active measures to preserve his confidences. Third, after publication, petitioner joined his attorney in enthusiastically promoting the book on television and radio shows. Based on these key facts, the district court determined that von Bulow had waived his attorney-client privilege.

Petitioner argues that this holding is erroneous because only the client—and not his attorney—may waive the privilege. Of course, the privilege belongs solely to the client and may only be waived by him. An attorney may not waive the privilege without his client's consent. Hence, absent a client's consent or waiver, the publication of confidential communications by an attorney does not constitute a relinquishment of the privilege by the client. *See, e.g., Schnell v. Schnall*, 550 F.Supp. 650, 653 (S.D.N.Y.1982) (no waiver of attorney-client privilege where attorney testified at SEC hearing without presence or authorization of client). See also Wigmore, supra, § 2325, at 633 (attorney's voluntary disclosures remain privileged unless impliedly authorized by client).

A client may nonetheless by his actions impliedly waive the privilege or consent to disclosure. And an attorney may, in appropriate circumstances, possess "an implied authority to waive the privilege on behalf of his client." *Drimmer*, 628 F.Supp. at 1251; Wigmore, supra, § 2325. Moreover, it is the client's responsibility to insure continued confidentiality of his communications. In *In re Horowitz*, 482 F.2d 72 (2d Cir.), *cert. denied*, 414 U.S. 867 (1973), Judge Friendly, speaking for the Court, warned: "[i]t is not asking too much to insist that if a client wishes to preserve the privilege under such circumstances, he must take some affirmative action to preserve confidentiality."

Applying these principles, it is quite clear that in finding that von Bulow waived his privilege the district court did not abuse its discretion. In light of petitioner's acquiescence in and encouragement of Reversal of Fortune's publication, Judge Walker properly concluded that von Bulow consented to his attorney's disclosure of his confidences and effectively waived his attorney-client privilege. Our discussion now turns to examine the breadth of that waiver.

B. The Scope of the Waiver

1. The Contents of the Published Conversations

The district court held that plaintiffs were entitled to discover "the entire contents of all conversations from which Dershowitz published extracts in Reversal of Fortune." The four relevant conversations between von Bulow and his attorneys were their initial one, and the ones regarding the bail hearing, appellate strategy, and von Bulow's decision to testify on his own behalf. Under that ruling, plaintiff is permitted to discover those parts of the four identified conversations not made public in the book. Petitioner argues that the district court's holding improperly broadened the fairness doctrine to include extrajudicial disclosures and that, accordingly, the discovery order cannot stand. We agree.

Relying on *United States v. Tellier*, 255 F.2d 441 (2d Cir.), *cert. denied*, 358 U.S. 821 (1958) and *Teachers Insurance & Annuity Association of America v. Shamrock Broadcasting Co.*, 521 F.Supp. 638 (S.D.N.Y.1981), the district judge based his decision on an extension of "[t]he principle that disclosure of a portion of a privileged conversation entitles an adversary to discovery of the matters discussed in the remainder of the conversation. . . . " The court reasoned that where reputation is at stake in a major case, it is tried today before the bar of public opinion, as well as in a courtroom. Judge Walker believed it unfair to permit a party to make use of privileged information as a sword with the public, and then as a shield in the courtroom. Thus, the trial judge found what is generally called a "waiver by implication", see Wigmore, supra, § 2327, at 635, based on fairness considerations.

These considerations—which underlie "the fairness doctrine"—aim to prevent prejudice to a party and distortion of the judicial process that may be caused by the privilege-holder's selective disclosure during litigation of otherwise privileged information. Under the doctrine the client alone controls the privilege and may or may not choose to divulge his own secrets. But it has been established law for a hundred years that when the client waives the privilege by testifying about what transpired between her and her attorney, she cannot thereafter insist that the mouth of the attorney be shut. *Hunt v. Blackburn*, 128 U.S. 464, 470–71 (1888). From that has grown the rule that testimony as to part of a privileged communication, in fairness, requires production of the remainder. McCormick On Evidence § 93, at 194–95 (2d ed. 1972).

Yet this rule protecting the party, the factfinder, and the judicial process from selectively disclosed and potentially misleading evidence does not come into play when, as here, the privilege-holder or his attorney has made extrajudicial disclosures, and those disclosures have not subsequently been placed at issue during litigation. In fact, the cases finding, as the district court did here, implied waivers on account of fairness involved material issues raised by a client's assertions during the course of a judicial proceeding.

Neither of the cases relied upon by the district court compel an opposite result. In *Tellier*, 255 F.2d 441, the government had called the defendant's attorney as its chief witness. The attorney testified to a conversation he had with defendant over the latter's objection. We held the conversation was not privileged because it was not intended to be confidential, but was meant to be passed on to third parties. This is quite different from the case at bar where von Bulow's conversations with attorney

Dershowitz were originally intended to be confidential, and were therefore privileged, at least prior to disclosure. *Teachers Insurance*, 521 F.Supp. 638, is also unsupportive of the district court's conclusion. In that case a party had voluntarily disclosed documents to the SEC that would otherwise have been privileged, and this was held to have waived the privilege. These disclosures made in a trial setting have no application to disclosures in a book made outside a litigation context.

Applying the fairness doctrine, we hold therefore that the extrajudicial disclosure of an attorney-client communication—one not subsequently used by the client in a judicial proceeding to his adversary's prejudice—does not waive the privilege as to the undisclosed portions of the communication. Hence, though the district court correctly found a waiver by von Bulow as to the particular matters actually disclosed in the book, it was an abuse of discretion to broaden that waiver to include those portions of the four identified conversations which, because they were not published, remain secret.[22]

2. Related Conversations With Dershowitz

The district court next ruled that von Bulow's waiver extended to subject matter areas related to the published conversations with Dershowitz.[23] This "subject matter waiver", which allows the attacking party to reach all privileged conversations regarding a particular subject once one privileged conversation on that topic has been disclosed, is simply another form of the waiver by implication rule discussed above. Like the "implied waiver", the subject matter waiver also rests on the fairness considerations at work in the context of litigation. *See Smith*, 538 F.Supp. at 979 ("It would be unfair to allow a client to assert the attorney-client privilege and prevent disclosure of damaging communications while allowing the client to disclose other selected communications solely for self-serving purposes.")

For this reason, it too has been invoked most often where the privilege-holder has attempted to use the privilege as both "a sword" and "a shield" or where the attacking party has been prejudiced at trial.

[22] FN1. Of course, it is conceivable that assertions before trial may mislead or prejudice an adversary at trial and thereby impede the proper functioning of the judicial system. For that reason plaintiff is entitled to attempt to demonstrate in subsequent proceedings that von Bulow's assertion of his attorney-client privilege is misleading or otherwise prejudicial. At such time, the district court may, in its discretion, reevaluate the scope of petitioner's waiver.

[23] FN2. It held that the waiver encompassed the following subject matter areas: (1) the initial meeting between von Bulow and his attorney Dershowitz; (2) the development of new evidence leads; (3) the potential drug use by von Bulow's family members; (4) von Bulow's bail application; (5) appellate strategy; (6) the acceptance of the prosecution's lab results at the first trial; (7) the weaknesses in the prosecution's case; (8) scientific and other investigations undertaken by the defense; (9) whether von Bulow should testify on his own behalf; (10) defendant's life story; (11) defendant's ability to refute the testimony of Maria and Alexander; (12) whether von Bulow placed insulin in the black bag or needle; and (13) likely questions, answers, and jury responses should von Bulow take the stand.

For example, in *Weil v. Investment/Indicators, Research & Management, Inc.*, 647 F.2d 18 (9th Cir.1981), the Ninth Circuit held that the client had waived its attorney-client privilege "only as to communications about the matter actually disclosed" because the disclosure occurred early in the proceedings, was made to opposing counsel rather than to the court, and was not demonstrably prejudicial to other party. Professor Wigmore's formulation of the subject matter waiver rule also contemplates the testimonial use of privileged information in the courtroom:

> The client's offer of his own or the attorney's testimony as to a specific communication to the attorney is a waiver as to all other communications to the attorney on the same matter. Wigmore, supra, § 2327, at 638.

But where, as here, disclosures of privileged information are made extrajudicially and without prejudice to the opposing party, there exists no reason in logic or equity to broaden the waiver beyond those matters actually revealed. Matters actually disclosed in public lose their privileged status because they obviously are no longer confidential. The cat is let out of the bag, so to speak. But related matters not so disclosed remain confidential. Although it is true that disclosures in the public arena may be "one-sided" or "misleading", so long as such disclosures are and remain extrajudicial, there is no legal prejudice that warrants a broad court-imposed subject matter waiver. The reason is that disclosures made in public rather than in court—even if selective—create no risk of legal prejudice until put at issue in the litigation by the privilege-holder. Therefore, insofar as the district court broadened petitioner's waiver to include related conversations on the same subject it was in error.

3. Related Conversations With Other Defense Attorneys

Again invoking the fairness doctrine, the district court found that von Bulow's waiver extended to his conversations with all other defense attorneys which relate to the subject matter disclosed in the book. Since we have already found that the publication of Reversal of Fortune did not result in a sweeping subject matter waiver, that waiver a fortiori cannot extend to von Bulow's other attorneys.

In *Wi-LAN, Inc. v. Kilpatrick Townsend & Stockton LLP*, 684 F.3d 1364 (Fed. Cir. 2012), the Federal Circuit cited *Von Bulow* in holding that the Ninth Circuit likely would apply a fairness balancing test to determine the scope of waiver. The court noted but did not decide the question whether Federal Rule of Evidence 502 applies to disclosures not made in the course of litigation, such as in pre-litigation demands and negotiations.

Selective and Partial Waiver

In *Von Bulow*, the client waived the privilege with respect to communications that were widely distributed in his counsel's book. The question was whether, under the circumstances, the client could waive the privilege with respect to some communications but not others. What if a client discloses privileged communications to a government agency investigating the client's affairs but does not consent to general disclosure of the documents? Could the client claim that the waiver was limited only to the government agency involved, and thus still assert the privilege against third parties, such as another government agency or plaintiffs in a civil action?

The court in *Westinghouse Electric Corporation v. Republic of the Philippines,* 951 F.2d 1414 (3d Cir. 1991), answered "no" to this question. During the administration of President Ferdinand Marcos, Westinghouse obtained a contract to build the Philippines' first nuclear power plant. Several years later, newspaper accounts alleged that Westinghouse obtained the contract by bribing government officials. Westinghouse retained the firm of Kirkland & Ellis to see if its representatives had actually bribed anyone.

Kirkland wrote two letters describing the findings of its investigation. At Westinghouse's request, it showed one of these letters to the Securities and Exchange Commission. Kirkland lawyers also described their findings verbally in meetings with SEC officials. The SEC concluded its investigation in 1983. President Marcos was deposed in 1986. The Justice Department thereafter restarted an old investigation of Westinghouse and a grand jury subpoenaed the Kirkland letters. Westinghouse eventually provided the letters to the Justice Department pursuant to a confidentiality agreement. In 1988, the new Philippine government sued Westinghouse, alleging a variety of misconduct regarding the power plant. The government requested that Westinghouse produce the Kirkland letters. Westinghouse refused, asserting that the letters were protected by the attorney-client privilege and the work-product doctrine.

The trial court rejected the assertion of attorney-client privilege, and the court of appeals affirmed. The court noted that in *Diversified Industries, Inc. v. Meredith,* 572 F.2d 596 (8th Cir.1977), the Eighth Circuit adopted a "limited waiver rule" under which a party in Westinghouse's position waived the privilege only as to the government. The Eight Circuit reasoned that any other rule would deter firms from investigating alleged misbehavior. The *Westinghouse* court disagreed. It argued that "selective waiver does not serve the purpose of encouraging full disclosure to one's attorney in order to obtain informed legal assistance; it merely encourages voluntary disclosure to government agencies, thereby extending the privilege beyond its intended purpose."

In rejecting the Eighth Circuit approach, the court distinguished between "two distinct types of waivers: selective and partial. Selective waiver permits the client who has disclosed privileged communications to one party to continue asserting the privilege against other parties. Partial waiver permits a client who has disclosed a portion of privileged communications to continue asserting the privilege as to the remaining portions of the same communications." The court noted that everyone agrees partial waiver raises concerns of fairness to opposing parties but that there is some disagreement as to whether selective waiver raises such concerns. The court did not rule on the point, but expressed its skepticism that selective waiver raised fairness concerns: "in our view, when a client discloses privileged information to a government agency, the private litigant in subsequent proceedings is no worse off than it would have been had the disclosure to the agency not occurred." For a similar result under California law, *see McKesson HBOC, Inc. v. Superior Court*, 115 Cal.App.4th 1229, 9 Cal.Rptr.3d 812 (2004).

The recently enacted Federal Rule of Evidence 502(a) is largely consistent with this view. It states that disclosure in a federal investigation or proceeding waives privilege with regard to undisclosed communications only if the waiver is intentional, the undisclosed communications pertain to the same subject matter as those disclosed, and fairness requires that the undisclosed and disclosed communications be considered together.

Though the trend is strongly against allowing selective waiver of either attorney-client privilege or work product protection, *United States v. Reyes*, 239 F.R.D. 591 (N.D. Ca. 2006) ("In accord with every appellate court that has considered the issue in the last twenty-five years, this Court holds that Brocade's Audit Committee, and their attorneys . . . cannot waive the attorney-client privilege selectively"), the issue is open in some courts (such as the Ninth Circuit) and a few cases allow selective disclosure. *See In re McKesson HBOC, Inc.*, 2005 WL 946455 (N.D. Cal. 2005).

Most notably, in *Regents of the University of California v. Superior Court*, 165 Cal.App.4th 672, 81 Cal.Rptr.3d 186 (2008), the court interpreted California's Evidence Code § 912, which provides that only disclosure "without coercion" counts as waiver, to allow selective waiver in cases where an enforcement agency offers an entity a break in exchange for cooperation including waiver of the privilege. The court held "the threat of regulatory action and indictment posed the risk of significant costs and consequences to the corporations such that they could cooperate with the Department of Justice's investigation without waiving the privilege."

---

3. DISCLOSURE WITHIN ANOTHER PRIVILEGED RELATIONSHIP

Disclosure of confidential communications generally waives the attorney-client privilege because disclosure is generally inconsistent with the lawyer-client confidentiality the privilege tries to protect. That is not always the case, however. What if a client discloses an attorney-client privileged communication within some other privileged relationship, as to a spouse, minister, or psychotherapist?

The general rule is that disclosure of a privileged communication within the scope of some other privilege is not a waiver. *E.g.* Cal. Evid. Code § 912(c). In *Solomon v. Scientific American, Inc.*, 125 F.R.D. 34 (S.D.N.Y. 1988), for example, a client wrote and sent to his lawyer a memorandum describing the facts regarding his sale of some stock. The client later sued the purchaser, which tried to obtain the memorandum, in part on the ground that the client had waived any privilege by disclosing it to third parties. The court rejected this claim, saying that

> On the record on this motion, the only persons to whom the privileged communication was shown to have been disclosed were plaintiff's wife and another of his attorneys, Mr. Ellis. Neither of those disclosures can be deemed a waiver, since both were consistent with the maintenance of the confidential attorney-client relationship. *See McCormick on Evidence* Sec. 91 (E. Cleary 3d ed. 1984) and cases cited; *see also* Supreme Court Standard 511 to Fed.R.Evid. (waiver not applicable "if the disclosure is itself a privileged communication"), which although not enacted by Congress "continues to have utility as a Standard," 2 J. Weinstein & M. Berger, *Weinstein's Evidence* 511–1 (1986).

One can see the reason for this rule. If your lawyer's advice causes you stress, you might wish to discuss the advice with your minister, spouse, or therapist. Because the rule effectively piggybacks an exception to waiver on other existing privileges, however, it can create distinctions among clients unrelated to the purpose of the rule. For example, a married heterosexual client would not waive the privilege by discussing his attorney's advice with his wife. In most jurisdictions that do not recognize same-sex marriage, a gay or lesbian client would waive the privilege by discussing such advice with his partner, because in most jurisdictions the marital privilege only extends to married persons.[24]

[24] California's Domestic Partner Rights and Responsibilities Act, which states that "registered domestic partners shall have the same rights, protections, and benefits, and shall be subject to the same responsibilities, obligations, and duties under law. . . . as are granted to and imposed upon spouses," presumably extends the privilege and thus this rule to domestic partners.

F. "COMMON INTEREST" EXCEPTION TO WAIVER

Sometimes two or more parties to an action will want to cooperate but will either be unwilling or unable to be represented as joint clients by the same lawyer. This situation commonly arises in criminal practice. Suppose two or more defendants are accused of a crime. They would like to cooperate with each other, to present a coordinated defense, but their interests either actually or potentially conflict. (For example, one defendant might find it advantageous to claim that the other pulled the trigger.)

This situation provides the setting for one of the most familiar exercises in game theory (indeed, in all of social science): the prisoner's dilemma. In this game, two prisoners are arrested for a serious crime. If they cooperate with one another by remaining silent each receives a relatively light penalty, say conviction for a minor crime that can be proved to a certainty. If one prisoner remains silent and the other confesses, the confessor receives no penalty and the silent prisoner receives a heavy one. If both confess, both receive a moderate penalty—higher than nothing but lower than if they had remained silent and been convicted. If the prisoners cannot cooperate, each has an incentive to confess in an effort to escape punishment, leading both to confess and receive a moderate penalty. If they can cooperate, in contrast, they obtain a light punishment.

A simple 2 x 2 diagram illustrates the problem. Payoffs to the row player are listed first; the payoffs represent years in prison, so a low number is better than a high one.

		Column Player	
		Cooperate	Defect
Row Player	Cooperate	1, 1	7, 0
	Defect	0, 7	5, 5

In the first cell (upper left), both defendants remain silent and get a minor penalty. In the second cell (upper right), the row player cooperates by staying silent but the column player defects and gets a break for providing evidence to the government. In the lower left cell, the reverse happens. The fourth cell is the most interesting one. If the players are fully informed each would know that the other would have an incentive to defect and provide evidence to the government in exchange for a deal. If each worried that the other would defect then each would have an incentive to defect first, leading to a worse outcome than cooperation. (Note here that by "worse" outcome we mean worse from the defendants' point of view; the prosecutor probably would see this as the best outcome.)

In this situation, cooperation benefits each defendant. Uncertainty as to whether the other defendant is cooperating might undercut cooperation, however, driving the defendants' outcome from cell one to cell four. A lawyer might facilitate cooperation by assuring each defendant that the other is not defecting.

One way to achieve such a result is for each defendant to hire the same lawyer, who can then take advantage of the joint client rule to facilitate cooperation between the defendants. As we will see in chapter 11.H, however, conflicts of interest may force each defendant to have his own lawyer. The joint client exception would then fall away and a lawyer wanting to facilitate cooperation would face the risk of waiving privilege and leaving her own statements open to discovery.

One way to get around this problem, and allow lawyers to facilitate coordination that might move the defendants from the lower-right cell to the upper-left, is for counsel to enter into what is commonly called a "joint defense agreement." This term is a bit of a misnomer, for it applies when several parties have a common legal interest and its purpose is to create an exception to the rule that disclosure of confidential communications waives the attorney-client privilege with respect to (at least) such communications. The following material discusses this exception in some detail.

In reading the following material, bear in mind that the common interest doctrine differs from joint representation. Joint representation refers to the arrangement whereby one lawyer represents more than one client at the same time and the clients agree to share information. The common interest doctrine does not entail full representation. It does not, for example, impose a traditional duty of loyalty running from a lawyer for *X* to other lawyers' clients who share a common legal interest with *X*. That is one of the main points of the next case. In addition, while in joint representation the common attorney is presumptively obliged to share with each client information material to the joint representation the common interest doctrine imposes no such default. The doctrine prevents a disclosure made within its parameters from counting as waiver of the attorney-client privilege but it creates no presumptive obligation to share information with other parties having a common legal interest.

Restatement of the Law Governing Lawyers § 76

UNITED STATES OF AMERICA V. STEPNEY

246 F. Supp. 2d 1069 (N.D. Cal. 2003)

PATEL, CHIEF JUDGE.

. . . . Defendants are charged with participation in the criminal enterprises of a street gang in the Hunter's Point area of San Francisco. In a series of three indictments, the government has charged a total of nearly thirty defendants with over seventy substantive counts relating to the operation of the gang over a period of several years. The number of defendants and the separate crimes charged render this case extraordinarily factually complex. Defense counsel report that they have already received discovery of over 20,000 pages of police reports, FBI memos, and other law enforcement materials.

In an effort to prepare coherent defenses efficiently, various defense counsel have sought to enter into joint defense agreements that would allow defendants to share factual investigations and legal work product. Out of concern for the Sixth Amendment rights of the defendants and the integrity of the proceedings, at the parties' initial appearance on October 15, 2001, the court ordered that any joint defense agreements be committed to writing and provided to the court for *in camera* review. No joint defense agreements were ever filed with the court pursuant to this order.

More than a year after the court's initial order, the attorney for one defendant moved to withdraw his representation on the grounds that he had entered into a joint defense agreement with another defendant who he had since come to believe was cooperating with the prosecution. Although the attorney seeking to withdraw did not believe that he had obtained confidential information from the cooperating defendant, he did believe that the joint defense agreement had created an implied attorney-client relationship that included a duty of loyalty. The attorney maintained that this duty of loyalty would prevent him from cross-examining the cooperating defendant, should he testify at trial.

The court denied the motion to withdraw after conducting a colloquy in which the cooperating defendant waived any attorney-client privilege with respect to information received by the moving attorney. The court also ruled that joint defense agreements do not create in one attorney a duty of loyalty toward the defendant with whom he collaborates. In an order dated November 22, 2002, the court set forth requirements that future joint defense agreements: (1) be in writing; (2) contain a full description of the extent of the privilege shared; (3) contain workable withdrawal provisions; and (4) be signed not only by the attorneys but also by the clients who hold the privileges at issue. . . .

DISCUSSION

I. *The Joint Defense Privilege Generally*

The joint defense privilege is commonly described as an extension of the attorney-client privilege. . . . Scholarly commentators have uniformly argued that the joint defense privilege differs sufficiently from the attorney-client privilege in both purpose and scope that the two should be viewed as entirely separate doctrines. . . . To inform the analysis of the proposed joint defense agreements, the court must first examine in detail the nature of the joint defense privilege.

1. *Protections for Attorney–Client Communications*

The attorney-client privilege limits only the power of a court to compel disclosure of attorney-client communications or otherwise admit the communications themselves into evidence. Outside the courtroom, the privilege does not provide grounds for sanctioning an attorney's voluntary disclosure of confidential communications to third parties. This is not to say that attorneys may freely reveal their clients' confidences should they so desire. Mechanisms other than the attorney-client privilege protect against voluntary disclosure of confidential communications by counsel. The ethical rules governing attorneys require that all information pertaining to a client's case be kept confidential. The comment to Model Rule of 1.6 discusses the relationship between the attorney-client privilege and the ethical duty of confidentiality:

> The principle of confidentiality is given effect in two related bodies of law, the attorney-client privilege (which includes the work product doctrine) in the law of evidence and the rule of confidentiality established in professional ethics. The attorney-client privilege applies in judicial and other proceedings in which a lawyer may be called as a witness or otherwise required to produce evidence concerning a client. The rule of client-lawyer confidentiality applies in situations other than those where evidence is sought from the lawyer through compulsion of law. The confidentiality rule applies not merely to matters communicated in confidence by the client but also to all information relating to the representation, whatever its source.

Id., R. 1.6 cmt. The ethical duty of confidentiality may be enforced by more than just sanctions against an offending attorney. In a criminal case, where an attorney violates this ethical duty by revealing a client's confidences to the government, a court may suppress the resulting evidence. Prosecutors may also be subject to sanctions where they have induced an attorney to violate her duty of confidentiality. Model Rules of Prof'l Conduct, R. 8.4(a).

In criminal cases, the Constitution also protects confidential attorney-client communications from the eyes and ears of the government. An intrusion by the government into an attorney-client relationship in order to obtain confidential information may be deemed a violation of a defendant's Sixth Amendment right to effective assistance of counsel or Fifth Amendment due process rights. In such a situation, a court may suppress evidence gathered as a result of the communication or, in egregious cases where the prejudice cannot otherwise be cured, dismiss the indictment.

These three doctrines—the evidentiary rule of attorney-client privilege, the ethical duty of confidentiality imposed on attorneys, and the ethical and constitutional requirements that the government not intrude upon the attorney-client relationship—serve the common end of keeping communications between attorney and client from disclosure either to adversaries or the finder of fact, thus encouraging the full and frank communications between attorney and client that are required for the adversarial system to function.

2. *The Evolution of the Joint Defense Privilege*

The joint defense privilege initially arose as an extension of the attorney-client privilege against court-ordered disclosure against confidential communications. Ordinarily, the attorney-client privilege will be deemed waived where a client discloses the contents of an otherwise privileged communication to a third party or where the communication occurs in the presence of third parties. . . . The joint defense privilege was adopted as an exception to this waiver rule, under which communications between a client and his own lawyer remain protected by the attorney-client privilege when disclosed to co-defendants or their counsel for purposes of a common defense.

Although established as an evidentiary rule which bound courts from compelling disclosure of certain evidence, the joint defense privilege was soon applied as an ethical doctrine which imposed on counsel a limited duty of confidentiality toward their client's co-defendants regarding information obtained in furtherance of a common defense.[25] In particular, courts have ruled that an attorney may be disqualified if her client's interests require that she cross-examine (or oppose in a subsequent action) another member of a joint defense agreement about whom she has learned confidential information.

In the first case to raise the issue, *Wilson P. Abraham Constr. Corp. v. Armco Steel Corp.,* 559 F.2d 250, 253 (5th Cir.1977), the Fifth Circuit addressed a motion to disqualify plaintiff's counsel brought by defendants in a civil antitrust action. In a prior criminal action against various steel mills for price fixing in which Armco had been charged, plaintiff's attor-

[25] FN2. Although courts have declared that attorneys operating under a joint defense agreement owe defendants other than their clients a limited duty of confidentiality, the ABA Committee on Ethics & Professional Responsibility has opined that the Model Rules of Professional Conduct do not impose such duties on an attorney. ABA Comm. on Ethics & Prof'l Responsibility, Formal Op. 395 (1995). The Committee nonetheless noted that courts had recognized an attorney's "fiduciary obligation" to other members of a joint defense agreement that could create a disqualifying conflict of interest. *Id.*

ney had represented another steel company also named as a defendant. In this capacity, he had conferred with representatives of other indicted companies, including Armco, at meetings designed to develop a joint defense. In its motion, Armco maintained that the attorney's obligation to maintain the confidences learned through the previous joint defense effort conflicted with his client's present interests and warranted his disqualification. The Fifth circuit agreed, finding:

> Just as an attorney would not be allowed to proceed against his former client in a cause of action substantially related to the matters in which he previously represented that client, an attorney should also not be allowed to proceed against a co-defendant of a former client wherein the subject matter of the present controversy is substantially related to the matters in which the attorney was previously involved, and wherein confidential exchanges of information took place between the various co-defendants in preparation of a joint defense.

Id. at 253.

Despite the analogy to attorney-client relationships, the *Abraham Construction* court did not treat the attorney's participation in a joint defense agreement as identical to formal representation of a client. Had plaintiff's attorney actually represented Armco, he would have been disqualified automatically on the irrebuttable presumption that he had gained confidences during the prior representation on a related matter. . . . Finding that there had been "no direct attorney-client relationship," the court refused to presume that plaintiff's attorney had obtained confidential information in the course of the joint defense. The court instead placed the burden on the party moving for disqualification to prove that the plaintiff's attorney had actually been privy to confidential information. *Abraham Constr.*, 559 F.2d at 253.

Subsequent courts have followed suit in requiring a showing that the attorney actually obtained confidences before disqualifying counsel. While a joint defense agreement does impose a duty of confidentiality, that duty is limited in that the showing required to establish a conflict of interest arising from prior participation in a joint defense agreement is significantly higher than that required to make out a conflict based on former representation of a client.

Finally, a few courts have assumed that the prosecution in a criminal case could violate a defendant's constitutional rights by receiving information from cooperating co-defendants (or their attorneys) that was obtained through a joint defense agreement.

II. *The Court's Power to Inquire into Joint Defense Agreements*

As a threshold matter, defendants object to the court's inquiries into joint defense agreements prior to any controversy arising that would require such disclosure. Defendants assert that there is no authority for requiring advance disclosure of joint defense agreements and that such disclosures inhibit their ability to represent their clients effectively. Defendants also object to the court's requirement that the joint defense agreements be committed to writing. The court therefore begins by addressing how its inherent supervisory powers permit inquiry into the circumstances of representation and imposition of procedural requirements on joint defense agreements in order to safeguard defendants' Sixth Amendment rights to conflict-free counsel.

"Under their supervisory power, courts have substantial authority to oversee their own affairs to ensure that justice is done." *United States v. Simpson,* 927 F.2d 1088, 1089 (9th Cir.1991). A court may exercise its supervisory powers to implement a remedy for the violation of a recognized statutory or constitutional right, or may take preemptive steps to avoid such violations by imposing procedural rules not specifically required by the Constitution or Congress. *United States v. Hasting,* 461 U.S. 499, 505 (1983); *Simpson,* 927 F.2d at 1090.

These supervisory powers unquestionably allow courts to require disclosure of the precise nature of a criminal defendant's representation to ensure that no conflict of interest exists that would deprive a defendant of his Sixth Amendment right to effective assistance of counsel. Courts have routinely intervened—prior to any controversy arising—where the circumstances of a criminal defendant's representation raises the potential for conflict of interest during the course of the proceedings, even before intervention is required by statutory or constitutional rule. . . .

As discussed above, joint defense agreements impose an ethical duty of confidentiality on participating attorneys, presenting the potential for conflicts of interest that might lead to the withdrawal or disqualification of a defense attorney late in the proceedings or the reversal of conviction on appeal. *See, e.g., United States v. Henke,* 222 F.3d 633, 643 (9th Cir.2000) (reversing defendants' convictions where trial court improperly denied defense counsel's motion to withdraw on the eve of trial). When a party to a joint defense agreement decides to cooperate with the government, the potential for disclosure of confidential information also threatens other defendants' Sixth Amendment rights. "Federal courts have an independent interest in ensuring that criminal trials are conducted within the ethical standards of the profession and that legal proceedings appear fair to all who observe them." *Wheat v. United States,* 486 U.S. 153, 160 (1988). Courts also "[have] an independent interest in protecting a fairly-rendered verdict from trial tactics that may be designed to generate issues on appeal." *United States v. Moscony,* 927 F.2d 742 (3d Cir.), *cert. denied,* 501 U.S. 1211 (1991). Given the high potential for mischief, courts are well justified in inquiring into joint defense agreements before problems arise.

The present case appears particularly likely to lead to conflicts caused by cooperation between defendants. Here, there are a large number of defendants, some of whom may not have known each other prior to their first appearance before this court. The charges span a variety of incidents over several distinct periods of time and allege roles of varying degrees of culpability. The interests of any two defendants are less likely to coincide precisely than in the case of two defendants accused of essentially equal participation in a single crime.[26] Where defendants do not have cohesive interests, the potential for conflict is, by definition, greater—as is the potential for cooperating with the government.

In addition to the lack of cohesion obvious from the face of the indictment, the unfolding of the present proceedings has provided further evidence that the defendants' interests are not generally united. A significant number of the defendants in this case have in fact entered guilty pleas and cooperated with the government. One of the cooperating defendants has been murdered and another has received threats. Whether or not these actions can be attributed to any defendants in this case, they have proven intimidating to other defendants seeking to plead guilty or cooperate with the government. These circumstances illustrate that defendants interests are not cohesive, indicating a far greater likelihood of conflict than in a case with fewer defendants and a more unified defense.

The threat that these agreements might pose to defendants' Sixth Amendment rights—and to the integrity of the proceedings—warrants the minimal disclosures that the court has thus far required and the restrictions imposed by this court. The court appreciates defendants' concern that disclosing who among them have signed a joint defense agreement might give the government insight into the trial strategies of various defendants. Defendants have not, however, asserted any legal grounds to prevent disclosure of joint defense agreements to the court. To the extent that joint defense agreements simply set forth the existence of attorney-client relationships—implied or otherwise—between various attorneys and defendants, the contents of such agreements do not fall within the attorney-client privilege. The court has nonetheless conducted its inquiry into joint defense agreements *in camera* in order to avoid offering the prosecution any hint of defense strategies.

Once disclosed to the court, a joint defense agreement may indicate a potential for future conflicts of interest that warrants further action. The present case certainly calls for inquiry.[27] As set forth below, the proposed

---

[26] FN3. This difference of interests between defendants is, in fact, likely to lead to the choice of separate representation with a joint defense agreement rather than joint representation.

[27] FN4. The joint defense agreements presented to this court may even create the type of representation on which the court must act under Federal Rule of Criminal Procedure 44(c). Rule 44(c)(2) requires that a federal court take active measures to safeguard defendants' Sixth Amendment rights when defendants jointly charged in a criminal indictment "are represented by the same counsel." Fed.R.Crim.P. 44(c)(1)(B), (2). While each of the jointly charged defendants in

joint defense agreement has heightened the court's concern that potential conflicts might arise in this particular case, or that the defendants have been substantially misinformed of their rights under the joint defense privilege. The court now turns to these areas of concern.

III. *Problems with the Proposed Joint Defense Agreements*

The proposed Joint Defense Agreement submitted by counsel contemplates "open and candid exchange of investigation leads and legal theories of defense." The agreement suggests that any defendant who is a party to the case will "meet to discuss the case and . . . candidly and openly address all charges and possible defenses." It provides in unqualified terms that "all counsel who sign this agreement will owe all defendants who sign this agreement a duty of confidentiality." It also provides that each attorney will owe each defendant a duty of loyalty. The agreement notes that individuals may withdraw from the agreement by notifying all remaining members, but that withdrawal does not relieve a party of the duties created by the agreement.

The proposed agreement submitted by defendants is problematic in at least two material respects. First, the proposed agreement purports to create a duty of loyalty on the part of signing attorneys that extends to all signing defendants. The proposed defense agreement also does not contain workable withdrawal provisions that adequately avoid the possibility of disqualification on the eve of trial, or even during trial.

A. *Ethical Obligations Imposed by the Privilege*

The proposed joint defense agreement explicitly imposes on signing attorneys not only a duty of confidentiality, but a separate general duty of loyalty to all signing defendants. Such a duty has no foundation in law and, if recognized, would offer little chance of a trial unmarred by conflict of interest and disqualification.

Joint defense agreements are not contracts which create whatever rights the signatories chose, but are written notice of defendants' invocation of privileges set forth in common law.[28] Joint defense agreements

---

the present case has his or her own separate attorney, the proposed joint defense agreement presented to this court purports to impose on *each* attorney duties of loyalty and confidentiality toward *each* defendant. As discussed below, the court finds little to distinguish this form of representation from multiple representation of all defendants who sign the agreement by a single team composed of all the attorneys—a situation in which this court would be obliged by statute to "take appropriate measures to protect each defendant's right to counsel" unless there is good cause to believe that no conflict of interest is likely to arise. Fed.R.Crim.P. 44(c)(2).

[28] FN5. No written agreement is generally required to invoke the joint defense privilege. The existence of a writing does establish that defendants are collaborating, thus guarding against a possible finding that a particular communication was made spontaneously rather than pursuant to a joint defense effort. *See United States v. Weissman,* 195 F.3d 96, 98–99 (2d Cir.1999) (finding no joint defense agreement in place at the time communication took place). A written joint defense agreement also protects against misunderstandings and varying accounts of what was agreed to by the attorneys and their clients.

therefore cannot extend greater protections than the legal privileges on which they rest. A joint defense agreement which purports to do so does not accurately set forth the protections which would be given to defendants who sign. In the present case, unless the joint defense privilege recognized in this Circuit imposes a duty of loyalty on attorneys who are parties to a joint defense agreement, the duty of loyalty set forth in the proposed agreement would have no effect other than misinforming defendants of the actual scope of their rights.

Courts have consistently viewed the obligations created by joint defense agreements as distinct from those created by actual attorney-client relationships.[29] As discussed above, courts have also consistently ruled that where an attorney represents a client whose interests diverge from a party with whom the attorney has previously participated in a joint defense agreement, no conflict of interest arises unless the attorney actually obtained relevant confidential information. This position is inconsistent with a general duty of loyalty owed to former clients, which would automatically preclude an attorney from subsequently representing a client with an adverse interest. Model Rules of Prof'l Conduct, R. 1.9.

To support the proposed imposition of a general duty of loyalty, defendants rely exclusively on the Ninth Circuit's opinion in *United States v. Henke,* 222 F.3d 633 (9th Cir.2000) (per curiam), which states that a joint defense agreement "establishes an implied attorney-client relationship with the co-defendant," *id.* at 637. Defendants' argument rests on the conclusion that by referring to an "implied attorney-client relationship," the Ninth Circuit implicitly expanded the joint defense privilege beyond the recognized protection against disclosure of confidential information learned through a joint defense agreement to impose on each attorney an

[29] FN6. Several courts have drawn parallels between joint defense agreements and the attorney-client relationship in passing prefatory remarks, rather than as legal conclusions drawn after thorough analysis of the scope of each relationship and the precise nature of the ethical duties involved. Bartel, *supra,* at 901. These statements should not be taken out of context, but must be examined in light of the issues decided by the particular court. Individual courts have recognized that the two types of relationships create privileges which are similar in some respects and different in others. The *Abraham Construction* court, for example, stated that in a joint defense arrangement, "the counsel of each defendant is, in effect, the counsel of all for the purposes of invoking the attorney-client privilege in order to shield mutually shared confidences." *Abraham Constr.,* 559 F.2d at 253. In the following paragraph, however, the court distinguished between the two types of relationships in holding that for parties to a joint defense agreement, "there is no presumption that confidential information was exchanged as there was no direct attorney-client relationship." *Id.*

In particular, an analogy between joint defense agreements and attorney-client relationships in the context of the evidentiary attorney-client privilege does not necessarily hold where the ethical obligations imposed by joint defense agreements are at issue. The Seventh Circuit, in upholding the district court's exclusion of a defendant's statements to a co-defendant's legal investigator pursuant to the attorney-client privilege, made the sweeping statement, "The attorney who thus undertakes to serve his client's co-defendant for a limited purpose becomes the co-defendant's attorney for that purpose." *United States v. McPartlin,* 595 F.2d 1321, 1337 (7th Cir.), *cert. denied,* 444 U.S. 833 (1979). In light of the narrow evidentiary issue before that court, the court does not read *McPartlin* to pass on whether joint defense relationships entail the full ethical obligations of the attorney-client relationship.

additional general duty of loyalty to her client's co-defendants. Defendants have cited no legal authority suggesting that joint defense agreements entail a duty of loyalty.

In *Henke,* three co-defendants participated in joint defense meetings in which confidential information was discussed. On the eve of trial, one defendant pleaded guilty and agreed to testify for the government. Counsel for the other two defendants each moved to withdraw on the grounds that the duty of confidentiality prevented them from cross-examining the former co-defendant and impeaching him with prior statements made in confidence. The cooperating co-defendant filed papers expressly stating that he did not waive the attorney-client privilege and would take legal action if the remaining defense counsel disclosed confidential information, even in an *ex parte* motion to withdraw.

The conflict addressed by the *Henke* court resulted from the attorney's duty to protect specific confidential information revealed during the course of a joint defense meeting, not from a broader duty of loyalty owed to the cooperating witness. Although the *Henke* court referred to joint defense agreements in terms of an "implied attorney-client relationship," the court's analysis focused exclusively on confidential information. Accepting that the cooperating witness had made statements at joint defense meetings which would contradict his testimony, the court noted that the remaining defense attorneys could neither introduce those statements nor seek out further evidence to support those statements without using the witness's confidences against him. In finding a conflict, the court did not rest on the attorneys' adverse position to the former party to the joint defense agreement, but relied instead on the fact that the defense attorneys would use or divulge specific pieces of privileged information.

Admittedly, there is a significant difference between the disclosure of confidential information and the use of confidential information without disclosure. Both the common law doctrine of attorney-client privilege and the ethical duty of confidentiality address only the disclosure of confidential information and not the use of confidential information, without disclosure, in a manner adverse to the client's interests. *See* 8 Wigmore, Evidence § 2292 (attorney-client privilege); Model Rules of Prof'l Conduct, R. 1.6 (duty of confidentiality). Any obligation on the part of an attorney not to use confidential information against a client arises from separate duties. *See* ABA Model Rules of Prof'l Conduct, R. 1.9(c) ("A lawyer who has formerly represented a client in a matter . . . shall not thereafter (1) use information relating to the representation to the disadvantage of the client. . . . "). An attorney might use information gained in confidence to structure an investigation for facts with which she could discredit the cooperating witness without ever disclosing the information and running afoul of either the attorney-client privilege or the duty of confidentiality.

The *Henke* court suggests that the duty to protect confidential information divulged under a joint defense agreement may extend beyond the duty not to disclose and include a duty not to use the information gained in a manner adverse to the interests of the client. *See, e.g. Henke,* 222 F.3d at 637–38 ("Had [the attorneys] pursued the material discrepancy in some other way, a discrepancy they learned about in confidence, they could have been charged with using it against their one-time client. . . . ").[30] This position is entirely consistent with the rule for disqualification established in *Abraham Construction* and followed by other courts: disqualification is proper where a party seeking disqualification can show that an attorney for another defendant actually obtained relevant confidential information through a joint defense agreement. Indeed, the *Henke* court unambiguously adopted the standard set forth in *Abraham Construction* by quoting that decision at length. *See Henke,* 222 F.3d at 637 (quoting *Abraham Constr.,* 559 F.2d at 253).

For the *Henke* court, a conflict of interest only arose where the attorney possessed relevant confidential information. Even the possession of some confidential information by an attorney would not require disqualification unless the defense of her client required disclosure or use of that information:

> There may be cases in which defense counsel's possession of information about a former co-defendant/government witness learned through joint defense meetings will not impair defense counsel's ability to represent the defendant or breach the duty of confidentiality to the former co-defendant. Here, however, counsel told the district court that this was not a situation where they could avoid reliance on the privileged information and still fully uphold their ethical duty to represent their clients.

---

[30] FN7. Defendants also assert in the joint defense agreement that any duty of confidentiality includes a duty of loyalty, relying on the Ninth Circuit's pronouncement in *Damron v. Herzog* that "it is anomalous to find that the duty of confidentiality does not have as its direct correlation a duty of loyalty." 67 F.3d 211, 215 (9th Cir.1995), *cert. denied,* 516 U.S. 1117 (1996) (citations omitted). Defendants apparently read this language to imply that whenever an attorney is under a duty of confidentiality to an individual, she is also under a general duty of loyalty.

When the above language is placed in context, however, it is clear that the *Damron* court referred to a far more limited duty. The court simply echoed the rule embraced by *Henke* and *Abraham Construction* that the law does not trust an attorney who actually possesses relevant confidences to proceed without using or disclosing them:

> Damron argues that Herzog's advice to the Wheatleys necessarily involved decisions based on confidential information, which inevitably created the risk of a breach.
>
> We agree that when an attorney engages in a conflict of interest on the same matter, he or she is in a position to act on the confidential information learned from the relationship with the first client, whether or not that information is actually disclosed or acted upon in advising the new client. Because this position creates such a grave risk of breach of confidence, it is anomalous to find that the duty of confidentiality does not have as its direct correlation a duty of loyalty.

Damron, 67 F.3d at 215 (citations omitted). Because the correlative "duty of loyalty" referred by the *Damron* court would not arise unless the attorney actually possessed confidential information, it is distinct from the general duty of loyalty owed former clients.

Henke, 222 F.3d at 638.

In distinguishing cases based on reliance on protected information, the *Henke* court specifically noted that joint defense meetings in and of themselves are not disqualifying. This refusal to extend a *per se* rule would not be possible if a general duty of loyalty existed to a cooperating former co-defendant, because the interests of the testifying witness in co-operating effectively would always be adverse to the interests of the remaining defendants in preventing or minimizing the witness's testimony.

Finally, the court notes that the cases on which the *Henke* court relied to reach its conclusion do not suggest a general duty of loyalty or a full attorney-client relationship between an attorney and all co-defendants who are party to a joint defense agreement. These cases address only whether the protections for confidential information are waived when the information is shared with co-defendants or their counsel who are parties to a joint defense arrangement. . . . The court finds no cases recognizing joint defense agreements as creating either a true attorney-client relationship or a general duty of loyalty.

There is good reason for the law to refrain from imposing on attorneys a duty of loyalty to their clients' co-defendants. A duty of loyalty between parties to a joint defense agreement would create a minefield of potential conflicts. Should any defendant that signed the agreement decide to cooperate with the government and testify in the prosecution's case-in-chief, an attorney for a non-cooperating defendant would be put in the position of cross-examining a witness to whom she owed a duty of loyalty on behalf of her own client, to whom she also would owe a duty of loyalty. This would create a conflict of interest which would require withdrawal. . . . Thus, the existence of a duty of loyalty would require that the attorneys for *all* noncooperating defendants withdraw from the case in the event that any *one* participating defendant decided to testify for the government.

A duty of loyalty would even require withdrawal where a defendant sought to put on a defense that in any way conflicted with the defenses of the other defendants participating in a joint defense agreement. An attorney with a duty of loyalty to defendants other than her client could not shift blame to other defendants or introduce any evidence which undercut their defenses. Nor could an attorney cross-examine a defendant who testified on his own behalf.

As these scenarios illustrate, a joint defense agreement that imposes a duty of loyalty to all members of the joint defense agreement eliminates the utility of employing separate counsel for each defendant and (for purposes of conflict analysis) effectively creates a situation in which all signing defendants are represented jointly by a team of all signing attorneys. The court certainly could not permit joint representation of defendants with such disjointed interests as those in the present case. Fed.R.Crim.P. 44(c)(2).

Disqualification of attorneys late in the proceedings benefits no one—it deprives defendants of counsel whom they know and trust and perhaps even chose; it forces delays while new counsel become acquainted with the case, which harm defendants, the prosecution, and the court. In the present case, where certain attorneys have acted as lead counsel for large groups of defendants on major issues, disqualification could prejudice all defendants, not simply those who are parties to the joint defense agreement. The potential for disqualification arising from joint defense agreements can be "used as a weapon in the hands of aggressive prosecutors" that discourages formation of the agreements. To avoid these problems, many defense attorneys draft joint defense agreements that explicitly disclaim any attempt to create an attorney-client relationship. [Craig S. Lerner, *Conspirators' Privilege and Innocents' Refuge: A New Approach to Joint Defense Agreements*, 77 Notre Dame L. Rev. 1449, 1507–08 & n. 246 (2002)]; Joint Defense Agreement, Am. Law Institute—Am. Bar Ass'n, Trial Evidence in the Federal Courts: Problems and Solutions, at 35 (1999) (providing that the agreement should not be read "to create an attorney-client relationship between any attorney and anyone other than the client of that attorney").

Because neither precedent nor sound policy supports imposing on attorneys who sign a joint defense agreement a general duty of loyalty to all participating defendants, the court finds the provisions of the proposed Joint Defense Agreement that purport to create a duty of loyalty unacceptable. Should defendants wish to enter into representation in which attorneys owe multiple defendants a general duty of loyalty, they would need to obtain approval of the court pursuant to Federal Rule of Criminal Procedure 44(c)(2).

B. *Withdrawal Provisions*

The proposed joint defense agreement provides that any member may withdraw from the agreement by giving notice to all other members. At the hearing on the proposed agreements, defense counsel suggested that signing defendants were willing accept the risk of conflict created by a withdrawing defendant by accepting the risk that counsel might be disqualified. Ordinarily, defendants seeking to enter into representation which holds potential conflicts of interest accept risks by waiving their rights to assert the conflict, rather than by steeling themselves to assert it as defense counsel suggests. The situation created by the joint defense agreement is no exception.

A first question arising as to the nature of an appropriate waiver is at what point in the proceedings defendants should waive their rights in order to avoid conflicts. Given the highly divergent interests of defendants in the present case, the court is entitled to require that waiver provisions be included in the joint defense agreement, so that defendants who participate are fully apprised of the potential for conflict and understand the consequences both of entering into the joint defense agreement and of withdrawing from it. The alternative—deferring action on waiver until one defendant decides to testify—fails to avoid the danger of disqualification entirely.

A second and more complicated question is what sort of waiver provisions would avoid the threat of conflict while adequately protecting defendants' right to cooperate on a joint defense. Defendants could conceivably waive potential conflicts through provisions in the joint defense agreement in one of two ways. One court has allowed defendants to waive potential conflict by agreeing in advance that no attorney will use any information obtained by reason of the confidentiality in cross-examining defendants. *United States v. Anderson,* 790 F.Supp. 231, 232 (W.D.Wash.1992). This method of waiving conflict, however, stands in tension with the general principle that where an attorney has actually obtained confidential information relevant to her representation of a client, the law presumes that she cannot avoid relying on the information—however indirectly or unintentionally—in forming legal advice and trial strategy. *See Henke,* 222 F.3d at 637–38 ("Had [the attorneys] pursued the material discrepancy in some other way, a discrepancy they learned about in confidence, they could have been charged with using it against their one-time client. . . . "). Because the cross-examining attorney still holds relevant confidences of the witness, it is not clear that she can truly operate free from conflict. The solution also compromises one defendant's right to a fully zealous attorney for another defendant's decision to testify. The waiver is less informed, as each defendant must waive the right to use the others' confidences before knowing what those confidences are.

The better form of waiver is suggested by the American Law Institute–American Bar Association in their model joint defense agreement, which provides:

> Nothing contained herein shall be deemed to create an attorney-client relationship between any attorney and anyone other than the client of that attorney and the fact that any attorney has entered this Agreement shall not be used as a basis for seeking to disqualify any counsel from representing any other party in this or any other proceeding; and no attorney who has entered into this Agreement shall be disqualified from examining or cross-examining any client who testifies at any proceeding, whether under a grant of immunity or otherwise, because of such attorney's participation in this Agreement; and the signatories and their clients further agree that a signatory attorney examining or cross-examining any client who testifies at any proceeding, whether under a grant of immunity or otherwise, may use any Defense Material or other information contributed

> by such client during the joint defense; and it is herein represented that each undersigned counsel to this Agreement has specifically advised his or her respective client of this clause and that such client has agreed to its provisions.

Joint Defense Agreement, Am. Law Institute—Am. Bar Ass'n, Trial Evidence in the Federal Courts: Problems and Solutions, at 35 (1999). Under this regime, all defendants have waived any duty of confidentiality for purposes of cross-examining testifying defendants, and generally an attorney can cross-examine using any and all materials, free from any conflicts of interest. This form of waiver also places the loss of the benefits of the joint defense agreement only on the defendant who makes the choice to testify. Defendants who testify for the government under a grant of immunity lose nothing by this waiver. Those that testify on their own behalf have already made the decision to waive their Fifth Amendment right against self-incrimination and to admit evidence through their cross-examination that would otherwise be inadmissible.

The conditional waiver of confidentiality also provides notice to defendants that their confidences may be used in cross-examination, so that each defendant can choose with suitable caution what to reveal to the joint defense group. Although a limitation on confidentiality between a defendant and his own attorney would pose a severe threat to the true attorney-client relationship, making each defendant somewhat more guarded about the disclosures he makes to the joint defense effort does not significantly intrude on the function of joint defense agreements. The attorney-client privilege protects "full and frank" communication because the attorney serves as the client's liaison to the legal system. Without a skilled attorney, fully apprised of her client's situation, our adversarial system could not function. Any secret a client keeps from his own counsel compromises his counsel's ability to represent him effectively and undermines the purpose of the attorney-client privilege.

Joint defense agreements, however, serve a different purpose. Each defendant entering a joint defense agreement already has a representative, fully and confidentially informed of the client's situation. The joint defense privilege allows defendants to share information so as to avoid unnecessarily inconsistent defenses that undermine the credibility of the defense as a whole. In criminal cases where discovery is limited, such collaboration is necessary to assure a fair trial in the face of the prosecution's informational advantage gained through the power to gather evidence by searches and seizures. Co-defendants may eliminate inconsistent defenses without the same degree of disclosure that would be required for an attorney to adequately represent her client. The legitimate value of joint defense agreements will not be significantly diminished by including a limited waiver of confidentiality by testifying defendants for purposes of cross-examination only.

CONCLUSION

For the foregoing reasons, the Court rules as follows:

(1) Any joint defense agreement entered into by defendants must be committed to writing, signed by defendants and their attorneys, and submitted *in camera* to the court for review prior to going into effect.

(2) Each joint defense agreement submitted must explicitly state that it does not create an attorney-client relationship between an attorney and any defendant other than the client of that attorney. No joint defense agreement may purport to create a duty of loyalty.

(3) Each joint defense agreement must contain provisions conditionally waiving confidentiality by providing that a signatory attorney cross-examining any defendant who testifies at any proceeding, whether under a grant of immunity or otherwise, may use any material or other information contributed by such client during the joint defense.

(4) Each joint defense agreement must explicitly allow withdrawal upon notice to the other defendants.

IT IS SO ORDERED.

CASE QUESTIONS

1. Is there a "joint defense privilege?"
2. How does a joint defense agreement (JDA) relate to rules of evidence?
3. How can a JDA create a conflict of interest?
4. What duties does a lawyer for one client in a JDA owe another client who discloses information subject to the JDA?
5. Suppose one client who is part of a JDA cooperates with the government at trial of another, non-cooperating JDA client. May the lawyer for the non-cooperating client use confidential information disclosed by the cooperating client to cross-examine that client? May such a lawyer disclose such information?
6. Does a prosecutor need to worry about improper disclosure from cooperating JDA clients? Why or why not?

Stepney is the most comprehensive opinion regarding joint defense agreements, but it is not clear how authoritative it is. For one thing, the opinion quotes language from the Ninth Circuit's opinion in *United States v. Henke,* 222 F.3d 633, 637 (9th Cir.2000) (per curiam), which (as Judge

Patel noted) states a joint defense agreement "establishes an implied attorney-client relationship with the co-defendant." A district judge has no power to correct a circuit court decision, and the Ninth Circuit may believe it meant what it said in *Henke*, rather than treating this language as loose dicta, as *Stepney* arguably does. And *Stepney* is a criminal case, in which conflicts of interest may raise problems of ineffective assistance of counsel that could force retrials every district judge would be keen to avoid. (chapter 7 discusses the relationship between conflicts and ineffective assistance of counsel). These should be considered open questions, but the analysis of *Stepney* is correct.

There is some reason to believe other courts will find *Stepney* persuasive. *United States v. Almeida*, 341 F.3d 1318 (11th Cir. 2003), is consistent with Judge Patel's analysis. Almeida was indicted for conspiring to distribute cocaine. One alleged co-conspirator was Ludwig "Tarzan" Fainberg. Almeida and Fainberg initially agreed to coordinate their defense, and their respective attorneys entered into an oral joint defense agreement. Over a two-year period, the parties worked extensively under this agreement, and shared much information. Fainberg changed his mind and pleaded guilty, however. As part of his plea, he agreed to cooperate with the government and testify against Almeida.

At trial, the government argued that Fainberg enjoyed an attorney-client privilege with respect to discussions with Almeida's counsel. The government claimed Almeida's attorney effectively represented both Almeida and Fainberg, and therefore suffered from a conflict of interest. The government asked the court to prohibit Almeida's counsel "from using any confidential information they had obtained from Fainberg during the two years in which the joint defense privilege was in operation" and to either obtain a conflict waiver from Almeida or disqualify his counsel from cross-examining Fainberg.

The trial court "found that a joint defense agreement existed and concluded that this agreement precluded Almeida's counsel from using any information obtained from Fainberg in connection with the joint defense." The court barred Almeida's lawyer from cross examining Fainberg based on Fainberg's communications or information derived from those communications. (The court did not require that Almeida get new counsel, however, nor did it rule that his original counsel had a conflict of interest.) Almeida was convicted of one count of conspiring to distribute cocaine.

After his conviction, Almeida obtained a privilege waiver from Fainberg. He then took Fainberg's deposition. At the deposition, Fainberg denied "conspiring with Almeida. . . . claimed that Almeida was 'not guilty' of the charges and that the Government concocted a case based upon Fainberg's 'macho talk' that 'nobody believed.' " Fainberg further testified "that he related this position to one of Almeida's lawyers during a joint defense strategy session, but that he had to change his testimony in order to get himself 'out of the situation.' " Evidence derived from Fainberg's statements tended to show that two government witnesses conspired to lie about Almeida and then, having got their stories straight, perjured themselves to obtain reduced sentences.

The trial court then conceded that its original ruling had been in error, but held that the error was harmless. The court of appeals reversed. It agreed that the trial court "abused its discretion when it precluded Almeida from utilizing the communications that Fainberg made to Almeida's attorneys while operating under the joint defense agreement." The court held that "Fainberg waived the privilege when he agreed to plead guilty and testify against Almeida in exchange for the Government's dismissal of several counts in the indictment." In the court's view,

> . . . . confidential communications made during joint defense strategy sessions are privileged. A duty of loyalty, however, does not exist in this situation and it is therefore improper to conclude that all of the attorneys in the joint defense strategy session represent all of the participating defendants. Any potential conflict of interest arises solely from the fact that when defendant B becomes a witness for the state, the attorney for defendant A must make sure that the attorney-client privilege is respected and that confidential communications are not revealed. The mere inability to utilize the privileged communications is not itself a manifestation of a conflict of interest, because no lawyer in the world could utilize those communications. Rather, the potential conflict of interest stems from the fact that defendant A's lawyer might be so tongue-tied (due to his fear of revealing the confidential communications made by defendant B) that his representation of defendant A suffers. Since the degree to which defendant A's lawyer is impaired may be de minimis, the rules [governing the effective assistance of counsel in cases of conflicted representation] might be inapplicable (or subject to modification) in this scenario. We need not decide the issue, however, because we hold that Fainberg waived his attorney-client privilege when he turned state's evidence, thereby entirely removing the possibility of a conflict of interest from the case. . . .
>
> We hold that when each party to a joint defense agreement is represented by his own attorney, and when communications by one co-defendant are made to the attorneys of other co-defendants, such communications do not get the benefit of the attorney-client privilege in the event that the co-defendant decides to testify on behalf of the government in exchange for a reduced sentence.[31] The district court's

[31] FN21. In the future, defense lawyers should insist that their clients enter into written joint defense agreements that contain a clear statement of the waiver rule enunciated in this case, thereby allowing each defendant the opportunity to fully understand his rights prior to entering into the agreement. See, e.g., Stepney, 246 F.Supp.2d at 1084–86 (requiring that a writ-

error prevented the introduction of crucial evidence that would have significantly undermined the credibility of three of the Government's key witnesses. There is a reasonable possibility that the jury would not have convicted Almeida but for the district court's erroneous exclusionary ruling. The error was not harmless, and Almeida's conviction is therefore VACATED and the case is REMANDED for a new trial.

PROBLEM 5–7

1. Suppose X, Y, and Z are indicted. X communicates with his lawyer, who passes the communication on to Y's lawyer, who tells Y. Suppose Y then decides to cooperate with the government, and tells the government what X's lawyer told Y's lawyer; what is the status of X's communication?
2. Suppose X tells Y something directly and then they both describe the conversation to their lawyers. Y then cooperates with the government. What is the status of the communication from X to Y?
3. Suppose X tells Y's lawyer something, and Y's lawyer passes the statement on to Y. What is the status of the communication?
4. Suppose Y testifies at trial against X. Under any of the preceding scenarios (and hearsay problems aside), may Y testify as to what he learned about what X said?
5. Suppose Y agrees to cooperate and testifies at trial against X, and that X's lawyer has privileged joint defense information from Y's lawyer. May X's lawyer use it to cross-examine Y?
6. Suppose Y agrees to cooperate and testifies at trial against X, and that X's lawyer has privileged joint defense information from Y's lawyer. May X's lawyer disclose that information to assist X's defense?

Stepney provides a good overview of common-interest exception issues, but does not cover them all. For example, suppose parties A and B are represented by Lawyers L1 and L2, respectively. A communication from A to L1 is plainly privileged; if the common interest exception applies it means that L1 may tell L2 about the communication without waiving A1's privilege. L2 then of course may tell B, in a communication

---

ten joint defense agreement include a provision that the attorney-client privilege is waived in the event that a co-defendant takes the stand against his accomplice, and citing the model joint defense agreement prepared by the American Law Institute and American Bar Association).

that will itself be covered by B's privilege. May L1 communicate directly to B (suppose L2 consents to such communications, as we will see later he would have to)? In addition, how common do the parties' interests have to be? Do they have to be identical or just mostly similar? Is legal similarity required or is factual similarity enough?

These questions were addressed in *In re Teleglobe Communications Corp.*, 493 F.3d 345 (3d Cir. 2007). Excerpts from the opinion follow:

"When co-clients and their common attorneys communicate with one another, those communications are 'in confidence' for privilege purposes. Hence the privilege protects those communications from compelled disclosure to persons outside the joint representation. Moreover, waiving the joint-client privilege requires the consent of all joint clients. *Restatement (Third) of the Law Governing Lawyers* § 75(2). A wrinkle here is that a client may unilaterally waive the privilege as to its own communications with a joint attorney, so long as those communications concern only the waiving client; it may not, however, unilaterally waive the privilege as to any of the other joint clients' communications or as to any of its communications that relate to other joint clients. *Id.* at cmt. e. . . .

Recognizing that it is often preferable for co-defendants represented by different attorneys in criminal proceedings to coordinate their defense, courts developed the joint-defense privilege. In its original form, it allowed the attorneys of criminal co-defendants to share confidential information about defense strategies without waiving the privilege as against third parties. Moreover, one co-defendant could not waive the privilege that attached to the shared information without the consent of all others. Later, courts replaced the joint-defense privilege, which only applied to criminal co-defendants, with a broader one that protects all communications shared within a proper 'community of interest' whether the context be criminal or civil. . . . Thus, the community-of-interest privilege allows attorneys representing different clients with similar legal interests to share information without having to disclose it to others. It applies in civil and criminal litigation, and even in purely transactional contexts. [citations omitted]

Two aspects of the modern community-of-interest privilege are noteworthy. First, to be eligible for continued protection, the communication must be shared with the *attorney* of the member of the community of interest. *Cf. Ramada Inns, Inc. v. Dow Jones & Co.*, 523 A.2d 968, 972 (Del. Super. Ct. 1986) (emphasizing that the relevant Delaware evidentiary rule protects communications disclosed to an attorney). Sharing the communication directly with a member of the community may destroy the privilege. Second, all members of the community must share a common legal interest in the shared communication. RICE § 4:35. Delaware Rule of Evidence 502(b)(3), which sets out the State's version of the community-of-interest privilege, incorporates both requirements (that the clients' separate attorneys share information and that the clients have a common legal interest):

> A client has a privilege to refuse to disclose and to prevent any other person from disclosing confidential communications[,] made for the purpose of facilitating the rendition of professional legal services to the client . . . [,] by the client or the client's representative or the client's lawyer or a representative of the lawyer to a lawyer or a representative of a lawyer representing another in a matter of common interest.

DEL. R. EVID. 502(b)(3).

The requirement that the clients' separate attorneys share information (and not the clients themselves) derives from the community-of-interest privilege's roots in the old joint-defense privilege, which (to repeat) was developed to allow *attorneys* to coordinate their clients' criminal defense strategies. *See Chahoon v. Commw.*, 62 Va. 822, 21 Gratt. 822, 1871 WL 4931, at *11 (1871). Because the common-interest privilege is an exception to the disclosure rule, which exists to prevent abuse, the privilege should not be used as a *post hoc* justification for a client's impermissible disclosures. The attorney-sharing requirement helps prevent abuse by ensuring that the common-interest privilege only supplants the disclosure rule when attorneys, not clients, decide to share information in order to coordinate legal strategies.

Similarly, the congruence-of-legal-interests requirement ensures that the privilege is not misused to permit unnecessary information sharing. In a leading case, a District Court in South Carolina explained the contours of the requirement:

> A community of interest exists among different persons or separate corporations where they have an identical legal interest with respect to the subject matter of a communication between an attorney and a client concerning legal advice. The third parties receiving copies of the communication and claiming a community of interest may be distinct legal entities from the client receiving the legal advice and may be a non-party to any anticipated or pending litigation. The key consideration is that the nature of the interest be identical, not similar, and be legal, not solely commercial. The fact that there may be an overlap of a commercial and a legal interest for a third party does not negate the effect of the legal interest in establishing a community of interest.

Duplan Corp. v. Deering Milliken, Inc., 397 F.Supp. 1146, 1172 (D.S.C. 1974).

The Restatement takes a more flexible approach than *Duplan* toward the similarity and types of interests that qualify as "common": "[T]he common interest . . . may be either legal, factual, or strategic in character. The interests of the separately represented clients need not be entirely congruent." *Restatement (Third) of the Law Governing Lawyers* § 76 cmt. e. Professor Rice criticizes *Duplan*'s strictness and cites a few cases announcing that the interest need not be identical (though maintaining, contrary to the Restatement, that the interest must be legal, rather than "factual or strategic"). RICE § 4:36 (citing, *e.g., SCM Corp. v. Xerox Corp.*, 70 F.R.D. 508, 524–25 (D. Conn. 1976) (Newman, J.) (holding that legal interests must be "demonstrably common" or the clients must have a "substantial" risk of shared exposure to justify privileged information-sharing)). Rice, however, still recognizes *Duplan* as the leading approach. *Id.* ("This . . . standard . . . coined in *Duplan* . . . has been widely followed."). The Delaware courts seem not to have taken a position on whether the common legal interest must be identical, and we need not resolve the congruence-of-legal-interests question here. For our purposes, it is sufficient to recognize that members of the community of interest must share at least a substantially similar legal interest."

The Delaware statute extends to communications by a client "to a lawyer or a representative of a lawyer representing another in a matter of common interest," which means communication from one client to the lawyer for another client would be privileged under Delaware law. Client-to-client communications, however, would not be privileged. *Accord United States v. Schwimmer,* 892 F.2d 237, 243 (2d Cir. 1990) (doctrine protects "communications passing from one party to the attorney for another party").

The common interest exception may create an issue for prosecutors or plaintiffs' attorneys faced with a defendant who chooses to withdraw from a JDA and cooperate with the other side. The cooperating defendant may disclose her own information but she has no power to waive the privilege for information disclosed by another party to the JDA. If prosecutors or plaintiffs' counsel receive such information they may be subject to penalties. These could range from disqualification, as happened in *Rico*, to dismissal of an indictment, which Judge Patel alludes to in *Stepney*.

The few courts to consider allegations of such disclosure have set a fairly strict standard for non-cooperating defendants who wish to pursue such a claim. In *United States v. Aulicino,* 44 F.3d 1102, 1117 (2d Cir.1995), the court held that absent evidence of deliberate governmental efforts to intrude on the attorney-client relationship a defendant must show "specific facts that indicate communication of privileged information to the prosecutor and prejudice resulting therefrom.' " *See also United*

States v. Salvagno, 306 F. Supp. 2d 258 (N.D. N.Y. 2004) (court refused to order hearing on claim of improper intrusion where government repeatedly admonished cooperating witness not to divulge joint defense information). One court employed a test that also asked whether any intrusion was intentional and substantially detrimental to the defense. *United States v. Hsia,* 81 F.Supp.2d 7 (D.D.C.2000).

An analogous issue may arise from entity representation in the civil context. Suppose an entity employee is suspected of wrongdoing for which the entity would be liable too. If counsel for the entity interviewed the employee, a proper "civil *Miranda* warning" would make clear that the entity and not the employee controlled the privilege covering the employee's statements. (Recall that the absence of such a warning might result in the lawyer owing duties to both the entity and the employee, in which case the client might control the privilege over the client's statements.)

If counsel suspected that the entity's interests would conflict with the interests of its employee, however, it would be common for the employee to retain his own lawyer, often paid by the entity. The employee's lawyer and entity counsel would then enter into a JDA. In this case, what happens if the entity wants to cooperate with the government, as was the case in *Perez*?

United States v. LeCroy, 348 F. Supp.2d 375 (E.D. Pa. 2004), dealt with that issue. J.P. Morgan and two employees received grand jury subpoenas. Morgan was represented by counsel and recommended counsel for two employees. The employees and their lawyers met twice with Morgan lawyers under a verbal JDA. Morgan then considered cooperating with the government. Its counsel informed counsel for the employees that Morgan wanted to interview them again, reserving the right to produce his interview notes to the government. The employees went ahead with two interviews on this basis. When they later objected to disclosure of notes taken by Morgan's counsel the court held that the JDA prevented disclosure of notes from the first two meetings but that Morgan modified it by reserving its rights to disclose and the employees acquiesced in the modification by agreeing to interviews on that basis. Morgan therefore could disclose notes from the second set of interviews but not the first. An interesting aspect of *Leroy* is that the government avoided possible disqualification of the prosecution team (which might have happened if the court rule Morgan was wrong to disclose the notes) by having a different team of attorneys litigate the privilege issue, with instructions not to discuss the matter with the prosecution team.

Common Interest in Transactions

"May parties negotiating a business transaction rely on a 'joint defense agreement' as the basis for refusing to produce privileged documents exchanged long before they are actually sued by a third party?" This was the question posed in *OXY Resources California, LLC v. Superior Court*, 115 Cal.App.4th 874 (2004). That case involved over 200 documents pertaining to a transaction between OXY Resources and EOG Resources. The parties expected the transaction would provoke litigation from a third party with an interest in the subject of the transaction.

The agreement recited that the parties "anticipate that the past and future ownership and operation of [assets exchanged by the parties] will present various legal and factual issues common to . . . the Parties, as anticipated potential defendants, acknowledge that they share a common interest in defending against Claims by Third Parties, and they may wish to make joint efforts in preparation against any defense of anticipated actions or proceedings." The transaction did provoke a lawsuit, and the parties objected to production of several documents dated both before and after the transaction closed.

The plaintiff moved to compel production of the documents. The trial court granted that motion as to documents dated after the transaction closed but denied it as to documents dated before the transaction closed. According to the trial court, "[d]ocuments exchanged by parties who have already committed in writing to negotiate a more detailed formal agreement are protected under the 'common interest' theory, as reasonably necessary to further the interests of both parties in finalizing negotiations."

The court of appeals reversed. It first noted that California does not recognize a common interest privilege as such, and that the Evidence Code forbids courts from creating new privileges. The court said "the common interest doctrine is more appropriately characterized under California law as a non-waiver doctrine, analyzed under standard waiver principles applicable to the attorney-client privilege and the work product doctrine." A party "seeking to rely on the common interest doctrine" therefore "does not satisfy its burden to justify a claim of privilege simply by demonstrating that a confidential communication took place between parties who purportedly share a common interest. Rather, the party seeking to invoke the doctrine must first establish that the communicated information would otherwise be protected from disclosure by a claim of privilege." Only if a basis for privilege is established is it necessary "to determine whether disclosing the information to a party outside the attorney-client relationship waived any applicable privileges."

The court concluded that, "[f]or the common interest doctrine to attach, most courts seem to insist that the two parties have in common an interest in securing legal advice related to the same matter—and that the communications be made to advance their shared interest in securing legal advice on that common matter [citations omitted].” The court specifically endorsed the use of the doctrine in the transactional context: “As one federal court has recognized, ‘[b]y refusing to find waiver in these [commercial] settings courts create an environment in which businesses can share more freely information that is relevant to their transactions. This policy lubricates business deals and encourages more openness in transactions of this nature.’ ” (quoting *Hewlett–Packard Co. v. Bausch & Lomb Inc.,* 115 F.R.D. 308, 311, (N.D.Cal.1987).)

Against this background, the court of appeals held that the joint defense agreement created a reasonable expectation of confidentiality, so that the parties had a reasonable expectation that even shared documents would be held in confidence. Sharing by itself therefore did not destroy any privilege that might otherwise exist. The court of appeals reversed the trial court with respect to 13 documents withheld solely on the basis of the joint defense agreement, with no underlying privilege established. As to the remaining documents, the court concluded that the trial court erroneously “relied on general statements that all of the withheld communications were on matters of common interest and were reasonably necessary to accomplish the purpose for which lawyers were consulted. These unspecified claims of a common interest, applied generally to over 200 communications, are insufficient to protect the disputed documents from disclosure.”

The court therefore remanded for further proceedings: “The trial court must first conclude that the information contained in the documents is protected from disclosure by the attorney-client privilege or the work product doctrine; it must then determine whether the disclosures were reasonably necessary to accomplish the purpose for which the parties consulted their attorneys in finalizing the negotiations.”

For a ruling consistent with *OXY Resources*, *see STI Outdoor v. Superior Court,* 91 Cal.App.4th 334 (2001). The *OXY Resources* court relied in part on *Hewlett–Packard Co. v. Bausch & Lomb Inc.* 115 F.R.D. 308 (N.D.Cal.1987). That case in turn was questioned persuasively in *Nidec Corp. v. Victor Co. of Japan*, 249 F.R.D. 575 (N.D. Cal. 2007). The privilege issue there was collateral to patent litigation in which JVC was a defendant. While the litigation was pending Matsushita, which owned the majority of JVC shares, sought to sell its JVC stock. Prospective buyers were understandably interested in whether the pending litigation would affect JVC. A Matsushita representative gave a lawyer for one prospective buyer, TPG, a summary of the litigation.

Nidec served a subpoena on TPG, seeking in part the production of this litigation summary. Matsushita moved to quash the subpoena, in part on the ground that the summary was privileged and disclosure to a prospective buyer did not waive the privilege. It cited *Hewlett–Packard* for this proposition.

The court disagreed: "the disclosures which concern the instant litigation, to be protected, must be made in the course of formulating a *common legal strategy*." It held that even though Matsushita might have shared the litigation summary to help convince prospective bidders to buy the majority of the selling company's shares, it "did not further a common legal strategy in connection with the instant litigation. It was not, for instance, a communication coordinating the defense of this case. . . . Thus, it was designed not to further a joint defense in this litigation, but to further a commercial transaction in which the parties, if anything, have opposing interests."

The *Nidec* Court distinguished *Hewlett Packard* on the ground that the interest at issue there involved expected joint litigation, with the seller defending allegedly infringing sales before the transaction date and the buyer defending such sales thereafter. The Court found no evidence of such a joint legal interest in the case before it, and it rejected any extension of *Hewlett Packard* to cases involving only joint commercial, rather than legal, interests.

Finally, though the common interest exception may apply to both litigation and transactions some authority holds there must be some identifiable event, concern, or issue that creates the interests held in common. In *In re Grand Jury Subpoena*, 274 F.3d 563, 574 (1st Cir. 2001), the court held that a joint defense agreement could not encompass general cooperation untethered to particular issues:

> Lawyer's affidavit avers that his three clients (Oldco, Roe, and Moe) entered into an oral joint defense agreement in 1990, at which time no particular litigation or investigation was in prospect. The agreement thereafter remained in effect, Lawyer says, attaching ex proprio vigore to all matters subsequently arising (including the current grand jury investigation). The law will not countenance a "rolling" joint defense agreement of this limitless breadth.
>
> The rationale for recognizing joint defense agreements is that they permit parties to share information pertinent to each others' defenses. *See Hunydee v. United States,* 355 F.2d 183, 185 (9th Cir. 1965). In an adversarial proceeding, a party's entitlement to this enhanced veil of confidentiality can be justified on policy grounds. But outside the context of actual or prospective litigation, there is more vice than virtue in such agreements. Indeed, were we to sanction the intervenors' view, we would create a judicially enforced code of silence, preventing attorneys from disclosing information obtained

> from other attorneys and other attorneys' clients. Common sense suggests that there can be no joint defense agreement when there is no joint defense to pursue. We so hold.

Though the court's language is broad enough to preclude recognition of the common interest exception in transactional settings, no such issue was before the court and its language is better read not to reach cases such as *OXY Resources*.

The Main Points to Recall From Chapter 5 Are:

- The attorney-client privilege is a rule of evidence; it is different from (and narrower than) the fiduciary duty of confidentiality.
- The privilege applies to communications, not facts. Disclosure of a fact does not waive the privilege as to a communication; communication of the fact does not privilege the fact itself.
- The communications must be between a lawyer and a client, in confidence, including through intermediaries reasonably necessary to further the purposes of the representation.
- When a lawyer represents an entity, the entity is the client and holds the privilege.
- There is no privilege as between joint clients but joint clients have a privilege as against everyone else.
- There is no privilege for communications furthering a crime or fraud, regardless whether the lawyer knows about the crime or fraud.
- Conduct inconsistent with maintaining confidentiality waives the privilege.
- Where a client waives strategically in litigation, the waiver extends to all communications on the subject matter of the communications the client wants to introduce.
- Disclosure within another privileged relationship, or to persons with whom a privilege-holder has a common legal interest, do not waive the privilege.
- Disclosure of a privileged communication to another party with a common legal interest is not waiver, but there is no separate privilege for such communications.

The following chart summarizes the main points regarding the duty of confidentiality and the attorney-client privilege.

	Duty of Confidentiality	Privilege
Covers	All information relating to representation not generally known	Confidential communications between attorney and client for purpose of providing legal services
Applies When	At all times	Rules of evidence apply
Effect	Forbids voluntary disclosure (but not disclosure requires by law) or use of information that harms client or benefits lawyer outside the practice of law	Prevents disclosure evidence rules otherwise could compel
Controlled by	Client	Client
Exceptions	Prevent death or serious bodily injury; prevent or rectify serious financial harm in which L's services have been used; self-defense (respond to allegation of representation-related misconduct); seek advice about compliance with rules; disclosure required by law	Communications in furtherance of a crime or fraud; joint clients; common interest exception to waiver

CHAPTER 6

THE WORK PRODUCT DOCTRINE

■ ■ ■

The work product doctrine is designed to prevent one party from free riding on another's confidential work. Because the doctrine is not based solely on confidentiality it differs from the duty of confidentiality and from privilege with respect to its scope, exceptions, and waiver.

Fed. R. Civ. P. 26(b)(3)
Cal. Code Civ. P. 2018
Restatement (Third) of the Law Governing Lawyers §§ 87–93

A. SCOPE

Work product generally includes everything you produce while working for a client. This broad category is divided into "opinion" work product and everything else, which is often called "fact" work product.

Opinion work product is that which reflects your impressions, opinions, research, conclusions, or theories.[1] Courts often construe this category to include things such as notes of a witness interview, so long as the notes did more than simply transcribe what the witness said. The attorney's selection, arrangement, characterization, and synthesis reflected in the notes is likely to qualify as opinion work product.[2] This distinction is sometimes phrased as a difference between "derivative" or "interpretive" material, which is derived from an attorney's thoughts or reflects an attorney's interpretations of facts, and purely "evidentiary" material that is neither derived from such thoughts nor reflects such interpretation. Work product protection extends to derivative or interpretive material but not purely evidentiary material. *Coito v. Superior Court*, 54 Cal.4th 480 (2012). Thus, under California law "a statement independently prepared by a witness does not become protected work product simply upon its transmission to an attorney," *id.* at 494, but where a statement is the result of an attorney interview it "would not exist but for the attorney's initiative, decision, and effort to obtain it" and it therefore is eligible for either absolute protection (if the statement is imbued with the attorney's thoughts and impressions of the case) or qualified protection (if not).

1 Cal. Code Civ. P. 2018.030; Fed. R. Civ. P. 26(b)(3)(B).

2 *Rico v. Mitsubishi*, 42 Cal.4th 807, 68 Cal.Rptr.3d 758 (2007).

Under federal law, opinion work product receives heightened protection that in practice is close to absolute.[3] Under California law, opinion work product is not discoverable under any circumstances.[4] (That is the "absolute" protection referenced in *Coito*.)

Other forms of work product are subject to discovery if the party asking for the material has a substantial need for it and cannot get the information in some other way without substantial hardship.[5] A statement from a witness who later died or forgot the relevant events would be an example of such a case.[6]

Under California law work product protection applies to everything you produce while working for a client. Under federal law the protection extends only to materials prepared in anticipation of litigation. Some federal courts extend the doctrine only to materials prepared primarily to assist in litigation. Others extend it to materials prepared because litigation is anticipated, a notionally broader category.[7]

B. EXCEPTIONS

Under California law a client's criminal or fraudulent activity does not vitiate work product protection in civil cases. Work product protection may be vitiated where the government investigates a client's criminal or fraudulent conduct and the lawyer is suspected of knowing participation in the activity.[8]

Federal cases are divided on whether work product protection is forfeited when a client engages in criminal or fraudulent activity. Because the lawyer holds the work product privilege, some cases hold that lawyers may assert the doctrine as to opinion work product even if the client engaged in criminal or fraudulent activity so long as the lawyer did not know of that activity.[9] Under this rule "fact" work product could be discovered in such a case, and even opinion work product might be discoverable if the lawyer were knowingly involved in the unlawful activity.

These exceptions do not apply to work product created after the fact to defend a client against charges of crime or fraud. They apply only to work by lawyers through which the crime or fraud was advanced.

---

[3] Fed. R. Civ. P. 26(b)(3); *Upjohn Co. v. United States*, 449 U.S. 383, 400–01 (1981).

[4] Cal. Code Civ. P. 2018.030(a).

[5] Fed. R. Civ. P. 26(b)(3)(A)(ii).

[6] *Smith v. Diamond Offshore Drilling, Inc.*, 168 F.R.D. 582 (1996).

[7] The "because litigation is anticipated" standard is endorsed in *United States v. Adlman*, 134 F.3d 1194 (2d Cir. 1998).

[8] Cal. Code Civ. P. § 2018.050.

[9] *In re Grand Jury Proceedings,* 867 F.2d 539 (9th Cir. 1989) (district court did not abuse its discretion in ordering innocent attorney to testify regarding fact but not opinion work product); *In re National Mortg. Equity Corp. Mortg. Pool Certificates Litig.*, 116 F.R.D. 297 (C.D. Cal. 1987).

C. WAIVER

Work product protection is waived if the work product is placed at issue[10] or disclosed to a testifying expert.[11] The common interest exception to waiver extends to work product as well as to privileged communications. Some authority holds that where parties collaborate on work product each contributing party must agree to waive protection for a waiver to be effective.[12] The rule may be different where work product is created for an entity and a constituent.[13]

Because the work product doctrine is designed to prevent one party from free riding on the work of another, however, it is not as concerned with confidentiality as the attorney-client privilege is. Limited disclosure of work product material does not waive the protection of the doctrine unless the disclosure is likely to reveal work product material to an opponent.[14]

	PRIVILEGE	WORK–PRODUCT DOCTRINE
PROTECTS	Confidential communications relating to representation	Mental impressions of counsel; other work done on behalf of client in preparation for litigation (California law protects all work for a client, including in transactions; federal protection extends only to work done in anticipation of litigation)
CONTROLLED BY	Client	Lawyer
EXCEPTIONS	Crime-fraud; self-defense; prevent death or harm	Crime-fraud (federal, but not California); self-defense

---

[10] *Holmgren v. State Farm Mut. Auto Ins. Co.*, 976 F.2d 573 (9th Cir. 1992).

[11] *Association of Irritated Residents v. Fred Schakel Dairy*, 2008 WL 2509735 (E.D.Cal. 2008); *Williamson v. Superior Court*, 21 Cal.3d 829, 148 Cal.Rptr. 39, 582 P.2d 126 (1978).

[12] *Armenta v. Superior Court*, 101 Cal.App.4th 525, 534, 124 Cal.Rptr.2d 273 (2002) ("Where . . . work product is the result of collaboration by counsel, all holders of the work product privilege must consent to waiver of the privilege.")

[13] *In re Grand Jury Subpoena*, 274 F.3d 563, 574 (1st Cir. 2001).

[14] *E.g. SEC v. Schroeder,* 2009 WL 1125579 (N.D. Cal. 2009) (disclosure of work product to independent auditor did not waive protection of doctrine); *SEC v. Roberts,* 254 F.R.D. 371 (N.D. Cal. 2008) (same); *Merrill Lynch & Co. v. Allegheny Energy*, 229 F.R.D. 441 (S.D.N.Y. 2004) (same).

D. THE ORIGINS OF THE DOCTRINE

HICKMAN V. TAYLOR

329 U.S. 495 (1947)

MR. JUSTICE MURPHY delivered the opinion of the Court.

This case presents an important problem under the Federal Rules of Civil Procedure as to the extent to which a party may inquire into oral and written statements of witnesses, or other information, secured by an adverse party's counsel in the course of preparation for possible litigation after a claim has arisen. Examination into a person's files and records, including those resulting from the professional activities of an attorney, must be judged with care. It is not without reason that various safeguards have been established to preclude unwarranted excursions into the privacy of a man's work. At the same time, public policy supports reasonable and necessary inquiries. Properly to balance these competing interests is a delicate and difficult task.

On February 7, 1943, the tug "J. M. Taylor" sank while engaged in helping to tow a car float of the Baltimore & Ohio Railroad across the Delaware River at Philadelphia. The accident was apparently unusual in nature, the cause of it still being unknown. Five of the nine crew members were drowned. Three days later, the tug owners and the underwriters employed a law firm, of which respondent Fortenbaugh is a member, to defend them against potential suits by representatives of the deceased crew members and to sue the railroad for damages to the tug.

A public hearing was held on March 4, 1943, before the United States Steamboat Inspectors at which the four survivors were examined. This testimony was recorded and made available to all interested parties. Shortly thereafter, Fortenbaugh privately interviewed the survivors and took statements from them with an eye toward the anticipated litigation; the survivors signed these statements on March 29. Fortenbaugh also interviewed other persons believed to have some information relating to the accident, and in some cases he made memoranda of what they told him.

At the time when Fortenbaugh secured the statements of the survivors, representatives of two of the deceased crew members had been in communication with him. Ultimately claims were presented by representatives of all five of the deceased; four of the claims, however, were settled without litigation. The fifth claimant, petitioner herein, brought suit in a federal court under the Jones Act on November 26, 1943, naming as defendants the two tug owners, individually and as partners, and the railroad.

One year later, petitioner filed 39 interrogatories directed to the tug owners. The 38th interrogatory read:

> "State whether any statements of the members of the crews of the Tugs 'J. M. Taylor' and 'Philadelphia' or of any other vessel were taken in connection with the towing of the car float and the sinking of the Tug 'John M. Taylor.'
>
> Attach hereto exact copies of all such statements if in writing, and if oral, set forth in detail the exact provisions of any such oral statements or reports."

Supplemental interrogatories asked whether any oral or written statements, records, reports, or other memoranda had been made concerning any matter relative to the towing operation, the sinking of the tug, the salvaging and repair of the tug, and the death of the deceased. If the answer was in the affirmative, the tug owners were then requested to set forth the nature of all such records, reports, statements, or other memoranda.

The tug owners, through Fortenbaugh, answered all of the interrogatories except No. 38 and the supplemental ones just described. While admitting that statements of the survivors had been taken, they declined to summarize or set forth the contents. They did so on the ground that such requests called "for privileged matter obtained in preparation for litigation," and constituted "an attempt to obtain indirectly counsel's private files." It was claimed that answering these requests "would involve practically turning over not only the complete files, but also the telephone records and, almost, the thoughts, of counsel.". . . .

The District Court for the Eastern District of Pennsylvania, sitting en banc, held that the requested matters were not privileged. . . . The Third Circuit Court of Appeals, also sitting en banc, reversed the judgment of the District Court. It held that the information here sought was part of the "work product of the lawyer," and hence privileged from discovery under the Federal Rules of Civil Procedure. . . .

In urging that he has a right to inquire into the materials secured and prepared by Fortenbaugh, petitioner emphasizes that the deposition-discovery portions of the Federal Rules of Civil Procedure are designed to enable the parties to discover the true facts, and to compel their disclosure wherever they may be found. It is said that inquiry may be made under these rules, epitomized by Rule 26, as to any relevant matter which is not privileged, and, since the discovery provisions are to be applied as broadly and liberally as possible, the privilege limitation must be restricted to its narrowest bounds.

On the premise that the attorney-client privilege is the one involved in this case, petitioner argues that it must be strictly confined to confidential communications made by a client to his attorney. And, since the materials here in issue were secured by Fortenbaugh from third persons, rather than from his clients, the tug owners, the conclusion is reached that these materials are proper subjects for discovery under Rule 26. . . .

[T]he memoranda, statements, and mental impressions in issue in this case fall outside the scope of the attorney-client privilege, and hence are not protected from discovery on that basis. It is unnecessary here to delineate the content and scope of that privilege as recognized in the federal courts. For present purposes, it suffices to note that the protective cloak of this privilege does not extend to information which an attorney secures from a witness while acting for his client in anticipation of litigation. Nor does this privilege concern the memoranda, briefs, communications, and other writings prepared by counsel for his own use in prosecuting his client's case, and it is equally unrelated to writings which reflect an attorney's mental impressions, conclusions, opinions, or legal theories.

But the impropriety of invoking that privilege does not provide an answer to the problem before us. Petitioner has made more than an ordinary request for relevant, nonprivileged facts in the possession of his adversaries or their counsel. He has sought discovery as of right of oral and written statements of witnesses whose identity is well known and whose availability to petitioner appears unimpaired. He has sought production of these matters after making the most searching inquiries of his opponents as to the circumstances surrounding the fatal accident, which inquiries were sworn to have been answered to the best of their information and belief. Interrogatories were directed toward all the events prior to, during, and subsequent to the sinking of the tug. Full and honest answers to such broad inquiries would necessarily have included all pertinent information gleaned by Fortenbaugh through his interviews with the witnesses. Petitioner makes no suggestion, and we cannot assume, that the tug owners or Fortenbaugh were incomplete or dishonest in the framing of their answers.

In addition, petitioner was free to examine the public testimony of the witnesses taken before the United States Steamboat Inspectors. We are thus dealing with an attempt to secure the production of written statements and mental impressions contained in the files and the mind of the attorney Fortenbaugh without any showing of necessity or any indication or claim that denial of such production would unduly prejudice the preparation of petitioner's case or cause him any hardship or injustice. For aught that appears, the essence of what petitioner seeks either has been revealed to him already through the interrogatories or is readily available to him direct from the witnesses for the asking.

The district court . . . simply ordered production on the theory that the facts sought were material and were not privileged as constituting attorney-client communications. . . . In our opinion, neither Rule 26 nor any other rule dealing with discovery contemplates production under such circumstances. That is not because the subject matter is privileged or irrelevant, as those concepts are used in these rules.

Here is simply an attempt, without purported necessity or justification, to secure written statements, private memoranda, and personal recollections prepared or formed by an adverse party's counsel in the course of his legal duties. As such, it falls outside the arena of discovery and contravenes the public policy underlying the orderly prosecution and defense of legal claims. Not even the most liberal of discovery theories can justify unwarranted inquiries into the files and the mental impressions of an attorney. Historically, a lawyer is an officer of the court, and is bound to work for the advancement of justice while faithfully protecting the rightful interests of his clients. In performing his various duties, however, it is essential that a lawyer work with a certain degree of privacy, free from unnecessary intrusion by opposing parties and their counsel.

Proper preparation of a client's case demands that he assemble information, sift what he considers to be the relevant from the irrelevant facts, prepare his legal theories, and plan his strategy without undue and needless interference. That is the historical and the necessary way in which lawyers act within the framework of our system of jurisprudence to promote justice and to protect their clients' interests. This work is reflected, of course, in interviews, statements, memoranda, correspondence, briefs, mental impressions, personal beliefs, and countless other tangible and intangible ways—aptly though roughly termed by the Circuit Court of Appeals in this case as the "work product of the lawyer." Were such materials open to opposing counsel on mere demand, much of what is now put down in writing would remain unwritten. An attorney's thoughts, heretofore inviolate, would not be his own. Inefficiency, unfairness, and sharp practices would inevitably develop in the giving of legal advice and in the preparation of cases for trial. The effect on the legal profession would be demoralizing. And the interests of the clients and the cause of justice would be poorly served.

We do not mean to say that all written materials obtained or prepared by an adversary's counsel with an eye toward litigation are necessarily free from discovery in all cases. Where relevant and nonprivileged facts remain hidden in an attorney's file, and where production of those facts is essential to the preparation of one's case, discovery may properly be had. Such written statements and documents might, under certain circumstances, be admissible in evidence, or give clues as to the existence or location of relevant facts. Or they might be useful for purposes of impeachment or corroboration. And production might be justified where the witnesses are no longer available or can be reached only with difficulty. Were production of written statements and documents to be precluded under such circumstances, the liberal ideals of the deposition-discovery portions of the Federal Rules of Civil Procedure would be stripped of much of their meaning. But the general policy against invading the privacy of an attorney's course of preparation is so well recognized and so essential to an orderly working of our system of legal procedure that a burden rests on the one who would invade that privacy to establish adequate reasons to justify production through a subpoena or court order. That burden, we believe, is necessarily implicit in the rules as now constituted.

Denial of production of this nature does not mean that any material, nonprivileged facts can be hidden from the petitioner in this case. He need not be unduly hindered in the preparation of his case, in the discovery of facts, or in his anticipation of his opponents' position. Searching interrogatories directed to Fortenbaugh and the tug owners, production of written documents and statements upon a proper showing, and direct interviews with the witnesses themselves all serve to reveal the facts in Fortenbaugh's possession to the fullest possible extent consistent with public policy. Petitioner's counsel frankly admits that he wants the oral statements only to help prepare himself to examine witnesses and to make sure that he has overlooked nothing. That is insufficient under the circumstances to permit him an exception to the policy underlying the privacy of Fortenbaugh's professional activities. If there should be a rare situation justifying production of these matters, petitioner's case is not of that type.

UPJOHN CO. V. UNITED STATES

449 U.S. 383 (1981)

JUSTICE REHNQUIST delivered the opinion of the Court.

Petitioner Upjohn Co. manufactures and sells pharmaceuticals here and abroad. In January, 1976, independent accountants conducting an audit of one of Upjohn's foreign subsidiaries discovered that the subsidiary made payments to or for the benefit of foreign government officials in order to secure government business. The accountants so informed petitioner Mr. Gerard Thomas, Upjohn's Vice President, Secretary, and General Counsel. Thomas is a member of the Michigan and New York Bars, and has been Upjohn's General Counsel for 20 years. He consulted with outside counsel and R. T. Parfet, Jr., Upjohn's Chairman of the Board. It was decided that the company would conduct an internal investigation of what were termed "questionable payments."

As part of this investigation [Upjohn sent a questionnaire to certain employees]. . . . Thomas and outside counsel also interviewed the recipients of the questionnaire and some 33 other Upjohn officers or employees. . . . [The IRS sought production of the questionnaire responses and notes the attorneys took in their interviews. The Court held responses to the questionnaires were protected by the attorney-client privilege.]

Our decision that the communications by Upjohn employees to counsel are covered by the attorney-client privilege disposes of the case so far as the responses to the questionnaires and any notes reflecting responses to interview questions are concerned. The summons reaches further, however, and Thomas has testified that his notes and memoranda of interviews go beyond recording responses to his questions. . . .

While conceding the applicability of the work product doctrine, the Government asserts that it has made a sufficient showing of necessity to overcome its protections. The Magistrate apparently so found. The Government relies on the following language in *Hickman:*

> "We do not mean to say that all written materials obtained or prepared by an adversary's counsel with an eye toward litigation are necessarily free from discovery in all cases. Where relevant and nonprivileged facts remain hidden in an attorney's file, and where production of those facts is essential to the preparation of one's case, discovery may properly be had. . . . And production might be justified where the witnesses are no longer available or can be reached only with difficulty."

329 U.S. at 511. The Government stresses that interviewees are scattered across the globe, and that Upjohn has forbidden its employees to answer questions it considers irrelevant. The above-quoted language from *Hickman,* however, did not apply to "oral statements made by witnesses . . . whether presently in the form of [the attorney's] mental impressions or memoranda." *Id.* at 329 U. S. 512. As to such material, the Court did

> "not believe that any showing of necessity can be made under the circumstances of this case so as to justify production. . . . If there should be a rare situation justifying production of these matters, petitioner's case is not of that type."

Id. at 329 U. S. 512–513. *See also Nobles, supra* at 422 U. S. 252–253 (WHITE, J., concurring). Forcing an attorney to disclose notes and memoranda of witnesses' oral statements is particularly disfavored, because it tends to reveal the attorney's mental processes, 329 U.S. at 329 U. S. 513 ("what he saw fit to write down regarding witnesses' remarks"); *id.* at 329 U. S. 516–517 ("the statement would be his [the attorney's] language, permeated with his inferences") (Jackson, J., concurring).

Rule 26 accords special protection to work product revealing the attorney's mental processes. The Rule permits disclosure of documents and tangible things constituting attorney work product upon a showing of substantial need and inability to obtain the equivalent without undue hardship. This was the standard applied by the Magistrate. Rule 26 goes on, however, to state that,

> "[i]n ordering discovery of such materials when the required showing has been made, the court shall protect against disclosure of the men-

tal impressions, conclusions, opinions or legal theories of an attorney or other representative of a party concerning the litigation."

Although this language does not specifically refer to memoranda based on oral statements of witnesses, the *Hickman* court stressed the danger that compelled disclosure of such memoranda would reveal the attorney's mental processes. It is clear that this is the sort of material the draftsmen of the Rule had in mind as deserving special protection. . . .

Based on the foregoing, some courts have concluded that no showing of necessity can overcome protection of work product which is based on oral statements from witnesses. . . . Those courts declining to adopt an absolute rule have nonetheless recognized that such material is entitled to special protection. . . .

We do not decide the issue at this time. It is clear that the Magistrate applied the wrong standard when he concluded that the Government had made a sufficient showing of necessity to overcome the protections of the work product doctrine. The Magistrate applied the "substantial need" and "without undue hardship" standard articulated in the first part of Rule 26(b)(3). The notes and memoranda sought by the Government here, however, are work product based on oral statements. If they reveal communications, they are, in this case, protected by the attorney-client privilege. To the extent they do not reveal communications, they reveal the attorneys' mental processes in evaluating the communications. As Rule 26 and *Hickman* make clear, such work product cannot be disclosed simply on a showing of substantial need and inability to obtain the equivalent without undue hardship.

While we are not prepared at this juncture to say that such material is always protected by the work product rule, we think a far stronger showing of necessity and unavailability by other means than was made by the Government or applied by the Magistrate in this case would be necessary to compel disclosure. Since the Court of Appeals thought that the work product protection was never applicable in an enforcement proceeding such as this, and since the Magistrate whose recommendations the District Court adopted applied too lenient a standard of protection, we think the best procedure with respect to this aspect of the case would be to reverse the judgment of the Court of Appeals for the Sixth Circuit and remand the case to it for such further proceedings in connection with the work product claim as are consistent with this opinion.

Accordingly, the judgment of the Court of Appeals is reversed, and the case remanded for further proceedings.

It is so ordered.

Ordinary and "Opinion" Work Product

Upjohn distinguishes "ordinary" work product information, which does not include or reflect an attorney's opinions and impressions of a matter, and "opinion work product," which does. Ordinary work product is protected from discovery unless the party requesting the information can show that it has a substantial need for the information and could not otherwise obtain it without undue hardship.

For example, suppose a party sent an investigator to interview a witness to an accident and the investigator recorded the interview. If the witness later could not recall what happened, or was unavailable for some reason, a court might allow another party to discover the tapes on the ground that the party had no other way to get the information. *See Smith v. Diamond Offshore Drilling, Inc.*, 168 F.R.D. 582 (1996) ("the statements sought by the Plaintiff in this case were taken just a few days after the accident, and, consequently, will be more accurate than any statements that could now be obtained from the same witnesses. Because the Plaintiff has a substantial need for the statements and cannot obtain their substantial equivalent by any means other than through the Defendant, the Court concludes that the Defendant must produce the statements."); *Teribery v. Norfolk & W. Ry. Co.,* 68 F.R.D. 46 (W.D. Pa. 1975). Other circumstances that have been found sufficient to overcome work product protection include the refusal of witnesses to testify and the destruction of documents, *In re Vitamins Antitrust Litig.*, 211 F.R.D. 1 (D. D.C. 2002), and the inability of witnesses to recall important events. *See Ehrlich v. Howe*, 848 F.Supp. 482 (S.D.N.Y. 1994); *Xerox Corp. v. IBM*, 64 F.R.D. 367 (S.D.N.Y. 1974).

In this example the relevant evidence included audio files, which, let us assume, do not contain or reflect the impressions of the lawyer or investigator who made them. (One could of course argue that the choice of questions to ask reflected the mental impressions of the investigator, but for now let's assume only obvious questions were asked). What if notes rather than audio files were at issue? The notes would be more likely to have been filtered through the mental impressions of the lawyer or investigator and thus would be more likely to be treated as "opinion" work product.

Upjohn did not hold that opinion work product can never be discovered, only that the standard for discovering it was stricter than the standard for discovering ordinary work product. Some courts have held on their own that opinion work product enjoys "absolute" protection, while others satisfy themselves with holding it enjoys "nearly absolute" protection. *E.g. Diamond Offshore Drilling*, 168 F.R.D. at 585. You get the point. It is almost impossible to discover opinion work product in federal court. In some states, protection for opinion work product is expressly made absolute. *See* Cal. Code Civ. P. 2018.030(a).

How far does opinion work product extend? Consider the following comment from the trial court in *Rico v. Mitsubishi*, 42 Cal.4th 807 (2007), which the Supreme Court quoted with approval. As you recall from the last chapter, the document in that case contained notes taken by a paralegal, who sat in on an interview between a lawyer and an expert witness:

> "As to the content of the document, although it doesn't contain overt statements setting forth the lawyer's conclusions, its very existence is owed to the lawyer's thought process. The document reflects not only the strategy, but also the attorney's opinion as to the important issues in the case. Directions were provided by Mr. Yukevich as to the key pieces of information to be recorded, and Mr. Yukevich also added his own input as to the important details, by inserting other words in the notes. The attorney's impressions of the case were the filter through which all the discussions at the conference were passed through on the way to the page. . . .
>
> This court determines that the attorney's directions to record only portions of the conference specific to the attorney's concerns in the litigation are sufficient to support the finding that the notes are covered by the absolute work product [doctrine], as the choices in statements to record show the thought process and are too intertwined with the document." Although the notes were written in dialogue format and contain information attributed to Mitsubishi's experts, the document does not qualify as an *expert's* report, writing, declaration, or testimony. The notes reflect the *paralegal's* summary along with *counsel's* thoughts and impressions about the case. The document was absolutely protected work product because it contained the ideas of Yukevich and his legal team about the case. (§ 2018.030, subd. (a).)

E. THE "PREPARED IN ANTICIPATION OF LITIGATION" REQUIREMENT

UNITED STATES V. ADLMAN

134 F.3d 1194 (2d Cir. 1998)

LEVAL, CIRCUIT JUDGE:

This appeal concerns the proper interpretation of Federal Rule of Civil Procedure 26(b)(3) ("the Rule"), which grants limited protection against discovery to documents and materials prepared "in anticipation of litigation." Specifically, we must address whether a study prepared for an attorney assessing the likely result of an expected litigation is ineligible for protection under the Rule if the primary or ultimate purpose of mak-

ing the study was to assess the desirability of a business transaction, which, if undertaken, would give rise to the litigation. We hold that a document created because of anticipated litigation, which tends to reveal mental impressions, conclusions, opinions or theories concerning the litigation, does not lose work-product protection merely because it is intended to assist in the making of a business decision influenced by the likely outcome of the anticipated litigation. Where a document was created because of anticipated litigation, and would not have been prepared in substantially similar form but for the prospect of that litigation, it falls within Rule 26(b)(3). . . .

Background

Sequa Corporation is an aerospace manufacturer with annual revenues of nearly $2 billion. Prior to 1989, Atlantic Research Corporation ("ARC") and Chromalloy Gas Turbine Corporation ("Chromalloy") were wholly-owned Sequa subsidiaries. Appellant Monroe Adlman is an attorney and Vice President for Taxes at Sequa.

In the spring of 1989, Sequa contemplated merging Chromalloy and ARC. The contemplated merger was expected to produce an enormous loss and tax refund, which Adlman expected would be challenged by the IRS and would result in litigation. Adlman asked Paul Sheahen, an accountant and lawyer at Arthur Andersen & Co. ("Arthur Andersen"), to evaluate the tax implications of the proposed restructuring. Sheahen did so and set forth his study in a memorandum (the "Memorandum"). He submitted the Memorandum in draft form to Adlman in August 1989. After further consultation, on September 5, 1989, Sheahen sent Adlman the final version. The Memorandum was a 58–page detailed legal analysis of likely IRS challenges to the reorganization and the resulting tax refund claim; it contained discussion of statutory provisions, IRS regulations, legislative history, and prior judicial and IRS rulings relevant to the claim. It proposed possible legal theories or strategies for Sequa to adopt in response, recommended preferred methods of structuring the transaction, and made predictions about the likely outcome of litigation.

Sequa decided to go ahead with the restructuring, which was completed in December 1989 in essentially the form recommended by Arthur Andersen. . . . The reorganization resulted in a $289 million loss. Sequa claimed the loss on its 1989 return and carried it back to offset 1986 capital gains, thereby generating a claim for a refund of $35 million.

In an ensuing audit of Sequa's 1986–1989 tax returns, the IRS requested a number of documents concerning the restructuring transaction. Sequa acknowledged the existence of the Memorandum, but cited work-product privilege as grounds for declining to produce it. On September 23, 1993, the IRS served a summons on Adlman for production of the Memorandum.

When Adlman declined to comply, the IRS instituted an action in the United States District Court for the Southern District of New York to enforce the subpoena. Adlman defended on the grounds that the Memorandum was protected by both the attorney-client and work-product privileges. The district court (Knapp, J.) in its first decision rejected Adlman's claim that the Memorandum was protected by attorney-client privilege, finding that Adlman had not consulted Arthur Andersen in order to obtain assistance in furnishing legal advice to Sequa. It rejected Adlman's claim of work-product privilege because the Memorandum was prepared for litigation based on actions or events that had not yet occurred at the time of its creation. The court granted the IRS's petition to enforce the summons. On appeal, we affirmed denial of Adlman's claim of attorney-client privilege. . . .

On remand, Adlman argued that the Memorandum was protected by Rule 26(b)(3) because it included legal opinions prepared in reasonable anticipation of litigation. Litigation was virtually certain to result from the reorganization and Sequa's consequent claim of tax losses. Sequa's tax returns had been surveyed or audited annually for at least 30 years. In addition, the size of the capital loss to be generated by the proposed restructuring would result in a refund so large that the Commissioner of Internal Revenue would be required by federal law to submit a report to the Joint Congressional Committee on Taxation. *See* 26 U.S.C.A. § 6405(a). Finally, Sequa's tax treatment of the restructuring was based on an interpretation of the tax code without a case or IRS ruling directly on point. In light of the circumstances of the transaction, Adlman asserted there was "no doubt that Sequa would end up in litigation with the IRS." Sequa's accountant at Arthur Andersen concurred, opining that "any corporate tax executive would have realistically predicted that this capital loss would be disputed by the IRS" because of the "unprecedented and creative nature of the reorganization, the fact that Sequa was continually under close scrutiny by the IRS and the size of the refund resulting from the capital loss."

The district court again rejected the claim of work-product privilege, concluding that the Memorandum was not prepared in anticipation of litigation. Adlman appeals.

Discussion

The work-product doctrine, codified for the federal courts in Fed.R.Civ.P. 26(b)(3), is intended to preserve a zone of privacy in which a lawyer can prepare and develop legal theories and strategy "with an eye toward litigation," free from unnecessary intrusion by his adversaries. *Hickman v. Taylor,* 329 U.S. 495, 510–11 (1947). Analysis of one's case "in anticipation of litigation" is a classic example of work product, *see NLRB v. Sears, Roebuck & Co.,* 421 U.S. 132, 154 (1975), and receives heightened protection under Fed.R.Civ.P. 26(b)(3). . . .

The first problem we face is to determine the meaning of the phrase prepared "in anticipation of litigation." The phrase has never been interpreted by our circuit; furthermore, courts and commentators have expressed a range of views as to its meaning. It is universally agreed that a document whose purpose is to assist in preparation for litigation is within the scope of the Rule and thus eligible to receive protection if the other conditions of protection prescribed by the Rule are met. The issue is less clear, however, as to documents which, although prepared because of expected litigation, are intended to inform a business decision influenced by the prospects of the litigation. The formulation applied by some courts in determining whether documents are protected by work-product privilege is whether they are prepared "primarily or exclusively to assist in litigation"—a formulation that would potentially exclude documents containing analysis of expected litigation, if their primary, ultimate, or exclusive purpose is to assist in making the business decision. Others ask whether the documents were prepared "because of" existing or expected litigation—a formulation that would include such documents, despite the fact that their purpose is not to "assist in" litigation. Because we believe that protection of documents of this type is more consistent with both the literal terms and the purposes of the Rule, we adopt the latter formulation.

1. *"Primarily to assist in" litigation.*

The "primarily to assist in litigation" formulation is exemplified by a line of cases from the United States Court of Appeals for the Fifth Circuit. In *United States v. Davis,* 636 F.2d 1028 (5th Cir.), *cert. denied,* 454 U.S. 862 (1981), the Fifth Circuit denied protection to documents made in the course of preparation of a tax return. This result was well justified as there was no showing whatsoever of anticipation of litigation. In what might be characterized as a dictum, or in any event a statement going far beyond the issues raised in the case, the court asserted that the Rule applies only if the "primary motivating purpose behind the creation of the document was to aid in possible future litigation."

We believe that a requirement that documents be produced primarily or exclusively to assist in litigation in order to be protected is at odds with the text and the policies of the Rule. Nowhere does Rule 26(b)(3) state that a document must have been prepared *to aid* in the conduct of litigation in order to constitute work product, much less *primarily or exclusively* to aid in litigation. Preparing a document "in anticipation of litigation" is sufficient.

The text of Rule 26(b)(3) does not limit its protection to materials prepared to assist at trial. To the contrary, the text of the Rule clearly sweeps more broadly. It expressly states that work-product privilege applies not only to documents "prepared . . . for trial" but also to those prepared "in anticipation of litigation." If the drafters of the Rule intended to limit its protection to documents made to assist in preparation for litigation, this would have been adequately conveyed by the phrase "prepared . . . for trial." The fact that documents prepared "in anticipation of litigation" were also included confirms that the drafters considered this to be a different, and broader category. Nothing in the Rule states or suggests that documents prepared "in anticipation of litigation" with the purpose of assisting in the making of a business decision do not fall within its scope. . . .

In addition to the plain language of the Rule, the policies underlying the work-product doctrine suggest strongly that work-product protection should not be denied to a document that analyzes expected litigation merely because it is prepared to assist in a business decision. Framing the inquiry as whether the primary or exclusive purpose of the document was to assist in litigation threatens to deny protection to documents that implicate key concerns underlying the work-product doctrine. . . .

2. *Prepared "because of" litigation.*

The formulation of the work-product rule used by the Wright & Miller treatise, and cited by the Third, Fourth, Seventh, Eighth and D.C. Circuits, is that documents should be deemed prepared "in anticipation of litigation," and thus within the scope of the Rule, if "in light of the nature of the document and the factual situation in the particular case, the document can fairly be said to have been prepared or obtained *because of* the prospect of litigation." Charles Alan Wright, Arthur R. Miller, and Richard L. Marcus, 8 *Federal Practice & Procedure* § 2024, at 343 (1994) (emphasis added).

The Wright & Miller "because of" formulation accords with the plain language of Rule 26(b)(3) and the purposes underlying the work-product doctrine. Where a document is created because of the prospect of litigation, analyzing the likely outcome of that litigation, it does not lose protection under this formulation merely because it is created in order to assist with a business decision.

Conversely, it should be emphasized that the "because of" formulation that we adopt here withholds protection from documents that are prepared in the ordinary course of business or that would have been created in essentially similar form irrespective of the litigation. It is well established that work-product privilege does not apply to such documents. . . .

Furthermore, although a finding under this test that a document is prepared because of the prospect of litigation warrants application of Rule 26(b)(3), this does not necessarily mean that the document will be protected against discovery. Rather, it means that a document is *eligible* for work-product privilege. The district court can then assess whether the party seeking discovery has made an adequate showing of substantial need for the document and an inability to obtain its contents elsewhere without undue hardship. The district court can order production of the portions of the document for which a litigant has made an adequate showing. The court can focus its attention on whether the document or any portion is the type of material that should be disclosed, while retaining the authority to protect against disclosure of the mental impressions, strategies, and analyses of the party or its representative concerning the litigation. . . . .

Adlman is in tension with *United States v. Textron, Inc.*, 577 F.3d 21 (1st Cir. 2009), which held that tax accrual workpapers do not enjoy work product protection. The papers at issue in that case identified debatable positions the defendant company had taken on its tax returns along with an estimated probability of succeeding against the IRS should it challenge those positions. In some cases the relevant papers listed the IRS as having a 100% chance of success should it choose to challenge a particular transaction.

The IRS requested those papers pursuant to a policy in which it requests such papers from companies that have engaged in a type of transaction the IRS has identified as a form of tax avoidance. The company asserted the attorney-client privilege and work product doctrines as a defense to production. The trial court found the privilege had been waived when the papers were given to the company's outside accounting firm. It upheld the work product assertion, however, citing *Adlman*. The court of appeals initially affirmed and then, on rehearing *en banc*, reversed.

According to the majority:

> It is not enough to trigger work product protection that the subject matter of a document relates to a subject that might conceivably be litigated. Rather, as the Supreme Court explained, "the literal language of [Rule 26(b)(3)] protects materials prepared for any litigation or trial as long as they were prepared by or for a party to the subsequent litigation." *Federal Trade Commission v. Grolier Inc.*, 462 U.S. 19, 25 (1983) (emphasis added). This distinction is well established in the case law. See, e.g., *NLRB v. Sears, Roebuck & Co.*, 421 U.S. 132, 138 (1975).
>
> Nor is it enough that the materials were prepared by lawyers or represent legal thinking. Much corporate material prepared in law offices or reviewed by lawyers falls in that vast category. It is only work done in anticipation of or for trial that is protected.

Confidentiality and work product

Because the work product doctrine is designed to prevent one party from free riding on the work of another, it is not as concerned with confidentiality as the attorney-client privilege is. Limited disclosure of work product material does not waive the protection of the doctrine unless the disclosure is likely to reveal work product material to an opponent. *E.g. SEC v. Schroeder,* 2009 WL 1125579 (N.D. Cal. 2009) (disclosure of work product to independent auditor did not waive protection of doctrine); *SEC v. Roberts,* 254 F.R.D. 371 (N.D. Cal. 2008) (same); *Merrill Lynch & Co. v. Allegheny Energy*, 229 F.R.D. 441 (S.D.N.Y. 2004) (same). This fact may be important to your everyday work. For example, it is common for lawyers to help third party witnesses draft declarations submitted to courts (if not for the lawyer to draft the declaration altogether). Are drafts of such declarations work product or are they discoverable? Some cases hold drafts retain work product protection even though shared with non-clients, so long as they are not shared widely or with adverse parties. *See Randleman v. Fid. Nat. Title Ins. Co.*, 251 F.R.D. 281, 285 (N.D. Ohio 2008)("the trend is to consider draft affidavits and communications with counsel relating to affidavits as covered by the attorney work product doctrine"). Such cases appear to reason that final versions of declarations are served on parties that may depose the declarant and test the declarant's assertions, while drafts are not advanced as evidence. Such arguments of course do not eliminate the possibility that a party might use a draft to impeach a witness's statements in a final version. Judges often have strong intuitions about such matters, and strictly controlling authority is often lacking, so a judge's "gut" reaction to such issues may well be decisive.

Some differences between federal and California work product rules

Unlike federal law, in California, work product protection is not limited to material prepared in anticipation of litigation. Cal. Code Civ. P. 2018.030. And, unlike the attorney-client privilege and federal work product doctrine, California recognizes no crime-fraud exception to work product protection in civil cases. *Id.* § 2018.050; *Rico v. Mitsubishi Motors, Corp.*, 42 Cal.4th 807 (2007); *State Comp. Ins. Fund v. Superior Court*, 91 Cal.App.4th 1080, 1091 (2001). Finally, under California law the protection of the work-product doctrine in criminal cases is limited to "core" or "opinion" work product—the opinions and impressions of counsel. *People v. Zamudio*, 43 Cal.4th 327, 355 (2008) (noting that Penal Code § 1054.6 makes applicable to criminal cases the protection of Code of Civil Procedure § 2018.030(a), pertaining to opinion work product, but not the more general provision of § 2018.030(b).)

Waiver by disclosure to testifying experts or when work product at issue

Although the FRCP implies near-absolute protection from disclosure for opinion work product, there is an exception. If counsel discloses opinion work product to an expert witness who relies on that work product in forming her opinion, the work product must be disclosed under the general rule requiring disclosure of all materials an expert considers in forming an opinion. *See, e.g., Association of Irritated Residents v. Fred Schakel Dairy*, 2008 WL 2509735 (E.D.Cal. 2008); *Williamson v. Superior Court*, 21 Cal.3d 829 (1978).

Even opinion work product may be subject to discovery when it is at issue in litigation. *Holmgren v. State Farm Mut. Auto Ins. Co.*, 976 F.2d 573 (9th Cir. 1992), for example, involved a dispute over production of an insurance adjustor's notes estimating the value of the claims arising from the drunk driving of one of State Farm's insureds. The notes had been made in connection with settlement demands made by the person injured by the insured.

State Farm eventually paid $40,000 to settle the underlying claim. The injured party then sued it for bad faith settlement practices. In the bad faith litigation, the injured party obtained an order for production of the adjuster's notes, which valued the claim at between $78,000 and $145,000. The court of appeals affirmed the district court's order requiring production of the notes and that court's admission of the notes as evidence, stating: "We agree with the several courts and commentators that have concluded that opinion work product may be discovered and admitted when mental impressions are *at issue* in a case and the need for the material is compelling."

The Main Points to Recall From Chapter 5 Are:

- Work product doctrine protects the tangible embodiment of your work for a client.
- Opinion work product is that which reflects your mental impressions and conclusions. Protection for opinion work product is nearly absolute.
- Fact work product includes that which does not embody such impressions and conclusions. It is protected subject to a balancing test in which the requesting party may demonstrate a need for disclosure.
- Under federal law work product protects only material created in anticipation of litigation. Under California law all work product is protected.

- Work product protection may be waived if the material is placed at issue or disclosed widely.

	Duty of Confidentiality	Attorney Client Privilege	Work Product Doctrine (Federal)	Work Product Doctrine (CA)
Covers	All information that relates to representation and which is not generally known	Confidential communications between attorney and client for purpose of providing legal services	Mental impressions of counsel ("opinion" work product) and other work done on behalf of client ("fact" work product) in preparation for litigation	All work for a client (no "in anticipation of litigation" requirement)
Held By	Client	Client	Attorney	Attorney
Applies When	At all times	Rules of evidence apply	Material is prepared in anticipation of litigation	At all times
Effect	Forbids voluntary disclosure (but not disclosure required by law) or use of information that harms client or benefits lawyer outside the practice of law	Prevents disclosure evidence rules otherwise would compel	Requires party seeking fact work product to demonstrate substantial need for disclosure and that disclosure would not work undue hardship on producing party. Standard for producing opinion work product is higher-close to absolute protection	Absolute protection for opinion work product; balancing test based on fairness for fact work product
Exceptions	Prevent death or serious bodily injury; self-defense (respond to allegation of representation-related misconduct); seek advice about compliance with rules; disclosure required by law	Communications in furtherance of a crime or fraud; joint clients	Crime-fraud; self-defense	None in civil proceedings; crime-fraud in government proceedings

CHAPTER 7

REQUIREMENTS OF AND RELATING TO THE DUTY OF CARE

■ ■ ■

The duty of care requires lawyers to act competently and diligently. Competence is defined as acting with reasonable care, a standard that should be familiar from tort law. Reasonable care is defined pragmatically by comparison to what a competent lawyer would do in similar circumstances. Similar circumstances include the type of matter in the relevant jurisdiction, typically a state. In areas of law that are uniquely federal, such as patent, copyright, or some securities law issues, a national standard may be appropriate.

The cases in this chapter cover the basic elements of duty of care violations, with an emphasis on civil liability. You should bear in mind, however, that neglect of client matters is the most common source of lawyer discipline. Richard A. Abel, LAWYERS IN THE DOCK 57–58 (2007). Neglect includes things like missed deadlines or hearing dates or the failure to investigate facts or line up needed experts. Substance abuse is often a factor in neglect cases. So is a high-volume, low margin business model, in which a lawyer takes on many small cases each of which generates a small profit.

It is also common for lawyers to take on work in areas they know little or nothing about. The lawyers want the business and reason they can learn the law while working on the matter. Sometimes that works out.[1] Sometimes it does not. Such situations can be particularly risky for junior lawyers. Our first case illustrates the point.

A. CIVIL MALPRACTICE

A plaintiff alleging malpractice must show the defendant attorney owed the plaintiff a duty, breached it (by conduct falling below the standard of care), and that this breach was the actual and legal cause of damage suffered by the plaintiff. Of these requirements the duty and causation elements are most frequently litigated. The following materials survey these requirements.

[1] Though even then there can be problems of misrepresentation—few lawyers pitch business by admitting their ignorance—and how to bill time spent learning things a more seasoned lawyer would know already

1. DUTY AND BREACH

Model Rules 1.1–1.2(c); 1.3–1.4
Cal. R. Prof. Conduct 3–110
Restatement of the Law Governing Lawyers §§ 16, 20, 48–49, 50, 52–56

The Chicken and the Egg: A Duty to Seek Supervision

There is a chicken-and-egg aspect to competence. Competence includes exercising good judgment and, as the Introduction notes, judgment rests heavily on experience. According to *Restatement* § 16 cmt d:

> The lawyer must be competent to handle the matter, having the appropriate knowledge, skills, time, and professional qualifications. The lawyer must use those capacities diligently, not letting the matter languish but proceeding to perform the services called for by the client's objectives, including appropriate factual research, legal analysis, and exercise of professional judgment.

But how do you get the experience needed to act competently without accepting representations that only experience could make you competent to handle? In general you do so by working with and for more senior lawyers and actively developing an experience base sufficient to make good judgments about your practice. Here is an example of how *not* to do that.

BEVERLY HILLS CONCEPTS, INC. V. SCHATZ AND SCHATZ, RIBICOFF AND KOTKIN

247 Conn. 48 (1998)

KATZ, ASSOCIATE JUSTICE.

. . . . This appeal arises from a malpractice action brought by Beverly Hills Concepts, Inc. (plaintiff) against the named defendant, the law firm, Schatz and Schatz, Ribicoff and Kotkin (Schatz & Schatz), and the individual defendants, attorneys Stanford Goldman, Ira Dansky and Jane Seidl.

Charles Remington, Wayne Steidle, and Jeannie Leitao, incorporated the plaintiff as a Massachusetts corporation in April, 1987. They sold fitness equipment with a distinctive color scheme and logo, as well as a plan for operating a fitness club for women. The plaintiff's system included everything an owner would need to run a club, including equipment, training, sales and marketing support, and advertising and promotional materials. The plaintiff incorporated in Connecticut on August 17, 1987, and opened a corporate headquarters in Rocky Hill. From its Rocky Hill headquarters, the plaintiff licensed purchasers to use its concept, and sold distributorships to investors who gained the exclusive right to sell the plaintiff's products and to sublicense its name within a regional territory.

In October, 1987, prompted by a legal problem regarding the plaintiff's trademark in California, Leitao contacted the law firm of Schatz & Schatz. On October 28, 1987, the plaintiff met with Goldman, a partner at Schatz & Schatz, and Seidl, an associate in the firm. Leitao advised them that she recently had filed a trademark application for the name "Beverly Hills Concepts" in Washington, D.C. Goldman assumed incorrectly that this meant that the plaintiff had a "federally registered trademark," which would have alleviated the need to register as a "business opportunity" pursuant to the Connecticut Business Opportunity Investment Act (act). General Statutes (Rev. to 1987) § 36–503 et seq. He told Leitao that Schatz & Schatz possessed expertise in the field of franchising, and that the firm was well qualified to handle the plaintiff's legal affairs. Goldman also said that he would be involved personally in the firm's representation of the plaintiff.

In fact, beginning in late 1987, Goldman turned the plaintiff's file over to Seidl, a junior associate, and Ira Dansky, a "contract" lawyer not yet admitted to the Connecticut bar. Neither Seidl nor Dansky possessed expertise in the law of franchising and business opportunities. Schatz & Schatz billing records revealed that Goldman spent only about two hours on the plaintiff's matter between December, 1987, and June, 1988.

Before turning the plaintiff's file over to Seidl, Goldman visited the plaintiff's headquarters in Rocky Hill and examined its distributorship and licensing agreements and promotional materials. Despite the plaintiff's request for guidelines regarding the sale of its equipment and "system" pending its franchise registration, Schatz & Schatz failed to advise the plaintiff that it was violating the act by selling fitness club packages without first registering with the state banking commissioner. Rather, after analyzing the plaintiff's documents, Goldman told Remington that the question of whether the plaintiff was offering business opportunities within the meaning of the act was a "gray area" of the law. . . .

In the winter of 1987–88, Seidl began drafting the plaintiff's franchise documents. On February 8, 1988, another Schatz & Schatz associate, who had been assigned the task of researching the franchise registration requirements of fourteen states, including Connecticut, informed Seidl that the plaintiff was not exempt from the registration requirements of the act.

That same day, Schatz & Schatz contacted the plaintiff's Washington, D.C., trademark attorney, who confirmed that the plaintiff's trademark application was pending, and that no federal registration had been issued. Under these circumstances, Schatz & Schatz lawyers should have realized that the plaintiff was not exempt from the filing requirements of the act. Yet no one from the defendant law firm apprised the plaintiff of that fact. . . .

[O]n June 28, 1989, the banking commissioner issued a cease and desist order and a notice of intent to fine the plaintiff up to $10,000 for each sale made in violation of the act. The commissioner further issued a stop order invalidating the plaintiff's postsale registration. On June 26, 1991, following hearings in September and November of 1989 and May of 1990, the commissioner issued a final cease and desist order, stating that the plaintiff had violated the act repeatedly by selling unregistered business opportunities in Connecticut. This malpractice action followed. . . .

We note first that the defendants do not challenge on appeal the trial court's determination that their failure to register the plaintiff with the banking commission constituted legal malpractice. Seidl shares the blame for that lapse.

The trial court also reasonably could have found that Seidl had engaged in legal malpractice because, in her position as a junior associate, she failed to seek appropriate supervision. Rule 1.1 of the Rules of Professional Conduct provides that: "A lawyer shall provide competent representation to a client. Competent representation requires the legal knowledge, skill, thoroughness and preparation reasonably necessary for the representation." The commentary to rule 1.1 provides in part that a lawyer who lacks relevant experience may "associate or consult with, a lawyer of established competence in the field in question. . . . " Having little experience in franchising, Seidl, therefore, could have rendered competent representation by seeking appropriate supervision. She failed to do so. She testified that she had sent both Goldman and Dansky copies of her work product. Seidl's pursuit of supervision, however, went no further. She stated that she had "assume[d] somebody was . . . watching, taking care of looking at my work." The trial court reasonably concluded that this passivity departed from the applicable standard of care.

Help! Getting Guidance Without Getting Fired

You probably have a lot in common with Jane Seidl. She was a junior lawyer who knew nothing about her franchise law assignment. You know more than nothing about some areas of law but nothing about others. And even what you have studied amounts only to what can be gleaned from a few hundred pages of reading on an entire topic. An expert you are not.

For that reason, you are almost certain to encounter early in your career assignments about which you know much less then you should. *Schatz & Schatz* tells you that you proceed at your own risk: If you make a mistake, it is no defense that you expected your boss to look out for you. You are liable for malpractice on your own. (Your employer might have a statutory obligation to indemnify you, but that would not mean you were not liable.) That means you have to seek guidance from senior lawyers who know how it is done. You could in theory learn enough of the law to be sure that you knew what you were doing, but it takes a long time to learn enough to be sure that you are not missing something, so that is a risky approach.

But it is hard to confess ignorance. You don't want to seem dumb or uncooperative; you want your boss to think of you as whip-smart, independent, and highly capable—the type of person who takes problems off her hands rather than adds to her workload. In other words, you want to be the type of person your boss wants to continue paying, and even give a raise to, rather than sending off to pursue other interests (which is the term you use when you get fired).

So, you must satisfy your duty of care, which implies asking for supervision and guidance, and you don't want to look ignorant. How do you reconcile these demands? The best way is to combine hard work and framing.

The hard work part is easy: Research the law thoroughly and pursue leads that look relevant until you confirm that they are or are not. A good way to judge whether you have gone far enough is to proceed until you notice your sources referring back to each other. Probably you will spend more time than you can justify billing to the client, which means you or your partner will have to discount it. If you have a billable hour requirement, that probably means extra work for you. Not great, but better than malpractice liability.

The framing part is designed to make it easier for you to seek guidance and for your boss to give it. Do your homework first. Then frame your request in terms of the senior lawyer's expertise, not your ignorance. Do not demand help, provide an opportunity for the senior lawyer to display their command of the subject and mentor an eager learner (you).

A couple of tips: (1) Try to obtain an exemplar of the senior lawyer's work (a brief or contract, for example) and study it. Use it as a baseline (unless you find out it is flawed) and compliment it as a way of approaching questions about its meaning. (2) Have one or two longish meetings, not 20 short question sessions. Though it is less obvious, this too, is part of framing.

Much as you try to frame your request for help as a benefit to the senior lawyer, in reality it is at least in part time she could spend doing something more productive. She therefore will experience it partly as a loss. Remember that people are loss averse and that the loss function is steepest at the beginning of the curve. (See the prospect theory chart in chapter 3.B.1.) In English, that means your boss will perceive you as more costly for her to deal with if you make three short trips to her office to ask one question than if you make one trip to ask three questions.

For more on this point *see* Richard Thaler, *Mental Accounting Matters*, http://faculty.chicagogsb.edu/richard.thaler/research/MentalAccounting.pdf.

Contracting for Competence

If you do not work in a firm with lawyers competent in the subject of your representation you might seek to obtain the support of a competent lawyer by contracting with someone outside your firm. There are some commercial risks with that strategy—the client might wonder why you are necessary, after all, and why he or she shouldn't just hire the lawyer you are hiring—but it is acceptable, and preferable to winging it.

Contracting outside the firm raises authority and confidentiality issues not raised by walking down the hall to consult a colleague. You should assume that whether to contract with the new lawyer is the client's call, even if you were to pay the new lawyer's fees, as you presumably would prefer not to do. Your client's consent is necessary both as a matter of agency and because you would have to explain the matter to the lawyer you propose to hire, which presumably requires the client's informed consent to your disclosure. The contract with the outside lawyer also might include a specified division of labor and responsibility, which raises issues under Rule 1.2.

The ABA addresses these issues in a new comment 6 to Model Rule 1.1, approved in 2012. The introduction of these principles to the rules may be taken as an indication of the increase in the number of cases where small firms or sole practitioners form alliances that allow them to provide services in comparatively complex individual matters without incurring the fixed costs that come with larger size.

You can't be liable for breaching a duty you don't have. That's the good news. The bad news is you may have duties without knowing it. Our second case illustrates how.

NICHOLS V. KELLER

15 Cal.App.4th 1672 (1993)

MARTIN, ACTING PRESIDING JUSTICE.

INTRODUCTION

Plaintiff appeals from summary judgments (Code Civ.Proc., § 437c) in a legal malpractice action arising from an industrial accident.

FACTS

In December 1987, Zurn Industries employed the 46–year–old plaintiff at a cogeneration plant construction project in Crow's Landing, Stanislaus County. Zurn was a subcontractor and Kiewit Industrial was the general contractor on the project. Plaintiff had been a union boilermaker for over 24 years. On December 7, plaintiff commenced work on the exterior of a large boiler. He was working on scaffolding approximately 50 feet above the ground. Plaintiff testified at deposition he was working on the uppermost level of scaffolding with no workers above him. However, a coworker declared there were individuals working on an unfinished catwalk above the plaintiff.

Sometime before noon, plaintiff completed a heliarc weld and removed his welding "hood," which left only a cloth cap on his head. Plaintiff then reached for his hard hat when something hit him on the head. Plaintiff dropped to his knees on the scaffolding, although he apparently did not lose consciousness. He never saw the object that hit him on the head. However, someone told him it was a piece of steel approximately four inches by four inches by one-quarter-inch thick.

A coworker transported plaintiff to a hospital emergency room in Patterson, California. Emergency room personnel X-rayed plaintiff's head and closed a scalp laceration with 16 stitches. The emergency room doctor released plaintiff to "light duty" work for a one-week period. Plaintiff returned to his regular work as a welder approximately one week after that.

On February 24, 1988, plaintiff and his wife met with defendant E. Paul Fulfer, an attorney with the defendant firm of Fulfer & Fulfer, to discuss plaintiff's accident and legal rights and remedies. At the conclusion of the meeting, defendant Fulfer had plaintiff sign a workers' compensation application for adjudication of claim. Fulfer executed the form as "applicant's attorney" and filed the application on plaintiff's behalf with the Stockton office of the Division of Industrial Accidents/California Department of Industrial Relations. The Stockton office received the document on February 26, 1988 (case No. STK068205). Defendant Fulfer then associated defendant Edward Keller, an attorney with defendant firm of LaCoste, Keller, Mello & Land, to prosecute the workers' compensation claim. Fulfer signed a formal pleading bearing the caption "association of attorneys" on January 20, 1989.

Defendant Keller met with plaintiff on March 28, 1988, and said he would represent plaintiff in his pending workers' compensation matter against Zurn Industries and Aetna Casualty and Surety Company. Defendant Keller continued to represent plaintiff in the workers' compensation proceeding until July 1989.

Sometime in 1989, plaintiff and his wife traveled from their home in Nevada to a workers' compensation medical appointment in the San Francisco area. On their return trip, they visited the Boilermakers Union Hall in Pittsburg, California. Plaintiff and his wife spoke with union employees Jim Wilson and Greg Bingham regarding plaintiff's accident at the cogeneration plant. They suggested plaintiff meet with another attorney and scheduled an appointment with James Butler of the law offices of William L. Veen in San Francisco. . . .

On July 7, 1989, plaintiff and his wife met with attorney Butler. According to plaintiff,

> "At this meeting I learned for the first time that a third-party claim could and very likely should have been brought in regards to my industrial injury in December 1987, and that my wife and I may have a legal claim against Edward C. Keller and Elbert Paul Fulfer, attorneys, who had failed to advise or inform us of these facts."

On March 21, 1990, plaintiff filed a complaint for damages in Stanislaus County Superior Court. Plaintiff named attorneys Keller, Fulfer, and their respective law firms as defendants. . . .

On December 17, 1990, defendant Fulfer and his law firm filed a motion for summary judgment. Defendants alleged . . . the attorney-client relationship, if any, which existed between defendant Fulfer and plaintiff was limited solely to the subject matter of plaintiff's workers' compensation claim . . . On December 19, 1990, defendant Keller and his law firm also filed a motion for summary judgment. . . . On January 31, 1991, the court filed a minute order granting defendants' motions for summary judgment. . . .

DISCUSSION

. . . . Actionable legal malpractice is compounded of the same basic elements as other kinds of actionable negligence: duty, breach of duty, causation, and damage. The elements of a cause of action for professional negligence are (1) the duty of the professional to use such skill, prudence and diligence as other members of the profession commonly possess and exercise; (2) breach of that duty; (3) a causal connection between the negligent conduct and the resulting injury; and (4) actual loss or damage resulting from the professional negligence. When these elements coexist, they constitute actionable negligence. On the other hand, absence of, or failure to prove, any of them is fatal to recovery. An attorney, by accepting employment to give legal advice or render legal services, impliedly agrees to use ordinary judgment, care, skill, and diligence in the performance of the tasks he or she undertakes.

The question of the existence of a legal duty of care in a given factual situation presents a question of law which is to be determined by the courts alone. Entry of summary judgment in favor of the defendant in a professional negligence action is proper where the plaintiff is unable to show the defendant owed such a duty of care. Absent the existence of a duty by the professional to the claimant, there can be no breach and no negligence. (*Goldberg v. Frye* (1990) 217 Cal.App.3d 1258, 1267–1268.). . . .

A significant area of exposure for the workers' compensation attorney concerns that attorney's responsibility for counseling regarding a potential third-party action. One of an attorney's basic functions is to advise. Liability can exist because the attorney failed to provide advice. Not only should an attorney furnish advice when requested, but he or she should also volunteer opinions when necessary to further the client's objectives. The attorney need not advise and caution of every possible alternative, but only of those that may result in adverse consequences if not considered.

Generally speaking, a workers' compensation attorney should be able to limit the retention to the compensation claim if the client is cautioned (1) there may be other remedies which the attorney will not investigate and (2) other counsel should be consulted on such matters. However, even when a retention is expressly limited, the attorney may still have a duty to alert the client to legal problems which are reasonably apparent, even though they fall outside the scope of the retention. The rationale is that, as between the lay client and the attorney, the latter is more qualified to recognize and analyze the client's legal needs. The attorney need not represent the client on such matters. Nevertheless, the attorney should inform the client of the limitations of the attorney's representation and of the possible need for other counsel.

An attorney's duty to his or her client depends on the existence of an attorney-client relationship. If that relationship does not exist, the fiduciary duty to a client does not arise. Except for those situations where an attorney is appointed by the court, the attorney-client relationship is created by some form of contract, express or implied, formal or informal. (*Fox v. Pollack* (1986) 181 Cal.App.3d 954, 959.) A member of the State Bar shall not contract with a client prospectively limiting the member's liability to the client for the member's professional malpractice. However, this rule is not intended to prevent a member from reasonably limiting the scope of the member's employment or representation. (Rules Prof. Conduct, rule 3–400(A), Discussion.)

In their motions for summary judgment, defendant attorneys maintained they agreed to undertake only a limited employment. Attorney

Fulfer asserted he agreed to represent plaintiff in the workers' compensation matter only and, even then, for two specific purposes: (1) to file a workers' compensation application on plaintiff's behalf and (2) to refer plaintiff to defendant Keller, so the latter could actually prosecute the workers' compensation claim on plaintiff's behalf. Attorney Keller argued the attorney-client relationship between the plaintiff and himself was solely for the purpose of representation in the workers' compensation claim. Keller claimed he owed only a duty to prosecute that claim and not to prosecute any possible third-party claim or to advise plaintiff as to the prosecution of such a claim. Defendants reiterate these positions on appeal.

In his opposition to the motions for summary judgment, plaintiff attached the declaration of attorney Yale Jones, a certified specialist in workers' compensation law. Jones declared attorney Fulfer acted below the standard of care of an attorney in the Stockton area by failing to (1) advise plaintiff of the different remedies available through the Workers' Compensation Appeal Board and through a civil action; (2) advise plaintiff of the statute of limitations applicable to plaintiff's third-party action; (3) advise plaintiff to consult another attorney concerning any available rights and remedies plaintiff might have against third parties; and (4) provide plaintiff with written advice regarding which rights defendant Fulfer would protect or which needed to be reviewed by other competent attorneys and what would happen in the event plaintiff did not protect those rights. Attorney Jones also declared defendant Keller acted below the standard of care for the same reasons. Declarant's opinion as to defendant Keller was based on a set of hypothetical facts.

Thus, defendants maintained they undertook limited duties to plaintiff and, as a matter of law, they owed him no duty to advise about possible third-party claims, while plaintiff's expert, Yale Jones, declared their duties were far more expansive and required both counsel to advise plaintiff about various workers' compensation and civil remedies, the applicable statute of limitations for a third-party action, the propriety of obtaining a "second opinion" as to available rights and remedies, and the precise scope of defendants' representation. The lower court's minute order concluded: "[I]t is undisputed that the representation was undertaken for the limited purpose of the workman's compensation claim. Furthermore, an attorney's obligation does not include a duty to advise on all possible alternatives no matter how remote or tenuous. [(*Davis v. Damrell* (1981) 119 Cal.App.3d 883, 889.)]"

A determination that defendants owe plaintiff no duty of care would negate an essential element of plaintiff's cause of action for negligence and would constitute a complete defense. Whether a duty of care exists is a question of law for the court and is reviewable de novo. All persons are required to use ordinary care to prevent injury to others from their conduct. (Civ.Code, § 1714, subd. (a); *Scott v. Chevron U.S.A.* (1992) 5 Cal.App.4th 510, 515.) A professional has a duty to use such skill, prudence and diligence as other members of the profession commonly possess and exercise. Legal duties are not discoverable facts of nature. Rather, they are merely conclusory expressions that, in cases of a particular type, liability should be imposed for damage done.

Foreseeability of harm, though not determinative, has become the chief factor in duty analysis. Confusion has arisen over the concept of foreseeability and the variety of roles it plays in tort law. Foreseeability is a question of fact for the jury in many contexts. However, in defining the boundaries of duty, foreseeability is a question of law for the court. The question of foreseeability in a "duty" context is a limited one for the court and is readily contrasted with the fact-specific foreseeability questions bearing on negligence (breach of duty) and causation posed to the jury or trier of fact.

It seems to us the foreseeability factor compels a finding of duty in cases of this type. A trained attorney is more qualified to recognize and analyze legal needs than a lay client, and, at least in part, this is the reason a party seeks out and retains an attorney to represent and advise him or her in legal matters. (2 Mallen & Smith, Legal Malpractice, *supra,* § § 19.5, 19.28, pp. 159–162, 229–233.) As Justice Brandeis observed a century ago:

> " 'The duty of a lawyer today is not that of a solver of legal conundrums: he is indeed a counsellor at law. Knowledge of the law is of course essential to his efficiency, but the law bears to his profession a relation very similar to that which medicine does to that of the physicians. The apothecary can prepare the dose, the more intelligent one even knows the specific for most common diseases. It requires but a mediocre physician to administer the proper drug for the patient who correctly and fully describes his ailment. The great physicians are those who in addition to that knowledge of therapeutics which is open to all, know not merely the human body but the human mind and emotions, so as to make themselves the proper diagnosis—to know the truth which their patients fail to disclose. . . . ' " (Mason, Brandeis: A Free Man's Life (1946) p. 80.)

What was true in 1893 is certainly true today in this increasingly complex and technologically advanced society in which we live. In the context of personal injury consultations between lawyer and layperson, it is reasonably foreseeable the latter will offer a selective or incomplete recitation of the facts underlying the claim; request legal assistance by employing such everyday terms as "workers' compensation," "disability," and "unemployment"; and rely upon the consulting lawyer to describe the array of legal remedies available, alert the layperson to any apparent legal problems, and, if appropriate, indicate limitations on the retention of counsel and the need for other counsel. In the event the lawyer fails to so advise the layperson, it is also reasonably foreseeable the layperson will fail to ask relevant questions regarding the existence of other remedies and be deprived of relief through a combination of ignorance and lack or failure of understanding. And, if counsel elects to limit or prescribe his representation of the client, i.e., to a workers' compensation claim only without reference or regard to any third party or collateral claims which the client might pursue if adequately advised, then counsel must make such limitations in representation very clear to his client. Thus, a lawyer who signs an application for adjudication of a workers' compensation claim and a lawyer who accepts a referral to prosecute the claim owe the claimant a duty of care to advise on available remedies, including third-party actions. . . .

CASE QUESTIONS

1. What are the elements of a malpractice claim?
2. What must a worker's compensation lawyer do to limit her duties to worker's compensation work?
3. How does the court describe legal duties (in contrast to facts of nature)?
4. What does the court consider the most important element of duty analysis?
5. What did Fulfer and Keller need to do to satisfy the standard of care?
6. What is the rule for limiting the scope of representation?

What You Say and What They Hear I

Nichols brings to mind a famous line from the movie *Cool Hand Luke*, starring Paul Newman: "What we have here is, failure to communicate." Nichols was a boilermaker. He was 46 when he was injured and had worked as a union boilermaker for 24 years (since he was 22). He probably did not graduate college. There is no reason to believe he was sophisticated in the ways of the legal world and the facts suggest he was not.

When Nichols met with E. Paul Fulfer he probably had no very clear idea of what he wanted from a lawyer. He knew he had been hit in the head with a steel plate and had been injured. He probably suspected, or at least hoped, that the law would give him some money for his injury. It is highly unlikely that he knew anything about the difference between workers' compensation and tort law. There is no reason to think he did, and the facts suggest he didn't. In his mind, Nichols went to Fulfer with a problem—his injury—hoping for a solution—money.

Fulfer seems to have had workers' compensation expertise. He had on hand the form Nichols needed to file a claim and he knew Keller, who prosecuted such claims. In his mind, Fulfer may have been a workers' compensation lawyer and little or nothing more. The same is true of Keller. But there is no reason to think Nichols would have understood what it meant to be a workers' compensation lawyer, or any other kind of lawyer, for that matter, rather than just a "lawyer."

In terms of the concepts you studied in the Introduction, *Nichols* may be explained as a case in which Fulfer and Keller perceived categories Nichols did not. They placed themselves in a subcategory—workers' comp lawyer—Nichols did not see. The Court's finding in favor of Nichols represents a judgment that may be described as holding that it is a lawyer's responsibility to identify such subcategories functionally in terms of what the lawyer will and will not do *in relation to the client's understanding of the client's problem.*[2]

The lesson of *Nichols,* therefore, is simple: When you as a lawyer have information a client does not, especially information about your own practice in relation to the facts the client brings to you, there is a risk of miscommunication. You may say that you will represent Nichols regarding a workers' compensation claim and no more. Nichols may hear only that you will represent him, and ignore the "and no more" because he has no idea of what more there might be. You do have an idea, and the point of *Nichols* is to place on you the burden of making clear to a client both that you will only represent him to a limited extent *and that he might have other claims you will not pursue but which he might wish to look into.* The burden of clear communication is on you, not the client. Speak up!

For an interesting case applying *Nichols* to class action lawyers, *see Janik v. Rudy, Exelrod & Zieff,* 119 Cal.App.4th 930 (2004). The court there cited *Nichols* in holding that class counsel's duties are defined by the duty of care and not limited by an order certifying a case as a class action. The court held

[2] From a policy perspective you can think of this point in two ways. From an economic point of view, it is cheaper for you to provide information that you have and clients may not than for clients to have to ask for your opinion. By hypothesis, they don't know what you do; they may not know to ask and it is inefficient to give them incentive to investigate information you already have. From a less instrumental point of view, recall the view of counsel depicted in *Barbara A. v. John G.* You are presumed to be the sophisticated, informed party, while the client is the dependent, uninformed party. Part of doing a good job for the client, *Nichols* tells us, is making sure the client's lack of information does not harm them, at least when it is easy for you to remedy that lack.

> In the context of a class action, both the representative plaintiffs and the absent class members . . . are entitled to assume that their attorneys will consider and bring to the attention of at least the class representatives additional or greater claims that may exist arising out of the circumstances underlying the certified claims that class members will be unable to raise if not asserted in the pending action. The class members are entitled to assume that their attorneys are attempting to maximize their recovery for the conduct they are challenging and that they are not, without good reason, failing to assert those claims that will do so. . . .

Under *Janik*, lawyers representing a class may be sued for failing to bring claims class members might reasonably expect them to bring.

Seeing Yourself as Others See You

One of the hardest things to do in the law, as in life, is to understand how others perceive you. You know what you think and mean, after all, and it is natural to think others will as well. Probably Fulfer and Keller thought Nichols understood the limits they intended to place on the duties they owed him. That didn't work out; they needed to do more.

It can be hard to understand that others' perceptions of you affect their choices and, therefore, may affect your choices. Yet that is a direct result of the fifth rule of judgment you read in the introduction: Strategy spaces are interdependent.

What exactly does that mean? For Fulfer and Keller it meant the duties they owed depended on what Nichols understood, not what was clear to them. Here is a game that illustrates clearly the notion that strategy spaces are interdependent. It is a game of simultaneous choices and it has a dominant solution. In English, that means there is a right answer, and to reach it you have to think in terms of (i) what is best for you; (ii) given what the other player does; which (iii) will be based on what the other play expects you to do. This setup is taken from Meghana Bhatt & Colin F. Camerer, *Self-referential thinking and equilibrium as states of mind in games: fMRI evidence*, 52 GAMES & ECON. BEHAVIOR 425 (2005):

You are player one. You get to choose either A, B, or C. Simultaneously, Player two gets to choose either AA or BB. After the choices are made, each player receives the payoffs indicated in the cell dictated by the choices. (I.e., if player one chooses A, and player two chooses AA, then player One gets 43 and player Two gets 10.) Assume the payoff figures are paid in dollars.

Player One's Payoffs

	AA	BB
A	43	85
B	94	57
C	68	39

Player Two's Payoffs

	AA	BB
A	10	37
B	44	60
C	73	6

This exercise may seem abstract, but a seasoned lawyer would recognize in an instant that they think in these terms all the time. For successful lawyers, it becomes second nature.

The Relationship Between Disciplinary Rules and the Duty of Care

There is no cause of action for violating a disciplinary rule. As *Nichols* demonstrates, however, the cause of action for legal malpractice requires a plaintiff to show that an attorney owed the plaintiff a duty of care and breached it. Disciplinary rules may be relevant to defining the scope and content of duties of care. (They also may be relevant to defining the scope and content of fiduciary obligations when the cause of action is for breach of fiduciary duty.)

For example, the plaintiff in *Mirabito v. Liccardo*, 4 Cal.App.4th 41 (1992), alleged that her late husband's attorney (also his second cousin) breached his fiduciary duties to the husband by inducing him to invest in ventures in which the attorney had an undisclosed personal interest. The attorney failed to advise his client to seek independent counsel regarding these investments and, though he personally guaranteed the investments, he forgot to mention that he had filed for bankruptcy around the time of at least one investment. As we will see later, these are serious mistakes.

The husband lost about $4 million, which the plaintiff sought from the attorney. At trial, the plaintiff sought to introduce evidence from attorneys who would testify, in part, that disciplinary rules required the defendant to disclose all facts relevant to the investment decision and to provide the plaintiff's late husband the opportunity to seek independent counsel. The defense moved to exclude this evidence. The trial court allowed the testimony, and the court of appeals affirmed this decision:

* * *

> Since [Plaintiff's] fraud claims were based, in part, upon [Lawyer's] alleged breach of his fiduciary duties, it was incumbent upon [Plaintiff] to establish what "duties" [Lawyer] was alleged to have breached. It is well established that an attorney's duties to his client

are governed by the rules of professional conduct. (*Day v. Rosenthal* (1985) 170 Cal.App.3d 1125, 1147.) Those rules, together with statutes and general principles relating to other fiduciary relationships, all help define the duty component of the fiduciary duty which an attorney owes to his client. (*David Welch Co. v. Erskine & Tulley* (1988) 203 Cal.App.3d 884, 890.)

Appellant [cites cases holding] the rules cannot be used to establish an attorney's civil liability. Neither of these cases is persuasive for the point appellant advances. Both cases merely hold that there is no independent cause of action for the breach of a disciplinary rule. Here, Edmond did not allege Leonard's violation of a rule as a separate cause of action. Rather, Edmond alleged Leonard had breached his fiduciary duties. Leonard's breach of his duties was then measured by his violation of the rules.[3]

* * *

For a contrary approach, *see Hizey v. Carpenter*, 119 Wash.2d 251 (1992) (jury in lawyer malpractice action could not be informed of rules of professional conduct either by instruction or through expert testimony).

2. CAUSATION AND DAMAGES

A malpractice plaintiff must show that but for the lawyer's negligence the plaintiff would have been better off. When the underlying matter involved litigation this element generally requires the malpractice plaintiff to hold a "trial within a trial," meaning the malpractice plaintiff must show he or she more likely than not would have prevailed in the underlying matter (or on an issue in that matter that would affect the client's result) had the lawyer not been negligent. That can be a tall order, and causation is often central to malpractice defenses. The same requirement applies when the underlying matter did not involve litigation, as the following case shows.

---

[3] FN2. At oral argument, appellant attempted to buttress her argument by pointing to a recent out-of-state case, *Lazy Seven Coal Sales, Inc. v. Stone & Hinds* (Tenn.1991) 813 S.W.2d 400. According to appellant, in *Lazy Seven*, the Tennessee Supreme Court held that state's rules of professional responsibility could not be used in a legal malpractice trial to prove an attorney's misconduct. We question appellant's reading of the case. We interpret *Lazy Seven* as holding simply that the violation of a rule of conduct, by itself, does not establish an attorney's malpractice. The *Lazy Seven* court implicitly approved the use of the rules of professional responsibility at trial when it stated, "the standards stated in the Code are not irrelevant in determining the standard of care in certain actions for malpractice. The Code may provide guidance in ascertaining lawyers' obligations to their clients under various circumstances, and conduct which violates the Code may also constitute a breach of the standard of care due a client."

In any event, we need not definitively interpret Tennessee law on this point. To the extent Lazy Seven conflicts with California law, we decline to follow it.

VINER V. SWEET

30 Cal.4th 1232 (2003)

KENNARD, J.

In a client's action against an attorney for legal malpractice, the client must prove, among other things, that the attorney's negligent acts or omissions caused the client to suffer some financial harm or loss. When the alleged malpractice occurred in the performance of transactional work (giving advice or preparing documents for a business transaction), must the client prove this causation element according to the "but for" test, meaning that the harm or loss would not have occurred without the attorney's malpractice? The answer is yes.[4]

I

In 1984, plaintiffs Michael Viner and his wife, Deborah Raffin Viner, founded Dove Audio, Inc. (Dove). The company produced audio versions of books read by the authors or by celebrities, and it did television and movie projects.

In 1994, Dove went public by issuing stock at $10 a share. In 1995, the Viners and Dove entered into long-term employment contracts guaranteeing the Viners, among other things, a certain level of salaries, and containing indemnification provisions favorable to the Viners. The Viners received a large share of Dove's common stock and all of its preferred cumulative dividend series "A" stock.

Thereafter, Michael Viner discussed with longtime friend David Povich, a partner in defendant law firm Williams & Connolly in Washington, D.C., the possibility of selling the Viners' interest in Dove. In the fall of 1996, Norton Herrick proposed buying the Viners' entire interest in Dove. Attorney Povich assigned the matter to his partner, defendant Charles A. Sweet, a corporate transactional attorney. Sweet was not a member of the California Bar and was not familiar with California law. During the negotiations with Herrick, Sweet learned that under the Viners' employment agreements with Dove, the latter owed the Viners a substantial amount of unpaid dividends on their preferred stock. Sweet also learned that the Viners wanted to preserve their right to engage in the television and movie businesses.

When the negotiations with Herrick were unsuccessful, Ronald Lightstone of Media Equities International (MEI) approached the Viners. Thereafter, in March 1997, the Viners and MEI entered into an agreement under which MEI was to invest $4 million, and the Viners $2 mil-

---

[4] FN1. Causation analysis in tort law generally proceeds in two stages: determining cause in fact and considering various policy factors that may preclude imposition of liability. (*Ferguson v. Lieff, Cabraser, Heimann & Bernstein* (2003) 30 Cal.4th 1037, 1045, 135 Cal.Rptr.2d 46, 69 P.3d 965; *PPG Industries, Inc. v. Transamerica Ins. Co.* (1999) 20 Cal.4th 310, 315–316, 84 Cal.Rptr.2d 455, 975 P.2d 652.) This case concerns only the element of cause in fact.

lion, to buy Dove stock. By May 1997, disputes arose, and the parties to the agreement each threatened litigation. That same month, Ronald Lightstone of MEI and Michael Viner, without defendant attorney Sweet's involvement, agreed that MEI would buy the Viners' stock in Dove and the Viners would terminate their employment with Dove.

Defendant attorney Sweet and Lightstone of MEI negotiated the final agreement, which the parties signed on June 10, 1997. The deal consisted of a securities purchase agreement and an employment termination agreement. Under the former, MEI agreed to buy a significant portion of the Viners' stock for more than $3 million. Under the latter agreement, the Viners' employment with Dove was terminated, mutual general releases were given, and Dove was to pay the Viners a total of $1.5 million over five years in monthly payments, with Dove's series "E" preferred stock to be held in escrow for distribution to the Viners if Dove defaulted on the monthly payments to them.

The employment termination agreement contained a noncompetition provision stating that the Viners would not " 'compete' in any way, directly or indirectly, in the audio book business for a period of four years" in any state in which Dove was doing business. The agreement also had a nonsolicitation provision that the Viners would not "directly or indirectly contract with, hire, solicit, encourage the departure of or in any manner engage or seek to employ any author or, for purposes of audio books, reader, currently under contract or included in the Company's book or audio catalogues for a period of four years.". . . .

Defendant attorney Sweet led the Viners to believe that the employment termination agreement gave them three years of monthly payments by Dove, retained the indemnity protection they had with Dove, and provided credit for work done before their departure from Dove. The Viners also thought that they could use their celebrity contacts for any work that did not compete with Dove's audiobook business and involvement in film and television productions, and that if Dove defaulted on the agreed-upon monthly payments to them, the noncompetition clauses would be voided. The contracts did not so provide.

Later, several arbitration proceedings took place to resolve disputes between the Viners and MEI, including a claim by the Viners that the noncompetition provision of the employment termination agreement violated Business and Professions Code section 16600's restrictions on noncompetition agreements. The arbitrator rejected the claim, and the superior court confirmed the arbitrator's decision. On June 3, 1998, the Viners brought a malpractice action against Attorney Sweet and the law firm of Williams & Connolly. Presented at trial were . . . seven claims. . . .

After deliberating five days, the jury found defendants liable . . . awarding the Viners $13,291,532 in damages. Defendants moved for judgment notwithstanding the verdict or in the alternative for a new trial, arguing that the trial court erred in not instructing the jury that the Viners needed to prove they would have received a better deal "but for" defendant attorney Sweet's negligence. The trial court denied both motions.

The Court of Appeal reduced the damage award to $8,085,732, but otherwise affirmed the judgment. . . .

We granted defendants' petition for review, and thereafter limited the issues to whether the plaintiff in a transactional legal malpractice action must prove that a more favorable result would have been obtained *but for* the alleged negligence.[5]

II

Defendants contend that in a transactional malpractice action, the plaintiff must show that *but for* the alleged malpractice, a more favorable result would have been obtained. Thus, defendants argue, the Viners had to show that without defendants' negligence (1) they would have had a more advantageous agreement (the "better deal" scenario), or (2) they would not have entered into the transaction with MEI and therefore would have been better off (the "no deal" scenario).

The Viners respond that in *Mitchell v. Gonzales* (1991) 54 Cal.3d 1041, this court repudiated the "but for" test of causation in tort cases alleging negligence. Not so. . . . *Mitchell* did not abandon or repudiate the requirement that the plaintiff must prove that, *but for* the alleged negligence, the harm would not have happened. On the contrary, *Mitchell* stated that jury instructions on causation in negligence cases should use the "substantial factor" test articulated in the Restatement Second of Torts (Restatement), and *Mitchell* recognized that "the 'substantial factor' test *subsumes* the 'but for' test." (*Mitchell v. Gonzales, supra,* 54 Cal.3d at p. 1052 italics added.). . . .

The text of Restatement section 432 demonstrates how the "substantial factor" test subsumes the traditional "but for" test of causation. Subsection (1) of section 432 provides: "Except as stated in Subsection (2), the actor's negligent conduct is *not a substantial factor* in bringing about harm to another *if the harm would have been sustained even if the actor had not been negligent.*" (Italics added.) Subsection (2) states that if "two forces are actively operating . . . and each of itself is sufficient to bring about harm to another, the actor's negligence may be found to be a substantial factor in bringing it about."

---

[5] FN2. The trial court refused defendants' requested instruction on "but for" causation. The court did instruct the jury that a cause of an injury "is something that is a substantial factor in bringing about" the harm. Because the Court of Appeal addressed this case as presenting the "pure question of law" of whether the legal requirement of showing "but for" causation applies at all to transactional malpractice cases, and because we limited our review to that issue, we have not framed our discussion in terms of instructional error.

Thus, in Restatement section 432, subsection (1) adopts the "but for" test of causation, while subsection (2) provides for an exception to that test. The situation that the exception addresses has long been recognized, but it has been given various labels, including "concurrent independent causes" (*Mitchell v. Gonzales, supra,* 54 Cal.3d at pp. 1049, 1052), "combined force criteria" (Robertson, *The Common Sense of Cause in Fact* (1997) 75 Tex. L.Rev. 1765, 1778), and "multiple sufficient causes" (Rest.3d Torts, Liability for Physical Harm (Basic Principles) (Tent. Draft No. 2, Mar. 25, 2002) § 27, com. b, p. 70).

This case does not involve concurrent independent causes, which are multiple forces operating at the same time and independently, each of which would have been sufficient by itself to bring about the harm. Here, the Viners argued that their losses were caused by defendants' negligence, the actions of MEI exploiting that negligence, the underlying economic situation, and "other factors." Because these forces operated in combination, with none being sufficient in the absence of the others to bring about the harm, they are not concurrent *independent* causes.[6] Accordingly, the exception stated in subsection (2) of Restatement section 432 does not apply, and this case is governed by the "but for" test stated in subsection (1) of Restatement section 432.[7]

The Court of Appeal here held that a plaintiff suing an attorney for transactional malpractice need not show that the harm would not have occurred in the absence of the attorney's negligence. We disagree. We see nothing distinctive about transactional malpractice that would justify a relaxation of, or departure from, the well-established requirement in negligence cases that the plaintiff establish causation by showing either: (1) *but for* the negligence, the harm would not have occurred, or (2) the negligence was a concurrent independent cause of the harm.

"When a business transaction goes awry, a natural target of the disappointed principals is the attorneys who arranged or advised the deal. Clients predictably attempt to shift some part of the loss and disappointment of a deal that goes sour onto the shoulders of persons who were responsible for the underlying legal work. Before the loss can be shifted, however, the client has an initial hurdle to clear. *It must be shown that the loss suffered was in fact caused by the alleged attorney malpractice.* It is far too easy to make the legal advisor a scapegoat for a variety of business misjudgments unless the courts pay close attention to the cause in fact element, and deny recovery where the unfavorable outcome was like-

[6] FN3. "Concurrent independent causes" should not be confused with "concurrent causes." The former refers to multiple forces operating at the same time and independently, each of which would have been sufficient by itself to bring about the harm. The latter refers simply to multiple forces operating at the same time.

[7] FN4. The requirement that the plaintiff prove causation should not be confused with the method or means of doing so. Phrases such as "trial within a trial," "case within a case," "no deal" scenario, and "better deal" scenario describe methods of proving causation, not the causation requirement itself or the test for determining whether causation has been established.

ly to occur anyway, the client already knew the problems with the deal, or where the client's own misconduct or misjudgment caused the problems. It is the failure of the client to establish the causal link that explains decisions where the loss is termed remote or speculative. Courts are properly cautious about making attorneys guarantors of their clients' faulty business judgment." (Bauman, *Damages for Legal Malpractice: An Appraisal of the Crumbling Dike and Threatening Flood* (1988) 61 Temp. L.Rev. 1127, 1154–1155, fns. omitted, italics added (hereafter Bauman, *Damages for Legal Malpractice*).)

In a litigation malpractice action, the plaintiff must establish that *but for* the alleged negligence of the defendant attorney, the plaintiff would have obtained a more favorable judgment or settlement in the action in which the malpractice allegedly occurred. The purpose of this requirement, which has been in use for more than 120 years, is to safeguard against speculative and conjectural claims. (*Mattco Forge, Inc. v. Arthur Young & Co.* (1997) 52 Cal.App.4th 820, 832–834.) It serves the essential purpose of ensuring that damages awarded for the attorney's malpractice actually have been caused by the malpractice.

The Court of Appeal here attempted to distinguish litigation malpractice from transactional malpractice in order to justify a relaxation of the "but for" test of causation in transactional malpractice cases. One of the distinguishing features, according to the court, was that in litigation a gain for one side necessarily entails a corresponding loss for the other, whereas in transactional representation a gain for one side does not necessarily result in a loss for the other. We question both the accuracy and the relevance of this generalization. In litigation, as in transactional work, a gain for one side does not necessarily result in a loss for the other side. Litigation may involve multiple claims and issues arising from complaints and cross-complaints, and parties in such litigation may prevail on some issues and not others, so that in the end there is no clear winner or loser and no exact correlation between one side's gains and the other side's losses. In addition, an attorney's representation of a client often combines litigation and transactional work, as when the attorney effects a settlement of pending litigation. The "but for" test of causation applies to a claim of legal malpractice in the settlement of litigation . . . even though the settlement is itself a form of business transaction.

Nor do we agree with the Court of Appeal that litigation is inherently or necessarily less complex than transactional work. Some litigation, such as many lawsuits involving car accidents, is relatively uncomplicated, but so too is much transactional work, such as the negotiation of a simple lease or a purchase and sale agreement. But some litigation, such as a beneficiary's action against a trustee challenging the trustee's management of trust property over a period of decades, is as complex as most transactional work.

It is true, as the Court of Appeal pointed out, that litigation generally involves an examination of past events whereas transactional work involves anticipating and guiding the course of future events. But this distinction makes little difference for purposes of selecting an appropriate test of causation. Determining causation always requires evaluation of hypothetical situations concerning what might have happened, but did not. In both litigation and transactional malpractice cases, the crucial causation inquiry is *what would have happened* if the defendant attorney had not been negligent. This is so because the very idea of causation necessarily involves comparing historical events to a hypothetical alternative.

The Viners also contend that the "but for" test of causation should not apply to transactional malpractice cases because it is too difficult to obtain the evidence needed to satisfy this standard of proof. In particular, they argue that proving causation under the "but for" test would require them to obtain the testimony of the other parties to the transaction, who have since become their adversaries, to the effect that they would have given the Viners more favorable terms had the Viners' attorneys not performed negligently. Not so. In transactional malpractice cases, as in other cases, the plaintiff may use circumstantial evidence to satisfy his or her burden. An express concession by the other parties to the negotiation that they would have accepted other or additional terms is not necessary. And the plaintiff need not prove causation with absolute certainty. Rather, the plaintiff need only " 'introduce evidence which affords a reasonable basis for the conclusion that it is more likely than not that the conduct of the defendant was a cause in fact of the result.' " (*Ortega v. Kmart Corp.* (2001) 26 Cal.4th 1200, 1205 quoting Prosser & Keeton on Torts, (5th ed.1984) § 41, p. 269, fns. omitted.) In any event, difficulties of proof cannot justify imposing liability for injuries that the attorney could not have prevented by performing according to the required standard of care. . . .

For the reasons given above, we conclude that, just as in litigation malpractice actions, a plaintiff in a transactional malpractice action must show that *but for* the alleged malpractice, it is more likely than not that the plaintiff would have obtained a more favorable result.

CASE QUESTIONS

1. What did the Viners claim Sweet did not do but should have done?
2. How were they harmed?
3. What must a malpractice plaintiff show to prove causation?
4. How does the court treat the "substantial factor" test?

5. What does the rule in *Viner* require you to prove? What evidence would you attempt to introduce to prove it?

6. Suppose the alleged malpractice involved litigation that was not resolved on the merits. (Suppose a lawyer missed the deadline for filing under the applicable limitations period, for example.) Would the malpractice plaintiff have to try the underlying case as part of the malpractice case?

PROBLEM 7–1

Suppose a malpractice plaintiff sued his lawyer for filing a claim too late. Suppose also that the lawyer could show that the client probably would have lost at trial, but the client could show that the defendant was risk averse and would have settled had a timely claim been filed. Does the malpractice plaintiff win on the ground that she lost the chance to settle or does she lose on the ground that she would have lost at trial?

3. LIMITATIONS AND TOLLING

Causation is an important defense for lawyers defending malpractice actions. The limitations period is often another. The limitations period on malpractice actions varies from state to state. In California, the limitations period is set by Code of Civil Procedure § 340.6(a), which provides:

> An action against an attorney for a wrongful act or omission, other than for actual fraud, arising in the performance of professional services shall be commenced within one year after the plaintiff discovers, or through the use of reasonable diligence should have discovered, the facts constituting the wrongful act or omission, or four years from the date of the wrongful act or omission, whichever occurs first. In no event shall the time for commencement of legal action exceed four years except that the period shall be tolled during the time that any of the following exist:
>
> (1) The plaintiff has not sustained actual injury;
>
> (2) The attorney continues to represent the plaintiff regarding the specific subject matter in which the alleged wrongful act or omission occurred;
>
> (3) The attorney willfully conceals the facts constituting the wrongful act or omission when such facts are known to the attorney, except that this subdivision shall toll only the four-year limitation; and
>
> (4) The plaintiff is under a legal or physical disability which restricts the plaintiff's ability to commence legal action.

Two questions relevant to the provisions of Section 340.6 are often litigated. The first is when an injury occurs, within the meaning of section (a)(1). The second is when a lawyer "continues to represent" a client within the meaning of Section (a)(2).

The general rule is that both provisions are construed broadly. Thus, "[a]ctual injury occurs when the client suffers any loss or injury legally cognizable as damages in a legal malpractice action based on the asserted errors or omissions." *Jordache Enters., Inc. v. Brobeck, Phleger & Harrison,* 18 Cal.4th 739 (1998). The Court reasoned that the injury requirement operates to ensure that the limitations period on a claim does not begin before the client suffered enough of an injury to allow a claim to be filed. The Court's use of the terms "loss" and "damage" therefore should not be read too literally; the *Jordache* court implied loss occurred when "the attorneys' alleged neglect allowed the insurers to raise an objectively viable defense" to the plaintiff's claim to insurance coverage. *See also Croucier v. Chavos*, 207 Cal.App.4th 1138 (2012)(lack of recovery on money judgment and transfer of assets rendering enforcement more difficult constituted injury sufficient to trigger commencement of limitations period).

Both the injury and continued representation issues were raised in *Fritz v. Ehrmann*, 136 Cal.App.4th 1374 (2006). Fritz alleged that Ehrmann negligently drafted a promissory note. Ehrmann asserted the statute of limitations as a defense. The relevant note was drafted and signed in 1995. It was secured by title to a motel, and it superseded an earlier note signed in 1983.

Fritz claimed malpractice on two issues. The first concerned prepayment of debt. The 1983 note gave the borrowers the right to pre-pay their debt. Fritz claimed the parties agreed in 1995 to eliminate this right in exchange for Fritz charging a lower interest rate but that Ehrmann failed to include this provision in the 1995 note.

The second issue concerned deferred interest. The 1983 note deferred to the end of the note's term some interest the borrowers owed. As of 1995, $182,474 in interest had been deferred. Fritz alleged that in preparing the 1995 Ehrmann included the new interest rate but said nothing about the deferred interest.

The borrowers prepaid principal in November 2000 and August 2001. They made a payment in January 2002, which they claimed was the final payment they owed. Fritz took that money but also took the position that the borrowers owed him the $182,474 in interest deferred under the original 1983 note.

In June 2002 the borrowers sued Fritz to clear title to the motel. Fritz cross-claimed for money he claimed was owed. Ehrmann represented Fritz in this dispute until April 2003, when Fritz got a new lawyer. In October 2003 Fritz settled with the borrowers for $100,000. In November 2003, he sued Ehrmann for malpractice.

Ehrmann argued that the limitations period expired before the malpractice claim was filed. He argued Fritz was injured over a year before the suit was filed and that he had not represented Fritz continuously for purposes of the tolling provision of Section 340.6(a)(2). Fritz argued the limitations period was tolled both because he had not suffered injury and because Ehrmann continued to represent him.

The court sided with Fritz on both issues. With respect to injury, it held

> "The mere breach of a professional duty, causing only nominal damages, speculative harm, or the threat of future harm-not yet realized-does not suffice to create a cause of action for negligence. . . . until the client suffers appreciable harm as a consequence of [the] attorney's negligence, the client cannot establish a cause of action for malpractice. . . . Under section 340.6, the one-year limitations period commences when the plaintiff actually or constructively discovers the facts of the wrongful act or omission, but the period is tolled until the plaintiff sustains actual injury."

The court contrasted actual injury, which causes the statute to accrue, with speculative or contingent damage, which does not: "[S]peculative and contingent injuries are those that do not yet exist, as when an attorney's error creates only a potential for harm in the future."

According to the court, Fritz had two types of injuries. First, he could have been injured by the borrowers' prepayment of principal, assuming he could not thereafter reinvest the principal and obtain a similar rate of return.[8] Second, he could have been injured by the failure to specify in the note that the deferred interest was to be repaid at the end of the term. Both injuries were speculative at the time Ehrmann prepared the note. The borrowers might never have had the funds or the inclination to prepay principal, and they might have paid the deferred interest in accord with the parties' original understanding without regard to any ambiguity in the second note.

As to whether the limitations period was tolled by continued representation, the court found "representation may be deemed continuous where a hiatus separates completion of a transaction on behalf of a client and resumption of legal activities after a problem arises, many years later. . . . " Because no legal work needed to be done on the note between 1995 and 2002, when the borrower claimed to have paid off the note, the

[8] The court maintained this position even though the borrower did prepay some principal and Fritz agreed to allow the prepayment. The court reasoned that the borrower's request to prepay evidenced their understanding that the terms of the old note continued to apply, and therefore did not implicate Ehrmann's alleged negligence. More fundamentally, the court found the prepayment created tax advantages for Fritz and he therefore suffered no net harm from the payments.

court treated Ehrmann as Fritz's lawyer for that period of time, plus a period thereafter where Ehrmann tried to resolve the dispute.

Continuous representation tolls the limitations period even if the client is aware of the act or omission at issue. *E.g. Laird v. Blacker*, 2 Cal.4th 606, 618 (1992). The reasoning is that this rule minimizes disruption of the attorney-client relationship that might occur because of malpractice—the lawyer can try to fix or minimize the problem without prejudicing the client's claim, and the client can allow the lawyer to do so without worrying about losing the claim.

Representation may continue for purposes of Section 340.6 even after a client has replaced one attorney with another. *Nielsen v. Beck*, 157 Cal.App.4th 1041 (2007), is such a case. Beck represented Nielson in an unlawful detainer matter. The bankruptcy court ruled against Nielson in September 2003. Nielson became dissatisfied with Beck's performance and replaced him with another lawyer. The substitution of attorney form was filed on August 26, 2004.

In September and October 2004, Nielson contacted Beck three times for advice concerning negotiations (which were conducted by successor counsel) relating to the bankruptcy claims. Beck billed Nielson one hour for the calls. Nielson sued Beck for malpractice in September 2005. The court held there was a factual issue as to when Beck stopped representing Nielson, and reversed the trial court's order granting summary judgment in favor of Beck. Conversely, a failure to withdraw from representation will not, by itself, toll the limitations period where the facts otherwise indicate the representation has ended. *Shapero v. Fliegel* 191 Cal.App.3d 842 (1987).

Disputes sometimes arise over when a plaintiff should have discovered the act or omission in question. For example, the plaintiff in *Gonzalez v. Kalu*, 140 Cal.App.4th 21 (2006), hired her lawyer to file a sexual harassment claim against her former employer (who fired her after receiving a demand letter from the lawyer). Kalu filed an administrative complaint in July of 2000, and allegedly told Ms. Gonzalez that the case would take a long time.

Ms. Gonzalez did not hear from Kalu again until June of 2003, when she went to his office to pick up her file. She then learned that nothing had happened on the administrative front, and he had never filed a civil action against her employer. She sued for malpractice, and the trial court dismissed on the ground that no reasonable juror could find that the limitations period had not run during the three years of silence.

The court of appeals reversed, finding that a reasonable juror could conclude that the lawyer represented Ms. Gonzalez during this time and that the tolling provision of Section 340.6(a)(2) therefore preserved her claim. The court stated that for purposes of Section 340.6, "in the event of an attorney's unilateral withdrawal or abandonment of the client, the representation ends when the client actually has or reasonably should have no expectation that the attorney will provide further legal services. . . . That may occur upon the attorney's express notification to the client that the attorney will perform no further services or, if the attorney remains silent, may be inferred from the circumstances."[9]

Is the limitations period tolled against a law firm even after the lawyer who committed malpractice leaves the firm? In *Beal Bank, SSB v. Arter & Hadden, LLP*, 42 Cal.4th 503 (2007), the California Supreme Court said: No. According to the Court:

> section 340.6, subdivision (a) defines the limitations period for '[a]n action against an attorney,' [and] the tolling provision in subdivision (a)(2) extends the limitations period only during ongoing representation by '[t]he attorney.' " Under ordinary rules of grammar, "[t]he attorney" in subdivision (a)(2) refers back to the "attorney" who is the target of the action in subdivision (a). . . . Thus, under the most natural reading of the statute, an action against an individual attorney is tolled so long as *that attorney* continues representation; conversely, an attorney's continued representation tolls an action only against that attorney.

The court concluded "the text implies an action against a law firm is tolled so long as *that firm* continues representation, just as an action against an attorney is tolled so long as *that attorney* continues representation, but representation by one attorney or firm does not toll claims that may exist against a different, unaffiliated attorney or firm." It also held that this conclusion was consistent with the purpose of the statute: "When a lawyer leaves a firm and takes a client with him, the firm's representation of the client ceases. There is no risk the firm will attempt to run out the clock on the statute of limitations by offering reassurances and blandishments about the state of the case. Conversely, the firm loses all ability to mitigate any damage to the client."

A Duty to Inform on Yourself?

Suppose you make a mistake and breach the duty of care. Does your duty of loyalty require that you inform your client that you may be liable to the client for malpractice? And, if so, how far do you have to go? May you (i) inform the client of the facts that would lead a reasonable person to conclude that you had breached the duty of care, or do you actually have to say (ii): "a court might find that I acted negligently; you should

---

[9] It is worth noting that Kalu stated that he normally advised clients in writing when a representation ended, but there was no evidence of such a writing in this case. The importance of making clear when representation is over is discussed in more detail in chapter 10.

consult a different lawyer about claims you might have against me." Or even worse (iii): "It is my view that I am liable to you, and you should consult a lawyer about the extent of that liability and the best way for you to proceed against me"?

The law is not as clear as one would like it to be, but the best answer is that (i) is not enough, (iii) would comply with the duty of loyalty but is not required, while the duty of loyalty would demand at least disclosure (ii). *E.g. Beal Bank, SSB v. Arter & Hadden, LLP*, 42 Cal.4th 503, 514 (2007) ("attorneys have a fiduciary obligation to disclose material facts to their clients, an obligation that includes disclosure of acts of malpractice").

As the New Jersey Supreme Court put it in *Circle Chevrolet Co. v. Giordano, Halleran & Ciesla*, 142 N.J. 280 (1995), *overruled on other grounds Olds v. Donnelly*, 150 N.J. 424 (1997):

> An attorney has an ethical obligation to advise a client that he or she might have a claim against that attorney, even if such advice flies in the face of that attorney's own interests. The Rules of Professional Conduct (RPC) provide that "[a] lawyer shall not represent a client if the representation of that client may be materially limited by the . . . lawyer's own interests, unless . . . the client consents after a full disclosure of the circumstances and consultation with the client." RPC 1.7(b)(2). The RPC also provides that "[a] lawyer shall explain a matter to the extent reasonably necessary to permit the client to make informed decisions regarding the representation." RPC 1.4(b). Thus, an attorney who realizes he or she has made a mistake must immediately notify the client of the mistake as well as the client's right to obtain new counsel and sue the attorney for negligence. Accordingly, application of the entire controversy doctrine to legal malpractice claims does not infiltrate the sanctity of the lawyer-client relationship because, notwithstanding the doctrine, the attorney is under an overriding ethical obligation to inform the client of the accrual of a probable claim against that attorney.

Accord Tallon v. Committee On Professional Standards, 447 N.Y.S.2d 50, 51 (1982) ("An attorney has a professional duty to promptly notify his client of his failure to act and of the possible claim his client may thus have against him. After making such disclosure, withdrawing from the case and advising his former client of his right to retain other counsel, an attorney may then settle any claim that his former client has against him."). Statutes may affect this duty in particular circumstances. For example, California Penal Code § 1240.1(a) provides that in cases where a defendant is entitled to appellate counsel it is the duty of trial counsel to advise the defendant whether grounds for appeal exist. The statute cautions, however, that trial counsel shall "admonish the defendant that he or she is not able to provide advice concerning his or her own competency, and that the State Public Defender or other counsel should be consulted for advice as to whether an issue regarding the competency of counsel should be raised on appeal."

Overlapping Causes of Action II

Does the limitations period of Section 340.6 apply to causes of action other than breach of the duty of care? What about breach of fiduciary duty, such as in *Welch v. Erskine & Tully*? The *Welch* court held that Section 340.6 did not apply to that case because the plaintiff did not allege malpractice.

The court in *Quintilliani v. Mannerino*, 62 Cal.App.4th 54 (1998), disagreed. The case involved an attorney who also acted as a concert promoter. The plaintiff brought several causes of action and the court had to determine whether Section 340.6 applied to them. The court found the source of the duty decisive: "Since most claims for breach of fiduciary obligations can be restated as a claim for attorney malpractice, and since the fiduciary obligations here arose out of the attorney-client relationship, we find that section 340.6 applies to such claims." *Accord Stoll v. Superior Court*, 9 Cal.App.4th 1362 (1992).

Plaintiff's counsel in *Quintilliani* chose to plead allegations of incompetence as both malpractice and breach of fiduciary duty. The case therefore might be distinguished from *Welch*, which is a paradigm breach of fiduciary duty case involving the self-interested use of client information. That fact probably explains why, as the *Quintilliani* court noted, the authorities cited in *Welch* "do not relate to legal malpractice actions. . . . " The *Quintilliani* court's conclusion—that "*Welch* should not be followed, since it did not cite any authority dealing with a breach of fiduciary duty in the context of attorney malpractice"—thus may be read narrowly to stand only for the proposition that a plaintiff cannot avoid the malpractice limitations period by calling a duty of care claim a cause of action for breach of fiduciary duty.

Yet the court's terse reasoning leaves open the broader reading that even core fiduciary duty claims are subject to the limitations period for malpractice. That reading also fits with the language of the statute, which applies to any action "against an attorney for a wrongful act or omission, other than for actual fraud . . . " Breaches of the duty of loyalty almost certainly involve wrongful acts or omissions. (The statute may *effectively* distinguish between violations of care and loyalty, however, because violations of the latter may be more likely to fall into either the exclusion of fraud claims or into one of the categories of tolling.)

The question of which limitations period to apply raises the general question of how to deal with overlapping causes of action, which we noted briefly in chapter 2. In a typical case a client might sue a lawyer on one or more of three theories. The first is breach of contract. Such a claim would lie if the lawyer expressly or impliedly promised to perform in a way the lawyer did not perform. The second is malpractice—negligence, as in *Viner*—and the third is breach of fiduciary duty.

It can be hard to distinguish between these claims, particularly because counsel for a client-plaintiff often will plead the same facts as a predicate for each claim and seek the same relief on each claim. In this regard, note that the *Quintilliani* court thought most breach of fiduciary duty claims could be restated as claims for malpractice. Regardless whether that statement is right as a purely empirical matter, doctrinally it is too broad. It fails to distinguish cases in which the lawyer deliberately advances his own interests, either at the client's expense or using the client's information, from cases of sheer inadvertence or incompetence. In other words, it fails to distinguish between the duty of care, which, as we saw in Part I, is not a true fiduciary duty, and the duty of loyalty, which is.

Some states will dismiss an action for breach of fiduciary duty that does no more than repeat allegations pleaded in support of a cause of action for malpractice (breach of the duty of care). *See Weil, Gotshal & Manges, LLP v. Fashion Boutique of Short Hills, Inc.*, 780 N.Y.S.2d 593, 596 (2004); *Majumdar v. Lurie*, 274 Ill.App.3d 267 (1995). Even states that do not dismiss fiduciary duty claims that duplicate malpractice claims may require a party seeking damages to show that, but for the fiduciary breach, the lawyer would have done a better job for them. A plaintiff operating under this rule must show that the breach caused the claimed damages, just as the party would in a malpractice case. *Kilpatrick v. Wiley, Rein & Fielding*, 909 P.2d 1283 (Utah App.1996).

Other states have no such rule, however, which may lead to decisions that seem to qualify the fiduciary duty cause of action but which in fact deal with duty of care-style claims. We saw two examples of such cases earlier, in connection with disgorgement. One of them, *Slovensky v. Friedman*, 142 Cal.App.4th 1518 (2006), refused to recognize a breach of fiduciary duty claim where a client received some recovery on a claim that was actually barred by the applicable statute of limitations. She nevertheless sued her counsel for allegedly lying to her and pressuring her to settle.

The *Slovensky* court seemed to reason that the client had no claim to begin with so her counsel's alleged misconduct did her no harm and, therefore, was not actionable. This reasoning is questionable (though understandable on the facts of the case). The no-harm premise disposes of the malpractice claim and (of course) a breach of fiduciary duty claim seeking damages. But it should not necessarily dispose of an equitable claim for disgorgement where a client can show a clear and serious breach of duty. *See, e.g., Restatement* §§ 37, 60(2). On the facts of *Slovensky,* disgorgement might be appropriate to reduce the incentive to (allegedly) lie to and browbeat clients into fee-generating settlements even if the client would have been worse off had her claim been subjected to stand-alone scrutiny rather than folded into a package settlement (which it was).

Burrow v. Arce, 997 S.W.2d 229 (Tx 1999), illustrates this reasoning, which hews more closely than *Slovensky* to the basic premises of agency law. The court there held: "[t]hough the historical origins of the remedy of forfeiture of an agent's compensation are obscure, the reasons for the remedy are apparent. The rule is founded both on principle and pragmatics. In principle, a person who agrees to perform compensable services in a relationship of trust and violates that relationship breaches the agreement, express or implied, on which the right to compensation is based. The person is not entitled to be paid when he has not provided the loyalty bargained for and promised. . . It is the agent's disloyalty, not any resulting harm, that violates the fiduciary relationship and thus impairs the basis for compensation. An agent's compensation is not only for specific results but also for loyalty. Removing the disincentive of forfeiture except when harm results would prompt an agent to attempt to calculate whether particular conduct, though disloyal to the principal, might nevertheless be harmless to the principal and profitable to the agent. The main purpose of forfeiture is not to compensate an injured principal, even though it may have that effect. Rather, the central purpose of the equitable remedy of forfeiture is to protect relationships of trust by discouraging agents' disloyalty." The extent of forfeiture lies in the court's discretion.

This distinction between causes of action for breach of loyalty and care matters in some cases, so it is important to understand the conceptual difference between the two, even if loose language in the cases blurs the distinction. The distinction may affect the burden of proof, the manner of proof, and the availability of punitive damages.

Burden of proof: When lawyers enter into contracts with existing clients, there is a risk that the lawyer will use her expertise and influence to cut a good deal for herself at the client's expense. Transactions between lawyers and existing clients therefore are subject to particularly rigorous scrutiny; such transactions are voidable by the client unless the lawyer can demonstrate that they are fair. *See, e.g., Restatement (Third) of the Law Governing Lawyers* § 18(1)(a). This allocation of burdens differs from normal contract or tort cases, in which the plaintiff would bear the burden of proof and persuasion on a fairness-related defense such as duress or unconscionability. In chapter 11.G, we study an example of a lawyer unable to meet this burden.

Manner of proof: The distinction between care and loyalty also may affect what evidence a plaintiff must present to establish a prima facie case. A plaintiff alleging a breach of the duty of care must establish the standard of care, which is generally a factual question regarding the practice in the relevant field and geographic area. Courts that see breach of fiduciary duty claims as essentially interchangeable with negligence claims require plaintiffs to produce expert testimony in support of the fiduciary duty claim. *E.g.*, *Aller v. Law Office of Carole C. Schriefer, P.C.*, 140 P.3d 23 (Colo. App. 2005).

Hoagland ex rel Midwest Transit, Inc. v. Sandberg, Phoenix & von Gontard, P.C., 385 F.3d 737, 743 (7th Cir. 2004), is a notable example of this line of authority. That case involved a claim by a receiver against a law firm that had represented a failed corporation. The receiver alleged the law firm had harmed the corporation by representing both the corporation and one of its officers in a derivative suit (one brought nominally on behalf of the corporation alleging harm to the corporation) that alleged the officer had looted the corporation. The receiver sought repayment by the firm of fees the corporation had paid it in connection with this matter.

The Seventh Circuit affirmed dismissal of the claim on the ground that the receiver had failed to present expert testimony to support his claim. Judge Posner wrote that, under Illinois law, a malpractice claim "requires (unless the lawyer's breach of duty is obvious even to a layperson, which is not contended) expert testimony regarding the standard of care *or loyalty* that the lawyer is alleged to have violated." (emphasis added). He rejected the argument that the receiver could pursue a disgorgement claim without such evidence:

> An attorney's throwing one client to the wolves to save the other is malpractice whatever the plaintiff chooses to call it. He cannot be permitted, by recharacterizing the claim—whether by calling the conflict of interest a breach of fiduciary obligation or by contending that his contract with the law firm contained an implied promise not to commit such conflicts—to get around the requirement of presenting expert testimony. That is the kind of formalist move that courts rightly reject. Illinois courts hold that "when a breach of fiduciary duty claim is based on the same operative facts as a legal malpractice claim, and results in the same injury, the later claim should be dismissed as duplicative." The fact that restitution was sought instead of conventional damages also does not alter the nature of the suit. Restitution is a remedy, at least when sought as here as reparations for a tort. It is often sought in lieu of damages. Asking for restitution doesn't change the cause of action.

385 F.3d at 743.

This language should be taken as accurately stating Illinois law, requiring dismissal of fiduciary duty claims that do no more than regurgitate malpractice claims. Logically, however, this reasoning is debatable. Suppose the interests of the corporation and the corporate officer conflicted so strikingly that the law firm could not have represented both in the derivative suit. Setting aside the question of who would have standing to complain of the conflict, in that event the firm would have been disqualified from representing at least the officer, a result economically equivalent to at least a partial forfeiture of fees. Why then should the receiver be denied disgorgement of at least some of the fees just because the conflict was litigated after the fact instead of up front?

One answer might be that in *Hoagland* the alleged disloyalty (the conflict of interest) is hard to understand—harder, at least, than a case where a lawyer trades on a client's information or fleeces the client. Expert testimony might well be required in *Hoagland* even if the court distinguished disgorgement of fees from a damages award.

Note the qualification in the parenthetical to the *Hoagland* opinion: expert testimony is required even in a fiduciary duty case "unless the lawyer's breach of duty is obvious even to a layperson." This exception to the general rule requiring expert testimony does not distinguish fiduciary duty claims from negligence claims: if the standard of care is obvious to a lay juror, a negligence plaintiff need not present expert testimony, either. As a factual matter, however, cases alleging true breaches of the duty of loyalty may be more likely to fall within this exception than are cases that try to dress up a duty of care claim as a duty of loyalty claim.

Availability of punitive damages. A claim for breach of the duty of care (malpractice) is a negligence claim for which punitive damages are not available. Cal. Civ. Code § 3294. In contrast, punitive damages are available for breach of fiduciary duties. California courts will award punitive damages if the fiduciary breach is "despicable." Thus, in *Ball v. Posey*, 176 Cal.App.3d 1209 (1986), the court affirmed a punitive damages award against a lawyer who exercised undue influence over an elderly client so he could convert her assets to his own use. In *American Airlines, Inc. v. Sheppard, Mullin, Richter & Hampton,* 96 Cal.App.4th 1017, 1051 (2002), the court affirmed the trial court's refusal to award such damages for a firm that accepted a representation that conflicted with its duties to a current client, but where the firm assiduously maintained that client's confidences.

As this brief survey shows, the relationship between claims based on the duty of care and those alleging "breach of fiduciary duty" is not as clear as it should be. The easiest way to make it as clear as it is going to be is to distinguish between fiduciary duty claims that are in fact disguised duty of care claims and true fiduciary duty claims—those alleging disloyal conduct. Don't rely on general statements that apply only in particular contexts, such as the one in *Quintilliani.*

4. FEE DISGORGEMENT

The problem of overlapping causes of action also implicates the remedy of disgorgement of fees. *Restatement* Section 37 states that "a lawyer engaging in a clear and serious violation of duty to a client may be required to forfeit some or all of the lawyer's compensation for the matter. Considerations relevant to the question of forfeiture include the gravity and timing of the violation, its willfulness, its effect on the value of the lawyer's work for the client, any other threatened or actual harm to the client, and the adequacy of other remedies."

This provision overlaps with, but is not the same as, malpractice liability. As comment a to Section 37 states,

> [a] lawyer's misconduct can constitute malpractice rendering the lawyer liable for any resulting damage to the client under the common law or, in some jurisdictions, a consumer-protection statute (see § 41, Comment *b*). Malpractice damages can be greater or smaller than the forfeited fees. Conduct constituting malpractice is not always the same as conduct warranting fee forfeiture. A lawyer's negligent legal research, for example, might constitute malpractice, but will not necessarily lead to fee forfeiture.

Section 37 therefore provides an alternative theory under which a client might pursue recovery from a lawyer who has breached a duty to the client.

Historically, disgorgement was an equitable remedy. The gist of the remedy was that a disloyal agent had to pay to the principal any profits earned through her disloyalty. That concept obviously relates most directly to claims for breach of the duty of loyalty. As the preceding note and the comment to *Restatement* § 37 show, however, the distinction between claims for breach of loyalty and care has not been drawn as cleanly as it could be. Disgorgement is therefore less closely associated with loyalty violations than this distinction would imply.

Jurisdictions disagree on whether clients seeking disgorgement must show they were harmed by the alleged breach of duty. For example, the California Supreme Court has held that a client not harmed by a fiduciary's unlawful conduct may not recover fees, even where the legal violation is clear. *Frye v. Tenderloin Housing Clinic, Inc.* 38 Cal.4th 23, 48 (2006). *See also Slovensky v. Friedman*, 142 Cal.App.4th 1518, 1521 (2006) (applying *Frye* to very different facts). In contrast, in *Huber v. Taylor*, 469 F.3d 67 (3d Cir. 2006), the Third Circuit interpreted Texas law to allow disgorgement even where the client could not show harm. *Burrow v. Arce*, discussed above, summarizes Texas law on this point. On the issue generally, *see* Charles W. Wolfram, *A Cautionary Tale: Fiduciary Breach As Legal Malpractice*, 34 HOFSTRA L. REV. 689, 699–701 (2006).

Factual differences between these cases may have contributed to the different legal rules. In *Frye*, the California Supreme Court dealt with a client who sought to recover fees obtained by a non-profit housing law clinic that had not registered with the state bar, as required by law. In *Huber*, the Third Circuit dealt with a claim that counsel had favored one set of clients over a different set of clients in order to maximize counsel's fee. The disfavored clients did not claim that they received less than they would have received from truly loyal counsel, only that their counsel acted disloyally by favoring other clients to further counsel's own interests.

You should think of disgorgement in relation to the facts of particular cases. In cases where a lawyer deliberately advances his self-interest either at the client's expense or using the client's information, standard principles of agency law hold that the lawyer must account to the client for the profits earned from the relevant conduct. *United States v. O'Hagan*, in chapter 4, is one example of such a case. *Beery v. State Bar*, in chapter 11.G, is another.

Finally, note that the text of Section 37 does not require that the breach of duty have been intentional in order to support a disgorgement remedy. The "willfulness" of the breach is a relevant factor, but not a condition. *See also Restatement (Second) of Agency* § 469 (1958).

B. CRIMINAL MALPRACTICE

Criminal malpractice works differently from civil malpractice. In most states a plaintiff alleging malpractice by a criminal lawyer must plead and prove that he or she was actually innocent of the crime alleged. This requirement bars many but not all claims involving criminal defense counsel, as the following materials show.

WINNICZEK V. NAGELBERG

394 F.3d 505 (7th Cir. 2005)

POSNER, CIRCUIT JUDGE:

The district court dismissed for failure to state a claim a diversity suit that charges breach of contract, legal malpractice, and breach of fiduciary duty, all in violation of Illinois law. The plaintiffs are Hilary Winniczek and his wife, Danuta; the defendant is a lawyer, Sheldon Nagelberg.

The complaint, our only source of facts, alleges the following. Winniczek was charged with a variety of federal criminal offenses arising from his participation in a scheme to help people obtain commercial drivers' licenses fraudulently. He hired a lawyer named Petro to represent him. Nagelberg got wind of the matter and advised the Winniczeks that Petro was inexperienced in federal criminal matters and they should fire

Petro and hire him; and they did so. Nagelberg then told them that Winniczek had a good defense to the criminal charges but that it would cost the Winniczeks $150,000 in fees, plus $20,000 in expenses, to present the defense. They paid him the $170,000 over the course of the year preceding the scheduled date of the criminal trial.

As soon as Nagelberg was fully paid, he told the Winniczeks that he wouldn't take the case to trial because Winniczek had made statements to the authorities when he was represented by Petro that scotched any defense he might have had, and as a result Winniczek had no choice but to plead guilty. Nagelberg then departed the scene and another lawyer represented Winniczek at the plea hearing. Winniczek pleaded guilty and was sentenced to 22 months in prison.

Winniczek does not claim to be innocent of the crimes for which he was convicted, and this dooms his claim for legal malpractice. (His wife, not having been represented by Nagelberg, obviously has no malpractice claim.) Under Illinois law, as that of other states, a criminal defendant cannot bring a suit for malpractice against his attorney merely upon proof that the attorney failed to meet minimum standards of professional competence and that had he done so the defendant would have been acquitted on some technicality; the defendant (that is, the malpractice plaintiff) must also prove that he was actually innocent of the crime . . . which Winniczek cannot prove. This "actual innocence" rule presumably has an exception for the case in which, although the defendant is guilty, he received an unlawful penalty; the existence of the exception [has been assumed in some cases] though we cannot find any case that actually discusses the question; but the exception would not be applicable to Winniczek either.

The "actual-innocence" rule differs from the rule applicable to malpractice arising out of civil matters. There the only requirement is, as in all tort cases, that the plaintiff prove he was injured by the defendant's negligence. If the malpractice involved the handling of a lawsuit, all he has to prove is that he would have won had it not been for the lawyer's negligence [citations omitted] It would be irrelevant that the negligence had consisted in failing to make a purely technical argument.

The reason for the difference is not that criminals are disfavored litigants, though there are hints of such a rationale in some cases. . . . It is that the scope for collateral attacks on judgments is broader in criminal than in civil matters. A criminal defendant can establish ineffective assistance of counsel, the counterpart to malpractice . . . and thus get his conviction vacated, by proving that had it not been for his lawyer's failure to come up to minimum professional standards, he would have been acquitted. He can do this even if, as in a case in which his only defense was that illegally seized evidence had been used against him, the ground for acquittal would have been unrelated to innocence. *Owens v. United*

States, 387 F.3d 607, 609–11 (7th Cir. 2004), and cases cited in *id.* at 611. Since a criminal defendant thus has a good remedy for his lawyer's malpractice—namely to get his conviction voided—he has less need for a damages remedy than the loser of a civil lawsuit, who would have no chance of getting the judgment in the suit set aside just because his lawyer had booted a good claim or defense.

This analysis shows that the logic of the "actual innocence" rule does not extend to a case in which the complaint is not that the plaintiff lost his case because of his lawyer's negligence, but that he was overcharged. The fact that one of the plaintiffs, namely Mrs. Winniczek, wasn't even charged with a crime merely underscores the district court's error. She is seeking restitution of money obtained from her by false pretenses or breach of an implied contract. [citations omitted] But so is Winniczek, in count one of the complaint, which is for breach of contract or, what need not be distinguished in this case (for all that is important is that the Winniczeks are complaining only about an overcharge, and not about the failure of Nagelberg to gain Winniczek an acquittal or a lighter sentence), breach of the fiduciary obligation that Nagelberg, as Winniczek's lawyer, owed him. [citations omitted] Only count two is for malpractice, and only that count is barred by the requirement, in a malpractice suit growing out of a criminal conviction, of proving actual innocence of the crime.

To see why count one is not about malpractice, imagine that Nagelberg had promised to represent Winniczek for a fee of $50,000, plus $25,000 in prepaid expenses of which any amount not expended was to be returned to Winniczek. Suppose further that Nagelberg had done a superb though ultimately unsuccessful job in representing Winniczek but had incurred expenses of only $5,000 and refused to refund the balance of the $25,000 in prepaid expenses. There would be no malpractice, in the sense of incompetent representation—and there would be nothing in the thinking behind the actual-innocence rule to suggest that Winniczek should not be allowed to enforce his contract just because he had been convicted.

So we are not surprised that the courts that have confronted this type of case—no Illinois court has—have held that the actual-innocence rule is not a bar. *Bird, Marella, Boxer & Wolpert v. Superior Court*, 106 Cal. App. 4th 419 (App. 2003); *Van Polen v. Wisch*, 23 S.W.3d 510, 516 (Tex. App. 2000); *Labovitz v. Feinberg, supra*, 713 N.E.2d at 385. As explained in *Bird, Marella*,

> "a fee dispute between a convicted criminal defendant client and his former counsel does not entail the policy considerations which arise from a malpractice suit. The client does not seek to shift the punishment for his criminal acts to his former counsel nor is the client's own criminal act the 'ultimate source of his predicament' as evidenced by the fact a client *acquitted* of the

> criminal charges against him could have suffered the same unlawful billing practices. . . . Furthermore a fee dispute between client and counsel does not give rise to the practical problems and pragmatic difficulties inherent in a malpractice action brought by a convicted criminal defendant client. . . . There is no difficulty in quantifying damages for a wrongful conviction or a longer prison sentence and there is no problem of applying a standard of proof within a standard of proof. A judgment for the client in a fee dispute is not inconsistent with a judgment for the People in the criminal case. And, there is no duplication of effort since a fee dispute obviously cannot be resolved through postconviction relief."

130 Cal.Rptr.2d at 789 (emphasis in original).

We expect that if and when such a case is presented to an Illinois court, it will decide it the same way. Nagelberg argues, however, that the Winniczeks' complaint alleges only malpractice (which the actual-innocence rule bars). But that is not correct. The complaint has two counts, remember, and only the second is captioned "professional negligence" (i.e., malpractice); the first is captioned "breach of contract/fiduciary duty." It is true that the narrative portion of count one accuses Nagelberg not only of overcharging and of charging for services not rendered but also of being careless, for example in failing to read the statements by Winniczek to the authorities that showed he had no defense. But the fact that a breach of contract is negligent rather than willful does not change the character of the breach. Sometimes a contract is broken willfully, sometimes unavoidably (circumstances beyond the promisor's control, but not rising to the level at which he would have a defense of impossibility or *force majeure*, might have prevented him from fulfilling his promise), and sometimes carelessly (the promisor should have realized he couldn't fulfill his promise—that he had bitten off more than he could chew). Since liability for breach of contract is, in general, strict liability . . . the cause, character, and mental element of the breach usually are immaterial.

The point is that in count one—unlike count two—the Winniczeks are not trying to blame Nagelberg for the fact that Winniczek was convicted; that would be a malpractice claim and, if it could be maintained (it could not, because of the actual-innocence rule), the measure of damages would be the cost to Winniczek of being convicted, imprisoned, and fined. [citations omitted] In count one the Winniczeks are trying to recover damages differently measured from what would be appropriate in a malpractice suit, where the wrong is not an overcharge but a conviction. The recovery of the overcharge is not barred by the actual-innocence rule. . . .

The dismissal of count two is affirmed, but the dismissal of count one is reversed and the case remanded for further proceedings consistent with this opinion.

CASE QUESTIONS

1. What causes of action are asserted here? Which does the "actual innocence" rule block?
2. What reasons support the actual innocence rule?
3. Why do those reasons apply to malpractice claims but not other claims?
4. In terms of actual conduct, what distinguished the two causes of action?

The "actual innocence" rule is the majority rule. *E.g., Wiley v. County of San Diego*, 19 Cal.4th 532 (1998). A criminal defendant who files a malpractice claim against her criminal defense counsel must plead and prove that she was exonerated of the criminal conviction. *Coscia v. McKenna & Cuneo*, 25 Cal.4th 1194 (2001). Departures do happen, though. The Colorado Supreme Court departed from this rule in *Rantz v. Kaufman*, 109 P.3d 132 (Colo. 2005).

Brooks v. Shemaria, 144 Cal.App.4th 434 (2006), held the actual innocence rule was not a bar to a suit arising out of a criminal defense lawyer's alleged failure to return the unearned portion of a retainer: "The primary right Brooks seeks to vindicate is the right to be billed in accordance with the terms of the retainer agreement, i.e., to have Shemaria's compensation governed by those terms. It has nothing to do with the quality of Shemaria's representation or with Brooks' guilt or innocence. The actual innocence requirement therefore does not apply."

The *Shemaria* court also held that the actual innocence rule did not bar a claim for negligent failure to seek the return of seized property, even though this claim related to the lawyer's competence:

> In his professional negligence claim concerning the return of property proceedings, Brooks does not seek to profit from his own wrong, even assuming, as we must, that Brooks actually committed the crime of which he was convicted. The property Brooks wanted returned, and which allegedly was lost through Shemaria's dereliction, was Brooks' property already. Brooks would not *profit* by merely regaining possession of what was already his, or by obtaining damages if the fail-

ure to regain possession was caused by Shemaria's lack of reasonable care.

For similar reasons, Brooks' claim does not seek to shift Brooks' own responsibility or punishment to Shemaria. Brooks does not challenge his conviction or sentence or seek damages for either of them. Rather, he seeks damages for the destruction of property that both the trial court and the sheriff determined should have been returned, not destroyed. And even if Brooks' criminal conduct is in some sense "the ultimate source of his predicament" (*Wiley*, *supra*, 19 Cal.4th at p. 540) (e.g., it is undoubtedly a but-for cause of the loss of his property), the court's and the sheriff's determinations that the property *should* have been returned strongly suggest that Brooks' criminal conduct was *not* the proximate cause of the property's destruction.

Moreover, there is no form of postconviction redress for the wrongs Brooks alleges. On the contrary, once Brooks' property was destroyed, it was "lost forever." (*Wiley*, *supra*, 19 Cal.4th at p. 543.)

Finally, Brooks' claim does not face the practical problems described by the Supreme Court. Quantifying damages will be a relatively straightforward matter of determining the value of the property that was lost as a result of Shemaria's alleged negligence. And there will be no need to weave together different standards of proof, because the reasonable doubt standard did not apply in the return of property proceedings at issue.

In sum, we are aware of no policy consideration that supports application of the actual innocence requirement here. We therefore conclude that it does not apply, so the trial court erred when it granted summary judgment on Brooks' claim for professional negligence concerning the return of property proceedings.

* * *

Powell v. Associated Counsel for the Accused, 125 Wash.App. 773 (2005), confirmed Judge Posner's intuition in *Winniczeck* that there must be an exception for an unlawful penalty. Powell pleaded guilty to a gross misdemeanor, for which the maximum sentence was one year. He was erroneously sentenced to 2.5 years in prison, and his attorney failed to catch the mistake. He was released after over 20 months in jail, and sued his attorneys for damages for the 8 months he served beyond the maximum sentence.

The attorneys moved to dismiss, citing the actual innocence rule. The trial court granted the motion, and the court of appeals reversed. According to the court, "Powell's situation is closer to that of an innocent person wrongfully convicted than of a guilty person attempting to take advantage of his own wrongdoing. Powell has no quarrel with having been incarcerated for the period of time justified by the gross misdemeanor that he pleaded guilty to having committed. . . . we decline to extend the innocence requirement to these facts, for to do so would not serve the public policy" of forcing the defendant to bear the full lawful brunt of his acts.

When does the limitations period begin running for a criminal malpractice claim? For claims requiring a plaintiff to show actual innocence, the California legislature has provided two-year limitations period that begins running when the plaintiff is exonerated. California Assembly Bill No. 316, 2009–10 Reg. Sess. § 2 (2009).

C. THE CONSTITUTIONAL STANDARD OF CARE IN CRIMINAL CASES: THE INEFFECTIVE ASSISTANCE OF COUNSEL DOCTRINE

We next turn from civil liability to the standard of care guaranteed by the constitutional right to counsel, which the Supreme Court has interpreted to require state-appointed counsel in certain criminal cases. The Court has held the right to counsel requires lawyers who meet a certain minimum level of competence, judged in part by prevailing professional standards and in part by whether the lawyer's conduct affected the result of a proceeding. Defendants who wish to challenge convictions often contend their counsel failed to provide effective representation, and the line of cases dealing with such claims is referred to as the "ineffective assistance of counsel" cases.

Ineffective assistance of counsel is neither a tort theory nor a theory of discipline. A lawyer may act ineffectively for a client who could not prove his or her actual innocence, and thus could not sustain a civil claim against the lawyer. Or a lawyer could act negligently but in a way that did not matter to the result of any proceeding, in which case the lawyer might be disciplined for negligent conduct but might escape civil liability under the actual innocence rule and might be held to be effective counsel under the second element of the *Strickland* test discussed below.

Ineffective assistance case law applies only where the constitutional right to counsel applies; the cases therefore do not apply to civil disputes. They are worth studying even for lawyers who do not practice criminal law, however, because they provide a window on the administration of justice in the United States and on the role lawyers play in enforcing both criminal statutes and the rights of the accused.

STRICKLAND V. WASHINGTON

466 U.S. 668 (1984)

JUSTICE O'CONNOR delivered the opinion of the Court.

This case requires us to consider the proper standards for judging a criminal defendant's contention that the Constitution requires a conviction or death sentence to be set aside because counsel's assistance at the trial or sentencing was ineffective.

I

A

During a 10–day period in September 1976, respondent planned and committed three groups of crimes, which included three brutal stabbing murders, torture, kidnaping, severe assaults, attempted murders, attempted extortion, and theft. After his two accomplices were arrested, respondent surrendered to police and voluntarily gave a lengthy statement confessing to the third of the criminal episodes. The State of Florida indicted respondent for kidnaping and murder and appointed an experienced criminal lawyer to represent him.

Counsel actively pursued pretrial motions and discovery. He cut his efforts short, however, and he experienced a sense of hopelessness about the case, when he learned that, against his specific advice, respondent had also confessed to the first two murders. By the date set for trial, respondent was subject to indictment for three counts of first-degree murder and multiple counts of robbery, kidnaping for ransom, breaking and entering and assault, attempted murder, and conspiracy to commit robbery. Respondent waived his right to a jury trial, again acting against counsel's advice, and pleaded guilty to all charges, including the three capital murder charges.

In the plea colloquy, respondent told the trial judge that, although he had committed a string of burglaries, he had no significant prior criminal record and that at the time of his criminal spree he was under extreme stress caused by his inability to support his family. He also stated, however, that he accepted responsibility for the crimes. The trial judge told respondent that he had "a great deal of respect for people who are willing to step forward and admit their responsibility" but that he was making no statement at all about his likely sentencing decision.

Counsel advised respondent to invoke his right under Florida law to an advisory jury at his capital sentencing hearing. Respondent rejected the advice and waived the right. He chose instead to be sentenced by the trial judge without a jury recommendation.

In preparing for the sentencing hearing, counsel spoke with respondent about his background. He also spoke on the telephone with respondent's wife and mother, though he did not follow up on the one unsuccessful effort to meet with them. He did not otherwise seek out character witnesses for respondent. Nor did he request a psychiatric examination, since his conversations with his client gave no indication that respondent had psychological problems.

Counsel decided not to present and hence not to look further for evidence concerning respondent's character and emotional state. That decision reflected trial counsel's sense of hopelessness about overcoming the evidentiary effect of respondent's confessions to the gruesome crimes. It also reflected the judgment that it was advisable to rely on the plea colloquy for evidence about respondent's background and about his claim of emotional stress: the plea colloquy communicated sufficient information about these subjects, and by forgoing the opportunity to present new evidence on these subjects, counsel prevented the State from cross-examining respondent on his claim and from putting on psychiatric evidence of its own.

Counsel also excluded from the sentencing hearing other evidence he thought was potentially damaging. He successfully moved to exclude respondent's "rap sheet." Because he judged that a presentence report might prove more detrimental than helpful, as it would have included respondent's criminal history and thereby would have undermined the claim of no significant history of criminal activity, he did not request that one be prepared.

At the sentencing hearing, counsel's strategy was based primarily on the trial judge's remarks at the plea colloquy as well as on his reputation as a sentencing judge who thought it important for a convicted defendant to own up to his crime. Counsel argued that respondent's remorse and acceptance of responsibility justified sparing him from the death penalty. Counsel also argued that respondent had no history of criminal activity and that respondent committed the crimes under extreme mental or emotional disturbance, thus coming within the statutory list of mitigating circumstances. He further argued that respondent should be spared death because he had surrendered, confessed, and offered to testify against a codefendant and because respondent was fundamentally a good person who had briefly gone badly wrong in extremely stressful circumstances. The State put on evidence and witnesses largely for the purpose of describing the details of the crimes. Counsel did not cross-examine the medical experts who testified about the manner of death of respondent's victims.

The trial judge found several aggravating circumstances with respect to each of the three murders. He found that all three murders were especially heinous, atrocious, and cruel, all involving repeated stabbings. All three murders were committed in the course of at least one other dangerous and violent felony, and since all involved robbery, the murders were for pecuniary gain. All three murders were committed to avoid arrest for the accompanying crimes and to hinder law enforcement. In the course of one of the murders, respondent knowingly subjected numerous persons to a grave risk of death by deliberately stabbing and shooting the murder victim's sisters-in-law, who sustained severe—in one case, ultimately fatal—injuries.

With respect to mitigating circumstances, the trial judge made the same findings for all three capital murders. First, although there was no admitted evidence of prior convictions, respondent had stated that he had engaged in a course of stealing. In any case, even if respondent had no significant history of criminal activity, the aggravating circumstances "would still clearly far outweigh" that mitigating factor. Second, the judge found that, during all three crimes, respondent was not suffering from extreme mental or emotional disturbance and could appreciate the criminality of his acts. Third, none of the victims was a participant in, or consented to, respondent's conduct. Fourth, respondent's participation in the crimes was neither minor nor the result of duress or domination by an accomplice. Finally, respondent's age (26) could not be considered a factor in mitigation, especially when viewed in light of respondent's planning of the crimes and disposition of the proceeds of the various accompanying thefts.

In short, the trial judge found numerous aggravating circumstances and no (or a single comparatively insignificant) mitigating circumstance. With respect to each of the three convictions for capital murder, the trial judge concluded: "A careful consideration of all matters presented to the court impels the conclusion that there are insufficient mitigating circumstances . . . to outweigh the aggravating circumstances." See *Washington v. State*, 362 So.2d 658, 663–664 (Fla.1978), (quoting trial court findings), *cert. denied*, 441 U.S. 937 (1979). He therefore sentenced respondent to death on each of the three counts of murder and to prison terms for the other crimes. The Florida Supreme Court upheld the convictions and sentences on direct appeal.

B

Respondent subsequently sought collateral relief in state court on numerous grounds, among them that counsel had rendered ineffective assistance at the sentencing proceeding. Respondent challenged counsel's assistance in six respects. He asserted that counsel was ineffective because he failed to move for a continuance to prepare for sentencing, to request a psychiatric report, to investigate and present character witnesses, to seek a presentence investigation report, to present meaningful arguments to the sentencing judge, and to investigate the medical examiner's reports or cross-examine the medical experts. In support of the claim, respondent submitted 14 affidavits from friends, neighbors, and relatives stating that they would have testified if asked to do so. He also submitted one psychiatric report and one psychological report stating that respond-

ent, though not under the influence of extreme mental or emotional disturbance, was "chronically frustrated and depressed because of his economic dilemma" at the time of his crimes.

The trial court denied relief without an evidentiary hearing, finding that the record evidence conclusively showed that the ineffectiveness claim was meritless. . . . The Florida Supreme Court affirmed the denial of relief. *Washington v. State*, 397 So.2d 285 (1981). . . . [Washington then filed a petition for a writ of habeas corpus, which was denied by the district court. The Court of Appeals for the 11th Circuit remanded the case to allow the district court to apply a standard the court of appeals announced.]

Petitioners, who are officials of the State of Florida, filed a petition for a writ of certiorari seeking review of the decision of the Court of Appeals. The petition presents a type of Sixth Amendment claim that this Court has not previously considered in any generality. The Court has considered Sixth Amendment claims based on actual or constructive denial of the assistance of counsel altogether, as well as claims based on state interference with the ability of counsel to render effective assistance to the accused. *E.g., United States v. Cronic*, 466 U.S. 648. With the exception *of Cuyler v. Sullivan*, 446 U.S. 335 (1980), however, which involved a claim that counsel's assistance was rendered ineffective by a conflict of interest, the Court has never directly and fully addressed a claim of "actual ineffectiveness" of counsel's assistance in a case going to trial. . . .

II

In a long line of cases that includes *Powell v. Alabama*, 287 U.S. 45 (1932), *Johnson v. Zerbst*, 304 U.S. 458 (1938), and *Gideon v. Wainwright*, 372 U.S. 335 (1963), this Court has recognized that the Sixth Amendment right to counsel exists, and is needed, in order to protect the fundamental right to a fair trial. . . .

[A] fair trial is one in which evidence subject to adversarial testing is presented to an impartial tribunal for resolution of issues defined in advance of the proceeding. The right to counsel plays a crucial role in the adversarial system embodied in the Sixth Amendment, since access to counsel's skill and knowledge is necessary to accord defendants the "ample opportunity to meet the case of the prosecution" to which they are entitled. . . .

Because of the vital importance of counsel's assistance, this Court has held that, with certain exceptions, a person accused of a federal or state crime has the right to have counsel appointed if retained counsel cannot be obtained. That a person who happens to be a lawyer is present at trial alongside the accused, however, is not enough to satisfy the constitutional command. The Sixth Amendment recognizes the right to the assistance of counsel because it envisions counsel's playing a role that is critical to the ability of the adversarial system to produce just results. An accused is entitled to be assisted by an attorney, whether retained or appointed, who plays the role necessary to ensure that the trial is fair.

For that reason, the Court has recognized that "the right to counsel is the right to the effective assistance of counsel." *McMann v. Richardson*, 397 U.S. 759, 771, n. 14 (1970). Government violates the right to effective assistance when it interferes in certain ways with the ability of counsel to make independent decisions about how to conduct the defense. [citations omitted] Counsel, however, can also deprive a defendant of the right to effective assistance, simply by failing to render "adequate legal assistance," *Cuyler v. Sullivan*, 446 U.S., at 344 (actual conflict of interest adversely affecting lawyer's performance renders assistance ineffective).

The Court has not elaborated on the meaning of the constitutional requirement of effective assistance in the latter class of cases—that is, those presenting claims of "actual ineffectiveness." In giving meaning to the requirement, however, we must take its purpose—to ensure a fair trial—as the guide. The benchmark for judging any claim of ineffectiveness must be whether counsel's conduct so undermined the proper functioning of the adversarial process that the trial cannot be relied on as having produced a just result. . . .

III

A convicted defendant's claim that counsel's assistance was so defective as to require reversal of a conviction or death sentence has two components. First, the defendant must show that counsel's performance was deficient. This requires showing that counsel made errors so serious that counsel was not functioning as the "counsel" guaranteed the defendant by the Sixth Amendment. Second, the defendant must show that the deficient performance prejudiced the defense. This requires showing that counsel's errors were so serious as to deprive the defendant of a fair trial, a trial whose result is reliable. Unless a defendant makes both showings, it cannot be said that the conviction or death sentence resulted from a breakdown in the adversary process that renders the result unreliable.

A

As all the Federal Courts of Appeals have now held, the proper standard for attorney performance is that of reasonably effective assistance. See *Trapnell v. United States*, 725 F.2d, at 151–152. The Court indirectly recognized as much when it stated in *McMann v. Richardson*, *supra,* 397 U.S., at 770, that a guilty plea cannot be attacked as based on inadequate legal advice unless counsel was not "a reasonably competent attorney" and the advice was not "within the range of competence demanded of attorneys in criminal cases." *See also Cuyler v. Sullivan*, *supra,* 446 U.S., at 344. When a convicted defendant complains of the ineffectiveness of counsel's assistance, the defendant must show that counsel's representation fell below an objective standard of reasonableness.

More specific guidelines are not appropriate. The Sixth Amendment refers simply to "counsel," not specifying particular requirements of effective assistance. It relies instead on the legal profession's maintenance of standards sufficient to justify the law's presumption that counsel will fulfill the role in the adversary process that the Amendment envisions. The proper measure of attorney performance remains simply reasonableness under prevailing professional norms.

Representation of a criminal defendant entails certain basic duties. Counsel's function is to assist the defendant, and hence counsel owes the client a duty of loyalty, a duty to avoid conflicts of interest. See *Cuyler v. Sullivan, supra*, 446 U.S., at 346. From counsel's function as assistant to the defendant derive the overarching duty to advocate the defendant's cause and the more particular duties to consult with the defendant on important decisions and to keep the defendant informed of important developments in the course of the prosecution. Counsel also has a duty to bring to bear such skill and knowledge as will render the trial a reliable adversarial testing process. See *Powell v. Alabama*, 287 U.S., at 68–69.

These basic duties neither exhaustively define the obligations of counsel nor form a checklist for judicial evaluation of attorney performance. In any case presenting an ineffectiveness claim, the performance inquiry must be whether counsel's assistance was reasonable considering all the circumstances. Prevailing norms of practice as reflected in American Bar Association standards and the like, e.g., ABA Standards for Criminal Justice 4–1.1 to 4–8.6 (2d ed. 1980) ("The Defense Function"), are guides to determining what is reasonable, but they are only guides. No particular set of detailed rules for counsel's conduct can satisfactorily take account of the variety of circumstances faced by defense counsel or the range of legitimate decisions regarding how best to represent a criminal defendant. Any such set of rules would interfere with the constitutionally protected independence of counsel and restrict the wide latitude counsel must have in making tactical decisions. Indeed, the existence of detailed guidelines for representation could distract counsel from the overriding mission of vigorous advocacy of the defendant's cause. Moreover, the purpose of the effective assistance guarantee of the Sixth Amendment is not to improve the quality of legal representation, although that is a goal of considerable importance to the legal system. The purpose is simply to ensure that criminal defendants receive a fair trial.

Judicial scrutiny of counsel's performance must be highly deferential. It is all too tempting for a defendant to second-guess counsel's assistance after conviction or adverse sentence, and it is all too easy for a court, examining counsel's defense after it has proved unsuccessful, to conclude that a particular act or omission of counsel was unreasonable. *Cf. Engle v.*

Isaac, 456 U.S. 107, 133–134 (1982). A fair assessment of attorney performance requires that every effort be made to eliminate the distorting effects of hindsight, to reconstruct the circumstances of counsel's challenged conduct, and to evaluate the conduct from counsel's perspective at the time. Because of the difficulties inherent in making the evaluation, a court must indulge a strong presumption that counsel's conduct falls within the wide range of reasonable professional assistance; that is, the defendant must overcome the presumption that, under the circumstances, the challenged action "might be considered sound trial strategy." There are countless ways to provide effective assistance in any given case. Even the best criminal defense attorneys would not defend a particular client in the same way. See Goodpaster, *The Trial for Life: Effective Assistance of Counsel in Death Penalty Cases*, 58 N.Y.U.L.Rev. 299, 343 (1983).

The availability of intrusive post-trial inquiry into attorney performance or of detailed guidelines for its evaluation would encourage the proliferation of ineffectiveness challenges. Criminal trials resolved unfavorably to the defendant would increasingly come to be followed by a second trial, this one of counsel's unsuccessful defense. Counsel's performance and even willingness to serve could be adversely affected. Intensive scrutiny of counsel and rigid requirements for acceptable assistance could dampen the ardor and impair the independence of defense counsel, discourage the acceptance of assigned cases, and undermine the trust between attorney and client.

Thus, a court deciding an actual ineffectiveness claim must judge the reasonableness of counsel's challenged conduct on the facts of the particular case, viewed as of the time of counsel's conduct. A convicted defendant making a claim of ineffective assistance must identify the acts or omissions of counsel that are alleged not to have been the result of reasonable professional judgment. The court must then determine whether, in light of all the circumstances, the identified acts or omissions were outside the wide range of professionally competent assistance. In making that determination, the court should keep in mind that counsel's function, as elaborated in prevailing professional norms, is to make the adversarial testing process work in the particular case. At the same time, the court should recognize that counsel is strongly presumed to have rendered adequate assistance and made all significant decisions in the exercise of reasonable professional judgment.

These standards require no special amplification in order to define counsel's duty to investigate, the duty at issue in this case. As the Court of Appeals concluded, strategic choices made after thorough investigation of law and facts relevant to plausible options are virtually unchallengeable; and strategic choices made after less than complete investigation are reasonable precisely to the extent that reasonable professional judgments support the limitations on investigation. In other words, counsel has a duty to make reasonable investigations or to make a reasonable decision that makes particular investigations unnecessary. In any ineffectiveness case, a particular decision not to investigate must be directly assessed for reasonableness in all the circumstances, applying a heavy measure of deference to counsel's judgments.

The reasonableness of counsel's actions may be determined or substantially influenced by the defendant's own statements or actions. Counsel's actions are usually based, quite properly, on informed strategic choices made by the defendant and on information supplied by the defendant. In particular, what investigation decisions are reasonable depends critically on such information. For example, when the facts that support a certain potential line of defense are generally known to counsel because of what the defendant has said, the need for further investigation may be considerably diminished or eliminated altogether. And when a defendant has given counsel reason to believe that pursuing certain investigations would be fruitless or even harmful, counsel's failure to pursue those investigations may not later be challenged as unreasonable. In short, inquiry into counsel's conversations with the defendant may be critical to a proper assessment of counsel's investigation decisions, just as it may be critical to a proper assessment of counsel's other litigation decisions.

B

An error by counsel, even if professionally unreasonable, does not warrant setting aside the judgment of a criminal proceeding if the error had no effect on the judgment. *Cf. United States v. Morrison*, 449 U.S. 361, 364–365 (1981). The purpose of the Sixth Amendment guarantee of counsel is to ensure that a defendant has the assistance necessary to justify reliance on the outcome of the proceeding. Accordingly, any deficiencies in counsel's performance must be prejudicial to the defense in order to constitute ineffective assistance under the Constitution.

In certain Sixth Amendment contexts, prejudice is presumed. Actual or constructive denial of the assistance of counsel altogether is legally presumed to result in prejudice. So are various kinds of state interference with counsel's assistance. *See United States v. Cronic*, 466 U.S., at 659, and n. 25. Prejudice in these circumstances is so likely that case-by-case inquiry into prejudice is not worth the cost. Moreover, such circumstances involve impairments of the Sixth Amendment right that are easy to identify and, for that reason and because the prosecution is directly responsible, easy for the government to prevent.

One type of actual ineffectiveness claim warrants a similar, though more limited, presumption of prejudice. In *Cuyler v. Sullivan*, 446 U.S., at 345–350, the Court held that prejudice is presumed when counsel is burdened by an actual conflict of interest. In those circumstances, counsel breaches the duty of loyalty, perhaps the most basic of counsel's duties.

Moreover, it is difficult to measure the precise effect on the defense of representation corrupted by conflicting interests. Given the obligation of counsel to avoid conflicts of interest and the ability of trial courts to make early inquiry in certain situations likely to give rise to conflicts, see, e.g., Fed.Rule Crim.Proc. 44(c), it is reasonable for the criminal justice system to maintain a fairly rigid rule of presumed prejudice for conflicts of interest. Even so, the rule is not quite the per se rule of prejudice that exists for the Sixth Amendment claims mentioned above. Prejudice is presumed only if the defendant demonstrates that counsel "actively represented conflicting interests" and that "an actual conflict of interest adversely affected his lawyer's performance." *Cuyler v. Sullivan, supra*, 446 U.S., at 350, 348 (footnote omitted).

Conflict of interest claims aside, actual ineffectiveness claims alleging a deficiency in attorney performance are subject to a general requirement that the defendant affirmatively prove prejudice. The government is not responsible for, and hence not able to prevent, attorney errors that will result in reversal of a conviction or sentence. Attorney errors come in an infinite variety and are as likely to be utterly harmless in a particular case as they are to be prejudicial. They cannot be classified according to likelihood of causing prejudice. Nor can they be defined with sufficient precision to inform defense attorneys correctly just what conduct to avoid. Representation is an art, and an act or omission that is unprofessional in one case may be sound or even brilliant in another. Even if a defendant shows that particular errors of counsel were unreasonable, therefore, the defendant must show that they actually had an adverse effect on the defense.

It is not enough for the defendant to show that the errors had some conceivable effect on the outcome of the proceeding. Virtually every act or omission of counsel would meet that test, *cf. United States v. Valenzuela–Bernal*, 458 U.S. 858, 866–867 (1982), and not every error that conceivably could have influenced the outcome undermines the reliability of the result of the proceeding. Respondent suggests requiring a showing that the errors "impaired the presentation of the defense." Brief for Respondent 58. That standard, however, provides no workable principle. Since any error, if it is indeed an error, "impairs" the presentation of the defense, the proposed standard is inadequate because it provides no way of deciding what impairments are sufficiently serious to warrant setting aside the outcome of the proceeding.

On the other hand, we believe that a defendant need not show that counsel's deficient conduct more likely than not altered the outcome in the case. This outcome-determinative standard has several strengths. It defines the relevant inquiry in a way familiar to courts, though the inquiry, as is inevitable, is anything but precise. The standard also reflects the profound importance of finality in criminal proceedings. Moreover, it comports with the widely used standard for assessing motions for new trial based on newly discovered evidence. Nevertheless, the standard is not quite appropriate.

Even when the specified attorney error results in the omission of certain evidence, the newly discovered evidence standard is not an apt source from which to draw a prejudice standard for ineffectiveness claims. The high standard for newly discovered evidence claims presupposes that all the essential elements of a presumptively accurate and fair proceeding were present in the proceeding whose result is challenged. *Cf. United States v. Johnson*, 327 U.S. 106, 112 (1946). An ineffective assistance claim asserts the absence of one of the crucial assurances that the result of the proceeding is reliable, so finality concerns are somewhat weaker and the appropriate standard of prejudice should be somewhat lower. The result of a proceeding can be rendered unreliable, and hence the proceeding itself unfair, even if the errors of counsel cannot be shown by a preponderance of the evidence to have determined the outcome.

Accordingly, the appropriate test for prejudice finds its roots in the test for materiality of exculpatory information not disclosed to the defense by the prosecution, *United States v. Agurs*, 427 U.S., at 104, 112–113, and in the test for materiality of testimony made unavailable to the defense by Government deportation of a witness, *United States v. Valenzuela-Bernal, supra*, 458 U.S., at 872–874. The defendant must show that there is a reasonable probability that, but for counsel's unprofessional errors, the result of the proceeding would have been different. A reasonable probability is a probability sufficient to undermine confidence in the outcome. . . .

The governing legal standard plays a critical role in defining the question to be asked in assessing the prejudice from counsel's errors. When a defendant challenges a conviction, the question is whether there is a reasonable probability that, absent the errors, the factfinder would have had a reasonable doubt respecting guilt. When a defendant challenges a death sentence such as the one at issue in this case, the question is whether there is a reasonable probability that, absent the errors, the sentencer—including an appellate court, to the extent it independently reweighs the evidence—would have concluded that the balance of aggravating and mitigating circumstances did not warrant death.

In making this determination, a court hearing an ineffectiveness claim must consider the totality of the evidence before the judge or jury. Some of the factual findings will have been unaffected by the errors, and factual findings that were affected will have been affected in different ways. Some errors will have had a pervasive effect on the inferences to be drawn from the evidence, altering the entire evidentiary picture, and some will have had an isolated, trivial effect. Moreover, a verdict or conclusion only weakly supported by the record is more likely to have been affected by errors than one with overwhelming record support. Taking the unaffected findings as a given, and taking due account of the effect of the errors on the remaining findings, a court making the prejudice inquiry must ask if the defendant has met the burden of showing that the decision reached would reasonably likely have been different absent the errors.

IV

A number of practical considerations are important for the application of the standards we have outlined. Most important, in adjudicating a claim of actual ineffectiveness of counsel, a court should keep in mind that the principles we have stated do not establish mechanical rules. Although those principles should guide the process of decision, the ultimate focus of inquiry must be on the fundamental fairness of the proceeding whose result is being challenged. In every case the court should be concerned with whether, despite the strong presumption of reliability, the result of the particular proceeding is unreliable because of a breakdown in the adversarial process that our system counts on to produce just results. . . .

Although we have discussed the performance component of an ineffectiveness claim prior to the prejudice component, there is no reason for a court deciding an ineffective assistance claim to approach the inquiry in the same order or even to address both components of the inquiry if the defendant makes an insufficient showing on one. In particular, a court need not determine whether counsel's performance was deficient before examining the prejudice suffered by the defendant as a result of the alleged deficiencies. The object of an ineffectiveness claim is not to grade counsel's performance. If it is easier to dispose of an ineffectiveness claim on the ground of lack of sufficient prejudice, which we expect will often be so, that course should be followed. Courts should strive to ensure that ineffectiveness claims not become so burdensome to defense counsel that the entire criminal justice system suffers as a result. . . .

V

Having articulated general standards for judging ineffectiveness claims, we think it useful to apply those standards to the facts of this case in order to illustrate the meaning of the general principles. The record makes it possible to do so. There are no conflicts between the state and federal courts over findings of fact, and the principles we have articulated are sufficiently close to the principles applied both in the Florida courts and in the District Court that it is clear that the factfinding was not affected by erroneous legal principles. *See Pullman–Standard v. Swint*, 456 U.S. 273, 291–292 (1982).

Application of the governing principles is not difficult in this case. The facts as described above, make clear that the conduct of respondent's counsel at and before respondent's sentencing proceeding cannot be found unreasonable. They also make clear that, even assuming the challenged conduct of counsel was unreasonable, respondent suffered insufficient prejudice to warrant setting aside his death sentence.

With respect to the performance component, the record shows that respondent's counsel made a strategic choice to argue for the extreme emotional distress mitigating circumstance and to rely as fully as possible on respondent's acceptance of responsibility for his crimes. Although counsel understandably felt hopeless about respondent's prospects, nothing in the record indicates, as one possible reading of the District Court's opinion suggests, that counsel's sense of hopelessness distorted his professional judgment. Counsel's strategy choice was well within the range of professionally reasonable judgments, and the decision not to seek more character or psychological evidence than was already in hand was likewise reasonable.

The trial judge's views on the importance of owning up to one's crimes were well known to counsel. The aggravating circumstances were utterly overwhelming. Trial counsel could reasonably surmise from his conversations with respondent that character and psychological evidence would be of little help. Respondent had already been able to mention at the plea colloquy the substance of what there was to know about his financial and emotional troubles. Restricting testimony on respondent's character to what had come in at the plea colloquy ensured that contrary character and psychological evidence and respondent's criminal history, which counsel had successfully moved to exclude, would not come in. On these facts, there can be little question, even without application of the presumption of adequate performance, that trial counsel's defense, though unsuccessful, was the result of reasonable professional judgment.

With respect to the prejudice component, the lack of merit of respondent's claim is even more stark. The evidence that respondent says his trial counsel should have offered at the sentencing hearing would barely have altered the sentencing profile presented to the sentencing judge. As the state courts and District Court found, at most this evidence shows that numerous people who knew respondent thought he was generally a good person and that a psychiatrist and a psychologist believed he was under considerable emotional stress that did not rise to the level of extreme disturbance. Given the overwhelming aggravating factors, there is no reasonable probability that the omitted evidence would have changed the conclusion that the aggravating circumstances outweighed the mitigating circumstances and, hence, the sentence imposed. Indeed, admission of the evidence respondent now offers might even have been harmful to his case: his "rap sheet" would probably have been admitted into evidence, and the psychological reports would have directly contradicted respondent's claim that the mitigating circumstance of extreme emotional disturbance applied to his case. . . .

Failure to make the required showing of either deficient performance or sufficient prejudice defeats the ineffectiveness claim. Here there is a double failure. More generally, respondent has made no showing that the justice of his sentence was rendered unreliable by a breakdown in the adversary process caused by deficiencies in counsel's assistance. Respondent's sentencing proceeding was not fundamentally unfair.

We conclude, therefore, that the District Court properly declined to issue a writ of habeas corpus. The judgment of the Court of Appeals is accordingly

Reversed.

. . . .

JUSTICE MARSHALL, dissenting.

The opinion of the Court revolves around two holdings. First, the majority ties the constitutional minima of attorney performance to a simple "standard of reasonableness." Second, the majority holds that only an error of counsel that has sufficient impact on a trial to "undermine confidence in the outcome" is grounds for overturning a conviction. I disagree with both of these rulings.

A

My objection to the performance standard adopted by the Court is that it is so malleable that, in practice, it will either have no grip at all or will yield excessive variation in the manner in which the Sixth Amendment is interpreted and applied by different courts. To tell lawyers and the lower courts that counsel for a criminal defendant must behave "reasonably" and must act like "a reasonably competent attorney," is to tell them almost nothing. In essence, the majority has instructed judges called upon to assess claims of ineffective assistance of counsel to advert to their own intuitions regarding what constitutes "professional" representation, and has discouraged them from trying to develop more detailed standards governing the performance of defense counsel. In my view, the Court has thereby not only abdicated its own responsibility to interpret the Constitution, but also impaired the ability of the lower courts to exercise theirs. . . .

B

I object to the prejudice standard adopted by the Court for two independent reasons. First, it is often very difficult to tell whether a defendant convicted after a trial in which he was ineffectively represented would have fared better if his lawyer had been competent. Seemingly impregnable cases can sometimes be dismantled by good defense counsel. On the basis of a cold record, it may be impossible for a reviewing court confidently to ascertain how the government's evidence and arguments would have stood up against rebuttal and cross-examination by a shrewd, well-prepared lawyer. The difficulties of estimating prejudice after the fact are exacerbated by the possibility that evidence of injury to the defendant may be missing from the record precisely because of the incompetence of defense counsel. In view of all these impediments to a fair evaluation of the probability that the outcome of a trial was affected by ineffectiveness of counsel, it seems to me senseless to impose on a defendant whose lawyer has been shown to have been incompetent the burden of demonstrating prejudice.

Second and more fundamentally, the assumption on which the Court's holding rests is that the only purpose of the constitutional guarantee of effective assistance of counsel is to reduce the chance that innocent persons will be convicted. In my view, the guarantee also functions to ensure that convictions are obtained only through fundamentally fair procedures. The majority contends that the Sixth Amendment is not violated when a manifestly guilty defendant is convicted after a trial in which he was represented by a manifestly ineffective attorney. I cannot agree. Every defendant is entitled to a trial in which his interests are vigorously and conscientiously advocated by an able lawyer. A proceeding in which the defendant does not receive meaningful assistance in meeting the forces of the State does not, in my opinion, constitute due process. . . .

CASE QUESTIONS

1. According to the opinions in *Strickland*, what purpose does the right to counsel serve?
2. How does the court define a "fair" trial?
3. Under *Strickland*, are the variables of the counsel's competence and prejudice to the defendant dependent or independent? (I.e, is it the case that strong evidence may make up for weak lawyering, and vice versa?)
4. What is the standard for judging competence?
5. What is the standard for judging prejudice?
6. How does the doctrine work if counsel is actually or constructively denied?
7. How does the doctrine work if defense counsel has a conflict of interest?

In *Rompilla v. Beard*, 545 U.S. 374 (2005), the Court found counsel ineffective in the penalty phase of a murder trial where counsel failed to investigate evidence of the defendant's childhood. Counsel in *Rompilla* interviewed the defendant and some of his family members, and reviewed reports from three psychiatrists. The defendant himself offered them no help, at one point ending a meeting regarding the penalty phase by saying he was "bored being here listening." He also falsely claimed to have had a "normal" childhood, and sent his counsel chasing false leads. The Court noted that the defendant's family members told counsel they did not know him well because he had spent so much time in prison. Counsel did not examine school and prison records, and did not pursue alcoholism as a theory of mitigation, though they knew defendant had been drinking at the time of the offense. In response to these arguments, the Court noted the state's argument that "the duty to investigate does not force defense lawyers to scour the globe on the off-chance something will turn up; reasonably diligent counsel may draw a line when they have good reason to think further investigation would be a waste." The Court concluded that there was "room for debate about trial counsel's obligation to follow at least some of these potential lines of inquiry."

Without resolving these arguments definitively, the Court found counsel acted unreasonably because counsel failed to examine the court file from the defendant's previous conviction. The prosecutors notified counsel that they intended to introduce evidence of the defendant's rape conviction, including the victim's testimony, to emphasize the defendant's violent nature. Counsel nevertheless only looked at the transcript on the eve of the sentencing hearing, and never looked at the rest of this file. The Court found it was "objectively unreasonable" for counsel not to review a readily available public record on which counsel had notice the prosecution intended to rely.

The majority opinion twice emphasized that the cost of investigation plays a role in evaluating whether counsel's conduct was reasonable. 545 U.S. at 375, n.4 & 378 n.8. Justice O'Connor's concurrence stressed that counsel did not make a strategic choice not to review the file. (For example, counsel did not forgo reading the file in order to pursue other, more promising leads.) Instead, counsel's failure to read the file "was the result of inattention, not reasoned strategic judgment."

With regard to the second element of the *Strickland* analysis, the Court noted that the file contained evidence showing Rompilla had a nightmarish childhood and suffered from "organic brain damage" that impaired significantly his cognitive functions. The Court concluded that this evidence might well have influenced the jury's view of Rompilla's culpability, and therefore undermined confidence in the penalty imposed.

Rompilla is consistent with *Wiggins v. Smith*, 539 U.S. 510 (2003), in which the Court found counsel ineffective on the ground that he conducted an inadequate investigation into the facts of his client's childhood (which included parental abandonment and sexual molestation, homelessness, rape in foster homes, and generally severe privation). The *Wiggins* court emphasized *Strickland's* statement that " 'strategic choices made after less than complete investigation are reasonable' only to the extent that 'reasonable professional judgments support the limitations on investigation.' " *Accord In re Hill*, 198 Cal.App.4th 1008 (2011)("Absent a reasonable investigation of all possible defenses and other reasonable preparation for trial, Hill's trial counsel did not have an adequate basis on which to make reasonable tactical decisions in planning and executing a defense strategy"). The Supreme Court has noted as well, however, that time itself is a scarce resource and defense attorneys are allowed to focus their efforts on certain matters even if doing so requires them to forgo investigation of other matters. *Herrington v. Richter*, 131 S.Ct. 760 (2011)("An attorney can avoid activities that appear "distractive from more important duties" and are "entitled to formulate a strategy that was reasonable at the time and to balance limited resources in accord with effective trial tactics and strategies").

In contrast, *Schriro v. Landrigan*, 550 U.S. 465 (2007), reversed an appellate court finding that counsel had been ineffective. At the penalty phase of his trial for felony murder Landrigan refused to allow his lawyer to present mitigating evidence, in the form of testimony from his biological mother and his ex-wife. Landrigan confirmed his refusal in a colloquy with the trial judge, in which he commented: "I think if you want to give me the death penalty, just bring it right on, I'm ready for it." Landrigan later changed his mind and petitioned for a writ of *habeas corpus* on the ground that his counsel was ineffective in not investigating the possibility that he suffered organic brain damage from his mother's use of drugs and alcohol during pregnancy. The Court distinguish *Rompilla* and *Wiggins* on the ground that the defendants in those cases did not affirmatively instruct counsel not to present mitigating evidence, and did not interfere with counsel's proffer to the court regarding what such evidence would show, as Landrigan did.

Cullen v. Pinholster, 131 S.Ct. 1388 (2011), rejected a habeas petition and distinguished *Rompilla* on the ground that where a habeas petition has been presented to a state court a federal court ruling on a subsequent petition may consider only the record presented to the state court, and may not consider new evidence. The Court further held that Pinholster's counsel had not acted ineffectively at the penalty phase of his trial when they chose to present mitigation evidence pertaining only to Pinholster's mother rather than to Pinholster himself. The Court noted this "'family sympathy'" mitigation defense "was known to the defense bar in California at the time and had been used by other attorneys." *Cf Harrington v. Richter*, 131 S.Ct. 760 (2011)(Under *Strickland* "[t]he question is whether an attorney's representation amounted to incompetence under "prevailing professional norms," not whether it deviated from best practices or most common custom").

In *Cullen* the Court distinguished *Rompilla* on the ground that it involved a first habeas petition rather than a petition already adjudicated on the merits in a state court proceeding, and thus subject to the particularly deferential review provided by the Antiterrorism and Effective Death Penalty Act (AEDPA), 28 U.S.C. §2254.[10] *See also Harrington v Richter*, 131 S.Ct. 760 (2011)(When a federal court reviews a state court's merits determination subject to AEDPA the "state court must be granted adeference and latitude that are not in operation when the case involves review under the *Strickland* standard itself"). *Harrington* also described the prejudice element of *Strickland* analysis as closely related to a standard that asks whether ineffective assistance more likely than not caused prejudice to the defendant, holding that "the difference between *Strickland*'s prejudice standard and a more-probable-than-not standard is slight and matters 'only in the rarest case.'"

Strickland and later cases are less willing to second-guess judgment calls than the failure to investigate (unless such failure was itself based on a strategic judgment). *Florida v. Nixon*, 543 U.S. 175 (2004), for example, involved a defendant, Nixon, accused of kidnapping a woman, tying her to a tree, and setting her on fire while still alive. Nixon confessed and his confession was corroborated by substantial evidence. His public defender urged Nixon to concede guilt at trial (Nixon having pleaded not guilty), in the hope the concession would make his penalty phase arguments more credible. Nixon was unresponsive, and neither approved nor disapproved this strategy. After Nixon was convicted and sentenced to death, new counsel argued that trial counsel was ineffective because he did not get express consent to the concession strategy. The Court disagreed. It found that counsel adequately consulted Nixon and, in light of Nixon's unresponsiveness, "counsel cannot be deemed ineffective for attempting to impress the jury with his candor and his unwillingness to engage in "a useless charade."

Nevertheless, bad judgments sometimes amount to ineffective assistance of counsel. In *Miller v. Anderson*, 255 F.3d 455 (7th Cir. 2001), the defendant was convicted of the rape, torture, and murder of a young woman. At trial, the prosecution presented an expert who testified that a hair found on the victim's body was "almost certainly" the defendant's. Miller's trial counsel chose only to cross-examine the government's expert

---

[10] Under AEDPA such a habeas petition may not be granted unless the initial state court review of the relevant issue "resulted in a decision that was contrary to, or involved an unreasonable application of, clearly established Federal law" or "resulted in a decision that was based on an unreasonable determination of the facts."

and not to find one of his own. In postconviction proceedings, a different defense lawyer retained an expert, more experienced than the government's expert, who opined that the hair belonged to the victim, not Miller. Trial counsel also failed to subpoena bank records that would have contradicted testimony that Miller had bought shotgun shells the day before the murder (he also failed to note that the shells bought were made by a different company than the shells that killed the victim).

According to Judge Posner, however,

> Most questionable of all the lawyer's fumbles was his decision to call a psychologist to testify that Miller was incapable of the kind of violence that had been perpetrated against the victim. The lawyer did this knowing that Miller had been previously convicted of kidnapping, rape, and sodomy and at the time of the crime for which he was being tried had been free on parole from a life sentence for kidnapping. The state brought these facts out on cross-examination of the psychologist and they not only destroyed the psychologist's credibility but almost certainly and perhaps decisively bolstered the jury's confidence in Miller's guilt. (The state had made no effort to place his prior convictions in evidence to demonstrate a *modus operandi.*) At the postconviction proceedings, the lawyer was unable to articulate a coherent reason for having put the psychologist on the stand, given the inevitability of the destruction of the psychologist and of Miller himself if the jury was told about the prior convictions. Nor did the Indiana courts give any reason for supposing it an even minimally intelligent tactic. The fact that it *was* a tactic obviously does not immunize it from review in a challenge to the lawyer's effectiveness. Tactics are the essence of the conduct of litigation; much scope must be allowed to counsel, but if no reason is or can be given for a tactic, the label "tactic" will not prevent it from being used as evidence of ineffective assistance of counsel . . .
>
> The minimally competent lawyer would have presented expert evidence that there was no physical evidence of Miller's presence at the crime scene, would have greatly undermined the hardware clerk's evidence, would not have undermined the alibi testimony of Miller's wife, would by forgoing psychological evidence (unlikely in any event to impress a jury) have kept the evidence of Miller's previous crimes from the jury, and would thus have forced the state to rely entirely on Wood's questionable testimony. The jury might have concluded that Wood was trying to save his life by portraying himself falsely as the tool of an older man. This is far from certain; indeed, we think the chance of an acquittal would still have been significantly less than 50 percent; but it would not have been a negligible chance, and that is enough to require us to conclude that the lawyer's errors of representation were, in the aggregate, prejudicial.

Actual denial of counsel is probably less common than ineffective practice by counsel, and it rarely if ever takes the form of a state refusal to give a defendant any lawyer at all in a case where the right to counsel applies. Denial can take other forms, however. In *Burdine v. Johnson*, 262 F.3d 336 (5th Cir. 2001), *cert. denied Cockrell v. Burdine*, 535 U.S. 1120 (2002), the court held that, where counsel slept in court while evidence of guilt was introduced against his client, the client had been denied counsel at a critical stage of trial and prejudice could be presumed under *Strickland*.

Recent cases make clear that *Strickland* applies to pretrial proceedings such as pleas and plea bargaining. In *Padilla v. Kentucky*, 130 S.Ct. 1473 (2010), the Supreme Court held that criminal defense lawyers must advise clients whether a guilty plea carries a risk of deportation, at least in those situations where the immigration consequences of a plea are clear. The court rejected a proposed distinction between a failure to advise a client on such consequences and incorrect advice on such consequences, which Padilla also alleged. The court did not reach the question whether Padilla was prejudiced by this failure. *Premo v. Moore*, 131 S.Ct. 733 (2011), rejected a *Strickland* challenge based on counsel's failure to move to suppress evidence before advising the defendant regarding a plea offer. The Court gave no indication that *Strickland* did not apply to advise to accept a plea.

In *Missouri v. Frye*, 132 S.Ct. 1399 (2012), the Supreme Court held that *Strickland* applies to cases in which ineffective assistance causes a defendant not to accept a plea rather than to plead guilty. The Court noted that "[n]inety-seven percent of federal convictions and ninety-four percent of state convictions are the result of guilty pleas." Thus, it held,

> The reality is that plea bargains have become so central to the administration of the criminal justice system that defense counsel have responsibilities in the plea bargain process, responsibilities that must be met to render the adequate assistance of counsel that the Sixth Amendment requires in the criminal process at critical stages.

Defense counsel in *Frye* had failed to communicate a plea offer that would have left the defendant in a better position than a later offer he did accept. The Court held "that, as a general rule, defense counsel has the duty to communicate formal offers from the prosecution to accept a plea on terms and conditions that may be favorable to the accused. . . When defense counsel allowed the offer to expire without advising the defendant or allowing him to consider it, defense counsel did not render the effective assistance the Constitution requires." With respect to the prejudice element of *Strickland* the Court held that

> [W]here a plea offer has lapsed or been rejected because of counsel's deficient performance, defendants must demonstrate a reasonable probability they would have accepted the earlier plea offer had they been afforded effective assistance of counsel. Defendants must also demonstrate a reasonable probability the plea would have been entered without the prosecution canceling it or the trial court refusing to accept it, if they had the authority to exercise that discretion under state law. To establish prejudice in this instance, it is necessary to show a reasonable probability that the end result of the criminal process would have been more favorable by reason of a plea to a lesser charge or a sentence of less prison time.

The Court remanded for reconsideration under this standard, noting that after the initial plea offer Frye had been arrested again for the same offense (driving without a license). That subsequent arrest, the Court noted, might create a question whether Frye ultimately would have been able to obtain the benefit of the original offer.

In *Lafler v. Cooper*, 132 S.Ct. 1376 (2012), the Court extended this rule to cases in which counsel provides deficient advice that leads a defendant to reject a plea offer. Counsel in that case had erroneously advised the defendant that he could not be convicted of attempted murder because the prosecution would be unable to prove intent to kill. The defendant had fired a gun at the victim's head and missed; the defendant then connected with three shots, each below the waist. The defendant was convicted at (concededly fair) trial and received a minimum sentence 3.5 times longer than then sentence that would have accompanied the charges in the plea offer.

In *Lafler* the Court rejected the government's argument that the concededly fair trial following rejection of the plea cured any *Strickland* violation:

> Far from curing the error, the trial caused the injury from the error. Even if the trial itself is free from constitutional flaw, the defendant who goes to trial instead of taking a more favorable plea may be prejudiced from either a conviction on more serious counts or the imposition of a more severe sentence

Lafler applied *Frye's* standard for establishing prejudice and also addressed the question of a remedy for a violation in such circumstances. *Lafler* holds that trial courts have discretion to fashion a remedy appropriate for the circumstances of particular cases. The Court mentioned resentencing in light of the plea offer or, possibly, vacating a conviction and ordering the prosecution to tender the plea offer again. It emphasized the trial court's discretion, however, holding the proper remedy on the facts of *Lafler* was to

[O]rder the State to reoffer the plea agreement. Presuming respondent accepts the offer, the state trial court can then exercise its discretion in determining whether to vacate the convictions andresentence respondent pursuant to the plea agreement, to vacate only some of the convictions and resentence respondent accordingly, or to leave the convictions and sentence from trial undisturbed.

Lafler also suggests that *Strickland* jurisprudence embraces two different conceptions of a fair trial, both of which may be found in *Strickland* itself. The first conception is that of right result: A trial is fair when it provides adequate assurance that the defendant convicted is actually guilty of the crime charged. On this view counsel's performance is secondary, relevant mostly insofar as it might bear on the question whether the prosecutors got the right person. The second conception is that of a fair fight: A trial is fair when both sides are represented by counsel who defend their interests with vigor. Particular cases tend to emphasize the conception consistent with the result of the case; *Lafler* confirms that each conception captures important purposes served by the doctrine:

> The goal of a just result is not divorced from the reliability of a conviction . . . but here the question is not the fairness or reliability of the trial but the fairness and regularity of the processes that preceded it, which caused the defendant to lose benefits he would have received in the ordinary course but for counsel's ineffective assistance

---

D. SPECIAL OBLIGATIONS OF PROSECUTORS

Model Rule 3.8; Restatement § 97(3)

Lawyers are generally allowed to argue positions that are supported by evidence and which arguably satisfy the elements of a claim or defense. A lawyer is permitted to allow a fact finder to decide whether the claim or defense is true, even if the lawyer personally knows of evidence that contradicts the claim and may overwhelm it. A lawyer has no obligation to make sure his or her opponent takes advantage of procedural devices that may benefit the opponent.

To one degree or another, prosecutors work under stricter rules. Comment 1 to Model Rule of Professional Conduct 3.8 states:

> A prosecutor has the responsibility of a minister of justice and not simply that of an advocate. This responsibility carries with it specific obligations to see that the defendant is accorded procedural justice, that guilt is decided upon the basis of sufficient evidence, and that special precautions are taken to prevent and to rectify the conviction of innocent persons.

The rule gives effect to this principle through specific obligations imposed on prosecutors. These include:

• A prosecutor may not bring charges he or she knows are not supported by probable cause;

• A prosecutor must make reasonable efforts to ensure an accused person has been advised of the right to counsel and how to obtain counsel, and has been given a reasonable opportunity to obtain counsel if the accused so desires;

• A prosecutor must not seek from an unrepresented person a waiver of important rights;

• A prosecutor must timely disclose all information the prosecutor knows of that tends to show the accused is not guilty or which tends to mitigate the level of guilt (though the prosecutor need not undertake a search for such evidence of which he or she does not have knowledge);

• A prosecutor must "refrain from making extrajudicial comments that have a substantial likelihood of heightening public condemnation of the accused and exercise reasonable care" to ensure that persons associated with the prosecutor make no such comments as well.

• A prosecutor who knows of new, credible, material evidence creating a reasonable likelihood that a convicted defendant did not commit the offense for which he or she was convicted must disclose the evidence to a court or other proper authority and (if the conviction was in the prosecutor's jurisdiction) must disclose the evidence to the defendant and investigate further.

• A prosecutor who knows of clear and convincing evidence showing that a defendant in the prosecutor's jurisdiction was convicted of a crime the defendant did not commit must seek to remedy the conviction.

With respect to the last two obligations, comment 9 to Model Rule 3.8 provides that a prosecutor does not violate rule 3.8 if the prosecutor in good faith makes the judgment that evidence does not satisfy the conditions of these obligations, even if the prosecutor's judgment letter proves to be wrong.

Two types of pretrial conduct illustrate unique aspects of the criminal justice system. The first concerns charging and plea bargaining. The Hon. Jed Rakoff, of the Southern District of New York, describes the importance of these elements:

> Beginning in the 1960s, and escalating thereafter, Congress and most state legislatures, largely in response to public pressure, decreed that those convicted of crimes would serve ever-longer prison sentences. In the federal system, for example, this trend took the form of mandatory minimum sentences, sentencing guidelines, and the abolition of parole. Faced with the knowledge that their clients, if

> convicted after trial, would be sentenced to very long periods of incarceration, prudent defense counsel increasingly sought to negotiate plea bargains that would allow their clients to obtain lower sentences by pleading guilty to lesser counts or narrower charges, or in exchange for other sentencing concessions. The direct result was to increase greatly the percentage of criminal cases resolved by guilty pleas; such pleas now account for ninety-seven percent of all federal criminal convictions and ninety-four percent of all state criminal convictions. The indirect results were to move primary responsibility for sentencing from the courts to the prosecutors and, concomitantly, to move the locus of the resolution of most criminal cases from the public forum of the courtroom to the private venue of the prosecutor's office.

Jed. S. Rakoff, Frye *and* Lafler*: Bearers of Mixed Messages*, 122 Yale L.J. Online 25 (2012), http://yalelawjournal.org/2012/06/18/rakoff.html.

The *Frye* and *Lafler* opinions discussed above extended the ineffective assistance of counsel doctrine to the plea bargaining process. Judge Rakoff questioned, however, whether these decisions would improve the quality of the plea bargaining process:

> [M]ost of the unfairness that occurs during the plea-bargaining process is, in my experience, not the result of defense counsel's ineffectiveness. Instead, it is the result of overconfidence on the part of prosecutors, whose evidence and sources, having never been put to the test of a trial, appear much stronger to the prosecutors than is objectively warranted. For example, a prosecutor, intent on ensnaring as many defendants as possible, is often more prone to credit a cooperator's testimony than a jury that has heard the cooperator cross-examined by effective defense counsel would be.
>
> *Frye* and *Lafler* do nothing to address this kind of problem. On the contrary, they may make it worse. *Frye* and *Lafler* could push defense attorneys toward urging their clients to take the first plea offered, even if counsel felt there was a realistic chance that a better deal might later be obtained; for otherwise, the defense attorney would risk facing a charge of ineffectiveness of counsel if the later plea bargain—or sentence after trial—proved more onerous than the initial offer. But the corollary of this result is that both the prosecutor and the defense counsel will be negotiating their deal at a time when neither fully understands the strengths or weaknesses of the case: a recipe for injustice.

PROBLEM 7–2

Judge Rakoff's assessment depicts plea bargaining as (in the terms used in this book) a situation in which defense counsel seek to "de-bias" prosecutors by pointing out possible weaknesses in the stories prosecutors have heard from law enforcement officials and cooperating witnesses. Does it seem plausible that prosecutors would have a tendency to credit such sources too much? If one believes that prosecutors, even those acting in good faith, nevertheless may not have an objective view of the facts, does that possibility affect your view of Model Rule 3.8(a)'s requirement that prosecutors bring only charges supported by probable cause? Is an "objective" view possible, are partial and incompletely informed views the only ones possible? And what, if anything, follows for legal ethics from your answers to these questions?

PROBLEM 7–3

Does Rule 3.8(a) prohibit a prosecutor from alluding in plea bargaining to more severe charges than he or she thought justified in order to achieve what the prosecutor felt was a more just plea? Does it forbid threats to bring such charges in order to achieve such a plea?

PROBLEM 7–4

What do you think of Judge Rakoff's suggestion that extending the *Strickland* doctrine to plea bargaining might make the process less just? How might you assess this risk? Would the behavior of civil litigators provide a useful analogue (and how might the difference between the ineffective assistance of counsel doctrine and civil liability doctrines affect the analogy)?

Prosecutors must disclose evidence tending to exculpate a defendant or mitigate his culpability. That obligation is established both by Rule 3.8(d) and Supreme Court cases interpreting the due process clause, commonly referred to as the *Brady* doctrine, for *Brady v. Maryland*, 373 U.S. 83 (1963), which held that "the suppression by the prosecution of evidence favorable to an accused upon request violates due process where the evidence is material either to guilt or to punishment, irrespective of the good faith or bad faith of the prosecution." Evidence is material "within the meaning of *Brady* when there is a reasonable probability that, had the evidence been disclosed, the result of the proceeding would have been different." A reasonable probability does not mean that the defendant "would more likely than not have received a different verdict with the evidence," only that the likelihood of a different result is great enough to "undermine[ ] confidence in the outcome of the trial." *Smith v. Cain*, 132 S.Ct. 627 (2012).

The ABA has opined that its disciplinary rule is broader than the *Brady* doctrine because "Rule 3.8(d) does not implicitly include the materiality limitation recognized in the constitutional case law. The rule requires prosecutors to disclose favorable evidence so that the defense can decide on its utility." ABA Formal Op. 09-454. Another difference is that *Brady*, though not Rule 3.8(d), entails a duty for prosecutors to learn what information, potentially subject to disclosure, is in the possession of other government actors, such as police officers. *Kyles v. Whitley*, 514 U.S. 419, 438 (1995).

Many charges of prosecutorial misconduct rest on the claim that a prosecutor failed to disclose information he or she was bound to disclose. Two cases illustrate such claims and also provide perspective on available remedies. *Imbler v. Pachtman,* 424 U.S. 409 (1976), holds that "in initiating a prosecution and presenting the state's case, the prosecutor is immune from a civil suit for damages under" 42 U.S.C. § 1983, which provides a damages remedy against any person who, acting under color of state law, has deprived a plaintiff of a constitutional right. Imbler had been convicted of murder and sentenced to death. A month before his execution the prosecutor, Pachtman, informed the governor of information bolstering Imbler's alibi defense and calling into question the veracity of the state's chief identification witness. Imbler later sued Pachtman under Section 1983, claiming the relevant information was known or available to Pachtman at trial. After reviewing the common law doctrine that prosecutors are immune from suits alleging wrongful indictment, reflected in cases such as *Yaselli v. Goff*, 12 F.2d 96 (1926), the Court extended that rule to Pachtman, noting that "a prosecutor stands perhaps unique, among officials whose acts could deprive persons of constitutional rights, in his amenability to professional discipline by an association of his peers."

Connick v. Thompson, 131 S. Ct. 1350 (2011), extended this immunity to local government entities such as district attorney's offices. That case involved a prosecutor's failure, admitted privately by the prosecutor and conceded by the district attorney's office, to reveal to the defense tests on a swatch of cloth taken from a robbery scene. The cloth was soaked with the robber's blood, but the blood on the cloth did not match the defendant's blood type. The defendants' conviction of the robbery led him not to testify in his own defense at a later trial where he was convicted of murder. One month before the date set for the defendant's execution, an investigator found the swatch of cloth and presented it to the district attorney, which petitioned for a stay of execution. Both the robbery and murder conviction were later reversed, and the defendant then sued the New Orleans District Attorney alleging an unlawful failure to train prosecutors in proper *Brady* procedures.

The Court rejected this failure-to-train theory, noting among other things that prosecutors attend law school, pass the bar, receive on-the-job training, and "are personally subject to an ethical regime designed to reinforce the profession's standards." The Court noted:

> Prosecutors are not only equipped but are also ethically bound to know what *Brady* entails and to perform legal research when they are uncertain. A district attorney is entitled to rely on prosecutors' professional training and ethical obligations in the absence of specific reason, such as a pattern of violations, to believe that those tools are insufficient to prevent future constitutional violations in "the usual and recurring situations with which [the prosecutors] must deal."

Imbler and *Connick* note the possibility of professional discipline, and *Imbler* notes the possibility of criminal prosecution, for prosecutorial misconduct. Several commentators contend that discipline is rare and therefore a weak deterrent to misconduct. Such claims must be assessed with care: one would want to know both how many times a prosecutor was disciplined and how many disciplinable acts prosecutors committed within a relevant jurisdiction and time period. Such data are hard to come by. One study, *Preventable Error: A Report on Prosecutorial Misconduct in California 1997-2009*, surveyed reported opinions and media accounts of 4,000 cases in which prosecutorial misconduct charges were made. The charges were rejected in about 3,000 of the cases and not ruled on in 282 others. Misconduct was found in 707 cases, a number the authors contrast with the 10 public disciplinary proceedings against prosecutors in California during the relevant period (of 4,741 total cases).

Brady obligations are, of course, not the only duties prosecutors must discharge. The following case illustrates a more general requirement that prosecutors act fairly, in a manner designed to adduce the truth. In reading it, ask yourself whether similar conduct by a defense attorney would either be likely to or would justify a similar response.

UNITED STATES V. LOPEZ-AVILA

678 F.3d 955 (9th Cir. 2012)

Before: JOHN T. NOONAN and CARLOS T. BEA, CIRCUIT JUDGES, and DONALD E. WALTER, SENIOR DISTRICT JUDGE.

ORDER

The opinion in this case was filed on January 12, 2012 and was published at Slip Op. 259. The government has filed a motion requesting that we amend the opinion to remove the name of Assistant U.S. Attorney Jerry Albert from the Federal Reporter. The government's motion is DENIED. . .

OPINION

BEA, CIRCUIT JUDGE:

. . . Defendant Aurora Lopez–Avila attempted to enter the United States from Mexico at the Nogales Port of Entry in Arizona. Upon a tip from an informant, customs officials searched her car and found 9.7 kilograms of cocaine behind the back seat cushion. Lopez–Avila was charged by indictment with possession with intent to distribute over 5 kilograms of cocaine . . .

Lopez–Avila initially pleaded guilty. At the guilty plea hearing, Lopez–Avila was asked a standard set of questions by a magistrate judge, including questions put to ascertain whether Lopez–Avila was knowingly and voluntarily entering a plea of guilty to the charges against her. The questioning included the following colloquy:

> COURT: In the last 48 hours have you had any drugs, prescription medication, or alcoholic beverage?
>
> DEFENDANT: No.
>
> COURT: Have you ever been treated for a mental condition?
>
> DEFENDANT: No.
>
> COURT: Ms. Lopez, has anyone threatened you or forced you to plead guilty?
>
> DEFENDANT: No.
>
> COURT: Has anyone made any promises to you as to what would happen in your case?
>
> DEFENDANT: No.[ ]

One month later, during a presentence interview, Lopez–Avila stated that she had been " 'forced' to commit this offense, or she would face dire consequences." Lopez–Avila had not earlier mentioned to defense counsel that she had been threatened to transport the contraband. Her counsel forthwith moved to withdraw the guilty plea in light of this new information. Following a hearing, the court granted the motion to withdraw the guilty plea.

The case proceeded to trial. Lopez–Avila conceded that she had been transporting contraband and therefore, as the district court later stated, "the whole issue in [the] case [was] whether [Lopez–Avila] was under duress, or threatened, or forced to commit this crime." The government's case-in-chief took approximately one-and-a-half days. During that time, according to the district court, there were "no big surprises" during the testimony of the government's three witnesses. Rather, "the government . . . was moving forward as it had expected as the evidence was being presented."

On the afternoon of the second day of trial, Lopez–Avila took the stand in her own defense. She testified she had been coerced to transport the drugs found in her car. During cross-examination, the prosecutor—Jerry Albert of the U.S. Attorney's office in Tucson—attempted to impeach Lopez–Avila's testimony regarding such coercion by asking questions regarding what Lopez–Avila had said during her initial guilty plea hearing. Defense counsel objected, and at sidebar defense counsel argued that there was "an agreement that this change of plea and her admitting guilt was not going to be a part of this record." The prosecutor stated that he wanted to use certain questions and answers from that hearing to impeach Lopez–Avila but that, pursuant to counsels' agreement, he would not "bring out [that] she pled guilty." In particular, the prosecutor requested that he be allowed to recite to Lopez–Avila the following question and answer from the initial guilty plea hearing:

COURT: Ms. Lopez, has anybody threatened you?

DEFENDANT: No.

The court overruled the objection and allowed the prosecution to proceed. The prosecution then asked Lopez–Avila about that exchange:

> Q: Do you recall testifying under oath on February 24th, 2010, and being asked *this question* by the Court—by the Magistrate Judge:
>
> Ms. Lopez, has anyone threatened you?
>
> And you gave—did you give the following answer:
>
> No
>
> Did you tell that under oath to Magistrate Judge Guerin?
>
> DEFENDANT: Yes.
>
> Q: Was that a lie?
>
> DEFENDANT: How is that? I don't understand.
>
> Q: Well, are you—you've now admitted that you in fact told the judge that *you were not threatened in this case.* And I'm asking you was your testimony on February 24th, 2010, while you were under oath, was that a lie? Did you lie to the judge about not being threatened?
>
> DEFENDANT: Yes.

(Emphasis added.)

Cross-examination proceeded for approximately forty more minutes, when the court took a brief recess. At the recess, defense counsel asked the prosecution for a copy of the transcript from the guilty plea hearing. Immediately upon reviewing the transcript, defense counsel noticed that the prosecutor had misquoted the magistrate judge's question to Lopez–

Avila, without notifying the court or defense counsel of his alteration. . . .

The defense immediately moved for a mistrial. Defense counsel contended that the prosecutor had made it seem as though Lopez–Avila had been asked whether she had been threatened *to commit the offense,* when the magistrate judge in fact had asked Lopez–Avila a different question: whether she had been threatened *to plead guilty.* The prosecutor admitted that his misquoting of the transcript had been intentional but claimed that his reading was a fair one: the transcript "didn't say threaten you to plead guilty. So I wasn't going to mention force you to plead guilty. That's not—I read exactly the way it was. And it's—to me, that says anyone threatened you? Period." But, of course, the prosecutor had *not* read the magistrate's question "exactly the way it was." AUSA Albert omitted an important ellipsis between the words "threatened you" and the end of the magistrate's question, which ellipsis would reveal that words were missing. Here, that missing phrase made all the difference.

The court agreed that the defense had the better reading of the real question and answer: that Lopez–Avila was answering whether she been threatened or forced to plead guilty and not whether she had been threatened or forced to commit any other act. The court told the prosecutor that "it would have been helpful to bring this to the court's attention at sidebar in advance." After a brief recess to consider the matter, the court concluded that it could not cure the error by giving a jury instruction. The court then declared a mistrial.

Following the mistrial order, defense counsel moved to dismiss the case on double jeopardy grounds. At the hearing on that motion, the court said that it was "very surprised the [prosecution] had attempted to present . . . that evidence in that way to this jury." However, the court denied the motion. It correctly stated that under *Oregon v. Kennedy,* 456 U.S. 667 (1982), the Double Jeopardy Clause bars retrial after a defendant requests a mistrial "only where the governmental conduct in question is intended to 'goad' the defendant into moving for a mistrial. Considering what had occurred at trial up to that point, the court found no evidence "that this was a strategy decision on [the prosecution's] part to abort the trial." Instead, the government "was moving forward as it had expected as the evidence was being presented," and the prosecutor's presentation of the edited transcript "was a deliberate strategy . . . to attempt to convict the defendant, or present evidence that [the prosecution] felt was supporting guilt rather than presenting evidence in order to go to a mistrial."

Lopez–Avila took an interlocutory appeal challenging the district court's denial of her double jeopardy motion. The district court divested itself of jurisdiction over the case and allowed the appeal to proceed because of its conclusion that the claim presented by this interlocutory appeal is "colorable." . . .

IV.

Lopez–Avila makes two arguments for why double jeopardy should bar retrial in this case: (1) retrial is barred under *Oregon v. Kennedy*'s "goading" exception to the usual rule that double jeopardy does not bar retrial where a mistrial is granted with the defendant's consent, and (2) retrial is barred by the Arizona Supreme Court's interpretation of its state constitutional protection against double jeopardy, which interpretation is incorporated into federal proceedings in Arizona through 28 U.S.C. § 530B. Both contentions fail. The Double Jeopardy Clause provides no bar to Lopez–Avila's retrial.

A.

[T]he Double Jeopardy Clause usually does not bar retrial when a mistrial is declared with the consent of the defendant. Instead, "[o]nly where the governmental conduct in question is intended to 'goad' the defendant into moving for a mistrial may a defendant raise the bar of double jeopardy to a second trial after having succeeded in aborting the first on his own motion." In adopting this standard, the Supreme Court expressly rejected the idea that double jeopardy would bar retrial when mere " 'bad faith conduct' or 'harassment' on the part of the judge or prosecutor" provoked the defense to ask for a mistrial. In other words, in the language of veteran trial lawyers, the Double Jeopardy Clause bars retrial when a prosecutor's misconduct aims to "burn" the jury, but not when he merely aims to convict the defendant by methods foul.

In practice, the *Kennedy* standard is rarely met. That is because " '[i]t doesn't even matter that [the prosecutor] knows he is acting improperly, provided that his aim is to get a conviction. The only relevant intent is intent to terminate the trial, not intent to prevail at this trial by impermissible means.' " . . .

As the district court found, all of the evidence led to the conclusion that the prosecutor's conduct was "deliberate," a "trial strategy" used to "attempt to convict the defendant." . . . Retrial is not barred by the Double Jeopardy Clause . . .

B.

Lopez–Avila's second argument is that the Double Jeopardy Clause bars retrial in light of 28 U.S.C. § 530B, which governs ethical standards for government lawyers. 28 U.S.C. § 530B states that "an attorney for the Government shall be subject to State laws and rules, and local Federal court rules, *governing attorneys* in each State where such attorney engages in that attorney's duties, to the same extent and in the *same manner as other attorneys* in that State." (Emphasis added). Lopez–Avila contends that this statute, which by its terms applies to "rules . . . governing attorneys," also means that the Arizona Supreme Court's interpretation of the Arizona Constitution's Double Jeopardy Clause applies in federal criminal proceedings in Arizona. Therefore, Lopez–Avila contends, an Arizona state Double Jeopardy case . . . applies in this proceeding. . . .

[R]egulations promulgated by the Department of Justice pursuant to § 530B(b) confirm that § 530B(a) "should not be construed in any way to alter federal substantive, procedural, or evidentiary law." 28 C.F.R. § 77.1(b). Lopez–Avila gives no reason why this regulation is invalid or does not apply to this case. Its application makes clear that the content of the federal Double Jeopardy Clause is not to be transmuted into Arizona's, by reference to § 530B. Finally, although no decision in our circuit has responded to this precise argument, other courts that have examined whether § 530B changes other substantive legal rules have unanimously rejected the claim.

In sum, we conclude that the Double Jeopardy Clause does not bar a retrial of Lopez–Avila under these circumstances. We therefore affirm the district court's denial of her motion to dismiss based on the Double Jeopardy Clause.

V.

We must note, however, that our conclusion on the double jeopardy question may not be the end of this matter. AUSA Jerry Albert represented to the trial court an altered version of the dialogue between the court and a witness at a hearing which had taken place in that same federal court. He presented a falsified version of an exchange as the true recitation of the transcript, until caught out by defense counsel. He did so to make it seem to the jury as if Lopez–Avila had lied under oath about being threatened *to commit the cocaine possession crime,* when she had plainly responded to a magistrate judge's question about whether she had been threatened *to enter a plea of guilty.* It is hard to see—and, from our vantage point as an appellate tribunal, we do *not* see-how a prosecutor could interpret a magistrate's question, "Has anyone threatened you or forced you to plead guilty?", asked at a run-of-the-mill guilty plea hearing, to mean "Has anyone threatened you *to commit this offense* or forced you to plead guilty?"

After the mistrial was granted, AUSA Albert maintained that his reading was plausible. Perhaps Albert truly thought this, or perhaps he thought that consistently maintaining this position would minimize the possibility of any potential sanctions against him. We have no way of knowing, as it is not our task to conduct a thorough investigation of Albert's conduct for disciplinary purposes. We do note that Albert's name does not appear on the prosecution's brief in our court, and he did not appear at oral argument before us. But whatever Albert's motivation, it is worth reminding him and all federal prosecutors of Justice Sutherland's famous statement that the dual obligation of a federal prosecutor in our justice system is to strike hard blows but to refrain from striking foul ones; to use legitimate means to attempt to secure a conviction without employing improper methods to do so. *Berger v. United States,* 295 U.S. 78, 88 (1935).

The mistake in judgment does not lie with AUSA Albert alone. We are also troubled by the government's continuing failure to acknowledge and take responsibility for Albert's error.

The Department of Justice has an obligation to its lawyers and to the public to prevent prosecutorial misconduct. Prosecutors, as servants of the law, are subject to constraints and responsibilities that do not apply to other lawyers; they must serve truth and justice first. Their job is not just to win, but to win fairly, staying within the rules. That did not happen here, and the district court swiftly and correctly declared a mistrial when Albert's misquotation was revealed.

When a prosecutor steps over the boundaries of proper conduct and into unethical territory, the government has a duty to own up to it and to give assurances that it will not happen again. Yet, we cannot find a single hint of appreciation of the seriousness of the misconduct within the pages of the government's brief on appeal. Instead, the government attempts to shift blame by stating that "the prosecutor gave the defense counsel an opportunity to stop the offending question before the prosecutor asked it," but "defense counsel did not realize, or even inquire about, how the question from the change of plea transcript had been redacted." Of course, as we have explained, Albert told the district court what he intended to *say.* Albert did not tell the court or opposing counsel that what he intended to say was not a full nor fair recitation of the magistrate's question to Lopez–Avila.

Finally, upon initial release of this opinion, the government filed a motion requesting that we remove Albert's name and replace it with references to "the prosecutor." The motion contended that naming Albert publicly is inappropriate given that we do not yet know the outcome of any potential investigations or disciplinary proceedings. We declined to adopt the government's suggestion and denied its motion. We have noticed that the U.S. Attorney's Office in Arizona regularly makes public the names of prosecutors who do good work and win important victories. If federal prosecutors receive public credit for their good works—as they should—they should not be able to hide behind the shield of anonymity when they make serious mistakes.

We recognize that this court is not the proper venue for direct discipline of Albert, so we will not state here that the blow struck by him necessarily was one so foul as to require some form of official sanction. We were not in district court to see what occurred; Albert has not appeared before us to explain himself; and this appeal is not directly about his misconduct, but rather about the question whether the Double Jeopardy Clause bars a new prosecution. However, we do not need a record greater or different than we have here to determine that Albert should not have misrepresented the transcript's question. Accordingly, we are in a position to do three things to ensure that this matter is handled properly following this disposition: we remand the case to allow the district court to consider dismissal with prejudice of the indictment as an exercise of its supervisory powers and to prevent other misconduct in the future; we instruct the district court to consider disciplinary options also pursuant to its supervisory powers; and we note that the Office of Professional Responsibility within the Department of Justice has the responsibility of investigating allegations of misconduct by federal prosecutors. Whether the circumstances attendant to Albert's misrepresentation attenuate or aggravate the misconduct is a matter as to which the trial judge or officials in the Office of Professional Responsibility are in a better position to determine. . . .

Lopez-Avila dealt with conduct during cross-examination. Prosecutors' conduct in the course of argument is subject to special scrutiny as well and probably presents a more common source of ethical issues. *People v. Shazier*, 2012 WL 6734681 (Cal. App. Dec. 27, 2012) illustrates this point. The court in that case reversed a finding that a defendant convicted of sexual conduct with minors was a sexually violent predator within the meaning of California law. The first trial on this question resulted in a hung jury. The second trial produced a finding for the prosecution, a result reversed on appeal due to prosecutorial misconduct in the form of the prosecutor's allusion to the consequences of such a finding (hospitalization rather than prison), in violation of an *in limine* ruling. The third trial produced a finding for the prosecution, again reversed on grounds of prosecutorial misconduct. The court of appeals held:

> Defendant's assertion of prosecutorial misconduct in this case is based on a series of incidents in which the prosecutor asked improper questions of the witnesses that elicited inflammatory answers, or made improper arguments to the jury.
>
> In considering the effect of the prosecutor's conduct, we are mindful that "[p]rosecutors . . . are held to an elevated standard of conduct. It is the duty of every member of the bar to "maintain the respect due to the courts" and to "abstain from all offensive personality." (Bus. & Prof. Code, § 6068, subds. (b) and (f).) A prosecutor is held to a standard higher than that imposed on other attorneys because of the unique function he or she performs in representing the interests, and in exercising the sovereign power, of the state. As the United States Supreme Court has explained, the prosecutor represents "a sovereignty whose obligation to govern impartially is as compelling as its obligation to govern at all; and whose interest, therefore, in a criminal prosecution is not that it shall win a case, but that justice shall

be done." Prosecutorial misconduct —often occurring during argument—may take a variety of forms. It may include (without limitation) mischaracterizing or misstating the evidence; referring to facts not in evidence; misstating the law, particularly where done in an effort to relieve the People of responsibility for proving all elements of a crime beyond a reasonable doubt; attacking the integrity of, or casting aspersions on defense counsel; intimidating witnesses; referring to a prior conviction of the defendant that was not before the jury; predicting that the defendant, if not found guilty, will commit future crimes; stating a personal opinion, such as an opinion that the defendant is guilty; or appealing to passions or prejudice, such as asking the jury to view the crime through the victim's eyes. . .

During closing argument, as it was nearing the end, the prosecutor said . . . imagine if you found the petition to be not true in this case. [Can] you explain this to people that you work with, or friends, or neighbors. What did you do? Well we found the petition to be not true. Oh, wow. That is interesting. Did the person—" . . .

We see no difference between the prosecutor's proposal here that a juror or jurors conduct a conversation with an imaginary friend explaining that by their verdict they loosed a dangerous predator on the public than saying directly to the jury, "your friends and neighbors will condemn you if you release him." Both are flagrant misconduct. Public opinion is not a proper consideration for a jury. This reasoning has been condemned as faulty since the time of ancient Greece. *Argumentum ad populum* is fallacious. A jury cannot be made to consider an appeal to the masses, with the notion that "a proposition is true because many or most believe it."

The Main Points to Recall From Chapter 7 Are:

- Lawyers owe clients a duty of care; it requires the lawyer to act with the diligence and skill normally exercised by competent lawyers in similar circumstances.
- A plaintiff alleging breach of the duty of care (negligence/malpractice) must show the lawyer owed her a duty, breached that duty, and thereby was the actual and proximate cause of harm to the client.
- Lawyers may be subject to other forms of civil sanction, such as fee disgorgement or damages for breach of fiduciary duty, in addition to liability for violating the duty of care.
- In most jurisdictions, criminal defendants must allege and demonstrate their actual innocence to prevail on a malpractice

claim against their criminal lawyer. This rule does not extend to claims based on something other than negligence.

- The Sixth Amendment test for ineffective assistance of counsel asks whether defense counsel's conduct was unreasonable *and*, if so, whether there is a reasonable probability that, but for counsel's unprofessional errors, the result of the proceeding would have been different.
- Prosecutors are subject to special obligations designed to ensure the impartial administration of justice.

CHAPTER 8

LIABILITY TO NON-CLIENTS

■ ■ ■

In some cases you may be liable to persons other than your clients. The most obvious way to create such liability is to violate a general legal rule applicable to everyone, such as by committing fraud. But there are other ways, too.

Historically, indirect liability to non-clients was limited by the doctrine of privity, which held that a tort plaintiff could only sue those with whom he or she had a direct relationship. The privity requirement has been relaxed over the years, however. You may now be liable if you invite a third party to rely on you and then frustrate that reliance, or you may be hired by a client to confer some benefit on a third person, who in some jurisdictions may sue you to enforce the obligations you owe to the client.

Some jurisdictions also recognize liability if you represent someone who owes a fiduciary duty to a third party, such as a guardian who owes such a duty to a ward, and your client harms the third party by committing a crime or fraud that in some way relates to your representation. This "pass through" form of liability is less common than the first two types. The following materials survey these types of liability.

A. DUTIES TO PARTIES RELATED TO CLIENTS

Restatement (Third) of the Law Governing Lawyers § 51

MEIGHAN V. SHORE

34 Cal.App.4th 1025 (1995)

EPSTEIN, ACTING P. J.

In this case we hold that when a husband and wife consult an attorney about a personal injury action against a third party on account of personal injury to one of them, and the other spouse has a potential claim for loss of consortium of which the attorney is or ought to be aware, the attorney has a duty to inform that spouse of the consortium cause of action. . . .

We emphasize the narrowness of our holding. It pertains to the peculiar tort of loss of consortium, where both spouses consult an attorney with respect to a personal injury suffered by one of them and the attorney knows or could readily ascertain that the other spouse has a potential claim for loss of consortium, and where that spouse is unaware of his or her rights.

Factual and Procedural Summary

The lawsuit was brought by Joan Meighan, wife of Dr. Clement Meighan, an anthropologist and member on the faculty of the University of California, Los Angeles. The respondent is Samuel Shore, an attorney. Since the case reaches us on summary judgment, we apply a strict construction of the evidence presented by respondent and a liberal reading of the proofs submitted by the appellant.

The information available to respondent indicated that Dr. Meighan had experienced chest pains on October 8, 1988, and was taken to a hospital. He was in the emergency room for about an hour, then transferred to the coronary care unit under "coronary precaution" orders. His initial cardiogram was abnormal, but did not definitively show that a heart attack was in progress or that heart damage had occurred. In fact, he was suffering a heart attack. The first abnormal heart enzyme study was taken the next morning, about 4 a.m. The first cardiogram to show heart damage was taken about 7 a.m. that morning. Mrs. Meighan was with her husband for two to three hours in the coronary care unit, on the evening of October 8. She left for home about 10 p.m. after being told by the attending physician that Dr. Meighan was not having a heart attack. Respondent concluded that Dr. Meighan had a viable medical malpractice claim against the hospital and the attending physician for failing to administer medication that might have limited the extent of damage from the heart attack he suffered during the 12–hour period, 7 p.m. October 8 to 7 a.m. October 9.

Had respondent inquired, he would have ascertained the following about Mrs. Meighan's knowledge and impressions. She "had been trained as a nurse." He also would have ascertained she knew that heart attacks are caused by blood clots, that medication is available to dissolve clots, and that it is only effective during the early hours of a heart attack. Dr. Meighan had had two previous bypass procedures, and appellant was concerned about his care. She was particularly concerned because, she understood, the on-call cardiologist did not appear and initiate therapy for three and one-half hours after being called. She was hysterical and afraid, and demanded that the nurses get a cardiologist to examine her husband.

Respondent did not ask appellant or her husband whether either of them had any medical training, and he assumed they had none. Appellant had not come in as a referred client, and based on "the evolution of the facts in the case, at the conclusion of the meeting" respondent "ruled out the possibility" that she might have a viable right to proceed against the defendant for loss of consortium and emotional distress. Whether or not respondent formed that opinion (as we shall discuss, the trial court rejected his disclaimer), he never discussed the subject with appellant or her husband. Appellant declared that before meeting her present counsel (who was substituted in February 1991), she "had no idea that I might have any claim at all. I have never heard of a spouse of a negligently-injured person having any possibility of suing in her own right. Mr. Shore never mentioned as [*sic*] such thing to me, or my husband, in my presence or to my knowledge. [¶] If I had known of any such spousal rights, I would have joined my husband in the medical malpractice lawsuit." Her husband's testimony is to the same effect.

According to appellant's declaration, after being released from the hospitalization and treatment that were the subject of the underlying lawsuit, Dr. Meighan suffered physically and she was required to take over many things that he used to do. He was unable to provide her with emotional and physical support that he previously had given. Their personal relationship was affected. Appellant declared that her husband, who had been very active despite two bypass operations, "has been unable to provide me with the same emotional support that I received before; his disability completely changed our lives. He was compelled to leave a job that he had had and had always loved for many, many years as a full Professor at UCLA due to his disability and his pervasive fear of another massive, and potentially fatal, heart attack.". . . .

Both appellant and Dr. Meighan spoke to respondent about the case at the initial interview. Respondent said he would accept the case, and handed over a retainer agreement. The agreement had a blank space in the body for the name of the client to be inserted; it was left blank. The sole "client" signature was that of Dr. Meighan.

Although respondent does not recall making the statement, appellant testified at deposition that he said, in effect, that he was representing her husband, and not her. She described the statement, or statements, in various ways at deposition. She said that respondent "said he was not representing me, only my husband, or words to that effect." He did not say why. She and her husband had been together on everything, so she assumed "we would be together on this, and he made it very clear we were not." Respondent said "that Clem was the one that was suing, not as a couple, or something like that." She realized "yes, it's probably, you know, since he's the one that was injured, I had nothing to do with it."

It is undisputed that appellant understood respondent was not representing her and she never thought that he was; she did not seek and he did not offer legal advice to her about a potential lawsuit on her behalf; she did not sign a retainer agreement by which respondent might be paid for such representation; and respondent did not act as her attorney. Nevertheless, respondent had several conversations with appellant in which they discussed legal matters, and in which he "repeatedly gave [her] legal advice"—presumably about the medical malpractice action on behalf of Dr. Meighan.

Appellant's suit against respondent is premised on his duty to inform her of her right to sue the health care providers for loss of consortium and for negligent infliction of emotional distress. Respondent moved for summary judgment. His moving papers presented two bases for that relief. First, he argued that since appellant was not his client, he owed her no duty. Second, he asserted that his decision not to pursue an action on her behalf was based on a reasonable and good faith exercise of discretion, and hence was not actionable under *Kirsch v. Duryea* (1978) 21 Cal.3d.303. The trial court expressly rejected the latter ground, stating that it was "specifically discounting the defendant's self serving declarations which the court does not believe and which this court is entitled to disregard. CCP Sec. 437c, subd. (e)." But it accepted the argument about lack of duty and, on that basis, granted summary judgment. (Appellant also moved for summary judgment. Her motion was denied.)

Discussion

I

A

This case is principally about duty. More precisely, it concerns the duty of an attorney to a person so closely related with the client as to be in legal privity with that person, yet not the client. "The determination of duty is primarily a question of law. It is the court's 'expression of the sum total of those considerations of policy which lead the law to say that the particular plaintiff is entitled to protection.' (Prosser, Law of Torts (4th ed. 1971) pp. 325–326.) Any number of considerations may justify the imposition of duty in particular circumstances, including the guidance of history, our continually refined concepts of morals and justice, the convenience of the rule, and social judgment as to where the loss should fall. While the question whether one owes a duty to another must be decided on a case-by-case basis, every case is governed by the rule of general application that all persons are required to use ordinary care to prevent others from being injured as the result of their conduct. However, foreseeability of the risk is a primary consideration in establishing the element of duty."

In this case, the foreseeability of harm to the plaintiff is so clear that it would be easy to pass over the issue of duty. Yet, to paraphrase Justice Kaus (*Williams v. State of California* (1983) 34 Cal.3d 18, 22,) we may not put the foreseeability cart before the duty horse. Foreseeability is an important element in the duty analysis, but it is not coterminous with the doctrine.

Plaintiff's lawsuit is for professional negligence, in the nature of attorney malpractice. That aspect of negligence consists of the failure of an attorney to "use such skill, prudence, and diligence as lawyers of ordinary skill and capacity commonly possess and exercise in the performance of the tasks which they undertake." [citations omitted]

To understand the application of duty in the context of this case, we begin with a discussion of the principal tort at issue—loss of consortium.

B

Loss of consortium has been described as "loss of conjugal fellowship and sexual relations." (*Rodriguez v. Bethlehem Steel Corp.* (1974) 12 Cal.3d 382, 385.) In somewhat more general terms, it has been referred to as the loss of "the noneconomic aspects of the marriage relation, including conjugal society, comfort, affection, and companionship." . . .

The statute of limitations for loss of consortium is one year from the date of the spouse's injury, and there is no tolling during the pendency of the spouse's personal injury action. It is undisputed that in this case the statute ran during the period respondent was representing Dr. Meighan.

Damages for loss of consortium are regarded as community property, as are other damages for personal injury suffered by a spouse. It is significant that the relationship between the spouses is one of privity. Thus, an unsuccessful personal injury suit by the physically injured spouse acts as an estoppel that bars the spouse who would claim damages for loss of consortium. . . .

The circumstance of privity bears on the duty of an attorney to the spouse of a physically injured client. But it does not make the spouse privy to the attorney-client contract. Nor is it determinative by itself of the issue of duty. We turn next to a fuller examination of duty in the context of the consortium tort.

C

At common law, the starting point is privity: an attorney was not liable for professional negligence to anyone other than the client whose cause he or she engaged to undertake. . . . California's journey away from this doctrine began nearly 40 years ago with the first of a pair of decisions by Chief Justice Gibson. These decisions have guided the development of California law, and of many other jurisdictions, ever since.

The first is *Biakanja v. Irving* (1958) 49 Cal.2d 647. The court dealt with a nonattorney notary who had drawn a will for a testator who wished to devise all of his property to the plaintiff. Because of the notary's negligence, the putative will was ineffective, and the plaintiff received only one-eighth of the estate through the law of intestate succession. She sued the notary for the difference. His defense was classic: he was not liable in negligence to anyone not in privity to his contract with the testator. Since that excluded the plaintiff, he argued, he was not liable to her for his error.

The argument was rejected. The court could have rejected it on a third party contract beneficiary theory, reasoning that plaintiff was the intended beneficiary of the contract between the notary and the testator. But it did not. Instead, the court formulated the five-point test by which the case is known:

> "The determination whether in a specific case the defendant will be held liable to a third person not in privity is a matter of policy and involves the balancing of various factors, among which are the extent to which the transaction was intended to affect the plaintiff, the foreseeability of harm to him, the degree of certainty that the plaintiff suffered injury, the closeness of the connection between the defendant's conduct and the injury suffered, the moral blame attached to the defendant's conduct, and the policy of preventing future harm."

Measured by these standards, the court had no difficulty in finding a duty by the notary.

The second case, *Lucas v. Hamm*, *supra*, 56 Cal.2d 583, is similar to *Biakanja*, except that the person engaged to draw the will was an attorney, and therefore did not commit a crime by unauthorized practice of law. The court reiterated its earlier reasoning and added a further consideration, since the defendant was an attorney: whether recognition of liability would impose an undue burden on the profession. The court concluded that it would not, "particularly when we take into consideration that a contrary conclusion would cause the innocent beneficiary to bear the loss." Thus, the lack of contract privity between the beneficiaries and the attorney engaged by the testator did not preclude the plaintiffs from maintaining an action in tort against the attorney. The court went on to conclude that the beneficiaries also were entitled to recover on a third party beneficiary theory. Reaching the merits of liability, the court found that the attorney was not culpable for running afoul of the hypertechnical rules against perpetuities and restraints on alienation. . . .

Later cases have refined the doctrine, explaining and applying it, and keeping it true to its original analysis. . . . . Mallen and Smith have undertaken a national survey of the cases. They acknowledge an abundance of authority for the privity rule, most notably in New York, but point out that the vast majority of the cases that adhere to it arise in factual situations where no jurisdiction would allow a plaintiff to recover. (1 Mallen & Smith, *supra*, § 7.10, pp. 376–379.) The modern trend, they conclude, "is to recognize the existence of a duty beyond the confines of those privy to the attorney-client contract." (*Op. cit. supra*, § 7.11, p. 381.) The trend manifests itself through two theories: the traditional third party beneficiary approach, and the California multicriteria test. The California approach, they find, "has been cited with approval and accepted with near unanimity by those jurisdictions which have examined the issue." (*Op. cit. supra*, at p. 383, and fn. 5; the authors cite decisions from 20 American jurisdictions, and 1 English precedent.). . . .

We are satisfied that, in California, professional liability is not dependent upon privity of contract, but the presence or absence of a client's intent that the plaintiff benefit from or rely upon the attorney's services is particularly significant in the determination of duty. Intended reliance may be express or implicit, obvious or subtle. In the final analysis, application of duty depends on the particular factual setting of the case. We now turn to a consideration of duty in the circumstances of this case.

D

It is significant that respondent's undoubted client, Dr. Meighan, had a community property interest in appellant's recovery for loss of consortium, just as appellant had an interest in his recovery of damages for medical malpractice. The consortium tort is so closely interwoven with the personal injury action that plaintiff and her husband were in privity with respect to it; a loss of the husband's lawsuit would have collaterally estopped his wife from prosecuting her action for loss of consortium. Respondent had an obligation to advise Dr. Meighan of these rights.

Unlike other cases in which it is obvious to the potential client that he or she must obtain other representation in order to pursue a claim in the event the consulted attorney should refuse to undertake the cause, in this case it cannot be assumed that appellant or her husband was aware of his or her rights under the tort, and in fact the evidence shows that they were not. More significantly, respondent did not refuse to undertake the representation; he accepted the case presented to him, but neglected or chose not to say anything about the consortium cause of action even though his declaration reveals he considered it and decided it was not worth pursuing.

While the Meighans were unaware of the full extent of their rights, it may be inferred they expected that, if respondent agreed to take the case, he would at least inform them of what they were. That surely was the expectation of Dr. Meighan, the acknowledged client. It also was the reasonable expectation of appellant.

There is one further circumstance: respondent's statement to appellant that he was representing Dr. Meighan, not her. Respondent argues that an attorney may refuse to represent a client and that malpractice liability cannot be affixed on the attorney who does so, even though, as a result, the potential client's rights are not prosecuted and thereby lost. We agree with that contention as a general proposition: a simple refusal to undertake representation, without any other facts (e.g., an undertaking to investigate the case, to advise about it, to make a referral, or delay during a critical period) cannot fix malpractice liability on the attorney.

Here, however, respondent has not established the clear picture he postulates. His statement to Mrs. Meighan was not made in the context of a *refusal* to represent her. There was, in fact, no discussion of her rights at all. For all that the record shows, it was simply an explanation to Mrs. Meighan of the reason she was not to sign the retainer agreement. Given the context of the consultation and the nature of the tort at issue, respondent's statement cannot foreclose her rights as a matter of law.

All of this points to a finding of a duty by respondent. The same conclusion is reached when the facts are analyzed under the *Biakanja* factors.

(1) *The extent to which the transaction was intended to affect Mrs. Meighan.* Mr. and Mrs. Meighan sought out respondent to take their "case," which they perceived as a lawsuit against certain of Dr. Meighan's health care providers. The normal expectation of persons in their position is that the attorney will advise them of their rights with respect to the injuries suffered. We infer they held that expectation. The marital community would benefit by any recovery of damages by either spouse; each had a community property interest in such recovery. Thus, while the retainer agreement did not expressly name appellant as a party to be benefited by respondent's services, the transaction necessarily affected her interests.

(2) *Foreseeability of harm to Mrs. Meighan.* It was entirely foreseeable that appellant would lose her rights to pursue an action for loss of consortium unless respondent at least alerted her to its existence before it became barred by the statute of limitations.

(3) *Certainty that Mrs. Meighan suffered injury.* It was inevitable that the cause of action would become barred upon the running of the statute of limitations without a suit commenced on behalf of appellant. That is what happened.

(4) *Closeness of connection between respondent's conduct and injury.* The effect was direct; no attenuation analysis is required.

(5) *Policy of preventing future harm.* The duty at issue was to inform Mrs. Meighan of the existence of her cause of action for loss of consortium. Respondent was not required to represent her in a lawsuit to recover for that tort. Had he given the warning, it would have been up to the Meighans to decide whether to pursue the claim; and if so, with what attorney. The harm is the loss of rights by reason of a failure to advise under circumstances where advice is reasonably expected. Requiring that it be given in these limited circumstances will discourage its loss by an uninformed failure to act. It also will reduce the prospect of secondary litigation, as in this case, over that failure.

(6) Finally, we consider the criterion added by *Lucas: whether recognition of liability under the circumstances would impose an undue burden on the profession*. We have emphasized the unusual setting of this case. That setting informs the narrowness of the duty: where husband and wife consult an attorney about a lawsuit over personal injury to one spouse and the other has a potential claim for loss of consortium, of which he or she is unaware, and the attorney agrees to represent the injured spouse, counsel has a duty to inform the other spouse of the potential consortium claim. Imposition of a duty in this limited situation will not impose an undue burden on the profession. To the contrary, it will vindicate the reasonable expectation of persons who seek legal advice about their rights, the providing of which is the unique office of an attorney.

We conclude that, in these circumstances, respondent had a duty to inform the Meighans of the existence of their rights under the consortium tort. If he thought it was without merit, or that pressing it would weaken Dr. Meighan's case, or if he simply did not want to handle it, he was perfectly free to act on those conclusions. What he was not free to do was to keep his evaluation entirely to himself, without warning the Meighans that the right existed and would be lost unless pursued. Had he done that, the Meighans could have made their own decision about whether they wished to pursue the action, and, if they did, whether they wanted to find other counsel who would represent both the malpractice and consortium causes of action.

CASE QUESTIONS

1. How is *Meighan* different from *Nichols v. Keller, supra* chapter 7.A.1?
2. What is privity?
3. What does the court say is "particularly important" in determining whether a lawyer owes a duty to a non-client?
4. How does this case compare with or contrast to *Lucas v. Hamm*, which the court cites?
5. What non-*Biakanja* facts are present and matter in this case?

In an omitted portion of the opinion, the *Meighan* court gave some examples of actions that create and do not create duties to third parties. In *Roberts v. Ball, Hunt, Hart, Brown & Baerwitz*, 57 Cal.App.3d 104 (1976), the court of appeals held a law firm owed a duty to a creditor who was shown an opinion letter the firm wrote with the knowledge that it would be shown to third parties to secure financing. On these facts, the letter created a reliance interest running from the creditor to the firm. The creation of a duty to enforce a reasonable reliance interest is consistent with Model Rule 2.3(a), permitting lawyers to write such letters, and with *Restatement* § 95, which is to the same effect.

In contrast, in *Goodman v. Kennedy*, 18 Cal.3d 335 (1976), the Supreme Court held a lawyer did not owe a duty to investors who bought stock from shareholders the lawyer had advised. The Court reasoned the lawyers had no relationship with the investors and therefore owed duties only to their clients, the selling shareholders. Any other rule, it held, would chill legal advice by forcing lawyers to hedge against the risk of unforeseeable and potentially unlimited liability.

In *Bily v. Arthur Young & Co.*, 3 Cal.4th 370, 389 (1992), the Supreme Court held that accountants were not liable to any person who might foreseeably be harmed by their malpractice. The court applied the "intent to benefit" approach of the Restatement Second of Torts, section 522, in limiting liability for negligent misrepresentations in an audit: the auditor's duty does not run to anyone who might see and rely upon its opinion, but only to those to whom or for whom the misrepresentations were made.

More recently, the court in *Hall v. Superior Court,* 108 Cal.App.4th 706 (2003), rejected an effort to extend *Meighan*. A young girl drowned in her paternal grandmother's swimming pool. The girl's mother was not present when the child drowned, but the girl's father and grandmother were. The parents separated after the drowning. Following the separation, the mother sued the grandmother for negligence. The father objected to the suit and threatened to divorce the mother if she did not drop it. The mother persisted with the claim, and the father filed for divorce. Shortly after that filing, the case settled for $210,000, which was paid by the grandmother's insurer.

The father then sued the mother and the mother's lawyer for half the settlement. He claimed he would not have objected to the suit if someone had told him the insurer would pay for it rather than his mother. The lawyer never represented the father, who tried to get around this fact by relying on *Meighan*. His argument was that his ex-wife's lawyer harmed him by not informing him that he had a stake in the claim and by not joining him as an indispensable party to the suit against his mother.

Noting in part that the father was present at the drowning while the mother was not, thus creating a potential conflict of interest between them, the court rejected this argument:

> Brent has ignored the material facts placing this case outside the scope of *Meighan.* Unlike the couple in *Meighan,* Estella and Brent never met together with Hall to seek advice about *their* potential claims arising from their daughter's death. Instead Estella contacted

and met with Hall alone to discuss *her* particular legal rights. At no point did Brent ever contact Hall to discuss the wrongful death case or his legal rights. Hall's sole client Estella had no expectation Brent would benefit from or rely on Hall's legal services. Nor is there any evidence Brent himself had any such expectation.

Based on the particular facts of this case, we conclude it would have imposed an undue burden on Hall to require him to contact Brent (who was not living with Estella) so he could advise Brent about his legal rights or suggest Brent contact another lawyer to do so. We are wary about extending an attorney's duty to persons who have not come to the attorney seeking legal advice and whom the attorney has never met. We recognize the awkward position Hall would have found himself in if he were required to seek out Brent and suggest he sue his mother. Beyond that, in this instance we seriously question whether Hall could have engaged in such a discussion with Brent without breaching his duty of loyalty to his existing client, Estella.

Triangular Duty Relationships

Lawyers often refer to relationships in which a lawyer acts for a client but also owes duties to a third party as "triangular relationships," and that phrase helps approach the problem of liability to non-clients. Think of your fiduciary duties to clients as existing on a vertical axis and your client's relationships to third parties as existing on a horizontal axis.

In general, the triangular duty problem arises when your representation of a client is related to your client's relations with some third party in such a way that recognizing a duty running from you to the third party advances the purposes of the representation. The *Restatement* recognizes such duties in three types of cases. The first type of case, described in Section 51(2), is when the lawyer or the client (with the lawyer's agreement) invites a third party to rely on the lawyer, as in the case of an opinion letter. This was the circumstance in *Roberts v. Ball, Hunt, Hart, Brown & Baerwitz* 57 Cal.App.3d 104 (1976), which the *Meighan* court cites.

The second type of case is based on the client's intention. Section 51(3) states that a lawyer owes a duty to a third party when the lawyer knows that the client intends the lawyer's services to benefit the third party; the imposition of the duty would not impair the lawyer's obligations to the client, and the absence of a duty would make it unlikely that the third party could enforce the lawyer's obligations to the client. The paradigm case here is where a client retains a lawyer to draft a will leaving assets to a third party, as was the case in *Lucas v. Hamm* 56 Cal.2d 583 (1961).

The third type of case is based on the client's status as one who acts on behalf and for the benefit of a third party. Examples include clients who act as trustees, guardians, executors, or in some other capacity where they owe a fiduciary duty to a third party. Section 51(4) recognizes a duty where a lawyer represents such a person, knows that action is necessary to prevent or rectify the consequences of a criminal or fraudulent act by the client, or a breach of duty in which the lawyer is involved, the third party cannot protect his or her own rights, and the imposition of such a duty would not impair the lawyer's ability to represent the client. Unlike the second type of case, status-based duties may arise regardless whether the client intends that the attorney act to benefit the third party.

The following diagram may help distill the principles set forth in the *Restatement*. You always owe fiduciary duties to your client, represented by the solid vertical line between lawyer and client. When the facts on the horizontal line between the client and the third party satisfy the conditions just discussed, the lawyer owes duties to, and may be sued by, the third party. That contingent duty is represented by the dashed diagonal line.

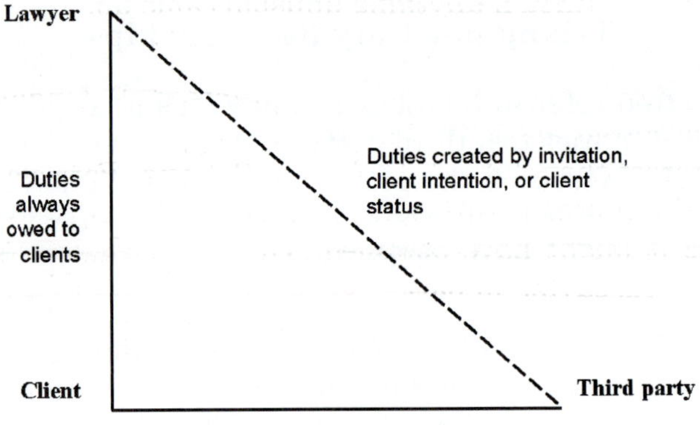

Client status or intention relative to third party

For a general discussion of this issue, *see* Geoffrey C. Hazzard, Jr., *Triangular Duty Relationships: An Exploratory Analysis*, 1 GEO. J. L. ETHICS 15 (1987).

Some cases extend liability beyond the scope suggested by the *Restatement*. In *Fickett v. Superior Court*, 27 Ariz.App. 793 (1976), for example, an attorney represented a guardian for an incompetent person. The guardian was replaced and the new guardian accused the old one of looting the estate. The new guardian sued counsel for the old guardian. Counsel moved for summary judgment, arguing that, since the new guardian did not allege counsel had not looted the estate himself or colluded with the old guardian to loot the estate, counsel could not be held liable for the old guardian's misconduct.

The trial court denied the motion and the court of appeals affirmed the denial. The appellate court thought the new guardian could maintain a suit on the theory that counsel was negligent in failing to discover the old guardian's misconduct. The court said "when an attorney undertakes to represent the guardian of an incompetent, he assumes a relationship not only with the guardian but also with the ward. If, as is contended here, petitioners knew or should have known that the guardian was acting adversely to his ward's interests, the possibility of frustrating the whole purpose of the guardianship became foreseeable as did the possibility of injury to the ward. In fact, we conceive that the ward's interests overshadow those of the guardian."

Morales v. Field, Degoff, Huppert & Macgowan, 99 Cal.App.3d 307 (1979), reached a similar result. Defendants represented Wells Fargo Bank, which was as executor of the will of Beatrice Morales and trustee of a trust that took assets under her will. Plaintiff Patricia Morales, Beatrice's daughter, was the only living beneficiary of the trust. When Beatrice died, defendants sent Patricia letters saying that she did not need to do anything in connection with the probate of the will and that they would keep her informed if anything unusual came up.

To settle a claim against the estate, Wells Fargo guaranteed a renegotiated loan Beatrice previously had guaranteed. Defendants represented both Wells Fargo and the principal debtors on the loans, creating a conflict of interest they did not disclose to Patricia. Patricia sued the law firm, claiming the settlement harmed her indirectly by denying the estate certain rights it might have obtained. The court of appeals allowed the suit to go forward, saying in part:

> An attorney who acts as counsel for a trustee provides advice and guidance as to how that trustee may and must act to fulfill his obligations to all beneficiaries. It follows that when an attorney undertakes a relationship as adviser to a trustee, he in reality also assumes a relationship with the beneficiary akin to that between trustee and beneficiary. . . . to require at a minimum that a trustee's attorney inform beneficiaries of his dual representation in transactions involving the trust can only have salutary results, such as the elimination of the need for lawsuits similar to the instant action.

99 Cal.App.3d at 316.

Other courts are less willing to extend duties to beneficiaries. In *Goldberg v. Frye*, 217 Cal.App.3d 1258 (1990), for example, the court held that a beneficiary of a trust could not sue counsel for the trustee for malpractice in connection with the administration of the trust. Curiously, the *Goldberg* court did not cite *Morales*. (One could attempt to reconcile the cases on the ground that *Goldberg* recognized that counsel for a trustee might create duties to beneficiaries by undertaking to represent them, and that counsel in *Morales* had written Patricia promising to keep her informed, but the *Goldberg* court did not make such an argument.)

Wells Fargo Bank, N.A. v. Superior Court, 22 Cal.4th 201 (2000), dealt with allegations of misconduct by the beneficiaries of a trust, the Boltwoods, against the trustees of the trust, one of whom was Wells Fargo. The Boltwoods demanded and received communications between Wells Fargo and its counsel relating to matters of trust administration. They also demanded communications relating to the charges of misconduct they had raised. Wells Fargo asserted that such communications were privileged.

The Supreme Court agreed. It rejected the Boltwood's claim that the privilege was trumped by the trustees' duties to report to the beneficiaries on the administration of the trust. The Court noted that most jurisdictions agreed with this claim, but it found no express statutory exception to the privilege for trustees, and held that it had no power to recognize implicit exceptions. The Court did not limit its holding to communications relating to the Boltwood's allegations of misconduct. It found Wells Fargo had been under no duty to disclose privileged communications relating to trust administration, either.

More generally, the Court also rejected the claim that the Boltwoods were co-clients of the trustee's counsel. According to the Court, "The attorney for the trustee of a trust is not, by virtue of this relationship, also the attorney for the beneficiaries of the trust. The attorney represents only the trustee." (quoting *Fletcher v. Superior Court*, 44 Cal.App.4th 773, 777 (1996)).

In *Borissoff v. Taylor & Faust*, 33 Cal.4th 523 (2004), the California Supreme Court dealt with a malpractice claim brought by a fiduciary of an estate against counsel hired by a previous fiduciary of the estate. The Court reasoned that counsel had been retained by the fiduciary in his capacity as a fiduciary, not personally, so that counsel's duties ran to the office of fiduciary of the trust. When the second fiduciary took over that office, he had standing to bring suit for breach of such duties. The Court correctly rejected the defendant's analogy between a successor fiduciary and a beneficiary of the trust.

Moeller v. Superior Court, 16 Cal.4th 1124 (1997), reached a parallel result regarding privilege. That case held that when one trustee replaces another, the successor trustee controls the privilege regarding communications between counsel and the predecessor trustee in his capacity as trustee (rather than in his personal capacity).

Johnson v. Superior Court, 38 Cal.App.4th 463 (1995), distinguished between cases in which a fiduciary hires counsel to help the fiduciary discharge her duties and cases in which a fiduciary hires counsel to find out what those duties are, or because the fiduciary thinks she has breached those duties. Summarizing both *Goldberg* and *Morales* in relation to this distinction, the court said

> We question whether an attorney who undertakes to represent a trustee or other fiduciary, by that fact alone, assumes a duty the breach of which will be actionable directly by the beneficiary. Even if such proposition can be supported generally, it cannot apply in a situation in which the interests of the fiduciary and the beneficiary are adverse.

38 Cal.App.4th at 474.

Finally, the court in *Chang v. Lederman*, 172 Cal.App.4th 67 (2009), declined to extend the *Lucas* analysis to a case in which a wife alleged a lawyer acted negligently in advising her husband not to modify his estate plan to leave more assets to his wife. (The original plan left most assets in trust for the husband's son from a prior marriage.) The court reasoned that cases extending a lawyer's duty to an intended beneficiary who lost assets due to the lawyer's mistake were different from Chang's case, in which the husband's initial estate plan was set up properly and the question was whether he intended to modify it to benefit Chang.

PROBLEM 8–1

Suppose you are approached by the trustee of a trust. The trustee says he is concerned he has invested trust assets imprudently; the investments seemed like a good idea at the time, but they did not pan out, and the trust has lost a lot of money. The trustee would like you to look into his conduct and write him a memorandum giving your opinion on whether he has breached his duties as trustee. If you undertake this representation, would you owe duties to the beneficiary of the trust?

All In The Family

Family members sometimes ask lawyers to help them out. That is one of the benefits of being a lawyer but it can lead to trouble, too. Greycas, Inc. v. Proud, *826 F.2d 1560 (7th Cir. 1987), is such a case.*

Timothy Proud was a lawyer. His brother-in-law, Wayne Crawford, ran a farm. Crawford needed money. He found a lender who would give him a loan secured by farm equipment. The lender wanted an opinion letter assuring them that the equipment was not subject to previous liens. Crawford asked Proud to write such a letter, which Proud did.

The letter said Proud had examined Illinois records to check UCC filings on the equipment and found none. That statement was false: Proud had not examined the records. He relied on Crawford, who assured him the equipment was not subject to any outstanding liens.

Crawford got the loan, went broke anyway, and committed suicide. When the lender discovered other creditors had priority on the farm equipment it sued Proud, who argued that he owed not duty to the lender. Proud lost and the court of appeals not only affirmed the verdict, on the ground Proud invited the lender to rely on him, but reported Proud to the Illinois bar. (Remember: Invited reliance creates an independent duty to the relying party.)

Crawford did not reveal his dire financial situation to Proud. Maybe if he had Proud would have known better than to rely on Crawford's account of his own situation. But either way Proud lied to someone he knew would rely on his lie and depended on his brother in law's word to make sure the lie would not come back to haunt him. Probably he would not have done the same for an ordinary client, but broke the rules for his family.

Tempting as it may be to help out a family member or to trust them, the family relationship is no defense to misconduct. And, surprisingly, family members may be more willing to set you up than ordinary clients, who might suspect that you would be more on guard with them.

> *A good rule for such situations comes from the eminent jurist B.B. King:*
>
> *"Nobody loves me but my mother,*
> *And she could be jivin' too"*

Invited reliance is the most common source of duties to third parties and it need not take the form of opinion letters. In *Moore v. Weinberg*, 383 S.C. 583, 681 S.E.2d 875 (2009), for example, the South Carolina Supreme Court held that a lawyer acting as escrow agent for a third party who lent money to the lawyer's client owed a duty to that third party *as an escrow agent* even though the lawyer performed no legal services for the third party. Weinberg represented Wheeler in litigation over the sale of Wheeler's business. $100,000 had been placed in escrow with the court pending resolution of the case. Wheeler told Moore, the lender, about the account. They agreed to use it as security for the loan Wheeler sought from Moore. Weinberg confirmed to Wheeler that the money was in the account. When the suit settled the clerk released the money to Weinberg who forgot that Wheeler had assigned his interest in the money to Moore. Weinberg therefore deducted his fees and paid the money out to Wheeler. Moore ultimately sued Weinberg for negligence in distributing the money.

According to the court, "Weinberg contends that allowing a cause of action against an attorney under these circumstances will intrude upon the attorney/client relationship and greatly hinder an attorney's ability to represent his client. In our view, Weinberg's argument misses the mark. Weinberg acted as the escrow agent and owed a fiduciary duty to Moore by virtue of this role. Therefore, it makes no difference that Weinberg was Wheeler's lawyer and represented him in other matters. Under the facts of this case, the duty arises from an attorney's role as an escrow agent and is independent of an attorney's status as a lawyer and distinct from duties that arise out of the attorney/client relationship."[1]

B. MISREPRESENTATION

Lawyers are not exempt from rules prohibiting ordinary fraud, and Model Rule 4.1 supplements the common law by forbidding you, in the course of representing a client, from knowingly making a false statement of material law or fact or failing to disclose a material fact when disclosure is needed to avoid assisting criminal or fraudulent conduct. These disclosure requirements are subject to the confidentiality requirements of Model Rule 1.6, but the exceptions to confidentiality in Model Rule 1.6(b)(1)–(3) will allow disclosure in many if not most cases to which Rule 4.1 might apply. The knowledge requirement of Rule 4.1 is narrower than some tort causes of action, such as negligent misrepresentation, and you should keep both tort and disciplinary rules in mind in reviewing the following materials.

Model Rules of Professional Conduct 4.1
Restatement (Third) of the Law Governing Lawyers §§ 56, 98

CICONE V. URS CORPORATION

183 Cal.App.3d 194 (1986)

MARTIN, ASSOCIATE JUSTICE.

This is an appeal from a judgment of dismissal following the sustaining of a general demurrer to an original cross-complaint without leave to amend.

On June 10, 1983, plaintiffs Gerald D. Lucas, Janice H. Lucas, and Lucas Family Trust filed a complaint alleging legal malpractice against defendants Frank J. Cicone and Frank J. Cicone Law Corporation et al. On October 25, 1983, defendants answered the complaint and filed a cross-complaint for comparative equitable indemnity, damages and puni-

---

[1] *Virtanen v. O'Connell,* 140 Cal. App. 4th 688, 693 (2006) provides useful advice for attorneys who choose to serve as escrow agent as well as counsel to a party to a transaction: "we caution that an attorney should be aware of the duties of an escrow holder before agreeing to act as one. When an attorney faces conflicting demands from his or her own client and another party to the escrow, the attorney cannot favor his or her own client and completely disregard the rights of the other party, to whom he or she owes a duty as an escrow holder. If the competing demands are not resolved, the law provides the attorney with a mechanism to avoid both the area between the rock and the hard place and tort liability, i.e., an interpleader action. However, the attorney cannot convert the escrowed property to his or her client's own use."

tive damages against URS Corporation, Arthur H. Stromberg and Richard W. Canady.

Cross-defendants filed general and special demurrers to the cross-complaint and a motion to strike the punitive damage allegations of the cross-complaint on December 23, 1983.

The demurrer and motion to strike were argued by counsel and submitted on January 26, 1984. On April 27, 1984, the lower court granted the general demurrer as to all causes of action without leave to amend. On June 26, 1984, the cross-complaint was dismissed with prejudice and judgment was entered in favor of the cross-defendants on June 27, 1984. This appeal followed.

FACTS

Cicone primarily challenges the trial court's decision to sustain the demurrers without leave to amend.

This case involves a legal malpractice suit brought against Cicone, an attorney, by plaintiffs, his former clients. Plaintiffs alleged Cicone was guilty of malpractice in conducting negotiations for the sale of plaintiffs' business, Advanced Production Service, Inc. (Advanced), to cross-defendant URS Corporation (URS). Cicone cross-complained against URS, its president and their attorney, Canady, for fraud, negligent misrepresentation, breach of good faith and fair dealing and equitable indemnity.

Cicone represents the factual allegations upon which the claims of fraud and deceit are based would be amended beyond those currently contained in the present cross-complaint to allege as follows:

In early September 1981, URS, through its president, Stromberg, reached a preliminary agreement with Gerald Lucas, President of Advanced, for URS to purchase from Lucas and his family the stock and assets of Advanced for $3.5 million cash. The final agreement was to be prepared by counsel for URS and, at Stromberg's request, it was to be executed by the parties in as short a period of time as was reasonable. Lucas then engaged Cicone to represent him and his family in consummating the transaction.

Shortly after entering into the preliminary agreement, Advanced gave the accountants and other personnel of URS full access to the books and records of Advanced, and the respective corporations' accountants and personnel were in frequent communication about Advanced's financial data.

Prior to October 13, 1981, URS presented Advanced with a proposed final agreement. The agreement provided in part that the sellers warranted the accuracy of an unaudited balance sheet of Advanced as of September 30, 1981, and included a warranty that Advanced had no liabilities other than those shown on the balance sheet. A number of other warranties in the agreement were stated to be made only to the best knowledge of sellers.

At a meeting on October 13, 1981, attended by Gerald Lucas, Cicone, Lucas' personal accountant R. Randall Richardson, Stromberg, and URS' attorney, Canady, Cicone advised Stromberg and Canady the sellers could not and would not guarantee the accuracy of the balance sheet. Canady, with Stromberg's tacit approval, replied the buyer understood and URS would deem the sellers to be guaranteeing the information in the balance sheet only to sellers' best knowledge.

Cicone would further allege that Canady's statement, made on behalf of Stromberg and URS, constituted a promise that URS would accept the balance sheet as correct only to the best of the sellers' knowledge. As Canady knew, that promise was false and was made without any intention of performing it, for cross-defendants intended to rely on the strict warranty contained in the written agreement. The promise was made for the purpose of inducing Cicone to rely on it and thereby to advise the sellers to follow through with the sale and to sign the final agreement. Cicone did rely on the promise and did advise the sellers to sign the agreement, and as a result the sellers did sign the agreement. Cicone's reliance on the promise was justifiable because the circumstances under which it was made gave him reason to believe it would be carried out and Cicone had no reason to disbelieve Canady.

The balance sheet was correct to the best of the sellers' knowledge. However, shortly after the transaction had been consummated, URS, through Stromberg, made a claim against the sellers based on a $200,000 understatement in the balance sheet of deferred tax liabilities, of which the sellers had been unaware. The sellers, through counsel other than Cicone, settled the claim without litigation for $125,000 and filed a legal malpractice action against Cicone. As a result, Cicone may incur liability to the sellers, and is required to defend a malpractice action, thereby incurring expense, losing time from his practice, and facing impairment of his professional reputation.

DISCUSSION

I. FRAUD AND DECEIT

. . . . In the third, fourth, fifth and sixth causes of action of the cross-complaint, Cicone attempts to allege causes of action for fraud and deceit.

Fraud

Fraud is an intentional tort, the elements of which are (1) misrepresentation; (2) knowledge of falsity; (3) intent to defraud, i.e., to induce reliance; (4) justifiable reliance; and (5) resulting damage. . . .

The lower court determined, inter alia, cross-defendants owed no duty to Cicone and therefore Cicone failed to state a cause of action. . . .

Duty

Cross-defendants argue a lack of duty owed to Cicone. However, this argument appears in relation to the causes of action for negligence and indemnity. More properly it could be stated, inferentially everyone has a duty to refrain from committing intentionally tortious conduct against another. Thus, a promise material to the contract which is made without any intention of performing it is deemed a misrepresentation of fact. (Civ.Code, §§ 1572, subd. (4), 1710, subd. (4); *Jacobs v. Freeman* (1980) 104 Cal.App.3d 177.)

Cicone alleges cross-defendants made a promise without disclosing they entertained no intention to perform said promise to deem the warranty of the financial statement as only to sellers' best knowledge and belief.

Although a duty to disclose a material fact normally arises only where there exists a confidential relation between the parties or other special circumstances require disclosure, where one does speak he must speak the whole truth to the end that he does not conceal any facts which materially qualify those stated. One who is asked for or volunteers information must be truthful, and the telling of a half-truth calculated to deceive is fraud. . . .

In California it is well established that an attorney may not, with impunity, either conspire with a client to defraud or injure a third person or engage in intentional tortious conduct toward a third person. Thus, the case law is clear that a duty is owed by an attorney not to defraud another, even if that other is an attorney negotiating at arm's length.

Thus, while duty is not an element of fraud in the traditional sense, a duty is owed to others to refrain from intentionally tortious conduct. Therefore, any inference arising from the lower court's decision that the element of duty bars Cicone's causes of action for fraud and deceit is not supported by law.

Misrepresentation

Cross-defendants assert the alleged misrepresentation is one of law and therefore not actionable. According to this theory, the allegations that Canady made "certain assurances and promises that the correct interpretation of the guarantee clause (or clauses) in [the] agreement was that it would be based upon sellers' best information and belief," amounts to nothing more than an allegation that Canady stated a legal opinion of how the terms of the contract would be interpreted in the future. . . .

It is true the representation must ordinarily be an affirmation of fact. (Civ.Code, § 1710, subd. (1).) A misrepresentation of law is ordinarily not actionable in the absence of a confidential relationship or other special circumstance. (4 Witkin, Summary of Cal. Law (8th ed. 1974) Torts, §§ 447, 451, pp. 2712, 2715.) The theory is either that everyone is bound to know the law, or that a statement regarding the law is a mere opinion on which one may not rely.

> " 'Wherever a party states a matter which might otherwise be only an opinion, and does not state it as the mere expression of his own opinion, but affirms it as an existing fact material to the transaction, so that the other party may reasonably treat it as a fact and rely and act upon it as such, then the statement clearly becomes an affirmation of fact within the meaning of the general rule, and may be a fraudulent misrepresentation.' (2 Pomeroy's Equity Jurisprudence, sec. 878.)" (*Crandall v. Parks* (1908) 152 Cal. 772, 776.)

Predictions or representations as to what will happen in the future are normally treated as opinion; but often they may be interpreted as implying knowledge of facts which makes the predictions probable. If the defendant does not know of such facts, the statement is an actionable misrepresentation. (See Rest.2d, Torts, § 539.) Thus, a statement by an architect that a building will not cost more than a certain amount may be regarded as an affirmation of fact. (*Barron Estate Co. v. Woodruff Co.* (1912) 163 Cal. 561, 574.) The same is true where an agent states his principal will advance money to harvest a crop, or where a corporation agent represents the corporation will lease certain property or locate a plant in a certain city. (*California C. & C. Corp. v. Carpenter* (1926) 77 Cal.App. 18, 27; *see also Eade v. Reich* (1932) 120 Cal.App. 32, 35.)

A statement of what the defendant or some third person intends to do relates to an existing state of mind, and is a representation of fact. (4 Witkin, Summary of Cal. Law, *op. cit. supra,* § 453, p. 2717.) Thus, a promise made without any intention to perform it may constitute fraud. In other words, a promise to do something necessarily implies the intention to perform, and where such intention is absent, there is a misrepresentation of fact, which is actionable fraud. (Civ.Code, § 1710, subd. (4).) A trier of fact may be justified in inferring from the circumstances surrounding the subsequent repudiation that defendant never intended to carry out the agreement when it was made. The subsequent repudiation relates back to the original promise. . . . .

Justifiable Reliance

Cross-defendants contend the allegation of the word "reasonable" is insufficient to allege justifiable reliance in this case. Cross-defendants declare: "[A]n attorney is not justified in relying on statements of law made by an adverse party or attorney in the course of arm's length negotiations." Cross-defendants urge us to hold any reliance by Cicone on the alleged misrepresentation was unjustifiable as a matter of law.

Whether reliance is justified is a question of fact for the determination of the trier of fact. The issue is whether the person who claims reliance was justified in relying on the representation in light of his own knowledge and experience. (*Gray v. Don Miller & Associates, Inc.* (1984) 35 Cal.3d 498, 503.) As Cicone points out:

> "Negligence in reliance upon a misrepresentation is not a defense where the misrepresentation was *intentionally* made to induce reliance upon it. (*Hefferan v. Freebairn* (1950) 34 Cal.2d 715 . . . ; *Smith v. Williams* (1961) 55 Cal.2d 617, 620. . . .) Only '[i]f the conduct of the plaintiff [in relying upon a misrepresentation] in the light of his own intelligence and information was manifestly unreasonable' will he be denied recovery. (*Hefferan v. Freebairn, supra,* 34 Cal.2d at p. 719.)" [citation omitted]

While the complaint has not been carefully drawn in this regard, it appears there is a reasonable possibility the paucity of facts regarding a justifiable reliance can be cured by amendment and the demurrer should not be sustained without leave to amend on this ground. . . .

II. NEGLIGENT MISREPRESENTATION

The seventh, eighth and ninth causes of action of the cross-complaint, incorporating various other allegations of the cross-complaint, are based on negligence. . . . "Where a defendant makes false statements, honestly believing them to be true, but without reasonable grounds for such belief, he may be held liable for negligent misrepresentation, a form of deceit." [citations omitted]. . . .

A "deceit" is defined in California law as "[t]he assertion, as a fact, of that which is not true, *by one who has no reasonable ground for believing it to be true*; . . . " (Civ.Code, § 1710, subd. (2), emphasis added.) Thus, where a defendant makes false statements honestly believing them to be true, but without reasonable grounds for such belief, he may be held liable for negligent misrepresentation, a form of deceit. [citations omitted]

Here, Cicone alleges cross-defendant Canady, an attorney, in his client's presence (the buyer) and in the presence of cross-complainant Cicone, an attorney, and his client (the seller) represented to Cicone and his client that the buyer would deem the seller to be guaranteeing the information in the unaudited balance sheet only to the seller's best knowledge and belief. This representation was made to induce Cicone to advise his client to close the sales transaction immediately, which was done. In an amended cross-complaint, Cicone would further allege that this representation was not true, that Canady had no reasonable basis for believing it to be true, that Cicone and his client were intended to and did, in fact, rely upon Canady's negligent representation with resulting damages.

. . .

In the present case, Cicone's reliance on Canady's alleged misrepresentation was the very purpose of the representation. Canady expected Cicone to advise his client to close the transaction; Cicone did so and the transaction was closed.

A duty of care under these facts logically follows from the holding in [*Roberts v. Ball, Hunt, Hart, Brown & Baerwitz*, (1976) 57 Cal. App. 3d 104]. . . . If the issuance of a legal opinion intended to secure a benefit for a client must be issued with due care towards third persons who the attorneys attempt or expect to influence on behalf of their clients, then a fortiori why should such a duty of care not exist toward the third party's attorney where an affirmative misrepresentation of fact is made directly to the attorney for the purpose of influencing his client?. . . .

Finally, persons such as Canady have, or can readily obtain, insurance for these risks.

Nor do we visualize any legitimate threat to the professional relationship between Canady and his client, the buyer, by imposing on Canady a duty of care toward Cicone under our facts. An attorney must take pains to avoid negligent misrepresentation of material facts in negotiating business transactions with third parties and their attorneys. All that is required to avoid negligent misrepresentation is that the attorney have some reasonable basis for believing the truthfulness of his or her representations. Imposing possible liability where such a basis is lacking will not prevent an attorney from devoting his entire energies to his client's interest. Neither will it require the attorney to assist opposing counsel in the performance of the latter's duties to his client. . . .

CASE QUESTIONS

1. What is the standard for distinguishing factual statements from other statements?
2. When is silence actionable, and when is it not actionable?
3. Is the court right to say that this case is like *Roberts*, which involved an opinion letter? Could you distinguish the cases?

PROBLEM 8–2

How could Canady have avoided this problem?

PROBLEM 8–3

Would Canady's client be liable for his alleged misstatement, or just Canady?

PROBLEM 8–4

Would Canady's client want him or not want him to make such statements? What client pressures are relevant to such a situation?

Cicone was followed in *Shafer v. Berger, Kahn, Shafton, Moss, Figler, Simon & Gladstone*, 107 Cal.App.4th 54 (2003). The Shafers were homeowners who contracted for renovations on their house. The contractor performed poorly and the Shafers sued him. The contractor tendered the case to his insurer to provide a defense. The insurer agreed to do so and selected a lawyer to represent the contractor. It reserved its rights to claim that the insurance policy did not cover the case because the plaintiff alleged intentional misconduct.

Because of this reservation of rights, the contractor demanded that the insurer pay for an attorney he selected to represent his interests. Under the rule of *San Diego Navy Federal Credit Union v. Cumis Ins. Society, Inc.*, 162 Cal.App.3d 358 (1984), the insurer would have to pay for such counsel to avoid the risk that the lawyer it selected would provide a weak defense against the intentional tort claims, thus pinning liability on grounds that would fall outside the scope of the insurance policy, saving the insurer money.

The insurer in *Shafer* did not want to pay for *Cumis* counsel so it retained a lawyer to advise it on coverage issues. That lawyer, Lance LaBelle, re-drafted the reservation of rights letter so that it did not mention the exclusion for intentional torts. That mooted the contractor's basis for demanding his own lawyer. By not reserving its right to claim that the policy did not cover intentional misconduct, however, the insurer effectively waived that defense and bound itself to insure such claims.

The homeowners won in arbitration and the arbitrators found the contractor was guilty of fraud. The homeowners then sued the insurer under a provision of the Insurance Code that allowed them to sue on the contractor's policy. LaBelle then told the homeowners that their claim based on the policy was weak because the arbitrators found the contractor committed intentional fraud and the policy did not extend to intentional acts. In other words, LaBelle took one coverage position with the contractor and a different position with the homeowners.

The homeowners eventually found out that the insurer had amended its reservation of rights and effectively agreed to insure the contractor against intentional acts. The homeowners then sued the insurer and LaBelle. They claimed LaBelle defrauded them by asserting to them that the policy excluded intentional misconduct when he had taken the contrary position before. LaBelle demurred to the claim, and the trial court sustained the demurrer without leave to amend.

The court of appeals reversed. Relying on *Cicone*, it related lawyer liability for fraud to agency law, and elaborated on the principle that agents are responsible for their own tortious acts:

" 'An agent or employee is always liable for his own torts, whether his employer is liable or not.' " "In other words, when the agent commits a tort, such as . . . fraud . . . , then . . . the agent [is] subject to liability in a civil suit for such wrongful conduct. '[I]f a tortious act has been committed by an agent acting under authority of his principal, the fact that the principal thus becomes liable does not, of course, exonerate the agent from liability.' ". . . .

"A lawyer communicating on behalf of a client with a nonclient may not . . . [¶] . . . knowingly make a false statement of material fact . . . to the nonclient. . . . " (Rest.3d, Law Governing Lawyers, § 98, p. 58.) "The law governing misrepresentation by a lawyer includes the criminal law (theft by deception), *the law of misrepresentation in tort law* and of mistake and fraud in contract law, and procedural law governing statements by an advocate. . . . Compliance with those obligations meets social expectations of honesty and fair dealing and facilitates negotiation and adjudication, which are important professional functions of lawyers." (*Id.*, com. b, pp. 58–59, citation omitted, italics added.) "A misrepresentation can occur through direct statement or through affirmation of a misrepresentation of another, as when a lawyer knowingly affirms a client's false or misleading statement." (*Id.*, com. c, p. 59.)

As one of our courts has stated: "In the context of fraudulent conduct by an attorney toward persons not his own clients, no preference is accorded to the attorney's professional status in the disposition of claims alleging fraud. If an attorney commits actual fraud in his dealings with a third party, the fact he did so in the capacity of attorney for a client does not relieve him of liability. While in general an attorney's professional duty of care extends only to dealings with his own client and to intended beneficiaries of the legal work performed, these limitations upon liability for negligence . . . do not apply to liability for fraud."

"In general, a lawyer who makes a fraudulent misrepresentation is subject to liability to the injured person when the other elements of the tort are established. . . . " (Rest.3d, Law Governing Lawyers, § 98, com. g, p. 61.) This rule "applies equally to statements made to a sophisticated person, such as to a lawyer representing another client, as well as to an unsophisticated person." (*Id.*, com. b, p. 59.) "Misrepresentation is not part of proper legal assistance; vigorous argument often is. Thus, lawyers are civilly liable to clients and nonclients for fraudulent misrepresentation, but are not liable for such conduct as using legally innocuous hyperbole or proper argument in negotiations . . . or presenting an argument to a tribunal in litigation." (*Id.,* § 56, com. f, p. 418.). . . .

" 'Although a duty to disclose a material fact normally arises only where there exists a confidential relation . . . or other special circumstances require disclosure, where one does speak he must speak the whole truth to the end that he does not conceal any facts which materially qualify those stated. . . . One who is asked for or volunteers information must be truthful, and the telling of a half-truth calculated to deceive is fraud.' " (*Pavicich v. Santucci* (2000) 85 Cal.App.4th 382, 397–398.) . . .

"A knowing misrepresentation may relate to a proposition of fact. . . . Certain statements, such as some statements relating to price or value, are considered nonactionable hyperbole or a reflection of the state of mind of the speaker and not misstatements of fact. . . . Whether a misstatement should be so characterized depends on *whether it is reasonably apparent that the person to whom the statement is addressed would regard the statement as one of fact* or based on the speaker's knowledge of facts reasonably implied by the statement or as merely an expression of the speaker's state of mind. Assessment depends on the circumstances in which the statement is made, including the past relationship of the negotiating persons, their apparent sophistication, the plausibility of the statement on its face, the phrasing of the statement, related communication between the persons involved, the known negotiating practices of the community in which both are negotiating, and similar circumstances. In general, a lawyer who is known to represent a person in a negotiation will be understood by nonclients to be making *nonimpartial* statements, in the same manner as would the lawyer's client." (Rest.3d, Law Governing Lawyers, § 98, com. c, pp. 59–60, italics added.)

American Bar Association Formal Ethics Opinion 06–439 elaborates on similar points and distinguishes statements of a client's position from statements of fact. Statements of position extend to things such as willingness to accept or pay certain amounts and assessments of the strength of a party's case or an opponent's case: "A buyer of products or services, for example, might overstate its confidence in the availability of alternate sources of supply to reduce the appearance of dependence upon the supplier with which it is negotiating." In contrast, a statement of fact would be one as to which there are standards a reasonable person could apply to reach a specific conclusion, particularly if the fact at issue is within the exclusive knowledge of one party and thus could not be investigated by the other party at its own initiative. An example here might be "a lawyer representing an employer in labor negotiations stating to union lawyers that adding a particular employee benefit will cost the company an additional $100 per employee, when the lawyer knows that it actually will cost only $20 per employee."

PROBLEM 8–5

Suppose you are negotiating a settlement for a client whom you know will accept any amount over $10,000 to settle the case. At the beginning of negotiations, you state your client will not accept a dime under $100,000. Have you made an actionable misrepresentation?

PROBLEM 8–6

Suppose you are negotiating the same settlement and you represent that your client (an entity) is nearly insolvent and cannot afford to pay more than $100,000. Suppose your client actually is solvent and could afford to pay more. Have you made an actionable misrepresentation? *See Siegel v. Williams,* 818 N.E.2d 510 (Ind.App. 2004).

You Don't Say

Restatement § 98 provides that lawyers may not knowingly make false statements of material fact or law to nonclients or fail to disclose information where required by law. When does the law require disclosure? Disclosure is sometimes required as a matter of law, often as one element of rules governing some status, such as that of a fiduciary. As we saw in chapter 2 and will see again in chapter 11, fiduciaries have duties to disclose material facts to their principals.

It is also common for lawyers or others to create disclosure obligations they would not otherwise have by undertaking to speak even when they have no duty to do so. Though silence absent a duty to disclose is not misleading, once you undertake to speak you must disclose whatever is necessary to avoid misleading the person you are speaking to. Voluntary disclosure of partial truths, in other words, may be fraud. The following cases exemplify the point.

For a case applying *Cicone* and *Schafer* to a claim of fraud by omission, *see Vega v. Jones, Day, Reavis & Pogue*, 121 Cal.App.4th 282 (2004). For cases similar to *Cicone and Shafer, see Hansen v. Anderson, Wilmarth & Van Der Maaten,* 630 N.W.2d 818, 825–826 (Iowa 2001) (allowing transactional lawyer accused of malpractice to seek indemnity from lawyer representing other transacting party, who allegedly made false statements in connection with the transaction: "once a lawyer responds to a request for information in an arm's-length transaction and undertakes to give that information, the lawyer has a duty to the lawyer requesting the information to give it truthfully. Such a duty is an independent one imposed for the benefit of a particular person or class of persons. . . .

[¶] Public policy favors a duty, running from an attorney representing a party to a commercial transaction, not to make fraudulent misrepresentations to an attorney representing the adverse party in the transaction."); *Fire Ins. Exch. v. Bell by Bell,* 643 N.E.2d 310, 312–13 (Ind. 1994) (insured could sue insurer and its attorney for misrepresenting amount of policy limit; "[t]he reliability of lawyers' representations is an integral component of the fair and efficient administration of justice. The law should promote lawyers' care in making statements that are accurate and trustworthy and should foster the reliance upon such statements by others"); *Slotkin v. Citizens Cas. Co. of New York*, 614 F.2d 301 (2d Cir.1979) (same).

State-law fraud rules are not the only source of worry in such cases. In many cases, lawyers make statements in transactions involving the purchase or sale of securities. Such lawyers may face liability under the federal securities laws. *Rubin v. Schottenstein, Zox & Dunn*, 143 F.3d 263 (6th Cir. 1998), is such a case.

Plaintiffs invested $153,000 in an Ohio company represented by Richard Barnhart of the Schottenstein firm. Plaintiffs alleged that, in connection with this investment, plaintiffs spoke with Barnhart regarding the company's financial position, including its relationship with its bank. Barnhart allegedly assured plaintiffs that the relationship was sound and that the bank would provide more funding for the company once the plaintiff invested. In reality, the plaintiffs alleged, the company was already in default of its agreements with the bank and the plaintiff's proposed investment would itself trigger another default. The plaintiffs invested, the bank froze the company's account (to get the money itself), and the company then filed for bankruptcy. The plaintiffs sued Barnhart under Section 10(b) of the Securities Exchange Act and SEC Rule 10b–5.

The Sixth Circuit reversed the district court's order granting summary judgment in favor of defendants and sent the case back for trial. Excerpts from the majority opinion follow:

"There is nothing special about Barnhart's status as an attorney that negates his Rule 10b–5 duty to disclose, a duty that ordinarily would devolve under Rule 10b–5 upon a third party under these circumstances. Although under Rule 10b–5(b) and its predecessor, "only those individuals who had an affirmative obligation to reveal what was allegedly omitted can be held liable as primary participants in the alleged deception[, a] duty to disclose naturally devolve[s] on those who h[ave] direct contacts with 'the other side.' " *SEC v. Coffey,* 493 F.2d 1304, 1315 (6th Cir.1974). "Direct contacts may take many forms. An accountant or lawyer, for instance, who prepares a dishonest statement is a primary participant in a violation even though someone else may conduct the personal negotiations with a security purchaser." *Id.* at 1315 n. 24. "A person undertaking to furnish information which is misleading because of a failure to disclose a material fact is a primary participant." *SEC v. Washington County Util. Dist.,* 676 F.2d 218, 223 (6th Cir.1982). Under the long-established precedents of this circuit, the conversations between Barnhart and the plaintiffs clearly were instances of "direct contacts" sufficient to give rise to a duty to disclose.

The defendants urge that "silence, absent a duty to disclose, does not violate" Rule 10b–5, and that *Coffey*'s direct-contacts analysis does not alter this rule. True enough. But here we are not confronted with Barnhart's silence; on the contrary, Barnhart spoke at length about the proposed investment both with Rubin and with Weiss. The question thus is not whether Barnhart's silence can give rise to liability, but whether liability may flow from his decision to speak to Rubin and Weiss concerning material details of the proposed investment, without revealing certain additional known facts necessary to make his statements not misleading. This question is answered by the text of Rule 10b–5(b) itself: it is unlawful for any person to "omit to state a material fact necessary in order to make the statements made, in the light of the circumstances under which they were made, not misleading. . . . " 17 C.F.R. § 240.10b–5(b).

In sum, while an attorney representing the seller in a securities transaction may not always be under an independent duty to volunteer information about the financial condition of his client, he assumes a duty to provide complete and nonmisleading information with respect to subjects on which he undertakes to speak. As the Seventh Circuit so aptly put the point, "[u]nder Rule 10b–5 . . . the lack of an independent duty does not excuse a material lie." *Ackerman v. Schwartz,* 947 F.2d 841, 848 (7th Cir.1991). When Barnhart consented to speak to Rubin and Weiss concerning the status of MDI's relationship with Star Bank, and about Star Bank's likely reaction to a substantial loan from Rubin and Cohen, he assumed a duty to speak fully and truthfully on those subjects. . . .

According to the defendants, "lawyers, unlike . . . other parties to securities transactions, have an obligation of confidentiality that is at the heart of the duties they owe their clients." It is perhaps symptomatic of the current debate over the state of legal ethics that the defendants would invoke the attorney's duty of confidentiality to justify what, if Rubin's and Weiss's affidavits are correct, amount to outright lies. . . . In any event, the mere fact that one party generally may not be entitled to rely on the advice of counsel for another party is an insufficient reason to ignore the statutory rule prohibiting "any person"—not excepting lawyers—from making material misrepresentations in connection with the sale of securities. The defendants' argument is no more persuasive when phrased as the principle that a party who is represented by counsel cannot rely on the opinion of the other party's attorney.

That principle, as a reading of the cases cited by the district court reveals, is limited to reliance on the opinions or research of the other party's attorney on points of law . . . The theory is that one's own lawyer ought to be able to detect and cure misleading statements of law from the other side. Extending the principle to factual representations would put an investor in far greater peril in speaking to an issuer's counsel than in speaking with the president of the company. In short, it would allow an attorney to mislead investors with impunity. We cannot endorse this perverse result. Admission to the bar, if anything, imposes a heightened, not a lessened, requirement of probity. Accordingly, we conclude that Rubin and Cohen have shown sufficient facts to entitle them to a trial on their misrepresentation-based claims."

A second source of liability is Rule 4.1's requirement that, subject to the confidentiality requirement of Rule 1.6, counsel may not "fail to disclose a material fact when disclosure is necessary to avoid assisting a criminal or fraudulent act by a client. . . . " *State ex rel Neb. State Bar Ass'n v. Addison*, 226 Neb. 585 (1987), exemplifies this rule in practice. Addison represented Medina, a personal injury plaintiff who had been struck by two cars after they collided. Each driver had a primary insurance policy; one driver had an additional policy with a $1 million policy limit. Medina incurred $112,836 in hospital bills. Addison negotiated with the hospital to release its claims against Medina in return for a percentage of the two primary insurance policies. During the negotiation Addison realized that the hospital administrator did not know about the $1 million umbrella policy, and was basing his decision on the incorrect belief that only the primary policies were available to Medina. The Nebraska disciplinary authorities found Addison had a duty to disclose the additional policy to the administrator, and that his failure to disclose violated the Nebraska rule equivalent to current Rule 4.1. Addison was suspended from practice for six months.

Similarly, the court in *Kentucky Bar Ass'n v. Geisler*, 938 S.W.2d 578 (Ky. 1997), affirmed discipline against an attorney who settled a personal injury case without informing the defendant that plaintiff had died. The court rejected counsel's defense—if the defendant wanted to know, he should have asked—and held instead that "candor and honesty necessarily require disclosure of such a significant fact as the death of one's client. Opposing counsel does not have to deal with his adversary as he would deal in the marketplace. Standards of ethics require greater honesty, greater candor, and greater disclosure, even though it might not be in the interest of the client or his estate."

A Duty to Correct Your Opponent's Mistake?

Model Rule 4.1 has some easy applications and some hard ones. Let's start with the easy ones first. Suppose you negotiate with a third party on behalf of your client. Suppose further you make a material misstatement of fact during the negotiations. You must correct the misstatement if possible within the parameters of Rule 1.6. Because Model Rule 1.6(b)(2) allows disclosure to prevent the client from accomplishing a fraud using your services, disclosure is permitted and thus required by Rule 4.1. Note that in a state such as California, which does not authorize such disclosure, the lawyer still would be prevented from assisting a client in committing a fraudulent act; in such a case the lawyer would be well advised to attempt to persuade the client to agree to disclosure and to withdraw from the representation before closing the deal if the client did not agree. At a minimum, the lawyer's advise should include a warning that the lawyer's misstatement likely would be attributed to the client under basic agency principles, thus exposing the client to the risk of liability as well.

Now suppose; (i) you do not make a misstatement; (ii) the parties have agreed on a material term; (iii) the non-client's lawyer (your counterpart on the other side) prepares a contract; (iv) that lawyer omits the term from the contract; and (v) you notice the omission but the other side does not. Must you notify the other side of their own mistake? The American Bar Association has said that you must. Informal Op. 86–1518 of the American Bar Association Committee on Ethics and Professional Responsibility treats this situation as involving a "scrivener's error" and concludes that by not disclosing you might raise "a serious question of violation of the duty" under Rule 1.2(d) not to assist a client in fraudulent conduct. The opinion also notes that Rule 4.1(b) requires disclosure (within the confines of Rule 1.6) to avoid assisting a client in committing a fraudulent act. And Rule 8.4(c) forbids lawyers from dishonest or fraudulent conduct. Indeed, the ABA opinion goes so far as to say the lawyer may correct the omission without notifying the client or obtaining client consent. It reaches this result, however, by treating disclosure as impliedly authorized by the client, on the theory that the client asked the lawyer simply to memorialize the agreement the client had reached. The opinion did not reach "the issue of the lawyer's duty if the client wishes to exploit the error."

What if we do reach that issue? What if you tell the client about the omission and the client grins gleefully, signs the agreement, and instructs you to say nothing and to return the signed agreement to the other side? The ABA's presumed consent does not apply in such a case, and in a state such as California that does not allow disclosure to prevent financial harm you presumably would be bound by the client's instruction to say nothing. Your options would be limited to carrying out the instructions or withdrawing.

Must you withdraw? Probably. The answer depends on whether delivering the agreement would amount to fraudulent conduct. Model Rule 1.16(a) provides that you must withdraw if continued representation would lead to a violation of the rules. Model Rule 1.1(d) defines fraud to include "conduct that is fraudulent under the substantive or procedural law of the applicable jurisdiction and has a purpose to deceive." Comment 5 to Rule 1.1 states that "[f]or purposes of these Rules, it is not necessary that anyone has suffered damages or relied on the misrepresentation or failure to inform." *Restatement (Second) of Contracts* § 161(d) provides that a failure to disclose a fact is equivalent to the assertion that a fact exists where a party knows "that disclosure of the fact would correct a mistake of the other party as to the contents or effect of a writing, evidencing or embodying an agreement in whole or in part."

It is important to note that this portion of the *Restatement* of contracts deals with defenses to a contract action, not with an affirmative claim for fraud. *Restatement (Second) of Contracts* Chapter 7 (Introductory note). In some cases contract law allows misrepresentation to serve as a defense even if the facts would not support an affirmative claim under tort law. The Model Rules do not distinguish between fraud as an affirmative claim and fraud as a defense, but the best reading of the Rule 1.1(d) definition would extend it to encompass both claims and defenses. *Restatement (Third) of the Law Governing Lawyers* § 98 cmt b ("The law governing misrepresentation by a lawyer includes the criminal law (theft by deception), the law of misrepresentation in tort law and of mistake and fraud in contract law, and procedural law governing statements by an advocate").

The discussion to this point has focused on a mistake regarding a term the parties previously had agreed on. What if the mistake concerns a point the parties have not specifically agreed on? General statements about this category of cases are probably risky. Some guidance may be found in *Brown v. County of Genesee*, 872 F.2d 169 (6th Cir. 1989), in which the court refused to vacate a settlement agreement in an employment case. The plaintiff's counsel demanded that the defendant pay plaintiff the highest amount she could have earned has she not suffered discrimination. Defendant's counsel asked that the demand be put in writing. The plaintiff's counsel then sent a written demand that plaintiff be paid at a particular level, which was one level below the highest for which she would have been eligible absent discrimination. Defendant's counsel suspected, but did not know directly from plaintiff or her counsel, that plaintiff simply misunderstood the pay scale.

The district court vacated the settlement but the court of appeals reversed. As a matter of contract law it held the mistake was unilateral and therefore provided no defense to the settlement agreement. On the question of defense counsel's duties, the court held that "absent some misrepresentation or fraudulent conduct, the [defendant] had no duty to advise the [plaintiff] of any such factual error, whether unknown or suspected." The court reasoned

> An attorney is to be expected to responsibly present his client's case in the light most favorable to the client, and it is not fraudulent for him to do so. . . . We need only cite the well-settled rule that the mere nondisclosure to an adverse party and to the court of facts pertinent to a controversy before the court does not add up to "fraud upon the court" for purposes of vacating a judgment under Rule 60(b). . . .

[citation omitted]

> Although the appellee may have negotiated for a higher settlement figure, the plaintiff's subjective and/or objective desires were of no consequence because the mistake or error of plaintiff's legal counsel in evaluating the wage levels available to [plaintiff] resulted from failing to examine and/or a misunderstanding of public records which were available to all individuals. . . . . [plaintiff's] counsel could have structured the settlement agreement so as to assure the highest possible wage rate to which she would have been entitled. [Plaintiff's] failure to formulate the settlement agreement in appropriate terms cannot be imputed as fraudulent or unethical conduct by the [defendant] where the fault, if any, was not attributable to it.

872 F.2d at 175–76. *Genesee* is interesting but should be used with caution. The facts gave defendant's counsel every reason (other than an overt statement by the other side) to know plaintiff had made a mistake, which makes it a relatively strong holding against any duty to correct. But the relevant salary schedule was publicly available, which tends to weaken the case for imposing such a duty.

PROBLEM 8–7

Here are a series of statements, inspired by Douglas Richmond, *Lawyers' Professional Responsibilities and Liabilities in Negotiations*, 22 GEO. J. L. ETHICS 249, 285–86 (2009). Which, if any are statements of fact? As to the others, what are they?

Suppose you represent a soft drink bottling company whose driver just ran into a bus full of children. The families jointly hire a lawyer and sue the soft drink company, the bus driver, and the city where the accident occurred. The soft drink company has a general insurance policy that covers the accident; the policy has a $10 million limit. You think the bus driver was partly at fault. The insurer has authorized you to spend all the money available under the policy (i.e., $10 million). Your client has told you he doesn't care how much the insurance company pays but he will not go a dime over the policy limit and wants the lowest price possible, because the public will tend to assume the relative settlement price shows the relative culpability of the defendants.

At a settlement conference you offer $8 million and the plaintiff demands $12 million. The settlement judge tells you it is obvious that the case should settle for $10 million. You say:

(A) "With respect, judge, the whole thing is the bus driver's fault and we plan to prove it. $8 million is more than generous and they should take it because it's more than they'll get from us at trial."

(B) "With respect, judge, $8 million is our best offer. We'll take our chances with the jury above that."

(C) "With respect judge, these people are getting a lot already from the city and the bus company; we can't go any higher and we won't go any higher."

(D) "With respect, judge, we're having trouble funding the $8 million and it's unreasonable to ask us for more; you can't get blood from a stone."

(E) "With respect, judge, my client just should not have to pay a dime more than $8 million; their case against us just is not worth it."

(F) "With respect, judge, the public is going to see these numbers and apportion blame accordingly; $8 million is already more than the blame we deserve and we're just not going to take more blame than we deserve."

Boundary Issues
What Are You Selling? Part III

The court in *Rubin v. Schottenstein, Zox & Dunn* characterized the issue it faced this way: "One fundamental question posed by this case is whether enterprising attorneys may gratuitously tout their clients' securities unconstrained by the general duty imposed by the securities laws not to make materially misleading statements in connection with the sale of such securities." The word "tout" is telling. In the court's view, Barnhart had crossed a line from practicing law to fronting for his client's fraudulent schemes. Viewed from that angle, the court's ruling is no surprise.

The point is a general one, and it is important to understand its full significance. Clients like lawyers who will dig into the client's business and come to understand it well. Indeed, the most effective (and prosperous) lawyers are often those who understand the client's business as well as the client does and also understand the law. Such lawyers can integrate legal advice with business advice in a way that makes sense to clients and leaves them far better off than they are with lawyers who just mouth legal rules.

But there is a risk to getting so close to a client. You can see the risk both in *Rubin* and in *Burton v. RJ Reynolds*, where the attorneys allowed themselves to be used as a conduit for research on smoking and health, in the hope that their involvement would bring the research under the cloak of the attorney-client privilege. The basic question is: what are you selling? Is it legal advice or is it the touting of your client's business or simply the hope that if you get paid your client's business documents will be privileged?

Lawyers often come between their clients and others, such as opposing litigants or business associates negotiating transactions. As lawyers get closer to clients, however, it is easy for lawyers to get farther from paradigm legal services such as writing briefs and negotiating. And the farther lawyers get from such services the more they run the risk of incurring liability for ordinary acts such as touting securities. There are few bright lines in this area (though the lines should have been clear enough in *Rubin*). The best way to think about the question is to ask yourself, with respect to any given task, what it is that you are selling. If the answer is anything other than services that most people would recognize as "lawyering," you should ask yourself if you really want to be selling it. The answer may be yes, or it may be no. Either way, you are better off asking and thinking things through than just charging ahead to advance your client's cause.

C. SECONDARY LIABILITY: AIDING AND ABETTING AND CONSPIRACY

Third parties who feel wronged by a client sometimes accuse lawyers of assisting the client in unlawful conduct. Whether lawyers are liable in such suits depends on what they are alleged to have done. In general, lawyers are not liable for advising clients on what the law is or what they may do under the law. For example, a lawyer generally would not be liable for correctly advising a client that the default measure of damages for breach of contract includes the plaintiff's expectation but not the defendant's profits, even if the numbers implied by such advice tempt the client to breach. At the other end of the continuum, a lawyer who knowingly submits false documents to a government agency to obtain benefits cannot defend a charge of aiding and abetting a crime just by saying "but I was representing my client." Most cases fall in between these two extremes. The line between lawful advising and unlawful conspiring may not always be clear, and lawyers must pay close attention to it. The following materials illustrate these points.

REYNOLDS V. SCHROCK

341 Or. 338 (2006)

BALMER, J.

This case requires us to determine whether a lawyer may be liable to a third party for aiding and abetting a client's breach of fiduciary duty, and, if the lawyer may be so liable, what circumstances must exist to impose liability. Plaintiff sued defendant for breach of fiduciary duty, and he also sued defendant's lawyer for his role in that alleged breach. The trial court entered summary judgment in the lawyer's favor, and the Court of Appeals reversed.

We allowed the lawyer's petition for review and now reverse the decision of the Court of Appeals. We hold that a lawyer may not be held jointly liable with a client for the client's breach of fiduciary duty unless the third party shows that the lawyer was acting outside the scope of the lawyer-client relationship. Because there is no evidence in the summary judgment record that the lawyer in this case was acting outside the scope of that relationship, the lawyer was entitled to judgment as a matter of law. We therefore reverse the decision of the Court of Appeals and affirm the trial court's summary judgment in favor of the lawyer.

I. FACTS

Plaintiff was a naturopathic physician, and defendant Donna Schrock was one of plaintiff's patients. Plaintiff and Schrock bought two parcels of land together. In 1999, Schrock filed two separate actions against plaintiff. The first action concerned the jointly owned land, and the second alleged that, in the course of the doctor-patient relationship, plaintiff had engaged in improper sexual conduct with Schrock. The two actions were consolidated, and the parties later settled them in an agreement negotiated and drafted by their respective lawyers, including Schrock's lawyer, defendant Charles Markley.

The settlement agreement provided, in part, that plaintiff would transfer his share of one of the two jointly owned properties (the "lodge property") to Schrock and that Schrock and plaintiff together would sell the second property (the "timber property") and transfer the proceeds to plaintiff. If the proceeds of the timber property sale were less than $500,000, then Schrock would pay plaintiff the difference and Schrock would grant plaintiff a security interest for that amount in the lodge property to secure the payment. If the proceeds of the timber property sale equaled or exceeded $500,000, then Schrock would owe plaintiff nothing and plaintiff would have no security interest in the lodge property.

After the parties signed the settlement agreement, plaintiff transferred his interest in the lodge property to Schrock. Markley then advised Schrock that, in his opinion, nothing in the settlement agreement expressly required her to retain the lodge property in anticipation of the possible creation of a security interest in plaintiff's favor. Schrock, with Markley's assistance and without plaintiff's knowledge, sold the lodge property to a third party before the parties sold the timber property. Markley asked the escrow officer handling the sale to keep the sale confidential. Markley also advised Schrock that she could revoke the consent that she had given earlier to plaintiff's plan to sell the jointly owned timber property. In Markley's view, plaintiff had failed to provide Schrock with information about the value of the timber property prior to arranging to sell it, contrary to a requirement in the settlement agreement, and that breach freed Schrock from any obligation to consent to the sale of the timber property. Based on Markley's advice, and with Markley's assistance, Schrock revoked her consent to the sale of the timber property.

II. PROCEEDINGS BELOW

Plaintiff sued Schrock and Markley over their actions in connection with the implementation of the settlement agreement. As to Schrock, plaintiff alleged, among other things, that the settlement agreement had created fiduciary duties between Schrock and plaintiff as joint venturers. Plaintiff asserted that Schrock, by selling the lodge property and revoking her consent to the sale of the timber property, had breached her fiduciary duty to plaintiff and the implied covenant of good faith and fair dealing that was part of the settlement agreement.[2] He further alleged that Schrock had converted his interest in the lodge property by selling that property and retaining the proceeds.

Plaintiff's complaint alleged that Markley was jointly liable with Schrock because he had aided and abetted Schrock's torts by giving her "substantial assistance and encouragement" in the commission of the torts and acting "in concert with [her] pursuant to a common design * * *." He also alleged that Markley had interfered with the contract (the settlement agreement) between plaintiff and Schrock. Plaintiff and Schrock later settled, leaving Markley as the only remaining defendant.

Markley moved for summary judgment, and the trial court granted his motion. . . . The Court of Appeals affirmed the trial court's judgment in Markley's favor on the conversion claim. The court, however, reversed the judgment on the breach of fiduciary duty claim. The Court of Appeals held that this court's precedents did not exempt a lawyer from liability for assisting in a client's breach of fiduciary duty and that the Court of Appeals' case law suggested that a lawyer for a fiduciary could be liable for knowingly aiding or assisting a fiduciary in a breach of duty. As noted, Markley sought review, which we allowed.

---

[2] FN3. Both the claim for breach of fiduciary duty and the claim for breach of the covenant of good faith and fair dealing arose from the duties that plaintiff and Schrock allegedly owed one another as a result of the settlement agreement. The parties and the courts below treated the claims as a single claim for breach of fiduciary duty, and we do as well.

III. ANALYSIS

We begin our analysis, as do the parties, with this court's decision in *Granewich v. Harding,* 329 Or. 47 (1999). . . . Although *Granewich* left unanswered the question of when a lawyer representing a client may be liable for the client's torts, that case usefully describes the circumstances in which a person who assists another in committing a tort ordinarily may be liable for resulting harm to a third party. *Granewich* stated that section 876 of the *Restatement (Second) of Torts* (*Restatement*) "reflect[s] the common law of Oregon" on that subject. Section 876 provides:

> "For harm resulting to a third person from the tortious conduct of another, one is subject to liability if he
>
> "(a) does a tortious act in concert with the other or pursuant to a common design with him, or
>
> "(b) knows that the other's conduct constitutes a breach of duty and gives substantial assistance or encouragement to the other so to conduct himself, or
>
> "(c) gives substantial assistance to the other in accomplishing a tortious result and his own conduct, separately considered, constitutes a breach of duty to the third person."

The parties agree that plaintiff's allegations do not state a claim under subsection (c) because plaintiff does not assert that Markley's "own conduct, separately considered, constitute[d] a breach of duty to [plaintiff]." The parties further agree, for purposes of this court's review, that Schrock owed a fiduciary duty to plaintiff and that she breached that duty. The specific issue thus is whether plaintiff can recover from Markley for acting in concert with Schrock or substantially assisting her in breaching the fiduciary duty that she owed to plaintiff.

Under *Granewich* and the *Restatement,* a person who acts "in concert with" or "gives substantial assistance or encouragement" to a fiduciary who breaches a duty to a third party may be liable for the resulting harm. Markley argues, however, that that general rule does not apply when a lawyer, in the context of a lawyer-client relationship, advises a client who breaches a fiduciary duty to a third party. The *Restatement* labels any such exemption from liability that the law otherwise would impose as a "privilege." *See Restatement* § 890 ("One who otherwise would be liable for a tort is not liable if he acts in pursuance of and within the limits of a privilege * * *."). We therefore consider whether the fact that Markley was acting as Schrock's lawyer when he engaged in the challenged conduct created a privilege that protects Markley from liability. If that status does create such a privilege, then we must consider the circumstances in which the privilege applies.

B. *Privilege Against Joint Liability for a Lawyer Assisting a Client's Breach of Fiduciary Duty*

This court has not considered previously what privileges, if any, protect a person from liability for substantially assisting another in a breach of fiduciary duty. However, several cases have considered privileges as they relate to claims for interference with contractual relations brought against advisors or agents who acted on behalf of another person or entity. Those cases are instructive, because, like the present case, they involve claims against a person for actions on behalf of a client or principal that allegedly harmed a third party.

[In these cases this court] protected from liability defendants who owed duties to an entity or person and who, in the course of performing those duties, harmed a third party. This court recognized a qualified privilege in those cases because it was necessary to protect important relationships between the defendant and the entity or person . . . That is, this court, in exercising its common-law authority to define tortious conduct, implicitly concluded that the effective performance of the duties arising from those relationships required that the person performing those duties have a qualified privilege from tort liability. . . .

Not every relationship between a person who breaches a contract or a fiduciary duty and one who substantially assists in such a breach necessarily justifies recognition of a privilege against liability. However, we think that the lawyer-client relationship is one that does. That is true, in our view, because safeguarding the lawyer-client relationship protects more than just an individual or entity in any particular case or transaction; it is integral to the protection of the legal system itself. *See Restatement (Third) of the Law Governing Lawyers* (*Restatement of Lawyers*) ch. 2, Introductory Note (2000) (citing "the importance to the legal system of faithful representation"); *id.* § 121 comment b (conflict rules protect "interests of the legal system" by preventing compromise of process of adversary litigation). Myriad business transactions, as well as civil, criminal, and administrative proceedings, require that the client have the assistance of a lawyer. And a variety of doctrines, from the rules against conflicts of interest to the confidential nature of lawyer-client communications, demonstrate the ways in which the legal system protects the lawyer-client relationship.

Moreover . . . a third party's claim against the lawyer that puts the lawyer at odds with the client will compromise the lawyer-client relationship. A lawyer who is sued for substantially assisting a client's breach of fiduciary duty becomes subject to divided loyalties. As this court has recognized, lawyers cannot serve their clients adequately when their own self-interest—in these examples, the need to protect themselves from potential tort claims by third parties—pulls in the opposite direction. Moreover, allowing a claim against the lawyer may raise issues of lawyer-client privilege, if the preparation of an adequate defense for the lawyer would require the disclosure of privileged communications.

To summarize the discussion above, this court's earlier decisions hold that a person may be jointly liable with another for substantially assisting in the other's breach of a fiduciary duty owed to a third party, if the person knows that the other's conduct constitutes a breach of that fiduciary duty. *Granewich,* 329 Or. at 57, 985 P.2d 788. Our tort case law also makes clear, however, that, if a person's conduct as an agent or on behalf of another comes within the scope of a privilege, then the person is not liable to the third party. In this case, we extend those well-recognized principles to a context that we have not previously considered and hold that a lawyer acting on behalf of a client and within the scope of the lawyer-client relationship is protected by such a privilege and is not liable for assisting the client in conduct that breaches the client's fiduciary duty to a third party. Accordingly, for a third party to hold a lawyer liable for substantially assisting in a client's breach of fiduciary duty, the third party must prove that the lawyer acted outside the scope of the lawyer-client relationship.

Several features of the rule regarding the circumstances in which a lawyer's conduct may be privileged are particularly important. First, the rule places the burden on the plaintiff to show that the lawyer was acting outside the scope of the lawyer-client relationship. . . . Second, the rule protects lawyers only for actions of the kind that permissibly may be taken by lawyers in the course of representing their clients. It does not protect lawyer conduct that is unrelated to the representation of a client, even if the conduct involves a person who is a client. . . . For the same reason, the rule does not protect lawyers who are representing clients but who act only in their own self-interest and contrary to their clients' interest. Similarly, this court would consider actions by a lawyer that fall within the "crime or fraud" exception to the lawyer-client privilege, OEC 503(4)(a), and Rule of Professional Conduct 1.6(b)(1), to be outside the lawyer-client relationship when evaluating whether a lawyer's conduct is protected. . . .

Courts in other jurisdictions also have limited a lawyer's joint liability for the wrongdoing of his or her clients to protect the lawyer-client relationship. In *Chem–Age Industries, Inc. v. Glover,* 652 N.W.2d 756, 774–75 (2002), the South Dakota Supreme Court concluded that a lawyer could not be jointly liable for aiding a client's breach of fiduciary duty if the lawyer was "[m]erely acting as a scrivener for a client" and that liability could be imposed only if the lawyer "rendered 'substantial assistance' to the breach of duty, not merely to the person committing the breach." 652 N.W.2d at 774. The Massachusetts Supreme Judicial Court rejected claims by trust beneficiaries that a trustee's lawyers could be liable for assisting the trustee's breach of fiduciary duty, holding that the beneficiaries had to "show that the [lawyer] knew of the breach and actively participated in it such that he or she could not reasonably be held to have acted in good faith." *Spinner v. Nutt,* 417 Mass. 549, 556 (1994). In a case involving the liability of an accountant for aiding and abetting a client's breach of fiduciary duty, the Minnesota Supreme Court, quoting *Restatement* section 876(b), noted that "most courts have recognized that 'substantial assistance' means something more than the provision of routine professional services" and found that allegations that alleged only that the accountant provides such "routine services" were insufficient to meet the "substantial assistance" requirement. *Witzman v. Lehrman, Lehrman & Flom,* 601 N.W.2d 179, 189 (Minn.1999).

In our view, the test that we hold applicable here—whether the lawyer's conduct fell outside the permissible scope of the lawyer-client relationship—often will lead to the same result as the tests adopted in the cases described above. It does so, however, in a more predictable and useful way, because it focuses on the scope of the lawyer-client relationship—and the legal rules, such as OEC 503(4)(a), that help define that scope—rather than on the fine line between "advice" and "assistance" or between "substantial assistance" and other assistance. We acknowledge that the test does not identify a bright line between liability and immunity, but it nevertheless uses concepts tied directly to the lawyer's role in representing the client and existing sources of law regarding the scope of that role.

C. *Application of the Privilege*

We now return to the facts of this case. Like the parties and the courts below, we assume for these purposes that Schrock breached a fiduciary duty to plaintiff and that Markley knowingly provided substantial assistance to her or acted in concert with her in so doing. We focus on whether Markley, as Schrock's lawyer, has a qualified privilege from liability to plaintiff for assisting in that breach of duty. Here, plaintiff had "the burden of negating [the] qualified privilege * * * as part of his affirmative case." [citation omitted] On summary judgment, therefore, plaintiff had the burden of producing evidence that would show that Markley's conduct was not privileged because it fell outside the permissible scope of his role as Schrock's lawyer. *See* ORCP 47 C (on summary judgment, "[t]he adverse party has the burden of producing evidence on any issue raised in the motion as to which the adverse party would have the burden of persuasion at trial").

Taken in the light most favorable to plaintiff, the summary judgment record shows that Markley took four actions that plaintiff asserts are relevant to his claims. First, Markley advised Schrock that the settlement agreement did not require her to retain the lodge property in anticipation of the possibility that plaintiff's security interest would attach to it and assisted her in selling it. Second, he called the escrow officer and asked her not to tell anyone about the pending sale of the property. Third, he assisted Schrock in revoking her consent to sell the timber property. Finally, he accepted substantial fees for performing legal work for Schrock, including the foregoing three actions.

Nowhere has plaintiff suggested, and nothing in the record indicates, that any aspect of Markley's advice and assistance to Schrock fell outside the scope of the lawyer-client relationship or the assistance that a lawyer properly provides for a client. There is no credible claim that Markley's conduct violated any applicable statute. No evidence in the summary judgment record suggests that Markley's or Schrock's conduct was criminal or fraudulent. Whether or not Markley's interpretation of the agreement was correct-a determination that we need not make here-the purpose of the privilege requires that lawyers be able to assess the legal problems that their clients bring to them and discuss the full range of available solutions. Moreover, lawyers must be able to assist their clients in implementing those solutions, to the extent that that assistance falls within the legitimate scope of the lawyer-client relationship. Although courts may not always agree with the legal advice that a lawyer provides, protecting a lawyer from liability to a third party for advising a client is essential to the administration of justice. . . .

Plaintiff argues that we should interpret Markley's acceptance of fees as a self-interested act that fell outside the scope of the qualified privilege. We disagree. Whether Markley took no fee or an hourly fee or a contingent fee is irrelevant to the central question whether his actions fell within the scope of the lawyer-client relationship. If anything, Markley's acceptance of a fee supports his claim that he was acting as Schrock's lawyer, although there is no evidence here that he was *not* acting as her lawyer.

The summary judgment record reveals no evidence from which a reasonable jury could find that Markley acted outside the scope of the lawyer-client relationship in his representation of Schrock. Markley's conduct therefore falls within the scope of the privilege that we have described above. The trial court was correct in granting Markley's motion for summary judgment.

CASE QUESTIONS

1. What must a plaintiff show to establish secondary liability against counsel in such a case?
2. Who has the burden of proof regarding the qualified privilege?
3. The court provides three examples of a sufficient showing. What are they?

In the *Granewich* case mentioned above the plaintiff was a minority shareholder in a small company. He alleged counsel for the company conspired with the majority shareholders to squeeze the plaintiff out of the company. The *Reynolds* Court distinguished *Granewich* on the ground that the lawyer defendant there was alleged to have represented the company but acted in concert with individual shareholders, thus acting outside the bounds of his role as an attorney for the company.

Not every state approaches secondary liability the same way. In *Joel v. Weber*, 602 N.Y.S.2d 383, 384 (1993), the court denied a motion to dismiss claims brought by a third party against a firm for aiding and abetting the allegedly tortuous conduct of the firm's client against the plaintiff. The court held that "[a]lthough mere negligence by an attorney in rendering advice to a client does not support a separate right of action by a third party allegedly injured by that advice, nevertheless, under New York law, an attorney may be liable to third parties for actions taken in furtherance of his role as counsel upon proof, as alleged in detail by the plaintiffs herein, of the existence of 'fraud, collusion, malice or bad faith'."

The plaintiff in *Skarbrevik v. Cohen, England & Whitfield*, 231 Cal.App.3d 692 (1991), alleged that Comis, counsel for a close corporation, aided and abetted the corporation's majority shareholders in diluting the plaintiff's interest in the company. The plaintiff alleged Comis conspired with the majority shareholders to amend the corporate bylaws to rescind the plaintiff's right to purchase a portion of any new issue of stock. In connection with this conspiracy, Comis prepared minutes for a shareholders meeting that never took place, and prepared and filed with the Secretary of State and the Department of Corporations documents memorializing actions that supposedly took place at this fictitious meeting.

Plaintiff asserted claims against Comis for negligence and conspiracy to defraud. The court held Comis could not be liable for negligence because he represented the corporate entity rather than any individual shareholder. Comis therefore owed plaintiff no duty in plaintiff's capacity as a shareholder; he owed duties only to the entity itself.

The court also rejected the plaintiff's conspiracy claim. It found substantial evidence that the majority shareholders breached their fiduciary duty to the plaintiff by diluting his interest and fraudulently concealed their plans to do so. It also found evidence sufficient for a jury to conclude that Comis assisted in this fraud. The court held, however, that Comis could not be liable for conspiring not to disclose the majority shareholders' plan because he did not himself owe a fiduciary duty to the plaintiff that would impose a disclosure obligation on him. The court distinguished fraudulent concealment from actual fraud, for which conspiracy liability might lie in an appropriate case.

Pacific Investment Management Company LLC v. Mayer Brown LLP, 603 F.3d 144 (2d Cir. 2010), provides a useful contrast to *Rubin v.*

Schottenstein, Zox & Dunn, 143 F.3d 263 (6th Cir. 1998), discussed above, and highlights the difference under the civil damage provisions of the federal securities laws between primary liability for misstatements and secondary liability. The case arose from the collapse of a brokerage firm called Refco. Plaintiffs alleged that Refco entered into a series of sham loan transactions to hide losses it suffered and that its lawyers facilitated these transactions and wrote misstatements about them in documents Refco used to sell securities to the public. The statements were issued in Refco's name, however, and were not attributed to the law firm.

The Second Circuit found this distinction decisive: "a secondary actor can be held liable in a private damages action brought pursuant to Rule 10b–5 only for false statements attributed to the secondary-actor defendant at the time of dissemination." Absent such attribution, the court held, a law firm could be held liable only for aiding and abetting a fraud, and the Supreme Court's decisions in *Central Bank of Denver, N.A. v. First Interstate Bank of Denver, N.A.*, 511 U.S. 164 (1994), and *Stoneridge Investment Partners, LLC v. Scientific–Atlanta, Inc.*, 552 U.S. 148 (2008), foreclosed civil damages actions under the federal securities laws for such aiding and abetting. State law remedies could remain viable even in the wake of this ruling, however.

Model Rule 1.2(d) forbids you from counseling a client to commit a crime or fraud or from assisting the client in doing so. It allows you to discuss the consequences of a client's plans or assist the client in determining what the law is. The rule presents some gray areas and some hard choices. The following materials explore both.

Model Rule of Professional Conduct 1.2(d)

UNITED STATES V. SARANTOS

455 F.2d 877 (2d Cir. 1972)

FEINBERG, CIRCUIT JUDGE:

Defendants Robert Sarantos and Constantine Makris appeal from judgments of conviction after a 15–day trial before Judge Inzer B. Wyatt and a jury in the United States District Court for the Southern District of New York. Sarantos was convicted on five counts of conspiring to make false statements to the Immigration and Naturalization Service (INS) and to defraud the United States Government in violation of 18 U.S.C. §§ 371, 1001, 1546. Makris was found guilty along with Sarantos on two of those counts. Sarantos was also convicted separately on seven counts of aiding and abetting others to make false statements to the INS in violation of 18 U.S.C. §§ 1001 and 2. Each defendant received a short prison sentence and a period of probation. On this appeal, Sarantos and Makris challenge various portions of the trial court's charge to the jury. We find no error and affirm their convictions.

I

Viewed in the light most favorable to the Government, the record reveals the following facts: Sarantos and Makris were participants in illegal plans to obtain permanent residence in this country for male Greek aliens. Defendants sought to take advantage of an immigration rule that permitted the alien spouse of a United States citizen to obtain an immigrant visa, which entitled the alien to enter the country as a permanent resident regardless of whether the yearly quota of immigrant visas allotted to the alien's country had been exhausted. To exploit this special exception to the quota system the participants employed a scheme generally involving two steps: First, a sham marriage was arranged between the Greek alien and a Puerto Rican women who was a United States citizen; and second, a visa petition was prepared over the wife's signature, stating falsely that the married couple was living together as man and wife.

Makris was essentially a marriage broker. He helped to locate Puerto Rican women who were interested in marrying Greek aliens in return for a fee. He also assisted in arranging sham marriages. Sarantos, an attorney, was involved in the second stage. The parties to the sham marriages visited his office shortly after the wedding ceremony. There the wife would sign a visa petition in blank, which Sarantos would later complete and file with the INS. In each case the petition stated falsely that the parties were living together as husband and wife. Sarantos also instructed wives who were called before the INS to say that they were living with their husbands but not to mention that they were paid to marry.

Although the Government failed to show that Sarantos was ever explicitly told that the couples were not living together, it did furnish abundant evidence that Sarantos was informed of the sham nature of the marriages: In some cases newlyweds required in his presence the aid of an interpreter or sign language because they shared no common language; divorce papers were executed simultaneously with immigration papers; Sarantos was told the wife was being paid a fee; and Sarantos was at least indirectly informed that the parties were not living together. The prosecution also established that several of the couples purported to be living in buildings owned or managed by other clients of Sarantos, which might be considered "safe" addresses; *i. e.,* the managers would be expected to tell an INS investigator that the couples were actually living together. On this evidence, the jury found Sarantos guilty not only of conspiracy but also of aiding and abetting the making of false statements to the INS.

II

Before the case went to the jury the trial court instructed the jurors on the elements of the crimes charged against Sarantos. The jury was told, among other things, that before they could find Sarantos guilty of aiding and abetting the making of false statements they must conclude that "he knew . . . [the statements] were false and that he wilfully and knowingly participated in furthering the conduct." After defining knowingly and wilfully as meaning that "one knows what he or she is doing, as distinguished from an inadvertent or careless act," the court further charged the jury that:

> . . . if you find that Mr. Sarantos acted with reckless disregard of whether the statements made were true or with a conscious effort to avoid learning the truth, this requirement is satisfied, even though you may find that he was not specifically aware of the facts which would establish the falsity of the statements.

The attorney for Sarantos objected to the charge on the ground that reckless disregard of the falsity of the statements or a conscious effort to avoid learning the truth did not amount to "knowledge." The trial court overruled the objection, and Sarantos now claims the court committed reversible error.

The charge on the issue of knowledge given by the district judge in this case was taken almost verbatim from a charge which we upheld recently in United States v. Egenberg, 441 F.2d 441, 444 (2d Cir. 1971), cert. denied, 404 U.S. 994 (U.S. Dec. 14, 1971), a case also involving 18 U.S.C. § 1001. The court in *Egenberg* in turn relied on another decision of this court in United States v. Abrams, 427 F.2d 86, 91 (2d Cir.), cert. denied 400 U.S. 832 (1970). We held in *Abrams* that there was sufficient evidence to convict an attorney of knowingly causing the making of a false statement in an affidavit which he completed over his client's signature and filed with the INS, and we stated:

> Although appellant may not have been specifically aware of what his client's plans for departure were, the jury could have found from the evidence that appellant acted with reckless disregard of whether the statements made were true and with a conscious purpose to avoid learning the truth.

Defendant offers a number of arguments why these decisions should not foreclose his objection to the charge. First is a frontal attack on *Abrams,* which defendant urges us to overrule. He contends that when an attorney is charged with aiding and abetting the making of a false statement it cannot be enough to show reckless disregard of its falsity. Otherwise, defendant claims, we radically alter the attorney-client relationship and make the attorney "an investigative arm of the government."

We stand by our decision in *Abrams*. Its purpose in cases such as this was to prevent an individual like Sarantos from circumventing criminal sanctions merely by deliberately closing his eyes to the obvious risk that he is engaging in unlawful conduct. Our ruling in *Abrams* was intended to foreclose this possible loophole, not to create a new crime as defendant suggests. Compare *Morissette v. United States*, 342 U.S. 246, 263 (1952). Construing "knowingly" in a criminal statute to include wilful blindness to the existence of a fact is no radical concept in the law. Nor can it be said that the *Abrams* decision changes the lawyer's role. We have not held, as appellant contends, that an attorney must investigate "the truth of his client's assertions" or risk going to jail. We have held, and continue to hold, that he cannot counsel others to make statements in the face of obvious indications of which he is aware that those assertions are not true. *Cf. United States v. Benjamin*, 328 F.2d 854, 862–863 (2d Cir.), cert. denied, 377 U.S. 953 (1964). . . .

Judgments affirmed.

For a similar result, *see United States v. Frank*, 494 F.2d 145 (2d Cir. 1974) (Friendly, J.). Defendants in that case were accused of defrauding and helping to defraud a client. Two lawyer defendants argued that they merely performed the sort of ordinary tasks lawyers perform all the time, and that the evidence was therefore insufficient to convict them. Here is Judge Friendly's response:

> Hemlock and Hoffer claim that the evidence is consistent with their having simply engaged in professional activities and that any wrongdoing was solely Frank's and Miller's. Hoffer makes the further argument that he was acting in a subordinate capacity and thus was even farther than Hemlock from the odoriferous stream of guilty knowledge. But too many red flags were flying to make these contentions plausible. It is useful to recall Judge Learned Hand's observation that 'the cumulation of instances, each explicable only by extreme credulity or professional inexpertness, may have a probative force immensely greater than any one of them alone.' United States v. White, 124 F.2d 181, 185 (2 Cir. 1941). We repeat also that lawyers cannot 'escape criminal liability on a plea of ignorance when they have shut their eyes to what was plainly to be seen,' United States v. Benjamin, 328 F.2d 854, 863 (2 Cir.), cert. denied, 377 U.S. 953 (1964).

In *United States v. Heredia*, 483 F.3d 913 (9th Cir. 2007), the Ninth Circuit recently considered *en banc* and reaffirmed its "deliberate ignorance" rulings and jury instruction, which trace to *United States v. Jewell*, 532 F.2d 697 (9th Cir. 1976). The holding in *Jewell*, which has been endorsed by all circuits except the Court of Appeals for the D.C. Circuit, is that " 'knowingly' in criminal statutes is not limited to positive knowledge, but includes the state of mind of one who does not possess positive knowledge only because he consciously avoided it."

Jury instructions stating this rule are sometimes called "ostrich instructions." Judge Richard Posner summarizes the rule regarding such instructions this way:

> It is not the purpose of the ostrich instruction to tell the jury that it does not need direct evidence of guilty knowledge in order to find such knowledge beyond a reasonable doubt. Still less is it to enable conviction of one who merely suspects that he may be involved with wrongdoers. At times during the oral argument of this appeal the government's able lawyer came close to suggesting that the proper office of the ostrich instruction is to enable conviction upon the basis of constructive notice—if a reasonable man who knew what [the defendant] knew would have inquired further and discovered the illegal activity, [the defendant] is an aider and abettor. Not so. Aider and abettor liability is not negligence liability. The abettor and aider must know that he is assisting an illegal activity. We add that if it were the purpose of the ostrich instruction to enable conviction for mere negligence, the instruction would be worded differently.
>
> The most powerful criticism of the ostrich instruction is, precisely, that its tendency is to allow juries to convict upon a finding of negligence for crimes that require intent. . . . The criticism can be deflected by thinking carefully about just what it is that real ostriches do (or at least are popularly supposed to do). They do not just fail to follow through on their suspicions of bad things. They are not merely careless birds. They bury their heads in the sand so that they will not see or hear bad things. They deliberately avoid acquiring unpleasant knowledge. The ostrich instruction is designed for cases in which there is evidence that the defendant, knowing or strongly suspecting that he is involved in shady dealings, takes steps to make sure that he does not acquire full or exact knowledge of the nature and extent of those dealings. A deliberate effort to avoid guilty knowledge is all the guilty knowledge the law requires.
>
> [The court later clarified that the "steps" it referred to could be purely mental]: the deliberate effort to avoid guilty knowledge that we said is all the guilty knowledge the law requires can be a mental, as well as a physical, effort—a cutting off of one's normal curiosity by an effort of will.

United States v. Giovannetti, 919 F.2d 1223 (7th Cir. 1990).

The Ethics Ostrich

What should you do if you are representing a client and begin to think that the client is breaking the law? What if the client is breaking the law and using your services to help do it?

Model Rule 1.2(d) prohibits you from counseling a client to engage in unlawful conduct and from assisting a client in such conduct. Model Rule 1.16(a) requires that you not represent a client if the representation will result in a violation of the rules of professional conduct or other law. If you are already representing such a client, then you must withdraw from the representation. (These rules can present complex problems, which we explore later in connection with the ethics of advocacy.) *Sarantos* and *Frank* show you that criminal laws are relevant to such situations, too.

Sometimes it is hard to know what a client is doing. They may not tell you everything; they may lie. You are not at risk from facts that you neither know nor, in the exercise of reasonable care, should know. But that does not mean you can turn a blind eye to facts that you do know, or which you should know based on information you have. If you see a red flag you cannot safely ignore it. If you stick your head in the sand, and hope that everything will work out for the best, you might wind up being charged with knowledge that you did not actually have but which you did avoid learning.

In some contexts it is an accepted part of practice for a lawyer not to acquire information she could acquire if she tried. Criminal defense counsel might not want to know if their client did it, for example. As we will see, the rules governing counsel in such cases differ based on what counsel knows. But criminal defense is a special case, in which the tradition of putting the government to its proof is very strong and the notion of the lawyer as the client's champion in an adversary contest is at its strongest. It is dangerous to extrapolate from that context to others, especially to cases in which a lawyer helps a client engage in future activity, or in a pattern of continuous activity, as in *Sarantos*. There is a big difference between defending someone on trial for something that has happened already and helping a client do that thing in the first place.

In other words, don't be an ethics ostrich. Sticking your head in the sand is dangerous as well as irresponsible. Especially for lawyers who help out *ex ante* rather than defend a client *ex post*, it will make you look sneaky, and therefore culpable. It will never do you any good.

D. ADVISING OR ASSISTING CLIENTS IN UNLAWFUL ACTIVITY

You may not advise clients to break the law or assist them in doing so but you may test the legality of laws (which might conflict with a superior law such as the constitution) or the legality of court orders. The line between testing and obeying is conceptually clear but may appear murky in some circumstances, as the following case illustrates.

MATTER OF KEVIN L. SCIONTI

630 N.E.2d 1358 (Ind. 1994)

PER CURIAM

Kevin L. Scionti, the Respondent here, was charged by disciplinary complaint with violating Rule 1.2(d) of the Rules of Professional Conduct for Attorneys at Law, pursuant to which an attorney shall not counsel a client to engage in conduct that the lawyer knows is criminal. Additionally, the complaint charges Respondent with violating Prof.Cond.R. 8.4(d) by engaging in conduct prejudicial to the administration of justice. . . .

Respondent was admitted to the Bar of this state on October 15, 1982, and is therefore subject to the disciplinary jurisdiction of this Court. Gary and Annette Smoot's marriage was dissolved by court order on April 25, 1990. The court granted Annette custody of the Smoot's minor son pursuant to a July 25, 1990 court order. Gary was granted visitation rights for every other weekend, commencing at 5:00 p.m. and ending 6:00 p.m. Sunday. On December 5, 1990, the Delaware County Prosecutor charged Annette with child molesting, a Class B felony. The purported victim was the Smoot's minor son. He remained in the custody of Annette during this time.

On September 20, 1991, Respondent entered his appearance on behalf of Gary in a post-dissolution proceeding challenging the terms and conditions of the July, 1990 custody order. Gary had previously retained attorney Donald Dunnuck to represent him, and Mr. Dunnuck's appearance continued.

On November 8, 1991, Gary picked up his minor son for visitation. He failed to return his son on November 10, 1991, on the advice of Respondent, thus violating the July, 1990 court order setting the terms and condition of visitation. Judge Thomas Newman of the Henry Superior Court signed an *ex parte* order on November 11, 1991, directing Gary to immediately return his son to his mother's custody. Respondent's request that the order be removed and his subsequent application for emergency custody were both denied by Judge Newman. On November 12, 1991, Annette was charged by information with intimidation and obstruction of justice, both Class D felonies, by the Delaware County Prosecutor. The charges alleged that Annette struck her minor son and coached him not to testify against her. During the period of time Gary unlawfully retained custody of his son, he maintained regular telephone conversations with Respondent and Mr. Dunnuck.

A contempt violation hearing regarding Gary's failure to return his son was held on November 22, 1991. At that time, Gary had not yet returned his son to Annette's custody. During hearing, the court heard the following testimony of Respondent:

Q: Mr. Scionti, there's been some testimony that you knowingly gave advice to Mr. Smoot to violate a Court Order. Is that correct?

A: Uh, that is correct.

Q: Could you explain to the Court the circumstances surrounding that advice, please?

. . . . .

A: That after consultation with the Delaware Prosecutor's Office, we were aware that a new information would be filed the 12th. . . . Uh, that we were aware that new charges would be filed the 12th, uh, and that we felt the presiding Judge of this Court or the criminal Court needed to be advised of that matter uh, before Gary returned the child to Annette, should that be what the Court decided to do.

. . . . .

Q: So you advised Mr. Smoot to [not return his son] despite the fact that there was a custody Order existing in this cause at that time. Yes or no?

A: Yes.

Q: And so on that basis, you advised Mr. Smoot to do that? Despite the Court Order. Yes?

A: Yes.

Q: And you knew that there was an Ex Parte Order that was signed by the Judge on the 12th. Yes?

A: I learned on the 12th that it had been signed on the 11th.

Q: And you still advised Mr. Smoot to stay in hiding with the child?

A: Until such time as this Court could hold a hearing or the criminal Court could hold a hearing. Yes.

Q: And you knew that there was an entry at some point made by this Court denying your Petition for an Ex Parte Petition for Emergency Custody. Yes?

A: Yes.

Q: And you still did not advise Mr. Smoot to return the child?

A: If I recall, on that date, the Judge had set this matter today, for hearing today and we advised Mr. Smoot that he would have to bring the child to Court today. I advised him to keep him until today. Yes.

Transcript of hearing on contempt citation, November 22, 1991, at 68, 69, 75, 76–77.

Gary testified at the hearing that Respondent and Mr. Dunnuck advised him, during a telephone conversation on November 8, 1991, to take his son and not return him.

At the conclusion of the hearing, the court found no justification for the violation of the orders, and thus found Gary to be in contempt. He was incarcerated in the Henry County Jail for ninety days. All pending criminal charges against Annette were dismissed on November 26, 1991.

We find that the evidence clearly and convincingly establishes that Respondent counseled his client to engage in conduct that Respondent knew was criminal, thereby violating Prof.Cond.R. 1.2(d). Respondent further violated Prof.Cond.R. 8.4(d) by engaging in conduct that is prejudicial to the administration of justice.

Respondent contends that a finding of violation of Prof.Cond.R. 1.2(d) is unwarranted because the offense Respondent's client committed derived from a civil action, and therefore a criminal violation was unforeseeable by Respondent. We find this argument unpersuasive. Respondent is a licensed attorney with several years of experience in private practice. It is thus not unreasonable to expect Respondent to be aware of Indiana law making interference with custody a criminal violation.

Respondent further relies on the comments to Prof.Cond.R. 8.4(d) and 1.2(d) as supportive of his assertion that he genuinely believed that the advice he provided to his client was justified by the circumstances as he knew them. The comment to Prof.Cond.R. 1.2(d) provides:

> A lawyer may counsel a client to make a good faith effort to determine the validity, scope, meaning, or application of the law.

The comment following Prof.Cond.R. 8.4(d) provides:

> A lawyer may refuse to comply with an obligation imposed by law on a good faith belief that no valid obligation exists.

Respondent, however, admits only that he believed his advice to his client was justified by the situation. Respondent does not claim that the legal obligations imposed by court order were invalid. Any doubts as to the validity of the original visitation order should have been dispelled in Respondent's mind after the trial court judge signed the *ex parte* order on November 12, 1991, reaffirming the substance of the original order, and after Respondent's request for withdrawal of that order and application for emergency custody were denied. Respondent's client was clearly legally obligated to return custody of his child to his ex-wife. That obligation was three times reaffirmed by the court through its November 11 order, its denial of Respondent's request to withdraw that order, and its denial of Respondent's application for emergency custody. Respondent's argument that his perceived invalidity of the order excused his client's noncompliance is therefore without merit.

Now that we have found misconduct, it is the duty of this Court to assess an appropriate sanction. In doing so, we examine several factors, including the duty violated, the lawyer's mental state, the actual or potential injury caused by the misconduct, and factors in aggravation and mitigation. *In re Clanin* (1993), Ind., 619 N.E.2d 269. In the absence of mitigating factors, Respondent's actions would reflect a complete disregard for the sanctity of the judicial process and thus would merit correspondingly significant sanction. However, we are cognizant of the fact that Respondent's misconduct was not motivated by personal gain and was directly attributable to his concern for the welfare of his client's minor son. Although his method of handling the situation is unacceptable and warrants our censure, Respondent's lack of sinister motives persuades us that he is not currently unfit to practice law. For these reasons, we conclude that a public reprimand is an appropriate sanction.

It is, therefore, ordered that the Respondent, Kevin L. Scionti, is hereby reprimanded and admonished for his misconduct set out above.

Costs of this proceeding are assessed against the Respondent.

SHEPARD, C.J., dissents, with SULLIVAN, J., concurring.

As a client, Gary Smoot might not have fully appreciated his legal duty to comply with the orders of courts. He likely relied on his lawyers, Donald Dunnuck and Kevin Scionti, whom we expect to know better. As a result of relying on his lawyers, Mr. Smoot spent 90 days in jail for his comtempt. Today, Mr. Smoot's lawyer gets a better deal—a simple reprimand. This differential in treatment is not justified by mitigating circumstances or by any expression of regret by respondent Scionti. Indeed, as he stood before Judge Newman explaining his advice to his client, Scionti did not express any apology. As he stands before us charged by the Disciplinary Commission and found by the hearing officer to have committed misconduct, Scionti continues to argue that he did not violate Rule 1.2 and that the Commission has not proven he did anything prejudicial to the administration of justice (a violation of Rule 8.2). I think it was prejudicial. The authority of our courts depends on lawyers and their clients obeying court orders. Mr. Scionti's conduct undermines that authority and for that reason he should be subject to more severe sanction.

No Matter Where You Go, There You Are II

What would you have done in this situation? If you really believed—and the police seemed to believe, too—that your client's former spouse was molesting the children, would you insist that the client return the children to that spouse? Would you think the child's well-being was more important than the order, and that—importantly—you were the right person to decide that? Would you just accept a disciplinary sanction as the price of doing the right thing? Are the ethical rules unvarying moral commands or are they just prices you have to pay for certain kinds of conduct, sort of like the speed limit, which you might well break if you thought you had a good reason?

The rules tell you a fair bit about how they see themselves, but only you can decide how you see them. You will make better judgments if you think such things through now, when you have the leisure to do so, instead of thinking of them for the first time when you confront a panicked client in a situation such as Smoot and Scionti faced.

Thinking Dynamically and Interactively IV

How would you describe the decision Scionti faced?

Drawing on the material you studied in the Introduction, we may think of *Scionti* as a case in which a lawyer does not understand how his advice will look to a judge. In other words, judges have many categories for lawyers, including a category called something like "rogue lawyer who counsels defiance of my orders." That might not be a category that ever occurred to Scionti, or at least not one he thought much about. And, like most people, he probably would have been very reluctant to think of himself in that category. He no doubt focused on Gary's problem and the seemingly very real risk of child abuse. On this reading, to misunderstand the categories available to another player in the game is to misunderstand the range of inferences one's conduct might raise, and thus fundamentally misunderstand one's position.

The prospect of harm to a child makes *Scionti* a hard case. Most Rule 1.2(d) cases are easier. The attorney in *In re Evans*, 759 N.E.2d 1064 (Ind. 2001), for example, was disciplined for filing a tax return he knew to be false. The client misstated the profit from a real estate transaction in which the lawyer was involved. Counsel in *Attorney Grievance Comm'n of Maryland v. Culver*, 381 Md. 241, 849 A.2d 423 (2004), represented a client who fell behind in paying fees. The lawyer advised the client to open credit card accounts, draw down cash advances to pay the fees, and then declare bankruptcy (in which the lawyer offered to represent him).

PROBLEM 8–8

Suppose you represent a client who suffered personal injuries for which he incurred medical expenses. Using a different lawyer, the client declared bankruptcy and the medical expense debts were discharged. The client then retained you to sue on the personal injury claim, for which the lawyer charged a 40% contingent fee. You file suit and submit a demand for settlement, which includes a demand for reimbursement of the medical expenses. You then learn those expenses have been discharged in bankruptcy. May you proceed to settle the claim without informing the defendant of this fact?

PROBLEM 8–9

Assume you represent a single mother whose landlord is trying to evict her for not paying her rent. She has not paid her rent for several months, in part because she has spent money on some minor repairs to the apartment that the landlord had promised to do but which he had not in fact done. Your client might be able to catch up enough on the rent to avoid eviction, but it would take her a couple of months at least. If she is evicted from this apartment she probably will not be able to find another, at least not in the near term.

The apartment is in shabby condition: the pipes in the kitchen and bathroom are corroded and leak slightly, the walls and carpet are moldy and filled with holes, mice are often scurrying about, and some wiring is partly exposed. The law in your jurisdiction implies a warranty of habitability that requires apartments to meet certain minimum standards. A breach of this warranty is a defense to an action for non-payment of rent, so if the court found such a breach your client probably could not be evicted, or at least not right now.

You do not believe the facts your client has given you are enough to persuade a judge that the implied warranty has been breached. But they are close. If the pipes gave way and flooded the apartment, or if the wiring shorted out and cut off electricity, or if there were rats running around instead of mice, you believe a judge would find a breach of the warranty and refuse to evict your client. May you advise your client:

(a) Of the law of implied warranty and of your view that her apartment is close to being in breach of it but that a court would probably say it was not in breach?

(b) Of what things would, in your opinion, have to happen for an implied warranty claim to be sustained?

(c) To go home and chip away at the corrosion on the pipes to determine its extent?

(d) To go home and run a lot of water through the pipes in the hope that they would give way and create a flood that would establish the defense?

(e) To go home and place bits of cheese behind the exposed wires, so the mice might try to chew through them?

(f) To buy a pet rat and let it loose?

E. SOME PROBLEMS IN ADVISING CLIENTS: TAX SHELTERS AND "TORTURE MEMOS"

Model Rules 1.2(d), 2.1

Lawyers often serve clients by advising them on future conduct rather than litigating about past conduct. The preceding materials surveyed the requirements of Model Rule 1.2(d) with respect to advice. Model Rule 2.1 requires that lawyers offer candid advice based on independent professional judgment. The rule states lawyers may refer to social, moral, and other factors not strictly related to the relevant law, but it does not require that a lawyer do so.

Advice often takes the form of an opinion letter. These letters may be divided into two types. One type of letter is directed to third parties, to assure them of some legal fact about the client. A letter stating that shares to be sold in a securities offering are properly issued, or that debt to be sold is a valid and binding obligation of the borrower are examples of such letters. So is the UCC report at issue in *Greycas v. Proud*, discussed in section A. These letters benefit clients by giving third parties assurance they can rely on in dealing with the client. And, of course, they give third parties possible claims against the lawyers if the lawyers act incompetently or in bad faith.

A second type of letter is directed to the client and aims to provide the client a basis for a defense against possible accusations of bad faith. Companies accused of patent infringement, for example, often seek letters opining either that a patent asserted against them is invalid or that they do not infringe it. They use these letters to defend against allegations that they infringed willfully, a finding that could increase the damages they owe if they are found liable for infringement. Lawyers sometimes seek opinion letters regarding the lawfulness of their conduct, which they may use to defend against allegations of bad faith.

A notable if extreme example of such letters involves tax shelters marketed by lawyers and accounting firms in the early 2000s. A tax shelter is an investment that generates more in tax savings than it costs. Shelters typically generate losses taxpayers can use to reduce their taxable income; shelter buyers therefore report lower taxable income and pay less in taxes than they would without the shelter. Paying less exposes taxpayers to the risk of underpayment penalties, which can be very high. A taxpayer will not be penalized, however, if there was a reasonable basis for the position taken in the tax return, and thus a reasonable cause for underpayment. *See* 26 U.S.C. § 6664(c)(1). Lawyers involved in these shelters attempted to provide taxpayers such cause, and thus insurance against penalties, by providing opinion letters stating the shelter was "more likely than not" permissible under the law.

The most notable instance of such activity involved Paul Daugerdas, a partner at Jenkens & Gilchrist's Chicago office. Mr. Daugerdas was both a lawyer and accountant. He allegedly marketed a particular tax shelter to very rich people, often those seeking to offset capital gains, and he and his firm issued "more likely than not" letters to shelter buyers, who were clients of the firm. Notwithstanding these letters, the shelters employed transactions that allegedly lacked economic substance and had no business purpose other than the reduction of the purchaser's tax liability. The shelters therefore did not comply with the tax laws and did not lawfully reduce the purchasers' tax liability.

Mr. Daugerdas allegedly knew these facts but marketed the shelters and issued the letters anyway. The opinion letters allegedly included statements Daugerdas knew to be false, such as:

> You [the client] entered into the Transactions . . . for substantial nontax business reasons, including (without limitation) your belief that the potential economic benefits of owning the Note [a promissory note provided as part of the shelter by the third-party buyer] outweighed the potential economic benefits of retaining the Remainder Interest, and a desire to maximize profits and minimize risks with respect to your various investment activities.

Daugerdas allegedly was paid slightly over $95 million between 1998 and 2002 for marketing such shelters, including issuing the opinion letters.

The preceding discussion uses the word "allegedly." That is because the facts recounted are taken from a federal indictment handed down against Mr. Daugerdas in 2009. The investigation leading to the indictment began long before that, as did civil suits brought by clients who bought the shelters. In 2002, clients whose shelters did not hold up when audited by the IRS began to sue a group of defendants including Jenkens & Gilchrest. In 2005 the defendants agreed to an $81.55 million settlement, of which the firm reportedly paid $5.25 million of its own money. In 2007 the firm settled a government investigation by agreeing to pay $76 million. The firm did not survive the turmoil; it closed its doors in March 2007.[3]

The paragraph quoted above provides insight to an important aspect of opinion letters: The facts. Letters are generally based on a particular set of facts set forth in some detail in the letter, and the assurance of the letter generally extends no farther than the facts recited. This fact (pardon the pun) implies two important things. First, lawyers must be sure either to verify the facts or to make plain that they rely on the clients' assurance that the facts are true. A lawyer who claims to have investigated facts he has not investigated, as in *Greycas*, is asking for trouble and has no defense when it arrives. The same is true of a lawyer who attempts to rely on client assurances when the lawyer knows or has reason to believe those assurances are false. To count, reliance must both be real (i.e., the lawyer does not actually know the assurances are false) and reasonable. Second, clients who misrepresent the facts cannot rely on opinion letters based on the misrepresentation. That is both because the letter generally will not provide assurance with respect to the true facts and because a client cannot rely in good faith on a letter the client knows to be predicated on a false assumption.

Limiting an opinion to the facts stated and allocating responsibility for verifying those facts are two ways lawyers try to make sure clients understand the limitations or qualifications that apply to their opinions. These steps also tend to limit the liability risk of the lawyer signing the opinion. At least in private practice, lawyers' desire to limit that risk often leads to letters so thoroughly qualified and so narrowly limited that the opinion itself takes up comparatively little space. Such limitations and qualifications reflect a tension in opinion letter practice: Clients want an opinion strong enough to suit their purpose, such as providing a defense, while lawyers want to an opinion weak enough to limit their potential liability to the client or third parties, including the government.

---

[3] The Internal Revenue Service has its own rules governing opinion letter practice. These rules define practice before the IRS to include rendering written advice regarding any transaction or arrangement having a potential for tax avoidance or evasion. Treasury Department Circular 230 § 10.2(a)(4). The rules provide in part that lawyers providing opinions that conclude there is a greater than 50% likelihood that a tax issue would be resolved in the client's favor: (i) must use reasonable efforts to identify and consider all relevant facts; (ii) must not rely on an unreasonable factual assumption, including one the lawyer knows to be incomplete or wrong; (iii) must not rely on an unreasonable factual representation from the client or anyone else; (iv) must relate the law to the relevant facts; (v) must not rely on unreasonable legal conclusions; (vi) must not contain internally inconsistent legal analyses or conclusions; (vii) must consider all significant federal tax issues and either state a conclusion regarding such issues or state that the lawyer cannot reach a conclusion; and (viii) must not take into account the chance that the client's return would not be audited. Requirement (vii) may be relaxed if the lawyer and client agree to limit the scope of the lawyer's analysis, unless the opinion concerns a transaction the IRS has identified as a tax avoidance transaction or concerns an arrangement the principal purpose of which is to avoid taxes. Additional rules apply to opinions a lawyer knows or has reason to know will be used to market transactions or arrangements.

Such tensions may produce tense negotiations and awkward wording reflecting these conflicting goals. For example, law is seldom perfectly certain, and where it is not lawyers should provide clients a sense of the relevant probabilities. ABA Model Rule 2.1, which requires lawyers to "exercise independent professional judgment and render candid advice," would seem to require as much.[4] Some clients may want a verbal report of the probabilities but not want to see the probabilities recounted in a letter; recounting a low probability that the client's actions are lawful might weaken the letter to the point of uselessness even if the lawyer subjectively believed in the opinion rendered. A lawyer likely discharges his duties by providing honest verbal advice (so long as the letter says or implies nothing to the contrary) but may want the qualification recounted in the letter anyway, as a way of managing his own financial risk.

Similarly, there often is a difference between the answer that is legally most correct (or least flawed) and an answer that can be supported by rational argument. Clients may want to take the most aggressive supportable position and may ask for a letter marking that boundary rather than a letter stating the most probable interpretation of the law. Comment 3 to Model Rule 2.1 may be relevant here; it provides that at least experienced clients may ask for purely technical advice and the lawyer may provide it without amplification.

Such considerations have played a role in arguments regarding memoranda relating to the treatment of prisoners written by lawyers in the Office of Legal Counsel (OLC), a department within the United States Department of Justice. The OLC interprets laws for the executive branch and sometimes for agencies. An OLC interpretation is binding in the sense that the Department of Justice will not prosecute an official for acting in accordance with the OLC's interpretation of a law, even if others in the Department of Justice, or new lawyers appointed after an election, disagree with that interpretation.

In 2001 and 2002, OLC lawyers were asked to opine on laws relevant to the government's response to the September 11, 2001 terrorist attacks on New York and Washington. The opinions took the form of memoranda from the Assistant Attorney General for the Office of Legal Counsel, Jay Bybee (now a judge on the Court of Appeals for the Ninth Circuit). Two such memoranda, dated August 1, 2002, illustrate some of the tensions relevant to advising clients. Each memorandum addressed interrogation techniques. The first memorandum responded to a request from the CIA "regarding the contours of the torture statute. This inquiry was prompted by the arrest of Abu Zubaydah. The CIA represented that Zubaydah was one of the highest ranking members of the al Qaeda terrorist organiza-

[4] The Daugerdas letter might seem to be an example of a probabilistic opinion—it opined only at the "more likely than not" level of certainty—but it is a bad example because the lawyers allegedly knew that they were facilitating an unlawful scheme and thus that the level of certainty they stated was false.

tion."[5] The CIA later requested an opinion on specific interrogation techniques it was considering. That request produced the second memorandum.[6]

The first memorandum was entitled "Standards of Conduct for Interrogation Under 18 U.S.C. §§ 2340–2340A." It recites that the OLC was asked for its opinion of "the standards of conduct under the Convention Against Torture and Other Cruel, Inhuman and Degrading Treatment or Punishment as implemented by Sections 2340–2340A of title 18 of the United States Code. 18 U.S.C. § 2340A makes torture a criminal act. 18 U.S.C. § 2340(1) defines torture to mean

> an act committed by a person acting under the color of law specifically intended to inflict severe physical or mental pain or suffering (other than pain or suffering incidental to lawful sanctions) upon another person within his custody or physical control.

18 U.S.C. § 2340(2) defines "severe mental pain or suffering" to mean:

> the prolonged mental harm caused by or resulting from—
>
> (A) the intentional infliction or threatened infliction of severe physical pain or suffering;
>
> (B) the administration or application, or threatened administration or application, of mind-altering substances or other procedures calculated to disrupt profoundly the senses or the personality;
>
> (C) the threat of imminent death; or
>
> (D) the threat that another person will imminently be subjected to death, severe physical pain or suffering, or the administration or application of mind-altering substances or other procedures calculated to disrupt profoundly the senses or personality; and

The memorandum, written in significant part by OLC attorney (and Berkeley Law professor) John Yoo, concluded:

> For an act to constitute torture as defined in Section 2340, it must inflict pain that is difficult to endure. Physical pain amounting to torture must be equivalent in intensity to the pain accompanying serious physical injury, such as organ failure, impairment of bodily function, or even death. For purely mental pain or suffering to amount to torture under Section 2340, it must result in significant psychological

---

[5] David Margolis, Memorandum for the Attorney General [&] the Deputy Attorney General, January 5, 2010 at 3.

[6] Margolis noted:

> the unclassified Bybee memo and the classified Bybee memo should be read together because these memos were intended to address the specific techniques discussed in the classified Bybee memo. Although the unclassified Bybee memo was capable of broad application, the classified Bybee memo addressed specific techniques applied to a specific individual under specific circumstances and advised the CIA, "If these facts were to change, this advice would not necessarily apply.

> harm of significant duration, e.g., lasting for months or even years. We conclude that the mental harm also must result from one of the predicate acts listed in the statute, namely: threats of imminent death; threats of infliction of the kind of pain that would amount to physical torture; infliction of such physical pain as a means of psychological torture; use of drugs or other procedures designed to deeply disrupt the senses, or fundamentally alter an individual's personality; or threatening to do any of these things to a third party.

As the opinion stated, the key statutory phrase in the definition of torture is the statement that acts are torture if they cause "severe physical or mental pain or suffering." Much of the criticism of the memorandum was directed at its reliance on a different statute that used the term "severe pain":

> Significantly, the phrase "severe pain" appears in statutes defining an emergency medical condition for the purpose of providing health benefits. . . . These statutes define an emergency condition as one "manifesting itself by acute symptoms of sufficient severity (including *severe pain)* such that a prudent lay person, who possesses an average knowledge of health and medicine, could reasonably expect the absence of immediate medical attention to result in—placing the health of the individual . . . (i) in serious jeopardy, (ii) serious impairment to bodily functions, or (iii) serious dysfunction of any bodily organ or part." [citation omitted] Although these statutes address a substantially different subject from Section 2340, they are nonetheless helpful for understanding what constitutes severe physical pain. They treat severe pain as an indicator of ailments that are likely to result in permanent and serious physical damage in the absence of immediate medical treatment. Such damage must rise to the level of death, organ failure, or the permanent impairment of a significant body function. These statutes suggest that "severe pain," as used in Section 2340, must rise to a similarly high level—the level that would ordinarily be associated with a sufficiently serious physical condition or injury such as death, organ failure, or serious impairment of body functions—in order to constitute torture.

Georgetown Professor David Luban has criticized the memorandum sharply on several grounds. Among these were:

> The memo ignored inconvenient Supreme Court precedents, misrepresented sources, and pulled the "organ failure or death" standard out of a Medicare statute on emergency medical conditions. . . . The Medicare statute lists severe pain as a possible symptom of a medical emergency, and Mr. Yoo flips the statute and uses the language of medical emergency to define severe pain. This was so bizarre that the OLC itself disowned his definition a few months after it became public. It is highly unusual for one OLC opinion to disown

> an earlier one, and it shows just how far out of the mainstream Mr. Yoo had wandered.

In a blog post Professor Luban elaborated on this reasoning:

> the fundamental trick used by the torture lawyers [was] pretending that the legal definition of 'torture' is something technical rather than "colloquial." Because it's technical, only lawyers can figure out what it means, using The Powerful Methods Of Legal Analysis.
>
> This is nonsense. The core definition of torture in both the U.S. torture statute and the Convention Against Torture is intentional infliction of "severe physical or mental pain or suffering." That's not a narrow or technical definition (although Congress went on to give a narrow definition to the mental pain or suffering part). . . . [Professor Luban surveyed four dictionary definitions of "torture" and concluded] the colloquial meaning of 'torture' is virtually the same as the legal definition. . . .
>
> In short: the fundamental trick really is nothing but a trick. The legal definition IS the colloquial definition. . . .
>
> The most famous use of this fundamental trick is in the Bybee Memo's notorious "organ failure or death" definition of "severe pain." "Severe pain" is of course a vague phrase, because there is no sharp boundary between pain that is severe and pain that is merely bothersome. But there's a difference between vague and obscure. "Severe pain" is not an obscure term, because everyone who has ever given birth to a baby, gotten kicked in the wrong place playing sports, broken a bone, or slipped a disc knows what it is.
>
> What about organ failure or death? Well, um, none of the living can report on the pain of death. And very few among us know what organ failure feels like. By using the fundamental trick, the Bybee Memo was able to ignore the colloquial meaning and make it seem as if "severe pain" is a technical term. Under the guise of providing interrogators with a workable test of the vague term "severe," Yoo and Bybee substituted a "technical" definition that only the dead could use.

David Luban, *The Fundamental Trick: Pretending That "Torture" is a Technical Term:* http://balkin.blogspot.com/2010/02/fundamental-trick-pretending-that.html (reprinted by permission of the author).

More generally, in his testimony Professor Luban argued that the memorandum wrongly tried to justify a position President Bush's administration wanted to take rather than simply informing the administration of what the law is (and was):

> There is a common misperception that lawyers are always supposed to spin the law in favor of their clients. That's simply not true. It is

true that in a courtroom, lawyers are supposed to argue for the interpretation of law that most favors their client. The lawyer on the other side argues the opposite, and the judge who hears the strongest case from both sides can reach a better decision.

But matters are completely different when a lawyer is giving a client advice about what the law means. Now there is nobody arguing the other side, and no judge to sort it out. For that reason, legal ethics rules require the lawyer-advisor to give an independent and candid opinion of what the law really requires. The ABA emphasizes that "a lawyer should not be deterred from giving candid advice by the prospect that the advice will be unpalatable to the client."

This is common sense. Otherwise, clients might go to their lawyers to say, "Give me an opinion that says I can do what I want"—and then duck responsibility by saying, "My lawyer told me it was legal." Then we would have a perfect Teflon circle: the lawyer says "I was just doing what my client instructed" and the client says "I was just doing what my lawyer approved.". . . . .

The authors [of the memo] may believe their conclusions represent the law as it should be. But the job of a legal opinion is to advise the client on the law as it is. If that dissuades the client from doing something the client wants to do, so be it. . . . The lawyer's job is emphatically not to enable clients to defy law by interpreting it oddly.

Testimony of David Luban Before the House Judiciary Committee, Subcommittee on the Constitution, Civil Rights, and Civil Liberties *Hearing on: "From the Department of Justice to Guantanamo Bay: Administration Lawyers and Administration Interrogation Rules, Part I"* May 6, 2008.[7]

For his part, Professor Yoo has written that the hard question facing the OLC lawyers was:

what interrogation measures fell short of the torture ban and could be used against al Qaeda leaders. . . . would limiting a captured terrorist to six hours' sleep, isolating him, interrogating him for several hours, or requiring him to exercise constitute "severe physical pain or suffering"?. . . .

Because the federal antitorture law used words rare in the federal code, no prosecutions had been brought under it, and it had never been interpreted by a federal court. We wrote the memo to give the executive branch guidance on these specifics. . . . .

OLC interpreted "severe" as a level of pain "equivalent in intensity to the pain accompanying serious physical injury, such as death, organ

[7] Professor Luban elaborates on these points and adds additional support for them in testimony before the Senate Senate Judiciary Committee, Subcommittee on Administrative Oversight and the Courts Hearing: "What Went Wrong: Torture and the Office of Legal Counsel in the Bush Administration" May 13, 2009.

> failure, or serious impairment of bodily functions." Many critics don't like this interpretation, preferring that it encompass more.
>
> OLC's first 2002 opinion did not make up this definition out of thin air. It applied a standard technique used to interpret ambiguous phrases in law. When Congress does not define its terms, courts commonly look in the United States Code for the use of similar language. The only other place where similar words appear is in a law defining health benefits for emergency medical conditions. . . . obviously, Congress's terminology here was not exactly on point, but it was the closest Congress had come to defining severe pain. It was an illustration of severe pain, not an effort to limit its definition.
>
> The point of the 2002 memo was to give clear guidance on the state of the law, not to give the administration political cover, much less paint a pretty picture for a broad range of sensibilities. . . .
>
> It should be clearly understood that neither the August 2002 memo nor the Justice Department advocated or recommended torture or any other interrogation tactics. Rather, OLC addressed this question: What is the meaning of "torture" under the federal criminal laws?
>
> The 2002 memo was, in effect, rewritten in 2004 to take out language about what torture was or wasn't, to placate the sensibilities of those who didn't like seeing the law of torture and harsh interrogation even discussed. Nothing of substance about the law had changed.

John Yoo, WAR BY OTHER MEANS 171–74 (2006) (reprinted in edited form by permission of the author).

Controversy over the memoranda prompted an investigation by the Department of Justice Office of Professional Responsibility (OPR). OPR prepared a draft report and delivered it to the Attorney General on December 23, 2008. OPR originally planned to release the report publicly on January 12, 2009.[8] It then received from Attorney General Michael Mukasey criticism regarding both the process of completing the report and the substance of the report. In response OPR prepared a second draft; it gave the draft to Bybee and Yoo and invited them to respond. OPR issued its final report in July 2009. The report found that "John Yoo and Jay Bybee engaged in professional misconduct by failing to provide 'thorough, candid, and objective' analysis in memoranda regarding the interrogation of detained terrorist suspects."[9]

The OPR report then went to Associate Deputy Attorney General David Margolis. In January 2010 he issued a final report that declined to

---

[8] The relevant parties disagreed about whether OPR planned to give Bybee and Yoo the opportunity to review the report and respond to its findings, though the final report on the matter concluded OPR did not plan to provide a draft of the report to Bybee and Yoo before releasing it publicly.

[9] Margolis Report at 1.

adopt the OPR findings. Margolis discussed several issues relevant to opinion letter practice and to advising clients more generally. One of those issues pertains to interpretation of Model Rule 2.1, mentioned above. In its second draft report, the OPR found Bybee and Yoo "failed to fulfill their duty to exercise independent legal judgment and to render candid legal advice, pursuant to D.C. Rule of Professional Conduct 2.1."[10] OPR described its Rule 2.1 analysis as follows:

> Although a number of courts have found attorneys to have violated Rule 2.1, the reported decisions and professional literature provided little guidance for application of the standard in this context. We therefore approached our Rule 2.1 analysis by considering, as a threshold matter, whether there was evidence that the client desired a particular result or outcome, and whether the attorney was aware of the desired result. If so, we looked for the following acts or omissions by the attorney, all of which we considered evidence that the attorney failed to meet the obligations of Rule 2.1:
>
> 1. Exaggerating or misstating the significance of authority that supported the desired result;
>
> 2. Ignoring adverse authority or failing to discuss it accurately and fairly;
>
> 3. Using convoluted and counterintuitive arguments to support the desired result,while ignoring more straightforward and reasonable arguments contrary to the desired result;
>
> 4. Adopting inconsistent reasoning or arguments to favor the desired result;
>
> 5. Advancing frivolous or erroneous arguments to support the desired result.
>
> OPR first draft at 126–27; OPR second draft at 134–35.[11]

Both Bybee and Yoo "objected to OPR's consideration of the 'threshold matter' of whether the attorneys were aware of the result that the client wanted."[12] They each argued "lawyers almost always know which answer to a legal question is consistent with the wishes of the client."[13] Bybee cited a document stating "guiding principles" for OLC lawyers, which several former lawyers had endorsed in 2004. This document stated that " '[a]lthough OLC's legal determinations should not seek simply to legitimate the policy preferences of the administration of which it is a part, *OLC must take account of the administration's goals and assist in their accomplishment within the law.'* Guiding Principles at 5 (emphasis

[10] *Id.* at 13.

[11] Quoted in Margolis Report at 13–14.

[12] *Id.* at 14.

[13] *Id.*

added)."[14] Margolis noted that "[i]n the final report, OPR (correctly, I believe) no longer characterized the attorney's knowledge of the client's desired result as a threshold matter under its Rule 2.1 analysis."[15] With regard to Model Rule 2.1, Margolis concluded

> The requirement in Rule 2.1 that an attorney exercise independent professional judgment must be read in conjunction with other obligations of the attorney and cannot mean that the attorney is supposed to exercise judgment independent of the client's objectives, but rather that the attorney should not provide dishonest advice to satisfy the client's objectives nor should the attorney provide advice when the attorney is encumbered by a conflicting personal interest or an inappropriate relationship with the client.[16]

With respect to memorandum's use of the Medicare statutes, Margolis reasoned:

> [T]he memo does not define "severe pain" as strictly limited to incidents resulting in organ failure or death. Rather, the memo advised that severe pain must rise to a "similarly high level," and that victims must suffer pain that is *"of the kind* that is *equivalent to* the pain that would be associated with serious physical injury so severe that death, organ failure, or permanent damage resulting in a loss of significant body function will likely result." (emphasis added). These qualifiers do not help much and could have been clearer, but the memo read carefully does not authorize interrogators to engage in any behavior that does not *in fact* cause serious physical injury, organ failure or death. More importantly, this definition was accompanied by the approval of specific techniques in the classified Bybee memo, and approval of the use of specific techniques to interrogate Zubaydah was the immediate purpose of the CIA's inquiry.[17]

Thus, Margolis found that "[w]hile the unclassified Bybee memo was not particularly helpful, I find that its issuance to a limited audience in conjunction with the narrower memo evidences a performance deficiency, but does not amount to professional misconduct."[18]

[14] *Id.* at 14–15. The Margolis report also cited an OPR interview with former OLC attorney Dan Levin, who was asked "Is it implicit in a situation like this that you're trying to accommodate the client?" He responded, "Well, I think you're always trying to find a legal way for them to do what they want to do."

[15] *Id.*

[16] *Id.* at 26. Elsewhere Margolis noted that the D.C. equivalent to Model Rule 1.2(d) was more directly applicable to the OPR's criticisms of the memoranda. *Id.* at 22. The D.C. rule states: "A lawyer shall not counsel a client to engage, or assist a client, in conduct-that the lawyer knows is criminal or fraudulent, but a lawyer may discuss the legal consequences of any proposed course of conduct with a client and may counselor assist a client to make a good-faith effort to determine the validity, scope, meaning, or application of the law."

[17] Margolis Report at 33.

[18] *Id.* at 34.

Margolis concluded by distinguishing good performance from misconduct. He cautioned:

> my decision not to adopt OPR's misconduct finding should not be misread as an endorsement of the subjects' efforts. OPR's analytical framework permits a finding of poor judgment when
>
> > a Department attorney chooses a course of action that is in marked contrast to the action that the Department may reasonably expect an attorney exercising good judgment to take. Poor judgment differs from professional misconduct in that an attorney may act inappropriately and thus exhibit poor judgment even though he or she may not have violated or acted in reckless disregard of a clear obligation or standard.
>
> I have found that Yoo and Bybee did not violate a clear obligation or standard. However, as I have noted, the standard that OPR identified is consistent with the action that the Department reasonably expects of its attorneys. In contradiction of that high standard, the unclassified Bybee memo consistently took an expansive view of executive authority and narrowly construed the torture statute while often failing to expose (much less refute) countervailing arguments and overstating the certainty of its conclusions. Even though the memorandum was intended for a limited audience, Yoo and Bybee certainly could have foreseen that the memorandum would someday be exposed to a broader audience, and their failure to provide a more balanced analysis of the issues created doubts about the *bona fides* of their conclusions. I appreciate . . . [that] the task at hand [was] to identify the line and not to build in a margin of comfort inside the line. However, this task did not necessarily demand a memorandum devoid of nuance, and I believe primarily that the unclassified Bybee memorandum overstates the certainty of its conclusions in a way the represents a "marked contrast to the action that the Department may reasonably expect an attorney exercising good judgment to take." Thus, I conclude that Yoo and Bybee exercised poor judgment by overstating the certainty of their conclusions and underexposing countervailing arguments."[19]

PROBLEM 8–10

One criticism of the OPR's draft report was that it failed to take into account that Bybee and Yoo were working: (i) at the request of the CIA; (ii) less than a year after the September 11, 2001 attacks and at a time when the level of intelligence "chatter" was "consistent with that which preceded" those attacks; (iii) to define the boundaries of the statute criminalizing torture with

---

[19] *Id.* at 68.

respect to imminent interrogation of a person described as an al Quaeda leader; (iv) who, the CIA was certain, had information he refused to divulge; (v) pertaining to terrorist networks overseas and plans to conduct future attacks against the United States or its interests. Should those facts matter in assessing the performance of Bybee and Yoo? If so, why? (Do they change the meaning of the law?) If not, why not?

PROBLEM 8–11

One defense of the memoranda was that they stated Bybee and Yoo's honest belief of what the torture statute and that other issues, such as whether lawful acts were nevertheless inhumane or would undermine America's standing in the world community, were issues of policy, not law. On this view, if the statute did not preclude "waterboarding" then Bybee and Yoo had no obligation, or indeed any special competence, to discuss the morality or desirability of the practice, or the practical consequences of using such a tactic. Do you agree with this view? Why or why not? How does your answer to this problem compare to your answer to Problem 7–10?

PROBLEM 8–12

Suppose David Luban is right to say the legal definition of torture and the colloquial definition of torture are the same. (That is, that legally torture means "severe physical or mental pain or suffering.") Using that definition, how would you advise CIA officials on what they could and could not do when interrogating persons suspected of, or suspected to have knowledge of, terrorist acts?

The Main Points to Recall From Chapter 8 Are:

- Lawyers may assume duties to third parties in addition to their clients; in such cases they must fulfill both sets of duties.
- The three most common ways lawyers assume such duties are based on (i) reliance by the third party invited by the lawyer or by the client with the lawyer's knowledge; (ii) the client's intention that the lawyer's services benefit the third party; (iii) in some cases in some jurisdictions, the client's status as a fiduciary owing duties to the third party.
- In dealing with third parties, lawyers also are subject to general legal rules, such as prohibitions on deceit.
- Regardless of third-party liability concerns, lawyers may not help clients commit unlawful acts.

- Lawyers cannot escape liability by sticking their heads in the sand to avoid problematic knowledge; willful ignorance of facts counts as knowledge of those facts.
- Lawyers may not assist clients in committing unlawful acts, but may advise clients with regard to good faith challenges to law.

CHAPTER 9

ASSUMING DUTIES

■ ■ ■

The relationship between lawyers and clients is based on assent. *See* Restatement (Second) Agency § 15 ("An agency relation exists only if there has been a manifestation by the principal to the agent that the agent may act on his account, and consent by the agent so to act."). Lawyers assume duties to clients through acts that give clients reason to believe the lawyer agrees to assume duties.

Though the lawyer-client relationship rests on assent it does not rest on formal contract law. The Restatement (Second) of Agency § 16 states that "[t]he relation of principal and agent can be created although neither party receives consideration." This fact means that payment of fees is neither a necessary nor a sufficient condition to create duties running from a lawyer to a client. It is not necessary because a lawyer may owe duties to a person who has no obligation to pay; it is not sufficient because a third party, such as an insurance company, may pay a lawyer to represent someone else. And, as mentioned earlier, agency principles are in some cases modified to take into account the social context in which lawyers deal with others, particularly clients.

Like the "bundle of sticks" you probably heard about in your property course, duties are not an all-or-nothing thing. Lawyers may assume all the duties a lawyer owes a client by agreeing to represent the client. Lawyers can also assume some duties without assuming others, however. For example, a lawyer who agrees to receive a confidence assumes a duty to protect that confidence. A lawyer who gives advice, with or without receiving a confidence, owes a duty of care to the extent of that advice.

The basic rule for assuming duties is that a lawyer owes a duty of confidentiality where she accepts confidential information in circumstances justifying the client in believing that she will keep the information confidential. If such a duty is formed it implies a duty of loyalty pertaining to the confidences—i.e., not to use them for the lawyer's gain. A lawyer assumes a duty of care to the extent she gives advice or reasonably may be perceived as having done so. *See, e.g., People ex rel Department of Corporations v. SpeeDee Oil Change Systems, Inc.*, 20 Cal.4th 1135 (1999).

Lawyers sometimes owe duties to persons who are not yet their clients but whose interests a lawyer seeks to represent. Class actions are the most common example. A class does not technically exist until a court certifies a case as a class action. Nevertheless, it is common to see courts say things such as that it is "well established that by asserting a representative role on behalf of a proposed class, representative plaintiffs and their counsel voluntarily accept a fiduciary obligation towards members of the putative class. Such a fiduciary obligation exists even before the class has been certified." *In re M & F Worldwide Corp. Shareholders Litig.*, 799 A.2d 1164, 1174 n.34 (Del. Ch. 2002). *See also Masztal v. City of Miami*, 971 So.2d 803, 808 (Fla.App. 2007).

Model Rule 1.18(a) defines a "prospective client" as a person who discusses a matter with a lawyer with an eye toward possibly forming an attorney-client relationship with that lawyer. The definition does not require that the relationship actually be formed, and we begin with that situation.

Restatement (Third) of the Law Governing Lawyers §§ 14–15
Model Rule of Professional Conduct § 1.18

A. DUTY OF CONFIDENTIALITY

1. CONFIDENCES RECEIVED FROM PROSPECTIVE CLIENTS WHO DON'T HIRE YOU

Sometimes clients shop around for lawyers. That is particularly likely to happen when the client is sophisticated and the matter at issue is important. One form of shopping involves what is often called a "beauty contest." A client will invite a few firms to interview for the job at hand. During these interviews, of course, the lawyers need to find out enough about the matter to give the client a sense of how the lawyer would approach it.

What is the status of information exchanged in such interviews? Model Rule 1.18 treats the client as a "prospective client" and prohibits counsel from revealing the information or using it except as permitted by Rule 1.9, the rule governing subsequent conflicts of interest. (Rule 1.18 is easier on lawyers than Rule 1.9 because Rule 1.18(c) provides for disqualification only when a lawyer receives from a prospective client information that could harm the prospective client significantly in the matter at hand.)

This rule presents the risk that a lawyer might be disqualified from representing a client who would like to hire her because she interviewed with a client who hired somebody else. In practical terms, this means a lawyer might lose a potentially lucrative case because of an interview from which she earned nothing.

That is what happened in *Bridge Products, Inc. v. Quantum Chem. Corp.*, 1990 WL 70857 (N.D. Ill. 1990). Bridge Products had to change lawyers while it was in litigation against Quantum. Bridge interviewed four firms, including Sidley & Austin. Bridge ultimately hired the firm of Katten, Muchin & Zavis. Here is the court's description of the interaction between Sidley and Bridge:

> There were two contacts of substance between Bridge and Sidley. The first of these was a telephone conversation between Deborah Stonebraker, Bridge's general counsel and Vice President of Legal Affairs, and James Cahan, a partner at Sidley. Stonebraker explained that Bridge was seeking new outside counsel to represent it in this case and gave Cahan a brief synopsis of the case's underlying facts and procedural status. It was decided to pursue the matter further and a meeting was scheduled for August 11, 1989. In the meantime, Sidley obtained the court file in the case in order to better prepare for the meeting.
>
> On the appointed date, Stonebraker and Bridge's chief executive officer, Edwin C. Parker, met with Cahan and another partner in Sidley's environmental group, J. Andrew Schlickman. The meeting lasted slightly over one hour. The parties of course discussed the status of the litigation as well as its underlying facts in great detail. But this was not all. Since the property at issue in this case is located in the state of Virginia, Bridge had also retained the services of the Virginia firm known as Hunton & Williams to represent it before the Virginia as well as the federal environmental protection agencies. Stonebraker and Parker state in sworn affidavits that they disclosed to Sidley some of their privileged communications to Hunton & Williams as well as some of Hunton & Williams' findings and plans regarding the strategy that was to be taken in dealing with the regulatory agencies. In addition, Bridge divulged information concerning (1) its own view as to proper trial strategy; (2) its opinion of Quantum as well as Quantum's view of the case; and (3) its conversations with Gardner regarding settlement as well as what Bridge was prepared to accept. Quantum does not dispute that this information was in fact divulged. Lastly, Parker and Stonebraker sought an initial opinion from Sidley with respect to how it thought the case had been handled so far and how, in general, Sidley would pursue the matter if hired. Sidley, in fact, did offer some preliminary observations along with advice and the meeting was adjourned.
>
> At the meeting, Sidley did nothing at all to indicate that the information that it was receiving from Parker and Stonebraker would not be held in confidence, or that it might be used against Bridge if it did not officially retain Sidley as outside litigation counsel. Indeed, Schlickman and Cahan informed Parker and Stonebraker that they

had already performed a conflicts check and that Bridge was clear. Finally, although the issue was not discussed, Bridge did not condition the August 11th meeting on Sidley's agreement not to bill the time. Parker and Stonebraker engaged in similar interviews on behalf of Bridge with McDermott, Will & Emory, Baker & McKenzie, and Katten, Muchin & Zavis.

Several months after Bridge hired the Katten, Muchin firm, Quantum also had to hire new counsel. It ultimately hired Sidley & Austin. Bridge then moved to disqualify Sidley based on the interview described above. The court granted the motion. Here are some excerpts from its opinion:

"[T]here was no formal attorney/client relationship between Bridge and Sidley. The parties never entered into an actual agreement, and Bridge never paid Sidley any money for its services. This, however, is far from conclusive because Bridge can still prove that there was an implicit attorney/client relationship which derived from the nature of the parties' interview. . . . a party seeking to establish an "implied attorney/client relationship" must demonstrate that (1) he "submitted confidential information to a lawyer," and (2) that he did so "with the reasonable belief that the lawyer was acting as the party's attorney." . . .

With respect to the first prong of the test, we conclude that confidential information was actually disclosed to Sidley by Bridge. The affidavits of Parker and Stonebraker initially establish, in part, that Bridge disclosed to Sidley its innermost strategies and desires regarding settlement, and some of the privileged communications it had had with both Gardner, Carton & Douglas and Hunton & Williams.

Sidley does not refute that these communications were made. Instead, it makes three counter arguments which attempt to negate the confidentiality of the information. First, it argues that the Parker and Stonebraker affidavits are too vague to prove the confidentiality of the information. Second, Sidley takes the position that any confidentiality in these communications was destroyed by the fact that Bridge, through its attorney Gardner, had already made many disclosures to Quantum concerning most aspects of the litigation. And third, Sidley argues that, in any event, confidentiality was destroyed by the fact that Parker and Stonebraker made similar disclosures to Gardner's other potential replacements, and not just Sidley. These arguments all fail, however.

Contrary to Quantum's first argument, Bridge's affidavits are sufficient to establish prima facie confidentiality. . . . "[i]t would defeat the very purpose of the disqualification motion—preserving client confidence—if in order to obtain disqualification any client were forced to reveal what had earlier been told to his or her lawyer." *Donohoe v. Consolidated Operating & Prod. Corp.,* 691 F.Supp. 109, 112 (N.D.Ill.1988). Thus, quoting the confidential disclosures is unnecessary. Rather, Bridge must merely raise an evidentiary inference that actual confidences were disclosed. . . .

Second, the fact that Bridge and Gardner had already made many disclosures to Quantum about the condition of the site and the possibility of settlement does not destroy confidentiality. As Bridge correctly points out in its reply, such disclosures were all made within the context of an adversarial proceeding. Quantum's affidavits do nothing to show that Gardner gave away Bridge's entire strategy simply by making specific disclosures regarding certain matters in conducting settlement negotiations.

Finally, the fact that Bridge made similar disclosures in interviews with three other law firms also does not destroy confidentiality. There is no indication that Bridge did not expect the same confidentiality to attach to these disclosures. Moreover, as will be discussed below, the law firms, including Sidley, could easily have avoided an implied attorney/client relationship had they wished to do so. . . .

The second prong of the test asks whether the confidential information was disclosed with the reasonable belief that there was an attorney/client relationship. We conclude that it was.

Sidley's argument on this prong focuses on the context of the meeting. In this regard, it asks us to view the August 11th meeting as part of a mere "beauty contest." Having apparently failed the swimsuit competition, Sidley does not wish to be saddled with the ethical encumbrances of an attorney/client relationship for which it never received any money.

The focus, however, must be on what Bridge, and not Sidley, reasonably believed. Sidley was one that knew of the ethics rules, and thus it was Sidley that was responsible for making clear to Bridge that the initial meeting was purely preliminary and that confidences would not necessarily be protected. This it did not do. Sidley did not have Bridge sign a conflicts waiver; this would have put Bridge on notice with respect to making confidential disclosures. Sidley did not even indicate whether Bridge would be billed for the meeting; such knowledge would also have made Bridge more wary of making indiscriminate disclosures. Thus, it is Sidley, and not Bridge, who must pay for this confusion by being deemed part of an implicit professional relationship and all the ethical responsibilities arising therefrom. . . . [1] [The court went on to hold that the mat-

[1] FN1. Quantum's reliance on *B.F. Goodrich Co. v. Formosa Plastics Corp.,* 638 F.Supp. 1050 (S.D.Tex.1986), is misplaced. There, the court first found that the preliminary interview at issue did not lead to a *direct* attorney/client relationship on the undisputed facts. Quantum cites this portion of the *Goodrich* case for the proposition that an initial interview will not lead to an *implicit* attorney/client relationship. Quantum's position, however, is undermined by the very next portion of the *Goodrich* opinion. Thus, the court continues: "The fact that the attorney-client

ters were substantially related and the Sidley firm's efforts to screen the affected attorneys did not preclude disqualification.]

In cases such as this, however, the law firms who are participating in interviews with the goal of obtaining new business are far from helpless. By putting their prospective clients on notice that there is no attorney/client relationship as yet, they can avoid the possibility of having one imposed on them by law because of the potential client's misperception about the safety of their confidential disclosures. Of course a law firm who is selling itself to a prospective client with the greatest of zeal will not find it easy to insert disclaimers into the all-important interview, but if it fails to do so in the interest of heightening its sales pitch, this court, at least, finds that it must live with the consequences, including potential disqualification in the future. We find our approach to be more faithful to Seventh Circuit precedent as well as the better rule of law. . . . For the foregoing reasons, the plaintiff's motion to disqualify Sidley & Austin from representing the defendant in this litigation on conflict-of-interest grounds is granted. It is so ordered."

With this in mind, how should you handle initial interviews? (One obvious point, which we will study in detail in chapter 11, is that you should never participate in an interview until you have run a conflicts check and determined that you could take the case if hired.)

It's not that I don't like you,
I just that like other people too—. . . .

The principles reflected in Bridge *present a dilemma for lawyers. On the one hand, if you are in an interview you want to impress the prospective client and win the job. To do that, you want to gain the client's trust and confidence. This interest gives you an incentive to accept confidences from the client and to use those confidences as the basis for demonstrating how you would handle the case.*

On the other hand, if the client picks someone else, as happened in Bridge, *you would not want the unsuccessful interview to prevent you from obtaining future business. As the opinion points out, you can struc-*

---

relationship had not yet been established does not mean that the . . . firm owed no duty whatever to Goodrich." *Id.* at 1052. The court goes on to set forth the criteria for the implied attorney/client relationship as espoused by the Seventh Circuit. While the *Goodrich* court ultimately concluded that there was no such implicit relationship on the facts of that case, that conclusion was based not on any inference drawn from the preliminarity of the negotiations, but rather on the finding that no actual confidences were divulged to the law firm.

ture the interview to keep this option open. You could have the prospective client sign a conflict waiver, or even just an acknowledgment that you disavow any duty of confidentiality with respect to the meeting, so that the prospective client understands that you reserve the right to use or disclose the information as you see fit. Neither of these steps will tend to make the prospective client trust you or rely on you.

Beauty contests therefore require you to calibrate your interests and make your position clear to the prospective client. As the Bridge opinion notes, absent some action on your part, the default assumption in such cases is that the client will expect you to keep confidential what is said in the interview. Courts will vindicate the reliance interests this assumption generates by preventing you from using or disclosing information, including by granting motions to disqualify, as happened in Bridge.

For further discussion of confidentiality in the beauty contest context, see Formal Opinion 2006–2 of the Committee on Professional and Judicial Ethics of the Association of the Bar of the City of New York (following Restatement § 15 and Model Rule 1.18 to conclude that a duty of confidentiality attaches unless the lawyer obtains a waiver, the information disclosed would not cause significant harm to the client, or the client acted strategically to taint the lawyer).

Similar issues may come up when an entity has a problem caused by allegations against a constituent. The constituent may believe entity counsel represents him and, if there is a reasonable basis for that belief, counsel may be disqualified from acting adversely to the constituent. *Perez v. Kirk & Carrigan*, 822 S.W.2d 261 (Tex.App. 1991), which you read in chapter 5.B, is such a case. If the constituent does not provide confidential information to counsel or receive advice from counsel, however, courts typically will deny a motion to disqualify. *See Harris v. Dillman*, 2008 WL 2694753 (E.D. Cal. 2008) (school superintendent who discussed allegations against him with counsel for district was not represented where he did not disclose confidential information or receive advice from counsel).

---

2. INTERNET COMMUNICATIONS

BARTON V. UNITED STATES DISTRICT COURT

410 F.3d 1104 (9th Cir. 2005)

KLEINFELD, CIRCUIT JUDGE.

We grant a writ of mandamus to prevent disclosure of communications by prospective clients to their lawyers.

Facts.

Plaintiffs sued SmithKline Beecham Corporation, which does business as GlaxoSmithKline. They claim injury from Paxil, a medication manufactured by SmithKline. Plaintiffs did not initiate contact with their lawyers by walking into the law office. Instead, the law firm posted a questionnaire on the internet, seeking information about potential class members for a class action the law firm contemplated.[2] The district court ordered plaintiffs to produce the four plaintiffs' answers to the questionnaire. Plaintiffs seek, and we grant, a writ of mandamus vacating the district court's order compelling production.

The law firm that now represents the plaintiffs posted a questionnaire relating to the antidepressant Paxil on the internet. Although the firm in its briefs calls the questionnaire an "intake" questionnaire, it did not call it that on the net. The law firm's presentation on the web does not say that those who answer the questionnaire are submitting themselves to the firm as potential clients.

The questionnaire is entitled "PAXIL WITHDRAWAL LITIGATION INITIAL CONTACT." Its introduction, in boldface, says that its purpose is "to gather information." The subject of the information is "potential class members," but responses are requested, not only from potential class members, but also from "loved ones" who would presumably include siblings, parents of adult children, and others who knew of another person's Paxil use, but who could not be plaintiffs in a lawsuit for damages from Paxil.[3]

---

[2] FN1. The district court did not certify a class. A large number of Paxil cases have been consolidated by the Judicial Panel on Multidistrict Litigation, with five plaintiffs, including the four who returned questionnaires, to go to trial first.

[3] FN4. The boldface text states, in full:

The purpose of this questionnaire is to gather information bout potential class members who have suffered withdrawal symptoms as a result of stopping the use of Paxil or decreasing the dose of Paxil in an effort to stop taking it. We will also use your contact information to keep you updated on developments of the litigation including whether a class is certified, either formally or for settlement purposes.

If you believe that you or a loved one has been adversely affected by GlaxoSmithKline, the makers of Paxil (generically known as Paroxetine), please fill out the form below:

The questionnaire asks for extensive information about use of Paxil and symptoms. At the end, it suggests that "you do not sign nor return" a form that GlaxoSmithKline might send requesting an authorization for release of medical records. Then, in order to cause the filled-out questionnaire to be emailed to the law firm, the person filling it out has to check a "yes" box. The "yes" box acknowledges that the questionnaire "does not constitute a request for legal advice and that I am not forming an attorney client relationship by submitting this information."[4]

The law firm, as it has acknowledged, was careful to avoid committing itself to an attorney-client relationship. It might (and did) receive many thousands of responses, and did not want to leave itself open to suits for malpractice to those who answered, such as for letting the statutes of limitations run.

More important than what the law firm intended is what the clients thought. Here, there is ambiguity. On the one hand, the form can be filled out by "a loved one" rather than by the potential client, and the person sending it in has to acknowledge that he is not requesting legal advice and is not forming an attorney client relationship by sending it in. The form also states that the person will not have retained an attorney until he signs a fee agreement and that "local counsel may be contacted for referral of this matter." The form states that its purpose is to "gather information about potential class members," not to consider accepting them as clients. On the other hand, the stated purpose of gathering "information about potential class members" suggests that the firm is indeed trolling for clients.

The manufacturer sought the four plaintiffs' questionnaires in discovery "to juxtapose against what they are now claiming in discovery to determine whether or not the two fit and whether there's any information that provides for fertile cross-examination at trial." The plaintiffs opposed production on the basis of the attorney-client privilege. No privilege relating to confidential medical disclosures is asserted, no doubt because the nature of the claims, damages from Paxil withdrawal, would make the medical information disclosed in the questionnaires discoverable, if the same questions were put fully to plaintiffs in interrogatories or depositions.

---

[4] FN5. The "yes" box acknowledgment states, in full:

I agree that the above does not constitute a request for legal advice and that I am not forming an attorney client relationship by submitting this information. I understand that I may only retain an attorney by entering into a fee agreement, and that I am not hereby entering into a fee agreement. I agree that any information that I will receive in response to the above questionnaire is general information and I will not be charged for a response to this submission. I further understand that the law for each state may vary, and therefore, I will not rely upon this information as legal advice. Since this matter may require advice regarding my home state, I agree that local counsel may be contacted for referral of this matter.

The district court concluded that the attorney-client privilege did not apply because the disclaimer established that the communications were not "confidential" and that checking the "yes" box waived the privilege. The district court acknowledged that under California law the privilege applied to pre-employment communications with an attorney by a prospective client with a view to employing the attorney. Although the district court did not label any part of its decision "findings of fact," its decision states that the law firm posted the questionnaire online to find potential clients, that the four individuals submitted answers "because they were seeking legal representation," and that as a result of submitting the questionnaires they obtained representation by the law firm.

What tipped the district court in favor of disclosure was the checked "yes box" disclaimer that included "I agree that the above does not constitute a request for legal advice and that I am not forming an attorney client relationship by submitting this information." The district court concluded that the plaintiffs' attorneys could not assert the attorney-client privilege against the defendants when they insisted on "a disclaimer of confidentiality" to protect themselves.

Analysis

. . . . What is "new" about the case is attorneys trolling for clients on the internet and obtaining there the kind of detailed information from large numbers of people that used to be provided only when a potential client physically came into a lawyer's office. Two things had to happen to bring this about: the change in law in the 1970s that permitted attorney advertising, and the sufficiently widespread use of the internet, within the past five or ten years, that makes internet advertising worthwhile. . . .

The first determination the district court made was whether, absent consideration of the disclaimer, the questionnaires were submitted "in the course of" an attorney-client relationship and thus ordinarily protected under California's attorney-client privilege. Concluding that they were, the district court next considered whether the disclaimer at the bottom of the questionnaire acted as a waiver of the protections afforded under the attorney-client privilege. This second step is where the district court clearly erred.

In considering the first step, the district court said that "[t]he four individuals who filled out the questionnaires, in turn, did so only because they were seeking legal representation with regard to the same matter. Indeed, by filling out the questionnaire, these four plaintiffs did, in fact, secure legal representation.". . . . It is not clear whether the district court intended the quoted sentence to be a finding of fact. If it did, then we would review it for clear error . . . . If it did not, we would come to the same conclusion ourselves.

That is not to say that the question whether the respondents were trying to secure legal services is without doubt. Arguing that they were is (1) the response of at least one of them that he was trying "to get in the class action," (2) the nature of the information they provided (detailed accounts of their psychological and physical symptoms and medical histories relating to Paxil), (3) the context of supplying information to lawyers who apparently were bringing a Paxil class action, and (4) the ultimate representation of these four plaintiffs. Arguing that they were not was (1) the elusive wording of the questionnaire, (2) the disclaimers, (3) the response of at least one of them that she was furnishing information and "if they needed me, call me," and (4) the law firm's statement that the lawyers were attempting to "gather information *about* potential class members," not that they were soliciting them as clients. The questionnaire is ambiguous, but the plaintiffs should not be penalized for the law firm's ambiguity. It is their privilege, not any right of the lawyers, that is at stake. A layman seeing the law firm's internet material would likely think he was being solicited as a potential client. In all likelihood, a very high proportion of questionnaire submitters completed the questionnaire "with a view to retention of" the law firm, and thus submitted them "in the course of" an attorney-client relationship.

Given this determination, a statement on the questionnaire that it is intended to be "confidential" is not required to protect the questionnaire from disclosure. Under California law, once it is determined that a communication was made in "the course of the lawyer-client" relationship, "the communication is presumed to have been made in confidence and the opponent of the claim of privilege has the burden of proof to establish that the communication was not confidential."

The opponent of the privilege in this case is GlaxoSmithKline, and it thus has the burden of showing that the answers to the questionnaires were not intended to be confidential. The district court found that GlaxoSmithKline had met this burden because of the disclaimer at the bottom of the questionnaire which disclaimed any formation of an attorney-client relationship. The district court clearly erred in treating the disclaimer of an attorney-client relationship as a disclaimer of confidentiality.

First, the district court based its conclusion on a misunderstanding that the law firm had made "a disclaimer of confidentiality." It did not. Neither the word "confidentiality" nor the substance of a disclaimer of confidentiality can be found in the online questionnaire. The text in the checked box to which the court referred is potentially confusing to clients (as their ambiguous responses suggest) and the law firm should have spoken clearly to the laymen to whom its website was addressed about what commitments it did and did not make. A risky and expensive trip to this court could have been avoided by a plain English explanation on the website. But the vagueness and ambiguity of the law firm's prose does not amount to a waiver of confidentiality by the client. Our focus is on the clients' right, not the lawyers.' And the words just do not say what the district court thought they said, that "confidentiality" was waived.

Second, the law in California requires that the attorney-client privilege apply, even though the plaintiffs filled out the questionnaires before the law firm represented them and with no assurance that it would. Under California law, a client's communication to a lawyer is confidential if made "in the course of that relationship," which by itself might seem to imply that communications prior to establishment of the relationship would not be privileged. But the phrase does not mean that the lawyer has to take the person on as a client before the privilege applies, because the word "client" is defined to mean a person who consults a lawyer for the purposes of "retaining the lawyer," "securing legal service," or securing "advice." All three can precede the lawyer's acceptance of the client.

The check box on the law firm's website protected the law firm by requiring the questionnaire submitter to disclaim a purpose of "request[ing] legal advice," and to acknowledge that the submitter is not "forming an attorney client relationship" by sending in the answers. But the box does not disclaim the purpose of "securing legal service." The questionnaire is designed so that a person filling it out and submitting it is likely to think that he is requesting that the law firm include him in the class action mentioned at the beginning of the form.

Prospective clients' communications with a view to obtaining legal services are plainly covered by the attorney-client privilege under California law, regardless of whether they have retained the lawyer, and regardless of whether they ever retain the lawyer. Under [*Beery v. State Bar*, 43 Cal. 3d 802 (1987)], "[t]he fiduciary relationship existing between lawyer and client extends to preliminary consultation by a prospective client with a view to retention of the lawyer, although actual employment does not result." Applying that principle, the California Supreme Court held in *Beery* that a lawyer was subject to discipline when a person, not then a client, came in to ask the lawyer about writing a will for him (but did not hire him to do it), and the lawyer talked the person into an investment that his fiduciary duty would prohibit him from selling to a client.

There is nothing anomalous about applying the privilege to such preliminary consultations. Without it, people could not safely bring their problems to lawyers unless the lawyers had already been retained. "The rationale for this rule is compelling," because "no person could ever safely consult an attorney for the first time with a view to his employment if the privilege depended on the chance of whether the attorney after hearing his statement of the facts decided to accept the employment or decline it." The privilege does not apply where the lawyer has specifically stated that he would not represent the individual and in no way wanted to be involved in the dispute, but the law firm did not do that in this case—it just made it clear that it did not represent the submitter *yet.* Under *People v. SpeeDee Oil Change Systems, Inc.,* [20 Cal. 4th 1135 (1999)], when the communication between a lawyer and possible client proceeds "beyond initial or peripheral contacts" to acquisition by the lawyer of information that would be confidential were there to be representation, the privilege applies.

In deciding that the district court plainly erred, and that a writ of mandamus must be granted, our judgment is not based on a mechanical application of verbal formulas. We are influenced by how fundamental the lawyer-client privilege is to the operation of an adversarial legal system. Potential clients must be able to tell their lawyers their private business without fear of disclosure, in order for their lawyers to obtain honest accounts on which they may base sound advice and skillful advocacy. There would be no room for confusion had the communication been in the traditional context of a potential client going into a lawyer's office and talking to the lawyer. The changes in law and technology that allow lawyers to solicit clients on the internet and receive communications from thousands of potential clients cheaply and quickly do not change the applicable principles.

GlaxoSmithKline cannot be permitted access to a communication that a plaintiff made confidentially to his lawyer in order to compare it to what the same individual said at a deposition. But that is exactly what GlaxoSmithKline seeks. It must be conceded that if a plaintiff says one thing to his lawyer, and says another at his deposition, keeping the first disclosure secret creates a risk to the honest and accurate resolution of the dispute. That risk is mitigated by the plaintiffs' lawyers ethical duties of candor toward the tribunal and fairness to the opposing party and counsel. The privilege does not mean that the plaintiffs may lie about their symptoms, or that their lawyers may allow them to lie. A lawyer can be disbarred for offering evidence that the lawyer knows to be false, failing to disclose a material fact when disclosure is necessary to prevent a fraud by the client, or assisting a witness to testify falsely. Most lawyers' sense of honor would prevent them from doing these things even if they were not at risk of losing their licenses if they did. These restraints of honor and ethics, rather than court-ordered disclosure of confidential communications, are the means that our system uses to deal with the risk of clients saying one thing to their lawyers and another to opposing counsel, the judge, or the jury.

CASE QUESTIONS

1. Whose perspective does the court say matters in this case? Why?

2. What test does the *SpeeDee Oil* court state for determining whether a pre-retention communication is privileged?

3. Did counsel in this case owe a duty of care to people who submitted forms from the website?

4. Can you conceive of websites that might create a duty of care in such circumstances? How?

In 2012 the ABA approved an amendment to Rule 1.18 and added a new comment 2 to that rule. The amendment alters the rule so that it extends to lawyers who "learn[ ] information from" a prospective client" rather than lawyers who "consult" with a client. The comment explains that the changed indicates that the rule applies to prospective clients who provide information by any means, including electronic communication. The rule therefore applies when a lawyer, either "in person" or through "advertising in any medium" invites "the submission of information about a potential representation without clear and reasonably understandable warnings and cautionary statements that limit the lawyer's obligations . . ." On the other hand, the rule does not extend to cases where "a person provides information to a lawyer in response to advertising that merely describes the lawyer's education, experience, areas of practice, and contact information, or provides legal information of general interest." The rule specifies that the rule does not extend to a person who contacts a lawyer in order to taint him or her with information that might cause the lawyer to be disqualified from a matter. That this comment exists tells you something about the potential for rules to be used as tactics.

For a general discussion of means by which firms that use the Web may or may not create web-based duties of confidentiality, *see* ABA Formal Opinion 10–457 (2010); California State Bar Standing Committee on Professional Responsibility and Conduct (COPRAC), Formal Op. 2003–001. The ABA opinion distinguishes websites that solicit information from potential clients from those that do not. It states:

> if a lawyer website specifically requests or invites submission of information concerning the possibility of forming a client-lawyer relationship with respect to a matter, a discussion, as that term is used in Rule 1.18, will result when a website visitor submits the requested information. If a website visitor submits information to a site that does not specifically request or invite this, the lawyer's response to that submission will determine whether a discussion under Rule 1.18 has occurred.

Barton deals with the question whether information submitted by a prospective client may be withheld from production. What if the issue is disqualification? COPRAC opinion 2005–168 dealt with a hypothetical in which a law firm represented a husband in connection with a divorce. His wife submitted confidential information to the firm through its website. The site contained a link entitled "What are my rights," which led to a page that asked "Wondering about a legal problem you have?" That page asked for contact information, a statement of facts regarding the problem, and for particular questions the user had. Before submitting the information, the wife was presented the following disclaimer:

Terms

- **I understand and agree** that I may receive a response to my inquiry from an attorney at Law Firm.
- **I agree** that by submitting this inquiry, I will not be charged for the initial response.
- **I agree** that I am not forming an attorney-client relationship by submitting this question. I also understand that I am not forming a confidential relationship.
- **I further agree** that I may only retain Law Firm or any of its attorneys as my attorney by entering into a written fee agreement, and that I am not hereby entering into a fee agreement. I understand that I will not be charged for the response to this inquiry.

The opinion concluded that the firm's page invited the wife to consult with the firm. Even assuming the disclaimer prevented formation of an attorney-client relationship, the opinion concluded "We do not believe that a prospective client's agreement to Law Firm's terms prevented a duty of confidentiality from arising on the facts before us, because Law Firm's disclosures to Wife were not adequate to defeat her reasonable belief that she was consulting Law Firm for the purpose of retaining Law Firm . . . . . An attorney-client relationship is not a prerequisite to a lawyer assuming a duty of confidentiality in such a situation."

Finding the "terms" language ambiguous and potentially confusing, the opinion rejected the notion that the disclaimer of a confidential relationship prevented the creation of a duty of confidentiality.

> Had Law Firm written its agreement with Wife with a plain-language reference that her submission would lack confidentiality, then that would have defeated a reasonable expectation of confidentiality. Accord, *Barton v. District Court* (9th Cir. 2005) 410 F.3d 1104, 1110 (Law firm should have spoken clearly to the laymen to whom its website was addressed about what commitments it did and did not make by a plain English explanation on the website). Without ruling out other possibilities, we note that had Wife agreed to the following, she would have had, in our opinion, no reasonable expectation of confidentiality with Law Firm: "I understand and agree that Law Firm

will have no duty to keep confidential the information I am now transmitting to Law Firm.

The opinion also noted that the firm could have avoided the problem by requiring that prospective clients submit enough information for the firm to check conflicts before submitting any confidential information.

The ABA opinion states that a person who knows a lawyer has declined to represent them or is representing an adversary has no reasonable basis to expect that the lawyer will keep communications from the person confidential. ABA Formal Op. 10–457 at 4–5. It further notes that websites may use clear and understandable disclaimers to avoid creating duties to prospective clients but that even such disclaimers may be ineffective if the website elsewhere undercuts them (as by promising confidentiality or rendering advice, for example).

---

3. CONFIDENCES FROM PARTIES RELATED TO CLIENTS

The duty of confidentiality extends to persons—even non-clients—who provide confidences to you under circumstances justifying them in believing that you will keep the information confidential. The following case illustrates how this might happen. This rule means that in assessing your own duties (and, as we shall see, your own risk of conflicts), you must pay attention both to all your clients and to any non-clients to whom you might owe a duty of confidentiality.

WESTINGHOUSE ELECTRIC CORPORATION V. KERR–MCGEE CORPORATION

580 F.2d 1311 (7th Cir. 1978)

SPRECHER, CIRCUIT JUDGE.

The novel issues on this appeal are (1) whether an attorney-client relationship arises only when both parties consent to its formation or can it also occur when the lay party submits confidential information to the law party with reasonable belief that the latter is acting as the former's attorney and (2) whether the size and geographical scope of a law firm exempt it from the ordinary ethical considerations applicable to lawyers generally.

The four separate appellants are some of the defendants in this antitrust case who were each denied their motions to disqualify the law firm of Kirkland and Ellis ("Kirkland") from further representing the plaintiff Westinghouse Electric Corporation ("Westinghouse"). Whether fortuitously or by design, on the same day, October 15, 1976, Kirkland, while representing the American Petroleum Institute ("API"), of which three of the appellants, Gulf Oil Corporation ("Gulf"), Kerr–McGee Corporation ("Kerr–McGee") and Getty Oil Company ("Getty"), were members, released a report which took an affirmative position on the subject of competition in the uranium industry, while simultaneously filing this lawsuit, representing Westinghouse, seeking to establish an illegal conspiracy in restraint of trade in the uranium industry. . . . .

I

On September 8, 1975, Westinghouse, a major manufacturer of nuclear reactors, notified utility companies that 17 of its long-term uranium supply contracts had become "commercially impracticable" under § 2–615 of the Uniform Commercial Code. In response, the affected utilities filed 13 federal actions, one state action, and three foreign actions against Westinghouse, alleging breach of contract and challenging Westinghouse's invocation of § 2–615. The federal actions were consolidated for trial in the Eastern District of Virginia at Richmond under MDL Docket No. 235.

As an outgrowth of its defense of these contract actions, Westinghouse on October 15, 1976, filed the present antitrust action against 12 foreign and 17 domestic corporations engaged in various aspects of the uranium industry.

Kirkland's representation of Westinghouse's uranium litigation has required the efforts of 8 to 14 of its attorneys and has generated some $2.5 million in legal fees.

Contemporaneously with its Westinghouse representation in the uranium cases, Kirkland represented API, using six of its lawyers in that project.

In October, 1975, Congress was presented with legislative proposals to break up the oil companies, both vertically by separating their control over production, transportation, refining and marketing entities, and horizontally by prohibiting cross-ownership of alternative energy resources in addition to oil and gas. Since this proposed legislation threatened oil companies with a potential divestiture of millions of dollars of assets, in November, 1975, the API launched a Committee on Industrial Organization to lobby against the proposals. On December 10, 1975, API's president requested that each company designate one of its senior executives to facilitate coordination of the Committee's activities with the individual companies.

The Committee was organized into five task forces. The Legal Task Force was headed by L. Bates Lea, General Counsel of Standard Oil of Indiana, assisted by Stark Ritchie, API's General Counsel.

On February 25, 1976, Ritchie wrote to Frederick M. Rowe, a partner in Kirkland's Washington office, retaining the firm to review the divestiture hearings and "prepare arguments for use in opposition to this type of legislation." On May 4, 1976, Ritchie added that the Kirkland firm's work for API "should include the preparation of possible testimony, analyzing the probable legal consequences and antitrust considerations of the proposed legislation" and "you should make an objective survey and study of the probable effects of the pending legislation, specifically including probable effects on oil companies that would have to divest assets." Ritchie noted that "(a)s a part of this study, we will arrange for interviews by your firm with a cross-section of industry personnel." The May 4 letter to Rowe concluded with:

> Your firm will, of course, act as an independent expert counsel and hold any company information learned through these interviews in strict confidence, not to be disclosed to any other company, or even to API, except in aggregated or such other form as will preclude identifying the source company with its data.

On May 25, 1976, Ritchie sent to 59 API member companies a survey questionnaire seeking data to be used by Kirkland in connection with its engagement by API. In the introductory memorandum to the questionnaire, Ritchie advised the 59 companies that Kirkland had "ascertained that certain types of data pertinent to the pending anti-diversification legislation are not now publicly available" and the API "would appreciate your help in providing this information to Kirkland. . . . " The memorandum included the following:

> Kirkland, Ellis & Rowe is acting as an independent special counsel for API, and will hold any company information in strict confidence, Not to be disclosed to any other company, or even to API, except in aggregated or such other form as will preclude identifying the source company with its data.

(Emphasis in original). The data sought was to assist Kirkland "in preparing positions, arguments and testimony in opposition to this type of legislative (divestiture)" and was not to be sent to API but rather to Kirkland.

Pursuant to the provision in Ritchie's May 4, 1976 letter to Rowe that interviews would be arranged with a cross-section of industry personnel, Nolan Clark, a Kirkland partner, interviewed representatives of eight oil companies between April 29 and June 15, 1976.

After going through several drafts, the final Kirkland report to API was released on October 15, 1976. The final report contains 230 pages of text and 82 pages of exhibits. References to uranium appear throughout the report and uranium is the primary subject of about 25 pages of text and 11 pages of exhibits. The report marshalls a large number of facts and arguments to show that oil company diversification does not threaten overall energy competition. In particular the report asserts that the relatively high concentration ratios in the uranium industry can be expected to decline, that current increases in uranium prices are a result of increasing demand, that oil company entry into uranium production has stimulated competition and diminished concentration, that oil companies have no incentive to act in concert to restrict coal or uranium production and that the historical record refutes any charge that oil companies have restricted uranium output. The report concludes that "the energy industries, both individually and collectively, are competitive today and are likely to remain so."

As noted at the outset of this opinion, the API report was issued on the same day as the present antitrust suit was filed against several defendants, including Gulf, Kerr–McGee and Getty.

The district court concluded that "(a) comparison of the two documents reveals a rather basic conflict in their contentions and underlying theories." The court also observed that "(p)erhaps in recognition of the diametrically opposing theories of the API report and the Westinghouse complaint, Kirkland does not attempt to rebut the oil companies' charges that it has simultaneously taken inconsistent positions on competition in the uranium industry."

Gulf, Kerr–McGee and Getty are substantial dues-paying members of API. Kerr–McGee and Getty are also represented on API's board of directors.

At Ritchie's request, the cross-section interviews were mainly arranged by Gerald Thurmond, Washington Counsel of Gulf Oil Company and a member of API's Antitrust Strategy Group. On May 11, 1976, Thurmond advised Gulf officials that Nolan Clark of Kirkland planned to visit them. Attached to Thurmond's letter were the questions "which will be covered" in the meeting.

The meeting was held on May 28, 1976 in Denver. Nolan Clark represented Kirkland. In attendance for Gulf were six vice presidents, a comptroller and a regional attorney. Also present was a Harvard professor who "also is working with API on the same subject." The meeting lasted more than two hours followed by lunch, during which discussions continued. After the meeting and in three letters from Gulf vice president Mingee to Clark dated August 10, 11 and 13, Gulf submitted specific information sought by Clark through the questionnaire and other written questions and in each letter Mingee stressed the confidential basis upon which the information was supplied.

Nolan Clark's interview with two Kerr–McGee vice presidents took place in Oklahoma City on June 9, 1976 and lasted about three hours. Clark was given considerable background information on Kerr–McGee's uranium industry, including mining locations, uranium conversion process, and pellet fabrication. On the subject of uranium marketing and pricing, one of the Kerr–McGee vice presidents described the escalating prices and tightening supplies in the current market, and the reasons behind the trends. Kerr–McGee sent its completed questionnaire to Clark on August 25, 1976.

Kirkland did not interview any Getty personnel. However, Getty received the confidential API questionnaire which requested it to estimate the value of its assets subject to proposed divestiture and its research and development outlays in alternative energy fields. Getty completed the questionnaire and mailed its data sheets to Nolan Clark on June 4, 1976, with the understanding that the data would be held in confidence.

II

The crux of the district court's determination was based upon its view that an "attorney-client relationship is one of agency to which the general rules of agency apply" and "arises Only when the parties have given their consent, either express or implied, to its formation." 448 F.Supp. at 1300 (emphasis supplied). Although some courts have stated that the attorney-client relation is one of agency and that the general rules of law applicable to agencies apply, in none of those cases was an agency principle applied to assist an attorney to avoid what would otherwise be an obligation to his client. . . . .

The district court abused its discretion in applying a narrow, formal agency approach to determining the attorney-client relation and in applying a different imputation of knowledge principle in the case of a large law firm than that "traditionally" and recently applied by this circuit to sole practitioners and smaller firms. *Schloetter v. Railoc of Indiana, Inc.*, 546 F.2d 706, 710 (7th Cir. 1976).

III

The client is no longer simply the person who walks into a law office. A lawyer employed by a corporation represents the entity but that principle does not of itself solve the potential conflicts existing between the entity and its individual participants.

Three district courts have held that each individual member of an unincorporated association is a client of the association's lawyer. In *Halverson v. Convenient Food Mart, Inc.*, 458 F.2d 927, 930 (7th Cir. 1972), we held that a lawyer who had represented an informal group of 75 franchisees "(b)ecause . . . (he) in effect had represented and benefited every franchisee, . . . could reasonably believe that each one of them was his client."

Here we are faced with neither an ordinary commercial corporation nor with an informal or unincorporated association, but instead with a nation-wide trade association with 350 corporate and 7,500 individual members and doing business as a non-profit corporation.

We need not make any generalized pronouncements of whether an attorney for such an organization represents every member because this case can and should be decided on a much more narrow ground.

There are several fairly common situations where, although there is no express attorney-client relationship, there exists nevertheless a fiduciary obligation or an implied professional relation:

(1) The fiduciary relationship existing between lawyer and client extends to preliminary consultation by a prospective client with a view to retention of the lawyer, although actual employment does not result.[5]

(2) When information is exchanged between co-defendants and their attorneys in a criminal case, an attorney who is the recipient of such information breaches his fiduciary duty if he later, in his representation of another client, is able to use this information to the detriment of one of the co-defendants, even though that co-defendant is not the one which he represented in the criminal case. *Wilson P. Abraham Const. Corp. v. Armco Steel Corp.*, 559 F.2d 250 (5th Cir. 1977) (disqualification case).

(3) When an insurer retains an attorney to investigate the circumstances of a claim and the insured, pursuant to a cooperation clause in the policy, cooperates with the attorney, the attorney may not thereafter represent a third party suing the insured nor indeed continue to represent the insurer once a conflict of interest surfaces.

(4) In a recent case, where an auditor's regional counsel was instrumental in hiring a second law firm to represent some plaintiffs suing the auditor and where the second firm through such relationship was in a position to receive privileged information, the second law firm, although having no direct attorney-client relationship with the auditor, was disqualified from representing the plaintiffs. *Fund of Funds, Ltd. v. Arthur Andersen & Co.*, 567 F.2d 225 (2d Cir. 1977).

(5) In a recent case in this circuit, a law firm who represented for many years both the plaintiff in an action and also a corporation which owned 20% Of the outstanding stock of the defendant corporation, was permitted to continue its representation of the plaintiff but was directed to disassociate itself from representing or advising the corporation owning 20% Of defendant's stock. *Whiting Corp. v. White Machinery Corp.*, 567 F.2d 713 (7th Cir. 1977).

[5] FN12. ABA Code of Professional Responsibility, EC 4–1: "Both the fiduciary relationship existing between lawyer and client and the proper functioning of the legal system require the presentation by the lawyer of confidences and secrets of one who has employed or sought to employ him." Cf. McCormick on Evidence (2d ed. 1972), § 88, p. 179: "Communications in the course of preliminary discussion with a view to employing the lawyer are privileged though the employment is in the upshot not accepted." See also, *Taylor v. Sheldon*, 172 Ohio St. 118, 173 N.E.2d 892, 895 (1961).

In none of the above categories or situations did the disqualified or disadvantaged lawyer or law firm actually represent the "client" in the sense of a formal or even express attorney-client relation. In each of those categories either an implied relation was found or at least the lawyer was found to owe a fiduciary obligation to the laymen.

The professional relationship for purposes of the privilege for attorney-client communications "hinges upon the client's belief that he is consulting a lawyer in that capacity and his manifested intention to seek professional legal advice." The affidavits before the district court established that: the Washington counsel for Gulf "was given to believe that the Kirkland firm was representing both API and Gulf;" Kerr–McGee's vice president understood a Kirkland partner to explain that Kirkland was working on behalf of API and also its members such as Kerr–McGee; and Getty's vice president stated that in submitting data to Kirkland he "acted upon the belief and expectation that such submission was made in order to enable (Kirkland) to render legal service to Getty in furtherance of Getty's interests."

A fiduciary relationship may result because of the nature of the work performed and the circumstances under which confidential information is divulged. The Supreme Court approved and transmitted to Congress in 1972 the Federal Rules of Evidence, which included among the lawyer-client privilege rules eventually eliminated by Congress, the following definition:

> A "client" is a person, public officer, or corporation, association, or other organization or entity, either public or private, who is rendered professional legal services by a lawyer, or who consults a lawyer with a view to obtaining professional legal services from him.

The professional relationship does not arise where one consults an attorney in a capacity other than as an attorney. The district court said that the Kirkland "firm's involvement was that of an expert consultant and researcher." The questionnaire sent to 59 oil company members of API represented to the recipients that the Kirkland firm "is acting as an independent special counsel for API." The API letter employing Kirkland expressly said that "(y)our firm will, of course, act as an independent expert counsel." The lobbying-type functions undertaken by Kirkland in this case are not foreign to lawyers and in fact are a common undertaking by Washington, D. C., lawyers. In soliciting confidences from API members, Kirkland did not disavow its capacity as attorneys but came expressly represented as lawyers.

The district court concluded that "the transmission by the oil companies of confidential information on their uranium industries and assets has given rise to justifiable fears that their disclosures will return to haunt them in the present litigation" and "(t)he acquired information appears to be closely related to the subject matter of the Westinghouse complaint." The court did not find violations of Canons 4 or 5 because it could not find an attorney-client relationship on the basis of the narrow agency rules applied. However the court did find a Canon 9 violation, but did not believe that such a violation alone should result in disqualification "especially in a case of the present complexity and magnitude" involving a two-city large law firm which had attempted to segregate the substantial number of lawyers working on each matter.

The lower court perceived that "an attorney should be disqualified under Canon 9 only when 'there is a reasonable possibility of improper professional conduct' and 'the likelihood of public suspicion or obloquy outweighs the social interests which will be served by a lawyer's continued participation in a particular case.' "

Gulf, Kerr–McGee and Getty each entertained a reasonable belief that it was submitting confidential information regarding its involvement in the uranium industry to a law firm which had solicited the information upon a representation that the firm was acting in the undivided interest of each company. Canons 4 and 5, as well as Canon 9, apply. If Kirkland's size and multi-city status had any effect, it was in the direction of encouraging the oil companies to divulge confidential information. Whereas they might show reluctance to entrust their substantial assets and future fortunes to a sole practitioner or small law firm, Kirkland's substance and reputation would tend to comfort any apprehensions and open the lines of communication. In any event, there is no basis for creating separate disqualification rules for large firms even though the burden of complying with ethical considerations will naturally fall more heavily upon their shoulders.

The fact that the two contrary undertakings by Kirkland occurred contemporaneously, with each involving substantial stakes and substantially related to the other, outbalances the client's interest in continuing with its chosen attorney. However, we believe that Westinghouse should have the option and choice of dismissing Gulf, Kerr–McGee and Getty from the antitrust case or discharging Kirkland as its attorney in the case. Substitute counsel has represented Westinghouse in the case since February 17, 1978, so that the impact of any change-over has been somewhat eased.

Affirmed in part; Reversed and Remanded in part.

CASE QUESTION

1. Whom did Kirkland & Ellis (K & E) represent?
2. To whom did it owe duties?

3. What was the basis for the expectation of confidentiality asserted in the case?
4. What body of law did the district court rely on?
5. Why was that reliance a mistake?
6. What categories of non-client duties did the appellate court enumerate?

B. DUTY OF CARE

You owe a duty of care if and to the extent you undertake to advise people about their matters. That is true even if you do not accept a case. As in *Nichols v. Keller*, the duty you create by giving advice may not be limited to the actual advice given; it may extend to advice a competent lawyer would have given in light of the advice that was given. The following case illustrates these points. It also illustrates the importance of communication, the ease of mistaken communication, and the consequences for counsel who miscommunicates.

TOGSTAD V. VESELY, OTTO, MILLER & KEEFE

291 N.W.2d 686 (Minn. 1980)

PER CURIAM

This is an appeal by the defendants from a judgment of the Hennepin County District Court involving an action for legal malpractice. The jury found that the defendant attorney Jerre Miller was negligent and that, as a direct result of such negligence, plaintiff John Togstad sustained damages in the amount of $610,500 and his wife, plaintiff Joan Togstad, in the amount of $39,000. Defendants (Miller and his law firm) appeal to this court from the denial of their motion for judgment notwithstanding the verdict or, alternatively, for a new trial. We affirm.

In August 1971, John Togstad began to experience severe headaches and on August 16, 1971, was admitted to Methodist Hospital where tests disclosed that the headaches were caused by a large aneurism on the left internal carotid artery. The attending physician, Dr. Paul Blake, a neurological surgeon, treated the problem by applying a Selverstone clamp to the left common carotid artery. The clamp was surgically implanted on August 27, 1971, in Togstad's neck to allow the gradual closure of the artery over a period of days.

The treatment was designed to eventually cut off the blood supply through the artery and thus relieve the pressure on the aneurism, allowing the aneurism to heal. It was anticipated that other arteries, as well as the brain's collateral or cross-arterial system would supply the required blood to the portion of the brain which would ordinarily have been provided by the left carotid artery. The greatest risk associated with this procedure is that the patient may become paralyzed if the brain does not receive an adequate flow of blood. In the event the supply of blood becomes so low as to endanger the health of the patient, the adjustable clamp can be opened to establish the proper blood circulation.

In the early morning hours of August 29, 1971, a nurse observed that Togstad was unable to speak or move. At the time, the clamp was one-half (50%) closed. Upon discovering Togstad's condition, the nurse called a resident physician, who did not adjust the clamp. Dr. Blake was also immediately informed of Togstad's condition and arrived about an hour later, at which time he opened the clamp. Togstad is now severely paralyzed in his right arm and leg, and is unable to speak.

Plaintiffs' expert, Dr. Ward Woods, testified that Togstad's paralysis and loss of speech was due to a lack of blood supply to his brain. Dr. Woods stated that the inadequate blood flow resulted from the clamp being 50% closed and that the negligence of Dr. Blake and the hospital precluded the clamp's being opened in time to avoid permanent brain damage. . . .

Dr. Blake and defendants' expert witness, Dr. Shelly Chou, testified that Togstad's condition was caused by blood clots going up the carotid artery to the brain. They both alleged that the blood clots were not a result of the Selverstone clamp procedure. In addition, they stated that the clamp must be about 90% closed before there will be a slowing of the blood supply through the carotid artery to the brain. Thus, according to Drs. Blake and Chou, when the clamp is 50% closed there is no effect on the blood flow to the brain.

About 14 months after her husband's hospitalization began, plaintiff Joan Togstad met with attorney Jerre Miller regarding her husband's condition. Neither she nor her husband was personally acquainted with Miller or his law firm prior to that time. John Togstad's former work supervisor, Ted Bucholz, made the appointment and accompanied Mrs. Togstad to Miller's office. Bucholz was present when Mrs. Togstad and Miller discussed the case.[6]

Mrs. Togstad had become suspicious of the circumstances surrounding her husband's tragic condition due to the conduct and statements of the hospital nurses shortly after the paralysis occurred. One nurse told Mrs. Togstad that she had checked Mr. Togstad at 2 a. m. and he was fine; that when she returned at 3 a. m., by mistake, to give him someone

[6] FN3. Bucholz, who knew Miller through a local luncheon club, died prior to the trial of the instant action.

else's medication, he was unable to move or speak; and that if she hadn't accidentally entered the room no one would have discovered his condition until morning. Mrs. Togstad also noticed that the other nurses were upset and crying, and that Mr. Togstad's condition was a topic of conversation.

Mrs. Togstad testified that she told Miller "everything that happened at the hospital," including the nurses' statements and conduct which had raised a question in her mind. She stated that she "believed" she had told Miller "about the procedure and what was undertaken, what was done, and what happened." She brought no records with her. Miller took notes and asked questions during the meeting, which lasted 45 minutes to an hour. At its conclusion, according to Mrs. Togstad, Miller said that "he did not think we had a legal case, however, he was going to discuss this with his partner." She understood that if Miller changed his mind after talking to his partner, he would call her. Mrs. Togstad "gave it" a few days and, since she did not hear from Miller, decided "that they had come to the conclusion that there wasn't a case." No fee arrangements were discussed, no medical authorizations were requested, nor was Mrs. Togstad billed for the interview.

Mrs. Togstad denied that Miller had told her his firm did not have expertise in the medical malpractice field, urged her to see another attorney, or related to her that the statute of limitations for medical malpractice actions was two years. She did not consult another attorney until one year after she talked to Miller. Mrs. Togstad indicated that she did not confer with another attorney earlier because of her reliance on Miller's "legal advice" that they "did not have a case."

On cross-examination, Mrs. Togstad was asked whether she went to Miller's office "to see if he would take the case of (her) husband * * *." She replied, "Well, I guess it was to go for legal advice, what to do, where shall we go from here? That is what we went for." Again in response to defense counsel's questions, Mrs. Togstad testified as follows:

> Q And it was clear to you, was it not, that what was taking place was a preliminary discussion between a prospective client and lawyer as to whether or not they wanted to enter into an attorney-client relationship?
>
> A I am not sure how to answer that. It was for legal advice as to what to do.
>
> Q And Mr. Miller was discussing with you your problem and indicating whether he, as a lawyer, wished to take the case, isn't that true?
>
> A Yes.

On re-direct examination, Mrs. Togstad acknowledged that when she left Miller's office she understood that she had been given a "qualified, quality legal opinion that (she and her husband) did not have a malpractice case."

Miller's testimony was different in some respects from that of Mrs. Togstad. Like Mrs. Togstad, Miller testified that Mr. Bucholz arranged and was present at the meeting, which lasted about 45 minutes. According to Miller, Mrs. Togstad described the hospital incident, including the conduct of the nurses. He asked her questions, to which she responded. Miller testified that "(t)he only thing I told her (Mrs. Togstad) after we had pretty much finished the conversation was that there was nothing related in her factual circumstances that told me that she had a case that our firm would be interested in undertaking."

Miller also claimed he related to Mrs. Togstad "that because of the grievous nature of the injuries sustained by her husband, that this was only my opinion and she was encouraged to ask another attorney if she wished for another opinion" and "she ought to do so promptly." He testified that he informed Mrs. Togstad that his firm "was not engaged as experts" in the area of medical malpractice, and that they associated with the Charles Hvass firm in cases of that nature. Miller stated that at the end of the conference he told Mrs. Togstad that he would consult with Charles Hvass and if Hvass's opinion differed from his, Miller would so inform her. Miller recollected that he called Hvass a "couple days" later and discussed the case with him. It was Miller's impression that Hvass thought there was no liability for malpractice in the case. Consequently, Miller did not communicate with Mrs. Togstad further.

On cross-examination, Miller testified as follows:

Q Now, so there is no misunderstanding, and I am reading from your deposition, you understood that she was consulting with you as a lawyer, isn't that correct?

A That's correct.

Q That she was seeking legal advice from a professional attorney licensed to practice in this state and in this community?

A I think you and I did have another interpretation or use of the term "Advice". She was there to see whether or not she had a case and whether the firm would accept it.

Q We have two aspects; number one, your legal opinion concerning liability of a case for malpractice; number two, whether there was or wasn't liability, whether you would accept it, your firm, two separate elements, right?

A I would say so.

Q Were you asked on page 6 in the deposition, folio 14, "And you understood that she was seeking legal advice at the time that she was in your office, that is correct also, isn't it?" And did you give this answer, "I don't want to engage in semantics with you, but my impression was that she and Mr. Bucholz were asking my opinion after having related the incident that I referred to." The next question, "Your legal opinion?" Your answer, "Yes." Were those questions asked and were they given?

MR. COLLINS: Objection to this, Your Honor. It is not impeachment.

THE COURT: Overruled.

THE WITNESS: Yes, I gave those answers. Certainly, she was seeking my opinion as an attorney in the sense of whether or not there was a case that the firm would be interested in undertaking.

Kenneth Green, a Minneapolis attorney, was called as an expert by plaintiffs. He stated that in rendering legal advice regarding a claim of medical malpractice, the "minimum" an attorney should do would be to request medical authorizations from the client, review the hospital records, and consult with an expert in the field. John McNulty, a Minneapolis attorney, and Charles Hvass testified as experts on behalf of the defendants. McNulty stated that when an attorney is consulted as to whether he will take a case, the lawyer's only responsibility in refusing it is to so inform the party. He testified, however, that when a lawyer is asked his legal opinion on the merits of a medical malpractice claim, community standards require that the attorney check hospital records and consult with an expert before rendering his opinion.

Hvass stated that he had no recollection of Miller's calling him in October 1972 relative to the Togstad matter. He testified that:

> A * * * when a person comes in to me about a medical malpractice action, based upon what the individual has told me, I have to make a decision as to whether or not there probably is or probably is not, based upon that information, medical malpractice. And if, in my judgment, based upon what the client has told me, there is not medical malpractice, I will so inform the client.

Hvass stated, however, that he would never render a "categorical" opinion. In addition, Hvass acknowledged that if he were consulted for a "legal opinion" regarding medical malpractice and 14 months had expired since the incident in question, "ordinary care and diligence" would require him to inform the party of the two-year statute of limitations applicable to that type of action.

This case was submitted to the jury by way of a special verdict form. The jury found that Dr. Blake and the hospital were negligent and that Dr. Blake's negligence (but not the hospital's) was a direct cause of the injuries sustained by John Togstad; that there was an attorney-client contractual relationship between Mrs. Togstad and Miller; that Miller was negligent in rendering advice regarding the possible claims of Mr. and Mrs. Togstad; that, but for Miller's negligence, plaintiffs would have been successful in the prosecution of a legal action against Dr. Blake; and that neither Mr. nor Mrs. Togstad was negligent in pursuing their claims against Dr. Blake. The jury awarded damages to Mr. Togstad of $610,500 and to Mrs. Togstad of $39,000. . . .

1. In a legal malpractice action of the type involved here, four elements must be shown: (1) that an attorney-client relationship existed; (2) that defendant acted negligently or in breach of contract; (3) that such acts were the proximate cause of the plaintiffs' damages; (4) that but for defendant's conduct the plaintiffs would have been successful in the prosecution of their medical malpractice claim.

This court first dealt with the element of lawyer-client relationship in the decision of *Ryan v. Long*, 35 Minn. 394 (1886). The Ryan case involved a claim of legal malpractice and on appeal it was argued that no attorney-client relation existed. This court, without stating whether its conclusion was based on contract principles or a tort theory, disagreed:

> (I)t sufficiently appears that plaintiff, for himself, called upon defendant, as an attorney at law, for "legal advice," and that defendant assumed to give him a professional opinion in reference to the matter as to which plaintiff consulted him. Upon this state of facts the defendant must be taken to have acted as plaintiff's legal adviser, at plaintiff's request, and so as to establish between them the relation of attorney and client.

Id. (citation omitted). More recent opinions of this court, although not involving a detailed discussion, have analyzed the attorney-client consideration in contractual terms. *See*, *Ronnigen v. Hertogs*, 294 Minn. 7, 199 N.W.2d 420 (1972); *Christy v. Saliterman*, *supra*. For example, the *Ronnigen* court, in affirming a directed verdict for the defendant attorney, reasoned that "(u)nder the fundamental rules applicable to contracts of employment * * * the evidence would not sustain a finding that defendant either expressly or impliedly promised or agreed to represent plaintiff * * *." 294 Minn. 11, 199 N.W.2d 422. The trial court here, in apparent reliance upon the contract approach utilized in Ronnigen and Christy, supra, applied a contract analysis in ruling on the attorney-client relationship question. This has prompted a discussion by the Minnesota Law Review, wherein it is suggested that the more appropriate mode of analysis, at least in this case, would be to apply principles of negligence, i.e., whether defendant owed plaintiffs a duty to act with due care. 63 Minn.L.Rev. 751 (1979).

We believe it is unnecessary to decide whether a tort or contract theory is preferable for resolving the attorney-client relationship question raised by this appeal. The tort and contract analyses are very similar in a case such as the instant one,[7] and we conclude that under either theory

[7] FN4. Under a negligence approach it must essentially be shown that defendant rendered legal advice (not necessarily at someone's request) under circumstances which made it reasonably foreseeable to the attorney that if such advice was rendered negligently, the individual re-

the evidence shows that a lawyer-client relationship is present here. The thrust of Mrs. Togstad's testimony is that she went to Miller for legal advice, was told there wasn't a case, and relied upon this advice in failing to pursue the claim for medical malpractice. In addition, according to Mrs. Togstad, Miller did not qualify his legal opinion by urging her to seek advice from another attorney, nor did Miller inform her that he lacked expertise in the medical malpractice area. Assuming this testimony is true, as this court must do [citation omitted], we believe a jury could properly find that Mrs. Togstad sought and received legal advice from Miller under circumstances which made it reasonably foreseeable to Miller that Mrs. Togstad would be injured if the advice were negligently given. Thus, under either a tort or contract analysis, there is sufficient evidence in the record to support the existence of an attorney-client relationship.

Defendants argue that even if an attorney-client relationship was established the evidence fails to show that Miller acted negligently in assessing the merits of the Togstads' case. They appear to contend that, at most, Miller was guilty of an error in judgment which does not give rise to legal malpractice. *Meagher v. Kavli*, 256 Minn. 54 (1959). However, this case does not involve a mere error of judgment. The gist of plaintiffs' claim is that Miller failed to perform the minimal research that an ordinarily prudent attorney would do before rendering legal advice in a case of this nature. The record, through the testimony of Kenneth Green and John McNulty, contains sufficient evidence to support plaintiffs' position.

In a related contention, defendants assert that a new trial should be awarded on the ground that the trial court erred by refusing to instruct the jury that Miller's failure to inform Mrs. Togstad of the two-year statute of limitations for medical malpractice could not constitute negligence. The argument continues that since it is unclear from the record on what theory or theories of negligence the jury based its decision, a new trial must be granted. *Namchek v. Tulley*, 259 Minn. 469 (1961).

The defect in defendants' reasoning is that there is adequate evidence supporting the claim that Miller was also negligent in failing to advise Mrs. Togstad of the two-year medical malpractice limitations period and thus the trial court acted properly in refusing to instruct the jury in the manner urged by defendants. One of defendants' expert witnesses, Charles Hvass, testified:

---

ceiving the advice might be injured thereby. *See, e. g., Palsgraf v. Long Island R. Co.*, 248 N.Y. 339, 162 N.E. 99, 59 A.L.R. 1253 (1928). Or, stated another way, under a tort theory, "(a)n attorney-client relationship is created whenever an individual seeks and receives legal advice from an attorney in circumstances in which a reasonable person would rely on such advice." 63 Minn.L.Rev. 751, 759 (1979). A contract analysis requires the rendering of legal advice pursuant to another's request and the reliance factor, in this case, where the advice was not paid for, need be shown in the form of promissory estoppel. See, 7 C.J.S., Attorney and Client, § 65; Restatement (Second) of Contracts, § 90.

Q Now, Mr. Hvass, where you are consulted for a legal opinion and advice concerning malpractice and 14 months have elapsed (since the incident in question), wouldn't and you hold yourself out as competent to give a legal opinion and advice to these people concerning their rights, wouldn't ordinary care and diligence require that you inform them that there is a two-year statute of limitations within which they have to act or lose their rights?

A Yes. I believe I would have advised someone of the two-year period of limitation, yes.

Consequently, based on the testimony of Mrs. Togstad, i.e., that she requested and received legal advice from Miller concerning the malpractice claim, and the above testimony of Hvass, we must reject the defendants' contention, as it was reasonable for a jury to determine that Miller acted negligently in failing to inform Mrs. Togstad of the applicable limitations period. . . .

Affirmed.

CASE QUESTIONS

1. Relative to experience with lawyers, what sort of a person is Mrs. Togstad?
2. How did she find Mr. Miller?
3. Why did he meet with her, given his field of practice?
4. Examine closely the testimony of Mrs. Togstad and Mr. Miller. Are they saying different things? How, precisely, do their descriptions of the meeting differ?
5. What theories of duty formation are relevant here?
6. Does it make a difference which theory the court endorses?
7. In hindsight, what distinction does Mr. Miller wish to draw? Is that a reasonable distinction to ask a lawyer to draw? How about a client?
8. In hindsight, what should Mr. Miller have done after Mrs. Togstad left his office?

But I didn't say that

Suppose Mrs. Togstad and Mr. Miller testified truthfully on what each said at their meeting. Even if Miller was right about the words he used, it would have been perfectly reasonable for an ordinary person such as Mrs. Togstad to interpret 'you don't have a case we are interested in taking" to mean "you don't have a case," period. After all, if she did have a case, why would Miller turn it down? Perhaps Mr. Miller did not understand how his comment might sound to a legally unsophisticated person. To Mrs. Togstad his advice meant that she shouldn't bother filing a medical malpractice claim, and she let the limitations period expire.

Miller also testified that he told Togstad he and his firm were not medical malpractice experts and that she should seek a second opinion promptly if she wanted one. Ironically, crediting that testimony might strengthen the view that Mr. Miller failed to see how Mrs. Togstad saw him. He might have thought the comment was a prudent and cautious one. But to Mrs. Togstad a second opinion might make little sense if she believed she already had received the assessment she came for. After all, if Mr. Miller was not qualified to judge the merits of her case why would he spend 45 minutes talking to her about it? Possibly Miller thought he was doing Bucholz a favor in listening to Mrs. Togstad's story, but if so he failed to make that clear to her and the possibility might not occur to her in a situation in which she was seeking guidance through unfamiliar terrain.

In terms of the theory of categorization explained in the Introduction, we may read the case as one in which Mrs. Togstad did not exactly miscategorize Mr. Miller—she came to him to evaluate whether she had a case and he at least seemed interested in evaluating it—but in which she did not apprehend the range of reasons relevant to a lawyer's decision to take a case or turn it down. To a lawyer, Miller's version of his statement—"there was nothing related in her factual circumstances that told me that she had a case that our firm would be interested in undertaking" might mean many things: The firm had enough profitable business at the moment, even if meritorious the case wasn't worth enough, Miller was shifting his practice to a different area, and so on. His classification of the case as not one his firm wanted might well reflect something other than his view of the merits.

Mrs. Togstad might not think about such reasons, however, and they certainly would be less available to her than to Mr. Miller. Her classification of his comment as a substantive assessment of the case was no doubt partly his responsibility—both seem to have understood that such an assessment was part of the reason for meeting—and that understanding would prime Mrs. Togstad to classify his comments as going to the merits of her case. In Bruner's terms, if Mrs. Togstad viewed lawyers as persons who advise on the merits of the claim, this perception made "advice" an accessible category for Mrs. Togstad when she considered what to make of what she heard.

Flatt v. Superior Court, 9 Cal.4th 275 (1994), features facts similar to *Togstad* but with a different result. The plaintiff in *Flatt* was William

Daniel. He contacted Gail Flatt to see if he had a malpractice case against a lawyer named Hinkle, who had represented him in his divorce. In their first meeting Daniel disclosed confidential information to Flatt and gave her documents concerning his claim. Flatt told him he "definitely" had a malpractice claim against Hinkle.

After this meeting Flatt performed a conflicts check and learned that her firm represented Hinkle in an unrelated matter. She wrote Daniel a letter stating the firm had a conflict and could not represent him; the letter did not caution him that he needed to line up a lawyer and decide what to do before the limitations period ran on his claim against Hinkle.

Daniel dawdled and the limitations period on his claim had run by the time he retained a lawyer to sue Hinkle. He then sued Flatt, claiming she breached a duty of care to him by not warning him of the limitations period. Flatt moved for summary judgment on the ground that she owed Daniel no duties. The trial court denied the motion and the court of appeals affirmed. The Supreme Court reversed. The majority reasoned as follows:

We have little quarrel with the reasoning of the majority of the Court of Appeal as to whether Daniel's status with respect to Flatt and her firm was that of a client. Given the shape of our law governing the nature of the attorney-client relationship, ably reviewed in the majority opinion—including its emphasis on the factual nature underlying the formation of the professional relation—we willingly indulge the assumption that, given the record before the superior court on defendants' motion for summary judgment, Daniel *might* have been Flatt's client; in any event, we agree with the Court of Appeal majority that issues of fact material to that question remained in dispute.[8] We disagree, however, with the majority's implicit assumption that the question of Daniel's client status is

[8] FN1. In concluding that, if credited, Daniel's version of events surrounding the July 27 meeting might support the inference that an attorney-client relationship had arisen, the Court of Appeal majority contrasted the results in *Fox v. Pollack* (1986) 181 Cal.App.3d 954, 226 Cal.Rptr. 532 (plaintiffs went to the office of the attorney representing their vendors to sign land sale papers; the attorney read the papers to them and asked if they understood them; plaintiffs later filed suit against the attorney, complaining that the documents varied from the oral agreement; *held,* the fact that plaintiffs "thought" defendant was their attorney was insufficient to create an attorney-client relationship unilaterally, absent some objective evidence of an agreement to represent) with that in *Miller v. Metzinger* (1979) 91 Cal.App.3d 31, 154 Cal.Rptr. 22 (reversing summary judgment for defendant attorney where client testified that, although no fee had been paid, attorney had agreed to obtain her medical records, evaluate her claim, and advise her as to the appropriate action and evidence suggested that attorney knew statute of limitations would expire less than a month before he referred the case to another attorney). (See also *Beery v. State Bar* (1987) 43 Cal.3d 802, 239 Cal.Rptr. 121, 739 P.2d 1289; *Westinghouse Elec. Corp. v. Kerr–McGee Corp.* (7th Cir.1978) 580 F.2d 1311.) The majority concluded that, based on Daniel's declaration of what occurred at the meeting with Flatt—including his assertion (contradicting his prior deposition testimony) that Flatt had given him "a little bit of an opinion" as to whether or not he had a valid claim against Hinkle—"an attorney-client relationship could rest upon the version of the interaction claimed by [Daniel]."

itself material to the dispositive legal issue raised by defendants' motion for summary judgment.

An attorney's duty of loyalty to a client is not one that is capable of being divided, at least under circumstances where the ethical obligation to withdraw from further representation of one of the parties is mandatory, rather than subject to disclosure and client consent. Although the principle upon which that conclusion rests is integral to the nature of an attorney's duty of loyalty itself, the result is also compelled by the highly practical dilemma that an advisory duty to the erstwhile client would impose on the attorney. In addition, our conclusion is motivated by an appreciation of the damage done to the existing client's sense of trust and security—features essential to the effective functioning of the fiduciary relationship—likely to follow from a conclusion that Flatt had a duty to advise Daniel under the facts of this case. . . .

Flatt's decision not to represent Daniel in light of her firm's ongoing representation of the Hinkle firm thus placed her in an ethical dilemma: on severing—as she must—the relationship with Daniel, what if any duty did she have to advise him respecting his contemplated lawsuit, advice that would almost inevitably harm Hinkle's interests to some extent? We have no difficulty in concluding that under these circumstances any advice to Daniel regarding the statute of limitations governing his claim against Hinkle would have run counter to the interests of an existing client of Flatt and her firm and of their obligation of undivided loyalty to him. We therefore conclude that she had no *duty* to give Daniel any such advice.[9]

Not only would the advisory duty argued for by Daniel have been contrary to the principle of attorney loyalty, it would as a practical matter have placed both Hinkle and Flatt in an insupportably awkward position, one that was bound to damage Hinkle's relationship with the firm and hobble the firm's effectiveness in representing him. It is not difficult to imagine Hinkle's reaction on learning that, in the course of severing her professional relationship, however infant, with Daniel, Flatt had advised Hinkle's would-be adversary of the statute of limitations governing the timing of his lawsuit and that, Flatt having refused to take his case, it was prudent to seek alternative counsel lest Daniel's claim against Hinkle be barred by the passage of time. . . .

Neither, we conclude, did Flatt have a duty under the circumstances to advise Daniel that it was prudent to seek other counsel promptly. Hav-

[9] FN6. We acknowledge, without having to decide in this case, the possibility that in a different factual situation—one involving, perhaps, the lapse of considerable time and the expenditure of substantial resources before discovery of the conflicting dual representation—an attorney's mere withdrawal from the second representation may not be sufficient in itself to resolve all ethical responsibilities. Whether a showing, for example, of substantial prejudice to the interests of the second client arising out of such facts would lead us to modify the rule we adopt in this case is a question whose answer must await another day.

ing sought an attorney to plead his case against Hinkle and having been turned down by Flatt, Daniel obviously knew that he had to continue the search for representation if he intended to pursue the claim. He admitted as much at his deposition. Although, as Justice Phelan pointed out in his dissent from the majority Court of Appeal opinion, it is prudent for any attorney not facing a conflict in representation like that here to routinely advise a client or potential client not to delay in finding alternative representation (see, e.g., Mallen and Smith, Legal Malpractice (3d ed. 1989) § 2.11, at pp. 114–115), we cannot hold Flatt liable for not having done so. Not only is the average client's understanding of the practical realities of obtaining representation to defend or vindicate interests adequate to protect against the risks at stake, but the insoluble ethical dilemma raised by imposing on a fiduciary a duty to provide advice that is against the interests of an existing client argues conclusively against a contrary holding. . . .

[Justice Kennard dissented:]

A lawyer who has conflicting responsibilities to two different clients is caught in a dilemma, because steps taken to protect the rights of one client may cause injury to the other. But the fact that the dilemma arose is surely not the fault of the *clients.* A lawyer assumes a duty of care to each client whom the lawyer agrees to represent; if the lawyer negligently breaches that duty, he or she should be liable to the client for any damage to the client caused by the breach. . . . .

Flatt's duty, if it existed, was a duty to use the skill, prudence, and diligence commonly possessed by other attorneys, not a duty to advise Daniel about the statute of limitations; but if Flatt did owe Daniel that duty of care, then Flatt's failure to advise Daniel of the statute of limitations may have been a breach of that duty. Thus, the two issues in this case are these: (1) whether Attorney Flatt owed a duty of care to Daniel; and (2) if so, whether that duty obligated Flatt to advise Daniel regarding the statute of limitations when Flatt withdrew from representation of Daniel. As discussed below, the majority's failure to separately address these two questions leads it to the wrong result. . . .

Flatt's duties . . . were not one-sided, because both Daniel and Hinkle were her clients. Flatt owed each of her clients a duty of care; her duty to one did not abrogate her duty to another. (See *Ishmael v. Millington* (1966) 241 Cal.App.2d 520, 526 [When a lawyer represents dual interests, "[t]he loyalty [the lawyer] owes one client cannot consume that owed to the other."].) To hold otherwise would turn the status of client into a meaningless label.

Even if, as the majority concludes, Flatt would have violated her duty of loyalty to her client Hinkle by giving advice to Daniel when she withdrew from representing him, that fact does not absolve her of her duty of care to Daniel and it does not exonerate her from liability if she has breached that duty. That Flatt may have been forced to choose between her responsibilities to two clients provides no justification for immunizing her from liability if she did not act with the skill, prudence, and diligence that other members of the profession would have exercised under the circumstances. Daniel did not create the conflict. He was deprived of the services of the counsel of his choice through no fault of his own. The majority has advanced no reason why he should bear the loss resulting from the attorney's resolution of the conflict. . . .

Because Flatt chose to resolve the conflict of interest between clients Daniel and Hinkle by withdrawing from her representation of Daniel,[10] her conduct was governed by the State Bar Rules of Professional Conduct, rule 3–700(A)(2), which requires that "[a] member shall not withdraw from employment until the member has taken reasonable steps to avoid reasonably foreseeable prejudice to the rights of the client. . . . " Oddly, the majority does not discuss this rule. . . .

Whether, on the facts of this case, Attorney Flatt breached her duty of care to Daniel by failing to advise him upon withdrawing from representation that the limitations period was running or that he should promptly seek replacement counsel is an issue to be resolved by expert evidence regarding the standard of care. . . . This issue could be resolved on summary judgment only if, by offering uncontroverted expert evidence, Flatt established that the reasonably prudent lawyer, withdrawing from representation of Daniel under these circumstances, would not have advised Daniel of the running of the statute of limitations or of the need to promptly obtain other counsel. . . .

Because the record contains no evidence showing what the standard of care would have required Flatt to do upon discovering the conflict of interest and withdrawing from her representation of Daniel, Flatt has failed to establish, as a matter of law, that her duty of care to Daniel did not obligate her to advise him regarding the statute of limitations. Therefore, Flatt has not demonstrated that her actions satisfied the standard of care she owed to Daniel, and Flatt is not entitled to summary judgment on this ground.

---

[10] FN4. Although the majority describes this as a case in which Flatt had "a mandatory and unwaivable duty *not* to represent [Daniel]," such is not the case. Flatt might well have been able to resolve the conflict of interest by withdrawing from her representation of Hinkle, rather than Daniel, so long as the conflict of interest arose inadvertently. (See *Truck Ins. Exchange v. Fireman's Fund Ins. Co.* (1992) 6 Cal.App.4th 1050, 1059–1060.) Moreover, there was another option available to Flatt: our Rules of Professional Conduct permit a lawyer to "[r]epresent a client in a matter and at the same time in a separate matter accept as a client a person or entity whose interest in the first matter is adverse to the client in the first matter" if both clients give their informed written consent to the dual representation. (Rules Prof.Conduct, rule 3–310(C)(3).) The record does not show why Flatt did not pursue either of these options.

PROBLEM 9–1

Which opinion in *Flatt* is more persuasive? Why?

For a case dealing with formation issues in the context of unbundled representation, *see Delso v. Trustees for Retirement Plan for Hourly Employees of Merck & Co., Inc.*, 2007 WL 766349 (D. N.J. 2007). There the court stated "the attorney-client relationship begins with a non-lawyer's reliance on the professional skills of an attorney, who, in turn, knows of this reliance and accepts responsibility for it," and held that an attorney who agreed to help a party with research and to "ghostwrite" some documents had created an attorney-client relationship.

C. ADVERTISING AND SOLICITATION

Model Rule of Professional Conduct 7.1–7.3

Advertising by lawyers is a simple subject that has produced a complicated body of law. The subject is simple because the legal and economic basics of advertising are simple. Advertising allows lawyers to provide potential clients with information about services and prices. Informed clients are better able to choose among lawyers in terms of both service and price. Consumers who are sensitive to price will favor relatively less expensive lawyers, and competition among lawyers will tend to keep prices down, at least relative to a world in which consumers have less information.[11]

Fraudulent advertisements are harmful of course (they create demand for a product or service out of proportion to its actual quality), but they can be regulated through ordinary prohibitions on fraud. Lawyers are always subject to civil penalties for fraud or coercion; disciplinary rules are not needed to impose such penalties (though they may be relevant in some ways, such as drafting jury instructions).

The relatively straightforward economics of lawyer advertising have nevertheless produced a complex body of law. That body of law goes beyond the simple prohibition of fraud, which Model Rule 7.1 forbids. For example, today Model Rule 7.2(a) permits advertising through written or recorded communications, though under Model Rule 7.2(b) a lawyer may not pay anyone for an endorsement and, under Rule 7.2(c), the ad must

---

[11] Licensing of lawyers restricts entry into the market, and thus the supply of legal services, so advertising might not drive price down to marginal cost, as in the economic model of perfect competition. On average, however, one would expect advertising to induce competition that would tend to increase the quality of service and decrease the price.

list the name and address of at least one lawyer for the firm who accepts responsibility for its content. Previous restrictions were stricter.

Rule 7.2 is limited to written or recorded communications and the rules distinguish between such fixed, static communications and real-time contact either in person, on the phone, or through electronic media such as text, chat, or e-mail. Rule 7.3(a) forbids lawyers from using such means to solicit business if making a profit is a significant motive for the solicitation. Communications from at least some public interest lawyers (at least those not planning to claim fees) and pro bono volunteers are not covered. (The rule also excludes communications with other lawyers, clients a lawyer has represented before, or with family members of the soliciting lawyer.) Rule 7.3(c) also requires that permitted solicitations be labeled "Advertising Material." Finally, Rule 7.4(a) allows lawyers to advertise that they do or do not do a particular kind of work but under Rule 7.4(d) a lawyer may not claim to be a specialist unless he or she has been certified as such by an organization approved by a state or accredited by the ABA and the name of the certifying organization is included in the advertisement.

To understand why these rules are so complex it helps to understand a bit of history. The current version of Model Rule 7.2 (and its predecessors) is the product of Supreme Court decisions that forced bar associations to abandon prohibitions on lawyer advertising, which they imposed for most of the 20th Century. These prohibitions were not the result of inertia, or respect for tradition. Lawyer advertising was common in the 19th Century. *See* LAWYER ADVERTISING AT THE CROSSROADS (ABA 1995) (hereinafter "Crossroads Report"). Abraham Lincoln, for example, ran modest classified ads, which promised that all business "will be attended to with promptness and fidelity."

Nevertheless, since 1908, when the American Bar Association adopted its original Canons of Ethics, states have severely restricted advertising by lawyers. Why? The ABA's 1995 study of the issue reports that the 1908 restrictions were neither a response to advertising abuses, nor of credible reports of harm to consumers, so the explanation probably lies elsewhere.

One conjecture is that bar associations adopted advertising restrictions as one part of a more general effort to restrict entry into the profession. Why restrict entry? One might offer a standard economic explanation: the fewer lawyers there are the more money each lawyer can make. More topical explanations are available, too. Rapid commercialization and industrialization in the latter part of the 19th Century, combined with widespread immigration and relatively easy standards for admission to the bar, produced a much bigger and more heterogeneous bar. Entry restrictions could be seen as a reaction to these developments—an effort to preserve the traditional demographics of the bar. Crossroads Report at 33.

A related explanation, succinctly offered by Professor Fred Zacharias, is that bar associations adopt rules against advertising so that lawyers will not look too bad (or at least not worse than they already may appear) in the eyes of the public.[12] Another possible explanation is that advertising regulations solve an adverse selection problem. The idea behind this argument is that lawyers who advertise are less scrupulous than others, yet advertising would direct clients to them, with the result that the shiftiest lawyers would have the most business, and the average quality of representation would suffer.

Barton v. State Bar, 209 Cal. 677 (1930), exemplifies the operation of rules in the first part of the 20th Century. California Rule of Professional Conduct 2 provided that "[a] member of The State Bar shall not solicit professional employment by advertisement or otherwise. This rule shall not apply to the publication of use of ordinary professional cards, or to conventional listings in legal directories."

Barton placed an ad in a daily newspaper, which read: "D. Barton. Advice free, all cases, all courts. Open eves. Room 907, 704 Market Street, phone Douglas 0932." He was found to have violated the rule, and appealed on the ground that the rule was unreasonable. According to Barton—writing in 1930!—"no amount of preaching can alter the cold, indisputable fact that the law has ceased to be a sacrosanct profession and has become a highly competitive business." The Court disagreed, even though it acknowledged that the only words in the advertisement that violated the rule were: "Advice free." (The Court did, however, reduce the recommended punishment from a three-month suspension to a reprimand.)

Matters stood roughly there until the 1970s. In *Virginia Pharmacy Board v. Virginia Citizens Consumer Council*, 425 U.S. 748 (1976), the Court struck down a statute that declared it was "unprofessional conduct" for a pharmacist to advertise the price of prescription drugs. The Court held that the First Amendment's protection of the freedom of speech extends to "commercial speech," a term that included the price advertisements by pharmacists that were at issue in that case. The Court rejected the state's justifications for the law, which included the claims that the regulations were necessary to maintain high standards of professionalism, to prevent pharmacists from cutting prices and then cutting corners to maintain their profit margins, which might harm consumers, and to maintain the status of pharmacists as skilled professionals rather than "shopkeepers," which supposedly attracted new entry into the profession and reinforced good professional habits among existing pharmacists.

[12] Fred C. Zacharias, *What Direction Should Legal Advertising Take?* http://ssrn.com/abstractID=829305.

These justifications were similar to the claims bar associations advanced to justify prohibitions on lawyer advertising. It was therefore predictable that the Court would face a challenge to those prohibitions. The very next term, in *Bates v. State Bar of Arizona*, 433 U.S. 350 (1977), the Court applied *Virginia Pharmacy Board* and struck down Arizona's ban on commercial advertising. The Court surveyed a large number of justifications for the ban (some of them extraordinarily weak, such as the claim that advertising would raise prices by raising overhead—do you see why that is such a bad argument?) and rejected each of them.

In dissent, Justice Powell argued that legal services are so individualized and subjective that they cannot be touted in categorical terms, and that it is not possible to determine whether a fee that is reasonable for one case is reasonable for another. At times his argument approached a striking sort of paternalistic nihilism, mixing the odd claim that no general treatment of the subject would be appropriate with the plea to wait until bar associations revised their rules.

The *Bates* Court focused on price advertising. The majority opinion claimed to reserve judgment on both advertisements touting the quality of a firm and on in-person solicitation, as opposed to conventional media ads, but portions of the opinion strongly hinted that states could regulate these types of communications. The Court confirmed this suggestion in two solicitation cases decided the following term, each written by Justice Powell, the dissenter in *Bates*.

Ohralik v. Ohio State Bar Association, 436 U.S. 447 (1978), affirmed a sanction based on Ohralik's in-person solicitation of two victims of an accident, one of whom he solicited in her hospital bed, though after consulting with her parents. Each person initially assented to be represented by Ohralik but then withdrew their assent. Ohralik sued them for breach of contract; they reported him to the state bar.

Justice Powell distinguished *Bates* on the ground that, "[u]nlike a public advertisement, which simply provides information and leaves the recipient free to act upon it or not, in-person solicitation may exert pressure and often demands an immediate response, without providing an opportunity for comparison or reflection." The Court held that Ohio had a valid interest in preventing fraud or "overreaching" (presumably meaning coercion). When Ohralik pointed out that he had not been found to have committed fraud or to have coerced anyone, the Court replied that Ohio could ban in-person solicitation as a prophylactic measure to prevent those harms.

In re Primus, 436 U.S. 412 (1978), involved group solicitation in South Carolina. Following media reports that South Carolina women on welfare were being sterilized as a condition to receiving further public assistance, a businessman called the South Carolina Council on Human Relations to investigate the charges. He set up a meeting of such women, which Ms. Primus, who was on retainer to the Council, attended. At this meeting, Ms. Primus advised the women that they might have a claim based on their sterilization. The American Civil Liberties Union later offered to pay for such a suit.

A local woman named Mary Etta Williams decided to sue. When Ms. Primus learned this, she wrote Ms. Williams, informing her of the ACLU's offer.[13] Ms. Williams had the letter with her when she went to her doctor to seek care for one of her children. The doctor's lawyer was in the office, and he persuaded Ms. Williams to sign a release in favor of the doctor. She showed him Ms. Primus's letter, which he copied. The state bar charged Ms. Primus with unlawful solicitation; she was found to have violated the bar's anti-solicitation rule and she received a private reprimand, which she appealed.

The Supreme Court reversed. It analogized Ms. Primus's actions to those at issue in *NAACP v. Button*, 371 U.S. 415 (1963), which protected the activities of the NAACP in holding meetings to advise Southern Blacks of their rights. The Court felt Ms. Primus's actions fell within the rule that "collective activity undertaken to obtain meaningful access to the courts is a fundamental right within the protection of the First Amendment." *Id.* at 425 (quoting *United Transportation Union v. Michigan Bar*, 401 U.S. 576, 585 (1971)). Noting that "[t]he ACLU engages in litigation as a vehicle for effective political expression and association, as well as a means of communicating useful information to the public," the Court concluded that Ms. Primus's "letter . . . to Mrs. Williams thus comes within the generous zone of First Amendment protection reserved for associational freedoms."

The Court distinguished *Ohralik* on the ground that

---

[13] The letter stated:

Mrs. Marietta Williams 347 Sumter Street Aiken, South Carolina 29801

Dear Mrs. Williams:

You will probably remember me from talking with you at Mr. Allen's office in July about the sterilization performed on you. The American Civil Liberties Union would like to file a lawsuit on your behalf for money against the doctor who performed the operation. We will be coming to Aiken in the near future and would like to explain what is involved so you can understand what is going on.

Now I have a question to ask of you. Would you object to talking to a women's magazine about the situation in Aiken? The magazine is doing a feature story on the whole sterilization problem and wants to talk to you and others in South Carolina. If you don't mind doing this, call me collect at 254–8151 on Friday before 5:00, if you receive this letter in time. Or call me on Tuesday morning (after Labor Day) collect.

I want to assure you that this interview is being done to show what is happening to women against their wishes, and is not being done to harm you in any way. But I want you to decide, so call me collect and let me know of your decision. This practice must stop.

About the lawsuit, if you are interested, let me know, and I'll let you know when we will come down to talk to you about it. We will be coming to talk to Mrs. Waters at the same time; she has already asked the American Civil Liberties Union to file a suit on her behalf.

Sincerely, s/ Edna Smith Edna Smith Attorney-at-law

> This was not in person solicitation for pecuniary gain. Appellant was communicating an offer of free assistance by attorneys associated with the ACLU, not an offer predicated on entitlement to a share of any monetary recovery. And her actions were undertaken to express personal political beliefs and to advance the civil-liberties objectives of the ACLU, rather than to derive financial gain.

Taken together, *Ohralik* and *Primus* created more lenient standards for regulations of solicitation directed to what could plausibly be called a political end than for regulations aimed at solicitation for ordinary, money-making litigation. The basic logic was that self-interest led to a greater risk of "overreaching" in the latter case than in the former, and thus greater leeway for state regulation.

Many questions remained, however. Some of these were answered in the 1980s. The Court clarified the test it would apply to regulations of "commercial speech," an imprecise term that safely encompassed Ohralik's behavior but not, probably, Primus's. Under *Central Hudson Gas & Electric Corp. v. Public Service Commission of New York*, 447 U.S. 557 (1980), as modified by *Board of Trustees of the State University of New York v. Fox*, 492 U.S. 469 (1989), regulations of commercial speech are permissible if the speech at issue: (i) is protected speech, which means it concerns lawful conduct and is not misleading; (ii) the government interest in regulating speech is substantial; (iii) the regulation directly advances the government's interest; and (iv) there is a reasonable fit between the scope of the regulation and the scope of the interest.

As both *Bates* and *Ohralik* state, the government always has a substantial interest in preventing fraud, coercion, or "overreaching." This point is one of the few to remain constant through the cases. Which other interests are substantial, however, and which are not? The answer is not as clear as one might hope.

In re R.M.J., 455 U.S. 191 (1982), dealt with a rule specifying (and limiting) the information lawyers could place in advertisements. The court held that the rule was unconstitutional as applied to advertisements that were possibly (and partly) in bad taste but were not misleading. Similarly, *Zauderer v. Office of Disciplinary Counsel*, 471 U.S. 626 (1985), rejected a state's claim that the dignity of the profession is a substantial state interest justifying advertising restrictions. The Court did not say that concerns for professional dignity could never justify a restriction, but it did not seem sympathetic to the argument.

Zauderer ran a newspaper ad aimed at women who had used the Dalkon Shield IUD. The ad recounted allegations made regarding the health effects of the Dalkon Shield and stated that the firm was representing women in such cases and would represent additional clients on a contingent fee basis. It also contained an illustration of the IUD. Zauderer received 200 inquiries, leading to the filing of 136 suits.

Ohio disciplinary authorities alleged that this ad, and another Zauderer had run offering to represent defendants accused of drunk driving on what amounted to a contingent fee basis, violated various anti-advertising rules. The drunken driving ad was alleged to advertise an unlawful service—contingent-fee representation in a criminal case. The IUD ad was alleged to say both too much—by including an illustration, which the rules prohibited, and too little—by failing to include two required disclosures: (i) whether the fee percentage would be calculated before or after costs; and (ii) that clients might be liable for costs. Zauderer was found liable for each ad, and appealed.

The Supreme Court struck down the state's restrictions on what Zauderer could not say but upheld the rules compelling disclosure. The Court found that the ads were not misleading and rejected the claim that the ads presented the "possibilities for overreaching, invasion of privacy, the exercise of undue influence, and outright fraud" that the Court had cited in upholding the restrictions on in-person solicitation that were at issue in *Ohralik*. As the Court put it

> appellant's advertisement—and print advertising generally—poses much less risk of over-reaching or undue influence. Print advertising may convey information and ideas more or less effectively, but in most cases, it will lack the coercive force of the personal presence of a trained advocate. In addition, a printed advertisement, unlike a personal encounter initiated by an attorney, is not likely to involve pressure on the potential client for an immediate yes-or-no answer to the offer of representation. Thus, a printed advertisement is a means of conveying information about legal services that is more conducive to reflection and the exercise of choice on the part of the consumer than is personal solicitation by an attorney. Accordingly, the substantial interests that justified the ban on in-person solicitation upheld in Ohralik cannot justify the discipline imposed on appellant for the content of his advertisement.

The Court also found that, unlike in-person solicitation, advertisements were visible and open to scrutiny in their original form; there would be no conflicting testimony about what the ad said, and thus no need to avoid such conflicts by prohibiting the ad.

As noted above, the Court rejected Ohio's claim that its restrictions justifiably maintained the dignity of the profession. The Court said "although the State undoubtedly has a substantial interest in ensuring that its attorneys behave with dignity and decorum in the courtroom, we are unsure that the State's desire that attorneys maintain their dignity in their communications with the public is an interest substantial enough to justify the abridgment of their First Amendment rights."

Finally, with regard to Ohio's requirement that the ads disclose certain information about contingent fees, the Court said

> In requiring attorneys who advertise their willingness to represent clients on a contingent-fee basis to state that the client may have to bear certain expenses even if he loses, Ohio has not attempted to prevent attorneys from conveying information to the public; it has only required them to provide somewhat more information than they might otherwise be inclined to present. . . .
>
> [T]he State has attempted only to prescribe what shall be orthodox in commercial advertising, and its prescription has taken the form of a requirement that appellant include in his advertising purely factual and uncontroversial information about the terms under which his services will be available. Because the extension of First Amendment protection to commercial speech is justified principally by the value to consumers of the information such speech provides . . . appellant's constitutionally protected interest in not providing any particular factual information in his advertising is minimal. . . .
>
> We do not suggest that disclosure requirements do not implicate the advertiser's First Amendment rights at all. We recognize that unjustified or unduly burdensome disclosure requirements might offend the First Amendment by chilling protected commercial speech. But we hold that an advertiser's rights are adequately protected as long as disclosure requirements are reasonably related to the State's interest in preventing deception of consumers. . . . The State's position that it is deceptive to employ advertising that refers to contingent-fee arrangements without mentioning the client's liability for costs is reasonable enough to support a requirement that information regarding the client's liability for costs be disclosed.

The reasoning in *Zauderer* promised great freedom for lawyers to advertise. For a while, that promise was realized. *Shapero v. Kentucky Bar Association*, 486 U.S. 466 (1988), held that Kentucky could not prevent a lawyer from sending solicitation letters targeted to homeowners facing foreclosure proceedings.[14] In response to the state's claim that it was protecting recipients who might feel overwhelmed by their legal problems, Justice Brennan's plurality opinion said "[t]he relevant inquiry is not whether there exist potential clients whose "condition" makes them susceptible to undue influence, but whether the mode of communication poses a serious danger that lawyers will exploit any such susceptibility." *Id.* at 465. The Court noted that, unlike *Ohralik*, the written solicitation in

---

[14] The letter stated

"It has come to my attention that your home is being foreclosed on. If this is true, you may be about to lose your home. Federal law may allow you to keep your home by ORDERING your creditor [sic] to STOP and give you more time to pay them

You may call my office anytime from 8:30 a. m. to 5:00 p. m. for FREE information on how you can keep your home

"Call NOW, don't wait. It may surprise you what I may be able to do for you. Just call and tell me that you got this letter. Remember it is FREE, there is NO charge for calling."

this case was available to be examined by bar officials and did not present the sort of risk of undue influence the *Ohralik* Court thought inherent in face-to-face solicitation.

Similarly, in *Ibanez v. Florida Department of Business and Professional Regulation*, 512 U.S. 136 (1994), the Court held that Florida could not discipline an attorney who was also a certified public accountant and certified financial planner, and who listed these certifications ("CPA" and "CFA") on her business cards, letterhead, and telephone listings. That result was consistent with *Peel v. Attorney Registration and Disciplinary Commission of Illinois*, 496 U.S. 91 (1990), which held that Illinois could not discipline an attorney for proclaiming that he was "certified as a civil trial specialist by the National Board of Trial Advocacy." In each case the Court noted that there was no evidence that the particular statements at issue were misleading and rejected the argument that such statements generally may be regulated as inherently misleading.

Only a year after *Ibanez*, however, in *Florida Bar v. Went For It*, 515 U.S. 618 (1995), the Court blurred what appeared to be a clear distinction between in-person solicitation, which could be prohibited under *Ohralik*, and generally distributed written matter, which could be regulated for falsity but not prohibited. Florida conducted a "two year study of the effects of lawyer advertising on public opinion," and then modified its anti-advertising rules.

One of the new rules forbid written solicitation regarding "an action for personal injury or wrongful death or otherwise relates to an accident or disaster involving the person to whom the communication is addressed or a relative of that person, unless the accident or disaster occurred more than 30 days prior to the mailing of the communication." In conjunction with another rule, pertaining to lawyer referral services, this rule created what the Court called a "brief 30–day blackout period after an accident during which lawyers may not, directly or indirectly, single out accident victims or their relatives in order to solicit their business." The law did not prohibit non-lawyers from contacting accident victims, so it created an imbalance some might find worrisome. An insurer could contact a victim and attempt to settle a claim and obtain a release, for example, but a lawyer could not contact the victim and advise them to sue instead.

Florida argued that the regulation was justified as an effort "to protect the flagging reputations of Florida lawyers by preventing them from engaging in conduct that, the Bar maintains, 'is universally regarded as deplorable and beneath common decency because of its intrusion upon the special vulnerability and private grief of victims or their families.' " Notwithstanding *Zauderer's* at best tepid response to the dignity of the profession as a justification for advertising restrictions, the *Went For It* Court treated this interest as substantial. The Court made this clear in rejecting the lawyers' claim that anyone who was offended by such a solicitation could simply throw it away:

> The purpose of the 30–day targeted direct mail ban is to forestall the outrage and irritation with the state licensed legal profession that the practice of direct solicitation only days after accidents has engendered. The Bar is concerned not with citizens' "offense" in the abstract . . . but with the demonstrable detrimental effects that such "offense" has on the profession it regulates.

The 5–4 decision in *Went For It* muddles significantly the constitutional aspect of lawyer anti-advertising rules. It is at odds with at least the implications of *Zauderer*, which questioned whether the dignity of the profession was sufficient to justify such rules. An unsympathetic but fair reading of the opinion is that it rests on the view that the state has a substantial interest in having the public think that lawyers as a class are better than they are—the lawyers who want to send such ads have the disposition to do so whether or not the ads are sent. A sympathetic but fair reading would hold that if lawyers cannot engage in targeted advertising they might find it easier to resist the temptation to engage in unseemly conduct.

The most parsimonious explanation of the opinion is that the self-interest of lawyers justifies restrictions on commercial speech so long as those restrictions are not too severe. (Recall that the ban lasted only 30 days after the accident.) Justice Kennedy made this point in dissent, quoting "the amicus brief filed by the Association of Trial Lawyers of America. There it is said that disrespect for the profession from this sort of solicitation (but presumably from no other sort of solicitation) results in lower jury verdicts." As he concludes, "to the extent the bar seeks to protect lawyers' reputations by preventing them from engaging in speech some deem offensive, the State is doing nothing more (as amicus the Association of Trial Lawyers of America is at least candid enough to admit) than manipulating the public's opinion by suppressing speech that informs us how the legal system works."

Where do all these cases leave us, particularly as law firm communications have moved onto the Internet and listservs, into chat rooms, and out through spam? A couple of points seem clear.

First, lawyers who plan litigation plausibly described as political have more leeway in both advertising and solicitation than do lawyers who are looking for more typical, garden-variety work. This point follows from the distinction between *Ohralik* and *Primus*, the logic of which applies across different forms of media.

Second, states can regulate solicitation more closely than advertising. Right off the bat, this distinction presents a definitional question. What is advertising and what is solicitation? One way to approach the question is to remember that *Ohralik* accepted the ban on solicitation on the ground that in-person contacts present a high risk that lawyers will coerce or dupe prospective clients and that verbal communications can produce messy swearing contests because they cannot be reproduced exactly in litigation or disciplinary hearings. Following this reasoning, communications that cannot be verified and which present a genuine risk of undue influence are solicitations and other communications are not. In more concrete terms, telephonic or in-person pitches to particular people would be solicitations; written pitches, or verbal pitches directed at large numbers of people would not.

This distinction fits the Model Rules reasonably well. Model Rule 7.2 states that lawyers "may advertise services through written, recorded or electronic communication, including public media." Model Rule 7.3(a), by contrast, states "[a] lawyer shall not by in-person, live telephone or real-time electronic contact solicit professional employment from a prospective client when a significant motive for the lawyer's doing so is the lawyer's pecuniary gain, unless the person contacted" is another lawyer or someone with a close relationship or prior professional relationship with the target of the solicitation.[15]

California law is similar. California Rule of Professional Conduct 1–400(a) defines a "communication" as any message or offer "concerning the availability for professional employment of a member or a law firm directed to any former, present, or prospective client." Rule 1–400(B) defines "solicitation" to include any communication:

> (1) Concerning the availability for professional employment of a member or a law firm in which a significant motive is pecuniary gain; and
>
> (2) Which is;
>
> > (a) delivered in person or by telephone, or
> >
> > (b) directed by any means to a person known to the sender to be represented by counsel in a matter which is a subject of the communication.

Rule 1–400(C) forbids lawyers from soliciting any "prospective client with whom the member or law firm has no family or prior professional relationship, unless the solicitation is protected from abridgment by the Constitution of the United States or by the Constitution of the State of California. A solicitation to a former or present client in the discharge of a member's or law firm's professional duties is not prohibited." It is worth noting that Rule 1–400(B)(2) overlaps with the rule against contacting a

---

[15] The prohibition on real-time electronic contact" was added in 2002. According to the Reporter's Memorandum explaining the change, it distinguishes between chat-room discussions and e-mail communications on the ground that the former pose the risks associated with in-person solicitation while the latter do not.

party one knows to be represented by counsel. Model Rule 4.2 and California Rule 2–100. Rule 2–100(C)(2) provides that you may discuss a matter with a represented person who is looking for a second opinion. Presumably this more particular rule would allow communications otherwise prohibited by Rule 1–400(B)(2).

Ironically enough, taken by themselves the California rules paint a misleading picture of California's anti-advertising rules. Pursuant to Rule 1–400(e), the Board of Governors of the state bar has defined 16 types of communications that are presumed to be misleading, and therefore in violation of the rule. As one might expect, many of these categories deal with things other than the truth or falsity of a communication.

Third, because communications that give recipients the time and privacy to think things over (breathing space, as it were), and which are preserved and thus available for future inspection, receive more lenient treatment than in-person pitches, lawyers who make approaches over the Internet may have slightly more latitude than those who limit themselves to traditional media. For example, unlike mailed solicitations, e-mail communications can be interactive at very low cost, and thus may partly substitute for personal contact but still be available for inspection and present a lower risk of undue influence.

This distinction is particularly important under California law, under which a communication is a solicitation only if it is made in person or by telephone, Rule 1–400(d)(1), unless it is directed at a represented party. In its Formal Opinion 2001–155, the California State Bar Standing Committee on Professional Responsibility and Conduct concluded that law firm websites are communications, not solicitations, even if they provide e-mail services:

> Although e-mail communication as part of web site technology permits faster responses and more interaction than is possible with other forms of written communication, it does not create the risk that the attorney might be able to use her persuasive ability and experience to influence unduly the potential client's thoughtful decision to hire her. Similarly, although e-mail can be transmitted through telephone lines, its resemblance to a telephone discussion ends with the mechanism of transmission. The static nature of an e-mail message allows a potential client to reflect, re-read, and analyze; the written form allows the potential client to share and discuss the communication with others and maintain a permanent record of its contents; and the mechanical steps involved in sending and receiving messages impose a measured pace on the interchange.

Formal Opinion 2004–166 extended this logic to communications targeted at chatrooms likely to involve potential clients as participants. This opinion provides an interesting example of tension that can arise between relatively clear statutory language, the relatively impersonal nature of communications in web forums such as chat rooms, and the concern that lawyers not appear undignified. The opinion offers the following hypothetical:

> Attorney, a personal injury lawyer, searches the Internet and discovers a chat room created for victims and families of a recent mass disaster. The purpose of the chat room is prominently stated on its home web page as "the provision of emotional support to victims of the recent mass disaster and their families by similarly affected persons."[16] After monitoring the conversation taking place in the chat room for a while, Attorney introduces herself as a lawyer and offers to answer any questions. Attorney hopes to prompt the chat room participants to hire her to perform legal services.

The opinion concludes that the attorney's messages are not solicitations under California law, because they are not made in person or by telephone. It draws on the reasoning of *Ohralik*, however, to conclude that the messages can be prohibited as communications "transmitted in [a] manner which involves intrusion, coercion, duress, compulsion, intimidation, threats, or vexatious or harassing conduct," in violation of Rule 1–400(D)(5). "Under our facts, Attorney's conduct is intrusive. Victims and family members who visit the chat room are there to seek emotional support, and do not expect to encounter a lawyer hoping to be retained.Attorney's participation in this particular chat room is therefore a violation of subdivision (D)(5) of the rule." In a footnote, however, the opinion states that the case would be different if the chat room were devoted to legal aspects of a mass disaster. In that event, "the same conduct exhibited by Attorney here would not involve intrusion."

There are risks to web-based approaches, of course. Anyone can access a website, which means a Nevada resident could easily read communications made by California lawyers. If a California lawyer's website provides general legal advice, such as the types of allegations being made against a particular drug, and invites users of that drug to contact the firm, is the California lawyer practicing law in Nevada? *See* Formal Opinion 2001–155. For a general survey of such issues, *see* J.T. Westermeier, *Ethics and the Internet*, 17 GEO. J. L. ETHICS 267 (2004).

An unusual aspect of lawyer advertising regulations is that (apart from solicitation cases involving genuine overreaching) they seem to be widely disregarded. Professor Fred Zacharias reviewed lawyer advertisements in the San Diego yellow pages. Out of 835 advertisements, he

[16] FN1. For purposes of this opinion, "chat room" refers to an Internet location where participants communicate with other participants electronically in real time. Unlike ordinary e-mail or electronic messages posted to a computer bulletin board or listserv, a chat room is designed to allow participants to exchange messages back and forth instantaneously. In addition, unlike "instant messaging," which typically involves real-time communication between only two people, a chat room typically allows several people or even a large group to communicate simultaneously.

found 257 actual or presumptive violations and many more possible violations. Nevertheless, though there was reason to believe this sample was representative of such ads over time, in the period following California's 1988 revision of its rules, Professor Zacharias found only three instances in which California lawyers had been disciplined for violating the anti-advertising rules.

Professor Zacharias concluded that the difference between the number of advertising rule violations (actual or probable) and the rarity of discipline could not be explained by either doubt as to the applicability of the rules or doubt as to whether they were constitutional. *What Lawyers Do When Nobody's Watching: Legal Advertising As A Case Study of the Impact of Underenforced Professional Rules*, 87 IOWA L. REV. 971 (2002). He suggested several reasons for this disparity. In a later work,[17] he offered the following as the main reason behind under-enforcement, quoting from a disciplinary official from Arizona:

> "We know that if we prosecute a lawyer for misleading advertising, we'll end up in litigation and the courts will probably end up finding the prosecution unconstitutional. Why waste the resources?"

D. ON (NOT) ADVANCING CLIENTS MONEY

Lawyers often represent people who need money fast. They may have been injured or wrongly fired and need to pay for food and rent, etc. Lawyers are an obvious possible source of funds, especially if the lawyer believes the client has a good claim and is willing to lend the client money in anticipation of recovery. Nevertheless, such loans are strictly prohibited under the Model Rules, which take the view that clients should not be forced or allowed to choose among lawyers on the basis of which lawyer offers them the most. Even a state that allows such loans in some circumstances, as California does, restricts loans to those made after an attorney-client relationship has been formed. The following case is typical of way the rule works.

---

[17] Fred C. Zacharias, *What Direction Should Legal Advertising Take?* http://ssrn.com/abstractID=829305

Model Rule of Professional Conduct 1.8(e)
Cal. R. Prof. Conduct 4–210

OKLAHOMA BAR ASSOCIATION V. SMOLEN

17 P.3d 456 (Okla. 2000)

HODGES, J.

¶ 1 Complainant, the Oklahoma Bar Association, alleged one count of misconduct warranting discipline against respondent attorney, Donald E. Smolen (Respondent). The complaint alleged that Respondent had violated rule 1.8(e) of the Oklahoma Rules of Professional Conduct (ORPC) . . .

¶ 3 During Respondent's representation of Mr. Miles in a case before the Workers' Compensation Court, Respondent loaned Mr. Miles $1,200. The check to Mr. Miles recited that the money was for travel expenses. Respondent admitted that the true purpose of the loan was for living expenses because Mr. Miles' home had been destroyed by fire. Without the loan, Mr. Miles indicated he would have to move to Indiana and would be unable to continue his medical treatment or make court appearances. At the time of the loan, Mr. Miles was receiving temporary total disability benefits of $426.00 a week from which Respondent's attorney fee was subtracted. Mr. Miles received $384.00 a week before loan payments.

¶ 4 Respondent's loan to Mr. Miles was interest free and without penalty or cost other than the amount of the principle. Mr. Miles was to repay the loan at $100.00 a week from his temporary total disability benefits. Mr. Miles made three $100.00 payments on the loan. One of the payments was returned to Mr. Miles resulting in his paying only $200.00 on the loan. Respondent agreed to forego further repayment until final settlement of the Workers' Compensation case.

¶ 5 When Mr. Miles became involved in other legal matters, he sought an attorney to handle the additional matters together with the workers' compensation claim. After learning of Mr. Miles search for a new attorney, Respondent terminated the attorney-client relationship with Mr. Miles. Thereafter, Mr. Miles hired Mr. Elias to represent him. During mediation over a fee dispute between Mr. Miles and Mr. Elias, the Tulsa County Bar Association learned of Respondent's loan and reported Respondent's conduct to the Oklahoma Bar Association.

¶ 6 Respondent admits the loan to Mr. Miles is not an isolated incident. He testified that he had consulted lawyers whose opinions are well respected in legal ethics, and it was their belief that Respondent's conduct would not violate rule 1.8(e). Respondent admits that his actions violate the express language of rule 1.8(e). However, Respondent submits that he has not violated the intent of rule 1.8(e), and that rule 1.8(e) unconstitutionally treats clients who need humanitarian loans differently than clients who receive advances of litigation expenses and court costs. . . .

¶ 10 Most authorities prohibit a lawyer from providing financial assistance to clients for living expenses during representation. In 1991, a draft of a provision of the Restatement of Law would have allowed a lawyer to make or guarantee a loan to a client "if the loan [was] needed to enable the client to withstand delay in litigation that otherwise might unjustly induce the client to settle or dismiss a case because of financial hardship rather than on the merits." However, in 1996 the American Law Institute Council decided the rule was ill-advised, and, in 1998, the provision was removed. The final draft of the Restatement would not allow a lawyer to make or guarantee a loan to a client except for litigation expenses and court costs. Rule 1.8(e) of the American Bar Association's Model Rules of Professional Conduct (Model Rules) adopted in 1983 prohibits a lawyer from advancing funds to a client for living expenses. A proposal to allow lawyers to advance clients funds for living expenses was rejected by the American Bar Association House of Delegates.

¶ 11 Twenty-nine states have adopted the current version of ABA Model Rule 1.8(e) which allows repayment of litigation costs to be contingent on the outcome of the case but forbids advances for living expenses. Fourteen other states follow the ABA Model Code of Professional Responsibility, adopted in 1969, or a version of the Model Rules or Model Code that requires the client remain liable for litigation expenses and court costs and prohibits advances for living expenses. Only eight states explicitly allow lawyers to advance or guarantee loans to clients for living expenses: Alabama, California, Louisiana, Minnesota, Mississippi, Montana, North Dakota, and Texas. . . .

¶ 13 We have has previously disciplined lawyers for providing financial assistance to clients for purposes other than litigation expenses and court costs. Several other courts addressing the question have also imposed discipline on lawyers for like conduct. In *Mississippi Bar v. Attorney HH,* the Mississippi Supreme Court expressed its concern that allowing a lawyer to advance funds to a client for living expenses would "generate unseemly bidding wars for cases and inevitably lead to further denigration of our civil justice system."

¶ 14 Respondent admits violating rule 1.8(e) but argues that he should not be disciplined because he did not violate the intent of the rule. What Respondent in reality requests is that we adopt an exception to the rule that allows attorneys to make loans to clients for necessary living expenses after the attorney-client relationship is established.

¶ 15 The rule against attorneys providing financial assistance to clients for living expenses is based on the common-law prohibitions against practice of champerty and maintenance.[18] The evils associated with champerty and maintenance intended to be prevented by rule 1.8(e)'s prohibition are: (1) clients selecting a lawyer based on improper factors, and (2) conflicts of interest, including compromising a lawyer's independent judgment in the case and creating the potentially conflicting roles of the lawyer as both lawyer and creditor with divergent interests.

¶ 16 Respondent argues that he advanced the funds only after the attorney-client relationship was established with repayment to be made from benefits which had already been awarded, and the loan was for humanitarian purposes. Thus, he posits that the evils of champerty and maintenance are absent here and that he should not be disciplined because he did not violate the intent of the rule. We reject this argument as have most other states. First, Mr. Miles' workers' compensation claim had not been completely resolved. He was receiving only temporary benefits at the time Respondent made the loan, and, at least, a potential settlement regarding permanent disability remained pending. Second, it would be unrealistic to conclude that even if Respondent does not publicize that he makes loans to clients for living expenses, potential clients would not learn of Respondent's practice from existing and past clients. Thus, potential clients may base their decision to retain Respondent on improper inducements. The fact that the loan was for humanitarian purposes may be a mitigating factor. Nonetheless, Respondent violated rule 1.8(e).

¶ 17 Given that the Restatement and the ABA have rejected the same exception tendered by Respondent and an overwhelming number of courts have also declined to adopt Respondent's proposed exception, we also decline to make the ad hoc exception to rule 1.8(e) advocated by Respondent. We are not unsympathetic to the plight of litigants. However, because of the potential ethical problems which can arise from a lawyer advancing clients money for living expenses, the explicit prohibition against such conduct in the Oklahoma Rules of Professional Conduct, we believe Respondent should be disciplined. . . .

CASE QUESTIONS

1. What is "champerty"? What is "maintenance"?
2. What justifications does the court offer for Rule 1.8(e)?

---

[18] FN35. 1 Geoffrey C. Hazard, Jr. & W. William Hodes, The Law of Lawyering' 1.8:601, at 273 (2d ed. 1998 Supp.); Michael R. Koval, *Living Expenses, Litigation Expenses, and Lending Money to Clients,* 7 Geo. J. Legal Ethics 1117 (1994). Champerty is "[a] bargain by a stranger with a party to a suit, by which such third person undertakes to carry on the litigation at his own cost and risk, in consideration of receiving, if successful, a part of the proceeds or subject sought to be recovered." Black's Law Dictionary 209 (5th ed.1979). "Maintenance" is "[a]n officious intermeddling in a suit which in no way belongs to one, by maintaining or assisting either party, with money or otherwise, to prosecute or defend it." *Id.* at 860.

3. What exception to the rule does the Court say that Smolen wants to establish? What is the Court's argument with regard to this proposed exception?

4. Under this holding, could the attorney write a letter to a commercial lender providing his estimate of the value of a case? Could the attorney guarantee a loan from a commercial lender?

PROBLEM 9–2

Analyze Rule 1.8(e) from an economic point of view. Are the concerns asserted to justify it valid? Who benefits from the rule? Does anyone lose?

PROBLEM 9–3

Is there a difference between advancing money for living expenses and advancing costs in litigation?

Alternative Funding Mechanisms

Lawyers cannot ethically advance clients cash (though lawyers can advance money for litigation expenses) but in some jurisdictions they can direct clients to third parties who fund litigation through a cash advance. Where permitted, such transactions are often referred to as "litigation loans." This name is somewhat misleading, because typically the advances do not have to be repaid unless the plaintiff borrower receives money from the case.

As Professor Julia McLaughlin defines the term, "six criteria typify a litigation loan: (1) a cash advance; (2) made by a non-party; (3) to a plaintiff in a personal injury civil action; (4) in exchange for an assigned share of the litigation proceeds, if any; (5) arising out of settlement or judgment; and (6) payable at the time of recovery." Julia H. McLaughlin, *Litigation Funding: Charting A Legal And Ethical Course*, 31 VT. L. REV. 156 (2007).

In *Fausone v. U.S. Claims, Inc.*, 915 So.2d 626 (Fla.App. 2005), the court described a case involving such a loan. Victoria Fausone was hit by a dump truck while riding her bicycle. She retained a law firm to represent her in this claim and in a second unrelated products liability claim.

"Beginning in October 2000, Ms. Fausone began selling interests in her lawsuits to organizations that buy such interests. These transactions are often referred to as 'litigation loans,' but the law does not regard them as loans because the corporation that gives money to the plaintiff has no right to recover from the plaintiff in the event that the lawsuit is unsuccessful. These transactions, however, are quite similar to any other nonrecourse loan secured by an interest in any form of transferable property.

Ms. Fausone first sold an interest in her lawsuit to Advance Legal Funding, L.L.C., of Biloxi, Mississippi. She received $3000 in October 2000 and agreed to pay Advance Legal Funding, L.L.C., $6000 if she received a settlement of her claim before May 1, 2001, or $9000 plus 18% interest if a settlement occurred thereafter. Thus, the interest rate on this transaction depended on the date of repayment, but was never less than 200%.

Ms. Fausone sold a similar interest to Advance Settlement Funding, Inc., of Silver Springs, Florida. She received $2000 in exchange for a repayment schedule that increased by $150 per month with a total not to exceed $4250. The annual rate of interest on this transaction for the first year was approximately 90% . . . .

In the summer of 2001, Ms. Fausone contacted U.S. Claims seeking additional money. In fairness to U.S. Claims, it should be emphasized that there is no evidence that it solicited Ms. Fausone. How or why she contacted them is not contained in the record. U.S. Claims provided more favorable terms for its litigation loans, and it helped Ms. Fausone consolidate her earlier loans. It helped her resolve the earlier loans at a significant discount.

U.S. Claims initially gave Ms. Fausone $18,000 in mid-August 2001, some of which was used to pay off the earlier loans. The purchase agreement was allegedly reviewed by Ms. Fausone's attorneys and transmitted to U.S. Claims by those lawyers. Her attorneys also provided U.S. Claims with information about her claim to assist U.S. Claims in deciding whether to advance her funds. Thereafter, Ms. Fausone returned to U.S. Claims on numerous other occasions between August 2001 and November 2002 to obtain advances in the total amount of approximately $30,000, secured by her personal injury claims. . . .

The agreement provides that if the proceeds of the claim are less than the money owed, then U.S. Claims is entitled to 100% of the proceeds, but that if no recovery is received, Ms. Fausone will have no obligation to make any payment unless failure of recovery is due to "fraud, misrepresentation, breach of warranty or failure to perform any covenant" by Ms. Fausone or her attorney. The agreement also forbids Ms. Fausone from selling any other portion of the proceeds of her claim to any other funding sources.

The agreement contains a repayment schedule. Based on the total amount advanced of $30,000, Ms. Fausone was required to repay $42,890 before November 14, 2002. After November 14, 2002, and before February 14, 2003, the amount increased to $46,808. After February 14, 2003, and before May 14, 2003, the amount increased to $50,937. Thus, although these terms were better than the earlier agreements, the interest rate for these loans was still well above the rates normally allowed for consumer transactions. . . . .

In mid–2003, U.S. Claims received notice from Ms. Fausone's attorney that her personal injury claim for her bicycle accident had settled for an amount in excess of $200,000 but that she had instructed him not to remit repayment to U.S. Claims. U.S. Claims sought to collect on the debt owed by Ms. Fausone, which, in accordance with the repayment schedule, totaled $50,937 at that time. Because Ms. Fausone refused to repay U.S. Claims, it initiated arbitration with the American Arbitration Association in Philadelphia.[19] Approximately two months later, Ms. Fausone filed a petition for declaratory judgment in Florida, arguing that the terms of her agreement with U.S. Claims were unconscionable, that she was being charged usurious interest, and that she should not be compelled to arbitrate. . . .

U.S. Claims filed a motion to dismiss or abate the Florida action pending arbitration. The trial court entered an order staying the claim pending arbitration. The case went to arbitration in February 2004 in Philadelphia. Ms. Fausone was offered the opportunity to appear by telephone, but she did not participate in the arbitration. U.S. Claims was awarded $72,117. Ms. Fausone then filed a motion in the Florida action to vacate the arbitration award, and U.S. Claims responded by filing a motion to confirm the award. A hearing was conducted on the motions in April 2004, at which time Ms. Fausone decided not to proceed with her motion to vacate. The trial court then entered an order granting U.S. Claims' motion to confirm the arbitration award.

According to the repayment schedule contained in the initial and amended agreements, this is the amount Ms. Fausone would be required to pay U.S. Claims if her payment was made after February 14, 2004, and before May 14, 2004. Although this was the amount awarded after arbitration, the arbitration award provided that if Ms. Fausone failed to pay by May 14, 2004, the amount owed would continue to increase in accordance with the payment schedule contained in the initial and amended agreements. After February 14, 2005, the amount increased to $102,007. It is unclear from the record whether this amount has continued to increase during the term of the arbitration and litigation. . . .

[Ms. Fausone] has not demonstrated that the purchase agreements could be invalidated by a Florida court. There appear to be no laws regulating such agreements in Florida. They are not treated like consumer loans. Accordingly, we must affirm the judgment on appeal and grant U.S. Claims' motion for attorneys' fees pursuant to the purchase agreement."

[19] [Eds note: The agreement provided for arbitration in Pennsylvania or Delaware and required Ms. Fausone to waive any objection to personal jurisdiction and to application of any law other than the law of Delaware.]

In contrast, courts in New York and Michigan have interpreted state usury laws to invalidate litigation loan agreements.[20] The New York court rewrote the agreement to yield a 16% interest rate. A court in Ohio interpreted state rules against champerty to invalidate such an agreement.[21]

Beyond litigation funding, ABA Formal Opinion 432 (2004) holds that criminal defense counsel may post bond for a client or arrange for it to be posted so long as the personal interest implicated by doing so presents no risk of limiting the lawyer's ability to represent the client. The Florida Supreme Court held a lawyer may give used clothing to an indigent client so long as the client does not have to "repay" the gift and it is not used to obtain employment. *Florida Bar v. Taylor*, 648 So.2d 1190 (Fla. 1994). The Mississippi Supreme Court ruled that a lawyer may advance a client money to pay health insurance premiums. *In re G.M.*, 797 So.2d 931 (Miss. 2001).

Disciplinary Rules and Competition

Why do you suppose the ABA and state disciplinary boards care if lawyers lend money to clients? After all, the money in that case goes from the lawyer to the client, not the other way around. One answer is simple paternalism: clients shouldn't pick lawyers based on who fronts them the most money. But is that answer sound? Money is what most clients are after anyway, and getting some sooner (even if they have to pay it back) may be better than getting it later. Some clients will have good reasons to need money quickly; they could be injured and unable to work, as in *Smolen*. Why should clients have to rely on other sources of money if the source best able to assess the value of their case—their lawyer—is willing to do so?

Another argument might be that loans from lawyers to clients create conflicts of interest. If a lawyer knows that she won't be repaid unless a client holds out for a larger settlement, the lawyer might have an incentive to pressure the client to reject an offer the client likes. In theory this is possible, of course, but similar pressures already exist in the contingent fee context, where lawyers might pressure clients to turn down settlements that would not be profitable for the lawyer. And this logic can run in the other direction too. Clients might feel pressured to accept inadequate settlements just to pay their then-due bills; a loan from a lawyer might tide the client over so the client could hold out for a fairer settlement or verdict.

---

[20] *Echeverria v. Estate of Lindner*, 801 N.Y.S.2d 233 (N.Y. Sup. 2005); *Lawsuit Fin. v. Curry*, 261 Mich.App. 579, 683 N.W.2d 233, 240 (2004).

[21] *Rancman v. Interim Settlement Funding Corp.*, 99 Ohio St.3d 121, 789 N.E.2d 217, 221 (2003).

Another, less appealing, explanation is that Rule 1.8(e) is anti-competitive. It is designed to keep lawyers from competing for clients on the basis of up-front cash. That means lawyers will get to keep money in the near term, which is good for them, and not worry that by doing so they will lose clients to other lawyers who are willing to serve as lenders. Is that a good basis for the rule?

Notice that this explanation is an example of a general feature of disciplinary rules. Mandatory rules, such as the prohibition on client loans, eliminate competition on the basis of the subject of the rule. Discretionary rules, such as the ability but not the duty to reveal client confidences, create competition by providing a basis on which lawyers can distinguish themselves from each other.

E. LIMITATIONS ON THE ABILITY TO FORM DUTIES OR REFUSE TO FORM DUTIES

In some circumstances lawyers have no discretion to take a case while in others their discretion to decline a case is limited. Model Rule 1.16(a)(1) provides a lawyer must decline a case if accepting it would result in a violation of the rules or some other law. Thus if accepting a matter would place a lawyer in a conflict of interest with a present client or (in a matter substantially related to earlier work) with a former client, the lawyer must decline the matter. Conversely, some state prohibitions against discrimination treat lawyers as other businesses—as "public accommodations"—and require that lawyers not decline representation on the basis of certain impermissible considerations, such as race or gender. The following case is a rare example of the enforcement of such a rule.

Model Rule of Professional Conduct 1.16(a)
Cal. R. Prof. Conduct 2–400

STROPNICKY V. NATHANSON

19 MDLR 39 (1997)

The Commonwealth of Massachusetts Commission Against Discrimination

CHARLES E. WALKER, JR., HEARING COMMISSIONER

Opinion: Findings of Fact, Conclusion of Law and Order of the Single Commissioner

I. PROCEDURAL HISTORY

On July 24, 1991, Complainant, Joseph Stropnicky, filed a complaint with this Commission charging Respondent, Judith Nathanson, with gender discrimination in a place of public accommodation in violation of G.L. c. 272, sec. 98. Specifically, Complainant alleged that he was denied legal services by Respondent, who conducts her practice out of an office in Lawrence, MA., because he is a man.

II. FINDINGS OF FACT

1. Complainant, Joseph Stropnicky, is a white male residing in Beverly, Massachusetts.

2. Respondent, Judith Nathanson, practices law for a profit as part of a partnership . . .

3. During the summer of 1991, Complainant was in the process of executing a divorce settlement agreement with his wife of eighteen years. He testified that his role throughout his marriage was non-traditional. During the early years of his eighteen year marriage, Complainant worked to support himself and his wife while she pursued a career in medicine. Once Complainant and his wife had children, he stayed home serving as homemaker and caregiver for seven years. After his second child's third birthday, he returned to school and acquired a teaching degree in biology. At the time of their divorce, Complainant was earning one-tenth of his wife's salary.

4. Philip Woodbury, the lawyer/mediator who drafted the settlement agreement advised Complainant to have the agreement reviewed by a private attorney. He provided Complainant with a list of attorneys, including Nathanson, and told him that Nathanson dealt aggressively with issues of concern to wives in divorce matters.

5. On or about July 21, 1991 Complainant phoned Respondent's office seeking to retain Attorney Nathanson to review his draft separation agreement. Nathanson's secretary informed him that Nathanson did not represent men in divorce proceedings. Complainant insisted on speaking with Nathanson and demanded that she return his call.

6. Nathanson returned Complainant's phone call and explained that she would not review Complainant's separation agreement because she only represented women in divorce proceedings. She maintained this position even after Complainant explained that the circumstances surrounding his divorce were those traditionally associated with women in divorce proceedings.

7. Following their telephone conversation, Complainant sent Nathanson a letter stating that her "women only" divorce practice was discriminatory. On July 24, 1991 he filed a discrimination complaint with this Commission.

8. In response to his letter, Nathanson wrote Complainant a letter, dated July 25, 1991, apologizing for offending him and offering to review his settlement agreement. He declined Nathanson's offer because he did not feel confident, given the circumstances, that she would, at this point, be able to represent his best interests. He executed the divorce settlement agreement without the benefit of counsel.

9. Complainant testified that Respondent's gender-based policy made him feel angry, humiliated, and defeated. He despaired of being unable to find an attorney who understood his special circumstances. Complainant stated that he always supported the goals of feminism and equal rights for women, but now feels betrayed by feminism. Complainant stated that he did not retain an attorney to review his separation agreement because of his negative experience with Respondent and now regrets his decision to proceed unrepresented.

10. Nathanson testified that she represented only women in divorce cases, in part, because she sought to devote her expertise to eliminating gender bias in the court system. She stated that the issues that arise in representing wives in divorce proceedings differ from those involved in representing husbands. By example, she noted that wives' attorneys emphasize the value of homemaker services and the limited future earning potential of homemakers re-entering the work force, while husbands' attorneys tend to minimize these issues.

11. The Supreme Judicial Court Gender Bias Study defines gender bias as follows: "Gender bias exists when decisions made or actions taken were based on preconceived or stereotypical notions about the nature, role or capacity of men and women. Myths and misconceptions about the economic and social realities of men's and women's lives and about the relative value of their work also underlie gender bias."

12. The issues of alimony, child support, and distribution of assets faced by Complainant at the time of his divorce were those traditionally associated with wives in divorce proceedings.

13. Nathanson testified that she needs to feel a personal commitment to her client's cause in order to function effectively as an advocate, and that in family law she has only experienced this sense of personal commitment in representing women. She testified that her female divorce clients derive a specific benefit from her limited practice. They feel comfortable sharing their anxieties and concerns with an advocate whom they trust to be wholeheartedly as well as intellectually committed to their interests. Nathanson believes that her practice of advancing arguments only on behalf of women enhanced her credibility with judges she appeared before in the family law courts.

14. Nathanson testified that all of her potential clients undergo a screening process. She does not make a final decision about whether to

represent a particular client in divorce proceedings without having spoken at length to the client about the matters in controversy and conferring with her partners. She would not represent women whose positions in divorce litigation were repugnant to her personal values. She testified that in other legal proceedings, not involving controversies between men and women, she has no ethical problem with representing men.

III. CONCLUSIONS OF LAW

A. Jurisdiction

G.L. c. 272, sec. 98 provides that "it is unlawful to make any distinction, discrimination or restriction on account of . . . sex . . . relative to the admission of any person to or his treatment in, any place of public accommodation, resort or amusement." The phrase "place of public accommodation, resort or amusement" is defined in G.L. c. 272 sec. 92A as "any place which is open to and accepts or solicits patronage of the general public." The Supreme Judicial Court has held that G.L. c. 272 is a remedial statute which should be given a 'broad, inclusive interpretation." [citations omitted]

The statute, "without limiting the generality of this definition," sets forth a non-exclusive list of examples of public accommodations, including "a gas station, garage, retail store or establishment, including those dispensing personal services." G.L. c. 272, sec. 92A. The courts and this Commission have extended the statute's reach to include entities not specifically cited in G.L. c. 272 in furtherance of the remedial purpose of the statute.

While this Commission has asserted jurisdiction over doctors' and dentists' offices as places of public accommodation, the issue of whether a law office is a place of public accommodation is one of first impression. In such instances, the Commission often looks to federal law for instruction in interpreting G.L. c. 151B. The Americans with Disabilities Act of 1990 (hereinafter "the ADA") specifically identifies a law office as a place of public accommodation. 42 U.S.C.A. sec. 12181(7)(F). For the Commission to impose an interpretation of G.L. c. 272 that is less inclusive than the ADA would be inconsistent with the remedial nature of the statute and the Supreme Judicial Court's instruction that it be given an expansive reading. It is clear that Respondent's law office is an "establishment" which "dispenses personal services" to the public and solicits the business of clients. There is no practical reason to determine why a law office should be viewed differently from the office of a doctor or dentist.

Respondent asserts that an attorney in private practice is a professional person, not a "place." Even though Respondent is an "individual," however, she conducts her business in a place and solicits patrons for that business. . . . Respondent operated all aspects of her business out of an office at 375 Common Street in Lawrence, MA and invited the general public, by way of advertising, to solicit her services there. I conclude that Respondent's place of business satisfies the criteria set forth in *Jaycees* and qualifies as a "place" within the meaning of the Massachusetts statute.

Respondent also contends that her business is not "public" within the meaning of the statute. She asserts that her selective screening of clients is indicative of the private nature of her business. Respondent further argues that law firms, unlike traditional "places of public accommodation" such as entertainment or retail establishments, generally invoke criteria above and beyond one's ability to pay the service fee to determine what business to accept. Thus, Respondent alleges, law offices are outside the scope of c. 272. I do not concur.

I conclude that the fact that Respondent provides a service and solicits the business of the general public is sufficient to place her business within the ambit of the statute. . . . that Nathanson advertised her services to the general public and invited potential clients to consult with her at her place of business renders her business a place of public accommodation within the meaning of the statute and requires her to abide by the Commonwealth's anti-discrimination laws pertaining to such establishments.

B. Liability

Complainant must establish a prima facie case of discrimination by showing: (1) He is a member of a protected category under the statute, (2) who was denied access to or restricted in the use of (3) a place of public accommodation. *Bachner* v. *Charlton's Lounge and Restaurant*, 9 MDLR 1288 (1984). Complainant is a member of a protected class by virtue of his gender. He has demonstrated that he was denied a consultation with and refused service by Respondent solely on the basis of his gender. Therefore, Complainant has established by direct evidence a case of discriminatory treatment.

Respondent does not dispute denying legal representation to Complainant solely on the basis of his gender. She does assert that it is not unlawful discrimination to limit one's professional practice to representing traditionally disadvantaged groups, including women. While I make no judgments about Respondent's motives in choosing to represent only women in divorce matters, I must conclude that the law does not allow her to deny service based solely on a potential client's gender.

By this ruling, I do not intend to regulate the areas of practice an attorney may choose to pursue. Nor do I intend to undermine those professional considerations attorneys traditionally rely upon in making business decisions. I conclude, simply, that an attorney or law office holding itself out as open to the public may not reject a potential client solely on the basis of gender or some other protected class. Thus, *e.g.*, Respondent may deny representation to a handicapped individual who wishes to pursue a discrimination claim based on disability on the grounds that the attorney has no expertise in that area of the law, but not because he or she chooses not to represent the handicapped.

This ruling does not impinge upon Nathanson's right to devote her practice to furthering the cause of women as she defines that cause. Had Nathanson concluded that the issues raised by Complainant's divorce action were not consistent with her specialty and area of interest and rejected Complainant on that basis, rather than solely because he is a man, the focus of this inquiry would be different. However, Nathanson never inquired into the nature or circumstances of Complainant's divorce case and stated only that she did not represent men in divorce cases. Had this case involved the rejection of a female or African–American on similar grounds, it would appear more starkly to be a violation of the spirit and intent of G.L. c. 272. Though this action involved discrimination against a male, I conclude that it constituted unlawful discrimination in violation of c. 272. . . .

Respondent asserts that this Commission is barred from adjudicating claims of this sort brought against attorneys because attorney conduct is regulated exclusively by the judiciary. . . . Respondent has cited no authority which requires me to conclude that attorneys or other regulated professions, such as medicine and dentistry, are exempt from compliance with the anti-discrimination laws of the Commonwealth with respect to selecting clients. Moreover, a close reading of the statute does not reveal any such intent by the legislature. To the contrary, the language in the statute and supporting case law require that the statute be given a broad and inclusive effect. I do not find that attorneys as a profession are exempt from the provisions of G.L. c. 272 merely because they are regulated in other respects by the state. . . .

IV. DAMAGES

Upon a determination that unlawful discrimination has occurred, the Commission is authorized to grant remedies to effectuate the purpose of the statute and to make the Complainant whole. This remedy may include damages for emotional distress. Complainant testified credibly that he felt defeated by Respondent's actions and despaired of finding an attorney who understood his circumstances. He testified that he felt angry, humiliated, and distracted as a result of Respondent's actions. I find that Complainant is entitled to damages for emotional distress in the amount of $5,000.00.

V. ORDER

Based on the foregoing Findings of Fact and Conclusions of Law, I hereby order the following relief:

(1) Respondent shall cease and desist from engaging in any discriminatory conduct in violation of G.L. c. 272, sec. 98.

(2) Respondent shall pay to the Complainant $5,000.00 in damages for emotional distress plus interest thereon at the statutory rate of 12% per annum from the date the complaint was filed until such date as payment is made and post-judgment interest begins to accrue.

PROBLEM 9–4

Should lawyers be allowed to specialize in representing only women or men in divorce matters? Is such specialization different from other sorts of specialization, such as a lawyer who only represents labor, or only management, in labor disputes, or a lawyer who only represents bidders (or targets) in takeover disputes?

PROBLEM 9–5

Suppose it is true that you just don't feel that you could represent zealously a man (woman) in such a matter. How would you handle an inquiry such as Stropnicky's? Could you require him to waive any duty of care claims as a condition of representing him? (*See* Cal. R. Prof. Conduct 3–400; Model Rule 1.8(h)(1); *Restatement* § 54(2)).

PROBLEM 9–6

In *Wishnatsky v. Rovner*, 433 F.3d 608 (2006), the court reinstated a civil rights complaint that alleged a law school clinic violated the plaintiff's free speech rights when it refused, partly on ideological grounds, to represent him. Wishnatsky had criticized the clinic for a case it brought objecting to the display of the Ten Commandments on government property. He publicly criticized the clinic and then wrote the clinic asking it to represent him in a suit seeking the removal of a depiction of the goddess Themis from a local courthouse. When the clinic refused Wishnatsky sued it, arguing that the refusal was impermissible viewpoint discrimination. "Excluding a prospective client from consideration for government-funded legal services simply because he has engaged in protected speech that the director of the program finds disagreeable," the court held, "violates [First Amendment] principles." How might the clinic have responded better?

The Main Points to Recall From Chapter 9 Are:

- Like the bundle of sticks that is property rights, attorney duties to clients are not all-or-nothing things; attorneys may assume some duties without assuming others.

- Attorneys assume duties of confidentiality when they willingly receive confidences in circumstances that justify the disclosing party in believing the attorney will keep the information confidential.
- Attorneys assume duties of care when and to the extent they undertake to advise or act on behalf of clients'.
- It is more likely that assuming a duty of care will entail assuming a duty of confidentiality than vice versa, but either is possible.
- An attorney may assume either or both duties even if no formal representation follows.
- In determining whether a lawyer has assumed duties, courts will tend to take the client's perspective on the parties' interaction, if only in determining whether factual disputes merit a trial.

CHAPTER 10

TERMINATING DUTIES

■ ■ ■

Model Rule of Professional Conduct 1.16(a)–(d) Restatement (Third) of the Law Governing Lawyers §§ 31–33

The basic rules governing termination of duties are themselves pretty simple. A client may terminate a lawyer (and thus duties) at will. A lawyer *may* terminate them if (i) the lawyer can terminate the relationship without material harm to the client; *or* (ii) there is good cause to do so; the notion of good cause includes a good reason for termination (such as nonpayment of fees or fundamental disagreement over objectives); so long as (iii) where a tribunal's consent to termination is necessary, the tribunal gives it. A lawyer *must* terminate them if any of the conditions of Rule 1.16(a) exist. Subject to some exceptions, the duty of confidentiality, you will recall, survives termination.

As always, though, even simple rule structures can present tricky problems. All representations end sometime. How do you know when that is? After settlement or trial? After time for appeal? After a contract is negotiated? What if you are advising an employer on how to deal with a problematic employee? Do the duties end if the employee is fired? What if the employee is not fired? Do the duties continue as long as the problem persists?

As these questions suggest, you need to know when your duties have ended, and you need to make sure the client knows that that is your position. A simple letter—"this concludes our representation in this matter, it has been a pleasure working with you," etc.—will do. (Why a letter? Can you think of a reason to write?) Lawyers may shy away from such letters, however, because they do not want to appear standoffish to clients, and would prefer for clients to think (in rough terms) that because you represent them already they might as well give a new matter to you.

The cases in this section highlight some aspects of these problems. In general, they reduce to three points: (1) It is easier to stay out of trouble than to get out of trouble, so make sure you want to create duties before you do; (2) when you want to get out, make sure everyone knows it; and (3) make sure the client is no worse off for your leaving than the client would have been had you stayed.

HANLIN V. MITCHELSON

794 F.2d 834 (2d Cir. 1986)

MESKILL, CIRCUIT JUDGE:

. . . In December 1976, Hermine Hanlin entered into a written partnership agreement with the four members of a singing group called "The Manhattans." The agreement provided not only that she would be an equal business partner with the four group members, but also that she would serve as the group's manager. Thus, in addition to receiving a share in the partnership's profits, Hanlin was also to receive a commission on the group's personal appearances and a percentage of the proceeds from its music publishing activities.

In 1981, shortly after the Manhattans received a Grammy award, there was a falling out between Hanlin and the group. Pursuant to a clause in the partnership agreement, the dispute went to arbitration in accordance with the arbitration laws of the State of New York. Hanlin retained California attorney Marvin Mitchelson to represent her in the arbitration proceedings. According to Hanlin, she entered into a verbal agreement with Mitchelson which required her to pay a flat fee of $25,000 in advance, plus expenses, and obligated him to handle the case "as far as it has to go." She paid him the $25,000 fee.

During hearings before a three member panel of the American Arbitration Association, the Manhattans' attorney questioned Hanlin about her withdrawal of $26,700 from a joint account she shared with Manhattans group member Kenneth Kelley. Hanlin had not previously informed Mitchelson of this withdrawal; he first learned of it during the arbitration hearings. In a subsequent affidavit, Mitchelson stated that he initially decided to " 'steer away' from the shoals of this potentially devastating testimony" for fear that the withdrawal would be considered a breach of Hanlin's fiduciary duty to the Manhattans and would harm her case against them. When Kelley asserted a formal counterclaim for the $26,700, however, Mitchelson urged the arbitrators to treat the counterclaim as beyond the proper scope of the arbitration.

The arbitral award, issued on December 23, 1982, directed the Manhattans to pay Hanlin $20,620 and directed Hanlin to pay Kelley $26,750. The award also declared that Hanlin had percentage interests in certain Manhattans contracts and directed the parties to execute assignments in connection with those interests. According to Hanlin, these assignments were never executed and the award to her was never confirmed.

Hanlin was unhappy with the arbitral award and urged Mitchelson to appeal it and to persuade the arbitral panel to correct alleged errors.

Mitchelson did obtain a "Clarification of Award," issued by the panel on February 18, 1983, which explained an apparent discrepancy between the award and one of the assignments.

Hanlin, still dissatisfied, continued to urge Mitchelson by telephone, mail and telegraph to appeal. Not satisfied with his response, she wrote to him on March 28, 1983, asking that he return the $25,000 fee she had paid. A lawyer in Mitchelson's Los Angeles office responded by letter on March 30, 1983, refusing to make any refund, stating that the arbitration award was "final and . . . not appealable," and offering "to assist any counsel you may choose with a legal case history or any other service which I can reasonably provide" if Hanlin wished to sue any of the individual defendants in New York. Hanlin responded by letter on April 6, 1983, asking for further advice about obtaining performance of the arbitral award without mentioning her earlier request for a refund.

Mitchelson himself wrote to Hanlin on April 21, 1983, saying that he had been unable to answer her letters because he had been involved in an automobile accident and had just been released from the hospital. Mitchelson reiterated that the arbitration was "binding" and explained why the award to Kelley might have been within the scope of the arbitration. He then offered to seek to reopen the arbitration, but added "I cannot act for you if you are going to be hostile and keep asking me to return fees to you." Mitchelson stated that Hanlin was not entitled to a fee refund, noting also that Hanlin owed his office $6,500 in "costs" for the arbitration.

On May 24, 1983, New York attorney Neal Rosenberg wrote to Mitchelson stating that he had "been retained by Ms. Hanlin in reference to the enclosed correspondence." The "correspondence" was apparently the series of letters described above in which Hanlin had urged an appeal and Mitchelson had declined to pursue one. Rosenberg disagreed with Mitchelson's assessment that the arbitral award could not have been appealed. He stated, however, that the deadline had passed for seeking an order to vacate or modify the award and asked Mitchelson to "advise us as to how you intend to resolve this matter." On June 21, 1983, an attorney in Mitchelson's office responded to Rosenberg, defending Mitchelson's "good faith opinion" that no appeal to the arbitral panel had been warranted and asserting that "any other relief," presumably including an appeal to a court, was beyond the scope of Mitchelson's representation of Hanlin.

On April 6, 1984, Hanlin filed the instant diversity action against Mitchelson in the district court seeking compensatory and punitive damages for "intimidation," negligence, defamation and malpractice. Mitchelson counterclaimed for the $6,500 in costs and expenses allegedly owed to him by Hanlin. . . .

When Hanlin's deposition of Mitchelson was aborted by Mitchelson's attorney, Hanlin moved the district court for an order compelling a continuation of the deposition. Mitchelson cross-moved for summary judgment on the remainder of Hanlin's complaint. Hanlin then moved for leave to amend her complaint to add claims under contract and negligence theories based on Mitchelson's alleged failure to confirm the arbitral award within the one year limitations period.

In an opinion by Judge Leisure, to whom the case had been reassigned, the court denied Hanlin's motion to compel discovery, denied leave to amend and granted summary judgment to Mitchelson, dismissing Hanlin's complaint. Hanlin appeals from the judgment entered December 12, 1985. . . .

Hanlin challenges the district court's grant of summary judgment on her negligence and malpractice claims and its denial of her motions for leave to amend her complaint and to compel discovery. . . .

The district court's third basis for denying leave to amend was that Hanlin's amended claims would be frivolous because the failure to confirm the award occurred after Hanlin had terminated Mitchelson's representation. We reject this notion for the following reasons.

It is not altogether clear that the attorney-client relationship between Hanlin and Mitchelson had terminated. The exchange of letters between Hanlin and Mitchelson's office certainly suggests that the relationship was strained. However, the letters, taken together, do not indicate conclusively that the relationship was at an end.

For example, when Hanlin demanded on March 28, 1983, that Mitchelson refund her fee, Mitchelson's office responded not be declaring the representation over but by justifying the fee and offering to assist New York counsel in preparing for suits against the individual Manhattans. Thereafter, on April 6, Hanlin wrote to Mitchelson again asking for legal advice, apparently still viewing him as her lawyer. Mitchelson responded on April 21, warning Hanlin about her "hostile" activity toward him but nevertheless offering to seek a reopening of the arbitration for her. The clear implication of the April 21 letter is that on that date Mitchelson, too, saw his attorney-client relationship with Hanlin as still intact. Even when Attorney Rosenberg wrote to Mitchelson stating that he had been retained by Hanlin at least as to the matter of the appeal, the response from Mitchelson's office, in addition to raising questions about the scope of Mitchelson's representation, not only defended past acts but also sought current information about Hanlin's arbitration-related activities, apparently recognizing some continued responsibility.

"As between attorney and client, no special formality is required to effect the discharge of the attorney. 'Any act of the client indicating an unmistakable purpose to sever relations is enough.' " *Costello v. Bruskin,*

58 A.D.2d 573 (2nd Dep't 1977) (quoting 3 N.Y.Jur., Attorney and Client, § 5). A client's malpractice suit against an attorney is enough to indicate that the client has terminated the relationship. *Id.*, at 116; *see also Lazzaro v. Kelly,* 87 A.D.2d 975 (4th Dep't 1982). Short of instituting a malpractice suit, however, a client may question her attorney's tactics, suggest alternatives and even consult another attorney without automatically terminating the attorney-client relationship. *See Bucaro v. Keegan, Keegan, Hecker & Tully, P.C.,* 483 N.Y.S.2d 564, 567–68 (Sup.Ct.1984). We have refused to find a termination even when the plaintiff and her newly retained attorney directly asked the first attorney to withdraw from the case. *Gonzalez y Barredo v. Schenck,* 428 F.2d 971, 974, 977–78 (2d Cir.1970).

We conclude that the status and scope of the attorney-client relationship here prior to the commencement of the instant suit are unresolved questions of fact. The termination of the relationship was not so clear as to render Hanlin's proposed amendment frivolous and, therefore, no proper basis appears for denying leave to amend.

Furthermore, even if the letter from Attorney Rosenberg did terminate the attorney-client relationship between Hanlin and Mitchelson, the fact of termination would not end the malpractice inquiry. Questions would still remain about Mitchelson's handling of the termination.

Ordinarily, for example, a withdrawing attorney must give a client "clear and unambiguous" notice of the attorney's intent to withdraw from representation. There is no indication on the record that such notice was ever given to Hanlin. Beyond this notice requirement, the Code of Professional Responsibility imposes a broader duty. The Code plainly states that "a lawyer shall not withdraw from employment until he has taken reasonable steps to avoid foreseeable prejudice to the rights of the client." N.Y.Jud.Law (App.) Code of Prof.Resp. DR 2–110(A)(2) (McKinney Supp.1986). *See also id.* at EC 2–32 ("Even when withdrawal is justifiable, a lawyer should protect the welfare of the client . . . endeavoring to minimize the possibility of harm."). Whether Mitchelson fulfilled these duties is another open question on this record. In any event, the termination of the attorney-client relationship here, if it occurred, did not necessarily bar the malpractice suit. Standing alone, termination would thus not be enough to render the proposed amendment frivolous or to justify the denial of leave to amend Hanlin's complaint. . . .

CASE QUESTIONS

1. What should Mitchelson have done to avoid confusion over whether he was still representing Hanlin?

2. What should he have done to avoid disagreements over his fee or whether he was obliged to pursue an appeal?
3. What test does the court adopt for determining when a client has terminated a representation?

For additional authorities discussing the problem of representation that continues after a lawyer believes it has ended, see the discussion of the limitations period for malpractice claims in Chapter 7.A.3.

Model Rule of Professional Conduct 1.16(b)–(c)

WHITING V. LACARA

187 F.3d 317 (2d Cir. 1999)

PER CURIAM:

Garrett R. Lacara appeals from two orders of Judge Spatt denying Lacara's motions to withdraw as counsel for plaintiff-appellee Joseph M. Whiting. Although the record before Judge Spatt justified denial of the motions, amplification of Whiting's position at oral argument persuades us to reverse.

In July 1996, appellee, a former police officer, filed a civil rights action against Nassau County, the Incorporated Village of Old Brooksville, the Old Brooksville Police Department, other villages, and various individual defendants. The action was based on the termination of his employment as an officer. He sought $9,999,000 in damages.

Appellee's initial counsel was Jeffrey T. Schwartz. In October 1996, Robert P. Biancavilla replaced Schwartz. A jury was selected in October 1997 but was discharged when Biancavilla withdrew from the case with appellee's consent. Whiting retained Lacara in December 1997. In June 1998, the district court partially granted defendants' summary judgment motion and dismissed plaintiff's due process claims. The court scheduled the remaining claims, one free speech claim and two equal protection claims, for a jury trial on August 18, 1998. On July 20, 1998, the district court denied appellee's motion to amend his complaint to add a breach of contract claim and another due process claim.

On August 6, 1998, Lacara moved to be relieved as counsel. In support, he offered an affidavit asserting that appellee "[had] failed to follow legal advice," that appellee "[wa]s not focused on his legal rights," and that appellee "demand[ed] publicity against legal advice." Lacara also asserted that appellee had failed to keep adequate contact with his office, was "not sufficiently thinking clearly to be of assistance at the time of trial," and would "be of little or no help during trial." Furthermore, Lacara stated that appellee had "demand[ed] that [Lacara] argue collateral issues which would not be allowed in evidence," demanded that Lacara continue to argue a due process claim already dismissed by the court, and drafted a Rule 68 Offer without Lacara's consent and demanded that he serve it on defendants. Finally, Lacara asserted that on July 30, 1998, Whiting had entered his office and, without permission, had "commenced to riffle [Lacara's] 'in box.' " Lacara stated that he had to call 911 when Whiting had refused to leave the office. Lacara offered to provide further information to the court in camera. Whiting's responsive affidavit essentially denied Lacara's allegations. Whiting stated that he would not be opposed to an order relieving counsel upon the condition that Lacara's firm refund the legal fees paid by Whiting.

On August 13, Judge Spatt denied Lacara's motion to withdraw as counsel. Judge Spatt subsequently issued a written order giving the reasons for denying appellant's motion. . . .

We review a district court's denial of a motion to withdraw only for abuse of discretion. District courts are due considerable deference in decisions not to grant a motion for an attorney's withdrawal. The trial judge is closest to the parties and the facts, and we are very reluctant to interfere with district judges' management of their very busy dockets. . . .

In addressing motions to withdraw as counsel, district courts have typically considered whether "the prosecution of the suit is [likely to be] disrupted by the withdrawal of counsel." . . . Considerations of judicial economy weigh heavily in favor of our giving district judges wide latitude in these situations, but there are some instances in which an attorney representing a plaintiff in a civil case might have to withdraw even at the cost of significant interference with the trial court's management of its calendar. For example, the Code of Professional Responsibility might mandate withdrawal where "the client is bringing the legal action . . . merely for the purpose of harassing or maliciously injuring" the defendant. Model Code of Professional Responsibility ("Model Code") DR 2–110(B)(1); N.Y. Comp.Codes R. & Regs.tit. 22, § 1200.15(b)(1). In such a situation, by denying a counsel's motion to withdraw, even on the eve of trial, a court would be forcing an attorney to violate ethical duties and possibly to be subject to sanctions.

Lacara does not claim that he faces mandatory withdrawal. Rather, he asserts three bases for "[p]ermissive withdrawal" under the Model Code: (i) Whiting "[i]nsists upon presenting a claim or defense that is not warranted under existing law and cannot be supported by good faith argument for an extension, modification, or reversal of existing law," Model Code DR 2–110(C)(1)(a); (ii) Whiting's "conduct [has] render[ed] it unreasonably difficult for [Lacara] to carry out employment effectively," DR 2–

110(C)(1)(d); and (iii) Whiting has "[d]eliberately disregard[ed] an agreement or obligation to [Lacara] as to expenses or fees," DR 2–110(C)(1)(f). Although the Model Code "was drafted solely for its use in disciplinary proceedings and cannot by itself serve as a basis for granting a [m]otion to withdraw as counsel," we continue to believe that "the Model Code provides guidance for the court as to what constitutes 'good cause' to grant leave to withdraw as counsel." However, a district court has wide latitude to deny a counsel's motion to withdraw, as here, on the eve of trial, where the Model Code merely permits withdrawal.

In the instant matter, we would be prepared to affirm if the papers alone were our only guide. Although Lacara has alleged a nonpayment of certain disputed fees, he has not done so with sufficient particularity to satisfy us that withdrawal was justified on the eve of trial. Moreover, there is nothing in the district court record to suggest error in that court's finding that "Whiting has been very cooperative and desirous of assisting his attorney in this litigation." To be sure, we are concerned by Lacara's allegation that appellee trespassed in his office and that appellant had to call 911 to get Whiting to leave. However, Whiting disputes Lacara's description of these events. Moreover, we strongly agree with the district court that, as the third attorney in this case, Lacara had ample notice that appellee was a difficult client.

Nevertheless, we reverse the denial of appellant's motion for withdrawal under Model Code DR 2–110(C)(1)(a). Among Lacara's allegations are that Whiting insisted upon pressing claims already dismissed by the district court and calling witnesses Lacara deemed detrimental to his case. At oral argument, Whiting confirmed Lacara's contention that Whiting intends to dictate how his action is to be pursued. Whiting was asked by a member of the panel:

> Are you under the impression that if we affirm Judge Spatt's ruling, you will be able to tell Mr. Lacara to make the arguments you want made in this case? . . . [T]hat, if Mr. Lacara says, "That witness doesn't support your case," and you don't agree with that, are you under the impression that if we affirm Judge Spatt's ruling you'll be able to force him to call that witness?

To which Whiting replied, "Yes I am."

Moreover, in his statements at oral argument, Whiting made it clear that he was as interested in using the litigation to make public his allegations of corruption within the Brookville police department as in advancing his specific legal claims. For example, Whiting thought it relevant to inform us at oral argument that police officers in the department were guilty of "illegal drug use, acceptance of gratuities, [and] ongoing extramarital affairs while they were on duty." Appellee stated that he wanted to call an officer to testify that the officer could not "bring up anything criminal about the lieutenant, the two lieutenants, or the chief, which could get them in trouble or make the department look bad." Finally, Whiting made clear that he disagreed with Lacara about the handling of his case partly because Whiting suspects that Lacara wants to cover up corruption. Appellee stated: "For some strange reason, Mr. Lacara states that he doesn't want to put certain witnesses on the stand. . . . The bottom line is he does not want to make waves and expose all of the corruption that's going on within this community."

Also, at oral argument, appellee continued to bring up the already-dismissed due process claims. He asserted: "They found me guilty of something which was investigated by their department on two separate occasions and closed as unfounded on two separate occasions." We thus have good reason to conclude that Whiting will insist that Lacara pursue the already dismissed claims at trial.

Finally, appellee indicated that he might sue Lacara if not satisfied that Lacara provided representation as Whiting dictated. After admitting that he did not consider Lacara to be the "right attorney" for him in this case, Whiting asserted that he deemed Lacara "ineffective." The following exchange also occurred:

> Question from Panel:
> If you think that Mr. Lacara is ineffective in representing you as you stand here now, doesn't Mr. Lacara face the prospect of a . . . malpractice suit, by you, against him, if he continues in the case?
>
> Appellee's Reply:
> Yes, I believe he absolutely does.
>
> Question from Panel:
> Then, isn't that all the more reason to relieve him? So that what you say is ineffective and is in effect a distortion of the attorney-client relationship, doesn't continue?
>
> Appellee's Reply:
> I believe I do have grounds to sue Mr. Lacara for misrepresentation. . . .

We believe that appellee's desire both to dictate legal strategies to his counsel and to sue counsel if those strategies are not followed places Lacara in so impossible a situation that he must be permitted to withdraw. . . . In this case, appellee's belief that he can dictate to Lacara how to handle his case and sue him if Lacara declines to follow those dictates leaves Lacara in a position amounting to a functional conflict of interest. If required to continue to represent Whiting, Lacara will have to choose between exposure to a malpractice action or to potential Rule 11 or other sanctions. To be sure, such a malpractice action would have no merit. However, we have no doubt it would be actively pursued, and even frivolous malpractice claims can have substantial collateral consequences.

As previously noted, the interest of the district court in preventing counsel from withdrawing on the eve of trial is substantial. Moreover, we would normally be loath to allow an attorney to withdraw on the eve of trial when the attorney had as much notice as did Lacara that he was taking on a difficult client. However, the functional conflict of interest developed at oral argument causes us to conclude that the motion to withdraw should be granted.

There may be places to get justice in this world; This is not one of them

Mr. Whiting wanted his lawyer to do unethical things and to sue him for malpractice if he didn't. That, and the claim that Mr. Whiting broke into his lawyer's office and wouldn't leave until the lawyer called 911, seems enough to confirm the court's view that he was a difficult client.

But the record reveals a much more common level of difficulty. Mr. Whiting sued because he was fired as a police officer. He demanded $10 million, which probably was not the expected salary he would have received for, say, another 20 years in the department. (Do the math.)

The court made clear that Mr. Whiting saw himself as the victim of a corrupt system he wanted to use his employment suit to expose. This corruption included cops who (i) took drugs; (ii) took bribes; and (iii) cheated on their spouses. True or not, these claims were not relevant to Mr. Whiting's employment dispute, though his insistence on pursuing them may provide some insight to his personality, which in turn may provide some understanding of why he got fired.

It is very common for clients to want to use lawsuits to get back at people they feel have hurt them. They see their problem as victimization rather than as particular causes of action and they want satisfaction—justice, as they see it—for their pain.

But the law generally does not offer vindication as such. In cases like Mr. Whiting's, clients get money, not apologies or judicial condemnation of their tormentors. They certainly don't get to use the judicial process to examine other people about misconduct unrelated to the claims and defenses of a case, such as the alleged taking of drugs and marital infidelity. Courtrooms are for resolving factual and legal disputes. They are not soapboxes for damning one's enemies.

Because this sort of client thinking is more common than the sort of overt demands and threats that persuaded the court to let Mr. Lacara with-

draw, it is more likely that you will have to deal with it in your practice and less likely that a court will let you walk away from it.

That means two things. First, choose your clients with care. It mattered to the court that Mr. Lacara should have known Mr. Whiting was a touch client to handle. "Assumed risk" counts. Second, you have to manage your client's expectations so they don't hurt themselves by insisting on things the system is not set up to provide.

The phrase "managing expectations" smacks of paternalism and, frankly, it is paternalistic. Some clients lack information and adjust their expectations when they get it. Others just want to use the court system to throw a tantrum. When clients act like children they need parents. A wise lawyer/parent will explain: "There may be places in this world where you get the kind of justice you are talking about. This is not one of them."

Suppose you accept an appointment to defend a client accused of sexually molesting a 12-year-old girl and making and selling pornographic images of the encounter. Suppose further that you diligently prepare the case until, just before trial, physical evidence is disclosed that convinces you that your client is guilty. Rather than cross-examine and attempt to discredit the chief witness against your client, the girl, should you move for leave to withdraw? *United States v. O'Connor*, 650 F.3d 839 (2d Cir. 2011), affirms denial of such a motion. The court cited with approval a passage from *United States v. Oberoi*, 331 F.3d 44, 47 (2d Cir. 2003), holding that it would be an abuse of discretion to deny a motion to withdraw if continued representation would lead to violation of a disciplinary rule.

Withdrawal and the Duty of Confidentiality

The opinion in *Lacara* reveals a great deal about the relationship between Lacara and his client. That information presumably was confidential and much of it presumably was privileged. How did it get into the record? Perhaps Whiting waived confidentiality by introducing such facts himself. If he didn't, though, the case poses the question of what a lawyer may say to a judge to persuade the judge to let her out of a case without violating the duty of confidentiality. That this issue can be serious is illustrated by California Rule of Court 3.1362, which requires a lawyer moving to withdraw from a case to submit a declaration stating "in general terms and without compromising the confidentiality of the attorney-client relationship" why the attorney filed a motion rather than a consent by the client to withdrawal or substitution.

The duty of confidentiality survives even termination of representation and therefore applies when a lawyer seeks to withdraw. Courts are not required to accept blanket assertions by an attorney that grounds for withdrawal exist. *Aceves v. Superior Court*, 51 Cal.App.4th 584, 592 (1996). They should, however, require the moving attorney to do no more than provide enough non-confidential detail to allow the court to understand the general nature of the grounds asserted. In *Aceves*, for example, a supervising public defender moved to allow a deputy public defender to withdraw:

> The supervising deputy asserted he was unable to relate the facts that generated the conflict without breaching client confidences. He did, however, declare the conflict was strictly between the client and the public defender's office, it was created by a statement from the client that had caused a complete breakdown of the attorney-client relationship and it had nothing to do with threats to witnesses as the People suggested.

The trial court in *Aceves* denied the motion on the ground that these disclosures provided insufficient information about the conflict to justify granting the motion. The public defenders office petitioned the court of appeal for a writ of mandate ordering the trial court to grant the motion; the court of appeal granted the writ.

Model Rule 1.6(b)(1) contains more confidentiality exceptions than does California law, but it is not clear that these exceptions expand a lawyer's ability to argue for withdrawal. A motion to withdraw is unlikely to be related to the prevention of death or substantial injury (Rule 1.6(b)(1)), and is not often seen as a means to prevent or rectify the commission of financial wrongdoing involving the lawyers services (Rules 1.6(b)(2)–(3)). Withdrawal certainly is not a request for advice concerning the lawyer's obligations, which are more likely the premise for such a motion (Rule 1.6(b)(4)), and a motion to withdraw is unlikely to be a response to an allegation by a client or third party (Rule 1.6(b)(5)), though disclosure would be appropriate if that ever were the case. Comment 3 to Model Rule 1.16 states that if a lawyer's request to withdraw is based on a client's demand that the lawyer act unprofessionally (as in *Lacara*), the lawyer may be "bound to keep confidential the facts that would constitute such an explanation." The comment states a lawyer's representation that "professional considerations" justify the motion "ordinarily should be accepted as sufficient." It offers no suggestion on what to do if a court does not accept such a statement.

Voluntary Withdrawal and Contingency Fees

In general, a lawyer may withdraw from a matter if the client doesn't pay his bill. Model Rule 1.16(b)(5); *Restatement* § 32(g). When appearing before a tribunal, however, a lawyer may only withdraw if the tribunal consents. Model Rule 1.16(c). As *Lacara* suggests, questions of judicial efficiency play an important and perhaps dominant role in such analysis.

Where a client has agreed to pay an hourly fee and does not pay it considerations of fairness and risk allocation tend to favor the lawyer. But when the lawyer has taken the case on a contingent fee basis, those considerations tend to cut the other way. *Haines v. Liggett Group, Inc.*, 814 F.Supp. 414 (D.N.J. 1993), exemplifies this point. The case involved three New Jersey law firms that formed a group to sue tobacco companies on health-related claims. The cases (there were several of them) dated to the early 1980s, an era in which tobacco companies litigated every case to the hilt and had not lost any of them. Things changed in the mid 1990s, but that was after the events related here.

The law firms signed contingent fee agreements with their individual clients. Under these agreements the firms paid the expenses of the lawsuits. At the time of the motion to withdraw, the firms had paid $1.2 million in out-of-pocket expenses (not counting over 1 million in-house photocopies) and put in over $5 million in unpaid attorney and paralegal time. Based on a comparable case, which yielded a $400,000 verdict, the firms estimated it would cost about $150,000 in expenses and $900,000 in time to take the case to trial.

One of the firms, Budd Larner, moved to withdraw from one of the cases on the ground that it was economically infeasible to continue and that its work already had produced a public benefit in the form of an important precedent. The court denied the motion. In part it held the firm had failed to specify the expenses it would incur for the particular case from which it wanted to withdraw. In part, however, the court felt the contingent fee agreement weighed against granting the motion. As the court put it:

* * *

"[T]his motion for withdrawal implicates concerns other than money. At stake is the ability of citizens to bring and maintain suits for the purpose of vindicating rights and receiving compensation for injuries, as well the ability of clients to rely upon the representation of and the agreements with their attorneys.

When an attorney agrees to undertake the representation of a client, he or she is under an obligation to see the work through to completion. . . . This obligation is not disposed of easily. As the court stated in *Kriegsman v. Kriegsman,* 150 N.J.Super. 474 (App.Div.1977):

> An attorney has certain obligations and duties to a client once representation is undertaken. These obligations do not evaporate because the case becomes more complicated or the work more arduous or the retainer not as profitable as first contemplated or imagined. Attorneys must never lose sight of the fact that the profession is a branch

of the administration of justice and not a mere money-getting trade. . . . The lawyer should not throw up the unfinished task to the detriment of his client. . . .

In cases when withdrawal would significantly impair a client's ability to find substitute counsel or to maintain the action, courts have refused to permit withdrawal despite the fact that representation has become unprofitable for the client's lawyers. . . . Such is the case here. If Budd Larner is permitted to withdraw from this case, it is unlikely that Haines will be able to find counsel to take Budd Larner's place. . . .

Also significant to the question of withdrawal is the fact that Budd Larner's representation is premised upon a contingency fee arrangement. . . . Having contracted with Haines on a contingency fee basis, Budd Larner cannot now walk away from the contract because the case may not generate the return it expected at the outset—either by judgment and/or additional clients. Contrary to Budd Larner's suggestion, profitably is not a "basic assumption" of a contingency fee contract. Although Budd Larner entered this contract with Haines because it believed the contract would be profitable, it also knew that in litigation—particularly litigation in which a law firm advances costs and forgoes fees until an expected judgment—there are uncertainties. As with all contingency fee arrangements, Budd Larner knowingly assumed the risk that its arrangement with Haines would not match its initial prediction of costs and returns. It is simply disingenuous to suggest that unilateral or bilateral mistake can be applied in such a context on the ground that cost has exceeded initial predictions."

* * *

Haines points out that you may not be able to withdraw from a matter when you want to. Even when you may withdraw, doing so may cost you money. The basic rules in a contingent fee case are: (1) Counsel may not recover anything if they unjustifiably withdraw; (2) they may recover the value of their services if they justifiably withdraw; (3) withdrawal compelled by the need to adhere to a mandatory ethical rule counts as justifiable for this purpose, but; (4) merely permissive withdrawal does not, unless the reasons for withdrawal survive a form of heightened scrutiny in which counsel demonstrates that recovery is justified; (5) withdrawal just because counsel thinks the case is meritless never counts as justified, nor does the client's rejection of a settlement recommended by counsel. And, (6) where permitted, recovery is still within the discretion of the trial court.

Estate of Falco, 188 Cal.App.3d 1004 (1987), exemplifies these points. Four sisters hired attorney G. Dana Hobart to contest their brother's will, which left them only a nominal sum. The bulk of his estate, almost $1 million, went to his secretary. Hobart was to be paid a percentage of the estate (not just the recovery) as a contingent fee.[1]

After investigating the case, Hobart decided the will challenge had no merit. He explained his reasons in a letter to the sisters and stated "I am asking that each of you communicate to me your immediate willingness to accept any settlement that I can put together. If you do not do so, I will be forced to withdraw from a [*sic*] case on the basis that it is unethical for me and Mr. Oshman to proceed with litigation that we consider to be without merit. . . . "

Hobart obtained a settlement offer of 50% of the estate, which he claimed he had authority to accept. He also informed his clients that he was taking a one-year sabbatical and would not be available for trial if they refused the offer. At least one client denied his authority to accept the settlement, which was not consummated. Two months before trial, Hobart and his firm moved to withdraw. The court granted the motion on the ground that "the attorney-client relationship is completely broken down."

The sisters eventually agreed to a settlement in which they would collectively receive 36% of the estate. Hobart then filed a petition seeking his costs and $48,000 in attorney's fees, as *quantum meruit* recovery. The court denied the petition. It noted that under *Fracasse v. Brent*, 6 Cal.3d 784 (1972), an attorney discharged with or without cause may maintain an action in *quantum meruit* to recover the value of the attorney's pre-discharge services. (*Fracasse* plays an important role in *General Dynamics*, the next case.)

But the *Falco* court found the situation is different when the attorney quits rather than being fired. *Falco* adopted the general rule that "recovery for services in quantum meruit is allowed only when the attorney has *justifiable* cause for withdrawing. An attorney who voluntarily abandons a case without good cause will be denied compensation." 188 Cal.App.3d at 1014.

The court of appeals rejected Hobart's claim that by granting the motion to withdraw the trial court found Hobart had cause to withdraw; it held that practical concerns might justify granting the motion even if

---

[1] FN2. According to the court, "[b]ased on the valuation of the decedent's estate of $918,924 stated in the Inventory and Appraisement, upon any settlement before trial under the terms of the contingent fee agreement, appellants' fees would have been one-third of the gross estate, or approximately $306,305. Had respondents settled for 50 percent ($459,462), respondents would have received $153,157 after paying appellants $306,305. In comparison, if appellants' fees were calculated on the basis of the clients' recovery, in a settlement before trial of 50 percent, the clients would receive $306,310 and the appellants' fee of one-third would total $153,152."

counsel had no cause to make it. The court also rejected Hobart's claim that he withdrew because his clients were uncooperative.[2]

The court also rejected the claim that a client's rejection of a settlement the attorney recommends justifies the attorney in withdrawing. "A client's right to reject settlement," the court said, "is absolute." Nevertheless, the court did find that if counsel negotiated a settlement the client initially rejected, and then accepted a substantially similar settlement after counsel withdrew, the client "should be required to make restitution to the attorney, under a theory of unjust enrichment. . . . "

With regard to Hobart's claim that he was ethically required to withdraw, the court held an attorney who withdraws for ethical reasons may recover fees but only if the attorney shows: (1) her withdrawal was mandatory or, if permissive, could survive heightened scrutiny by the trial court;[3] (2) the "overwhelming and primary motivation" for withdrawal was "the obligation to adhere to . . . statute or state bar rules; (3) the action was commenced in good faith; (4) after counsel withdrew the client obtained some recovery; and (5) counsel's work contributed to that recovery.[4] The trial court had determined that the sister's case was not, in fact meritless, which meant Hobart was not under an obligation to withdraw.

For a good and more recent discussion of these rules (and of a letter-writing war between lawyers and clients), *see Rus, Miliband & Smith v. Conkle & Olesten*, 113 Cal.App.4th 656 (2003).[5]

---

[2] In doing so the court provided an important practice tip: don't write intemperate letters to your client. "It is clear from the record that there was mutual animosity between appellants and respondents. The harsh tone of Hobart's letters to respondents understandably did not improve their compatibility." No matter how good it might feel at the time to write such letters, they always look bad later.

[3] The *Falco* court explained in a footnote: "In cases involving permissive withdrawal it is within the discretion of the trial court, with heightened scrutiny consistent with the standards articulated here, to determine whether counsel's withdrawal was justified for the purpose of awarding fees."

[4] The court noted in a footnote: "Subsequent recovery cannot, in itself, rebut counsel's allegations of cause for withdrawal on the basis of a meritless case, for the simple reason that counsel may *only* recover if their client subsequently recovers. However, the amount of the recovery and the facts which gave rise to the clients obtaining the recovery are valid considerations to be weighed by the trial court in determining whether counsel's withdrawal was justified."

[5] The *Rus* court added this gloss on *Falco*'s reasoning:

To allow an attorney under a contingency fee agreement to withdraw without compulsion and still seek fees from any future recovery is to shift the time, effort and risk of obtaining the recovery (economists would refer to these things as the "costs" of obtaining recovery) from the attorney, who originally agreed to bear those particular costs in the first place, to the client. The withdrawing attorney gets a free ride as to many of the headaches of litigation which he or she otherwise would have had to endure: answering the client's phone calls, showing up for depositions, responding to discovery, fending off summary judgment motions, preparing for trial, fending off in limine motions, picking a jury, fending off motions for nonsuit, judgment notwithstanding the verdict and new trial if he or she does win, and then, at the end of it all, protecting the fruits of victory by responding to an appeal. It is a very tough row which a contingency fee attorney originally agrees to hoe. Thus it is unassailably unfair to allow him or her to escape that labor absent the most compelling of permissive reasons-reasons that, as *Falco* indicated, must pass heightened scrutiny . . . Indeed, as a matter of policy, any other rule creates perverse incentives. The first attorney to represent a client would have reason to do as little as possible

---

GENERAL DYNAMICS CORPORATION V. SUPERIOR COURT

7 Cal.4th 1164 (1994)

ARABIAN, JUSTICE.

We granted review to consider an attorney's status as "in-house" counsel as it affects the right to pursue claims for damages following an allegedly wrongful termination of employment. Specifically, we are asked to decide whether an attorney's status as an employee bars the pursuit of implied-in-fact contract and retaliatory discharge tort causes of action against the employer that are commonly the subject of suits by *non*-attorney employees who assert the same claims. . . .

I

Andrew Rose, an attorney, began working for General Dynamics Corporation (hereafter General Dynamics) as a 27–year–old contract administrator at its Pomona plant in 1978. He progressed steadily within the organization, earning repeated commendations and, after 14 years with the company, was in line to become a division vice-president and general counsel. On June 24, 1991, he was fired, abruptly and wrongfully.

So Rose alleged in the complaint for damages that began this litigation. The complaint also alleged that although the stated reason for his discharge was a loss of the company's confidence in Rose's ability to represent vigorously its interests, the "real" reasons motivating his firing had more to do with an attempt by company officials to cover up widespread drug use among the General Dynamics work force, a refusal to investigate the mysterious "bugging" of the office of the company's chief of security, and the displeasure of company officials over certain legal advice Rose had given them, rather than any loss of confidence in his legal ability or commitment to the company's interests.

The complaint relied on two main theories of relief. First, it alleged that General Dynamics had, by its conduct and other assurances, impliedly represented to Rose over the years that he was subject to discharge only for "good cause," a condition that the complaint alleged was not present in the circumstances under which he was fired. Second, the complaint alleged that Rose was actually fired for cumulative reasons, all of which violated fundamental public policies: in part because he spearheaded an investigation into employee drug use at the Pomona plant (an investigation, the complaint alleged, that led to the termination of more than 60 General Dynamics employees), in part because he protested the compa-

---

and then jump on the hint of first client noncooperation to maximize recovery with a minimum of hassle.

ny's failure to investigate the bugging of the office of the chief of security (allegedly a criminal offense and, since it involved a major defense contractor, a serious breach of national security), and in part as a result of advising General Dynamics officials that the company's salary policy with respect to the compensation paid a certain class of employees might be in violation of the federal Fair Labor Standards Act, possibly exposing the firm to several hundred million dollars in backpay claims.

General Dynamics filed a general demurrer to the complaint, asserting that Rose had failed to state a claim for relief. Because he had been employed as an in-house *attorney,* the company contended, Rose was subject to discharge at any time, "for any reason or for no reason." The trial court overruled the demurrer and the Court of Appeal denied General Dynamics's ensuing petition for a writ of mandate, ruling that, at least at the pleading stage, the complaint was sufficient to survive a general demurrer as to both theories of relief.

II

The last two decades have seen a marked rise in the number and professional stature of so-called in-house or corporate counsel. . . . The growth in the number and role of in-house counsel has brought with it a widening recognition of the descriptive inadequacy of the nineteenth century model of the lawyer's place and role in society—one based predominantly on the small-to middle-sized firm of like-minded attorneys whose economic fortunes were not tethered to the good will of a single client—and of the social and legal consequences that have accompanied that transformation. Unlike the law firm partner, who typically possesses a significant measure of economic independence and professional distance derived from a multiple client base, the economic fate of in-house attorneys is tied directly to a single employer, at whose sufferance they serve. Thus, from an economic standpoint, the dependence of in-house counsel is indistinguishable from that of other corporate managers or senior executives who also owe their livelihoods, career goals and satisfaction to a single organizational employer. . . .

Moreover, the professional relationship between the in-house attorney and the client is not the "one shot" undertaking—drafting a will, say, or handling a piece of litigation—characteristic of the outside law firm. Instead, the corporate attorney-employee, operating in a heavily regulated medium, often takes on a larger advisory and compliance role, anticipating potential legal problems, advising on possible solutions, and generally assisting the corporation in achieving its business aims while minimizing entanglement in the increasingly complex legal web that regulates organizational conduct in our society. This expansion in the scope and stature of in-house counsel's work, together with an inevitably close professional identification with the fortunes and objectives of the corporate employer, can easily subject the in-house attorney to unusual pressures to conform to organizational goals, pressures that are qualitatively different from those imposed on the outside lawyer. . . .

III

If there is a unifying theme in this conflict, it is the claim of General Dynamics that our opinion in *Fracasse v. Brent* (1972) 6 Cal.3d 784 (*Fracasse*) is dispositive of *all* issues tendered against it by Rose in his complaint. . . .

In *Fracasse,* an attorney entered into a contingent fee contract with a client to represent her as a plaintiff in a personal injury lawsuit. Not long afterward—and before any recovery had been made on her behalf—the client decided to end the relationship. She discharged the attorney, and retained other counsel to pursue her claim. The former attorney then filed a declaratory relief action against her, alleging that he had been discharged without cause and in breach of the contingency fee agreement, and seeking a judgment that he was entitled to his one-third contingency fee as a percentage of any sum ultimately recovered by his former client. . . .

[W]e concluded that "a client should have both the right and the power at any time to discharge his attorney with or without cause". . . . Our holdings in that case were expressly founded on the recognition that a client who retains an attorney to prosecute a personal injury action under a contingent fee agreement "may and often is very likely to be a person of limited means for whom the contingent fee arrangement offers the only realistic hope of establishing a legal claim.". . . . We had such concerns in mind when we wrote that the contingent fee client " 'must rely almost entirely upon the good faith of the attorney who alone can make an informed estimate of the value of the client's legal right and of the expense and effort necessary to enforce it.' " [citation omitted] " 'The client,' " we observed, " 'may frequently be forced to choose between continuing the employment of an attorney in whom he has lost faith, or risking the payment of double contingency fees equal to the greater portion of any amount eventually recovered. . . . ' " (*Ibid.*) . . .

[The Court reaffirmed] the unilateral right of the client to sever the professional relationship at any time and for any reason [but went on to hold that rule] does not mean, however, that the "absolute" right of the personal injury client to discharge unilaterally his attorney permits *all* clients to terminate the attorney-client relationship under *all* circumstances without consequence. The sources of contract and tort claims in wrongful termination cases are analytically distinct from the circumstances confronting the contingent-fee plaintiff that propelled our analysis in *Fracasse*.. . . .

Additionally, General Dynamics' claim of an unqualified immunity from any liability for terminating in-house counsel is inconsistent with the law in other areas, notably claims grounded in alleged violations of antidiscrimination laws and statutory rights to public collective bargaining. . . . While the "unfettered" right of the client to discharge his attorney at any time *is* an important value that should be upheld in most cases, the legal *consequences* of such an act will vary, depending on the strength of competing interests that are present in a particular case.

IV

As the name suggests, an implied-in-fact contract claim as a limitation on an employer's historical at-will power to terminate one of its employees is rooted in the conduct of the parties to the employment relationship itself. As such, it is a branch of the law of contracts and subject to the time-honored notion that contractual bargains ought to be enforced unless there is some imperative—generally rooted in policies external to the employment relationship—that prevents a court from doing so. At this stage of the litigation, General Dynamics' facial challenge to Rose's implied-in-fact contract claim does not attack the factual accuracy of the allegations of the complaint. It would, of course, be inappropriate to do so in a demurrer testing the legal sufficiency of the plaintiff's theory of relief.

Instead, General Dynamics' challenge is simply a corollary to its claim that our opinion in *Fracasse* applies globally to immunize an employer from *any* liability as a consequence of terminating an attorney-employee. . . . Perhaps the overriding distinction between *Fracasse* and this case lies in the allegations of the complaint that the plaintiff was hired as a "career oriented" employee with an expectation of permanent employment, provided his performance was satisfactory; that he was promised job security and substantial retirement benefits; that he regularly received outstanding performance reviews, promotions, salary increases, and commendations throughout his 14–year tenure; and that the company abruptly terminated him without adhering to its published discharge procedures.

These pleadings, we conclude, adequately allege that a "course of conduct, including various oral representations, created a reasonable expectation" that the plaintiff would not be terminated without good cause. The factual allegations of the complaint being sufficient to withstand a general demurrer, we see no reason in policy, at least at the outset, why the plaintiff's status as an in-house attorney should operate to defeat his contract claim. It is true, as we have just affirmed, that General Dynamics has a right to discharge any member of its general counsel's staff in whom it has lost confidence. That right does not mean, however, that it may do so without honoring antecedent contractual obligations to discharge an attorney-employee only on the occurrence of specified conditions. . . .

We agree that, as creatures of contract, implied-in-fact limitations on a client-employer's right to discharge in-house counsel are not likely to present issues implicating the distinctive values subserved by the attorney-client relationship. Such suits can thus for the most part be treated as implied-in-fact claims brought by the nonattorney employee. . . .

V

A

We turn next to an evaluation of Rose's claim that he was discharged for multiple reasons, each of which violated a "fundamental polic[y] that [is] delineated in constitutional or statutory provisions" of the law of this state. Unlike implied-in-fact contract claims, which, as discussed above, arise out of the conduct and expectations of the parties to the employment relationship, so-called public policy wrongful discharge claims are pure creatures of law. . . .

In California, refinements in the doctrine of wrongful discharge in violation of public policy have engrafted two prominent restraints on the vitality of such claims. The first is the requirement . . . that the public policy at issue must be one that is not only "fundamental" but is clearly established in the Constitution and positive law of the state. The second restriction . . . is the requirement that, even though established by positive law, the policy subserved by the employee's conduct must be a truly *public* one, that is, "affect[ing] a duty which inures to the benefit of the *public at large* rather than to a particular employer or employee."

There is a third characteristic . . . "decisions recognizing a tort action for discharge in violation of public policy *seek to protect the public, by protecting the employee* who refuses to commit a crime [citations] . . . , who reports criminal activity to proper authorities [citations], or who discloses other illegal, unethical, or unsafe practices [citation]". . . .

B

This foundational *public* rationale is especially important in the case of the attorney-employee. Perhaps the defining feature of professionals as a class is the extent to which they embody a dual allegiance. On the one hand, an attorney's highest duty is to the welfare and interests of the client. This obligation is channeled, however, by a limiting and specifically *professional* qualification: attorneys are required to conduct themselves *as such,* meaning that they are bound at all events not to transgress a handful of professional ethical norms that distinguish their work from that of the nonattorney.

Some (but not all) of these professional norms incorporate important *public* values. Lawyers are given wide professional license in part because of ethical restraints on their discretion designed to further (or at least not endanger) the public weal. The minimal ethical standards that distinctively define the lawyer as a professional are, of course, those embodied in the codes of ethics, and, in California, in the Rules of Professional Conduct. These standards are in turn linked by their nature and goals to important values affecting the public interest at large. It is through this chain of ethical duty that lawyers and their work are affected with a public interest. Out of this duality of allegiance—for the interests of the client on the one hand, but within the bounds of ethical norms on the other—a genuine moral dilemma may arise.

This is especially so in the context of the large commercially driven corporation whose essential objectives are largely defined by the desire to maximize profitability. In such a business culture, the in-house professional may be trapped between a laudable desire to further the goals of the client-employer and restrictions on conduct imposed by the ethical norms prescribed by the Rules of Professional Conduct. Of course, the potential for such a dilemma is common to outside counsel as well. But, unlike their in-house counterparts, outside lawyers enjoy a measure of professional distance and economic independence that usually serves to lessen the pressure to bend or ignore professional norms. Here again, the distinguishing feature of the in-house attorney is a virtually complete dependence on the good will and confidence of a single employer to provide livelihood and career success. . . .

C

There is a substantial counterargument against permitting the pursuit of a retaliatory discharge *tort* claim by in-house counsel, one that also inheres in the essential nature of the attorney's professional role. Indeed, in the handful of reported cases dealing with the question, a majority of courts have refused to permit the maintenance of such suits on the ground that they pose *too great* a threat to the attorney-client relationship. . . . .

Those courts that have declined to permit in-house counsel to pursue retaliatory discharge claims . . . have rested their conclusion on two distinct grounds: First, because the fiducial qualities of their professional calling pervade the attorney-client relationship, "lawyers are different." It is essential to the proper functioning of the lawyer's role that the client be assured that matters disclosed to counsel in confidence remain sacrosanct; to permit in-house attorneys to file suit against their clients can only harm that relationship. Second, to the extent that the retaliatory discharge tort rests on underpinnings designed to secure fundamental public policies, a tort remedy for in-house counsel is redundant—such attorneys are under an ethical obligation to sever their professional relationship with the erring client in any event—meaning, in the case of in-house counsel, resigning their employment.

D

If the . . . reasoning and conclusions [of these courts] can be faulted, it is because one searches in vain for a principled link between the ethical duties of the in-house attorney and the courts' refusal to grant such an employee a tort remedy under conditions that directly implicate those professional obligations. As more than one critic of these opinions has pointed out, both cases appear to reflect not only an unspoken adherence to an anachronistic model of the attorney's place and role in contemporary society, but an inverted view of the consequences of the in-house attorney's essential professional role. . . .

Within their area of professional competence, in-house attorneys, more than other organizational employees, are imbued with ethical constraints on the direction their efforts may legitimately take. Among other strictures on their conduct, they may not be a party to the commission of a crime, destroy evidence or suborn perjury. They are forbidden to do these things by the very ethical codes that define their professional identity. It is a short step from this premise to the conclusion that in-house lawyers ought to have access to a judicial remedy in those instances in which their employment is terminated for adhering to the requirements of just such a mandatory professional duty, either by an *affirmative act* required by the ethical code or statute or by resisting a demand of the employer on the ground that it is unequivocally *barred* by the professional code. . . .

In addition, the emphasis . . . on the "remedy" of the in-house attorney's duty of "withdrawal" strikes us as illusory. Courts do not require nonlawyer employees to quietly surrender their jobs rather than "go along" with an employer's unlawful demands. Indeed, the retaliatory discharge tort claim is designed to encourage and support precisely the *opposite* reaction. Why, then, did the courts in these three cases content themselves with the bland announcement that the only "choice" of an attorney confronted with an employer's demand that he violate his professional oath by committing, say, a criminal act, is to voluntarily withdraw from employment, a course fraught with the possibility of economic catastrophe and professional banishment?

Whatever the reason, the withdrawal "remedy" fails to confront seriously the extraordinarily high cost that resignation entails. More importantly, it is virtually certain that, without the prospect of limited judicial access, in-house attorneys—especially those in mid-career who occupy senior positions—confronted with the dilemma of choosing between adhering to professional ethical norms and surrendering to the employer's unethical demands will almost always find silence the better part of valor. Declining to provide a limited remedy under defined circumstances will thus almost certainly foster a degradation of in-house counsel's professional stature.

E

In addition to retaliatory discharge claims founded on allegations that an in-house attorney was terminated for refusing to violate a mandatory ethical duty embodied in the Rules of Professional Conduct, judicial access ought logically extend to those limited circumstances in which in-house counsel's *nonattorney* colleagues would be permitted to pursue a retaliatory discharge claim *and* governing professional rules or statutes expressly remove the requirement of attorney confidentiality. Thus, in determining whether an in-house attorney has a retaliatory discharge claim against his or her employer, a court must first ask whether the attorney was discharged for following a mandatory ethical obligation prescribed by professional rule or statute. . . . [6]

If, on the other hand, the conduct in which the attorney has engaged is merely ethically *permissible,* but not *required* by statute or ethical code, then the inquiry facing the court is slightly more complex. Under these circumstances, a court must resolve *two* questions: First, whether the employer's conduct is of the kind that would give rise to a retaliatory discharge action by a *non* attorney employee . . . second, the court must determine whether some statute or ethical rule, such as the statutory exceptions to the attorney-client privilege codified in the Evidence Code (see *id.,* §§ 956–958) specifically permits the attorney to depart from the usual requirement of confidentiality with respect to the client-employer and engage in the "nonfiduciary" conduct for which he was terminated. . . .

Except in those rare instances when disclosure is explicitly permitted or mandated by an ethics code provision or statute, it is never the business of the lawyer to disclose publicly the secrets of the client. In any event, where the elements of a wrongful discharge in violation of fundamental public policy claim cannot, for reasons peculiar to the particular case, be fully established without breaching the attorney-client privilege, the suit must be dismissed in the interest of preserving the privilege. . . .

We reject any suggestion that the scope of the privilege should be diluted in the context of in-house counsel and their corporate clients. Members of corporate legal departments are as fully subject to the demands of the privilege as their outside colleagues. It is likely, however, that many

---

[6] FN6. As our discussion makes evident, in California, these ethical prescriptions are those embodied in the state's Rules of Professional Conduct and certain provisions of the Business and Professions Code (e.g., §§ 6068, 6090.5–6107). We expressly decline to adopt as a predicate for retaliatory discharge claims by in-house counsel either the Model Rules of Professional Conduct or the Model Code of Professional Responsibility, both of which have "no legal force of their own" (1 Hazard & Hodes, The Law of Lawyering, *supra,* § 206, at p. 477) and neither of which has been adopted by this court. Although the question is not before us in this case, we suggest that ethical issues arising in retaliatory discharge claims filed in California by out-of-state in-house attorneys against their employers and based on extrastate conduct will be resolved under governing choice-of-law rules.

of the cases in which in-house counsel is faced with an ethical dilemma will lie outside the scope of the statutory privilege. . . . .

VI

Applying the principles developed above to the complaint in this case, it is evident that . . . plaintiff's first claim—for breach of an implied-in-fact just-cause agreement—adequately pleads the essential elements of the cause of action. It is less clear, however, that the allegations in support of relief under plaintiff's retaliatory discharge theory are sufficient. Plaintiff nowhere alleges that the conduct which allegedly led to his termination was required or supported by any requirement of our Rules of Professional Responsibility or a relevant statute. This omission is not surprising, however, in light of the fact that no court of this state has previously addressed the precise question presented by this case in a published opinion. In drawing up the complaint, plaintiff apparently proceeded on the assumption that the scope of retaliatory discharge claims by in-house counsel is coextensive with that of other corporate employees. We have, of course, concluded that that view is too expansive.

In light of our ruling, we believe the fairest resolution is to direct that the matter be remanded to the trial court and that plaintiff be permitted to amend his complaint against General Dynamics in accordance with the views we have expressed. It should go without saying that nothing we have said is intended to intimate in any way a view of the merits of this action.

CONCLUSION

The judgment of the Court of Appeal is affirmed and the cause is remanded to that court with directions to order further proceedings in accordance with the views expressed herein.

CASE QUESTIONS

1. The *General Dynamics* court discusses the relationship between legal ethics and diversification of a lawyer's client base; what is that relationship?
2. Under what circumstances may a terminated in-house lawyer bring a breach of contract claim?
3. Under what circumstances may such a lawyer bring a tort claim for wrongful discharge?

Privilege and Confidences in *General Dynamics*

The *General Dynamics* Court held that a terminated in-house lawyer may bring a tort cause of action if (and only if) "some statute or ethical rule, such as the statutory exceptions to the attorney-client privilege . . . specifically permits the attorney to depart from the usual requirement of confidentiality with respect to the client-employer and engage in the 'nonfiduciary' conduct for which he was terminated." This holding has a serious problem.

You will of course recognize that this passage mixes together two things that are very different: The attorney-client privilege and the duty of confidentiality. It is wrong to say that the privilege creates exceptions to the duty. It does not. The privilege has exceptions, codified in the Evidence Code, but these exceptions permit an attorney to disclose information compelled by the processes of some proceeding, as with a trial subpoena. That an exception to the privilege might apply in a proceeding does not authorize an exception to the *duty* of confidentiality: That a lawyer might be compelled to disclose a confidence does not mean she may volunteer it.

One can understand why the Court might have mixed and matched these concepts. At the time *General Dynamics* was decided, there were literally no exceptions to the duty of confidentiality codified in California Business and Professions Code § 6068(e). Today (2010), that provision allows for disclosure only when reasonably necessary to prevent a criminal act likely to result in death or substantial bodily injury. If terminated in-house lawyers could only disclose confidences as permitted by the duty, rather than the evidentiary privilege, then the cause of action would be largely illusory: few if any lawyers are terminated based on conduct that would pose a risk of death or substantial bodily injury.

For this reason, in order to make the *General Dynamics* rule more than an illusory victory, it is tempting to interpret the opinion as creating an exception to the duty of confidentiality that is coterminous with exceptions to the attorney-client privilege. That probably is the best reading of what the Court intended, but that reading faces significant problems.

The relationship between the *General Dynamics* holding and the duty of confidentiality was relevant to *Fox Searchlight Pictures, Inc. v. Paladino*, 89 Cal.App.4th 294 (2001). Gia Paladino was an in-house lawyer employed by Fox. She had a three-year contract. Shortly before the contract term was up, her supervisor told Paladino it would not be renewed. Her supervisor said Fox would not renew the contract because a film project on which Paladino had worked had not gone well. Paladino believed Fox was unhappy with her frequent use of maternity leave.

Paladino retained counsel to sue Fox for wrongful termination. Her lawyers sent Fox a draft of the complaint to determine whether Fox would claim that it disclosed Fox's confidences. On reading the draft, Fox sued Paladino, alleging she had breached duties she owed Fox by disclosing its confidences to her counsel. On the *General Dynamics* issue, the Court held "in-house counsel may disclose ostensible employer-client confidences to her own attorneys to the extent they may be relevant to the preparation and prosecution of her wrongful termination action against her former client-employer. . . . The attorneys for the in-house counsel are themselves bound by the rules of confidentiality and attorney-client privilege. Thus, disclosure to them is not a public disclosure. . . . "

The *Paladino* court noted that the language of California's duty of confidentiality, codified in Business and Professions Code § 6068(e), makes no exceptions for suits brought by lawyers against former employers. The court nevertheless concluded that Section 6068(e) should be read "in light of" the exceptions to the attorney-client privilege.

The court's analysis should not be generalized. If California's duty of confidentiality were qualified by exceptions to the attorney-client privilege, then a longstanding debate over whether California should allow lawyers to disclose client confidences in certain circumstances would have been entirely pointless. Section 6068(e)(2), allowing disclosure of confidences in certain circumstances, was added without any indication that Evidence Code exceptions might be relevant. For these reasons *Paladino* is best read as a case that does its best to make the rule of *General Dynamics* more than a "practical joke" rather than as a reliable exposition of the duty of confidentiality generally.

The Ethical Significance of Client Diversification

The *General Dynamics* court distinguished in-house lawyers from those who work in private firms on the ground that the former have only one client—the entity—and therefore are more vulnerable to economic pressure from the client than are the latter. That statement is probably true as a descriptive matter, but the general principle behind it is more important than the description.

Suppose a client wants you to do something you do not want to do. All else being equal, it will be easier for you to resist the client's pressure to do the wrong thing if you have a diversified list of clients than it will be if a large fraction of your business comes from the client in question. Why? No matter how ethical you may be, the costlier it is to do the right thing the harder it is to do the right thing. If your choice is between helping a client break the law and making your lease payment for the month, or making partner, or even paying your child's tuition, you will feel more pressure to go along with the client than you would if your economic circumstances were secure. If the client represents a small or even only a middling fraction of your business, then you will find it easier to resign (or be fired), and thereby avoid professional trouble. Remember Rule Two: Always be prepared to walk away.

If you practice in a firm, this rule means that you should not be satisfied if you land a big client that will pay you enough fees to make a good living. You will want to keep looking for clients who will stay with you if the big client has to go. If you practice in-house, diversification will take a slightly different form. You will not be in a position to solicit new clients, but you will be in a position to make friends with other lawyers—both at other companies and at private firms—who might give you a place to go if you find that you need to leave your employer.

The easier it is to walk away, the more likely you are to do it if you need to.

The Main Points to Recall From 10 Are:

- Lawyers must withdraw from representation if that representation will result in the violation of an ethics rule or other law.
- Lawyers not before a tribunal may withdraw from representation but must not prejudice their clients in doing so.
- Lawyers before a tribunal may withdraw if they do not prejudice their clients *and* the tribunal assents.
- Clients may terminate lawyers at any time, for any reason or no reason at all.
- Clients who terminate in-house lawyers for a bad reason may be held liable for doing so.

CHAPTER 11

CONFLICTS OF INTEREST

■ ■ ■

Conflicts of interest exist when you have a personal or professional interest that is at odds with your client's interests and your duties to your client. Conflicting personal interests include things like an economic stake in the subject of the representation. Conflicting professional interests generally take the form of duties owed to another client. Conflicts present harder problems than may seem apparent at first glance. We will study these problems in detail in this chapter, but it is important to get off on the right foot: In conflict analysis, timing is (almost) everything. *When* a conflict arises usually determines which duties it implicates and which disciplinary rules apply. The relevant distinction is between successive and contemporaneous representation of adverse interests.

This diagram depicts the basic difference between contemporaneous and subsequent conflicts.

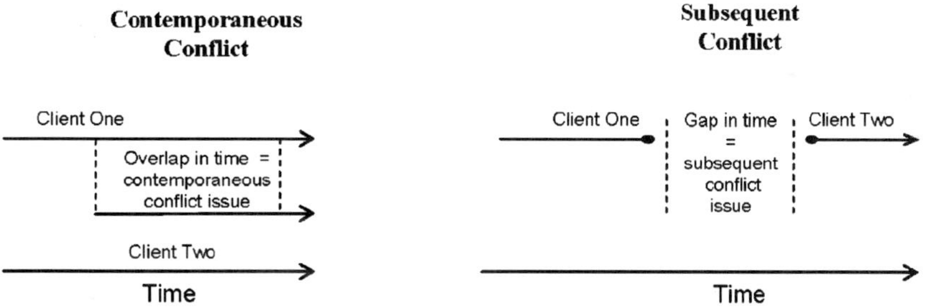

The California Supreme Court explained the distinction in terms of fiduciary duties in *Flatt v. Superior Court*, 9 Cal.4th 275, 278 (1994):

> Where the potential conflict is one that arises from the *successive* representation of clients with potentially adverse interests, the courts have recognized that the chief fiduciary value jeopardized is that of client *confidentiality.* Thus, where a former client seeks to have a previous attorney disqualified from serving as counsel to a successive client in litigation adverse to the interests of the first client, the governing test requires that the client demonstrate a "*substantial relationship*" between the subjects of the antecedent and current representations.

The "substantial relationship" test mediates between two interests that are in tension in such a context—the freedom of the subsequent client to counsel of choice, on the one hand, and the interest of the former client in ensuring the permanent confidentiality of matters disclosed to the attorney in the course of the prior representation, on the other. Where the requisite substantial relationship between the subjects of the prior and the current representations can be demonstrated, access to confidential information by the attorney in the course of the first representation (relevant, by definition, to the second representation) is *presumed* and disqualification of the attorney's representation of the second client is mandatory; indeed, the disqualification extends vicariously to the entire firm. [citations omitted]

The interest implicated and the governing test is different, however, where an attorney's potentially conflicting representations are *simultaneous.* In such a situation—perhaps the classic case involving an attorney's interests in conflict with those of the client—the courts have discerned a distinctly separate professional value to be at risk by the attorney's adverse representations. The primary value at stake in cases of simultaneous or dual representation is the attorney's duty—and the client's legitimate expectation—of *loyalty,* rather than confidentiality. And because the substantial relationship test is founded on the need to protect against the improper use of client *secrets*—a concern that often is not implicated by the simultaneous representation of clients in *unrelated* matters—and applies "where the representation of a former client has been terminated and the parameters of such relationship . . . fixed," such a test "does not set a sufficiently high standard by which the necessity for disqualification should be determined" in cases involving dual representation. (*Cinema 5 Ltd. v. Cinerama, Inc.* (2d Cir.1976) 528 F.2d 1384, 1387.)

In evaluating conflict claims in dual representation cases, the courts have accordingly imposed a test that is more stringent than that of demonstrating a substantial relationship between the subject matter of successive representations. Even though the simultaneous representations may have *nothing* in common, and there is *no* risk that confidences to which counsel is a party in the one case have any relation to the other matter, disqualification may nevertheless be *required.* Indeed, in all but a few instances, the rule of disqualification in simultaneous representation cases is a *per se* or "automatic" one. [citations omitted]

The reason for such a rule is evident, even (or perhaps especially) to the nonattorney. A client who learns that his or her lawyer is also representing a litigation adversary, even with respect to a matter *wholly unrelated* to the one for which counsel was retained, cannot long be expected to sustain the level of confidence and trust in counsel that is one of the foundations of the professional relationship. All legal technicalities aside, few if any clients would be willing to suffer the prospect of their attorney continuing to represent them under such circumstances. As one commentator on modern legal ethics has put it: "Something seems radically out of place if a lawyer sues one of the lawyer's own present clients in behalf of another client. Even if the representations have nothing to do with each other, so that no confidential information is apparently jeopardized, the client who is sued can obviously claim that the lawyer's *sense of loyalty* is askew." (Wolfram, Modern Legal Ethics (1986 ed.) § 7.3.2, p. 350, italics added.) It is for that reason, and not out of concerns rooted in the obligation of client confidentiality, that courts and ethical codes alike prohibit an attorney from simultaneously representing two client adversaries, even where the substance of the representations are unrelated.[1]

Thus a basic dichotomy we will explore in this chapter.

With regard to *current* clients: (1) you may not represent one client in a matter in which that client is directly adverse to another current client, even if the two representations are completely unrelated; and (2) should you choose to do business with a current client you will need to (a) make sure they know you do not act for them in the transaction; (b) advise them to get another lawyer regarding the transaction and give them a chance to do so; and (c) be prepared to demonstrate the substantive fairness of the transaction.

With regard to *former* clients you must not (1) act adversely to them in a matter substantially related to the prior representation; (2) use or disclose information learned in the representation in a manner adverse to the former client unless the information has become generally known.

Conflicts of interest doctrine encompasses two other major issues. The first concerns presumptions regarding what you know and imputa-

---

[1] FN4. There are, of course, exceptions even to this rule. The principle of loyalty is for the *client's* benefit; most courts thus permit an attorney to continue the simultaneous representation of clients whose interests are adverse as to unrelated matters provided full disclosure is made and both agree in writing to waive the conflict. (See, e.g., Steinberg & Sharpe, *Attorney Conflicts of Interest: The Need for a Coherent Framework* (1990) 66 Notre Dame L.Rev. 1, 3, fn. 7, and materials cited.) But this class of cases is a rare circumstance, typically involving corporate clients, and overcoming the presumption of "prima facie impropriety" is not easily accomplished. (See, e.g., *Cinema 5, Ltd. v. Cinerama, Inc., supra,* 528 F.2d at p. 1387; *United States v. Nabisco* (E.D.N.Y.1987) 117 F.R.D. 40, 44); Restatement of the Law Governing Lawyers (Tent. Draft No. 4, *supra*) § 213, p. 160 (reporter's note to com. *e*). It is not, in any event, one that concerns us in this case, given Flatt's understandable decision not to represent Daniel in his contemplated lawsuit against Hinkle and his firm. There was thus no occasion here for disclosure and client waiver of the conflict.

tion of that knowledge either from your firm to you or from you to your firm. The basic rule traditionally has been that if one lawyer in a firm has a conflict of interest precluding representation then no other lawyer in the firm may undertake that representation. There is an exception to this rule if the conflict is personal to a lawyer but other lawyers in the firm were unaffected by the conflict, as might happen if one lawyer was philosophically opposed to a representation but other lawyers in the firm were not. The basic rule still holds for contemporaneous conflicts because the rules governing such conflicts are designed to enforce the duty of loyalty, which both a lawyer and a firm owe to clients.

Imputation works differently when only confidences are at stake. The basic rules regarding presumed knowledge and imputation of knowledge are:

(a) If you do work in which a reasonable lawyer would have acquired confidential information regarding a client you will be deemed to have acquired such information regardless whether you actually learned it—the presumption that you acquired such information is not rebuttable; this presumption means you may not act adversely to a former client in a matter substantially related to your prior work for that client; this prohibition applies to you regardless whether you are at the firm where you did the work or have moved to another firm;

(b) Confidential information you learn while working at a firm is imputed to every other lawyer then working at the firm and their knowledge is imputed to you while you work at the firm; this presumption is not rebuttable;

(c) If you leave a firm you may rebut the presumption that you knew what other lawyers at the firm knew; to do so you must show that while at the firm you did not actually acquire confidential information relating to some matter and did no work in which a reasonable lawyer would be expected to have acquired confidential information regarding the matter;

(d) If you leave the firm, the firm may rebut the presumption that other lawyers there knew the information you knew about some matter; to do so the firm must show that no lawyer remaining at the firm retains confidential information regarding the matter;

(e) If you move from one firm to another the law varies on what happens to the firm that hires you: (1) Under the traditional rule and the law applied in some jurisdictions, confidential information you possess from your prior work is imputed to the new firm as if you learned it while working there; (2) There is an exception to this rule if you worked for the government before joining the new firm; in such cases the firm may rebut the presumed imputation of your information to other lawyers in the firm by effectively screening you from any matter related to your prior work; (3) Even if you joined the new firm from another private firm, some jurisdictions, and Model Rule 1.10, allow your new firm to rebut this presumption by effectively screening you from a matter in which other lawyers in the firm act adversely to your former client, even in a matter substantially related to your work for that client; (4) Other jurisdictions allow screening only if you did not perform substantial work on the relevant matter while at a prior firm.

This is a lot of information; do not worry if not all of it makes sense to you now. You will study each point in detail as you read through this chapter.

The second major issue concerns transactions with current clients. As fiduciaries, lawyers are subject to strict oversight of such transactions, which must be on terms fair and reasonable to the client and which are disclosed in terms the client can understand. The client also must be given a reasonable opportunity to consult independent counsel about the transaction, and the client must give written consent to the transaction.

A. CONFLICTS ARISING FROM CONCURRENT REPRESENTATION

Model Rule 1.7(a)(1) forbids you from representing a client if the representation will be directly adverse to another, current client. A conflict exists even if the two matters are completely unrelated. The only questions are whether the client is current and, if so, whether the representation would be directly adverse to the current client. The following materials explore these two points.

1. WHICH CLIENTS ARE CURRENT?

Restatement of the Law Governing Lawyers §§ 121–22, 128
Model Rule of Professional Conduct 1.7(a)(1)

TRUCK INS. EXCHANGE V. FIREMAN'S FUND INS. CO.

6 Cal.App.4th 1050 (1992)

REARDON, ASSOCIATE JUSTICE.

The underlying lawsuit was commenced in February 1990. Kaiser Cement Corporation, Kaiser Gypsum Company, Inc. (collectively, Kaiser), and Truck seek contribution from FFIC and other insurers to defend and indemnify Kaiser against third-party asbestos-related bodily injury lawsuits. Truck alleged that it alone had undertaken the defense of Kaiser and had expended more than $11,300,000 in defense costs and almost

$1,300,000 in indemnity expenses for those claims.[2] A key issue in the coverage cases is the terms of insurance policies issued by FFIC between 1939 and 1964. At the time the lawsuit was initiated, Truck was represented by the law firm of Ropers, Majeski, Kohn, Bentley, Wagner & Kane (Ropers).

On January 11, 1991, the trial court granted FFIC's motion to disqualify Ropers. Truck then asked Crosby to represent it. The Crosby firm had represented Truck and its affiliated companies in numerous other matters.

When Truck contacted Crosby concerning the instant case, Crosby ran a computerized conflicts check and found that for several months it had been defending Fireman's Fund Credit Union—an entity related to FFIC—in two wrongful termination suits. Crosby concedes that defending Fireman's Fund Credit Union made FFIC Crosby's client.

In a letter dated January 18, 1991, Crosby informed FFIC of Truck's desire for representation by Crosby and inquired of FFIC if it objected to Crosby representing Truck in the insurance coverage case. (See Rules Prof.Conduct, rule 3–310(B).) As an alternative, Crosby informed FFIC that to eliminate any conflict, it was willing to withdraw from the two wrongful termination cases, to help transfer those cases smoothly to new counsel, and to waive any fee for its past services. FFIC objected to the concurrent representation, did not provide written consent, and stated its desire to have Crosby continue as its attorney in the wrongful termination cases. Crosby, nonetheless, accepted representation of Truck.

On February 19, 1991, Crosby moved to withdraw as counsel for Fireman's Fund Credit Union in the wrongful termination cases. On March 7, Crosby notified the court that substitute counsel had been retained in each of those cases, that the case files had been transferred, and that other steps were being taken to insure an orderly transition of the matters.

Meanwhile, also on February 19, 1991, FFIC filed its motion to disqualify Crosby from representing Truck against FFIC in this case while it concurrently represented FFIC in the wrongful termination cases. In support of its motion, FFIC argued that a law firm may not sue a present client without that client's written consent; that FFIC did not consent to Crosby representing Truck; that Crosby thereby breached its duty of loyalty toward FFIC; and that a per se rule of disqualification applied.

Truck, on the other hand, argued that since Crosby had withdrawn as counsel for FFIC in the wrongful termination cases, FFIC was now only Crosby's former client. The issue, Truck contended, was therefore whether Crosby's former representation of FFIC in those cases was sub-

[2] FN2. By the time the trial court heard the motion to disqualify Crosby, Truck's defense costs in Kaiser's asbestos-related bodily injury cases had risen to more than $17,000,000.

stantially related to the present case so as to give Crosby access to confidential information now helpful to Truck. Truck argued that since there was no factual or legal connection between this and the wrongful termination cases, Crosby possessed no confidential information that could be misused to FFIC's prejudice.

Before the March 14, 1991, hearing on the motion, the trial court issued a tentative ruling indicating its intent to grant FFIC's motion to disqualify Crosby. The trial court found that Crosby was already representing FFIC when it undertook to represent Truck, as well as when FFIC filed its motion to disqualify Crosby. The court explained that an attorney may not represent an interest adverse to a current client without that client's approval, even if the attorney withdraws from the other cases before the motion to disqualify is heard.

During the hearing, the court acknowledged that this case presented a "hybrid" situation involving "an existing [representation] with an intent to depart." The court recognized that conflict problems of large compartmentalized law firms and insurance companies differ from those of sole practitioners representing private individuals, but it saw no reason why different rules should apply. Clarifying its tentative ruling, the court stated that absent a recognized exception, the per se disqualification rule used in concurrent representation cases applied. The court reaffirmed its order disqualifying Crosby.

II. DISCUSSION

A. *Standard of Review*

When reviewing an order granting or denying a motion to disqualify, a reviewing court defers to the trial court's decision, absent an abuse of discretion. . . . In the instant case, the trial court applied a per se standard of disqualification based upon the finding of "concurrent" representation. Truck contends that the trial court applied an incorrect standard and, in doing so, failed to exercise its discretion which is required under the "former" representation standard.

B. *The Rule*

Rule 3–310, effective May 27, 1989, provides in relevant part: "(B) A member shall not concurrently represent clients whose interests conflict, except with their informed written consent. . . . " The rule is clear in prohibiting an attorney from representing two or more clients at the same time whose interests conflict, unless there is informed written consent.

The undisputed facts before the trial court established that Crosby, knowing that it was representing FFIC in the wrongful termination cases, nevertheless agreed to begin representing Truck against FFIC in the insurance coverage case. In doing so, Crosby did not obtain the informed written consent of FFIC, and proceeded with its representation of Truck after such consent was explicitly denied. There was, therefore, concurrent representation of clients whose interests conflict, with no informed written consent.

On its face, rule 3–310(B) was violated.

C. *Withdrawal as a Cure for Rule Violation*

Also undisputed is the fact that prior to the hearing on FFIC's motion to disqualify, Crosby had withdrawn from its representation of FFIC in the wrongful termination cases. Truck argues that this withdrawal rendered FFIC a former client and that, as such, the less severe former representation standard (see *Global Van Lines v. Superior Court* (1983) 144 Cal.App.3d 483) rather than the standard governing concurrent representation, should have been applied. We disagree.

In cases involving the representation of a client against a former client, "the initial question is 'whether the former representation is "substantially related" to the current representation.' (See *Trone v. Smith* (9th Cir.1980) 621 F.2d 994, 998, and authorities cited therein.)" (*Global Van Lines v. Superior Court, supra,* 144 Cal.App.3d at p. 488, fn. omitted). "Substantiality is present if the factual contexts of the two representations are similar or related." (*Trone v. Smith* (9th Cir.1980) 621 F.2d 994, 998.) If a substantial relationship exists, courts will presume that confidences were disclosed during the former representation which may have value in the current relationship. Thus, actual possession of confidential information need not be proven when seeking an order of disqualification. (*Civil Service Com. v. Superior Court* (1984) 163 Cal.App.3d 70, 79–80.)

In contrast, in the concurrent representation context "[t]he principle precluding representing an interest adverse to those of a current client is based not on any concern with the confidential relationship between attorney and client but rather on the need to assure the attorney's undivided loyalty and commitment to the client. [Citations.]" This distinction between former representation and concurrent representation, and the distinct concerns at issue, are well recognized: "In contrast to representation undertaken adverse to a *former* client, representation adverse to a *present* client must be measured not so much against the similarities in litigation, as against the duty of undivided loyalty which an attorney owes to each of his clients." (*Unified Sewerage Agency, etc. v. Jelco Inc.* (9th Cir.1981) 646 F.2d 1339, 1345, emphasis in original; see also *Cinema 5, Ltd. v. Cinerama, Inc.* (2d Cir.1976) 528 F.2d 1384, 1386.) If this duty of undivided loyalty is violated, "public confidence in the legal profession and the judicial process" is undermined. (*See In re Yarn Processing Patent Validity Litigation* (5th Cir.1976) 530 F.2d 83, 89.)

Since Crosby unquestionably owed a duty of loyalty and commitment to FFIC, was that duty satisfied by Crosby's withdrawal of representation of FFIC before the hearing on the motion to disqualify? Simply put, may the automatic disqualification rule applicable to concurrent representation be avoided by unilaterally converting a present client into a former client prior to hearing on the motion for disqualification? We answer each question in the negative and hold, consistent with all applicable authority, that a law firm that knowingly undertakes adverse concurrent representation may not avoid disqualification by withdrawing from the representation of the less favored client before hearing. [citations omitted] Indeed, Truck's position to the contrary has been repeatedly rejected by numerous authorities in no uncertain terms. . . .

In its brief, we are told by Truck that the "proper rule under these circumstances is set forth in *Florida Insurance Guaranty Association, Inc. v. Carey Canada,* 749 F.Supp. 255, 261 (S.D.Fla.1990)," from which the following language is extracted: "When counsel, upon discovery and absent consent, immediately withdraws from a concurrent adverse representation, the proper disqualification standard is expressed in the former representation rule. Otherwise, to require disqualification for the *mere happenstance of an unseen concurrent adverse representation*—where the representations are not substantially related and client confidences are not endangered—would unfairly prevent a client from retaining counsel of choice and would penalize an attorney who had done no wrong." (*Florida Ins. Guar. Ass'n, Inc. v. Carey Canada* (S.D.Fla.1990) 749 F.Supp. 255, 261, emphasis added.) We agree with Truck that "the proper rule under the circumstances" is announced in *Carey Canada* but it certainly is not the rule Truck purports to glean from that case.

In *Carey Canada,* a law firm (Shackleford) was separately representing Florida Insurance Guaranty Association (FIGA) and Carey Canada in a nonconflicting context. When several insurers of Carey Canada became insolvent, FIGA was mandated by state law to step "into the shoes of the insolvent insurers" and thus became "the object of Carey Canada's asbestos related claims." When FIGA filed an action seeking declaratory relief to resolve its obligations with Carey Canada, Shackleford appeared on behalf of Carey Canada after withdrawing from representation of FIGA. FIGA moved to disqualify and the court *granted* the motion concluding that there had not been an immediate withdrawal "upon discovery of the conflict of interest and failure to obtain consent." Significantly, in explaining the language relied on by Truck, the court stated: "The option of dismissing FIGA, obviously, would not be available to Shackleford if Carey Canada were a new client that had come along subsequent to the conflict arising. [Citation.]"

Under our facts, there was no "mere happenstance of an unseen concurrent adverse representation." There was nothing happenstance or unseen in terms of concurrent adverse representation when Crosby agreed to represent Truck against its client, FFIC. In agreeing to represent Truck, Crosby knew that it was undertaking concurrent adverse representation and that it was doing so without the consent of FFIC. Under no circumstances can this activity be characterized as inadvertent, happenstance, or unseen. Whether the withdrawal of representation of FFIC was, therefore, immediate or delayed, is of no consequence because, under *Carey Canada*, the option of dismissing FFIC 'obviously, would not be available. . . .' . . . .

Truck finally contends that the automatic disqualification rule is harsh when applied to large law firms organized into specialty practice groups representing institutional clients where such situations may arise "inadvertently." Two observations seem appropriate: (1) there was nothing inadvertent when the firm agreed to represent Truck while representing FFIC; (2) to the extent this argument implies or suggests that the duty of loyalty owed a client of a large law firm is somehow less than that owed to the client of a smaller firm or sole practitioner, we summarily reject the implication.

We conclude, therefore, as follows: that the undisputed facts establish adverse concurrent representation within the meaning of rule 3–310(B); that withdrawing from representation of FFIC before the hearing on the motion to disqualify did not convert concurrent representation into prior representation for purposes of assessing the conflict; that the trial court applied the correct standard of automatic disqualification because of the adverse concurrent representation; that the motion to disqualify was properly granted. . . .

CASE QUESTIONS

1. When did the Crosby firm breach its duty of loyalty?
2. Could the Crosby firm have withdrawn from representing Fireman's Fund before accepting Truck, rather than just before the hearing?
3. What result if the Crosby firm heard about the Ropers firm being disqualified and withdrew from representing Fireman's Fund just in case Truck turned to Crosby to replace Ropers?

As *Truck Insurance* suggests, an attorney who drops one client to try to take on another violates the duty of loyalty, too. *See also American Airlines, Inc. v. Sheppard, Mullin, Richter & Hampton*, 96 Cal.App.4th 1017, 1037, 117 Cal.Rptr.2d 685 (2002) ("a lawyer may not avoid breaching the duty of loyalty which the concurrent representation rule is designed to avoid by unilaterally converting a present client into a former client. In fact, such conversion may itself be a breach of loyalty.")

Cal West Nurseries v. Superior Court, 129 Cal.App.4th 1170, 1171, 29 Cal.Rptr.3d 170 (2005), extends *Truck's* "hot potato" rule. A firm represented client A in one matter and was then retained to represent client B in another, unrelated matter. B's interests in that matter were adverse to A and to two other parties, C and D, as to whom the firm had no conflict. Client A objected to the firm's representation of B and the firm withdrew from representing B as against A. The firm wanted to continue representing B as against C and D but client A objected to that representation as well. The court of appeals held that the firm could not represent B against C and D.

First Clients First?

Suppose a firm concurrently represents two clients with adverse interests, who signed up with the firm at different times. May the client who signed up second disqualify the firm from representing the client who signed up first?

Opinions vary. In *Friskit, Inc. v. RealNetworks, Inc.*, 2007 WL 1994204 (N.D. Cal. 2007), the court said: No. Foley & Lardner represented Friskit Inc. in patent litigation for several years. Realnetworks was a defendant in that litigation. Rob Glaser was Chairman of the Board and CEO of Realnetworks; he also owned 32.4% of that company's stock. He hired Foley & Lardner to represent him in unrelated litigation in New York. At the time, he did not know that Foley & Lardner represented Friskit against Realnetworks.

When Glaser learned that Foley was counsel against Realnetworks, he sought to intervene in the Realnetworks case for purposes of disqualifying Foley as counsel for Friskit. The court granted his motion to intervene on the ground that Realnetworks was not Foley's client, and therefore might not have standing to assert Glaser's conflict claim.

The court denied Glaser's motion to disqualify, holding "[i]t is implicit under the California cases, and the Rules of Professional Conduct, that the duty of loyalty runs to the existing client, and is not subordinate to any duty owed a later-acquired client. That duty bars the attorney from taking on a representation that conflicts with that of the existing client. To enforce that duty by disqualifying the attorney from representing his existing client would turn the duty of loyalty on its head."

In contrast, the courts in *TransPerfect Global, Inc. v. MotionPoint* Corp., 2012 WL 2343908 (N.D. CA 2012) and *Fujitsu Ltd. v. Belkin Intern., Inc.*, 2010 WL 5387920 (N.D. CA 2010), held that the second client to retain a firm does have standing to disqualify the first. These courts reasoned that California courts have not distinguished between first and second clients in disqualification cases and have granted motions to disqualify filed by the second client.

Concurrent conflicts are generally easy to spot. If A sues B and your conflicts check shows that you currently represent A then accepting B as a client would create a concurrent conflict. Things are not always that easy, however. Two types of situations present the problem of who counts as a current client for conflicts purposes: frequent but intermittent representation, and a current source of confidential information.

The first problem occurs when you represent a client commonly but not continuously. Suppose you represent a client on discrete matters that come up every three or four months. The client calls and asks you a question, you research the question for a day or two, you give the client an answer, you send a bill, and it gets paid. You have no formal retainer and, apart from the day or two it takes to answer the question, you do no work for the client. Is that client a "current client" for purposes of the conflict rules only on the days you do work for it or for some other period of time? The answer might matter a lot, especially if you were asked to represent a party adverse to this client.

In *IBM v. Levin*, 579 F.2d 271, 274 (3d Cir. 1978), the trial court disqualified a firm representing a plaintiff who was suing IBM for alleged violations of the antitrust laws. On several occasions before and after the antitrust suit was filed, the firm had advised IBM on discrete labor matters. The firm had no matter pending for IBM on the date the antitrust suit was filed. For this reason, the firm argued that in filing the antitrust suit it did not take action contrary to the interests of a current client. (Because the two suits were unrelated, it also would not have violated the conflict rules pertaining to former clients, which we study below.)

The court of appeals rejected this argument:

> The [district] court found as a fact that at all relevant times CBM had an on-going attorney-client relationship with both IBM and the plaintiffs. This assessment of the relationship seems entirely reasonable to us. Although CBM had no specific assignment from IBM on hand on the day the antitrust complaint was filed and even though CBM performed services for IBM on a fee for service basis rather than pursuant to a retainer arrangement, the pattern of repeated retainers, both before and after the filing of the complaint, supports the finding of a continuous relationship

IBM v. Levin suggests that when you work for a client on a routine but not strictly continuous basis you run the risk of having a court treat that client as a current client for conflicts purposes even if you have no matter pending for that client at the time you want to accept representation adverse to that client's interests. Courts will tend to adopt a client's-eye-view of such situations.

From a conflicts point of view, it is in your interest to make clear to the client—in writing—whether you consider the representation to be continuous or a series of discrete representations, with nothing going on in between. That course will protect you against conflicts risks but it may make the client think you are not very loyal to their interests, which may make the client look elsewhere for representation. That is a tension you must learn to negotiate; it has no discrete, silver-bullet solution.

The second type of problem can arise when a firm represents a client and has some interest not arising from an attorney-client relationship but which is adverse to the client. *William H. Raley, Co. v. Superior Court*, 149 Cal.App.3d 1042 (1983), exemplifies this problem. In that case the Grey, Cary firm represented the owner of a property who sued a lessee for alleged breaches of the lease. The lessee was a corporation, whose stock was owned by a trust. The trustee of that trust was a bank. A Grey, Cary partner was a director of the bank and a member of the committee responsible for discharging the bank's obligations when it acted as trustee. This committee appointed the corporation's directors and was responsible for running its affairs.

When the lawyer for the corporation learned that a Grey, Cary partner was a bank director and member of the relevant committee, he moved to disqualify the firm on conflict of interest grounds. The trial court denied a motion to disqualify the firm but the court of appeals reversed. The court held that "a conflict of interest may arise [1] where an attorney's relationship with a person or entity creates an expectation that the attorney owes a duty of fidelity. It may also arise [2] where the attorney has acquired confidential information in the course of such a relationship which will be, or may appear to the person or entity to be, useful in the attorney's representation in an action on behalf of a client." The court concluded that "In effect, [the lawyer's] fiduciary relationship with [the corporation and the trust] through his positions with the Bank and the Committee, on the one hand, and his partnership status with Gray, Cary, on the other hand, places Gray, Cary on both sides of Carroll's lawsuit."

---

2. WHICH INTERESTS ARE DIRECTLY ADVERSE?

A good rule of thumb is that parties are adverse when they are across the table from each other in negotiations or across the courtroom in litigation. As a general matter other forms of adversity, such as exists between firms that compete in a market, do not count. They might be considered indirectly adverse interests. As comment six to Model Rule 1.7 states, "simultaneous representation in unrelated matters of clients whose interests are only economically adverse, such as representation of competing economic enterprises in unrelated litigation, does not ordinarily constitute a conflict of interest and thus may not require consent of the respective clients."

But the "across the table" rule of thumb and the "indirect adversity" concept do not explain all the cases. Consider the following.

NORTH STAR HOTELS CORP. V. MID–CITY HOTEL ASSOCIATES

118 F.R.D. 109 (D. Minn. 1987)

JANICE M. SYMCHYCH, UNITED STATES MAGISTRATE.

The above matter came before the undersigned United States Magistrate on November 25, 1987 upon defendant's motion to disqualify plaintiff's counsel, Faegre & Benson. Michael Stern, Esq., appeared on behalf of defendant; Jerry Snider, Esq., appeared on behalf of plaintiff. The motion was taken under advisement.

I. BACKGROUND

Plaintiff filed this action in federal district court on September 4, 1987, alleging breach of a management agreement contract between the parties and seeking damages and declaratory relief. Pursuant to the agreement, plaintiff managed and operated the Minneapolis Hilton Hotel, which is owned by defendant. Jerry Snider of Faegre & Benson represented plaintiff in connection with this management contract beginning in December, 1986. Defendant was represented by David Mylrea of the Estes, Parsinen & Levy law firm. Several weeks ago, Mr. Mylrea informed defendant that his law firm would have to withdraw from representation because of the possibility Mr. Mylrea would be required to testify during this litigation. Thereafter, defendant retained the law firm of Fredrikson & Byron through Michael Stern as counsel.

Defendant brought this motion to disqualify after Faegre & Benson refused to voluntarily withdraw from its representation of North Star. Defendant claims that Faegre & Benson's representation of North Star creates a conflict of interest with respect to two of Faegre's other clients, St. Louis Centre Partners and Burnsville Woods Partnership. An explanation of the partnerships' structures is helpful in elucidating this alleged conflict.

Mid–City Hotel Associates, the defendant in this lawsuit, is a partnership comprised of two general partners, Harry A. Johnson and Helen Johnson, each of whom own 10 percent. The remaining 80 percent is owned by the Johnson's children as limited partners. As a general partner, Harry A. Johnson is personally liable for any potential judgment not satisfied from partnership assets.

St. Louis Centre Partners is a general partnership involved in developing real estate in the vicinity of Highway 100 and Excelsior Boulevard, a project estimated at $80 million dollars. Faegre & Benson has represented St. Louis Centre Partners since its inception. Three general partners own St. Louis Centre: AP Development has a one percent ownership interest; Rosewood Corporation, a client of Faegre & Benson, has a 49.5 percent ownership interest; and Pineapple Management has a 49.5 percent ownership interest. Faegre & Benson represents both Rosewood Corporation and St. Louis Centre Partners with respect to all legal documents and business dealings with third parties. Pineapple Management is a Subchapter S corporation, 96 percent of which is owned by Harry A. Johnson.

Faegre & Benson also currently represents Burnsville Woods Partnership in its development of a $20 million dollar apartment complex in Burnsville. Rosewood Corporation and HAJ Construction each has a 50 percent ownership interest in the partnership. HAJ Construction is a Subchapter S corporation owned entirely by Harry A. Johnson. The parties concur that both HAJ Construction and Pineapple Management have been separately represented by Howard Cox of the Moss & Barnett law firm in negotiations with St. Louis Centre and Burnsville Woods. In addition, Mr. Cox represented Harry A. Johnson individually in setting up his corporations. It is equally clear, however, that Faegre & Benson has been the sole counsel for the St. Louis Centre and Burnsville Woods Partnerships as entities.

Burnsville Woods Partnership has formally requested that Faegre & Benson withdraw from representation of North Star in the instant litigation. In addition, counsel for defendant represents that on November 30, 1987, Harry Johnson was denied a letter of credit which was predicate to a certain real estate closing for Burnsville Woods. He asserts that the letter of credit was denied on account of a lis pendens filed by Faegre & Benson in connection with this litigation.

Defendant argues that Faegre & Benson's representation of North Star is directly adverse to the interests of two of its other clients, St. Louis Centre and Burnsville Woods; or, in the alternative, will materially limit its representation of them. The undersigned has been persuaded by defendant's arguments and will, therefore, grant the motion.

II. DISCUSSION

On November 1, 1987, the United States District Court amended Local Rule 1 to state that the professional conduct of attorneys licensed to practice in the district court shall be governed by the Minnesota Rules of Professional Conduct. The pertinent provision here is [Minnesota's Rule 1.7(a), which conforms to the Model Rule].

The factual context of this case makes application of the foregoing rule extremely difficult. Both parties represented to the court that they have diligently searched for legal precedent, but have found no case law bearing squarely on the issues raised. The undersigned has also found none. Therefore, the following analysis relies on the application of the spirit of the MRPC to the facts of this lawsuit, and other precedent.

The parties agree that the conflict of interest here does not involve the stuff of typical disqualification motions: there is no contention by defendant that Faegre & Benson is simultaneously or sequentially representing adverse parties on substantially related matters; or that confidences and secrets of one client will be improperly available to the advantage of another; or that the alleged conflict in any way bears on the substantive matters here in dispute. Rather, the issue is the potential financial impairment of two of Faegre & Benson's clients because of its representation of North Star against Mid–City in this lawsuit. By its very nature, the overriding function of the present lawsuit is to collect money damages from defendant. The assets of the general partner being sued, Harry Johnson, include substantial holdings in two real estate development partnerships represented by Faegre & Benson. Faegre & Benson represents a plaintiff who has the potential for collecting a large judgment which would be financially adversarial to its other clients. If the suit is successful, a judgment for which Harry Johnson is personally liable puts the other two clients at a direct financial risk. Furthermore, to the extent Harry Johnson may be personally liable, his diminished personal assets will make him less able to accommodate his personal guarantees of several millions of dollars of St. Louis Centre and Burnsville Woods partnerships' debt. Given these facts, Faegre & Bensons's representation of North Star in this action is "directly adverse" to the financial interests of its two partnership clients, within the meaning of MRPC 1.7(a).

Plaintiff raises multiple arguments in support of its position that no conflict exists. First, it claims that Harry Johnson is not a client and, therefore, it owes him no duty under the Rules. Simply because Faegre & Benson does not represent HAJ Construction or Pineapple Management does not preclude finding of a conflict. Rather, the court must look beyond the issue of formal representation and determine whether the relationship between Harry Johnson's role as a partner in defendant and his role in the partnership clients of Faegre & Benson has the potential to adversely impact the interests of the law firm's partnership clients. The somewhat sparse authority on this issue makes clear that the fact itself of an adverse party's membership in another organization or entity represented by a law firm cannot and does not determine the conflict issue. Rather, the significance of that individual's position as a member in such an entity must be examined. *Glueck v. Jonathan Logan, Inc.,* 653 F.2d 746 (2nd Cir.1981). Harry Johnson is a key principal in St. Louis Centre,

Burnsville Woods, and Mid–City. He is inferentially a man of some financial substance; $3 million dollars in personal loan guarantees demonstrates a likelihood that in the event of an adverse judgment in this action, plaintiff will look to him for payment. As assets belonging to him, Harry Johnson's interests in the two partnerships represented by Faegre & Benson could be impaired or reduced. His financial position is clearly significant to the two partnerships represented by Faegre & Benson.

Defendant acknowledges that if the composition of the various partnerships was different—if, for example, Harry Johnson was merely one of many limited partners, or if he had a significantly lesser interest in his Subchapter S corporations—that the outcome most probably should be different. *Cf. Glueck,* 653 F.2d at 749. It is true that in situations where an adverse party is merely a "vicarious client" by virtue of his membership in an organization which a law firm represents, the risks associated with simultaneous representation of adverse interests are minimal. *Shadow Isle, Inc. v. American Angus Association,* No. 84–6126–CV–SJ–6 (W.D.Mo. Sept. 22, 1987) (Westlaw, Allfeds file [1987 WL 17337]). The facts in this case indicate that Harry Johnson is a cornerstone of both the St. Louis Centre and Burnsville Woods partnerships, and as such Faegre & Benson's representation of North Star in a suit against Mid–City poses a direct financial threat to Faegre & Benson's other two clients.

Plaintiff also argues that Johnson should be forced to accept the consequences of the business structures under which he chose to operate, and cannot now claim that a potential judgment against his Mid–City partnership will negatively impact his obligations to his Subchapter S corporations, for which he is not subject to personal liability. It is true that for liability purposes he is bound by the business forms he chose. The issue before the court, however, is not Harry Johnson's liability; rather, it is the scope of a law firm's duties and loyalties to those it represents under the MRPC.

The district court is empowered to exercise its discretion to responsibly supervise the members of the bar. . . . The court is sensitive to the fact that motions for disqualification may serve to improperly delay proceedings and to deny a party the counsel of its choice. [citations omitted] Such motions are to be closely scrutinized for this reason. Here, the facts of record, the conduct of defendant's counsel, and the novel, but difficult issues involved cause the court to conclude that this motion is properly motivated and brought for honorable purposes. Although the traditional disqualification issues which arise in multiple representation cases are not present here, there is a sufficient adversity to two of Faegre & Benson's existing clients as to require disqualification. Although financial adversity has not yet been held to fall squarely within MRPC Rule 1.7(a), there is nothing precluding it from doing so. The unique issue here should not itself operate to preclude disqualification. Any doubt as to whether a law firm should be disqualified is to be resolved in favor of disqualification. *Coffelt v. Shell,* 577 F.2d 30, 32 (8th Cir.1978).

After a careful analysis, the undersigned, therefore, concludes that Faegre & Benson should be disqualified from its representation of North Star in this action. A law firm simply should not seek to compensate one client from the pockets of another. . . . defendant's motion to disqualify plaintiff's counsel, Faegre & Benson, from its representation in this lawsuit is GRANTED

As *North Star Hotels* suggests, whether interests are "directly adverse" requires judgments based on the facts of particular cases. Some points are clear. A lawyer may be directly adverse to a client's interests even if the lawyer does not oppose the client in litigation. *MGM, Inc. v. Tracinda Corp.*, 36 Cal.App.4th 1832, 1835 (1995), is an example.

The Christensen, White firm represented MGM stock in a transaction where Pathe Communications bought MGM. The firm also represented MGM in what the law firm referred to as "a long-dormant class action." Pathe (which had changed its name to MGM) later sued some of the key figures involved in the sale, alleging they misled Pathe about MGM's finances.

Credit Lyonnais (CLBN) financed the transaction. It sued the same defendants. The Christensen firm represented the defendants in the Credit Lyonnais action, though not the Pathe/MGM action. Pathe/MGM moved to disqualify the firm, which argued that its representation of the defendants in the CLBN action was not adverse to MGM. The court rejected the argument and granted the motion. It reasoned:

> while the two actions may be based on separate transactions; i.e., the merger of MGM and Pathe and the financing of CLBN, and involve separate legal theories; i.e., the duty to disclose to shareholders and the duty to make accurate representations to a lending institution to induce it to enter into a financing agreement, both are based on the same factual allegations. . . . both MGM and CLBN are challenging the merger. Each plaintiff will be trying to prove that [the defendants] acted in their individual interests and engineered a scheme to inflate the value of MGM so that they could make money from the sale of their shares in MGM. Every time Christensen White attempts to disprove this theory against their clients in the CLBN action, it will affect the MGM action. Also, of necessity, Christensen White must attempt to support the credibility of Silbert, a former director and shareholder of MGM, with respect to his participation during the negotiations for the merger. In effect, Christensen White will be rep-

resenting a former shareholder and director against the interests of the former corporate client.

Courts also may find direct adversity where representation of one client will adversely affect a potential claim another client has but has not brought. In *GATX/Airlog Co. v. Evergreen Int'l Airlines, Inc.*, 8 F.Supp. 2d 1182 (N.D. Cal. 1998), *order vacated as moot* 192 F.3d 1304, 1305 (9th Cir. 1999), the Mayer, Brown firm represented GATX, which converted passenger aircraft into cargo aircraft. GATX contracted with Evergreen to convert four planes for it. The Bank of New York (BNY) eventually became the beneficial owner of one of those planes.

The FAA originally approved the GATX conversion design but then declared it had made a mistake and restricted the amount of cargo the planes could carry. The restricted amount was not enough to justify the cost of operating the planes. Evergreen sent a demand letter to GATX, which retained Mayer, Brown to defend it and filed a declaratory relief action. In 1997, GATX and BNY negotiated an agreement to toll the limitations period on claims BNY might have against GATX.

Mayer, Brown represented BNY in unrelated matters. BNY moved to intervene in the Evergreen litigation for the purpose of disqualifying Mayer, Brown. The court granted the motion:

> MBP's representation of GATX was adverse to BNY. MBP spent the entire time between May 1997 and February 1998 advancing assertions in pleadings and dispositive motions that could provide GATX with defenses to claims by BNY and the other aircraft owners. MBP then sought discovery to support those assertions. Because BNY is the current owner of a plane that was converted for Evergreen, any defenses to Evergreen's claims are probably dispositive of BNY's claims. The Evergreen action, which was filed in mid–1996, is even more intimately entwined, then, with BNY's case. Finally, MBP did not reveal the conflict to its two clients until January 1998. MBP has never received a waiver from BNY.
>
> MBP argues that its representation was not adverse to BNY until BNY actually filed suit against GATX. This argument, however, lacks merit. MBP does accurately point out that the cases cited by the Court in *Flatt* all involved simultaneous suits. MBP contends that BNY was not a "party" until BNY filed suit against GATX in January 1998. . . . BNY should be considered a "party" from the time MBP represented GATX while GATX negotiated the May 1997 Tolling Agreement with BNY, and attempted to negotiate a settlement. MBP admits, as it must, that it knew of BNY's claims since that time.

"Positional" Conflicts

What if instead of parties who oppose each other in litigation, or who have conflicting economic interests, a case involves parties who have different interests relative to some legal rule? This problem is known as a "positional conflict," that is, a conflict arising from different positions on some legal question rather than different legal or economic interests. If you think about it for a moment, you will see that the distinction between positional legal interests and other types of conflicts is not very clean. A ruling on a legal issue, for example, can cause a party to lose money (including by losing a court case) just as much as losing a particular case or a particular contract could.

Nevertheless, the general rule is that positional conflicts do not create direct adversity for purposes of Rule 1.7(a). Comment 24 to that rule says "[o]rdinarily a lawyer may take inconsistent legal positions in different tribunals at different times on behalf of different clients. The mere fact that advocating a legal position on behalf of one client might create precedent adverse to the interests of a client represented by the lawyer in an unrelated matter does not create a conflict of interest." The comment goes on to say, however, that positional conflicts can be real conflicts for purposes of the rule "if there is a significant risk that a lawyer's action on behalf of one client will materially limit the lawyer's effectiveness in representing another client in a different case; for example, when a decision favoring one client will create a precedent likely to seriously weaken the position taken on behalf of the other client."

Williams v. Delaware, 805 A.2d 880 (2002), presented a true positional conflict. Bernard J. O'Donnell represented Williams and another client, both of whom appealed to the Delaware Supreme Court from convictions that led to capital sentences. Here are some excerpts from the opinion:

> O'Donnell asserts that, on appeal, Williams could raise an arguable issue that the Superior Court erred when it concluded it was required to give "great weight" to the jury's 10–2 recommendation in favor of the death penalty for Williams. O'Donnell contends, however, that he may have a conflict in presenting this argument because he has advocated a contrary position on behalf of a different client in another capital murder appeal pending before this Court. In *Garden v. State*, Nos. 125 & 162, 2001, O'Donnell argued in his opening brief that the Superior Court erred when it *failed* to give great weight to the jury's 2–10 vote rejecting the imposition of the death penalty for Garden.
>
> O'Donnell is concerned that his representation of both clients on this issue will create the risk that an unfavorable precedent will be created for one client or the other. O'Donnell also is concerned that it may invite questions about his credibility with this Court and his clients'

> perception of his loyalty to each of them. The State agrees that O'Donnell has a conflict of interest that disqualifies him from representing Williams in this appeal.
>
> In determining whether a positional conflict requires a lawyer's disqualification, the question is whether the lawyer can effectively argue both sides of the same legal question without compromising the interests of one client or the other. The lawyer must attempt to strike a balance between the duty to advocate any viable interpretation of the law for one client's benefit versus the other client's right to insist on counsel's fidelity to their legal position.
>
> Under the circumstances presented in Williams' case, we find that O'Donnell has identified and demonstrated the existence of a disqualifying positional conflict. It would be a violation of the Delaware Rules of Professional Conduct for O'Donnell to advocate conflicting legal positions in two capital murder appeals that are pending simultaneously in this Court. Both the United States Constitution and the Delaware Constitution guarantee each of O'Donnell's clients a right to the effective assistance of counsel in a direct appeal following a capital murder conviction. Given his clients' disparate legal arguments, O'Donnell's independent obligations to his clients may compromise the effectiveness of his assistance as appellate counsel for one or both clients, unless his motion to withdraw is granted.

Although positional conflicts are most often thought of in terms of concurrent clients, such issues can come up with regard to former clients. A lawyer might advocate a position for a client and then, after that representation was over, attack the same position for another client. Because conflict analysis for former clients focuses on confidentiality, such situations are unlikely to violate Rule 1.9 or lead to disqualification. (Note that this conflict has to do with general legal positions, not with the work the lawyer did for the first client. If a lawyer performed work for one client and then turned around and attacked that very work for another client, courts would view the situation as posing more than a mere positional conflict. We have seen just such a case; do you remember which one?)

3. LIMITATIONS ON COUNSEL'S ABILITY TO REPRESENT ZEALOUSLY

Even if a representation is not directly adverse to a current client, a lawyer still has a conflict if there is a significant risk that the lawyer's ability to represent a client would be materially limited by a lawyer's duties to another current or former client, to a third person, or by a personal interest of the lawyer. The following case exemplifies the first of these potential issues.

Model Rule of Professional Conduct 1.7(a)(2)

FIANDACA V. CUNNINGHAM

827 F.2d 825 (1st Cir. 1987)

COFFIN, CIRCUIT JUDGE.

This opinion discusses two consolidated appeals related to a class action brought by twenty-three female prison inmates sentenced to the custody of the warden of the New Hampshire State Prison. The suit challenges the state of New Hampshire's failure to establish a facility for the incarceration of female inmates with programs and services equivalent to those provided to male inmates at the state prison. After a bench trial on the merits, the district court held that the state had violated plaintiffs' right to equal protection of the laws and ordered the construction of a permanent in-state facility for plaintiffs no later than July 1, 1989. It also required the state to provide a temporary facility for plaintiffs on or before November 1, 1987, but prohibited the state from establishing this facility on the grounds of the Laconia State School and Training Center ("Laconia State School" or "LSS"), New Hampshire's lone institution for the care and treatment of mentally retarded citizens.

One set of appellants consists of Michael Cunningham, warden of the New Hampshire State Prison, and various executive branch officials responsible for the operation of the New Hampshire Department of Corrections ("state"). They challenge the district court's refusal to disqualify plaintiffs' class counsel, New Hampshire Legal Assistance ("NHLA"), due to an unresolvable conflict of interest. *See* N.H. Rules of Professional Conduct, Rule 1.7(b). They also seek to overturn that portion of the district court's decision barring the establishment of an interim facility for female inmates at LSS, arguing that this prohibition is unsupported either by relevant factual findings, *see* Fed.R.Civ.P. 52(a), or by evidence contained in the record.

The other group of appellants is comprised of the plaintiffs in a separate class action challenging the conditions and practices at the Laconia State School, including the New Hampshire Association for Retarded Citizens ("NHARC") and the mentally retarded citizens who currently reside at LSS (the "*Garrity* class"). This group sought unsuccessfully to intervene in the relief phase of the instant litigation after the conclusion of the trial, but prior to the issuance of the court's final memorandum order. *See* Fed.R.Civ.P. 24. On appeal, these prospective intervenors argue that the district court abused its discretion in denying their motion.

We begin by presenting the relevant facts and then turn to our analysis of the legal issues raised by each of these appeals.

I. *Factual Setting.*

This case began in June, 1983, when plaintiffs' appellate counsel, Bertram Astles, filed a complaint on behalf of several female inmates sentenced to the custody of the state prison warden and incarcerated at the Rockingham County House of Corrections. NHLA subsequently became co-counsel for plaintiffs and filed an amended complaint expanding the plaintiff class to include all female inmates who are or will be incarcerated in the custody of the warden. In the years that followed, NHLA assumed the role of lead counsel for the class, engaging in extensive discovery and performing all other legal tasks through the completion of the trial before the district court. Among other things, NHLA attorneys and their trial expert, Dr. Edyth Flynn, twice toured and examined potential facilities at which to house plaintiffs, including buildings at the Laconia State School, the New Hampshire Hospital in Concord, and the Youth Development Center in Manchester.

Pursuant to Fed.R.Civ.P. 68, the state offered to settle the litigation on August 1, 1986, in exchange for the establishment of a facility for female inmates at the current Hillsborough County House of Corrections in Goffstown. The state had already negotiated an agreement with Hillsborough County to lease this facility and expected to have it ready for use by the end of 1989. Plaintiffs rejected this offer, however, primarily because the relief would not be available for over three years and because the plan was contingent on Hillsborough County's ability to complete construction of a new facility for the relocation of its prisoners. Plaintiffs desired an in-state facility within six to nine months at the latest and apparently would not settle for less.

The state extended a second offer of judgment to plaintiffs on October 21, 1986. This offer proposed to establish an in-state facility for the incarceration of female inmates at an existing state building by June 1, 1987. Although the formal offer of judgment did not specify a particular location for this facility, the state informed NHLA that it planned to use the Speare Cottage at the Laconia State School. NHLA, which also represented the plaintiff class in the ongoing *Garrity* litigation, rejected the offer on November 10, stating in part that "plaintiffs do not want to agree to an offer which is against the stated interests of the plaintiffs in the *Garrity* class." The state countered by moving immediately for the disqualification of NHLA as class counsel in the case at bar due to the unresolvable conflict of interest inherent in NHLA's representation of two classes with directly adverse interests. The court, despite recognizing that a conflict of interest probably existed, denied the state's motion on November 20 because NHLA's disqualification would further delay the trial of an important matter that had been pending for over three years. It began to try the case four days later.

The *Garrity* class filed its motion to intervene on December 11, ten days after the conclusion of the trial on the merits. The group alleged that it had only recently learned of the state's proposal to develop a correctional facility for women at the Laconia State School. The members of the class were concerned that the establishment of this facility at the school's Speare Cottage, which they understood to be the primary building under consideration, would displace 28 residents of the school and violate the remedial orders issued by Chief Judge Devine in *Garrity,* 522 F.Supp. at 239–44, as well as N.H.Rev.Stat.Ann. ch. 171–A. The district court denied the motion to intervene on December 23, assuring the applicant-intervenors that it would "never approve a settlement which in any way disenfranchises patients of LSS or contravenes the letter or intent of [Chief Judge] Devine's order in *Garrity*."

Meanwhile, the court agreed to hold up its decision on the merits pending the conclusion of ongoing settlement negotiations, permitting the principal parties to spend the month of December, 1986, engaged in further efforts to settle the case. Within approximately one week after the conclusion of the trial, the parties reached an understanding with regard to a settlement agreement which called for the establishment of a "fully operational facility at the present site of the Laconia State School for the incarceration of female inmates by November 1, 1987." The agreement also provided that all affected residents of LSS would receive appropriate placements at least two months prior to the opening of the correctional facility. After negotiating this agreement, NHLA moved to withdraw as class co-counsel on December 11 and attorney Astles signed the settlement agreement on plaintiffs' behalf. The state, however, refused to sign the agreement.

This collapse of the post-trial settlement efforts prompted Judge Loughlin, the district judge in the instant case, and Chief Judge Devine, the *Garrity* trial judge, to convene a joint settlement conference on December 22, 1986. At this conference, plaintiffs formally withdrew their consent to the original settlement agreement in light of the state's refusal to abide by the agreement. Both parties agreed, nevertheless, to try once again to settle the matter in a manner acceptable to all concerned and to report to the en banc court by January 12, 1987. Judge Loughlin, apparently believing that NHLA's conflict of interest prevented its effective performance as plaintiffs' class counsel, granted NHLA's pending motion to withdraw the day after the joint settlement conference. NHLA, however, had reconsidered its withdrawal from the case in light of the state's failure to sign the settlement agreement and it immediately petitioned the court to be reinstated as class counsel. The court denied the motion for reinstatement, reasoning that the "doctrine of necessity," its purported justification for denying the state's earlier disqualification motion in the face of NHLA's conflict of interest, no longer had force because the case had been tried to a conclusion.

The district court finally announced its decision on the merits on January 13, 1987. Finding that the conditions of confinement, programs, and services available to New Hampshire female prisoners are not on par with the conditions, programs, and services afforded male inmates at the New Hampshire State Prison, the court held that such gender-based, inferior treatment violates the Equal Protection clause of the Fourteenth Amendment. As a primary remedy, it ordered the state to establish "a permanent facility comparable to all of the facilities encompassed at the New Hampshire State Prison . . . to be inhabited no later than July 1, 1989." In crafting a temporary remedy, it reiterated that "there shall not be a scintilla of infringement upon the rights and privileges of the *Garrity* class," and proceeded to rule that the state had to provide plaintiffs with "a building comparable to the Speare Building," but that such facility "shall not be located at the Laconia State School or its environs." This appeal resulted.

II. *Appeal of State Department of Corrections.*

As noted above, the state challenges the district court's decision on two independent grounds. First, it claims that the court should have disqualified NHLA as plaintiffs' class counsel prior to the commencement of the trial. Second, it contends that the court's proscription of the use of a site at the Laconia State School is unsupported either by relevant findings of fact or by evidence contained in the record. Because we find in favor of the state on its first claim and remand for a new trial on the issue of an appropriate remedy, we confine ourselves to an analysis of the disqualification issue.

A. *Refusal to Disqualify for Conflict of Interest.*

The state's first argument is that the district court erred in permitting NHLA to represent the plaintiff class at trial after its conflict of interest had become apparent. As we recognized in *Kevlik v. Goldstein,* 724 F.2d 844 (1st Cir.1984), a district court is vested with broad power and responsibility to supervise the professional conduct of the attorneys appearing before it. It follows from this premise that "[w]e will not disturb the district court['s] finding unless there is no reasonable basis for the court's determination." We must determine, therefore, whether the court's denial of the state's disqualification motion amounts to an abuse of discretion in this instance.

The state's theory is that NHLA faced an unresolvable conflict because the interests of two of its clients were directly adverse after the state extended its second offer of judgment on October 21, 1986. The relevant portion of New Hampshire's Rules of Professional Conduct states:

> A lawyer shall not represent a client if the representation of that client may be materially limited by the lawyer's responsibilities to another client . . . unless:

(1) the lawyer reasonably believes the representation will not be adversely affected; and

(2) the client consents after consultation and with knowledge of the consequences.

* * *

N.H. Rules of Professional Conduct, Rule 1.7(b).

The comment to Rule 1.7 prepared by the ABA goes on to state:

Loyalty to a client is also impaired when a lawyer cannot consider, recommend or carry out an appropriate course of action for the client because of the lawyer's other responsibilities or interests. The conflict in effect forecloses alternatives that would otherwise be available to the client.

N.H. Rules of Professional Conduct, Rule 1.7, comment. In this case, it is the state's contention that the court should have disqualified NHLA as class counsel pursuant to Rule 1.7 because, at least with respect to the state's second offer of judgment, NHLA's representation of the plaintiff class in this litigation was materially limited by its responsibilities to the *Garrity* class.

We find considerable merit in this argument. The state's offer to establish a facility for the incarceration of female inmates at the Laconia State School, and to use its "best efforts" to make such a facility available for occupancy by June 1, 1987, presented plaintiffs with a legitimate opportunity to settle a protracted legal dispute on highly favorable terms. As class counsel, NHLA owed plaintiffs a duty of undivided loyalty: it was obligated to present the offer to plaintiffs, to explain its costs and benefits, and to ensure that the offer received full and fair consideration by the members of the class. Beyond all else, NHLA had an ethical duty to prevent its loyalties to other clients from coloring its representation of the plaintiffs in this action and from infringing upon the exercise of its professional judgment and responsibilities.[3]

NHLA, however, also represents the residents of the Laconia State School who are members of the plaintiff class in *Garrity*. Quite understandably, this group vehemently opposes the idea of establishing a correctional facility for female inmates anywhere on the grounds of LSS. As counsel for the *Garrity* class, NHLA had an ethical duty to advance the interests of the class to the fullest possible extent and to oppose any settlement of the instant case that would compromise those interests. In

[3] FN4. The fact that the conflict arose due to the nature of the state's settlement offer, rather than due to the subject matter of the litigation or the parties involved, does not render the ethical implications of NHLA's multiple representation any less troublesome. Among other things, courts have a duty to "ensur[e] that at all stages of litigation . . . counsel are as a general rule available to advise each client as to the particular, individualized benefits or costs of a proposed settlement." *Smith v. City of New York,* 611 F.Supp. 1080, 1090 (S.D.N.Y.1985).

short, the combination of clients and circumstances placed NHLA in the untenable position of being simultaneously obligated to represent vigorously the interests of two conflicting clients. It is inconceivable that NHLA, or any other counsel, could have properly performed the role of "advocate" for both plaintiffs and the *Garrity* class, regardless of its good faith or high intentions. Indeed, this is precisely the sort of situation that Rule 1.7 is designed to prevent.

Plaintiffs argue on appeal that there really was no conflict of interest for NHLA because the state's second offer of judgment was unlikely to lead to a completed settlement for reasons other than NHLA's loyalties to the *Garrity* class. We acknowledge that the record contains strong indications that settlement would not have occurred even if plaintiffs had been represented by another counsel. . . . The question, however, is not whether the state's second offer of judgment would have resulted in a settlement had plaintiffs' counsel not been encumbered by a conflict of interest. Rather, the inquiry we must make is whether plaintiffs' counsel was able to represent the plaintiff class unaffected by divided loyalties, or as stated in Rule 1.7(b), whether NHLA could have reasonably believed that its representation would not be adversely affected by the conflict. Our review of the record and the history of this litigation—especially NHLA's response to the state's second offer, in which it stated that "plaintiffs do not want to agree to an offer which is against the stated interests of plaintiffs in the *Garrity* case"—persuade us that NHLA's representation of plaintiffs could not escape the adverse effects of NHLA's loyalties to the *Garrity* class.

Both the district court and plaintiffs on appeal have also advanced the belief that "necessity" outweighed the adverse effects of NHLA's conflict of interest in this instance and justified the denial of the state's pretrial disqualification motion. . . .

Absent some evidence of *true* necessity, we will not permit a meritorious disqualification motion to be denied in the interest of expediency unless it can be shown that the movant strategically sought disqualification in an effort to advance some improper purpose. Thus, the state's motivation in bringing the motion is not irrelevant; as we recognized in *Kevlik,* "disqualification motions can be tactical in nature, designed to harass opposing counsel." *Id.* However, the mere fact that the state moved for NHLA's disqualification just prior to the commencement of the trial is not, without more, cause for denying its motion. *See id.* There is simply no evidence to support plaintiffs' suggestion that the state "created" the conflict by intentionally offering plaintiffs a building at LSS in an effort "to dodge the bullet again" with regard to its "failure to provide in-state housing for the plaintiff class." We do not believe, therefore, that the state's second offer of judgment and subsequent disqualification motion were intended to harass plaintiffs. Rather, our reading of the record indicates that a more benign scenario is more probable: the state made a good faith attempt to accommodate plaintiffs by offering to establish a correctional facility in an existing building at the Laconia State School and, once NHLA's conflict of interest with regard to this offer became apparent, the state moved for NHLA's disqualification to preserve this settlement option.

As we are unable to identify a reasoned basis for the district court's denial of the state's pre-trial motion to disqualify NHLA from serving as plaintiffs' class counsel, we hold that its order amounts to an abuse of discretion and must be reversed.

B. *Proper Remedy.*

In light of the district court's error in ignoring NHLA's conflict of interest, we believe it necessary to remand the case for further proceedings. We must consider a further question, however: must the district court now start from scratch in resolving this dispute? The state argues that the court's failure to disqualify NHLA is plain reversible error, and therefore requires the court to try the matter anew. We subscribe to the view, however, that merely "conducting [a] trial with counsel that should have been disqualified does not 'indelibl[y] stamp or taint' the proceedings." *Warpar Manufacturing Corp. v. Ashland Oil, Inc.,* 606 F.Supp. 866, 867 (N.D.Ohio, E.D.1985) (quoting *Firestone Tire & Rubber Co. v. Risjord,* 449 U.S. 368, 376, 101 S.Ct. 669, 674, 66 L.Ed.2d 571 (1981)). With this in mind, we look to the actual adverse effects caused by the court's error in refusing to disqualify NHLA as class counsel to determine the nature of the proceedings on remand. [citations omitted]

We do not doubt that NHLA's conflict of interest potentially influenced the course of the proceedings in at least one regard: NHLA could not fairly advocate the remedial option—namely, the alternative of settling for a site at the Laconia State School—offered by the state prior to trial. The conflict, therefore, had the potential to ensure that the case would go to trial, a route the state likely wished to avoid by achieving an acceptable settlement. Nevertheless, we do not see how a trial on the merits could have been avoided given the manner in which the case developed below. Judge Loughlin stated on the record that he would not approve a settlement infringing on the rights of LSS residents, and under Rule 23(e), any settlement of this class action required his approval to be effective. It seems to us, therefore, that even if some other counsel had advised plaintiffs to accept the state's offer for a building at LSS, a trial on the merits would have been inevitable.

With respect to the merits of the equal protection issue, the state has been unable to identify any way in which the court's error adversely affected its substantial rights at trial. The state admits that it had long recognized the need to establish an in-state facility for female inmates comparable to the state prison and that it had already taken steps in this direction by negotiating an agreement for the use of the present Hillsborough County House of Correction beginning in 1989. The evidence adduced at trial confirmed what both parties had known all along—that female state inmates do not enjoy services, programs, and conditions of confinement similar to those afforded the male inmates at the state prison—and this evidence led the court to conclude that the state had violated plaintiffs' right to equal protection of the laws. . . .

For these reasons, we hold that, with regard to the merits of the case, the district court's failure to disqualify NHLA constitutes harmless error at most, Fed.R.Civ.P. 61, and we affirm the district court's holding that the state violated plaintiffs' rights to equal protection of the laws.

The situation is different, however, with respect to the remedy designed by the district court. We believe that it would be inappropriate to permit the court's remedial order—which includes a specific prohibition on the use of LSS—to stand in light of the court's refusal to disqualify NHLA. The ban on the use of buildings located on the grounds of LSS is exactly the sort of remedy preferred by NHLA's *other* clients, the members of the *Garrity* class, and therefore has at least the appearance of having been tainted by NHLA's conflict of interest. Consequently, we hold that the district court's remedial order must be vacated and the case remanded for a new trial on the issue of the proper remedy for this constitutional deprivation. . . .

Criminal defendants sometimes argue that prosecutors have personal interests that threaten to deny the defendant a fair trial. Such claims were presented in *Hollywood v. Superior Court,* 43 Cal.4th 721, 723 (2008) and *Haraguchi v. Superior Court*, 43 Cal.4th 706, 708 (2008).

Haraguchi involved a prosecutor who wrote a novel about a prosecutor who was trying to decide whether to prosecute a rape case involving an intoxicated victim. The book was published about the time the author/prosecutor was set to proceed with the trial of a person accused of raping an intoxicated woman. The defendant moved to recuse the prosecutor on the ground that her personal interest in seeing the book succeed deprived the defendant of a fair trial

California Penal Code § 1424 provides that such motions "may not be granted unless the evidence shows that a conflict of interest exists that would render it unlikely that the defendant would receive a fair trial." The trial court denied the motion on the ground that the book was not based on the defendant's case and that it was only a coincidence that the book was published near the time of trial. The Supreme Court affirmed the trial court (reversing the court of appeals), and strongly reaffirmed that rulings on disqualification motions are reviewed for an abuse of discretion only.

In *Hollywood* the prosecutor had cooperated with a director and his associates who wanted to make a movie about the case the prosecutor was handling. The defendant was at large, and the prosecutor cooperated in the hope that publicizing the crime would lead to the defendant's capture. The defendant was captured, and before trial he sought an order recusing the prosecutor. The defendant argued the prosecutor had a conflict because the prosecutor had (i) unlawfully disclosed confidential information to the filmmakers; (ii) cooperated in the making of a movie that portrayed the defendant in an inflammatory and inaccurate way; (iii) received incidental benefits from distribution of the movie; and (iv) tied his legacy to obtaining a conviction. The defendant also argued the totality of these circumstances justified recusal.

The trial court denied the motion, the court of appeals reversed, and the Supreme Court reversed the court of appeals. As in *Haraguchi*, the Court held the trial court's order would be reviewed for abuse of discretion (even though the prosecution sought the death penalty). The Supreme Court affirmed the trial court's rejection on the merits of each of the defendant's conflict theories. (The Court noted that the prosecutor had no present financial interest in the movie by the time of trial.)

4. REMEDIES FOR CONCURRENT CONFLICTS

Most reported cases of concurrent conflicts involve attorneys who want to represent a party in litigation. When courts find that a conflict exists, the most common remedy for the conflict is to disqualify the attorney from participating in the pending litigation. Though common, (and contrary to the language used in some cases), disqualification is not quite automatic. As the court said in *William H. Raley Co. v. Superior Court*, 149 Cal.App.3d 1042 (1983), the exercise of the power of disqualification

> requires a cautious balancing of competing interests. The court must weigh the combined effect of a party's right to counsel of choice, an attorney's interest in representing a client, the financial burden on a client of replacing disqualified counsel and any tactical abuse underlying a disqualification proceeding against the fundamental principle that the fair resolution of disputes within our adversary system requires vigorous representation of parties by independent counsel unencumbered by conflicts of interest.

The *Raley* court also said that disqualification orders are reviewed for an abuse of discretion, a standard that reaffirms that courts may decline to disqualify counsel when the facts suggest that disqualification is not appropriate.

Research Corp. Techs, Inc. v. Hewlett–Packard Co., 936 F.Supp. 697, 698 (D. Ariz. 1996), provides a relatively rare example of a court declining to disqualify a law firm caught in a contemporaneous conflict. A large law firm, McDermott, Will & Emery, acquired a smaller one, called Willian Brinks. The Willian firm represented a company called Research Corporation Technologies in a patent suit against Hewlett–Packard.

From 1979 through 1995 McDermott had represented HP on tax matters. The partner who did the work left the firm in 1995, though, and HP followed her to her new firm. McDermott did no work for HP from June 1995 to March 1996. On March 1, 1996 HP announced it would acquire the Willian firm, effective April 1. On March 28 an HP attorney contacted a lawyer at McDermott asking a discrete tax question. McDermott responded and followed up in a call on April 3. Meanwhile, on April 1 the Willian/McDermott merger took effect, at which point McDermott became Research Corporation's lawyer against HP in the patent case while representing HP regarding the discrete tax question.

When McDermott realized it had a conflict it took steps to screen the patent lawyers and the tax lawyers from each other. It also contacted HP, explained the conflict, and asked for a conflict waiver. HP declined and moved to disqualify McDermott from the patent case. The court found McDermott in violation of Model Rule 1.7 but refused to disqualify the firm. Excerpts from the opinion follow:

* * *

"The burden is on the moving party to show "sufficient reason why an attorney should be disqualified from representing [a] client," and, "[w]henever possible the courts should endeavor to reach a solution that is least burdensome upon the client or clients." [*Alexander v. Superior Court,* 685 P.2d 1309, 1313 (Az.Sup.Ct. 1984)]. Disqualification can result in increased expenses, delay in resolution of the proceedings and deprivation of choice of counsel. *See SWS Financial Fund A v. Salomon Bros. Inc.,* 790 F.Supp. 1392, 1400 (N.D.Ill.1992). Thus, "[o]nly in extreme circumstances should a party to a lawsuit be allowed to interfere with the attorney-client relationship of [an] opponent." *Alexander,* 141 Ariz. at 161, 685 P.2d at 1313.

The purposes behind the ethical rules favor an approach which does not automatically require disqualification. As noted by the court in *SWS Financial Fund,* ER 1.7(a) has two purposes: (1) it protects against disclosure of client confidences, especially where the matters are substantially related, and (2) it safeguards loyalty within the attorney-client relationship. Here, the parties concede the representations are separate and distinct, and, although some breach of the duty of loyalty to Hewlett–Packard has occurred, Hewlett–Packard cannot reasonably argue that its "expectations of loyalty were so cavalierly trampled that disqualification is warranted as a sanction."

In determining whether disqualification is required, courts have examined various factors, including (1) the nature of the ethical violation, (2) the prejudice to the parties, including the extent of actual or potential delay in the proceedings, (3) the effectiveness of counsel in light of the violations, and (4) the public's perception of the profession. In addition, whether or not a motion to disqualify has been used as a tactical device or a means of harassment should also be considered.

Because the Ninth Circuit has not expressly adopted a rule of automatic disqualification, and based on the well-reasoned decisions disfavoring a rule requiring automatic disqualification, the Court finds that the better rule is to consider the facts and circumstances of each case, including the particulars of the ethical violation itself, in determining whether the harsh sanction of disqualification is warranted.

As to the MW & E conflict, the nature of the ethical violation is not egregious. Although the violation should not have occurred, it was inadvertent. As soon as the respective MW & E attorneys realized that a problem existed, approximately two weeks after the concurrent representation occurred, they took precautions to safeguard against disclosure of any confidences. Moreover, disqualification would result in more prejudice to Research Corp. than any potential prejudice to Hewlett–Packard resulting from denial of disqualification. The [patent] litigation team has spent nineteen months preparing this case. Much of that time would have to be duplicated by substitute counsel in the event of disqualification, notwithstanding local counsel's expertise in the area of patent litigation. In addition, granting the motion would result in Research Corp.'s losing its chosen counsel and would delay the ultimate conclusion of these proceedings. In contrast, the prejudice to Hewlett–Packard is minimal.

Perhaps most importantly, nothing indicates that any confidential information related to the pending action has been received by the Lupo–Lever litigation team as a result of Hewlett–Packard's brief March/April 1996 contacts with the MW & E tax attorneys. Counsel for Hewlett–Packard was invited to submit under seal for in camera inspection any documentation showing that Research Corp. has gained an advantage against Hewlett–Packard as a result of MW & E's representation of Hewlett–Packard. Although Hewlett–Packard did submit a response to the Court's invitation, Hewlett–Packard did not come forward with any showing that Research Corp. has gained an advantage in the present patent litigation as a result of any past or present representation of Hewlett–Packard by MW & E.

Finally, the Court perceives neither any reduction in the effectiveness of counsel as a result of the violation, nor any negative effects on the public's perception of the profession. The situation presented here cannot reasonably be viewed as MW & E dropping Hewlett–Packard "like a hot potato" in favor of a more lucrative client. *Picker Int'l, Inc. v. Varian Assocs., Inc.*, 670 F.Supp. 1363, 1365 (N.D.Ohio 1987), *aff'd,* 869 F.2d 578 (Fed.Cir.1989).

Therefore, in consideration of all of the above, the Court finds that disqualification of MW & E as Research Corp.'s counsel under the facts and circumstances presented here would be inappropriate."

* * *

Harm vs. Risk II
Civil Liability (or Sanctions) and Concurrent Conflicts

An attorney who creates a concurrent conflict of interest generally violates Model Rule 1.7. Most of the time a court will grant a motion to disqualify the attorney as well. What about civil liability? Although it is common to speak of concurrent conflicts as breaches of the duty of loyalty there is an important difference between the disciplinary rules, disqualification practice, and tort liability for breach of fiduciary duty.

The risk of harm is sufficient to establish a concurrent conflict for purposes of discipline or disqualification. The "basic prohibition of conflicts of interest" in the *Restatement* states that a conflict of interest exists "if there is a substantial risk that the lawyer's representation of the client would be materially and adversely affected by the lawyer's own interests or by the lawyer's duties to another current client, a former client, or a third party." Restatement (Third) of the Law Governing Lawyers § 121.

In contrast, *Restatement* §§ 49 and 53 make clear that civil liability for breach of fiduciary duty requires that the lawyer have caused harm to the client. Violation of a conflicts rule therefore does not entail civil liability even though the rule violation will be relevant to the plaintiff's claim in most jurisdictions. (Recall, though, that a serious rule violation may justify disgorgement of fees. Restatement § 37.)

Nevertheless, even in an ordinary malpractice claim a conflict of interest provides a plaintiff an opportunity to tell a compelling story. Rather than merely presenting a decision as a mistake, plaintiff's counsel can use a conflict to weave a narrative of betrayal that could make even an innocuous mistake (or even just a close call) look sinister. Although *Palsgraf v. Long Island R. Co.*, 248 N.Y. 339 (1928), teaches every first-year student that there is no such thing as "negligence in the air," working while under a conflict provides a liability-friendly context for disappointed clients to spin down the road.

---

5. STANDING AND INTERLOCUTORY APPEAL

May a party that has never had an attorney-client relationship with a particular lawyer prevail on a motion to disqualify that lawyer? In general the answer is "no," but courts in some cases have created an exception to this rule.

Regarding the general rule, suppose party A is involved in litigation with two other parties, B and C, who are represented by the same lawyer, L. Suppose A wants to pursue a strategy of playing B and C off against each other, in the hope that conflicts between them will inure to A's benefit. Suppose further that L's joint representation of B and C frustrates this strategy? May A move to disqualify L?

Great Lakes Constr., Inc. v. Burman, 186 Cal.App.4th 1347, 1350 (2010), illustrates the general answer: "No." The Burmans hired Hampton Builders for a remodeling project and Hampton subcontracted the work to Ted Kipers. The subcontract bound Kipers to indemnify Hampton for certain things. Mrs. Burman was unhappy with the work and posted statements on the Internet to that effect. Hampton sued her for libel and for the unpaid contract price; the Burmans cross-complained for various things and Kipers asserted causes of actions against Hampton as well. Hampton then cross-complained against Kipers, based in part on the indemnity provisions in the subcontract.

The Burmans and Kipers hired the same lawyer to represent them. After taking some discovery Hampton moved to disqualify the lawyer on the ground that the interests of the Burmans (who complained about the work) and Kipers (who did the work) conflicted. The trial court granted the motion but the court of appeals reversed. The court held "[a] 'standing' requirement is implicit in disqualification motions. Generally, before the disqualification of an attorney is proper, the complaining party must have or must have had an attorney-client relationship with that attorney."

The *Great Lakes Construction* court noted an exception to this general rule allowing a party who has a reasonable expectation that a lawyer will preserve the party's confidential information standing to bring a disqualification motion even if the party and the lawyer never formed a full-fledged attorney-client relationship, *see DCH Health Servs. Corp. v. Waite*, 95 Cal.App.4th 829, 830 (2002), but found the exception irrelevant to the case. *See also Dino v. Pelayo*, 145 Cal.App.4th 347, 348 (2006) (requiring party to have confidential or fiduciary relationship with attorney as prerequisite for any motion to disqualify that attorney).

Other courts have recognized an exception where "the ethical breach so infects the litigation in which disqualification is sought that it impacts the moving party's interest in a just and lawful determination of her claims." *Colyer v. Smith,* 50 F.Supp.2d 966, 969 (C.D.Cal.1999)(stating rule but finding no non-client standing on the facts of the case). *In Concat LP v. Unilever*, PLC, 350 F.Supp.2d 796 (N.D.Cal. 2004), the court disqualified a firm that represented with respect to estate matters an individual who held an ownership interest in a company that sued another client of the firm for patent infringement. The individual client also participated in negotiations between the plaintiff and defendant companies. The court reasoned that the individual client's assets, and disclosure of those assets, were "inextricably intertwined with the business and financial matters of" the company accused of infringement. This holding is notable for appearing to use confidentiality concerns to establish standing and then applying the duty of loyalty standard (forbidding adversity even in unrelated matters) to the substantive conflict issue.

Two related issues concern who may appeal a disqualification order and when they may appeal it. Under California law, either a client or a disqualified lawyer has standing to appeal the disqualification order. *See A.I. Credit Corp. v. Aguilar & Sebastinelli*, 113 Cal.App.4th 1072, 1077 (2003) ("Disqualified attorneys themselves have standing to challenge orders disqualifying them"). A client may appeal from an order denying a motion to disqualify, as well. *Meehan v. Hopps* 45 Cal.2d 213 (1955); *Apple Computer, Inc. v. Superior Court,* 126 Cal.App.4th 1253 (2005). California courts have held that disqualification orders are collateral to the merits of a case and therefore may be appealed immediately. (Orders denying disqualification motions are also appealable on the alternative ground that they deny requests for injunctive relief—an order precluding counsel from participating in a case.)

In contrast, federal law does not allow for interlocutory appeals of disqualification orders as a matter of right. 28 U.S.C. § 1291 provides that federal appellate courts have jurisdiction only over "final decisions" of district courts. Case law provides an exception to this rule for "collateral orders," which are those that "finally determine claims of right separable from, and collateral to, rights asserted in the action, [and are] too important to be denied review and too independent of the cause itself to require that appellate consideration be deferred until the whole case is adjudicated," *Cohen v. Beneficial Indus. Loan Corp.,* 337 U.S. 541, 546 (1949), but the Supreme Court has held that disqualification orders do not fall within that exception in either criminal cases, *Flanagan v. United States,* 465 U.S. 259 (1984), or civil cases, *Richardson–Merrell, Inc. v. Koller*, 472 U.S. 424 (1985).

28 U.S.C. § 1292(b) provides an alternative method for interlocutory review. It gives district judges the discretion to certify an otherwise unappealable order as suitable for appeal if the order "involves a controlling question of law as to which there is substantial ground for difference

of opinion and [if] an immediate appeal from the order may materially advance the ultimate termination of the litigation. . . . " If the district court so certifies, the court of appeals has the discretion to hear the interlocutory appeal. Courts have construed this provision narrowly, *e.g., In re Cement Antitrust Litig.*, 673 F.2d 1020, 1021 (9th Cir. 1982), and it provides little hope for disqualified counsel. *See Elantec Semiconductor, Inc. v. Cooper*, 1999 WL 33921316 (N.D. Cal. 1999).

Some circuits allow a party to seek a writ of mandamus ordering a district court to change an order granting or disqualifying counsel. *E.g., Christensen v. United States Dist. Court*, 844 F.2d 694, 697 & n. 5 (9th Cir.1988). Mandamus is a discretionary remedy based on several factors, including

> whether (1) the party seeking the writ has no other means, such as a direct appeal, of attaining the desired relief, (2) the petitioner will be damaged in a way not correctable on appeal, (3) the district court's order is clearly erroneous as a matter of law, (4) the order is an oft-repeated error, or manifests a persistent disregard of the federal rules, and (5) the order raises new and important problems, or issues of law of first impression.

Id. at 697.

What Law Applies? Disqualification Practice in Federal Court

If a party moves to disqualify an attorney in a federal case, does state or federal law apply? There is some conflicting case law on the issue, but the best answer is that federal law applies and would govern in the case of a conflict with state law. Many district courts adopt state rules of professional conduct as part of their local rules, however, so district courts often cite state law as a basis for a ruling and courts of appeal follow suit. The district court opinion in *Silicon Graphics, Inc. v. ATI Techs., Inc.*, 741 F.Supp.2d 970 (W.D.Wis. 2010), illustrates these points:

"The next question is whether the Wisconsin Supreme Court rules have any role in resolving motions to disqualify filed in federal court. There is surprisingly little discussion of that question in this circuit. Plaintiff points out that this court has cited the Wisconsin Supreme Court rules in the past in resolving other motions for disqualification. In addition, plaintiff says [two Seventh Circuit cases arising from Illinois] are consistent with a policy of deference to state law because the rule in those cases is the same as the rule in Illinois, the state where [those cases] arose. However, neither side cites any cases in which the court of appeals or a district court discussed the extent to which state rules should be considered in a motion for disqualification. . . . .

Despite the lack of a clear holding in this circuit, I agree with defendants that federal law is controlling. As a general matter, federal courts apply state law to "substantive" questions when state law created the underlying cause of action. *Bevolo v. Carter,* 447 F.3d 979, 982 (7th Cir.2006). In addition, federal courts may "borrow" state law principles when federal law is silent on a particular question. *E.g., Owens v. Okure,* 488 U.S. 235, 239(1989) (federal courts may refer to statute of limitations under state law when federal law does not provide one). However, the Supreme Court has held that "[t]he state code of professional responsibility does not by its own terms apply to sanctions in the federal courts." *In re Snyder,* 472 U.S. 634, 645 (1985). This is because a federal court's authority to regulate lawyer conduct in its own cases comes from its inherent power, not from a particular state rule. *Id. See also In re Finkelstein,* 901 F.2d 1560, 1564 (11th Cir.1990) ("It is axiomatic that federal courts admit and suspend attorneys as an exercise of their inherent power."). If decisions whether to sanction a lawyer for misconduct are decided under federal law, it follows that "[m]otions to disqualify are . . . decided under federal law" as well. *FDIC v. United States Fire Insurance Co.,* 50 F.3d 1304, 1311–12 (5th Cir.1995). *See also United States v. Miller,* 624 F.2d 1198, 1200–01 (3d Cir.1980) ("Supervision of the professional conduct of attorneys practicing in a federal court is a matter of federal law."); 30 *Moore's Federal Practice* § 808.06[2][b], at 808–80 (3d. ed. 2010) ("Screening is a good example in which courts tend to refer to the emerging body of federal law rather than to the state law."). If that were not the case, district courts could not grant motions filed by lawyers who are not admitted to the state bar to practice in federal court.

Plaintiff cites *In re County of Los Angeles,* 223 F.3d 990, 995 (9th Cir.2000), in which the court stated, "we apply state law in determining matters of disqualification," but this decision seems to be an outlier. The court's only support for the proposition was *Paul E. Iacono Structural Engineer, Inc. v. Humphrey,* 722 F.2d 435, 439 (9th Cir.1983), in which the court upheld a local rule of a district court that required lawyers to comply with the state rules of professional conduct on the ground that "district courts are free to regulate the conduct of lawyers appearing before them." Thus, *Humphrey* simply stands for the principle that district courts have discretion to develop their own standards for the conduct of lawyers appearing before them and that it is not an abuse of discretion to include state rules as part of these standards. 30 *Moore's Federal Practice* § 802.01, at 802–6 (3d ed.2010) (noting that "[m]ost district courts regulate attorney conduct by local rules"). Any other interpretation would be contrary to *Cord v. Smith,* 338 F.2d 516, 524 (9th Cir.1964), in which the court rejected the view that state rules of professional conduct bind federal courts.

Humphrey is consistent with the view of other courts that have acknowledged that the federal standard may be informed by multiple sources, including state ethical rules. . . . However, the Court of Appeals for the Seventh Circuit does not seem to have taken this approach in the context of motions for disqualification. Although plaintiff says that the court of appeals was simply applying the Illinois rules in cases such as [the Illinois-based cases mentioned above], the court did not actually mention state law in that decision. In fact, plaintiff does not cite *any* cases involving a motion for disqualification in which the court of appeals relied on or even discussed a state's rules of conduct. Rather, the court has emphasized that the standard for disqualification 'has been developed through the prior caselaw of the Seventh Circuit.' [citation omitted] This may be a recognition that considering multiple sources of law could lead to conflict and confusion. 30 *Moore's Federal Practice* § 802.02, at 802–9 (3d ed. 2010) (stating that there are 'inherent problems' with federal court's reliance on state rules because of lack of clarity regarding result when state rules conflict with other sources).

The natural inference to be drawn from the court's silence regarding state rules of professional conduct is that the federal standard does not incorporate state rules and that district courts should not use those rules as supplemental authority, at least when there is a conflict between the two. Although district courts in Wisconsin, including this one, have cited the state rules in deciding motions for disqualification, this means little because the standards are the same in many respects. In this case, there is a clear difference between [the relevant state rule] and the federal standard."

The Main Points to Recall From Chapter 11(A) Are:

- The main value at stake in simultaneous representation is the duty of loyalty.
- Lawyers may not simultaneously represent directly adverse interests, even in unrelated matters.
- Directly adverse usually (but not quite always) means parties are across the table from each other.
- Lawyers also may not represent a client if their ability to do so is materially limited by an obligation to another current or former client, or by an obligation to a third person, or by a personal interest.

B. CONFLICTS ARISING FROM REPRESENTATION ADVERSE TO A FORMER CLIENT

As noted at the beginning of this chapter, when a lawyer opposes a former client the rules are more concerned about confidentiality than loyalty. Loyalty concerns are not completely absent from such cases—they tend to appear when a lawyer attacks his or her own work, for example—but they are not as pronounced as they are in concurrent conflict cases. Confidentiality presents a potential chicken-and-egg problem: A lawyer's former client has a right not to have its confidential information disclosed or used against it, and it would be odd to force the client to disclose the information to protect that right. Courts also are wary of swearing contests between former clients who claim they did disclose some information to their former lawyers and lawyers who claim the opposite.

The law deals with both concerns through the "substantial relationship" test, which holds lawyers may not oppose former clients in matters substantially related to the subject matter of the lawyer's previous representation. Under this test courts do not require former clients to prove they conveyed to their former lawyer information that might be used against them in a later matter in which the lawyer opposes them. The former client need only prove the former matter is substantially related to the latter. In slightly more precise terms, the former client must show that a reasonably competent lawyer doing whatever was needed to accomplish the goals of the first representation would have learned information material to the second representation. If the client does so, then the lawyer is conclusively presumed to have received such information in the first representation and, in the usual case, is disqualified from the second representation.

"Substantial relationship" is not a precise term, however, and neither, for that matter, is the concept of the subject matter of a representation. Litigation over former client conflicts is therefore common and sometimes heated. The following materials survey some of the most commonly contested points.

Model Rule of Professional Conduct 1.9
Restatement § 132

ANALYTICA, INC. V. NPD RESEARCH, INC.

708 F.2d 1263 (7th Cir. 1983)

POSNER, CIRCUIT JUDGE.

Two law firms, Schwartz & Freeman and Pressman and Hartunian, appeal from orders disqualifying them from representing Analytica, Inc.

in an antitrust suit against NPD, Inc. Schwartz & Freeman also appeals from an order directing it to pay NPD some $25,000 in fees and expenses incurred in prosecuting the disqualification motion; and NPD cross-appeals from this order, contending it should have got more.

John Malec went to work for NPD, a closely held corporation engaged in market research, in 1972. His employment agreement allowed him to, and he did, buy two shares of NPD stock, which made him a 10 percent owner. It also gave him an option to buy two more shares. He allowed the option to expire in 1975, but his two co-owners, in recognition of Malec's substantial contributions to the firm (as executive vice-president and manager of the firm's Chicago office), decided to give him the two additional shares—another 10 percent of the company—anyway and they told Malec to find a lawyer who would structure the transaction in the least costly way.

He turned to Richard Fine, a partner in Schwartz & Freeman. Fine devised a plan whereby the other co-owners would each transfer one share of stock back to the corporation, which would then issue the stock to Malec together with a cash bonus. Because the stock and the cash bonus were to be deemed compensation for Malec's services to the corporation, the value of the stock, plus the cash, would be taxable income to Malec (the purpose of the cash bonus was to help him pay the income tax that would be due on the value of the stock), and a deductible business expense to the corporation. A value had therefore to be put on the stock. NPD gave Fine the information he needed to estimate that value—information on NPD's financial condition, sales trends, and management—and Fine fixed a value which the corporation adopted. Fine billed NPD for his services and NPD paid the bill, which came to about $850, for 11 1/2 hours of Fine's time plus minor expenses.

While the negotiations over the stock transfer were proceeding, relations between Malec and his co-owners were deteriorating, and in May 1977 he left the company and sold his stock to them. His wife, who also had been working for NPD since 1972, left NPD at the same time and within a month had incorporated Analytica to compete with NPD in the market-research business. She has since left Analytica; Mr. Malec apparently never had a position with it.

In October 1977, several months after the Malecs had left NPD and Analytica had been formed, Analytica retained Schwartz & Freeman as its counsel. Schwartz & Freeman forthwith complained on Analytica's behalf to the Federal Trade Commission, charging that NPD was engaged in anticompetitive behavior that was preventing Analytica from establishing itself in the market. When the FTC would do nothing, Analytica decided to bring its own suit against NPD, and it authorized Schwartz & Freeman to engage Pressman and Hartunian as trial counsel. The suit was filed in June 1979 and charges NPD with various antitrust offenses, including abuse of a monopoly position that NPD is alleged to have obtained before June 1977.

In January 1980 NPD moved to disqualify both of Analytica's law firms. Evidentiary hearings on the motion were held intermittently between April 1980 and May 1981. At one stage the law firms voluntarily withdrew, but when the judge told them that he was minded to make them pay the fees and expenses that NPD had incurred in prosecuting the motion they moved to vacate the order granting their motion to withdraw. The motion to vacate was granted and the hearings resumed. In June 1981 the judge disqualified both firms and ordered Schwartz & Freeman to pay NPD's fees and expenses. Analytica has not appealed the orders of disqualification, having retained substitute counsel to prosecute its suit against NPD. . . .

For rather obvious reasons a lawyer is prohibited from using confidential information that he has obtained from a client against that client on behalf of another one. But this prohibition has not seemed enough by itself to make clients feel secure about reposing confidences in lawyers, so a further prohibition has evolved: a lawyer may not represent an adversary of his former client if the subject matter of the two representations is "substantially related," which means: if the lawyer could have obtained confidential information in the first representation that would have been relevant in the second. It is irrelevant whether he actually obtained such information and used it against his former client, or whether—if the lawyer is a firm rather than an individual practitioner—different people in the firm handled the two matters and scrupulously avoided discussing them.

There is an exception for the case where a member or associate of a law firm (or government legal department) changes jobs, and later he or his new firm is retained by an adversary of a client of his former firm. In such a case, even if there is a substantial relationship between the two matters, the lawyer can avoid disqualification by showing that effective measures were taken to prevent confidences from being received by whichever lawyers in the new firm are handling the new matter. [citations omitted] The exception is inapplicable here; the firm itself changed sides.

Schwartz & Freeman's Mr. Fine not only had access to but received confidential financial and operating data of NPD in 1976 and early 1977 when he was putting together the deal to transfer stock to Mr. Malec. Within a few months, Schwartz & Freeman popped up as counsel to an adversary of NPD's before the FTC, and in that proceeding and later in the antitrust lawsuit advanced contentions to which the data Fine received might have been relevant. Those data concerned NPD's profitability, sales prospects, and general market strength—all matters potentially germane to both the liability and damage phases of an antitrust suit charging NPD with monopolization. The two representations are thus substantially related, even though we do not know whether any of the information Fine received would be useful in Analytica's lawsuit (it might just duplicate information in Malec's possession, but we do not know his role in Analytica's suit), or if so whether he conveyed any of it to his partners and associates who were actually handling the suit. If the "substantial relationship" test applies, however, "it is not appropriate for the court to inquire into whether actual confidences were disclosed," *Westinghouse Elec. Corp. v. Gulf Oil Corp.,* [588 F.2d 221, 224 (7th Cir. 1978)] unless the exception noted above for cases where the law firm itself did not switch sides is applicable, as it is not here. . . .

Schwartz & Freeman argues, it is true, that Malec rather than NPD retained it to structure the stock transfer, but this is both erroneous and irrelevant. NPD's three co-owners retained Schwartz & Freeman to work out a deal beneficial to all of them. All agreed that Mr. Malec should be given two more shares of the stock; the only question was the cheapest way of doing it; the right answer would benefit them all. *Cf.* Coase, *The Problem of Social Cost,* 3 J. Law & Econ. 1 (1960). The principals saw no need to be represented by separate lawyers, each pushing for a bigger slice of a fixed pie and a fee for getting it. Not only did NPD rather than Malec pay Schwartz & Freeman's bills (and there is no proof that it had a practice of paying its officers' legal expenses), but neither NPD nor the co-owners were represented by counsel other than Schwartz & Freeman. Though Millman, an accountant for NPD, did have a law degree and did do some work on the stock-transfer plan, he was not acting as the co-owners' or NPD's lawyer in a negotiation in which Fine was acting as Malec's lawyer. As is common in closely held corporations, Fine was counsel to the firm, as well as to all of its principals, for the transaction. If the position taken by Schwartz & Freeman prevailed, a corporation that used only one lawyer to counsel it on matters of shareholder compensation would run the risk of the lawyer's later being deemed to have represented a single shareholder rather than the whole firm, and the corporation would lose the protection of the lawyer-client relationship. Schwartz & Freeman's position thus could force up the legal expenses of owners of closely held corporations.

But it does not even matter whether NPD or Malec was the client. In Westinghouse's antitrust suit against Kerr–McGee and other uranium producers, Kerr–McGee moved to disqualify Westinghouse's counsel, Kirkland & Ellis, because of a project that the law firm had done for the American Petroleum Institute, of which Kerr–McGee was a member, on competition in the energy industries. Kirkland & Ellis's client had been the Institute rather than Kerr–McGee but we held that this did not matter; what mattered was that Kerr–McGee had furnished confidential information to Kirkland & Ellis in connection with the law firm's work for the Institute. . . . If NPD did not retain Schwartz & Freeman—though we think it did—still it supplied Schwartz & Freeman with just the kind of confidential data that it would have furnished a lawyer that it had retained; and it had a right not to see Schwartz & Freeman reappear within months on the opposite side of a litigation to which that data might be highly pertinent. . . .

The "substantial relationship" test has its problems, but conducting a factual inquiry in every case into whether confidences had actually been revealed would not be a satisfactory alternative, particularly in a case such as this where the issue is not just whether they have been revealed but also whether they will be revealed during a pending litigation. Apart from the difficulty of taking evidence on the question without compromising the confidences themselves, the only witnesses would be the very lawyers whose firm was sought to be disqualified (unlike a case where the issue is what confidences a lawyer received while at a former law firm), and their interest not only in retaining a client but in denying a serious breach of professional ethics might outweigh any felt obligation to "come clean." While "appearance of impropriety" as a principle of professional ethics invites and maybe has undergone uncritical expansion because of its vague and open-ended character, in this case it has meaning and weight. For a law firm to represent one client today, and the client's adversary tomorrow in a closely related matter, creates an unsavory appearance of conflict of interest that is difficult to dispel in the eyes of the lay public—or for that matter the bench and bar—by the filing of affidavits, difficult to verify objectively, denying that improper communication has taken place or will take place between the lawyers in the firm handling the two sides. Clients will not repose confidences in lawyers whom they distrust and will not trust firms that switch sides as nimbly as Schwartz & Freeman. . . .

CASE QUESTIONS

1. Why does it not matter whether NPD was Schwartz & Freeman's client?
2. Why is antitrust litigation substantially related to a corporate stock transaction?
3. What is the purpose of the subsequent conflict rule?

The lawyers in *Analytica* dealt with NPD in the stock transaction and then were involved in antitrust litigation against NPD. What if counsel represented a client and then went on to represent other clients in the same industry, but not in a matter directly adverse to their old client?

Maritrans GP Inc. v. Pepper, Hamilton & Scheetz, 529 Pa. 241, 602 A.2d 1277, 1279 (1992), presents such a case.

Pepper, Hamilton represented Maritrans on a broad range of labor matters for several years. It also represented Maritrans in certain corporate finance matters. The principal Pepper lawyer responsible for labor matters was named Messina. According to the court:

> During the course of their labor representation of Maritrans, Pepper and Messina became "intimately familiar with Maritrans' operations" and "gained detailed financial and business information, including Maritrans' financial goals and projections, labor cost/savings, crew costs and operating costs." This information was discussed with Pepper's labor attorneys, and particularly with Messina, for the purpose of developing Maritrans' labor goals and strategies. In addition, during the course of preparing Maritrans' public offering, Pepper was furnished with substantial confidential commercial information in Maritrans' possession—financial and otherwise—including projected labor costs, projected debt coverage and projected revenues through the year 1994, and projected rates through the year 1990. Pepper and Messina, during the course of their decade-long representation of Maritrans, came to know the complete inner-workings of the company along with Maritrans' long-term objectives, and competitive strategies in a number of areas including the area of labor costs, a particularly sensitive area in terms of effective competition. In furtherance of its ultimate goal of obtaining more business than does its competition, including the New York-based companies, Maritrans analyzed each of its competitors with Pepper and Messina. These analyses included an evaluation of each competitor's strengths and weaknesses, and of how Maritrans deals with its competitors.

At some point, Pepper began to represent several of Maritrans's New York competitors in labor negotiations. These clients were negotiating with a different union than the one Maritrans dealt with, but, Maritrans alleged, if these clients succeeded in lowering wages and benefits paid to union workers then these clients would have lower costs and would be able to compete more effectively with Maritrans. Pepper took the position that its representation of these clients posed at most "business conflicts" and not "legal conflicts," so that they owed neither fiduciary nor ethical duties to Maritrans not to represent these clients. Pepper and Maritrans agreed that Pepper would not accept as clients more competitors of Maritrans, and that the firm would create an ethical screen between lawyers representing Maritrans and lawyers representing its competitors. This deal did not work, and Maritrans sued Pepper for damages and an injunction to keep it from representing Maritrans's competitors. Excerpts from the opinion follow:

Discovery procedures produced evidence as follows: (i) testimony by principals of the New York companies to the effect that the type of information that Pepper and Messina possess about Maritrans is of the type considered to be confidential commercial information in the industry and that they would not reveal that information about their companies to their competitors; (ii) testimony by principals of the New York companies that they were desirous of obtaining Maritrans' confidential commercial information; (iii) testimony by principals of the New York companies that labor costs are the one item that make or break a company's competitive posture; (iv) an affidavit from the United States Department of Labor attesting that, contrary to defendant Messina's sworn testimony at the first preliminary hearing in February, 1988, Maritrans' labor contracts are not on file with the Department of Labor and thus not available under the Freedom of Information Act; and other information as well. . . .

Pepper and Messina argue that a preliminary injunction was an abuse of discretion where it restrains them from representing a former client's competitors, in order to supply the former client with a "sense of security" that they will not reveal confidences to those competitors where there has been no revelation or threat of revelations up to that point. We disagree. Whether a fiduciary can later represent competitors or whether a law firm can later represent competitors of its former client is a matter that must be decided from case to case and depends on a number of factors. One factor is the extent to which the fiduciary was involved in its former client's affairs. The greater the involvement, the greater the danger that confidences (where such exist) will be revealed. Here, Pepper and Messina's involvement was extensive as was their knowledge of sensitive information provided to them by Maritrans. We do *not* wish to establish a blanket rule that a law firm may not later represent the economic competitor of a former client in matters in which the former client is not also a party to a law suit. But situations may well exist where the danger of revelation of the confidences of a former client is so great that injunctive relief is warranted. This is one of those situations. There is a substantial relationship here between Pepper and Messina's former representation of Maritrans and their current representation of Maritrans' competitors such that the injunctive relief granted here was justified. It might be theoretically possible to argue that Pepper and Messina should merely be enjoined from revealing the confidential material they have acquired from Maritrans but such an injunction would be difficult, if not impossible, to administer. . . . As fiduciaries, Pepper and Messina can be fully enjoined from representing Maritrans' competitors as that would create too great a danger that Maritrans' confidential relationship with Pepper and Messina would be breached.

Here, the trial court did not commit an abuse of discretion. On these facts, it was perfectly reasonable to conclude that Maritrans' competitive position could be irreparably injured if Pepper and Messina continued to represent their competitors and that Maritrans' remedy at law, that is their right to later seek damages, would be difficult if not impossible to sustain because of difficult problems of proof, particularly problems related to piercing what would later become a confidential relationship between their competitors and those competitors' attorneys (Pepper and Messina). The trial court already had to struggle with the problem of confidentiality in this regard. . . . In short, equitable principles establish that injunctive relief here was just and proper. Damages might later be obtained for breach of fiduciary duties and a confidential relationship, but that remedy would be inadequate to correct the harm that could be prevented by injunctive relief, at least until the court could examine the case in greater detail. . . .

CASE QUESTIONS

1. Pepper claimed this was a "business conflict" rather than a "legal conflict." Is there a difference? What is it?
2. What standard does the court establish to determine when a firm may not represent competitors of a former client?
3. What facts in this case seem like the best prospects for establishing a rule limiting the scope of the case?
4. With regard to subsequent conflicts, what is the relationship between ethical rules and fiduciary violations?

Suppose you have jointly represented a husband and wife on several matters over the years. These include the purchase of a business, the purchase of a home, and a personal injury action in which you asserted claims for each spouse. The spouses have separated and began divorce proceedings. May you represent one spouse against the other? *Johnson v. Superior Court*, 159 Cal.App.3d 573 (1984), said "yes" where the lawyer in question had represented the husband on business matters and then represented the wife in a divorce proceeding.

Direct and Indirect Representation: California's "Modified Substantial Relationship Test"

California courts have added a doctrinal gloss to the substantial relationship test. *H.F. Ahmanson & Co. v. Salomon Bros, Inc.*, 229 Cal.App.3d 1445, 1449 (1991), began to develop it. Ahmanson hired Salomon, an investment-banking firm, to advise it regarding Ahmanson's purchase of the Bowery Savings Bank. During the acquisition, Salomon advised Ahmanson to cancel certain agreements Bowery had with the FDIC; Salomon claimed they had a negative value of $25 million. A few days after the deal closed, Salomon admitted it had made a mistake. The agreements had a positive value of $30 million. Salomon hired the Wachtell, Lipton firm to defend it against an expected claim by Ahmanson.

Bowery previously had hired the Wachtell, Lipton firm to advise it regarding the credit risk aspects of its agreements with the FDIC. When Ahmanson learned this, it moved to disqualify Wachtell from representing Salomon on the ground that the representation was adverse to Wachtell's former client, Bowery. The trial court denied the motion, and the court of appeals affirmed.

> the rule followed in California is that the attorney's possession of confidential information will be presumed only when a substantial relationship has been shown to exist between the former representation and the current representation, *and* when it appears by virtue of the nature of the former representation or the relationship of the attorney to his former client confidential information material to the current dispute would normally have been imparted to the attorney. (emphasis added).

The court's use of the conjunctive "and" may be read to weaken the substantial relationship test. The court's language implies that matters may be substantially related but counsel still would not have received information requiring disqualification from a subsequent matter. The *Ahmanson* court analyzed three variables relevant to the conflict claim: factual similarity, legal similarity, and the extent of the lawyer's involvement in the first representation. It found that Wachtell's initial representation of Bowery was limited to advising it on credit risk, which was different from the interest rate risk as to which Salomon had made its mistake. It therefore agreed with the trial court that the matters were not substantially related.

Jessen v. Hartford Cas. Ins. Co., 111 Cal.App.4th 698, 702 (2003), stressed the nature of the lawyer's relationship with a client as well as the relationship of one matter to another. The court held it would presume that a lawyer who "was personally involved in providing legal advice and services to the former client" received confidential information from that client. In that case,

> there cannot be any delving into the specifics of the communications between the attorney and the former client in an effort to show that the attorney did or did not receive confidential information during the course of that relationship. As a result, disqualification will depend upon the strength of the similarities between the legal problem involved in the former representation and the legal problem involved in the current representation.

On the other hand, the court held, "where the former attorney-client relationship is peripheral or attenuated instead of direct" no such presumption would apply unless a former client presented additional evidence showing the lawyer probably acquired confidential information material to a subsequent representation.

As to the substantial relationship test itself, the *Jessen* court noted that,

> According to *Flatt,* a "substantial relationship" exists whenever the "subjects" of the prior and the current representations are linked in some rational manner. In the lexicon of the law, the words "subject" and "subject matter" mean more than the strict facts, claims, and issues involved in a particular action. . . .
>
> limiting the comparison of the two representations to their precise legal and factual issues might operate unrealistically to the detriment of the first client. Depending upon the nature of the attorney's relationship with the former client, in the office or in the courtroom, the attorney may acquire confidential information about the client or the client's affairs which may not be directly related to the transaction or lawsuit at hand but which the attorney comes to know in providing the representation to the former client with respect to the previous lawsuit or transaction. For example, whether a lawsuit is settled or contested may depend upon a myriad of considerations about the client's affairs which might not be subject to discovery but which nonetheless determine the client's course of action, such as a decision to settle an action or a particular claim or issue because of the potential for unrelated adverse ramifications to the client were the case to go to trial. The same might be true about the client's internal operations or policies, such as one which favors the settlement of lawsuits filed in some locales but not others based upon the client's history or perceptions about the inclinations of juries (or the capabilities of the bench) in the particular venues. . . .
>
> We therefore ascribe to the word "subjects" a broader definition than the discrete legal and factual issues involved in the compared representations. We consider the "subject" of a representation as including information material to the evaluation, prosecution, settlement or accomplishment of the litigation or transaction given its specific legal and factual issues. Thus, successive representations will be "substan-

tially related" when the evidence before the trial court supports a rational conclusion that information material to the evaluation, prosecution, settlement or accomplishment of the former representation given its factual and legal issues is also material to the evaluation, prosecution, settlement or accomplishment of the current representation given its factual and legal issues."

Do the normal rules apply when a lawyer jointly represents two parties in one representation, and then represents one party against the other in a substantially related subsequent representation? (Recall that this was the situation in *Brennan's, Inc. v. Brennan's Restaurants, Inc.*, 590 F.2d 168 (5th Cir. 1979), in Chapter 4.A.1.) That also was the situation in *Knight v. Ferguson*, 149 Cal.App.4th 1207 (2007). Knight wanted to open a restaurant. She sought to form a partnership with Steven Sponder for that purpose. Complications cropped up, and Knight wanted to talk to a litigator.

Knight's sister and brother-in-law, the Fergusons, recommended their lawyer, Wideman. Knight met with Wideman, in part to plan litigation strategy against Sponder. Sponder ultimately dropped out of the deal and the Fergusons agreed to take his place; they provided the financing Knight needed to start the restaurant. Knight eventually sued the Fergusons, who cross-claimed against her. The Fergusons hired Wideman to represent them against Knight. Knight moved to disqualify him on the ground that he had represented her in connection with the same proposed venture.

Wideman declared that he had only met once with Knight. He said the Fergusons had been present at the meeting, as had Knight's lawyer, Eric Burkhardt. He contended that he received no information from Knight that was confidential as against the Fergusons. Knight testified that she met with Wideman three times, and that she expected him to be her litigation counsel. Burkhardt testified that he thought Wideman was representing both the Fergusons and Knight. The trial court granted the motion to disqualify Wideman, and the court of appeals affirmed:

The Fergusons claim that Wideman's consultations with Knight were remote and peripheral. We disagree. They occurred at a critical stage, when Knight was creating the business entity which is at the heart of this action. Facts about Knight's difficulties with Sponder could be used to the Fergusons' advantage. In their cross-complaint, the Fergusons allege that Knight's partnership with Sponder "fell apart," and that Knight asked them to "take her partner's [Sponder's] place and participate in the ownership and management. . . . " Knight's discussions with Sponder are therefore linked to issues in this action.

The Fergusons claim that Knight did not prove that Wideman obtained confidential information. The "aggrieved client" need only satisfy a "low threshold of proof" and does not have to prove the attorney actually received confidential information. . . .

The Fergusons were always present during Knight's consultations with Wideman. They argue that Knight's discussions with Wideman were therefore neither privileged nor confidential. At oral argument, Wideman claimed that because those discussions were not confidential, his representing the Fergusons cannot prejudice Knight. Wideman sells himself short. He is a lawyer with wide litigation experience. He was aware of Knight's business concerns and aspirations. However good his intentions, he cannot help but use his expertise to exploit those concerns. The Fergusons' presence at the meetings is beside the point.

Where an attorney acquires knowledge about the former client's "attitudes," practices, business customs, "litigation philosophy," strengths, weaknesses or strategy, disqualification may be required for that reason alone. (*Jessen*, *supra*, 111 Cal.App.4th at p. 712.) Moreover, in addition to the meetings he had with Knight, Wideman also communicated with Burkhardt to develop a strategy which anticipated future litigation and led to the removal of Sponder as a partner. This, in turn, set the framework for the Fergusons to take over his partnership interest. . . .

Moreover, even if the attorney-client evidentiary privilege does not apply, the result does not change. (*Western Continental Operating Co. v. Natural Gas Corp.* (1989) 212 Cal.App.3d 752, 761 (*Western Continental Operating Co.*).) "[T]he pertinent issue is the propriety of an attorney's representation adverse to a former client. Our courts have distinguished the rule against representing conflicting interests from the attorney-client evidentiary privilege noting that the former is broader than the latter." (*Id.* at pp. 761–762.) Thus, even where the issue of disclosure of privileged information is absent, an attorney is properly disqualified for violating the separate and independent " '. . . duty not to represent conflicting interests. . . . " (*Id.* at p. 762.) ' " '. . . The evidentiary privilege and the ethical duty not to disclose confidences both arise from the need to encourage clients to disclose all possibly pertinent information to their attorneys, and both protect only the confidential information disclosed. The duty not to represent conflicting interests . . . is an outgrowth of the attorney-client relationship itself, which is confidential, or fiduciary, in a broader sense. Not only do clients at times disclose confidential information to their attorneys; they also repose confidence in them. The privilege is bottomed only on the first of these attributes, the conflicting-interests rule, on both.' [Citation.]" ' [Citations & Fn. omitted.]" (*Ibid.*)

A lawyer has a duty not to " 'do anything which will injuriously affect his former client.' " (*People ex. rel. Deukmejian v. Brown* (1981) 29 Cal.3d 150, 156.) "Where the lawyer switches sides and represents the former client's adversary in the same matter, everything the lawyer does for the new client necessarily will injuriously affect the former client." (*City Nat. Bank v. Adams* (2002) 96 Cal.App.4th 315, 329.)

Knight testified that she believed that Wideman was her "litigation counsel." She had the right to "repose confidence" in him and to expect that his loyalty to her would not be compromised.

PROBLEM 11–1

Can the court's reasoning be reconciled with the language from *Flatt v. Superior Court*, quoted at the beginning of this chapter, stating that the primary duty at issue in subsequent conflict cases is that of confidentiality while the primary duty at issue in contemporaneous conflict cases is loyalty? How is the Court using loyalty here?

Subsequent Conflicts and Confidences Obtained Other Than Through Representation

Oaks Mgm't Corp. v. Superior Court, 145 Cal.App.4th 453 (2006) dealt with the problem of confidences acquired by a lawyer acting in a non-lawyer capacity. Several years before the litigation was filed, the defendant in that case had borrowed money from a partnership. One of the partners was a lawyer who represented the plaintiff in the litigation. The defendant argued that the partnership obtained his personal financial information in connection with the loan transaction, and the lawyer therefore had access to confidential information that would help the plaintiff in the litigation.

The defendant insisted that *William H. Raley Co. v. Superior Court* 149 Cal.App.3d 1042 (1983), compelled disqualification of plaintiff's counsel. As noted in part A, however, *Raley* dealt with a situation best characterized as a contemporaneous conflict, and thus a conflict implicating the duty of loyalty rather than the duty of confidentiality. The *Oaks Management* court drew this distinction, and then offered the following test for cases in which only confidentiality is at issue:

> We agree [the defendant] had a reasonable expectation of privacy in the financial information he revealed to [the partnership] to obtain loans, but when no attorney-client relationship exists "[m]ere exposure to the confidences of an adversary does not, standing alone, warrant disqualification." (*In re Complex Asbestos Litigation* (1991) 232

> Cal.App.3d 572, 589.) "Such a rule would nullify a party's right to representation by chosen counsel any time inadvertence or devious design put an adversary's confidences in an attorney's mailbox."
>
> Rather, "[s]ince the purpose of a disqualification order must be prophylactic, not punitive, the significant question is whether there exists *a genuine likelihood that the status or misconduct of the attorney in question will affect the outcome of the proceedings before the court.* Thus, disqualification is proper where, as a result of a prior representation or through improper means, there is a reasonable probability counsel has obtained information the court believes would likely *be used advantageously against an adverse party during the course of the litigation.*. . . Disqualification is inappropriate . . . simply to punish a dereliction that will likely have *no substantial continuing effect on future judicial proceedings.*" (*Gregori* [*v. Bank of America* (1989) 207 Cal.App.3d 291] at pp. 308–309, 254 Cal.Rptr. 853, italics added.). . . .
>
> When an attorney cannot use confidential information gleaned from a nonclient to his or her disadvantage, the adversarial system would not be compromised by allowing the attorney to represent the opposing party. A "no harm, no foul" rule is applicable. . . .

The court went on to note that in the litigation the defendant's counsel inadvertently had produced financial data about the defendant that were more recent than the information the defendant had provided the partnership to which the plaintiff's counsel belonged. The court concluded that, even if plaintiff's counsel could get some benefit from knowing about the defendant finances, counsel got that benefit through the inadvertent production, so that information obtained through the partnership could cause the defendant no incremental harm.

In this regard, the court also offered the following observation on "the appearance of impropriety" as a ground for disqualification:

> To any extent the court felt there was arguably an appearance of impropriety, in California that is not a sufficient ground for disqualification of an attorney. " 'Canon 9 of the American Bar Association Model Code of Professional Responsibility (hereafter Canon 9) provides that: "A lawyer should avoid even the appearance of professional impropriety." ' . . . 'California has not adopted Canon 9, either in the Rules of Professional Conduct . . . or in the Business and Professions Code. . . . ' " (*Hetos Investments, Ltd. v. Kurtin* (2003) 110 Cal.App.4th 36, 47.) " 'Despite the many references to the appearances standard in our case law, and despite occasional judicial statements that "[d]isqualification is proper . . . to avoid any appearance of impropriety" [citation], there is no California case in which an attorney has been disqualified *solely* on this basis. Invariably, Canon 9 has been relied upon to disqualify counsel only where

the appearance of impropriety arises in connection with a tangible dereliction.' "

The Main Points to Recall From Chapter 11(B) Are:

- The main value at stake when you act adversely to a former client is confidentiality.
- You may not act adversely to a former client in a matter substantially related to your prior work for that client.
- Under the substantial relationship test you are conclusively presumed to know things a reasonably competent lawyer would have learned in performing the work you did; it does not matter whether you actually learned such information.

C. CONFLICTS IN CRIMINAL CASES

Conflicts doctrine in criminal cases differs from the doctrine in civil cases in two respects: A prosecutor can raise a conflict of interest on the part of defense counsel, and "active" conflict that adversely affects representation is a ground for finding counsel ineffective under *Strickland*, a standard that is somewhat easier to meet than the normal *Strickland* rule. This section elaborates on these differences.

WHEAT V. UNITED STATES

486 U.S. 153 (1988)

CHIEF JUSTICE REHNQUIST delivered the opinion of the Court.

The issue in this case is whether the District Court erred in declining petitioner's waiver of his right to conflict-free counsel and by refusing to permit petitioner's proposed substitution of attorneys.

I

Petitioner Mark Wheat, along with numerous codefendants, was charged with participating in a far-flung drug distribution conspiracy. Over a period of several years, many thousands of pounds of marijuana were transported from Mexico and other locations to southern California. Petitioner acted primarily as an intermediary in the distribution ring; he received and stored large shipments of marijuana at his home, then distributed the marijuana to customers in the region.

Also charged in the conspiracy were Juvenal Gomez–Barajas and Javier Bravo, who were represented in their criminal proceedings by attorney Eugene Iredale. Gomez–Barajas was tried first and was acquitted on drug charges overlapping with those against petitioner. To avoid a second trial on other charges, however, Gomez–Barajas offered to plead guilty to tax evasion and illegal importation of merchandise. At the commencement of petitioner's trial, the District Court had not accepted the plea; Gomez–Barajas was thus free to withdraw his guilty plea and proceed to trial.

Bravo, evidently a lesser player in the conspiracy, decided to forgo trial and plead guilty to one count of transporting approximately 2,400 pounds of marijuana from Los Angeles to a residence controlled by Victor Vidal. At the conclusion of Bravo's guilty plea proceedings on August 22, 1985, Iredale notified the District Court that he had been contacted by petitioner and had been asked to try petitioner's case as well. In response, the Government registered substantial concern about the possibility of conflict in the representation. After entertaining some initial discussion of the substitution of counsel, the District Court instructed the parties to present more detailed arguments the following Monday, just one day before the scheduled start of petitioner's trial.

At the Monday hearing, the Government objected to petitioner's proposed substitution on the ground that Iredale's representation of Gomez–Barajas and Bravo created a serious conflict of interest. The Government's position was premised on two possible conflicts. First, the District Court had not yet accepted the plea and sentencing arrangement negotiated between Gomez–Barajas and the Government; in the event that arrangement were rejected by the court, Gomez–Barajas would be free to withdraw the plea and stand trial. He would then be faced with the prospect of representation by Iredale, who in the meantime would have acted as petitioner's attorney. Petitioner, through his participation in the drug distribution scheme, was familiar with the sources and size of Gomez–Barajas' income, and was thus likely to be called as a witness for the Government at any subsequent trial of Gomez–Barajas. This scenario would pose a conflict of interest for Iredale, who would be prevented from cross-examining petitioner and thereby from effectively representing Gomez–Barajas.

Second, and of more immediate concern, Iredale's representation of Bravo would directly affect his ability to act as counsel for petitioner. The Government believed that a portion of the marijuana delivered by Bravo to Vidal's residence eventually was transferred to petitioner. In this regard, the Government contacted Iredale and asked that Bravo be made available as a witness to testify against petitioner, and agreed in exchange to modify its position at the time of Bravo's sentencing. In the likely event that Bravo were called to testify, Iredale's position in representing both men would become untenable, for ethical proscriptions would forbid him to cross-examine Bravo in any meaningful way. By failing to do so, he would also fail to provide petitioner with effective assistance of counsel. Thus, because of Iredale's prior representation of Gomez–Barajas and Bravo and the potential for serious conflict of interest, the Government urged the District Court to reject the substitution of attorneys.

In response, petitioner emphasized his right to have counsel of his own choosing and the willingness of Gomez–Barajas, Bravo, and petitioner to waive the right to conflict-free counsel. Petitioner argued that the circumstances posited by the Government that would create a conflict for Iredale were highly speculative and bore no connection to the true relationship between the co-conspirators. If called to testify, Bravo would simply say that he did not know petitioner and had no dealings with him; no attempt by Iredale to impeach Bravo would be necessary. Further, in the unlikely event that Gomez–Barajas went to trial on the charges of tax evasion and illegal importation, petitioner's lack of involvement in those alleged crimes made his appearance as a witness highly improbable. Finally, and most importantly, all three defendants agreed to allow Iredale to represent petitioner and to waive any future claims of conflict of interest. In petitioner's view, the Government was manufacturing implausible conflicts in an attempt to disqualify Iredale, who had already proved extremely effective in representing Gomez–Barajas and Bravo.

After hearing argument from each side, the District Court noted that it was unfortunate that petitioner had not suggested the substitution sooner, rather than two court days before the commencement of trial. The court then ruled:

> "[B]ased upon the representation of the Government in [its] memorandum that the Court really has no choice at this point other than to find that an irreconcilable conflict of interest exists. I don't think it can be waived, and accordingly, Mr. Wheat's request to substitute Mr. Iredale in as attorney of record is denied." App. 100–101.

Petitioner proceeded to trial with his original counsel and was convicted of conspiracy to possess more than 1,000 pounds of marijuana with intent to distribute, in violation of 21 U.S.C. § 846, and five counts of possessing marijuana with intent to distribute, in violation of § 841(a)(1).

The Court of Appeals for the Ninth Circuit affirmed petitioner's convictions, 813 F.2d 1399 (1987), finding that, within the limits prescribed by the Sixth Amendment, the District Court has considerable discretion in allowing substitution of counsel. The Court of Appeals found that the District Court had correctly balanced two Sixth Amendment rights: (1) the qualified right to be represented by counsel of one's choice, and (2) the right to a defense conducted by an attorney who is free of conflicts of interest. Denial of either of these rights threatened the District Court with an appeal assigning the ruling as reversible error, and the Court of Appeals concluded that the District Court did not abuse its discretion in declining to allow the substitution or addition of Iredale as trial counsel for petitioner.

Because the Courts of Appeals have expressed substantial disagreement about when a district court may override a defendant's waiver of his attorney's conflict of interest, we granted certiorari. . . .

II

The Sixth Amendment to the Constitution guarantees that "[i]n all criminal prosecutions, the accused shall enjoy the right . . . to have the Assistance of Counsel for his defence." In *United States v. Morrison,* 449 U.S. 361, 364 (1981), we observed that this right was designed to assure fairness in the adversary criminal process. Realizing that an unaided layman may have little skill in arguing the law or in coping with an intricate procedural system, *Powell v. Alabama,* 287 U.S. 45, 69 (1932); *United States v. Ash,* 413 U.S. 300, 307 (1973), we have held that the Sixth Amendment secures the right to the assistance of counsel, by appointment if necessary, in a trial for any serious crime. *Gideon v. Wainwright,* 372 U.S. 335 (1963). We have further recognized that the purpose of providing assistance of counsel "is simply to ensure that criminal defendants receive a fair trial," *Strickland v. Washington,* 466 U.S. 668, 689 (1984), and that in evaluating Sixth Amendment claims, "the appropriate inquiry focuses on the adversarial process, not on the accused's relationship with his lawyer as such." *United States v. Cronic,* 466 U.S. 648, 657, n. 21 (1984). Thus, while the right to select and be represented by one's preferred attorney is comprehended by the Sixth Amendment, the essential aim of the Amendment is to guarantee an effective advocate for each criminal defendant rather than to ensure that a defendant will inexorably be represented by the lawyer whom he prefers. . . .

The Sixth Amendment right to choose one's own counsel is circumscribed in several important respects. Regardless of his persuasive powers, an advocate who is not a member of the bar may not represent clients (other than himself) in court. Similarly, a defendant may not insist on representation by an attorney he cannot afford or who for other reasons declines to represent the defendant. Nor may a defendant insist on the counsel of an attorney who has a previous or ongoing relationship with an opposing party, even when the opposing party is the Government. The question raised in this case is the extent to which a criminal defendant's right under the Sixth Amendment to his chosen attorney is qualified by the fact that the attorney has represented other defendants charged in the same criminal conspiracy.

In previous cases, we have recognized that multiple representation of criminal defendants engenders special dangers of which a court must be aware. While "permitting a single attorney to represent codefendants . . . is not *per se* violative of constitutional guarantees of effective assistance of counsel," *Holloway v. Arkansas,* 435 U.S. 475, 482 (1978), a court confronted with and alerted to possible conflicts of interest must take adequate steps to ascertain whether the conflicts warrant separate counsel. See also *Cuyler v. Sullivan,* 446 U.S. 335 (1980). As we said in *Holloway:*

> "Joint representation of conflicting interests is suspect because of what it tends to prevent the attorney from doing. . . . [A] conflict may . . . prevent an attorney from challenging the admission of evidence prejudicial to one client but perhaps favorable to another, or from arguing at the sentencing hearing the relative involvement and culpability of his clients in order to minimize the culpability of one by emphasizing that of another."

Petitioner insists that the provision of waivers by all affected defendants cures any problems created by the multiple representation. But no such flat rule can be deduced from the Sixth Amendment presumption in favor of counsel of choice. Federal courts have an independent interest in ensuring that criminal trials are conducted within the ethical standards of the profession and that legal proceedings appear fair to all who observe them. Both the American Bar Association's Model Code of Professional Responsibility and its Model Rules of Professional Conduct, as well as the rules of the California Bar Association (which governed the attorneys in this case), impose limitations on multiple representation of clients. See ABA Model Code of Professional Responsibility DR5–105(C) (1980); ABA Model Rules of Professional Conduct, Rule 1.7 (1984); Rules of Professional Conduct of the State Bar of California, Rules 5 and 7, Cal.Bus. & Prof.Code Ann. § 6076 (West 1974). Not only the interest of a criminal defendant but the institutional interest in the rendition of just verdicts in criminal cases may be jeopardized by unregulated multiple representation.

For this reason, the Federal Rules of Criminal Procedure direct trial judges to investigate specially cases involving joint representation. In pertinent part, Rule 44(c) provides:

> "[T]he court shall promptly inquire with respect to such joint representation and shall personally advise each defendant of his right to the effective assistance of counsel, including separate representation. Unless it appears that there is good cause to believe no conflict of interest is likely to arise, the court shall take such measures as may be appropriate to protect each defendant's right to counsel."

Although Rule 44(c) does not specify what particular measures may be taken by a district court, one option suggested by the Notes of the Advisory Committee is an order by the court that the defendants be separately represented in subsequent proceedings in the case. 18 U.S.C.App., p. 650. This suggestion comports with our instructions in *Holloway* and in *Glasser v. United States,* 315 U.S. 60 (1942), that the trial courts, when alerted by objection from one of the parties, have an independent duty to ensure that criminal defendants receive a trial that is fair and does not contravene the Sixth Amendment.

To be sure, this need to investigate potential conflicts arises in part from the legitimate wish of district courts that their judgments remain intact on appeal. As the Court of Appeals accurately pointed out, trial courts confronted with multiple representations face the prospect of being "whip-sawed" by assertions of error no matter which way they rule. If a district court agrees to the multiple representation, and the advocacy of counsel is thereafter impaired as a result, the defendant may well claim that he did not receive effective assistance. *See, e.g., Burger v. Kemp,* 483 U.S. 776 (1987). On the other hand, a district court's refusal to accede to the multiple representation may result in a challenge such as petitioner's in this case. Nor does a waiver by the defendant necessarily solve the problem, for we note, without passing judgment on, the apparent willingness of Courts of Appeals to entertain ineffective-assistance claims from defendants who have specifically waived the right to conflict-free counsel. . . .

Thus, where a court justifiably finds an actual conflict of interest, there can be no doubt that it may decline a proffer of waiver, and insist that defendants be separately represented. As the Court of Appeals for the Third Circuit stated in *United States v. Dolan,* 570 F.2d 1177, 1184 (1978):

> "[W]hen a trial court finds an actual conflict of interest which impairs the ability of a criminal defendant's chosen counsel to conform with the ABA Code of Professional Responsibility, the court should not be required to tolerate an inadequate representation of a defendant. Such representation not only constitutes a breach of professional ethics and invites disrespect for the integrity of the court, but it is also detrimental to the independent interest of the trial judge to be free from future attacks over the adequacy of the waiver or the fairness of the proceedings in his own court and the subtle problems implicating the defendant's comprehension of the waiver."

Unfortunately for all concerned, a district court must pass on the issue whether or not to allow a waiver of a conflict of interest by a criminal defendant not with the wisdom of hindsight after the trial has taken place, but in the murkier pre-trial context when relationships between parties are seen through a glass, darkly. The likelihood and dimensions of nascent conflicts of interest are notoriously hard to predict, even for those thoroughly familiar with criminal trials. It is a rare attorney who will be fortunate enough to learn the entire truth from his own client, much less be fully apprised before trial of what each of the Government's witnesses will say on the stand. A few bits of unforeseen testimony or a single previously unknown or unnoticed document may significantly shift the relationship between multiple defendants. These imponderables are difficult enough for a lawyer to assess, and even more difficult to convey by way of explanation to a criminal defendant untutored in the niceties of legal ethics. Nor is it amiss to observe that the willingness of an attorney to obtain such waivers from his clients may bear an inverse relation to the care with which he conveys all the necessary information to them.

For these reasons we think the district court must be allowed substantial latitude in refusing waivers of conflicts of interest not only in those rare cases where an actual conflict may be demonstrated before trial, but in the more common cases where a potential for conflict exists which may or may not burgeon into an actual conflict as the trial progresses. In the circumstances of this case, with the motion for substitution of counsel made so close to the time of trial, the District Court relied on instinct and judgment based on experience in making its decision. We do not think it can be said that the court exceeded the broad latitude which must be accorded it in making this decision. Petitioner of course rightly points out that the Government may seek to "manufacture" a conflict in order to prevent a defendant from having a particularly able defense counsel at his side; but trial courts are undoubtedly aware of this possibility, and must take it into consideration along with all of the other factors which inform this sort of a decision.

Here the District Court was confronted not simply with an attorney who wished to represent two coequal defendants in a straightforward criminal prosecution; rather, Iredale proposed to defend three conspirators of varying stature in a complex drug distribution scheme. The Government intended to call Bravo as a witness for the prosecution at petitioner's trial. The Government might readily have tied certain deliveries of marijuana by Bravo to petitioner, necessitating vigorous cross-examination of Bravo by petitioner's counsel. Iredale, because of his prior representation of Bravo, would have been unable ethically to provide that cross-examination.

Iredale had also represented Gomez–Barajas, one of the alleged kingpins of the distribution ring, and had succeeded in obtaining a verdict of acquittal for him. Gomez–Barajas had agreed with the Government to plead guilty to other charges, but the District Court had not yet accepted the plea arrangement. If the agreement were rejected, petitioner's probable testimony at the resulting trial of Gomez–Barajas would create an ethical dilemma for Iredale from which one or the other of his clients would likely suffer.

Viewing the situation as it did before trial, we hold that the District Court's refusal to permit the substitution of counsel in this case was within its discretion and did not violate petitioner's Sixth Amendment rights. Other district courts might have reached differing or opposite conclusions with equal justification, but that does not mean that one conclusion was "right" and the other "wrong". The District Court must recognize a presumption in favor of petitioner's counsel of choice, but that presumption may be overcome not only by a demonstration of actual conflict but by a showing of a serious potential for conflict. The evaluation of the facts and circumstances of each case under this standard must be left primarily to the informed judgment of the trial court. The judgment of the Court of Appeals is accordingly *Affirmed.*

JUSTICE MARSHALL, with whom JUSTICE BRENNAN joins, dissenting.

The Court's resolution of the instant case flows from its deferential approach to the District Court's denial of petitioner's motion to add or substitute counsel; absent deference, a decision upholding the District Court's ruling would be inconceivable. Indeed, I believe that even under the Court's deferential standard, reversal is in order. . . .

At the time of petitioner's trial, Iredale's representation of Gomez–Barajas was effectively completed. As the Court notes, Iredale had obtained an acquittal for Gomez–Barajas on charges relating to a conspiracy to distribute marijuana. Iredale also had negotiated an agreement with the Government under which Gomez–Barajas would plead guilty to charges of tax evasion and illegal importation of merchandise, although the trial court had not yet accepted this plea arrangement. Gomez–Barajas was not scheduled to appear as a witness at petitioner's trial; thus, Iredale's conduct of that trial would not require him to question his former client. The only possible conflict this Court can divine from Iredale's representation of both petitioner and Gomez–Barajas rests on the premise that the trial court would reject the negotiated plea agreement and that Gomez–Barajas then would decide to go to trial. In this event, the Court tells us, "petitioner's probable testimony at the resulting trial of Gomez–Barajas would create an ethical dilemma for Iredale."

This argument rests on speculation of the most dubious kind. The Court offers no reason to think that the trial court would have rejected Gomez–Barajas' plea agreement; neither did the Government posit any such reason in its argument or brief before this Court. The most likely occurrence at the time petitioner moved to retain Iredale as his defense counsel was that the trial court would accept Gomez–Barajas' plea agreement, as the court in fact later did. Moreover, even if Gomez–Barajas had gone to trial, petitioner probably would not have testified. The record contains no indication that petitioner had any involvement in or information about crimes for which Gomez–Barajas might yet have stood trial. The only alleged connection between petitioner and Gomez–Barajas sprang from the conspiracy to distribute marijuana, and a jury already had acquitted Gomez–Barajas of that charge. It is therefore disingenuous to say that representation of both petitioner and Gomez–Barajas posed a serious potential for a conflict of interest.

Similarly, Iredale's prior representation of Bravo was not a cause for concern. The Court notes that the prosecution intended to call Bravo to the stand at petitioner's trial and asserts that Bravo's testimony could well have "necessitat[ed] vigorous cross-examination . . . by petitioner's counsel." *Ibid.* The facts, however, belie the claim that Bravo's anticipated testimony created a serious potential for conflict. Contrary to the Court's inference, Bravo could not have testified about petitioner's involvement in the alleged marijuana distribution scheme. As all parties were aware at the time, Bravo did not know and could not identify petitioner; indeed, prior to the commencement of legal proceedings, the two men never had heard of each other. Bravo's eventual testimony at petitioner's trial related to a shipment of marijuana in which petitioner was not involved; the testimony contained not a single reference to petitioner. Petitioner's counsel did not cross-examine Bravo, and neither petitioner's counsel nor the prosecutor mentioned Bravo's testimony in closing argument. All of these developments were predictable when the District Court ruled on petitioner's request that Iredale serve as trial counsel; the contours of Bravo's testimony were clear at that time. Given the insignificance of this testimony to any matter that petitioner's counsel would dispute, the proposed joint representation of petitioner and Bravo did not threaten a conflict of interest.

Moreover, even assuming that Bravo's testimony might have "necessitat [ed] vigorous cross-examination," the District Court could have insured against the possibility of any conflict of interest without wholly depriving petitioner of his constitutional right to the counsel of his choice. Petitioner's motion requested that Iredale either be substituted for petitioner's current counsel or be added to petitioner's defense team. Had the District Court allowed the addition of Iredale and then ordered that he take no part in the cross-examination of Bravo, any possibility of a conflict would have been removed. Especially in light of the availability of this precautionary measure, the notion that Iredale's prior representation of Bravo might well have caused a conflict of interest at petitioner's trial is nothing short of ludicrous. . . .

JUSTICE STEVENS, with whom JUSTICE BLACKMUN joins, dissenting.

This is not the first case in which the Court has demonstrated "its apparent unawareness of the function of the independent lawyer as a guardian of our freedom." *Walters v. National Assn. of Radiation Survivors,* 473 U.S. 305, 371 (1985) (STEVENS, J., dissenting) (footnote omitted). But even under the Court's paternalistic view of the citizen's right to select his or her own lawyer, its analysis of this case is seriously flawed. As Justice MARSHALL demonstrates, the Court exaggerates the significance of the potential conflict. Of greater importance, the Court gives inadequate weight to the informed and voluntary character of the clients' waiver of their right to conflict-free representation. Particularly, the Court virtually ignores the fact that additional counsel representing petitioner had provided him with sound advice concerning the wisdom of a waiver and would have remained available during the trial to assist in the defense. Thus, this is not a case in which the District Judge faced the question whether one counsel should be substituted for another; rather the question before him was whether petitioner should be permitted to have *additional* counsel of his choice. I agree with Justice MARSHALL that the answer to that question is perfectly clear.

Accordingly, although I agree with the Court's premise that district judges must be afforded wide latitude in passing on motions of this kind,[4] in this case it is abundantly clear to me that the District Judge abused his discretion and deprived this petitioner of a constitutional right of such fundamental character that reversal is required.

CASE QUESTIONS

1. Why does the prosecutor have standing to challenge a defendant's choice of counsel?
2. Could the problems the court specifies be solved by holding defendants to their waiver of a conflict?
3. Could the prosecutors ethically have moved to disqualify Iredale just because he won a previous case in a related matter?

PROBLEM 11–2

A and B are indicted for various fraudulent schemes. At the time of A's trial, B is a fugitive. A's attorney, C, wins an acquittal for A on most charges, but A is convicted on one felony count. C persuades the trial judge to give A a light sentence by arguing that B was the real mastermind of the scheme. According to C, A was just a pawn taken in by B, who was the consummate con artist. B is then captured. Impressed by the light sentence A received, B wishes to retain C to defend him at trial. He intends to argue that he is innocent. The prosecution moves to disqualify C on the ground that her previous defense of A precludes her from arguing for B's innocence, therefore creating an unwaivable conflict of interest. B is willing to waive any conflict. Should C be disqualified? *See United States v. Stites*, 56 F.3d 1020, 1022 (9th Cir. 1995).

PROBLEM 11–3

A and B are indicted for unlawful possession of firearms. C represents them both at trial. A is acquitted and B is convicted. B's conviction is later

---

[4] FN* In my view, deference to the trial judge is appropriate in light of his or her greater familiarity with such factors as the ability of the defendant knowingly and voluntarily to waive a potential conflict (including the possibility that a codefendant may be exerting undue influence over the defendant), the character of the lawyers, the particular facts of the case, and the availability of alternative counsel of a like caliber.

reversed on appeal. The government retries B, who again hires C to represent him. The government moves to disqualify C on the ground that it might call A to testify that B possessed a gun. If it did, the government contends, C would not be able to cross-examine A, her former client, and this conflict disables her from representing B. A and B are willing to waive any conflict, and A submits an affidavit claiming to have no knowledge of B possessing a gun. Citing *Wheat*, the trial court disqualifies C. Should this decision be affirmed? *See United States v. Lanoue*, 137 F.3d 656, 659 (1st Cir. 1998).

PROBLEM 11–4

Suppose counsel for a defendant believes he owes a duty of confidentiality to a third party from whom he received information. The third party is a potential witness for the defendant but, because counsel believes he owes the witness a duty of confidentiality, counsel does not call the witness. The defendant is convicted. As it turns out, counsel was mistaken: Under applicable law he did not owe the witness a duty of confidentiality. What is counsel's status under *Strickland* and its progeny? *See Tueros v. Greiner*, 343 F.3d 587, 588 (2d Cir. 2003).

PROBLEM 11–5

A is indicted for murder. He is represented by B. B's partner previously represented C, a third party whom A and B suspect actually committed the murder. A and B have no evidence that C committed the murder, but they suspect C because C has a record of violence, a history of bad relations with the victim, and, at the time of the murder, was living (on parole) in the town where the murder occurred. B wishes to continue representing A, who is willing to waive any conflict of interest. Should the court remove B from the case? *See People v. Jones*, 33 Cal.4th 234, 236 (2004).

PROBLEM 11–6

Suppose defense counsel is disqualified under *Wheat*, the defendant is convicted, and an appellate court later rules that counsel should not have been disqualified. Suppose the defendant files a petition for a writ of *habeas corpus* arguing that his conviction should be reversed. What must he show to prevail on his claim? *See Rodriguez v. Chandler*, 382 F.3d 670, 671 (7th Cir. 2004).

Conflicts of Interest and the *Strickland* Standard

Two cases are important to understanding the relationship between conflicts of interest and *Strickland* analysis. The first, *Cuyler v. Sullivan*, 446 U.S. 335, 348 (1980), was decided before *Strickland*. *Cuyler* involved two attorneys who represented three defendants accused of the same murder. One defendant, Sullivan, was tried before the others and was convicted. The defense rested at the close of the prosecution's case.

Sullivan petitioned for a writ of habeas corpus. He claimed that his attorneys pulled their punches at trial in order to help the other two defendants (who were acquitted in separate trials) in their later trials. He argued that his attorneys' conflict denied him the effective assistance of counsel. The Supreme Court rejected this argument. It held that trial judges are not obliged to inquire whether counsel jointly representing defendants has a conflict of interest. It also held that courts will not presume prejudice when a defendant asserts a conflict, except in the presumably rare case where the defendant raises the issue and the court refuses to consider it. In other cases, rather than presume prejudice from a conflict, the *Cuyler* court held that "[i]n order to establish a violation of the Sixth Amendment, a defendant who raised no objection at trial must demonstrate that an actual conflict of interest adversely affected his lawyer's performance." That standard was adopted in *Strickland*.

Mickens v. Taylor, 535 U.S. 162 (2002), is the second case. Defense counsel in *Mickens* was appointed to represent a defendant accused of murdering one of the lawyer's other clients. Counsel had a conflict by virtue of his continuing duty to preserve the confidences of his (now) former client, but counsel did not raise this conflict. The judge who appointed him noticed it, however, and the question in *Mickens* was whether to apply the *Sullivan* test or a rule of automatic reversal. The Court held that the *Sullivan* test applied ("it was at least necessary, to void the conviction, for petitioner to establish that the conflict of interest adversely affected his counsel's performance.").

In the course of the majority opinion, Justice Scalia noted that *Sullivan* referred to "active" conflicts and

> stressed the high probability of prejudice arising from multiple concurrent representation, and the difficulty of proving that prejudice. . . . Not all attorney conflicts present comparable difficulties. . . . we do not rule upon the need for the *Sullivan* prophylaxis in cases of successive representation. Whether *Sullivan* should be extended to such cases remains, as far as the jurisprudence of this Court is concerned, an open question.

The Main Points to Recall From Chapter 11(C) Are:

• Counsel laboring under an actual conflict of interest that adversely affects their performance are presumed ineffective; prejudice need not be shown.

• Courts may decline to allow defendants to waive conflicts, and prosecutors may complain of conflicts on the defense side of a case.

D. IMPUTATION OF KNOWLEDGE AND SCREENING

Model Rule of Professional Conduct 1.10–1.11
Restatement §§ 123–124

Subsequent conflict problems sometimes involve lawyers who have moved from one firm, where they worked for the former client, to another, where they want to work for someone whose interests are adverse to the former client. The basic rules governing such situations were summarized at the beginning of this chapter and we explore them in more detail here.

The phenomenon of firm-hopping lawyers raises several questions. The answers can be illustrated with the following example. Suppose there are two lawyers, *A* and *B*. In January they each work at Firm *X*. While at Firm *X*, Lawyer *A* represents IBM in antitrust matters. Lawyer *B* does no work for IBM and knows nothing of its matters. In December, Lawyer *A* moves to Firm *Y* and Lawyer *B* moves to firm *Z*. The following diagram depicts these changes and the applicable rules:

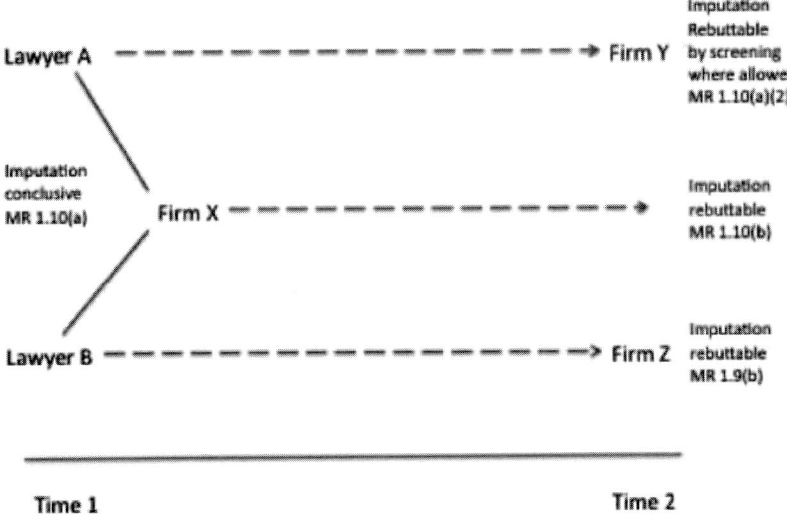

In English, while *A* and *B* work at Firm *X*, the information *A* has is imputed to everyone else in the firm, including *B*. *B* therefore cannot accept work adverse to one of *A*'s clients even though *B* in reality knows nothing about the client or its matters. That is the practical effect of Model Rule 1.10(a), which provides that when lawyers work in a firm none of them may represent a client that any one of them would be prohibited from representing under Rules 1.7 or 1.9.

Things change when either *A* or *B* switches firms. (For completeness the chart above assumes they both switch but either switch causes changes.) Suppose *A* moves to Firm *Y*. At that point *A* presumptively taints Firm *Y*, with the result that no lawyer in Firm *Y* may be adverse to one of *A*'s former clients on a matter substantially related to *A*'s prior work for that client. The Model Rules, and some states, allow this presumption to be rebutted through an appropriate screen keeping *A* from any involvement in such a matter. An appropriate screen means one that complies with Model Rule 1.10(a)(2) and any additional requirement a jurisdiction may impose.

As to Firm *X*, when *A* leaves the firm's position depends on whether any lawyer remaining at the firm has any material knowledge regarding the matters of *A*'s clients. If so, then their knowledge continues to be imputed to Firm *X* and, to the extent of such knowledge, it has the same conflicts it had before. If not, however, then under Model Rule 1.10(b) Firm *X* may accept matters adverse to *A*'s former clients, even if those matters are substantially related to the work *A* did for those clients while at Firm *X*.

What if *B* leaves? Under Model Rule 1.9(b), when *B* leaves Firm *X* she is no longer conclusively presumed to have knowledge of *X*'s matters; she may rebut the presumption by submitting an affidavit stating that she acquired no such knowledge. If *B* successfully rebuts the presumption, she does not taint her new firm, *Z*.

Although easy to state, experience shows these rules take a while to sink in. The following materials exemplify them and provide you a chance to see them in action.

---

1. IMPUTATION FROM FIRM TO LAWYER

ADAMS V. AEROJET–GENERAL CORP.

86 Cal.App.4th 1324, 104 Cal.Rptr.2d 116 (2001)

CALLAHAN, J.

. . . . In the mid–1980's, defendant Aerojet General Corporation (Aerojet) retained the Sacramento law firm of Holliman, Hackard & Taylor (Holliman Hackard) for advice on land use issues. Attorney Michael Hackard was a partner in Holliman Hackard during that time. Included among the subjects on which Holliman Hackard provided legal advice were (1) whether Aerojet's existing hazardous waste treatment, storage and disposal facilities were in compliance with local ordinances; (2) the installation of a contamination treatment facility to remove chemicals from groundwater serving the certain wells; (3) replacing a disposal practice whereby ammonium perchlorate was disposed of by way of open controlled burning from a waste incinerator; and (4) the closure of an on-site landfill on Aerojet's property, which involved drawing groundwater samples to determine whether any environmental contamination had resulted from the landfill use. During the course of this representation, Aerojet provided Holliman Hackard with confidential information regarding chemical contamination on Aerojet's property and surrounding areas, Aerojet's litigation strategy with respect to environmental contamination issues, and Aerojet's strategy for addressing the concerns of the public regarding contamination on the site.

Although Hackard was a principal at the firm, the billing records of Holliman Hackard reveal that he did not perform any work on Aerojet matters. Moreover, according to the declarations before the trial court, Hackard had no discussions with the attorneys at Holliman Hackard regarding Aerojet matters and was not made privy to any information, confidential or otherwise, about Aerojet. According to his declaration, Hackard departed the Holliman Hackard firm in 1989, without taking any files or written materials about Aerojet with him.

In March of 1998, numerous residents and occupants of the area surrounding Aerojet's disposal site filed the current suit against Aerojet and other defendants, alleging negligence, strict liability, trespass, nuisance, fraudulent concealment, unfair business practice, and intentional infliction of emotional distress. The plaintiffs were represented by three law firms, one of which was Hackard's new law firm of Hackard, Holt & Heller (Hackard Holt).

The first amended complaint in the underlying suit alleges that since 1951, defendants have released and improperly used and disposed of toxic chemicals, resulting in contamination of the groundwater and surrounding soils. It further alleges that defendants contaminated the soil with perchlorate and other toxic chemicals; that, moreover, defendants knew of the hazardous conditions they had created and nevertheless subjected plaintiffs to the danger of exposure to these substances without warning them of the health dangers, thereby willfully and intentionally concealing knowledge of the contamination.

Within days after the suit was filed, attorneys for Aerojet wrote to Hackard and requested that he and his firm disqualify themselves as counsel for plaintiffs, because the substantial relationship between Holliman Hackard's former representation of Aerojet and the present suit placed Hackard in a position adverse to a former client. Hackard declined, asserting that he had no personal involvement in the representation of Aerojet or possession of confidential information relevant to the present lawsuit. Aerojet then brought this motion to disqualify Hackard Holt from this litigation.

The court ordered Hackard and the Hackard Holt firm disqualified from the case. Invoking the "imputed knowledge" rule, i.e., that knowledge acquired by one member of a firm of lawyers is imputed to all members of the firm (*Rosenfeld Construction Co. v. Superior Court* (1991) 235 Cal.App.3d 566, 573), the court ruled that the knowledge acquired by Hackard's former partners about Aerojet must be imputed to Hackard. The court also found there was a substantial relationship between the subject matter of Holliman Hackard firm's prior representation and the present suit. "Therefore, there is a conclusive presumption that confidential information passed to Michael Hackard, as a partner in [Holliman Hackard], and he and his present firm must be disqualified." Plaintiffs filed this appeal from the order. . . .

II

Rule 3–310 and the Substantial Relationship Test

Disqualification in the present case turns upon application of rule 3–310(E) of the Rules of Professional Conduct of the State Bar of California (rule 3–310(E)), which provides, in pertinent part: "A member shall not, without the informed written consent of the . . . former client, accept employment adverse to the . . . former client where, by reason of the representation of the . . . former client, the member has obtained confidential information material to the employment." . . .

If Hackard himself had been personally involved with the Holliman Hackard firm's work on Aerojet matters during his tenure with the firm in the 1980's, this appeal would be easily resolved. Holliman Hackard's former representation of Aerojet clearly has a substantial relationship to the present lawsuit . . . . factual issues are similar if not identical (disposal of waste and chemical contamination in and around the Aerojet site); legal issues are related (toxic tort liability and the duty to warn the public); and Hackard's prior work on the case would have placed him in a position to be exposed to confidential information belonging to Aerojet. Viewing the evidence in the light most favorable to the trial court's ruling, we would be duty-bound to affirm the disqualification order. . . .

Here, however, there is no indication of Hackard's personal involvement in Aerojet matters, nor any direct evidence that he was exposed to client secrets during the time his former firm rendered services to Aerojet. Did the Aerojet work performed by Hackard's colleagues in the former firm stain him irretrievably with the taint of conflict, requiring his automatic disqualification? The answer depends on how far we extend the doctrine of imputed knowledge.

III

Imputed Knowledge and Vicarious Disqualification

It is now firmly established that where the attorney is disqualified from representation due to an ethical conflict, the disqualification extends to the entire firm . . . at least where an effective ethical screen has not been established. . . . The rule of vicarious disqualification is based upon the doctrine of imputed knowledge: " 'The imputed knowledge theory holds that knowledge by any member of a law firm is knowledge by all of the attorneys in the firm, partners as well as associates.' " [citations omitted] Courts have based this rule on the practical impossibility of a private law firm creating an "ethical wall" around an attorney who has been exposed to confidential information about the former client by screening him off from the firm's representation of the former client's adversary. Therefore, once the attorney is shown to have had probable access to former client confidences, the court will impute such knowledge to the entire firm, prohibiting all members of the firm from participating in the case. . . .

This case does not present a standard application of the imputed knowledge doctrine, however, because here the court applied the concept in reverse: instead of imputation from attorney to the remainder of the firm, the court here ruled that, once a connection was shown between the *former firm's* representation and the issues involved in the current lawsuit, the knowledge acquired by the former firm was "imputed" back to the attorney, mandating his automatic disqualification even after his departure from the firm, without inquiry as to whether the attorney was reasonably likely to have obtained confidential information.

To burden an attorney with such presumptive knowledge based solely on his former membership in a law firm which represented the former client, as Aerojet urges, would require a significant extension of the doctrine of imputed knowledge beyond that recognized by any existing case law. For the reasons which follow, we conclude such an extension would be inconsistent with both the policy objectives behind rule 3–310(E) and the *Ahmanson* [substantial relationship] test. Further, it would ignore certain undeniable realities regarding today's practice of law.

IV

Applying Rule 3–310(E) to Successive Representation

Our starting point is the text of rule 3–310(E): "A *member* shall not, without the informed written consent of the client or former client, accept employment adverse to the client or former client where, by reason of the representation of the client or former client, *the member* has obtained confidential information material to the employment." (Italics added.) The rule implements the ethical imperative of Business and Professions Code section 6068, subdivision (e), which states that it is the obligation of every attorney "[t]o maintain inviolate the confidence, and at every peril to himself or herself to preserve the secrets, of his or her client."

Rule 3–310(E) addresses the individual attorney, not the law firm. Its purpose is to ensure "permanent confidentiality of matters disclosed *to the attorney* in the course of the prior representation" . . . We therefore agree with the conclusion of the State Bar Committee on Professional Responsibility that, "[a]s written, rule 3–310(E) *refers to a 'member' and not to the member's law firm.* Rule 1–100(B)(2) defines the term 'member' as 'a member of the State Bar of California.' " (Cal. Compendium on Professional Responsibility, State Bar Formal Opinion No.1998–152, p. IIA–415, italics added (Formal Opinion No. 1998–152).) Both rule 3–310(E) and Business and Professions Code section 6068 thus presuppose that attorney-client confidences are acquired by *individual attorneys,* not by law firms in general. . . .

The vicarious disqualification rule has been established as a prophylactic device to protect the sanctity of former client confidences where a law firm with a member attorney who has acquired knowledge of confidential information material to the current controversy would otherwise be permitted to represent the former client's adversary. "No amount of assurances or screening procedures, no 'cone of silence,' could ever convince the opposing party that the confidences would not be used to its disadvantage. . . . No one could have confidence in the integrity of a legal process in which this is permitted to occur without the parties' consent." (*Cho v. Superior Court* (1995) 39 Cal.App.4th 113, 125 fn. omitted.) As the State Bar Committee observes: "the absence of an effective means of oversight combined with the law firm's interest as an advocate for the current client in the adverse representation are factors that tend to undermine a former client's trust, and in turn the public's trust, in a legal system that would permit such a situation to exist without the former client's consent." (Formal Opn. No.1998–152, *supra,* at p. IIA–418.)

Once an attorney departs the firm, however, a blanket rule to prevent future breaches of confidentiality is not necessary because the departed attorney no longer has presumptive access to the secrets possessed by the former firm. The court need no longer rely on the fiction of imputed knowledge to safeguard client confidentiality. Instead, the court may undertake a dispassionate assessment of whether and to what extent the attorney, during his tenure with the former firm, was reasonably likely to have obtained confidential information material to the current lawsuit. . . .

A rule of automatic disqualification such as that applied by the trial court would mean that an attorney who has had direct, personal contact with the former client may switch sides in subsequent litigation without adverse consequence if the court finds that his prior involvement was "minimal," yet an attorney who had *no contact whatever* with the former client can be disqualified if the court finds his *former firm's* relationship with the same client was substantially related to the new litigation, regardless of whether the attorney personally acquired any material confidential information. We do not believe rule 3–310(E) was intended to produce such an anomaly.

Disqualification based on a conclusive presumption of imputed knowledge derived from a lawyer's past association with a law firm is out of touch with the present day practice of law. Gone are the days when attorneys (like star athletes) typically stay with one organization throughout their entire careers. Partners with one law firm may join a competing firm or splinter off and form their own rival firm; former defense lawyers may become plaintiffs' specialists and vice versa; law firms (like marriages) dissolve, often acrimoniously, members striking off on their own and taking divergent paths. We have seen the dawn of the era of the "mega-firm." Large law firms (like banks) are becoming ever larger, opening branch offices nationwide or internationally, and merging with other large firms. Individual attorneys today can work for a law firm and not even know, let alone have contact with, members of the same firm working in a different department of the same firm across the hall or a different branch across the globe.

A rule under which a nonrebuttable presumption of imputed knowledge from an attorney's former firm follows him to whichever firm he subsequently joins would also pose insurmountable practical problems in screening for conflicts. When an attorney joins a new law firm, he normally discloses the names of former clients who will create a conflict for the new firm if it takes the opposing side in future litigation. But there is no way, when an attorney joins a new firm, that he or she can provide that new firm with notice of "imputed knowledge"—that is, names of clients and the nature of their matters the attorney never knew about or worked on while at the former firm. Application of the imputed knowledge doctrine under these circumstances would mean that the attorney's association with the new firm would automatically subject him and the new firm to disqualification without anyone knowing it.

Any construction of rule 3–310(E) which would create an ethical conflict based on that which is unknown to both the attorney and his new firm would not only impair the attorney's freedom to change firms but would have far-ranging disruptive repercussions on the client as well. Consider, for example, the impact of such a rule on a client who selects a law firm to handle major litigation, only to learn well into the progress of the suit that the hiring of a new attorney has resulted in the firm's summary disqualification because of a matter the new hiree's former firm handled of which he personally was not even aware.

We conclude that a rule which disqualifies an attorney based on imputed knowledge derived solely from his membership in the former firm and without inquiry into his actual exposure to the former client's secrets sweeps with too broad a brush, is inconsistent with the language and core purpose of rule 3–310(E), and unnecessarily restricts both the client's right to chosen counsel and the attorney's freedom of association. It also clashes with the principle that applying the remedy of disqualification " 'when there is no realistic chance that confidences were disclosed [to counsel] would go far beyond the purpose' of the substantial relationship test." . . .

V

The Appropriate Test

In crafting a standard applicable to a situation such as that posed here, we find helpful guidance in the American Bar Association Model Rules of Professional Conduct (4th ed. 1999) (ABA Model Rules). . . .

We conclude that disqualification should not be ordered where there is no reasonable probability the firm-switching attorney had access to confidential information while at his or her former firm that is related to the current representation. We therefore hold that where there is a substantial relationship between the current case and the matters handled by the firm-switching attorney's former firm, but the attorney did not personally represent the former client who now seeks to remove him from the case, the trial court should apply a modified version of the "substantial relationship" test. . . . The court's task, under these circumstances, is to determine whether confidential information material to the current representation would normally have been imparted to the attorney during his tenure at the old firm. In answering this question, the court should focus on the relationship, if any, between the attorney and the former client's representation. It should consider any time spent by the attorney working on behalf of the former client and "the attorney's possible exposure to formulation of policy or strategy" in matters relating to the current dispute. . . . The court should also take into account whether the attorney worked out of the same branch office that handled the former litigation, and/or whether his administrative or management duties may have placed him in a position where he would have been exposed to matters relevant to the current dispute. . . .

Finally, in light of the paramount importance of maintaining the inviolability of client confidences, where a substantial relationship between the former firm's representation of the client and the current lawsuit has been shown (as is the case here), the attorney whose disqualification is sought should carry the burden of proving that he had no exposure to confidential information relevant to the current action while he was a member of the former firm. (See ABA Model Rules, rule 1.9, Comment [7], p.

139.) That burden requires an affirmative showing and is not satisfied by a cursory denial.

VI

Application to the Trial Court's Ruling

The trial court . . . believed disqualification was mandatory because a substantial relationship existed between the work done by Hackard's *former firm* and his representation of plaintiffs in this suit. In other words, disqualification was based not on a particularized analysis of Hackard's relationship to Aerojet matters while at Holliman Hackard, but on a conclusive presumption derived from Hackard's mere *membership* in the former firm. "A trial court abuses its discretion when it applies the wrong legal standards applicable to the issue at hand. [citation omitted]" Since the trial court employed the wrong test, an abuse of discretion has been shown. . . .

On remand, the court should focus not only on the relationship between Hackard and the Holliman Hackard firm's representation of Aerojet, but whether Hackard's responsibilities as partner and principal, as well as his relationship with other members of the Holliman Hackard firm, placed him in a position where he was reasonably likely to have obtained confidential information relating to the current case. Prior to ruling on the disqualification motion the court, in its discretion, and with an eye toward avoiding satellite litigation and unwarranted annoyance, embarrassment, burden, or expense . . . may allow further limited discovery reasonably calculated to produce admissible evidence with respect to these issues.

SCOTLAND, P.J.

I agree with much of the majority's analysis, but disagree with the result.

. . . . As emphasized by the majority in this case, disqualification of an attorney from undertaking representation adverse to a client of the attorney's former law firm does not require proof that the attorney *actually* possesses confidential information about that client which is material to the current dispute. It merely must appear from the nature of the relationship between the attorney's former law firm and the client that confidential information material to the current dispute against the client " 'would normally have been imparted to the attorney' ". . . .

As the majority properly points out, this rule does not mean an attorney always is disqualified from representing a new client in an action brought against a party that had been represented by a law firm to which the attorney previously was a member. If the attorney can establish, to the trial court's satisfaction, that information about the opposing party substantially related to the matter at issue in the new lawsuit would *not* normally have been imparted to the attorney while he or she was a member of the law firm that had represented the opposing party, there is no basis to impute that information to the attorney and, thus, no basis to disqualify the attorney. . . .

Depending on the circumstances, discovery may be necessary in order to present the trial court with facts essential to determine whether the attorney was in a position with the former law firm such that confidential information about the former law firm's client that is material to the current dispute against that client normally would have been imparted to the attorney. This means that, assuming the former law firm still exists, the parties may have to engage in problematic and expensive discovery regarding the inner workings of the firm (e.g., how it assigned and handled the case; how litigation strategy was formed and discussed among partners and associates; whether members of the firm chat about cases in the hallway where their discussions could be overheard by others in the firm who are not directly involved in the litigation; whether billing records show the attorney charged any time to the client, etc.). In addition, such discovery would draw into this controversy a law firm that otherwise is not involved in the litigation, causing it to expend time and suffer the burden of responding to litigation in which it has no interest and will gain no benefit.

For this reason, I conclude that the attorney seeking to avoid disqualification should have a formidable burden to present a compelling prima facie showing that either (1) the prior representation of the opposing party by the attorney's former law firm did not have a substantial relationship to the matters at issue in the current lawsuit, or (2) the nature of the former relationship between the law firm and the opposing party was such that confidential information material to the current dispute normally would not have been imparted to the attorney.

I also conclude that the attorney cannot make such a prima facie showing merely by declaring that he or she does not recall having any discussions regarding confidential information about the opposing party while affiliated with the former law firm or that the attorney has never received such information. . . .

Moreover, because of its problematic nature, I conclude that discovery should be permitted only after the attorney makes the aforesaid prima facie showing. . . . unlike the majority, I conclude that remand is inappropriate because, as I shall explain, Hackard failed to make a prima facie showing that the nature of the relationship between Hackard's former law firm and Aerojet was such that confidential information material to the current dispute normally would not have been imparted to Hackard.

. . . . Hackard's former law firm was a small office of seven to ten attorneys, of which Hackard was a name partner and Aerojet was a major client. It is inconceivable that, in such a small firm with only three partners, there would not have been discussions among all the attorneys, particularly the partners, about material matters relating to the representation of a major, sustaining client like Aerojet. It takes no imagination to recognize that confidential information which would be useful to someone later suing Aerojet normally would be imparted during discussions about billing matters or billing rates, during casual conversations at social occasions with Aerojet principals, or in the many other types of contacts among attorneys in the firm that would not constitute direct representation and would not show up on billing records. The client was too big, the firm too small, and the matters at issue too closely related to say there is no conflict. . . .

In light of the important public policy at stake in this dispute, Hackard's declaration that he did not recall having "any" discussions with attorneys at his former law firm regarding Aerojet and that, while a shareholder of his former law firm, he never performed any work on Aerojet files, never met with Aerojet representatives, and "never received *any* information" about Aerojet's practices and procedures was too conclusory to rebut the presumption of imputed knowledge derived from the commonsense conclusion that, in light of the size of Hackard's former law firm and his status as one of three named partners, confidential information about its major client, Aerojet, material to the current dispute normally would have been imparted to Hackard. Likewise, declarations of his partners in the former law firm stating that they "do not recall" discussing with Hackard any matters relating to Aerojet are insufficient to rebut the presumption of imputed knowledge.

Consequently, I would affirm the order of disqualification.

Conflicts are imputed from lawyers to firms; are they imputed from support staff (such as secretaries, legal assistants, etc.) to lawyers? The answer is "no" unless the person in question has actual knowledge of confidential information that would create a conflict. *In re Complex Asbestos Litig.*, 232 Cal.App.3d 572, 595–96 (1991).

---

2. IMPUTATION FROM LAWYERS TO (NEW) FIRMS: SCREENING

As mentioned above, Model Rule 1.10(a)(2) allows a firm that has acquired a new lawyer to rebut the presumption of shared confidences by implementing an effective screen. Under this provision the lawyer may be allocated no part of the fee from the matter creating the conflict (though partners may take a general draw), the former client must be notified and given a description of the screening procedures allowing with affirmations that the procedures are being followed, and the screening firm must respond promptly to queries from the former client and updated its affirmations of compliance at reasonable intervals. The following case discusses both the state of screening as of mid 2010 and some of the elements of an effective screen.

KIRK V. FIRST AMERICAN TITLE INS. CO.

183 Cal.App.4th 776 (2010)

When an attorney obtains confidential information from a client, that attorney is prohibited from accepting a representation adverse to the client in a matter to which the confidential information would be material. In this case, we are not concerned with the issue of disqualifying the attorney possessing the material client confidences from representing an adverse party; it is conceded that the attorney is disqualified from doing so. Instead, we are concerned with the issue of the vicarious disqualification of the attorney's entire law firm. We conclude that, under the circumstances of this case, *automatic* vicarious disqualification is not required, and that, instead, there is a *rebuttable* presumption that the attorney's knowledge of client confidences is imputed to the firm, which can be refuted by evidence that the law firm adequately screened the attorney from the others at the firm representing the adverse party. In addition, as the disqualified attorney has left the firm, the trial court's examination of the screen's adequacy should be on a retrospective, not prospective, basis.

FACTUAL AND PROCEDURAL BACKGROUND

1. *The Underlying Litigation*

The instant attorney disqualification dispute arose in the context of four related class actions brought against First American Title Insurance Company and related First American entities (collectively, First American). Each class action is based on different allegations, although they each challenge business practices of First American as violative of, among other things, various consumer protection laws. . . . . The first of these four actions was filed on February 25, 2005. In each case, the plaintiffs were represented by the Bernheim Law Firm and the Kick Law Firm (collectively, plaintiffs' counsel). Collectively, we refer to the cases as the related class actions.

First American was represented by Bryan Cave, LLP. Three attorneys at Bryan Cave, Joel D. Siegel, Charles Newman, and Jason Maschmann (the First American team), were primarily responsible for the defense of the related class actions. Newman was first retained as counsel for First American in 1997; he defended against the related class actions from their initial filing. Together, the First American team has defended First American in 80 class actions across the country, and has also been retained to give legal advice to First American. The attorneys on the First American team are very familiar with, and have good rapport with, First American's in-house counsel, officers, and management employees. They "are uniquely and extensively knowledgeable about First American's personnel, products, services, data systems, history and organization on a national basis, including . . . California."

The related class action litigation is large, time-consuming, and expensive. . . . . The First American team defended multiple depositions and reviewed hundreds of thousands of pages of documents. By April 2009, First American had incurred over $5.5 million in attorney's fees in the related class actions and another $1 million in additional expenses. The related class actions are extremely complex and have been aggressively litigated.

2. *Plaintiffs' Counsel Contact Gary Cohen*

At one time, Gary Cohen had been Deputy Commissioner and General Counsel at the California Department of Insurance. In October 2007, he was chief counsel for Fireman's Fund Insurance Company. During that month, plaintiffs' counsel spoke by telephone with Cohen and solicited his services as a consultant in the related class actions, apparently due to his experience at the Department of Insurance.

After introductions by a mutual acquaintance, a 17–minute phone call took place between Cohen and plaintiffs' counsel. While it is clear that some portion of the conversation was devoted to Cohen's experience and qualifications, it is *undisputed* that plaintiffs' counsel, during this conversation, conveyed confidential information to Cohen material to the related class actions. Indeed, Attorney Bernheim specifically told Cohen that plaintiffs' counsel would be discussing confidential information. While the precise content of the information disclosed is not identified, plaintiffs' counsel conveyed attorney work product to Cohen, including plaintiffs' theories of the case, and their concerns regarding defense strategy and tactics. Plaintiffs' counsel also disclosed their estimates of the value of the cases.

Cohen expressed his interest in the related class actions, but indicated that he had to obtain permission from his employer before he could work with plaintiffs' counsel. A series of e-mails followed, the upshot of which was that Cohen declined the consultant position because it was possible that Fireman's Fund had provided Directors and Officers coverage to one or more of the First American entities. Cohen did not, however, cut off all communication with plaintiffs' counsel. Instead, when plaintiffs' counsel asked if, despite Cohen's inability to become plaintiffs' consultant, plaintiffs' counsel could "make contact with [Cohen] one more time regarding [his] thoughts," Cohen responded that he would telephone plaintiffs' counsel later.

Nothing further happened relevant to this matter for more than a year. Then, on December 8, 2008, the law firm of Sonnenschein Nath & Rosenthal LLP (Sonnenschein) issued a press release announcing that Cohen would join its San Francisco office as a partner in its insurance regulatory practice group on January 5, 2009.

Upon learning that Cohen would be leaving Fireman's Fund-and the possible conflict associated with that employment-plaintiffs' counsel again e-mailed Cohen and reasserted their interest in hiring him as an expert consultant. On January 12, 2009, after Cohen had moved to Sonnenschein, Cohen responded, stating that he would do a conflicts check and asking for one of the complaints to be sent to him by e-mail. The next day, plaintiffs' counsel sent to Cohen edited versions of the complaints (reducing them to what plaintiffs' counsel believed to be the main issues). Less than a half-hour later, Cohen responded, "It turns out that the firm does represent First American, so I'm afraid that I won't be able to be of any help. I haven't read the attachments to your email and will delete them without having read them." There was no further contact between Cohen and plaintiffs' counsel.

3. *The First American Team Moves to Sonnenschein*

On February 2, 2009, the First American team moved from Bryan Cave to Sonnenschein. Siegel moved to Sonnenschein's Los Angeles office, while Newman and Maschmann moved to Sonnenschein's St. Louis office. None of the First American team moved to the San Francisco office, where Cohen was located. Nor does it appear that any of them were part of the insurance regulatory practice group, in which Cohen practiced.

On February 3, 2009, First American filed substitutions of counsel in the related class actions, reflecting that Sonnenschein was now handling its defense, although the three main attorneys representing First American did not change. On February 4, 2009, plaintiffs filed a case management statement in which they "objected" to the representation of First American by Sonnenschein, due to their prior confidential consultation with Cohen. Until that point, the First American team had been unaware of Cohen's prior contacts with plaintiffs' counsel. That day, Siegel contacted John Koski, a partner in Sonnenschein's Chicago office who serves as the firm's General Counsel and sits on the firm's Ethics Committee. Koski discussed the matter with Siegel and Newman, and "had a separate, private discussion" with Cohen. Thereafter, Koski established an ethical screen around Cohen. That night, Koski sent a memorandum to all attorneys, paralegals, and secretaries at Sonnenschein, setting forth "mandatory screening procedures" for the related class actions.

The screening memorandum recites that it was created to "formalize and memorialize the procedures necessary to assure that no confidences or secrets relating to the [related class actions] will be disclosed, even inadvertently, to [the First American team] or any other Sonnenschein lawyer who may be asked to work on the [related class actions]." The memorandum indicated that the failure to observe the procedures would subject the offender to discipline. The memorandum provided that: (1) Cohen could not work on the related class actions; (2) no attorney or paralegal who may work on the related class actions may discuss them with Cohen; (3) Cohen may not be given non-public documents pertaining to the related class actions; (4) Cohen shall not access any documents on Sonnenschein's computer network pertaining to the related class actions; and (5) no fees from any work related to the related class actions would be apportioned to Cohen. . . .

5. *The Disqualification Motion*

On March 18, 2009, plaintiffs moved to disqualify Sonnenschein from further representation of the First American defendants, based on plaintiffs' counsel's prior confidential communications with Cohen. Sonnenschein opposed the motion, although it retained independent counsel to prepare the opposition in order to preserve its ethical wall. Much of the dispute centered on whether plaintiffs' counsel actually conveyed confidential information to Cohen; this is not an issue on appeal. As to whether the entire Sonnenschein firm should be vicariously disqualified, Sonnenschein relied on the ethical screening wall it had constructed. Both Cohen and Siegel submitted declarations indicating their compliance with the ethical screening wall. First American also submitted the declaration of its Senior Vice President and national litigation counsel, who testified to the key experience of the First American team and their irreplaceability. Specifically, he stated that it would cost First American millions of dollars to retain new counsel sufficiently prepared to defend the related class actions, "although it would be impossible for new counsel to attain the level of knowledge and proficiency of First American's current attorneys."

6. *Order Granting Disqualification*

The trial court ultimately granted the motion for disqualification. In its order, the trial court indicated that, "[n]o one is to blame for this situation except perhaps the itinerant nature of attorneys that has developed over the last fifteen years." The trial court found that plaintiffs' counsel disclosed confidential and privileged attorney work product information to Cohen during the initial 17–minute telephone call, a conclusion not challenged on appeal.

As to vicarious disqualification, the court reviewed applicable case law, and concluded that, when an attorney possesses disqualifying confidential client information, vicarious disqualification of the law firm is *au-*

tomatic, regardless of any ethical screening wall created. The trial court further concluded, however, that even if California law permitted the use of ethical walls in this context, "there is evidence that the wall Sonnenschein erected has not been a complete success.". . . .

Additionally, the trial court indicated that the balance of interests weighed in favor of disqualification. The court recognized "the substantial financial burden disqualification places on [First American], who will have to obtain new counsel and bring them up the learning curve on these very complex cases that have been litigated over a number of years." However, the court found that two competing policy interests outweighed these concerns. Specifically, the court relied on the need for vigorous representation of parties by independent counsel unencumbered by conflicts of interest, and the preservation of public trust in the scrupulous administration of justice and the integrity of the bar.

First American and Sonnenschein filed timely notices of appeal. . . . .

2. *Historical Development of the Law Regarding Vicarious Disqualification*

Generally speaking, the Rules of Professional Conduct govern attorney discipline; they do not create standards for disqualification in the courts. Nonetheless, as will be seen in our discussion, courts analyzing questions of disqualification often look to the Rules of Professional Conduct for guidance. California Rules of Professional Conduct, rule 3–310(E) provides, "A member shall not, without the informed written consent of the client or former client, accept employment adverse to the client or former client where, by reason of the representation of the client or former client, the member has obtained confidential information material to the employment." While the Model Rules of Professional Conduct promulgated by the American Bar Association (ABA) address the issue of *vicarious* disqualification (see ABA Model Rules Prof. Conduct, rule 1.10), the California Rules of Professional Conduct do not. Thus, in California, vicarious disqualification rules are the result of decisional law. *City and County of San Francisco v. Cobra Solutions, Inc.* (2006) 38 Cal.4th 839, 847.) It is useful for our analysis that we first discuss the development of California law in this area in some detail.

3. *Distillation of the Current State of the Law*

In very brief summary, the history of the law of vicarious disqualification appears to be as follows: (1) appellate courts initially concluded vicarious disqualification was not automatic, but instead subject to a balancing test; (2) [*Henriksen v. Great American Savings & Loan, supra,* 11 Cal.App.4th 109 (1992)] concluded the burden of rebutting the presumption of imputed knowledge simply could not be established in the case of a tainted attorney who represented one party and switched sides in the same case; (3) the Supreme Court favorably cited *Henriksen* and appeared to state a rule of automatic vicarious disqualification any time material confidential information was presumed to be held by the tainted attorney [(*Flatt v. Superior Court,* 9 Cal.4th 275 (1994)]; (4) the Supreme Court subsequently suggested that whether vicarious disqualification can be avoided by a proper ethical wall was still an open question [*People ex rel Department of Corporations v. SpeeDee Oil Change Systems, Inc.,* 20 Cal. 4th 1135, 1152 (1999)]; and (5) the Supreme Court has never directly addressed the issue on the merits.

Given this history, we conclude that it is improper to rely on *Flatt* as creating an absolute rule of vicarious disqualification in California. Instead, we believe that neither *Flatt* nor *SpeeDee Oil* addressed the issue of whether vicarious disqualification is absolute, and the state of the law is that as initially expressed by the appellate courts: (1) a case-by-case analysis based on the circumstances present in, and policy interests implicated by, the case; (2) tempered by the *Henriksen* rule that vicarious disqualification should be automatic in cases of a tainted attorney possessing actual confidential information from a representation, who switches sides in the same case.

We do not doubt that vicarious disqualification is the *general* rule, and that we should presume knowledge is imputed to all members of a tainted attorney's law firm. However, we conclude that, in the proper circumstances, the presumption is a rebuttable one, which can be refuted by evidence that ethical screening will effectively prevent the sharing of confidences in a particular case.

4. *Other Considerations Support This Conclusion*

While we believe our interpretation of the law follows from our analysis of its historical development, this much seems clear: the Supreme Court has not considered and definitively decided whether the presumption of imputed knowledge can be rebutted in a non-governmental attorney context with evidence of an ethical wall. We therefore consider three factors which lead us to conclude ethical walls should be recognized in California: (1) changing realities in the practice of law which undermine the rationale for an automatic rule of vicarious disqualification; (2) California's favorable experience with ethical walls in other circumstances; and (3) an understanding of policy considerations which supports the recognition of ethical walls in the proper cases.

a. *Changing Realities are Undermining the Rationale for an Automatic Rule of Vicarious Disqualification*

(1) *Courts Are Recognizing the Changing Circumstances*

As expressed by the Supreme Court, the vicarious disqualification rule is based on a recognition of "the everyday reality that attorneys, working together and practicing law in a professional association, share each other's, and their clients', confidential information." [CO] This "is not so much a conclusive presumption that confidential information has passed as a pragmatic recognition that the confidential information will work its way to the nontainted attorneys at some point." (*Goldberg v. Warner/Chappell Music, Inc.* (2005) 125 Cal.App.4th 752, 765.)

But several cases have questioned this paradigm as representing an outdated view of the practice of law. . . . The instant case illustrates the changing landscape of legal practice—we are concerned with the tainted attorney working in a different geographical office and in a different practice group from the attorneys with responsibility for the litigation. These are not attorneys discussing their cases regularly, passing each other in the hallways, or at risk of accidentally sharing client confidences at lunch. In a situation where the "everyday reality" is no longer that all attorneys in the same law firm actually "work[ ] together," there would seem to be no place for a rule of law based on the premise that they do.[5]

(2) *Other Jurisdictions Are Also Recognizing and Adapting to the Changing Reality*

Other states are very nearly split evenly as to whether to permit ethical screening of attorneys moving from one private law firm to another. Twelve states have adopted rules of professional conduct permitting such screening with no limitations based on the scope of the disqualified attorney's prior involvement in the representation. . . . An additional twelve states have adopted rules permitting screening when the disqualified attorney was not substantially involved in the prior representation, or under other similar limitations on the attorney's prior involvement.[6]

---

[5] FN21. We note here that amici in support of plaintiffs argue that while the paradigm may be changing for large law firms, the vast majority of California attorneys practice in small firms, and judicial recognition of a rule permitting ethical screening may lead attorneys in small firms to attempt ethical screening in situations in which it cannot be accomplished successfully. We therefore wish to emphasize that we are not adopting a broad rule permitting ethical screening in all cases. In this case, we are simply holding that, consistent with prior authority, *in the proper situation,* ethical screening may be sufficient to rebut the presumption of imputed knowledge. That some attorneys may attempt ethical screening in practices where it could not possibly work is not a sufficient basis to prohibit ethical screening in situations where it may; this is particularly the case when the unnecessary vicarious disqualification of an entire law firm would work a severe hardship on the client deprived of counsel of its choice.

[6] FN22. Moreover, 36 states and the District of Columbia permit ethical screening when the confidential information was conveyed by a former *prospective* client, although these rules generally apply only when the attorney took reasonable measures to avoid exposure to more information than was reasonably necessary to determine whether to accept the representation—a circumstance which arguably did not occur in the instant case. (Alaska Rules Prof. Conduct, rule 1.18; Ariz. Rules Prof. Conduct, rule 1.18; Ark. Rules Prof. Conduct, rule 1.18; Colo. Rules Prof. Conduct, rule 1.18; Conn. Rules Prof. Conduct, rule 1.18; Del. Rules Prof. Conduct, rule 1.18; D.C. Rules Prof. Conduct, rule 1.18; Fla. Bar Rules 4–1.18; Ill. Rules Prof. Conduct, rule 1.18; Ind. Rules Prof. Conduct, rule 1.18; Iowa Court Rules, rule 32:1.18; Ky.Supr. Ct. Rules, rule 3.130(1.18); La. Rules Prof. Conduct, rule 1.18; Me. Rules Prof. Conduct, rule 1.18; Md. Rules Prof. Conduct, rule 1.18; Minn. Rules Prof. Conduct, rule 1.18; Mo. Rules Prof. Conduct, rule 4–1.18; Mont. Rules Prof. Conduct, rule 1.20; Neb. Rules Prof. Conduct, § 3–501.18; Nev. Rules Prof. Conduct, rule 1.18; N.H. Rules Prof. Conduct, rule 1.18; N.J. Rules Prof. Conduct, rule 1.18;

That nearly half of the states have chosen to permit some level of ethical screening in the non-governmental attorney context demonstrates a growing understanding that law is often practiced in firms in which effective screening is possible. In 2009, the ABA Model Rules of Professional Conduct were modified to permit screening of a tainted (non-former-governmental) attorney at a private law firm. ABA Model Rule 1.10 had, for many years, provided for the vicarious disqualification of a law firm when a lawyer in that firm would be prohibited from representing the client due to a conflicting former representation. In February 2009, however, the ABA modified Model Rule 1.10 to permit the law firm to accept the representation if the disqualified lawyer is timely and adequately screened. (ABA Model Rules Prof. Conduct, rule 1.10(a)(2).) This change was made after the ABA Standing Committee on Ethics and Professional Responsibility had inquired of states permitting screening and learned that their experience demonstrated "that properly established screens are effective to protect confidentiality." (ABA Standing Committee on Ethics and Professional Responsibility, Recommendation 109 (February 16, 2009) p. 11.). . . .

b. *California's Experience in Other Contexts Suggests that Ethical Screening in Private Law Firms Can Be Effective*

It is undisputed that the presumption of imputed knowledge is uniformly rebuttable and may be overcome by a proper ethical screen when the issue arises in the context of government and former government attorneys.[7] Yet if ethical screening can, in any given case, be considered effective to screen a former government attorney in a private law firm, it gives rise to the question why screening cannot be equally effective to screen a private attorney in the same private law firm. The effectiveness of the screening process depends on the policies implemented by the law firm, not on the former employment of the screened attorney.

N.M. Rules Prof. Conduct, rule 16–118; N.Y. Rules Prof. Conduct, rule 1.18; N.C. Rules Prof. Conduct, rule 1.18; Ohio Rules Prof. Conduct, rule 1.18; 5 Okla. Stats. § Rule 1.18 (OSCN 2010) Appendix 3–A; Or. Rules Prof. Conduct, rule 1.18; Pa. Rules Prof. Conduct, rule 1.18; R.I. Rules Prof. Conduct, rule 1.18; S.C. Rules Prof. Conduct, rule 1.18; S.D. Rules Prof. Conduct, rule 1.18; Utah Rules Prof. Conduct, rule 1.18; Vt. Rules Prof. Conduct, rule 1.18; Wash. Rules Prof. Conduct, rule 1.18; Wis.Supr. Ct. Rules, rule 20:1.18; Wyo. Rules Prof. Conduct, rule 1.18.)

[7] FN24. In cases of a tainted attorney working in a government office, the courts have concluded the following policy considerations justify the use of only a rebuttable presumption of imputed knowledge: (1) public sector attorneys do not have a financial interest in the matters on which they work, so have less of an incentive than private attorneys to breach client confidences; (2) public sector attorneys do not recruit clients or accept fees, so have no financial incentive to favor one client over another; (3) disqualification increases the costs for public entities, raising the possibility that litigation decisions will be driven by financial considerations rather than the public interest; and (4) automatic vicarious disqualification will restrict the government's ability to hire attorneys with relevant private sector experience. (*City of Santa Barbara v. Superior Court, supra,* 122 Cal.App.4th at pp. 24–25, 18 Cal.Rptr.3d 403.) We note that, except for the last consideration, none of the other three could possibly apply in the context of a *former* government attorney working in a *private* law firm. Nonetheless, courts have not hesitated to apply only a rebuttable presumption of imputed knowledge in those cases as well. (*Chambers v. Superior Court, supra,* 121 Cal.App.3d at pp. 898–901, 175 Cal.Rptr. 575.)

There is another context in which a rebuttable presumption of imputed knowledge—and therefore, the use of ethical screens—has been adopted, that of the tainted *non-attorney employee.* When a tainted non-attorney employee of a law firm, possessing confidential case information, moves to an opposing law firm, vicarious disqualification of the opposing law firm is not necessary if the employee is effectively screened. [*In re Complex Asbestos Litig.,* 232 Cal. App. 3d 572 (1991).] The same rule applies to a non-retained expert, who is then employed by the opposing side. (*Shadow Traffic Network v. Superior Court* (1994) 24 Cal.App.4th 1067, 1084–1085.) Indeed, a rebuttable presumption applies *within an expert firm,* allowing an expert firm to ethically screen an expert who interviewed with a plaintiff from an expert retained by the defendant in the same matter. (*Western Digital Corp. v. Superior Court* (1998) 60 Cal.App.4th 1471, 1485.)

In all of these situations-government employees, former government employees, non-attorney employees, experts, and expert firms-the presumption of imputed knowledge is rebuttable, not conclusive. Moreover, the use of a rebuttable presumption is not justified as a "necessary evil" in order to advance important policy considerations. Instead, the rebuttable presumption is accepted because it is believed that, under the proper circumstances, ethical screening can work. There is no legitimate reason to believe that the same screening could not work in the context of private attorneys at a private firm. For example, in *City of Santa Barbara v. Superior Court,* [122 Cal.App.4th 17, 27 (2004)] the court upheld an ethical wall in a government office, and stated, "*Like all attorneys,* [the tainted attorney] knows that her participation and use of confidential information against a former client would subject her to a host of problems including tort liability and state bar discipline. Such conduct would be a recipe for financial and professional suicide. We are confident that an attorney's oath and the severe consequences that would inexorably flow from a breach thereof, coupled with [an effective] 'ethical wall,' are sufficient to safeguard the former clients' confidences and preserve the integrity of the judicial process." (Emphasis added.) We agree. These same considerations, and a proper ethical wall, can also be sufficient in the case of a tainted private attorney at a private firm.

c. *Policy Considerations*

Plaintiffs argue that there should be an irrebuttable presumption of imputed knowledge and automatic disqualification in order to "preserve public trust in the scrupulous administration of justice and the integrity of the bar."[8] We agree that preservation of the public trust is a policy con-

[8] FN27. Additionally, amici in support of plaintiffs argue that even if an ethical wall may be factually effective, the presence of a tainted attorney at opposing counsel's firm gives rise to an appearance of impropriety which the courts should not countenance. California courts, however, are in agreement that the mere *appearance* of a conflict is not sufficient to justify disqualifying an attorney from a representation. (See *In re Jasmine S.* (2007) 153 Cal.App.4th 835, 843,

sideration of the highest order. However, it is *just one* of the many policy interests which must be balanced by a trial court considering a disqualification motion, and we are not prepared to say that this interest *always* outweighs the opposing party's right to counsel of its choice. We reiterate the policy considerations to be taken into consideration in a motion for disqualification: (1) a client's right to chosen counsel; (2) an attorney's interest in representing a client; (3) the financial burden on a client to replace disqualified counsel; (4) the possibility that tactical abuse underlies the disqualification motion; (5) the need to maintain ethical standards of professional responsibility; and (6) the preservation of public trust in the scrupulous administration of justice and the integrity of the bar.

In this regard, we find persuasive the following analysis of the ABA Standing Committee on Ethics and Professional Responsibility: "[F]raming the issue of imputation as a choice between client protection and lawyer mobility presents a false choice. Clients *must* be protected, and their confidence (as well as that of the public) in their lawyers' promise to keep their secrets must be preserved. The question is not *whether* but *how* that should be accomplished. No one contends that the lawyer himself may represent others against a former client on substantially related matters after moving to a new firm. [The Model Rules are] unequivocal on this subject. In addition, no one disputes that the confidentiality duty continues after termination of the client-lawyer relationship. If a lawyer breaches that duty, she is subject to discipline, whether she has changed firms or not. Screening is a mechanism to give effect to the duty of confidentiality, not a tool to undermine it." (ABA Standing Committee on Ethics and Professional Responsibility, Recommendation 109 (February 16, 2009) pp. 10–11; italics in original.) The Standing Committee further noted, "Although much of the debate over lateral screening has been focused on the concerns of the clients of the lateral's former firm, there is a parallel set of interests: after a transferring lawyer has been hired, every imputed disqualification based on the unavailability of screening results in a client that loses its law firm of choice. The harm to all such clients is real, not theoretical. Often the disqualification of a firm, based upon an imputed conflict of a newly-hired lawyer, occurs after a manner is well under way and the affected client has spent substantial sums in fees. Typically, such clients have played no part in the circumstances that led to the imputed disqualification, yet they suffer the cost, disruption, and delay resulting from it. [¶]. . . . Thus, clients have interests on both sides of the screening question. Screening does not solve all such problems, but reduces them to situations where the interests of the former

---

63 Cal.Rptr.3d 593; *Hetos Investments, Ltd. v. Kurtin, supra,* 110 Cal.App.4th at p. 40, 1 Cal.Rptr.3d 472; *Gregori v. Bank of America* (1989) 207 Cal.App.3d 291, 306–307, 254 Cal.Rptr. 853.)

clients cannot adequately be addressed by the screening mechanism." (*Id.* at pp. 11–12.). . . .

In short, the general policy concern of "client protection" is not merely the interest in protecting client confidences which would weigh in favor of vicarious disqualification in all cases. It is, instead, a two-fold concern, which also implicates the interest in protecting a client who has established a longstanding relationship with counsel, and is at risk of losing that attorney by means of vicarious disqualification, through no fault of the client (or the client's attorney). A properly established ethical screen can satisfy both concerns-protecting client confidences from being used against the client by the tainted attorney's new firm, while still protecting the opposing client's longstanding attorney-client relationship.

In the days prior to large law firms, when there was limited firm-to-firm mobility, the latter concern was rarely implicated in cases involving vicarious disqualification. Now, however, with the proliferation of multi-office "mega-firms," frequent firm mergers, and attorneys increasingly changing firms throughout their careers, clients are at greater risk of finding their longstanding attorney-client relationships challenged due solely to their counsel's changing affiliations.

We hasten to add that we are not here attempting to effect a balancing of the policy interests in this case-this will be a matter for the trial court on remand. We do conclude, however, that, in certain cases, the public trust in the scrupulous administration of justice is not advanced (and, in fact, may be undermined) by an order disqualifying a party's long-term counsel due to the presence of another attorney in a different office of the same firm, who possesses only a small amount of potentially relevant confidential information, *and* has been *effectively* screened.

5. *The Elements of an Effective Screen*

Once the moving party in a motion for disqualification has established that an attorney is tainted with confidential information, a rebuttable presumption arises that the attorney shared that information with the attorney's law firm.The burden then shifts to the challenged law firm to establish "that the practical effect of formal screening has been achieved. The showing must satisfy the trial court that the [tainted attorney] has not had and will not have any involvement with the litigation, or any communication with attorneys or [ ]employees concerning the litigation, that would support a reasonable inference that the information has been used or disclosed."

The specific elements of an effective screen will vary from case to case, although two elements are necessary: First, the screen must be timely imposed; a firm must impose screening measures when the conflict first arises.[9] It is not sufficient to wait until the trial court imposes screening measures as part of its order on the disqualification motion. Second, it is not sufficient to simply produce declarations stating that confidential information was not conveyed or that the disqualified attorney did not work on the case; an effective wall involves the imposition of *preventive measures* to guarantee that information will not be conveyed. "To avoid inadvertent disclosures and establish an evidentiary record, a memorandum should be circulated warning the legal staff to isolate the [tainted] individual from communications on the matter and to prevent access to the relevant files." (*In re Complex Asbestos Litigation, supra,* 232 Cal.App.3d at p. 594.)

"The typical elements of an ethical wall are: [1] physical, geographic, and departmental separation of attorneys; [2] prohibitions against and sanctions for discussing confidential matters; [3] established rules and procedures preventing access to confidential information and files; [4] procedures preventing a disqualified attorney from sharing in the profits from the representation; and [5] continuing education in professional responsibility." (*Henriksen, supra,* 11 Cal.App.4th at p. 116, fn. 6.) We briefly discuss the first four of these elements. We stress, however, that the inquiry before a trial court considering the efficacy of any particular ethical wall is *not* to determine whether all of a prescribed list of elements (beyond timeliness and the imposition of prophylactic measures) have been established; it is, instead, a case-by-case inquiry focusing on whether the court is satisfied that the tainted attorney has not had and will not have any improper communication with others at the firm concerning the litigation. . . .

An additional element favorably acknowledged in caselaw is that the disqualified attorney has no supervisory powers over the attorneys involved in the litigation, and vice-versa. This is similar to the factor discussed above, that the tainted attorney receive no compensation from the matter. If the attorneys handling the matter are *supervising* the tainted attorney; the tainted attorney may feel an obligation to assist the supervising attorneys in their representation. Likewise, if the tainted attorney is supervising the attorneys involved in the litigation, there could be concerns that the tainted attorney sets policies that might bear on the subordinates' handling of the litigation.

Although not discussed in the caselaw, we believe one additional factor, commonly noted in ethical rules governing imputed conflicts, should also be considered by trial courts in their analysis: notice to the former

---

[9] FN31. "[S]creening should be implemented before undertaking the challenged representation or hiring the tainted individual." (*In re Complex Asbestos Litigation, supra,* 232 Cal.App.3d at p. 594, 283 Cal.Rptr. 732.)

client.[10] ABA Model Rules for Professional Conduct, rule 1.10(a)(2), provides that, when a disqualified attorney is timely screened, "written notice [must be] promptly given to any affected former client to enable the former client to ascertain compliance with the provisions of this Rule, which shall include a description of the screening procedures employed; a statement of the firm's and of the screened lawyer's compliance with these Rules; a statement that review may be available before a tribunal; and an agreement by the firm to respond promptly to any written inquiries or objections by the former client about the screening procedures[. Additionally,] certifications of compliance with these Rules and with the screening procedures are [to be] provided to the former client by the screened lawyer and by a partner of the firm, at reasonable intervals upon the former client's written request and upon termination of the screening procedures.". . . .

We note that these are the "typical elements" of a wall. Each of these elements need not necessarily be present for an ethical wall to be sufficient to rebut the presumption of imputed knowledge. Any ethical wall must ultimately be judged by whether it is sufficient to meet its purpose: satisfying the trial court that the tainted attorney has not had and will not have any involvement with, or communication concerning, the litigation which would support a reasonable inference that confidential information was or will be disclosed.

6. *The Trial Court Erred in Ruling Vicarious Disqualification was Automatic*

In sum, we have concluded that, when a tainted attorney moves from one private law firm to another, the law gives rise to a rebuttable presumption of imputed knowledge to the law firm, which may be rebutted by evidence of effective ethical screening. However, if the tainted attorney was actually involved in the representation of the first client, and switches sides in the same case, no amount of screening will be sufficient, and the presumption of imputed knowledge is conclusive.

When considering a motion to disqualify a law firm on the basis of imputed knowledge, in a case where the presumption is rebuttable, a trial court should consider, on a case-by-case basis, whether the ethical screening imposed by the firm is effective to prevent the transmission of confidential information from the tainted attorney. Moreover, the court should consider all of the policy interests implicated by the disqualification motion, in determining how to exercise its discretion. In this case, the trial court concluded that automatic vicarious disqualification was the rule; this was error.

---

[10] FN36. As with the other elements, notice is not an element required in all cases in order for an ethical wall to rebut the presumption of imputed knowledge and prevent disqualification of the law firm.

However, the trial court also concluded that, even if ethical screening were permissible, the ethical screening wall in this case was breached and it was therefore ineffective. . . . that finding is not supported by the record, the court's conclusion that the ethical wall was ineffective [therefore] cannot stand. . . . Under normal circumstances, we would stop here and remand for the trial court to consider whether the provisions of Sonnenschein's ethical wall were *adequate* to rebut the presumption of imputed knowledge. The circumstances, however, have changed.

7. *Effect of Cohen's Departure From Sonnenschein*

On First American's motion, we have taken additional evidence on appeal. (Code Civ. Proc., § 909.) That evidence indicates that Cohen is no longer employed by Sonnenschein. This changes the inquiry the trial court is to make on remand.

The purpose of a disqualification order is prophylactic, not punitive. That is, the issue is whether there is a genuine likelihood that allowing the attorney to remain on the case will affect the outcome of the proceedings before the court. When considering vicarious disqualification of a firm based on the presence of a tainted attorney, the issue is whether there is a likelihood that other attorneys at the firm may receive and use the information possessed by the tainted attorney in the pending action.

However, once the tainted attorney has left the firm, vicarious disqualification is not necessary "where the evidence establishes that no one other than the departed attorney had any dealings with the client or obtained confidential information." (*Goldberg v. Warner/Chappell Music, Inc., supra,* 125 Cal.App.4th at p. 755.) Thus, the inquiry is no longer a prospective one, but a retrospective one. The trial court should not consider the *risk* of transmitting information from the tainted attorney to those involved in the challenged representation, but, instead, whether the tainted attorney *actually* conveyed confidential information. (*Id.* at p. 762; cf. *Adams v. Aerojet–General Corp., supra,* 86 Cal.App.4th at p. 1335.) As part of its inquiry, however, the trial court may consider the elements of the ethical wall constructed by Sonnenschein, as the strength of the wall may well be relevant to a determination of whether it is likely that confidential information was actually conveyed.

In this case, Cohen was present at the Sonnenschein firm for approximately one year. On remand, the trial court must determine whether Cohen's activities at the firm actually resulted in the improper transmission, directly or indirectly, of confidential information from Cohen to the First American team, or any other member of the Sonnenschein firm who may have worked on the related class actions. If (1) the Sonnenschein firm can overcome the rebuttable presumption that confidential information was transmitted, by offering sufficient evidence that confidential information was not, in fact, transmitted;[11] and (2) the trial court, in the exercise of its discretion, concludes that the implicated policy considerations favor allowing Sonnenschein to remain as counsel, the trial court should deny the motion for disqualification. If, however, the trial court concludes that (1) Sonnenschein has not sufficiently rebutted the presumption that confidential information was transmitted, or (2) despite a finding that confidential information was not transmitted, the competing policy considerations nonetheless mandate disqualification of the entire firm under the circumstances, the trial court should grant the motion for disqualification. We express no opinion on the resolution of any of these questions, which are for the trial court to determine in the first instance.

DISPOSITION

The order of disqualification of the Sonnenschein firm is reversed. The matter is remanded to the trial court for further proceedings not inconsistent with the views expressed herein. Each party shall pay its own costs on appeal.

CASE QUESTIONS

1. Was Cohen ever hired to represent the plaintiffs against First American?
2. Was Cohen at Sonnenschein by the time the appeal was decided?
3. What presumption does the court say may be rebutted by screening?
4. When does disqualification remain "automatic"?
5. What are the typical elements of an effective screen?
6. Does a firm have to employ all of them?
7. What rule governs imputation to a firm when the tainted attorney or attorneys have left the firm?

Kirk can be construed narrowly or broadly. The narrow view is that the case is basically one of confidences imparted during an initial interview that did not result in full-fledged representation; Model Rule 1.18 has allowed screening in such cases for some time. The broader view is that the opinion makes clear that, at least in California, a firm may use a proper screen to rebut the presumption of shared confidences when it hires a new lawyer from another firm.

---

[11] FN38. In this regard, we note that Sonnenschein did not provide declarations of all members of the First American team, nor a declaration from John Koski, the Sonnenschein partner who established the ethical wall after a "private discussion" with Cohen. Clearly, every Sonnenschein attorney who worked on the related class actions, as well as any other member of the Sonnenschein firm whom Cohen is claimed to have had reason or occasion to discuss information obtained from plaintiffs' counsel, should provide testimonial evidence. (*SpeeDee Oil, supra,* 20 Cal.4th at p. 1152, fn. 5, 86 Cal.Rptr.2d 816, 980 P.2d 371.)

As *Kirk* notes, after much debate the ABA adopted a general screening provision in February 2009. It is too early to tell whether this decision will lead to widespread adoption by states. Firms have long been able to employ screens to rebut the presumption of imputation from government attorneys who move to private practice. Model Rule 1.11 allows for screening in such cases, so long as the firm promptly notifies the government agency in question. Failure to comply with the notice provisions, however, can forfeit the protection screening procedures might otherwise provide. *See United States v. Philip Morris, Inc.*, 741 F.Supp.2d 970 (D. D.C. 2004).

Kirk retained the presumption of "automatic" disqualification when an attorney who has worked on a matter moves to the firm working on the opposite side of the same matter. Many courts have refused to recognize screens as rebutting the presumption of imputed knowledge in such "side switching" cases. For a recent case allowing a screen to rebut the presumption even where a lawyer switched sides, *see Silicon Graphics, Inc. v. ATI Techs., Inc.*, 741 F.Supp.2d 970 (W.D.Wis. 2010). The court relied on *Cromley v. Board of Education of Lockport Township High School District* 205, 17 F.3d 1059 (7th Cir.1994), "and other cases decided by the Court of Appeals for the Seventh Circuit in which the court has held that law firms may avoid imputation through appropriate screening mechanisms regardless of the scope of the work performed for the former client by the disqualified lawyer."

Keep a List of Matters and Clients and Make it Clear

Because your knowledge may be imputed to a firm that hires you it is critical that you keep a list of matters and clients about which you have confidential information. If you have confidential information from non-clients, as in *Westinghouse*, this list must include such non-clients as well. If you do not have an accurate list then your new firm may be blindsided with disqualification motions based on your prior work. That is hardly getting off on the right foot. (It is one thing for a firm to assume the risk of losing work as a cost of hiring you; it is a very different thing for a firm to find out it will lose work only *after* hiring you.)

It is important for this list to be clear. *Lennartson v. Anoka–Hennepin Indep. School Dist. No. 11,* 662 N.W.2d 125, 126 (Minn.2003), illustrates why. Susanne Fisher was a junior associate at a firm that represented a plaintiff suing a school district for sexual harassment by two district employees. While the case was pending, she moved to the firm that represented the district. According to the court, "[i]n her 'conflicts and screening report,' Fischer disclosed that she had done 'isolated work' in the Lennartson case, which she elaborated to mean she had filled in for [her boss] on one deposition and had no involvement before or after that deposition."

"Isolated work" is not a precise term. Ms. Fischer took only one deposition but she deposed the supervisor of the men who allegedly harassed her client. He was probably an important witness and a competent lawyer would have learned the case well before deposing him. As noted above, Ms. Fischer would be presumed to have learned what a reasonably competent lawyer would have learned in doing the work she did, which means she would be presumed to know a lot. So while the deposition might be "isolated" in the sense that it probably took only one day, courts likely would not treat the deposition as "isolated work" in terms of the information Ms. Fischer would need to have had to do her job.

As things turned out, Ms. Fischer's description of her work apparently led the firm to believe she had done nothing significant on the case and the firm therefore could rebut the presumption of shared confidences by screening her from the matter. (Minnesota's rules allow screening for lawyers who have some confidential information from their prior work but only if that information is unlikely to be significant in the later matter.) The firm was ultimately disqualified, putting both Ms. Fischer and the lawyer who screened her for conflicts in a potentially (and perhaps actually) awkward position.

You may be wondering how you could give a prospective employer enough information to run a meaningful conflicts check without disclosing confidential information in violation of Rule 1.6. Good question. The answer is that before the ABA acted in 2012, lawyers simply acted as if an exception were implied by necessity. They provided as little information as they could while providing enough for a prospective employer to run a conflicts check. In 2012 the ABA approved Rule 1.6(b)(7), which allows disclosure a lawyer reasonably believes necessary "to detect and resolve conflicts of interest arising from the lawyer's change of employment or from changes in the composition or ownership of a firm" so long as disclosure does not prejudice clients.

Conflicts and the "Common Interest" Exception to Privilege Waiver

You will recall from chapter 5 that attorneys representing clients with a common legal interest often enter into joint representation agreements, so that they may invoke the common interest exception to waiver and thereby share privileged information without waiving the privilege. What happens if a lawyer who is party to and receives information under such an agreement moves to a firm that opposes the interests of one of the other parties to the agreement (though not the lawyer's client)? Must all parties to the agreement consent to the lawyer's move in order for the firm to avoid disqualification? Working from the other direction, suppose a lawyer (L_1) has information from a previous representation about Client X, and the lawyer joins an agreement to which some other lawyer currently opposing Client X (L_2) is a party. Does L_1's information taint L_2?

There is little authority on such questions, but there is some reason to believe the answer to the first question is "yes" while the answer to the second is "no." *In re Gabapentin Patent Litig.*, 407 F. Supp. 2d 607, 608 (D. N.J. 2005), involved two lawyers, Scott Lindvall and Patricia Clarke. They worked at a firm called Darby & Darby, and while there represented the Ivax Corporation, a defendant in a patent infringement matter. The litigation involved several defendants and Ivax was party to a joint defense agreement among them. Pursuant to this agreement, Lindvall and Clarke obtained privileged information from counsel for the other defendants. Darby & Darby stopped representing Ivax in 2003.

In 2005, Lindvall and Clarke decided to move to the Kaye Scholer firm. At the time, that firm represented Pfizer, the patentee who was the plaintiff in the Gabapentin action, in some matters. Kaye Scholer did not then represent Pfizer in the Gabapentin case but it knew that it might be asked to do so. Kaye Scholer obtained Ivax's consent to Lindvall and Clarke's moving to Kaye Scholer, subject to the firm's promise that it would screen them from two matters (including the Gabapentin case) as to which Pfizer was adverse to Ivax. Kaye Scholer did not seek the consent of other parties to the Gabapentin joint defense agreement. It took the position that it did not need the consent of these parties because Lindvall and Clarke never represented them.

Lindvall and Clarke moved to Kaye Scholer in April 2005. In September 2005, Pfizer substituted Kaye Scholer in as counsel for Pfizer in the Gabapentin case. Defendants who were parties to the joint defense agreement (including Ivax) then moved to disqualify Kaye Scholer on the ground that Lindvall and Clarke were prohibited from representing Pfizer in the matter and that their disqualification tainted the entire firm.

The court agreed. It held that Ivax had consented to the representation but that the consent of the other parties to the Gabapentin joint defense agreement was required as well. Excerpts from its opinion follow:

> The . . . Defendants argue that, based on the JDA and their actions pursuant thereto, disqualification of Kaye Scholer is still required because, unlike Ivax, they did not consent to waive the right to assert this conflict of interest. Neither Kaye Scholer nor Mr. Lindvall and Ms. Clarke dispute that Mr. Lindvall and Ms. Clarke acquired knowledge of the co-defendants' confidential information when participating in joint defense meetings. Rather, Kaye Scholer argues that it owes its ethical obligations only to Ivax because only Ivax was Mr. Lindvall's and Ms. Clarke's former client; that Ivax waived its right to object to Kaye Scholer's representation of Pfizer; and that its ethical screen, the efficacy of which is unchallenged, is sufficient to

> protect the co-defendants' confidences. The necessary import of Kaye Scholer's position is that Ivax, as one party to a joint defense agreement, can unilaterally waive the right to object to a conflict of interest for all other parties to the same agreement, as long as a screen is in place to protect the co-defendants' confidences. In assessing this position, the Court must consider whether the JDA (and actions taken pursuant thereto) created a fiduciary relationship or implied attorney-client relationship among all the parties thereto and their respective counsel, thus placing the co-defendants in a position to seek disqualification of Kaye Scholer. . . .
>
> An examination of the terms of the JDA reveals a clear intent that any voluntarily-shared information would remain confidential and be protected by the attorney-client privilege. For example, the JDA states that the signatories are required to "take all steps necessary to maintain the privileged and confidential nature of the information." The terms of the JDA and the undisputed performance thereunder are sufficient for the Court to conclude that an implied attorney-client relationship arose between Mr. Lindvall and Ms. Clarke, as counsel for Ivax, and the other First–Wave Defendants, by virtue of their joint participation in the defense of the Gabapentin matter. . . .
>
> Although there is no reason to doubt the efficacy of Kaye Scholer's screen or the integrity of Kaye Scholer, Mr. Lindvall and Ms. Clarke in complying with that screen, screening in this circumstance is insufficient. It is undisputed that Mr. Lindvall and Ms. Clarke had primary responsibility for Ivax's defense in the same matter (the Gabapentin action) in which Kaye Scholer now seeks to represent plaintiff Pfizer. As counsel for Ivax, they were privy to actual confidences of the other First–Wave Defendants. Out of these circumstances arose a fiduciary and implied attorney-client relationship between Mr. Lindvall and Ms. Clarke and the other First–Wave Defendants. The Court concludes that these relationships must be imputed to Kaye Scholer as well.

Essex Chem. Corp. v. Hartford Accident & Indem. Co., 993 F.Supp. 241 (D. N.J. 1998), reached a different result. In August 1993, Essex sued its insurers seeking a declaration that their insurance polices covered certain environmental claims. The Home Insurance Company was one of Essex's primary insurers. In 1996, Home and the other defendant insurers entered into a joint defense agreement. Home was represented in this matter by the Skadden firm.

In May 1988, Skadden had represented Essex in connection with a takeover attempt. Essex learned of this during the deposition of a former in-house attorney and, in 1997, filed a motion to disqualify Skadden as well as the five other defense firms representing the other insurers who were parties to the JDA.

Skadden withdrew voluntarily. The magistrate granted the motion as to the other firms. The Magistrate Judge stated: " 'I presume that such confidential and privileged information has been shared between all participants to the Joint Defense Agreement, despite defense counsel's certifications to the contrary.' The Magistrate Judge therefore concluded that allowing defense counsel to remain posed indirectly the same risk that Skadden's representation posed directly."

The district court reversed. Excerpts from its opinion follow:

> The law governing imputation of knowledge and disqualification is decidedly less clear where, as here, a party seeks to disqualify all counsel for all members of a joint defense consortium where a firm representing one member has previously represented a now-adverse party in a substantially related matter. . . .
>
> In a formal ethics opinion, the American Bar Association Committee on Ethics and Professional Responsibility addressed the obligations of a lawyer who represented a client who was a member of a joint defense consortium, subsequently changed firms, and was asked to file suit against other members of the consortium in a matter related to the former representation. *See* ABA Comm. on Ethics and Professional Responsibility, Formal Op. 395 (1995). The Committee opined that to the extent the attorney had received confidential information regarding other members of the defense consortium, the attorney might owe an obligation to his former client not to disclose such confidences, based on the client's obligation to the other members. As to whether the attorney had any direct obligation to other consortium members who, by virtue of the terms of the defense consortium agreement were not his clients, but from whom the attorney had received confidences, the Committee stated: "Lawyer would almost surely have a fiduciary obligation to the other members of the consortium, which might well lead to his disqualification." *Id.* In opining that the attorney would "almost surely" have a fiduciary obligation, the ABA did not state whether under the RPC's the attorney bore any ethical obligation to the other consortium members. . . .
>
> The Court finds that the Magistrate Judge's application of an irrebuttable presumption of shared confidences among Skadden and all defense counsel was improper. . . . In effect, the Magistrate Judge applied an irrebuttable presumption of shared confidences between Skadden and all defense counsel, making a double imputation

> of knowledge: first from the Skadden attorneys involved in the 1988 litigation to all Skadden attorneys, then from Skadden to all defense counsel. In so ruling, the Magistrate Judge refused to consider defendants' certifications stating that no Essex confidences had been relayed from Skadden to other defense counsel, declared that defendants' invocation of the joint defense privilege would render rebuttal impossible and deemed any showing of shared confidences unnecessary based on his finding that the Joint Defense Agreement created an implied attorney-client relationship between Essex and each member of the defense counsel group.
>
> Numerous courts . . . have rejected a per se rule of double imputation. As those authorities explained, under a per se rule of double imputation, knowledge acquired by one attorney is imputed to all attorneys associated in his firm; that same knowledge is then re-imputed to any attorney in a second firm with whom any member of the first firm becomes associated, based on multiple irrebuttable presumptions that members of the respective firms have shared client confidences. . . .
>
> [W]here knowledge is not actual, but imputed based on the presumption that members of a firm share confidences, automatic re-imputation of that same knowledge to another attorney with whom the vicariously disqualified attorney collaborated is unreasonable. The common thread among the cited authorities is their requirement of a painstaking factual analysis before disqualifying an attorney given the risk of interminable disqualification posed by an imputation-on-imputation rule. Such an analysis requires the trial court to ascertain the material facts in a manner consistent with effectuating any legitimately claimed privilege. The Magistrate Judge's efforts here fell short of what is appropriate.

The court remanded for a hearing on whether other firms representing parties to the JDA had received confidential information from Skadden; the hearing was to include "an examination of the provisions of the Joint Defense Agreement, which defendants have not submitted, and which will define and outline the relationship and obligations among the members of the defense consortium."

Information Transmitted to Non–Lawyers: The Expert Witness Problem

What happens if one party retains an expert as a consultant, whose identity is not disclosed, and who is then contacted by the opposing party?

This situation arose in *Shandralina G. v. Homonchuk*, 147 Cal.App.4th 395, 398 (2007). In February 2005, Defendant's counsel retained a Dr. Landers to consult with them regarding malpractice allegations asserted by Shandralina G.

In July 2005, shortly before the time for designating experts, one of Shandralina's lawyers contacted Landers to ask if he would consult with them. Landers apparently had forgotten that he had signed up with the defense, for he told plaintiff's counsel he would work with them. They then sent him some of Shandralina's medical records. When defense counsel learned of this, they moved to disqualify Shandralina's lawyers, asserting that their contact with Landers created a rebuttable presumption that he had provided them confidential information about the defense. The trial court granted the motion.

The court of appeals reversed. It held that the party seeking disqualification must show that the non-attorney whose conduct is the basis for the motion actually obtained confidential information. (Because *Shandralina* involved an expert, we will just use that term.) Once the moving party shows the expert received confidential information, the rule depends on whether the moving party is able to discover from the expert the contents of her communications with the lawyers for the opposing party.

If the party seeking disqualification can discover from the expert what information the expert conveyed to the other side, then no presumption that such information was conveyed will attach. The party seeking disqualification will bear the burden of proving that the expert both received confidential information and disclosed it to the other side.

If the expert has severed all ties with the moving party, however, and refuses to communicate with them, then the court presumes that the expert conveyed confidential information to the other side and the burden shifts to the party whose disqualification is sought to rebut that presumption. (Note that unlike the substantial relationship test for attorney disqualification, this presumption is rebuttable.)

The logic of this distinction is that the presumption makes sense only when the moving party has no ability to secure the evidence it needs to establish its right to disqualification. If it can secure such evidence, the presumption is not needed. Thus, the court reversed the disqualification order because "there was no legal impediment to Doctor's ability to obtain evidence from Landers on the content of the conversation to satisfy the burden of proof."

E. NON-CLIENT INFORMATION AND AFFILIATED ENTITIES

One of the harder problems in conflicts analysis comes up when a firm has information from an entity that has a business relationship with the firm's client but is not itself the client. For example, may a firm represent a parent company and simultaneously act adversely to a subsidiary of that company? Cases in this area tend to turn on the facts; general rules are hard to discern.

For example, the court in *Morrison Knudsen Corp. v. Hancock, Rothert & Bunshoft, LLP*, 69 Cal.App.4th 223, 226 (1999), affirmed disqualification of a law firm that represented a plaintiff suing a corporate subsidiary of a company that bought insurance from an insurer the firm also represented. The court did not consider the situation to create a contemporaneous conflict but, on the facts of the case, it concluded that in representing the insurance company the firm received information about how the corporate parent company dealt with litigation. The corporate parent controlled the legal affairs of the subsidiary. In representing the insurer, the firm learned information about patterns and practices the corporate parent employed in dealing with litigation, which could be useful in predicting how the parent would deal with the litigation in which the firm was adverse to the subsidiary.

The court discussed two approaches to the parent/subsidiary problem mentioned above. One of these was outlined in Formal Opinion 1989–113 of the California state bar's committee on professional responsibility and conduct. The opinion concluded that as a default matter a corporate parent and its subsidiary are separate entities and a lawyer does not act disloyally to one by acting adversely to the other. In some situations, however, the facts might imply that such adversity exists. The opinion discussed the "alter ego exception," under which two corporations that satisfy corporate law standards for being treated as the alter ego of each other should be treated as one corporation for conflicts purposes. Facts relevant to this inquiry include "the separateness of the entities involved, whether corporate formalities are observed, [and] the extent to which each entity has distinct and independent managements and board of directors. . . . "

A second approach traces to ABA Formal Opinion 95–390, which stated companies need not be alter egos of each other to be treated as one for conflicts purposes. It is enough if the facts show that representation of one company entailed the receipt of confidential information from the other in circumstances creating an obligation not to use the information to harm any member of the corporate family.

The *Morrison Knudsen* court favored the second approach, which it referred to as the "unity of interests test." According to the court,

> The alter ego test . . . was not developed to deal with conflict issues and in our view it does not work very well in conflicts cases. It involves many considerations which are irrelevant in conflicts cases, and omits others which may be highly relevant. Thus, while the test may be one standard among others for judging corporate relationships in conflicts cases, we do not think it can properly be viewed as the *sole* standard. . . .
>
> Many of the factors used to determine whether corporations are alter egos may have little or no bearing on whether they should be treated as one entity for purposes of attorney conflicts of interest. Undercapitalization, for example, is viewed as a "highly relevant factor" in alter ego cases but is not emphasized in any of the conflict of interest authorities. Undercapitalization, financial misrepresentation, commingling of assets and the like are important in alter ego cases because the alter ego rules were developed primarily for the protection of creditors. Such considerations, however, are not at the heart of the problem when the issue is whether the corporation should be protected from its attorneys. . . .
>
> Another reason why the alter ego test is a less than optimal solution is that it does not encompass considerations which may be central to an alleged conflict. It seems to us, for example, that where, as here, an attorney has received information from one affiliate which is substantially related to a claim against another affiliate, the attorney should ordinarily be disqualified from advancing that claim against the other affiliate. . . . Something different, and in general something less, than an alter ego finding may justify the treatment of corporate affiliates as one entity for conflict purposes. . . .

Faughn v. Perez, 145 Cal.App.4th 592, 595 (2006), illustrates the importance of facts to this analysis. There the court reversed an order disqualifying an attorney, Silberberg, who represented a woman in a medical malpractice case against a hospital and other defendants. The claims were based on injuries to an infant and her mother during childbirth. Silberberg entered the case in 2005. The defendant hospital was owned by a nonprofit corporation, which owned about 40 hospitals in California, Nevada, and Arizona. Between 2000 and 2003, the parent corporation had retained Silberberg to defend other hospitals it owned (but not the defendant hospital in this case) in five childbirth malpractice cases.

The record showed that the parent company controlled the defense in all its cases, including this case and the cases Silberberg had defended. On the other hand, the record suggested that individual hospitals played some role in managing their defenses, and that the parent company's policies might vary among different regions, and that the defendant hospital in this case was in a different region than the hospitals Silberberg had defended. The court found the defendant had not established a substantial relationship between Silberberg's previous representations and his suit against the hospital.

In *Volkswagen Aktiengesellschaft v. Novelty, Inc.*, 247 F. Supp. 2d 1076, 1077 (S.D. Ind. 2003), in contrast, the court disqualified a lawyer, Woodard, who had once represented Continental, a firm that investigated trademark infringement for trademark owners. Volkswagen was a large client of Continental. One of Woodard's assignments for Continental involved researching defenses raised by a third party, Galyan, which Volkswagen had accused of trademark infringement. In this capacity he dealt both with Continental and Volkswagen personnel.

After Woodard stopped representing Continental and (as the court found) Volkswagen, he was hired by Novelty, Inc. to defend a trademark action brought by Volkswagen. The court found the matters substantially related: "VW's case against Galyan's, like its action against Novelty, was for trademark infringement and dilution, specifically involving VW's interest in its logo and nomenclature pertaining to the 'Beetle' and the 'Bug.' Pl.Ex. B–1, Complaint. This is enough to create a presumption that the law firm conducting the research and investigation, and participating in the strategizing of issues relating to VW's action against Galyan's, "could have obtained confidential information in the first representation that would have been relevant in the second."

The Main Points to Recall From Chapter 11(D)–(E) Are:

- The main value at stake in subsequent representation is the duty of confidentiality.
- Lawyers may not represent a client in a matter adverse to a former client if the current matter is substantially related to the former matter.
- Whether matters are substantially related depends on the facts of the two matters and the relationship of those facts to the legal issues at stake.
- Receipt of confidential information from non-clients may create conflicts where the information is substantially related to a subsequent matter and the source of the information had a reasonable expectation that it would not be used against them.
- For conflict purposes, separate entities are considered separate unless the facts of a particular case justify treating them as one for conflicts purposes; corporate law doctrines are not dispositive.

- The basic rules regarding presumed knowledge and imputation of knowledge are:

(a) If you do work in which a reasonable lawyer would have acquired confidential information regarding a client you will be deemed to have acquired such information regardless whether you actually learned it—the presumption that you acquired such information is not rebuttable; this presumption means you may not act adversely to a former client in a matter substantially related to your prior work for that client; this prohibition applies to you regardless whether you are at the firm where you did the work or have moved to another firm;

(b) Confidential information you learn while working at a firm is imputed to every other lawyer then working at the firm and their knowledge is imputed to you while you work at the firm; this presumption is not rebuttable;

(c) If you leave a firm you may rebut the presumption that you knew what other lawyers at the firm knew; to do so you must show that while at the firm you did not actually acquire confidential information relating to some matter and did no work in which a reasonable lawyer would be expected to have acquired confidential information regarding the matter;

(d) If you leave a firm the firm may rebut the presumption that other lawyers there knew the information you knew about some matter; to do so the firm must show that no lawyer remaining at the firm retains confidential information regarding the matter;

(e) If you move from one firm to another the law varies on what happens to the firm that hires you: (1) Under the traditional rule and the law applied in some jurisdictions, confidential information you possess from your prior work is imputed to the new firm as if you learned it while working there; (2) There is an exception to this rule if you worked for the government before joining the new firm; in such cases the firm may rebut the presumed imputation of your information to other lawyers in the firm by effectively screening you from any matter related to your prior work; (3) Even if you joined the new firm from another private firm, some jurisdictions, and Model Rule 1.10, allow your new firm to rebut this presumption by effectively screening you from a matter in which other lawyers in the firm act adversely to your former client, even in a matter substantially related to your work for that client; (4) Other jurisdictions allow screening only if you did not perform substantial work on the relevant matter while at a prior firm.

F. CLIENT CONSENT

Under Model Rules 1.7(b)(4) and 1.9(a) clients may consent to allow their lawyer or former lawyer to undertake a matter the conflicts rules otherwise would bar her from taking so long as the consent is informed and confirmed in writing. Under the Model Rule 1.7(b) consent to concurrent conflicts may be sought only if a lawyer reasonably believes he could fulfill his obligations to both clients. Rule 1.7(b)(3) creates an exception to consent; it provides parties opposing each other in litigation cannot consent to have the same lawyer represent each of them.

Consent does not relieve a lawyer of her duties of loyalty, care, and confidentiality. A lawyer still owes those duties to their full extent, and may face civil liability for breach of those duties. And consent is only as good as the information on which it is based. A lawyer who does not give the client full information about the nature of a conflict and the advantages and disadvantages of consenting to a conflict may find that courts or disciplinary officials refuse to recognize the consent. Conversely, if a client knows all that information the client's consent might be found valid even if a lawyer failed to provide adequate disclosure.

The following cases explore these concepts. The first shows the parameters of consent. The second shows how not to obtain consent. The third shows how to do things right, including how to obtain consent to a future conflict that was not certain to occur at the time consent was given.

Restatement (Third) of the Law Governing Lawyers § 122

KLEMM V. SUPERIOR COURT

75 Cal.App.3d 893, 142 Cal.Rptr. 509 (1977)

GEO. A. BROWN, PRESIDING JUSTICE.

The ultimate issue herein is to what extent one attorney may represent both husband and wife in a noncontested dissolution proceeding where the written consent of each to such representation has been filed with the court.

Dale Klemm (hereinafter "husband") and Gail Klemm (hereinafter "wife") were married and are the parents of two minor children. They separated after six years of marriage, and the wife filed a petition for dissolution of the marriage in propria persona. There was no community property, and neither party owned any substantial personal property. Both parties waived spousal support. The husband was a carpenter with part-time employment.

At the dissolution hearing Attorney Catherine Bailey appeared for the wife. It developed that Bailey is a friend of the husband and wife and because they could not afford an attorney she was acting without compensation. The attorney had consulted with both the husband and wife and had worked out an oral agreement whereby the custody of the minor children would be joint, that is, each would have the children for a period of two weeks out of each month, and the wife waived child support.

The trial judge granted an interlocutory decree and awarded joint custody in accord with the agreement. However, because the wife was receiving aid for dependent children payments from the county, he referred the matter of child support to the Family Support Division of the Fresno County District Attorney's office for investigation and report.

The subsequent report from the family support division recommended that the husband be ordered to pay $25 per month per child (total $50) child support and that this amount be paid to the county as reimbursement for past and present A.F.D.C. payments made and being made to the wife. Bailey, on behalf of the wife, filed a written objection to the recommendation that the husband be required to pay child support.

At the hearing on the report and issue of child support on April 25, 1977, Bailey announced she was appearing on behalf of the husband. She said the parties were "in agreement on this matter, so there is in reality no conflict between them." No written consents to joint representation were filed. On questioning by the court the wife evinced uncertainty as to her position in the litigation. The wife said, "She (Bailey) asked me to come here just as a witness, so I don't feel like I'm taking any action against Dale." The judge pointed out that she (the wife) was still a party. When first asked if she wanted Bailey to continue as her attorney she answered "No." Later she said she would consent to Bailey's being relieved as her counsel. She then said she didn't believe she could act as her own attorney but that she consented to Bailey's representing the husband. After this confusing and conflicting testimony and a request for permission to talk to Bailey about it, the judge ordered, over Bailey's objection, that he would not permit Bailey to appear for either the husband or the wife because of a present conflict of interest and ordered the matter continued for one week.

At the continued hearing on May 2, 1977, Bailey appeared by counsel, who filed written consents to joint representation signed by the husband and wife and requested that Bailey be allowed to appear for the husband and wife (who were present in court). The consents, which were identical in form, stated:

> "I have been advised by my attorney that a potential conflict of interest exists by reason of her advising and representing my ex-spouse as well as myself. I feel this conflict is purely technical and I request Catherine Bailey to represent me."

The court denied the motion, and the husband and wife have petitioned this court for a writ of mandate to direct the trial court to permit such representation. . . . The California cases are generally consistent [in] permitting dual representation where there is a full disclosure and informed consent by all the parties, at least insofar as a representation pertains to agreements and negotiations prior to a trial or hearing. . . . Where, however, a fully informed consent is not obtained, the duty of loyalty to different clients renders it impossible for an attorney, consistent with ethics and the fidelity owed to clients, to advise one client as to a disputed claim against the other.

Though an informed consent be obtained, no case we have been able to find sanctions dual representation of conflicting interests if that representation is in conjunction with a trial or hearing where there is an actual, present, existing conflict and the discharge of duty to one client conflicts with the duty to another. As a matter of law a purported consent to dual representation of litigants with adverse interests at a contested hearing would be neither intelligent nor informed. Such representation would be per se inconsistent with the adversary position of an attorney in litigation, and common sense dictates that it would be unthinkable to permit an attorney to assume a position at a trial or hearing where he could not advocate the interests of one client without adversely injuring those of the other.

However, if the conflict is merely potential, there being no existing dispute or contest between the parties represented as to any point in litigation, then with full disclosure to and informed consent of both clients there may be dual representation at a hearing or trial.

In our view the case at bench clearly falls within the latter category. The conflict of interest was strictly potential and not present. The parties had settled their differences by agreement. There was no point of difference to be litigated. The position of each inter se was totally consistent throughout the proceedings. The wife did not want child support from the husband, and the husband did not want to pay support for the children. The actual conflict that existed on the issue of support was between the county on the one hand, which argued that support should be ordered, and the husband and wife on the other who consistently maintained the husband should not be ordered to pay support.

While on the face of the matter it may appear foolhardy for the wife to waive child support, other values could very well have been more important to her than such support such as maintaining a good relationship between the husband and the children and between the husband and herself despite the marital problems thus avoiding the backbiting, acrimony and ill will which the Family Relations Act of 1970 was, insofar as possible, designed to eliminate. It could well have been if the wife was forced to choose between A.F.D.C. payments to be reimbursed to the county by the husband and no A.F.D.C. payments she would have made the latter choice.

Of course, if the wife at some future date should change her mind and seek child support and if the husband should desire to avoid the payment of such support, Bailey would be disqualified from representing either in a contested hearing on the issue. (Rules of Prof. Conduct, rule 4–101; *Goldstein v. Lees* (1975) 46 Cal.App.3d 614.) There would then exist an actual conflict between them, and an attorney's duty to maintain the confidence of each would preclude such representation. . . .

We hold on the facts of this case, wherein the conflict was only potential, that if the written consents were knowing and informed and given after full disclosure by the attorney, the attorney can appear for both of the parties on issues concerning which they fully agree. . . .

Finally, as a caveat, we hasten to sound a note of warning. Attorneys who undertake to represent parties with divergent interests owe the highest duty to each to make a full disclosure of all facts and circumstances which are necessary to enable the parties to make a fully informed decision regarding the subject matter of the litigation, including the areas of potential conflict and the possibility and desirability of seeking independent legal advice. (*Ishmael v. Millington* (1966) 241 Cal.App.2d 520.) Failing such disclosure, the attorney is civilly liable to the client who suffers loss caused by lack of disclosure. (*Lysick v. Walcom, supra*, 258 Cal.App.2d 136.) In addition, the lawyer lays himself open to charges, whether well founded or not, of unethical and unprofessional conduct. (*Arden v. State Bar, supra,* 52 Cal.2d 310.) Moreover, the validity of any agreement negotiated without independent representation of each of the parties is vulnerable to easy attack as having been procured by misrepresentation, fraud and overreaching. (*Gregory v. Gregory* (1949) 92 Cal.App.2d 343.) It thus behooves counsel to cogitate carefully and proceed cautiously before placing himself/herself in such a position. . . .

It is ordered that a peremptory writ of mandate issue directing the trial court to reconsider Bailey's motion to be allowed to represent both husband and wife, that the court determine if the consent given by each was knowing and informed after a full disclosure by the attorney, and to decide the motion in accordance with the principles set forth in this opinion.

IMAGE TECH SERVICES, INC. V. EASTMAN KODAK CO.

820 F.Supp. 1212 (N.D. Cal. 1993)

CAULFIELD, DISTRICT JUDGE.

Defendant Eastman Kodak Company ("Kodak") brings a motion to disqualify plaintiffs' counsel, the Coudert Brothers Law Firm ("Coudert"). Upon consideration of the briefs and arguments of the parties, and good cause appearing therefrom, Kodak's motion to disqualify the Coudert firm is GRANTED.

FACTS AND BACKGROUND

The Coudert firm has provided legal services to Eastman Chemical, one of Kodak's three major operating divisions, for the last six years. These services have covered a vast array of legal matters, including competition law questions, joint ventures, contract issues, tax issues, and questions concerning environmental law. Coudert preformed this work out of the Washington, D.C., New York, Paris, Brussels, Hong Kong and Singapore offices. For purposes of this motion, it is undisputed that the work performed by Coudert for Eastman Chemicals did not involve issues directly relevant to this litigation.[12]

The facts and procedural background of this litigation have been amply recorded in the orders issued by this court, as well as the decisions of the Ninth Circuit Court of Appeals and the United States Supreme Court. For purposes of the present motion, it is sufficient to note that in 1991, Kodak appealed to the United States Supreme Court a judgment of the Ninth Circuit reversing and remanding the order of Judge William Schwarzer dismissing plaintiffs' federal antitrust claims. Coudert was asked by James Hennefer, counsel for the ISOs, to participate in the briefing before the Supreme Court. The ISOs primary contact with the Coudert firm was Douglas Rosenthal. A conflicts check performed by Coudert disclosed that the firm had an ongoing relationship with Eastman Chemical and Kodak Pathe. The work for Eastman Chemical was performed primarily by Coudert's Hong Kong office. Mr. Rosenthal asked Owen Nee, the managing partner of Coudert's Hong Kong Office, to disclose the conflict to the Eastman Chemical representatives, and obtain their consent to Coudert's representation of the ISOs.

Mr. Nee planned to discuss the conflict during a separately arranged meeting on other business with Barry Falin, Director of Business Development for the Filter Products Organization of Eastman Chemicals, and Michael Chung, Manager of the Filter Products Organization. In prepara-

[12] FN1. Coudert also represented a separately incorporated independent French subsidiary of Kodak, Kodak Pathe. For purposes of this opinion, the court deems Coudert's representation of Pathe irrelevant. *See,* State Bar of California Standing Committee on Professional Responsibility and Conduct, Formal Opinion No. 1989–113 (Parent and subsidiary corporations are separate entities, therefore, representation of a wholly owned subsidiary, let alone a separately incorporated subsidiary, does not create a conflict of interest).

tion for that meeting, Mr. Nee discussed with Mr. Rosenthal what information was to be given to the Eastman Chemical business representatives. Mr. Rosenthal telefaxed Mr. Nee on July 13, 1991 as follows:

> I have seen your fax of today and have spoken both to Ken Katz and Steve Hudspeth. I am authorized by both of them to affirm we trust your judgment about what to say, *in passing,* about our involvement in the Kodak Supreme Court case, when you meet with officials of Kodak Chemical dealing with China this Monday.
>
> As a small modification to your proposed statement, might I suggest the following:
>
> Our *San Francisco* office *is going to participate in a brief contrary to the interests of the Kodak Corporation in the Supreme Court Appeal;* and after review of the matter *we have determined that the China representation is sufficiently distant that the actions of the San Francisco office do not constitute a conflict of interest.* (emphasis added)[13]

After the meeting took place on July 23, 1991, Mr. Nee wrote Mr. Rosenthal and Mr. Hudspeth informing them that he "explained the matter in the form [they] sent to [him] by [their] telefax on July 12, 1991." Neither the documents submitted in opposition to Kodak's motion, nor the declaration of Mr. Nee, reflect that Coudert advised Falin and Chung of the nature of the conflict, the potential exposure to Kodak, or even that Kodak was a party to the Supreme Court action. Mr. Nee's telefax goes on to state that Messrs. Falin and Chung approved of Coudert's representation of the ISOs. Neither Messrs. Falin and Chung recall any such conversations. Mr. Chung testified specifically that even if he had been so informed, he did not recall Mr. Nee disclosing that Coudert would represent the ISOs at the district court level, or explaining the potential exposure Kodak faced in this action.

On September 20, 1991, Kodak was served with Respondent's Brief in the U.S. Supreme Court appeal. The brief identified Coudert as co-counsel for the ISOs. There is some dispute about when Coudert disclosed to Kodak that it would participate in the district court trial on remand. However, the parties agree that on July 30, 1992, Gordon Spivack of Coudert's New York office informed Gary Vangraafeiland, Senior Vice President and General Counsel of Eastman Kodak, that Coudert would participate in the preparation and trial of the ISO case in this court. Coudert filed a formal notice of appearance in this court on October 9, 1992. . . .

At the time Coudert was invited to participate in the brief before the Supreme Court in 1991, Coudert was actively representing Eastman

[13] FN4. Coudert's San Francisco office participated in two *amicus* briefs to the Supreme Court. Coudert's Washington, D.C. office "participated" in the brief for respondents on the merits before the Supreme Court.

Chemicals in a variety of international matters. Therefore, Coudert's representation of the ISOs conflicted with the interests of its existing client, Kodak. In 1991, Rule 3–310(B) provided that "[a] member shall not concurrently represent clients whose interests conflict, except with their informed written consent. . . . " Coudert admits that it failed to obtain written consent from Kodak before representing the ISOs.

Since Coudert failed to obtain written consent as required under former California Rule 3–310(B), Coudert failed to obtain consent. Even if written consent was not required, the court finds that Coudert failed to obtain "informed consent" under *Unified Sewerage Agency, etc. v. Jelco, Inc.,* 646 F.2d 1339 (9th Cir.1981). . . . Plaintiffs offer the declaration of Mr. Nee, in which he states that during a July 1992 meeting with Barry Falin and Michael Chung, businessmen who were managers at Eastman Chemical in Hong Kong, he disclosed to Eastman Chemical the representation of the ISOs. Coudert's own characterization of the disclosures fails to meet the requirements announced in *Jelco. Jelco,* as in this case, involved an issue of representation adverse to a present client. In reviewing the obligations of counsel as to present clients, the Ninth Circuit stressed that "representation adverse to a *present* client must be measured not so much as against the similarities in litigation, as against the duty of undivided loyalty which an attorney owes to each of his clients." *Jelco,* 646 F.2d at 1345.

The *Jelco* court held that to avoid disqualification under Disciplinary Rule DR5–105(B) of the Code of Professional Responsibility of the State of Oregon, an attorney must satisfy DR5–105(C)'s two conditions: "First, each client must consent to the multiple representation after full disclosure of the risks. Second, it must be 'obvious' that the attorney can adequately represent the interests of each client." As to the consent prong of this analysis, the court cited *In re Boivin,* 271 Or. 419, 533 P.2d 171 (1975), as the leading Oregon case on the meaning of "consent" in Cannon 5 of the disciplinary rules of the State Bar of Oregon. In *Boivin,* the court stated that consent must be informed consent, made after full disclosure of all material facts:

> To satisfy the requirement of full disclosure by a lawyer before undertaking to represent two conflicting interests, it is *not sufficient that both parties be informed of the fact that the lawyer is undertaking to represent both of them, but he must explain to them the nature of the conflict of interest in such detail so that they can understand the reasons why it may be desirable for each to have independent counsel,* with undivided loyalty to the interests of each of them.

Boivin, 533 P.2d at 174 (emphasis added).

Plaintiffs argue that the consent obtained from Mr. Falin was informed and, moreover, that Kodak's decision to continue to employ Coudert, even after the current motion was filed, is indicative of Kodak's consent. The court disagrees. . . . By Coudert's own admission, Messrs. Falin and Chung were told only that the San Francisco office of Coudert was going to participate in a brief before the Supreme Court adverse to Kodak's interests. Coudert did not explain how the representation would be adverse to Kodak's interest, nor did Coudert inform Kodak of the fact that Coudert's New York and San Francisco offices were actually going to appear on the brief before the Supreme Court. In fact, the July 13, 1991 telefax and Mr. Nee's declaration do not state that Mr. Nee told Messrs. Falin and Chung that Kodak was a party to the action before the Supreme Court, the nature of the underlying action, or the potential exposure to Kodak, should the ISOs prevail. . . .

The form, content and nature of the disclosure to Messrs. Falin and Chung was deficient under the standards for informed consent. Under both the California and ABA Rules of Professional Conduct, Coudert owes its client, Kodak, the highest level of undivided loyalty. Coudert's duties to disclose any representation adverse to the interests of Kodak cannot be fulfilled by mentioning "in passing" participation in a brief contrary to the interests of the client without stating the details of *why* the interests are contrary. The exposure Kodak faces in this action is substantial. Coudert's failure to fully disclose that exposure, as well as the extent of its participation in this action, falls short of the "undivided loyalty" it owes to its client. The details are essential to informed consent so that the client can weigh and measure the nature of the contrary interests and give informed consent based upon knowledge of material facts. . . .

While plaintiffs' argument that multinational clients (such as Kodak) will often consult international law firms (such as Coudert) on discreet legal issues is well taken, plaintiffs have cited to no California or Ninth Circuit authority creating an exception to the rules about representation adverse to an existing client because of these factors. Whether a matter is international, multinational or domestic, the standard of conduct for explanation of material facts underlying a potential conflict of interest is the same. The duty to the client of undivided loyalty and necessity of informed client consent to adverse representation applies internationally no matter how difficult the communication hurdles. Law is a profession of service premised upon representation of the client with the highest duty of loyalty and the deepest regard for the trust of the client. Therefore, policy requires the disqualification of Coudert.

Waivers generally pertain to conflicts that exist when the waiver is sought. Sometimes, however, a lawyer may see that a conflict that does not presently exist might arise in the future. Prudent lawyers will try to deal with this possibility up front, by informing the client or clients of the risk that a conflict could arise, making clear what the lawyer intends to do if the conflict does arise, and seeking consent to the intended course of action. "Advance waiver" is the term used to describe consent in such circumstances. In essence it means the client agrees to waive a conflict that does not presently exist but might arise in the future.

Advance waivers are enforceable (generally in the form of defenses to disqualification motions when a conflict does arise) in proportion to the quality of information on which the consent is based. In general, the clearer and more detailed the description of a possible conflict is the more likely it is that an advance waiver of that conflict will be enforced. General, open-ended waivers of future conflicts that are not described well enough for the client to understand them are unlikely to be enforced. Particularly when a lawyer jointly represents clients whose interests may diverge, it is important that the lawyer disclose whether the advance waiver extends to the case in which it is sought. In other words, if the lawyer wants to continue to represent one client in the event a conflict develops with a second client, the lawyer needs to make clear that he or she seeks consent to act adversely to the second client in the case at hand; it would be wise (and fair) to point out specifically that in such an event the lawyer could use the second client's confidences against him. The following case presents an example of a reasonably specific advance waiver.

ZADOR CORP. V. KWAN

31 Cal.App.4th 1285 (1995)

ELIA, ASSOCIATE JUSTICE:

Zador Corporation appeals after the trial court disqualified Heller, Ehrman, White & McAuliffe (Heller) from serving as Zador's counsel. For reasons we shall explain, we reverse.

[Zador was a corporation owned by the Young family. Zador bought some property from a partnership in which Jame Claitor and Roy Bolton were principals. The partnership transferred the property to C.K. Kwan, acting as agent for the Young family. Kwan then transferred the property to Zador.

The sales agreement provided that Zador was to transfer 15% of its interest in the property to Claitor or an entity he designated. In 1990, Bolton sued Zador, Kwan, and Claitor,] claiming that he was an intended third party beneficiary of the agreement relating to the 15 percent interest. Bolton also alleged that defendants fraudulently transferred the property to a wholly-owned Zador subsidiary. Zador cross-complained against the seller partnership, and its partners, including Claitor and Bolton. Zador alleged that the sellers sold the property at a grossly inflated price thereby divesting Zador of its assets.

On May 1, 1990, Zador asked Heller to defend it. Heller had represented the Young family for about 10 years. When Kwan learned of the lawsuit, he requested indemnity from Zador because he acted as Zador's agent. On May 23, 1990, Heller met with Kwan and Amelia Mak, Zador's Hong Kong in-house counsel. It was confirmed that Heller would represent Kwan and Zador in the action.

On June 22, 1990, Kwan met with Heller. Heller presented Kwan with a waiver and consent form. Heller told Kwan that the conflicts letter was standard. Heller stated that clients were required to sign such a letter when Heller represented multiple parties in the same litigation.

The letter provided, in pertinent part:

> "Based on the information that has been provided to us, we do not believe that our representation currently involves any actual conflict of interest. You should be aware, however, that our representation may in the future involve actual conflicts of interests if the interests of the Co-defendants become inconsistent with your interests. Should that occur, we will endeavor to apprise you promptly of any such conflict so that you can decide whether you wish to obtain independent counsel.
>
> "Multiple representation may result in economic or tactical advantages. You should be aware, however, that multiple representation also involves significant risks. First, multiple representation may result in divided or at least shared attorney-client loyalties. Although we are not currently aware of any actual or reasonably foreseeable adverse effects of such divided or shared loyalty, it is possible that issues may arise as to which our representation of you may be materially limited by our representation of the Co-defendants.
>
> "Furthermore, because we will be jointly retained by both you and the Co-defendants in this matter, in the event of a dispute between you and the Co-defendants, the attorney-client privilege generally will not protect communications that have taken place among all of you and attorneys in our firm. Moreover, pursuant to this 'Joint Client' arrangement, anything you disclose to us may be disclosed to any of the other jointly represented clients.
>
> "In the event of a dispute or conflict between you and the Co-defendants, there is a risk that we may be disqualified from representing all of you absent written consent from all of you at that time. We anticipate that if such a conflict or dispute were to arise, we would continue to represent the subsidiary companies of Miramar Hotel & Investment Co., Ltd. (the 'Companies'), whose legal interests in this matter are aligned, notwithstanding any adversity between you and the Companies' interests. Among the Companies are Zador (California) Corporation, Zador Corporation N.V. and YCS Invest-

ments. *Accordingly, we are now asking that you consent to our continued and future representation of the Companies and agree not to assert any such conflict of interest or to seek to disqualify us from representing the Companies, notwithstanding any adversity that may develop.* By signing and returning to us the agreement and consent set forth at the end of this letter, you will consent to such arrangement and waive any conflicts regarding that arrangement. Notwithstanding such waiver and consent, depending on the circumstances, there remains some degree of risk that we would be disqualified from representing any of you in the event of a dispute.

"Notwithstanding these risks, you have advised us that in this matter at the present time you do not desire to seek other counsel but instead you desire that we represent multiple interests of yourself and the Co-defendants. Because the interests of the Co-defendants may become inconsistent with your interests, under the ethical standards discussed below we are required to bring this matter to your attention and to obtain your consent, as well as the consent of the Co-defendants, before representing you in the matter described above. . . .

"Accordingly, we request that you signify your informed written consent by signing and returning this letter to us. We encourage you to seek independent counsel regarding the import of this consent, if you so desire, and we emphasize that you remain completely free to seek independent counsel at any time even if you decide to sign the consent set forth below. . . . "

After spending twenty minutes studying the form, Kwan signed it. After this meeting, Kwan met with Heller several times to discuss the case. Heller interviewed Kwan, discussed Kwan's answer to the complaint, and prepared and responded to interrogatories on Kwan's behalf.

With respect to the interrogatories, Kwan had informed the Youngs that $4 million was a reasonable value for the Platt Property. However, according to the interrogatory response, "the Platt property had a value far less than the approximately $4.1 million price paid by Zador. . . . " Kwan objected to submitting this response. He believed $4.1 million was a fair price. However, at Heller's urging, Kwan endorsed the interrogatory response.

On August 7, 1990, Heller reviewed documents produced by Bolton. The documents suggested Kwan might have received money from the sellers during the Platt Property transaction. On August 8, 1990, Heller attorneys met with each other to discuss this information. On August 13, 1990, Heller informed Kwan that this information suggested a possible conflict between his interests and Zador's interests. Heller told Kwan that he needed to retain separate counsel. Kwan agreed. Kwan also reaffirmed his consent to Heller's continued representation of Zador.

In an August 20, 1990, letter, Heller confirmed its discussion with Kwan. Among other things, the letter stated, "*Consistent with your agreement and consent dated June 22, 1990, which you have recently reaffirmed, we will continue to represent the Co-defendants in this lawsuit.*" (Emphasis added.)

On August 22, 1990, Wilson, Sonsini, Goodrich & Rosati (Wilson) advised Heller it was representing Kwan. Wilson requested a meeting with Heller. At the meeting, Wilson requested that Zador indemnify Kwan. Wilson said that if Zador sued Kwan, Wilson would move to disqualify Heller.

In a September 26, 1990, letter, Heller denied Kwan's request for indemnity. Heller explained that Kwan may have conspired to defraud Zador. However, Heller added that "If at some point in the future it becomes clear that Dr. Kwan did not act in complicity with James Claitor, Roy Bolton and the other Cross-defendants, and is otherwise entitled to indemnity, we can revisit the indemnity issue at that time."

After a year of negotiations over the indemnity issue, the parties signed an indemnity agreement. Indemnity was limited to the extent that "Kwan has acted in good faith and in a manner he reasonably believed to be in the best interests of Zador." The indemnity agreement specifically referred to the possibility that Kwan may have "breached any of his duties" to Zador and expressly contemplated the possibility of litigation between Kwan and Zador.

Heller also drafted and signed a Joint Defense Agreement with Wilson. In the agreement, it was acknowledged that Zador and Kwan had a "certain mutuality of interest in a joint defense. . . . " Zador, however, ultimately refused to sign the agreement.

In February 1991, Claitor cross-complained against Kwan for indemnity and contribution. The cross-complaint sought to transfer Claitor's liability to Zador to Kwan, among others.

In July 1992, Claitor was deposed. In his deposition, Claitor implicated Kwan in the conspiracy to defraud Zador. Heller invoked Kwan's duty to cooperate under the indemnity agreement and demanded an explanation. On April 15, 1993, Kwan and Wilson met with Heller. At the meeting, Kwan acknowledged that he had in fact profited from the Platt Property deal.

In July 1993, Zador formally withdrew from the indemnity agreement with Kwan. It also demanded refund of the sums it had paid for Kwan's separate defense.

On August 17, 1993, Heller amended its cross-complaint to name Kwan as a cross-defendant. Heller's claims against Kwan were based in part on the allegation that the Platt Property was overvalued.

In December 1993, Kwan moved to disqualify Heller. In January 1994, the trial court concluded that there was a substantial relationship between Heller's prior representation of Kwan and the current litigation. Accordingly, the motion to disqualify was granted.

Zador petitioned for a writ of mandate to this court. On March 1, 1994, we denied Zador's petition on the ground that Zador had an adequate legal remedy. On March 8, 1994, Zador filed its notice of appeal. On March 22, 1994, Zador petitioned for a writ of supersedeas or other appropriate stay order. On April 12, 1994, we entered an order staying proceedings below pending disposition of this appeal.

Standard of Review

The authority to disqualify an attorney stems from the trial court's inherent power "[t]o control in furtherance of justice, the conduct of its ministerial officers, and of all other persons in any manner connected with a judicial proceeding before it, in every matter pertaining thereto." [citation omitted]. . . . In reviewing a disqualification motion, we will uphold the trial court's decision absent an abuse of discretion. . . . "The trial court's exercise of this discretion is limited by the applicable legal principles and is subject to reversal when there is no reasonable basis for the action." [citation omitted]

Discussion

Appellant contends the trial court erred in granting the disqualification motion. Before addressing this contention, we first review the pertinent legal principles.

"The relation between attorney and client is a fiduciary relation of the very highest character, and binds the attorney to most conscientious fidelity-*uberrima fides.*" Among other things, the fiduciary relationship requires that the attorney respect his or her client's confidences. It also means that the attorney has a duty of loyalty to his or her clients.

Because of this fiduciary relationship, it is improper for an attorney to assume a position which is inconsistent with the interest of present of former clients. . . . In deciding whether disqualification is required, the "substantial relationship" test is often utilized. . . .

However, when the prior representation involves joint clients, and the subsequent action relates to the same matter, the substantial relationship test adds nothing to disqualification analysis. This is because a substantial relationship between the former representation and the subsequent action is *inherent* in such situations. In other words, clients A and B are jointly represented by C until C discovers a conflict between the legal position of A and B. Client B retains separate counsel. Client A then sues Client B. In these circumstances, a substantial relationship will always exist between C's prior representation of B and the litigation between A and B. Accordingly, in this situation, the substantial relationship test does not "test" anything. It should not determine whether C should be disqualified from representing A.

In addition, although the substantial relationship test determines whether confidences were likely disclosed, in a joint client situation, confidences are necessarily disclosed. . . . Accordingly, in such circumstances, the propriety of disqualification is not dependent upon the substantial relationship test. Rather, it generally turns upon the scope of the clients' consent. . . .

[I]nformed written consent is required before an attorney can jointly represent clients in the same matter. California Rules of Professional Conduct, Rule 3–310(C)(1) requires an attorney to obtain each client's informed written consent before accepting representation of more than one client in a matter in which the interests of the clients potentially conflict. Similarly, Rule 3–310(C)(2) requires an attorney to obtain each client's informed written consent before accepting or continuing representation of more than one client in a matter in which the interests of the clients actually conflict. . . .

As the drafters of the rules explain, "Subparagraphs (C)(1) and (C)(2) are intended to apply to all types of legal employment, including the concurrent representation of multiple parties in litigation or in a single transaction or in some other common enterprise or legal relationship. . . . In such situations, for the sake of convenience or economy, the parties may well prefer to employ a single counsel, but a member must disclose the potential adverse aspects of such multiple representation (e.g., Evid.Code, § 962) and must obtain the informed written consent of the clients thereto pursuant to subparagraph (C)(1). Moreover, if the potential adversity should become actual, the member must obtain the further informed written consent of the clients pursuant to subparagraph (C)(2)."

The Rules of Professional Conduct also require informed written consent before an attorney accepts "employment adverse to the client or former client where, by reason of the representation of the client or former client, the member has obtained confidential information material to the employment." (Cal.Rules of Prof.Conduct, Rule 3–310(E).). . . .

In this case, Heller advised Kwan that it would represent Kwan only if Kwan signed a detailed waiver. Kwan studied the form for twenty minutes and then signed it. By signing the form, Kwan waived the attorney-client privilege. Kwan was also advised that Heller would continue to represent Zador if a conflict existed. Kwan was advised that he had the right at any time to obtain separate counsel. Kwan also agreed to the following provision, "Accordingly, we are now asking that you consent to our continued and future representation of the Companies and agree not to assert any such conflict of interest or seek to disqualify us from representing the Companies, *notwithstanding any adversity that may develop.*" (Emphasis added.)

Subsequently, after reviewing documents produced by Bolton, Heller decided a possible conflict existed. It advised Kwan to retain separate counsel. Kwan agreed. Heller also asked Kwan to reaffirm his consent to Heller's continued representation of Zador. Kwan *again agreed.* Heller confirmed this agreement in writing: "*Consistent with your agreement and consent dated June 22, 1990, which you have recently reaffirmed, we will continue to represent the Co-defendants in this lawsuit.*" (Emphasis added.) Kwan raised no objections.

In July 1992, Claitor was deposed. In his deposition, Claitor implicated Kwan in the conspiracy to defraud Zador. Heller invoked Kwan's duty to cooperate under the indemnity agreement and demanded an explanation. On April 15, 1993, Kwan and Wilson met with Heller. At the meeting, Kwan acknowledged that he had in fact profited from the Platt Property deal.

In July 1993, Zador formally withdrew from the indemnity agreement with Kwan. It also demanded refund of the sums it had paid for Kwan's separate defense. On August 17, 1993, Zador amended its cross-complaint to name Kwan as a cross-defendant. Zador's claims against Kwan were based in part on the allegation that the Platt Property was overvalued. Finally, in December 1993, Kwan moved to disqualify Heller.

As these events show, Kwan consented to Heller's continued representation of Zador. The waiver and consent form was detailed. Kwan agreed not to disqualify Heller "*notwithstanding any adversity that may develop.*" (Emphasis added.) When adversity did develop, Kwan obtained separate counsel but reaffirmed his agreement to the consent form and to Heller's continued representation of Zador.

Kwan contends he did not consent to being sued by Zador. He states that he did not believe that "any adversity" included the possibility of a lawsuit. We are not persuaded. In these circumstances, involving legal disputes between former joint clients, we believe that "any adversity" quite naturally includes litigation.

California law does not require that every possible consequence of a conflict be disclosed for a consent to be valid. . . . The State Bar of California has reached a similar conclusion. In Formal Opinion 1989–115, the issue was whether a blanket waiver of the client's right to disqualify was ethically proper. In that matter, lead counsel requested local counsel's trial assistance. Local counsel represented several clients whose interests were presently or potentially adverse to lead counsel's client. Local counsel agreed to assist lead counsel but only if lead counsel's client waived its right to disqualify local counsel in any matter in which local counsel represented parties adverse to lead counsel's client. The Committee decided such blanket waivers were not per se improper. The Committee noted, "In addition, the nature of the subsequent conflict of interest may range from simply representing two clients in entirely unrelated matters to actually representing both sides in the same dispute. While a court would doubtless preclude a lawyer from representing both sides simultaneously [fn. omitted], the Committee believes that in such situation, *if the original waiver was informed, local counsel could withdraw from its representation of lead counsel's client and continue to represent its own client even if otherwise confidential information would be used against lead counsel's client.*" (*Id.* at p. 2, emphasis added.)

Accordingly, we conclude that Kwan consented to Heller's continued representation of Zador "notwithstanding any adversity" that developed. The consent form was detailed. Kwan subsequently reaffirmed his consent. In September 1990, Wilson said it would move to disqualify Heller if Zador sued Kwan. Thus, over three years before the motion to disqualify was filed, it was recognized that litigation between Zador and Kwan might ensue. . . .

Although we review the trial court's findings under an abuse of discretion standard, that standard does not assist us when the trial court employed the wrong legal analysis. . . . In this case, the trial court applied the substantial relationship test to disqualify Heller. In these circumstances, that test was not determinative. Because Kwan consented to Heller's continued representation of Zador "notwithstanding any adversity that developed," the trial court should have denied the disqualification motion.

CASE QUESTIONS

1. Was the conflict between Zador and Kwan contemporaneous or subsequent?
2. What role does the substantial relationship test play in this analysis?
3. What is the best fact for Heller's position that the consent was informed?
4. What is the best fact for Kwan's position?

In *Zador*, the Heller firm reaffirmed Kwan's consent to Heller's continued representation of Zador even after Heller advised Kwan that there was a risk of a conflict between Zador and Kwan such that Heller should stop representing Kwan, who should then get another lawyer. Was this reaffirmation necessary to the result in the case, or was Kwan's original consent sufficient?

This question was presented in *Visa U.S.A., Inc. v. First Data Corp.*, 241 F. Supp. 2d 1100, 1102 (N.D. Cal.2003), another case involving the Heller firm. First Data Corporation wanted to retain Heller to represent it in a matter, but there was a chance that First Data could find itself in a position adverse to Visa U.S.A., a major client of the Heller firm. The retainer agreement contained the following waiver language:

> Our engagement by you is also understood as entailing your consent to our representation of our other present or future clients in "transactions," including litigation in which we have not been engaged to represent you and in which you have other counsel, and in which one of our other clients would be adverse to you in matters unrelated to those that we are handling for you. In this regard, we discussed [Heller's] past and on-going representation of Visa U.S.A. and Visa International (the latter mainly with respect to trademarks) (collectively, "Visa") in matters which are not currently adverse to First Data. Moreover, as we discussed, we are not aware of any current adversity between Visa and First Data. Given the nature of our relationship with Visa, however, we discussed the need for the firm to preserve its ability to represent Visa on matters which may arise in the future including matters adverse to First Data, provided that we would only undertake such representation of Visa under circumstances in which we do not possess confidential information of yours relating to the transaction, and we would staff such a project with one or more attorneys who are not engaged in your representation. In such circumstances, the attorneys in the two matters would be subject to an ethical wall, screening them from communicating from [sic] each other regarding their respective engagements. We understand that you do consent to our representation of Visa and our other clients under those circumstances.

Visa and First Data soon found themselves in adverse positions on an unrelated matter. Visa retained the Heller firm in that matter, and First Data moved to disqualify the firm. First Data tried to distinguish *Zador* on the ground that Kwan had reaffirmed his consent once the nature of the conflict was known, which had not happened in *First Data*. The court rejected this argument: "An advance waiver of potential future conflicts, such as the one executed by First Data and Heller, is permitted under California law, even if the waiver does not specifically state the exact nature of the future conflict. . . . The only inquiry that need be made is whether the waiver was fully informed. . . . In some circumstances, a second waiver will be warranted, but only if the attorney believes that the first waiver was insufficiently informed. There is no case law requiring a second disclosure in all circumstances for an advance waiver to be valid. . . . "

It's Not Just A Letter, It's An Exhibit

When you write letters or e-mails in practice you are never writing just for yourself. You are rarely writing only for you and your recipient.

One implication of Rule of Survival Three—assume everything you do and say will become publicly known—is that you are also writing for future factfinders who might have to decide whether you have discharged your legal obligations. You should write with them in mind as well as your client.

This general rule is particularly important with regard to conflict waiver letters. If you need your client's consent to proceed with a representation you must write a letter that not only provides your client an adequate basis for deciding on your request but also persuades future third parties that you did so. The letter in *Image Technical Services* is a case study in how not to do that. The letters in *Zador* and *First USA* are better but not perfect.

Here are some rules of thumb for writing exhibit letters in general, and conflict waivers in particular.

1. Use simple words. Even if you are writing to a sophisticated client it will do no harm. For busy judges and lay jurors, it will be a relief. Remember, if a factfinder can't understand what you said they are more likely to think your client couldn't either.

2. Be clear. Simple words will help you clarify your thinking. Don't muddle it up with obfuscation, hedges, repetition, or the like.

3. Lay it all out. Don't try to hide facts or risks your client might run by agreeing to your request. Tell the client what you want, what risks, if any, you perceive to the client, the probability that such risks will occur (if you have a sense of that), and tell them that because you have an interest in getting the answer you want they should think about consulting disinterested counsel. In the context of a conflict waiver, the first point (what you want) means that you should tell the client what it is you want to do and what that means for the client. Will you sue them? Will you negotiate against them? What can they expect?

4. Don't minimize or hide disadvantages to consent. Never trivialize consent, as did the letter in *Image Technical*. If a client is not aware of a risk to consent and you are, tell the client.

5. Don't advise the client on your request. It is the client's call to make, not yours. Because you have an interest in the outcome you are not in a position to provide disinterested advice, and biased advice is unlikely to do either you or the client any good.

Waivers Involving Entities and Entity Constituents

You know that under Model Rule 1.13 counsel for an entity represents the entity itself, not its representatives, such as officers or directors.

Counsel may represent both the entity and one of its representatives, however, if conflict of interest rules permit. In some cases, counsel would need to obtain a waiver of conflicts to proceed with joint representation, and that waiver presents its own conflicts problem.

Suppose an officer wants counsel to represent both him and the entity, and the officer also has the power to sign documents on the entity's behalf. Because the entity is a legal fiction it can only act through representatives, who therefore may have the power to commit the entity to things that are in the officer's interests but not the entity's. When an officer wants joint representation he might be tempted to sign a conflict waiver even though the entity would be better off with its own lawyer. For that reason, conflict waivers in such situations must be signed by a representative of the entity other than the representative who will be jointly represented. Model Rule 1.13(g). The need for such a rule highlights the tricky nature such representations can present, and the corresponding need for counsel to proceed carefully.

On advance waivers generally, *see* Richard W. Painter, *Advance Waiver of Conflicts*, 13 GEO. J. OF LEGAL ETHICS 289 (2000).

G. TRANSACTIONS WITH CLIENTS

Lawyers sometimes do business with clients. That is dangerous. Lawyers sometimes receive gifts from clients. That is dangerous, too, if the gift is substantial. (A bottle of wine for a nice victory is OK.) The danger inheres in presumptions rooted in agency law, which require that an agent deal fairly with his or her principal.

Model Rule 1.8(a) exemplifies such a presumption translated into disciplinary rule form. It forbids you from doing a deal with a client or acquiring an interest (such as a lien) adverse to a client unless the transaction or terms on which the interest is acquired are fair and disclosed in writing to the client, the client is advised in writing that he or she may wish to consult an independent lawyer regarding the transaction, (and is given reasonable time to do so) and the client consents in a signed writing that sets forth the essential terms of the transaction and the lawyer's role in it, including whether the lawyer represents the client in the transaction.

These provisions apply even if the subject of the business transaction is unrelated to the subject of the representation. They generally do not apply to transactions in goods or services the client offers to the general public and in which the lawyer trades on that basis. (I.e., if you represent the local electric company your utility bill is not a fiduciary issue.) Similarly, Model Rule 1.8(c) forbids you from soliciting a substantial gift from a client or from preparing a document (such as a will) conveying such a gift, unless you are related to the client. The following materials examine these and related issues.

Model Rule of Professional Conduct 1.8
Cal. R. Prof. Conduct 3–300

BEERY V. STATE BAR

43 Cal.3d 802 (1987)

By The Court

In this proceeding, we review the recommendation of the State Bar of California that petitioner Robert L. Beery be suspended from the practice of law for five years, that execution of suspension be stayed, and that petitioner be placed on probation for a period of five years on conditions which include actual suspension for a period of three years and until restitution in the amount of $35,000 has been made.

The recommendation is based on a single incident of misconduct: petitioner entered into a business transaction with a client under circumstances which violated rules 5–101 and 5–102 of the Rules of Professional Conduct and sections 6103 and 6106 of the Business and Professions Code. Petitioner contends that the record does not support the finding of an attorney-client relationship at the time of the business transaction, that he did not willfully violate any rules of professional conduct or provisions of the Business and Professions Code, and that the recommended discipline is excessive.

Review of the record generated by the State Bar Court leads us to conclude that discipline is warranted and that the recommended discipline is appropriate, except that the period of actual suspension will be two years rather than three.

FACTS

Petitioner was admitted to the practice of law in the State of California in 1965. He has no prior disciplinary record.

The charge against petitioner stems from his representation of Richard Coss. In November 1974 petitioner incorporated American Steel Painting Corporation, which had been formed by Coss and an individual named Miller, and which was engaged in painting steel bridges and other steel structures. In February 1975 petitioner represented the company in a dispute with the State of California regarding bidding procedures.

Coss was injured in an automobile collision in June 1975, as a result of which he was paralyzed from the waist down and confined to a wheelchair. Coss retained defendant and two of defendant's law associates,

Maurice Nelson and Daniel Gardner, to represent him on a contingency fee basis in litigation against parties who might be liable for his injuries. Petitioner assisted in the initial investigation of the accident scene but the bulk of the litigation and negotiation work was performed by Nelson and Gardner. Petitioner monitored the progress of the litigation and maintained communications with Coss.

The personal injury action was settled in two stages in 1979 and 1980 for a total of approximately $250,000, of which Coss received approximately $150,000. Petitioner's share of the contingent fee amounted to approximately $20,000. In December 1980 Coss asked the advice of Maurice Nelson, who had handled the disbursement of settlement proceeds, regarding investing the money which Coss was then receiving. Coss, who was not sophisticated in financial matters, wanted a high rate of return but also was concerned about safeguarding principal. Nelson recommended United States Treasury securities, which were then yielding a high rate of interest.

In late December of 1980, Coss telephoned petitioner and asked for petitioner's advice regarding investments, saying he wanted a "fixed income." Coss considered petitioner both his attorney and his friend and had a high regard for petitioner's business acumen. Petitioner mentioned money markets, cash management accounts, and bonds. During the following weeks Coss placed two more telephone calls to petitioner to discuss investments and also, at the urging of Coss's wife, to discuss the possible drafting of a will. A meeting was arranged for February 25, 1981, in petitioner's law office in San Francisco. During one of the telephone conversations, in response to a casual inquiry about what he had been doing, petitioner said he was involved in a very interesting and exciting business venture using satellite technology.

During the meeting on February 25, petitioner told Coss that Coss could "buy into" the satellite venture and that it was a "good investment." Petitioner said Coss could invest $35,000.[14] Petitioner offered to personally guarantee Coss's investment. Coss said he would talk to his wife about it. Petitioner also discussed preparation of a will for Coss. Petitioner explained three different ways a will could be structured. Coss said he wanted everything to go to his wife if she survived him or, if not, to his two children in equal shares. Coss provided petitioner with the birth dates of his children but did not specifically direct petitioner to prepare a will.

The business venture which petitioner recommended to Coss was C & D Satellite Systems, Inc. (hereafter Satellite), which petitioner had incor-

[14] FN2. Coss testified that petitioner said there was $75,000 "available to invest" and that he (petitioner) would be investing $40,000. The hearing panel made no finding on whether petitioner represented he was personally investing $40,000. There was no evidence that petitioner made a loan to or invested in the satellite venture at that time.

porated the previous year. The principals of the corporation were petitioner, Thomas Benoit, and Leonard Sheffman. Benoit was the president and worked in sales and marketing, as did Sheffman. Petitioner handled legal matters and procured financing. A fourth individual, Donald May, was in charge of engineering. The business of Satellite was to install and operate computer-controlled, satellite-based entertainment and security functions for hotels and other commercial establishments. The principals had invested approximately $5,000 in Satellite, most of which had been consumed by administrative expenses. Petitioner's law office was used as Satellite's business address.

In September 1980 Satellite had entered into a contract to install a system in the Sands Hotel in San Diego. This was the first and only such contract which Satellite obtained. Sands was obligated to pay a fixed amount per room per month for a period of 10 years, with an option to renew for an additional 10 years, but payment was required only upon proof that all elements of the system were operating properly. The projected revenue to Satellite was $9,000 per month. To purchase the equipment for the project, Satellite borrowed $250,000 from Commercial Western Finance Corporation (hereafter Commercial). The loan was secured by Benoit's residence and by shares owned by petitioner in a ranching venture.

Satellite installed the equipment in the Sands Hotel in December 1980 but it did not function properly. Donald May informed Benoit that $30,000 to $35,000 would be needed to purchase additional equipment to make the system work as promised. Benoit passed this information along to petitioner, who knew that Commercial would not advance the money, nor would any other professional lender.

After the meeting with petitioner on February 25, Coss explained to his wife what petitioner had told him about Satellite. A few days later petitioner telephoned and asked if he could meet Coss and his wife at their home in Rocklin on Sunday morning, March 1. Coss and his wife agreed.

Petitioner arrived with a document dated February 26, 1981, and signed by Thomas Benoit for Satellite. The document provided that Satellite would pay to Coss the sum of $35,000, in equal monthly installments of principal and interest at the rate of 22 percent per annum, commencing on February 26, 1981, and payable on the 26th day of each month. The note did not specify the amount of the monthly payments, the rate of amortization, or the total number of payments. The note provided that the whole amount would become due on default and that the interest rate would then "be automatically adjusted to the maximum rate allowable by California law." The same document provided for an assignment by Satellite to Coss of the sum of $35,000 plus interest as specified in the note "of the money due or to become due under the contract dated September 8,

1980, from the Sands Hotel . . . with full power and authority to collect said sum as it becomes due."

When Coss reminded petitioner of his promise to guarantee repayment, petitioner wrote across the bottom of the document: "This note shall be paid in full within one year from the date hereof, and is personally guaranteed by the undersigned Robert L. Beery." Coss then accepted the document and wrote a check to Satellite in the amount of $35,000 which he gave to petitioner.

Petitioner did not explain his own relationship with Satellite except to say that he was "helping it get set up" and "hustling on the deal." Coss believed that petitioner was acting as his attorney in recommending the loan to Satellite and would not have entered into the transaction had he believed otherwise. Petitioner did not advise Coss that Coss could or should discuss the transaction with another lawyer or with an investment counselor. Petitioner did not tell Coss what Satellite planned to do with the money or that Satellite was having problems with the installation at the Sands Hotel. Petitioner did not mention that the money could not have been borrowed from a commercial lender.

Satellite's installation at the Sands Hotel never performed as promised and no money was ever paid to Satellite under the contract. A settlement was reached under which the Sands Hotel purchased some of the equipment from Satellite for $30,000. Satellite used the money to pay suppliers and paid nothing to Coss. Satellite defaulted on its loan from Commercial, which foreclosed on the security pledged by petitioner and Benoit. Coss, who had received nothing from Satellite or from the Sands Hotel, retained another attorney and brought suit against petitioner on his guarantee of the promissory note. Petitioner did not contest the action and a default judgment was entered against him. By this time petitioner had closed his office in San Francisco and was living in Nevada. Petitioner never paid any portion of the judgment. At the hearing he testified that he did not have the money to pay the judgment.

The hearing panel found that a lawyer-client relationship existed between petitioner and Coss at the time of the discussions of investment and the loan to Satellite, that the transaction was neither fair nor reasonable to Coss, that petitioner concealed material facts from Coss, that Coss was not given reasonable opportunity to seek the advice of independent counsel and did not consent in writing to the transaction, that petitioner represented conflicting interests without advising Coss of the existence of the conflict and without obtaining the written consent of any of the parties, and that a fiduciary relationship existed between petitioner and Coss at all times in issue. The panel concluded that petitioner had willfully violated rules 5–101 and 5–102(B) of the Rules of Professional Conduct and sections 6103 and 6106 of the Business and Professions Code and that petitioner's "conduct in the premises was dishonest."

The review department by motion adopted the decision of the hearing panel, noting that "in view of the degree of actual suspension recommended, it would be appropriate for the Supreme Court to include in its order in this matter a requirement that the Respondent comply with the provisions of Rule 955, California Rules of Court within the time directed by the Supreme Court." Three referees voted against the motion on the ground that the degree of discipline recommended appeared excessive.

I

. . . . Petitioner urges us to adopt his version of events and to reject the findings of the hearing panel. He maintains that his testimony is more plausible than Coss's because if a will had been discussed he would have billed Coss for his advice and would have followed through with preparation of a will. He maintains that Coss relied on Maurice Nelson for investment advice and did not want or need petitioner's advice. He also maintains that the record, taken as a whole, "reflects a collusive effort by Mr. and Mrs. Coss, aided by witness Maurice J. Nelson, to invade the client's Security Fund, through fraud and perjury."

Petitioner's contention is lacking in merit. Having carefully reviewed the entire record, we find no indication of perjury or attempted fraud on the part of Coss. The failure to bill Coss for the will discussion does not establish that it never took place. Having just collected a large contingency fee for representing Coss, petitioner may have intended to perform the additional service without charge. Also, Coss testified that he intended to discuss the matter with his wife before directing petitioner to prepare a will and then simply put off making a decision on the subject. Petitioner may have postponed billing until a will was actually prepared, or he may have been reluctant to bill in view of his use of the same meeting to solicit funds from Coss. The question of whether Coss solicited petitioner's advice is a straightforward conflict in testimony. The hearing panel, having observed the witnesses as they testified, was in the best position to judge credibility and petitioner has failed to demonstrate error in the findings unanimously adopted by the panel. . . .

The evidence amply supports the existence of an attorney-client relationship at the time of the loan transaction. "The fiduciary relationship existing between lawyer and client extends to preliminary consultation by a prospective client with a view to retention of the lawyer, although actual employment does not result." (*Westinghouse Elec.Corp. v. Kerr–McGee Corp.* (7th Cir.1978) 580 F.2d 1311, 1319, fn. omitted.) "When a party seeking legal advice consults an attorney at law and secures that advice, the relation of attorney and client is established *prima facie*." (*Perkins v. West Coast Lumber Co.* (1900) 129 Cal. 427, 429.) "The absence of an agreement with respect to the fee to be charged does not prevent the relationship from arising." (*Miller v. Metzinger* (1979) 91 Cal.App.3d 31, 39.) Coss sought and obtained petitioner's legal advice regarding preparation of a will at the same time that petitioner induced Coss to enter into the business transaction, and so an attorney-client relationship existed at that time.

Even apart from the will consultation, it would appear that the attorney-client relationship which existed during prosecution of the personal injury suit had not effectively terminated in relation to this business transaction. Given that petitioner had acted as attorney for Coss's business even before the personal injury litigation, that the same fund of money was involved in both the personal injury litigation and the business transaction, that Coss began soliciting petitioner's investment advice even before the final distribution of the litigation proceeds, and that nothing ever occurred which would signal to Coss an end of the attorney-client relationship, petitioner owed Coss the duties which attend the relationship of attorney and client.

II

Next petitioner contends that the loan to Satellite was "purely a business matter" and that he did not willfully violate any rules of professional conduct.

"All business dealings between an attorney and client in which the attorney benefits are closely scrutinized for unfairness on the attorney's part [citations] and attorneys have been disciplined for inducing clients to invest in enterprises without fully apprising them of the risks. [Citations.]" (*Yokozeki v. State Bar* (1974) 11 Cal.3d 436, 445, fn. 4.)

"While an attorney is not prohibited from having business transactions with his client, yet, inasmuch as the relation of attorney and client is one wherein the attorney is apt to have very great influence over the client, especially in transactions which are a part of or intimately connected with the very business in reference to which the relation exists, such transactions are always scrutinized by courts with jealous care, and are set aside at the mere instance of the client, unless the attorney can show by extrinsic evidence that his client acted with full knowledge of all the facts connected with such transaction, and fully understood their effect; and in any attempt by the attorney to enforce an agreement on the part of the client growing out of such transaction, the burden of proof is always upon the attorney to show that the dealing was fair and just, and that the client was fully advised. [Citations.] In the words of Lord Eldon, he must make it manifest that he gave to his client 'all that reasonable advice against himself that he would have given him against a third person.' " [citations omitted]

The attorney-client relationship is a fiduciary relation of the very highest character imposing on the attorney a duty to communicate to the client whatever information the attorney has or may acquire in relation to the subject matter of the transaction. . . . "The essence of a fiduciary or confidential relationship is that the parties do not deal on equal terms, because the person in whom trust and confidence is reposed and who accepts that trust and confidence is in a superior position to exert unique influence over the dependent party." (*Barbara A. v. John G.* (1983) 145 Cal.App.3d 369, 383.) An attorney's violation of the duty arising in a fiduciary or confidential relationship warrants discipline even in the absence of an attorney-client relationship. [citations omitted]. . . .

In *Worth v. State Bar,* supra, 17 Cal.3d 337, an attorney obtained $25,000 from the 77–year–old mother of his law partner by representing that she would be a limited partner in a real estate venture. The attorney failed to explain that he owned only one of the three parcels needed for the venture and thereafter he failed to complete a certificate of limited partnership. Discipline was imposed because "[a]n attorney who accepts the responsibility of a fiduciary nature is held to the high standards of the legal profession whether or not he acts in his capacity of an attorney."

In *Clancy v. State Bar,* supra, 71 Cal.2d 140, an attorney obtained $1,000 from a woman he had represented in connection with a personal injury claim, the probate of her deceased husband's estate, and application for a widow's pension from the Veteran's Administration. According to the woman's testimony, the attorney had represented that the money would be invested in G.I. mortgages. The attorney denied making the representation but resolution of this conflict was found to be unnecessary: "We do not agree with petitioner that 'the one crucial and determinative fact to be resolved' in this proceeding is what petitioner said to Mrs. Ragsdale. Rather, in our view, the fact that determines his culpability is what he left unsaid, i.e., his failure to disclose that he needed funds for his own use because of his pressing financial obligations and his inability to obtain funds elsewhere." . . . "Petitioner admittedly initiated the transaction, and whether he subjectively regarded it as a loan to him or an investment in him, he failed to fully and fairly disclose that the ultimate object of the investment was a temporary solution to his financial problems. He has not sustained his burden of showing that the transaction was 'at arm's length' [citation], and the record amply supports the finding that he 'used his position as an attorney for Mrs. Ragsdale and his knowledge of her lack of understanding of financial matters and her trust and confidence in him to obtain money from her fraudulently for his personal use without full, fair and truthful disclosure of the purpose for which the funds were to be used, and of his then existing financial condition which, if it had been disclosed, would have thwarted his purpose in acquiring these funds.' "

Petitioner's conduct was similar to that of the attorneys in the cases just cited. He solicited funds from Coss knowing that Coss placed great trust in him, that Coss was unsophisticated in financial matters, and that safety of the funds was a matter of the highest importance to Coss, a young man with a family to support who had recently suffered an injury leaving him paralyzed from the waist down and unable to perform his previous occupation of painter. Petitioner did not fully disclose his relationship with Satellite, nor did he advise Coss that Satellite had almost no invested capital, that the equipment installed at the Sands Hotel was not working properly, or that funds were unobtainable from commercial lenders. Petitioner did not suggest that Coss seek independent advice regarding the transaction. Petitioner guaranteed Satellite's note but only after Coss reminded him of his oral promise to do so. Petitioner failed to disclose that he would have no funds to make good on the guarantee if the Sands Hotel project failed. In short, this was not an arm's length business deal, material facts were concealed, and there is ample precedent for imposing discipline.

An attorney may be disciplined by disbarment or suspension for a willful violation of the rules of professional conduct. . . . Knowledge of the provision violated need not be shown nor is ignorance a defense: willful breach is established by evidence showing the attorney acted or omitted to act purposely. . . . Petitioner characterizes his own conduct as a negligent failure to comply with a purely technical requirement that he disclose his status as a principal of Satellite and that he obtain Coss's consent to his acting in a dual capacity. In so doing petitioner ignores the substance of the wrong he committed, which was an abuse of the trust reposed in him by his failure to disclose fully and fairly the highly risky nature of the enterprise for which he was soliciting funds. The manner in which the transaction was presented to Coss was carefully designed to place it in the most favorable light and to disclose none of the information which could have discouraged Coss from accepting. Petitioner knew what he was doing and intended to commit the acts. (*Abeles v. State Bar* (1973) 9 Cal.3d 603, 611.) Petitioner's conduct could not have been other than willful. . . .

CASE QUESTIONS

1. What problem does Mr. Beery share with Marvin Mitchelson in *Hanlin v. Mitchelson*, from Chapter 10?
2. What standard governs advice lawyers give to clients in lawyer-client transactions?
3. What right does a client presumptively have with regard to such transactions?
4. What must a lawyer do to rebut the presumption of undue influence?
5. Suppose Mr. Beery had made good on his personal guarantee; would that have mattered?

6. Suppose you had to demonstrate that a transaction with a client complied with your fiduciary obligations. How would you do it?

Generally it is clear when lawyers engage in transactions with clients within the meaning of the relevant disciplinary rules. But there are gray areas. For example, suppose you wish to represent a client and obtain a lien on some property securing your fee in the event the client fires you and then prevails. (This is called a "charging lien.") If you negotiate that provision up front, before assuming fiduciary duties, does the lien create an interest adverse to the client, and thus bring the fee agreement within the ambit of rules governing transactions with clients?

Interpreting California's Rule 3–300, in *Fletcher v. Davis*, 33 Cal.4th 61 (2004), the California Supreme Court said: Yes. The case involved a business, Master Washer (MW) evicted from its rented premises for failure to pay rent. The landlord refused to allow MW to enter the premises and reclaim its equipment, without which it could not operate. MW retained counsel to defend the eviction action and to file its own claim for conversion of its equipment.

MW and its counsel, Freddie Fletcher, negotiated an oral fee agreement under which MW would pay Fletcher $200 per hour plus costs. In lieu of a retainer, MW agreed to give Fletcher a lien on any judgment or settlement it received from the landlord plus an unspecified percentage "bonus" if the recovery was "large." Fletcher tried MW's conversion claim but the result was a mistrial. MW then fired him and hired another lawyer, who obtained a $504,000 judgment for MW.

Fletcher sued MW and its principals for distributing this sum in violation of his lien rights. The Supreme Court noted:

"[W]e have characterized as adverse an attorney's purchase of a note secured by a first deed of trust on property that was the subject of the litigation the attorney was engaged to pursue and on which the clients had a note secured by the second deed of trust; an attorney's acquisition of a writ of execution against the husband's property to secure payment of fees in a domestic dispute and the attorney's subsequent decision to levy on his own writ instead of the writ of his client, the wife; and an attorney's acquisition from the client of a note secured by a deed of trust in real property in order to secure payment of legal fees.

We have contrasted the above transactions with an unsecured promissory note, which 'gives an attorney only a right to proceed against the client's assets in a contested judicial proceeding at which the client may dispute the indebtedness. The note allows the attorney to obtain a judgment, and to seek to enforce the judgment against the client's assets, if any. It does not give the attorney a *present* interest in the client's property which the attorney can summarily realize.'

An attorney's charging lien on the proceeds of the litigation falls somewhere between these extremes. . . . we agree with Davis and Fischbach that it was reasonably foreseeable the charging lien could become detrimental to the client. Although a charging lien does not grant an attorney the power to summarily extinguish the client's interest in any recovery, a charging lien could significantly *impair* the client's interest by delaying payment of the recovery or settlement proceeds until any disputes over the lien can be resolved. For example, when there is a dispute over the existence or amount of an attorney's charging lien, the attorney can prevent the judgment debtor or the settling party from remitting the recovery to the client until the dispute is resolved. Alternatively, when the settlement draft is made jointly payable to the client and the attorney, the attorney may refuse to endorse the check until the dispute is resolved.[15] Even when the proceeds have been deposited in the client's trust account, the attorney may withhold an amount equivalent to the disputed portion. In each of these instances when the charging lien is disputed, the client's recovery will be 'tied up until everyone involved can agree on how the money should be divided . . . or until one or the other brings an independent action for declaratory relief.'

In sum, a charging lien grants the attorney considerable authority to detain all or part of the client's recovery whenever a dispute arises over the lien's existence or its scope. That would unquestionably be detrimental to the client. . . . A charging lien is therefore an adverse interest within the meaning of rule 3–300 and thus requires the client's informed written consent.[16] [§ 43 of] the Restatement Third of the Law Governing Lawyers is in accord. . . .

Finally, our holding that an attorney's charging lien to secure payment of hourly fees is adverse within the meaning of rule 3–300 does not compromise the public policy in favor of attorney liens. Rule 3–300 does not bar attorneys from obtaining liens on future recoveries. The rule merely requires the attorney who wishes to obtain such a lien to explain the transaction fully, to offer fair and reasonable terms, to provide a copy of the agreement, to give the client an opportunity to seek independent legal advice, and to secure the client's written consent. This is not a great deal more than is now required for most fee agreements: attorneys are

---

[15] FN2. Indeed, the attorney *must* do so in order to preserve the charging lien. (*In the Matter of Feldsott* (Review Dept.1997) 3 Cal. State Bar Ct. Rptr. 754, 758, 1997 WL 672661.)

[16] FN3. [The Court cited an opinion of the Los Angeles County Bar Association holding that Rule 3–300 does not apply to liens to secure contingent fees.] We are presented here only with a lien to secure hourly fees and thus do not decide whether rule 3–300 applies to a contingency-fee arrangement coupled with a lien on the client's prospective recovery in the same proceeding. (Cf. Bus. & Prof.Code, § 6147.)

required, with limited exceptions, to put most fee agreements in writing and explain fully the terms of the agreement. . . .

We therefore conclude that an attorney who secures payment of hourly fees by acquiring a charging lien against a client's future judgment or recovery has acquired an interest that is adverse to the client, and so must comply with the requirements of rule 3–300.[17] Fletcher failed to comply with the rule. Accordingly, Fletcher's lien may not be enforced in this proceeding. . . . "

The California State Bar Committee on Professional Responsibility and Conduct has taken the position that the rule of *Fletcher* is limited to cases in which counsel charges an hourly fee, and does not apply to contingent fee arrangements. Coprac Op. 2006–107.

Sugarman v. State Bar, 51 Cal.3d 609, 611 (1990), provides perspective on the adverse interest rule. Sugarman represented a company called Sundance, which owed him $30,000 in unpaid fees. Sugarman also represented Sundance's president, Bagdrasarian, in his individual capacity. Sundance acquired the right to buy another firm and asked Sugarman to represent it in the transaction. Sugarman told the Sundance directors that he could not afford to do more work for the company until he was paid what he was already owed. The board told him he would be paid in 30 days, but Sugarman said he could not wait.

Bagdarasian offered to pay Sugarman $15,000 from Bagdarasian's own money. The deal was that Sugarman would repay Bagdarasian in installments, as Sugarman received payment from Sundance. Sugarman agreed, so long as the two executed a note to make it a "real" transaction. The loan went through, but Sugarman later declared bankruptcy and listed Bagdarasian as a creditor. The Court held that the predecessor to Rule 3–300 applies even where a client extends a loan to an attorney in lieu of fees: " 'All dealings between an attorney and his client that are beneficial to the attorney will be closely scrutinized with the utmost strictness for any unfairness.' " Sugarman was suspended from practice for three years, on terms guaranteeing actual suspension for at least one year.

---

[17] FN4. Fletcher also contends that Business and Professions Code sections 6147 and 6148, which regulate contingency-fee and hourly-fee contracts between attorneys and their clients, impliedly preempt the field of attorney-client transactions, and that section 6148, subdivision (d)(4) in particular exempted his fee agreement with Master Washer, a corporation, from any requirement of a writing. As demonstrated above, however, an agreement to secure client payment with an interest in client property imposes risks and consequences beyond those inherent in a fee agreement. A finding that regulation of the former is preempted by regulation targeted at the latter would render rule 3–300 meaningless, even though the drafters of the rule expressly contemplated that these provisions would have complementary effects. . . .

Contrast *Sugarman* with *Fergus v. Songer*, 150 Cal.App.4th 552 (2007). Songer wanted to enforce a judgment he had obtained against the owner of a hotel. He hired Fergus to do so, on a contingency-fee basis. Fergus succeeded in forcing the sale of the hotel, which Songer wanted to buy. Songer had little money, however, and the hotel needed extensive repairs.

Fergus offered to advance money to Songer in exchange for raising Fergus's contingent fee percentage from 45% of the recovery to 50%. He prepared a letter memorializing the terms but Songer never signed it. Fergus advanced money to Songer by drawing down a line of credit secured by the home he owned with his wife. She agreed to this plan only if she and Fergus became 50% partners with Songer.

Songer bought the hotel for $910,000 and later re-sold it for $4.8 million. He refused to pay Songer the contingent fee, rightly claiming that the initial contingent fee agreement was voidable for failure to comply with the requirements of Business & Professions Code § 6147, and the modification was unsigned (and would have fallen anyway with the voiding of the original agreement).

The court of appeals agreed with these arguments but found Fergus's wife had a separate claim against Songer based on her claim that he agreed to become 50% partners in the hotel in exchange for her agreement to allow the community home to be used as collateral for the advances to Songer. According to the court, "Wife was not an attorney and was not bound by section 6147 or rule 3–300. She was innocent of any wrongdoing. No evidence suggests that she was aware of Fergus's failure to comply with legal requirements or that she, in any way, participated in a scheme to do an impermissible 'end run' around section 6147 or rule 3–300. In reliance upon the partnership agreement, wife parted with valuable consideration: she put her home at risk to obtain funds to refurbish the hotel and render it operational so that it could be sold."

Market Baselines, Transaction Costs, and the Economics of Client Transactions

Transactions with clients are risky. As *Beery* suggests, if you engage in a transaction with a client the transaction is voidable by the client unless you are able to demonstrate that the client was fully informed regarding all material aspects of the transaction, and willingly entered into it, *and* that the transaction was substantively fair to the client.

Proving that a transaction was fair can be very hard to do, especially if the subject of the transaction is something that does not have a fixed value that is easy to ascertain. How does one show the fairness of the terms of an investment in such a novel venture as in-room movies were at the time *Beery* was decided? For that matter, suppose you sold a client an antique car, or a house in a vacation resort. How would you show that such transactions were fair?

The best way to think about this question is to take an arms-length market transaction as a baseline and compare that transaction to the one between lawyer and client. To take a simple example, if Microsoft stock is selling at $100 per share and the lawyer buys Microsoft stock from the client at $100 per share, it would be easy to say that the transaction is fair because the market sets an objective benchmark price for the transaction. By parity of reasoning, a transaction between a lawyer and a client at $70 per share would be suspect.

This example raises two questions. One is what happens if there is not an active market in the subject of the transaction. That was the case in *Beery*. The simple fact that no commercial lender would put more money into Beery's venture suggests that there was no market transaction to be had. To the extent such transactions serve as the baseline for fairness analysis, the absence of such a baseline implies that the lawyer—who has the burden of proving the transaction fair—is not going to be able to carry that burden. (You could get an economist to testify that she thought the transaction was fair, and the other side could get one to testify to the contrary; whether that would be good enough for you depends on whether you feel comfortable consigning your fate to a fact-finder evaluating a swearing contest.) If there is no market for transactions of the type a lawyer and client engage in, then one has to ask why the transaction occurred. A natural inference in the fiduciary context is that it occurred because the lawyer exercised his influence to the detriment of the client.

But then why would lawyers and clients ever transact? If there is a market for a transaction, the client could just go into the market. If there is not, the transaction is highly suspicious, and risky for the lawyer. How could lawyer-client transactions ever be justified? One answer is that a transaction might save on transaction costs. Even if there is a market for some transactions, and therefore a baseline against which the transaction might be measured, it might be costly for buyers and sellers to find each other. A lawyer and client have already found each other, and if they are willing to engage in a transaction at the market price they can save on search costs by dealing with each other rather than trying to find someone else.

That is a cogent economic explanation but it is incomplete. Prudent lawyers will want to take steps to verify that the transaction is fair, which means performing some sort of market comparison. That is costly in and of itself. And a prudent lawyer will advise a client to at least consider obtaining separate legal counsel for the transaction, which is costly, too, and which the client might not have to do if the client dealt with someone else. Even in the best of circumstances, the potential costs of ensuring the fairness (and appearance of fairness) of a lawyer-client transaction will erode some of the cost savings clients might get from dealing with lawyers, which leads back to the question of why such transactions make sense from the client's point of view. Probably the best rule to follow is never to engage in a client transaction unless you have a simple, convincing answer to that question.

Doing It Right

The transaction-cost baseline approach just described works well for business transactions but it does not fit as well in cases where the client is not looking for someone to transact with in general but wants to confer a gift, such as a bequest in a will, on a lawyer. By hypothesis in such cases there are no substitute transactions to serve as baselines. How, then, can fairness be established? The answer is that everything rests on the procedure by which the gift was memorialized and, in particular, whether the attorney can rebut the presumption that the gift was the product of undue influence and then, if necessary, defeat whatever evidence a plaintiff might introduce to establish such influence.

Franciscan Sisters Health Care Corp. v. Dean, 448 N.E.2d 872, 873 (1983), provides an example of an attorney who was able to rebut the presumption that a bequest by his client was void. Excerpts of the opinion follow:

Defendant John R. Dean prepared Mrs. Elizabeth Messmer's final will on February 7, 1978. After making two small specific bequests the will further provided:

"All the rest and residue of my estate, personal and mixed, I give, devise and bequeath in equal parts among them to St. Elizabeth Hospital of Danville, Illinois and my long time friend and advisor John R. Dean, or his heirs."

Mrs. Messmer died in St. Elizabeth Hospital on April 10, 1979, at the age of 97, and the will was admitted to probate shortly after Mrs. Messmer's death. The hospital's and Dean's shares were each worth approximately $130,000. The plaintiff, Franciscan Sisters Health Care Corporation, doing business as St. Elizabeth Hospital, filed suit, seeking to invalidate the entire will, alleging that Dean as the attorney who drafted the instrument had presumptively exercised undue influence in obtaining his legacy. Mr. Dean admitted in his pleadings and stipulated at trial that a presumption of his undue influence over the testator had been raised.

Finding that Dean had not overcome the presumption of undue influence, the circuit court of Vermilion County invalidated the will. Dean appealed that decision and argued before the appellate court that the trial court had misunderstood the effect of the presumption and that the evidence he presented rebutted it. . . .

Mr. Dean had known Mrs. Messmer long prior to the day the contested will was prepared. They had known each other socially for over 20 years. He acted as Mrs. Messmer's lawyer for the last few years of her life. Dean and his family had vacationed with the testator, dined with her, and visited her on holidays.

After preparation of the will in Mr. Dean's office on February 7, 1978, Dean went down the hall to the offices of attorney Edward Litak. Dean informed Litak that he had prepared a will for a client in which he, Dean, was quite a substantial beneficiary and that he wanted Litak and his secretary, Julie Hembrey (18 years old) to witness the will and to talk to the testator about it.

Dean then went back to his office and brought Mrs. Messmer to Litak's office. After introducing Mrs. Messmer to Mr. Litak, he left the office. Mr. Litak and Ms. Hembrey spent the next 15 to 20 minutes asking Mrs. Messmer if she understood what she was doing and if she knew that Mr. Dean was receiving a substantial amount.

Both Mr. Litak and Ms. Hembrey testified that they believed that at the time Mrs. Messmer executed the will she was of sound mind, acting freely and voluntarily, and under no duress of any kind. The will was executed in Litak's office after their conversation. Ms. Hembrey then went and notified Mr. Dean, who subsequently returned to Litak's office. Mrs. Messmer and Mr. Dean then left together.

This court has defined undue influence to be "any improper * * * urgency of persuasion whereby the will of a person is overpowered and he is induced to do or forbear an act which he would not do or would do if left to act freely." (Powell v. Bechtel (1930), 340 Ill. 330, 338.) To set aside a will, this court has found that the undue influence "must be of such a nature as to destroy the testator's freedom concerning the disposition of his estate and render his will that of another." (Breault v. Feigenholtz (1973), 54 Ill.2d 173, 181.) It is important to understand what one faces when suing to invalidate a will that complies with the statutory prerequisites.

Mr. Dean does not dispute the fact that because he drafted the will and stands to gain a substantial legacy from it, a presumption of undue influence has been raised. At issue here is what is required to rebut such a presumption and whether that requirement was met.

In Diederich v. Walters (1976), 65 Ill.2d 95, 100–03 (hereafter Diederich), this court addressed the approach taken in courts of this State concerning the effect of presumptions:

"The determination of whether a jury should be instructed as to the existence of a presumption must be made by the trial court in the context of the facts and circumstances of each case with reference to the applicable law, the evidence, other instructions and the particular nature and procedural effect of the presumption itself. With regard to the procedural effect of presumptions, most jurisdictions in this country follow the rule that a rebuttable presumption may create a prima facie case as to the particular issue in question and thus has the practical effect of requiring the party against whom it operates to come forward with evidence to meet the presumption. However, once evidence opposing the presumption comes into the case, the presumption ceases to operate, and the issue is determined on the basis of the evidence adduced at trial as if no presumption had ever existed. (See 1 Jones, Evidence sec. 3:8 (6th ed. 1972).) The burden of proof thus does not shift but remains with the party who initially had the benefit of the presumption. . . .

The amount of evidence that is required from an adversary to meet the presumption is not determined by any fixed rule. A party may simply have to respond with some evidence or may have to respond with substantial evidence. If a strong presumption arises, the weight of the evidence brought in to rebut it must be great. . . .

The potential for abuse is great where an attorney drafts a will and stands to benefit from that will. Clients may often depend upon their attorneys for both financial and legal advice. As the relationship of attorney-client grows, a sense of trust develops and is strengthened between the two parties. This trust can be abused by an unscrupulous attorney, and we feel it is usually unnecessary for lawyers to prepare clients' documents under which they benefit. Almost always, a third party is available who can intervene and provide a disinterested perspective.

We therefore feel that as matter of public policy an attorney in such a situation must provide "clear and convincing" evidence to rebut the presumption of undue influence once it has been raised.

We now find that measured by a "clear and convincing" standard, the evidence brought forward by Mr. Dean was sufficient to rebut the presumption of undue influence. . . .

It was established that although the testator was old, she was alert and intelligent. She managed her own personal and business affairs prior to and during the period in which the contested will was executed.

Both Mr. Litak and Ms. Hembrey concluded that the will represented Mrs. Messmer's wishes. It is important to recall that this assessment was made after considerable questioning of Mrs. Messmer, in the office of Mr. Litak without Mr. Dean being present. Litak asked the testator what her relation to Dean was; whether the substantial gift to Dean was in accordance with her wishes; and whether Dean or anyone else had suggested the gift or pressured her into making it. Litak and Hembrey were convinced that she was aware that Mr. Dean was made a substantial beneficiary under the will and that is what she wanted to do. We conclude that the evidence Mr. Dean presented is sufficient to overcome the presumption of undue influence. In accord with Thayer's theory in effectively rebutting the presumption, the "bubble" has burst and the presumption of undue influence has vanished.

Sufficient evidence has been produced to rebut the presumption of undue influence as a matter of law. However, the judge as the trier of fact must now weigh the evidence and consider any and all reasonable inferences that can be drawn from these facts, including the possible inference of undue influence. Our decision here affirms the appellate court, which held that after the presumption is rebutted as a matter of law "[w]hat remains is a factual question, and we remand the cause to the trial judge as trier of fact to assess the strength of the evidence." (102 Ill.App.3d 61, 70.) We direct that the circuit court hear additional evidence as to whether Mr. Dean in fact exercised undue influence on Mrs. Messmer in the drafting of her will which provided a substantial beneficial interest to him.

See also In re Bleil's Estate, 96 Cal.App. 283, 285 (1929) ("The presumption of undue influence which attached to the attorney solely because he was the attorney for the testatrix was not positive in character. In order that the presumption become absolute, evidence of activity, persuasion, or instigation on the part of the attorney, directed toward the execution of the will in his favor, is an indispensable prerequisite.").

The Main Points to Recall From Chapter 11(F)–(G) Are:

- Clients may consent to representation that otherwise would be prohibited by conflict rules so long as the attorney reasonably believes he or she will be able to satisfy her obligations to each client and each client consents after being fully informed of what they are consenting to and how their consent will affect their interests.
- Consent may be given when a conflict arises or in advance.
- Lawyers may engage in transactions with clients if the transaction terms are fair (i.e., they are the same as the client would get in a disinterested, market transaction); the lawyer discloses to the client all relevant information; and advises the client as he or she would advise a client doing a transaction with someone else.

H. PARTICULAR PROBLEMS INVOLVING INSURERS

Insurance companies are a very common source of business for some lawyers. One type of representation involves an insurance company hiring a lawyer to represent an insured who has been involved in an accident. In such a case the insurance policy will require the insurance company (subject to certain exclusions) both to defend and indemnify the insured. Where the insured is sued because of the accident, the defense obligation will include an obligation to pay for a lawyer. Typically the lawyer will be selected and paid by the insurance company.

This structure presents three issues. The first is whether the lawyer represents only the insured or both the insured and the insurance company. Jurisdictions vary on their default rule on this question. The second is whether the insured is at risk from a lawyer who is paid by, and may have a long relationship with, the insurer. Model Rule 1.8(f) allows a lawyer to accept payment from a non-client if the client gives informed consent, the lawyer's independent judgment is not compromised, and the client's confidences are maintained. These conditions are generally satisfied in such situations but independence of judgment can be an issue, as the first case demonstrates. Finally, a particular kind of conflict of interest arises if an insurer pays to defend an insured while reserving the right to claim later that the insurance policy did not cover the relevant matter. The following materials explore these issues.

PURDY V. PACIFIC AUTO. INS. CO.

157 Cal.App.3d 59 (1984)

L. THAXTON HANSON, ASSOCIATE JUSTICE.

Plaintiffs David E. Purdy and Thomas C. Wood, Trustee for David E. Purdy, Bankrupt, filed a complaint alleging bad faith refusal to settle and professional negligence (legal malpractice). Named as defendants were the insurer, Pacific Automobile Insurance Company, a corporation (hereinafter Pacific), and Pacific's attorney, Roger W. Roberts, as well as two law firms in which Roberts was a partner during the actionable events, Parker, Stanbury, McGee and Roberts and Roberts, Mead & Harrison, and various Does. . . .

On Saturday, May 15, 1970, plaintiff Purdy, Marion "Buck" Partin, and various members of their respective families, went for an overnight campout on a dry lake in San Bernardino County. These two men had known each other since childhood in Missouri, and had renewed their association in California when both were employed by Philco–Ford in Newport Beach.

The campers arrived at the southwest end of Saugy Dry Lake in the late afternoon, and set up camp. Purdy had driven to the lake on Partin's motorcycle, but once there commenced operation on the dry lake bed of a motorcycle he had never driven before, a Yamaha owned by Carl Partin, Buck's cousin. Buck mounted a Harley–Davidson motorcycle owned by George Henricks, and also drove out on the dry lake bed. Neither Purdy nor Partin were wearing helmets. The two motorcycles collided violently; both men were injured, but more particularly Partin, who sustained severe and permanent injuries, including brain damage.Both men suffered some degree of amnesia after the accident, and there was initial difficulty in determining how the collision had occurred. There were no actual eyewitnesses to the accident.

On May 5, 1971, Partin filed suit against Purdy, Carl Partin (the owner of the Yamaha) and Carl Partin's business, Partin Limestone Products, Inc. Partin was insured for liability by defendant insurer, Pacific. The policy limit was the sum of $100,000. Upon commencement of the Partin suit, Carl Partin notified Pacific, and Pacific undertook the defense of all three defendants named therein. Pacific's claims manager, Kenneth Bonar, was in charge of the matter. He hired Attorney Roger W. Roberts and his firm, Parker, Stanbury, McGee and Roberts, to defend.

Pacific had obtained a statement from Purdy on November 16, 1970, in which Purdy declared that he and Partin had separated on the lake bed and that Purdy had been heading back toward the campsite at the southwest end of the dry lake when the collision occurred. Purdy was suffering from some retrograde amnesia, and did not remember seeing Partin just before the collision. A supplemental statement was taken from Purdy on December 7, 1971. In it, Purdy declared that he was heading back toward the campsite, driving southwest, when he heard Partin's cycle behind him, and heard it accelerate just before the two motorcycles impacted. Purdy gave a similar account in his deposition. Purdy's version of events was the foundation for the defense theory that Partin had caused the accident by accelerating and cutting in front of Purdy just before the collision.

However, it became abundantly clear by November 1972, when Partin's attorney made his first demand for settlement at policy limits, that Purdy's version of events was not supported by a substantial body of other evidence that had become known to Pacific. There appeared to be a gap in time, between Purdy's last recollection of heading back toward the camp and the collision. A number of witnesses who did not observe actual impact, nevertheless placed the collision point at the western side of the lake, and recalled that both drivers were headed away from the campsite, not toward it, at the time of the accident. The accounts of these witnesses were supported by a photograph taken of the tracks of the two cycles and the angle of impact.

On November 3, 1971, Pacific received the most comprehensive account to date of the accident, in a statement given by Garold Partin. Partin declared that prior to the accident, both cycles were headed away from the campsite; that Partin was *ahead* of Purdy on the Harley–Davidson and was driving at a moderate rate of speed, while Purdy was travelling much faster on the Yamaha. The collision had occurred, according to Garold Partin, when Purdy's vehicle overtook the Partin vehicle; this witness had observed the point of impact, on the left of the Harley–Davidson right behind the driver's seat. The seat had in fact been pushed up, as if the wheel of the Yamaha had struck it.

Garold Partin's statement was the subject of a letter written by Pacific's Bonar to Pacific's attorney, Roberts, in November 1971. Bonar conceded that Garold Partin's account was very revealing about what had actually occurred at Saugy Lake. Attorney Roberts concurred in this estimate; in a letter to Bonar on November 14, 1971, Roberts declared that it appeared that Purdy had overtaken Partin and had in fact caused the collision by misjudging the distances involved. Garold Partin's account of the accident was validated in May 1972 in a report of Truesdail Laboratories, Inc., the expert accident reconstruction firm retained by Pacific. On May 30, 1972, Attorney Roberts noted this fact in a letter to Bonar.

It had long been apparent that due to Partin's severe injuries that any jury verdict for Partin would greatly exceed the $100,000 limit. Attorney Roberts had at least twice, in letters to Bonar dated September 30, 1971 and January 25, 1972, referred to this state of affairs, as evidence was accumulating that the defense theory was incorrect and the possibility that Partin would be found contributorily negligent was diminishing.

A mandatory settlement conference on the Partin–Purdy suit was held on November 15, 1972, and was attended by both Bonar and Roberts. Partin's attorney offered to settle the entire claim for the policy limits of $100,000. Bonar, who had the authority to settle to the policy limits, refused to do so.

Shortly thereafter, Bonar discovered that Partin's counsel had deposed Truesdail Laboratories' engineer, Ralph Engdahl, learning that Engdahl had come to the conclusion that Partin had not been contributorily negligent, but that Purdy had caused the accident. Partin's counsel had Engdahl served with a subpoena for trial.

The second offer of settlement was made by Partin's attorney in a letter to Attorney Roberts on December 11, 1972. Bonar instructed Roberts to refuse to settle, and Roberts communicated the refusal to Partin's counsel by letter dated December 21, 1972. Pacific refused to settle, even though it now appeared that the opinion of their expert Engdahl about how the accident had occurred was shared by another expert hired by Partin, Fred Cady of Blewett & Associates. Bonar testified at trial that even knowing that Purdy's account of the accident would be disputed by two experts on accident reconstruction, he was still confident that "some" expert would be found by Attorney Roberts to support Purdy's version of events.

The third and final offer of settlement was made by Partin's counsel at a chambers conference on January 15, 1973, just prior to the commencement of trial. Bonar refused to settle. Attorney Roberts made a strategic attempt to obtain bifurcation of liability from the other issues in litigation, but failed.

The case went to trial, and on February 2, 1973, the jury returned a verdict for Partin against Purdy in the sum of $325,000. Judgment was entered February 5, 1973. Bonar continued to reject the idea that Purdy had been responsible for the accident, and sought a new trial. When that was denied, Pacific took an appeal from the judgment, a judgment subsequently affirmed by the Court of Appeal on January 13, 1975. Pacific ultimately paid the $100,000 sum but that left the major part of the judgment outstanding against Purdy. (Carl Partin's liability was limited to $15,000, as the owner of the vehicle involved in the collision).

Expert testimony was presented at the present trial below concerning Pacific's refusal to settle by an experienced personal injury defense lawyer, David Canter, and by claims analyst Kenneth McBride. These experts were of the opinion that by the time the *first* offer of settlement was made, in November 1972, it was clear from the evidence already gathered and known to Pacific that a verdict for Partin in excess of the policy limits was highly probable, and that Pacific's refusal to settle at that time or thereafter was not reasonable.

There was also considerable testimony at the present trial indicating that Purdy was never told of the first offer of settlement; was told of the second offer only shortly before it expired and was not given an opportunity to express any opinion about that offer; was never advised of the accumulated evidence that he, not Partin, had been responsible for the accident; and was never advised of the third and final offer of settlement. Just prior to trial, on January 2, 1973, Attorney Roberts had received a letter from Purdy, dated December 28, 1972, in which Purdy requested "very strongly" that the case be settled within policy limits. Bonar was advised of Purdy's position, but testified that knowing that Purdy wanted the litigation ended had no impact on his evaluation of the situation.

Purdy testified at trial concerning his long friendship with Partin, both in Missouri and California. The verdict rendered against Purdy, memorialized the fact, as it were, that Purdy was responsible for Partin's severe injuries. This was very distressing to Purdy. He stated that, "It hurt then, and it hurts now, and it always will." After the verdict, Purdy testified, he was shunned by friends and co-workers the two men had had in common.

Purdy, also injured in the accident, was unable to work and in 1971 lost his job at Philco–Ford. By the time of trial, in January of 1973, he was about $7,000 or $8,000 in debt, but even after the adverse judgment he had no intention of filing bankruptcy. In September 1972, he began new employment as a district manager for a newspaper, supervising about fifty carriers.

Purdy testified that in October 1974, he learned that although the appeal was still pending in Partin v. Purdy, the balance of the judgment unpaid could be enforced by Partin against any assets Purdy had at any time. On October 30, 1974, Purdy reluctantly filed his petition to be adjudicated a bankrupt, and listed the Partin judgment as the major outstanding debt. Purdy testified that had it not been for the Partin judgment, he never would have found it necessary to declare bankruptcy, but there was simply no way that he could pay off even a portion of the outstanding judgment owed to Partin. There was further testimony by Purdy that the fact of his bankruptcy filing had caused him humiliation and anxiety in connection with his present employment, and that he had difficulty thereafter in obtaining ordinary credit. . . .

THE LEGAL MALPRACTICE ACTIONS

Both plaintiff Purdy and his plaintiff trustee have appealed from adverse judgments rendered below concerning their causes of action for professional negligence (legal malpractice) against Pacific's attorney, Roberts, and the law firms in which he was a partner during the actionable events. (Attorney Roberts changed his partnership arrangements shortly before the third and final offer of settlement was rejected by Pacific). . . .

Both plaintiffs specifically alleged that the gravamen of their complaint against the lawyers for Pacific was that they had "negligently failed to effectuate a settlement" of the Partin suit, and that had they performed with professional skill at the standard required of them, the settlement would have been made and the harm avoided. The trial court awarded the lawyer defendants judgment on the pleadings against plaintiff trustee, and nonsuited Purdy on his cause against the lawyers at the conclusion of his evidence. . . .

In the case at bench . . . there were in fact two clients, the insurance carrier and the insured. We recognize that traditionally, where an insurance carrier is called upon to defend its insured, the attorney retained by the carrier for this purpose owes the same fiduciary duty to the insured as he or she would had the insured made the selection of counsel. The attorney's primary duty has been said to be to further the best interests of the insured.

In *American Mut. Liab. Ins. Co. v. Superior Court* (1974) 38 Cal.App.3d 579, 592, the "triangular" aspect of the representation afforded the insured by the insurer's lawyers is described as a coalition for a common purpose, a favorable disposition of the claim-with the attorney owing duties to both clients. As a practical matter, however, there has been recognition that, in reality, the insurer's attorneys may have closer ties with the insurer and a more compelling interest in protecting the insurer's position, whether or not it coincides with what is best for the insured. (See *U.S. Fid. & Guar. Co. v. Louis A. Roser Co.* (8th Cir.1978) 585 F.2d 932, 938, fn. 5.)

The problem arises when the attorney knows, or should know, that a conflict has appeared between the insurer and the insured as to the most beneficial course of action indicated by the developing circumstances. It has long been the law in this state that when a conflict develops, the *insurer* cannot compel the insured to surrender control of the litigation, and must, if necessary, secure independent counsel for the insured. . . . The conflict situation was also thoroughly discussed in *Lysick v. Walcom* (1968) 258 Cal.App.2d 136, placing a duty squarely on the attorney for the insurer to withdraw from representation or make full disclosure to both clients in the event of a conflict between them, or risk exposure to liability for harm resulting from his failure so to act, as well as to a charge of professional misconduct.

In the instant case, the record discloses that Purdy had in fact employed independent counsel as of December 1972, prior to the last offer of settlement; and that counsel strongly urged settlement of the Partin suit. Pacific, however, retained control of the litigation—to Purdy's disadvantage. The fact that Purdy did have independent counsel at a crucial stage of the settlement negotiations undoubtedly explains why the causes of action against the lawyer defendants herein were not refined to charges of failing to disclose a conflict between the insurer and insured.

Both Purdy and his trustee specified that the professional negligence of the lawyer defendants consisted of their failure to effectuate a settlement of the Partin litigation. . . . Concededly, the lawyer defendants did not order or even strongly urge Pacific to settle, perhaps because they knew such conduct would be fruitless. The correspondence between the lawyer defendants and Pacific indicates, however, that the lawyer defendants were aware of (1) the accumulating evidence of Purdy's responsibility for the accident and (2) the potential for an excess verdict, and communicated that awareness to Pacific. The practical problem was that Pacific, with a total exposure of only $100,000, apparently decided to gamble on a favorable outcome at trial, in disregard of what was most beneficial to their insured and the claimant.

There were no allegations in the trustee's cause of action against the lawyer defendants of conspiracy or of the commission of any intentional torts. In the absence of such allegations or of failure to act properly with respect to disclosure of the conflict of interest, we hold as a matter of law that the cause of action by the trustee against the lawyer defendants was fatally defective due to failure to plead sufficient proximate cause. . . .

CASE QUESTIONS

1. Whom did Roberts represent?
2. Who made decisions regarding settlement offers?
3. What did Roberts tell Purdy about settlement?
4. Describe Roberts's relationship to Pacific, and then to Purdy.
5. Describe Purdy's relationship with Partlin.
6. What allegations might have overcome the court's causation ruling?

Purdy illustrates two important points. The first is that an insurer's interests may differ from the insured's interests, and the difference may create an untenable situation for an attorney, such as Roberts, representing both parties. At a minimum, the conflict discussed in *Purdy* required Roberts to disclose to Purdy that Pacific's interests diverged from his own; more practically the divergence was so severe that Purdy needed to get separate counsel (and Roberts needed to withdraw from representing him or terminate the joint client relationship in some other manner). The second point is that causation is an important element in a malpractice case. Purdy's claim (brought by the trustee in bankruptcy) asserts that Roberts committed malpractice because Pacific refused to settle for an offer at the limits of Pacific's policy. Purdy's claim failed because lawyers cannot force clients to settle and there was no evidence that Roberts conspired with Pacific against Purdy or failed to disclose a conflict. Causation still would have been an issue had Roberts failed to discuss conflicts with Purdy because even if that failure cost Purdy the chance to demand independent counsel who could pressure Pacific to settle there could be no guarantee that such pressure would work.

Insurance policies generally require insurers to (i) defend actions based on events covered by the policy and (ii) indemnify the insured for losses for which the insured is liable based on covered events. For example, if you have automobile insurance, your policy probably requires your insurer to pay for damages you cause if you are responsible for an accident and to pay your costs of defense based on any suit arising from the accident.

This seemingly simple structure is both extremely common and much more complicated than it seems at first glance. When an insurance company hires a lawyer to defend an insured, who is the client? All jurisdictions agree that the insured is a client. After all, the insured is the person the lawyer is hired to defend. But the insurance company has client-like characteristics, too. The insurance company will generally choose the lawyer, have at least some ability to control the defense (deciding whether to settle and for how much, for example), and pay the lawyer.

Jurisdictions differ on the question whether the insurance company is a client in this situation. In *Pine Island Farmers Coop v. Erstad & Riemer, P.A.*, 649 N.W.2d 444, 445 (Minn. 2002), the court noted the problem and chose a default rule of insured-only representation, subject to modification by the parties:

> Liability insurance contracts grant the insurer rights to participate in and, in some areas, control the defense of claims against the insured. . . . As a result, defense counsel and the insurer inevitably share information about claims. With defense counsel and the insurer in frequent contact over the details of the litigation, the insurer has ample opportunity to inform defense counsel how different approaches to the claim might affect its interests. When the interests of the insurer differ from those of the insured, defense counsel who represents both may find itself in what we have called "an exceedingly awkward position."
>
> The danger is that, if a conflict of interest does arise, the nature of the tripartite relationship makes it likely that defense counsel will tend to favor the interests of the insurer at the expense of those of the insured. As one commentator has stated, defense counsel "may be tempted to help the client [the insurer] who pays the bills, who will send further business, and with whom long-standing personal relationships have developed." Ronald E. Mallen & Jeffrey M. Smith, 4 *Legal Malpractice* § 29.16, at 325 (5th ed.2000). Similarly, the Eighth Circuit Court of Appeals explained:
>
> > Even the most optimistic view of human nature requires us to realize that an attorney employed by an insurance company will slant his efforts, perhaps unconsciously, in the interests of his real client—the one who is paying his fee and from whom he hopes to receive future business—the insurance company.
>
> *United States Fid. & Guar. Co. v. Louis A. Roser Co.,* 585 F.2d 932, 938 n. 5 (8th Cir.1978).
>
> As these authorities suggest, it may be rather difficult for defense counsel who represents both the insured and the insurer to provide the insured with "the same 'undeviating and single allegiance' that he would owe to the insured if retained and paid by [the insured]." In this way, permitting dual representation can cause damage to the relationship between defense counsel and the insured by eroding the

> insured's trust and confidence in defense counsel's ability to faithfully represent his or her interests. . . .
>
> Based on these considerations, we hold that, in the absence of a conflict of interest between the insured and the insurer, the insurer can become a co-client of defense counsel based on contract or tort theory if two conditions are satisfied. First, defense counsel or another attorney must consult with the insured, explaining the implications of dual representation and the advantages and risks involved. Second, after consultation, the insured must give its express consent to the dual representation.

Purdy adopts a different default rule. It holds that in such cases counsel represents both the insurer and the insured. That statement might be read to imply that the insurer and insured have equal claims on counsel's loyalty. But the *Purdy* court also said the "attorney's primary duty has been said to be to further the best interests of the insured." How would you reconcile those statements if you were hired by an insurer to represent an insured?

The best answer is not that your actions would depend on the issue. To take just one example, suppose an insurer hires you to represent an insured and you learn the insured lied on his policy application, thus defrauding the insurer and providing a possible defense for the insurer as against the insured? May you or must you inform the insurer about the insured's fraud? COPRAC Opinion 1995–139 holds that you represent both the insured and insurer but that

> if an insured reveals matters to the attorney in confidence, and these matters are not intended to be heard by the insurer, the attorney may not reveal them to the insurer, regardless of the relationship between them. . . . The same analysis applies to any secrets of the insured/client learned by the attorney during the course of the representation.
>
> . . . even where the attorney has a close ongoing relationship with an insurer, and from a business perspective considers insurer an important "client," in any particular representation it is the obligation to protect the *insured's* confidences and secrets which is paramount. . . . This is true even where the attorney comes to believe that the insured has fraudulently created a situation in which coverage appears to exist where it actually does not.

The opinion goes on to state that if you evaluate the information at issue and conclude that you would have a duty to inform the insurer of it if you represented the insurer alone, then you have a conflict and must withdraw.

Which brings up the next question: What happens when there is a conflict, and how might a conflict come up? We'll take the second question first. The confidential information example just given is one way a conflict might arise. More commonly, a conflict may arise because of a coverage dispute. What is that?

Any given incident may relate to an insurance policy in one of three ways: it is either not covered at all, covered, or within the scope of coverage but excluded. Suppose you have an automobile insurance policy and (1): your house burns down in a fire. The fire is not covered by the auto policy (though it may, of course, be covered by a homeowner's policy). Now suppose (2): you accidentally hit someone at a stop sign. The accident is covered by the policy. Now suppose (3): you intentionally run down your professional responsibility teacher with your car, killing him. That accident would fall within the scope of coverage in the sense that it would have to do with your car, but it would almost certainly be excluded: the policy would not cover you for deliberate harm you caused using the car. To simplify things, let's call examples (1) and (3) "not covered" and example (2) "covered."

Now let's take a more realistic example. Suppose you are an insurer, and you have issued to the owner of a building a policy that covers general business liability (personal injury or property damage) but which excludes both intentional misconduct and liability for harm to the environment. The owner leases the building to a dry cleaning business, which is accused of polluting nearby groundwater. The owner (your insured) asks you to defend and indemnify it against regulatory and other liability based on the actions of its tenant. What do you do? Here is a description of the resulting problem, from *Armstrong Cleaners, Inc. v. Erie Ins. Exch.*, 364 F. Supp. 2d 787, 801 (S.D. Ind. 2005).

The problem here is one that arises often when a liability insurer cannot be confident at the outset of litigation whether the insured's actions are covered by the liability insurance policy. An insurer who faces such uncertainty has four options. First, it may decide to ignore its doubts and simply provide a defense and coverage under the policy. Second, an insurer that is confident the claim is not covered may simply deny coverage and a defense, leaving the insured to fend for himself. If the insurer turns out to be wrong on the issue of coverage, though, the insurer will be estopped from challenging the insured's handling of the underlying case, will be held liable for costs of defense and settlement/judgment up to policy limits, and may also be held liable for punitive damages for bad faith denial of claims. [citations omitted]

The third and fourth options offer a middle ground. The insurer can file a declaratory judgment action for a judicial determination of its obligations under the policy, or it can defend its insured under a reservation of rights. [citations omitted] Either of these two actions will preserve an insurer's right to challenge later the extent of coverage without being estopped by a judgment in the underlying action. [citation omitted]

If the insurer follows either of these latter two options, the insurer and its insured go forward together to defend the underlying litigation, but with at least a simmering potential conflict in their interests. The problem arises because liability insurance policies typically give the insurer control over the defense of the underlying litigation. In cases where the handling of the underlying litigation may affect whether the claim is covered or not covered, the conflict of interests may be sufficiently clear and immediate that one attorney cannot represent the interests of both the insurer and the insured.

The classic example in Indiana law is a lawsuit by a person who has been shot and injured by the insured. The victim alleges in Count One that the insured shot him intentionally and in the alternative in Count Two that the insured shot him negligently. Under a typical liability insurance policy, coverage is available for negligent acts but not for intentional acts. The insurer therefore would benefit from either a defense verdict or a finding of intentional wrongdoing. The insured, on the other hand, would benefit from either a defense verdict or a finding of negligence. Absent informed consent of both the insurer and the insured, an attorney trying to represent both the insured and the insurer would face an insurmountable conflict of interest. [citation omitted]

Let's pause here to make sure this situation is clear. As we noted earlier, a claim is either not covered, covered, or excluded. You can diagram the situation this way:

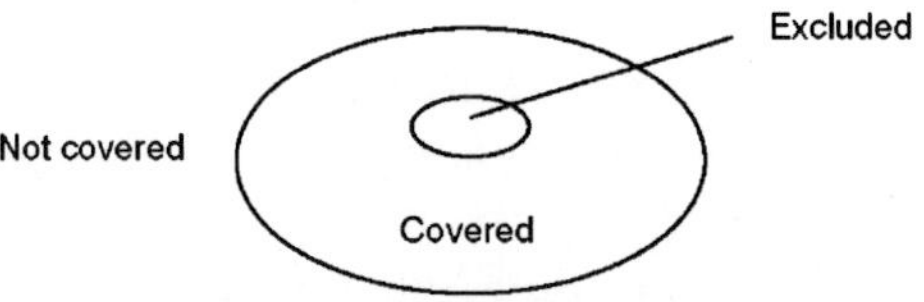

The insurer has to indemnify the insured for losses that are covered but not excluded. The insurer does not have to pay indemnity for either uncovered or excluded acts. This structure can create a sort of schizophrenia for the insurer: it's best (cheapest) option is to claim either that nothing within the policy happened or that it happened deliberately. That can create a conflict for counsel: the insured might prefer a negligence finding while the insurer might prefer a finding of willful misconduct. That conflict could affect a wide variety of decisions at trial, from how to examine witnesses to whether to ask for special verdict forms. Not every case is that hard, of course. Let's return to *Armstrong*:

At the same time, not every reservation of rights poses a conflict for defense counsel. If the coverage dispute turns on issues that are independent of the issues in the underlying lawsuit, one lawyer selected by the insurer can handle the underlying litigation, and the insured and insurer can resolve the coverage dispute separately. [citations omitted]

How should courts, insurers, and policyholders distinguish between reservations of rights that create conflicts requiring informed consent by the insured and those that do not? The problem is governed at its core by the Rules of Professional Conduct that address conflicts of interest where an attorney has multiple clients or where a third party is paying the attorney to represent a client (such as the insured). . . .

The governing Rule of Professional Conduct is Rule 1.7(a). As amended effective January 1, 2005, the rule provides that unless the client gives informed consent, a lawyer shall not represent a client if the representation involves a "concurrent conflict of interest." A concurrent conflict of interest exists if "there is a significant risk that the representation of one or more clients will be materially limited by the lawyer's responsibilities to another client, a former client or a third person or by a personal interest of the lawyer." Ind. R. Prof. Cond. 1.7(a)(2).

Under this standard, attorneys, parties, and courts cannot resort to easy rules of thumb. . . . "There is no talismanic rule that allows a facile determination of whether a disqualifying conflict of interests exists. Instead, the potential for conflict requires a careful analysis of the parties' respective interests to determine whether they can be reconciled . . . or whether an actual conflict of interest precludes insurer-appointed defense counsel from presenting a quality defense for the insured." [citations omitted]

Whether the potential conflict of interest is sufficient to require the insured's consent is a question of degree that requires some predictions about the course of the representation. If there is a reasonable possibility that the manner in which the insured is defended could affect the outcome of the insurer's coverage dispute, then the conflict may be sufficient to require the insurer to pay for counsel of the insured's choice. Evaluating that risk requires close attention to the details of the underlying litigation. The court must then make a reasonable judgment about whether there is a significant risk that the attorney selected by the insurance company will have the representation of the insureds significantly impaired by the attorney's relationship with the insurer.

Erie argues here that the rule is simple: If the underlying lawsuit alternatively alleges covered and non-covered conduct by the insured (such as the intentional v. negligent shooting cases), then the conflict requires independent counsel. If the underlying lawsuit does not alternatively allege both covered and non-covered conduct on the part of the insured, then the insurer's reservation of rights does not create a conflict entitling the insured to select his own attorney. This simple test, however, loses sight of the broader principle, which Erie itself has correctly identified: "The conflict of interest arises because the manner in which the defense of the insured is conducted could be outcome determinative of the insurer's coverage defense, and to the Policy's duty to indemnify." That standard comes closer to the applicable standard from Rule 1.7(a)(2), a significant risk that the representation will be materially limited by the attorney's responsibilities to a third person such as the insurer. The shooting example, with its either-or choice between intentional and negligent conduct, poses a clear and easy application of that standard. The standard, however, cannot be confined to only its easiest and clearest applications. Rule 1.7(a)(2) sweeps more broadly and looks more generally at the risk that an attorney's representation of one client will be impaired by her relationship with another client or another entity paying the bill. The court therefore examines the undisputed facts concerning the coverage issues Erie has raised and their relationship to the likely course of the underlying litigation against the Armstrongs.

The balance of the *Armstrong* opinion is an analytical *tour de force.* Read it if you would like a good example of how a court should decide whether a material limitation conflict exists.

But we still have not identified what happens when there is a conflict between the insurer and insured such that control of the defense of the action might affect whether a claim was covered. What happens when that situation arises? *Cumis* counsel.

Cumis counsel refers to an attorney chosen by the insured but paid by the insurer. The name comes from *San Diego Navy Fed. Credit Union v. Cumis Ins. Soc'y*, 162 Cal.App.3d 358, 360 (1984). The *Cumis* court reasoned as follows:

> In the usual tripartite relationship existing between insurer, insured and counsel, there is a single, common interest shared among them. Dual representation by counsel is beneficial since the shared goal of minimizing or eliminating liability to a third party is the same. A different situation is presented, however, when some or all of the allega-

> tions in the complaint do not fall within the scope of coverage under the policy.
>
> In such a case, the standard practice of an insurer is to defend under a reservation of rights where the insurer promises to defend but states it may not indemnify the insured if liability is found. In this situation, there may be little commonality of interest. . . . Although issues of coverage under the policy are not actually litigated in the third party suit, this does not detract from the force of these opposing interests as they operate on the attorney selected by the insurer, who has a dual agency status. . . .
>
> We conclude the Canons of Ethics impose upon lawyers hired by the insurer an obligation to explain to the insured and the insurer the full implications of joint representation in situations where the insurer has reserved its rights to deny coverage. If the insured does not give an informed consent to continued representation, counsel must cease to represent both. Moreover, in the absence of such consent, where there are divergent interests of the insured and the insurer brought about by the insurer's reservation of rights based on possible noncoverage under the insurance policy, the insurer must pay the reasonable cost for hiring independent counsel by the insured. The insurer may not compel the insured to surrender control of the litigation.

Rules governing when an insured has a right to *Cumis* counsel have been codified in California Civil Code § 2860.

There is one last piece of the puzzle to put in place. If the insurance company thinks a claim might not be covered, why bother defending it at all? If it is not covered, then no defense was ever required. The answer is simple, and important: the duty to defend a claim is broader than the duty to indemnify for losses attributable to the claim. This answer poses a new question: if a complaint alleges both covered and non-covered claims, how are defense costs allocated between those claims?

The California Supreme Court answered this question in *Buss v. Superior Court*, 16 Cal.4th 35 (1997). *Buss* involved a business dispute that led to a complaint alleging 27 causes of action being filed against Buss and entities related to him. Among these was a cause of action for defamation, which Buss's insurer concluded was the only claim that plausibly fell within the scope of Buss's insurance policies.

That case settled, but it led to a complaint by Buss against his insurer, and a cross-complaint by the insurer against Buss. The gist of Buss's claim was that the insurer wrongly denied that it had a duty to defend the entire action; the gist of the insurer's claim was that Buss wrongly denied that the insurer could recover defense costs that it had paid for work unrelated to the defamation claim. The trial court ruled against Buss on both his claim and the insurer's; the court of appeals affirmed. On the relevant questions, the Supreme Court largely sided with the insurer:

> The insurer's duty to indemnify runs to claims that are actually covered, in light of the facts proved. By definition, it entails the payment of money in order to resolve liability. It arises only after liability is established.
>
> By contrast, the insurer's duty to defend runs to claims that are merely potentially covered, in light of facts alleged or otherwise disclosed. It entails the rendering of a service, viz., the mounting and funding of a defense in order to avoid or at least minimize liability. It arises as soon as tender is made. It is discharged when the action is concluded. It may be extinguished earlier, if it is shown that no claim can in fact be covered. If it is so extinguished, however, it is extinguished only prospectively and not retroactively: before, the insurer had a duty to defend; after, it does not have a duty to defend further.
>
> Obviously, the insurer's duty to defend is broader than its duty to indemnify. But, just as obviously, it is not unlimited. It extends beyond claims that are actually covered to those that are merely potentially so—but no further. . . .
>
> in a "mixed" action, in which some of the claims are at least potentially covered and the others are not, the insurer has a duty to defend as to the claims that are at least potentially covered, having been paid premiums by the insured therefor, but does not have a duty to defend as to those that are not, having not been paid therefor. This conclusion is in line with the "general rule" that "[w]hen a complaint in an action . . . states different causes of action . . . against the insured, one of which is within . . . coverage . . . and others of which may not be, the insurer is bound to defend *with respect to those which, if proved, would be within . . . coverage*." . . .
>
> Despite the foregoing, we have nevertheless held that, in a "mixed" action, the insurer has a duty to defend the action in its entirety. . . . We cannot justify the insurer's duty to defend the entire "mixed" action contractually, as an obligation arising out of the policy, and have never even attempted to do so. To purport to make such a justification would be to hold what we cannot-that the duty to defend exists, as it were, in the air, without regard to whether or not the claims are at least potentially covered. . . . we can, and do, justify the insurer's duty to defend the entire "mixed" action prophylactically, as an obligation imposed by law in support of the policy. . . .

> As to the claims that are at least potentially covered, the insurer may not seek reimbursement for defense costs. . . . . Under the policy, the insurer has a duty to defend the insured as to the claims that are at least potentially covered. With regard to defense costs for these claims, the insurer has been paid premiums by the insured. It bargained to bear these costs. To attempt to shift them would upset the arrangement. . . . As to the claims that are not even potentially covered, however, the insurer may indeed seek reimbursement for defense costs.

The Strategy of Judgment: Pleading Into or Out of Coverage

Insurance is an important part of litigation strategy. As the discussion in *Buss* suggests, the strategic implications of insurance begin with the drafting of the complaint. Imagine you are counsel for a plaintiff you believe has committed intentional misconduct. Should you allege only intentional misconduct or add a fall-back claim for negligent misconduct? (This question arose in *Greycas*; do you recall how it was resolved there?)

The defendant's insurance situation, and thus the availability of insurance money to pay your client, depends on your drafting choices. If you allege only intentional misconduct the defendant's insurer may take the position that the complaint alleges no covered claims. (Intentional wrongdoing is generally excluded from insurance coverage.). Limiting the complaint to intentional torts would mean the defendant would have to pay his or her own defense costs, which might make them more willing to settle. It would also mean, however, that the defendant would have to pay any settlement or judgment out of his own pocket, without help from an insurer. Adding the negligence count would mean that the defendant's insurer would subsidize his costs of defense, which might make for a tougher, more drawn-out fight, but it would also mean that the insurance proceeds might be available to pay a settlement or judgment. Complicating this analysis is the rule that the duty to defend is broader than the duty to indemnify, which means that even alleging only intentional torts might not avoid facing a funded defense if the jury could find for the plaintiff on a negligence theory.

Which strategy is best? There is no universally correct answer. It depends on the circumstances. Can you see which circumstances are key?

The Main Points to Recall From Chapter 11(H) Are:

- Attorneys hired by an insurer to defend an insured represent the insured.

- They may also represent the insurer, if the facts justify that conclusion and conflicts rules permit it. In some jurisdictions dual representation is the default position, in others it is not.
- Such attorneys may not slight the interests of the insured to advance the interests of an insurer.
- Conflicts are common in such cases, particularly if some claims are covered by an insurance policy while others are excluded.
- In such cases, some jurisdictions allow insureds to retain their own counsel at the expense the insurer.

I. THE PROHIBITION ON TRYING A CASE YOU (OR ANOTHER LAWYER IN YOUR FIRM) TESTIFY IN

Model Rule of Professional Conduct 3.7

Our final conflict of interest principle is found in Model Rule 3.7, which forbids you from trying a case in which you are likely to be a necessary witness unless your expected testimony is uncontested (such as authenticating a document nobody questions), you are testifying to the value of your own services (as you might do if you sued a client for a fee), or if disqualifying you would work a hardship on your client. You may try the case if another lawyer in your firm is likely to testify, unless the testimony creates a conflict of interest under Model Rules 1.7 or 1.9 (which would be imputed to you under Model Rule 1.10(a)). Some courts have been concerned that these rules may be used tactically and therefore have construed them strictly. The following case illustrates that approach.

MURRAY V. METROPOLITAN LIFE INSURANCE COMPANY

583 F.3d 173 (2d Cir. 2009)

DENNIS JACOBS, CHIEF JUDGE:

Plaintiffs in this class action were policyholders of Metropolitan Life Insurance Company when it was a mutual insurance company. They complain that they were misled and shortchanged in the transaction by which the company demutualized in 2000. Nine years after the action was commenced and five weeks before trial was scheduled to begin, plaintiffs moved to disqualify the lead counsel for Metropolitan Life Insurance Company and MetLife, Inc. ("MetLife"), Debevoise & Plimpton LLP ("Debevoise"). The grounds alleged related to that firm's representation of MetLife in the underlying demutualization. The United States District Court for the Eastern District of New York (Platt, *J.*) granted the motion to disqualify on September 1; the district court then stayed its order and immediately certified the issue to this Court pursuant to 28 U.S.C. § 1292(b). We accepted the certification. . . .

The district court disqualified Debevoise on the ground that its representation of MetLife in the 2000 demutualization made it counsel to the policyholders as well. On appeal, plaintiffs urge affirmance on that ground, and also on the independent ground that the witness-advocate rule requires disqualification because four Debevoise lawyers who worked on the demutualization will give testimony adverse to MetLife at trial.

[The court concluded that under the entity client principle the Debevoise firm did not represent individual policyholders by virtue of its representation of MetLife]. . . .

Plaintiffs make the separate argument that disqualification of Debevoise is proper by virtue of the witness-advocate rule set out in Rule 3.7 of the New York Rules of Professional Conduct. Subsection (a) of the Rule provides, with certain exceptions, that "[a] lawyer shall not act as an advocate before a tribunal in a matter in which the lawyer is likely to be a witness on a significant issue of fact." N.Y. R. Prof'l Conduct § 3.7(a). Subsection (b) is broader, as it addresses imputation: "A lawyer may not act as an advocate before a tribunal in a matter if . . . another lawyer in the lawyer's firm is likely to be called as a witness on a significant issue other than on behalf of the client, and it is apparent that the testimony may be prejudicial to the client." *See* N.Y. R. Prof'l Conduct § 3.7(b)(1).

Rule 3.7 lends itself to opportunistic abuse. "Because courts must guard against the tactical use of motions to disqualify counsel, they are subject to fairly strict scrutiny, particularly motions" under the witness-advocate rule. *Lamborn v. Dittmer,* 873 F.2d 522, 531 (2d Cir.1989). The movant, therefore, "bears the burden of demonstrating specifically how and as to what issues in the case the prejudice may occur and that the likelihood of prejudice occurring [to the witness-advocate's client] is substantial." "Prejudice" in this context means testimony that is "sufficiently adverse to the factual assertions or account of events offered on behalf of the client, such that the bar or the client might have an interest in the lawyer's independence in discrediting that testimony."

As this definition suggests, the showing of prejudice is required as a means of proving the ultimate reason for disqualification: harm to the integrity of the judicial system. We have identified four risks that Rule 3.7(a) is designed to alleviate: (1) the lawyer might appear to vouch for his own credibility; (2) the lawyer's testimony might place opposing counsel in a difficult position when she has to cross-examine her lawyer-adversary and attempt to impeach his credibility; (3) some may fear that the testifying attorney is distorting the truth as a result of bias in favor of his client; and (4) when an individual assumes the role of advocate and witness both, the line between argument and evidence may be blurred, and the jury confused. *Ramey v. Dist. 141, Int'l Ass'n of Machinists &*

Aerospace Workers, 378 F.3d 269, 282–83 (2d Cir.2004) (internal citations and alterations omitted). These concerns matter because, if they materialize, they could undermine the integrity of the judicial process.

In imputation cases (Rule 3.7(b)), the witness is not acting as trial counsel; these concerns are therefore "absent or, at least, greatly reduced." *Ramey,* 378 F.3d at 283 (internal quotation marks omitted); *see also* A.B.A. Model Rules of Prof'l Conduct § 3.7 cmt. 5 ("Because the tribunal is not likely to be misled when a lawyer acts as advocate in a trial in which another lawyer in the lawyer's firm will testify as a necessary witness, [Model Rule 3.7(b)] permits the lawyer to do so except in situations involving a conflict of interest."). Accordingly, disqualification by imputation should be ordered sparingly, *see Kubin v. Miller,* 801 F.Supp. 1101, 1114 (1992), and only when the concerns motivating the rule are at their most acute.

Therefore, we now hold that a law firm can be disqualified by imputation only if the movant proves by clear and convincing evidence that [A] the witness will provide testimony prejudicial to the client, and [B] the integrity of the judicial system will suffer as a result. This new formulation is consistent with our prior efforts to limit the tactical misuse of the witness-advocate rule. *See, e.g., Lamborn,* 873 F.2d at 531.

A

In this case, four Debevoise lawyers are likely to be called to testify at trial. Three of them are transactional lawyers who are not and will not be trial advocates; the fourth, a litigator, is a member of the trial team, but will not act as an advocate before the jury. None of these witnesses, then, is properly considered trial counsel for purposes of Rule 3.7(a). *See Ramey,* 378 F.3d at 283 ("The advocate-witness rule applies, first and foremost, where the attorney representing the client *before a jury* seeks to serve as a fact witness *in that very proceeding.*") (first emphasis added). If the rule applies here at all, therefore, it will be subsection (b) (imputation), and plaintiffs do not contend otherwise.

B

The parties dispute whether the Debevoise lawyer-witnesses will give testimony so prejudicial to MetLife that the integrity of the judicial system may be threatened and disqualification warranted. Our review of the record suggests that the Debevoise witnesses will do little more than authenticate documents and confirm facts that do not appear to be in dispute. For example, plaintiffs state that they intend to use the testimony of Wolcott Dunham, a Debevoise transactional lawyer, to show that MetLife "intentionally or recklessly omitted material facts from the prospectus." A review of the cited deposition excerpts, however, reveals only that Dunham testified that it was inaccurate to characterize a policyholder's interest in the company as "ownership." MetLife argues that this testimony is not adverse to its position in this litigation. Plaintiffs assert that MetLife is wrong, but do not explain why.

Plaintiffs contend that they will use the testimony of James Scoville, another Debevoise transactional lawyer, to establish that "MetLife revealed that a significant portion of the value of the Demutualization that it had said was set aside for policyholders was in fact earmarked for new stockholders." A review of the cited deposition testimony, however, shows that Scoville testified only to what various written documents clearly state. It appears that at most Scoville will be asked to authenticate those documents. And the same is true for the remaining witnesses.

We doubt that, on this record, the testimony at issue is sufficiently prejudicial to MetLife to warrant disqualification. We recognize, however, that we are not in a good position to answer this question; and there is no finding by the district court on this issue of fact.

Even if we assume that some portion of the Debevoise lawyers' testimony will be adverse to MetLife (when considered in a context that we cannot fully evaluate or appreciate on this interlocutory appeal), plaintiffs have failed to establish the clear and convincing evidence of prejudice necessary to justify the extreme remedy of disqualification by imputation.

First (as noted above), the concerns motivating Rule 3.7 are attenuated where, as here, the witness-"advocate" is *not* someone who will be trying the case to the jury. Therefore, plaintiffs seeking disqualification under Rule 3.7(b) must make a considerably higher showing of prejudice than would be required under Rule 3.7(a). From the outset, then, we are inclined to conclude that disqualification is inappropriate in this case.

Second, MetLife's desire to keep Debevoise as its trial counsel, plainly evidenced by MetLife's position in this appeal, militates strongly against a finding of prejudice. This appeal has been prosecuted in large part by MetLife's in-house lawyers, who have argued to this Court that disqualification was improper and that Debevoise should be reinstated, notwithstanding that Debevoise non-advocate lawyers are scheduled to testify as fact witnesses during trial. We are reluctant to conclude that MetLife, a sophisticated client with sophisticated in-house counsel, has a radically defective understanding of the case after nine years of litigation.

C

Even if plaintiffs could convince us that allowing Debevoise to remain as MetLife's trial counsel poses some threat to the integrity of the judicial process, we must also consider whether that vital interest may be harmed by disqualification. Parties have a well-recognized and entirely reasonable interest in securing counsel of their choice. Prospective jurors, who must leave their homes and occupations to serve, have an interest in judicial efficiency, an interest that we respect. Other litigants, whose pending matters are affected or delayed by developments in other cases, are also harmed by the uncertainties caused by disqualification. And the public in general has an interest in the swift and orderly administration of justice.

In this case, disqualification would require MetLife to retain new counsel. Appreciable time and money would be spent to bring new counsel to the state of readiness that Debevoise attained after more than nine years of work. And other circumstances intensify the harm to MetLife: several billions of dollars are at stake, the legal issues are complex, pre-trial litigation has been ongoing for more than nine years, and disqualification occurred on the eve of trial.

Finally, plaintiffs' lengthy and unexcused delay in bringing its motion to disqualify weighs against disqualification. When plaintiffs filed this lawsuit in 2000, they knew that Debevoise had represented MetLife during demutualization and that it would continue to represent MetLife in this litigation. But plaintiffs did not move to disqualify even when, seven years later, the district court ruled that plaintiffs were clients of Debevoise. Instead, plaintiffs waited until after settlement negotiations broke down, five weeks before trial was scheduled to begin, to finally file their motion.Plaintiffs' delay, which suggests opportunistic and tactical motives, magnifies the harms to the judicial system that already inhere in any disqualification by imputation, abuse the expectations of jurors, and has the general tendency to impair rather than promote confidence in the integrity of the judicial system.

The foregoing reasons, which weigh against finding an adverse impact on the integrity of the judicial system, reinforce our conclusion that plaintiffs have failed to show by clear and convincing evidence that any of the Debevoise lawyers' testimony would be so prejudicial to MetLife that the integrity of the judicial system would be threatened. Consequently, the witness-advocate rule does not justify disqualification in this case.

CONCLUSION

Based on the foregoing analysis, we reverse the disqualification order and reinstate Debevoise as trial counsel to MetLife in the underlying securities litigation.

CHAPTER 12

RELATIONS WITH THIRD PARTIES ON BEHALF OF CLIENTS

■ ■ ■

As a lawyer you will often deal with third parties who have information you need. You must distinguish parties who are represented with respect to the matter you are working on from parties who are not represented.

Unless part of a good-faith undercover investigation, you may not communicate with a represented person without the consent of their lawyer—their own consent will not do. You may communicate with an unrepresented person but if your client's interests differ from theirs or are reasonably likely to do so you may not give them legal advice except the advice to get their own lawyer.

Finally, in gathering evidence you may not suppress evidence or advise a third party to do so. You must respect the legal rights of third parties and not do things designed to burden or harass them.

A. REPRESENTED PERSONS

Model Rule 4.2 provides that when you represent a client in a matter you may not contact a person represented by counsel with respect to the matter unless you have the permission of that person's lawyer. The person's own permission is not good enough; their lawyer's permission is required. This rule presents several surprisingly tricky issues, such as when a matter arises, how the scope of a matter is defined, and whether a given entity constituent is considered to be represented by entity counsel.

This last issue raises another. Model Rule 3.4(f) provides that you may not request any person to decline voluntarily to provide information to a party unless that person is your client or a relative, employee, or other agent of your client. The two issues are linked by a common scenario: Under Rule 4.2 counsel for an entity may represent certain entity employees but does not automatically represent former employees. Former employees often have relevant information, however, so both sides of a case may want to interview or depose them. Subject to conflict of interest rules, entity counsel may offer to represent a former employee and, if the employee agrees to such representation, entity counsel may advise the former employee not to cooperate with requests for information made by another party. If the former employee does not agree, however, entity counsel may not ask the former employee to refuse to cooperate with such requests.

The following materials explore these issues.

Model Rules of Professional Conduct 4.2, 3.4(f)
Restatement of the Law Governing Lawyers §§ 99–100, 102

SNIDER V. SUPERIOR COURT

113 Cal.App.4th 1187 (2003)

NARES, J.

In this petition for writ of mandate (petition) we are presented with the question whether the trial court properly disqualified attorney Dale Larabee from representing petitioner David Snider because of his contacts with two employees, one a sales manager and the other a director of production, of respondent Quantum Productions, Inc. The court found that Larabee violated California's State Bar Rules of Professional Conduct, rule 2–100 that provides in part:

"(A) While representing a client, a member shall not communicate directly or indirectly about the subject of the representation with a *party* the member *knows to be represented by another lawyer in the matter,* unless the member has the consent of the other lawyer.

"(B) For purposes of this rule, a '*party*' includes:

"(1) *An officer, director, or managing agent of a corporation* or association, and a partner or managing agent of a partnership; or

"(2) An association member or *an employee of an association, corporation, or partnership, if the subject of the communication is any act or omission of such person in connection with the matter which may be binding upon or imputed to the organization for purposes of civil or criminal liability or whose statement may constitute an admission on the part of the organization."* (Italics added.)

We conclude that there was no violation of rule 2–100 as the contacted employees were not "represented parties" within the scope of that rule as (1) they were not "officer[s], director[s] or managing agent[s]" of the organization; (2) the subject matter of the communications was not an act or omission of the employees that could be binding or imputed to the organization; and (3) they were not employees whose statements might constitute admissions on behalf of the organization. We further conclude that if the employees were subject to rule 2–100, the court still erred in ordering the disqualification of Larabee as the evidence did not show that he had actual knowledge the employees were represented parties. Accordingly, we grant Snider's petition and order the superior court to vacate its order disqualifying Larabee and his firm from representing Snider in this action.

We emphasize, however, that counsel desiring to contact an employee of a represented organization should endeavor to ensure, prior to the contact, that the employee, either because of his or her status within the organization or the subject matter of the proposed communication, does not come within the scope of rule 2–100. Further, once contact is made, counsel should at the outset pose questions designed to elicit information that would determine whether the employee comes within rule 2–100's scope and should not ask questions that could violate the attorney-client privilege. By the same token, if organizations do not want employees within the scope of rule 2–100 to have contact with opposing counsel, it is incumbent upon them to take proactive measures to ensure that the employees and opposing counsel understand the organization's position. Ethical violations and unnecessary litigation over such ex parte contacts would largely be obviated by prudent actions taken by counsel and organizations in applying rule 2–100.

FACTUAL AND PROCEDURAL BACKGROUND

A. *Factual Background*

Snider was employed by Quantum, an event design and construction company, as a sales manager. In 2002 Snider resigned and formed Gardenia Design Group (Gardenia), which Quantum alleged was in direct competition with Quantum. Quantum also alleged that Snider misappropriated confidential and secret business information from Quantum and used that information to compete with Quantum. In July 2002 Quantum filed a complaint against Snider and Gardenia, alleging misappropriation of trade secrets, breach of contract, intentional interference with contractual relations and prospective economic advantage, and unfair competition. Snider denies Quantum's allegations.

B. *Procedural Background*

1. *The motion to disqualify*

In the joint trial readiness report filed with the court prior to trial, Quantum listed as a percipient witness, among others, its employee Toni Lewis. Snider and Gardenia listed as percipient witnesses, among others, Lewis and Laura Janikas, also a Quantum employee.

Thereafter, between the joint trial readiness conference and trial, Larabee contacted Lewis and Janikas to talk with them about the pending case. When counsel for Quantum discovered the contacts, he brought a motion for a trial continuance and to disqualify Larabee from representing Snider (motion to disqualify).

In support of the motion to disqualify, Quantum submitted the declaration of its president, Pam Navarre, as well as declarations from Janikas and Lewis. In Navarre's declaration she stated that Quantum employs approximately 40 people. She stated that she and Quantum's vice-president, Bill Hardt, were the only executive-level personnel at the company. She further stated that below the executives in the company were two sales managers, a director of operations, and a director of production. Janikas was a sales manager, and her duties included selling Quantum's goods and services and supervising two subordinate employees. She was also responsible for enforcing Quantum's rules, policies and procedures. Janikas had the authority to direct all work by others in the company in relation to the goods and services she contracted to provide on behalf of Quantum. According to Navarre, the position of sales manager was a position of great confidence in the company and she relied on the counsel and input of Janikas in making corporate policies and decisions. Navarre did not describe Lewis's position at Quantum.

In her declaration, Janikas described her work for Quantum as including "management responsibilities." She stated that she had been aware of the litigation for months but had not discussed it at length with her superiors. She stated that in January 2003 Larabee called her at home on two occasions and left messages for her. She returned one of his calls and left a message for Larabee. Larabee was able to reach her on her work cellular phone. According to Janikas, she talked to Larabee for about 10 minutes.

Janikas stated that Larabee "asked [her] many questions about this lawsuit, and made [her] feel like [she] was on the witness stand." He asked her if she knew the "real reason" why Quantum had sued Snider. She replied that she understood that he had been sued because he breached his contract with Quantum. Larabee asked if she had seen Snider's contract with Quantum. She replied that she had not. Larabee asked her if she had signed a contract. She replied that she had, as had all other employees. Larabee asked her what she thought the contract meant, and Janikas attempted to explain it to him. Larabee asked Janikas if Quantum sold wedding services before Snider quit. She responded that it did. Larabee also asked her about a meeting of key employees in October 2001. Larabee also asked her if she took a pay cut after September 11, 2001, and whether that made her want to leave Quantum. He asked her "many more questions" that she could not remember. At the end of the conversation Larabee asked her if Quantum's counsel had ever called and talked to her. She responded that he had not.

In her declaration, Lewis stated that she was the director of productions for Quantum, and described her work there, which included supervising the production department and its 19 employees. Larabee first called her before Christmas 2002. He left a message on her work cellular phone number saying that he wanted to meet her. Larabee left several additional messages for her and she eventually returned his calls in January 2003. She agreed to meet with him at his offices, but she did not make the appointment. According to Lewis, Larabee never asked her if counsel represented her.

Larabee filed a declaration in opposition to Quantum's motion. In that declaration he stated that he had no intention of calling Janikas or Lewis as witnesses in the case. He also confirmed that he never spoke with Lewis concerning the case; his only conversations with her were unsuccessful attempts to set up a meeting. He stated that he had asked both Janikas and Lewis if counsel for Quantum had talked to them about trial testimony and they both stated that they had not. Before contacting them, he asked Snider what duties and responsibilities they had. Snider told Larabee that they were salespeople with no corporate responsibility. Based upon this he concluded that they were not within the "control group" of Quantum's management and he did not believe that they could bind or make an admission on behalf of the organization. Larabee only wanted to ask them about matters of which they had percipient knowledge, particularly about a meeting in the Fall of 2001 when Navarre told the employees that business was bad and that if they wanted to look for another job they could do so. Larabee admitted asking Janikas if she had any idea why Snider had been sued. According to Larabee, she stated that she did not.

Larabee also stated that he told Janikas and Lewis that he was Snider's counsel and they did not have to talk to him if they did not want to. He stated that Lewis had called him back as many times as he called her and that she wanted to talk to Larabee. According to Larabee, Lewis also contacted Snider on her own and told Snider that she had to rewrite her declaration multiple times because Quantum's attorneys did not like it and that they "told her what to say."

Larabee also stated that he did not believe that there was an attorney-client relationship between Quantum's attorney and Lewis and Janikas. He stated that he waited until after the trial readiness conference to contact them as he wanted to give counsel a chance to tell the employees not to talk to him.

Larabee submitted an expert declaration from Dennis Schoville, an attorney, in which he opined that Larabee did not violate rule 2–100. However, the court did not consider that document because it was filed late.

2. *The court's ruling*

In February 2003 the court granted Quantum's motion to disqualify Larabee as Snider's counsel. . . .

DISCUSSION

On this petition Snider asserts that the court erred in ordering disqualification as (1) Larabee did not know the employees were represented by counsel; (2) the employees he contacted did not come within the terms of rule 2–100; (3) the court should not have disqualified another member of his firm; and (4) Quantum was not prejudiced by the contacts. We grant Snider's petition. . . .

II. *Were Janikas and Lewis Employees Subject to Rule 2–100?*

A. *Policies Concerning Rule Against Ex Parte Contact*

"Contact with represented parties is proscribed to preserve the attorney-client relationship from an opposing attorney's intrusion and interference." (*Jackson v. Ingersoll–Rand Co.* (1996) 42 Cal.App.4th 1163, 1167.) "Moreover, with regard to the ethical boundaries of an attorney's conduct, a bright line test is essential. As a practical matter, an attorney must be able to determine beforehand whether particular conduct is permissible; otherwise, an attorney would be uncertain whether the rules had been violated until . . . he or she is disqualified. Unclear rules risk blunting an advocate's zealous representation of a client." [citation omitted] Further, rule 2–100 must be interpreted narrowly because "a rule whose violation could result in disqualification and possible disciplinary action should be narrowly construed when it impinges upon a lawyer's duty of zealous representation." (*Continental Ins. Co. v. Superior Court* (1995) 32 Cal.App.4th 94, 119 (*Continental*).)

B. *Covered Employees*

To determine whether Larabee violated rule 2–100 by contacting Janikas and Lewis, we must first determine whether they were "covered employees," i.e., those with whom contact was proscribed under rule 2–100. In order to decide this issue we must look to the development of the rule preventing ex parte contact with employees of represented entities, reviewing California authority, American Bar Association (ABA) Model Rule 4.2, and out-of-state authority.

1. *California authority*

Former rule 7–103 provided:

> "A member of the State Bar shall not communicate directly or indirectly with a party whom he knows to be represented by counsel upon a subject of controversy, without the express consent of such counsel. This rule shall not apply to communications with a public officer, board, committee or body."

In 1977 a committee of the Los Angeles County Bar Association interpreted former rule 7–103 in a formal opinion. In that opinion, the committee stated that there was "nothing unethical in an attorney interviewing a nonmanagement employee of an adverse party who may be a witness without the consent of that party's attorney. . . . " (Cal. Compendium on Prof. Responsibility, L.A. County Bar Assn. Formal Opn. No. 369 (Nov. 23, 1977) p. 69.) The committee found the test to be "the extent to which the employees are 'closely identified with management of the company.' " Thus, at that time, former rule 7–103 was interpreted to allow ex parte contact with a represented organization's employees unless they were members of the organization's "control group." (*Continental, supra,* 32 Cal.App.4th at p. 114.) An organization's control group has been stated as consisting of " ' "officers and agents . . . responsible for directing [the company's] actions in response to legal advice." ' " (*Bobele v. Superior Court* (1988) 199 Cal.App.3d 708, 712.)

However, in 1981 the United States Supreme Court issued its decision in *Upjohn Co. v. United States* (1981) 449 U.S. 383, 390 (*Upjohn*), wherein the high court held that "the corporate attorney-client privilege extends not only to communications between corporate counsel and members of the control group, but also to communications with middle and low level corporate employees." (*Continental, supra,* 32 Cal.App.4th at p. 114.) . . .

[T]he court in *Mills Land & Water Co. v. Golden West Refining Co.* (1986) 186 Cal.App.3d 116 (*Mills*) upheld the disqualification of an attorney under former rule 7–103 for making ex parte contact with the opposing organization's former president, who had remained on its board of directors. In doing so, the Court of Appeal rejected the "control group" test to determine the propriety of ex parte contacts with employees of represented organizations. As the court in *Mills* stated: "The question is not simply whether [the former president] was in a position to bind [the organization] in some fashion. His position makes him potentially privy to privileged information about the litigation." Thus, the court in *Mills* adopted the "blanket" rule regarding ex parte contacts . . . prohibiting ex parte contact with any current employees of an organization. . . . Two years later, in 1988, rule 7–103 was repealed and the current rule 2–100 was adopted. . . .

The parameters of rule 2–100(B) are stated succinctly in *Triple A Machine Shop, Inc. v. State of California* (1989) 213 Cal.App.3d 131, 140 (*Triple A*): "[R]ule 2–100 permits opposing counsel to initiate ex parte contacts with . . . present employees (other than officers, directors or managing agents) who are not separately represented, so long as the communication does not involve the employee's act or failure to act in connection with the matter which may bind the corporation, be imputed to it, or constitute an admission of the corporation for purposes of establishing liability." In that case, the Court of Appeal, while not discussing in detail the reach of the new rule 2–100, rejected the previous blanket prohibition and held that the government attorney's ex parte contact with the defendant's assistant facilities manager was not improper.

Although the drafters of rule 2–100 and the court in *Nalian* characterize rule 2–100 as prohibiting contact only with members of an organization's "control group," the actual text of paragraph (B)(2) suggests that rule may be a bit broader than that. It is true that paragraph (B)(1) states the control group test: officers, directors and managing agents of the organization may not be contacted for any purpose. However, paragraph (B)(2) focuses on the subject matter of the communication and arguably applies to employees outside of an organization's control group if the subject matter of the conversation is the employee's act or failure to act in connection with the matter at issue, *and* that act or failure to act could bind the organization, be imputed to it, *or* if the employee's statement could constitute an admission against the organization.

With regard to statements that could constitute admissions on the part of the organization, Evidence Code section 1222 provides in part: "Evidence of a statement offered against a party is not made inadmissible by the hearsay rule if: [¶] (a) The statement was made by a person authorized by the party to make a statement or statements for him concerning the subject matter of the statement." This has been interpreted in California as only applying to high-ranking organizational agents who have actual authority to speak on behalf of the organization.

2. *Model Rule 4.2*

ABA Model Rules of Professional Conduct, rule 4.2 (ABA Model Rule 4.2), provides for a proscription against certain ex parte contacts with employees of represented organizations, similar to California's former rule 7–103:

> "In representing a client, a lawyer shall not communicate about the subject of the representation with a party the lawyer knows to be represented by another lawyer in the matter, unless the lawyer has the consent of the other lawyer or is authorized to do so by law or a court order."

Although ABA Model Rule 4.2 is stated in general terms, the comment to that rule provides further guidance as to its scope and application to employees. At the time rule 2–100 was adopted, the comment to ABA Model Rule 4.2 read substantially the same as California rule 2–100(B)(1) and (2), providing in part that:

> "[i]n the case of an organization, this Rule prohibits communications by a lawyer for one party concerning the matter in representation with persons having a managerial responsibility on behalf of the organization, and with any other person whose act or omission in connection with that matter may be imputed to the organization for purposes of civil or criminal liability or whose statement may constitute an admission on the part of the organization."

However, the comments to ABA Model Rule 4.2 were substantially revised when the ABA Model Rules were revised in 2002. As amended, the relevant portion of the comment reads:

> "In the case of a represented organization, this Rule prohibits communications with a constituent of the organization who supervises, directs or regularly consults with the organization's lawyer concerning the matter or has authority to obligate the organization with respect to the matter or whose act or omission in connection with the matter may be imputed to the organization for the purposes of civil or criminal liability."

The revisions to the comment were meant "to 'clarif[y] application of the Rule to organizational clients.' " (*Palmer v. Pioneer Inn Associates, Ltd.* (2002) 59 P.3d 1237, 1242 (*Palmer*).) The phrase "whose statement may constitute an admission on the part of the organization" was omitted from the comment "because it had been misapplied to situations when an employee's statement could be admissible against the organizational employer, when the clause was only ever intended to encompass those few jurisdictions with a law of evidence providing that statements by certain employees of an organization were not only admissible against the organization but could not thereafter be controverted by the organization."

3. *Out-of-state authority*

In interpreting ABA Model Rule 4.2 and their own rules governing attorney ethics, state and federal courts have come up with various tests to determine which employees of represented organizations may be contacted by opposing counsel. On one end is the "blanket" test, which prohibits contact with any current or former employees of an organization. At the other end is the " 'control group' test, which covers only high-level management employees. Several tests fall in the middle, including a party-opponent admission test, a case-by-case balancing test, and a 'managing-speaking agent' test." Given the comments of the drafters of California rule 2–100 and its text, California did not intend to adopt a blanket prohibition on communications with an organization's employees. However, cases adopting the restrictive "control group" test, and those adopting a more middle-ground approach, provide authority helpful to our analysis of whether Janikas and Lewis were employees covered by the terms of rule 2–100.

One case has defined the "control group" that is subject to the proscription against ex parte contact as the "litigation control group," which consists of " 'agents and employees responsible for, or significantly involved in, the determination of the organization's legal position in the matter. . . . ' " (*Michaels v. Woodland* (1997) 988 F.Supp. 468, 471.) The court in that case also noted that fact witnesses are not a part of the control group. Another case has defined the control group as being " 'limited to those managerial employees with authority to commit the organization to a position regarding the subject matter of representation.' " (*Johnson v. Cadillac Plastic Group, Inc.* (1996) 930 F.Supp. 1437, 1442.) "Examples of the types of employees capable of committing an organization are those 'whose duties include making litigation decisions' or 'answering the type of inquiries posed.' [Citation.]" These definitions of "control group" are consistent with California's, those " ' "high level employees responsible for directing [the company's] actions in response to legal advice." ' " (*Bobele, supra,* 199 Cal.App.3d at p. 712, 245 Cal.Rptr. 144.)

Courts adopting the control group test conclude that it "serves the policies of preserving the availability of witnesses, reducing discovery costs by permitting informal interviews of a broad range of employees, and affording the best opportunity for pre-litigation fact investigation. The test has become disfavored following the *Upjohn* decision, because the control group test is narrower than the attorney-client privilege rule approved in that case. Also, it lacks predictability because it is not always clear which employees fall within the 'control group.' " (*Palmer, supra,* 59 P.3d at p. 1245. fns. omitted.)

Cases that have taken a more middle-ground approach attempt to reconcile the competing interests of attorneys seeking discovery and the legitimate concerns of an organization to protect privileged matter. Closest to the blanket rule is the "party-opponent admission" test. Under this test, contact is proscribed with "any employee whose statement might be admissible as a party-opponent admission." (*Palmer, supra,* 59 P.3d at p. 1243.) Courts adopting the party-opponent admission test relied upon the language of the former comment to ABA Model Rule 4.2 and concluded "that the former comment's reference to 'admissions' was clearly meant to incorporate the rules of evidence governing admissions." (*Palmer, supra,* 59 P.3d at p. 1243.) Supporters of this test reason that it gives " 'a sound practical cast to the rule: those who can hurt or bind the organization *with respect to the matter at hand* are off limits except for formal discovery or except with the consent of the entity's lawyer.' " (*Brown v. St. Joseph County* (N.D.Ind.1993) 148 F.R.D. 246, 254.) In jurisdictions that would interpret the evidentiary rule broadly, "it essentially covers all or almost all employees, since any employee could make statements concerning a matter within the scope of his or her employment, and thus could potentially be included within the rule." (*Palmer, supra,* 59 P.3d at p. 1243, fn. omitted.)

However, this interpretation of the former comment's reference to employees whose statements can be considered evidentiary "admissions" is of doubtful validity today given the deletion of that portion of the comment to ABA Model Rule 4.2 and the explanation given for that deletion. Moreover, in jurisdictions that follow the traditional common law rule, such as California, an employee's admission would be "imputed to the employer only if the employee *had authority to speak on the employer's behalf.*" (Comment, *Ethical Limitations on Investigating Employment Discrimination Claims: The Prohibition on Ex Parte Contact with a Defendant's Employees* (1991) 24 U.C. Davis L.Rev. 1243, 1274–1275 & fn. 159, italics added; Evid.Code, § 1222.) "These jurisdictions interpret the common law rule restrictively, typically imputing to the employer only the statements of high-ranking executives and spokespersons." (Comment, *supra,* 24 U.C. Davis L.Rev. at. pp. 1275–1276.) As discussed, *ante,* California follows this restrictive interpretation of what employee statements constitute admissions on the part of their organizational employer.

The "managing-speaking agent" test evolved in response to the *Upjohn* decision. Jurisdictions following this test "reasoned that the protection afforded an organization under the no-contact rule should be commensurate with that afforded by the attorney-client privilege." (*Palmer, supra,* 59 P.3d at p. 1244; *Wright by Wright v. Group Health Hosp.* (1984) 103 Wash.2d 192 [691 P.2d 564] (*Wright*).) *Wright,* the leading case adopting this test, held that the managing-speaking agent test restricts the no-contact rule to those employees having "managing authority sufficient to give them the right to speak for, and bind, the corporation." (*Wright, supra,* 691 P.2d at p. 569.) This test would not bar contact with managers whose responsibilities are unrelated to the representation at issue. (*Id.* at p. 570; Comment, *supra,* 24 U.C. Davis L.Rev. at p. 1288, fn. 224.)

Some courts have adopted a "case-by-case balancing" test. (*Palmer, supra,* 59 P.3d at pp. 1245–1246.) "Under this test, the particular facts of the case must be examined to determine what informal contacts may be appropriate in light of the parties' specific needs. Factors to be considered are the claims asserted, the employee's position and duties, the employer's interests in protecting itself, and the alternatives available to the party seeking an informal interview." (*Ibid.; Baisley v. Missisquoi Cemetery Ass'n* (1998) 167 Vt. 473, 708 A.2d 924.) However, this test offers little guidance in advance as to whether it is proper to conduct an ex parte interview and has only been applied when an attorney seeks guidance from a court in advance of the contact. (*Palmer, supra,* 59 P.3d at p. 1246.)

Finally, there is what has been called the "alter ego" or "New York" test. (*Palmer, supra,* 59 P.3d at p. 1246.) Under this test, a New York court held the no-contact rule applied to "corporate employees whose acts or omissions in the matter under inquiry are binding on the corporation (in effect, the corporation's 'alter egos') or imputed to the corporation for purposes of its liability, or employees implementing the advice of counsel." (*Niesig v. Team I* (1990) 76 N.Y.2d 363, 558 N.E.2d 1030, 1035.) This test "would clearly permit direct access to employees who were merely witnesses to an event for which the corporate employer is sued." (*Id.* at pp. 1035–1036.)

C. *Analysis of Janikas's and Lewis's Status at Quantum*

1. *Paragraph (B)(1)*

To determine whether Lewis and Janikas were within the ambit of rule 2–100, we must first determine whether they were officers, directors or "managing agents" of Quantum. The parties agree that neither were officers or directors. The dispute lies in whether they were managing agents of Quantum.

Quantum concedes that paragraph (B)(1) refers to Quantum's "control group," i.e., "officers and agents . . . responsible for directing [the company's] actions in response to legal advice." (*Upjohn, supra,* 449 U.S. at p. 391; *Nalian, supra,* 6 Cal.App.4th at p. 1259, fn. 1, quoting & citing *Upjohn.*) Quantum nevertheless goes on to argue that a broad interpretation must be given to the term "managing agent," one that would include Lewis and Janikas even if they were mid- or lower-level employees, in order to protect the attorney-client privilege. This argument is unavailing.

In support of its proposition that the term "managing agent" refers to mid- or low-level employees, Quantum relies on authority that predates rule 2–100, including *Mills, Upjohn,* and Formal Opinion No. 410, and ignores the fact that the drafters of rule 2–100 expressly rejected such a broad no-contact rule. Rather, we must look to the meaning of the term "managing agent" and the intent of the drafters of rule 2–100 to determine whether it applied to Janikas and Lewis.

Snider contends that the definition of "managing agent" in rule 2–100 is the same as that in Civil Code section 3294, subdivision (b), which requires wrongdoing by an "officer, director, or managing agent" before punitive damages will be awarded against an organization for an employee's act. In *White v. Ultramar* (1999) 21 Cal.4th 563, 573 (*White*), a wrongful termination action, the California Supreme Court defined "managing agent" for the purposes of organizational liability for punitive damages as including only an employee that "exercises substantial discretionary authority over decisions that ultimately determine corporate policy." The high court later restated the test in different terms, holding that a managing agent is an employee that "exercise[s] substantial discretionary authority over significant aspects of a corporation's business." In reaching this conclusion, the high court stated that the Legislature placed the term managing agent "next to the terms 'officer' and 'director,' intending that a managing agent be more than a mere supervisory employee." The court also rejected a broader definition of managing agent, stating that, "[i]f we equate mere supervisory status with managing agent status, we will create a rule where corporate employers are liable for punitive damages in most employment cases."

We conclude that the definition of managing agent in *White* applies equally well to rule 2–100(B)(1). First, like Civil Code section 3294, the term "managing agent" immediately follows the terms "officer" and "director," indicating an intention to limit the term to high-level management, not mere supervisory employees. This is so because in interpreting statutes (and rules) we seek to " 'ascertain common characteristics among things of the same kind, class, or nature when they are cataloged in legislative enactments.' [Citation.]" (*White, supra,* 21 Cal.4th at p. 573.)

Further, the history behind rule 2–100's adoption supports a narrow reading to the term. The drafters specifically stated that they intended that rule 2–100 would adopt the "control group" test. While the language of paragraph (B)(2) may be broader than that test (as we discuss, *post*), paragraph (B)(1) adopts that test, given the terms employed. A "managing agent" that exercises substantial discretionary authority over organizational policy making is consistent with the definition of control group members, those " ' "officers and agents . . . responsible for directing [the company's] actions in response to legal advice." ' " (*Bobele, supra,* 199 Cal.App.3d at p. 712.)

Quantum asserts that it would be improper to use the definition of managing agent adopted in the *White* case because that case sought to limit the award of punitive damages against organizations, whereas rule 2–100 is designed to protect the attorney-client privilege, which requires a broader definition. We reject this contention. First, it ignores the *White* court's discussion of the grouping of the words "officer, director or managing agent." Rule 2–100 and Civil Code section 3294 use the exact same grouping. Further, to support this proposition Quantum again relies upon *Mills* and *Upjohn,* authority that the drafters of rule 2–100 rejected in adopting the final language for paragraph (B)(1). In fact, the drafters of rule 2–100 expressly intended that the number of "covered employees" be limited in scope. Thus, the policy reasons behind the definition of "managing agent" enunciated in *White* are consistent with the policies behind rule 2–100. In sum, we conclude that the term "managing agent" in rule 2–100 refers to those employees that exercise substantial discretionary authority over decisions that determine organizational policy.

Applying this definition to Janikas and Lewis, there is no evidence in the record demonstrating that they fit within the definition of managing agents. Quantum's president Navarre describes Janikas as a supervisory employee that could enforce Quantum's policies, and that she relied upon Janikas when she (Navarre) was setting corporate policy. However, Navarre does *not* state that Janikas had the discretion and authority to set corporate policy as to any issues, much less the matter involved in this litigation. Indeed, she states that she and the company's vice-president are the only executive-level persons at Quantum. Navarre stated nothing in her declaration concerning Lewis's status at Quantum. Therefore,

Janikas and Lewis did not fall within the terms of paragraph (B)(1) of rule 2–100.

2. *Paragraph (B)(2)*

Quantum argues that Janikas and Lewis were improperly contacted because they fell within the terms of paragraph (B)(2) of rule 2–100, as each was an employee whose "act or omission . . . in connection with the matter . . . may be binding upon or imputed to the organization for purposes of civil or criminal liability or whose statement may constitute an admission on the part of the organization." This argument is unavailing.

Preliminarily, this argument fails because there is no evidence that the subject matter of the contacts with the employees was concerning "any act or omission of such person in connection with the matter." The interview with Janikas did not concern her own actions or omissions concerning the dispute, but her percipient knowledge and understanding of events surrounding the dispute. In fact, Quantum does not, and the trial court did not, address this issue.

Quantum focuses on the second category in paragraph (B)(2) of rule 2–100, those employees whose statements "may constitute an admission on the part of the organization." However, as discussed, *ante,* this category only applies to "high-ranking executives and spokespersons" with the authority to speak on behalf of the organization. This interpretation is again consistent with the drafters of rule 2–100's rejection of the broader interpretation of the no-contact rule under former rule 7–103, and their desire to limit prohibited contact to only the organization's control group.

It is also consistent with the California Supreme Court and the drafters' intent to follow the comment to Model Rule 4.2 and the language of *D.I. Chadbourne, supra,* 60 Cal.2d 723, in their final revisions to this portion of rule 2–100(B)(2). The comment to Model Rule 4.2 was revised, omitting that portion discussing admissions by employees. In doing so, it was made clear that the original comment, upon which paragraph (B)(2) was based, was to be given a narrow interpretation, limited to "those few jurisdictions with a law of evidence providing that statements by certain employees of an organization were not only admissible against the organization but could not thereafter be controverted by the organization." (*Palmer, supra,* 59 P.3d at p. 1242, fn. omitted.) *D.I. Chadbourne* used language that applied to rule 2–100(B)(2) would limit its application to high-ranking management who speak for the organization.

It does appear that rule 2–100(B)(2) could apply to persons outside the "control group" if in fact the management-level employee was given actual authority to speak on behalf of the organization or could bind it with regard to the subject matter of the litigation. Despite the comments of the drafters of rule 2–100, this portion of the rule appears to follow the "managing-speaking agent" test: those employees "hav[ing] managing authority sufficient to give them the right to speak for, and bind, the corporation." (*Wright, supra,* 691 P.2d at p. 569.) This interpretation best reconciles the language of the statute and the drafters' intent to narrowly circumscribe the type of employees who would be covered by the rule.

The fact remains, however, that even under this test there was no evidence presented that Janikas or Lewis had authority from Quantum to speak concerning this dispute or any other matter, or that their actions could bind or be imputed to Quantum concerning the subject matter of this litigation. In sum, the evidence presented by Quantum does not demonstrate that Janikas and Lewis were employees subject to the terms of rule 2–100(B)(2).

3. *Protection for employees privy to attorney-client information*

Quantum argues that Larabee violated rule 2–100 and disqualification was proper because he violated Quantum's attorney-client relationship and received "confidential" information concerning the litigation. . .

[T]here was no evidence presented that Larabee actually violated the attorney-client privilege existing between Quantum and its counsel. There was no evidence presented that Quantum's counsel had any communications with Janikas or Lewis prior to Larabee's contacts and attempted contacts with them. Indeed, Janikas admitted both in her conversation with Larabee and in her declaration that she had never spoken with counsel for Quantum at the time of Larabee's contact. Lewis's declaration is silent on this issue.

Quantum argues that Larabee admitted "Lewis told him that corporate counsel coached her testimony." However, this misstates the record. Larabee stated in his declaration that Lewis, on her own, contacted *Snider* and told him that counsel for Quantum made her rewrite her declaration several times and "told her what to say." This does not establish violation of the attorney-client privilege by Larabee. It further is not a violation of rule 2–100 as the rule is not intended to prevent the parties themselves from communicating with respect to the subject matter of the representation.

Quantum also points to Larabee's questioning of Janikas as to why Quantum sued Snider. We agree that this question was ill advised if Larabee did not know if the employee was privy to confidential communications with counsel. However, if Janikas had been privy to attorney-client protected information and it was disclosed to Larabee, Quantum would still have a remedy, regardless of whether Janikas came within the terms of rule 2–100. If an attorney violates the attorney-client privilege "the court may disqualify him or her from further participation in the case [citation] and, under certain circumstances, may exclude improperly obtained evidence or take other appropriate measures to achieve justice and ameliorate the effect of improper conduct." (*Triple A, supra,* 213 Cal.App.3d at p. 144, 261 Cal.Rptr. 493.) However, Janikas has not asserted in her declaration that she was privy to such information or that she divulged it to Larabee.

Quantum points to Larabee's questions concerning a "key company meeting" Janikas attended. However, again there is no indication that counsel was present at that meeting and that confidential attorney-client information was discussed. . .

Quantum argues that because Janikas states in her declaration that Larabee asked her "many more questions I cannot remember right now," there might have been confidential information disclosed. However, this is mere speculation that cannot support a finding of a violation of rule 2–100, or disqualification of counsel.

With regard to Quantum's concerns that there could be a breach of the attorney-client privilege if attorneys were allowed to contact employees of a represented organization without advance permission, two points. First, organizations such as Quantum can instruct their employees to contact them before speaking to opposing counsel or they "can send the other party a letter warning that their employees are represented by counsel in the matter, and may not be interviewed under rule 2–100 without the consent of counsel." (*Jorgensen v. Taco Bell Corp.* (1996) 50 Cal.App.4th 1398, 1403 (*Jorgensen*).)

Additionally, . . . [i]f there were an actual breach of the attorney-client privilege through contacts made with employees who fall outside the scope of rule 2–100, an organization would still have remedies outside of rule 2–100 to remedy such a violation. Thus, organizations are still protected from disclosure of attorney-client privileged information even though opposing counsel may contact non-"control group" or non-"managing-speaking agent" employees of those organizations.

Nevertheless, to avoid potential violations of the attorney-client privilege, an attorney contacting an employee of a represented organization should question the employee at the beginning of the conversation, before discussing substantive matters, about the employee's status at that organization, whether the employee is represented by counsel, and whether the employee has spoken to the organization's counsel concerning the matter at issue. If a question arises concerning whether the employee would be covered by rule 2–100 or is in possession of privileged information, the communication should be terminated. Once a dispute arises that could lead to litigation, it is also incumbent upon an organization and its counsel to take proactive measures to protect against disclosure of privileged information by informing employees and/or opposing counsel their position concerning communications between employees and opposing counsel. The exercise of caution and prudence on both sides will avoid much of the potential for violations of rule 2–100 or breach of attorney-client relationships.

D. *Attorney Larabee's Knowledge*

Even if Quantum could demonstrate that Janikas or Lewis were subject to the terms of rule 2–100, we still would not conclude there was a violation of rule 2–100 as Quantum did not demonstrate that Larabee had actual knowledge that Janikas and Lewis were deemed "represented parties" under that rule. . . .

Quantum argues that it is enough that Larabee should have known that Janikas and Lewis were employees subject to rule 2–100, that there was a duty to inquire of opposing counsel, and if an agreement could not be reached as to the contact, Larabee was required to submit the matter to a court to make the determination. These arguments are unavailing.

[A]ctual knowledge is required before an attorney can be held to have violated rule 2–100. Nor does rule 2–100 require advance permission of opposing counsel or an order from the court prior to contacting employees that are not within the scope of 2–100. . . .

We emphasize, however, that in cases where an attorney has reason to believe that an employee of a represented organization might be covered by rule 2–100, that attorney would be well advised to either conduct discovery or communicate with opposing counsel concerning the employee's status before contacting the employee. A failure to do so may, along with other facts, constitute circumstantial evidence that an attorney had actual knowledge that an employee fell within the scope of rule 2–100. It might further provide support for a more drastic sanction if a violation of rule 2–100 is found. Further, as discussed, *ante,* once actual contact is made, an attorney should first ask questions that would establish the employee's status within an organization before moving to substantive questions.

Here, however, there is no evidence that Larabee knew that these employees were within Quantum's "control group," that they were "managing-speaking agents" of Quantum, or that he sought to question them about their own actions or omissions that could be binding on or imputed to the organization. In fact, Larabee's information from his client Snider was that they were no more than salespersons. Counsel for Quantum did not tell Larabee that it deemed these employees to be represented parties. Larabee's conversation with Janikas did not reveal anything that would indicate otherwise, necessitating an end to the conversation. Larabee was never able to talk substantively to Lewis. In short, there is no evidence that in this case Larabee had actual knowledge that Janikas and Lewis were "represented parties" under rule 2–100. Without such actual knowledge, there can be no violation of rule 2–100.

III. *Disqualification of Counsel*

Because we have concluded that attorney Larabee's contacts with Janikas and Lewis did not violate rule 2–100 and that he did not otherwise breach the attorney-client privilege, there were no proper grounds for the disqualification order, and the court abused its discretion in granting Quantum's motion.

CASE QUESTIONS

1. What makes someone a managing agent?
2. Was Janikas or Lewis a harder call under this standard, or were they equally easy/hard?
3. What mental state is required to find a violation of the rule?
4. The court specified what attorneys should do to avoid a violation; what did it say?

PROBLEM 12–1

Suppose Larabee had contacted a current employee, that the employee began describing their responsibilities at Quantum, and that Larabee had said he wasn't interested in what they did, just what they knew. If the employee turned out to fall within the scope of Rule 2–100, would Larabee have violated the rule?

Model Rule 4.2 does not prohibit contact with *former* employees (unless, of course, those employees either have a separate attorney-client relationship with counsel for the entity or if they have a lawyer of their own). It follows that you may interview former employees without asking permission from counsel for the entity.

Nevertheless, it does not follow that anything goes in such interviews. Rule 4.4, for example, requires that counsel not use methods of obtaining evidence that violate the legal rights of third persons. Though the rule speaks of "methods" the comments make clear that the rule extends to prohibit counsel from trying to obtain privileged or work product information no matter what method they use. (The privilege, you will recall, will belong to the entity, not the employee, who may have no power to waive it.)

It does not follow, however, that counsel may not interview former employees who possess privileged or work product information. Counsel may do so but must take reasonable steps not to acquire such information. *Muriel Siebert & Co., Inc. v. Intuit Inc.*, 8 N.Y.3d 506 (2007) provides an example of the right approach. In that case, Siebert sued Intuit. Siebert later fired its Chief Operating Officer, Demigny, who knew about the subject matter of the suit and had cooperated extensively in drafting the complaint. Siebert's lawyer informed Intuit's lawyer that Demigny was no longer under Siebert's control. The lawyers agreed he should be deposed. Before the deposition, Intuit's lawyers interviewed Demigny; they did not tell Siebert's lawyers about the interview.

At the beginning of this interview, Intuit's lawyers warned Demigny:

> that he should not disclose any privileged or confidential information, including any conversations with Siebert's counsel, or offer any information concerning Siebert's legal strategy. Dermigny was further cautioned that if, during the interview, he was asked a question that could potentially lead to the disclosure of such information, he should so advise Intuit's attorneys and decline to answer the question. Intuit's attorneys then questioned Dermigny about the underlying facts of the case, but did not elicit any privileged information nor inquire about Siebert's litigation strategy.

Siebert later moved to disqualify Intuit's counsel, asserting that the interview was improper. The trial court agreed that New York's disciplinary rule had not been violated but disqualified counsel because of an appearance of impropriety. The court of appeals reversed, citing defense counsel's warnings as a basis for concluding that the interview did not improperly seek privileged information.

The New York Court of Appeals (the highest court) affirmed: "In this case, Intuit's attorneys properly advised Dermigny of their representation and interest in the litigation, and directed Dermigny to avoid disclosing privileged or confidential information. They also directed Dermigny not to answer any questions that would lead to the disclosure of such information. Dermigny stated that he understood the admonitions and, on this record, no such information was disclosed. Thus, there is no basis for disqualification."

It is common for a law firm representing a company to offer to represent current and former employees as well, with fees paid by the company. So long as there is no conflict of interest between the company and the constituent such representation is permissible, and companies often favor it as a tactic to control or at least manage the flow of information from the company to its litigation opponents. The no-contact rule is one source of such control.

One court recently faulted this procedure, however, and disqualified the firm that employed it. The court in *Rivera v. Lutheran Medical Center*, 866 N.Y.S.2d 520 (2008), found that by contacting (at the client's request) current and former employees the law firm violated the prohibition on soliciting clients. (See chapter 9.C.) According to the court, "These witnesses are not parties to the litigation in any sense and there is no chance that they will be subject to any liability. They were clearly solicited . . . to gain a tactical advantage in this litigation by insulating them from any informal contact with plaintiff's counsel." In addition, sitting as a trial judge in *Apple, Inc. v. Motorola, Inc.*, No. 1:11-cv-08540 (N.D. Ill April 21, 2012), Judge Posner held that a law firm that volunteered to represent (free of charge) an inventor who was a witness in a patent did not form a bona fide attorney client relationship with the witness in part because "[t]he only plausible motive for an Apple lawyer to volunteer his services—free of charge—would be to coach [the witness] so that he wouldn't say anything damaging to Apple in his deposition." The Court emphasized that the retainer agreement between the firm and witness gave Apple control of the privilege. *Cf In re Grand Jury Subpoena*, in chapter 5.B, *supra*.

A good rule of legal ethics is to never try to do indirectly what you could not do yourself. The rule is relevant to dealing with third parties. Rule 4.2 applies to lawyers, not clients, who can always talk to each other. A client who wants to do so might also like to talk to her lawyer first, to get advice about what she should say and not say. Advice is permissible, but scripting the client so heavily that the conversation is in fact between the lawyer and the opposing party is not. Where do you draw the line between advice and scripting? The California State Bar Committee on Professional Responsibility and Conduct offered the following thoughts in its Opinion 1993–131:

> When the content of the communication to be had with the opposing party originates with or is directed by the attorney, it is prohibited by rule 2–100. Thus, an attorney is prohibited from drafting documents, correspondence, or other written materials, to be delivered to an opposing party represented by counsel even if they are prepared at the request of the client, are conveyed by the client and appear to be from the client rather than the attorney. An attorney is also prohibited from sending the opposing party materials and simultaneously sending copies to the party's counsel. Providing copies to opposing counsel does not diminish the prohibited nature of the communications with the opposing party.
>
> An attorney is also prohibited from scripting the questions to be asked or statements to be made in the communications or otherwise using the client as a conduit for conveying to the represented opposing party words or thoughts originating with the attorney.
>
> When the content of the communication to be had with the opposing party originates with and is directed by the client, it is permitted by rule 2–100. Thus, an attorney may confer with the client as to the

strategy to be pursued in, the goals to be achieved by, and the general nature of the communication the client intends to initiate with the opposing party as long as the communication itself originates with and is directed by the client and not the attorney.

To similar effect, *see* ABA Formal Op. 11-461 (lawyers may advise clients that they are entitled to communicate directly with opposing client and may advise clients on substance and strategy but may not overreach, as by advising client to attempt to elicit confidential information from opposing client); N.Y.City Ethics Op. 2002–3 (2002) (lawyer may assist client who "conceives of the idea" of communicating with represented party but may not encourage client to elicit confidential information).

The no-contact rule traces its origins to principles of etiquette among 19th-Century lawyers. John Leubsdorf, *Communicating With Another Lawyer's Client: The Lawyer's Veto and the Client's Interest*, 127 U. PA. L. REV. 683, 684 (1979). That explains why, unusually among such rules, it grants power to the lawyer, not the client. As we will see in a moment, a lawyer violates the rule by communicating with a represented person who is perfectly willing to waive any rights they have but whose lawyer has not consented to the communication.

For a seemingly simple provision, the no-contact rule generates a surprising number of issues. One issue is when a "matter" arises, in connection with which a person might be represented. For example, suppose an employee believes she has been sexually harassed and hires a lawyer to look into her claim. The lawyer is not sure and hires an investigator to interview the alleged harasser to see if his story confirms hers. Suppose the employee is someone who would be considered represented by counsel for the entity employer: Does the no-contact rule extend to investigations to determine whether there is a claim? If the (now former) employee files suit seven months after the interview, should her counsel be disqualified for violating the rule?

Jorgensen v. Taco Bell Corp., 50 Cal.App.4th 1398 (1996), held that on these facts there was no "matter" in which the alleged harasser could be represented, and that in any event counsel for the prospective plaintiff did not "know" the harasser to be represented, so the rule was not violated. In contrast, the court disqualified counsel for the plaintiff in *Inorganic Coatings, Inc. v. Falberg*, 926. F. Supp. 517 (E.D. Pa. 1996), who sent a demand letter to a prospective defendant, drafted a complaint, spoke to counsel for the prospective defendant and then, later that same day, spoke at length with the prospective defendant himself. Presumably the case may be distinguished from *Jorgenson* on the ground that the decision to file suit plainly had been made and the filing itself was imminent. *Cf. Johnson v. Cadillac Plastic Group, Inc.,* 930 F.Supp. 1437 (D. Colo. 1996)

("the protections of Rule 4.2 attach only once an 'adversarial relationship' sufficient to trigger an organization's right to counsel arises.")

The scope of a matter presents a related issue. A person represented for one matter is not represented with respect to everything they have said and done. The Rule does not prevent communications with them regarding a matter different from the one on which they are represented.

Several courts have taken a narrow view of the scope of a matter. In *People v. Santiago*, 925 N.E.2d 1122 (Ill. 2010), the Illinois Supreme Court held that prosecutors did not violate Rule 4.2 when they interviewed in a criminal investigation a woman who was represented by counsel in a (civil) child protection matter even though both cases were based on the same harm to the woman's young daughter. According to the court,

> "had the drafters of Rule 4.2 intended the parameters of the rule to be defined from a fact perspective rather than a case perspective, the drafters would have included language to that effect. In fact, other rules in the Illinois Rules of Professional Conduct do use the broader phrases 'same or substantially related matter' or "the subject matter" of the representation. . . . because the drafters of Rule 4.2 did not include the words "subject matter" or "same or a substantially related" matter in the rule, we presume that the omission was deliberate. We therefore decline to adopt such a broad reading of Rule 4.2."

See also United States v. Ford, 176 F.3d 376 (6th Cir. 1999) (no violation of the rule when prosecutors placed an informant in the cell of a prisoner represented by counsel in connection with his recent conviction on money-laundering charges because prosecutors were interested in obtaining evidence regarding the prisoner's alleged threats against the prosecutors and judge in the money-laundering trial: "Since prosecutors were investigating an offense other than the offense for which Defendant was indicted, the contact does not pertain to the 'subject matter of the representation' as Rule 4.2 states."). *Cf. Miller v. Material Sciences Corp.*, 986 F.Supp. 1104 (N.D. Ill. 1997) (no violation of Rule 4.2 when lawyer contacted former controller of a firm lawyer was suing for securities fraud where former controller stated he was represented by counsel in an SEC investigation but not in the civil case the lawyer inquired about).

What constitutes "communication" may present issues as well. Speaking to or corresponding with a represented party falls within the scope of the rule, but what about simple observation? The trial court in *Hill v. Shell Oil Co.*, 209 F.Supp.2d 876 (N.D. Ill. 2002), found no violation where counsel for a putative class of black customers of Shell Oil videotaped the operations of certain Shell stations to gather evidence to support their claim that the stations required black customers, but not white customers, to pre-pay for gasoline. The court found a discernable continuum in the cases from clearly impermissible to clearly permissible conduct. Lawyers (and investigators) cannot trick protected employees into doing things or saying things they otherwise would not do or say. They cannot normally interview protected employees or ask them to fill out questionnaires. They probably can employ persons to play the role of customers seeking services on the same basis as the general public. They can videotape protected employees going about their activities in what those employees believe is the normal course. That is akin to surveillance videos routinely admitted.

Here we have secret videotapes of station employees reacting (or not reacting) to plaintiffs and other persons posing as consumers. Most of the interactions that occurred in the videotapes do not involve any questioning of the employees other than asking if a gas pump is prepay or not, and as far as we can tell these conversations are not within the audio range of the video camera. These interactions do not rise to the level of communication protected by Rule 4.2.

In contrast, counsel in *Midwest Motor Sports v. Arctic Cat Sales, Inc.*, 347 F.3d 693 (8th Cir. 2003) hired an investigator who visited the showroom of the plaintiff (a terminated dealer) and who was instructed to question a manager at the showroom. The manager was not there but the investigator did speak to a salesman. The investigator also spoke to a manager at the showroom of another distributor, which was not a party to the suit. The court affirmed the disqualification of the lawyer who hired the investigator.

Similarly, in *Microsoft Corp. v. Alcatel Bus. Systems*, 2007 WL 4480632 (D. Del. 2007), the court disqualified a patent litigation firm that bought and had installed in its offices a telecommunications system that allegedly infringed its client's patents. One of the technicians who installed the system identified himself as an employee of the prospective infringement defendant. Attorneys for the firm questioned him about the configuration and use of the system, but they obtained no confidential information. The court found the attorneys managed only "to get objective information about the accused products, without the glaze of litigation stratagems that usually accompanies the discovery process." Nevertheless, it found the technician was a represented person and ordered as a sanction that the lawyers who interviewed the technician and an expert who learned of the technician's comments not be allowed to participate in the case.

Social networking sites present a modern variation on these themes. You should presume that a lawyer would violate Rule 4.2 by sending a "friend" request to a person the lawyer knows to be represented by counsel in a matter, at least if the purpose of the request was to gather information from the person's webpage. *See* Ass'n of the Bar of the City of New

York Formal Op. 2010–2 n.4. A lawyer's attempt to disguise his or her identity presumably would violate rules 4.1 and 8.4(c). *Id.*

Cases involving entities present particular issues. Suppose an opposing party is an entity with in-house lawyers but which is represented by outside counsel in the matter at hand. Would you violate the no-contact rule if you contacted the in-house attorneys rather than outside counsel? ABA Opinion 06–443 states that such contact does not violate the rule unless the in-house lawyer is part of the group specified in comment seven to Rule 4.2, i.e., a person who "supervises, directs or regularly consults with the organization's lawyer concerning the matter or has authority to obligate the organization with respect to the matter or whose act or omission in connection with the matter may be imputed to the organization for purposes of civil or criminal liability." *See also Restatement* § 100.

Another issue concerns what happens if an employee would be deemed represented by entity counsel for purposes of Rule 4.2 but would not in fact want such representation. *United States v. Talao*, 222 F.3d 1133 (9th Cir. 2000), exemplifies this problem. Lita Ferrer was the bookkeeper for a company under investigation for violating various labor laws. She received a subpoena to testify before the grand jury. Her employer instructed her to consult with the company's counsel, Christopher Brose. Brose called Ferrer and arranged to meet her the following day, before her scheduled testimony.

Ferrer then went to the U.S. Attorney's office and asked to see a prosecutor. She then asked to change the date of her testimony. She wanted a new date so she could avoid Brose: his presence, she said, would make her feel pressured to perjure herself. She was told the date could not be changed, but that Brose would not be with her during her testimony. The next day, Ferrer met with Brose; later that day, she then ran into two prosecutors in the hallway outside the grand jury room and told them she no longer wanted Brose to represent her; she felt his representation pressured her to lie.[1] The prosecutors interviewed Ferrer, who explained that her boss had lied to both investigators and to Brose.

The trial court found that the prosecutors had violated California's no-contact rule. The Ninth Circuit reversed. The court agreed with the Second Circuit's *Hammad* ruling (discussed below) that the no-contact rule applies to pre-indictment, non-custodial communications, but found that the prosecutors did not violate the rule:

> When a corporate employee/witness comes forward to disclose attempts by the corporation's officers to coerce her to give false testimony, the prohibition against *ex parte* contacts does little to support an appropriate attorney-client relationship. Once the employee

---

[1] The passive voice here is deliberate. The court of appeals made clear that Ferrer felt that her boss was actively pressuring her to lie, and that the presence of her boss's lawyer would reinforce that pressure.

> makes known her desire to give truthful information about potential criminal activity she has witnessed, a clear conflict of interest exists between the employee and the corporation.
>
> Under these circumstances, corporate counsel cannot continue to represent both the employee and the corporation. Indeed, Brose made clear in his testimony at the evidentiary hearing before the district court that if Ferrer had approached him with information adverse to the interests of the corporation he would have advised her that she should retain her own lawyer. Under these circumstances, because the corporation and the employee cannot share an attorney, *ex parte* contacts with the employee cannot be deemed to, in any way, affect the attorney-client relationship between the corporation and its counsel. In this setting, the corporation's interest, therefore, clearly does not provide the basis for application of the rule.

The *Talao* court concluded with two useful observations. The first was a caution against accepting too readily an employee's claim that counsel for an entity was conspiring with entity management to force the employee to lie. According to the court:

> Indeed, it is not unknown for corporate employees involved in alleged wrongdoing to attempt to gain favor with U.S. Attorneys by claiming that corporate officials or corporate counsel directed them to act unlawfully. Clients are sometimes willing to throw lawyers to the wolves when they believe that doing so will let them avoid prosecution or a longer prison sentence. Claims of lawyer misconduct made under such circumstances should be viewed with a most critical eye.

A word to the wise: Sometimes clients want help because they are being pressured to lie, sometimes they want cover for their own lawlessness. If setting up their lawyer gives them cover, they may well choose that option. The *Talao* court's second observation tells prosecutors what to do if an entity constituent comes to them with a story like Ferrer's:

> [T]he U.S. Attorney here did the right thing in advising Ferrer that she had a right to be represented by an attorney and giving her the opportunity to contact substitute counsel. When a person who has been represented by institutional counsel perceives a conflict in that representation and approaches a prosecutor or investigator, the prosecutor or investigator should do as Harris did here: advise the person of his right to obtain substitute counsel. Furthermore, we do not mean to suggest that government officials have a license to approach an employee and initiate communications whenever there is a possible conflict of interest between the employee and the corporation for whom the employee works. In this case, Ferrer initiated the communications with the U.S. Attorney's office, and Harris responded properly by clarifying her ethical duties [by checking with a supervisor] and advising Ferrer of her right to counsel

---

The No–Contact Rule and Undercover Investigations

Model Rule 8.4(a) prohibits lawyers from using third parties to do things the rules prohibit lawyers from doing themselves. Combined with Rules 4.1, prohibiting materially false statements, and Rule 4.2, forbidding contact with represented parties without the permission of the relevant lawyer, that rule presents a potential problem for lawyers who want to gather evidence through informal means.

In at least three types of cases courts tend to allow lawyers to use investigators to obtain evidence without admitting that they are investigating a potential claim. The first two types involve civil rights cases, in which lawyers may employ "testers" to see if a potential defendant does in fact discriminate on an impermissible basis, and intellectual property cases, in which investigators may purchase "knockoff" goods to establish the basis for an infringement claim. *See* New York County Lawyers' Association Committee on Professional Ethics Opinion No. 737 (May 23, 2007).

That opinion states "there is no nationwide consensus" on the degree to which lawyers may use what the opinion calls "dissemblance," by which it means use investigators who pretend to be ordinary consumers when they are not. The opinion suggests non-government lawyers may use dissemblance in civil rights or intellectual property cases to obtain evidence that is not otherwise available of a continuing or immediately impending violation of the law so long as the lawyers violate no rule of professional conduct (other than, arguably, Rules 4.1 and 8.4(c)), do not violate the legal rights of third parties, and do not seek to elicit privileged information. That is a fair summary of the current state of the law. The opinion of the Bar of the City of New York mentioned above notes this opinion and distinguishes it with respect to the topic of informal discovery utilizing social networking cites on the ground that informal discovery on such sites does not typically require dissemblance or other misleading conduct. Ass'n of the Bar of the City of New York Formal Op. 2010–2

The third type of case involves government lawyers who work with undercover law enforcement officials to gather evidence of crimes. *United States v. Hammad*, 858 F.2d 834 (2d Cir. 1988), has received considerable attention for its holding that Rule 4.2 applies to prosecutors who participate in pre-indictment investigations. The prosecutor in that case prepared and provided to an informant a sham subpoena, which the informant then used as a pretext for a conversation with a target of the investigation; the prosecutor knew the target was represented by counsel in the matter. The FBI videotaped the conversation. The target was later indicted and moved to suppress the tapes of the meeting on the ground that the prosecutor had violated New York's version of the no-contact rule.

The Second Circuit held the prosecutor had violated New York's version of the no-contact rule. It reasoned that "the prosecutor issued a subpoena for the informant, not to secure his attendance before the grand jury, but to create a pretense that might help the informant elicit admissions from a represented suspect. Though we have no occasion to consider the use of this technique in relation to unrepresented suspects, *see United States v. Martino,* 825 F.2d 754 (3d Cir. 1987), we believe that use of the technique under the circumstances of this case contributed to the informant's becoming that alter ego of the prosecutor. Consequently, the informant was engaging in communications proscribed by" the rule.

The *Hammad* court concluded that trial courts have discretion to suppress evidence obtained through violation of the no-contact rule. It reversed the trial court's suppression order in that case, however, on the ground that "the government should not have its case prejudiced by suppression of its evidence when the law was previously unsettled in this area." To date, no reported federal case has suppressed evidence as a sanction for violation of the no-contact rule.

The only reported case to both have found a violation of the rule in the context of a pre-indictment non-custodial investigation, and to have excluded evidence obtained by means of the violation, is *State v. Miller,* 600 N.W.2d 457 (Minn. 1999). The case involved an investigation of a landfill operator suspected of fraudulent billing practices. A county attorney named Stassen was assigned to assist with investigation of possible civil violations; a second county attorney, Skelly, was later assigned to assist with criminal issues.

Stassen met with representatives of the landfill, including Robert Miller, the general manager, and Joe Dixon, the lawyer for the landfill. The case was then turned into a criminal investigation, with Skelly in charge. County and federal officials then cooperated in executing a search warrant at the landfill's offices. Staff members notified Miller, who was not then in the office, that a search was under way.

When Miller arrived at the office, he was given a copy of the search warrant and told he was not under arrest. An investigator asked to interview him. Miller agreed, but said he first wanted to fax the search warrant to Dixon, which he did.

While Miller was being interviewed, Dixon called one of the investigators, stated that he represented the landfill, and asked that no statements be taken from employees until he arrived. The investigator refused to terminate the interview with Miller or to notify Miller that Dixon wanted to speak to him. The investigator also said that Dixon would not be allowed into the offices while the warrant was being executed, because the offices were considered a crime scene. After this conversation, the investigator telephoned Skelly, who opined that the investigators did not have to terminate the interview with Miller and did not have to permit Dixon to enter the search area.

Miller was eventually indicted and moved to suppress statements taken during the interview on the ground that they were taken in violation of Rule 4.2. The trial court and court of appeals agreed, and granted his motion. The Supreme Court affirmed:

> We do not perceive that the application of MRPC 4.2 should be limited, in a criminal context, to contacts with an attorney's client after the client has been charged. Adverse counsel's contacts with an attorney's client can be disruptive and deleterious to the attorney's relationship with a client irrespective of whether the client has been charged with a crime, and the need for an attorney's counsel in an adverse interview is certainly no less before the client is charged than after. We hold that the appropriate analysis is to look at alleged violations on a case-by-case basis, examining the totality of the circumstances of the contact to determine if it went beyond appropriate and commonly accepted investigatory activity of police to implicate issues relating to the fair administration of justice on the part of the prosecuting attorney. . . .
>
> [T]he question is whether there is a rational basis to conclude that a change in the nature of the investigation from civil to criminal justifies allowing the prosecutor's contact with appellant as "authorized by law," when contact was clearly prohibited by MRPC 4.2 when the proceeding was civil in nature. We believe there is none. While we are not unmindful of the severity of the sanction of suppression of evidence developed in a police investigation, in circumstances where, as here, not only has the proscription of MRPC 4.2 prohibiting contact with a represented client been violated, the record reflects a systematic isolation of the client from his attorney by refusing to terminate the non-custodial interview despite the attorney's request and prohibiting the attorney from speaking with the client.
>
> We interpret the "authorized by law" exception to MRPC 4.2 to mean that legitimate investigative processes may go forward without violating MRPC 4.2 even when the target of the investigation is represented by counsel, but when the process goes beyond fair and legitimate investigation and is so egregious that it impairs the fair administration of justice, it is not "authorized by law."
>
> While we are not unmindful of the harshness of the trial court sanction that "[t]he proper remedy for this violation is to exclude the portion of the statements [sic] made after [Dixon] requested that the officers not interview [appellant]," we believe it appropriately reflects the seriousness of the ethical violation and the prejudice to appellant.

The No–Contact Rule and Class Actions

How does the no-contact rule work when a plaintiff files suit against an entity, such as a corporation, and seeks to certify a class that includes current employees of the entity? Suppose, for example, that a former employee sues a company for failing to pay overtime and alleges that this failure to pay is a continuing policy. Can the company's counsel talk to current employees (who are prospective class members) about the case? Does it matter if a court has not yet certified the case as a class action?

The court in *Atari, Inc. v. Superior Court*, 166 Cal.App.3d 867 (1985), answered some of these questions. The plaintiffs filed suit alleging various employment-related claims on behalf of a class of former Atari employees. The trial court entered an order allowing plaintiff's counsel to communicate with persons who would be members of the class if one were certified (to let them know that the case had been filed and gather any information they might have), but not allowing the employer to engage in such communications. The court of appeals reversed this prohibition, reasoning that it would be unfair to allow plaintiffs' counsel but not Atari's lawyers access to prospective class members: "Absent a showing of actual or threatened abuse," the court held, "both sides should be permitted to investigate the case fully." The court refused to accept "the suggestion that a potential (but as yet unapproached) class member should be deemed `a party . . . represented by counsel' even before the class is certified; we respectfully disagree to this extent with the federal courts which apparently would accept it. . . ." Though *Atari* rejects the broad claim that members of an *uncertified* class are represented by counsel for purposes of the no-contact rule, courts will pay attention to the circumstances of particular cases and might be willing to grant orders that would limit or preclude certain kinds of contact.

Judges regulate communications with class members more extensively if a class is certified. For an overview of the practical aspects of this question, *see* Manual on Complex Litigation § 21.12. In particular, once a class has been certified, even conditionally, you should assume that Model Rule 4.2 and state law equivalents, such as California's Rule 2-100, forbid contact with putative class members absent the consent of class counsel. *E.g. Hernandez v. Vitamin Shoppe Indus, Inc.*, 174 Cal. App. 4th 1441 (2009).

A final issue relates to unbundled representation: Is a client assisted by a lawyer who provides only limited services "represented" within the meaning of Rule 4.2 or "unrepresented" within the meaning of Rule 4.3? Colorado added a comment to its Rule 4.2, stating that a party representing himself but to whom limited representation has been provided is considered "unrepresented" for purposes of Rule 4.2 unless the lawyer who wants to communicate with that party "has knowledge to the contrary." This approach has the virtue of being practical, and is likely to be followed elsewhere. For an opinion reaching this result, *see McMillan v. Shadow Ridge at Oak Park Homeowners' Ass'n*, 165 Cal.App.4th 960 (2008), in which a party who appeared for herself but who had retained counsel for particular, limited purposes first confirmed to opposing counsel that she represented herself and then moved to disqualify him for violation of the no-contact rule after he spoke to her about scheduling matters.

The following case illustrates that the rule against contacting represented parties extends to passive as well as active communication; it also illustrates a separate rule, stated in Model Rule 8.5(a), that a lawyer may be disciplined by his or her licensing jurisdiction for conduct occurring outside that jurisdiction. The same rule provides that a lawyer offering services in a jurisdiction may be disciplined by that jurisdiction even if the lawyer is not licensed there. Rule 8.5(b)(1) provides that for conduct in connection with a matter pending before a tribunal the rules of the jurisdiction in which the tribunal sits govern. (Note that those rules may incorporate other rules as well.) Rule 8.5(b)(2) provides a choice of law provision for other cases; it states that the rules of the jurisdiction in which conduct occurs govern that conduct unless the predominant effect of the conduct is felt in a different jurisdiction, in which case that jurisdiction's rules apply.

Model Rule of Professional Conduct 8.5

IN RE HOWES

123 N.M. 311 (1997)

PER CURIAM:

In early August 1988, Billy Wilson (Wilson) was shot and killed in an apartment house in Washington, D.C. On August 23, 1988, Darryl Smith (defendant) was arrested for this murder and subsequently gave a lengthy videotaped statement to police, in which he admitted being at the scene of the murder but claimed that the murder had actually been committed by a Larry Epps.

Public Defender Jaime S. Gardner was appointed to represent defendant, and respondent, who was at all material times an attorney licensed by this Court, represented the United States. . .

On August 24, 1988, defendant appeared for presentment in the Superior Court of the District of Columbia and was ordered held without bond until a preliminary hearing could be held. On September 6, 1988, respondent moved the court to release defendant on his own recognizance pending further investigation of the case. Prior to defendant's release, respondent indicated to the public defender that he would like to speak with defendant about the case; however, she refused permission unless respondent was willing to offer her client complete immunity, which he was not willing to offer.

Between September 26 and October 5, 1988, defendant contacted District of Columbia Metropolitan Police Detective Donald R. Gossage (detective) on several occasions and made statements to him about the Wilson murder and two other murders. The detective told respondent about these statements. Respondent had no personal experience with a defendant who contacted police to discuss his own case, but office policy permitted him to deal with witnesses who were represented by counsel in other cases without notifying their attorneys. Respondent discussed the situation with the chief of the felony section, who told him to advise the detective that if defendant were to initiate further contact with the detective, the detective could listen but that he was not to initiate contact with defendant. There was no discussion about whether to notify the public defender. Respondent relayed the message to the detective and told him as well to make notes of anything defendant might say, so that any inconsistent statements could be used for impeachment purposes.

The public defender first learned of these contacts with her client through testimony presented at his preliminary hearing on October 5, 1988. . . Defendant's attorney complained in open court about the contacts with her client made without her knowledge and asked the court to issue a directive that there be no further contacts with defendant. Respondent stated that he expected no further contacts with defendant but added that "if he wants to call us, we will take his call." The court issued no directive but observed on the record that the public defender would undoubtedly instruct her client that such contacts were not in his best interest.

Between October 5 and November 1, 1988, however, defendant continued his efforts to contact the detective from the jail. He left messages for the detective on his beeper and even spoke with him on several occasions regarding the Wilson murder and the other two cases (wherein he was not charged and, therefore, not represented by counsel.) Respondent was aware that defendant was talking about the Wilson murder to the detective but did not notify the public defender or obtain her permission for the detective to discuss the case with her client.

On November 18, 1988, the detective was in respondent's office working with him on the Wilson murder case when respondent himself received a call from defendant on his private line. Respondent had never given his private number to defendant, although he had given it to the detective. At respondent's request, the detective listened in on an extension. Although defendant was advised that he did not have to speak with defendant and the detective and that his lawyer would not be happy, he proceeded to talk about the Wilson case for approximately six minutes while respondent and the detective listened and took notes. Defendant called back about ten minutes later and spoke with respondent and the detective for another fifteen minutes, although he was again reminded that the public defender would be unhappy with him. At the conclusion of this call, the detective agreed to visit defendant at the jail. Although respondent's notes indicate that defendant now was focusing almost exclusively on the Wilson murder, the public defender was advised neither of the calls nor of the impending visit with her client.

The detective had been advised by respondent that because defendant was initiating the calls, the constitutionality and the voluntariness of the statements were established and that he should "let Darryl talk" but refrain from posing questions of his own. After the call to his own office and the appointment for the detective to visit personally with defendant, respondent consulted with the chief and deputy chief of the felony section, who advised him that the detective should take a partner with him to the jail and give defendant his Miranda warnings before proceeding with the interview.

While the deputy chief recalled that there may have been some discussion of the ethical proprieties of communicating directly with defendant, the chief of the felony section acknowledged in his testimony that his primary concern in advising respondent was whether the evidence would be constitutionally admissible. The deputy chief did not recollect that respondent advised either himself or the chief that he had personally spoken with defendant. It is also clear from the record that the chief's advice as to any ethical considerations was more directed at the contacts the detective was having with defendant rather than to any calls respondent might be receiving. The chief acknowledged that his understanding of the rules regarding professional responsibility would probably not have affected his advice, because he "didn't think the D.C. bar rules had much to say about how the police behaved."

On November 21, 1988, the detective and a partner visited with defendant at the jail and gave Miranda warnings, but defendant refused to sign the form because, he said, it would make his lawyer angry. The meeting was terminated.

On November 25 or 26, 1988, respondent received four more collect calls from defendant from the jail, all of which he accepted. He reminded defendant that his attorney had already complained to the court about his contacts with representatives of the government but permitted defendant to continue to speak with him nonetheless. Respondent asked no questions but listened to everything defendant had to say. While his notes again indicate that defendant was now speaking only of the Wilson murder, respondent did not advise defendant's attorney of these calls.

Defendant was indicted for the murder of Wilson on December 8, 1988. The public defender subsequently sought to have defendant's statements to respondent and the detective suppressed and/or the indictment dismissed on the basis of prosecutorial misconduct. The motion was denied by written order dated July 10, 1989, but the judge referred the matter of respondent's possible violation of DR 7–104 of the Code of Professional Responsibility to the District of Columbia Board of Professional Responsibility.

The Board of Professional Responsibility for the District of Columbia at that time had disciplinary jurisdiction over any attorney who engaged in the practice of law in the District of Columbia on a *pro hac vice* basis, but in 1988 the relevant rule did not apply to an AUSA practicing pursuant to 28 USC § 517. For this reason, the case was referred to the office of New Mexico's disciplinary counsel in May 1990.

Rule 16–805, NMRA subjects a lawyer admitted to practice in New Mexico to the disciplinary authority of this Court, even though he or she may be engaged in practice elsewhere. Both respondent and his employer, the United States Department of Justice (DOJ), filed federal suits challenging this Court's jurisdiction to conduct this disciplinary proceeding. Both suits were resolved in favor of this court's jurisdiction. . . .

The hearing committee and the disciplinary board concluded that respondent had violated Rule 16–402 by directly communicating about the subject of the representation with a party he knew to be represented by another lawyer in the matter without the consent of the other lawyer and without authorization of law to do so. . .

The issues raised by respondent in his appeal are (a) whether he was entitled to rely on the advice of his supervisor and thus should be excused for any violation of Rule 16–402 under the provisions of Rule 16–502(B); (b) whether he "communicated" with defendant within the meaning of Rule 16–402; (c) whether any communication that occurred was "authorized by law;" (d) whether his actions were authorized under federal Constitutional principles that override New Mexico's Rules of Professional Conduct; and (e) whether, even if a violation occurred, disciplinary action should be taken against him. . . .

Respondent . . . argues that he did not violate Rule 16–402 because the evidence in the case shows that he simply listened to defendant. Since there was no questioning of defendant, he reasons, he did not "communicate" with defendant. We disagree.

While certainly one purpose of Rule 16–402 is to prevent attorneys from utilizing their legal skills to gain an advantage over an unsophisticated lay person, an equally important purpose is to protect a person represented by counsel "not only from the approaches of his adversary's lawyer, but from the folly of his own well-meaning initiatives and the generally unfortunate consequences of his ignorance." *People v. Green,* 274 N.W.2d 448, 459 (1979) (quoting Justice Levin's dissent).

The law and Rule 16–402 also recognize that once an attorney has been retained or appointed to represent a litigant, that attorney's responsibility is to act on behalf of the client and to protect the client from compromising his or her case by inadvertently waiving a viable defense or from disclosing privileged information. The attorney cannot fulfill this responsibility when opposing counsel freely comes into contact with the client without the attorney's knowledge.

By not contacting defendant's attorney and by encouraging defendant to talk to him and to the detective without her advice, respondent violated Rule 16–402 and the principles behind it.

> The principle is not so much, important as that is, to preserve the civilized decencies, but to protect the individual, often ignorant and uneducated, and always in fear, when faced with the coercive police power of the State. The right to the continued advice of a lawyer, already retained or assigned, is his real protection against an abuse of power by the organized State. It is more important than the preinterrogation warnings given to defendants in custody. These warnings often provide only a feeble opportunity to obtain a lawyer, because the suspect or accused is required to determine his need, unadvised by anyone who has his interests at heart. The danger is not only the risk of unwise waivers of the privilege against self-incrimination and of the right to counsel, but the more significant risk of inaccurate, sometimes false, and inevitably incomplete descriptions of the events described.

People v. Hobson, 348 N.E.2d 894, 899 (1976).

To argue that one does not violate Rule 16–402 if one does not ask questions or impart information borders on sophistry. People do not compromise their positions or waive their defenses by listening to an attorney; they do so by talking while the attorney listens.

"Communication" and "interrogation" are not synonymous, and it is "communication" that is prohibited by Rule 16–402. One can communicate interest and concern simply by indicating a willingness to listen. Since criminal defendants who are in custody often attempt to seek out and explain themselves to persons in authority under the generally misguided notion that they can extricate themselves from an unfortunate situation, the apparent willingness of a detective and a prosecutor to consider a defendant's version of the facts can be a particularly compelling message. "The influence of the prosecutor's presence is immeasurable."

People v. Green, 274 N.W.2d 448, 456 (quoting Justice Moody, concurring in part and dissenting in part). Respondent and the detective were well aware that defendant was attempting to discuss the evidence in his own case in order to help himself and they used his false hope to their advantage. Even if they asked no questions of defendant, by granting him an audience they tacitly encouraged him to keep talking.

While a lack of overreaching by a prosecutor in this situation may be a mitigating factor, it does not excuse compliance with the standard prescribed by Rule 16–402. . . .

We therefore reject respondent's argument that an attorney does not violate Rule 16–104 unless he or she is an active participant in a conversation with a represented opponent regarding the subject matter of the representation.

III. Whether respondent communications were "authorized by law" within the meaning of Rule 16–402.

Respondent next contends that even if he is found to have "communicated" with defendant, there is no violation of Rule 16–402 because any communication he might have had was "authorized by law." . . .

The cases cited by respondent in support of his first theory do little to bolster his position, as the cases concern the issue of whether statements made to a prosecutor by a represented defendant should be suppressed rather than the issue of whether the prosecutor violated the ethical prohibition against contact with a represented party. . . .

Respondent's reliance upon the holdings in suppression decisions as justification for his conduct is misplaced, as these cases generally do not define an attorney's ethical responsibilities. If they mention disciplinary rules at all, it is primarily to make clear that the rules are not ordinarily available to a criminal defendant in fashioning a personal remedy for himself or herself. . . .

Respondent has chosen to ignore the body of case law which has held that even where an attorney's actions do not violate constitutional standards, they may still be in violation of Rule 7–104(A) and/or Rule 16–402. . .

Suppose one of your employees, such as a secretary or legal assistant, sues you for employment law violations. The complaint served on you shows that they have a lawyer. May you talk to them about it? *In re Knappenberger*, 338 Or. 341 (2005), says no, even if you seek to talk to them as their employer rather than as (i) a lawyer on (ii) the other side.

B. UNREPRESENTED PERSONS

Model Rule 4.3 provides that when you deal with unrepresented persons (such as witnesses, for example) on behalf of a client you may not state or imply that you are disinterested. If you know or reasonably should know the person misunderstands whom you represent and what you are doing (your "role" in a matter), you must correct the misunderstanding. If you know or reasonably should know the person's interests do or might conflict with your client's interests, then you may not give them legal advice unless it is the advice to consult their own lawyer. Issues under this rule arise in surprising and ambiguous ways, as the next case demonstrates.

Model Rule of Professional Conduct 4.3
Restatement of the Law Governing Lawyers § 103

HOPKINS V. TROUTNER

134 Idaho 445 (2000)

TROUT, CHIEF JUSTICE.

This is an appeal from an order setting aside a Release of All Claims and Indemnity Agreement and Stipulation for Dismissal with Prejudice. The district judge found that there had been overreaching by Defendant Arthur "Art" Troutner's (Troutner) attorney, Brian K. Julian (Julian), in negotiating a Release and Indemnity Agreement with Plaintiff Joseph S. Hopkins (Hopkins).

Hopkins filed a complaint against Troutner on June 17, 1997, asserting causes of action for assault and battery, intentional infliction of emotional distress, negligent infliction of emotional distress and invasion of privacy. Hopkins' claims stem from alleged physical and sexual abuse he suffered from Troutner as a minor child. On April 10, 1998, the district judge granted Hopkins' attorneys' motion for leave to withdraw from the case. Shortly after his attorneys withdrew from the case, Hopkins was contacted by representatives of Troutner and was given Julian's telephone number to call. Hopkins then called Julian several times and conducted settlement negotiations by telephone.

Hopkins expressed to Julian a desire to settle the case and stated that he would do so for less than the offers of judgment tendered to other plaintiffs in similar cases filed against Troutner. Julian's affidavit filed in this case provided the following description of their discussion:

> He then solicited what I believe to be the value of this case, after informing me that he would certainly take much less than the Offer of

Judgment previously filed herein to the other Plaintiffs. I told him, in my opinion, the case was worth $3,000.00 to $4,000.00.

Hopkins then demanded $6,000, for which Julian advised him he would have to get settlement authority. The next day, Julian telephonically offered $5,500 to Hopkins, which Hopkins accepted.

Hopkins then went to Julian's office where Julian presented the Release and Indemnity Agreement. Julian explained that the documents would forever dismiss Hopkins' cause of action and that Hopkins could seek legal counsel if desired. Hopkins signed the Release and Indemnity Agreement and then accepted and cashed the settlement check of $5,500. The parties then submitted to the court a Stipulation for Dismissal pursuant to the Release and Indemnity Agreement and the district judge signed an Order of Dismissal with Prejudice on April 21, 1998.

Attorney M. Karl Shurtliff entered his appearance on behalf of Hopkins on April 21, 1998. On April 24, 1998, Hopkins . . . filed a Motion to Set Aside Release of all Claims and Indemnity Agreement and Stipulation for Dismissal with Prejudice on May 22, 1998, asserting the theories of incapacity, duress, undue influence and overreaching.

The district judge . . . granted Hopkins' motion pursuant to Rule 60(b)(6) on the basis of overreaching. More specifically, the district judge found the following two statements in Julian's affidavit supported the judge's conclusion that there had been overreaching: (1) "He then solicited what I believed to be the value of this case, after informing me that he would certainly take much less than the offer of judgment previously filed herein to the other Plaintiffs"; and (2) "I told him, in my opinion, the case was worth $3,000 or $4,000." Troutner then filed this appeal.

We decline to overturn the district judge's decision to grant Hopkins relief because the judge clearly perceived the issue as one of discretion, acted within the outer boundaries of his discretion and consistently with applicable legal standards, and reached his decision by an exercise of reason.

Idaho courts have not had occasion to define overreaching in the context of an attorney's conduct for the purposes of Rule 60(b). During argument, Hopkins' attorney cited, over objection, the Comment to ABA Model Rule of Professional Conduct 4.3, which provides:

> An unrepresented person, particularly one not experienced in dealing with legal matters, might assume that a lawyer is disinterested in loyalties or is a disinterested authority on the law even when the lawyer represents a client. During the course of a lawyer's representation of a client, the lawyer should not give advice to an unrepresented person other than the advice to obtain counsel.

MODEL RULES OF PROFESSIONAL CONDUCT Rule 4.3 cmt. (1995). The comments to the Rules of Professional Conduct have not been adopted in Idaho and are not binding authority. However, this is not a bar disciplinary proceeding and it was appropriate for the district judge to consider the Comment to Rule 4.3 as instructive authority among the applicable legal standards; no different than case law from other jurisdictions or the Restatement. The district judge thus acted well within the boundaries of his discretion and consistently with the legal standards applicable in concluding that there was overreaching.

Finally, we examine whether the district judge reached his decision through an exercise of reason. The following statement by the district judge reflects his analysis of what was impermissible about Julian's conduct and why that supported a decision to set aside the order of dismissal:

> I'm not sure I know precisely what overreaching is, because I think it's more on the equitable side of the Court's jurisdiction and less on the legal side. Again I think Mr. Julian has been honest, not unethical and straightforward in this case. But I think when—if he were to have said, "You need to get your own—form your own opinion about that, or find somebody to give you an opinion about that. My client would only pay you three or $4,000," that's different. But Mr. Hopkins was asking him, "What's this case worth?" Under circumstances that should have led, I think, Mr. Julian to believe that his answer was going to be relied upon by Mr. Hopkins.

The district judge, through an exercise of reason, concluded that Julian did not merely state a factual matter to Hopkins. Instead, Julian inappropriately offered Hopkins legal advice upon which Julian should have expected Hopkins to rely since he was unrepresented at the time. The district judge's reasoned analysis thus satisfies the third element of the abuse of discretion test.

The district judge's decision to grant Hopkins relief from the Release of All Claims and Indemnity Agreement and Stipulation for Dismissal with Prejudice pursuant to I.R.C.P. 60(b)(6) is hereby affirmed. We award costs on appeal to respondent.

JUSTICE SCHROEDER, dissenting.

I respectfully dissent from the opinion of the Court. In this case Hopkins made the decision to represent himself. He was competent to understand the nature of the proceedings in which he was involved. It is unrealistic under these circumstances to characterize the statements of Troutner's attorney as legal advice to Hopkins. It was a method of stating how much his client would pay as part of the negotiations initiated by Hopkins. Regardless, even treating the statements as legal advice, the settlement still should not be set aside.

There is no showing that Hopkins relied upon the statements of Troutner's attorney. In fact, the record establishes that he did not. Hopkins insisted on more money than the attorney said the case was worth, and he obtained substantially more money in the settlement than the attorney initially said the case was worth.

There is no showing that Hopkins was harmed. Nothing in the record establishes that the settlement amount did not fall within the range of reasonableness.

Finally, despite the order of the district court that Hopkins return the settlement amount, at the date of the hearing before this Court he had not done so. He has kept the benefits of the settlement but avoided the binding effect of the settlement.

In sum, to justify setting aside the settlement there should be a showing of reliance, harm and fair conduct by the person seeking to avoid the settlement. None of these elements has been shown.

Stating a Position, Stating a Fact, or Giving Advice?

Sometimes small differences in wording create big differences in meaning. One difference important in various contexts is between stating a position and either stating a fact or giving advice. Had Julian said: "it is our position your case is worth $3,000 or $4,000 dollars" he would neither have stated a fact nor given advice. (Technically he would have asserted as fact that his client held that position, but judges and other lawyers know positions may change.) Had he said "we are willing to pay you $3,000," as the court suggested he might have done, he might have been deemed to state a fact about his client's state of mind—that the client was in fact willing to pay that much—but he would not have given advice. When Julian said it was his opinion that the case was worth $3,000 or $4,000 he might have thought that by qualifying his numbers as only his opinion he had avoided making a factual statement about the value of the case. But a lawyer's advice sometimes takes the form of an opinion, so the qualification did not solve all his problems and indeed left him open to the criticism you read in the opinion.

Words are deeds; choose them carefully.

Model Rule of Professional Conduct 3.4(f)
Restatement (Third) of the Law Governing Lawyers § 116(3)–(4)

KENSINGTON INTERNATIONAL LTD. V. REPUBLIC OF CONGO

2007 WL 2456993 (S.D.N.Y.) *aff'd* (2008)

Kensington is a financial institution in the business of, among other things, investing in debt and equity instruments issued by domestic and foreign entities. Congo is a sovereign nation located in Africa. Cleary is an international law firm with offices in several cities including New York, Washington, and Paris.

In the underlying case, Kensington sought recognition and enforcement of a final money judgment rendered against Congo by the High Court of Justice, Queen's Bench Division, Commercial Court in London. Further to that end, on September 30, 2004, the Court granted Kensington's motion against Congo for partial summary judgment, entered a money judgment of $56,911,991.47, and certified the judgment as final pursuant to Rule 54(b). Thereafter, Kensington began taking discovery in aid of execution of the judgment.

Among those subpoenaed in this process was non-party witness Medard Mbemba, a citizen of France and Congo with residences in France and the Ivory Coast and an office in Washington, D.C. Mbemba, through his company, African Partners, was involved in various business dealings with the Congolese government and its officials and agencies, including aspects of the shipping and oil and gas industries. Kensington hoped Mbemba possessed knowledge of the whereabouts of Congo's assets and served on him a subpoena which noticed a deposition for December 23, 2004 in Washington, D.C.

Mbemba's native language is French. Though he does not speak English, his son, Frank Mbemba, does. Frank Mbemba accepted service of the subpoena on December 6, 2004. At some point thereafter, Mbemba consulted with a friend who was an attorney about his obligations under the subpoena; the friend informed him that he was required to testify and suggested an attorney in the United States who could accompany him. After considering the cost of counsel, Mbemba decided he would attend alone. His son communicated with Arnon Siegel, an attorney at Dechert, to coordinate a date and place for the deposition. . . .

[O]n January 28, 2005, Frank Mbemba called Siegel and told him his father was with him in Washington and would appear for deposition on Friday, February 4, 2005. Mbemba was scheduled to be in Washington until Saturday, February 5 and would not return for several months. Siegel informed an attorney at Cleary, Boaz Morag, of the scheduled deposition (and of the fact that Mbemba was not represented by counsel). Morag replied by email and by phone that neither he nor any other Cleary attorney familiar with the case could attend the deposition on February 4, complained of the short notice, and asked that it be rescheduled; Siegel refused, claiming there was no other suitable time during Mbemba's limited stay in Washington. Though Morag proposed that the deposition be held at a later date in France, no agreement was reached on that score, and Siegel informed Morag the deposition would occur as scheduled. As early as Monday, January 31, 2005, Morag informed Siegel of his intention to have the Court intervene to postpone the deposition, but no application was ever made.

On Monday, January 31, and again on Wednesday, February 2, 2005, Morag contacted Jean–Pierre Vignaud, a partner in Cleary's Paris office, to update him on the status of the Mbemba deposition. Vignaud is a member of Cleary's ten-member worldwide executive committee and, though he had no prior substantive role in the instant case, he is the relationship partner for Congo and has, and is known for having, extensive connections with Congo's political leadership. At Morag's request, Vignaud contacted Mbemba on February 3. First, he emailed Mbemba at the address listed on the African Partner's website. The message, in translation, stated:

> Dear Sir:
>
> Our firm represents the interests of the Republic of Congo in a number of legal proceedings involving certain creditors, particularly in the United States.
>
> My colleagues in our New York office have just learned that you agreed to . . . give a deposition concerning your knowledge of commercial or financial transactions of the Republic of Congo and assets belonging to the Republic in the United States and outside the United States.
>
> I wish to call your attention to the very particular nature of depositions in U.S. procedural law. These depositions are given under oath, and it is extremely rare to agree to submit to this procedure without preparation or the assistance of an attorney who is completely familiar with the case. My colleague, Boaz Morag of our New York office will be at a hearing the whole day on Friday and therefore will not be able to assist you on that occasion. Under these circumstances, giving a deposition without the assistance of an attorney who is familiar with the case seems to us to present very serious risks and inconveniences that I will leave to you to assess. In any event, I suggest you urgently contact Boaz Morag . . . or myself at the number below.

He also placed two calls to the Washington D.C. contact number on the African Partner's website, leaving one voice mail message.

On Thursday, February 4, 2005, sometime before 4 p.m. EST, Mbemba called Vignaud at his office in France (10 p.m. C.E.T.) The call was forwarded to Vignaud's home or cell phone. Mbemba recalled at his deposition the following about the conversation:

> A: [Vignaud] said we have learned that you are going to go and meet with a lawyer for Kensington in order to give a deposition, and I'm talking now to you in your capacity as Congolese patriot and I want you to understand that these steps are going to affect the stability of Congo. . . .
>
> A: I told him I did not know the matter. I said that if my deposition is going against the interests of my country, then I am against giving the deposition, I'm saying no out of patriotism. And [Vignaud] said yes it is dangerous for your country. So, I said I do not know the United States and I do not know customs there and lawyers. I do not have a lawyer so he said well, this is one more reason you should not go. So, he asked that my son take the initiative to cancel this appointment. So, I said you are a lawyer. If you are trying to defend the interests of Congo, tell your colleagues that I will not go. . . .
>
> Q: Did you understand Mr. Vignaud to be telling you not to go to this deposition?
>
> A: Yes, that's what he said, not to come.

Mbemba recalled at his deposition that Vignaud said

> "I want to inform you that your deposition can hurt the Congo," specifically that these are people who buy loans at percent of their value and who are very dangerous. Then they hire lawyers and they can destabilize the economies of countries, and I'm warning you so that you'll know and not participate in this kind of a game because it is a bad thing for your country. I [Mbemba] said bad for the government or for the population or for certain persons? He [Vignaud] said bad for the population. I said, sir, Mr. Vignaud, I don't have the honor of knowing you and I'm telling you that I will not go to this lawsuit. Not because this is what you are telling me to do, but out of patriotism.

When asked whether he felt Vignaud was trying to persuade him not to attend, Mbemba replied, "It is not an impression, he told me as such not to go."

Mbemba testified that he knew Vignaud to be someone with "privileged connections to . . . the authorities in Congo." When asked if he felt threatened by Vignaud's statements, Mbemba replied, "So, when somebody tells you that something is bad for your country and that I feel obliged to warn you, yes, it sounds like a threat." It was Mbemba's state of mind, even before he spoke with Vignaud, that testifying against Congo in a matter over Congo's debt was "dangerous."

Following the call to Mbemba, Vignaud called Morag to tell him to notify Dechert that Mbemba was not testifying. Morag informed Vignaud that he thought it would be better if Mbemba called Dechert directly and asked Vignaud to convey as much to Mbemba. Vignaud called Mbemba, this time at the Watergate Hotel where Mbemba was staying.

In this, the second conversation, Vignaud asked Mbemba if he would communicate his intention directly to Dechert through his son. Mbemba said he did not want to get his son further involved and asked that Cleary contact Dechert; Vignaud agreed to have an email sent to Dechert. Mbemba recalls he asked Vignaud, "What kind of danger am I in if I don't go? I mean, what will happen? Nothing, he said, nothing.". . . . In neither of the conversations did Vignaud mention the need or the possibility of rescheduling the deposition.

At 4 p.m. on Thursday, Morag sent the following email to Siegel:

> M. Mbemba contacted our firm this afternoon and asked us to relay to you his intention not to appear tomorrow. He stated that he had been unaware of the precise nature of the proceeding tomorrow and now that he understands that he will be asked questions under oath on a number of subjects, he stated that he feels uncomfortable appearing without having consulted with a lawyer, which he has not apparently done. He said that he travels to the United States often and there should be another occasion to schedule the deposition.

Upon receiving the email, Siegel contacted Frank Mbemba who confirmed that his father would not appear for his deposition. Siegel informed Frank that the subpoena required his father by law to appear at the deposition. Frank then spoke with Mbemba and convinced him to testify at the deposition for two reasons. First, because the law required him to testify. Second, Mbemba testified Frank said "Dad, you know very well that you are not protecting the Congolese people. You are protecting a group of individuals that you know and that I know, and you'll be protecting them. You want to be in politics, you have to be transparent everywhere." Frank Mbemba called Siegel back and told him that his father had changed his mind and would attend the deposition, and Siegel so informed Morag by email that the deposition would go forward as planned.

The following morning, Friday, February 3, Vignaud—having received the Siegel email from Morag—attempted to call Mbemba several times and spoke with him once, just before Mbemba was to leave for his deposition. Mbemba recounts the conversation:

> ['W]e have just learned that you are going for the deposition in spite of what we discussed. It's incredible that somebody would go make a deposition without a lawyer.['] At that moment I remembered-I remembered at that moment that Congo has been using Vignaud as a lawyer for the last 20 or 30 years. We lost lots of lawsuits. We could

> have paid all this public debt instead of paying Mr. Vignaud. I said to Mr. Vignaud thank you very much but do you know how old I am?—and I tell him how old I was—therefore, I am old enough to be able to make my own decisions. And then I hung up on him. . . .

Mbemba went to the deposition. Vignaud attempted to reach Mbemba at the Watergate two more times after Mbemba had already left.

Needless to say, Vignaud's account of the substance of the phone calls differs considerably. While he denies much of what transpired, his admissions are far more telling and, in all but the most technical sense, seem to contradict his denials. To the extent his denials contradict Mbemba's testimony, the Court credits Mbemba's testimony as it finds it is more consistent and believable; Mbemba had little to gain from testifying falsely, either at his deposition or when he voluntarily appeared in court. . . .

The Court finds that sanctions are appropriate here. It so holds because it finds that the evidence clearly demonstrates Cleary's attorneys acted without legal justification and in fact acted to delay or obstruct the post-judgment discovery process in this case. . . .

The sequence of events relevant to this motion begins with Cleary in a jam: it wanted Morag to attend Mbemba's deposition but, because of the late notice from Mbemba as to his availability and Dechert's refusal to reschedule, he could not. Morag's initial impulse to seek a protective order to prevent the deposition was the proper one and evidences Cleary's intention to postpone the deposition. Perhaps Cleary decided that there were no legitimate grounds to seek a protective order; perhaps it feared a court would inquire as to whether Cleary had a sufficient interest in attending the deposition of a non-party witness to warrant delay of the deposition; or perhaps it never had any intention of going to court. But in any event, the record is clear that, in forgoing the legal means at its disposal for postponing or defining the terms of the deposition, Cleary made a choice to achieve its goals through illegitimate means: contacting Mbemba directly and persuading him to avoid the deposition. . . .

Had Cleary done as it claimed and only informed Mbemba of the nature of depositions and the prudence of obtaining counsel-even if its motives were not entirely altruistic-the Court would not find Cleary acted solely in bad faith. But a review of the findings of fact shows Cleary did much more than disinterestedly inform Mbemba of American legal custom.

Cleary's story begins to falter with the selection of Vignaud as the attorney to contact Mbemba. . . . Vignaud was selected in the hope that he could assert influence over Mbemba. As a well known figure in Congo, he could make a convincing argument that the deposition was "us vs. them" and force Mbemba to pick a side. A Cleary associate in New York who speaks conversational French could not, with adequate gusto, inspire

Mbemba to join the fight against the "vulture creditors" threatening Congo's stability. Nor could anyone but Vignaud even create the impression that acquiescence in his demands might yield a benefit; disobedience, a penalty. In a case where innuendo was needed in place of explicit commands, Vignaud appears to have been the only man for the job. . . .

Vignaud delivered on the promise of his influence. His first act, the February 3 email from to Mbemba, standing alone, would probably not suffice to show bad faith. It does, however, begin a theme for the remainder of the communications with Mbemba: the blurring of the line between Congo's interest and Mbemba's. . . . Mbemba, through his testimony firmly establishes that Cleary acted in bad faith in trying to persuade him not to attend the deposition. . . .

Having successfully persuaded Mbemba not to attend the deposition, Cleary then attempted to have Mbemba call Dechert himself to cancel. Doing so might possibly insulate Cleary from Mbemba's ultimate decision not to attend, but Mbemba refused. The resulting communique demonstrates Cleary's attempt to obscure what actually transpired between Vignaud and Mbemba and suggests the law firm had something to hide. . . .

Vignaud's several attempts to contact Mbemba, particularly on the morning of the deposition, show an urgency uncharacteristic of an attorney who disinterestedly seeks to inform a witness of the dangers of being deposed without counsel. As Vignaud saw it, Mbemba's choice to testify on February 4 was a problem for Congo, not a problem for Mbemba. . . . A phone call to Mbemba made in good faith would have had as its aim *Mbemba's* interests, not Congo's. The reason why nonparty witnesses elect to consult with attorneys prior to depositions is to protect themselves, not one of the parties to the litigation. Vignaud's admissions make plain that he was at all times acting solely in Congo's interest and he testified Congo's interest did not include having Mbemba represented at the deposition, thus undercutting Cleary's proffered reason for the communications in the first place. . . .

Sanctions serve three purposes: (1) to prevent a party from benefitting from its own improper conduct, (2) to provide specific deterrents, and (3) to provide general deterrence. . . . Cleary did not benefit from its own improper conduct. But Cleary is an ideal candidate for specific deterrence. It has shown a willingness to operate in the murky area between zealous advocacy and improper conduct, and here it crossed the line. Cleary, through two of its attorneys, sought to interfere with the legitimate post-judgment discovery process in this case by attempting in bad faith in furtherance of its own interests to dissuade Mbemba from attending the properly noticed deposition. This conduct is inconsistent with counsel's obligations under the Federal Rules of Civil Procedure and recognized ethical strictures. *See, e.g., Harlan v. Lewis,* 982 F.2d 1255, 1259

(8th Cir.1993) (upholding the district court's imposition of sanctions where it found that defense counsel attempted to dissuade a non-party witness from giving testimony); ABA Model Rules of Prof'l Conduct R. 3.4(f) (prohibiting a lawyer from "requesting a person other than a client to refrain from voluntarily giving relevant information to another party"); *id.* at R. 3.4 Cmt. 1 ("Fair competition in the adversary system is secured by prohibitions against destruction or concealment of evidence, improperly influencing witnesses, obstructive tactics in discovery procedure, and the like."); Restatement (Third) of the Law Governing Lawyers § 116(3) (2000) (stating a "lawyer may not unlawfully induce or assist a prospective witness to evade or ignore process obliging the witness to appear to testify").

This case is far from over, and sanctions are necessary to remind Cleary that it has obligations beyond representing its client. Accordingly, Cleary is hereby sanctioned pursuant to the Court's inherent authority. Cleary is directed to pay to Kensington the reasonable costs and attorney's fees incurred by Kensington in connection with this motion. This sanction is imposed as a formal reprimand and should be circulated to all attorneys at Cleary. Sanctions here will also serve as a general deterrent to other law firms and perhaps as an entreaty as well: civil litigation can be high stakes, zealously litigated, aggressively fought, *and* civil.

The Second Circuit affirmed Judge Preska's order. The court's opinion turns largely on credibility determinations: the court believed Mr. Mbemba and not Mr. Vignaud. In part the court reached this view by comparing Mr. Vignaud's stated aims to his actual language and his actions. He said he wanted to warn Mr. Mbemba about risks to Mr. Mbemba but he talked about the Congo and he never offered to provide Mr. Mbemba his own lawyer. Because his conduct did not match his story very well the court found the story suspicious.

This technique is common. People often offer explanations in litigation that are inconsistent with their actions at the time in question. The inconsistencies always call the explanation into question. In general, the tighter the fit between the litigation explanation and the contemporaneous conduct, the stronger the story, and vice versa.

It is also worth noting that the e-mail from Cleary to Dechert stating that the deposition was off was misleading in what it implied but failed to disclose. That it was misleading in light of the full record suggested to the court that Cleary had a reason to mislead—i.e., that it had to something to cover up. Shading the truth looks shady, and implies that you have something to be shady about.

PROBLEM 12–2

It would be nice if no one ever asked you to do something like signal a witness such as Mr. Mbemba that your client would prefer he not volunteer his testimony. It would be nice, but unrealistic. The court suggests that had Cleary drawn a line at a particular point the court would not have concluded that it acted in bad faith. What was that point? More practically, suppose you were asked to write a letter to Mr. Mbemba in this case. What could it ethically say? Try writing it to test your grasp of the case.

C. RECEIVING EVIDENCE

Model Rule 4.4(a) governs means and methods of obtaining evidence. You may not use means that have no substantial purpose other than to embarrass, delay, or burden another person. You may not use methods that violate the legal rights of a third person. Traditionally this latter prohibition has been read to extend to rights provided by law, in particular to privilege and work product material, rather than to contractual rights, such as might be created by an employee's non-disclosure agreement. The law on this point is not extensive, however, and some uncertainty remains.

Rule 4.4(b) pertains to documents pertaining to a matter that you know or reasonably should know have been sent to you inadvertently. (This situation is very similar to the inadvertent waiver issues discussed in chapter 5.E.1). The rule requires you to notify the sender of the document promptly. It does not require that you not read the document but, as discussed in chapter 5, doing so puts you at risk of disqualification if a court concludes the document contains privileged information and you should not have read it.

Issues raised by these rules are common and complex, as the following materials illustrate.

Model Rule of Professional Conduct 4.4

PILLSBURY, MADISON & SUTRO V. SCHECTMAN

55 Cal.App.4th 1279, 64 Cal.Rptr.2d 698 (1997)

LAMBDEN, J.

Steven Schectman and Law Offices of Pinnock & Schectman (Schectman) appeal from the order granting a preliminary injunction requiring them to turn over documents that were removed from Pillsbury, Madison & Sutro (PM & S).

PM & S brought an action against Schectman for specific recovery of personal property and for temporary, preliminary, and permanent injunctive relief. The complaint alleges Schectman gained possession of confidential personnel documents removed from the offices of PM & S without its consent. Schectman represents current and former PM & S employees in connection with employment law claims against PM & S. PM & S also filed applications for a writ of possession, a temporary restraining order, and an order to allow expedited discovery.

Pursuant to stipulation of the parties, the court appointed a special master to review the documents and to make a recommendation to the court as to whether they are legally protectible. The special master found none of the documents violated any attorney-client privilege or constituted work product and none was of a trade secret nature. The special master found a number of documents were intended to be confidential, specifically those involving communications within the human resources department relating to employees. . .

After extensive briefing and oral argument, the court ruled PM & S owned the documents and most, if not all of them, were intended to be confidential and were understood by the employees at PM & S to be confidential documents. The court found the documents were not directed to any of the former employees concerning their individual status as employees of PM & S but, rather, were documents relating to the performance of their duties while employed by the firm. The court also found the documents included original writings as well as copies of documents and were unique rather than fungible property. The court further found the documents were removed improperly from PM & S and wrongfully possessed by Schectman as the agent of whomever it was who improperly removed the documents.

Under the authority of the claim and delivery of personal property statutes (Claim and Delivery Statutes) (Code Civ. Proc., §§ 511.010–516.050) and those providing for injunctions (id., § 526 et seq.), along with the court's inherent authority to administer the resolution of disputes, the court issued an order requiring Schectman to surrender originals and copies of documents removed from PM & S, and not previously delivered to the court, as well as any documents summarizing, quoting from, or otherwise recording information concerning the nature or contents of those documents. The order is a continuing one, requiring Schectman to turn over any documents coming into his possession unless received pursuant to a legitimate discovery request or other court order. The court stated it would turn over the documents to counsel for PM & S and ordered PM & S to post a bond of $5,000. The court specifically noted its order did not constitute a determination of the merits of any discrimination claim brought by Schectman. . . .

II.

Turning to the merits of the appeal, Schectman claims the cases relied upon by PM & S and the court . . . should be disregarded. . . Schectman argues there should be no protection of documents not involving any personal privacy interest. He relies on "[t]he legion of cases" in the trade secret area where relief is denied to employers whose employees have taken documents that fail to rise to the level of trade secrets. For example, in *American Paper & Packaging Products, Inc. v. Kirgan* (1986) 183 Cal.App.3d 1318, the court held that although customer lists could be protectible trade secrets, the plaintiff's customer lists were not protectible since the information contained in them was generally known in the trade and already being used by good faith competitors. As discussed below, trade secret law protects an interest distinct from the documents themselves and does not apply here.

Schectman relies on *FMC Corp. v. Capital Cities/ABC, Inc.* (7th Cir. 1990) 915 F.2d 300, a First Amendment case, where a television station obtained possession of originals and copies of a defense contractor's documents. FMC brought an action for conversion and misappropriation of its business information resulting from the station's refusal to return copies of the FMC documents. In reviewing these claims, the court applied California law. The court affirmed the dismissal of FMC's misappropriation of confidential business information claim on the ground that confidential business information could be misappropriated only by a direct business competitor, since the thrust of the misappropriation tort is the pirating of the fruits of another's labors and passing them off as one's own. As to the conversion claim, the court noted the gravamen of the tort of conversion is the deprivation of the possession or use of one's property. However, in response to the station's First Amendment claims, the court stated the station was free "to retain copies of any of FMC's documents in its possession (and to disseminate any information contained in them) in the name of the First Amendment." The court thus found a public policy exception to the general rules protecting property interests. No such exception is presented here.

Schectman also relies on *Church of Scientology v. Armstrong* (1991) 232 Cal.App.3d 1060. The church brought an action against its former member, Armstrong, alleging he converted to his own use confidential archive materials and disseminated them to unauthorized persons. Armstrong asserted the defense of justification, alleging he gave the documents to his attorney because he believed his life was threatened by the church. The trial court found Armstrong's conduct was justified. The Court of Appeal affirmed, relying on sections of the Restatement Second of Torts, which allow a person to make intentional invasions of another's interests when the actor reasonably believes such other person intends to cause a confinement or a harmful or offensive contact to the actor. The evidence indicated church investigators shoved Armstrong, struck his elbow with a car, and attempted to run him off the road. No similar conduct, and thus no possibility of justification, appears in this case.

Schectman has failed to cite any authority contrary to the foregoing cases condemning self-help evidence gathering by employees for use in contemplated litigation against their soon-to-be former employers. The facts here, involving the wrongful possession of confidential documents for use in anticipated litigation against PM & S . . . raise an issue distinctly within the court's inherent authority to administer the resolution of disputes, and no policy exception to that authority is presented by this case. There is no underlying First Amendment issue, as was the case in *FMC Corp. v. Capital Cities/ABC, Inc.*, supra, 915 F.2d 300. Nor is there any justification based upon evidence of threats of physical harm, as in *Church of Scientology v. Armstrong*, supra, 232 Cal.App.3d 1060.

Schectman's reliance on cases involving trade secrets is also misplaced. No one has claimed these documents are trade secrets. . . The documents taken by Schectman . . . are not shown to have any intrinsic value to anyone other than their owner, except possibly by their use in a potential lawsuit, where such use would come squarely within the ambit of the Civil Discovery Act of 1986 (Stats. 1986, ch. 1334, § 2, p. 4700) (Discovery Act) and the Evidence Code.

. . . the Discovery Act as amended and interpreted has subsumed the entire field pertaining to the gathering of evidence in preparation for trial. The fact counsel still conduct much pretrial preparation and discovery without judicial assistance does not mean parties to litigation can operate outside the applicable parameters of the Discovery Act or may violate other laws or common law strictures in their zeal to pursue litigation.

. . . Discovery in the litigation context presupposes ownership of documents will remain with whomever holds title, while allowing access to the trier of fact, and litigants, in specifically delineated legal proceedings. . . . Schectman's assertion of an interest or justification superior to any interest grounded "solely on the basis of ownership" is not readily distinguished from a pickpocket's interest in a stranger's purse. Whether or not he might be able to articulate an end justifying the means he proposes-which is no less than to lay claim to documents which do not arguably "implicate any personal privacy interest"-he would still fail to state a sufficient reason to subvert society's interest in preserving private property, as well as maintaining the jurisdiction of the courts to administer the orderly resolution of disputes. The trial court properly rejected these claims under the authority of the Claim and Delivery Statutes, which are based not only upon fundamental common law concepts of property ownership and conversion, but also upon a recognition of the court's inherent authority to administer disputes over possession of chattels.

Accordingly, although it is enough to conclude there was no abuse of discretion in granting the injunction in this case, we will state clearly our agreement with those courts which have refused to permit "self-help" discovery which is otherwise violative of ownership or privacy interests and unjustified by any exception to the jurisdiction of the courts to administer the orderly resolution of disputes. Any litigant or potential litigant who converts, interdicts or otherwise purloins documents in the pursuit of litigation outside the legal process does so without the general protections afforded by the laws of discovery and risks being found to have violated protected rights. The least sanction cognizable in these circumstances would appear to be the one chosen by the trial court here: the return to the status quo existing at the time the documents were taken.

Accordingly, we conclude Schectman has failed to show any abuse of discretion in the issuance of the preliminary injunction. The order is affirmed and the request for stay denied.

CASE QUESTIONS

1. Were the documents at issue subject to the attorney-client privilege or work product doctrine?
2. The court distinguished the *Capital Cities*, and *Church of Scientology* cases, which Schechtman had cited. What were the distinctions?
3. What relief did the lower court order?

Property, Confidentiality, and Informal Investigations

It is very common for corporate employees either to sign confidentiality agreements or to agree to employment policies that include confidentiality obligations that go beyond the default rules of agency or other laws. It is also very common for such employees to quit or be fired. And, finally, it is common for such employees to take with them information they obtained during their employment and which is subject to such agreements or policies. For that reason, former employees are a prime source of investigation for plaintiffs' attorneys who suspect corporate misconduct. They are a prime source of concern to companies who might be sued for alleged misconduct.

This combination of factors can create risks for lawyers conducting investigations. The rules and cases provide less guidance than one might hope for, especially if other factors come into play, such as the payment of consulting or other fees to former employees. The report of a special master in *Carpenters Health and Welfare Fund v. The Coca Cola Company*,

587 F.Supp.2d 1266 (N.D. Ga. 2008), illustrates the point. The suit was a class action alleging that Coca Cola violated the federal securities laws. Four months after the complaint was filed, two former Coke employees contacted plaintiffs' counsel and offered to help with the case. Each had been fired from Coke.

When he was fired, one of the two former employees had taken with him over 3,000 documents, some of which were marked confidential. He told plaintiffs' counsel about the documents. Counsel eventually hired the two former employees as consultants to work on the case. They were guaranteed $75,000 plus $200 per hour for any time they worked on the case. After signing the agreement, the employee who had taken the documents gave them to class counsel, who referred to some of them in an amended complaint.

Plaintiffs' counsel moved the court to certify a class and to appoint plaintiffs' counsel as class counsel. Coke argued that counsel should not be appointed to represent the class because counsel had, in effect, bought documents that had been stolen from Coke. Counsel responded that (i) they had nothing to do with stealing the documents, which were taken before they ever heard of the former employees; (ii) they paid the former employees for time as consultants, which had been held permissible (*see Centennial Mgmt. Servs., Inc. v. Axa Re Vie*, 193 F.R.D. 671, 682 (D. Kan. 2000)); and (iii) the payments furthered the public policy of supporting whistleblowers who reveal corporate misconduct.

The special master rejected these arguments and recommended that the court refuse to appoint counsel to represent the class. The master found relevant Model Rule 4.4(a), which "provides in part that a lawyer shall not use methods of obtaining evidence that violate the rights of his client or third parties." It cited "[n]umerous cases [that] embody these concepts."*

The master also found instructive New Jersey Ethics Opinion 680, which addressed a situation in which a client took from opposing counsel's briefcase documents supporting the client's case. The Committee concluded that if the lawyer had participated in the theft he would have violated Rule 4.4 ("[i]t is well established that an attorney may not do indirectly that which is prohibited directly"), and, consequently, that "the lawyer cannot be involved in the subsequent review of evidence obtained improperly by the client." The opinion concluded that "[f]or a lawyer to

* These cases included *Florida Bar v. McCaghren*, 171 So.2d 371 (Fla. 1965) (sanctioning and suspending counsel for ignoring red flags regarding wrongly obtained evidence); *In re Knight*, 129 Vt. 428, 281 A.2d 46 (1971) (attorney suspended for failing to withdraw from an unlawful plan of another to create evidence adverse to an opposing party); Ariz. State Bar Comm. on Rules of Prof'l Conduct, Op. 88–8 (1988) (lawyer who learns of client's secret recording of her husband's conversations has no duty to report her but may not use any information on the tape); *Tennessee Bar Assoc. v. Freemon*, 50 Tenn.App. 567, 362 S.W.2d 828 (1961) (lawyer sanctioned despite his being unaware of client's plan to entrap the opposing party but nevertheless goes to motel and takes pictures of client's wife).

allow a client's improper actions taken in the context of litigation to benefit that client in such litigation would constitute 'conduct that is prejudicial to the administration of justice' under RPC 8.4(d)." NJ Eth. Op. 680, WL 33971 (Jan. 16, 1995).

The master concluded:

> Here Class Counsel satisfy the requirements relating to competency, experience, and resources. They have vigorously and skillfully prosecuted this case now for over seven years. Their knowledge of the relevant substantive legal principles is more than adequate. The question here, though, is whether acquiring and paying for Company Documents and apparently never even to this day recognizing that such actions were wrong so impair their ability to fairly and adequately represent the interests of the class that they must be found to be inadequate Class Counsel under Rules 23(a)(4) and (g). . . .
>
> Here the conduct is serious, relates to the prosecution of this case, and raises a number of potential ethical and policy issues. Moreover, this matter was brought to the attention of Class Counsel over a year ago. Had they addressed this issue head-on recognizing the impropriety of the arrangement they made with [the former employee who stole the documents] that might well have served to mitigate the circumstances. But they did not. Instead, they turned a blind eye to the terms of the Consulting Agreement pursuant to which they paid for the Company Documents and continue even now to make unfounded arguments which only obfuscate this issue. The result is that one is left with the belief that Plaintiffs' Counsel have not been candid and have instead been evasive relative to this serious matter.
>
> Accordingly, I find that Plaintiffs' Class Counsel cannot be found to be adequate counsel in this case. . . .

The district court ultimately rejected the special master's recommendation and found the lawyers in question adequate to serve as class counsel. The case had settled by that time, however, and the district court's decision should be viewed in light of the general tendency of courts to favor settlements. It is not clear what the district court would have done in different circumstances, and the special master's report reflects a possible perspective on this issue.[2]

---

[2] *See also* New York State Bar Association Ethics Opinion 700 (attorney contacted by former employee of adversary who reported adversary had altered documents produced in discovery should not adduce additional disclosures, should not take advantage of unsolicited disclosures, and should notify opposing counsel that disclosure had been made; attorney might ask court to determine whether alleged alteration waived privilege).

This combination of circumstances implicates several different rules. First, like any lawyer class counsel is obliged to pursue their client's claims competently and diligently. Model Rule 1.3; Cal. R. Prof. Conduct 3–110. Interviewing witnesses is one thing a competent and diligent lawyer does. Second, third party witnesses who have confidentiality obligations may face legal risks for cooperating with investigating lawyers. Such lawyers may not advise witnesses on those risks, other than to advise them to obtain counsel of their own. Model Rule 4.3. (In some cases the investigating lawyer may assist a witness in retaining such a lawyer and may pay for such a lawyer, subject to applicable conflict of interest rules, such as Model Rule 1.8(f) or Cal. R. Prof. Conduct 3–310(f).)

Third, as noted above the investigating lawyer may not seek to obtain privileged or work product information. Model Rule 4.4(a), cmt. 1.[3] But what is an investigating lawyer to make of the requirement that she not violate the "legal rights of a third party"? What are those rights? The comment states that they are too many and varied to catalogue, but it is reasonably clear that the prohibition includes general restrictions on conduct created by the law rather than by the third party's employment contracts. An investigating lawyer may not wiretap a third party or break into their home or business in pursuit of evidence.

What, then, of the confidentiality agreement? The Model Rules do not address this topic specifically. The most relevant provision is Section 102 of the *Restatement*, which provides that an investigating lawyer may not seek to obtain information when he reasonably should know that the witness in question owes to a third party a duty of confidentiality that is "imposed by law." The comments to this section make clear that it does not extend to contractual obligations that exceed such baseline legal rules. The most general baseline rule is the duty of confidentiality imposed by Agency law. *See Restatement (Third) of Agency* § 8.05. As you will recall from chapter 1, that provision allows an agent to disclose information of the principal in service of the superior interests of a third party. Whether that exception applies will depend on the facts of the case at hand.

Are documents different from information generally? Logically there is no difference, and the *Restatement of Agency* disavows any difference between a breach of duty accomplished by memory and a breach accomplished through the delivery of documents. *Restatement (Third) of Agency* § 8.05. At least one employer, however, has asserted that an investigating lawyer may interview former employees but is precluded from obtaining documents on the ground that to do so is to receive stolen property.

Finally, what about the money? A lawyer may not ethically offer a witness money contingent on the content of the witnesses' testimony.

[3] There is no California equivalent to Model Rule 4.4(a).

Model Rule 3.4(b) prohibits lawyers from "offer[ing] an inducement to a witness that is prohibited by law." Comment 3 to that provisions distinguishes payments for expenses from fees paid for testifying. *See also* Cal. R. Prof. Conduct 5–310(b) (prohibiting "compensation to a witness contingent upon the content of the witness's testimony"). Lawyers may, however, compensate witnesses for costs they incur in connection with a matter, including the cost of their time. ABA Formal Opinion 96–402; COPRAC Opinion 1997–149.

Suppose you are involved in a case in which an adverse witness is not represented by counsel. You depose the witness and learn she has a Facebook page and liberally grants "friend" requests to gain access to that page. You know a third party who knows the witness well enough to, probably, gain access to the page through a "friend" request. May you have the third party send such a request and then access the page yourself? Philadelphia Bar Association Professional Guidance Committee Opinion 2009–2 answers that question: "no." New York City Bar Association Ethics Opinion 2010–2 opines that real names (of a lawyer or employee) may be used to make such requests but false names may not.

Now, suppose you represent a woman who wants to divorce her husband. She decided to seek a divorce after she discovered on the couple's home computer evidence that her husband had an e-mail account she had not previously known about. Guessing her husband's password, she logged into this account and discovered e-mails proving that her husband was a serial adulterer. She printed the e-mails, placed them in a folder, and continues logging in every few days to read messages in the account. Suppose she tells you what she has done (and continues to do). Her conduct raises several questions. First, may you or must you notify the husband or, supposing he is represented, his counsel, of your client's spying? If the e-mail snooping relates to a pending case must you notify the court?

These questions are best taken in reverse order. Model Rule 3.3(b) provides that a lawyer who: (i) represents a client in an adjudicative proceeding; (ii) knows; (iii) that a person (here, the client) has engaged in; (iv) criminal or fraudulent conduct; (v) related to the proceeding "shall take reasonable remedial measures, including, if necessary, disclosure to the tribunal." Whether the rule imposes such an obligation in this situation depends on whether the e-mail snooping is criminal or fraudulent. That is a question of substantive law, to which statutes such as the Stored Communications Act, 18 U.S.C. §§ 2701–12, or the Computer Fraud and Abuse Act, 18 U.S.C. § 1030. Substantive law on such questions is not as clear as one might like, however, *compare Jennings v. Jennings*, 736 S.E.2d 242 (S.C.) (wife's daughter-in-law did not violate Stored Communications Act by obtaining password to husband's e-mail to gain evidence of adultery because preserved versions of e-mails already read were not protected under the Act) *with Theofel v. Farey–Jones,* 359 F.3d 1066, 1075 (9th Cir.2004)(Stored Communications Act does protect such e-mails). The substantive law must be correlated with the relevant disciplinary rule, of course. The Ninth Circuit's interpretation of the Stored Communications Act would not support a disclosure duty in a state, such as California, that has no mandatory disclosure obligation corresponding to Model Rule 3.3(b).

If disclosure is not mandatory under Rule 3.3(b) it is not clear that it would be permissible under any other rule. The client's activity is not "inadvertent" delivery of evidence, so the text of Model Rule 4.4(b) does not apply to this situation. So held the New York State Bar Association's Committee on Professional Ethics (Op. 945, 11/7/2012). The opinion notes that information regarding the client's activities is confidential information within the meaning of Rule 1.6 and concludes that Rule 4.4(b) creates no exception to that rule in this circumstance. This opinion follow the ABA's Opinion 11-460, which holds a lawyer does not have a duty *under the rules* to inform opposing counsel that the lawyer's client has copied potentially privileged communications between opposing counsel and his or her client. The ABA cautioned that case law in particular jurisdictions may impose such a duty. *See also* Az. Op 01-04 (same).

Next, suppose your client wants you to read the e-mails. May you do so? In this case the risks will vary according to the content of the communications. If the communications are otherwise privileged, you would be at risk of disqualification if you read them, regardless of any other consequences under the rules. (Recall the result in *Rico v. Mitsubishis* in chapter 5.) The California Committee on Professional Responsibility and Conduct has issued a proposed opinion (Interim Number 06-04) that would extend the rules of *Rico* and *State Fund, supra,* to material deliberately sent to a lawyer by a third party as well material as to sent inadvertently. A lawyer therefore would have to read no more of the material than necessary to ascertain its privileged character and then stop reading and notify opposing counsel. This proposed opinion deals only with material sent by a third party, however, and therefore does not address the client confidentiality issue raised in the last paragraph.

One could also argue, for example, that to read the e-mails would be to intrude into a privileged relationship of the opposing party, in violation of Rule 4.4(a). *See* ABA Op. 460 n.6. That conclusion is debatable, however, because Rule 4.4(a) prohibits the use of "methods" of obtaining evidence that violate the rights of a third party. In this case the client employed the unscrupulous method without the lawyer's sanction. One might argue that reading such e-mails was not itself an improper method. One might also argue that to read the e-mails would be to benefit from the client's misconduct and thus to assist the client in a crime or fraud, though this argument presumes both that the underlying intrusion was criminal or fraudulent and that such *ex post* examination counts as assistance. Neither proposition is self-evident.

Finally, what about use in court or a proceeding under court authority, such as making one of the e-mails an exhibit at a deposition? The evidence in this hypothetical situation is not false, so Rule 3.3(a) would not preclude its use, and the evidence might well fall within a hearsay exception (as an admission) or, possibly, might be useful to prove the nature of the relationship between the husband and a paramour even if not asserted for the truth of particular statements. *White v. White,* 344 N.J. Super. 211 (2001), denied a motion to quash such evidence on the ground that they were collected in violation of the New Jersey law against wiretapping. The court found the law applied only to communications being sent or received, not stored. One can imagine courts issuing orders against the use of evidence so acquired, however, if only to avoid creating an incentive for future litigants to employ such methods.

D. EMBARRASSING OR BURDENING OTHERS

As noted above, Model Rule 4.4(a) forbids you from using on behalf of a client means that have no substantial purpose other than embarrassing others. Cases dealing this rule are, fortunately, rare. When they arise the most interesting question may be more sociological than legal—why did the lawyer do what he did rather than whether the conduct violates the rule. Bear that distinction in mind as you read the next case.

IDAHO STATE BAR V. WARRICK

137 Idaho 86 (2002)

WALTERS, JUSTICE.

This is an attorney disciplinary case. Steven Warrick appeals from a decision rendered by the Professional Conduct Board of the Idaho State Bar ("ISB") finding that Warrick violated Idaho Rule of Professional Conduct ("I.R.P.C") 4.4(a) concerning expressions of bias and I.R.P.C. 3.3(a)(4), relating to presentation of false evidence. We uphold the Board's findings. We impose on Warrick a sanction of thirty days suspension from the practice of law. We further order that Warrick pass the Multistate Professional Responsibility Examination as a condition for reinstatement to active practice. Finally, we award costs to the ISB for this proceeding.

FACTS AND PROCEDURAL BACKGROUND

Steven Warrick was admitted to the practice of law in Idaho in 1983. He was elected as the Elmore County Prosecutor in 1996 and served until

April 1, 1998. As such, Warrick was in charge of prosecuting Ronald E. Calfee, a.k.a. Ted Hulsey Hungate ("Calfee") for one count of felony trafficking of methamphetamine, a case from which both counts of Warrick's alleged misconduct stem. . . .

On February 18, 1998, Warrick was at the Elmore County law enforcement building, which houses the jail where Calfee was incarcerated. Warrick wrote the words "waste of sperm" and "scumbag" next to Calfee's name on the inmate control board. . . . .

As a result of the incidents in Elmore County, complaints against Warrick were filed with the Idaho State Bar. The ISB proceeded with a formal disciplinary action. In Count I of the ISB's complaint, ISB alleged that Warrick violated I.R.P.C. 4.4(a) and 8.4(d) for writing offensive words on the inmate board at the Elmore County Jail about a defendant he was prosecuting. . . . [Both parties moved for summary judgment against Warrick. The Professional Responsibility Board granted the ISB's motion with regard to Rule 4.4 and Warrick's motion with respect to Rule 8.4.]

Warrick argues that the Board erred by granting summary judgment to ISB and finding that he violated I.R.P.C. 4.4(a) by writing the words "waste of sperm" and "scumbag" on the inmate control board. To support this argument, Warrick asserts that he was not representing any client at the time of the incident and the rule contemplates acts by a lawyer during the course of his representation of a client. He contends that there was no communication or means directed by him to inmate Calfee or to a third person intended to embarrass Calfee or a third person.

To the contrary, ISB argues that it is irrelevant whether Calfee was embarrassed or injured by the words written on the inmate control board. ISB contends that there does not have to be an actual showing of bias and that the rule only requires a demonstration that Warrick intended to appeal to or engender bias. ISB asserts that the focus of I.R.P.C. 4.4 is upon professionalism not upon injuries that may be sustained by a recipient of the communication. . . . .

I.R.P.C. 4.4 states, in relevant part:

Rule 4.4—Respect for Rights of Third Persons

In representing a client, a lawyer shall not:

(a) use means that have no substantial purpose other than to embarrass, delay, or burden a third person, including conduct intended to appeal to or engender bias against a person on account of that person's gender, race, religion, national origin, or sexual preference, whether that bias is directed to other counsel, court personnel, witnesses, parties, jurors, judges, judicial officers, or any other participants.

The Idaho Rules of Professional Conduct are based upon the Model Rules of Professional Conduct recommended by the American Bar Association. The ABA comments to Model Rule 4.4 state that the model rule focuses upon "the substantial 'purposes' of the action rather than its effect." ABA Annot. Model Rules of Prof'l Conduct R. 4.4 cmt. (1996). The former ABA Rule 4.4 focused on effect and forbade an attorney from acting when the attorney knows or it is obvious that the action would harass or maliciously injure another. *Id.* The Board in this case properly considered the purpose rather than the effect of Warrick's conduct. In partially granting ISB's motion for summary judgment, the Board found that

> the clear evidence shows that Warrick wrote derogatory and offensive words, that this conduct had no substantial purpose other than to embarrass the inmate and appeal to or engender bias in the local law enforcement officers for whom the offensive words were intended.

We find that this is a clear violation of I.R.P.C. Rule 4.4(a). . . .

The Board's determination is based upon undisputed facts. Warrick admitted that he wrote the words "scumbag" and "waste of sperm" on the inmate control board next to Calfee's name. At the time, Warrick was representing the state of Idaho in a criminal action being prosecuted against Calfee as a party. Warrick contended that the words were meant to humor the law enforcement officers and that only a few people saw the words and the words were never conveyed to or seen by Calfee.

Although Warrick claims he meant the words for humor, the conduct was inappropriately aimed at Calfee, a party in a pending action being prosecuted by Warrick on behalf of the State. Despite the fact that Calfee did not see the words, nor were the words conveyed to Calfee, their purpose could only have been to demean Calfee in the eyes of others. The evidence shows that Warrick clearly used means that had no substantial purpose other than to embarrass Calfee and was intended to engender bias in the local law enforcement personnel.

This Court holds that the Board properly granted summary judgment to ISB on Warrick's violation of I.R.P.C. 4.4(a). . . .

In its brief on appeal, ISB asserted that Warrick's inappropriate comments with regard to Calfee violated I.R.P.C. 8.4(d), as well as rule 4.4(a), since his actions were prejudicial to the administration of justice. However, at oral argument ISB counsel conceded that if this Court found a violation of I.R.P.C. 4.4(a) with respect to Count I, that there was not a need to address this additional allegation. Therefore, this Court will not discuss whether there was a violation of I.R.P.C. 8.4(d).

PROBLEM 12–3

Why do you suppose Warrick wrote what he did on the board? Was the court right to say he acted as a lawyer on behalf of a client rather than as an ordinary person?

The Main Points to Recall From Chapter 12 Are:

- You may not communicate about a matter with a party you know to be represented unless that party's lawyer consents or a court authorizes you to do so.
- You may communicate with an unrepresented party, but you must not imply that you are neutral; you must make sure they know your agenda.
- You may not advise an unrepresented person whose interests conflict with your client's interests, but you may tell them to get their own lawyer.
- You may not use methods of investigation, such as wiretapping or burglary, that violate the rights of third parties created by law.
- You may not seek by any means privileged or work product information and should take reasonable steps to avoid acquiring such information.
- You may not employ methods that embarrass or unduly burden third parties.

CHAPTER 13

RELATIONS WITH YOUR FIRM

■ ■ ■

If you practice with a firm or partnership you are an agent of the firm or partnership as well as an agent of your clients. You owe the firm the standard duties of loyalty and care any agent owes any principal. Disciplinary rules prohibiting you from lying or misappropriating money apply to your dealings with your firm as well as with the firm's clients.

As a junior lawyer the Model Rules exempt you from discipline for relying on a senior lawyer's (1) reasonable resolution of (2) an arguable legal question. The California rules contain no such provision, however, and even the model rules offer no defense against unreasonable resolutions or unambiguous (and thus not arguable) legal commands.

A. FIDUCIARY OBLIGATIONS TO A FIRM

Restatement § 9(2) provides that a lawyer employed by an entity is subject to applicable laws governing that entity. In the case of partnerships or LLPs, that law includes fiduciary obligations to the partnership. Model Rule 8.4(c) provides it is professional misconduct to engage in conduct—any conduct—involving dishonesty, fraud, deceit, or misrepresentation. The conduct does not have to be in connection with the representation of a client. The two provisions together can make conduct toward your firm or your partners a matter for professional discipline, as the following case illustrates.

Restatement (Third) of the Law Governing Lawyers § 9
Model Rule of Professional Conduct 8.4

MATTER OF DISCIPLINARY PROCEEDINGS AGAINST CURRAN

180 Wis.2d 540, 509 N.W.2d 429 (1994)

PER CURIAM

This is an appeal of the Board of Attorneys Professional Responsibility (Board) from the recommendation of the referee that the court suspend the license of Attorney John C. Curran to practice law in Wisconsin for six months as discipline for professional misconduct. That misconduct consisted of Attorney Curran's having paid himself a management fee in connection with the construction of a building he and his law partners built without informing his partners of those payments, diverting to his own account a law firm client's payment for legal services and issuing that client unwarranted credits on its legal bills with the law firm and diverting to his own use the payment he received for legal services he rendered for the daughter of a client. The Board took the position that Attorney Curran's misconduct warrants more severe discipline than that recommended by the referee; specifically, the Board contended that the misconduct warrants a license suspension of at least two years. Attorney Curran cross-appealed from the referee's report, contending that the circumstances surrounding his misconduct render a 30–day license suspension appropriate discipline.

The court determines that the seriousness of Attorney Curran's misconduct established in this proceeding warrants the suspension of his license to practice law for two years. His dealings with his law partners in a business venture and with his firm in respect to client fees involve a pattern of deceit and a repeated breach of his fiduciary duty for purposes of personal financial gain.

Attorney Curran was licensed to practice law in Wisconsin in 1971 and practices in Milwaukee. He has not previously been the subject of a disciplinary proceeding. The parties stipulated to the facts and the referee, Attorney Rose Marie Baron, made the following findings in respect to Attorney Curran's professional misconduct.

Attorney Curran formed a law partnership with two other attorneys in 1975. The partnership agreement was renewed in 1981 and other attorneys were added. Attorney Curran left that law firm in August, 1989 at the request of three of the partners, in part because of his conduct considered in this proceeding.

Beginning in 1987, Attorney Curran and two of his partners owned an office building they had built in Waukesha. During its construction, Attorney Curran was responsible for managing the construction account and paid himself a $50,000 construction management fee from the account without the authorization of either of the partners and did not inform either of them of the amount of that fee or that he had taken it. Attorney Curran deposited the $50,000 into his personal bank account. In addition, from July, 1987 through January, 1989, Attorney Curran paid himself a monthly $350 management fee from the office building checking account. He deposited those payments, totaling $6,300, into his personal banking account and did not inform either of the partners in writing as to the amount of the fees or the time of their payment.

In another matter, Attorney Curran's law firm did legal work for a construction company the president of which was a personal friend of Attorney Curran. In February, 1988, Attorney Curran sent the company president a letter asking him to make all checks for legal services payable directly to him. For the next two years, Attorney Curran received $81,300 in payments from the construction company for various legal services and did not put those fees into the law firm's overhead account but deposited them into his personal bank account. At various times up to August, 1989, Attorney Curran issued credits totaling approximately $109,000 on the construction company's and its president's legal bills without informing his partners.

In a third matter, Attorney Curran provided legal services to a client, who was president of a corporation, and the client's family. Rather than having the law firm bill the client directly for the services he provided, Attorney Curran directed his secretary to manually prepare nine billing statements to the client's corporation identifying the services as "miscellaneous legal services." Those services involved Attorney Curran's overseeing a lawsuit in California related to the client's daughter's divorce and amounted to $15,000, $9,900 of which Attorney Curran deposited into his personal bank account. He placed the remainder into the law firm's account to cover costs and expenses the firm had advanced. Attorney Curran never informed any of his partners that he was depositing the $9,900 into his personal bank account.

Upon leaving the law firm in August, 1989, Attorney Curran resolved all monetary issues in respect to these matters. In the stipulation in this proceeding, Attorney Curran acknowledged that the facts to which he stipulated constitute a violation of the Rules of Professional Conduct for Attorneys.

On the basis of those facts, the referee concluded that Attorney Curran engaged in conduct involving dishonesty, fraud, deceit or misrepresentation, in violation of SCR 20:8.4(c), in respect to each of the matters. As discipline, the referee recommended that the court suspend Attorney Curran's license to practice law for six months. Although not explicitly set forth as factors she considered in determining the discipline to recommend, the referee noted in her report that there had been a lack of "collegial atmosphere" in Attorney Curran's law firm, as well as "considerable tension" among the partners. The referee stated that she was not convinced Attorney Curran intended to defraud his partners when he withdrew the construction management fee from the building escrow account but she determined that his doing so constituted deceit. She said, "By failing to disclose his intent to withdraw this large sum of money, Mr. Curran concealed or perverted the truth for the purpose of misleading his partners."

The referee explicitly rejected Attorney Curran's attempt to justify having the construction company client pay fees directly to him rather than to the law firm by his claim that the gross receipts of legal fees he contributed to the law office overhead account were substantially greater than any other attorney's in the office. The referee also rejected Attorney Curran's contention that he did not receive any of the $109,000 in credits he issued to a client and his construction company; the referee noted that the client gave Attorney Curran a quit claim deed to a condominium in exchange for a $13,000 credit on the balance owed to the law firm.

In its appeal, the Board argued that Attorney Curran's breach of his fiduciary duty to his law partners by diverting some $160,000 from the partnership and his unauthorized withdrawal of approximately $56,000 from funds in the building project without the consent of his partners in that venture warrant a license suspension of at least two years. The Board took the position that lawyers in a partnership have the same fiduciary duty to one another—loyalty, disclosure, accounting—as persons in a non-lawyer partnership. Further, the Board contended, Attorney Curran's misappropriation of law partnership funds is no less serious than the misappropriation of funds belonging to a client, citing the court's statement in *Disciplinary Proceedings Against Casey,* 174 Wis.2d 341, 341–42 (1993), that the court would treat the two no differently.

Although the referee did not specifically indicate what factors, if any, she considered in mitigation of the seriousness of Attorney Curran's misconduct or the severity of the discipline to be imposed for it, the Board set forth the following factors that would render a two-year license suspension rather than license revocation appropriate discipline to impose under these circumstances: once his misappropriation of law firm funds was discovered, Attorney Curran did not attempt to mislead the Board or any court; he has not previously been disciplined for professional misconduct; when he was removed from the partnership, he lost his financial interest in that partnership and the building where the firm was located.

For his part, Attorney Curran argued that less severe discipline than that recommended by the referee is warranted for the reason that there had been ongoing disputes between himself and his former law partners, who he claimed were attempting to enrich themselves and control clients of the firm. He also contended that of the three partners involved in the building project, he was the only one who had anything to do with the financing, design and construction of the office building and, accordingly, the fees he took from that project were, in his words, "reasonable and appropriate". Those arguments have no merit in respect to mitigating the seriousness of Attorney Curran's misconduct.

Also without merit are Attorney Curran's assertions that his former partners violated their professional duty to bring his conduct to the attention of the Board and themselves breached several provisions of the agreement by which he withdrew from the law firm. There is nothing in the record to substantiate those allegations and the referee made no findings of fact in that regard. The court also emphatically rejects Attorney

Curran's assertion that the Rules of Professional Conduct for Attorneys are not intended to apply business relationships between lawyers but govern only an attorney's conduct in representing a client and in the practice of law.

In his conduct established in this proceeding, Attorney Curran has demonstrated a fundamental dishonesty in the pursuit of his profession which puts at risk those who would employ him to represent their interests as well as the courts he serves. Of particular concern is his attempt to justify his misconduct by recourse to what he perceives to have been injustices perpetrated upon him by those whose funds and fees he misappropriated. The six-month license suspension recommended by the referee is an inadequate measurement of the seriousness of that misconduct. . . .

IT IS ORDERED that the license of John C. Curran to practice law in Wisconsin is suspended for a period of two years, commencing February 21, 1994.

Curran was a partner in his own firm. Would the same rules have applied to him as a low-level associate, a position you may find yourself in after graduation? Yes. Partners may have greater opportunities to engage in fiduciary breaches, as Curran did, but it does not follow that associates have no such duties, or that they could breach the ones they have with impunity.

Johnson v. Brewer & Pritchard, P.C., 73 S.W.3d 193 (Tex. 2002), illustrates the point. James Chang was an associate at Brewer & Pritchard. He had a friend named Henry King. King's father and members of a delegation from China were injured in a helicopter crash. Chang talked to two partners in the firm about representing the crash victims; he reasoned he might have an advantage in getting the case because of his friendship with King.

One of the partners told Chang how to structure a contingent fee agreement if he needed to. He also talked to Chang about referring the case to another firm, how to structure a referral fee, and which personal injury firms might do a good job with the referral. Chang and his friend then met with several personal injury lawyers. One of these lawyers, Nick Johnson, was a friend of Chang's from law school; through Chang, he was also a friend of Henry King.

Five days after the crash, Henry King signed a contingent fee agreement with Nick Johnson. Chang was present either at or shortly before the signing. Johnson then "flipped" the case to Jamail & Kolius, a well-known personal injury firm with whom Chang and King previously had met. Johnson's referral fee was 50% of the Jamail firm's net fee. Chang told Brewer & Pritchard that the firm had "lost out" to the Jamail firm. He claimed not to know how that firm got the case. Chang left Brewer & Pritchard about two months later for another firm.

The personal injury suit settled a little over a year later, in October, 1996. Nick Johnson's fee was $3,000,000. In that same month, Brewer & Pritchard sued Johnson and Chang. (In October, 1997, Chang formed a partnership with Johnson.) The firm alleged that Chang had breached his fiduciary duties to the firm, and that Johnson had aided in the breach. Here are relevant excerpts from the opinion:

Brewer & Pritchard asserts that throughout Chang's employment, he owed a fiduciary duty to put the firm's interests above his own and to refrain from taking actions detrimental to the firm. The firm alleges that Chang "seize[d] for himself what he perceived to be a lucrative business opportunity," thereby breaching a fiduciary duty. Brewer & Pritchard also asserts that it had policies forbidding associates from practicing law for their own account, engaging in employment of any kind other than their employment with the firm, or referring cases without securing a referral fee for Brewer & Pritchard. The firm contends that its actual damages for Chang's breach of fiduciary duty are the amount of the referral fee that Nick Johnson obtained in connection with the helicopter crash.

Johnson and Chang argue that as a matter of law Chang owed no fiduciary duty to Brewer & Pritchard. They assert that Chang had no employment agreement with Brewer & Pritchard and that an associate does not owe a fiduciary duty to his or her firm "merely as a result" of being employed. . . .

We have no difficulty in concluding that under common-law agency principles, an associate owes a fiduciary duty not to accept a fee or other compensation for referring a matter to a lawyer or law firm other than the associate's employer without the employer's consent. The more difficult question is whether an associate can be said to have breached a fiduciary obligation to his or her employer when the associate undertakes to pursue the representation of a party on behalf of his or her employer, then participates in referring the potential client to other counsel with no compensation, benefit, or other advantage to the associate. There is evidence in the case before us that Chang specifically undertook to act as Brewer & Pritchard's agent in obtaining an agreement from the helicopter crash victims to represent them. Brewer & Pritchard also offered summary judgment evidence that its associates were not permitted to practice law for their own account or engage in employment of any kind other than their employment with that firm.

There are a number of competing considerations in deciding whether to impose a fiduciary duty under such circumstances. One of these is that under Texas rules of ethics governing lawyers, an attorney may agree to represent a client even though the attorney is not competent to handle the matter, as long as another lawyer who is competent is associated with the prior consent of the client. Brewer & Pritchard argues that it would have been entitled to a substantial referral fee if Chang had "signed up" the helicopter crash victims with that firm, rather than Nick Johnson, even if Brewer & Pritchard had no intention of actually handling the case but instead intended to immediately refer it to other lawyers.

However, on balance, we think it unwise to impose an absolute fiduciary duty upon associates of a law firm to abstain from directing those with legal needs to a firm other than the associate's employer. If one of the parties injured in the helicopter crash had been Chang's mother, should Brewer & Pritchard have a cause of action for breach of fiduciary duty if Chang referred her to an experienced personal injury lawyer without securing a referral fee for Brewer & Pritchard? The answer to that question should be no.

There could be many reasons why it would be in a potential client's best interest for an associate to suggest that they seek representation from a firm other than the firm for whom the associate works. For example, suppose that an existing client of a firm asks an associate if that firm handles corporate and tax matters. The associate says yes, and tells her employer that she will try to secure representation of the client in these matters. The client meets with the tax and business lawyers of the firm, but afterwards asks the associate for a frank evaluation of whether lawyers at another firm who handle such matters on a more regular basis and to the exclusion of other practice areas might be better suited. The associate should not be faced with breaching a fiduciary duty to the firm that employs her by giving an answer that leads the client to another firm.

There is evidence in this case that Brewer & Pritchard had little or no experience with personal injury claims and had never taken to trial a claim involving catastrophic personal injuries. A firm's legitimate interest in demanding loyalty from its associates should not outweigh competing considerations of the public's interest in encouraging lawyers to assist those who need legal advice in securing the most appropriate representation for the particular type of case and market competition.

Brewer & Pritchard contends that its policy forbidding an associate from referring a case to another lawyer or firm without compensation to Brewer & Pritchard gives rise to a fiduciary duty. We disagree. The firm's referral policy may have been a contractual condition of Chang's employment, an issue we need not decide since Brewer & Pritchard has not sued Chang for breach of contract. But a contractual obligation does not generally give rise to a fiduciary duty. The court of appeals in [citation omitted] correctly held that although an agreement between lawyers recited that one would be "an 'associate' of [the other's] law firm 'for purposes of the agreement,' " there was no fiduciary duty in handling settlement proceeds arising from the matter covered by the agreement "simply because of their business ties." An employee may agree in a contract with his or her employer not to make any referrals at all to another firm or lawyer, even if the employee receives no referral fee or other payment. But we will not elevate such a consensual, contractual duty into a fiduciary duty imposed by law.

Nor do we today set forth a broad rule governing all employees who might divert a business opportunity from their employer without receiving any compensation or benefit in return. We need not and do not decide whether there may be a fiduciary duty in other contexts. We hold only that an associate may participate in referring a client or potential client to a lawyer or firm other than his or her employer without violating a fiduciary duty to that employer as long as the associate receives no benefit, compensation, or other gain as a result of the referral. However, an associate owes a fiduciary duty not to accept or agree to accept profit, gain, or any benefit from referring or participating in the referral of a client or potential client to a lawyer or firm other than the associate's employer. . . .

[The court remanded to the trial court to determine whether Chang received such a benefit.]

CASE QUESTIONS

1. What is the relationship between the contract and fiduciary claims in this case? How is a contract duty different from a fiduciary duty?
2. What limitation does the court place on an associate's ability to refer work away from his or employer?

Johnson states a liability rule similar to the rule set forth in the *Restatement (Third) of Agency* § 8.02, which states: "An agent has a duty not to acquire a material benefit from a third party in connection with transactions conducted or other actions taken on behalf of the principal or otherwise through the agent's use of the agent's position."

PROBLEM 13–1

Suppose that you are an associate at a firm and a relative asks you to represent them in connection with a car accident. May you do so? Do you have any obligations to your firm in this regard?

PROBLEM 13–2

Note that in Texas a lawyer may represent a client in a matter in which the lawyer has no expertise but can refer the client to counsel with such expertise. (See MR 1.5(e)) What would you tell a prospective client to explain how the representation would work?

B. MOBILE LAWYERS

In the modern economy it is common for lawyers to move from one firm to another. It is increasingly common for such moves to prompt litigation in which departing lawyers are accused of breach of contract, breach of fiduciary duty, and, more recently, theft of trade secrets (especially in the form of client lists). As *Curran* shows, such claims are significant both for the financial risk they present and, though less commonly, for the potential for discipline. Lawyer departures also may reduce a firm's profits and possibly lead to dissolution. Either prospect is something you should take into account to the extent possible when choosing among firms. Though it is not possible to obtain perfect knowledge of how vulnerable a firm is to the departure of a few key people, there are some signs to look for. The following materials survey these points.

Restatement (Third) of the Law Governing Lawyers § 9(3)

1. BASIC RESTRICTIONS

GRAUBARD MOLLEN DANNETT & HOROWITZ V. MOSKOVITZ

86 N.Y.2d 112 (1995)

KAYE, CHIEF JUDGE.

This appeal focuses on a modern-day law firm fixture: the revolving door. With charges of faithless deserting partners and countercharges of a vindictive abandoned firm, the key question becomes whether departing partners can "solicit" clients of the firm. Here we decide only that plaintiff law firm's allegations of breach of fiduciary duty, breach of contract and fraud are sufficient to withstand summary dismissal, which was the conclusion also reached by the trial court and Appellate Division.

The following factual account is drawn largely from the assertions of plaintiff law firm, the nonmovant, and denied in material part by defendants. As alleged in the amended complaint, defendant-appellant Irving Moskovitz, along with Seymour Graubard, in 1949 founded plaintiff law firm. Over the next 40 years, the firm grew to 35 lawyers, with four senior partners—Graubard, Moskovitz, Raymond Horowitz and Emmanuel Dannett. Defendant Peter Schiller joined the firm in 1949 and became a partner in 1956; defendant John Young arrived in 1964 and became a partner in 1971. Control of the firm, however, was centered in the four seniors (who initiated most of the business), especially Moskovitz, the firm's managing partner for 33 years, until 1982.

In 1959, Moskovitz brought into the firm as a client F. Hoffman LaRoche & Co., Ltd. and affiliates (Roche), a worldwide pharmaceutical group headquartered in Switzerland. Legal services for Roche were mainly in the area of international taxation, Moskovitz's specialty, although the firm also handled corporate and litigation matters for the client. In the late 1980s, billings to Roche exceeded $1 million per year.

Concerned with developing a plan both for transition of management to the junior partners and for retirement of the seniors, the firm in 1981 retained an outside consultant and in 1982 adopted a "Phasing Out and Retirement Program." The agreement provided for a three-year "phase-down" during which the four senior partners were to receive decreasing compensation percentages and a return of their capital, and then annual benefits for five years after their retirement. The retirement agreement included the following "Clarifications," reading:

> "3. It is the spirit of the program that, during retirement, and even afterward, each of the retirees will not do anything to impair the firm's relationship with its existing clients and business.
>
> "4. The partners recognize that efforts towards institutionalization of the business of the firm is essential to the firm's continuing prosperity. In particular, the partners approaching phase-down and retirement will integrate, to the extent possible, relationships between the firm's clients and the other partners."

At the time the agreement was presented, according to plaintiff, Moskovitz additionally assured the junior partners that the seniors would do all they could to secure the firm's future and to institutionalize clients, particularly key clients, by integrating them with other partners in the firm. Some time after the agreement was approved in April 1982, however, Moskovitz approached Graubard and suggested starting a new partnership with Horowitz, a proposal Graubard rejected. Soon thereafter, the firm signed a $1.5 million lease on new office space and moved into its new quarters.

At the end of the three-year phase-down, having received back his capital as well as compensation exceeding that provided in the retirement agreement, Moskovitz—then 73 years old—became "of counsel" to the firm. However, he soon became unhappy with the law firm and contacted legal search consultants (Alan Roberts & Associates) regarding a possible move, with his tax partners Schiller and Young, to another law firm. Moskovitz told Roberts that his client Roche would accompany him if it approved the new firm. On November 30, 1987 Roberts put Moskovitz in touch with LeBoeuf Lamb Leiby & MacCrae, a New York based firm, and a four-month negotiation ensued, culminating on April 29, 1988 in defendants' announced resignation from plaintiff law firm to join LeBoeuf.

According to plaintiff, LeBoeuf would not finalize any arrangement with defendants unless Roche approved the transfer of its business. Moskovitz likewise wanted to ensure that he would continue to represent Roche if he moved to LeBoeuf. In March 1988 Moskovitz asked Roche's tax director whether the company had any objection to representation by LeBoeuf if he were to move there. Defendants' meetings with Roche and with LeBoeuf became nearly contemporaneous: on March 4, defendants met with LeBoeuf partners at the Metropolitan Club and later that same week, Moskovitz met with Roche's domestic general counsel. On at least one occasion, in April 1988, Moskovitz arranged for the head of LeBoeuf's tax department to meet with Roche's general counsel. Furthermore, plaintiff firm was engaged in settlement negotiations of a tax audit matter for Roche from late 1987 and continuing into the first quarter 1988 with potentially serious financial consequences. Moskovitz asked for and received assurances from a Roche executive that he would continue to handle the matter if he joined LeBoeuf.

Defendants had planned to remain at the firm for two months beyond their announced resignation, continuing to draw their compensation, but one week later—on May 6—the firm locked them out of their offices and sued them for fraud, breach of fiduciary duty, breach of contract and unjust enrichment, seeking damages exceeding $10 million based upon lost revenues of the Roche account and $30 million in punitive damages.[1] Defendants, consequently, began their association with LeBoeuf on May 9 and Roche immediately had its files transferred there.

Analysis

Urging that he be granted summary judgment, Moskovitz posits three issues: *first,* as a matter of public policy, is there a breach of fiduciary duty when a withdrawing partner, prior to announcing his resignation, "solicits" firm clients; *second,* is a contractual requirement that an attorney try to "integrate" or "institutionalize" clients into the firm legally enforceable; and *third,* is a cause of action for fraud stated by alleging that a promisor, at the time of making certain representations, lacked any intention to perform them. For the reasons that follow, we answer all three questions in the affirmative.

---

[1] FN1. Moskovitz points out that the Roche business sent to LeBoeuf quickly dwindled below the aggregate compensation paid defendants. By 1993, all three defendants had left LeBoeuf.

Breach of Fiduciary Duty

Both sides acknowledge the principle that law partners, no less than any other business or professional partners, are bound by a fiduciary duty requiring "the punctilio of an honor the most sensitive" (*Meinhard v. Salmon,* 249 N.Y. 458, 464; *see also, Duane Jones Co. v. Burke,* 306 N.Y. 172, 188–189). Both sides acknowledge as well the principle that an attorney stands in a fiduciary relation to the client (*Matter of Kelly v. Greason,* 23 N.Y.2d 368, 375).

Translating principles into practice, however, presents a far greater problem.

Moskovitz insists that the venerable principle of fiduciary duty among law partners must in today's marketplace give way to the higher value of attorney responsibility to clients: keeping them informed of matters that affect them, allowing them counsel of their choice, and incident to that choice assuring unrestricted attorney mobility. He emphasizes that he had a direct, personal relationship with Roche, as its lawyer, for more than 30 years and therefore had not simply a right but actually an affirmative obligation to tell Roche, particularly in the midst of a serious tax matter he was handling for the client, that he was considering joining another law firm and ascertain whether it might have a conflict of interest there—and he did no more than that.

It is unquestionably difficult to draw hard lines defining lawyers' fiduciary duty to partners and their fiduciary duty to clients. That there may be overlap, tension, even conflict between the two spheres is underscored by the spate of literature concerning the current revolving door law firm culture. . . .

One respected commentator opines that, while a departing partner's preresignation negotiations with firm clients in most businesses would probably constitute breach of the common-law obligation of loyalty to the firm, in the case of law practice, "the public policy favoring client freedom of choice in legal representation should override the firm's proprietary interest in holding its clientele" [citation omitted]

We agree with the trial court and Appellate Division, however, that as a matter of principle, preresignation surreptitious "solicitation" of firm clients for a partner's personal gain—the issue posed to us—is actionable. Such conduct exceeds what is necessary to protect the important value of client freedom of choice in legal representation, and thoroughly undermines another important value—the loyalty owed partners (including law partners), which distinguishes partnerships (including law partnerships) from bazaars.

What, then, is the prohibited "solicitation"? As the trial court recognized, in classic understatement, the answer to that question is not "self-evident."

Given the procedural posture of the case before us, plainly this is not an occasion for drawing the hard lines. Factual variations can be crucial in determining whether an attorney's duties have been breached, and we cannot speculate as to what conclusions will follow from the facts yet to be found in the case before us. We can, however, set out certain broad parameters, as the trial court did.

At one end of the spectrum, where an attorney is dissatisfied with the existing association, taking steps to locate alternative space and affiliations would not violate a partner's fiduciary duties. That this may be a delicate venture, requiring confidentiality, is simple common sense and well illustrated by the eruption caused by defendants' announced resignation in the present case. As a matter of ethics, departing partners have been permitted to inform firm clients with whom they have a prior professional relationship about their impending withdrawal and new practice, and to remind the client of its freedom to retain counsel of its choice. . . .

At the other end of the spectrum, secretly attempting to lure firm clients (even those the partner has brought into the firm and personally represented) to the new association, lying to clients about their rights with respect to the choice of counsel, lying to partners about plans to leave, and abandoning the firm on short notice (taking clients and files) would not be consistent with a partner's fiduciary duties. . . .

Although the trial court harbored the belief that discovery would facilitate resolution of this dispute as a matter of law, and therefore invited renewal of plaintiff's cross motion for summary judgment, the volumes of depositions and affidavits have not in fact clarified the issues. With Moskovitz pointing to evidence that his preresignation conduct was nothing more than appropriate client informational service, and plaintiff law firm pointing to evidence that he was engaged in improper solicitation of Roche for his own benefit, no conclusion can be drawn at this juncture as to where on the spectrum this case falls. Plainly Moskovitz's summary judgment motion was correctly denied.

Breach of Contract

Having concluded that there is an issue of fact with respect to the alleged breach of fiduciary duty, the same result follows as to the breach of contract claim, where the core of appellant's legal challenge before us—that the supervening public policy favors client freedom of choice—is essentially the same. The retirement agreement provision in issue in no way compromised the freedom of clients to choose their counsel or the freedom of appellant to practice law. The provision simply obliged the firm's senior partners to use their "best efforts" to expose firm clients to the work of other attorneys in the firm, as they deemed appropriate, in the hope that, with retirement of the seniors on the horizon, such familiarity would breed longevity in the relationship.

Given Moskovitz's insistence that the client looked only to him, and would never have remained with the firm after his departure, whether the promised "best efforts" were in fact used is a disputed issue that must be determined at trial.

Fraud

Plaintiff's cause of action for fraud—alleging that Moskovitz made false representations to the partnership prior to its approval of the retirement agreement with no intention of complying with those representations—similarly states a claim that survives summary judgment.

A cause of action for fraud may arise when one misrepresents a material fact, knowing it is false, which another relies on to its injury (*see, Ochs v. Woods,* 221 N.Y. 335, 338). A false statement of intention is sufficient to support an action for fraud, even where that statement relates to an agreement between the parties. . . .

Plaintiff charges that Moskovitz represented orally to the partnership that he and the other seniors would act to ensure the future of the firm by integrating and institutionalizing the clients when he never intended to do so and indeed was even considering the formation of a new partnership. Although (as the Trial Judge recognized) plaintiff may ultimately have difficulty persuading a fact finder of its assertions by clear and convincing evidence, a cause of action has been stated. And as with the claims for breach of fiduciary duty and breach of contract, material fact issues preclude summary judgment.

Accordingly, the order of the Appellate Division should be affirmed, with costs, and the certified question answered in the affirmative.

Sizing Up Firms: Grabbers and Pushers

In addition to the fiduciary lessons it teaches, *Graubard* offers some lessons about law firm life that are useful, especially to new lawyers. Some firms have been around so long that they are institutions, and their founding members are long forgotten. Other firms, generally very small ones, are essentially support structures for their founding members. At institutional firms, lawyers come and go and, even if departures affect profits in a given year, the institution will go on. At smaller firms centered around one or two big rainmakers, the firm is quite likely to dissolve (or at least shrink a lot) when the rainmakers retire.

But there are a lot of firms in the middle, too, and they can be hard to figure out. A firm such as the Graubard firm could go either way when its founding or senior partners retire. If the senior partners are the type of people who cling closely to franchise clients such as Roche, enjoying to the fullest the money and influence that comes from having a big book of business, then it will be harder for more junior lawyers to develop relationships with such clients than would it would be if the senior partners passed the client on to the next generation. And if the client's representatives do not have a close relationship with more junior lawyers in the firm they are more likely to shop for new counsel elsewhere when the senior lawyer retires than they would be if they did have such relationships.

One can over-simplify the world by dividing senior lawyers in such firms into two camps: grabbers and pushers. Grabbers hold tightly to clients and don't like other lawyers developing too much influence with the client. Pushers are happy to hand the client off to more junior lawyers (keeping in touch as much as the client relationship requires) and spend their time trolling for new clients. Pushers tend to grow institutions; grabbers do not.

From the new lawyer's perspective, it is useful to watch the way senior lawyers behave. If they are grabbers, it is important to know how the firm plans to handle the inevitable day when the senior lawyer starts to wind down. As *Graubard* shows, grabbers make for hard transitions. In extreme cases, they can put the viability of a firm at risk. Pushers cause fewer problems when they retire because they have in effect been in transition away from the existing client base all the while. More simply, in firms where it matters at all (meaning other than very large or very small firms) grabbers create risks for new lawyers while pushers create opportunities.

All that being said, it is useful to remember the advice attributed to a very prominent senior lawyer at a New York firm. When asked by a summer associate what he thought would happen to the firm when he retired, he replied: "That's up to you."

---

2. SOLICITING FORMER CLIENTS AND FORMER COLLEAGUES

Suppose a lawyer or group of lawyers leaves Firm A to establish Firm B. Suppose they want to recruit some of their former colleagues to leave Firm A and join them at B. May they do so? Are there limits on what they can do? The next case addresses these issues.

REEVES V. HANLON

33 Cal.4th 1140 (2004).

BAXTER, J.

Plaintiffs Robert L. Reeves and Robert L. Reeves & Associates, A Professional Law Corporation, brought the instant lawsuit against defendants Daniel P. Hanlon, Colin T. Greene, and Hanlon & Greene, A Professional Corporation (H & G). The operative complaint included the following allegations: In 1995, Reeves's law firm, which emphasized immigration law and litigation, employed Hanlon as an attorney. In 1997, the firm employed Greene as an associate attorney. In 1998, Reeves entered into an agreement with Hanlon whereby Hanlon could earn an equity position in a law firm to be formed; thereafter, the firm's name was changed to "Reeves and Hanlon, Professional Law Corporation."

On or about June 30, 1999, both Hanlon and Greene resigned from Reeves's firm without notice or warning. They improperly persuaded plaintiffs' employees to join H & G, personally solicited plaintiffs' clients to discharge plaintiffs and to instead obtain services from H & G, misappropriated plaintiffs' trade secrets, destroyed computer files and data, and withheld plaintiffs' property, including a corporate car. The complaint asserted 14 causes of action, including intentional interference with contractual relationships, interference with prospective business opportunity, conspiracy to interfere with prospective economic advantage, misappropriation of confidential information in violation of the UTSA, unauthorized use of a corporate car, and destruction of corporate property. . . .

[T]he trial court issued a statement of decision concluding that Hanlon and Greene had assumed fiduciary duties to plaintiffs and that they had engaged in interference with contracts and prospective business opportunity, and misappropriation of trade secrets. The court determined that, for more than five months prior to their departure, Hanlon and Greene had accessed plaintiffs' password-protected computer database to print out confidential name, address, and phone number information on 2,200 clients and had fomented dissatisfaction among plaintiffs' personnel. Although Greene had been chair of plaintiffs' litigation department and Hanlon had been responsible for over 500 client matters when they abruptly resigned without notice, they left no status reports or list of matters or deadlines on which they had been working. Nor did they attempt to cooperate with plaintiffs on a notice to clients. Shortly before resigning, Greene intentionally erased extensive computer files in plaintiffs' computer server containing client documents and form files used by plaintiffs. The evening of their resignations, defendants personally solicited plaintiffs' key employees. As a result, plaintiffs lost nine employees over the next 60 days, six of them joining defendants' new firm. Defendants also began a campaign to solicit plaintiffs' clients, contacting at least 40 clients by telephone without offering them a choice of counsel. All of this had been "intentionally done . . . to disrupt [plaintiffs'] ongoing business." Although historically, plaintiffs typically lost only one or two clients a month, plaintiffs lost 144 clients to defendants over the next 12 months.

The trial court found that defendants' conduct caused damage to plaintiffs in the total amount of $182,180.18 as follows: (1) 144 of plaintiffs' clients who transferred to H & G did not pay $62,540.50 in fees that they owed to plaintiffs; (2) plaintiffs suffered $36,000 in lost future business revenue; (3) plaintiffs incurred $61,639.68 in expenses to mitigate damages, including $41,630.49 for informing clients that the firm was still in business and $20,009.19 for recruiting replacement employees; and (4) defendants were unjustly enriched in the amount of $22,000 due to the misappropriation of confidential client information. The court, however, declined to award punitive damages, finding that defendants did not act with malice, oppression or fraud, but instead acted out of "immaturity" and "an apparent get-rich-quick mentality at the expense of [plaintiffs]." The court reduced the damages award to $150,000 pursuant to the parties' stipulation [capping damages at $150,000]. . . .

A. Intentional Interference with At–Will Employment Relations

Preliminarily, we state what is not at issue here. We have not been asked to review the propriety of the determinations by the trial court and the Court of Appeal that defendants are liable to plaintiffs for their tortious interference with plaintiffs' *client* relations and prospective *client* opportunities. Accordingly, we accept in full the Court of Appeal's conclusion that "[t]here is direct evidence that [Hanlon's and Greene's] departure was calculated to cripple the Reeves firm's ability to provide legal services: they left abruptly, damaged computer files, removed firm property, and failed to provide adequate guidance concerning their open cases. There is also evidence indicating that Hanlon and Greene phoned far more clients than the 40 or so clients they admitted to contacting, and [that] they exploited these clients' lack of facility with English and ignored their rights concerning the selection of counsel [citation]."

While the issue here does concern defendants' interference with plaintiffs' employee relations, we emphasize the following matters also are not in dispute. First, it is not disputed that the nine employees who left Reeves's firm, including the six who joined H & G, had employment relationships with plaintiffs that they could terminate at will. Second, we accept as undisputed the Court of Appeal's conclusion that the record contains substantial evidence that defendants "mounted a campaign against the Reeves firm involving destruction of computer records, misuse of confidential information, and unethical conduct, of which the cultivation of employee discontent was only a component. This campaign unfairly impaired the Reeves firm's ability to retain its employees." Third, we accept the Court of Appeal's additional determination that the record contains substantial evidence that plaintiffs incurred expenses, above the historical baseline, of $20,009.19 for employee recruitment to mitigate damages. . . .

What is disputed is the Court of Appeal's legal conclusion that "an employer may recover for interference with the employment contracts of its at-will employees by a third party when the third party does not show that its conduct in hiring the employees was justifiable or legitimate." . . . .

Where no unlawful methods are used, public policy generally supports a competitor's right to offer more pay or better terms to another's employee, so long as the employee is free to leave. . . . as the Restatement Second of Torts explains, if a party to a contract with the plaintiff is free to terminate the contractual relation when he chooses, "there is still a subsisting contract relation; but any interference with it that induces its termination is primarily an interference with the future relation between the parties, and the plaintiff has no legal assurance of them. As for the future hopes he has no legal right but only an expectancy; and when the contract is terminated by the choice of [a contracting party] there is no breach of it. The competitor is therefore free, for his own competitive advantage, to obtain the future benefits for himself by causing the termination. Thus, he may offer better contract terms, as by offering an employee of the plaintiff more money to work for him or by offering a seller higher prices for goods, and he may make use of persuasion or other suitable means, all without liability." (Rest.2d Torts, § 768, com. i.). . . .

Consistent with the decisions recognizing that an intentional interference with an at-will contract may be actionable, but mindful that an interference as such is primarily an interference with the future relation between the contracting parties, we hold that . . . to recover for a defendant's interference with an at-will employment relation, a plaintiff must plead and prove that the defendant engaged in an independently wrongful act—i.e., an act "proscribed by some constitutional, statutory, regulatory, common law, or other determinable legal standard"—that induced an at-will employee to leave the plaintiff. Under this standard, a defendant is not subject to liability for intentional interference if the interference consists merely of extending a job offer that induces an employee to terminate his or her at-will employment.

We now address whether application of the principles we announce today calls for affirmance of the $20,009.19 award against defendants. We conclude it does. Here, it is undisputed that Hanlon and Greene engaged in unlawful and unethical conduct in mounting a campaign to deliberately disrupt plaintiffs' business.

Greene had been chair of plaintiffs' litigation department, and Hanlon had been responsible for over 500 client matters, and both had assumed fiduciary duties to plaintiffs. When the two abruptly resigned without notice, they left no status reports or list of pending matters or deadlines on which they were working. Not only did they leave without providing such information, they acted unlawfully to delete and destroy plaintiffs' computer files containing client documents and forms. Additionally, Hanlon and Greene misappropriated confidential information, improperly solicited plaintiffs' clients, and cultivated employee discontent. While the computer files and the confidential information all appear to have pertained to plaintiffs' clients, not their employees, and while Hanlon and Greene waited until after their resignations to offer jobs to plaintiffs' employees, we cannot conclude the trial court abused its discretion in finding that defendants' unlawful and unethical actions were designed in part to interfere with and disrupt plaintiffs' relationships with their key at-will employees. . . . .

B. Violations of the UTSA

At trial, the court found that defendants violated the UTSA (Civ. Code, § 3426 et seq.) by misappropriating plaintiffs' confidential client list and, pursuant to Civil Code section 3426.3, subdivision (b), awarded plaintiffs $22,000 (representing a royalty fee of $10 for each of the 2,200 clients on the list). Defendants argue the Court of Appeal erroneously affirmed the trial court on this matter.

Under the UTSA, a client list qualifies as a "[t]rade secret" if it "[d]erives independent economic value, actual or potential, from not being generally known to the public or to other persons who can obtain economic value from its disclosure or use" and "[i]s the subject of efforts that are reasonable under the circumstances to maintain its secrecy." (Civ. Code, § 3426.1, subd. (d); see, e.g., *Morlife, Inc. v. Perry* (1997) 56 Cal.App.4th 1514, 1520–1522.) A violation of the UTSA occurs when an individual misappropriates a former employer's protected trade secret client list, for example, by using the list to solicit clients (*American Credit Indemnity Co. v. Sacks* (1989) 213 Cal.App.3d 622, 632–633 (American Credit)) or to otherwise attain an unfair competitive advantage (see *Morlife*, supra, 56 Cal.App.4th at p. 1523).

Here, defendants do not dispute that plaintiffs' client list derived independent economic value from not being generally known or that plaintiffs took reasonable efforts to maintain the list's secrecy under the circumstances. Instead, defendants claim the trial court erroneously found violations of the UTSA based on their mailing of a professional announcement to the clients appearing on that list.

Under defendants' authorities, although an individual may violate the UTSA by using a former employer's confidential client list to solicit clients, the UTSA does not forbid an individual from announcing a change of employment, even to clients on a protected trade secret client list. As one decision explains, merely announcing a new business affiliation, without more, is not prohibited by the UTSA definition of misappropriation because such conduct is "basic to an individual's right to engage in fair competition." (*American Credit*, supra, 213 Cal.App.3d at p. 636; cf.

Aetna Bldg. Maintenance Co. v. West (1952) 39 Cal.2d 198, 204 [stating the common law rule].)

We have no quarrel with defendants' authorities, but find they support the trial court's determinations that defendants violated the UTSA by using the trade secret client data in an improper manner "to directly solicit clients" and for defendants' "own pecuniary gain to the detriment and damage of" plaintiffs. There is substantial evidence in the record supporting these findings, including testimony that defendants used the data to solicit a number of plaintiffs' clients directly by telephone. Additionally, there is substantial evidence showing that defendants' business announcement caused plaintiffs' clients, many of whom lacked fluency in English, to believe Reeves had died or his firm had gone out of business, and that plaintiffs had to conduct their own mail campaign to reassure clients their firm remained able to serve them.[2] Because defendants' conduct as such was not in furtherance of their right to engage in fair competition, the authorities they cite do not support a different result.

CASE QUESTIONS

1. What must a plaintiff show to maintain a claim for interference with an at-will employment contract?
2. Did the plaintiff here satisfy this requirement? How?
3. What are the elements of a trade secret?
4. What acts of misappropriation were alleged here?
5. What acts does the court imply would not have constituted misappropriation?

Conduct similar to that described in *Reeves* may lead to discipline, including disbarment. *See Maryland Attorney Grievance Comm'n v. Keiner,* Md., Misc. Docket AG No. 24, 8/19/11 ("Disbarment is the appropriate sanction for an attorney who violated Maryland Lawyers' Rules of Professional Conduct 1.4(a) and (b) and 8.4 (a)–(d), by wrongfully deleting

[2] FN9. Prior to defendants' departure, plaintiffs' firm went by the name of "Reeves and Hanlon, Professional Law Corporation." The business announcement defendants mailed out informed plaintiffs' clients of the formation of "Hanlon & Greene, A Professional Corporation," but made no mention of Robert Reeves's continuing practice.

In recognition of the principle that the professional obligation of attorneys to their clients requires attorneys to provide for an orderly transition in the event of an employment change, Formal Opinion No. 1985–86 of the State Bar Standing Committee on Professional Responsibility and Conduct provides that departing attorneys should cooperate with their former employers to arrange for the issuance of a joint notice to clients. Here, defendants prepared and distributed their business announcement without seeking plaintiffs' input or approval.

and altering his law firm's clients' electronic computer files in an effort to make viable cases appear closed for lack of merit. The attorney engaged in such conduct in order to conceal the cases from the firm, with the intent of pursuing the cases on his own once he started his own law practice. The attorney also wrongfully used the firm's resources in an effort to solicit new clients for his proposed law practice).

---

3. THE TRADE SECRETS PROBLEM

Reeves exemplifies two trends. The first, which began some time ago, is that lawyers no longer stay at one firm for their whole careers but move from one firm to another. The second trend, of which *Reeves* is a prominent part, is that lawyers now commonly litigate departures from firms in the same way clients litigate employee departures. Tort litigation for breach of fiduciary duty, interference with contract or prospective economic advantage, unfair competition, and misappropriation of trade secrets are now unexceptionable if not common.

Such suits tend to revolve around two questions: What can a departing lawyer take with her and what can she do to facilitate her departure? The first question can be thought of as a property issue: Who owns what information? The second can be thought of as an unfair competition issue: Which actions amount to a fair fight for business and which are impermissible?

The property question is most likely to focus on trade secrets. (Copyright litigation is conceivable, but not as yet common in the reported cases.) *Reeves* refers to the California implementation of the Uniform Trade Secrets Act. The UTSA defines a trade secret as follows:

> "Trade secret" means information, including a formula, pattern, compilation, program device, method, technique, or process, that: (i) derives independent economic value, actual or potential, from no being generally known to, and not being readily ascertainable by proper means by, other persons who can obtain economic value from its disclosure or use, and (ii) is the subject of efforts that are reasonable under the circumstances to maintain its secrecy.

The UTSA provides for injunctive relief or damages for misappropriation of a trade secret. The Act defines misappropriation to mean

> (i) acquisition of a trade secret of another by a person who knows or has reason to know that the trade secret was acquired by improper means; or (ii) disclosure or use of a trade secret of another without express or implied consent by a person who (A) used improper means to acquire knowledge of the trade secret; or (B) at the time of disclosure or use knew or had reason to know that his knowledge of the

trade secret was (I) derived from or through a person who has utilized improper means to acquire it; (II) acquired under circumstances giving rise to a duty to maintain its secrecy or limit its use; or (III) derived from or through a person who owed a duty to the person seeking relief to maintain its secrecy or limit its use; or (C) before a material change of his position, knew or had reason to know that it was a trade secret ad that knowledge of it had been acquired by accident or mistake.

Finally, the UTSA defines "improper means" to include "theft, bribery, misrepresentation, breach or inducement of a breach of duty to maintain secrecy, or espionage through electronic or other means."

Reeves treated a client list as a trade secret. It qualified this holding, however, by distinguishing between the use of the list to "solicit" clients, which would qualify as misappropriation, and use of the list merely to announce a change in employment status.

This aspect of the holding was consistent with dicta in *Moss, Adams & Co. v. Shilling,* 179 Cal.App.3d 124, 126 (1986). *Moss Adams* involved two accountants who left their employer to start their own firm. After hours one night, they took home the rolodex belonging to the firm's receptionist. They copied from the rolodex the names and addresses of clients for whom they had worked during the previous year. To each person on this list, they mailed an announcement:

> "John D. Shilling and Cynthia L. Kenyon, formerly with Moss Adams, are pleased to announce the formation of a new partnership: Shilling, Kenyon & Co. [,] Certified Public Accountants[,] Lloyds Bank Building[,] One Almaden Blvd., Suite 1110[,] San Jose, CA 95113[,] (408) 295–3822[.]"

The accounting firm sued Shilling and Kenyon for misappropriation of trade secrets, interference with prospective economic advantage, interference with contractual relations, breach of contract, breach of fiduciary duty, and unfair competition. The court affirmed a grant of summary adjudication in favor of Shilling and Kenyon.

In dicta consistent with *Reeves,* the *Moss Adams* court said "The mailing of such an announcement does not constitute solicitation and therefore is not unfair competition." The holding of *Moss Adams* differed from *Reeves,* however. The court held that Shilling and Kenyon had not misappropriated trade secrets because they only copied the names of clients for whom they had worked, and those names were not trade secrets.

Subsequent courts have rejected this distinction. *Morlife, Inc. v. Perry,* 56 Cal.App.4th 1514, 1517 (1997), which is cited in *Reeves,* is the key case. It involved employees of a roofing company who left to start a competing firm. One of the employees took with him a collection of customer business cards he had accumulated over the years. He used those cards to contact prospective customers. The roofing company sued under the UTSA, and the employees cited *Moss Adams* in their defense. The court rejected the argument:

> [T]he distinction *Moss, Adams* makes between former employees who personally dealt with customers and former employees who did not rests on an unsound premise. There is no legitimate reason for characterizing differently the conduct of a former employee who uses customer information personally developed for the employer during the period of employment from the use of the very same information developed by a co-worker who had no customer contact. Creating an artificial distinction between the conduct of these two employees under the rubric of commercial impracticality in not being able to "wipe clean" one former employee's memory constitutes an unjustified abandonment of legitimate regulation of competitive activity, and ignores the paramount interest in protecting information meeting the definitional criteria of a trade secret.
>
> Furthermore, in absolving former sales personnel from disclosing or using customer information that would otherwise qualify as a trade secret to solicit business, the court in *Moss, Adams* did not appropriately recognize that information developed by an employee concerning the employer's customers represents an investment of time and money *on the part of the employer*, justifying a grant of trade secret protection against exploitation by the former employee. . . . In the case of a former employee who attempts to use personal customer contacts for personal benefit upon going into competition with the former employer, "[i]t is this personal acquaintance and additional influence of the friendship developed during his employment . . . which makes solicitation of former customers by appellant *so unfair to his former employer*. . . .
>
> *Moss, Adams* was decided before the UTSA became effective. That court was unencumbered by the legislatively-mandated definition of misappropriation now contained in the UTSA. Under the UTSA, simple disclosure or use may suffice to create liability. It is no longer necessary, if it ever was, to prove that the purpose to which the acquired information is put is outweighed by the interests of the trade secret holder or that use of a trade secret cannot be prohibited if it is infeasible to do so. Thus, despite the apparent solace appellants may find from the reasoning in *Moss, Adams,* its premise is inapposite to commercial interactions occurring after the effective date of the UTSA.

Following judicial rejection of the *Moss Adams* distinction, UTSA litigation in such cases will focus on distinguishing permissible notification from impermissible misappropriation by solicitation.

Reeves involves lawyers leaving one firm to set up their own competing firm. Similar problems can arise when lawyers move from one firm to another firm that already exists. In such a case there may be less need to solicit employees of the former firm to come work as support staff at the new firm (and thus less risk of liability for interference with contract) but there will be a greater need to provide the new firm with information that will let it assess whether it wants to hire you. For an extensive discussion of fiduciary obligations in this context, *see Gibbs v. Breed, Abbott & Morgan*, 710 N.Y.S.2d 578 (2000).

---

4. AGREEMENTS RESTRICTING PRACTICE

Lawyers may not enter into agreements restricting their right to practice law after they leave a firm. This rule covers two main types of agreements. The first, covered by Model Rule 5.6(A), limits the lawyer's ability to compete with his or her prior firm in a particular type of practice and/or location. These agreements resemble ordinary covenants not to compete. The second type of agreement, covered by Model Rule 5.6(b), generally is proposed by an opposing party and restricts the lawyer from representing a particular person or members of a group of persons with similar claims. These are not covenants not to compete; they instead are meant to prevent the lawyer from prosecuting further claims against a party, presumably to lessen the possibility of such claims by denying claimants a lawyer with experience bringing them. Both these prohibitions are taken very seriously, as the following materials illustrate. We begin, however, with an unusual case allowing a non-competition restriction to be enforced.

Restatement § 13
Model Rule of Professional Conduct 5.6(a)
Cal. R. Prof. Conduct 1–500

HOWARD V. BABCOCK

6 Cal.4th 409 (1993)

MOSK, JUSTICE.

We granted review to decide whether an agreement between law partners is enforceable if it requires withdrawing partners to forego certain contractual withdrawal benefits if they compete with their former law firm. We conclude that an agreement among law partners imposing a reasonable toll on departing partners who compete with the firm is enforceable.

I

In 1982, partners in the law firm of Parker, Stanbury, McGee, Babcock & Combs executed a partnership agreement. Article X of the agreement provided in pertinent part that: "Should more than one partner, associate or individual withdraw from the firm prior to age sixty-five (65) and thereafter within a period of one year practice law . . . together or in combination with others, including former partners or associates of this firm, in a practice engaged in the handling of liability insurance defense work as aforesaid within the Los Angeles or Orange County Court system, said partner or partners shall be subject, at the sole discretion of the remaining non-withdrawing partners to forfeiture of all their rights to withdrawal benefits other than capital as provided for in Article V herein"

Article V provided that a general partner who withdraws from the partnership shall be paid his or her capital interest, and a sum "equal to the share in the net profit of the firm that the withdrawn . . . partner would have received during the first twelve months following the withdrawal . . . if he had remained with the firm . . . during the said twelve month period." Plaintiffs Howard, Moss and Loveder and defendants Babcock, Combs, Kinnett, Waddell, Bergsten and Schaertel signed the partnership agreement.

In January 1984, participating partners Loveder and Schaertel were elevated to general partners and Osborne and Cicotte were admitted as participating partners. Strickroth and Mori were admitted as participating partners in 1985 and Barrett was admitted as a participating partner in 1986. The partnership agreement was not amended, nor did the new partners admitted after 1982 ever sign it.

On December 8, 1986, plaintiffs (Howard, Moss, Loveder and Strickroth) notified the remaining members of the firm that they were terminating their relationship with the firm, and that they would begin practice in competition with the firm in January 1987. They asserted that article X was unenforceable. Defendants notified plaintiffs that they would withhold a portion of plaintiffs' withdrawal benefits because of plaintiffs' violation of article X. Plaintiffs replied that the partnership agreement was no longer effective, and published notice of dissolution of the firm, effective December 31, 1986.

On January 2, 1987, plaintiffs entered business in Orange County as a general partnership under the name of Howard, Moss, Loveder & Strickroth, handling, among other cases, liability defense work for insurance companies and self-insured companies. Defendants operated as a new general partnership under the name of Parker, Stansbury, McGee, Babcock & Combs.

The assets of the original Parker firm on December 31, 1986, included the capital of the firm, namely, the profits shown on the balance sheet;

the accounts receivable, that is, work performed and billed, but in which the bill had not been paid; and the unfinished business, that is, open files that required additional work that would be billed in the future.

Defendants tendered payment to plaintiffs for their share of the capital of the firm, but refused to compensate them for the accounts receivable or to acknowledge that they had any interest in the work in progress or unfinished business of the firm.

Clients of the original Parker firm substituted the Howard firm in approximately 200 cases. . . .

[The trial court found that] all that the plaintiffs were entitled to was their share of the profits for 1986. They were not entitled to any payment for goodwill or any share of the profits after 1986. . . . The court filed an interlocutory judgment ordering plaintiffs to provide defendants with an accounting of the net profits plaintiffs had billed or collected from clients who wanted plaintiffs to continue work in progress when plaintiffs left the Parker firm. . . . The trial court then entered the final judgment prepared by defendants, ordering plaintiffs to pay defendants the sum of $382,686, and finding that defendants owed plaintiffs nothing. . . .

California has a settled policy in favor of open competition. Nonetheless, it has long been the law of this state that a partnership agreement may provide against competition by withdrawing partners in a limited geographical area. . . . Thus Business and Professions Code section 16602, derived from Civil Code former section 1675, provides: "Any partner may, upon or in anticipation of a dissolution of the partnership, agree that he will not carry on a similar business within a specified county or counties, city or cities, or a part thereof, where the partnership business has been transacted, so long as any other member of the partnership, or any person deriving title to the business or its goodwill from any such other member of the partnership, carries on a like business therein."

This statutory language has been relied on in enforcing covenants not to compete among partners practicing in the professions, including accountants and physicians. In fact, these agreements typically do not actually prohibit competition, but rather place a price on competition. . . .

Until recent years, no court has considered the applicability of Business and Professions Code section 16602 to the legal profession. Now, however, a conflict has developed in the Courts of Appeal over the issue. . . .

Our first duty in interpreting a statute is to be guided by the words that appear on the face of the enactment. Business and Professions Code section 16602 speaks in general terms, providing that "any partner" may agree not to compete with members of the partnership upon dissolution. Nothing in its language conveys an exception to its terms for lawyers, nor have the parties or amicus curiae directed us to any legislative history indicating that the statute was intended to apply to all partners except those who happened to be lawyers. . . .

Accordingly, finding no ambiguity in the terms of the statute, and finding no demonstrated legislative intent to create a silent exception for lawyers, we may apply the statute "according to its terms without further judicial construction." [citation omitted] Thus, we conclude that the statute applies to partners in law firms.[3]

This conclusion does not end our inquiry, however. This court has the authority to prescribe rules of professional conduct for attorneys as part of its inherent power to regulate the practice of law. It is in our power to impose a higher standard of conduct on lawyers than that applicable to other professionals.

The Court of Appeal, plaintiffs, and the State Bar of California, as amicus curiae, maintain that we have already promulgated a rule of professional conduct imposing just such a higher standard, a rule that prohibits partners in law firms from entering into noncompetition agreements. They refer us to rule 1–500 of the Rules of Professional Conduct (rule 1–500).[4]

Rule 1–500 provides: "(A) A member shall not be a party to or participate in offering or making an agreement, whether in connection with the settlement of a lawsuit or otherwise, if the agreement restricts the right of a member to practice law, except that this rule shall not prohibit such an agreement which: (1) Is a part of an employment, shareholders', or partnership agreement among members provided the restrictive agreement does not survive the termination of the employment, shareholder, or partnership relationship; or (2) Requires payments to a member upon the member's retirement from the practice of law; or (3) Is authorized by Business and Professions Code sections 6092.5, subdivision (i) or 6093 [providing for authority of State Bar Court to impose conditions of probation on disciplined attorneys]. (B) A member shall not be a party to or participate in offering or making an agreement which precludes the reporting of a violation of these rules."

We are not persuaded that this rule was intended to or should prohibit the type of agreement that is at issue here. An agreement that as-

---

[3] FN4. We are not called upon to discuss noncompetition agreements affecting employees, as opposed to partners.

[4] FN5. Rule 1–500 is based on American Bar Association (ABA), Model Code of Professional Responsibility, former Disciplinary Rule 2–108 (1 Witkin, Cal. Procedure (3d ed. 1985) Attorneys, § 50, p. 70), now numbered rule 5.6 of the ABA Model Rules of Professional Conduct. Rule 5.6 provides: "A lawyer shall not participate in offering or making: (a) a partnership or employment agreement that restricts the rights of a lawyer to practice after termination of the relationship, except an agreement concerning benefits upon retirement; or (b) an agreement in which a restriction on the lawyer's right to practice is part of the settlement of a controversy between private parties." The ABA rules may be helpful in interpreting the California rules.

sesses a reasonable cost against a partner who chooses to compete with his or her former partners does not restrict the practice of law. Rather, it attaches an economic consequence to a departing partner's unrestricted choice to pursue a particular kind of practice.

We agree [with an appellate court holding that] an agreement between law partners that a reasonable cost will be assessed for competition is consistent with rule 1–500. Rejecting an interpretation of rule 1–500 like that proffered by plaintiffs here, the court [in that case] stated: "We do not construe rule 1–500 in such a narrow fashion. . . . The rule does not . . . prohibit a withdrawing partner from agreeing to compensate his former partners in the event he chooses to represent clients previously represented by the firm from which he has withdrawn. Such a construction represents a balance between competing interests. On the one hand, it enables a departing attorney to withdraw from a partnership and continue to practice law anywhere within the state, and to be able to accept employment should he choose to do so from any client who desires to retain him. On the other hand, the remaining partners remain able to preserve the stability of the law firm by making available the withdrawing partner's share of capital and accounts receivable to replace the loss of the stream of income from the clients taken by the withdrawing partner to support the partnership's debts. Concluding that the agreement was not invalid on its face, the court held that the validity of the agreement depended on whether it "amounts to an agreement for liquidated damages or an agreement resulting in a forfeiture.". . . .

[O]ur interpretation of the rule must be illuminated by our recognition that a revolution in the practice of law has occurred requiring economic interests of the law firm to be protected as they are in other business enterprises. We are confident that our recognition of a new reality in the practice of law will have no deleterious effect on the current ability of clients to retain loyal, competent counsel of their choice.

"The traditional view of the law firm as a stable institution with an assured future is now challenged by an awareness that even the largest and most prestigious firms are fragile economic units. . . . " Not the least of the changes rocking the legal profession is the propensity of withdrawing partners in law firms to "grab" clients of the firm and set up a competing practice. [citations omitted] In response, many firms have inserted noncompetition clauses into their partnership agreements. These noncompetition clauses have grown and flourished, despite, or in defiance of, the consistent holding of many courts across the nation that a noncompetition clause violates the rules of professional conduct of the legal profession. It is evident that these agreements address important business interests of law firms that can no longer be ignored.

The firm has a financial interest in the continued patronage of its clientele. The firm's capital finances the development of a clientele and the support services and training necessary to satisfactorily represent the clientele. In earlier times, this investment was fairly secure, because the continued loyalty of partners and associates to the firm was assumed. But more recently, lateral hiring of associates and partners, and the secession of partners from their firms has undermined this assumption. Withdrawing partners are able to announce their departure to clients of the firm, and many clients defect along with the attorneys with whom they have developed good working relationships. The practical fact is that when partners with a lucrative practice leave a law firm along with their clients, their departure from and competition with the firm can place a tremendous financial strain on the firm. . . .

Recognizing these sweeping changes in the practice of law, we can see no legal justification for treating partners in law firms differently in this respect from partners in other businesses and professions.

We are aware that many courts have interpreted the rules of professional conduct of their states, often stated in identical or very similar terms with the language of our rule 1–500, as prohibiting all agreements restricting competition among lawyers, including those that merely assess a cost for competition. . . .

Upon reflection, we have determined that these courts' steadfast concern to assure the theoretical freedom of each lawyer to choose whom to represent and what kind of work to undertake, and the theoretical freedom of any client to select his or her attorney of choice is inconsistent with the reality that both freedoms are actually circumscribed. Putting aside lofty assertions about the uniqueness of the legal profession, the reality is that the attorney, like any other professional, has no right to enter into employment or partnership in any particular firm, and sometimes may be discharged or forced out by his or her partners even if the client wishes otherwise. . . .

Moreover, the contemporary changes in the legal profession to which we have already alluded make the assertion that the practice of law is not comparable to a business unpersuasive and unreflective of reality. Commercial concerns are now openly recognized as important in the practice of law. Indeed, we question whether any but the wealthy could enter the profession if it were to be practiced without attention to commercial success. In any event, no longer can it be said that law is a profession apart, untouched by the marketplace. Not only has law firm culture changed but, as in other businesses, lawyers now may advertise their services and may even communicate by letter with persons unknown to them, suggesting the possibility of employment. Thus the general rules and habits of commerce have permeated the legal profession.

The same relaxation of the traditional rule against treating a law practice as comparable to a business can be seen in the development of the rules regarding sale of goodwill in a law firm. Although in 1988 the court in *Fraser v. Bogucki* (1988) 203 Cal.App.3d 604, rejected the concept of sale of goodwill in a law practice because it would treat clients as a commodity, the rules of professional conduct have since been amended expressly to permit the sale of goodwill in certain circumstances. (See Rules Prof. Conduct, rule 2–300.) Of course the rule requires notification to clients that the practice has been sold and that they have the right to hire new counsel, but the change does undercut the pristine view that clients are not deemed to be assets with a financial value.

Further, we question the premise that an agreement such as is at issue here would necessarily discourage withdrawing partners from continuing to represent clients who choose to employ them. Unless the penalty were unreasonable, it is more likely that the agreement would operate in the nature of a tax on taking the former firm's clients—a tax that is not unreasonable, considering the financial burden the partners' competitive departure may impose on the former firm. The sum to be forfeited by the withdrawing partners may be seen as comparable with a liquidated damage clause, an accepted fixture in other commercial contexts. . . .

We are confident that the interest of the public in being served by diligent, loyal and competent counsel can be assured at the same time as the legitimate business interest of law firms is protected by an agreement placing a reasonable price on competition. We hold that an agreement among partners imposing a reasonable cost on departing partners who compete with the law firm in a limited geographical area is not inconsistent with rule 1–500 and is not void on its face as against public policy. . . .

KENNARD, JUSTICE, dissenting.

Although the law is a business in the sense that an attorney in a law firm earns a living by practicing law, it is also and foremost a profession, with all the responsibilities that word implies. The ethical rule that this court is called upon to interpret exists to enforce the traditional and sound view that service to clients, including protection of the clients' ability to employ the attorneys they have come to trust, is more important than safeguarding the economic interests of established attorneys and law firms. I would enforce the rule according to the ordinary meaning of its terms to bar all agreements by which established firms seek to protect themselves against competition from attorneys who leave the firm.

I cannot accept that the practice of law has been so altered that it is now irretrievably profit-centered rather than client-centered. If ethical rules for attorneys must accommodate the "realities" of practicing law, then those realities ought to include this court's insistence that attorneys serve more than their own interests and accomplish more than amassing fees. Protection of the public and preservation of public respect for the law require no less.

Here, the judgment of the trial court, which upheld the restrictive covenant, directed plaintiffs, the former partners, to pay the law firm 82.5 percent of the profits derived from work plaintiffs performed *after* the termination of the partnership. To order an attorney to surrender 82.5 percent of the income obtained from representing clients is to restrict the attorney's practice of law in any meaningful sense of the word. The economic disincentives flowing from such an order may encourage the lawyer to give up the clients, "thereby interfering with the lawyer-client relationship and, more importantly, with clients' free choice of counsel."

The majority maintains that its interpretation of ethical standards is justified because an economic "revolution" has occurred in the practice of law. It asserts that its holding is warranted because law firms, including those that are large and prestigious, are adversely affected by withdrawing partners "grabbing" clients, law firms are intentionally ignoring the rules of ethics in any event, law firms have a financial interest in their clients, the law firm's capital financed the development of the clientele, law firms may be economically injured by the loss of clients, and other businesses and professions are permitted to have anti-competition agreements. I have no quarrel with the majority's assertions that former partners sometimes "take" clients from law firms, that law firms have a financial interest in their clientele, or that law firms may be economically injured by the loss of clients.

But the purpose of rules of professional ethics is to restrain and guide the conduct of attorneys and to protect the public, not to protect the financial interests of law firms. Accordingly, I cannot accept the majority's view that the protection of law firms justifies devaluing the rights of clients. There is no reason to assume that the controlling partners of established law firms have a moral entitlement to protection from competition.

CASE QUESTIONS

1. What were the relevant restrictions of the agreement?
2. Who did the trial court order to pay what to whom?
3. What interests does the majority think are balanced by such agreements?

PROBLEM 13–3

The *Howard* Court decided that CRPC 1–500 did not invalidate the agreement at issue. What agreements does that rule apply to?

Howard v. Babcock is somewhat unusual in enforcing an agreement that creates a disincentive for lawyers to take on new clients. *Law Offices of Ronald J. Palagi v. Howard*, 275 Neb. 334 (2008), is more representative. Palagi employed Stephen Howard under an agreement that promised Howard 15% of the fees on cases he handled. The agreement also provided an additional 5% payment in exchange for Howard's agreement to this term:

> The parties acknowledge that the clients listed on the client list may exercise their right to choose [Howard] as their attorney in the event [Howard's] association with The Firm is terminated. . . . If clients of [Law Offices] request that [Howard] represent them, then [Howard] may decide to represent them, but all attorney fees generated on such matters would be paid to [Law Offices], and no attorney fees will be paid to [Howard].

Howard did leave the firm, and he challenged this clause as it applied to two cases. The Nebraska Supreme Court found the clause unenforceable. It relied in part the Nebraska version of Model Rule 5.6 and held that, based on that rule and

> similar ethics rules in effect throughout the country, "[c]ourts do not enforce any agreement involving the employment of lawyers that appears to have restrictive and thus anticompetitive tendencies." This is so whether the restriction on competition is direct or indirect. The prohibition against restrictive covenants in agreements between lawyers is generally reasoned to be necessary to ensure the freedom of clients to select counsel of their choice. Courts and commentators note a distinction between the business principles which govern commercial enterprises and the ethical principles that govern the practice of law and find that because " ' "clients are not merchandise" ' " and " ' "[l]awyers are not tradesmen," ' " restrictive covenants may not " ' "barter in clients." ' " Because the client's freedom of choice is the paramount interest the ethics rules attempt to serve, courts reason that any disincentive to competition is as detrimental to the public interest as an outright prohibition on competition. Thus, cases almost uniformly hold that financial disincentive provisions in attorney agreements are unenforceable as against public policy.

Payment on Dissolution

Jewel v. Boxer, 156 Cal.App.3d 171 (1984), involved the dissolution of a partnership ("JBE") in which Jewel, Boxer, Elkind, and Leary were partners. The partners did not have a written agreement specifying what would happen to fees on matters pending when JBE was dissolved. (Indeed, they had no written agreement at all.)

After JBE was dissolved, Jewel and Leary formed a new firm, as did Boxer and Elkind, who also took three associates with them.

> Shortly after dissolution, each former partner sent a letter to each client whose case he had handled for the old firm, announcing the dissolution. Enclosed in the letter was a substitution of attorney form, which was executed and returned by each client retaining the attorney who had handled the case for the old firm. The new firms represented the clients under fee agreements entered into between the client and the old firm.

As a result of this procedure, Boxer and Elkind handled most of the personal injury and workers' compensation cases pending at JBE at the time of its dissolution. Jewel and Leary handled some of those cases and the rest of the old firm's other types of cases.

Jewel and Leary claimed that the post-dissolution fees Boxer and Elkind received from cases they took with them from JBE were assets of JBE and therefore were to be divided among the JBE partners. They filed a complaint demanding an accounting of those fees.

The trial court agreed that fees earned after JBE dissolved were assets of JBE. The court divided those assets among the partners on the basis of quantum meruit, however, rather than on the basis of each partner's ownership interest.

The court of appeals reversed. It held:

> that in the absence of a partnership agreement, the Uniform Partnership Act requires that attorneys' fees received on cases in progress upon dissolution of a law partnership are to be shared by the former partners according to their right to fees in the former partnership, regardless of which former partner provides legal services in the case after the dissolution. The fact that the client substitutes one of the former partners as attorney of record in place of the former partnership does not affect this result . . . . . absent a contrary agreement, any income generated through the winding up of unfinished business is allocated to the former partners according to their respective interests in the partnership

The appellate court remanded the case with instructions to the trial court to allocate post-dissolution fees "based upon the respective interests in the former partnership."

The court of appeals rejected the trial court's reliance on *Fracasse v. Brent* 6 Cal.3d 784, 786 (1972), which held that a client has an absolute right to discharge an attorney employed under a contingent fee contract, the attorney then being entitled only to the reasonable value of the services rendered before discharge. It held "the right of a client to the attorney of one's choice and the rights and duties as between partners with respect to income from unfinished business are distinct and do not offend one another. Once the client's fee is paid to an attorney, it is of no concern to the client how that fee is allocated among the attorney and his or her former partners."

The court of appeals also found that cases pending at dissolution were unfinished business of JBE even though the clients later substituted attorneys: "the substitutions of attorneys here did not alter the character of the cases as unfinished business of the old firm. To hold otherwise would permit a former partner of a dissolved partnership to breach the fiduciary duty not to take any action with respect to unfinished partnership business for personal gain."

As the court framed the issues, substitution before dissolution might invoke the rule of *Fracasse*. It would also imply, however, that the partners were competing with the firm before dissolution, which would provide the basis for a breach of loyalty claim by the partnership. As the court put it:

There are sound policy reasons for applying the rule against extra compensation [i.e., compensation for post-dissolution work higher than that implied by the partnership interest] to law partnerships. The rule prevents partners from competing for the most remunerative cases during the life of the partnership in anticipation that they might retain those cases should the partnership dissolve. It also discourages former partners from scrambling to take physical possession of files and seeking personal gain by soliciting a firm's existing clients upon dissolution.

Boxer and Elkind argue that application of the rule in the present context will discourage continued representation of clients by the attorney of their choice, as former partners will not want to perform all of the postdissolution work on a particular case while receiving only a portion of the income generated by such work. Of course, this is all the former partners would have received had the partnership not dissolved. Additionally, the former partners will receive, in addition to their partnership portion of such income, their partnership share of income generated by the work of the other former partners, without performing any postdissolution work in those cases. On balance, the allocation of fees according to each partner's interest in the former partnership should not work an undue hardship as to any partner where each partner completes work on the partnership's cases which are active upon its dissolution. . . . .

Undue hardship should be prevented by two basic fiduciary duties owed between the former partners. First, each former partner has a duty to wind up and complete the unfinished business of the dissolved partnership. This would prevent a partner from refusing to furnish any work and imposing this obligation totally on the other partners, thus unfairly benefiting from their efforts while putting forth none of his or her own. Second, no former partner may take any action with respect to unfinished business which leads to purely personal gain. [citations omitted] Thus, the former partners are obligated to ensure that a disproportionate burden of completing unfinished business does not fall on one former partner or one group of former partners, unless the former partners agree otherwise.

It is unlikely that the partners, in discharging their mutual fiduciary duties, will be able to achieve a distribution of the burdens of completing unfinished business that corresponds precisely to their respective interests in the partnership. But partners are free to include in a written partnership agreement provisions for completion of unfinished business that ensure a degree of exactness and certainty unattainable by rules of general application. If there is any disproportionate burden of completing unfinished business here, it results from the parties' failure to have entered into a partnership agreement which could have assured such a result would not occur. The former partners must bear the consequences of their failure to provide for dissolution in a partnership agreement.

Jewell prompted some dynamic thinking by law firms facing dissolution. *In re Brobeck, Phleger & Harrison LLP*, 408 B.R. 318 (N.D. Cal. 2009), dealt with a firm whose partners executed a "Jewel waiver" as part of their plan dissolving the firm. The waiver stated:

> Except as specifically set forth below, neither the Partners nor the Partnership shall have any claim or entitlement to clients, cases or matters ongoing at the time of the dissolution of the Partnership oth er than the entitlement for collections of amounts due for work performed by the Partners and other Partnership personnel on behalf of the Partnership prior to their departure from the Partnership. The provisions of this Section 9(e) are intended to expressly *waive, opt out of and be in lieu of any right any Partner or the Partnership may have to 'unfinished business'* of the Partnership, as that term is defined in *Jewel v. Boxer*. . . .

The firm dissolved because it was in financial trouble, and its creditors filed a petition for involuntary bankruptcy. The bankruptcy trustee challenged the waiver as part of an effort to recover for the bankruptcy estate fees from work in progress when the firm dissolved. The trustee first argued the waiver was ineffective under the Revised Uniform Partnership Act (RUPA); the court rejected that argument, holding the waiver complied both with *Jewel* and with the RUPA.

The trustee also challenged the waiver as a constructive fraudulent transfer, which is a bankruptcy term for transfers of assets made within a year preceding bankruptcy and at a time the firm was insolvent, for less than reasonably equivalent value. The trustee claimed the firm got nothing for waiving its rights to future revenues under *Jewel*. The court agreed. It rejected the defendant's main argument—that the firm received value for the waiver because the waiver facilitated an orderly transition of cases, thereby fulfilling the firm's duty to ensure its clients would not be harmed by its dissolution—on the ground that individual attorneys owed such duties anyway and would have been required to discharge them with or without the waiver.

Brobeck involved a waiver executed on the eve of dissolution, when the firm was insolvent. A waiver included in a partnership agreement from the outset, or added at a time the firm was solvent or more than one year before bankruptcy, presumably would not be subject to the arguments the trustee successfully made in that case.

C. SUPERIOR–SUBORDINATE RELATIONS

An ethical and attentive supervisor is one of the greatest blessings a junior attorney can have. An unethical or inattentive supervisor can be one of the greatest curses. Much of the material in this book aims to help you understand which type of supervisor you have and to deal with any problems that may arise as a result. There also are specific rules governing the responsibilities of junior and senior attorneys. Model Rule 5.1(a) requires managing attorneys to take reasonable steps to assure the firm's lawyers adhere to the rules, and Rule 5.1(b) requires supervising attorneys to do the same for the lawyers they supervise. Under Rule 5.1(c), a supervising lawyer is responsible for the violations of a junior lawyer if the supervisor ratifies the conduct constituting the violation or is aware of the conduct at a time when its consequences can be avoided but fails to take remedial action. As to junior lawyers (i.e., you), Rule 5.2(a) makes clear that the rules apply to you in full notwithstanding your relative lack of experience. Rule 5.2(b) provides a partial exception; under it you are not responsible for a violation if you relied on a senior attorney's reasonable resolution of an arguable issue. Unreasonable resolutions or inarguable issues, however, eliminate this exception.

Relationships between junior and senior lawyers do not always fit the model of a traditional firm, and firms themselves are changing in response to client demand and competition. One change is that in recent years (especially following the recession of 2008) firms have become more hesitant to incur the fixed costs of hiring an associate full time, with the expectation of at least a year or two of continuous employment, and more willing to make one-off purchases of associate time for a particular project, with no guarantee and perhaps no expectation of future work. Such shifting contractual structures can present interesting questions of responsibility and liability, as the next case shows.

Model Rules of Professional Conduct 5.1–5.2
Restatement § 11
California Labor Code §§ 2802, 2865

KRAMER V. NOWAK

908 F.Supp. 1281 (E.D. Pa. 1995)

LOUIS H. POLLAK, DISTRICT JUDGE.

I. Background

This case arises out of two previous pieces of litigation. The first was an action brought in federal court in New Jersey by Lightning Lube, Inc. against Witco Corporation, in which Lightning Lube alleged violations of RICO and federal antitrust law, as well as fraud, breach of contract, and tortious interference. In that action, Lightning Lube was represented by Steven Kramer and Jeffrey Nowak of the law firm Steven M. Kramer & Associates. Lightning Lube ultimately recovered a judgment in the sum of $11.5 million. The second action was a malpractice suit brought by Ralph Venuto, Lightning Lube's President, against Mr. Kramer. This action, apparently, was resolved through arbitration. . . . [T]he action appears to have focused on an allegation that Kramer negligently represented Lightning Lube, preventing it from recovering a significantly larger judgment in its suit against Witco. According to Kramer, the malpractice claim resulted in an arbitral award against him in the sum of $440,000.

Following Kramer's defeat in the malpractice action, he filed the present action, a suit against his former associate Jeffrey Nowak. . . . The complaint alleges that the arbitral judgment "was based upon conduct engaged in by Mr. Nowak while he was an independent contractor for the plaintiff in the case entitled *Lightning Lube, Inc. v. Witco Corp.*, 802 F.Supp. 1180 (DNJ). The conduct consisted of miscalculation of prejudgment interest." Complaint, ¶ 5. Based on this description of Nowak's alleged misconduct, Kramer asserts a claim for contribution, in which Kramer seeks to shift a portion of the arbitral award onto Nowak. Kramer further asserts claims for negligence and for breach of contract.

II. The Present Motion

Nowak has moved to dismiss or, in the alternative, for summary judgment. Nowak argues that he was Kramer's employee and not, as Kramer asserts, an independent contractor. Nowak also argues that (1) the contribution claim must be dismissed because there has been no finding that Nowak and Kramer were joint tortfeasors, (2) the negligence claim must be dismissed because the complaint does not assert any duty owed by Nowak and because the claim is barred by the statute of limitations, and (3) the breach of contract claim must be dismissed because the complaint does not assert that Nowak failed to fulfill a specific contractual provision. . . .

III. Facts Alleged

The factual allegations contained in the complaint are extremely skimpy, consisting of the single sentence quoted in full above: "The conduct consisted of the miscalculation of prejudgment interest." Nonetheless, affidavits submitted by both parties flesh out the background and details of this event.

According to Nowak, the two parties first met in July 1988, while Nowak was in his final semester at Rutgers University Law School in Newark, New Jersey. Kramer was a practicing lawyer with offices in Philadelphia and New York and had placed an advertisement seeking a law student to work on a large antitrust matter—*Lightning Lube, Inc. v. Witco Corp.*—pending in federal court. Nowak responded to the advertisement, was interviewed by Kramer in Kramer's Philadelphia office, and was hired by Kramer. At Kramer's instruction, Nowak then began working out of the client's office in Mt. Laurel, New Jersey. Nowak worked at Lightning Lube's office from June 1988 until shortly after the conclusion of the litigation sometime in 1993 or 1994.

By June 1989, Nowak had been admitted to the New Jersey bar, and Kramer placed Nowak's name on his letterhead as an associate of the firm "Steven M. Kramer & Associates." The letterhead also lists Lightning Lube's address—where Nowak worked—as the firm's New Jersey office. In addition to arranging that Lightning Lube provide office space to Nowak, Kramer also arranged that Lightning Lube pay Nowak's salary directly. Kramer nonetheless maintained strict supervision over Nowak's work. Every day, Nowak prepared a log detailing the work he had done that day; the log was faxed to Kramer's New York office. All documents prepared by Nowak for the litigation were also faxed to Kramer for his approval. One fact to be noted about the relationship of the two parties is that Kramer often directed Nowak to sign Kramer's name to documents to be filed in the district court in New Jersey. Thus, the documents Nowak filed in the Lightning Lube litigation contain only Kramer's signature.

Among the many papers Nowak prepared for the Lightning Lube litigation was a motion for prejudgment interest. This motion was prepared after the jury returned a judgment of approximately $11.5 million in compensatory damages and $50 million in punitive damages in favor of Lightning Lube. Both Kramer and Nowak agree that Kramer instructed

Nowak to prepare the motion. Kramer claims that he "completely delegated the task to Mr. Nowak." Nowak disputes this characterization. . .

Despite the disagreement over the degree of supervision exerted by Kramer over the prejudgment interest motion, it is agreed that Kramer directed Nowak to prepare it. Further, the motion bears Kramer's name, Nowak having signed it, as was the usual procedure between them.

The motion prepared by Nowak sought approximately $4 million in prejudgment interest. . . . Judge William G. Bassler of the District of New Jersey reduced the damages award, declining to accept the punitive damages award and cutting down the compensatory damages award by $2 million. As a result of these decisions, Judge Bassler approved prejudgment interest in the amount of $2 million, rather than the $4 million requested by Lightning Lube. Represented by Kramer, Lightning Lube appealed several aspects of the district court ruling, but did not appeal the determination of prejudgment interest.

IV. The Relationship Between Kramer and Nowak

. . . Although I conclude that Nowak has established that he was Kramer's employee, the additional materials submitted by the parties persuade me that this conclusion does not mandate dismissal. . . . Under New Jersey case law . . . "[t]he relationship of master and servant exists 'whenever the employer retains the right to direct the manner in which the business shall be done, as well as the result to be accomplished, or in other words, not only what shall be done, but how it shall be done.' " In short, "the determinative factor, according to all the adjudications, is the control retained."

Nowak has produced considerable evidence that Kramer maintained control over Nowak's work. . . . A law firm associate is generally considered the firm's employee. *See* Leonard Gross, *Ethical Problems of Law Firm Associates,* 26 Wm. & Mary L.Rev. 259 (1985); Cindy Holland, Comment, *The Liabilities and Ethical Responsibilities of a Law Firm Associate,* 16 J.Legal Prof. 241 (1991).

Kramer does not dispute any of these facts. Rather, Kramer points to the fact that Lightning Lube paid Nowak's salary as evidence of Nowak's independent contractor status. However, Kramer himself had apparently arranged that Nowak's salary would be paid by his client. That Lightning Lube paid Nowak does not cast doubt on the evidence that Kramer controlled Nowak's work. There is no evidence that Kramer's supervision of Nowak's day-to-day working life was at all affected because Lightning Lube paid Nowak directly, rather than indirectly through a fee payment to Kramer. Based on the record before the court, it is clear that Nowak was Kramer's employee.

Nowak asserts that this conclusion dictates that the case be dismissed. In support of this assertion, Nowak points to the well-established principle of respondeat superior, under which an employer can be deemed legally responsible for the torts committed by employees acting in the scope of their employment. Yet the principle of respondeat superior only establishes an employer's liability with regard to third persons injured by the employee's wrongdoing. The principle of respondeat superior does not immunize employees from breaches of duty committed within the scope of employment.

The Restatement (Second) of Agency provides that "[a]n agent is subject to liability for loss caused to the principal by any breach of duty." Restatement (Second) of Agency § 401. The Restatement includes no exception for acts performed in the scope of employment. On the contrary, it states "[A] servant, who, while acting within the scope of employment, negligently injures a third person, although personally liable to such person, is also subject to liability to the principal if the principal is thereby required to pay damages." *Id.*, cmt. d. Under the Restatement, an employer may also sue an employee for contribution and breach of contract. *Id.* ("Where the negligence of both principal and agent combine in causing loss to a third person, the principal has a right to contribution in states in which this is permitted between tortfeasors."); *id.*, § 400.

Thus, while the determination that Nowak was Kramer's employee is relevant to certain issues considered below, it does not require that the suit be dismissed. . . .

VI. Kramer's Tort Claim

. . . Despite the many failings of the complaint, I construe the negligence allegation as asserting the following: that Nowak, as Kramer's employee, owed Kramer the various duties owed by an agent to his principal. These duties include what the Restatement of Agency terms the "duty of care and skill." Restatement (Second) of Agency § 379. Under this principle, "a paid agent is subject to a duty to the principal to act with standard care and with the skill which is standard in the locality for the kind of work which he is employed to perform and, in addition, to exercise any special skill that he has." *Id.*, § 379(1). Nowak allegedly violated this duty in calculating the prejudgment interest motion. . . .

2. Whether a Law Firm Partner May Sue an Associate for Negligence

An attorney's overriding duty is to the client. . . Because of the importance of the duty owed by attorneys to their clients, a court should be very cautious about concluding that, in representing a client, an attorney may also owe duties to persons other than the client. Kramer's tort claim—alleging that Nowak, in his work for Lightning Lube, breached a duty owed to Kramer—asks this court to recognize a duty owed by subordinate attorneys to their supervisors, the breach of which can subject the subordinate to liability for negligence.

Unfortunately, very few cases have examined whether associates in a law firm may be liable to the firm or the firm's partners for negligence in fulfilling their employment duties. One commentator has stated that "[l]awsuits between associates and law firms are virtually nonexistent, in part because malpractice insurance policies cover both the partners and the associates of the law firm." Leonard Gross, *Ethical Problems of Law Firm Associates,* 26 Wm. & Mary L.Rev. 259, 315 n. 22 (1985). . . .

The only case that has examined the question thoroughly is *Pollack v. Lytle,* 120 Cal.App.3d 931 (1981). In *Pollack,* a divided panel of the California court of appeals concluded that an attorney could bring a claim for breach of fiduciary duty and fraud against another attorney he had hired to assist in the prosecution of a medical malpractice claim. In the underlying medical malpractice litigation, William Pollack represented the plaintiff. During the course of his representation, Pollack realized that the case would require expert testimony from a neurological surgeon. Aware that Pollack was having difficulty finding a surgeon to serve as expert, Robert Lytle approached Pollack and falsely represented that he had a close friend who was a neurological surgeon and who would be willing to testify on plaintiff's behalf on the condition that Lytle be made trial counsel. Pollack agreed to this arrangement. Lytle then bungled the case in a variety of ways, preventing the client from accepting a $250,000 settlement and losing a jury verdict through his trial errors. Following defeat in the medical malpractice action, the plaintiff sued Pollack for legal malpractice. While the legal malpractice suit was pending, Pollack sued Lytle for breach of fiduciary duty, breach of contract, legal malpractice, and for a declaration of a right to indemnity. The trial court sustained Lytle's demurrer and Pollack appealed.

A divided appellate court reversed. The opinion of the court began its analysis by concluding that Lytle had been Pollack's agent in the prosecution of the underlying action. Making liberal use of the Restatement (Second) of Agency, the court then listed the duties owed by agents to their principals: the duty to provide diligent and faithful service, the duty to use reasonable care and skill, and the duty not to compete with the principal. The court found that Lytle's conduct in the litigation had breached these duties. . . .

Concluding that ordinary principles of tort and agency law dictated a finding of liability in favor of Pollack, the court then examined whether public policy counseled against imposing liability on an attorney for a breach of duty owed to another attorney. The court found that although an attorney's primary duty must be to the client, this duty was not compromised by imposing liability for breach of the duties owed to the principal attorney:

> Admittedly, [the associate attorney] remains bound to act in the best interests of the client, but this creates no unavoidable conflict.

> Should he find that the principal attorney's actions to date pose a potential danger to the client's best interests, the agent-associate is duty bound to make the fullest disclosure of these material facts to the principal attorney. Since the principal attorney and the associate each owes the duty of loyalty to the client, the disclosure of information which reveals a potential danger to the client's interests will normally prompt the principal attorney to act in protection of those interests. However, should the principal attorney choose to ignore the client's interests, the agent-associate remains free to terminate the agency relationship and withdraw as associate counsel. Furthermore, the associate attorney's duty to exercise reasonable professional care, skill and diligence on behalf of the client is precisely equivalent to the duty he owes his principal in dealing with the subject matter of the agency. Accordingly, public policy considerations do not mandate that an associate attorney remain free from liability for a breach of the duty owed to his principal. To the contrary, whether associate counsel is brought in from outside the principal attorney's office or is the junior associate in a firm of attorneys, the problems inherent in allowing an agent-associate to act in conflict with or contradiction of the principal attorney are manifest. Holding that an associate attorney owes no duty to anyone but the client would create the potential for a battle of wills over promotion of the client's interests, a situation which could well redound to the client's detriment, for the determination of a client's best interests is at best a subjective value judgment upon which reasonable minds could differ. Moreover, in view of the principal attorney's liability for the acts of subordinate counsel under the doctrine of respondeat superior, it would be manifestly unfair to relieve an agent-associate of accountability to his principal.

Id. at 942–43. The *Pollack* court thus concluded that public policy allows suits between supervising and associate attorneys for three reasons: (1) because no conflict arises between an associates' dual duties to their clients and to their employers, (2) because unnecessary conflicts between associates and partners would arise if associates owed their supervisors no duties, and (3) because imposing liability on associates to partners for the associate's negligence is the necessary corollary to the liability of partners to clients for an associate's negligence.

Dissenting, Justice Johnson concluded that the duty owed by an attorney to a client is unduly threatened by recognizing duties owed by attorneys to their employers. In reaching this conclusion, Justice Johnson drew on a series of cases in which California courts held that an attorney who takes over a case in the midst of litigation owes no duty to the predecessor attorney. . . .

The *Pollack* majority . . . concludes that there can be no genuine conflicts between the duty an associate owes to the client and the duties owed to the firm; these duties, the court states, are "precisely equivalent." I agree with dissenting Justice Johnson that conflicts of duty are quite possible if attorneys are deemed to owe duties to those other than their clients. For instance, a law firm may choose to devote more resources to cases that appear likely to generate high revenues than to cases with less money-making potential. An associate instructed to devote her time to the high-revenue case may be faced with a conflict between the duty she owes her employer and the duty she owes her low-revenue clients. . . .

The conclusion that attorneys may experience conflicting duties owed to employers and clients does not, however, lead to the conclusion that only a duty to clients should be recognized. Under general principles of agency law, an agent may have duties both to the principal and to third persons, such as customers. *See* Restatement (Second) of Agency §§ 320–62 (setting out the duties and potential liabilities of agents to third persons) and §§ 376–431 (setting out the duties and potential liabilities of agents to principals). Employees in many fields, such as medicine, teaching, and psychotherapy, owe strong and legally cognizable duties to those they serve. Recognition of these duties, however, does not mean that employees in these fields owe no duties to anyone else. To hold that an agent attorney owes a duty only to the client, and is not subject to liability to a principal attorney, would be to create an exception to the general principles of agency law that would apparently be unique to the legal profession.

The effect of creating such an exception would be to immunize from liability the torts committed by subordinate attorneys against their employers. Associate attorneys would only need to be concerned with misconduct which rises to the level that a client would regard as malpractice. Yet examples of misconduct performed in legal representation can be imagined in which the primary injury is suffered by the employer, not the client. For instance, an associate blunder in a case generating considerable publicity could cause the law firm to suffer a loss to its reputation more damaging than the harm done to the client. Of course, the threat of termination and the promise of advancement provide associates considerable incentives to perform their jobs well. Yet these incentives are present in all other fields of employment, while employees in other fields also have the deterrent provided by the possibility of suit brought by their employers. Because I can find no reason why lawyer employees—and no others—should be exempt from the possibility of suit brought by their employers, I conclude that, under generally applicable principles of agency, supervising attorneys may sue subordinate attorneys for their negligence in representing clients. . .

3. Whether the Complaint States a Cause of Action for Negligence

. . . Kramer affirmed and ratified Nowak's calculation by authorizing the motion to be filed with the court under Kramer's name. *See* Restatement of Agency § 82–104 (discussing effects of a principal's ratification of an agent's negligence). As the Restatement (Second) of Agency states: "*Unless he has been authorized to act in the manner in which he acts,* the agent who subjects the principal to liability because of a negligent or other wrongful act is subject to liability to the principal for the loss which results therefrom." Restatement (Second) of Agency § 401 cmt. d (emphasis added). It would appear that in delegating to Nowak the preparation of a motion bearing Kramer's signature, Kramer authorized Nowak to act as he did and thus that Nowak is not subject to liability for the preparation of the motion.

One can, however, imagine a case in which the negligence of a subordinate attorney in preparing a motion would not be apparent upon the reasonable inquiry of the signing attorney. It is true that Kramer has neither alleged nor brought forward any evidence to suggest that this is such a case. . . . [but] summary judgment is as yet inappropriate because Kramer may have construed plaintiff's motion as one for dismissal rather than summary judgment. In order to survive this motion, Kramer must produce evidence that creates a genuine issue of fact as to (1) whether Kramer ratified Nowak's alleged negligence and (2) whether the miscalculation of prejudgment interest could have been discovered through the reasonable inquiry required by Rule 11. The former addresses the nature of the relationship between Kramer and Nowak—and thus whether, in delegating the task of calculating the prejudgment interest, Kramer authorized Nowak to act as he did, thus relieving Nowak of liability. The latter addresses the difficulty of discovering the miscalculation—and thus whether Kramer violated his nondelegable duty to reasonably investigate the law and facts upon which the motion bearing his name was based. . . . .

Note the court's (quite correct) rejection of Nowak's claim that because his firm would be liable for his negligence, he could not be. It seems to be a standard misconception that vicarious liability—the principle that a principal is liable for harm an agent causes within the course and scope of his employment—works in reverse, exculpating the agent. It does not. Judge Posner put the point this way:

> a lawyer cannot insulate himself from a malpractice suit by incorporating. But neither can an individual who uses his position in a business corporation to commit a tort. Suppose a corporate employee in furtherance of his employment bribes the purchasing officer of one of his corporation's customers. The customer (if harmed by the bribe) can sue the corporation—but he can also sue the employee who did the bribing. "It is a common misunderstanding that the principle of limited liability protects the shareholders and officers of a corpora-

tion for liability for their own wrongful acts. It does not. It protects them from derivative liability, that is, from being called to account for the wrongs of the corporation."

Hoagland ex rel. Midwest Transit, Inc. v. Sandberg, Phoenix & von Gontard, P.C., 385 F.3d 737, 742 (7th Cir. 2004)

For a California case involving an action against a senior attorney who was not a partner (and thus was an employee), see *Cassady v. Morgan, Lewis & Bockius*, 145 Cal.App.4th 220, 223 (2006). Cassady was a lawyer who had worked at several different firms while representing a client, who followed him from firm to firm. The client then sued Cassady and Morgan, Lewis for breach of contract, breach of fiduciary duty, malpractice, and related claims. Cassady eventually sued Morgan, Lewis for indemnity. The court of appeals held that Cassady bore the burden of demonstrating that the defense costs for which he claimed reimbursement were incurred in defending acts that occurred while he worked at Morgan, Lewis.

What Do You Mean It's a Service Business?

While we are on the topic of practical advice, a few comments on law as a service business are appropriate. Lawyers don't sell widgets, they serve their clients' needs; junior lawyers serve the needs of senior lawyers as well. Many ethical problems stem from the tension between providing a service, which implies responding to and meeting demands as fast, efficiently, and fully as you can, and adhering to ethical rules. A major goal of this text is to introduce that tension to you and give you a sense of how to handle it.

It should be obvious, though, that the tension between service and ethics does not exhaust the notion of providing good service, which you have to do if you want to do well as a lawyer. What does it mean to provide good service and how, as a practical matter, do you do it?

A famous study at Bell Labs provides useful advice on these questions. As reported in an article by Professor William D. Henderson, *Are We Selling Results or Resumes?: The Underexplored Linkage Between Human Resource Strategies and Firm–Specific Capital*, Indiana Legal Studies Research Paper 105, Bell Labs studied its own engineers to determine why some were more productive than others.

The study presented some interesting design problems. One was to identify the subject group—who determined who was a star? The researchers eventually polled engineers themselves, to get a peer assessment, the managers for whom they worked, and, eventually, customers for whom they worked. Once the researchers identified the star group, they drew up three general categories of 45 different cognitive, personal, and social characteristics. They then tested both the stars and some average employees; they found no correlation between the 45 categories and being a star.

Undaunted, the researchers spent the next two years studying the engineers. They eventually came up with a set of nine work *strategies* they believed distinguished star from ordinary performers. Professor Henderson summarizes the findings, in order of relative importance:

> "(1) *Taking initiative.* Top performers took responsibility above and beyond their stated jobs, volunteering for new activities and promoting new ideas;
>
> (2) *Networking.* Top performers were deft at tapping into coworkers' expertise and shared their own knowledge with those that needed it;
>
> (3) *Self–Management.* Top performers were very good at regulating their own work commitments, time, performance level, and career growth;
>
> (4) *Perspective.* Top performers understood their jobs within the larger context of the organization and could analyze problems from the viewpoint of customers, managers and team members;
>
> (5) *Followership.* Although perceived by others as leaders, top performers excelled at setting aside their own agendas and using their talents to help other leaders accomplish the organization's goals;
>
> (6) *Teamwork.* Top performers were more willing to assume joint 'ownerhsip' of goals setting, group commitments, work activities, schedules, and defusing conflict among group members;
>
> (7) *Leadership.* Top performers had the ability to formulate, state, and build consensus on common goals and then work to accomplish them;
>
> (8) *Organizational Savvy.* Top performers recognized and thus could navigate competing interests within an organization
>
> (9) *Show-and-tell.* Top performers typically had the ability to present their ideas persuasively in written or oral form."

Henderson also notes that average workers drew the wrong lessons from the success of star performers.

> For example, average performers tended to invert the order of priority and thus focus on organizational savvy and show-and-tell, which they surmised was the key . . . similarly, middle performers tended to view initiative (the most important work strategy) as doing tasks that will get noticed by superiors, whereas top performers viewed it as action and follow-through that help coworkers or the organization succeed. Likewise, middle performers viewed networking as staying

"in the loop" on office gossip and getting to know people who could help their careers. Top performers, in contrast, viewed networking as a bartering system in which the cost of admission was technical expertise, and staying in required a sincere commitment to be reciprocal over the long term.

MATTER OF HOWES

123 N.M. 311 (1997)

[For the facts of the case see chapter 12.A]

I. The applicability of Rule 16–502(B) to respondent's actions.

Respondent first argues that New Mexico's Rule 16–502(B) should control the resolution of this case. This rule states that "a subordinate lawyer does not violate the Rules of Professional Conduct if that lawyer acts in accordance with a supervisory lawyer's reasonable resolution of an arguable question of professional duty." It is respondent's contention that he was a "subordinate lawyer" within the meaning of this rule and that, as such, he was not only entitled but also obligated to rely upon the advice given to him by the chief and deputy chief of the felony section with respect to the calls generated by defendant. Consequently, he asserts, his actions must be excused. Respondent's position fails for several reasons.

First of all, Rule 16–502(B) must be read in connection with Rule 16–502(A), which directs that "a lawyer is bound by the Rules of Professional Conduct notwithstanding that the lawyer acted at the direction of another person." The ABA Comment to Model Rule 5.2 makes it clear that the rule, taken as a whole, is not meant to immunize attorneys from accountability for their misconduct.[5]

Respondent has cited no cases, and we are aware of none, which hold for the proposition that an attorney may be exonerated from the consequences of his or her misconduct simply on the basis that the unethical acts were committed upon another's instructions or authorization. The few reported cases on this topic uphold the theory that an attorney is always answerable for his or her own actions. As one court has noted:

> When others are involved in misconduct with counsel, degrees of culpability may vary, but ultimate responsibility does not. Counsel simply cannot delegate to others their own duty to act responsibly . . . [in] the end, each member of the bar is an officer of the court.

---

[5] FN3. The ABA Comment begins with the admonition that "although a lawyer is not relieved of responsibility for a violation by the fact that the lawyer acted at the direction of a supervisor, that fact may be relevant in determining whether a lawyer had the knowledge required to render conduct a violation of the Rules."

> His or her first duty is not to the client or the senior partner, but to the administration of justice.

Roberts v. Lyons, 131 F.R.D. 75, 84 (E.D.Pa.1990) citing *Coburn Optical Indus., Inc. v. Cilco,* 610 F.Supp. 656, 661 (M.D.N.C.1985); *see also McCurdy v. Kansas Dep't of Transp.,* 21 Kan.App.2d 262 (1995) ("[A] lawyer is not relieved of his or her responsibility for a violation of the rules of professional conduct just because he or she acted at the direction of a supervisor," citing the Comment to Rule 5.2).

Even more compelling, however, is that in this instance there was no "arguable question of professional duty" needing resolution. Respondent has argued that various memoranda generated in-house at the Department of Justice prior to his actions took the position that federal prosecutors are not bound by state disciplinary rules prohibiting communication with represented persons and has submitted these documents as exhibits to the record. We are not persuaded that an attorney's employer, even though that employer may be an attorney or an arm of the United States government, can create an "arguable question of professional duty" within the meaning of Rule 16–502(B) by the simple mechanism of unilaterally declaring that a particular rule of conduct is burdensome and should not apply to its employees.

In further support of his position that such an arguable question exists, respondent has cited numerous articles on the subject of whether or not federal prosecutors should be bound by state ethical rules. While we recognize that a debate currently rages regarding the applicability of ABA Model Rule 4.2 to federal prosecutors, all of the articles cited by respondent were published between 1990 and 1996 and were no doubt occasioned in part by former Attorney General Richard Thornburgh's *Memorandum* of June 8, 1989, which discussed the applicability of Rule 4.2 to federal prosecutors and which itself was issued after respondent's acts of misconduct. Respondent's duty to refrain from communicating with a represented criminal defendant is not subject to argument. According to the ABA Comment to Model Rule 5.2, if a question of ethical duty can be answered in only one way, "the duty of both lawyers is clear and they are equally responsible for fulfilling it."

Even if one were to accept the premise that an arguable question of professional duty with respect to Rule 16–402 existed in November 1988, it is apparent from the record of these proceedings that the discussions respondent had with the chief of the felony section regarding defendant's calls bore only a tangential relationship to respondent's ethical duties. The chief testified under oath that his "primary concern as a supervisor was whether the evidence was constitutionally admissible" and that he "would have focused on the constitutional issues involved in contacts between a defendant and a law enforcement representative; that is, I would have been focusing on his Fifth Amendment right to be silent, his Sixth

Amendment right to counsel." Additionally, it is not clear from the testimony of the chief and deputy chief that they were even aware that respondent himself was communicating with defendant. Clearly respondent was not seeking advice as to his ethical obligations to defendant and to the public defender; any passing consideration of these duties which may have arisen was secondary to the primary question of how to obtain admissible evidence from defendant.

Rule 16–502 cannot and does not excuse respondent's conduct. . . .

The Main Points to Recall From Chapter 13 Are:

- You owe duties to your firm, as an agent of your firm, as well as to your client.
- You must discharge both sets of duties simultaneously.
- For purposes of discipline you may rely on reasonable judgment calls of supervising attorneys.
- If you need supervision or assistance of a more experienced attorney to discharge your duty of care to a client, the duty of care requires you to get it.

CHAPTER 14

SOME ECONOMICS OF PRACTICE

■ ■ ■

Money gets people's attention. Disciplinary rules governing how you deal with money are strict and tend to be strictly enforced. Penalties for breaking those rules are harsh.

The basic rules require that you only charge a reasonable fee. Like most standards relying on the term "reasonable," this one incorporates a multi-factor test that is not notably precise. Other rules depend on whether money in your possession belongs to you or your client. (Lawyers often hold money belonging to clients, as when they receive a retainer in advance or accept a check in settlement of a case, all or part of which is to be paid to the client.) You must segregate your own money from your client's money and never intermingle the two. You must never take money you have not earned, and when you take money you have earned you must make clear how you earned it.

A. FEES

Model Rule 1.15(a) requires that you hold client property in your possession separate from your own property. The rule requires that money belonging to a client or third party be kept in an account (called a trust account) separate from your firm's general business account or your personal account. Rule 1.15(b) forbids you from depositing your own money in the trust account unless the deposit is to pay service charges on the account and is in an amount no greater than such charges. Rule 1.15(c) requires that all advance payments for fees or expenses be placed in the trust account and withdrawn (generally to be deposited in your firm's general operating account) only when fees are earned or expenses incurred. To make sense of these rules it helps to understand what different types of fee arrangements exist, and we start with a basic survey of those types.

1. WHAT TYPES OF FEES ARE THERE?

Model Rule of Professional Conduct 1.15
Cal. R. Prof. Conduct 4–100
Cal. Code Civ. P. § 1021
Cal. Bus & Prof. Code § 6091

Within certain bounds, such as the requirement that fees be reasonable, lawyers and clients are free to negotiate fee terms acceptable to them. These terms are important because there are different types of fees, and the type of fee at issue may affect analysis of whether the fee was reasonable. Clarity is key, and it is your job to be clear.

As described by the court in *In re Montgomery Drilling Co.*, 121 B.R. 32 (Bkrtcy.E.D. Cal. 1990), there are three basic types of fees:

> Essentially, three types of retainers exist, being (1) Classic or True Retainers, (2) Security Retainers, and (3) Advance Payment Retainers. Classic Retainers refer to the payment of a sum of money to secure availability over a period of time. Entitlement to the fee exists whether or not services are ever rendered. . . . The other two types of retainers are the Security Retainers and Advance Payment Retainers. The Security Retainer is typified by the fact that the retainer will be held by the attorneys to secure payment of fees for future services that the attorneys are expected to render. In such an agreement, the money given as a retainer is not present payment for future services. Rather, it remains property of the Debtor until the attorney applies it to charges for services actually rendered, and any unearned funds are returned to the Debtor.
>
> The third type of retainer, the Advance Payment Retainer, is an agreement whereby the Debtor pays, in advance, for some or all of the services that the attorney is expected to perform on the Debtor's behalf. This type of retainer differs from the Security Retainer in that ownership to the funds is intended to pass to the attorney at the time of payment. Under California law, the issue of whether ownership of these funds passes to the attorney upon receipt is largely undecided. See *Katz v. Workers' Compensation Appeals Board,* 30 Cal.3d 353, 356 fn. 2 (1981); *Baranowski v. State Bar,* 24 Cal.3d 153, 164 (1979).

The distinctions among these types of fees are very important. If money is yours, as with a true retainer, then the client has no entitlement to it and you do not have to deposit it in a client trust account. You can put it in your account or the firm's general account (assuming you comply with your duties to your firm) and use it as you see fit. If it is not yours, as with a security retainer, you must segregate the money in a trust account and withdraw it only when you have earned it. Failure to do so is a serious ethical violation.

T & R Foods, Inc. v. Rose, 47 Cal. App. 4th Supp. 1, 4 (1996), which recites the *Montgomery Drilling* language, exemplifies the point. In that case a client paid a lawyer a $25,000. The lawyer died and the client sued to recover the unearned portion of that money (over $24,000). The question was whether the fee agreement was a true retainer, in which case the money belonged to the lawyer as soon as he got it and the client had no interest in it, or an advance payment retainer, in which case the money belonged to the client, with the lawyer (and his estate) holding it in trust for the client.

The retainer agreement stated "[o]n employment, we request a $25,000 retainer. Fees will be charged against the retainer. The retainer is to be replenished monthly to maintain a $25,000 credit toward fees." According to the court, "[t]his language clearly shows that the $25,000 retainer was not a classic retainer, but rather an advance payment retainer. We conclude therefore that rule 4–100 required such funds to be segregated until earned."

Some cases limit the ability of lawyers to contract with clients to treat advance payments as true retainers. In other words, a contract term stipulating that a payment is earned on receipt is not effective if the payment is for the lawyer's work in a particular matter rather than simply to secure the lawyer's availability, as is the case with the true retainer. *See Matthew v. State Bar*, 49 Cal.3d 784, 789 (1989) (faulting lawyer for refusing to return unearned portion of retainer dubbed "non-refundable" in parties' agreement); *In re Phillips,* 4 Cal. State Bar Ct. Rptr. 315 (2001) (same).

California law is not fully clear on whether an advance payment retainer must be placed in a trust account. There is an unquestionable duty to account for such funds, however, *In the Matter of Fonte,* 2 Cal. State Bar Ct. Rptr. 752, 756–758 (1994), and placing such funds in a trust account is the simplest way to discharge that duty.

Related issues may arise if there is a dispute over who is entitled to money the lawyer holds. Suppose a lawyer settles a case for a client she represents pursuant to a contingent fee agreement and receives $1 million from the defendant. Suppose further that the lawyer and client disagree about how the lawyer's share of the fee should be calculated under the agreement. What are the lawyer's obligations with respect to the $1 million? Alternatively, suppose the lawyer is aware that the client promised a third party a share of the client's recovery in exchange for assistance with the case. (Suppose the client speaks poor English and the third party serves as a translator and advisor.) Suppose the lawyer receives the $1 million and the client instructs the lawyer to pay the client the client's full share, without regard to the claims of the third party. What are the lawyer's duties then?

Model Rule 1.15(d) provides that when a lawyer receives money, as in these examples, the lawyer must notify the client and any third person who has an interest in the money (or other property) and deliver to the client or third person any money or property they are "entitled to receive." Rule 1.15(e) provides that if there is a dispute about who is entitled to what the lawyer must distribute any portion of the money or property that is not in dispute and segregate the property as to which there is a dispute, generally by keeping it in the lawyer's trust account. This provision applies both to disputes in which the lawyer has a claim and disputes solely between a client and a third party.

In the first hypothetical problem, therefore, a lawyer could pay from her trust account to her general operating account any amount of the fee that both she and the client agreed the lawyer was owed. Thus, suppose the dispute was whether the lawyer's contingent percentage was 20% or 30%. Assuming both the client and lawyer agreed the lawyer was entitled to at least 20% the lawyer could transfer that amount to her operating account but could not transfer the incremental 10%. That would have to stay in the trust account until the dispute was resolved.

As to the second hypothetical problem, the comment to Rule 1.15(e) provides that the standard for assessing disputes between a client and a third party is whether the third party's claim is frivolous. If it is not, the lawyer must hold the money and not pay it to the client. When there is a substantial dispute, the lawyer may file an action to have a court resolve it. *See, e.g.*, Wisconsin State Bar Professional Ethics Comm., Op. E–09–01.

Trust Account Basics

What's all this about a trust account? The *Handbook on Client Trust Accounting for California Attorneys* offers the following summary:

> All funds you receive from or hold for a client must be deposited into a bank account that is clearly labeled as a client trust bank account.
>
> When you receive other properties on behalf of a client, you have to identify what you've received in your written records, actually label the properties to identify the owner, and immediately put them into a safe deposit box or some other place of safe keeping. . . . .
>
> Whenever you receive money or other property on behalf of a client, you have to promptly notify that client of that fact.

> You can't *deposit* any money belonging to you or your law firm into any of your client trust bank accounts (except for the small amounts of money necessary to cover bank charges). This is known as commingling.
>
> You can't *keep* any money belonging to you or your law firm (other than money for bank charges) in any of your client trust bank accounts. This is also known as commingling. That means that when you're holding client money that includes your fees, you have to take those fees out of the client trust bank account *as you earn them.* It's not a matter of your convenience; you are ethically required to withdraw your money from that account as soon as you reasonably can. (In fact, it would be a good idea for you to withdraw your fees on a regular basis, perhaps when you do your monthly reconciliation. . . .)
>
> Money held in a client trust bank account becomes yours and not the client's as soon as, in the words of rule 4–100(A)(2), your "interest in that portion becomes fixed." BUT—and this is a big but—you can't withdraw any fees that the client disputes. As far as you're concerned, from the moment a client disputes your fee, that money is frozen in the client trust bank account until the fee dispute is resolved. As soon as your interest becomes fixed and is not in dispute, you are obligated to withdraw that money promptly from the client trust bank account. . . .
>
> When your clients ask you for money or other properties that you're holding for them, you must deliver them promptly.
>
> When clients ask you how much money you're holding for them or what you've done with the money while you've had it, you must tell them.
>
> When the State Bar asks you how much money you're holding for the client or what you've done with it while you've had it, you must tell the State Bar.
>
> For at least five years after disbursement you have to keep complete records of all client money, securities or other properties that are entrusted to you.

In addition, if a client gives you a small amount of money, or a large amount of money for a very short time, such that the cost of allocating interest to the client would exceed the amount of interest, you must place the money in a common client account. Cal. Bus. & Prof. Code §§ 6211–6213. Interest on that account—called an "IOLTA" account ("Interest on Lawyer's Trust Account") is paid to the state bar, which uses it to fund various programs. If client money can generate sufficient interest to make allocation of that interest sensible, of course, then the interest belongs to the client. It is never yours.

Although you may have only one client trust account, each client's money is her own. You may never use the money of one client to pay another. And, if you follow the rules of trust accounting, you should never be in a position where you will need to.

In re Sather, 3 P.3d 403, 405 (Colo. 2000), illustrates the importance of making sure up front that you and the client understand how a payment will be treated. In that case the Colorado Supreme Court dealt with an attorney who accepted a $20,000 flat fee in advance of filing a civil rights suit. The attorney later declared personal bankruptcy and was suspended from practice. He acknowledged his client was entitled to a partial refund of fees but he failed to refund the fees promptly, as required by Colorado's rule 1.16.

The court interpreted Colorado's Rule 1.15 to establish a default rule under which "an attorney earns fees by conferring a benefit on or performing a legal service for the client. . . . thus an attorney cannot treat advance fees as property of the attorney and must segregate all advance fees by placing them into a trust account until such time as the fees are earned." The court also held that "[a]n attorney cannot label advance fees "non-refundable" because it misleads the client and risks impermissibly burdening the client's right to discharge his attorney, in violation of Colo. RPC 8.4(c) and 1.16(d)." Excerpts from the opinion follow:

The rule requiring that an attorney segregate funds advanced by the client from the attorney's own funds serves important interests. As a fiduciary to the client, one of an attorney's primary responsibilities is to safeguard the interests and property of the client over which the attorney has control. Requiring the attorney to segregate all client funds—including advance fees—from the attorney's own accounts unless and until the funds become the attorney's property protects the client's property from the attorney's creditors and from misuse by the attorney. Thus, Colo. RPC 1.15(a) and (f) further the attorney's fiduciary obligation to protect client property.

In addition to protecting client property, requiring an attorney to keep advance fees in trust until they are earned protects the client's right to discharge an attorney. *See* Colo. RPC 1.16(d) cmt. ("A client has a right to discharge an attorney at any time, with or without cause, subject to liability for payment for the lawyer's services."). Upon discharge, the attorney must return all unearned fees in a timely manner, even though the attorney may be entitled to quantum meruit recovery for the services that the attorney rendered and for costs incurred on behalf of the client.

If an attorney suggests to a client that any pre-paid or advance funds are "non-refundable" or constitute the attorney's property regardless of how much or how little work the attorney performs for the client, then the client may fear loss of the funds and may refrain from exercising his right to discharge the attorney. Because the unearned portion of the advance fees must be kept in trust and cannot be treated as the attorney's property until earned, the client will not risk forfeiting fees for work to be performed in the future if the client chooses to discharge his attorney. Thus, the requirement that the attorney place advance fees in trust protects the client's right to discharge his attorney. . . .

When a client pays an attorney before the attorney provides legal services, the crucial issue becomes whether funds are "earned on receipt" and may be treated as the attorney's property, or whether the fees are unearned, in which case the funds must be segregated in a trust account under Colo. RPC 1.15. As one publication aptly framed this dilemma:

The basic question is, Whose money is it? If it's the client's money in whole or in part, it is subject to the trust account requirements. If it is the lawyer's money, placing it into a trust account would violate the anti-commingling rule.

. . . . We hold that an attorney earns fees only by conferring a benefit on or performing a legal service for the client. Unless the attorney provides some benefit or service in exchange for the fee, the attorney has not earned any fees and, with a possible exception in very limited circumstances, the attorney cannot treat advance fees as her property. . . .

Some forms of advance fees or retainers appropriately compensate an attorney when the fee is paid because the attorney makes commitments to the client that benefit the client immediately. Such an arrangement is termed a "general retainer" or "engagement retainer," and these retainers typically compensate an attorney for agreeing to take a case, which requires the attorney to commit his time to the client's case and causes the attorney to forego other potential employment opportunities as a result of time commitments or conflicts. Although an attorney usually earns an engagement retainer by agreeing to take the client's case, an attorney can also earn a fee charged as an engagement retainer by placing the client's work at the top of the attorney's priority list. Or the client may pay an engagement retainer merely to prevent the attorney from being available to represent an opposing party. . . . In all of these instances, the attorney is providing some benefit to the client in exchange for the engagement retainer fee.

In contrast to engagement retainers, a client may advance funds—often referred to as "advance fees," "special retainers," "lump sum fees," or "flat fees"—to pay for specified legal services to be performed by the attorney and to cover future costs. . . . We note that unless the fee agreement expressly states that a fee is an engagement retainer and explains how the fee is earned upon receipt, we will presume that any advance fee is a deposit from which an attorney will be paid for specified legal services. . . .

In the case of both advance fees and engagement retainers, the attorney performs a service or provides a benefit to the client in exchange for the fee. We recognize that we have not previously explained the ethical principle that determines when an attorney may treat funds paid as engagement retainers or advance fees as property of the attorney. Because this principle is a crucial element of the attorney-client relationship, we make our interpretation of the underlying ethical principle explicit: an attorney earns a fee only when the attorney provides a benefit or service to the client. . . . Under Colo. RPC 1.15(a) and (f), all client funds—including engagement retainers, advance fees, flat fees, lump sum fees, etc.—must be held in trust until there is a basis on which to conclude that the attorney "earned" the fee; otherwise, the funds must remain in the client's trust account because they are not the attorney's property.

With respect to fees mutually agreed to be "earned on receipt," an attorney must describe in writing the nature of the benefit being provided to a specific client in order to claim some portion or all of an engagement retainer as earned when paid. . . . That is, an attorney cannot treat a fee as "earned" simply by labeling the fee "earned on receipt" or referring to the fee as an "engagement retainer." *See Wong v. Michael Kennedy, P.C.,* 853 F.Supp. 73, 81 (E.D.N.Y.1994). Rather, the attorney must explain in detail the nature of the benefit being conferred on the client, whether it is the attorney's guarantee of availability, prioritization of the client's work, or some other appropriate consideration. . . .

Having discussed the ethical principle requiring that attorneys maintain in trust all advance fees until the attorney earns the fees, we address Sather's characterization of his fee as "non-refundable." Because fees are always subject to refund under certain conditions, labeling a fee "non-refundable" misleads the client and may deter a client from exercising their rights to refunds of unearned fees under Colo. 1.16(d). Thus, we hold that attorneys cannot enter into "non-refundable" retainer or fee agreements. . . .

Attorney fees are always subject to refund if they are excessive or unearned. . . . A fee agreement that suggests that advance fees are "non-refundable" undermines the client's understanding of her rights and may discourage a client from seeking refunds to which the client may be entitled. . . .

In addition to misinforming the client, "non-refundable fees" may discourage the client from discharging his attorney for fear that the client will not be able to recover advance fees for which the attorney has yet to perform any work. *See Cooperman,* 611 N.Y.S.2d 465. Because the label is inaccurate and misleading, and discourages a client from exercising the right to discharge an attorney, we hold that attorneys may not enter into "non-refundable fee" agreements or otherwise communicate to their clients that the fees are "non-refundable." . . .

We acknowledge that in some instances a client may agree with an attorney to allow the attorney to treat funds paid in advance of legal services or other consideration as property of the attorney and thus not subject to the trust account requirements. . . .

In the limited circumstances in which an attorney earns fees before performing any legal services (i.e., engagement retainers) or where an attorney and client agree that the attorney can treat advance fees as the attorney's property before the attorney earns the fees by supplying a benefit or performing a service, the fee agreement must clearly explain the basis for this arrangement and explain how the client's rights are protected by the arrangement. In either of these situations, however, an attorney's fees are always subject to refund if excessive or unearned, and an attorney cannot communicate otherwise to a client. . . .

The following chart summarizes the three basic types of fees (though they go by more than three names), who owns them, and how they should be treated.

	True Retainer	**Security Retainer**	**Advance Payment**
Purpose	Secure availability (no work required)	Provide lawyer assurance that money will be there when earned	Pay lawyer up front for work to be performed later (may be flat fee or partial fee)
Belongs to	Lawyer, on receipt	Client; lawyer takes only when earned	Jurisdictions differ; Lawyer in CA but client under *Sather*
Deposit in	Firm or lawyer's account	Trust account only	Jurisdictions differ; advisable to deposit in trust account in all jurisdictions.

2. THE THIRD RAIL: TAKING WHAT YOU HAVEN'T EARNED

Here's a tip: Never, ever, **EVER** take client money you have not earned. Doing so is the third rail of legal ethics. The only question is how bad things will be. Consider:

MATTER OF WARHAFTIG

106 N.J. 529 (1987)

PER CURIAM

In this disciplinary proceeding, arising out of a presentment filed by the District XII Ethics Committee, respondent is charged with invading trust account funds by withdrawing anticipated legal fees in advance of real-estate closings. The Disciplinary Review Board (DRB or Board) concluded that respondent had engaged in unethical conduct, but that knowing misappropriation had not been established by clear and convincing evidence. The Board therefore recommended that respondent be publicly reprimanded. Because we conclude that respondent's conduct clearly constituted knowing misappropriation under *In re Wilson,* 81 *N.J.* 451 (1979), we decline to adopt the DRB's recommendation, and instead order that respondent be disbarred.

I

The charges filed against respondent were the result of a random compliance audit conducted by the Office of Attorney Ethics pursuant to *Rule* 1:21–6(c). The audit took place in November and December, 1983, and covered the two-year period ending on October 31st of the same year. The audit findings were summarized in the Board's Decision and Recommendation:

The audit disclosed that respondent

> continually issued checks to his own order for fees in pending real estate matters. He would replace the "advance" when the funds were received for the real estate closing [audit report at 3].

In one case, a real estate closing occurred on September 19, 1983. Funds totalling $70,722.33 were deposited into respondent's trust account on September 20, 1983. In another case, a real estate closing took place on October 28, 1983. The funds totalling $150,686.27 were deposited into his trust account on October 31, 1983. However, respondent had issued a check to his order for $910 on June 16, 1983 which represented his fee of $455 for each of these two closings. The audit report revealed other instances where respondent similarly took advance fees. A summary of these instances follows:

Fees Taken In Advance of Closings

Days in Advance

	1–30	30–60	60–90	90–120	120
Number of Instances	6	9	3	2	2
Total Withdrawn	$2,600	3,935	1,110	910	910

* * * * * *

Respondent maintained his own lists of fees taken in advance. This list contained the names of clients and the amounts he anticipated earning from these clients in pending real estate closings. As a closing occurred and the fee was earned, respondent would delete the client's name and fee. When an anticipated closing fell through, respondent would replace the fee he had earlier advanced to himself.

* * *

When respondent received notice of the audit, he contacted his accountant who advised him that if his trust account was short he should immediately replace the funds. Respondent borrowed $11,125 from accounts in the names of his two teenage sons and deposited the money into his trust account to cover the withdrawn fees. Respondent made this deposit about five days before the originally scheduled audit date of October 4, 1983.

The auditor was not able to determine which clients' monies respondent had taken because of the size of respondent's real estate practice. Money continually flowed in and out of the trust account. Respondent, at the ethics hearing, maintained that he never failed to make the proper disbursements at the closings and that no one ever lost money as a result of his practice. He discontinued this practice in September 1983 when he received notice of the audit.

At the Ethics Committee hearing, respondent explained that his withdrawal of advance fees from the trust account was necessitated by the "gigantic cash flow burden" he experienced beginning in the early 1980's. Such pressures were the result of a precipitous decline in his real-estate practice. At the same time, an additional strain on respondent's finances was created by his wife's having to undergo treatment for cancer, and by his son's need for extensive psychiatric counseling. According to respondent, only a small portion of these expenses was covered by insurance.

Respondent was also questioned at the hearing as to whether he knew, at the time the advance-fee scheme was implemented, that his conduct constituted an ethical violation. Respondent stated:

> I was aware that what I was doing was wrong, and I was also aware that no one was being hurt by what I was doing. And what I was doing, especially by keeping lists like this, was making sure that nobody would get hurt by what I was doing.
>
> * * *
>
> My perspective on the taking of the money was it was wrong, it was a violation of the rules. But I was so certain that no one could possibly be hurt by it that I didn't feel that I was stealing, certainly not stealing.

In a presentment filed on June 28, 1985, the Ethics Committee concluded that respondent had failed to comply with the record-keeping provisions of *Rule* 1:21–6; that several checks he had drawn on business accounts were dishonored for insufficient funds; that he had made false entries in his trust account records, contrary to *DR* 9–102; and that he had misappropriated clients' funds, also a violation of *DR* 9–102. Specifically, the presentment stated that "[r]espondent's conduct was clearly unethical in that he did deliberately and repeatedly take funds from his trust account equal to anticipated fees." The panel therefore recommended that respondent be publicly disciplined, but directed the attention of the DRB to several mitigating factors it found to be present in the case.

The DRB adopted these conclusions in its decision. Acknowledging that "[a] knowing act is required before any taking of funds warrants * * * disbarment [,]" the Board observed:

> Respondent believed that the funds taken by him were fees that he would invariably receive from real estate transactions. The modest amounts taken were exactly those that he anticipated. Although his business account had frequent overdrafts, there is absolutely no indication in this record that respondent ever used trust funds to cover them.
>
> * * *
>
> Respondent while acknowledging that his premature withdrawal of fees was improper, did not perceive it as misappropriation of clients' funds. He advanced to himself only such monies to which he had a colorable interest.

The Board concluded that the record did not support a finding that knowing misappropriation had occurred in this case. The Board, in recommending a public reprimand, also noted the existence of several mitigating factors: respondent's discontinuance of the practice at issue; his cooperation with the Office of Attorney Ethics; the acknowledgment of his wrongdoing; and the fact that no clients were actually injured by respondent's conduct. . . .

II

In recommending public discipline, the DRB recognized that *In re Wilson, supra,* which requires the disbarment of an attorney who knowingly misappropriates his clients' funds, controls the outcome of this case. However, the Board emphasized a perceived distinction between respondent's conduct, which it characterized as the "premature withdrawal of * * * monies to which he had a colorable interest[,]" and the knowing misappropriation described in *Wilson, supra.* Apparently, the Board was persuaded by respondent's contention that while he was aware that he was violating a Disciplinary Rule, he "didn't feel that [he] was stealing * * *."

The distinction drawn by the DRB cannot be sustained under the *Wilson* rule. As we stated in *In re Noonan,* 102 *N.J.* 157, 160 (1986), knowing misappropriation under *Wilson* "consists simply of a lawyer taking a client's money entrusted to him, knowing that it is the client's money and knowing that the client has not authorized the taking." We have consistently maintained that a lawyer's subjective intent, whether it be to "borrow" or to steal, is irrelevant to the determination of the appropriate discipline in a misappropriation case. In *Wilson, supra,* we articulated the reason for this strict approach:

> Lawyers who "borrow" may, it is true, be less culpable than those who had no intent to repay, but the difference is negligible in this connection. Banks do not rehire tellers who "borrow" depositors' funds. Our professional standards, if anything, should be higher. Lawyers are more than fiduciaries: they are representatives of a profession and officers of this Court. [81 *N.J.* at 458, 409 *A.*2d 1153.]

It is clear that respondent's conduct constituted knowing misappropriation as contemplated by *Wilson.* Through the use of the advance-fee mechanism, he took funds from his trust account before he had any legal right to those monies. These "fees" were taken by respondent before he received any deposits in connection with the relevant real-estate closings. Thus, he was effectively borrowing monies from one group of clients in order to compensate himself, in advance, for matters being handled for other clients. Respondent made these withdrawals with full recognition that his actions had not been authorized by his clients, and that he was therefore violating the rules governing attorney conduct. . . .

The DRB also based its decision on the existence of several mitigating factors. Our review of the record, in light of the plain language of *Wilson* and our subsequent decisions, compels the conclusion that these factors should be given little weight. The Board noted the fact that no client was injured by respondent's conduct, and that he replaced the funds he had misappropriated. However, we have emphasized in the past that the absence of client losses is irrelevant in a misappropriation case. The Board also pointed to respondent's having been a member of the Bar since 1968, and the evidence of his good character adduced at the ethics hearing. However, as we made clear in *Wilson, supra,* the prior outstanding record of an attorney cannot diminish the seriousness of misappropriation of client funds:

> This offense against common honesty should be clear even to the youngest; and to distinguished practitioners, its grievousness should be even clearer. [81 *N.J.* at 460, 409 *A.*2d 1153.]

The DRB also observed that respondent, in the three years since the audit occurred, had discontinued the practice of taking advance fees, and that recurrence of this practice would be extremely unlikely. Here again, our holding in *Wilson, supra,* makes consideration of this factor improper. Finally, the Board took note of respondent's cooperation with the investigation, and his acknowledgment of his guilt. While we acknowledge respondent's candor in admitting his wrongful conduct, we cannot accord it any significance as a mitigating factor.

In concluding that respondent's mishandling of his clients' trust funds requires that he be disbarred, we again confront the harsh results of the *Wilson* rule. We note the very real hardship that beset respondent's family and apparently led to his wrongful conduct. It is especially tragic that these unfortunate circumstances contributed to conduct requiring the disbarment of an attorney who, for the better part of his career, has conducted himself in an exemplary fashion.

Yet, we are also mindful that our primary purpose here is not to punish attorneys, but to protect the public. . . . . In our view, the overriding need "to preserve the confidence of the public in the integrity and trustworthiness of lawyers[,]" requires that we continue to apply the strictest discipline in misappropriation cases. Anything less would undermine the effectiveness of the *Wilson* rule and erode public confidence in the integrity of the legal profession.

Finally, while we understand that respondent's conduct was in large part the result of financial pressures caused by serious illness within his family, it appears that respondent had other sources of funds available to him. By his own admission, as soon as he was informed of the audit, respondent restored the deficit in his trust account with $11,125 borrowed from bank accounts in his sons' names. Respondent should have considered the availability of other sources of funds when his financial difficulty first arose. Instead, he misappropriated monies belonging to his clients, despite his knowledge that this practice constituted a violation of the rules governing attorney conduct.

In view of our conclusion that respondent knowingly misappropriated client funds, we order that he be disbarred. Respondent shall reimburse the Ethics Financial Committee for appropriate administrative costs.

Cash Flow, Cost Structures, Ethical Problems

Was Warhaftig a bad guy? Does he deserve to be disbarred? Would you trust him with your real estate deal? If you look at these questions abstractly—with an eye on the reputation of lawyers generally rather than just on Warhaftig—maybe these questions will seem easy. But Warhaftig himself seems less culpable than, for example, James O'Hagan, who stole from a client and traded on inside information to cover up the theft.

If you think Warhaftig is not a truly bad person, but a person who made a bad choice under extremely trying conditions, and then had the bad luck to be caught in a random audit of his trust account, then you have to ask why he did it. From an economic point of view the answer is that Warhaftig's costs were too high in relation to his income. He could not wait for deals to close; he had bills to pay. He "knew" he would not hurt anyone and, unlike many people who say such things, he didn't.

Warhaftig's example offers a lesson, which is no less true for being familiar. If you don't want to face the choice of paying for your spouse's cancer treatment or following the rules of professional conduct, then don't live or work at the limits of your income. Give yourself a cushion to work with. You might need it someday.

The disciplinary and fiduciary rules governing transactions between lawyers and clients do not apply to negotiations between the parties over whether to form an attorney-client relationship. Because the fiduciary relation is the product of an agreement, it cannot precede it, at least not unless the lawyer has taken steps to assume such duties before reaching a formal agreement. Such rules therefore do not govern the initial fee negotiations between a lawyer and client.

But what about changes to the initial agreement? At the point either the lawyer or the client might want to make a change, the lawyer is a fiduciary and subject to fiduciary duty rules and disciplinary rules. Does that mean that if the lawyer raises her fees once a year, she must treat the increase as equivalent to a new agreement with an existing client? Could such treatment be avoided by writing the initial agreement to reserve the right to make changes later on?

The basic rule is that agreements reached at the beginning of representation or within a reasonable time thereafter are enforceable as made. Any modification beyond a reasonable time is voidable at the option of the client unless the lawyer can show that the agreement and the circumstances in which it was made were fair and reasonable to the client. *Restatement (Third) of the Law Governing Lawyers* §§ 18(1); 38(1).

Maksym v. Loesch, 937 F.2d 1237, 1239 (7th Cir. 1991) (Posner, J.), illustrates this principle. Dolores Loesch was a widow. Her late husband, Fred, left two wills; one left Fred's estate to his two daughters from a previous marriage and the other (later) will left it to Dolores. The daughters contested the later will, and Dolores hired Walter Maksym to represent her. She signed a fee agreement providing that for basic services he would be paid 2.5% of the fair market value of the estate. For additional services, including defending the will contest, he would be paid $100 per hour on top of the 2.5% figure.

Dolores later fired Maksym because she thought he moved too slowly. She paid him $10,000, but under the formula set forth in the retainer agreement he was owed $126,000. Maksym sued Dolores for the balance of his fee. She defended in part on the theory that "because lawyers are fiduciaries all contracts between lawyers and their present or even prospective clients are presumptively fraudulent if the lawyer benefits from the contract."

The court rejected that claim:

> The purpose of the rule is to protect the reasonable expectations of the person who reposes confidence in an agent who, he has been led to believe, will treat his affairs with the same solicitude with which the agent would treat the agent's own affairs. The creation of these expectations is not instantaneous, and we may assume therefore that a retention agreement signed shortly after the first meeting between the parties is not subject to the rule of presumptive impropriety. It is quite otherwise if the agreement is signed months later . . . when, as is common, the fiduciary relationship has flowered without benefit of a written agreement. At that point the lawyer or other fiduciary has an ascendancy over his client, a position of trust, that may enable him to drive too hard a bargain; and it is against this danger that the presumption is directed.
>
> The danger was not present here. According to the facts . . . Mrs. Loesch first discussed representation with Maksym "in or about October, 1978," the retainer agreement was signed on October 19, and representation commenced then. . . . there is no reason to think that Maksym performed any significant work on the matters for Mrs. Loesch before the retainer agreement was signed. Mere preliminary discussions—the courtship leading up to the agreement—are not enough to bring the presumption of voidability into play.

Contrast *Loesch* with *Perez v. Pappas*, 98 Wash.2d 835 (1983), where an attorney re-negotiated his fee on the eve of settlement, taking a cash payout rather than the previously agreed percentage. The court found the attorney breached his fiduciary duty to the plaintiff "in renegotiating the fee for his services without full disclosure and in failing to give a written accounting," but that the attorney cured the breach by refunding the difference between the two fee amounts.

3. REASONABILITY OF FEES

Model Rule 1.5(a) provides that you may not charge or collect an unreasonable fee. It sets forth eight factors to assess reasonability. Rule 1.5(b) provides the scope of the representation and the basis for the fee must be communicated to the client, preferably in writing. (Some state provisions, such as California Business & Professions Code §§ 6147–6148, make this preference a requirement in some circumstances.) Rule 1.5(c) and (d) allow contingent fees except in divorce or criminal matters, and require that the fee agreement be written and signed by the client, and that the client informed how costs will be dealt with under the agreement.

The following materials explore these rules. The first case raises the question whether a lawyer inexperienced in one field may charge a client for learning the field.

Model Rules of Professional Conduct 1.5, 1.15, 1.16(d)
Restatement of the Law Governing Lawyers §§ 34–43; 18

MATTER OF FORDHAM

423 Mass. 481, 668 N.E.2d 816 (1996)

O'CONNOR, JUSTICE.

This is an appeal from the Board of Bar Overseers' (board's) dismissal of a petition for discipline filed by bar counsel against attorney Laurence S. Fordham. On March 11, 1992, bar counsel served Fordham with a petition for discipline alleging that Fordham had charged a clearly excessive fee in violation of S.J.C. Rule 3:07, DR 2–106, as appearing in 382 Mass. 772 (1981), for defending Timothy Clark (Timothy) in the District Court against a charge that he operated a motor vehicle while under the influence of intoxicating liquor (OUI) and against other related charges. Fordham moved that the board dismiss the petition and the board chair recommended that that be done. Bar counsel appealed from the chair's decision to the full board, and the board referred the matter to a hearing committee. . . .

After five days of hearings, and with "serious reservations," the hearing committee concluded that Fordham's fee was not substantially in excess of a reasonable fee and that, therefore, the committee recommended against bar discipline. Bar counsel appealed from that determination to the board. By a vote of six to five, with one abstention, the board accepted the recommendation of the hearing committee and dismissed the petition for discipline. Bar counsel then filed in the Supreme Judicial Court for Suffolk County (county court) a claim of appeal from the board's action. . . .

On March 4, 1989, the Acton police department arrested Timothy, then twenty-one years old, and charged him with OUI, operating a motor vehicle after suspension, speeding, and operating an unregistered motor vehicle. At the time of the arrest, the police discovered a partially full quart of vodka in the vehicle. After failing a field sobriety test, Timothy was taken to the Acton police station where he submitted to two breathalyzer tests which registered .10 and .12 respectively.

Subsequent to Timothy's arraignment, he and his father, Laurence Clark (Clark) consulted with three lawyers, who offered to represent Timothy for fees between $3,000 and $10,000. Shortly after the arrest, Clark went to Fordham's home to service an alarm system which he had installed several years before. While there, Clark discussed Timothy's arrest with Fordham's wife who invited Clark to discuss the case with Fordham. Fordham then met with Clark and Timothy.

At this meeting, Timothy described the incidents leading to his arrest and the charges against him. Fordham, whom the hearing committee described as a "very experienced senior trial attorney with impressive credentials," told Clark and Timothy that he had never represented a client in a driving while under the influence case or in any criminal matter, and he had never tried a case in the District Court. The hearing committee found that "Fordham explained that although he lacked experience in this area, he was a knowledgeable and hard-working attorney and that he believed he could competently represent Timothy. Fordham described himself as 'efficient and economic in the use of [his] time.' . . .

"Towards the end of the meeting, Fordham told the Clarks that he worked on [a] time charge basis and that he billed monthly. . . . In other words, Fordham would calculate the amount of hours he and others in the firm worked on a matter each month and multiply it by the respective hourly rates. He also told the Clarks that he would engage others in his firm to prepare the case. Clark had indicated that he would pay Timothy's legal fees." After the meeting, Clark hired Fordham to represent Timothy.

According to the hearing committee's findings, Fordham filed four pretrial motions on Timothy's behalf, two of which were allowed. One motion, entitled "Motion in Limine to Suppress Results of Breathalyzer Tests," was based on the theory that, although two breathalyzer tests were exactly .02 apart, they were not "within" .02 of one another as the regulations require. See 501 Code Mass.Regs. § 2.56(2) (1994). The hearing committee characterized the motion and its rationale as "a creative, if not novel, approach to suppression of breathalyzer results." Although the original trial date was June 20, 1989, the trial, which was before a judge without jury, was held on October 10 and October 19, 1989. The judge found Timothy not guilty of driving while under the influence.

Fordham sent the following bills to Clark:

"1. April 19, 1989, $3,250 for services rendered in March, 1989.

"2. May 15, 1989, $9,850 for services rendered in April, 1989.

"3. June 19, 1989, $3,950 for services rendered in May, 1989.

"4. July 13, 1989, $13,300 for services rendered in June, 1989.

"5. October 13, 1989, $35,022.25 revised bill for services rendered from March 19 to June 30, 1989.

"6. November 7, 1989, $15,000 for services rendered from July 1, 1989 to October 19, 1989."

The bills totaled $50,022.25, reflecting 227 hours of billed time, 153 hours of which were expended by Fordham and seventy-four of which were his associates' time. Clark did not pay the first two bills when they became due and expressed to Fordham his concern about their amount. Clark paid Fordham $10,000 on June 20, 1989. At that time, Fordham assured Clark that most of the work had been completed "other than taking [the case] to trial." Clark did not make any subsequent payments. Fordham requested Clark to sign a promissory note evidencing his debt to Fordham and, on October 7, 1989, Clark did so. In the October 13, 1989, bill, Fordham added a charge of $5,000 as a "retroactive increase" in fees. On November 7, 1989, after the case was completed, Fordham sent Clark a bill for $15,000.

Bar counsel and Fordham have stipulated that all the work billed by Fordham was actually done and that Fordham and his associates spent the time they claim to have spent. They also have stipulated that Fordham acted conscientiously, diligently, and in good faith in representing Timothy and in his billing in this case. . . .

The board dismissed bar counsel's petition for discipline against Fordham because it determined, relying in large part on the findings and recommendations of the hearing committee, that Fordham's fee was not clearly excessive. Pursuant to S.J.C. Rule 3:07, DR 2–106(B), "a fee is clearly excessive when, after a review of the facts, a lawyer of ordinary prudence, experienced in the area of the law involved, would be left with a definite and firm conviction that the fee is substantially in excess of a reasonable fee." The rule proceeds to list eight factors to be considered in ascertaining the reasonableness of the fee:

"(1) The time and labor required, the novelty and difficulty of the questions involved, and the skill requisite to perform the legal service properly.

"(2) The likelihood, if apparent to the client, that the acceptance of the particular employment will preclude other employment by the lawyer.

"(3) The fee customarily charged in the locality for similar legal services.

"(4) The amount involved and the results obtained.

"(5) The time limitations imposed by the client or by the circumstances.

"(6) The nature and length of the professional relationship with the client.

"(7) The experience, reputation, and ability of the lawyer or lawyers performing the services.

"(8) Whether the fee is fixed or contingent."

In concluding that Fordham did not charge a clearly excessive fee, the board adopted, with limited exception, the hearing committee's report. The board's and the hearing committee's reasons for dismissing the petition are as follows: Bar counsel and Fordham stipulated that Fordham acted conscientiously, diligently, and in good faith in his representation of the client and his billing on the case. Although Fordham lacked experience in criminal law, he is a "seasoned and well-respected civil lawyer." The more than 200 hours spent preparing the OUI case were necessary, "in part to educate [Fordham] in the relevant substantive law and court procedures," because he had never tried an OUI case or appeared in the District Court. The board noted that "[a]lthough none of the experts who testified at the disciplinary hearing had ever heard of a fee in excess of $15,000 for a first-offense OUI case, the hearing committee found that [Clark] had entered into the transaction with open eyes after interviewing other lawyers with more experience in such matters." The board also thought significant that Clark "later acquiesced, despite mild expressions of concern, in [Fordham's] billing practices." Moreover, the Clarks specifically instructed Fordham that they would not consider a guilty plea by Timothy. Rather they were interested only in pursuing the case to trial. Finally, Timothy obtained the result he sought: an acquittal.

Bar counsel contends that the board's decision to dismiss the petition for discipline is erroneous on three grounds: First, "[t]he hearing committee and the Board committed error by analyzing only three of the factors set out in DR 2–106(B)(1)–(8), and their findings with regard to these criteria do not support their conclusion that the fee in this case was not clearly excessive"; second, the board "misinterpreted [DR 2–106's] prohibition against charging a clearly excessive fee by reading into the rule a 'safe harbor' provision"; and third, "by allowing client acquiescence as a complete defense." . . .

The first factor listed in DR 2–106(B) requires examining "[t]he time and labor required, the novelty and difficulty of the questions involved, and the skill requisite to perform the legal service properly." Although the hearing committee determined that Fordham "spent a large number of hours on [the] matter, in essence learning from scratch what others . . . already know," it "[did] not credit Bar Counsel's argument that Fordham violated DR 2–106 by spending too many hours." The hearing committee reasoned that even if the number of hours Fordham "spent [were] wholly out of proportion" to the number of hours that a lawyer with experience in the trying of OUI cases would require, the committee was not required to conclude that the fee based on time spent was "clearly excessive." It was enough, the hearing committee concluded, that Clark instructed Fordham to pursue the case to trial, Fordham did so zealously and, as stipulated, Fordham spent the hours he billed in good faith and diligence. We disagree. . . .

In considering whether a fee is "clearly excessive" within the meaning of S.J.C. Rule 3:07, DR 2–106(B), the first factor to be considered pursuant to that rule is "the novelty and difficulty of the questions involved, and the skill requisite to perform the legal service properly." DR 2–106(B)(1). That standard is similar to the familiar standard of reasonableness traditionally applied in civil fee disputes. . . . Based on the testimony of the four experts, the number of hours devoted to Timothy's OUI case by Fordham and his associates was substantially in excess of the hours that a prudent experienced lawyer would have spent. According to the evidence, the number of hours spent was several times the amount of time any of the witnesses had ever spent on a similar case. We are not unmindful of the novel and successful motion to suppress the breathalyzer test results, but that effort cannot justify a $50,000 fee in a type of case in which the usual fee is less than one-third of that amount.

The board determined that "[b]ecause [Fordham] had never tried an OUI case or appeared in the district court, [Fordham] spent over 200 hours preparing the case, in part to educate himself in the relevant substantive law and court procedures." Fordham's inexperience in criminal defense work and OUI cases in particular cannot justify the extraordinarily high fee. It cannot be that an inexperienced lawyer is entitled to charge three or four times as much as an experienced lawyer for the same service. A client "should not be expected to pay for the education of a lawyer when he spends excessive amounts of time on tasks which, with reasonable experience, become matters of routine." *Matter of the Estate of Larson,* 103 Wash.2d 517, 531 (1985). "While the licensing of a lawyer is evidence that he has met the standards then prevailing for admission to the bar, a lawyer generally should not accept employment in any area of the law in which he is not qualified. However, he may accept such employment if in good faith he expects to become qualified through study and investigation, as long as such preparation would not result in unreasonable delay or expense to his client." Model Code of Professional Responsibility EC 6–3 (1982) . . .

DR 2–106(B) provides that the third factor to be considered in ascertaining the reasonableness of a fee is its comparability to "[t]he fee customarily charged in the locality for similar legal services." The hearing committee made no finding as to the comparability of Fordham's fee with the fees customarily charged in the locality for similar services. However, one of bar counsel's expert witnesses testified that he had never heard of a fee in excess of $15,000 to defend a first OUI charge, and the customary flat fee in an OUI case, including trial, "runs from $1,000 to $7,500." Bar counsel's other expert testified that he had never heard of a fee in excess of $10,000 for a bench trial. In his view, the customary charge for a case similar to Timothy's would vary between $1,500 and $5,000.

One of Fordham's experts testified that she considered a $40,000 or $50,000 fee for defending an OUI charge "unusual and certainly higher by far than any I've ever seen before." The witness had never charged a fee of more than $3,500 for representing a client at a bench trial to defend a first offense OUI charge. She further testified that she believed an "average OUI in the bench session is two thousand [dollars] and sometimes less." Finally, that witness testified that she had "heard a rumor" that one attorney charged $10,000 for a bench trial involving an OUI charge; this fee represented the highest fee of which she was aware. The other expert witness called by Fordham testified that he had heard of a $35,000 fee for defending OUI charges, but he had never charged more than $12,000 (less than twenty-five per cent of Fordham's fee).

Although finding that Fordham's fee was "much higher than the fee charged by many attorneys with more experience litigating driving under the influence cases," the hearing committee nevertheless determined that the fee charged by Fordham was not clearly excessive because Clark "went into the relationship with Fordham with open eyes," Fordham's fee fell within a "safe harbor," and Clark acquiesced in Fordham's fee by not strenuously objecting to his bills. The board accepted the hearing committee's analysis apart from the committee's reliance on the "safe harbor" rule.

The finding that Clark had entered into the fee agreement "with open eyes" was based on the finding that Clark hired Fordham after being fully apprised that he lacked any type of experience in defending an OUI charge and after interviewing other lawyers who were experts in defending OUI charges. Furthermore, the hearing committee and the board relied on testimony which revealed that the fee arrangement had been fully disclosed to Clark including the fact that Fordham "would have to become familiar with the law in that area." It is also significant, however, that the hearing committee found that "[d]espite Fordham's disclaimers concerning his experience, Clark did not appear to have understood in any real sense the implications of choosing Fordham to represent Timothy. Fordham did not give Clark any estimate of the total expected fee or the number of $200 hours that would be required." The express finding of the hearing committee that Clark "did not appear to have understood in any real sense the implications of choosing Fordham to represent Timothy" directly militates against the finding that Clark entered into the agreement "with open eyes."

That brings us to the hearing committee's finding that Fordham's fee fell within a "safe harbor." The hearing committee reasoned that as long as an agreement existed between a client and an attorney to bill a reasonable rate multiplied by the number of hours actually worked, the attorney's fee was within a "safe harbor" and thus protected from a challenge that the fee was clearly excessive. The board, however, in reviewing the hearing committee's decision, correctly rejected the notion "that a lawyer may always escape discipline with billings based on accurate time charges for work honestly performed."

The "safe harbor" formula would not be an appropriate rationale in this case because the amount of time Fordham spent to educate himself and represent Timothy was clearly excessive despite his good faith and diligence. Disciplinary Rule 2–106(B)'s mandate that "[a] fee is clearly excessive when, after a review of the facts, a lawyer of ordinary prudence, experienced in the area of the law involved, would be left with a definite and firm conviction that the fee is substantially in excess of a reasonable fee," creates explicitly an objective standard by which attorneys' fees are to be judged. We are not persuaded by Fordham's argument that "unless it can be shown that the 'excessive' work for which the attorney has charged goes beyond mere matters of professional judgment and can be proven, either directly or by reasonable inference, to have involved dishonesty, bad faith or overreaching of the client, no case for discipline has been established." Disciplinary Rule 2–106 plainly does not require an inquiry into whether the clearly excessive fee was charged to the client under fraudulent circumstances, and we shall not write such a meaning into the disciplinary rule.

Finally, bar counsel challenges the hearing committee's finding that "if Clark objected to the numbers of hours being spent by Fordham, he could have spoken up with some force when he began receiving bills." Bar counsel notes, and we agree, that "[t]he test as stated in the DR 2–106(A) is whether the fee 'charged' is clearly excessive, not whether the fee is accepted as valid or acquiesced in by the client." Therefore, we conclude that the hearing committee and the board erred in not concluding that Fordham's fee was clearly excessive. . . .

In charging a clearly excessive fee, Fordham departed substantially from the obligation of professional responsibility that he owed to his client. The ABA Model Standards for Imposing Lawyer Sanctions § 7.3 (1992) endorses a public reprimand as the appropriate sanction for charging a clearly excessive fee. We deem such a sanction appropriate in this case. Accordingly, a judgment is to be entered in the county court imposing a public censure. The record in this case is to be unimpounded.

PROBLEM 14–1

Does *Fordham* mean you may not charge your clients to learn the law? What does that imply for you as you start your career?

PROBLEM 14–2

If a partner in a firm tells you to write down all your time and let him or her decide whether to reduce it, may you follow that instruction? If you notice the partner never reduces your hours, but always bills the client in full, must you say something to the partner? What?

Ratification?

Suppose an attorney and client enter into a fee agreement that would be unconscionable, and thus unreasonable for purposes of the model rules, but that the parties then perform the agreement over a long period of time. For example, suppose a lawyer enters into a contingency agreement with a musician in a case where the lawyer attempts to secure song royalties for the musician, taking a percentage of each royalty payment for a fee. Does the client's acceptance of the benefits of the agreement ratify it, thus making it enforceable even if it would not have been enforced absent such acceptance? *See King v. Fox*, 7 N.Y.3d 181 (2006) (ratification is possible with full disclosure); *cf. Blattman v. Gadd*, 112 Cal.App. 76 (1931) (rejecting ratification).

Fordham rejects the idea that a bill is reasonable so long as the lawyer bills for work actually done, rather than falsely claiming to have done work, at rates agreed to by the client. This holding implies that client consent is not a defense to an unreasonable fee. *In re Martin*, 374 S.C. 164 (2007), presents a variation on this principle in the entity client context. Martin represented an insurer in several matters. An officer of the insurance company directed Martin to bill time he had spent on certain matters to other matters on which he had done no work. According to the

Court, "the officer was terminated by the company based on alleged payments on fictitious claims generated by an adjuster in the State of Kentucky. He subsequently pled guilty in federal court to a criminal offense related to his activities, but not related to the activities of respondent nor the averments in the indictment against respondent."

Martin was indicted for mail fraud but the indictment was dismissed. He had been suspended on an interim basis when the indictment was filed, and was ultimately suspended from practice for six months, retroactive to the date of the interim suspension. This light punishment no doubt reflects the Court's acceptance of the claim that Martin did in fact follow the instructions of an officer for the insurer. The officer was not his client, however, the insurer was. Billing records that might not mislead the officer might mislead other client constituents, and thus might facilitate misconduct by the officer to the detriment of the client. Thus, while Martin's explanation may seem perfectly plausible on its face it mistakes an agent of the client for the client. Falsely attributing work done on one matter to another matter would be unacceptable even for an individual client. Though in that case there might be no risk of misleading the client, the client might use the false records to mislead others.

When faced with such a request it is always a good idea to ask yourself why someone wants you to create a false record. If there were no reason, why would they ask you to do it? And if there is a reason, it likely will point to someone who could be harmed by the lie. Such harm is not necessary for a violation of Rule 1.5, but it does make it more likely that the lie will be uncovered and some action taken against you. Remember the mail fraud indictment against Martin, which might well have been the product of a complaint by someone at the insurance company who did not know of the officer's instructions to Martin, or by someone to whom the officer lied. It was good for Martin that the indictment was dismissed, but it would have been much better had it never been brought.

***Ex post or ex ante*?**

What if an agreement is reasonable when the parties enter into it but becomes unreasonable over time? Is it enforceable because it was reasonable at the outset, or unenforceable because unreasonable when current payments are made?

The court in *Holmes v. Loveless*, 122 Wash. App. 470 (2004), opted for *ex post* review. In 1970 Holmes and Kruger's law firm began representing a real estate developer named Loveless. In 1972 Loveless and a partner developed a mall in Alaska. Holmes and Kruger agreed to do the legal work on the mall in return for a discounted rate through 1974 (after which they would charge their regular rates) plus 5% of any cash distributions from the joint venture that developed the mall. Loveless had entered into similar agreements with the firm before, and the 5% term was negotiated. (The firm took it rather than a 7% ownership stake.)

The joint venture began making cash distributions in the early 1980s. By 2001 the venture had paid the firm $380,000. It then notified the firm that it would not longer make payments, and simultaneously paid a large distribution to Loveless and his partner. The firm sued to enforce the agreement. The trial court ruled for the firm. The court of appeals reversed. It reasoned:

> Holmes may have provided services valuable to the joint venture, but he assumed very little risk in the agreement. Other employment was not precluded, and the discount was only provided for a limited time. His firm still covered its overhead expenses. In comparison with *Bauermeister,* the return to Holmes has been enormously favorable, and he has not demonstrated any special circumstances, such as particular expertise or unusual demands on his time, that would justify continued enforcement of the agreement. While the 5 percent provision may have been reasonable at the outset given the small percentage it represented of the development's total revenue, at this point over thirty years later, the amount of fee reduction does not justify further enforcement of the agreement.

Retainers and Reasonability

The type of retainer you charge affects analysis of whether your fee is reasonable. Fordham charged by the hour. The firm in *Ryan v. Butera, Beausang, Cohen & Brennan*, 193 F.3d 210 (3d Cir. 1999), earned $1 million for one month's work, consisting of revising one complaint, and was allowed to keep it. The difference was in the type of retainer and the economic factors that made that retainer make sense.

The Butera firm was hired to represent Raymark, a company emerging from bankruptcy and facing over 68,000 cases in which plaintiffs claimed they were hurt by asbestos Raymark produced. Raymark wanted lawyers who could handle such a large volume of relatively complex cases, and it needed lawyers that could get past its history of not paying its fees (see above re: Bankruptcy). It offered the Butera firm $1 million up front as a non-refundable retainer plus a set amount to be paid quarterly as work was performed and a fixed amount per day of trial.

The firm agreed. Beausang sent a letter to Raymark acknowledging receipt of the $1 million and stating that "[g]iven the significant impact on my practice, I would not have accepted this engagement had this fee not been fully earned and non-refundable." The Raymark representative signed and returned that letter as "acknowledged and agreed."

The relationship lasted about ten weeks before Raymark fired the firm. During that time, the firm recorded 335.5 hours of work for Raymark and incurred out-of-pocket expenses of approximately $37,000. After firing the firm Raymark sued to recover the $1 million.

The trial court ruled for the firm, reasoning that Raymark had spent $1 million to buy the "opportunity" to use Beausang's services at capped costs. The court compared this agreement to an options contract, where the option is worth *something,* though less than the fully-realized opportunity. The court also found the agreement similar to *Brobeck, Phleger & Harrison v. Telex Corp.,* 602 F.2d 866 (9th Cir.1979), a well-known case in which the Ninth Circuit affirmed the enforceability of a fee agreement that yielded a $1 million payment for a firm that only filed with the Supreme Court a petition for writ of certiorari and provided some settlement advice. The trial court found that, as in *Brobeck,* Raymark was a sophisticated client that wanted to attract highly qualified counsel and did so through a negotiated fee agreement.

The court of appeals affirmed, noting "[i]n *Brobeck* and here, the attorneys clearly were paid very well, but the context of the payments and the fact that the clients received some intangible benefits in retaining the attorneys meant that the courts could conclude that the compensation in each case was not so high as to be inequitable and unfair."

Fee Agreement Formalities

Model Rule 1.5(b) expresses a preference for written fee agreements but does not require them. Rule 1.5(c), however, requires that contingent fee agreements be in writing and be signed by the client. Similarly, if a fee modification were treated as transaction with a client, Model Rule 1.8(a)(1) would require a writing.

Like Rule 1.5(c), California Business & Professions Code § 6147 requires that contingent fee agreements be in writing and, except for health-care cases (where fees are fixed by § 6146) that they include a statement that the "fee is not set by law but is negotiable between attorney and client." In contrast to Rule 1.5(b), however, Business & Professions Code § 6148(a) requires a writing for all fee agreements where the total cost to the client is expected to exceed $1,000. Failure to comply with either provision renders the fee agreement voidable at the client's option, leaving the attorney with a claim for reasonable fees. Section 6148(d) excludes many important categories of clients from this provision, however, including corporations.

---

4. DIVISION OF FEES AMONG LAWYERS

Rule 1.5(e) allows referral fees if the referring lawyer either assumes joint responsibility for a matter or the division of fees is proportionate to the lawyers' work. In either case the client must agree to the division of fees, the agreement must be confirmed in writing, and the total fee must be reasonable. Some states vary these provisions, as with the California requirement that a client affirmatively consent in writing to the division of fees. The rules are strictly enforced, as the following case illustrates.

Model Rule 1.5(e)
Cal. R. Prof. Conduct 2–200

CHAMBERS V. KAY

29 Cal.4th 142 (2002)

BAXTER, J.

This matter arises from a dispute between two attorneys over contingent fees generated from the successful prosecution of a client's lawsuit against third parties. Rule 2–200(A)(1) of the California Rules of Professional Conduct (all further references to rules are to these rules), which this court approved to protect the public and to promote respect and confidence in the legal profession, provides in pertinent part that a member of the State Bar "shall not divide a fee for legal services with a lawyer who is not a partner of, associate of, or shareholder with the member unless . . . [t]he client has consented in writing thereto after a full disclosure has been made in writing that a division of fees will be made and the terms of such division. . . . " Here, the plaintiff attorney seeks a division or apportionment of fees despite noncompliance with the rule's written client consent requirement. We conclude, based on the uncontroverted record before us, that rule 2–200(A)(1) is binding on plaintiff and precludes him from sharing in the subject fees. Accordingly, we affirm the judgment of the Court of Appeal.

Factual and Procedural Background

Attorneys Arthur Chambers and Philip Kay had separate law practices in San Francisco. They had individual office letterheads; Kay listed his home law office on 43d Avenue as his professional address, while Chambers listed his office address as 1388 Sutter Street, suite 510. Kay also maintained a separate professional liability insurance policy for his practice. Except perhaps as otherwise noted below, Chambers and Kay did not list each other as employees or partners in any official documents.

In 1992 and 1993, Kay paid Chambers $200 per month to use a conference room in Chambers's office on Sutter Street for depositions and client meetings. Kay used Chambers's office telephone service, law library, and postage and copy machines. Kay also maintained files and a computer in the office, rented a monthly space in the building parking lot, and was listed as a cotenant on the building directory. Chambers assisted Kay with his work on a few cases. Additionally, Chambers's staff regularly provided assistance to Kay with case-related documents.

In 1992, at Kay's request, Chambers began serving as cocounsel in a sexual harassment action that Kay had previously filed on behalf of his client, Rena Weeks, against Martin Greenstein and the law firm of Baker & McKenzie (hereafter *Weeks* or the *Weeks* case). Chambers's responsibilities in the case included maintaining the files, conducting discovery that Kay assigned to him, conferring with Weeks in the office, and appearing as cocounsel on her behalf at pretrial hearings. Both Chambers and Kay were listed in the *Weeks* case pleadings as plaintiff's counsel, at the Sutter Street office address, and Chambers advanced costs and expenses of $3,356.32 in the case. Chambers, however, continued to work on other cases he had at the time.

During discovery in *Weeks*, a dispute arose between Chambers and Kay over the disclosure of certain documents and Chambers's alleged efforts to persuade Weeks to settle. On September 29, 1993, Kay notified Chambers by letter that Chambers was removed effective immediately from the *Weeks* case with the client's approval. Kay's letter confirmed that Chambers would "receive the compensation agreed upon," that is: in the event the case was settled before depositions, "16.5% of the attorney's fees called for under my agreement with [Weeks], which is 40% of the monies recovered"; thereafter, an "increase to 28%" of the fees specified under the agreement with Weeks; and reimbursement of the costs Chambers had advanced to date. Kay sent a copy of the letter to Weeks, but never sought or obtained her written or oral consent to the proposed fee division with Chambers.

Chambers sent a letter to Kay accepting his compensation offer. On September 30, 1993, Kay filed a "Notice of Association and Disassociation of Counsel" in *Weeks*, stating that Alan B. Exelrod had been "associated as counsel of record" in place of Chambers.

On November 1, 1993, Kay wrote to Chambers complaining of his "malfeasance" and violation of fiduciary duties to Weeks. Kay reiterated that Chambers would receive the "payment as originally agreed upon of one-sixth of the attorney's fees of forty-percent (40%)" recovered in *Weeks* upon submission of his time records. Unlike the September 29 letter, this letter did not show a copy to the client.

The *Weeks* case eventually was tried to a jury, resulting in a large award of compensatory and punitive damages for Weeks and a significant award of attorney fees.[1] Counsel for Kay then wrote to Chambers informing him that his "failure to perform legal services" in the *Weeks* case, the "wholly improper accounting" provided in his attorney fees billing statement, and unforeseen "changed circumstances" all served "as a basis for abrogation of any agreement" between them as to a fee division. This letter contained an offer to compensate Chambers for his services in *Weeks* in the amount of $200 per hour for the total number of hours specified in his prior billing statement. Chambers declined Kay's offer and proposed mediation of their fee dispute.

The judgment in favor of Weeks, including the attorney fee award, was affirmed on appeal in 1998. After that judgment was satisfied and Kay obtained his attorney fees, Chambers initiated this action alleging one cause of action for breach of contract and one common count. The trial court granted summary judgment in favor of Kay on grounds that: (1) the parties' alleged agreement for a division of fees violated rule 2–200 and therefore was unenforceable; and (2) the governing statutes of limitations (Code Civ. Proc., §§ 337, 339) barred the common count seeking quantum meruit recovery. The Court of Appeal reversed the judgment in favor of Kay on the quantum meruit claim, but otherwise affirmed the judgment. We granted Chambers's petition for review.

Discussion

Both the trial court and the Court of Appeal below determined that Chambers cannot prevail on his breach of contract cause of action because it is premised on a fee-splitting agreement that failed to comply with rule 2–200. Chambers challenges those determinations on the grounds that: (1) rule 2–200 governs fee divisions between attorneys only where "pure referral fees" are at issue and therefore does not apply here; (2) even if rule 2–200 is not limited in application to pure referral fees, the arrangement here falls within the rule's express exemption for fees divided between a member of the State Bar and "a partner of, associate of, or shareholder with" the member; and (3) in any event, noncompliance with rule 2–200 does not render the fee-splitting agreement invalid and unenforceable. Additionally, Chambers contends that the Court of Appeal erred in concluding that a quantum meruit award could not be predicated on the apportionment of the contingent fee paid to Kay. We shall address these issues in order.

---

[1] Eds. Note: The initial damages award was $50,000 in compensatory damages for emotional distress and $7.1 million in punitive damages, $6.9 million against the firm and $250,000 against the defendant partner, Martin Greenstein. The trial court reduced the punitive damage award against the firm to $3.5 million and let stand the punitive award against Greenstein. The court also awarded $1.8 million in fees. The reduced damages award was affirmed on appeal; the order awarding attorney's fees also was affirmed, but the amount of the award was reversed on the ground that it had not been justified adequately. *Weeks v. Baker & McKenzie*, 63 Cal.App.4th 1128 (1998).

A. *Applicability of Rule 2–200*

As noted, rule 2–200 states that a member of the State Bar "*shall not divide a fee for legal services with a lawyer* who is not a partner of, associate of, or shareholder with the member" unless the requirements specified in the rule have been met. (Rule 2–200(A), italics added.) Significantly, the rule does not limit its application to "pure referral fees" (hereafter referral fees), in which one lawyer receives " 'a percentage of a contingent fee for doing nothing more than obtaining the signature of a client upon a retainer agreement while the lawyer to whom the case is referred performs the work.' " (*Moran v. Harris* (1982) 131 Cal.App.3d 913, 921.) Nor does it purport to categorically exempt fee divisions among attorneys who work jointly on behalf of a client. Rather, rule 2–200's language, reasonably read, appears to encompass any division of fees where the attorneys working for the client are not partners or associates of each other, or are not shareholders in the same law firm. . . . .

B. *Rule 2–200's Exemption for Partners and Associates*

Rule 2–200, by its terms, does not restrict the division of fees between a State Bar member and a lawyer who is "a partner of, associate of, or shareholder with" that member. We next consider Chambers's contention that, although he and Kay maintained separate law practices when acting as Weeks's cocounsel, their arrangement to divide fees in *Weeks* was not subject to restriction because Chambers was Kay's partner or associate.

Chambers first argues that, once he and Kay put their names jointly on pleadings in the *Weeks* case, made joint court appearances on Weeks's behalf, and acted as "true *co-counsel*" in the lawsuit, they functioned as partners within the meaning of rule 2–200's exemption. He additionally asserts that the agreement between Kay and him to work jointly, to contribute to the lawsuit's costs, and to defer any compensation for work performed for several years removed their agreed fee division from the ambit of rule 2–200. We disagree. Although rule 2–200 does not define the terms "partner" and "associate," the rule's language and history indicate these terms are not meant to apply in the circumstances established here.

Rule 1–100(B)(1)(a) defines a " '[l]aw [f]irm' " as "two or more lawyers whose activities constitute the practice of law, and who share its profits, expenses, and liabilities." The record in this case indisputably establishes that although Chambers and Kay shared certain office space and facilities, with Kay paying Chambers for their use, the two maintained independent law practices with separate identities, separate addresses of record with the State Bar, and separate clients, expenses, and liabilities. Thus, even though Chambers and Kay worked together in *Weeks* and a few other cases, they were not members of the same law firm as defined by the Rules of Professional Conduct.

Although the rules omit a definition of the term "partner," Chambers and Kay were not in a partnership and were not each other's partner as those terms are commonly understood. The Corporations Code defines a partnership as "an association of two or more persons to carry on as coowners a business for profit under Section 16202, predecessor law, or comparable law of another jurisdiction." (Corp. Code, § 6101, subd. (7).) Generally, a partnership connotes co-ownership in partnership property, with a sharing in the profits and losses of a continuing business. (*Nelson v. Abraham* (1947) 29 Cal.2d 745, 749.) Here, no evidence suggests that Chambers and Kay acted as co-owners of a law firm or law office, or that they contemplated sharing in the profits and losses of a continuing business engaged in the practice of law.

In *Bank of California v. Connolly* (1973) 36 Cal.App.3d 350, the Court of Appeal explained that "[a] joint venture exists where there is an 'agreement between the parties under which they have a community of interest, that is, a joint interest, in a common business undertaking, an understanding as to the sharing of profits and losses, and a right of joint control.' " (*Id.* at p. 364.) In comparing joint ventures with partnerships, the court commented that "the incidents of both relationships *are the same in all essential respects.*" (*Ibid.*, italics added.) Here, Chambers asserts that the *Weeks* case essentially represented a joint venture in which he and Kay agreed to work together, share in the costs, and defer any compensation for work performed for several years in the hopes of splitting profits when the case was concluded. In Chambers's view, rule 2–200's partner exemption properly applies because, as joint venturers, he and Kay functioned as partners for that single transaction. We disagree.

Whereas a partnership ordinarily involves a continuing business for an indefinite or fixed period of time, it is commonly understood that a joint venture is usually formed for a single business transaction or enterprise. But while rule 2–200 expressly exempts fee divisions between attorneys who are partners, it makes no mention of an exemption for fee divisions between attorneys who are joint venturers. . . . even assuming Chambers correctly characterizes his relationship with Kay as a joint venture . . . it would be unreasonable to construe the exemption for partners as implying an additional exemption for joint venturers. . . . Indeed, not only would the implied exemption severely limit rule 2–200's application to fee divisions involving attorneys working jointly, but it would seem to eliminate the rule's application to all fee divisions, including those involving referral fees.

We next consider whether Chambers was Kay's "associate" within the meaning of rule 2–200. Although rule 2–200 does not define what it means by the term, the Rules of Professional Conduct elsewhere provide that an associate is "an employee or fellow employee who is employed as a lawyer." (Rule 1–100(B)(4).)

Here, the record is undisputed that Chambers was never Kay's salaried employee and that Chambers did not expect Kay to pay him a salary or other wages as compensation for his work in *Weeks*. On the contrary, all of the evidence shows that the parties agreed Chambers would be compensated based solely on a percentage of any contingent fee that Weeks paid to Kay. The evidence also establishes that Chambers advanced costs in the *Weeks* case, reflecting additional conduct inconsistent with his claim to have been Kay's employee. Viewed together, these uncontroverted facts establish a "division of fees" governed by rule 2–200, not an agreement to employ Chambers as an associate. (State Bar Formal Opn. No. 1994–138, p. 2.)

While Kay may have controlled Chambers's involvement in the *Weeks* case and supervised his work, it remains undisputed that Chambers's compensation was linked to the client's ultimate payment of a contingent fee. That being the case, Kay's authority over Chambers's involvement in the case did not transmute the parties' compensation arrangement from one based on a division of fees to one reflecting an employer-employee relationship. . . .

C. *The Effect of Noncompliance with Rule 2–200*

[N]othing in the record contradicts Kay's evidence that no one ever sought or obtained Weeks's oral or written consent to the fee sharing, or suggests that Weeks was even aware of her right of consent. Hence, we now address Chambers's contention that he is entitled to a division of fees obtained in the *Weeks* case despite noncompliance with the rule's written consent requirement.

Rule 2–200 unambiguously directs that a member of the State Bar "*shall not divide a fee for legal services*" unless the rule's written disclosure and consent requirements and its restrictions on the total fee are met. Yet Chambers, in effect, seeks the aid of this court in dividing the fees of a client without satisfaction of the rule's written consent requirement. We decline such aid. . . .

Margolin [*v. Shemaria*, 85 Cal.App.4th 891, 895 (2000)], a case involving a pure referral fee, explained the purpose of rule 2–200's notice and consent requirements as follows: "Just as a client has a right to know how his or her attorney's fees will be determined, he or she also has a right to know the extent of, and the basis for, the sharing of such fees by attorneys. Knowledge of these matters helps assure the client that he or she will not be charged unwarranted fees just so that the attorney who actually provides the client with representation on the legal matter has 'sufficient compensation' to be able to share fees with the referring attorney. Disclosure of these matters to the client should be in writing because the client should not be expected to mentally retain such information throughout the pendency of the case." (*Margolin*, *supra*, 85 Cal.App.4th at p. 903.) Moreover, "[r]equiring the client's written consent to fee sharing impresses upon the client the importance of his or her consent, and of the right to reject the fee sharing." (*Ibid.*)

We agree with this statement of rule 2–200's purpose. We further conclude that the rule's written disclosure and consent requirements remain equally important where, as here, the division of fees accompanies or is prompted by a division of the legal services provided to the client. As part of their professional obligations, attorneys are required to "keep a client reasonably informed about significant developments relating to the employment or representation, including promptly complying with reasonable requests for information and copies of significant documents when necessary to keep the client so informed." (Rule 3–500; see also Bus & Prof. Code, § 6068, subd. (m) [attorneys have a duty "to keep clients reasonably informed of significant developments in matters with regard to which the attorney has agreed to provide legal services"].)

A division of fees may reflect each participating attorney's responsibilities in a case or fees may be charged for multiple attorney participation in the case without regard to the particular services each attorney performs. Such information may affect the client's level of confidence in the attorneys and is indispensable to the client's ability to make an informed decision regarding whether to accept the fee division and whether to retain or discharge a particular attorney. As in the case of referral fees, requiring the client's written consent to fee divisions among participating attorneys impresses on the client the importance of consent and the right to reject a fee division. All in all, Chambers fails to persuade us that the protection afforded by the rule's written consent requirement is any less necessary or beneficial where, as here, attorneys from separate law firms seek to divide both the work and the fees in a particular matter.

Were we to hold that the fee obtained in *Weeks* may be divided as Chambers and Kay agreed, with no indication that the required client consent was either sought or given, we would, in effect, be both countenancing and contributing to a violation of a rule we formally approved in order "to protect the public and to promote respect and confidence in the legal profession." (Rule 1–100(A), 1st par.; Bus. & Prof. Code, § 6076.) Such a result would be untenable as well as inconsistent with the policy considerations that motivated the adoption of rule 2–200. . . .

D. *Quantum Meruit Recovery*

After holding that rule 2–200 precluded recovery for breach of the fee-sharing agreement, the Court of Appeal determined that Chambers nonetheless was entitled to recover in quantum meruit for the reasonable value of the legal services he had provided before his discharge from the *Weeks* case. Here, Chambers contends that the Court of Appeal erred in concluding that a quantum meruit award could not be predicated upon an apportionment of the contingent fee.

. . . . According to Chambers, a trial court remains free to award the entire fee provided for in a fee-sharing agreement as a proper quantum meruit determination where, as here, the amount specified in the agreement is based on the understanding that that attorney's services were completed. In essence, Chambers contends that, notwithstanding the absence of the required written client consent, he should be allowed to accomplish indirectly a division of fees under the guise of a quantum meruit claim. We reject the contention. None of the authorities Chambers identifies addressed quantum meruit recovery in the context of an improper fee division. . . . We perceive no legal or policy justification for finding that the fee the parties negotiated without the client's consent furnishes a proper basis for a quantum meruit award in this case.

Conclusion and Disposition

We recognize, as did the Court of Appeal below, that this fee dispute is between attorneys only and that the client is not a party. Nonetheless, rule 2–200 aims to protect clients by requiring, inter alia, the attorney's written disclosure and the client's written consent to nonexempt fee divisions. Although Chambers complains that Kay should not be permitted to take advantage of his own disregard of the Rules of Professional Conduct, we are not persuaded that this circumstance justifies or otherwise excuses Chambers's equally disturbing neglect of rule 2–200 and the policy considerations that motivated its adoption. Chambers could have protected his interests, and at the same time fulfilled the beneficial purposes of the rule and acted in Weeks's best interests, by requesting proof of her written consent to the fee division before committing himself to her case.

The judgment of the Court of Appeal is affirmed.

Chambers holds that an attorney may not recover a fee under an agreement that divides fees in violation of the rules of professional conduct but that the attorney may recover the value of his or her services in *quantum meruit*. (Which, you will recall, is an equitable action rather than an action for breach of contract.) It also holds that the terms of the agreement may not be the basis for calculating the amount of the *quantum meruit* recovery, because this would grant by the back door of equity relief that is denied through the front door of contract.

The Court elaborated on *quantum meruit* recovery two years later in *Huskinson & Brown, LLP v. Wolf*, 32 Cal.4th 453 (2004). Like *Chambers*, that case involved an agreement to divide fees to which the client had not provided written consent. Huskinson & Brown was a malpractice defense firm. A client, Ms. Sanchez, brought it a malpractice claim, which it referred to Appell & Wolf in exchange for that firm's oral promise to pay Huskinson & Brown 25% of any fees it recovered. Appell & Wolf prosecuted the case, though Huskinson & Brown put in 20 hours of work and paid an expert witness $800.

Appell & Wolf obtained a $250,000 judgment for the client and collected its fees. It then refused to pay 25% of those fees to Huskinson & Brown, which in turn sued Appell & Wolf, alleging causes of action including breach of contract, unjust enrichment, and *quantum meruit*. The Court held the Huskinson firm could proceed on the *quantum meruit* claim. Excerpts from the opinion follow (all citations omitted)

Quantum meruit refers to the well-established principle that "the law implies a promise to pay for services performed under circumstances disclosing that they were not gratuitously rendered." To recover in quantum meruit, a party need not prove the existence of a contract but it must show the circumstances were such that "the services were rendered under some understanding or expectation of both parties that compensation therefor was to be made" Here, the quantum meruit award reflects the trial court's implicit determination that plaintiff did not gratuitously offer the services covered by that award and that all parties herein expected plaintiff would be compensated for its work in the event attorney fees were recovered in Sanchez's case. Nonetheless, defendants contend, in essence, that they owe plaintiff nothing because allowing recovery on an implied promise to pay for plaintiff's services is tantamount to permitting a division of client fees, in contravention of rule 2–200.[2]

By its terms, the rule expressly prohibits attorneys from "divid[ing] a fee for legal services" when certain requirements, such as written client consent to the fee division after a full written disclosure of its terms, have not been met. Notably, however, rule 2–200 does not purport to restrict attorney compensation on any basis other than a division of fees. Nor does it suggest that attorneys or law firms are categorically barred from making or accepting client referrals, from agreeing to a division of labor on a client's case, or from actually working on a case where labor is divided.

The question arises whether a quantum meruit award for services rendered in reliance on a fee-sharing agreement that lacks written client consent constitutes a division of fees within the rule's contemplation. We think not. True, a quantum meruit award as such would serve to compensate for legal services that have been performed pursuant to an agreement rendered unenforceable under rule 2–200. But when based on the

---

[2] FN3. Defendants argue: "Even assuming that [plaintiff] did provide the services [it] alleged, they were provided after the case was referred to [defendants] and were provided either voluntarily, as Sanchez was a friend, *or were provided with the expectation that [plaintiff] would receive a percentage fee.*" (Italics added.) To the extent defendants maintain here that plaintiff volunteered the 20 hours of legal services covered by the trial court's quantum meruit award, defendants forfeited that issue by failing to raise it in the Court of Appeal.

reasonable value of those services, such an award involves no apportionment of the fees that the client paid or has agreed to pay and therefore is not a fee division subject to rule 2–200's client disclosure and consent requirements.

Formal Opinion No. 1994–138 of the State Bar Standing Committee on Professional Responsibility and Conduct (State Bar, Formal Opinion No. 1994–138) clarifies that rule 2–200 does not apply where there is no direct division of client-paid fees. For example, if a law office that works directly with a client agrees to pay an "outside" lawyer $50 per hour for his or her services, and bills that work to the client at $70, the proposed compensation would not trigger rule 2–200's requirements because the outside lawyer would not be paid a percentage of the fees collected from the client. (State Bar, Formal Opn. No. 1994–138, *supra,* at pp. 3–4.) That is, "the amount paid to the outside lawyer is not tied to specific legal fees received by the law office." (*Id.* at p. 4.) Like an hourly fee arrangement, an award of compensation based on the number of hours plaintiff worked on Sanchez's case would not divide or be otherwise tied to the specific legal fees she paid. . . .

Allowing recovery in quantum meruit would not discourage compliance with rule 2–200. Attorneys who negotiate contingent fee-sharing agreements, which take into account the risk that the client pays no fee if the client does not prevail in his or her case, understandably prefer to receive their negotiated fees rather than the typically lesser amounts representing the reasonable value of the work performed. Consequently, even if quantum meruit recovery is available when the absence of client notification or consent renders a fee-sharing agreement unenforceable, such attorneys have no less incentive to comply with rule 2–200. The facts of this case illustrate the point precisely. If the parties had obtained Sanchez's written consent to the agreed fee sharing as rule 2–200 requires, plaintiff might have received $18,497.91 in fees. As determined by the trial court, however, the reasonable value of plaintiff's 20 hours of legal services was only $5,000. Because the negotiated fee far exceeds the amount of quantum meruit recovery, we may logically assume that, notwithstanding the availability of quantum meruit recovery, plaintiff and all other similarly situated law firms and attorneys remain fully motivated to see that all of their future fee-sharing agreements comply with rule 2–200.

The Legislature's regulation of fee agreements between attorneys and clients favors the availability of quantum meruit recovery. Business and Professions Code section 6147 requires attorneys who represent clients on a contingent fee basis to obtain signed, written fee agreements from their clients. (*Id.,* subd. (a).) Similarly, Business and Professions Code section 6148 generally requires attorneys in noncontingent fee cases to procure signed, written contracts from clients reflecting rates, fees, and charges whenever it is reasonably foreseeable that their legal expenses will exceed $1,000. (*Id.,* subd. (a).)

Like rule 2–200, both Business and Professions Code provisions operate to ensure that clients are informed of and agree to the terms by which the attorneys who represent them will be compensated. But while both statutes provide that a failure to comply with their requirements renders an agreement voidable at the client's option, both also specify that, where an agreement is voided, the attorney remains "entitled to collect a reasonable fee." (Bus. & Prof.Code, §§ 6147, subd. (b), 6148, subd. (c).) Allowing quantum meruit recovery when two law firms negotiate a fee-sharing agreement without complying with rule 2–200's written client consent requirement is consistent with the Legislature's policy determination that, even if a particular fee or compensation agreement is not in writing or signed by the client, a law firm laboring under such an agreement nonetheless deserves reasonable compensation for its services.

Permitting quantum meruit recovery as between law firms is also consistent with case law holding or otherwise recognizing that attorneys may recover from their clients the reasonable value of their legal services when their fee contracts or compensation agreements are found to be invalid or unenforceable for other reasons. . . .

Where services are rendered under a contractual compensation arrangement that is unenforceable as against public policy, but the subject services are not otherwise prohibited, quantum meruit may be allowed. . . . On this last point, we emphasize once again that rule 2–200 does not purport to categorically prohibit attorneys from making or accepting client referrals, from agreeing to divide the labor on a client's case, or from working on cases with attorneys from other law firms. By its terms, the rule merely bars attorneys who engage in such conduct from dividing client fees among themselves when certain requirements, such as written client consent to the fee division, have not been met.

Finally, we have found cases in which courts have disallowed quantum meruit recovery to attorneys who violated one of the Rules of Professional Conduct. Those cases, however, involved violations of a rule that proscribed the very conduct for which compensation was sought, i.e., the rule prohibiting attorneys from engaging in conflicting representation or accepting professional employment adverse to the interests of a client or former client without the written consent of both parties. . . . Here, of course, rule 2–200 does not bar the services plaintiff rendered on Sanchez's behalf; it simply prohibits the dividing of Sanchez's fees because she was not provided written disclosure of the fee-sharing agreement and her written consent was not obtained.

Huskinson approved a suit for *quantum meruit* by one lawyer against another for work done for their common client even if the plaintiff had no contract claim. Does its holding extend to suits against the client as well as the other lawyer? In *Srong v. Beydoun*, 166 Cal.App.4th 1398 (2008), the court of appeal held it does not. The court reasoned that Rule 2–200 is designed to protect clients and that "It makes no sense to allow an attorney whose only connection to the client is through an unenforceable fee-sharing agreement to recover fees directly from that client."

Finally, suppose a lawyer and client agree to a contingent fee and the lawyer then brings in a second lawyer with whom he agrees to divide the contingent fee (in an agreement approved in writing by the client). Suppose further that the client likes the second lawyer better and fires the first lawyer. Suppose finally the second lawyer claims the entire contingent fee. Has the first lawyer any claims against the second? *Olsen v. Harbison,* 191 Cal.App.4th 325 (2010), says "no." In that case the first lawyer alleged claims against the second for quantum meruit, breach of contract, fraud and deceit, and interference with contractual relations. The court of appeals affirmed summary adjudication for the second lawyer on the fraud and interference claims on the ground that they were barred by California's litigation privilege. It affirmed summary adjudication of the quantum meruit and contract claims on the ground that the first lawyer expected to be paid by the client (from the proceeds of the litigation, if any) not by the second lawyer, and that the first lawyer's services were for the benefit of the client, not the second lawyer. The court distinguished *Huskinson* on the ground that, unlike cases where a lawyer has no direct claim against the client, the first lawyer had such a claim and could pursue it directly (because the division of fees was properly approved, it presented no impediment to such a claim).

B. (THE PROHIBITION ON) SELLING YOURSELF OFF

As noted in chapter 13.B.4, Model Rule 5.6(b) forbids you from agreeing to restrict your practice as part of a settlement on behalf of a client. Such arrangements are proposed more often than you might think. They tend to involve cases in which a common fact pattern affects a large number of claimants under circumstances where a class action either cannot be maintained or is less desirable than a series of individual actions. Defendants in such cases sometimes offer to settle a case by paying the client's claim and offering to pay the lawyer to not bring any further cases. Either offering or accepting such a payment is a serious violation of the rules, as the following case illustrates.

Model Rule 5.6(b); Cal. R. Prof. Conduct 1–500

FLORIDA BAR V. RODRIGUEZ

959 So.2d 150 (Fla. 2007)

PER CURIAM

[Francisco Ramon Rodriguez] was a shareholder in the law firm of Friedman, Rodriguez, Ferraro, and St. Louis. The firm was hired to represent twenty clients who sought to sue DuPont Corporation for damages allegedly resulting from use of the DuPont product Benlate, a fungicide that was suspected of causing severe crop damage and was recalled from the market in March 1991. The partners in the firm were Paul D. Friedman, Diane D. Ferraro, Roland R. St. Louis, and Francisco R. Rodriguez. The Florida Bar brought separate disciplinary actions against the four named partners of the firm alleging that they committed misconduct by engaging in a secret "engagement agreement" with the DuPont Corporation, solely for their own financial benefit, while they were representing the clients in the Benlate cases against DuPont.[3] Based on the partners' separate acts of misconduct, they received different sanctions. . . .

With regard to Rodriguez, a referee made the following findings and recommendations.

The Firm, DuPont, and the Engagement Agreement. In 1996, the firm represented twenty different plaintiffs in property damages claims against DuPont arising from the use of Benlate. St. Louis, who was the lawyer who brought in the clients for the firm, had primary responsibility for communicating with the clients. Rodriguez's primary role in the Benlate cases was to act as first chair if any of the cases went to trial and to handle significant hearings.

The firm discovered that in the case for one of its clients, Davis Tree Farm, DuPont had concealed its testing of Benlate in Costa Rica. The test plants exhibited significant damage and DuPont ordered the plants to be destroyed. The firm subsequently filed a motion to strike DuPont's pleadings in the Davis Tree Farm case. The trial court judge orally ruled that she would enter an order striking DuPont's pleadings and entered a judgment in favor of Davis Tree Farm.

---

[3] [Eds Note: The Court elsewhere said "St. Louis and Rodriguez were the firm's principal actors in developing and executing the secret engagement agreement. As will be discussed herein, Rodriguez's misconduct is less egregious than St. Louis's misconduct. St. Louis negotiated the engagement agreement for the firm, placed his financial interests above those of his clients with regard to DuPont, and lied to Judge Wilson and the Bar regarding the secret engagement agreement. This Court disbarred St. Louis. *Florida Bar v. St. Louis*, 967 So.2d 108 (Fla. 2007)."]

After the judge made this oral ruling, DuPont approached the firm to try to settle the Davis Tree Farm case, as well as the other Benlate cases the firm was handling. DuPont's attorney negotiated with Rodriguez and St. Louis. At this point, Rodriguez learned that DuPont was requesting as a condition of settlement a restriction on the firm's right to practice. DuPont's counsel stated that settlement of the firm's cases would include resolving the Davis Tree Farm case before the trial judge issued her written order, as well as requiring the firm not to use the fees earned to fund future litigation against DuPont. The firm engaged in research to determine whether it was ethical for the firm to engage in such an agreement. The firm's researcher informed Rodriguez that the law was unclear, but it appeared that DuPont's objective could be achieved by engaging the firm after the firm finished representing the twenty Benlate clients.

DuPont eventually made offers of settlement to nineteen of the Benlate plaintiffs, but not to Davis Tree Farm. The firm was prepared to recommend that the clients accept the offers because the firm believed the offers exceeded what the clients could have reasonably expected to recover if their respective cases had gone to trial. While Rodriguez initially rejected DuPont's request for the firm not to bring future Benlate cases against the corporation, St. Louis told DuPont that in order to have a restriction on the firm's right to practice, DuPont would have to pay the firm. DuPont made settlement of the nineteen Benlate plaintiffs' claims contingent on the settlement of the Davis Tree Farm case.

On August 7, 1996, the trial judge's written order striking DuPont's pleadings arrived in the mail. Settlement negotiations continued and when DuPont's offer reached $30,000,000, the spokeswoman for Davis Tree Farm agreed to accept the offer. Although Rodriguez believed settlement negotiations were complete, DuPont then made the settlement of the nineteen Benlate clients contingent on the firm agreeing to sign an "engagement agreement" that would preclude the firm from bringing future cases against DuPont. Again, Rodriguez declined to enter into such an agreement until the firm's representation of the clients was complete. The firm resisted DuPont's condition until the appointed mediator made it clear that DuPont would retract the offer unless the firm signed such an engagement agreement. The mediator, who had substantial experience in mass tort cases and had been appointed as the Special Master to handle discovery disputes in Benlate-related litigation in Dade County, advised Rodriguez that in these situations, parties would sometimes make an engagement agreement.

After much discussion about the settlement amounts that the firm was going to recommend that the clients accept from DuPont, the firm and DuPont negotiated the restrictions on the right to practice. DuPont agreed to pay the firm $6,445,000 in exchange for the firm's agreement not to pursue future claims against DuPont and for the firm to possibly perform future work for DuPont on an hourly basis. Thus, the $59,000,000 offered to the Benlate plaintiffs and the $6,445,000 offered to the firm through the engagement agreement constituted separate funds. Rodriguez did not participate in drafting the engagement agreement. However, he did not object to the agreement, he agreed with its terms, and he testified that he "negotiated very hard for the $6,445,000." Further, language in the engagement agreement stated that it was contingent upon the effectiveness of the settlement agreement with the Benlate clients.

The referee found that, at this point, Rodriguez became an agent of DuPont, and his allegiance to both DuPont and his Benlate clients created a conflict of interest. Further, the referee found that the firm placed its interest above that of the Benlate clients because (1) the firm avoided the risks and expenses of protracted litigation and possible appeals; (2) the firm received fees from these cases, some of which had fatal flaws; (3) the firm received significant amounts of attorney's fees from the settlements; (4) the firm accepted a guaranteed $6,445,000 in exchange for not pursuing future cases against DuPont; and (5) the firm could return to the "very successful full time practice" of working on an hourly basis with DuPont as an added client.

The referee found that the attorneys of the firm knew or should have known that negotiations for settlements were not concluded until the clients had accepted DuPont's offers and, if the offers were rejected, they would have to resume negotiations. Yet, DuPont's agreement with the firm was conditioned on the consummation of the settlement agreement between DuPont and the firm's clients. The referee found that the statement in the engagement agreement that the firm had "completed the negotiations" indicated that the firm had a desire, if not an intent, not to have any further discussions with DuPont on behalf of its clients.

On August 8, 1996, the parties appeared before the trial judge and announced that a settlement for the Benlate clients had been reached and requested that the judge vacate and seal the order striking DuPont's pleadings. The parties did not inform the judge about the engagement agreement. Also, because all but two of the Benlate clients had the right to accept or reject the settlement, DuPont insisted that the clients only be told the amount that they were being offered to settle their respective cases. DuPont further insisted that the clients keep the amount they received confidential. To enforce these conditions, ten percent of the settlement amounts were to be held in escrow for two years and, should any breach of confidentiality occur, approximately $6,000,000 of the clients' settlement monies would be lost. Rodriguez never told the clients about the engagement agreement. He claimed that because DuPont had insisted on confidentiality, he believed a breach of that confidentiality would result in the clients losing ten percent of the settlement. However, because the settlement agreement between the clients and DuPont was separate from the engagement agreement between the firm and DuPont, the referee found that the confidentiality provisions of the settlement agreement were between the clients and DuPont, and did not bind the firm. Thus, disclosure of the engagement agreement to the clients would not have jeopardized the escrow funds.

The referee found that by not disclosing the agreement, Rodriguez was protecting the firm's interest in $6,445,000, "his own interest in $1,440,000," and DuPont's economic interests in "not having disclosed to the world that it had done some very bad things to its clientele and got caught doing them." Because there was ongoing Benlate litigation occurring around the nation, the latter information potentially could have caused DuPont serious harm.

Rodriguez testified that the money he would receive from the agreements never entered his mind. However, the referee found this to be unlikely because (1) Rodriguez admitted that he found the amounts offered to the clients to be "staggering"; (2) Rodriguez testified that the Benlate clients were clients with "no hope" and would obtain no money had their cases gone to trial; and (3) Rodriguez "received in excess of $4,700,000 from the settlements."

Aftermath of the Settlement and Engagement Agreements. After the terms of the settlement and engagement agreements were agreed upon, St. Louis traveled around the state to meet with clients and convince them to accept DuPont's settlement agreement. St. Louis told the clients that if they did not accept the settlement offer, the firm would no longer represent them. On August 12, 1996, the firm received $6,445,000. Thereafter, on August 16, 1996, the firm received $59,000,000 from DuPont. When one client refused to settle, Rodriguez filed a motion to withdraw representation and a charging lien. At the hearing on this motion, Rodriguez did not tell the judge about the engagement agreement. Rather, he claimed that he wished to withdraw because the client wanted to eliminate Rodriguez's fee. Eventually, the client accepted DuPont's offer and Rodriguez resumed the attorney-client relationship with the client. Rodriguez did withdraw from representing Fred Haupt, another client who refused to settle. Haupt eventually settled with DuPont through his own means.

1997 Bar Investigation. In 1997, based on the complaint of one of the Benlate plaintiffs, the Bar conducted an investigation into allegations that the firm did not explain to its clients the $59,000,000 original settlement agreement, and that a possible conflict of interest had occurred between the various Benlate clients. The individual who filed the complaint, Robert L. Beasley, alleged that the firm was coercing clients into accepting DuPont's offers, the clients were being held hostage by the firm, and the firm was keeping the interest earned from the clients' settlement funds. Rodriguez contacted attorney Robert Batsel to represent him during this initial Bar investigation, which included a meeting with Bar representatives. Rodriguez and Batsel subsequently testified that the Bar did not ask any questions that called for them to disclose the engagement agreement to the Bar. Rodriguez and Batsel believed the meeting concerned whether there was an improper aggregate settlement with the Benlate clients. Eventually, this earlier disciplinary proceeding resulted in a consent judgment in 1998.

The Instant Complaint. The Bar filed the instant complaint in 2003. Before the referee in these proceedings, Batsel testified that during the 1997 meeting the Bar representatives never posed a question that required Rodriguez to disclose the engagement agreement. Batsel testified that if the Bar had asked questions regarding the engagement agreement during that 1997 investigation, Batsel would have counseled Rodriguez to disclose the agreement. The instant referee found Batsel's testimony credible. Further, the referee found that Rodriguez and Batsel did not conspire to deceive the Bar. The referee did find, however, that Rodriguez should have disclosed the engagement agreement on his own accord during the 1997 investigation.

Findings as to Guilt. Based on these facts, the referee recommended that Rodriguez be found guilty of violating Rules Regulating the Florida Bar 4–1.4(a) (informing client of status of representation), 4–1.4(b) (duty to explain matters to client), 4–1.5(a) (prohibited fees), 4–1.7(a) (representing a client whose interests are adverse to another client), 4–1.7(b) (duty to avoid limitation on independent professional judgment), 4–1.8(a) (business transaction with or acquiring interest adverse to client), 4–1.9(a) (conflict of interest as to former clients), 4–1.16(a)(1) (declining or terminating representation), 4–5.1(c) (responsibilities of a partner for rules violations), 4–5.6(b) (restriction on lawyer's right to practice), and 4–8.4(a) (lawyer shall not violate or attempt to violate the Rules of Professional Conduct). In making these recommendations, the referee specifically rejected the following defenses raised by Rodriguez: (1) he was only following the advice of counsel; (2) he believed he was acting in his clients' best interests; (3) client confidentiality prevented him from disclosing the engagement agreement to the Benlate clients and the Bar; (4) the Bar is at fault in this matter; and (5) DuPont is responsible for these acts of misconduct.

Disciplinary Recommendations. In aggravation, the referee found the sole factor of multiple offenses. In mitigation, the referee found (1) Rodriguez's lack of a disciplinary history; (2) his remorse; (3) his inexperience in handling settlements of multiple-plaintiff mass tort cases; (4) his interim rehabilitation; (5) the length of time during which Rodriguez has had to deal with various proceedings and negative publicity arising out of the DuPont settlement; (6) the emotional, financial, and physical stress Rodriguez has suffered for over eight years as a result of his misconduct; (7) the excellent results Rodriguez obtained for the Benlate clients;[4] and (8) Rodriguez's character and outstanding reputation in the community. . . .

Rodriguez's misconduct does not rise to the same level of egregiousness as that of his former partner St. Louis. *See Fla. Bar v. St. Louis*, 967 So. 2d 108 (Fla. 2007) (disbarring St. Louis). St. Louis engaged in additional acts of misconduct, such as drafting the engagement agreement, signing the engagement agreement on behalf of the firm, deliberately lying to a circuit court judge, making dishonest written statements to Bar representatives, and specifically refusing to advise certain clients in response to their inquiries. Nevertheless, Rodriguez still engaged in extremely serious misdeeds. He was scheduled to serve as first chair if any of the Benlate cases went to trial and he was responsible for the significant hearings. Yet to satisfy his own greed, he engaged in actions that directly conflicted with the interests of his clients. He became an agent for DuPont while still representing his Benlate clients against DuPont. In fact, due to the funds that were held in escrow to prevent any breach of confidentiality, the firm represented the Benlate plaintiffs as a fiduciary (the escrow agent) for two years after signing the engagement agreement. Thus, Rodriguez was representing adverse interests because he was on retainer to DuPont during that two-year period.

Davis Tree Farm was the only client aware of the engagement agreement. The other nineteen clients believed that Rodriguez was representing only their interests. However, Rodriguez's interests were clearly divided. When one client refused to settle, Rodriguez filed a motion to withdraw and filed a charging lien. Rodriguez alleged that he wished to withdraw because the client wanted to eliminate Rodriguez's fee. Rodriguez did not disclose the engagement agreement to the judge. Further, Rodriguez withdrew from representing another client who refused to settle.

When Rodriguez entered into the engagement agreement, he violated rule 4–5.6(b)(restriction on the right to practice). The rule was adopted by this Court in 1986. *See Fla. Bar re Rules Regulating Fla. Bar*, 494 So. 2d 977, 1069 (Fla. 1986). The rule was firmly established by the time Rodriguez entered into the engagement agreement ten years later in 1996. Further, the rule is clear and unambiguous in its language:

Restrictions on right to practice

A lawyer shall not participate in offering or making . . .

---

[4] FN2. In contrast to the referee's finding, this Court has repeatedly refused to find a mitigating factor based on a respondent's assertion that he engaged in misconduct in order to produce benefits for his client or a third party. . . . Thus, we disapprove the referee's finding of this factor in mitigation.

> (b) an agreement in which a restriction on the lawyer's right to practice is part of the settlement of a controversy between private parties.

R. Regulating Fla. Bar 4–5.6(b)(1986). Attorneys who engage in such engagement agreements receive severe sanctions, even when the misconduct is far less egregious than that in the instant case. *See In re Brandt*, 331 Ore. 113 (Or. 2000) (imposing thirteen- and twelve-month suspensions on two lawyers, one with a prior disciplinary record and the other without, for entering into a side agreement with the adversary to act as legal counsel); *In re Hager*, 812 A.2d 904 (D.C. 2002) (suspending for one year a lawyer who, while representing fifty clients against a manufacturer, secured a side agreement with the manufacturer involving restricting his right to practice, dropping the pending case, and maintaining confidentiality). In light of the severe sanctions imposed on attorneys who have engaged in side agreements and Rodriguez's serious misconduct, we conclude that a two-year suspension is the appropriate sanction.

The Court mentioned that the partner who drafted the unlawful engagement agreement, St. Louis, was disbarred. It also mentioned that other partners who were less involved were disciplined as well. What were their fates?

Ferraro received a public reprimand and made restitution of $425,000 to the clients. *Florida Bar v. Ferraro*, 839 So.2d 700 (Fla. 2003) (table citation). The sanction was based on the referee's finding that Ferraro had "absolutely nothing to do with the settlement negotiations with DuPont" and did not even know about the engagement agreement until well after her former partners received the prohibited funds. Also, Ferraro agreed to testify against her former partners. Due to these facts, the referee ultimately recommended a public reprimand, after finding that a suspension or disbarment was not appropriate.

Friedman did not know about the engagement agreement until after it had been executed. Thus, he had a comparatively smaller role in the firm's misconduct than St. Louis and Rodriguez. Also, Friedman cooperated with the Bar and he paid restitution before his disciplinary case was reviewed by this Court. However, Friedman partook in the financial benefits of the unethical engagement agreement, exposed the Benlate clients to potential harm by engaging in the conflict of interest, and acquiesced in the firm lying to the clients. He did not take any measures to inform clients or repudiate the engagement agreement. In fact, as Secretary–Treasurer of the firm, Friedman received the prohibited funds from DuPont. Therefore, Friedman's misconduct merited a ninety-day suspension and payment of restitution in the amount of $910,000. *Fla. Bar v. Friedman*, 940 So.2d 428 (Fla. 2006) (table citation).

Getting Too Cute

As the *Rodriguez* Court describes the situation, Rodriguez and his partners learned that DuPont had suppressed evidence, a fact that could be very damaging to DuPont in other Benlate cases. DuPont wanted the firm out of the Benlate litigation business and was willing to pay a premium to get it out. Some of the premium went to the firm but, the facts suggest, some of it went to the clients, too. One could see how Rodriguez might have seen the engagement agreement as making everybody better off.

Suppose DuPont had been a bit less direct in its approach. Suppose that, instead of so overtly trying to buy off the firm, DuPont's counsel had approached St. Louis and Rodriguez and said, in substance:

> We've come to respect your talent as litigators, and your knowledge of Benlate issues. This litigation will end at some point. When it does, we want to retain you ourselves, so that you can advise us on how not to get into such a mess again. We would of course compensate your at a level commensurate with your unique experience. We believe in value billing, and have no doubt that your advice would be worth millions to us.
>
> We of course cannot enter into such a relationship at this time. Hopefully, however, this litigation will be over soon, so we can continue our relationship on that different basis.
>
> Now, about our settlement offer to your clients. . . .

Once a lawyer accepted such a proposal, Rule 1.9 would prevent it from representing any plaintiff against a company such as DuPont on matters substantially related to the lawyer's advice. And, of course, that is exactly what the client wants: to use the conflict rules to do an end run around the rule against agreements limiting practice.

Is this form of the proposal lawful? How would you handle it?

C. UPL

Laws in each state prohibit the unlicensed practice of law. Determining whether a person has a license is easy. Defining the scope of the practice of law is hard. That definition is important because it defines the things you may do free from competition by non-lawyers who, among other things, have not had to invest in law school and therefore do not have to charge rates sufficient to earn a return on that investment (or just pay off debt incurred in making it). Basic economics tells us that when an activity generates high profits people have an incentive to enter the market in which those profits are earned. The license requirement is a barrier to such entry, which is one reason the definition of "the practice of law" has been under pressure from various sources.

The following materials consider these points, and the forces that continue to affect the production and consumption of legal services. We begin, however, with some very practical rules and advice relevant to students: The rules concerning application and admission to the bar.

How to Apply for Admission to the Bar (and How Not to)

Tell the truth on your application for admission to any bar you apply to. Hopefully this reminder is not necessary, but you should know that the consequences for false statements (either false assertions or materially incomplete and therefore misleading assertions) may well be worse than the consequences of any history you might truthfully disclose. Among other self-evident reasons, bar applicants generally bear the burden of showing that they have the character necessary to practice law. Any questions regarding candor will significantly impair an applicant's ability to bear this burden.

Model Rule 8.1(a) forbids you from making a false statement of material fact on your application. Model Rule 8.1(b) requires you to disclose facts necessary to correct a misapprehension of which you are aware. (The same rules apply to lawyers in disciplinary proceedings.) The wording of many bar applications calls for extensive disclosure and affirmative representations that may turn an omission into an affirmatively false statement.

For example, the applicant in *Application of Zatik*, 126 Ohio St.3d 397 (2010), disclosed on his bar application two misdemeanor convictions for underage alcohol possession, his use of a false ID to purchase alcohol, and his adjudication as a juvenile delinquent based on these offenses plus a residential burglary. The application also asked whether he had "ever failed to answer fully and truthfully all questions on an application for admission to any educational institution?" He had answered in the negative, but in fact he had failed to disclose his convictions on his application to law school. His answer on the bar application was therefore false. The Ohio Board of Commissioners on Character and fitness "recognized that the applicant's criminal convictions and juvenile adjudication, which occurred while he was in his teens, were not likely to interfere with his admission to the bar," but concluded the applicant "needed a 'period of maturation' to develop the honesty, trustworthiness, and reliability necessary for successful admission to the bar." The Board therefore recommended

that the applicant not be allowed to sit for the bar for two years, a rec-

ommendation adopted by the Supreme Court. (Had he taken out loans to finance his legal education, they presumably would have to be paid, somehow, during this period.)

Your burden to show that you possess the character necessary to practice law extends beyond candor. It may even lead to the denial of an application based on charges dismissed on procedural grounds. In *Friedman v. Connecticut Bar Examining Committee,* 77 Conn.App. 526 (2003), for example, the applicant had been accused of cheating on an examination in law school. The student discipline committee found the applicant had cheated and recommended a penalty; the law school dean reversed the sanctions on procedural grounds (undue delay in bringing the charge). The school reported the charge to the Connecticut bar, however, and the Bar Examining Committee held a hearing on the merits of the cheating allegation. The applicant testified in his defense and a student (who had testified previously as well) testified against him.

The Bar Examining Committee found the student had cheated and therefore recommended that he be denied admission. The court of appeal affirmed, noting that it was the applicant's burden to establish his fitness and that the Committee was entitled to believe the student testifying against the applicant rather than the applicant. The court noted in passing that the applicant had disclosed on his bar application that he had been charged with cheating but not convicted; the court questioned the accuracy of that statement: "Query whether it would have been more accurate to respond that the student discipline committee had found against him, but that this decision was reversed due to the delay in bringing the charges to a hearing."

Just as opinions vary on many moral issues, opinions may vary to some extent on the types of conduct that call into question your character and fitness to practice law. Some acts, such as those involving the unlawful use of force or fraud, are universally condemned and accepted as a potentially proper basis for denying admission. The severity of the conduct and any evidence of rehabilitation will be relevant.

Other acts might be debated. In 2009, for example, New York denied admission to an applicant who had failed to pay his student loans after graduation, thus letting the outstanding loan balance increase from $270,000 to $435,000 over four years. The applicant's personal history was remarkable, including the early death of his father and repeated abandonment by his mother. An investigative subcommittee of the Committee on Character and Fitness found

> Applicant's determination to pursue a postsecondary education remarkable particularly in light of the fact that Applicant did not go to junior high or high school. Applicant obtained a GED and took out his first student loans to attend community college to take precollege, foundational courses including, English, math and basic study skills.

> Applicant attended SUNY Albany from 1992 to 1995 and graduated with [a] B.A. degree. From1995 to 1997, Applicant attended SUNY Buffalo and obtained a Masters in Education. From 2000 to 2004, Applicant attended Hastings College of Law, University of California and obtained his J.D. degree. Applicant finished his last three credits needed for law school while attending the University of London where he also obtained an LL.M. degree in December of 2004. Applicant paid for his education by taking out both private and government sponsored student loans which totaled approximately $270,000.00 when he completed his education.
>
> Applicant has spent the last four years trying to get a license to practice law. Applicant disclosed in the interview that he is provided testing accommodations for a learning disability. He was unable to sit for the Florida Bar as planned in July of 2005 due to what appears to be an unfortunate administrative glitch. He stated that he was delayed in taking the New York State bar exam because accommodations for his handicap were originally denied and that after being granted the accommodations he took the exam three times before passing in February of 2008. Applicant took the California bar exam in July of 2008 but failed by a few points. During this four year delay Applicant has been unable to make substantial payments toward his student loans, but has no other delinquent debt.

In November 2009, the New York Supreme Court, Appellate Division, affirmed the Committee's decision. The court found the applicant's "recalcitrance in dealing with the lenders has been and continues to be incompatible with a lawyer's duties and responsibilities as a member of the bar. . . . " (The quoted documents may be found through links in Jonathan D. Glater, *Again, Debt Disqualifies Applicant From the Bar*, NEW YORK TIMES November 19, 2009, available at http://www.nytimes.com/2009/11/27/business/27lawyer.html.)

Some differences of opinion may introduce constitutional considerations into the licensing decision. In *Hallinan v. Committee of Bar Examiners*, 65 Cal.2d 447 (1966), for example, the California Committee of Bar Examiners refused to certify an applicant fit to practice law. The Committee cited the applicant's criminal convictions based on acts of civil disobedience he committed in connection with the Civil Rights Movement of the 1960s and the applicant's history of getting into fistfights. The California Supreme Court reversed.

With regard to the civil disobedience aspect of the Committee's decision, the Court cited the United States Supreme Court's decision in *Schware v. Board of Bar Examiners*, 353 U.S. 232 (1957), which held an applicant's history of ideological activism, including some violations of the law, was not enough to justify denying admission to an otherwise qualified applicant. The Court held:

> A State can require high standards of qualification, such as good moral character or proficiency in its law, before it admits an applicant to the bar, but any qualification must have a rational connection with the applicant's fitness or capacity to practice law. . . . Obviously an applicant could not be excluded merely because he was a Republican or a Negro or a member of a particular church. Even in applying permissible standards, officers of a State cannot exclude an applicant when there is no basis for their finding that he fails to meet these standards, or when their action is invidiously discriminatory.

The California Supreme Court concluded that "[t]he purposes of investigation by the bar into an applicant's moral character should be limited to assurance that, if admitted, he will not obstruct the administration of justice or otherwise act unscrupulously in his capacity as an officer of the court." (The court dealt with the fistfights on essentially factual grounds.)

Ideologically motivated conduct still may lead to denial of an application for admission to the bar, however. The case of Matthew Hale is a recent notable example. In *Hale v. Committee on Character and Fitness for the State of Illinois*, 335 F.3d 678 (7th Cir. 2003), the court described the facts as follows:

> Hale's avowed mission in life is to bring about the hegemony of the white race, the legal abolition of equal protection, and the deportation of non-white Americans by non-violent means. With these goals in mind, Hale attended Southern Illinois University School of Law, graduating with a J.D. and passing the Illinois bar exam in 1998. In his application for admission to the Illinois State Bar, Hale disclosed his active role in promoting racism and anti-Semitism.
>
> Hale's application was referred to a single member of the Committee on Character and Fitness of the Third Judicial District of the State of Illinois (Third District Committee), pursuant to Rule 5.1(a) of the Rules of Procedure of the Board of Admissions and the Committee on Character and Fitness (the Rules of Procedure). This member advised the Board that he was not prepared to recommend that Hale be admitted to practice law in Illinois.
>
> In accordance with Rule 5.2(a) of the Rules of Procedure, the Chairperson of the Third District Committee assigned Hale's application to a three-person "Inquiry Panel" for further review. On December 18, 1998, in a 2–1 written decision, the Inquiry Panel recommended that the Committee refuse to approve Hale's admission to practice law in Illinois. The Committee rejected the argument that Hale was merely an applicant with distasteful views that were nonetheless protected under the First Amendment. Instead, it said, Hale's active commitment to bigotry under "any civilized standards of decency" demonstrated a "gross deficiency in moral character, particularly for lawyers who have a special responsibility to uphold the rule of law for all

persons." In short, the Committee believed that Hale was likely to commit acts of various kinds in the future that were inconsistent with membership in the bar.

The Inquiry Panel's recommendation that Hale not be certified resulted in the automatic creation by the Committee of a five-member "Hearing Panel" to determine with finality whether Hale should be certified for admission to practice law. The Panel held a hearing on April 10, 1999, at which multiple witnesses testified that Hale possessed the requisite character and fitness to practice law. Hale himself testified before the Panel, and asserted that he was prepared to comply with the Rules of Professional Conduct. He also indicated, however, that he believed that the Rules applied only while he worked as an attorney, and not while he practiced his religion.

On June 30, 1999, the Hearing Panel denied Hale's application. It began by drawing a distinction between Hale's First Amendment right to express ideas and his right to become a member of the Illinois bar, commenting that the case was "not about Mr. Hale's First Amendment rights. The issue here is whether Mr. Hale possesses the requisite character and fitness for admission for the practice of law." The Hearing Panel based its decision that Hale had not satisfied his burden of proving that he possessed the requisite character and fitness on several findings. First, the Hearing Panel believed that Hale's outspoken intent to continue discriminating in his private life, especially taken together with negative character evidence such as academic probation, an order of protection, and a list of arrests (not convictions), was inconsistent with the Rules of Professional Conduct. The Hearing Panel was also concerned about Hale's refusal to repudiate a 1995 letter he wrote in response to published commentary in support of affirmative action, in which Hale referred to the female author's "rape at the hands of a nigger beast." The letter, the Hearing Panel found, was insulting, inappropriate, and showed a "monumental lack of sound judgment" that would put Hale "on a collision course with the Rules of Professional Conduct." Finally, the Hearing Panel concluded that Hale was not candid and open with it during the hearing.

After this denial Hale petitioned the Illinois Supreme Court for review. The Court denied the petition. *In re Hale*, 243 Ill. 174 (1999). Hale then petitioned the United States Supreme Court for a writ of *certiorari* granting review. It was denied as well. The Seventh Circuit, in the case quoted above, affirmed a district court order denying review of the Committee's decision on grounds of abstention.

One Illinois Supreme Court judge dissented from that Court's refusal to hear the case. He described the issues as follows:

> The crux of the Committee's decision to deny petitioner's application to practice law is petitioner's open advocacy of racially obnoxious beliefs. The Hearing Panel found that petitioner's "publicly displayed views are diametrically opposed to the letter and spirit" of the Rules of Professional Conduct. The Inquiry Panel found that, in regulating the conduct of attorneys, certain "fundamental truths" of equality and nondiscrimination "must be preferred over the values found in the First Amendment." Petitioner contends that the Committee's use of his expressed views to justify the denial of his admission to the bar violates his constitutional rights to free speech. That constitutional question deserves explicit, reasoned resolution by this court. Instead, the court silently accepts the conclusion of the Committee, which asserted that "[t]his case is not about Mr. Hale's First Amendment rights." To the contrary, this case clearly impacts both the first amendment to the federal Constitution and article I, section 4, of the Illinois Constitution.
>
> In addition, the Committee's ruling on petitioner's application presents a second important issue which this court should address. The Committee seems to hold that it may deny petitioner's application for admission to the bar without finding that petitioner has engaged in any specific conduct that would have violated a disciplinary rule if petitioner were already a lawyer. The Committee merely speculates that petitioner is "on a collision course with the Rules of Professional Conduct" and that, if admitted, he will *in the future* "find himself before the Attorney Registration and Disciplinary Commission." I believe this court should address whether it is appropriate for the Committee to base its assessment of an applicant's character and fitness on speculative predictions of future actionable misconduct.
>
> The question also arises: If all of petitioner's statements identified by the Committee had been made after obtaining a license to practice law, would he then be subject to disbarment? That is to say, is there one standard for admission to practice and a different standard for continuing to practice? And, if the standard is the same, can already-licensed lawyers be disbarred for obnoxious speech?
>
> The Illinois Supreme Court is the licensing authority for all Illinois lawyers. Its rules cover all aspects of admission to the bar and professional conduct thereafter. It has the power to license, regulate, and to disbar. The issues presented by Mr. Hale's petition are of such significant constitutional magnitude that they deserve a judicial review and determination by this court.

In re Hale, 243 Ill.Dec. 174 (1999) (Heiple, J., dissenting).

In 2004 Hale was tried and convicted for soliciting the murder of a federal judge who had ruled against him in a trademark dispute.

A license to practice law is needed only if you are practicing law, which raises the question of what does and does not constitute legal practice. The following materials survey answers to that question and some implications of those answers.

UNAUTHORIZED PRACTICE OF LAW COMMITTEE V. PARSONS TECHNOLOGY, INC.

1999 WL 47235 (N.D.Tex. 1999).

SANDERS, SENIOR J.

The Plaintiff, the Unauthorized Practice of Law Committee ("the UPLC"), is comprised of six Texas lawyers and three lay citizens appointed by the Supreme Court of Texas. The UPLC is responsible for enforcing Texas' unauthorized practice of law statute, Tex. Gov't Code §§ 81.101–.106 (Vernon's 1998) ('the Statute").[5]

The Defendant, Parsons Technology, Inc., ("Parsons") is a California corporation, whose principal place of business is Iowa, and is engaged in the business of developing, publishing and marketing software products, such as *Quicken Financial Software, Turbo Tax,* and *Webster's Talking Dictionary*. Parsons has published and offered for sale through retailers in Texas a computer software program entitled *Quicken Family Lawyer,* version 8.0, and its updated version *Quicken Family Lawyer '99* ("QFL").

QFL is the product at the center of this controversy. In its most recent version, QFL offers over 100 different legal forms (such as employment agreements, real estate leases, premarital agreements, and seven different will forms) along with instructions on how to fill out these forms. QFL's packaging represents that the product is "valid in 49 states including the District of Columbia;" is "developed and reviewed by expert attorneys;" and is "updated to reflect recent legislative formats." The packaging also indicates that QFL will have the user "answer a few questions to determine which estate planning and health care documents best meet [the user's] needs;" and that QFL will "interview you in a logical order,

---

[5] FN1. Tex. Gov't Code § 81.101 defines the practice of law, as follows:

(a) In this chapter the "practice of law" means the preparation of a pleading or other document incident to an action or special proceeding or the management of the action or proceeding on behalf of a client before a judge in court as well as a service rendered out of court, including the giving of advice or the rendering of any service requiring the use of legal skill or knowledge, such as preparing a will, contract, or other instrument, the legal effect of which under the facts and conclusions involved must be carefully determined.

(b) The definition in this section is not exclusive and does not deprive the judicial branch of the power and authority under both this chapter and the adjudicated cases to determine whether other services and acts not enumerated may constitute the practice of law.

tailoring documents to your situation." Finally, the packaging reassures the user that "[h]andy hints and comprehensive legal help topics are always available."

The first time a user accesses QFL after installing it on her computer the following disclaimer appears as the initial screen:

> This program provides forms and information about the law. We cannot and do not provide specific information for your exact situation.
>
> For example, we can provide a form for a lease, along with information on state law and issues frequently addressed in leases. But we cannot decide that our program's lease is appropriate for you.
>
> Because we cannot decide which forms are best for your individual situation, you must use your own judgment and, to the extent you believe appropriate, the assistance of a lawyer.

This disclaimer does not appear anywhere on QFL's packaging. Additionally, it does not appear on subsequent uses of the program unless the user actively accesses the "Help" pull-down menu at the top of the screen and then selects "Disclaimer."

On the initial use of QFL, or anytime a new user name is created, QFL asks for the user's name and state of residence. It then inquires whether the user would like QFL to suggest documents to the user. If the user answers "Yes," QFL's "Document Advisor" asks the user a few short questions concerning the user's marital status, number of children, and familiarity with living trusts. QFL then displays the entire list of available documents, but marks a few of them as especially appropriate for the user based on her responses.

When the user accesses a document, QFL asks a series of questions relevant to filling in the legal form. With certain questions, a separate text box explaining the relevant legal considerations the user may want to take into account in filling out the form also appears on the screen. As the user proceeds through the questions relevant to the specific form, QFL either fills in the appropriate blanks or adds or deletes entire clauses from the form. For example, in the "Real Estate Lease—Residential" form, depending on how the user answers the question regarding subleasing the apartment, a clause permitting subleasing with the consent of the landlord is either included or excluded from the form.

If a user selects a "health care document" (i.e., a living will, an advance health care directive, or a health care power of attorney) the following screen appears:

> Health Care laws vary from state to state. Your state may not offer every type of health care document.

> Family Lawyer assumes that you wish to have a health care document based on the laws of your state.
>
> When you select a living will, health care power of attorney, or advance health care directive, Family Lawyer will open the appropriate document based on your state.

When a Texas user selects a health care document a form entitled "Directive to Physicians and Durable Power of Attorney for Health Care" appears.

In addition to the separate text boxes providing question and form specific information, at any time throughout the program, the user may access various other help features which provide additional legal information. . . .

The UPLC filed this action in state court alleging that the selling of QFL violates Texas' unauthorized practice of law statute, Tex. Gov't Code § 81.101 and seeking, among other things, to enjoin the sale of QFL in Texas. Parsons subsequently removed this case to this Court. Both parties now seek summary judgment. The UPLC argues that Parsons has violated the Statute as a matter of law. Parsons responds that the mere selling of books or software cannot violate the statute because some form of personal contact beyond publisher-consumer is required by a plain reading of the Statute. Alternatively, if the statute is not construed to require some form of personal relationship, Parsons argues that the application of the Statute to the mere sale and distribution of QFL would infringe upon Parsons' speech rights under the United States and Texas Constitutions. Parsons also argues that the Statute, if utilized to prevent the sale and distribution of QFL, should be void for vagueness. . . .

III. ANALYSIS

B. *The Violation of the Texas Unauthorized Practice of Law Statute.*

The UPLC moves for summary judgment because it claims, as a matter of law, the sale and distribution of QFL violates the Statute. The UPLC argues that QFL gives advice concerning legal documents and selects legal documents for users, both of which involve the use of legal skill and knowledge, and this constitutes the practice of law. Additionally, the UPLC argues that the Defendant's forms are misleading and incorrect. In sum, the UPLC alleges that QFL acts as a "high tech lawyer by interacting with its 'client' while preparing legal instruments, giving legal advice, and suggesting legal instruments that should be employed by the user." In other words, QFL is a "cyber-lawyer."

No one disputes that the practice of law encompasses more than the mere conduct of cases in the courts. *See In re Duncan,* 65 S.E. 210 (S.C.1909) (finding that the practice of law includes "the preparation of legal instruments of all kinds, and, in general, all advice to clients, and all action taken for them in matters connected with the law."). However, a comprehensive definition of just what qualifies as the practice of law is "impossible," and "each case must be decided upon its own particular facts." *Palmer v. Unauthorized Practice of Law Committee,* 438 S.W.2d 374, 376 (Tex.App.—Houston 1969, no writ); *see also State Bar of Michigan v. Cramer,* 249 N.W.2d 1, 7 (Mich.1976) ("any attempt to formulate a lasting, all encompassing definition of 'practice of law' is doomed to failure.").

The UPLC, in arguing that the publication and sale of QFL constitutes the unauthorized practice of law, relies on two Texas Court of Appeals cases, *Palmer v. Unauthorized Practice of Law Committee,* 438 S.W.2d 374 (Tex.App.—Houston 1969, no writ), and *Fadia v. Unauthorized Practice of Law Committee,* 830 S.W.2d 162 (Tex.App.—Dallas 1992, writ denied).

Palmer held that the sale of will forms containing blanks to be filled in by the user, along with instructions, constituted the unauthorized practice of law. The *Palmer* court observed that the form sold by Mr. Palmer was "almost a will itself" and that the form purported to make specific testamentary bequests. The court feared that the unsuspecting layman "by reading defendants' advertisements, by reading the will form, and by reading the definitions that are attached, . . . [would be] led to believe that defendants' will 'form' is in fact only a form and that all testamentary dispositions may be thus standardized." The *Palmer* court held that the preparation of legal instruments of all kinds involves the practice of law. The *Palmer* court further held that the exercise of judgment in the proper drafting of legal instruments, or even the selecting of the proper form of instrument, necessarily affects important legal rights, and thus, is the practice of law.

In *Fadia,* the *pro se* defendant sold and distributed a manual entitled "You and Your Will: A Do–It–Yourself Manual." The defendant in *Fadia* attempted to get around *Palmer's* conclusion that the selling of a will manual constitutes the unauthorized practice of law, by arguing that the court should reject *Palmer* in light of recent state court decisions requiring some form of personal contact or relationship between the alleged unauthorized lawyer and the putative client in order to violate the unauthorized practice of law statute. The court rejected the defendant's argument, stating that it would not overrule *Palmer* and if there were to be a pre-requisite of personal contact between the parties, such a change to the Statute would have to come from the legislature and not the courts. The *Fadia* court went on to hold that because a will secures legal rights and its drafting involves the giving of advice requiring the use of legal skill or knowledge, the preparation of a will involves the practice of law. Since the selection of the proper legal form also affects important legal rights, the court reasoned that it too constituted the practice of law.

Therefore, since the will manual both purported to advise a layman on how to draft a will and selected a specific form for the layman to use, the court determined that the Defendant's selling of a will manual qualified as the unauthorized practice of law.

As already mentioned, the *Palmer* court found that the preparation of legal instruments of all kinds involves the practice of law. The Texas Supreme Court has since held that the mere advising of a person as to whether or not to file a form requires legal skill and knowledge, and therefore, would be the practice of law.

Based on the interpretations of the Statute by the Texas courts, QFL falls within the range of conduct that Texas courts have determined to be the unauthorized practice of law. For instance, QFL purports to select the appropriate health care document for an individual based upon the state in which she lives. QFL customizes the documents, by adding or removing entire clauses, depending upon the particular responses given by the user to a set of questions posed by the program. The packaging of QFL represents that QFL will "interview you in a logical order, tailoring documents to your situation." Additionally, the packaging tells the user that the forms are valid in 49 states and that they have been updated by legal experts. This creates an air of reliability about the documents, which increases the likelihood that an individual user will be misled into relying on them. This false impression is not diminished by QFL's disclaimer. The disclaimer only actively appears the first-time the program is used after it is installed, and there is no guarantee that the person who initially uses the program is the same person who will later use and rely upon the program.

QFL goes beyond merely instructing someone how to fill in a blank form. While no single one of QFL's acts, in and of itself, may constitute the practice of law, taken as a whole Parsons, through QFL, has gone beyond publishing a sample form book with instructions, and has ventured into the unauthorized practice of law.

Parsons attempts to avoid the conclusion that it is guilty of the unauthorized practice of law by arguing that the Statute requires personal contact or a lawyer-client relationship. Parsons bases its argument first on the language of the Statute, which it contends requires that the prohibited services must be provided "on behalf of a client" in order to be the practice of law.

Even assuming that Parsons is correct that paragraph (a) of the Statute requires the prohibited services to be completed "on behalf of" a client, paragraph (a) of the Statute is not an exclusive definition of the unauthorized practice of law. Paragraph (b) of the Statute gives the Court the authority to determine that other acts constitute the unauthorized practice of law. Therefore, a judge could legitimately determine, under the authority granted in paragraph (b), that services provided to the public as a whole, as opposed to a singular client, qualify as the practice of law.

Next, Parsons argues that this Court should require a personal relationship between the party charged with the unauthorized practice of law and the party who benefits from the "advice" since this is the logic of almost every other court to consider the issue. . . . However, as noted above, the *pro se* defendant in *Fadia* made this exact argument and the Texas Court of Appeals rejected it. . . .

Parsons' arguments to the contrary notwithstanding, QFL is far more than a static form with instructions on how to fill in the blanks. For instance, QFL adapts the content of the form to the responses given by the user. QFL purports to select the appropriate health care document for an individual based upon the state in which she lives. The packaging of QFL makes various representations as to the accuracy and specificity of the forms. In sum, Parsons has violated the unauthorized practice of law statute. . . .

The opinion in *Parsons* was vacated after the Texas legislature amended the definition of the "practice of law" to exclude "the design, creation, publication, distribution, display, or sale, including publication, distribution, display, or sale by means of an Internet web site, of written materials, books, forms, computer software, or similar products if the products clearly and conspicuously state that the products are not a substitute for the advice of an attorney." *See Unauthorized Practice of Law Committee v. Parsons Technology, Inc.*, 179 F.3d 956 (5th Cir. 1999).

CASE QUESTIONS:

1. What did QFL do?
2. Did individual acts of QFL constitute UPL?
3. What defense did Parsons assert?
4. Were the representations about QFL false?

For a similar case, *see Franklin v. Chavis*, 371 S.C. 527, 529 (2007), in which the South Carolina Supreme Court found that an insurance agent engaged in the unlicensed practice of law when an elderly acquaintance (and former client) of his asked him to help her draft a will. The woman gave the agent information about how she wanted the will to read. He used "Quicken Lawyer" software to generate the will for her; his role was limited to inputting the information she had given him, in response to queries generated by the software. According to the court:

> The preparation of legal documents constitutes the practice of law when such preparation involves the giving of advice, consultation, explanation, or recommendations on matters of law. Even the preparation of standard forms that require no creative drafting may constitute the practice of law if one acts as more than a mere scrivener. The purpose of prohibiting the unauthorized practice of law is to protect the public from incompetence in the preparation of legal documents and prevent harm resulting from inaccurate legal advice. *Housing Auth. of City of Charleston v. Key*, 352 S.C. 26 (2002); *see also In re: Baker*, 85 A.2d 505, 514 (N.J. 1951) ("The amateur at law is as dangerous to the community as an amateur surgeon. . . . ").
>
> The novel question here is whether respondent's actions in filling in the blanks in a computer-generated generic will constitute the practice of law. Respondent selected the will form, filled in the information given by Ms. Weiss, and arranged the execution of the will at the hospital. Although these facts are not in themselves conclusive, the omission of facts indicating Ms. Weiss's involvement is significant. There is no evidence Ms. Weiss reviewed the will once it was typed. The will was not typed in her presence and although respondent relates the details of what Ms. Weiss told him to do, there is no indication he contemporaneously recorded her instructions and then simply transferred the information to the form.
>
> We construe the role of "scrivener" in this context to mean someone who does nothing more than record verbatim what the decedent says. We conclude respondent's actions in drafting Ms. Weiss's will exceeded those of a mere scrivener and he engaged in the unauthorized practice of law.

PROBLEM 14–3

Do you agree with the conclusion of the *Chavis* court? Should Chavis be punished for this violation? What should the punishment be? Should Chavis's role in drafting the will render it invalid?

The Economics of Licensing

Probably you are in law school in order to practice law or, more precisely, train yourself to obtain a license to practice law (and then practice it well). That lawyering is a licensed profession is economically significant, and you should understand why. The economics of licensing will affect your career, because they affect the profession itself.

States that require you to attend law school, pass a bar exam, and pay a fee in order to practice law create barriers to entry. Those barriers impose costs on you, costs you have to recover for this to be an economically rational endeavor, and which you will therefore try to build into your fee schedules. Both the restriction on supply and the cost to licensed lawyers will tend to increase the costs clients pay for legal services.

A corollary point is that uniform license standards fit poorly with the demands of heterogeneous consumers. Especially when licensing is done by members of the licensed group—lawyers themselves—the bar may be set too high for consumers who need relatively simple service. Other losers from licensing include workers who could provide a level of service that would satisfy demand for relatively simple tasks but who cannot clear the (excessively high) licensing hurdle. Legal assistants, who do much routine work within firms, provide an example here.

If licensing succeeds in restricting entry then lawyers will make higher profits than they would in a freely competitive market. Higher profits tend to attract entry by non-lawyers who could provide substitute services but who have not passed the bar. That is why we see pressure on lawyers' profits from accountants who prepare tax returns, real estate specialists who close transactions, legal assistants who help fill out simple forms, and even interactive software, which helps people do simple legal tasks themselves.

Software might not be a perfect substitute for a real lawyer (such as you hope to be), you might say, but even if that claim is true (software is never tired or distracted or hung over, after all) that is only part of the relevant question. An economically rational consumer would want to know whether the increased expertise a real lawyer might offer would make a difference to them. Sometimes it will, but there is no reason to think it will in every case.

These points combine to form an argument you would do well to remember. The basic structure is simple. Licensing creates barriers to entry. Barriers to entry create supracompetitive profits for licensed lawyers. Supracompetitive profits attract entry efforts by persons seeking to earn such profits. Such efforts put pressure on the state to create exceptions to the licensing system, especially for persons who are demonstrably competent at discrete tasks lawyers can also perform. Successful entry drives revenues down to competitive levels. That means if you cannot offer clients a comparative advantage over non-lawyers who offer services that might substitute for yours, you cannot earn supracompetitive profits and may not be able to recover your investment in becoming a lawyer.

All this raises a question: what is "the practice of law" anyway? Is there really any such thing? Or is there only a set of things lawyers commonly do but which other people could do, too, if they had the chance? Could a good actor give as good a closing argument as a good lawyer? Could a good economist defend as well against an antitrust claim? This question is discussed in the following reading. Keep in mind that whatever you say the practice of law is, the line you draw creates real costs and benefits for real people, only some of whom are law students.

[Footnotes omitted]

Federal Trade Commission
Washington, DC 20580

Department Of Justice
Washington, DC 20530

December 20, 2002

Task Force on the Model Definition
of the Practice of Law
American Bar Association
750 N Lake Shore Drive
Chicago, IL 60611

Re: Comments on the American Bar Association's Proposed Model Definition of the Practice of Law

Dear Members of the Task Force:

The United States Department of Justice ("DOJ") and the Federal Trade Commission ("FTC") submit this letter in response to the Task Force's solicitation for public comments regarding its proposed Model Definition of the Practice of Law. The DOJ and the FTC understand the definition to be a proposed statute, regulation, or court rule, and submit these comments pursuant to that understanding. . . .

[W]e urge the ABA not to adopt the current proposed Definition, which, in our judgment, is overbroad and could restrain competition between lawyers and nonlawyers to provide similar services to American consumers. If adopted by state governments, the proposed Definition is likely to raise costs for consumers and limit their competitive choices. There is no evidence before the ABA of which we are aware that consumers are hurt by this competition and there is substantial evidence that they benefit from it. Consequently, we recommend that the proposed Model Definition be substantially narrowed or rejected. . . .

The Proposed Model Definition

The proposed Model Definition would define "the practice of law" as:

> [T]he application of legal principles and judgment with regard to the circumstances or objectives of a person that require the knowledge and skill of a person trained in the law.

Under subsection (c) of the Definition, "a person is presumed to be practicing law when engaging in any of the following conduct on behalf of another:"

> (1) Giving advice or counsel to persons as to their legal rights or responsibilities or to those of others;
>
> (2) Selecting, drafting, or completing legal documents or agreements that affect the legal rights of a person;
>
> (3) Representing a person before an adjudicative body, including, but not limited to, preparing or filing documents or conducting discovery; or
>
> (4) Negotiating legal rights or responsibilities on behalf of a person.

"Whether or not they constitute the practice of law," the proposed subsection (d) of the Model Definition would permit as an exception:

> (1) Practicing law authorized by a limited license to practice;
>
> (2) *Pro se* representation;
>
> (3) Serving as a mediator, arbitrator, conciliator or facilitator; and
>
> (4) Providing services under the supervision of a lawyer in compliance with the Rules of Professional Conduct.

A separate comment states that "for a person's conduct to be considered the practice of law, there must be another person toward whom the benefit of that conduct is directed. . . . The conduct also must be targeted toward the circumstances or objectives of a specific person. Thus, courts have held that the publication of legal self-help books is not the practice of law." The Definition further notes that nonlawyers engaged in the practice of law could be subject to civil and criminal penalties.

The proposed Model Definition is overly broad because it would prohibit nonlawyers from offering a number of services that they currently provide in competition with lawyers to the benefit of consumers. These services arguably would include those that relate to real estate closing and related matters; wills, trusts and estates; and numerous other areas. Many of these services, while not "requir[ing] the knowledge and skill of a person trained in the law," appear nonetheless to fall within the Model Definition's list of four types of conduct that are presumed to be "the practice of law."

Lay real estate closings are an area with which the DOJ and the FTC have much recent experience, and they provide a specific and fertile example of how the proposed Model Definition would result in significant consumer harm. The proposed Model Definition has the potential to prohibit or to limit the lay provision of real estate closing services. . . . realtors routinely fill out and explain purchase and sale agreements, the basic agreements into which buyers enter as the first steps toward buying a home. They may explain to consumers the ramifications of failing to have the home inspection done on time, the meaning of the mortgage contingency clause, and other portions of the agreement. They may also negotiate these clauses during the purchase process. Realtors often explain what is required by state law to obtain a smoke detector certificate, a termite certificate, and other certificates required by law for the purchase and sale of a home. . . . .

Other forms of lawyer-nonlawyer competition outside of the real estate context also could be eliminated or reduced by the proposed Model Definition. In the area of wills, trusts and estates, consumers use inexpensive electronic software to complete wills, trusts, and other legal documents. This software might be considered the practice of law under the proposed Model Definition because these applications assist in the "selection" and "drafting" of certain documents, and provide legal information and/or advice. Even though the software is produced for a mass audience and the proposed Model Definition indicates that conduct "must be targeted toward the circumstances or objectives of a specific person" in order to be the practice of law, we are concerned that a state agency or court could conceivably view the interactive nature of these programs as rising to the level of legal practice.

Consumers also obtain information or assistance regarding wills and trusts from other lay sources. Hospitals and other organizations essentially compete with lawyers by providing living will forms that prospective patients may complete. In some cases, these forms might be "selected" and "drafted" by the hospital and given to the patient by their physician. This practice arguably would be considered "the practice of law" under the proposed Model Definition.

While it is impossible to develop an exhaustive list of all of the instances of lawyer-nonlawyer competition that might be eliminated as a result of the proposed Model Definition, other examples include:

- Tenants' associations informing renters of landlords' and tenants' legal rights and responsibilities, often in the context of a particular landlord-tenant problem;
- Experienced lay employees advising their employer about what their firm must do to comply with state labor laws or safety regulations;

- Income tax preparers and accountants interpreting federal and state tax codes, family law code, and general partnership laws, and providing advice to their clients that incorporates this legal information; and
- Investment bankers and other business planners providing advice to their clients that includes information about various laws.

The proposed Model Definition arguably would cover each of these practices, and thus could preclude or inhibit nonlawyers from continuing to provide such services if the proposed Model Definition were to be adopted by any state. Moreover, to the extent the Model Definition is vague and ambiguous, the possibility exists that state agencies or courts will prohibit procompetitive conduct that the Task Force did not intend to include within the scope of the Model Definition of the practice of law. . . .

When nonlawyers compete with lawyers to provide services that do not require formal legal training, consumers may consider all relevant factors in selecting a service provider, such as cost, convenience, and the degree of assurance that the necessary documents and commitments are sufficient. The use of lay services also can reduce costs to consumers. Evidence suggests that the use of lay real estate closers provides a lower cost alternative for consumers. Additionally, although accountants and tax preparers do not typically itemize the legal-related services included in their services, it is probable that the cost of retaining an attorney for those same services would often be higher. Advice and information about the laws from tenants' associations and other advocacy organizations is often free. Will writing and other legal form fill software packages can be significantly less expensive than hiring an attorney to draft the will or other legal document. These services plainly benefit consumers. . . .

The DOJ and the FTC are unaware of any showing of likely harm that would justify a broad definition of "the practice of law" that would effectively preclude many nonlawyers from providing efficient services that are beneficial to consumers and serve the public interest. The agencies have not seen any factual evidence demonstrating that consumers are actually hurt by the availability of lay services. Many of the proposed state bar agency unauthorized practice of law opinions that our agencies have reviewed set forth no factual evidence and little evaluation of how the ability of lay services had actually hurt consumers. . . .

For consumers, the services of a licensed lawyer may well be desirable in many situations. A consumer might choose to hire an attorney to answer legal questions, provide legal advice, research the case law, negotiate disputes, or offer various protections. Consumers who hire attorneys may get better service and representation than those who do not. This is, however, no reason to eliminate lay service providers as an alternative.

Rather, the choice of hiring a lawyer or a nonlawyer should rest with the consumer.

Your Comparative Advantage and the Thesis of This Course

There is little question that many persons, and even many software programs, can in fact substitute effectively for routine tasks that lawyers now perform. With respect to such services, over the course of your career you should expect to see continued entry by non-lawyers, and therefore downward pressure on the fees you can charge. Other than actual argument in court—and probably not even as to that—there really is no single discrete act that lawyers do that some non-lawyers could not do as well if they took the time to learn it.

Is all this cause for despair? Has law school been a horrible mistake? No. In addition to strictly legal knowledge (which QFL has), there are two things you have that most non-lawyers do not. One is the ability to apply a large number of different types of knowledge to solve concrete legal problems. Though they do not use the terminology very often, case law is run through with applied everything: economics, sociology, literature, logic, history, philosophy, and more. You may not be more expert than a specialist in any one of these fields, but you will have more experience *applying* the basic learning of that field, in conjunction with learning from other relevant fields, in order to solve a concrete problem. The second thing you have is a habit of mind that can select what is relevant and analyze it dynamically and interactively in relation to some problem that needs to be solved.

In other words, what you have that software does not is legal judgment. When you work through the practice of law and try to identify what is unique to it, that may be all you find left. It is therefore your comparative advantage, and thus literally your stock in trade.

UPL and Multi-State Practice
Model Rule of Professional Conduct 5.5

Thus far we have been discussing the "practice of law" by people or programs who are not lawyers. But UPL regulations are state regulations, and they require that a person be licensed to practice *in the state in which the rule applies.* A lawyer licensed in New York is not thereby entitled to practice in California, and vice versa.

In an era of low communication and travel costs, this rule can present problems. Especially among larger firms it is extremely common for lawyers to ply their trade in a number of different places. If you represent a client in San Francisco and are flying to New York to depose a third-party witness, and during a layover in Chicago you return a telephone call from a client in Seattle, are you practicing law in any or all of California, Illinois, Washington, or New York? Would it matter if the California dispute was in private arbitration, rather than court? Would it matter if the matter was not litigation at all, but negotiation of a business deal among persons located in these places?

The Model Rules provide some guidance. Under Model Rule 5.5(a), you may not practice in a jurisdiction in violation of that jurisdiction's rules and you may not help anyone else to practice in violation of such rules. Under Rule 5.5(b) you may not establish a continuous presence in a jurisdiction in which you are not admitted or represent to others that you are admitted in places you are not. Rule 5.5(c) provides that a lawyer admitted in one jurisdiction (and not disbarred or suspended) may work temporarily in a jurisdiction where they are not admitted if they work with a lawyer who is admitted and actively participates in the representation, or if their work relates to a proceeding and the lawyer is or reasonably expects to be authorized to appear in the proceeding (or, in the case of alternative dispute resolution proceedings, if the proceedings arise from or relate to the lawyer's practice in a jurisdiction where he or she is admitted).

The case law answer to these questions is not very clear. The leading case is *Birbrower, Montalbano, Condon & Frank, P.C. v. Superior Court*, 17 Cal.4th 119 (1998). The case involved a New York firm, Birbrower, retained to represent ESQ, a California corporation located in Santa Clara County. ESQ had a contractual dispute with Tandem computers. Birbrower lawyers traveled to California on several occasions, spending a significant amount of time there.

ESQ and Tandem settled their dispute, and ESQ then sued Birbrower for malpractice. The suit was filed in California. Birbrower counterclaimed for fees it claimed it was owed. ESQ sought summary judgment on the counterclaim, arguing that the Birbrower attorneys were not licensed to practice in California and therefore had violated California Business and Professions Code section 6125. That section, like most UPL statutes, provides that "No person shall practice law in California unless the person is an active member of the State Bar."

The trial court granted ESQ's motion on UPL grounds. It also stated that Birbrower might be able to recover that portion of the fees billed for work done by attorneys while they were physically located in New York. The trial court left open the possibility that the firm could recover in equity (quantum meruit) for the value of its work. The court of appeals agreed that Birbrower could not recover for work performed in California, and held that the firm also could not recover for work performed by attorneys physically located in New York. The court also agreed that the firm could seek to recover the value of its work on an equitable claim.

The Supreme Court affirmed the order granting summary judgment. It rejected the firm's argument that the statute was intended only to keep non-lawyers from practicing law, as well as the firm's claim that arbitration (as opposed to in-court proceedings) should not be considered "the practice of law." The Court held that Birbrower could recover fees under the agreement "for the limited legal services it performed for ESQ in New York to the extent they did not constitute practicing law in California, even though those services were performed for a California client." The Court allowed Birbrower to pursue its claim for quantum meruit.

Justice Kennard dissented. She argued that a factual issue remained regarding whether the arbitration should count as "the practice of law." In her view:

* * *

> The majority focuses its attention on the question of whether the New York lawyers had engaged in the practice of law *in California,* giving scant consideration to a decisive preliminary inquiry: whether, through their activities here, the New York lawyers had engaged in the practice of law *at all.* In my view, the record does not show that they did. In reaching a contrary conclusion, the majority relies on an overbroad definition of the term "practice of law." I would adhere to this court's decision in *Baron v. City of Los Angeles* (1970) 2 Cal.3d 535, 86 Cal.Rptr. 673, 469 P.2d 353, more narrowly defining the practice of law as the representation of another in a judicial proceeding or an activity requiring the application of that degree of legal knowledge and technique possessed only by a trained legal mind. Under this definition, this case presents a triable issue of material fact as to whether the New York lawyers' California activities constituted the practice of law. . . .

To this the majority replied:

> If we were to carry the dissent's narrow interpretation of the term "practice law" to its logical conclusion, we would effectively limit section 6125's application to those cases in which nonlicensed out-of-state lawyers appeared in a California courtroom without permission. . . . Indeed, the dissent's definition of "practice law" . . . substantially undermines the Legislature's intent to protect the public from those giving unauthorized legal advice and counsel.

* * *

Birbrower does little to clarify what acts count as the practice of law. It does stand for the proposition that a lawyer practicing law while physically located in a state cannot recover under a fee agreement for such work unless the lawyer is either admitted to the bar of that state or falls within an exception to the state's UPL rules (such as a court ordering admission *pro hac vice* for a particular case).

The Rule Against Sharing Fees With Non–Lawyers and the Prohibition on Non–Lawyer Equity Investment

Model Rule 5.4 is titled "Professional Independence of a Lawyer." The rule's provisions aim to keep lawyers' judgment from being distorted or corrupted by the interests of people who are not subject to the rules of professional conduct or other rules governing lawyers.

Rule 5.4(a) provides that neither a lawyer nor a law firm may "share legal fees with a nonlawyer" unless payments are to the heirs or estate of a deceased lawyer (as a partnership agreement or an agreement for purchase of a deceased lawyer's practice may provide), to a firm's employees as part of a profit-sharing or retirement plan, or part of a court-awarded fee shared with a non-profit organization that recommended or retained a firm. The prohibition on sharing fees sometimes overlaps with UPL issues. *Cleveland Bar Association v. Nosan*, 108 Ohio St.3d 99 (2006), exemplifies such a case. Nosan was a lawyer who reached an agreement with FSMC, a company that advised consumers on how to deal with debt problems. The Ohio Supreme Court described the arrangement this way:

> In 1997, when respondent began working with the company, FSMC associated with attorneys to offer consumers help in managing their financial problems. FSMC leased office space for the associated attorneys, arranged advertising for their services, and provided support staff. In exchange for these business expenses, the attorney shared clients' legal fees with FSMC.
>
> Respondent entered into this arrangement with FSMC. He kept office space in Cleveland and Akron where a nonlawyer intake interviewer would meet with a financially troubled client and, using computer software, determine whether to recommend a debt-repayment plan or bankruptcy. The interviewer would also explain the services that respondent and FSMC offered, review the client's financial records, and set up a payment plan. On the few occasions that the client could not afford to repay the debts, the intake officer would refer the client to respondent to explore bankruptcy options.
>
> Documents supplied to the consumers-turned-respondent's-clients bore his "Bernard J. Nosan, Esq., Attorney at Law" letterhead; however, respondent did not prepare the documents or any forms that were used by his intake staff. In addition, respondent rarely talked with any of the clients who signed up for the debt-management ad-

> vice that the intake interviewer provided in conjunction with FSMC. In fact, respondent could recall at the panel hearing only a few times that he had had any personal contact with the many clients whom he supposedly represented.
>
> Respondent charged his clients a fee for establishing their repayment plan. Upon payment, he deposited the fees into his client trust account and wrote two checks: one to FSMC for 75 percent of the collected fee and the other to himself for the remaining 25 percent. Respondent and FSMC took their fees before any creditors were paid, requiring the client to bank that sum first.

On these facts, the Ohio Supreme Court affirmed a disciplinary board's finding that Nosan violated Ohio rules substantively equivalent to Model Rules 5.4(a) and 5.5. *See also Richland County Bar Association v. Akers*, 106 Ohio St.3d 337 (2005) (affirming suspension of lawyer who left his practice to teach elsewhere but allowed secretary to continue to use his name to conduct certain business and divided fees with her for work she performed).

Rule 5.4(a) also may overlap with Rule 7.2(b), which forbids lawyers from paying another to recommend the lawyer's services. Some cases present factual issues that could have been avoided by clarifying and documenting the facts more carefully at the outset of a representation rather than in the middle or at the end. *Son v. Margolius, Mallios, Davis, Rider & Tomar*, 349 Md. 441 (1998), is such a case. A man named Danny Son was changing a flat tire on the side of the road when he was hit by a truck. He was in a coma for some time. (He lived but was rendered quadraplegic in the accident.) Danny and his wife, Tae, were Korean–Americans. English was not their primary language and they were more comfortable dealing with members of the Korean community than with the broader community.

Tae contacted a woman named Jenny Park for assistance in finding a lawyer for Danny. Ms. Park "was well known in the Korean community generally as someone who helped people of Korean heritage deal with problems of one kind or another. She was also known to Ms. Son, who had worked as a bookkeeper for Ms. Park for about two months in 1987, when Ms. Son first came to Maryland. Ms. Park said that she had been helping other Koreans for about 15 years and in a variety of ways, including helping them find a lawyer when they needed one. . . . "

Apparently while Mr. Son was incapacitated, Ms. Park and Mr. and Mrs. Son signed a consulting agreement providing for Ms. Park to receive 5% of any settlement before trial. The litigation settled before trial for $4,850,000. Ms. Park requested and received $242,500 from the law firm (which received the $4.8 million and paid the money to the relevant claimants, including itself and Mr. and Mrs. Son). The Sons later divorced and Mr. Son contested the payment to Ms. Park. He claimed the consulting agreement was void because (i) Ms. Park had engaged in barratry; the law firm (ii) improperly used Ms. Park to solicit the case from Ms. Son (which would violate a Maryland statute similar to Model Rule 7.3(a)); (iii) improperly divided its contingent fee with Ms. Park, in violation of Rule 5.4(a); and (iv) improperly paid Ms. Park for her referral, in violation of the Maryland equivalent of Rule 7.2(b).[6]

The trial court granted summary judgment in favor of the law firm and Ms. Park on the barratry claim, and the court of appeal affirmed this ruling.[7] The court found Ms. Park did not intermeddle but helped members of the Korean community who asked for help. Absent affirmative intermeddling, the court held, it did not matter that she received a fee. The court also found the firm did not use Ms. Park to solicit the case, noting that Ms. Park and Ms. Son called the firm, rather than the firming calling them. The court reversed on the other two claims, however, finding that factual issues precluded summary judgment in favor of the firm. The court stated the rule succinctly:

> A lawyer may, of course, if properly authorized, pay money otherwise due to the client from a judgment or settlement to a third person on the client's behalf. The settlement sheet in this case shows many such payments. What a lawyer may *not* do under Rule 5.4(a), unless one of the three exceptions applies, is share part of his or her own fee with a non-lawyer. The question, in that regard, is whether the $242,500 payment to Ms. Park falls within the first category or the second . . . . . [The court found issues of fact on this question.] If a trier of fact were to conclude from the evidence that [the lawyer] indeed agreed to pay, and did pay, Ms. Park a part of his firm's fee, the trier of fact could also find that the payment was made "for recommending the lawyer's services," which would constitute a violation of [the Maryland equivalent to Rule 7.2(b)]."[8]

The court reversed the grant of summary judgment on these issues and remanded for resolution of the factual disputes. The court also held that even if the firm had violated Rules 5.4 and 7.2, on these facts the violations did not justify forfeiture of the firm's entire fee; only the amount paid to Ms. Park was at stake.

---

[6] The solicitation claim also implicated Model Rule 8.4(a), which forbids a lawyer from using an intermediary to violate a disciplinary rule.

[7] The Maryland Supreme Court distinguished among (i) barratry, which required a consistent pattern of stirring up litigation; (ii) maintenance, in which a third party assisted a party to maintain a suit in which a third party had no interest; and (iii) champerty, a species of maintenance in which a third party agreed to fund litigation in return for a stake in the subject of the claim (a fractional interest in property, for example). 709 A.2d at 119–120.

[8] FN6. The law firm had drafted a term sheet detailing how it would distribute the settlement funds but omitting the payment to Ms. Park. The court stated in a footnote: "Even if, in substance, the arrangement did not constitute an improper fee split, it was wholly inappropriate for Mr. Stein not to reveal the payment to Ms. Park on the settlement sheet."

Rule 5.4(b) provides lawyers may not establish partnerships with non-lawyers if any partnership activity constitutes the practice of law. Rule 5.4(d) extends this rule to prohibit lawyers from forming professional corporations in which nonlawyers are equity owners, officers or directors, or otherwise have the power to control the professional judgment of the lawyers in the corporation. This provision has been criticized by those who believe firms may need and should have access to capital provided by non-lawyer investors. *E.g.* Edward S. Adams and John H. Matheson, *Law Firms on the Big Board?: A Proposal for Nonlawyer Investment in Law Firms*, 86 *California Law Review* 1 (1998). In 2000 the American Bar Association rejected a proposal to allow "multidisciplinary practice" involving equity participation by non lawyers (such as financial or accounting professionals). The debate over the prohibition on non-lawyer investment continues, however, spurred on in part by the increasingly international nature of certain practice segments. In 2009 the ABA included multidisciplinary practice as a topic for discussion by its "Ethics 20/20 Commission." For a summary of the issues, *see* Paul D. Paton, *Multidisciplinary Practice Redux: Globalization, Core Values, and Reviving the MDP Debate in America*, 78 FORD. L. REV. 2193 (2010).

The Main Points to Recall From Chapter 14 Are:

- Fees must be reasonable.
- Client sophistication and the candor of your explanation are important in determining reasonability.
- You may not take possession of client funds until you have earned them, either by work or (properly documented) availability.
- Meddling with client funds virtually guarantees severe discipline; it is the third rail of ethics.
- You may not offer or accept an agreement restricting your own right to practice or the right to practice of another lawyer.
- You bear the burden of demonstrating your qualifications for admission to the bar.
- Material misstatements or omissions in connection with a bar application violate the rules and may lead to consequences worse than would attend the misstated or omitted facts.
- The unlicensed practice of law is illegal, but it is very hard to define what the practice of law is.

- You may not divide fees with, accept equity investment from, or cede control of your practice to, non-lawyers.

CHAPTER 15

RELATIONS WITH OTHER LAWYERS

■ ■ ■

The Model Rules require you to report to disciplinary officials misconduct by other lawyers that calls into question their fitness to practice law. This rule is meant to enforce the profession's commitment to self-regulation and to prevent blackmail. (Can you see why?) Self-regulation may serve two purposes: weeding out bad lawyers who pose a risk to clients and others and rectifying injustices even where there is no risk that the reported lawyer would commit future misconduct. Our first case below illustrates such facts.

The reporting requirement is limited, however, by the duty of confidentiality. Model Rule 1.6 trumps Model Rule 8.3. Because the duty of confidentiality is broad and has comparatively few exceptions, this is a significant limitation on the self-reporting obligation. The first case in this chapter elaborates on these rules (watch for the court's explanation of why the confidentiality obligation did not apply to the case).

In addition to this reporting requirement, lawyers who are not in the same firm sometimes work together. Their liability situation depends on whether they are co-agents for a common client or one is the sub-agent of the other. Co-agents are hired independently by a client but work together for the client. They are not liable for each other's acts. A sub-agent is a person hired by an agent to help the agent do his job. An agent is liable for the acts of her sub-agent, who of course is personally liable as well.

A. REPORTING (AND GETTING IN TROUBLE BY THREATENING TO REPORT) MISCONDUCT

Model Rules of Professional Conduct 8.3–8.4
Cal. Bus. & Prof. Code § 6090.5
Cal. R. Prof. Conduct 1-500(B)

In reading the following case bear in mind the rules of prosecutorial ethics described in chapter 7.D. The Gary Deegan referenced in this case was the lawyer whose failure to produce exculpatory evidence was at issue in *Connick v. Thompson*, discussed in that chapter.

IN RE MICHAEL G. RIEHLMANN

891 So.2d 1239 (La. 2005)

Respondent is a criminal defense attorney who was formerly employed as an Assistant District Attorney in the Orleans Parish District Attorney's Office. One evening in April 1994, respondent met his close friend and law school classmate, Gerry Deegan, at a bar near the Orleans Parish Criminal District Court. Like respondent, Mr. Deegan had been a prosecutor in the Orleans Parish District Attorney's Office before he "switched sides" in 1987. During their conversation in the bar, Mr. Deegan told respondent that he had that day learned he was dying of colon cancer. In the same conversation, Mr. Deegan confided to respondent that he had suppressed exculpatory blood evidence in a criminal case he prosecuted while at the District Attorney's Office. Respondent recalls that he was "surprised" and "shocked" by his friend's revelation, and that he urged Mr. Deegan to "remedy" the situation. It is undisputed that respondent did not report Mr. Deegan's disclosure to anyone at the time it was made. Mr. Deegan died in July 1994, having done nothing to "remedy" the situation of which he had spoken in the bar.

Nearly five years after Mr. Deegan's death, one of the defendants whom he had prosecuted in a 1985 armed robbery case was set to be executed by lethal injection on May 20, 1999. In April 1999, the lawyers for the defendant, John Thompson, discovered a crime lab report which contained the results of tests performed on a piece of pants leg and a tennis shoe that were stained with the perpetrator's blood during a scuffle with the victim of the robbery attempt. The crime lab report concluded that the robber had Type "B" blood. Because Mr. Thompson has Type "O" blood, the crime lab report proved he could not have committed the robbery; nevertheless, neither the crime lab report nor the blood-stained physical evidence had been disclosed to Mr. Thompson's defense counsel prior to or during trial. Respondent claims that when he heard about the inquiry of Mr. Thompson's lawyers, he immediately realized that this was the case to which Mr. Deegan had referred in their April 1994 conversation in the bar. On April 27, 1999, respondent executed an affidavit for Mr. Thompson in which he attested that during the 1994 conversation, "the late Gerry Deegan said to me that he had intentionally suppressed blood evidence in the armed robbery trial of John Thompson that in some way exculpated the defendant."

In May 1999, respondent reported Mr. Deegan's misconduct to the ODC. In June 1999, respondent testified in a hearing on a motion for new trial in Mr. Thompson's armed robbery case. During the hearing, respondent testified that Mr. Deegan had told him that he "suppressed exculpatory evidence that was blood evidence, that seemed to have excluded Mr. Thompson as the perpetrator of an armed robbery." Respondent also admitted that he "should have reported" Mr. Deegan's misconduct, and that while he ultimately did so, "I should have reported it sooner, I guess."

On September 30, 1999, respondent gave a sworn statement to the ODC in which he was asked why he did not report Mr. Deegan's disclosure to anyone at the time it was made. Respondent replied:

> I think that under ordinary circumstances, I would have. I really honestly think I'm a very good person. And I think I do the right thing whenever I'm given the opportunity to choose. This was unquestionably the most difficult time of my life. Gerry, who was like a brother to me, was dying. And that was, to say distracting would be quite an understatement. I'd also left my wife just a few months before, with three kids, and was under the care of a psychiatrist, taking antidepressants. My youngest son was then about two and had just recently undergone open-heart surgery. I had a lot on my plate at the time. A great deal of it of my own making; there's no question about it. But, nonetheless, I was very, very distracted, and I simply did not give it the important consideration that it deserved. But it was a very trying time for me. And that's the only explanation I have, because, otherwise, I would have reported it immediately had I been in a better frame of mind. [emphasis added]

On January 4, 2001, the ODC filed one count of formal charges against respondent, alleging that his failure to report his unprivileged knowledge of Mr. Deegan's prosecutorial misconduct violated Rules 8.3(a) (reporting professional misconduct), 8.4(c) (engaging in conduct involving dishonesty, fraud, deceit, or misrepresentation), and 8.4(d) (engaging in conduct prejudicial to the administration of justice) of the Rules of Professional Conduct. The ODC subsequently amended the formal charges to delete the alleged violation of Rule 8.4(c).

On March 5, 2002, respondent answered the amended formal charges and admitted some of the factual allegations therein, but denied that his conduct violated the Rules of Professional Conduct. Specifically, respondent asserted that Rule 8.3(a) "merely requires that an attorney possessing unprivileged knowledge of a violation of this Code shall report such knowledge to the authority empowered to investigate such acts. It is undisputed that respondent did report his knowledge of Deegan's statements to Thompson's attorneys, with the clear understanding that this information would be reported to the District Attorney and the Court, undeniably authorities empowered to investigate Deegan's conduct."

When this matter proceeded to a formal hearing before the committee, respondent testified that his best recollection of his conversation with Mr. Deegan in 1994 "is that he told me that he did not turn over evidence to his opponents that might have exculpated the defendant." Nevertheless, when asked whether he recognized during the barroom conversation that Mr. Deegan had violated his ethical duties, respondent replied, "Well, certainly." Respondent admitted that he gave the conversation no further thought after he left the bar because he was "distracted" by his own personal problems. . .

DISCUSSION

In this matter we are presented for the first time with an opportunity to delineate the scope of an attorney's duty under Rule 8.3 to report the professional misconduct of a fellow member of the bar. Therefore, we begin our discussion with a few observations relating to the rule and its history.

The American legal profession has long recognized the necessity of reporting lawyers' ethical misconduct. . . This court first adopted Rule 8.3 on December 18, 1986, effective January 1, 1987. Louisiana's rule is based on ABA Model Rule 8.3; however, there are several differences between the Model Rule and the Louisiana Rule that was in effect in 2001, at the time the formal charges were filed in this case. Most significantly, Model Rule 8.3 requires a lawyer to report the misconduct of another lawyer only when the conduct in question "raises a substantial question" as to that lawyer's fitness to practice. Louisiana's version of Rule 8.3 imposed a substantially more expansive reporting requirement, in that our rule required a lawyer to report all unprivileged knowledge of any ethical violation by a lawyer, whether the violation was, in the reporting lawyer's view, flagrant and substantial or minor and technical. . .

We now turn to a more in-depth examination of the reporting requirement in Louisiana. At the time the formal charges were filed in this case, Louisiana Rule 8.3(a) provided:

> A lawyer possessing unprivileged knowledge of a violation of this code shall report such knowledge to a tribunal or other authority empowered to investigate or act upon such violation.

Thus, the rule has three distinct requirements: (1) the lawyer must possess unprivileged knowledge of a violation of the Rules of Professional Conduct; (2) the lawyer must report that knowledge; and (3) the report must be made to a tribunal or other authority empowered to investigate or act on the violation. We will discuss each requirement in turn.

Knowledge

. . . [A]bsolute certainty of ethical misconduct is not required before the reporting requirement is triggered. The lawyer is not required to conduct an investigation and make a definitive decision that a violation has occurred before reporting; that responsibility belongs to the disciplinary system and this court. On the other hand, knowledge requires more than a mere suspicion of ethical misconduct. We hold that a lawyer will be found to have knowledge of reportable misconduct, and thus reporting is required, where the supporting evidence is such that a reasonable lawyer under the circumstances would form a firm belief that the conduct in question had more likely than not occurred. As such, knowledge is measured by an objective standard that is not tied to the subjective beliefs of the lawyer in question.

When to Report

Once the lawyer decides that a reportable offense has likely occurred, reporting should be made promptly. Arthur F. Greenbaum, The Attorney's Duty to Report Professional Misconduct: A Roadmap for Reform, 16 GEO. J. LEGAL ETHICS 259, 298 (Winter 2003). The need for prompt reporting flows from the need to safeguard the public and the profession against future wrongdoing by the offending lawyer. Id. This purpose is not served unless Rule 8.3(a) is read to require timely reporting under the circumstances presented.

Appropriate Authority

Louisiana Rule 8.3(a) requires that the report be made to "a tribunal or other authority empowered to investigate or act upon such violation." The term "tribunal or other authority" is not specifically defined. However, as the comments to Model Rule 8.3(a) explain, the report generally should be made to the bar disciplinary authority. Therefore, a report of misconduct by a lawyer admitted to practice in Louisiana must be made to the Office of Disciplinary Counsel.

DETERMINATION OF RESPONDENT'S MISCONDUCT AND APPROPRIATE DISCIPLINE

Applying the principles set forth above to the conduct of respondent in the instant case, we find the ODC proved by clear and convincing evidence that respondent violated Rule 8.3(a). First, we find that respondent should have known that a reportable event occurred at the time of his 1994 barroom conversation with Mr. Deegan. Stated another way, respondent's conversation with Mr. Deegan at that time gave him sufficient information that a reasonable lawyer under the circumstances would have formed a firm opinion that the conduct in question more likely than not occurred. Regardless of the actual words Mr. Deegan said that night, and whether they were or were not "equivocal," respondent understood from the conversation that Mr. Deegan had done something wrong. Respondent admitted as much in his affidavit, during the hearing on the motion for new trial in the criminal case, during his sworn statement to the ODC, and during his testimony at the formal hearing. Indeed, during the sworn statement respondent conceded that he would have reported the matter "immediately" were it not for the personal problems he was then experiencing. Respondent also testified that he was surprised and shocked by his friend's revelation, and that he told him to remedy the situation. There would have been no reason for respondent to react in the manner he did had he not formed a firm opinion that the conduct in question more likely than not occurred. The circumstances under which the conversation took place lend further support to this finding. On the same day that he learned he was dying of cancer, Mr. Deegan felt compelled to tell his best friend about something he had done in a trial that took place nine years earlier. It simply defies logic that respondent would now argue that he could not be sure that Mr. Deegan actually withheld Brady evidence because his statements were vague and non-specific.

We also find that respondent failed to promptly report Mr. Deegan's misconduct to the disciplinary authorities. As respondent himself acknowledged, he should have reported Mr. Deegan's statements sooner than he did. There was no reason for respondent to have waited five years to tell the ODC about what his friend had done.

In his answer to the formal charges, respondent asserts that he did comply with the reporting requirement of Rule 8.3(a) because he promptly reported Mr. Deegan's misconduct to the District Attorney and the Criminal District Court through the attorneys for the criminal defendant, John Thompson. Respondent has misinterpreted Rule 8.3(a) in this regard. The word "tribunal" must be read in the context of the entire sentence in which it appears. The proper inquiry, therefore, is what authority is "empowered" to act upon a charge of attorney misconduct. In Louisiana, only this court possesses the authority to define and regulate the practice of law, including the discipline of attorneys. . . In turn, we have delegated to disciplinary counsel the authority to investigate and prosecute claims of attorney misconduct. . . Therefore, respondent is incorrect in arguing that he discharged his reporting duty under Rule 8.3(a) by reporting Mr. Deegan's misconduct to Mr. Thompson's attorneys, the District Attorney, and/or the Criminal District Court. It is undisputed that respondent did not report to the appropriate entity, the ODC, until 1999. That report came too late to be construed as "prompt."

Having found professional misconduct, we now turn to a discussion of an appropriate sanction. In considering that issue, we are mindful that the purpose of disciplinary proceedings is not primarily to punish the lawyer, but rather to maintain the appropriate standards of professional conduct, to preserve the integrity of the legal profession, and to deter other lawyers from engaging in violations of the standards of the profession. . .

Respondent's actions violated the general duty imposed upon attorneys to maintain and preserve the integrity of the bar. . . we find that respondent's conduct was merely negligent. Accordingly, Standard 7.3 of the ABA's Standards for Imposing Lawyer Sanctions provides that the appropriate baseline sanction is a reprimand.

The only aggravating factor present in this case is respondent's substantial experience in the practice of law. As for mitigating factors, we adopt those recognized by the disciplinary board, placing particular emphasis on the absence of any dishonest or selfish motive on respondent's part. Notwithstanding these factors, however, respondent's failure to report Mr. Deegan's bad acts necessitates that some sanction be imposed. Respondent's knowledge of Mr. Deegan's conduct was sufficient to impose on him an obligation to promptly report Mr. Deegan to the ODC. Having failed in that obligation, respondent is himself subject to punishment. Under all of the circumstances presented, we conclude that a public reprimand is the appropriate sanction.

Accordingly, we will reprimand respondent for his actions.

Conclusion

Reporting another lawyer's misconduct to disciplinary authorities is an important duty of every lawyer. Lawyers are in the best position to observe professional misconduct and to assist the profession in sanctioning it. While a Louisiana lawyer is subject to discipline for not reporting misconduct, it is our hope that lawyers will comply with their reporting obligation primarily because they are ethical people who want to serve their clients and the public well. Moreover, the lawyer's duty to report professional misconduct is the foundation for the claim that we can be trusted to regulate ourselves as a profession. If we fail in our duty, we forfeit that trust and have no right to enjoy the privilege of self-regulation or the confidence and respect of the public. . .

VICTORY, J., dissenting.

I dissent from the majority opinion and would impose a harsher sanction on Respondent.

Sounding Boards

Mr. Riehlmann explained that he failed to report Mr. Deegan's misconduct because he was stunned to learn his friend had committed such misconduct, because he learned that fact at the same time he learned his friend had terminal cancer, and because his own life was overflowing with important and stressful events, including divorce and major surgery on his two-year-old son. Those facts did not justify his failure to report but one can understand how they might affect anyone's judgment.

Think about how you might react in such a situation. One possible effect would simply be to shut down mentally: to not think about Deegan's confession because it added stress levels already intolerably high. A report occurring before Deegan's death, for example, might lead to him fielding inquiries from disciplinary officials as his health deteriorated sharply. Some people might find that prospect untroubling—even for a friend as close as a sibling—but others might find it distressing enough to want to avoid thinking about reporting Deegan. After he died, of course, that prospect would be gone but by then one might have become accustomed to not reporting and one might worry that disciplinary officials would find fault in the failure to report while Deegan was alive and could be questioned about the case (recall that Deegan did not tell Riehlmann the name of the case in which Deegan withheld evidence). The longer the failure to report continued, the more costly reporting might seem, and thus the easier it would seem to do nothing. One could double down, in other words, by doing nothing where action was required.

Another reaction might be not to avoid thinking about Deegan's disclosure altogether but to assign it a relatively low priority compared to the challenges of getting through a difficult period in one's own life. "I'll deal with that when things calm down" might be a natural reaction, albeit one that leads to doubling down through inaction. Try as you might to cultivate dynamic, interactive, and probabilistic thinking, life will throw obstacles to such thinking in your way.

Both reactions might be summarized as failing to achieve the proper perspective with respect to the disclosure. How does one maintain perspective, and thus guard against doubling down, either actively or passively? One important way is to find persons whose judgment you trust to serve as a sounding board, providing you with their view of situations you are in. Ideally such people will know you well enough to know your own strengths and weaknesses, including your disposition toward risk, and will share enough of your values to provide both empathetic and dispassionate reactions. Riehlmann could have used advice from someone like that.

Model Rule 1.6(b)(4) allows disclosure to secure legal advice about compliance with the rules, though not all states have such an exception (California does not, as of this writing, for example) and not all dilemmas or problems involve compliance with rules. In such cases one must be careful not to say too much. But even with such a qualification in place, one of the most important things you can do to stay safe is actively to find such people and cultivate relationships with them that allow you to use them as sounding boards. (Often that means serving in that role yourself.)

Perspective may not come easily, and it may not come at all unless you actively work to achieve it. Finding a good sounding board is an important part of that work.

Sometimes lawyers fail to report misconduct in contexts suggesting the failure was part of a larger understanding through which the client might agree not to report misconduct in exchange for money from a llawyer who had engaged in misconduct. Because Rule 1.6 trumps rule 8.3 clients often have control in such situations, but in some cases they do not.

For example, in *In re Himmel*, 125 Ill. 2d 531 (1988), the court disciplined James H. Himmel, a lawyer retained by Tammy Forsberg to sue her former lawyer, John R. Casey. Ms. Forsberg suffered an injury and Mr. Casey obtained a $35,000 settlement for her. Under their retainer Casey was entitled to 1/3 of this amount but he kept all of it. Ms. Forsberg hired Himmel to get her money from Casey. She agreed to pay him 1/3 of any sum greater than the amount Casey owed her. Himmel negotiated a $75,000 settlement with Casey. As part of this agreement Forsberg agreed not to initiate any criminal, civil, or attorney disciplinary action against Casey. Himmel stood to gain $17,000 or more if Casey honored the agreement. Casey paid Forsberg an additional $10,400 but he eventually breached the agreement, Forsberg sued him, and judgment was entered against Casey. Himmel took no fee for his work on the matter.

The Illinois bar investigated the complaint against Casey, who eventually consented to being disbarred. The bar then proceeded against Himmel for failing to report Casey. The bar, and eventually the Illinois Supreme Court, concluded that Himmel had unprivileged information regarding Casey because Forsberg had brought her mother and her fiancé to meetings with Himmel. Because they were not clients, the Court found, those discussions were not privileged. The disciplinary board that initially heard the case found that Himmel "had been practicing law for 11 years, had no prior record of any complaints, obtained as good a result as could be expected in the case, and requested no fee for recovering the $23,233.34."

Himmel argued that his client had not wanted him to report Casey and that he had done the best job that could be done. The Supreme Court rejected both arguments, holding "A lawyer may not choose to circumvent the rules by simply asserting that his client asked him to do so." Concluding that both Himmel and Forsberg "stood to gain financially by agreeing not to prosecute or report Casey for conversion," the Court suspended Himmel from practice for a year.

California has no equivalent to Model Rule 8.3, so California lawyers have no ethical duty to report the misconduct of other lawyers. Attorneys *may* report misconduct, of course, and their reports are covered by a statutory litigation privilege, which means they cannot be sued for defamation or other torts based on the report itself. Cal. Civ. Code § 47. (The report may not, however, disclose client confidences. *See* Business & Professions Code § 6068(e).)

Things are a bit more complicated than this, however. Suppose you know another attorney has engaged in serious misconduct. May you take advantage of that misconduct to help your own client? May you threaten to report the attorney to gain leverage for your client? Would doing so make you complicit in the first attorney's wrongdoing?

Because Model Rule 8.3 does not require a report where Rule 1.6 protects the relevant information, it is in theory possible that a lawyer could promise not to report a violation in return for a higher settlement payment than a client would receive without such a promise. That is arguably what happened in *Himmel*, after all. Consider what the result in that case would be had Ms. Forsberg's mother and fiance not been privy to some communications with Himmel.

Some states forbid such settlements directly. For example, California Business & Professions Code §6090.5 provides:

(a) It is cause for suspension, disbarment, or other discipline for any member, whether as a party or as an attorney for a party, to agree or seek agreement, that:

(1) The professional misconduct or the terms of a settlement of a claim for professional misconduct shall not be reported to the disciplinary agency.

(2) The plaintiff shall withdraw a disciplinary complaint or shall not cooperate with the investigation or prosecution conducted by the disciplinary agency.

(3) The record of any civil action for professional misconduct shall be sealed from review by the disciplinary agency.

(b) This section applies to all settlements, whether made before or after the commencement of a civil action.

Similarly, California Rule of Professional Conduct 1-500(B) provides "[a] member shall not be a party to or participate in offering or making an agreement which precludes the reporting of a violation of these rules."

B. CLAIMS BETWEEN LAWYERS

The introductory materials to this chapter asked what happens when (i) a client hires two lawyers not in the same firm to work on a case; (ii) one lawyer suggests to the client that she hire an additional lawyer; or (iii) the client hires one lawyer who then hires another to help out.

The basic rules are that two lawyers each hired by the client are co-agents. They are responsible for their own conduct but not for the mistakes of their co-counsel. But if a lawyer hires another lawyer to perform some task, the second lawyer is a sub-agent of the first, who is liable to the client for the second lawyer's mistake. The original lawyer then has a claim for indemnity from the sub-agent.

It is important to be clear up front about what relationship each lawyer has to each other and to the client. The following cases illustrate the point.

WHALEN V. DEGRAFF, FOY, CONWAY, HOLT–HARRIS & MEALEY

863 N.Y.S.2d 100 (2008)

STEIN, J.

Plaintiff initially retained defendant to recover her interest in a partnership, Pearcove Associates, LP. Defendant ultimately secured a judgment in the amount of $1,235,976 against Julius Gerzof. In January 1995, before the judgment was satisfied, Gerzof died a resident of Florida.

In April 1995, defendant sought the assistance of Scott Cagan, a Florida attorney who was then with the firm of Bailey, Hunt, Jones and Besto (hereinafter Bailey), in preserving plaintiff's rights as against Gerzof's Florida estate. Initially, as pertinent here, defendant simply requested that Cagan determine whether an estate had been opened and advise as to the time in which it would be necessary to make a claim against the estate and the manner of doing so. Shortly thereafter, Bailey advised defendant that an estate had not yet been opened and that Bailey would take no further actions regarding the estate until instructed to do so by defendant. In August 1995, defendant notified plaintiff that defendant had retained Bailey "to follow the Gerzof estate and file any claims . . . required with respect to [her] judgment against Julius Gerzof."

In the meantime, defendant was negotiating with the Gerzof estate attorneys to attempt to settle plaintiff's judgment. Defendant learned that an estate was opened in early 1996 and instructed Bailey to file a notice of claim in late February 1996. On or about February 23, 1996, defendant sent Bailey the information necessary to file the notice of claim. The Gerzof estate attorneys advised defendant in early 1998 that a notice of claim had not been filed within the required time; consequently, they withdrew all offers of settlement and ended negotiations. Ultimately, plaintiff was unable to satisfy any of her judgment from the substantial assets of the estate. . . .

Plaintiff contends that defendant is liable for damages resulting from Bailey's failure to file the notice of claim either on the basis that defendant had a nondelegable duty to file such notice of claim or based upon defendant's negligent supervision of Bailey. Defendant maintains that its duty to plaintiff was completely met when it retained Bailey to file the notice of claim and that it was entitled to rely on Bailey to perform that act.

The general rule is that "[a] firm is not ordinarily liable . . . for the acts or omissions of a lawyer outside the firm who is working with the firm lawyers as co-counsel or in a similar arrangement" (Restatement [Third] of Law Governing Lawyers § 58, Comment *e*), as such a lawyer is usually an independent agent of the client. Here, however, defendant solicited Cagan and Bailey and obtained their assistance without plaintiff's knowledge. Although plaintiff was later advised that Bailey had been retained by defendant, she had no contact with Bailey and did not enter into a retainer agreement with that firm. Defendant concedes that plaintiff completely relied on defendant to take the necessary steps to satisfy her judgment against Gerzof. Under these circumstances, defendant assumed responsibility to plaintiff for the filing of the Florida estate claim and Bailey became defendant's subagent (*see* Restatement [Third] of Law Governing Lawyers § 58, Comment *e*). Therefore, defendant had a duty to supervise Bailey's actions (*see* Restatement [Third] Agency § 3.15; Restatement [Second] Agency §§ 5, 406)

While plaintiff would ordinarily be required to submit an affidavit of an expert setting forth the applicable standard of care in order to obtain summary judgment in her favor . . . no such affidavit is necessary here because it is undisputed that defendant knew of the deadline for filing the notice of claim and took no steps whatsoever to even inquire as to the status of that filing between February 1996 and January 1998. . . . Thus, plaintiff's motion for summary judgment should have been granted to the extent of awarding her judgment as a matter of law with respect to defendant's negligence in failing to supervise Bailey.

The basic rules of co-agency and sub-agency are clear enough but some cases raise collateral issues regarding these rules. *Musser v. Provencher*, 28 Cal.4th 274 (2002), provides an example. Musser was a family law attorney representing a wife in a divorce action. She consulted Provencher, a bankruptcy specialist, for advice on how to handle the husband's bankruptcy. Provencher gave bad advice, which Musser followed, harming her client. The client then sued Musser for malpractice. Musser settled with the client and then sued Provencher for indemnification.

Provencher defended on the ground that public policy forbids equitable indemnification (rather than contractual indemnification, such as insurance) for legal malpractice. Some cases had held that where one attorney replaces another the predecessor attorney may not seek indemnification from her successor. These cases reasoned that the successor might want to establish malpractice damages based on the predecessor's actions, and the prospect of an indemnity obligation running to the predecessor attorney might deter the successor attorney from doing so, thus creating a conflict between the successor and the client. The cases also reasoned that a successor attorney might need to disclose confidential communications to defend himself, but that the California confidentiality rules provide no exception allowing disclosure in such cases.

The Court rejected these arguments and allowed Musser's suit to proceed. It found no reason to believe the prospect of having to indemnify co-counsel would create a conflict of interest. And as the client had agreed to waive her confidentiality rights with respect to the indemnity claim, the Court found no confidentiality bar to such a suit.

In contrast, in *Beck v. Wecht*, 28 Cal.4th 289 (2002), the question was whether one lawyer may sue co-counsel for breach of fiduciary duty on the theory that co-counsel's negligence cost the first lawyer money. The clients in this case hired Daniel Beck to sue General Motors on a product defect theory. With the clients' agreement, Beck then brought L.L. McBee and Ronald Wecht into the case. McBee had extensive knowledge of the product in question, and Wecht served as local counsel. McBee and Beck agreed to divide the contingent fee Beck had agreed to with the clients, with each giving a portion of his fee to Wecht.

The case went to trial. During trial GM offered to settle for $6 million. The clients told McBee and Wecht to accept the offer. McBee was supposed to do that but he never did. The jury returned a defense verdict and the clients got nothing. They sued McBee for failing to follow their order to accept settlement, and they sued Wecht on the theory that he was a joint venturer with McBee. The clients did not sue Beck, who had been marginalized by the time of trial.

McBee settled with the clients. His settlement included a payment of $224,000 to Beck in return for Beck's release of any claims against McBee. Wecht denied that he was a joint venturer with McBee, but his insurer paid $1.4 million to settle the claims against him. Beck then sued Wecht for breach of fiduciary duty. He claimed as damages the fee he would have received if McBee had followed the clients' instructions and settled the case.

The trial court granted summary judgment in favor of Wecht on the ground that he owed Beck no fiduciary duty, and the Supreme Court affirmed. The Court held that to recognize such a duty running from one co-counsel to another might create conflicts of interest that could harm clients.

In reaching this conclusion the Court discussed three cases. The first was *Pollack v. Lytle*, 120 Cal.App.3d 931 (1981). Pollock had filed a medical malpractice case but was having a hard time finding an expert witness to support his liability theory. He alleged that Lytle came to him (lying about his qualifications) claiming to have an expert who would support the client's case but only if Lytle were involved. Lytle then represented the expert at a deposition Pollock did not attend. Pollock later alleged that the expert's testimony did not support the client's proximate causation theories but Lytle falsely told Pollock that it did. Based on that advice, Pollock claimed, he advised the client not to settle the case. The case tried and produced a defense verdict. Lytle then advised the client to sue Pollock for malpractice; Pollock sued Lytle for breach of fiduciary duty, seeking indemnification from Lytle for any liability Pollock had to the client. The court of appeals allowed Pollock to proceed on this theory.

The *Beck* Court overruled *Pollock*. It found two other cases persuasive. The first of these was *Saunders v. Weissburg & Aronson*, 74 Cal.App.4th 869 (1999). Saunders and Weissburg both represented a group of hospitals suing the Medicare system over payments. The case settled, with each hospital approving the settlement. Saunders then sued Weissburg, alleging that he had recommended to the group a settlement that favored certain hospitals over others and which yielded Weissburg a higher fee at Saunders' expense. The court of appeals affirmed summary judgment for Weissburg on the theory that he owed Saunders no duty to urge on the clients a settlement that maximized Saunders' fees. Instead, Saunders owed the clients a duty to exercise his best judgment in their interests. The court held that to recognize a duty running to co-counsel in such circumstances threatened to distort this independent judgment.

The second case cited approvingly by the *Beck* court was *Mason v. Levy & Van Bourg,* 77 Cal.App.3d 60 (1978). In that case Mason transferred two cases to the Van Bourg firm with the agreement that he would share in the contingent fee the client had agreed to pay. The Van Bourg firm did not bring the cases within the limitations period and Mason sued for the fee he claimed he would have received had the cases been brought. The court of appeals held Van Bourg owed Mason no duties. To hold otherwise, it reasoned, would cause successor counsel to worry about whether they would be sued rather than thinking about what was best for the client. A client might wish to accept a low settlement on the referred claims, for example, in return for concessions on other claims or in other areas. In such a case, the court believed lawyers such as Van Bourg should be free to exercise their best judgment.

Beck itself presented no such conflict. The clients and Beck both complained that McBee should have followed the clients' instruction to accept the $6 million settlement. (And the clients had waived any assertion of privilege, another concern raised in *Beck* and in *Musser*.) Nevertheless, the Court held:

> Beck's effort to distinguish his case on the facts raises a fundamental question. Should this issue—whether co-counsel owe one another a fiduciary duty to conduct their joint representation in a manner that does not diminish or eliminate the fees each expects to collect—be decided on a case-by-case basis? We think not. The better approach, we conclude, is a bright-line rule refusing to recognize such a fiduciary duty. Accordingly, we disapprove *Pollack v. Lytle, supra,* 120 Cal.App.3d 931, insofar as it is inconsistent with the views expressed herein.

CASE QUESTIONS

1. How is *Beck* different from *Provencher?*
2. Recall that *Pollock* was the California case cited by the court in *Kramer v. Nowak*, 908 F.Supp. 1281 (E.D. Pa. 1995). How does *Beck* affect *Kramer*? Are the facts of *Kramer*—a senior lawyer suing a junior associate in the same firm—closer to *Beck* or to *Provencher*?
3. What is the rule of *Beck*? What is the reason for that rule?

The Main Points to Recall From Chapter 15 Are:

- The Model Rules impose a duty to report misconduct that calls into question a lawyer's honesty, trustworthiness, or fitness to practice.
- What a lawyer knows is judged by admitted knowledge and inferences any reasonable lawyer must have drawn from that knowledge.

- Some jurisdictions, such as California, do not impose a duty to report misconduct but do condemn threats to report used as leverage to gain advantage.
- When a client hires two lawyers not in the same firm to work on the client's matter, the lawyers are co-agents. They are responsible for their own conduct but not for each other's.
- When a lawyer hires another lawyer to help the former discharge his or her obligations to a client, the second lawyer is a sub-agent of the first. The former lawyer is liable to the client for errors based on the sub-agent's advice. The sub-agent may be liable to the former lawyer for the sub-agent's mistakes.

CHAPTER 16

ETHICS IN ADVOCACY

■ ■ ■

This chapter proceeds in rough chronological order through the life of a lawsuit. That life often begins with pre-filing demands. Demands often point out undesirable side effects of litigation, such as adverse publicity. There is a difference between pointing out such a side effect and attempting to leverage it to the point that advocacy shades into extortion. Our first case illustrates these points.

To file a case or make a factual representation to a tribunal a lawyer should conduct an adequate investigation into the facts. Inevitably lawyers rely on clients for some and perhaps most of the facts. The line between reasonable reliance on a client's assurances and negligent assertion of facts may be hard to determine. Watching out for red flags—contradictions between the client's account and seemingly reliable evidence (such as checks the client cashed)—count as red flags. Our second case illustrates these points.

Lawyers who appear before tribunals owe a duty of candor to the tribunal. They cannot lie to the tribunal, knowingly introduce perjured testimony, or knowingly fail to cite directly adverse precedent from the controlling jurisdiction that is not cited by opposing counsel. ("Knowingly" is an important qualification. It is common for lawyers to avoid learning whether their client is telling the truth precisely to get around this rule.) Lawyers appearing before a tribunal cannot suppress evidence or obstruct access to it. Lawyers also may not use or threaten to use the legal system for improper purposes, such as extortion or harassment to obtain some advantage collateral to a supposed claim.

A. THE SCOPE OF LEGITIMATE DEMANDS

We first examine three subjects relevant to initiating a case: Liability for threatening to file litigation, liability for filing baseless litigation, and liability for filing litigation to gain a collateral advantage, which is one that could not be obtained through the litigation itself.

Parties often threaten to file litigation before they file it. The threats often come in the form of "demand" or "cease and desist" letters. To one degree or another the threats take the form: "If you do not do *X* then my client is going to sue you." The *X* may be to stop doing some act, such as pirating sound recordings, or to pay some amount of money as compensation for an alleged wrong.

Particularly when only money is demanded there may be a thin line between lawful demands and unlawful extortion. Where that line falls depends on the facts, of course, and also on policies designed to protect parties who litigate (or threaten to do so) in good faith. The following case examines how that line gets located. It is worth bearing in mind that demands for something other than money can create liability, too. Such demands are more likely to appear in abuse of process cases, which are examined in Section C below.

Cal. Civ. Code § 47
Cal. Code Civ. P. 425.16

FLATLEY V. MAURO

39 Cal.4th 299 (2006)

MORENO, J.

Plaintiff Michael Flatley, a well-known entertainer, sued defendant D. Dean Mauro, an attorney, for civil extortion, intentional infliction of emotional distress and wrongful interference with economic advantage. Flatley's action was based on a demand letter Mauro sent to Flatley on behalf of Tyna Marie Robertson, a woman who claimed that Flatley had raped her, and on subsequent telephone calls Mauro made to Flatley's attorneys, demanding a seven-figure payment to settle Robertson's claims.

Mauro filed a motion to strike Flatley's complaint under the anti-SLAPP statute. (Code Civ. Proc., § 425.16.) He argued that the letter was a prelitigation settlement offer and therefore Flatley's complaint arose from Mauro's exercise of his constitutionally protected right of petition. The trial court denied the motion. The Court of Appeal held that, because Mauro's letter and subsequent telephone calls constituted criminal extortion as a matter of law, and extortionate speech is not constitutionally protected, the anti-SLAPP statute did not apply. Therefore, it affirmed denial of Mauro's motion to strike. We granted Mauro's petition for review.

We conclude that . . . a defendant whose assertedly protected speech or petitioning activity was illegal as a matter of law, and therefore unprotected by constitutional guarantees of free speech and petition, cannot use the anti-SLAPP statute to strike the plaintiff's complaint. Applying this principle in the specific circumstances of the case before us, we agree with the Court of Appeal's conclusion. Mauro's communications constituted criminal extortion as a matter of law and, as such, were unprotected by constitutional guarantees of free speech or petition. Therefore, the anti-SLAPP statute does not apply. Accordingly, we affirm the decision of the Court of Appeal.

I. FACTS AND PROCEDURAL HISTORY

Michael Flatley is a performer and dance impresario who owns "the stock of corporations that present live performances by Irish dance troupes throughout the world." On March 4, 2003, Tyna Marie Robertson sued Flatley in Illinois for battery and intentional infliction of emotional distress based on allegations that Flatley had raped her in his hotel suite in Las Vegas on the night of October 19–20, 2002. Robertson was represented by D. Dean Mauro, an Illinois attorney. Robertson and Mauro then appeared on television, where Robertson described the alleged rape "in extremely lurid detail."

On March 6, 2003, Flatley filed his complaint in the present action in California against Mauro, Robertson and Doe defendants. In a second amended complaint, Flatley alleged five causes of action for civil extortion, defamation, fraud, intentional infliction of emotional distress, and wrongful interference with prospective economic advantage. The civil extortion, intentional infliction of emotional distress and wrongful interference causes of action were alleged against all defendants; the defamation and fraud causes of action were alleged against Robertson alone.

Mauro answered with a general denial and asserted various affirmative defenses including that Flatley's claims were barred by section 425.16, the anti-SLAPP statute. On August 1, 2003, Mauro filed a motion to strike Flatley's complaint under that statute.

Flatley's opposition to the motion argued that Mauro's communications constituted criminal extortion and were therefore not protected by the anti-SLAPP statute. He argued further that he could demonstrate a probability of prevailing on the merits. In support of his opposition, Flatley filed several declarations, including his own and those of his personal secretary, Thomas Trautmann, and his attorneys, John Brandon, Bertram Fields, and Richard Cestero.

The declarations submitted by Flatley set forth the following scenario: Flatley met Robertson in Las Vegas sometime before October 2002. Robertson was very friendly and Flatley gave her the telephone number of his personal secretary, Thomas Trautmann (Trautmann) in the event she wanted to reach Flatley.

In October 2002, Robertson called Trautmann to arrange a rendezvous with Flatley. On October 19, 2002, Robertson arrived at Flatley's two-bedroom suite in the Venetian Hotel in Las Vegas. She was told that one room was for Flatley and the other was for Trautmann. Robertson put her belongings in Flatley's bedroom. She did not request alternate accommodations or protest the accommodations offered.

That evening, Flatley and Robertson had dinner together. Upon returning to Flatley's hotel room, Robertson excused herself to the bathroom. Flatley disrobed and got into bed. Robertson reappeared, nude, and entered Flatley's bed, where she remained for the night. According to Flatley, everything that transpired between him and Robertson that night was consensual. At no time did Trautmann, who was in the next room with the door open, hear any cry or complaint of any kind.

The next morning, Robertson entered the common area of the suite, and kissed Flatley in Trautmann's presence. Her demeanor was relaxed and happy. She ate breakfast with Flatley, speaking affectionately to him and cordially to Trautmann. Upon leaving, she kissed Flatley again and said she hoped to see him again.

On January 2, 2003, Mauro sent a letter addressed to Flatley that was received by Flatley's attorney, John Brandon. . . .

Attached to the letter were 51 pages of material, including a draft of Robertson's complaint against Flatley, Robertson's medical records pertaining to treatment for the alleged rape, certificates of achievement awarded to Mauro, newspaper articles chronicling Mauro's multimillion-dollar cases and settlements, and the curricula vitae of Mauro's experts.

Among the attachments was a letter Robertson wrote to the Las Vegas Police Department on November 17, 2002. The letter refers to a telephone call she had made to the police department on November 14 in which she reported the rape. She asked that the letter, which described the rape, be added to the earlier report because she "did not get an adequate opportunity to explain." She added, however, that she had no "interest in seeing the Initial Incident Complaint form," because she was "a private person, and this is not something about which I can openly or freely explain to people." She also wrote that she could not at that time go into "more specific, or graphic details" because she was not "in any condition to relive this."

The record does not show that Robertson provided any additional information to the police, or that the police took any action regarding her allegation. According to Flatley's and Trautmann's declarations, no one in the Las Vegas Police Department contacted either Flatley or his representatives about the allegation and Flatley remained unaware of the allegation until Brandon received Mauro's letter.

Upon receipt of Mauro's letter, Brandon immediately called Mauro. Mauro gave Brandon a deadline of January 30, 2003, "to offer sufficient payment." On January 9, 2003, Mauro telephoned Brandon to complain that he had not heard from Flatley or Flatley's representatives. Brandon explained that he was not handling the matter but offered to pass along any message. Mauro told him that he would not extend the January 30, 2003, deadline. He added: "I know the tour dates; I am not kidding about this; it will be publicized every place he [Flatley] goes for the rest of his life." He added that dissemination of the story "would be immediate to any place where he [Flatley] and the troupes are performing everywhere in the world."

On January 10, 2003, Mauro again called Brandon, who was in a meeting, and left a message with Brandon's secretary. The message read: "Dean Mauro needs a call back in one-half hour, otherwise they are going public." When Brandon returned Mauro's call, Mauro "complained that people were investigating the matter before contacting him and were doing so in an intimidating manner. He said that if he did not receive a call by 8 p.m. Central Standard Time . . . , he would 'go public and the January 30 deadline is gone.' " He said, "I already have the news media lined up" and would "hit him [Flatley] at every single place he tours." Brandon read this back to Mauro to confirm its accuracy.

When Brandon asked Mauro why he was concerned about Flatley's attorneys investigating Robertson's claim before making an offer, Mauro stated that this "case is like an insurance claim where the adjuster would call the lawyer to acknowledge the attorney's lien." Brandon asked Mauro if acknowledging the lien was a problem. Mauro said "never mind about that, just pass on the message." Brandon conveyed the message to Bertram Fields, the attorney handling the matter for Flatley.

Fields called Mauro later that day. Mauro told Fields he knew how to "play hardball" and that if Flatley did not pay an acceptable amount, he and Robertson would "go public." Mauro said he would ensure that the story would follow Flatley wherever he or his troupes performed and would "ruin" him. Fields asked Mauro how much he was demanding and Mauro replied "it would take seven figures."

Fields reported Mauro's conduct to the FBI and arranged for Flatley to give the FBI a voluntary interview without the presence of counsel. Hoping to allow the FBI more time to investigate, Fields wrote Mauro asking him to extend the deadline. Mauro extended the deadline by one day in a letter that complained that Fields had failed to return Mauro's numerous messages. "You have my personal cell phone number, on 24 hours daily, and we still have received no substantive conversation of any kind for nearly a month."

Flatley did not pay Robertson and Mauro.

Mauro's reply to Flatley's opposition to the motion to strike argued that his January 2, 2002 letter was a prelitigation settlement offer in furtherance of his constitutional right of petition and, therefore, protected by section 425.16, subdivision (e)(1) and (4). . . .

II. DISCUSSION

The anti-SLAPP statute, section 425.16, allows a court to strike any cause of action that arises from the defendant's exercise of his or her constitutionally protected rights of free speech or petition for redress of grievances. . . . because not all speech or petition activity is constitutionally protected, not all speech or petition activity is protected by section 425.16. . . . section 425.16 cannot be invoked by a defendant whose assertedly protected activity is illegal as a matter of law and, for that reason, not protected by constitutional guarantees of free speech and petition. A contrary rule would be inconsistent with the purpose of the anti-SLAPP statute as revealed by its language. . . .

We conclude, therefore, that where a defendant brings a motion to strike under section 425.16 based on a claim that the plaintiff's action arises from activity by the defendant in furtherance of the defendant's exercise of protected speech or petition rights, but either the defendant concedes, or the evidence conclusively establishes, that the assertedly protected speech or petition activity was illegal as a matter of law, the defendant is precluded from using the anti-SLAPP statute to strike the plaintiff's action. . . .

Mauro argues: "All litigation-related speech, lawful or not, is in furtherance of petition or free speech rights." Thus, he argues, even assuming his letter was extortion, it is nonetheless protected by Code of Civil Procedure section 425.16 because it falls within subdivision (e)(1) and (2).[1] In advancing this argument, he invokes the litigation privilege set forth in Civil Code section 47, subdivision (b). He argues, first, that section 425.16 protects litigation communication to the same degree that such communication is protected by the litigation privilege and then reasons from this premise that section 425.16 must also protect unlawful litigation-related communication because the litigation privilege does.[2]

"The principal purpose of [Civil Code] section [47, subdivision (b)] is to afford litigants and witnesses [citation] the utmost freedom of access to the courts without fear of being harassed subsequently by derivative tort

---

[1] Section 425.16, subdivision (e) provides as follows: "(e) As used in this section, 'act in furtherance of a person's right of petition or free speech under the United States or California Constitution in connection with a public issue' includes: (1) any written or oral statement or writing made before a legislative, executive, or judicial proceeding, or any other official proceeding authorized by law; (2) any written or oral statement or writing made in connection with an issue under consideration or review by a legislative, executive, or judicial body, or any other official proceeding authorized by law; (3) any written or oral statement or writing made in a place open to the public or a public forum in connection with an issue of public interest; (4) or any other conduct in furtherance of the exercise of the constitutional right of petition or the constitutional right of free speech in connection with a public issue or an issue of public interest."

[2] Civil Code section 47, subdivision (b) states in relevant part: "A privileged publication or broadcast is one made: [¶] . . . [¶] (b) In any (1) legislative proceeding, (2) judicial proceeding, (3) in any other official proceeding authorized by law, or (4) in the initiation or course of any other proceeding authorized by law and reviewable pursuant to Chapter 2 (commencing with Section 1084) of Title 1 of Part 3 of the Code of Civil Procedure. . . . "

actions.". . . . To accomplish these objectives, the privilege is "an 'absolute' privilege, and it bars all tort causes of action except a claim of malicious prosecution." The litigation privilege has been applied in "numerous cases" involving "fraudulent communication or perjured testimony." The privilege has also been held to apply to "statements made prior to the filing of a lawsuit."

Seizing upon these principles, Mauro maintains that section 425.16 similarly protects any prelitigation-related communications even if that communication constitutes extortion. Assuming without deciding that the litigation privilege may apply to such threats, we conclude that they are nonetheless not protected under the anti-SLAPP statute because the litigation privilege and the anti-SLAPP statute are substantively different statutes that serve quite different purposes, and it is not consistent with the language or the purpose of the anti-SLAPP statute to protect such threats.

There is, of course, a relationship between the litigation privilege and the anti-SLAPP statute. Past decisions of this court and the Court of Appeal have looked to the litigation privilege as an aid in construing the scope of subdivision (e)(1) and (2) with respect to the first step of the two-step anti-SLAPP inquiry—that is, by examining the scope of the litigation privilege to determine whether a given communication falls within the ambit of subdivisions (e)(1) and (2). . . .

The litigation privilege is also relevant to the second step in the anti-SLAPP analysis in that it may present a substantive defense the plaintiff must overcome to demonstrate a probability of prevailing. . . . .

Notwithstanding this relationship between the litigation privilege and the anti-SLAPP statute, as we have observed, the two statutes are not substantively the same. In *Jarrow Formulas, Inc. v. LaMarche, supra,* 31 Cal.4th 728, we declined to create a categorical exemption from section 425.16 for malicious prosecution actions even though such claims are exempt from the litigation privilege. We rejected the plaintiff's "attempted analogy between the litigation privilege and the anti-SLAPP statute" as "inapt," explaining "the litigation privilege is an entirely different type of statute than section 425.16. The former enshrines a substantive rule of law that grants absolute immunity from tort liability for communications made in relation to judicial proceedings [citation]; the latter is a procedural device for screening out meritless claims [citation]."

Nor do the two statutes serve the same purposes. The litigation privilege embodied in Civil Code section 47, subdivision (b) serves broad goals of guaranteeing access to the judicial process, promoting the zealous representation by counsel of their clients, and reinforcing the traditional function of the trial as the engine for the determination of truth. Applying the litigation privilege to some forms of unlawful litigation-related activity may advance those broad goals notwithstanding the "occasional unfair result" in an individual case.

Section 425.16 is not concerned with securing for litigants freedom of access to the judicial process. The purpose of section 425.16 is to protect the valid exercise of constitutional rights of free speech and petition from the abuse of the judicial process (§ 425.16, subd. (a)), by allowing a defendant to bring a motion to strike any action that arises from any activity by the defendant in furtherance of those rights. (§ 425.16, subd. (b)(1).) By necessary implication, the statute does not protect activity that, because it is illegal, is not in furtherance of constitutionally protected speech or petition rights. . . .

Civil Code section 47 does not operate as a limitation on the scope of the anti-SLAPP statute. The fact that Civil Code section 47 may limit the liability of a party that sends to an opposing party a letter proposing settlement of proposed litigation does not mean that the settlement letter is also a protected communication for purposes of section 425.16. Therefore, we reject Mauro's contention that, because some forms of illegal litigation-related activity may be privileged under the litigation privilege, that activity is necessarily protected under the anti-SLAPP statute. . . .

"Extortion is the obtaining of property from another, with his consent . . . induced by a wrongful use of force or fear. . . . " (Pen. Code, § 518.) Fear, for purposes of extortion "may be induced by a threat, either: [¶] . . . [¶] 2. To accuse the individual threatened . . . of any crime; or, [¶] 3. To expose, or impute to him . . . any deformity, disgrace or crime[.]" (Pen. Code, § 519.) "Every person who, with intent to extort any money or other property from another, sends or delivers to any person any letter or other writing, whether subscribed or not, expressing or implying, or adapted to imply, any threat such as is specified in Section 519, is punishable in the same manner as if such money or property were actually obtained by means of such threat." (Pen. Code, § 523.)

Extortion has been characterized as a paradoxical crime in that it criminalizes the making of threats that, in and of themselves, may not be illegal. . . . Moreover, threats to do the acts that constitute extortion under Penal Code section 519 are extortionate whether or not the victim committed the crime or indiscretion upon which the threat is based and whether or not the person making the threat could have reported the victim to the authorities or arrested the victim. . . .

Attorneys are not exempt from these principles in their professional conduct. Indeed, the rules of professional conduct specifically prohibit attorneys from "threaten[ing] to present criminal, administration, or disciplinary charges to obtain an advantage in a civil dispute." (Cal. Rules of Prof. Conduct, rule 5–100(A).) . . .

Extortion is not a constitutionally protected form of speech. [citations omitted] The purpose of the anti-SLAPP statute, of course, is to protect "the valid exercise of the constitutional rights of speech and petition for the redress of grievances." (§ 425.16, subd. (a).) Flatley argues that the letter Mauro sent on behalf of Robertson, and his subsequent telephone calls to Flatley's attorneys, constituted extortion as a matter of law and, therefore, the trial court correctly dismissed Mauro's motion to strike Flatley's action as a SLAPP. (*Paul, supra,* 85 Cal.App.4th at pp. 1366–1367.) Mauro maintains that his activity on behalf of Robertson amounted to no more than the kind of permissible settlement negotiations that are attendant upon any legal dispute or, at minimum, that a question of fact exists regarding the legality of his conduct precluding a finding that it was illegal as a matter of law. . . .

At the core of Mauro's letter are threats to publicly accuse Flatley of rape and to report and publicly accuse him of other unspecified violations of various laws unless he "settled" by paying a sum of money to Robertson of which Mauro would receive 40 percent. In his follow-up phone calls, Mauro named the price of his and Robertson's silence as "seven figures" or, at minimum, $1 million.

The key passage in Mauro's letter is at page 3 where Flatley is warned that, unless he settles, "an in-depth investigation" will be conducted into his personal assets to determine punitive damages and this information will then **"BECOME A MATTER OF PUBLIC RECORD, AS IT MUST BE FILED WITH THE COURT. . . . [¶] Any and all information, including Immigration, Social Security Issuances and Use, and IRS and various State Tax Levies and information will be exposed**. We are positive the media worldwide will enjoy what they find." This warning is repeated in the fifth paragraph: **"[A]ll pertinent information and documentation, if in violation of any U.S. Federal, Immigration, I.R.S., S.S. Admin., U.S. State, Local, Commonwealth U.K., or International Laws, shall immediately [be] turned over to any and all appropriate authorities."** Finally, Flatley is warned that once the lawsuit is filed additional causes of action "shall arise" including "Defamatory comments, Civil Conspiracy, Reckless Supervision" which are "just the beginning" and that "ample evidence" exists "to prove each and every element for all these additional causes of action. Again, these actions allow for **Punitive Damages."**

At the top of the final page of the letter is the caption: **"<u>FIRST & FINAL TIME-LIMIT SETTLEMENT DEMAND</u>."** Beneath it a paragraph warns that there shall be **"<u>no continuances nor any delays.</u>"** At the bottom of the page, beneath Mauro's signature, a final paragraph warns Flatley that, along with the filing of suit, press releases will be disseminated to numerous media sources and placed on the Internet. . .

Evaluating Mauro's conduct, we conclude that the letter and subsequent phone calls constitute criminal extortion as a matter of law. These communications threatened to "accuse" Flatley of, or "impute to him," "crime[s]" and "disgrace" (Pen. Code, § 519, subds. 2, 3) unless Flatley paid Mauro a minimum of $1 million of which Mauro was to receive 40 percent. That the threats were half-couched in legalese does not disguise their essential character as extortion. . . . .

Whether Flatley in fact committed any violations of these various laws is irrelevant. Moreover, the threat to disclose criminal activity entirely unrelated to any alleged injury suffered by Mauro's client "exceeded the limits of respondent's representation of his client" and is itself evidence of extortion. That Mauro did not specify these other criminal offenses is of no import—"the accusations need only be such as to put the intended victim of the extortion in fear of being accused of some crime." Indeed, the very vagueness of the accusation serves the dual purpose of "magnifying the fear of his victim" and "protect[ing]" the extortionist "in the event of the failure to accomplish his extortion and . . . prosecution."

Mauro also threatened to accuse Flatley of raping Robertson unless he paid for her silence. Mauro argues that this threat cannot be the basis of a finding of extortion because Robertson had already reported the rape to the Las Vegas police department by the time the letter was sent. In the circumstances of this case, we reject his argument for the following reasons. . . . Flatley's complaint alleged that the purpose of Robertson's telephone call to the Las Vegas Police Department was not to file an actual crime report but simply to "create a 'sham' record of a police report that would make her threats more ominous. . . . [S]he wanted to prevent the police from taking any action that might make the matter public, since any public report of police action would necessarily spoil Robertson's scheme to extort a payment from [Flatley] to avoid such publicity."

These allegations are supported by the declarations of Mauro and Trautmann that they were never contacted by the police in connection with the alleged rape before Mauro sent his letter to Flatley's lawyers, and the absence of any evidence that the police ever took any action on the complaint. Moreover, Robertson's letter to the Las Vegas Police Department and Mauro's statements to the media after he filed Robertson's lawsuit—that she did not return to Las Vegas to pursue her complaint because she was too traumatized—support the conclusion that whatever complaint Robertson made to the Las Vegas police was insufficient to trigger a police investigation.

Mauro's declaration did not deny that he was aware that the Las Vegas police had not launched an investigation into Robertson's allegations when he sent the letter to Flatley. Yet, the letter was careful to include the number of a police report made to the Las Vegas Police Department as if to hold a police investigation over Flatley's head. Thus, as Flatley alleges, the incomplete police report appears to have existed only to make the threat of disclosure more ominous and the need to "settle" with Robertson and Mauro all the more urgent. Under these circumstances, the fact that Robertson may have made some report to the police did not render her threat to publicly accuse Flatley of rape unless he paid her and Mauro any less extortionate. (*People v. Umana* (2006) 138 Cal.App.4th 625, 640 ["Although section 519, subdivision 2, speaks in terms of *accusing* the victim of a crime, there is no reasonable basis for drawing a distinction between the initial accusation of a crime and continued pursuit of a criminal charge"].)

Moreover, in addition to the threats to accuse Flatley publicly of rape and violations of other laws, Mauro also alleged that he had in his possession "ample evidence" to support claims against Flatley for defamation and civil conspiracy and that these were "just the beginning." At minimum, these were threats that Flatley would be exposed to various kinds of opprobrium and he would be disgraced thereby unless he met Mauro's demands. (Pen. Code, § 519, subd. 3 [threat "to impute" "disgrace" sufficient to establish extortion].)

Lastly, any doubt as to extortionate character of the letter is dispelled by the accounts from Brandon and Fields of Mauro's telephone calls to them within a week of having sent the letter. In his very first conversation with Brandon, Mauro did not discuss the particulars of the claim or express an interest in negotiations but simply stated a deadline for Flatley "to offer sufficient payment." In a follow-up phone call, he objected to Flatley's investigation of Robertson's allegation and threatened to withdraw the January 30 deadline, thus further demonstrating that it was never his intention to engage in settlement negotiations. Instead, the insistent theme of his conversations with Flatley's lawyers is the immediate and extensive threat of exposure if Flatley failed to make a sufficient offer of money. This culminates in Mauro's threat to "go public" and "ruin" Flatley if the January 30 deadline was not met. We conclude that Mauro's conduct constituted criminal extortion as a matter of law in violation of Penal Code sections 518, 519 and 523.

Accordingly, because the activity forming the basis of Mauro's motion to strike Flatley's action was extortion as a matter of law and, therefore, not constitutionally protected activity for purposes of section 426.15, we further conclude that the trial court did not err when it denied Mauro's motion to strike.

CASE QUESTIONS

1. What does this case hold?

2. What is the relationship between the anti-SLAPP statute (CCP § 425) and the litigation privilege (Civil Code § 47)?

3. What made the letter an act of extortion?

PROBLEM 16–1

Re-write the letter to be as aggressive as lawfully possible.

Demand Letter Boomerang

Flatley rejected Mauro's demand letter, and in February 2003 Mauro sued Flatley in Illinois, where Ms. Robertson lived. Flatley sued Robertson and Mauro in Los Angeles one month later. Mauro dismissed Ms. Robertson's lawsuit later that year.

After the California Supreme Court's ruling, Mauro settled with Flatley. Media reports state Mauro paid Flatley $400,000 and apologized. The Illinois bar suspended Mauro for one year; a dissenter argued for disbarment.

Further media reports indicate Ms. Robertson did not respond to Flatley's suit and a default judgment for $11 million was entered against her. Efforts to enforce the judgment apparently led to a contempt citation issued in Los Angeles and her arrest for contempt (in Chicago) in December 2008.

Compare *Flatley* to *Sussman v. Bank of Israel*, 56 F.3d 450 (2d Cir. 1995). North American Bank ("NAB") was a New York bank with ties to Israel. NAB failed. Its deposits had been insured by the Bank of Israel ("BOI"), which paid NAB's depositors. BOI then filed suit in Israel against various persons associated with NAB. The defendants included one former NAB director and the estate of another. These defendants filed a response in the Israeli action, alleging in part that Israeli finance officials had kept them in the dark and misled them about NAB's condition.

After filing these responses, the defendants hired Nathan Lewin, a lawyer in Washington, D.C. Lewin drafted a complaint on their behalf, naming BOI and various other Israeli persons and entities (including the Israeli finance ministry) as defendants. Lewin then sent letters

> to several Israeli government officials, including then-Prime Minister Yitzchak Shamir, then-Minister of Finance Yitzchak Moda'i, and BOI Governor Michael Bruno, warning them of [the clients'] intention to bring the present suit, and proposing settlement discussions. After de-

scribing the general nature of the charges contained in the draft complaint, the letter stated:

> "This is a matter of extreme urgency because, in the absence of any satisfactory resolution of our differences, the lawsuit will be filed in New York within the next ten days. The agencies of the Government of Israel that are engaged in an effort directed against our clients are also pressing a trial in the Jerusalem District Court that is scheduled to begin shortly.
>
> If this controversy erupts into public view with the filing of our lawsuit and the inception of the Israeli proceeding, it will not only result in a grave injustice to individuals who have been among Israel's most constant and generous supporters, but will seriously damage foreign investment in Israel in the future.

The letter further asserted that Lewin's clients were at most honorary directors of NAB and had relied on BOI to monitor its operations. It concluded:

> In addition to the loss of their investments, which amounted to millions of dollars, our clients estimate that they have been forced to spend in excess of one million dollars fighting baseless claims made in the Israeli courts. Our lawsuit in federal court in New York will seek recovery against the Ministry of Finance, the Bank of Israel and individual government officials for these losses and for other harm caused to our clients.
>
> Our clients have heretofore been reluctant to take the step of filing suit because a full airing of this outrageous conduct by the Government of Israel will surely deter many potential foreign investors who might otherwise be interested in lending financial resources to Israel. However, the enormity of this injustice and the relentless prosecution of the case in Jerusalem leaves them no option.
>
> If you believe that discussions on this subject can lead to a fruitful and mutually satisfactory resolution, I am prepared to come to Jerusalem promptly to meet with you.

Lewin ultimately filed suit in New York. The suit was dismissed on *forum non conveniens* grounds. Invoking FRCP 11, the district court also entered a $50,000 sanction against Lewin, in part for filing a suit for an improper purpose.

The Court of Appeals for the Second Circuit reversed. It found the New York suit was not frivolous and had not been filed for an improper purpose. On the latter point the court commented:

> Mere warnings by a party of its intention to assert nonfrivolous claims, with predictions of those claims' likely public reception, are not improper.

Nor do we think it was appropriate for the district court to find that Lewin's prelitigation letters were evidence that the New York complaint was filed for an improper purpose. It is hardly unusual for a would-be plaintiff to seek to resolve disputes without resorting to legal action; prelitigation letters airing grievances and threatening litigation if they are not resolved are commonplace, sometimes with salutary results, and do not suffice to show an improper purpose if nonfrivolous litigation is eventually commenced.

PROBLEM 16–2

Is *Sussman* consistent with *Flatley*?

B. FOUNDATION FOR ASSERTING CLAIMS: PRE-FILING INVESTIGATION AND MALICIOUS PROSECUTION

We now turn to rules pertaining to the foundation you must have before submitting a claim to a tribunal or making a factual representation to a tribunal. Arising from the wave of foreclosures associated with the economic recession that began in 2008, the first case is an extreme illustration of the general principle that economic pressures on both clients and lawyers can create a tension between the investigation lawyers might like to do and the investigation clients are willing to pay for. In reading it remember your previous encounters with a high-volume, low-margin business model, in chapter 2.B. In reading this case bear in mind that the client, HBSC, was sanctioned by the bankruptcy court but did not appeal the sanction.

IN RE TAYLOR

655 F.3d 274 (3rd Cir. 2011)

FUENTES, CIRCUIT JUDGE

This case is an unfortunate example of the ways in which overreliance on computerized processes in a high-volume practice, as well as a failure on the part of clients and lawyers alike to take responsibility for accurate knowledge of a case, can lead to attorney misconduct before a court. It arises from the bankruptcy proceeding of Mr. and Ms. Niles C. and Angela J. Taylor. The Taylors filed for a chapter 13 bankruptcy in September 2007. In the Taylors' bankruptcy petition, they listed the bank HSBC, which held the mortgage on their house, as a creditor. In turn, HSBC filed a proof of claim in October 2007 with the bankruptcy court.

We are primarily concerned with two pleadings that HSBC's attorneys filed in the bankruptcy court—(1) the request for relief from the automatic stay which would have permitted HSBC to pursue foreclosure proceedings despite the Taylors' bankruptcy filing and (2) the response to the Taylors' objection to HSBC's proof of claim. We are also concerned with the attorneys' conduct in court in connection with those pleadings. We draw our facts from the findings of the bankruptcy court.

1. The proof of claim (Moss Codilis law firm)

To preserve its interest in a debtor's estate in a personal bankruptcy case, a creditor must file with the court a proof of claim, which includes a statement of the claim and of its amount and supporting documentation. In October 2007, HSBC filed such a proof of claim with respect to the Taylors' mortgage. To do so, it used the law firm Moss Codilis.[3] Moss retrieved the information on which the claim was based from HSBC's computerized mortgage servicing database. No employee of HSBC reviewed the claim before filing.

This proof of claim contained several errors: the amount of the Taylors' monthly payment was incorrectly stated, the wrong mortgage note was attached, and the value of the home was understated by about $100,000. It is not clear whether the errors originated in HSBC's database or whether they were introduced in Moss Codilis's filing. [HSBC ultimately corrected these errors in an amended court filing.] This dispute has now been resolved in favor of the Taylors.

2. The motion for relief from stay

At the time of the bankruptcy proceeding, the Taylors were also involved in a payment dispute with HSBC. HSBC believed the Taylors' home to be in a flood zone and had obtained "forced insurance" for the property, the cost of which (approximately $180/month) it passed on to the Taylors. The Taylors disputed HSBC's position and continued to pay their regular mortgage payment, without the additional insurance costs. HSBC failed to acknowledge that the Taylors were making their regular payments and instead treated each payment as a partial payment, so that, in its records, the Taylors were becoming more delinquent each month.

Ordinarily, the filing of a bankruptcy petition imposes an automatic stay on all debt collection activities, including foreclosures. However, pursuant to 11 U.S.C. § 362(d)(1), a secured creditor may file for relief from the stay "for cause, including the lack of adequate protection of an interest in property" of the creditor, in order to permit it to commence or continue foreclosure proceedings. Because of the Taylors' withheld insurance payments, HSBC's records indicated that they were delinquent. Thus, in

[3] [2] Moss Codilis is not involved in the present appeal. However, it is worth noting that the firm has come under serious judicial criticism for its lax practices in bankruptcy proceedings. "In total, [the court knows] of 23 instances in which [Moss Codilis] has violated [court rules] in this District alone." *In re Greco*, 405 B.R. 393, 394 (Bankr. S.D. Fla. 2009); *see also In re Waring*, 401 B.R. 906 (Bankr. N.D. Ohio 2009).

January 2008, HSBC retained the Udren Firm to seek relief from the stay.

Mr. Udren is the only partner of the Udren Firm; Ms. Doyle, who appeared for the Udren Firm in the Taylors' case, is a managing attorney at the firm, with twenty-seven years of experience. HSBC does not deign to communicate directly with the firms it employs in its high-volume foreclosure work; rather, it uses a computerized system called NewTrak (provided by a third party, LPS) to assign individual firms discrete assignments and provide the limited data the system deems relevant to each assignment.[4] The firms are selected and the instructions generated without any direct human involvement. The firms so chosen generally do not have the capacity to check the data (such as the amount of mortgage payment or time in arrears) provided to them by NewTrak and are not expected to communicate with other firms that may have done related work on the matter. Although it is technically possible for a firm hired through NewTrak to contact HSBC to discuss the matter on which it has been retained, it is clear from the record that this was discouraged and that some attorneys, including at least one Udren Firm attorney, did not believe it to be permitted.

In the Taylors' case, NewTrak provided the Udren Firm with only the loan number, the Taylors' name and address, payment amounts, late fees, and amounts past due. It did not provide any correspondence with the Taylors concerning the flood insurance dispute.

In January 2008, Doyle filed the motion for relief from the stay. This motion was prepared by non-attorney employees of the Udren Firm, relying exclusively on the information provided by NewTrak. The motion said that the debtor "has failed to discharge arrearages on said mortgage or has failed to make the current monthly payments on said mortgage since" the filing of the bankruptcy petition. It identified "the failure to make . . . post-petition monthly payments" as stretching from November 1, 2007 to January 15, 2008, with an "amount per month" of $1455 (a monthly payment higher than that identified on the proof of claim filed earlier in the case by the Moss firm) and a total in arrears of $4367. (It did note a "suspense balance" of $1040, which it subtracted from the ultimate total sought from the Taylors, but with no further explanation.) It stated that the Taylors had "inconsequential or no equity" in the property. The motion never mentioned the flood insurance dispute.

Doyle did nothing to verify the information in the motion for relief from stay besides check it against "screen prints" of the NewTrak infor-

[4] [5] LPS is also not involved in the present appeal, as the bankruptcy court found that it had not engaged in wrongdoing in this case. However, both the accuracy of its data and the ethics of its practices have been repeatedly called into question elsewhere.

mation. She did not even access NewTrak herself. In effect, she simply proofread the document. It does not appear that NewTrak provided the Udren Firm with any information concerning the Taylors' equity in their home, so Doyle could not have verified her statement in the motion concerning the lack of equity in any way, even against a "screen print." . . .

In February 2008, the Taylors filed a response to the motion for relief from stay, denying that they had failed to make payments and attaching copies of six checks tendered to HSBC during the relevant period. Four of them had already been cashed by HSBC.

3. The claim objection and the response to the claim objection

In March 2008, the Taylors also filed an objection to HSBC's proof of claim. The objection stated that HSBC had misstated the payment due on the mortgage and pointed out the dispute over the flood insurance. . .

In the same month, Doyle filed a response to the objection to the proof of claim. The response did not discuss the flood insurance issue at all. However, it stated that "[a]ll figures contained in the proof of claim accurately reflect actual sums expended . . . by Mortgagee . . . and/or charges to which Mortgagee is contractually entitled and which the Debtors are contractually obligated to pay." This was indisputably incorrect, because the proof of claim listed an inaccurate monthly mortgage payment (which was also a different figure from the payment listed in Doyle's own motion for relief from stay).

4. The claim hearings

In May 2008, the bankruptcy court held a hearing on both the motion for relief and the claim objection. HSBC was represented at the hearing by a junior associate at the Udren Firm, Mr. Fitzgibbon. At that hearing, Fitzgibbon ultimately admitted that, at the time the motion for relief from the stay was filed, HSBC had received a mortgage payment for November 2007, even though both the motion for stay and the response to the Taylors' objection to the proof of claim stated otherwise. Despite this, Fitzgibbon urged the court to grant the relief from stay, because the Taylors had not responded to HSBC's [Requests for Admissions on this issue] (which included the "admission" that the Taylors had not made payments from November 2007 to January 2008). It appears from the record that Fitzgibbon initially sought to have the RFAs admitted as evidence even though he knew they contained falsehoods.[5]

[5] Appellees now claim that "[i]t is clear from the record, that Mr. Fitzgibbon honestly disclosed to the Court that these checks had just been received by [the] Udren [Firm] and that the only issue was that of flood insurance." (App'ee Br. 16.) However, this disclosure did not occur until after Fitzgibbon had attempted to enter the RFAs, which made contrary claims, as evidence, and debtor's counsel raised the issue. As the bankruptcy court described it, "[Fitzgibbon] first argued that I should rule in HSBC's favor . . . On probing by the court, he acknowledged that as of the date of the continued hearing, he had learned that [the Taylors] had made every payment." (App. 196, emphasis added.) In a Rule 9011/11 proceeding such as the present one,

The bankruptcy court denied the request to enter the RFAs as evidence, noting that the firm "closed their eyes to the fact that there was evidence that . . . conflicted with the very admissions that they asked me [to deem admitted]. They . . . had that evidence [that the assertions in its motion were not accurate] in [their] possession and [they] went ahead like [they] never saw it." The court noted: Maybe they have somebody there churning out these motions that doesn't talk to the people that—you know, you never see the records, do you? Somebody sends it to you that sent it from somebody else. "I really find this motion to be in questionable good faith," the court concluded.

After the hearing, the bankruptcy court directed the Udren Firm to obtain an accounting from HSBC of the Taylors' prepetition payments so that the arrearage on the mortgage could be determined correctly. At the next hearing, in June 2008, Fitzgibbon stated that he could not obtain an accounting from HSBC, though he had repeatedly placed requests via NewTrak. He told the court that he was literally unable to contact HSBC—his firm's client—directly to verify information which his firm had already represented to the court that it believed to be true.

At the end of the June 2008 hearing, the court told Fitzgibbon: "I'm issuing an order to show cause on your firm, too, for filing these things . . . without having any knowledge. And filing answers . . . without any knowledge." Thereafter, the court entered an order sua sponte dated June 9, 2008, directing Fitzgibbon, Doyle, Udren, and others to appear and give testimony concerning the possibility of sanctions.

5. The sanctions hearings

The order stated that the purpose of the hearing included "to investigate the practices employed in this case by HSBC and its attorneys and agents and consider whether sanctions should issue against HSBC, its attorneys and agents." Among those practices were "pressing a relief motion on admissions that were known to be untrue, and signing and filing pleadings without knowledge or inquiry regarding the matters pled therein." The order noted that "[t]he details are identified on the record of the hearings which are incorporated herein." In ordering Doyle to appear, the order noted that "the motion for relief, the admissions and the reply to the objection were prepared over Doyle's name and signature." However, this order was not formally identified as "an order to show cause."

The bankruptcy court held four hearings over several days, making in-depth inquiries into the communications between HSBC and its lawyers in this case, as well as the general capabilities and limitations of a system like NewTrak. Ultimately, it found that the following had violated

---

one would expect the challenged parties to be scrupulously careful in their representations to the court.

Rule 9011: Fitzgibbon, for pressing the motion for relief based on claims he knew to be untrue; Doyle, for failing to make reasonable inquiry concerning the representations she made in the motion for relief from stay and the response to the claim objection; Udren and the Udren Firm itself, for the conduct of its attorneys; and HSBC, for practices which caused the failure to adhere to Rule 9011.

Because of his inexperience, the court did not sanction Fitzgibbon. However, it required Doyle to take 3 CLE credits in professional responsibility; Udren himself to be trained in the use of NewTrak and to spend a day observing his employees handling NewTrak; and both Doyle and Udren to conduct a training session for the firm's relevant lawyers in the requirements of Rule 9011 and procedures for escalating inquiries on NewTrak. The court also required HSBC to send a copy of its opinion to all the law firms it uses in bankruptcy proceedings, along with a letter explaining that direct contact with HSBC concerning matters relating to HSBC's case was permissible.[6]

B. The District Court's Decision

Udren, Doyle, and the Udren Firm (but not HSBC) appealed the sanctions order to the District Court, which ultimately overturned the order. The District Court's decision was based on three considerations: that the confusion in the case was attributable at least as much to the actions of Taylor's counsel as to Doyle, Udren, and the Udren Firm; that the bankruptcy court seemed more concerned with "sending a message" to the bar concerning the use of computerized systems than with the conduct in the particular case; and that, since Udren himself did not sign any of the filings containing misrepresentations, he could not be sanctioned under Rule 9011. Although HSBC had not appealed, the District Court overturned the order with respect to HSBC, as well.

The United States trustee then appealed the District Court's decision to this court.

II.

Rule 9011 of the Federal Rules of Bankruptcy Procedure, the equivalent of Rule 11 of the Federal Rules of Civil Procedure, requires that parties making representations to the court certify that "the allegations and other factual contentions have evidentiary support or, if specifically so identified, are likely to have evidentiary support." A party must reach this conclusion based on "inquiry reasonable under the circumstances."

[6] [10] Taylor's counsel was also ultimately sanctioned and removed from the case. Counsel did not perform competently, as is evidenced by the Taylors' failure to contest HSBC's RFAs. She also made a number of inaccurate statements in her representations to the court. However, it is clear that her conduct did not induce the misrepresentations by HSBC or its attorneys. As the bankruptcy court correctly noted, "the process employed by a mortgagee and its counsel must be fair and transparent without regard to the quality of debtor's counsel since many debtors are unrepresented and cannot rely on counsel to protect them."

The concern of Rule 9011 is not the truth or falsity of the representation in itself, but rather whether the party making the representation reasonably believed it at the time to have evidentiary support. . . .

A. Alleged literal truth

As an initial matter, the appellees' insistence that Doyle's and Fitzgibbon's statements were "literally true" should not exculpate them from Rule 9011 sanctions. First, it should be noted that several of these claims were not, in fact, accurate. There was no literal truth to the statement in the request for relief from stay that the Taylors had no equity in their home. Doyle admitted that she made that statement simply as "part of the form pleading," and "acknowledged having no knowledge of the value of the property and having made no inquiry on this subject." Similarly, the statement in the claim objection response that the figures in the original proof of claim were correct was false.

Just as importantly, appellees cite no authority, and we are aware of none, which permits statements under Rule 9011 that are literally true but actually misleading. If the reasonably foreseeable effect of Doyle's or Fitzgibbon's representations to the bankruptcy court was to mislead the court, they cannot be said to have complied with Rule 9011. See *Williamson v. Recovery Ltd. P'ship*, 542 F.3d 43, 51 (2d Cir. 2008) (a party violates Rule 11 "by making false, misleading, improper, or frivolous representations to the court") (emphasis added).

In particular, even assuming that Doyle's and Fitzgibbon's statements as to the payments made by the Taylors were literally accurate, they were misleading. In attempting to evaluate whether HSBC was justified in seeking a relief from the stay on foreclosure, the court needed to know that at least partial payments had been made and that the failure to make some of the rest of the payments was due to a bona fide dispute over the amount due, not simple default. Instead, the court was told only that the Taylors had "failed to make regular mortgage payments" from November 1, 2007 to January 15, 2008, with a mysterious notation concerning a "suspense balance" following. A court could only reasonably interpret this to mean that the Taylors simply had not made payments for the period specified. As the bankruptcy court found, "[f]or at best a $540 dispute, the Udren Firm mechanically prosecuted a motion averring a $4,367[ ] post-petition obligation, the aim of which was to allow HSBC to foreclose on [the Taylors'] house." Therefore, Doyle's and Fitzgibbon's statements in question were either false or misleading.

B. Reasonable inquiry

We must, therefore, determine the reasonableness of the appellees' inquiry before they made their false representations. Reasonableness has been defined as "an objective knowledge or belief at the time of the filing of a challenged paper that the claim was well-grounded in law and fact."

Ford Motor Co. v. Summit Motor Prods., Inc., 930 F.2d 277, 289 (3d Cir. 1991) (internal quotations omitted). The requirement of reasonable inquiry protects not merely the court and adverse parties, but also the client. The client is not expected to know the technical details of the law and ought to be able to rely on his attorney to elicit from him the information necessary to handle his case in the most effective, yet legally appropriate, manner.

In determining reasonableness, we have sometimes looked at several factors: "the amount of time available to the signer for conducting the factual and legal investigation; the necessity for reliance on a client for the underlying factual information; the plausibility of the legal position advocated; . . . whether the case was referred to the signer by another member of the Bar . . . [; and] the complexity of the legal and factual issues implicated." *Mary Ann Pensiero, Inc. v. Lingle*, 847 F.2d 90, 95 (3d Cir. 1988). However, it does not appear that the court must work mechanically through these factors when it considers whether to impose sanctions. Rather, it should consider the reasonableness of the inquiry under all the material circumstances. "[T]he applicable standard is one of reasonableness under the circumstances"

Central to this case, then, is the degree to which an attorney may reasonably rely on representations from her client. An attorney certainly "is not always foreclosed from relying on information from other persons." In making statements to the court, lawyers constantly and appropriately rely on information provided by their clients, especially when the facts are contained in a client's computerized records. It is difficult to imagine how attorneys might function were they required to conduct an independent investigation of every factual representation made by a client before it could be included in a court filing. While Rule 9011 "does not recognize a `pure heart and empty head' defense," a lawyer need not routinely assume the duplicity or gross incompetence of her client in order to meet the requirements of Rule 9011. It is therefore usually reasonable for a lawyer to rely on information provided by a client, especially where that information is superficially plausible and the client provides its own records which appear to confirm the information.

However, Doyle's behavior was unreasonable, both as a matter of her general practice and in ways specific to this case. First, reasonable reliance on a client's representations assumes a reasonable attempt at eliciting them by the attorney. That is, an attorney must, in her independent professional judgment, make a reasonable effort to determine what facts are likely to be relevant to a particular court filing and to seek those facts from the client. She cannot simply settle for the information her client determines in advance—by means of an automated system, no less—that she should be provided with.

Yet that is precisely what happened here. "[I]t appears," the bankruptcy court observed, "that Doyle, the manager of the Udren Firm bankruptcy department, had no relationship with the client, HSBC." By working solely with NewTrak, a system which no one at the Udren Firm seems to have understood, much less had any influence over, Doyle permitted HSBC to define—perilously narrowly—the information she had about the Taylors' matter. That HSBC was not providing her with adequate information through NewTrak should have been evident to Doyle from the face of the NewTrak file. She did not have any information concerning the Taylors' equity in the home, though she made a statement specifically denying that they had any.

More generally, a reasonable attorney would not file a motion for relief from stay for cause without inquiring of the client whether it had any information relevant to the alleged cause, that is, the debtor's failure to make payments. Had Doyle made even that most minimal of inquiries, HSBC presumably would have provided her with the information in its files concerning the flood insurance dispute, and Doyle could have included that information in her motion for relief from stay—or, perhaps, advised the client that seeking such a motion would be inappropriate under the circumstances.

With respect to the Taylors' case in particular, Doyle ignored clear warning signs as to the accuracy of the data that she did receive. In responding to the motion for relief from stay, the Taylors submitted documentation indicating that they had already made at least partial payments for some of the months in question. In objecting to the proof of claim, the Taylors pointed out the inaccuracy of the mortgage payment listed and explained the circumstances surrounding the flood insurance dispute. Although Doyle certainly was not obliged to accept the Taylors' claims at face value, they indisputably put her on notice that the matter was not as simple as it might have appeared from the NewTrak file. At that point, any reasonable attorney would have sought clarification and further documentation from her client, in order to correct any prior inadvertent misstatements to the court and to avoid any further errors. Instead, Doyle mechanically affirmed facts (the monthly mortgage payment) that her own prior filing with the court had already contradicted.

Doyle's reliance on HSBC was particularly problematic because she was not, in fact, relying directly on HSBC. Instead, she relied on a computer system run by a third-party vendor. She did not know where the data provided by NewTrak came from. She had no capacity to check the data against the original documents if any of it seemed implausible. And she effectively could not question the data with HSBC. In her relationship with HSBC, Doyle essentially abdicated her professional judgment to a black box. . . .

This was not a matter of extreme complexity, nor of extraordinary deadline pressure. Although the initial data the Udren Firm received was not, in itself, wildly implausible, it was facially inadequate. In short, then, we find that Doyle's inquiry before making her representations to the bankruptcy court was unreasonable.

In making this finding, we, of course, do not mean to suggest that the use of computerized databases is inherently inappropriate. However, the NewTrak system, as it was being used at the time of this case, permits parties at every level of the filing process to disclaim responsibility for inaccuracies. HSBC has handed off responsibility to a third-party maintainer, LPS, which, judging from the results in this case, has not generated particularly accurate records. LPS apparently regards itself as a mere conduit of information. Appellees, the attorneys and final link in the chain of transmission of this information to the court, claim reliance on NewTrak's records. Who, precisely, can be held accountable if HSBC's records are inadequately maintained, LPS transfers those records inaccurately into NewTrak, or a law firm relies on the NewTrak data without further investigation, thus leading to material misrepresentations to the court? It cannot be that all the parties involved can insulate themselves from responsibility by the use of such a system. In the end, we must hold responsible the attorneys who have certified to the court that the representations they are making are "well-grounded in law and fact." . . .

D. The Udren Firm and Udren's individual liability

We also find that it was appropriate to extend sanctions to the Udren Firm itself. Rule 11 explicitly allows the imposition of sanctions against law firms. In this instance, the bankruptcy court found that the misrepresentations in the case arose not simply from the irresponsibility of individual attorneys, but from the system put in place at the Udren Firm, which emphasized high-volume, high-speed processing of foreclosures to such an extent that it led to violations of Rule 9011.

However, we do not find that responsibility for these failures extends specifically to Udren, whose involvement in this matter was limited to his role as sole shareholder of the firm. . .

G. Conclusion

We appreciate that the use of technology can save both litigants and attorneys time and money, and we do not, of course, mean to suggest that the use of databases or even certain automated communications between counsel and client are presumptively unreasonable. However, Rule 11 requires more than a rubber-stamping of the results of an automated process by a person who happens to be a lawyer. Where a lawyer systematically fails to take any responsibility for seeking adequate information from her client, makes representations without any factual basis because they are included in a "form pleading" she has been trained to fill out, and ignores obvious indications that her information may be incorrect, she cannot be said to have made reasonable inquiry. Therefore, we find that the bankruptcy court did not abuse its discretion in imposing sanctions on Doyle or the Udren Firm itself. However, it did abuse its discretion in imposing sanctions on Udren individually.

We next turn to the question of an adequate legal foundation to bring a case, captured in the doctrine of tort liability for malicious prosecution. That doctrine covers cases in which a suit is filed without adequate grounds to file it. In part this is a factual question, of course, and to this extent the doctrine overlaps with the preceding case. In part this question concerns the legal basis for a claim, however, and that is the focus of the next case. In reading it bear in mind that malicious prosecution is different from threats, which may be unlawful even if no suit is filed, and from the abuse of process tort, which covers cases in which a suit is filed to gain some collateral benefit the plaintiff could not obtain through litigation.

SHELDON APPEL CO. V. OLIKER

47 Cal.3d 863 (1989)

ARGUELLES, JUSTICE.

. . . In August 1978, three of A & O's clients-M.J. Choppin, J.P. Kinzer, Jr., and Donald Miller (collectively, CKM)-sold a 42–unit apartment building to Sheldon Appel. During the negotiations which preceded the signing of the escrow agreement, Sheldon Appel represented that it would do a "first class" job of converting the building into condominiums and selling the units, and CKM ultimately agreed to sell the building for $2.75 million cash plus "47% of the excess, if any, of gross sales receipts to [Sheldon Appel] of the condominium units over 3,750,000 dollars." . . . neither the sale agreement nor the escrow agreement contained any provision expressly declaring that the property was to constitute security for Sheldon Appel's obligations.

Shortly after the close of escrow on February 5, 1979, CKM learned that Sheldon Appel was offering to sell the entire building in bulk for $4 million. . . . The sale of the building in bulk would have produced a quick profit for Sheldon Appel, sparing it the effort and expense associated with the sale of individual units. At the same time, however, CKM feared that such a sale would deprive it of its anticipated share of the profits attributable to the sale of the apartments as individual units rather than as a single piece of property.

After learning of Sheldon Appel's bulk sale offer, CKM consulted its attorneys, defendant A & O. On February 23, 1979, A & O filed a complaint on behalf of CKM against Sheldon Appel, seeking a declaration of CKM's rights under the sales contract and the imposition of an equitable lien on the property in question; at the same time, A & O recorded a notice of lis pendens on the property on behalf of CKM.

A little more than a month thereafter, on March 30, 1979, Sheldon Appel filed a motion to expunge the notice of lis pendens, contending that CKM's action did not affect "title to or right of possession of" the real property in question and thus that the lis pendens was not valid; in addition to expungement, the motion sought an award of attorneys' fees as a sanction for CKM's alleged misuse of the lis pendens procedure. Three weeks later, on April 19, 1979, the trial court granted the motion and expunged the lis pendens . . . Eventually, all of the causes of action in CKM's original lawsuit were terminated in Sheldon Appel's favor.

During the period between the recording of the lis pendens and its expungement, Sheldon Appel abandoned its plan to make a bulk sale of the apartment building and began to sell individual condominium units, incurring extra interest costs because of the cloud on the title resulting from the lis pendens. On December 4, 1979, after Sheldon Appel had sold enough condominiums to generate receipts in excess of $3.75 million but had not paid any of the excess to CKM, A & O filed a new action on CKM's behalf seeking damages for breach of contract.

On January 3, 1980, Sheldon Appel filed an answer to the breach of contract action and, at the same time, filed a cross-complaint against both CKM and A & O seeking damages for malicious prosecution. In support of its malicious prosecution claim, Sheldon Appel alleged that CKM and A & O had knowingly asserted an untenable lien claim and recorded an impermissible lis pendens to force it to sell individual units.

The trial court severed the malicious prosecution cross-complaint from the breach of contract complaint, and the contract action went to trial first. On April 24, 1984, CKM obtained a judgment of over $720,000 against Sheldon Appel in the breach of contract action. Sheldon Appel's cross-complaint for malicious prosecution then proceeded to a separate trial. . . .

At trial, the court, over objection, permitted an attorney called by Sheldon Appel to testify as an expert witness on the question of the legal tenability of the prior action. The court also admitted evidence with respect to the adequacy of the legal research that had been performed by A & O prior to the filing of the initial complaint and the recording of the lis pendens. John Zemanek, an attorney employed by A & O who at that point had been a member of the bar for less than a year, had prepared and filed the complaint and had recorded the notice of lis pendens on behalf of CKM. Zemanek initially reported spending slightly over four hours performing all of these tasks, but later testified that he had spent more time than he had reported. Sheldon Appel asserted that Zemanek had spent unreasonably little time researching the legal basis for the lien claim. . . . the jury found in favor of Sheldon Appel on the malicious prosecution action, and awarded it $82,000 in compensatory damages and $1 million in punitive damages.[7]

II

The common law tort of malicious prosecution originated as a remedy for an individual who had been subjected to a maliciously instituted criminal charge, but in California, as in most common law jurisdictions, the tort was long ago extended to afford a remedy for the malicious prosecution of a civil action. Under the governing authorities, in order to establish a cause of action for malicious prosecution of either a criminal or civil proceeding, a plaintiff must demonstrate "that the prior action (1) was commenced by or at the direction of the defendant and was pursued to a legal termination in his, plaintiff's, favor; (2) was brought without probable cause; and (3) was initiated with malice."

Although the malicious prosecution tort has ancient roots, courts have long recognized that the tort has the potential to impose an undue "chilling effect" on the ordinary citizen's willingness to report criminal conduct or to bring a civil dispute to court, and, as a consequence, the tort has traditionally been regarded as a disfavored cause of action. In a number of other states, the disfavored status of the tort is reflected in a requirement that a plaintiff demonstrate some "special injury" beyond that ordinarily incurred in defending a lawsuit in order to prevail in a malicious prosecution action. Even in jurisdictions, like California, which do not impose a special-injury requirement, the elements of the tort have historically been carefully circumscribed so that litigants with potentially valid claims will not be deterred from bringing their claims to court by the prospect of a subsequent malicious prosecution claim.

III

A & O's challenge to the trial court's treatment of the probable cause element in this case implicates four interrelated issues . . .

A. *Role of Court and Jury in the Probable Cause Determination*

A & O's initial and broadest contention is that the trial court committed a fundamental error in effectively leaving the determination of the probable cause issue to the jury rather than resolving that question itself. We conclude that the objection is well taken. . . .

The "malice" element of the malicious prosecution tort relates to the subjective intent or purpose with which the defendant acted in initiating the prior action, and past cases establish that the defendant's motivation

[7] The jury found both A & O and its client, CKM, liable for malicious prosecution, but the trial court entered judgment notwithstanding the verdict in favor of CKM, and Sheldon Appel has not pursued an appeal from the judgment in CKM's favor.

is a question of fact to be determined by the jury. By contrast, the existence or absence of probable cause has traditionally been viewed as a question of law to be determined by the court, rather than a question of fact for the jury. . . .

The question whether, on a given set of facts, there was probable cause to institute an action requires a sensitive evaluation of legal principles and precedents, a task generally beyond the ken of lay jurors, and courts have recognized that there is a significant danger that jurors may not sufficiently appreciate the distinction between a merely unsuccessful and a legally untenable claim. To avoid improperly deterring individuals from resorting to the courts for the resolution of disputes, the common law affords litigants the assurance that tort liability will not be imposed for filing a lawsuit unless *a court* subsequently determines that the institution of the action was without probable cause. [citations omitted] If the court determines that there was probable cause to institute the prior action, the malicious prosecution action fails, whether or not there is evidence that the prior suit was maliciously motivated. . . .

[U]nder a proper understanding of the probable cause element there were no disputed questions of fact relevant to probable cause to be submitted to the jury in this case, and for that reason it is clear that the trial court erred in submitting the issue to the jury in any form. . . .

[T]he court's error was in large part a product of long-standing confusion in the case law over both the substantive content of the probable cause standard and the underlying facts which are relevant to the probable cause determination. While, as we have just discussed, the probable cause determination has always been considered a question of law for the court, the cases have also made clear that if the facts upon which the defendant acted in bringing the prior action "are controverted, they must be passed upon by the jury before the court can determine the issue of probable cause. . . . 'What facts and circumstances amount to probable cause is a pure question of law. Whether they exist or not in any particular case is a pure question of fact. The former is exclusively for the court, the latter for the jury.' " [citations omitted]. . . .

B. *Objective or Subjective Nature of Probable Cause Element*

The instruction on probable cause given in this case was derived from much-quoted dictum contained in the Court of Appeal opinion in *Tool Research & Engineering Corp. v. Henigson* (1975) 46 Cal.App.3d 675. . . . The *Tool Research* court quite properly rejected the plaintiff's contention that probable cause to institute an action exists only if an attorney is "convinced that the trier of fact would accept the evidence in favor of the cause [he represents]" making it clear that the appropriate question is simply whether the prior action was legally "tenable."

In the course of rejecting that contention, however, the *Tool Research* court included broad dictum which purported to set forth a general definition of the probable cause element for all cases in which an attorney is the subject of a malicious prosecution action. The court stated in this regard: "*An attorney has probable cause to represent a client in litigation when, after a reasonable investigation and industrious search of legal authority, he has an honest belief that his client's claim is tenable in the forum in which it is to be tried. [Citations.] The test is twofold. The attorney must entertain a subjective belief in that the claim merits litigation and that belief must satisfy an objective standard.*" (Emphasis added.) . . .

The *Tool Research* "subjective belief" dictum alters the probable cause element in a fundamental respect. Under that dictum, even if a trial court finds that, on the basis of the facts known to the defendant attorney, the prior lawsuit *was* objectively reasonable-and thus that the malicious prosecution plaintiff was *not* subjected to an unjustified lawsuit-the court could not properly terminate the action in favor of the defendant so long as the plaintiff presented any evidence raising a question as to whether the defendant attorney subjectively believed in the tenability of the claim. And because the issue of the attorney's subjective belief or nonbelief in legal tenability would rarely be susceptible of clear proof and, when controverted, would always pose a factual question, the dictum would in many cases effectively leave the ultimate resolution of the probable cause element to the jury, rather than to the court.

Although past decisions of our own court are not as clear as they might be with respect to the "objective" versus "subjective" nature of the probable cause element . . . we find that, properly understood, the decisions do not support the *Tool Research* court's conclusion that the defendant's subjective belief *in the legal tenability* of the prior action is a necessary element of probable cause. As we explain, while our decisions do indicate that in some cases the defendant's subjective belief may be relevant to the probable cause issue, in all of the cases the "belief" in question related to the defendant's belief in, or knowledge of, *a given state of facts,* and not to the defendant's belief in, or evaluation of, *the legal merits of the claim*. . . .

When there is a dispute as to the state of the defendant's knowledge and the existence of probable cause turns on resolution of that dispute . . . the jury must resolve the threshold question of the defendant's factual knowledge or belief. . . . when . . . there is evidence that the defendant may have known that the factual allegations on which his action depended were untrue, the jury must determine what facts the defendant knew before the trial court can determine the legal question whether such facts constituted probable cause to institute the challenged proceeding. . . . the jury's factual inquiry into the defendant's belief or knowledge is not properly an inquiry into "whether [the defendant] thought the facts to constitute probable cause" [citations omitted] when the state of the defendant's factual knowledge is resolved or undisputed, it is the court which decides whether such facts constitute probable cause or not.

Accordingly, when, as in this case, the facts known by the attorney are not in dispute, the probable cause issue is properly determined by the trial court under an objective standard; it does not include a determination whether the attorney subjectively believed that the prior claim was legally tenable. . .

If the trial court concludes that the prior action was not objectively tenable, evidence that the defendant attorney did not subjectively believe that the action was tenable would clearly be relevant to the question of malice. Inasmuch as an attorney who does not have a good faith belief in the tenability of an action will normally assume that a court is likely to come to the same conclusion, the malicious prosecution tort will continue to deter attorneys from filing actions which they do not believe are legally tenable.

Furthermore, the probable cause element, as so defined, imposes no improper or unjustified hardship on a malicious prosecution plaintiff. If a court finds that the initial lawsuit was in fact objectively tenable, the court has determined that the fundamental interest which the malicious prosecution tort is designed to protect—"the interest in freedom from *unjustifiable* and *unreasonable* litigation" (1 Harper et al., The Law of Torts, supra, ï 4.2, p. 407, emphasis added)—has not been infringed by the initial action. Under such circumstances, it is not unfair to bar a plaintiff's suit for damages even if the plaintiff can show that its adversary's law firm did not realize how tenable the prior claim actually was, since the plaintiff could properly have been put to the very same burden of defending an identical claim if its adversary had simply consulted a different, more legally astute, attorney. This is a classic case of "no harm, no foul."

C. *Irrelevance of Attorney Research to Probable Cause*

As noted above, in addition to suggesting that a plaintiff may establish an absence of probable cause by demonstrating that the defendant attorney did not subjectively believe in the tenability of the prior claim, the *Tool Research* court further suggested that a plaintiff might prove a lack of probable cause by showing that the attorney had failed to conduct "a reasonable investigation and industrious search of legal authority . . . " before instituting the prior action. . . .

We conclude that the *Tool Research* decision significantly and improperly altered the probable cause element by suggesting that an attorney's reasonable investigation and industrious search of legal authority is an essential component of probable cause. This portion of the *Tool Research* dictum again shifts the focus of the probable cause inquiry from the objective tenability of the prior claim to the adequacy of the particular defendant's performance as an attorney. Furthermore, this component is not only fundamentally incompatible with the objective nature of the probable cause determination, but it is also at odds with a consistent line of California decisions which have made clear that an attorney's duty of care runs primarily to his own client rather than to the client's adversary, and which-on the basis of important policy considerations-have precluded the adversary from maintaining a negligence cause of action against its opponent's attorney. Allowing inadequate research to serve as an independent basis for proving the absence of probable cause on the part of an attorney would tend to create a conflict of interest between the attorney and client, tempting a cautious attorney to create a record of diligence by performing extensive legal research, not for the benefit of his client, but simply to protect himself from his client's adversaries in the event the initial suit fails.

As we have explained above, if the trial court concludes that, on the basis of the facts known to the defendant, the filing of the prior action was objectively reasonable, the court has necessarily determined that the malicious prosecution plaintiff was not subjected to an unjustified lawsuit. When the court has made such a determination, there is no persuasive reason to allow the plaintiff to go forward with its tort action even if it can show that its adversary's attorney did not perform as thorough an investigation or as complete a legal research job as a reasonable attorney may have conducted. Permitting recovery on such a basis would provide the plaintiff with a windfall; since the prior action was objectively tenable, the plaintiff could properly have been put to the very same burden of defense if its adversary had simply hired more thorough counsel. . . .

D. *Expert Testimony and Probable Cause*

The trial court's confusion as to the proper role of the court and the jury in the probable cause determination also led to yet another error in this case. As noted above, the court, over objection, permitted attorneys to be called as expert witnesses to give their opinions as to whether a reasonable attorney would conclude that the claims advanced in the prior action were tenable. In light of our earlier discussion, explaining that the objective tenability of the prior action is a question of law to be determined by the court, it is clear that the trial court erred in admitting this evidence. . . .

IV

Although it is sometimes necessary to submit preliminary factual questions to the jury when there is a dispute as to facts which the defendant knew when he instituted the prior action, in this case there was no dispute as to facts of which A & O was aware when it brought the prior action on its client's behalf. It was uncontroverted that CKM informed A & O of the details of the earlier real estate transactions and Sheldon

Appel's post-purchase bulk sale offer, and that A & O filed the declaratory relief complaint and recorded the lis pendens on the basis of those facts. Under these circumstances, it was the responsibility of the trial court to determine whether Sheldon Appel had established that A & O acted without probable cause in filing the lis pendens and the lien claim.

We need not remand the matter to the trial court, however, for we are as in good a position as that court to resolve the determinative legal question-namely, whether there was probable cause to file the lis pendens and the supporting lien claim. In resolving that issue, however, we must first clarify by how stringent a standard probable cause should be tested.

A number of early cases, discussing the probable cause issue in relation to a claim of a malicious prosecution of a criminal charge, defined probable cause as "a suspicion founded upon circumstances sufficiently strong to warrant a reasonable man in the belief that the charge is true." In the context of an action alleging malicious prosecution of a prior civil suit, however, it has long been recognized that it is not "true charges" but rather legally tenable claims for relief that the law seeks to protect

In addressing the somewhat related question as to the appropriate standard for determining the frivolousness of an appeal in *In re Marriage of Flaherty* (1982) 31 Cal.3d 637 we concluded that an appeal could properly be found frivolous only if "any reasonable attorney would agree that the appeal is totally and completely without merit." In arriving at that standard, we reasoned that "any definition [of frivolousness] must be read so as to avoid a serious chilling effect on the assertion of litigants' rights. . . . Counsel and their clients have a right to present issues that are arguably correct, even if it is extremely unlikely that they will win. . . . " (*Ibid.*) . . .

[W]e believe that the less stringent *Flaherty* standard more appropriately reflects the important public policy of avoiding the chilling of novel or debatable legal claims. That policy is no less applicable to the institution of actions at the trial stage than to the pursuit of appeals, and . . . we do not believe there is any reason to afford litigants and their attorneys less protection from subsequent tort liability than it is to shield them from court-imposed sanctions within the initial action. . . . [T]he *Flaherty* standard-modified to fit this context, i.e., whether any reasonable attorney would have thought the claim tenable-may make it clearer that in evaluating whether or not there was probable cause for malicious prosecution purposes, a court must properly take into account the evolutionary potential of legal principles. (See, e.g., Rest.2d Torts, § 675, com. f.)

Applying the appropriate probable cause standard to the facts of this case, we conclude that the dissenting justice in the Court of Appeal was correct in finding that the lien claim pursued by A & O, although not ultimately successful, was legally tenable and thus that there was probable cause to support both the lien claim and the lis pendens. At the time the lien claim was filed, there was at least one prior California decision which had suggested that a vendor's lien, under Civil Code section 3046, might well be available to protect the interests of a seller of real property under facts somewhat comparable to the circumstances in this case and, in addition, there were a variety of decisions which had recognized the right of a court to impose an equitable lien on property-even in the absence of an express contractual security provision-to effectuate the intent of the parties or to prevent unjust enrichment. . . . Accordingly, we conclude that the prior action was not instituted without probable cause.

V

The judgment of the Court of Appeal is reversed, and the case is remanded with directions to order the entry of judgment in favor of A & O on the malicious prosecution claim.

CASE QUESTIONS

1. What are the elements of the malicious prosecution tort?
2. What is probable cause, for purposes of the tort?
3. What is malice, and how does it relate to probable cause?
4. Why do some jurisdictions impose special injury requirements for the tort?

C. THE PURPOSE OF LITIGATION: THE ABUSE OF PROCESS TORT

The abuse of process tort is sometimes confused with the malicious prosecution tort but the two torts differ in important ways. An abuse of process claim requires the plaintiff to show a suit was filed in an effort to obtain some remedy other than the remedies the law provides for the cause of action asserted. The following case illustrates this difference, and illustrates as well important differences in the way people may perceive litigation.

SELTZER V. MORTON

336 Mont. 225 (2007)

JUSTICE JAMES C. NELSON delivered the Opinion of the Court.

This appeal follows a civil jury trial conducted in the District Court of the Eighth Judicial District, Cascade County. The Plaintiff, W. Steve

Seltzer ("Seltzer"), filed suit against Steve Morton ("Morton"), Dennis A. Gladwell ("Gladwell"), and Gibson, Dunn & Crutcher, L.L.P., ("GDC") (collectively "Defendants"), claiming that they had committed the torts of malicious prosecution and abuse of process. In the first phase of trial, the jury found in favor of Seltzer and awarded $1.1 million in compensatory damages. At this time, the jury also determined that the Defendants should be subjected to a punitive sanction. In the second phase of trial, the jury assessed punitive damages in the amount of $100,000.00 against Morton, $150,000.00 against Gladwell, and $20 million against GDC. The District Court reviewed the punitive damages verdicts, pursuant to both Montana statutory law and federal caselaw, and issued an order reducing the sanction against GDC to $9.9 million.

Seltzer has filed an appeal, arguing that the District Court erred in reducing the punitive damages verdict. The Defendants have filed a cross-appeal, arguing that the court erred by not further reducing the punitive damages verdict. Additionally, the Defendants have presented numerous other cross-appeal issues that were raised during trial and in post-verdict motions. . . . We affirm in all respects.

FACTUAL AND PROCEDURAL BACKGROUND

Seltzer is, among other things, a professional appraiser and authenticator of Western American artwork ("Western art"). In late 2000 or early 2001, at the request of an art auction house, he rendered his opinion as to the authenticity of a watercolor painting that Morton owned. Morton subsequently demanded that Seltzer recant his opinion. When he refused to do so, GDC filed a multi-count lawsuit against Seltzer. That lawsuit, which was eventually dismissed with prejudice, is the subject of this litigation.

Morton's painting, which was at the center of the underlying suit against Seltzer, bears a signature indicating that it is the work of Charles M. Russell ("Russell"). However, Seltzer and a number of other art experts believe the painting is actually the work of Seltzer's grandfather, Olaf Carl Seltzer ("O. C. Seltzer"). . . . Although both Russell and O.C. Seltzer are recognized as fine Western artists, Russell's work is more widely known and significantly more valuable.

Morton's painting, which is known as "Lassoing a Longhorn," depicts action and figures similar to that of other works by both Russell and O.C. Seltzer. . . . In its lower left corner, the painting bears a signature, a bison skull marking, and a date, all in heavy black ink, purporting that the painting is a 1913 work by Russell. The signature style is similar to that used by Russell in 1913. Additionally, a bison skull insignia resembling that in the painting is a hallmark accompaniment to Russell's signatures. The painting currently measures 16 1/2 by 22 3/4 inches.

There is no record or known information regarding the painting's origin, ownership, or whereabouts from 1913 to 1939. In November of 1939, the Newhouse Galleries in New York, New York, sold the painting to Amon Carter of Fort Worth Texas. The Amon Carter Museum's records listed the dimensions of the painting in 1939 as 20 5/8 by 26 3/4 inches-approximately 4 inches wider and 4 inches longer than the current dimensions of the painting. These same dimensions were cited in a 1966 book, discussed below, which catalogued the Museum's collection of Russell works. There is no evidence that the Amon Carter Museum ever authenticated or obtained independent authentication of the painting as a work of Russell.

In February of 1972, the Amon Carter Museum sold the painting to the Kennedy Galleries of New York, New York. In March of 1972, the Kennedy Quarterly, a publication featuring Western art then owned by the Kennedy Galleries, featured a print of the painting and listed its dimensions as 16 1/2 by 22 3/4 inches-the same as the current dimensions. There is no evidence that the Kennedy Galleries ever authenticated or obtained independent authentication of the painting as a work of Russell.

Morton and his brother, Frank, purchased the painting from the Kennedy Galleries in May of 1972 for $38,000.00. Other than obtaining verbal assurances from officials of the Kennedy Galleries, the Mortons neither requested nor obtained any proof or independent verification that the painting was an authentic Russell.

In 1998, Morton contacted Bob Drummond ("Drummond"), the Director of the Coeur d'Alene Art Auction, inquiring about the possibility of selling the painting at the Auction's annual Western art auction. Drummond advised Morton that the Coeur d'Alene Art Auction could sell the "choice C.M. Russell painting" at a "very good price." In August of 2000, Drummond notified Morton that the painting would likely "fetch a record price" at auction. Later that month, at Morton's request, Drummond appraised the fair market value of the painting as $650,000.00. Drummond is an experienced art appraiser familiar with the works of Russell. However, his aforementioned statements to Morton and his appraisal were premised on the assumption that the painting was an authentic Russell. He had not authenticated or obtained independent authentication of the painting as a Russell.

In late 2000 or early 2001, Morton decided to proceed with the sale of the painting by way of auction. However, Drummond's partner in the Coeur d'Alene Art Auction, Stuart Johnson, suspected that the painting was a work of O.C. Seltzer. Accordingly, Johnson recommended that Drummond consult with Seltzer before attempting to sell the painting as an authentic Russell.

Seltzer resides in Great Falls, Montana, which is the home of the C.M. Russell Art Museum. He is the world's foremost expert on the works of O.C. Seltzer, and to a lesser extent, an expert on the works of C.M. Russell. As noted above, Seltzer is a professional authenticator and appraiser of Western artwork. Particularly, he has long been engaged, upon request, in the business of authenticating the works of O.C. Seltzer throughout the country. In addition, Seltzer is a highly accomplished artist, having received numerous honors and awards at the prestigious C.M. Russell Art Auction held annually in Great Falls.

When Seltzer was contacted by Drummond, he expressed his opinion that, given the style and technique of the painting, it was clearly and obviously not an authentic Russell. Seltzer had seen a photograph of the painting in a 1979 edition of Horizon Magazine and had immediately determined that it was a work of O.C. Seltzer. In Seltzer's opinion, the distinguishing characteristics of the painting, as shown in the photograph, were obvious to a knowledgeable eye and there was therefore no need to inspect the painting itself prior to rendering his opinion. Viewing the original painting at trial in the instant suit, Seltzer pointed out what he had seen clearly in the photograph—i.e., that the color features and finely detailed sagebrush, action figures, and other details, were characteristic of O.C. Seltzer's work and uncharacteristic of Russell's work around 1913. In conjunction with this testimony, Seltzer also presented four O.C. Seltzer works which contain a steer that is virtually identical to that portrayed in "Lassoing a Longhorn."

To gather further information regarding the painting's authenticity, Stuart Johnson recommended that Drummond also contact Ginger Renner, who is the premier expert on the works of Russell, and to a lesser extent, the works of O.C. Seltzer. Ms. Renner is the widow of Frederic Renner, who was previously considered the premier expert on Russell's artwork. She was significantly involved in her late husband's work and she has carried on that work in the field of Russell art and Western art in general. In accordance with her expertise, she is considered a reliable authenticator of C.M. Russell art. . . . [A]t Drummond's request in late 2000 or early 2001, [Ms. Renner] examined a transparency reproduction of the painting. She then rendered her opinion that it was plainly the work of O.C. Seltzer and that the signature had been altered in some manner.

Given the expert opinions of Seltzer and Ginger Renner regarding "Lassoing a Longhorn," Drummond contacted Morton in January of 2001 and told him that the Coeur d'Alene Art Auction would not attempt to sell the painting as an authentic Russell because it was apparently a work of O.C. Seltzer. Later that month, Morton called Seltzer to discuss the issue. Seltzer generally explained the bases of his opinion regarding the painting's authenticity. . . .

On January 30, 2001, Morton took the painting from his home in California to Ginger Renner's home in Arizona. Ms. Renner examined the painting and immediately told Morton that, given the palette and style, it was unquestionably the work of O.C. Seltzer. The next day, Morton sent Ms. Renner a handwritten letter expressing his thanks and his "state of shock" upon learning her opinion of the painting's authenticity. In this letter, Morton also requested that she provide him a letter formally expressing her professional opinion in order to help him determine a course of action.

The Defendants did not disclose this letter during discovery proceedings in the underlying suit against Seltzer or in the instant suit. When Seltzer eventually moved for sanctions in the instant action to address this conduct, the District Court found that the letter was "unquestionably within the scope" of Seltzer's requests for production in the underlying suit, his requests for production in the instant suit, and the court's Order to Compel in the instant suit. The court also found that the letter "unquestionably goes to the heart of the claims and defenses at issue in this case" and that the Defendants' failure to disclose it was "the second incidence in this action of a failure to produce a highly relevant document adverse to their defense." Further, the court found that the letter "plainly indicates that Morton recognized [Renner's] opinion as credible." Finally, the court found that the failure to disclose "impaired Seltzer's ability to depose key witnesses . . . [and] impaired his ability to meaningfully follow up and investigate." Consequently, the court adjudicated the following facts as a discovery sanction:

> [Following his consultation with Ms. Renner,] Steve Morton at all times knew and believed that Ginger Renner was a recognized and credible expert on the works of both C.M. Russell and O.C. Seltzer. Steve Morton thereafter had no reason to believe that Ginger Renner's analysis or opinion was premature, flawed, or otherwise insufficient in any way. Consequently, as of January 31, 2001, Steve Morton knew that Ginger Renner's opinion created a serious and credible question as to whether the subject painting was in fact an authentic work of C.M. Russell.

The Defendants have not appealed the court's findings or the sanction imposed.

In February of 2001, at a cost of $200.00 to Morton, Ginger Renner sent him a formal letter stating in pertinent part:

> In my opinion ["Lassoing a Longhorn"] is a painting by the Montana artist, Olaf C. Seltzer. In every aspect, the palette, the draftsmanship is typical of the work of Seltzer. In light of the years of my experience with the work of Charles M. Russell there is nothing about this watercolor that would lead me to believe it was the work of C.M. Russell. . . .

In March of 2001, Morton's attorney, Joshua Rievman of New York, wrote a letter to the Kennedy Galleries stating, inter alia:

> In the past month the Mortons have been shocked to learn that the painting is not a work by Russell. Rather, two recognized experts on Western Art have concluded that the painting is obviously a work by an artist named Olaf Seltzer and that this must have been clear to any reputable dealer in the 1970's. As a result, the Painting, which was projected to fetch approximately $700,000 at auction, is likely worth, at best, only a tenth of this amount.
>
> The Mortons consider Kennedy Galleries' fraudulent (or, at the very least, negligent) misrepresentations to be an extremely serious matter and intend to hold Kennedy Galleries liable for the damages they have suffered.

During discovery proceedings in the underlying suit against Seltzer and the instant suit, the Defendants failed to disclose this letter. Seltzer moved for sanctions in this case and the District Court found that this letter was highly relevant and adverse to the defense [and imposed monetary sanctions]. . . .

Later in March of 2001, in a written response to this letter, the Kennedy Galleries, through its attorney, asserted its belief that the painting was an authentic Russell. It further asserted that the painting's "provenance" was "unassailable" because it had been purchased from the Amon Carter Museum and because Frederic Renner's 1966 book had listed the painting in the catalogue of Russell works then owned by the Amon Carter Museum.[8] However, the Kennedy Galleries provided no proof of authenticity, authentication analysis, or refutation of the credentials or opinions of Ginger Renner and Seltzer. . . .

Thereafter, despite having admitted his knowledge that the painting was not an authentic Russell, Morton twice attempted to sell the painting as an authentic Russell. First, in June of 2001, he requested that the Kennedy Galleries sell the painting on his behalf. Despite its previous assertions regarding the painting's authenticity, the Kennedy Galleries notified Morton that it would not attempt to sell "Lassoing a Longhorn" as an authentic Russell. Second, in July of 2001, Morton consigned the painting to Christie's Auction House in Los Angeles, California, for sale. Christie's returned the painting to Morton and notified him in writing that "this is not a work we can offer for sale."

By correspondence in July of 2001, Morton's counsel notified Seltzer, Ginger Renner, and Bob Drummond that the Mortons had "conducted a very thorough search for and analysis of relevant authorities" regarding

[8] [2] As Seltzer testified, the terms "provenance" and "authenticity" have distinct meanings when properly used in reference to artwork: the term "provenance" refers to a work's history of ownership, while the term "authenticity" refers to the source that created the work.

the painting. This letter described the provenance of the painting from 1939 to 2001 and also noted that Frederic Renner had included the painting in his 1966 catalogue of works then owned by the Amon Carter Museum. In conclusion, the letter summarily stated: "It is clear that the results of our investigation . . . conclusively establish the authenticity of the painting. With this issue now behind us, the Mortons are moving forward to sell the painting with a renewed confidence in its authenticity."

Although asserting this "renewed confidence," the Mortons had discovered no new information indicating that the painting was an authentic Russell; no new information refuting the acknowledged expert opinions of Ginger Renner and Seltzer; and no new information explaining or resolving the acknowledged discrepancy with the painting's dimensions. . . .

Thereafter, Morton secured new counsel-Dennis Gladwell of GDC. In September of 2001, Gladwell sent Seltzer a correspondence resembling a formal litigation interrogatory seeking responses to ten pointed questions regarding the basis of Seltzer's opinion of the painting. The GDC letterhead on which this correspondence was written indicated that GDC was a large international law firm with offices in Irvine, Los Angeles, Century City, San Francisco, and Palo Alto, California; Dallas, Texas; Denver, Colorado; New York, New York; Washington, D.C.; Paris, France; and London, England.

In response, Seltzer sent a letter referring Gladwell back to Seltzer's original letter in which he had stated his qualifications and his opinion. Seltzer also stated: "You keep referring back to Fred Renner's book and his opinion, etc. He made a mistake and realized that he had some years later."

Thereafter, Morton submitted the painting to a paper conservator, Margot Healey of Los Angeles, California, for analysis. She found [no evidence that the paper on which the painting was done had been altered or repaired]. . . . As Ms. Healey merely examined the painting to determine whether it had been physically altered, her analysis did not constitute an authentication of the painting as a Russell. Nevertheless, Gladwell then sent a letter to Seltzer, Ginger Renner, the Kennedy Galleries, and the Amon Carter Museum, stating that "the opinions of Ms. Renner and Mr. Seltzer were found to be unsubstantiated" by the paper conservator's report.

Then, in April of 2002, Gladwell sent a demand letter to Ginger Renner and Seltzer, stating:

1. Each of you will draft a letter to our specifications completely recanting and withdrawing any statement you have previously made regarding the authenticity of the painting currently owned by Mr. Morton.

> 2. In the letter, among other admissions you will make, you will admit that you did not perform a detailed examination of the painting and that your "opinion" was merely conjecture on your part.
>
> 3. You will agree to compensate Mr. Morton for the difference between what the painting sells for today, after we have tried to remove the cloud from its provenance, and what it could have sold for two years ago prior to your defamatory remarks about its authenticity.
>
> 4. Independently, you will reimburse Mr. Morton for the time, expense, embarrassment, grief and anxiety he has expended in trying to recover from your actions. The price: an additional $50,000 beyond the loss in value of the painting. Mr. Morton gave you every chance to withdraw your damaging comments over the better part of eight months during last year. Each of you elected to ignore his pleas or simply dismissed them. You will not have that luxury this time around. We expect immediate cooperation on the drafting of your "withdrawal of opinion" or litigation will be filed without any further discussion. And, given the opportunity afforded you to rectify this wrong, and your refusal to do so, punitive damages will be requested.

Seltzer did not respond.

Thereafter, Gladwell sent an email to William Claster, a partner in GDC, stating:

> We may need to open a new matter to pursue this painting issue I discussed. Erin [Alexander] has agreed to help. . . . The nature of the action will be injunctive relief, defamation of title, declaratory relief. . . . You and I will be the partners. I plan to bill very little time. But all billing will be through the firm as per normal protocol. We will probably put in less than 20–30 hours. You will recall that Steve [Morton] is President of the Bob Hope Desert Classic so I want to do it.

Gladwell was acquainted with Morton through prior representation. At the time of this email, Gladwell was a retired former partner on "of counsel" status with GDC. Consequently, pursuant to GDC's internal policy, Gladwell was required to obtain the permission of a partner who would be formally assigned to and ultimately responsible to the firm for the case. Claster was a partner authorized to grant Gladwell permission to proceed with the matter. Erin Alexander, referenced in the aforementioned email, was an associate member of GDC. Claster ultimately authorized Gladwell to proceed with the proposed litigation on behalf of GDC.

In May of 2002, Gladwell sent a letter to Seltzer and Ginger Renner again threatening litigation. Gladwell attached a proposed declaration for Seltzer and Ms. Renner to sign, which stated, inter alia:

3. Although I did not inspect the original, I offered the view that this painting may actually be a Seltzer and that the Russell signature could have been forged.

4. By this statement, which was made only casually in conversation, I did not intend to imply that the painting was a fake, a duplicate, a forgery or copy or a Seltzer with an altered signature. It was simply a statement of "possibility" that could apply to any painting including a Russell.

5. I am in no position either to authenticate the provenance of Mr. Morton's painting as an original Russell or to deny its provenance. That would require a careful examination of the painting, and perhaps other ink, paper and brush-stroke tests, none of which I performed.

6. It is unfortunate that my statement has been misinterpreted.

I declare under penalty of perjury under the laws of the States of (Arizona or Montana) that the foregoing is true and correct and that I executed this Declaration on

______, 2002, at ______.

Again, Seltzer did not respond.

On July 16, 2002, William Claster, Gladwell, and Erin Alexander, under the caption and authority of GDC, along with Montana attorney Oliver Goe of the law firm Browning, Kaleczyc, Berry & Hoven, P.C., filed a Complaint against Seltzer, on behalf of Morton and his brother Frank, in the United Stated District Court for the Montana District, Great Falls Division. . . . The Complaint requested relief in the form of declaratory relief, injunctive relief, general damages, special damages, punitive damages, costs, and attorney fees. As for compensatory damages sought, the Complaint alleged that Seltzer's stated opinion had caused the painting's value to be reduced "from the range of $650,000.00 to $800,000.00" down to "something under $50,000.00."

As noted above, GDC sued Seltzer on behalf of both Morton and his brother Frank. However, Frank Morton never authorized GDC to file suit on his behalf. He testified on this subject prior to trial in the instant case, and the parties stipulated that his testimony was true and required no proof. . . .

Seltzer retained counsel and served formal discovery requests seeking disclosure and production of all non-privileged documents concerning the authenticity of the painting. The Defendants responded that they had produced all such information. However, they did not disclose two non-privileged letters-i.e., the correspondence from Morton to Ginger Renner and the correspondence that Morton's former counsel, Joshua Rievman, had sent to the Kennedy Galleries. As noted above, the latter correspondence contained key admissions, including: (1) "the Mortons have been shocked to learn that the painting is not a work by Russell. Rather, two recognized experts on Western Art have concluded that the painting is obviously a work by an artist named Olaf Seltzer"; and (2) "The Mortons consider Kennedy Galleries' fraudulent (or, at the very least, negligent) misrepresentations to be an extremely serious matter and intend to hold Kennedy Galleries liable for the damages they have suffered."

Thereafter, Seltzer filed a Motion for Summary Judgment. In support of this Motion, he obtained and filed affidavits of 10 individuals (including himself and Ginger Renner) who had expertise regarding the works of Russell and O.C. Seltzer. Each of these affidavits expressed the opinion that the painting was not an authentic Russell. Shortly thereafter, the Mortons and their attorneys admitted, in a letter to the Kennedy Galleries, that they had not yet secured "a first class expert on Russell who can testify confidently" that the painting was is an authentic Russell. They also admitted that unless they could do so soon, "the law suit is probably over." Later that December, Gladwell acknowledged in an internal GDC email that "the Mortons may be . . . unable to pursue the current litigation . . . since we have no trial expert and as yet, have been unable to establish a complete provenance . . . and we are quickly running out of time."

On January 8, 2003, Gladwell sent a demand letter to the Kennedy Galleries and the Amon Carter Museum, stating:

> [T]en declarations have been filed by Mr. Seltzer claiming that the painting is a forgery. Despite repeated requests, neither of [you] have produced an expert who can testify that the painting is a genuine C.M. Russell. . . .
>
> Accordingly, demand is hereby made that you provide the Mortons with an authentic C.M. Russell whose value, at today's auction prices, would sell for $650,000. The Mortons will tender Lassoing a Longhorn to the Museum or the Galleries, as soon as a new Russell has been selected.

Nearly one month later, on February 6, the U.S. District Court dismissed the suit against Seltzer with prejudice pursuant to an unconditional stipulation of the parties necessitated by Morton's and Gladwell's acknowledged awareness that they could not prevail on the merits. In defending himself against this lawsuit, Seltzer incurred over $45,000.00 in legal fees.

Seltzer subsequently filed suit against the Mortons, Gladwell, GDC associate Erin Alexander, GDC, and Oliver Goe, alleging malicious prosecution and abuse of process. Frank Morton was dismissed, pursuant to a stipulation by the parties, following his deposition wherein he testified that he had never spoken with Gladwell before the suit against Seltzer was filed; that he had never spoken with any other GDC attorney before the suit against Seltzer was filed; and, most importantly, that he had never authorized GDC to file suit against Seltzer on his behalf. Additionally, the District Court granted summary judgment in favor of Erin Alexander and Oliver Goe and thus dismissed them from the suit.[9] In the first phase of trial, the jury found in favor of Seltzer on both his asserted causes of action, awarding $1.1 million in compensatory damages. In the second phase of trial, the jury awarded punitive damages in the amount of $100,000.00 against Morton, $150,000.00 against Gladwell, and $20 million against GDC. . . .

The District Court issued an order reviewing the punitive damages verdicts. . . . In applying federal due process jurisprudence, the court concluded that the punitive verdicts against Morton and Gladwell were not constitutionally excessive, but also concluded that the verdict against GDC did not comport with due process and therefore had to be reduced to $9.9 million. Seltzer then filed an appeal with this Court, after which the Defendants filed a cross-appeal.

DISCUSSION

Are the Defendants entitled to judgment as a matter of law on Seltzer's abuse-of-process claim?

In *Brault v. Smith,* 209 Mont. 21, 28–29 (1984), this Court held: "Essential to proof of abuse of process is (1) an ulterior purpose and (2) a willful act in the use of the process not proper in the regular conduct of the proceeding." *Brault* also indicated that an abuse of process entails "an attempt by the plaintiff to use process to coerce the defendant to do some collateral thing which he could not be legally and regularly compelled to do." Here, the Defendants moved the District Court for judgment as a matter of law on Seltzer's abuse-of-process claim. The court denied this motion.

On appeal, the Defendants present two arguments in seeking judgment on Seltzer's abuse-of-process claim. First, the Defendants contend that they are entitled to judgment because Seltzer "based his abuse-of-process claim *solely* on the filing of the complaint" in the underlying suit, and the mere filing of an unfounded lawsuit cannot, as a matter of law, establish an abuse of process. (Emphasis supplied by Defendants.)

We must reject the factual assertion contained in this argument because it is contrary to the record before us. The record clearly establishes that Seltzer did not base his abuse-of-process claim on the isolated fact

[9] FN3. Seltzer did not contest Goe's Motion for Summary Judgment because, inter alia, the Defendants had not provided Goe with the pertinent factual information regarding the underlying suit. Seltzer did contest Erin Alexander's Motion for Summary Judgment; however, the court ruled in Alexander's favor because, inter alia, the evidence showed that "she acted exclusively in a subordinate support role under the direction of one or more other more senior attorneys" at GDC.

that the Defendants filed a lawsuit against him. He based his claim on the Defendants' purpose in bringing the suit, as well as their conduct of utilizing the suit as an instrument of coercion, rather than a legitimate means to resolve a genuine dispute. Indeed, Seltzer's Complaint in this suit explicitly specified an alleged "ulterior motive" and Defendants' *use* of the lawsuit as the basis for the abuse-of-process claim-i.e., Seltzer alleged that the Defendants used the lawsuit "to attempt to force Seltzer to untruthfully recant his opinion." . . . the District Court's Final Pre–Trial Order reiterated these allegations as the basis for Seltzer's abuse-of-process claim. This Order also identified more specific grounds for this particular claim-i.e., it stated that Seltzer contended the Defendants had no intention of taking the underlying case to trial and that they simply utilized the lawsuit as a means to force Seltzer to recant his opinion so as to enable them to sell the painting as an authentic Russell to an unsuspecting buyer.

Furthermore, Seltzer presented evidence and argument at trial demonstrating that it was the Defendants' ulterior purpose and their intentional *use* of the underlying lawsuit-not merely the filing of the Complaint-which formed the basis for his abuse-of-process claim. Among other things, Seltzer presented the letters he received from GDC prior to the instigation of the lawsuit, wherein the Defendants threatened to file suit and seek punitive damages if he did not recant, under oath, his professional opinion regarding the authenticity of the painting. Seltzer utilized this evidence to demonstrate that the Defendants' subsequent instigation of legal process was one element of an ongoing course of intimidating and coercive conduct; that the lawsuit was in fact intentionally employed as a coercive device; and that the Defendants' conduct was therefore an abuse of process.

Seltzer also presented evidence and argument that the Defendants, while in the course of leveraging the underlying suit against him for nearly seven months, further abused legal process when they undermined the discovery proceedings by intentionally withholding pertinent documents, thereby impairing Seltzer's ability to defend himself. . . . In short, the record directly refutes the Defendants' premise that Seltzer "based his abuse-of-process claim *solely* on the filing of the complaint" in the underlying suit. Accordingly, we reject the Defendants' argument that they are entitled to judgment on Seltzer's abuse-of-process claim on this basis.

Second, the Defendants argue that they are entitled to judgment as a matter of law on Seltzer's abuse-of-process claim pursuant to this Court's statement in *Brault* that an abuse of process entails "an attempt by the plaintiff to use process to coerce the defendant to do some collateral thing which he could not be legally and regularly compelled to do." Here, Defendants assert, Seltzer failed to present proof that they attempted to make him perform some "collateral" act. Again, we find this assertion contrary to the record.

Seltzer's testimony demonstrated that he genuinely believed the painting was not an authentic Russell and that his statements were specifically intended to convey that opinion. Seltzer also . . . presented evidence that the Defendants invoked legal process in order to coerce him to lie about his professional opinion under oath. Yet, the stated purpose for which the Defendants invoked legal process was not to obtain this sworn declaration from Seltzer. Rather, the Defendants' Complaint, which Seltzer also presented as evidence in this case, professed to seek adjudication on the merits of the conflict so as to obtain an injunction, a declaratory judgment, and damages for loss allegedly caused by Seltzer's statements regarding the painting. Thus, the record demonstrates that Seltzer did in fact present proof that the Defendants used legal process "to coerce [him] to do some collateral thing which he could not be legally and regularly compelled to do." Moreover, the District Court, in reviewing the punitive damages award, found that

> the manifest and acknowledged objective of the lawsuit was not to obtain an adjudication of the merits of the asserted claims, but rather to threaten Seltzer and force a negotiated retraction and disavowal of his opinion thereby enabling the Mortons to sell the painting at full market value as an authentic Russell.

Accordingly, having found the Defendants' underlying assertion contrary to the record, we reject the argument that they are entitled to judgment as a matter of law on Seltzer's abuse-of-process claim. . . . "

[The Supreme Court affirmed judgment for plaintiff on his abuse of process claim. It also affirmed the modified punitive damage award of $9.9 million against the Gibson, Dunn firm. The following is an excerpt from that portion of the opinion]

We conclude that . . . GDC's conduct was highly reprehensible. This conduct evinced an indifference to and a reckless disregard of Seltzer's financial, psychological, and physical wellbeing, as well as his personal and professional reputation. None of the conduct at issue was accidental; GDC acted with actual malice, as found by the jury, and GDC does not contest that finding. As a direct result of GDC's malicious conduct, Seltzer suffered severe emotional distress which resulted in debilitating physical trauma; he suffered serious damage to his impeccable personal and professional reputation which he had built up over his lifetime; and he incurred over $45,000.00 in attorney fees in defending himself for nearly seven months. While the record does not contain extensive evidence regarding Seltzer's financial means, it does demonstrate that he was in a position of relative financial vulnerability. It is established that an adverse compensatory damages award of roughly $700,000.00, as sought in the underlying Complaint, would have forced Seltzer into bankruptcy.

Additionally, while he was able to hire counsel to defend himself, Seltzer lacked the funds to pay his attorney's hourly fee at that time. As the District Court found, Seltzer had a "relative lack of resources to defend himself." . . .

Abusive conduct toward an individual which causes the type of harm at issue here merits considerable punishment regardless of the setting in which it takes place. However, the fact that GDC utilized the judicial system as a tool to accomplish intimidation and oppression makes this behavior uniquely egregious. As the District Court stated:

> Although no less damaging, it may have been less reprehensible if a legal layman had devised and attempted to execute this scheme. However, it is even more reprehensible that a highly experienced trial attorney [of GDC] not only condoned this conduct, but in fact devised it, recommended it to the lay client, and aggressively prosecuted it on the client's behalf. As embodied in the Rules of Professional Conduct, lawyers have a special and essential professional responsibility to vigilantly safeguard against abusive litigation practices that impair or defeat the administration of justice rather than facilitate it. At its core, this case involved an extremely abusive, malicious, and oppressive litigation practice devised and executed by a prominent and experienced lawyer who had a professional gate-keeping duty to know better and discourage such abuses. . . .

At oral argument, counsel for GDC attempted to minimize the reprehensibility of the firm's conduct by arguing that litigation is a common occurrence and the "essence of the system" is to reach a verdict on the merits. Among other things, counsel argued:

> Clients bring demands letters to me every day . . . and sometimes they settle, sometimes they say: "Bring it on. In a court of law you're going to lose." . . . I believe that, in court, ya know, "bring it on"—if they've got a good lawsuit, a jury will find one way, if they don't, a jury will find the other way. And that's the essence of the system.

We take exception to this notion. The "essence" of our judicial system is not simply the resolution of disputes; rather, it is the resolution of *legitimate* disputes. Baseless lawsuits prosecuted in furtherance of ulterior motives have no place in our courts. Moreover, the sort of saber-rattling, chest-thumping approach typified by the comment of GDC's counsel, trivializes the devastating effects on the health, reputations, and fortunes of the real people who are maliciously and abusively sued. For the ordinary citizens who are the victims of such a lawsuit, it may be the most horrific experience of their lives. Indeed, those effects are not merely the collateral damage of some run-of-the-mill litigation battle between attorneys. Rather, the defendants in such cases are the innocent casualties of the war. That is why the "essence of the system" with respect to such lawsuits is to provide recourse for the victim and levy punishment against the perpetrator by way of actions for abuse of process and malicious prosecution. Thus, the "essence of the system" was evident in the instant suit by Seltzer's recovery of compensatory damages and the jury's assessment of a severe punitive sanction against GDC.

In short, GDC's use of the judicial system amounts to legal thuggery. This behavior is truly repugnant to Montana's foundational notions of justice and is therefore highly reprehensible. Thus, in accordance with Montana's legitimate interest in punishment and deterrence, we conclude that a particularly severe sanction comports with due process.

CASE QUESTIONS

1. What are the elements of the abuse of process cause of action?
2. How do they differ from the malicious prosecution tort?
3. What fact in *Seltzer* was most probative for the plaintiff?
4. What defense did the Gibson, Dunn firm and the Court reject as inconsistent with the essence of the judicial system?

Framing Legal Ethics: Context and Community

"Legal thuggery" is not a term you see very often. Less often still is it used of prestigious law firms such as Gibson, Dunn. The Court was obviously very unhappy with the conduct it described. Part of that unhappiness may have stemmed from the discovery misconduct alluded to in the opinion. The failure to produce relevant and highly probative documents always casts a shadow over your conduct and can lead courts to construe doubt against you. But the sanctions were against the clients, not the firm, and there is no reason to believe discovery misconduct accounts for the reference to "thuggery," which was directed at the firm, not the clients.

So why the anger? A complex question, no doubt, but context and community might explain part of it. The key is to consider those concepts in light of the elements of the tort.

A plaintiff alleging abuse of process must show the defendant used process for some ulterior purpose. As a practical matter, that means the plaintiff must show the defendant was trying to obtain through legal process something other than what they claimed to seek through that process and, generally, which they could not get without that process.

In *Seltzer,* the Mortons claimed they were not trying to obtain some collateral benefit. To the contrary, they argued, they filed suit precisely to establish their contention that the painting at issue was a genuine Russell. The Court did not accept this claim. It instead found that Seltzer had shown that the Mortons pursued the collateral goal of getting Seltzer to recant his opinion. Why did the Court perceive a difference between a judicial finding that the painting was a Russell and a statement by Seltzer recanting his opinion that it wasn't?

A plausible conjecture is that the context of the case—the world of high-priced art—led the Court to distinguish between judicial process and expert opinion, and thus to discount the Mortons (facially plausible) claim. The Mortons were trying to sell the painting. Suppose there were a limited number of auction houses that could do a good job with such a sale. Suppose further that such houses have their own reputational stake in their auctions: No one wants to be known as having sold a fraud. On these suppositions the houses might reasonably balk at selling a picture whose provenance was disputed by the leading experts in the field, as both the Coeur d'Alene Art Auction and Christie's did in this case.

In this context, perhaps the Court might reasonably distinguish between the force of a judicial determination of authenticity and the force of Seltzer's opinion. The Court might presume that auction houses would place more weight on Seltzer's view than on that of a judge or jury, so that a judicial determination would not in fact achieve what the Court saw as the Mortons' main goal of selling the painting. (After all, if you ran a high-end auction house would you trust a determination of a judge or jury over the opinion of the same sort of art experts you routinely used to vouch for the authenticity of paintings you sell?)

If the Court thought this way then it might be quite willing to believe the Mortons were less interested in what the courts did than it what they could be used to make Seltzer do. The Court might well presume that a sophisticated firm would grasp this distinction, too, and therefore brush aside logical arguments based on the elements of the abuse of process tort. The firm's excellence in knowing "what is really going on" in its cases would therefore work against it.

The importance of community is less conjectural. The Court stated it flatly in rejecting the argument that demand letters and litigation are common ways to resolve disputes. The Court's discussion carries an important lesson.

Counsel for Gibson, Dunn was no doubt right to say that he received demand letters every day. In some communities such letters, like litigation itself, is just one way of talking about a problem. If two people have different positions on some issue, and the positions are not obviously frivolous, then litigation is simply one among many options for sorting things out.

"Talking" is too anodyne, of course, for litigation unlike conversation may end in a court order. But the fact remains that in many lines of business demand letters and lawsuits are a way of life not occasions for panic and terror. Many lawyers and business executives think of a court fight as a perfectly ordinary way of reconciling differing positions.

With this in mind, think for a moment about the Mortons' position. Try to frame the situation from their point of view: They had bought the painting from a reputable gallery and it had been listed in a catalogue of Russell's work written by Frederic Renner, the leading expert on Russell's work. Mr. Seltzer's opinion was based on having seen a picture of the painting in a magazine several years earlier, not on examination of the painting itself. Ms. Renner's opinion counted against the Mortons, of course, but then she disagreed with her late husband. For persons who live in a world where litigation is a form of conversation, a demand letter might seem a natural (if, on these facts, aggressive) option to settle such a dispute.

The Court rejected this entire conception of the judicial process. It seemed to think of demand letters and litigation as extraordinary measures, not ordinary conversation. In part, probably, this conception related to a frame of Mr. Seltzer the Court seemed to adopt. In this frame Mr. Seltzer was an earnest, honest, art appraiser, innocent of worlds in which litigation is just a way of talking. People in this world did not "take positions," they said what they thought and refused to say what they did not think, even under pressure. He was, in essence, a combination of the straight-talking cowboy and the quintessential "little guy" fighting corrupt forces from far-away cities. (Remember, to say this is a frame is not to say it is wrong.)

Looking through that frame one can see how the Court might perceive Gibson, Dunn as a legal thug trying to bully Mr. Seltzer into lying so the Mortons could make money (by, implicitly, pawning off their Seltzer as a Russell). As the result of the case shows, that was a dangerous frame to be seen through.

Different communities frame situations differently. In addition to its legal holdings, *Seltzer* stands for the proposition that those differences matter. When you work within a community—in litigation between two large firms, for example—you must know the community's norms and folkways and translate them into the relevant frames for viewing your conduct and the conduct of those you deal with. That is part of seeing yourself as others see you, and of judging your own behavior accordingly.

When you work between communities, you must do more. You must not only understand the frames relevant to your world but those relevant to the other communities you deal with. You must understand how someone like Mr. Seltzer might perceive demand letters and draft affidavits (or, as importantly, how they might persuade a judge or jury that they perceived such things). Such understanding requires an active effort to empathize with different norms and perspectives. To fail to see yourself as others see you is to risk being caught in a frame in which your zealous representation is a court's thuggery.

D. CANDOR TOWARD A TRIBUNAL

Model Rule 3.3(a)(1) forbids you from making a false statement of fact or law to a tribunal and requires you to correct a false statement of fact or law you previously made. This rule is relatively straightforward but still may present tricky issues, as the following case illustrates.

Model Rule of Professional Conduct 3.3(A)(1)

COLORADO V. CASEY

948 P.2d 1014 (Colo. 1997)

PER CURIAM

In December 1994, S.R., a teenager, and her mother, met with the senior partner at the law firm where the respondent was an associate. In August 1994, S.R. attended a party held in the home of third parties. The police were called and they cited several persons at the party with trespassing and underage drinking. S.R. gave the police a driver's license in her possession that had been issued to her friend, S.J. A criminal summons charging trespass was issued to S.R. in the name of her friend, S.J. Since she was not aware of the summons in her name, S.J. failed to attend the first court hearing and a bench warrant was issued in her name. S.R., posing as S.J., later appeared to reset the matter. S.R. was arrested, jailed, and later released under the name of S.J.

After being assigned the case by the senior partner, the respondent wrote to the Colorado Springs City Attorney's Office, and advised the City Attorney, falsely, that he represented S.J., when he actually represented S.R. He requested and obtained discovery using S.J.'s name. He also notified the court clerk of his entry of appearance in the S.J. case. The senior partner "consulted and advised" the respondent, but the hearing board did not make findings as to when this occurred or as to the details of the conversation.

On February 14, 1995, the respondent appeared at a pretrial conference scheduled for S.J. His client, S.R., waited outside during the hearing. Although he spoke with an assistant city attorney about the case, the respondent did not reveal his client's true identity. The assistant city attorney agreed to dismiss the S.J. matter. The respondent presented the city's motion to dismiss the case and the court entered an order of dismissal on February 14, 1995.

Prior to the pretrial conference, S.J. called the respondent about the case. The respondent told her that he intended to get the trespassing charge dismissed, but that S.J. would then have to petition on her own to get the criminal record sealed. He also told S.J. the date and time of the pretrial hearing.

After the case was dismissed, the respondent met with his client and her mother, and S.J. and her stepfather. S.J. was upset that the respondent had spoken with the assistant city attorney outside of S.J.'s presence and she wanted to know if her name had been cleared. The respondent took S.J. and her stepfather outside, and explained that the trespassing charge had been dismissed and that his client would pay the court costs. The respondent admitted that S.J. would nevertheless have a criminal record and that she would have to petition the court to have her criminal record sealed. S.J.'s stepfather subsequently called his lawyer who reported the events to the district attorney.

The respondent stipulated that the foregoing conduct violated Colo. RPC 1.2(d) (counseling a client to engage, or assisting a client, in conduct that the lawyer knows is criminal or fraudulent) [criminal impersonation]; Colo. RPC 3.3(a)(1) (knowingly making a false statement of material fact or law to a tribunal); Colo. RPC 3.3(a)(2) (failing to disclose a material fact to a tribunal when disclosure is necessary to avoid assisting a criminal or fraudulent act by the client); Colo. RPC 8.4(c) (engaging in conduct involving dishonesty, fraud, deceit or misrepresentation); Colo. RPC 8.4(d) (engaging in conduct prejudicial to the administration of justice); and C.R.C.P. 241.6(3) (violating the highest standards of honesty, justice or morality).

The hearing panel approved the hearing board's recommendations that the respondent be suspended for forty-five days and be required to take and pass the MPRE. The respondent has excepted to the panel's action. He contends that a public censure rather than suspension is appropriate, primarily because his mental state at the time of the misconduct was at most "negligent," rather than "knowing" as found by the hearing board.

The respondent portrays his situation as involving a close question between the loyalty he owed his client, and his duty to the court. He apparently seeks to invoke the status of a "subordinate lawyer," as addressed in Colo. RPC 5.2:

> Rule 5.2. Responsibilities of a Subordinate Lawyer
>
> (a) A lawyer is bound by the Rules of Professional Conduct notwithstanding that the lawyer acted at the direction of another person.

> (b) *A subordinate lawyer does not violate the Rules of Professional Conduct if that lawyer acts in accordance with a supervisory lawyer's reasonable resolution of an arguable question of professional duty.*

(Emphasis added.) He asserts that before he succeeded in getting the trespass charge dismissed, he studied the applicable ethical rules. Colo. RPC 1.6 provides in part:

> (a) A lawyer shall not reveal information relating to representation of a client unless the client consents after consultation, except for disclosures that are impliedly authorized in order to carry out the representation, and except as stated in paragraphs (b) and (c).
>
> (b) A lawyer may reveal the intention of the lawyer's client to commit a crime and the information necessary to prevent the crime.

However, Colo. RPC 3.3, which the respondent admits to having violated, states:

> Rule 3.3. Candor Toward the Tribunal
>
> (a) A lawyer shall not knowingly:
>
> (1) make a false statement of material fact or law to a tribunal;
>
> (2) fail to disclose a material fact to a tribunal when disclosure is necessary to avoid assisting a criminal or fraudulent act by the client;
>
> . . . .
>
> (b) *The duties stated in paragraph (a) continue to the conclusion of the proceeding, and apply even if compliance requires disclosure of information otherwise protected by Rule 1.6.*

(Emphasis added). Colo. RPC 3.3(a)(2) applies because of his initial appearance before the court in which he represented, falsely, that he was appearing on behalf of the named defendant, S.J. At the pretrial conference he presented the motion to dismiss to the court resulting in the case being dismissed. The respondent had the duty to disclose to the court that his client was impersonating S.J. in the criminal proceedings.

Further, Colo. RPC 3.3(b) clearly resolves the respondent's claimed dilemma in that it provides that the duty to be truthful to the court applies even if to do so requires disclosure of otherwise confidential information. It is not "arguable" that the respondent's duty to his client prevented him from fulfilling his duty to be truthful to the court. *See id.* The protection afforded by Colo. RPC 5.2(b) for a subordinate who acts in accordance with a supervisory lawyer's direction is not available to the respondent. However, as discussed below a good-faith, but unsuccessful, attempt to bring an ethical problem to a superior's attention to receive guidance may be a mitigating factor.

We conclude that the hearing board's findings with respect to the respondent's mental state are supported by the record. The board stated:

> Respondent's conduct and violations of the Rules of Professional Conduct was not done negligently, but instead reveals a course of knowing conduct over an appreciable period of time, resulting in false and material information being submitted to the court, which without any remedial action being taken by the Respondent, caused both potential injury to a party to the legal proceeding and an adverse effect on the legal proceeding.

The Terminology section of the Rules of Professional Conduct states, " 'Knowingly,' 'known,' or 'knows' denotes actual knowledge of the fact in question. *A person's knowledge may be inferred from circumstances.*" (Emphasis added.) We agree with the board that the respondent engaged in "a course of knowing conduct over an appreciable period of time, resulting in false and material information being submitted to the court."

Under the ABA *Standards for Imposing Lawyer Sanctions* 6.12 (1991 & Supp.1992) (ABA *Standards*):

> Suspension is generally appropriate when a lawyer knows that false statements or documents are being submitted to the court or that material information is improperly being withheld, and takes no remedial action, and causes injury or potential injury to a party to the legal proceeding, or causes an adverse or potentially adverse effect on the legal proceeding.

The hearing board found the following factors in mitigation: the absence of a prior disciplinary record, *see id.* at 9.32(a); full and free disclosure to the board or a cooperative attitude in the disciplinary proceedings, *see id.* at 9.32(e); inexperience in the practice of criminal law, *see id.* at 9.32(f); and the expression of remorse, *see id.* at 9.32(*l*). . . .

We conclude that the record supports an additional factor in mitigation, although not included in ABA *Standards* 9.32. The respondent tried to bring his claimed ethical dilemma to the senior partner for his advice. The record indicates that the senior partner failed to provide adequate guidance to the respondent.

While we have determined that Colo. RPC 5.2(b) does not entitle the respondent to immunity, an attempt to obtain guidance from a senior partner and a failure of a senior partner to suggest a reasonable and ethical course of conduct for the respondent could be a factor to be considered in mitigation. Here, the board's finding that the senior partner "consulted and advised" the respondent, without detail about the advice, if any, given is inadequate to allow us to conclude that the consultation is a mitigation factor.

We conclude that the respondent's misconduct is serious enough to warrant a short suspension. The respondent's professed confusion regarding his professional responsibilities confirms that he should be required to take and pass the MPRE. Accordingly, we accept the board's and panel's recommendations. However, three members of the court would impose a more severe sanction. . . .

PROBLEM 16–3

Think back to the notion of dynamic and interactive thinking outlined in the Introduction, and the concepts of game theory we have studied. From a game theoretic perspective, there was an obvious flaw in the course Casey pursued. What was it?

PROBLEM 16–4

What do you suppose was said in Casey's conversations with the partner? Why didn't the conversation produce the (legally) "right" result?

Model Rule 3.3(b) requires you to disclose authority in the controlling jurisdiction which you know to be directly adverse to your client's position and which is not cited by your opponent. Note this rule is not limited to controlling authority but extends to authority in the controlling jurisdiction. In other words, if you are in a California court and know of a California appellate decision that satisfies the requirement of the rule you must disclose that decision even if it is not strictly binding on the court; it does not have to be a Supreme Court decision or a decision otherwise decisive in your case. As explained by the Alaska Court of Appeals in *Tyler v. State*, 47 P.3d 1095, 1108 (Alaska Ct. App. 2001), the Rule requires a lawyer to "disclose legal authorities that the court should, in fairness, consider when making its decision, even when these authorities are adverse to the lawyer's position." The *Tyler* court fined an attorney for failing to cite an Alaska Supreme Court case in which the attorney was counsel (and thus unquestionably knew about) even though the Supreme Court case was plausibly distinguishable from the case in which the sanction was issued.

The District Court in *Massey v. Prince George's County*, 918 F.Supp. 905, 908 (D. Md. 1996), adds a note of common sense advice about prudent practice in such situations. In rejecting an argument that a case did not have to be cited because it was distinguishable, the court said:

> . . . careful lawyering demands greater sensitivity. In this district, whenever a case from the Fourth Circuit comes anywhere close to being relevant to a disputed issue, the better part of wisdom is to cite it and attempt to distinguish it. The matter will then be left for the judge to decide. While Respondents may still in time be judged unsuccessful in their attempt to distinguish the case, they will never be judged ethically omissive for failing to cite it

Put differently, the more you would like not to cite a case, the more important it is that you cite it.

---

1. HANDLING EVIDENCE

Model Rule 3.4(a) provides a lawyer may not obstruct another party's access to evidence, may not alter, conceal, or destroy material having potential value as evidence, and may not encourage others to do any of these things. These straightforward principles present difficult questions. Suppose that in a criminal matter you discover clothes with blood on them. May you test the blood to see if it belongs to the victim or to your client, even if in doing so you destroy some portion of the blood? The following materials survey the rules governing such situations.

Model Rule of Professional Conduct 3.4
ABA Criminal Justice Standard 4–4.6
Restatement (Third) of the Law Governing Lawyers § 119

PEOPLE V. MEREDITH

29 Cal.3d 682 (1981)

TOBRINER, J.

Defendants Frank Earl Scott and Michael Meredith appeal from convictions for the first degree murder and first degree robbery of David Wade. Meredith's conviction rests on eyewitness testimony that he shot and killed Wade. Scott's conviction, however, depends on the theory that Scott conspired with Meredith and a third defendant, Jacqueline Otis, to bring about the killing and robbery. To support the theory of conspiracy the prosecution sought to show the place where the victim's wallet was found, and, in the course of the case this piece of evidence became crucial. The admissibility of that evidence comprises the principal issue on this appeal.

At trial the prosecution called Steven Frick, who testified that he observed the victim's partially burnt wallet in a trash can behind Scott's residence. Scott's trial counsel then adduced that Frick served as a defense investigator. Scott himself had told his former counsel that he had taken the victim's wallet, divided the money with Meredith, attempted to burn the wallet, and finally put it in the trash can. At counsel's request, Frick then retrieved the wallet from the trash can. Counsel examined the wallet and then turned it over to the police.

The defense acknowledges that the wallet itself was properly admitted into evidence. The prosecution in turn acknowledges that the attorney-client privilege protected the conversations between Scott, his former counsel, and counsel's investigator. Indeed the prosecution did not attempt to introduce those conversations at trial. The issue before us, consequently, focuses upon a narrow point: whether under the circumstances of this case Frick's observation of the *location* of the wallet, the product of a privileged communication, finds protection under the attorney-client privilege.

This issue, one of first impression in California, presents the court with competing policy considerations. On the one hand, to deny protection to observations arising from confidential communications might chill free and open communication between attorney and client and might also inhibit counsel's investigation of his client's case. On the other hand, we cannot extend the attorney-client privilege so far that it renders evidence immune from discovery and admission merely because the defense seizes it first.

Balancing these considerations, we conclude that an observation by defense counsel or his investigator, which is the product of a privileged communication, may not be admitted unless the defense by altering or removing physical evidence has precluded the prosecution from making that same observation. In the present case the defense investigator, by removing the wallet, frustrated any possibility that the police might later discover it in the trash can. The conduct of the defense thus precluded the prosecution from ascertaining the crucial fact of the location of the wallet. Under these circumstances, the prosecution was entitled to present evidence to show the location of the wallet in the trash can; the trial court did not err in admitting the investigator's testimony. . . .

On the night of April 3, 1976, Wade (the victim) and Jacqueline Otis, a friend of the defendants, entered a club known as Rich Jimmy's. Defendant Scott remained outside by a shoeshine stand. A few minutes later codefendant Meredith arrived outside the club. He told Scott he planned to rob Wade, and asked Scott to go into the club, find Jacqueline Otis, and ask her to get Wade to go out to Wade's car parked outside the club.

In the meantime, Wade and Otis had left the club and walked to a liquor store to get some beer. Returning from the store, they left the beer in a bag by Wade's car and reentered the club. Scott then entered the club also and, according to the testimony of Laurie Ann Sam (a friend of Scott's who was already in the club), Scott asked Otis to get Wade to go back out to his car so Meredith could "knock him in the head."

When Wade and Otis did go out to the car, Meredith attacked Wade from behind. After a brief struggle, two shots were fired; Wade fell, and Meredith, witnessed by Scott and Sam, ran from the scene.

Scott went over to the body and, assuming Wade was dead, picked up the bag containing the beer and hid it behind a fence. Scott later returned, retrieved the bag, and took it home where Otis and Meredith joined him.

We now recount the evidence relating to Wade's wallet, basing our account primarily on the testimony of James Schenk, Scott's first appointed attorney. Schenk visited Scott in jail more than a month after the crime occurred and solicited information about the murder, stressing that he had to be fully acquainted with the facts to avoid being "sandbagged" by the prosecution during the trial. In response, Scott gave Schenk the same information that he had related earlier to the police. In addition, however, Scott told Schenk something Scott had not revealed to the police: that he had seen a wallet, as well as the paper bag, on the ground near Wade. Scott said that he picked up the wallet, put it in the paper bag, and placed both behind a parking lot fence. He also said that he later retrieved the bag, took it home, found $100 in the wallet and divided it with Meredith, and then tried to burn the wallet in his kitchen sink. He took the partially burned wallet, Scott told Schenk, placed it in a plastic bag, and threw it in a burn barrel behind his house.

Schenk, without further consulting Scott, retained Investigator Stephen Frick and sent Frick to find the wallet. Frick found it in the location described by Scott and brought it to Schenk. After examining the wallet and determining that it contained credit cards with Wade's name, Schenk turned the wallet and its contents over to Detective Payne, investigating officer in the case. Schenk told Payne only that, to the best of his knowledge, the wallet had belonged to Wade.

The prosecution subpoenaed Attorney Schenk and Investigator Frick to testify at the preliminary hearing. When questioned at that hearing, Schenk said that he received the wallet from Frick but refused to answer further questions on the ground that he learned about the wallet through a privileged communication. Eventually, however, the magistrate threatened Schenk with contempt if he did not respond "yes" or "no" when asked whether his contact with his client led to disclosure of the wallet's location. Schenk then replied "yes," and revealed on further questioning that this contact was the sole source of his information as to the wallet's location.

At the preliminary hearing Frick, the investigator who found the wallet, was then questioned by the district attorney. Over objections by counsel, Frick testified that he found the wallet in a garbage can behind Scott's residence.

Prior to trial, a third attorney, Hamilton Hintz, was appointed for Scott. Hintz unsuccessfully sought an *in limine* ruling that the wallet of the murder victim was inadmissible and that the attorney-client privilege precluded the admission of testimony concerning the wallet by Schenk or Frick.

At trial Frick, called by the prosecution, identified the wallet and testified that he found it in a garbage can behind Scott's residence. On cross-examination by Hintz, Scott's counsel, Frick further testified that he was an investigator hired by Scott's first attorney, Schenk, and that he had searched the garbage can at Schenk's request. Hintz later called Schenk as a witness: Schenk testified that he told Frick to search for the wallet immediately after Schenk finished talking to Scott. Schenk also stated that Frick brought him the wallet on the following day; after examining its contents Schenk delivered the wallet to the police. Scott then took the stand and testified to the information about the wallet that he had disclosed to Schenk.

The jury found both Scott and Meredith guilty of first degree murder and first degree robbery. It further found that Meredith, but not Scott, was armed with a deadly weapon. Both defendants appeal from their convictions.

Defendant Scott concedes, and we agree, that the wallet itself was admissible in evidence. Scott maintains, however, that Evidence Code section 954 bars the testimony of the investigator concerning the location of the wallet. (2) We consider, first, whether the California attorney-client privilege codified in that section extends to observations which are the product of privileged communications. We then discuss whether that privileged status is lost when defense conduct may have frustrated prosecution discovery. . . .

Scott's statements to Schenk regarding the location of the wallet clearly fulfilled the statutory requirements. Moreover, the privilege did not dissolve when Schenk disclosed the substance of that communication to his investigator, Frick. Under Evidence Code section 912, subdivision (d), a disclosure which is "reasonably necessary" to accomplish the purpose for which the attorney has been consulted does not constitute a waiver of the privilege. If Frick was to perform the investigative services for which Schenk had retained him, it was "reasonably necessary," that Schenk transmit to Frick the information regarding the wallet.[10] Thus, Schenk's disclosure to Frick did not waive the statutory privilege. . . .

The statutes codifying the attorney-client privilege do not, however, indicate whether that privilege protects facts viewed and observed as a direct result of confidential communication. To resolve that issue, we turn first to the policies which underlie the attorney-client privilege, and then

[10] FN3 Although prior cases do not consider whether section 912, subdivision (d) applies to an attorney's investigator, the language of that subdivision covers the circumstances of the instant case. An investigator is as "reasonably necessary" as a physician or psychiatrist . . . Because the investigator, then, is a person encompassed by the privilege, he stands in the same position as the attorney for purposes of the analysis and operation of the privilege; the investigator cannot then disclose that which the attorney could not have disclosed. . . . Thus, the discussion in this opinion of the conduct of defense counsel, and of counsel's right to invoke the attorney-client privilege to avoid testifying, applies also to a defense investigator.

to the cases which apply those policies to observations arising from a protected communication.

The fundamental purpose of the attorney-client privilege is, of course, to encourage full and open communication between client and attorney. . . .

Judicial decisions have recognized that the implementation of these important policies may require that the privilege extend not only to the initial communication between client and attorney but also to any information which the attorney or his investigator may subsequently acquire as a direct result of that communication. In a venerable decision involving facts analogous to those in the instant case, the Supreme Court of West Virginia held that the trial court erred in admitting an attorney's testimony as to the location of a pistol which he had discovered as the result of a privileged communication from his client. That the attorney had observed the pistol, the court pointed out, did not nullify the privilege: "All that the said attorney knew about this pistol, or where it was to be found, he knew only from the communications which had been made to him by his client confidentially and professionally, as counsel in this case. And it ought therefore, to have been entirely excluded from the jury. It may be, that in this particular case this evidence tended to the promotion of right and justice, but as was well said in *Pearce* v. *Pearce*, 11 Jar. 52, in page 55, and 2 De Gex & Smale 25–27: 'Truth like all other good things may be loved unwisely, may be pursued too keenly, may cost too much.' " (*State of West Virginia* v. *Douglass* (1882) 20 W. Va. 770, 783.)

This unbearable cost, the *Douglass* court concluded, could not be entirely avoided by attempting to admit testimony regarding observations or discoveries made as the result of a privileged communication, while excluding the communication itself. Such a procedure, *Douglass* held, "was practically as mischievous in all its tendencies and consequences, as if it has required [the attorney] to state everything, which his client had confidentially told him about this pistol. It would be a slight safeguard indeed, to confidential communications made to counsel, if he was thus compelled substantially, to give them to a jury, although he was required not to state them in the words of his client." . . . .

The foregoing decisions demonstrate that the attorney-client privilege is not strictly limited to communications, but extends to protect observations made as a consequence of protected communications. We turn therefore to the question whether that privilege encompasses a case in which the defense, by removing or altering evidence, interferes with the prosecution's opportunity to discover that evidence. . . . [11]

[11] FN7 We agree with the parties' suggestion that an attorney in Schenk's position often may best fulfill conflicting obligations to preserve the confidentiality of client confidences, investigate his case, and act as an officer of the court if he does not remove evidence located as the result of a privileged communication. We must recognize, however, that in some cases an exami-

When defense counsel alters or removes physical evidence, he necessarily deprives the prosecution of the opportunity to observe that evidence in its original condition or location. As amicus Appellate Committee of the California District Attorney Association points out, to bar admission of testimony concerning the original condition and location of the evidence in such a case permits the defense in effect to "destroy" critical information; it is as if, he explains, the wallet in this case bore a tag bearing the words "located in the trash can by Scott's residence," and the defense, by taking the wallet, destroyed this tag. To extend the attorney-client privilege to a case in which the defense removed evidence might encourage defense counsel to race the police to seize critical evidence. . . . .

We therefore conclude that courts must craft an exception to the protection extended by the attorney-client privilege in cases in which counsel has removed or altered evidence. Indeed, at oral argument defense counsel acknowledged that such an exception might be necessary in a case in which the police would have inevitably discovered the evidence in its original location if counsel had not removed it. Counsel argued, however, that the attorney-client privilege should protect observations of evidence, despite subsequent defense removal, unless the prosecution could prove that the police probably would have eventually discovered the evidence in the original site.

We have seriously considered counsel's proposal, but have concluded that a test based upon the probability of eventual discovery is unworkably speculative. Evidence turns up not only because the police deliberately search for it, but also because it comes to the attention of policemen or bystanders engaged in other business. In the present case, for example, the wallet might have been found by the trash collector. Moreover, once physical evidence (the wallet) is turned over to the police, they will obviously stop looking for it; to ask where, how long, and how carefully they would have looked is obviously to compel speculation as to theoretical future conduct of the police.

We therefore conclude that whenever defense counsel removes or alters evidence, the statutory privilege does not bar revelation of the original location or condition of the evidence in question.[12] We thus view the

---

nation of evidence may reveal information critical to the defense of a client accused of crime. If the usefulness of the evidence cannot be gauged without taking possession of it, as, for example, when a ballistics or fingerprint test is required, the attorney may properly take it for a reasonable time before turning it over to the prosecution. [*State v. Olwell*, (1964) 394 P.2d 681, 684–85.] Similarly, in the present case the defense counsel could not be certain the burnt wallet belonged in fact to the victim: in taking the wallet to examine it for identification, he violated no ethical duty to his client or to the prosecution. (See generally, *Legal Ethics and the Destruction of Evidence* (1979) 88 Yale L. J. 1665.)

[12] FN8 In offering the evidence, the prosecution should present the information in a manner which avoids revealing the content of attorney-client communications or the original source of the information. In the present case, for example, the prosecutor simply asked Frick where he

defense decision to remove evidence as a tactical choice. If defense counsel leaves the evidence where he discovers it, his observations derived from privileged communications are insulated from revelation. If, however, counsel chooses to remove evidence to examine or test it, the original location and condition of that evidence loses the protection of the privilege. Applying this analysis to the present case, we hold that the trial court did not err in admitting the investigator's testimony concerning the location of the wallet. . . .

CASE QUESTIONS

1. Absent the court's ruling, would Schenk have been able to assert the privilege to refuse to answer "yes" or "no" to whether his investigator found the wallet based on a client communication?
2. If Frick had observed the wallet but not moved it, would Schenk have had to tell the prosecutors about it?
3. Under the Court's rule, could Frick have examined the wallet and left it at the scene but covered it up with garbage to make it harder to find?

PROBLEM 16–5

The Court's resolution of this issue requires defense counsel to weigh some competing probabilities. What are they?

PROBLEM 16–6

Suppose the evidence in question had been a knife with some blood on it, seized from the possession of a defendant. Suppose further the prosecution wanted to test the blood to see if it matched the blood of a murder victim. Suppose finally that there was only a little spot of blood, such that only one test could be performed. (I.e., there was not enough for both the prosecution and defense to run their own tests.) How should the prosecution proceed? How does the ruling in *Meredith* bear on this question? *See People v. Bolden,* 29 Cal.4th 515 (2002).

---

found the wallet; he did not identify Frick as a defense investigator or trace the discovery of the wallet to an attorney-client communication.

In other circumstances, when it is not possible to elicit such testimony without identifying the witness as the defendant's attorney or investigator, the defendant may be willing to enter a stipulation which will simply inform the jury as to the relevant location or condition of the evidence in question. When such a stipulation is proffered, the prosecution should not be permitted to reject the stipulation in the hope that by requiring defense counsel personally to testify to such facts, the jury might infer that counsel learned those facts from defendant. (Cf. *People* v. *Hall* (1980) 28 Cal.3d 143, 152 [167 Cal.Rptr. 844, 616 P.2d 826].)

2. DISCOVERY CONDUCT

Most cases do not press novel theories or seek to win approval of new legal rules. Most cases work within the confines of existing law, because most litigants would rather win early (in the trial court) than suffer a loss and await possible vindication on appeal, possibly years after losing. That is one way of looking at an important point: Trial court litigation is as much about the facts as the law, if not more so. Gathering the facts consumes most of the time spent in litigation.

The process of fact gathering (you may recall from your civil procedure class) is called discovery. And the discovery process has been the occasion for both many disciplinary actions and for many case sanctions—either in the form of monetary penalties or in the form of orders dismissing cases or claims or holding some facts to be established. Such "issue sanctions" can fundamentally alter the results of a case. In addition, Model Rule 3.4(d) provides that you may not make a frivolous discovery request or fail to make reasonably diligent efforts to comply with a proper request. The following section explores some of these topics.

REDWOOD V. DOBSON

476 F.3d 462 (7th Cir. 2007)

EASTERBROOK, CHIEF JUDGE.

This is a grudge match. Harvey Cato Welch represented Erik Redwood in a criminal prosecution for battery. Redwood was convicted and maintains that Welch is at fault. Redwood wants Welch to sign an affidavit confessing that he supplied ineffective assistance; he believes that with such an affidavit he could have his criminal record expunged. Welch, who believes that his legal work met professional standards, has refused to fall on his sword for Redwood's benefit. Redwood has retaliated by insulting Welch in public, calling him, among other things, a "shoe-shine boy." Redwood is white and Welch black; Welch believes that this phrase, when spoken to an adult, is a racial slur.

During October 1998 a scuffle occurred after Redwood again called Welsh a "shoe-shine boy." Redwood filed a battery suit in state court; Welch filed a defamation counterclaim and asked the State's Attorney to prosecute Redwood for inciting a breach of the peace. Erik Redwood was represented in that litigation by attorney Jude Redwood, his wife, who also is a plaintiff in the federal suit. Elizabeth Dobson, an Assistant State's Attorney, decided that Erik Redwood had committed a hate crime by using a demeaning term that led to a physical confrontation. Officer Troy Phillips of the Urbana Police Department presented the evidence to the grand jury, which returned an indictment. Attorney Marvin Gerstein, representing Welch in the civil litigation, later wrote to Jude Redwood suggesting that, if the litigation could be resolved amicably, he would try to persuade Dobson to dismiss the criminal charge. The Redwoods rejected that offer. The civil case went to trial; while the jury was deliberating, the parties reached a settlement. Meanwhile the criminal prosecution had been dismissed on the ground that the state's hate-crime law does not apply to speech that does not threaten immediate physical injury. See *People v. Redwood,* 335 Ill.App.3d 189 (4th Dist.2002).

While the prosecutor's appeal in the criminal prosecution was pending, the Redwoods filed this federal action against Dobson, Welch, Gerstein, Phillips, and the City of Urbana. The complaint, signed by Jude Redwood as counsel (she is also a plaintiff, alleging loss of consortium) accuses the five defendants of violating the first amendment by discriminating against Erik Redwood's religion (which, he maintains, leads him to "teach truth and righteousness to all persons, including defendant Harvey Welch", a curious euphemism for personal insults) and of conspiracy to maintain a malicious prosecution. . . .

Urbana settled the litigation for nuisance value. After extended discovery, the district court granted summary judgment for the four other defendants. Phillips prevailed as a result of the absolute immunity that applies to witnesses in criminal proceedings. See *Briscoe v. LaHue,* 460 U.S. 325 (1983). The Redwoods have abandoned their claims against him but appeal with respect to the remaining three defendants. The Redwoods also appeal from the denial of their motion for sanctions in discovery, Gerstein has filed a cross-appeal to protest the district court's denial of his motion for attorneys' fees, and both sides ask us to award sanctions for what they call frivolous arguments in this court.

Dobson, Welch, and Gerstein are right to label most of the Redwoods' appellate arguments as frivolous. . . .

The only reason why the Redwoods' appeal is not wholly frivolous is that the district court dismissed the state-law claims on the merits rather than relinquishing supplemental jurisdiction. A court that resolves all federal claims before trial normally should dismiss supplemental claims without prejudice. 28 U.S.C. § 1367(c)(3). That both sides have allowed animosity to get the better of legal judgment, however, implies the wisdom of bringing the contretemps to a conclusion in a single forum. . . .

A profusion of motions and cross-motions for sanctions—and the conduct underlying some of these motions—demonstrates the extent to which counsel have allowed personal distaste to displace dispassionate legal analysis. Most depositions are taken without judicial supervision. Witnesses often want to avoid giving answers, and questioning may probe sensitive or emotionally fraught subjects, so unless counsel maintain professional detachment decorum can break down. That happened here; the results were ugly.

Gerstein's deposition was taken by Charles L. Danner on behalf of both Redwoods, though Jude Redwood attended and sometimes acted as counsel in addition to her role as a plaintiff. Gerstein's counsel was Roger Webber, though Gerstein himself peppered the transcript with legal arguments. The deposition began badly when Danner spent the first 30 pages or so of the transcript exploring Gerstein's criminal record—mostly vehicular violations. Danner made no effort to explain how these questions could lead to admissible evidence, and they got under Gerstein's skin. After Gerstein spontaneously refused to answer some of the questions (remarking "That's none of your business"), Webber began instructing Gerstein not to answer.

Webber gave no reason beyond his declaration that the questions were designed to harass rather than obtain information—which may well have been their point, but Fed.R.Civ.P. 30(d) specifies how harassment is to be handled. Counsel for the witness may halt the deposition and apply for a protective order, see Rule 30(d)(4), but must not instruct the witness to remain silent. "Any objection during a deposition must be stated concisely and in a non-argumentative and non-suggestive manner. A person may instruct a deponent not to answer only when necessary to preserve a privilege, to enforce a limitation directed by the court, or to present a motion under Rule 30(d)(4)." Fed.R.Civ.P. 30(d)(1). Webber violated this rule repeatedly by telling Gerstein not to answer yet never presenting a motion for a protective order. The provocation was clear, but so was Webber's violation.

Danner then turned to Gerstein's troubles with the state bar, another topic whose relevance (or ability to lead to relevant evidence) has never been explained. Gerstein was censured for misconduct in 1991 and suspended for a month in 2002. Although the reasons are matters of public record, Danner demanded that Gerstein confess them in the deposition; Gerstein professed inability to remember, and when Danner inquired whether Gerstein had been ordered to obtain psychiatric counseling or anger-management therapy, Webber again told him not to answer. Richard Klaus, representing Dobson, opined that Danner had committed a misdemeanor under Illinois law by asking questions about Gerstein's mental health.

What happened next must be set out in full to be believed:

Q [by Danner]. Mr. Gerstein, have you ever engaged in homosexual conduct?

MR. WEBBER: Objection, relevance. MR. KLAUS: I join.

MR. WEBBER: I believe it violates Rule 30, and I'm instructing him not to answer the question.

A. I'm not answering the question. MR. KLAUS: I join the objection.

Q. Mr. Gerstein, are you involved in any type of homosexual clique with any other defendants in this action?

MR. WEBBER: Same objection. Same instruction.

MR. KLAUS: I join the objection.

Gerstein would have been entitled to stalk out of the room. Webber justifiably could have called off the deposition and applied for a protective order (plus sanctions). Fed.R.Civ.P. 26(c), 30(d)(3), (4). Instead he told Gerstein not to answer, which was untenable as no claim of privilege had been advanced.

After a brief recess, Gerstein acquired "amnesia" and started playing word games.

Q. During the last recess that we had that we just reconvened from, did you consult with your attorney concerning this deposition?

Instead of asserting the attorney-client privilege, a genuine reason not to answer (though perhaps consultation would have violated an order that the deposition be conducted without such conferences), Gerstein played dumb.

A. I don't understand the question.

Q. We just had a recess.

A. I understand that.

Q. Do you understand that? During that recess period, did you take that time to consult with your attorney regarding this deposition?

A. I don't know what you mean by the word consult.

Q. Did you speak with your attorney regarding this deposition?

A. I don't think so. I don't know.

Q. Do you know how—did you write anything to your attorney during that recess?

A. Write anything?

Q. Correct.

A. No.

Q. Did you speak with your attorney during that recess?

A. I had words with my attorney. We exchanged a conversation.

Q. Were those conversations-or strike that. Did any of the comments in that conversation or those conversations refer to any aspect of this deposition?

A. I can't recall.

The deposition fills a further 98 pages of transcript, unedifying to the end. At one point Danner asked whether the secretary who had typed the letter in which Gerstein offered to ask Dobson to dismiss the criminal prosecution was married; Webber instructed Gerstein not to answer. Danner asked whether the secretary had children; before Webber could leap in, Gerstein replied that she did. What this—indeed, what most of Danner's questions—had to do with the legal proceeding against Gerstein is unfathomable. Plaintiffs say that Gerstein once gave Danner "the finger," and though the transcript does not reflect that gesture the proceedings were heated enough that this could well have happened. (Gerstein does not deny this accusation; a video tape of the deposition was made, but we have not consulted it.)

Danner's conduct of this deposition was shameful—not as bad as the insult-riddled performance by Joe Jamail that incensed the Supreme Court of Delaware, see *Paramount Communications Inc. v. QVC Network Inc.,* 637 A.2d 34, 52–57 (Del.1994), but far below the standards to which lawyers must adhere. Gerstein, Webber, and Klaus were goaded, but their responses—feigned inability to remember, purported ignorance of ordinary words (the "consult" episode was not the only one), and instructions not to respond that neither shielded a privilege nor supplied time to apply for a protective order—were unprofessional and violated the Federal Rules of Civil Procedure as well as the ethical rules that govern legal practice.

At one point, after Jude Redwood said that, because this was a deposition rather than a trial, Danner was entitled to fish for evidence whether or not the answers would be admissible, Klaus replied: "[T]his is not a discovery deposition. There's no such distinction or dichotomy under the federal rules. Everything that is asked here must meet the standard of the federal rules of evidence." Klaus either did not know, or did not care, that discovery may be used to elicit information that will lead to relevant evidence; each question and answer need not be one that could be one that would itself be proper at trial. But Danner's questions had ventured so far beyond the pale that overstatement on the other side was inevitable.

When the Redwoods sought sanctions in the district court, the judge declared that everyone had behaved badly and that, because Danner was the greater offender, no sanctions would be appropriate. The district judge remarked that it was "ludicrous" for the Redwoods to argue that lawyers may not instruct witnesses not to answer. Given Rule 30(d)(1), however, the Redwoods had (and have) a meritorious position on this issue.

Mutual enmity does not excuse the breakdown of decorum that occurred at Gerstein's deposition. Instead of declaring a pox on both houses, the district court should have used its authority to maintain standards of civility and professionalism. It is precisely when animosity runs high that playing by the rules is vital. Rules of legal procedure are designed to defuse, or at least channel into set forms, the heated feelings that accompany much litigation. Because depositions take place in law offices rather than courtrooms, adherence to professional standards is vital, for the judge has no direct means of control.

Sanctions are in order, but they need not be monetary. See Fed.R.Civ.P. 30(d)(3), 37(a)(4), (b)(2). Because the arguments pro and con have been fully ventilated in this court, and none of the attorneys has asked for a hearing under Fed. R.App. P. 46(c), we see no need to drag out this controversy with a remand. Attorneys Danner, Gerstein, and Webber are censured for conduct unbecoming a member of the bar; attorney Klaus is admonished. (We differentiate in this way because a censure is the more opprobrious label, see *In re Charges of Judicial Misconduct,* 404 F.3d 688, 695–96 (2d Cir.2005), and Klaus's misconduct is substantially less serious than that of the other lawyers.) Any repetition of this performance, in any court within this circuit, will lead to sterner sanctions, including suspension or disbarment. . . .

What the Rules Say and What Really Happens: Customary Practice and Deviations From It

Defending the deposition in *Redwood v. Dobson* was tough duty. Roger Webber, the lawyer who drew that duty, freely instructed his witness not to answer questions on the ground that the questions aimed to harass rather than discover information. The court agreed that the questions were harassing but pointed out that under FRCP 30 harassment is not a proper basis for instructing a witness not to answer a question. Why then, with the rule so clear, did Webber not only make the instructions on the record but later declare that he did so to protect his client from harassment? Why did the trial court say it was "ludicrous" for Redwood to argue that the instructions were proper?

The answer is that the procedure specified under FRCP 30 is not very practical. It places the burden of ending harassment on the party being harassed, which must incur the cost of preparing the motion for a protective order and arguing it, with a chance but not a certainty of receiving a fee award covering that cost (as a sanction against the harasser) if the motion is granted. As a practical matter, no experienced lawyer would make such a motion without a very clear record showing that the court needed to intervene to protect the witness from misconduct. It is conceivable that one question would be enough to make such a showing (the question regarding homosexual conduct is an example of such a question) but even then a pattern of improper questions would be useful in fleshing out the parameters of the order counsel for a witness would seek.

As a practical matter, therefore, under the approach specified in the FRCP and applied in *Redwood v. Dobson,* a harassing party would get a few improper questions answered while counsel for the witness waited for the record to be clear enough so that the court's anger at being dragged into a discovery dispute would be directed at the questioner rather than the witness.

For these reasons, the type of instructions Webber gave are likely to be more common than motions for a protective order even after *Redwood v. Dobson*. Most questioners would not want a deposition adjourned for motion practice any more than most witnesses. In most cases both sides would prefer give and take over instructions, leading to negotiated resolutions that allowed the deposition to proceed relatively efficiently, albeit through means not complying fully with the FRCP.

Such extra-legal give and take does not lead to anarchy because in most cases each side values their reputation highly and does not want to tarnish it in the eyes of the court by taking an unreasonable position in a discovery dispute. Reputational concerns are in this sense as powerful as the FRCP in constraining misbehavior and may be more powerful. In practice, lawyers spend considerable time and effort to ensure that they appear to be more reasonable than their opponents with respect to any given discovery dispute.

The instructions Webber gave illustrate a more general and very important point. In some areas the custom of practice—what lawyers usually do, by tacit agreement and without running to judges—deviates from what the rules say should happen. Such deviations do not mean the rules are irrelevant. They are always there should one party choose to deviate from custom and seek strict enforcement of the rules. That move is always available to the players in the game, though it comes at a cost: A lawyer who makes it is likely to find that in the future other lawyers will be less likely to rely on sensible customary practices in dealing with him, and more likely to insist on (relatively costly) strict compliance with the rules.

You therefore need to treat custom carefully and take affirmative steps to understand the forces that sustain it. If you find yourself in a situation where custom is likely to break down, as in a grudge match such as *Redwood* or in dealing with a lawyer who is unlikely to deal with you or a particular jurisdiction again (and therefore might not care as much about reputational harm from obstreperous conduct) you need to think carefully about how much you should rely on custom and how much you should invoke the letter of the law.

PROBLEM 16–7

Suppose you are the lawyer taking the deposition in which the following exchange occurs (the deponent is Mr. Liedtke):

A. [Mr. Liedtke] I vaguely recall [Mr. Oresman's letter]. . . . I think I did read it, probably.

. . . .

Q. (By Mr. Johnston [Delaware counsel for QVC]) Okay. Do you have any idea why Mr. Oresman was calling that material to your attention?

MR. JAMAIL: Don't answer that.

How would he know what was going on in Mr. Oresman's mind?

Don't answer it.

Go on to your next question.

MR. JOHNSTON: No, Joe—

MR. JAMAIL: He's not going to answer that. Certify it. I'm going to shut it down if you don't go to your next question.

MR. JOHNSTON: No. Joe, Joe—

MR. JAMAIL: Don't "Joe" me, asshole. You can ask some questions, but get off of that. I'm tired of you. You could gag a maggot off a meat wagon. Now, we've helped you every way we can.

MR. JOHNSTON: Let's just take it easy.

MR. JAMAIL: No, we're not going to take it easy. Get done with this.

MR. JOHNSTON: We will go on to the next question.

MR. JAMAIL: Do it now.

MR. JOHNSTON: We will go on to the next question. We're not trying to excite anyone.

MR. JAMAIL: Come on. Quit talking. Ask the question. Nobody wants to socialize with you.

MR. JOHNSTON: I'm not trying to socialize. We'll go on to another question. We're continuing the deposition.

MR. JAMAIL: Well, go on and shut up.

MR. JOHNSTON: Are you finished?

MR. JAMAIL: Yeah, you—

MR. JOHNSTON: Are you finished?

MR. JAMAIL: I may be and you may be. Now, you want to sit here and talk to me, fine. This deposition is going to be over with. You don't know what you're doing. Obviously someone wrote out a long outline of stuff for you to ask. You have no concept of what you're doing.

Now, I've tolerated you for three hours. If you've got another question, get on with it. This is going to stop one hour from now, period. Go.

MR. JOHNSTON: Are you finished?

MR. THOMAS: Come on, Mr. Johnston, move it.

MR. JOHNSTON: I don't need this kind of abuse.

MR. THOMAS: Then just ask the next question.

Q. (By Mr. Johnston) All right. To try to move forward, Mr. Liedtke, . . . I'll show you what's been marked as Liedtke 14 and it is a covering letter dated October 29 from Steven Cohen of Wachtell, Lipton, Rosen & Katz including QVC's Amendment Number 1 to its Schedule 14D–1, and my question—

A. No.

Q.—to you, sir, is whether you've seen that?

A. No. Look, I don't know what your intent in asking all these questions is, but, my God, I am not going to play boy lawyer.

Q. Mr. Liedtke—

A. Okay. Go ahead and ask your question.

Q.—I'm trying to move forward in this deposition that we are entitled to take. I'm trying to streamline it.

MR. JAMAIL: Come on with your next question. Don't even talk with this witness.

MR. JOHNSTON: I'm trying to move forward with it.

MR. JAMAIL: You understand me? Don't talk to this witness except by question. Did you hear me?

MR. JOHNSTON: I heard you fine.

MR. JAMAIL: You fee makers think you can come here and sit in somebody's office, get your meter running, get your full day's fee by asking stupid questions. Let's go with it.

(JA 6002–06).

What should you do?

PROBLEM 16–8

Why do you suppose Mr. Jamail, the attorney defending the deposition, said what he said? How would you answer influence your own behavior in the deposition? Hint: Did Mr. Johnston ever get an answer to his question?

Answers may harass as well as questions. In *GMAC Bank v. HTFC Corp.*, 248 F.R.D. 182 (E.D. Pa. 2008), the court imposed sanctions against both a witness and his lawyer for obscene answers and other harassing conduct during a deposition. The court provided an example of this conduct:

> Q. [T]his is your loan file, what do Mr. and Mrs. Fitzgerald do for a living?
>
> A. I don't know. Open it up and find it.
>
> Q. Look at your loan file and tell me.
>
> A. Open it up and find it. I'm not your fucking bitch.
>
> Q. Take a look at your loan application.
>
> A. Do it yourself. Do it yourself. You want to do this in front of a judge. Would you prefer to [do] this in front of a judge? Then, shut the fuck up.
>
> Q. Sir, take a look-
>
> A. I'm taking a break. Fuck him. You open up the document. You want me to look at something, you get the document out. Earn your fucking money asshole. Isn't the law wonderful. Better get used to it. You'll retire when I'm done.

The court sanctioned the witness for this and similar conduct and for refusing to provide answers. It sanctioned his counsel because counsel "sat idly by as a mere spectator to [the client's] abusive, obstructive, and evasive behavior; and when he did speak, he either incorrectly directed the witness not to answer, dared opposing counsel to file a motion to compel, or even joined in [the client's] offensive conduct." The lawyer, Zaccardi, protested that he had tried to restrain his clients but had done so off the record. The court accepted this assertion but imposed sanctions anyway: "It is true that any attorney can be blindsided by a recalcitrant client who engages in unexpected sanctionable conduct at a deposition. An attorney faced with such a client cannot, however, simply sit back, allow the deposition to proceed, and then blame the client when the deposition process breaks down."

PROBLEM 16–9

What should Zaccardi have done to rein in an obviously difficult client? One answer is that he should not have snickered at the witness' obscene answers and should not have seemed to challenge GMAC to file a motion to compel. (Any even remotely experienced lawyer should have realized the judge would be very angry at the transcript and would grant the motion in a heartbeat.) But the court seemed more bothered by what Zaccardi did not do than by what he did. The court stated:

> It is true that, in most instances, Ziccardi did not actively counsel Wider on the record to provide evasive or incomplete answers or to refuse to answer questions. What is remarkable about Ziccardi's conduct is not his actions, but rather his failure to act. Despite the pervasiveness of Wider's evasive and incomplete answers and his repeated failure to answer questions, Ziccardi failed to take remedial steps to curb his client's misconduct.

The court did not specify what remedial steps it had in mind. Bearing in mind that Zaccardi owed a duty of loyalty even to so difficult a client as Mr. Wider, what should he have done?

Witness Coaching

Model Rule 3.4(b) provides that you may not counsel a witness to testify falsely or assist a witness in doing so. Witnesses are prepared by their counsel before depositions or trial. Preparation includes describing to the witness what a deposition or trial is about, describing the rules governing the proceedings, and informing the witness of topics likely to be covered in an examination. In the real world, it also includes what most people would call "coaching." In rough terms that means suggesting to witnesses that they limit their answers to the extent possible and not engage in open-ended dialogue; it also means suggesting to witnesses the best way to answer various questions. The *Restatement (Third) of the Law Governing Lawyers* §116 reporter's note to cmt. b (2000), lists permissible forms of preparation and states that preparation may include "rehearsal of testimony" as well as suggestions by the lawyer of a "choice of words that might be employed to make the witness's meaning clear."

Most lawyers qualify their coaching by emphasizing that clients must tell the truth and not perjure themselves. So qualified, coaching does not run afoul of the prohibition on introducing perjured testimony. It is still problematic, though, because it blurs the line between the witness' testimony, which is either on facts or expert opinion, and the lawyer's advocacy. The content of preparation conversations is often privileged, of course, so opposing counsel often try to explore the perimeters of the witness' preparation by asking questions about how long the witness met with counsel to prepare, whether the witness reviewed any documents, whether the documents refreshed the witness' recollection, and what the documents were. All but the last question are routine and have to be answered; practice varies on whether parties and judges believe the selection of documents to show a witness constitutes work product and therefore is protectable.

The limit to coaching is, or at least should be, that once the examination begins the witness is on his or her own. Opposing counsel is free to probe the witness' understanding of what he or she says, and possibly to unravel the effects of coaching. That limit is lost if lawyers actually coach witnesses during their testimony. That would not happen in trial, where a judge could observe, comment on, and forbid coaching.

Judges are not present at depositions but they are willing to sanction lawyers for overt coaching during depositions. That happened in *Tucker v. Pacific Bell Mobile Services*, 186 Cal.App.4th 1548 (2010), where during her testimony a witness looked at a notepad on which her lawyer wrote notes to her. The trial court sanctioned the lawyer for misuse of the discovery process and the court of appeal affirmed. Had counsel reviewed testimony with the witness during a break in the deposition the conversation would have been privileged, and the lawyer's notes to the witness presumably were privileged as well, but feeding answers to a witness during examination denies the opposing party the chance to test the witness' own knowledge or to probe why a witness may have testified differently after a break than before.

Federal Rule of Civil Procedure 30(e)(1)(B) allows witnesses to review their deposition transcripts and, "if there are changes in form or substance, to sign a statement listing the changes and the reasons for making them." In *Norelus v. Dennys, Inc.*, 628 F.3d 1270 (11th Cir. 2010), counsel for plaintiff in a sexual harassment case submitted a 63–page document making 868 changes to the plaintiff's deposition testimony. In affirming sanctions the district court imposed under 28 U.S.C. § 1927 (giving courts discretionary power to sanction attorneys who unreasonably prolong proceedings), the court of appeals held that for counsel to submit a "novella-length errata sheet making a slew of material changes in their client's deposition testimony was improper." The court held the district court did not abuse its discretion in concluding that counsel acted unreasonably in pursuing the plaintiff's claim after submitting a document that should have signaled unmistakably that there was no claim to pursue. As the court put it, "[w]hen the truth was thrust in [counsels'] faces, they stubbornly ignored it and kept on litigating."

Sanctions for failure to provide discovery have become more common over time. The increase is partly due to the development of electronic means of creating, transmitting, and storing information. Electronic data are easy to store but the volume of stored data can be so large, and the means of storing it can be so complex, that mistakes can and often do happen. Sometimes, of course, parties simply try to falsify or destroy evidence, which can lead to terminating sanctions (judgment for or against a party), monetary sanctions, or both.

A recent notable example of such sanctions is the over $9 million sanction levied against Qualcomm, Inc., for failure to comply with its discovery obligations in a patent case it brought against Broadcom, Inc. *Qualcomm Inc. v. Broadcom Corp.,* 548 F.3d 1004, 1026 (Fed.Cir.2008). The trial court also ruled that the patents Qualcomm asserted were unenforceable due to its inequitable conduct in litigation.

After levying the sanction the trial court ordered a large number of lawyers to show cause why they should not be personally sanctioned for this misconduct. The sanctions litigation went on for almost two years. The magistrate initially referred six lawyers to the California State Bar for possible discipline. This reference was mooted when the trial judge reversed the magistrate's holding that counsel could not use privileged communications to defend themselves. The second time around the magistrate chose not to issue any sanctions but offered the following observations on the discovery failures in the case:

> The Court was not presented with any evidence establishing that either in-house lawyers or outside counsel met in person with the appropriate Qualcomm engineers (those who were likely to have been involved in the conduct at issue and who were likely to be witnesses) at the beginning of the case to explain the legal issues and discuss appropriate document collection. Moreover, outside counsel did not obtain sufficient information from any source to understand how Qualcomm's computer system is organized: where emails are stored, how often and to what location laptops and personal computers are backed up, whether, when and under what circumstances data from laptops are copied into repositories, what type of information is contained within the various databases and repositories, what records are maintained regarding the search for, and collection of, documents for litigation, etc. Finally, no attorney took supervisory responsibility for verifying that the necessary discovery had been conducted (including ensuring that all of the correct locations, servers, databases, repositories, and computers were correctly searched for potentially relevant documents) and that the resulting discovery supported the important legal arguments, claims, and defenses being presented to the court. These fundamental failures led to the discovery violations.[13]

---

[13] Order Declining to Impose Sanctions Against The Responding Attorneys and Dissolving the Order to Show Cause, No. 05 cv 1958, at 4 (4/21/10).

The court also noted "a lack of agreement amongst the participants regarding responsibility for document collection and production."[14] Outside counsel believed in-house attorneys and legal assistants would take the lead while the client's employees apparently believed otherwise. From the perspective of outside counsel, this misunderstanding led to a situation in which counsel had responsibility for discovery but not authority to do what needed to be done to comply. This misalignment of authority and responsibility is dangerous and is likely to become more common as sophisticated clients insist on using their own staff or selected third-party vendors to conduct discovery. You would be wise not to accept responsibility for discovery unless you also had the authority to conduct it.

Sometimes lawyers simply get too cute and try to be too clever about their client's discovery obligations. The following case illustrates this risk.

WASHINGTON STATE PHYSICIANS INSURANCE EXCHANGE & ASSOCIATION V. FISONS CORP.

122 Wash.2d 299 (1993)

ANDERSEN, CHIEF JUSTICE.

[In 1986 Jennifer Pollock, a two-year-old girl, suffered seizure causing permanent brain damage. The seizures were caused by an excess of a drug called theophylline. Jennifer's parents sued her doctor, James Klicpera, who had prescribed the drug, and Fisons Corporation, which made it. Dr. Klicpera cross-complained against Fisons. After three years of litigation, Dr. Klicpera settled with the Pollocks.

Over a year after the settlement, Dr. Klicpera's attorney received from an anonymous source a letter showing that Fisons knew of problems with theophylline administered to children. Fisons sent the letter to several physicians, but not Dr. Klicpera. The letter had not been produced in response to document requests directed to Fisons.

The Pollocks and Dr. Klicpera moved for discovery sanctions against Fisons. A special master denied the motion but ordered Fisons to produce documents relating to theophylline. (The trial court later denied motions to reverse the special master's decision denying sanctions.) The next day, Fisons produced approximately 10,000 documents to the attorneys for the Pollocks and Dr. Klicpera.

These documents included a 1985 memorandum that reported on toxicity problems with theophylline and which referred to the then current recommended dosage as a significant "mistake" or "poor clinical judgment." The memorandum noted that the physician who oversaw dosage

---

[14] *Id.*

recommendations was heavily invested in stocks of companies that produced the drug. Finally, the memorandum noted that the drug's toxicity risks had not been reported in the principal journal for the doctors who prescribed it, and that many physicians therefore might not be aware of the "alarming increase in adverse reactions such as seizures, permanent brain damage and death." This memorandum had not been produced in discovery.

On April 27, 1990, shortly after the 1985 memo was revealed, the drug company settled with the Pollocks for $6.9 million. Dr. Klicpa and his insurer (which had paid the settlement to the Pollocks) asked the trial court to sanction Fisons for discovery abuse. They claimed that interrogatories and requests for production should have led to the discovery of the "smoking gun" documents, but that these documents were not revealed to the doctor until one of them was anonymously delivered to his attorneys.]

On its face, Rule 26(g) requires an attorney signing a discovery response to certify that the attorney has read the response and that after a reasonable inquiry believes it is (1) consistent with the discovery rules and is warranted by existing law or a good faith argument for the extension, modification or reversal of existing law; (2) not interposed for any improper purpose such as to harass or cause unnecessary delay or needless increase in the cost of litigation; and (3) not unreasonable or unduly burdensome or expensive, given the needs of the case, the discovery already had, the amount in controversy, and the importance of the issues at stake in the litigation.

Whether an attorney has made a reasonable inquiry is to be judged by an objective standard. Subjective belief or good faith alone no longer shields an attorney from sanctions under the rules. In determining whether an attorney has complied with the rule, the court should consider all of the surrounding circumstances, the importance of the evidence to its proponent, and the ability of the opposing party to formulate a response or to comply with the request. . . .

The trial court then denied sanctions, in part because: (1) The evidence did not support a finding that the drug company *intentionally* misfiled documents to avoid discovery; (2) neither the doctor nor the child had formally moved for a definition of "product" and neither had moved to compel production of documents or answers before requesting sanctions; (3) the conduct of the drug company and its counsel was consistent with the customary and accepted litigation practices of the bar of Snohomish County and of this state; and (4) the doctor failed to meet his burden of proving that the "evidence of discovery abuse is so clear that reasonable minds could not differ on the appropriateness of sanctions."

The trial court erred in concluding as it did. . . . intent need not be shown before sanctions are mandated. A motion to compel compliance with the rules is not a prerequisite to a sanctions motion. Conduct is to be measured against the spirit and purpose of the rules, not against the standard of practice of the local bar. Furthermore, the burden placed on the doctor by the trial court in this regard was greater than that mandated under the rule. . . .

The drug company was persistent in its resistance to discovery requests. Fair and reasoned resistance to discovery is not sanctionable. Rather it is the misleading nature of the drug company's responses that is contrary to the purposes of discovery and which is most damaging to the fairness of the litigation process.

The specific instances alleged to be sanctionable in this case involve misleading or "non" responses to a number of requests which the doctor claims should have produced the smoking gun documents themselves or a way to discover the information they contained.

The two smoking gun documents reportedly were contained in files which related to Intal, a cromolyn sodium product, which was manufactured by Fisons and which competed with Somophyllin. The manager of medical communications had a thorough collection of articles, materials and other documents relating to the dangers of theophylline and used the information from those materials to market Intal, as an alternative to Somophyllin Oral Liquid. The drug company avoided production of these theophylline-related materials, and avoided identifying the manager of medical communications as a person with information about the dangers of theophylline, by giving evasive or misleading responses to interrogatories and requests for production. . . .

The first discovery documents directed to the drug company were prepared by the child's attorney and were dated September 26, 1986. The interrogatories contained a short definition section stating in part:

> The term "the product" as used hereinafter in these interrogatories shall mean the product which is claimed to have caused injury or damage to JENNIFER MARIE POLLOCK as alleged in pleadings filed on her behalf, namely, to wit: "Somophyllin" oral liquid.

Clerk's Papers, at 4103.

These first interrogatories requested information about "the product" which is manufactured by the drug company, Fisons, as well as about theophylline, a drug entity which is the primary ingredient of the drug company's product Somophyllin Oral Liquid. The interrogatory regarding theophylline was answered by the drug company, as were the interrogatories about "the product".

Somophyllin and its primary ingredient, theophylline, were not distinguished in discussions between the attorneys or in drug company literature. The printed package insert for Somophyllin Oral Liquid (Exhibit

93) and marketing brochures refer to the names Somophyllin and theophylline interchangeably. . . .

The drug company's responses to discovery requests contained the following general objection:

> *Requests Regarding Fisons Products Other Than Somophyllin Oral Liquid.* Fisons objects to all discovery requests regarding Fisons products other than Somophyllin Oral Liquid as overly broad, unduly burdensome, harassing, and not reasonably calculated to lead to the discovery of admissible evidence.

See, e.g., Clerk's Papers, at 7399.

Theophylline is not a Fisons "product". Furthermore, because theophylline is the primary ingredient in Somophyllin Oral Liquid, any document focusing on theophylline would, necessarily, be one *regarding* Somophyllin Oral Liquid.

In November 1986 the doctor served his first requests for production on the drug company. Four requests were made. Three asked for documents concerning Somophyllin. Request 3 stated:

> 3. Produce genuine copies of any letters sent by your company to physicians concerning theophylline toxicity in children.
>
> The drug company's response was:
>
> Such letters, *if any,* regarding Somophyllin Oral Liquid will be produced at a reasonable time and place convenient to Fisons and its counsel of record.

Clerk's Papers, at 8458.

Had the request, as written, been complied with, the first smoking gun letter (exhibit 3) would have been disclosed early in the litigation. That June 30, 1981 letter concerned theophylline toxicity in children; it was sent by the drug company to physicians. . . .

The drug company's responses and answers to discovery requests are misleading. The answers state that all information *regarding* Somophyllin Oral Liquid which had been requested would be provided. They further imply that all documents which are relevant to the plaintiffs' claims were being produced. They do not specifically object to the production of documents that discuss the dangers of theophylline, but which are not within the Somophyllin Oral Liquid files. They state that there is no relevant information within the cromolyn sodium product files.

It appears clear that no conceivable discovery request could have been made by the doctor that would have uncovered the relevant documents, given the above and other responses of the drug company. The objections did not specify that certain documents were not being produced. Instead the general objections were followed by a promise to produce requested documents. These responses did not comply with either the spirit or letter of the discovery rules and thus were signed in violation of the certification requirement.

The drug company does not claim that its inquiry into the records did not uncover the smoking gun documents. Instead, the drug company attempts to justify its responses by arguing as follows: (1) The plaintiffs themselves limited the scope of discovery to documents contained in Somophyllin Oral Liquid *files*. (2) The smoking gun documents were not intended to relate to Somophyllin Oral Liquid, but rather were intended to promote another product of the drug company. (3) The drug company produced all of the documents it agreed to produce or was ordered to produce. (4) The drug company's failure to produce the smoking gun documents resulted from the plaintiffs' failure to specifically ask for those documents or from their failure to move to compel production of those documents. (5) Discovery is an adversarial process and good lawyering required the re-sponses made in this case.

If the discovery rules are to be effective, then the drug company's arguments must be rejected.

First, neither the child nor the doctor limited the scope of discovery in this case. Attorneys for the child, the doctor and the drug company repeatedly referred to both theophylline and Somophyllin Oral Liquid. There was no clear indication from the drug company that it was limiting all discovery *regarding* Somophyllin Oral Liquid to material from that product's file. Nor was there any indication from the drug company that it had information about theophylline, which is not a Fisons' "product", or information *regarding* Somophyllin Oral Liquid that it was not producing because the information was in another product's file. The doctor was justified in relying on the statements made by the drug company's attorneys that all relevant documents had been produced and he cannot be determined to have impliedly, albeit unknowingly, acquiesced in limiting the scope of discoverable information.

Second, the drug company argues that the smoking gun documents and other documents relating to theophylline were not documents *regarding* Somophyllin Oral Liquid because they were intended to market another product. No matter what its initial purpose, and regardless of where it had been filed, under the facts of this case, a document that warned of the serious dangers of the primary ingredient of Somophyllin Oral Liquid is a document *regarding* Somophyllin Oral Liquid.

Third, the discovery rules do not require the drug company to produce only what it agreed to produce or what it was ordered to produce. The rules are clear that a party must *fully* answer all interrogatories and all requests for production, unless a specific and clear objection is made. If the drug company did not agree with the scope of production or did not want to respond, then it was required to move for a protective order. In this case, the documents requested were relevant. The drug company did not have the option of determining what it would produce or answer, once discovery requests were made.

Fourth, the drug company further attempts to justify its failure to produce the smoking guns by saying that the requests were not specific enough. Having read the record herein, we cannot perceive of *any* request that could have been made to this drug company that would have produced the smoking gun documents. Unless the doctor had been somehow specifically able to request the June 30, 1981, "dear doctor" letter, it is unlikely that the letter would have been discovered. Indeed the drug company claims the letter was not an official "dear doctor" letter and therefore was not required to be produced.

Fifth, the drug company's attorneys claim they were just doing their job, that is, they were vigorously representing their client. The conflict here is between the attorney's duty to represent the client's interest and the attorney's duty as an officer of the court to use, but not abuse the judicial process. . . .

Like CR 11, CR 26(g) makes the imposition of sanctions mandatory, if a violation of the rule is found. Sanctions are warranted in this case. What the sanctions should be and against whom they should be imposed is a question that cannot be fairly answered without further factual inquiry, and that is the trial court's function. While we recognize that the issue of imposition of sanctions upon attorneys is a difficult and disagreeable task for a trial judge, it is a necessary one if our system is to remain accessible and responsible. . . .

The trial court's denial of sanctions is reversed and the case is remanded for a determination of appropriate sanctions.

CASE QUESTIONS

1. In what way were Fison's discovery responses misleading?
2. Why couldn't Fisons's counsel state an objection to a request and then state that Fisons would comply with only the part of the request to which it did not object?
3. Did the court find that the conduct of Fisons's counsel violated the standards of practice for lawyers in the relevant field and area?

PROBLEM 16–10

Try to articulate the reasoning of Fisons's lawyers. What were they thinking?

Both *Qualcomm* and *Fisons* imply an important corollary to the practical rule that the more you do not want to cite a case the more important it is that you cite it: Aside from legitimate privilege or work product issues, the more you do not want to produce a document the more important it is that you produce it.

3. INTRODUCING PERJURIOUS TESTIMONY

Model Rule 3.3(a)(3) forbids you from offering testimony you know to be false and requires you to take steps to remedy the introduction of testimony you did not know was false when given but later learn to have been false. Remediation may require disclosure to a tribunal, and this obligation trumps the confidentiality requirements of Rule 1.6. The remediation obligation continues until a matter is over. A lawyer may refuse to offer evidence he or she reasonably believes (but does not know) to be false, unless the evidence is the testimony of a defendant in a criminal case. The following chart illustrates these points, with a couple of additions to take account of variations in state law.

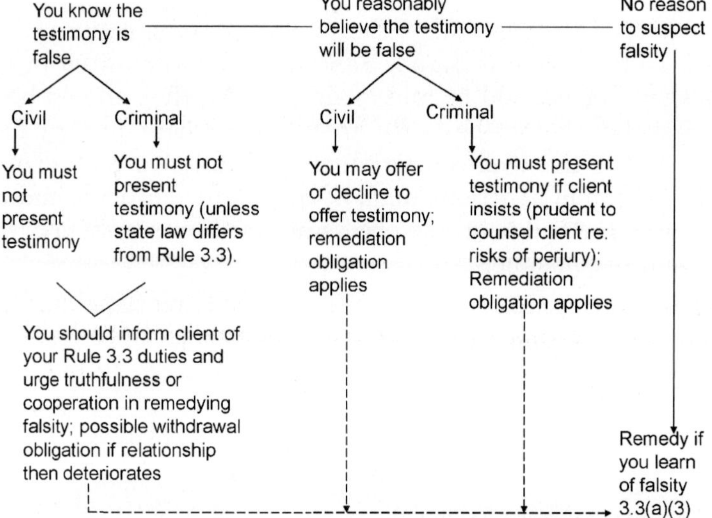

The chart creates a continuum based on your knowledge. The choices range from cases where you know proffered testimony to be false to cases in which you reasonably believe testimony to be false but do not actually know that it is false, to cases where you have no reason to know testimony is false. The latter case is the easiest because if you have no reason to disbelieve your client's testimony you would not and could not do anything to stop it. Your obligation in that case is limited to an obligation to remedy the introduction of testimony you later learn was false, as required by Rule 3.3(a)(3).

At the other end of the continuum, where you know testimony to be false, the Rule forbids you from introducing it in either a civil or criminal case. The chart divides the two because some states allow criminal defendants to "testify in the narrative," a procedure in which the defendant testifies but the lawyer does not ask him or her questions and does not argue the false testimony to the jury. The procedure is not common in civil cases (indeed, the author knows of no cases where it has been allowed). The first case below, *People v. Johnson,* endorses this narrative approach and surveys the possible solutions to the perjury problem. States that allow narrative testimony likely will not require lawyers to disclose to a tribunal that the client has committed perjury, so the endorsement of the narrative approach likely relieves lawyers of their obligation to remedy the testimony.[15] (Comment 7 to Rule 3.3 states the obligations of the rule are subordinate to such local rules.)

In the middle of the continuum, you have good reason to believe the client's testimony will be false but you do not actually know it will be false. Rule 3.3(a)(3) provides that you "may refuse" to offer such evidence "other than the testimony of a defendant in a criminal matter." The chart therefore divides your choices in civil and criminal cases.

What if only part of your client's testimony would be false? Comment 6 to Rule 3.3 states "[i]f only a portion of a witness's testimony will be false, the lawyer may call the witness to testify but may not elicit or otherwise permit the witness to present the testimony that the lawyer knows is false." The Rule offers no guidance on how you should refuse to permit a client to testify while on the stand, particularly without destroying the client's credibility with respect to matters as to which the client testifies truthfully.

The net result of these rules is that choices are arrayed from left to right; with one exception the farther to the left a choice is the less likely it is that you will have to try a case involving evidence you know or believe to be false. Rule 3.3 forbids you to introduce false evidence in any case; civil cases are on the left because the narrative approach probably will not be used in such cases. Criminal cases are one step to the right because some states allow narrative testimony. Civil cases in which you believe but do not know evidence to be false are one step further to the right because you have discretion to decline to introduce evidence in such cases. You have no such discretion in criminal cases where you reasonably be-

---

[15] Massachusetts Rule of Professional Conduct 3.3(e) is illustrative. It provides in relevant part:

> If a criminal trial has commenced and the lawyer discovers that the client intends to testify falsely at trial, the lawyer need not file a motion to withdraw from the case if the lawyer reasonably believes that seeking to withdraw will prejudice the client. If, during the client's testimony or after the client has testified, the lawyer knows that the client has testified falsely, the lawyer shall call upon the client to rectify the false testimony and, if the client refuses or is unable to do so, the lawyer shall not reveal the false testimony to the tribunal. In no event may the lawyer examine the client in such a manner as to elicit any testimony from the client the lawyer knows to be false, and the lawyer shall not argue the probative value of the false testimony in closing argument or in any other proceedings, including appeals.

lieve but do not know testimony to be false, and that category is therefore to the right of civil cases. The net result in that category is the same as in the last set of cases, where the issue of introducing false testimony does not come up because you have no reason to think the evidence is false. You are not free from the Rule in such cases, however, because the remediation obligation covers each category of cases (with the probable exception of states that allow narrative testimony).

The following materials elaborate on these rules.

Model Rule of Professional Conduct 3.3
Restatement (Third) of the Law Governing Lawyers § 120

PEOPLE V. JOHNSON

62 Cal.App.4th 608 (1998)

KREMER, PRESIDING JUSTICE.

Anthony L. Johnson was convicted of numerous violent sexual offenses, kidnappings and robberies. He was sentenced to 5 consecutive life terms plus 440 years. On appeal, he contends he was denied his right to testify in his own defense. . . . We conclude the court erred in denying Johnson his constitutional right to testify but find the error harmless beyond a reasonable doubt. . . . .

FACTS

The evidence shows Johnson kidnapped, robbed and committed brutal sexual offenses against seven different women over a period of several years. Six of the offenses involved a distinctive modus operandi of approaching the victim very late at night as she was getting out of her car or shortly thereafter,forcing her back into the driver's seat while the assailant sat in the back seat, threatening to kill the victim if she did not obey, directing her to drive the car only a short distance (i.e., a matter of blocks), having her park the car and then pulling her into the back seat where he sexually assaulted her. . . .

Two of the victims identified Johnson in a line-up. DNA evidence recovered in five of the cases matched Johnson with a random match probability of 1 in 3,600,000. Additionally, Johnson's fingerprints were recovered from two of his victim's vehicles, including one of the two cases where no DNA evidence was recovered. As to the one remaining victim where there was neither DNA nor fingerprint evidence, blood testing indicated Johnson could not be excluded as a donor of the sperm found in the victim and a pubic hair with characteristics similar to Johnson's pubic hair was found in the victim's car.

Johnson did not present any evidence except a stipulation that, if called to the stand, a police detective would testify he interviewed a witness who saw a person matching the description of the victim who was attacked near the college campus followed by a Black man (Johnson is Black) but did not pay much attention to them as they both appeared to be "homeless types."

We set out in more detail the circumstances surrounding his denial of his right to testify. At trial, after the prosecution had completed its case-in-chief, defense counsel requested and was granted an in camera hearing. Johnson was present during the in-chambers conference. Defense counsel told the court he had "an ethical conflict" with Johnson about Johnson's desire to take the stand and testify. Defense counsel explained, "I cannot disclose to the court privileged communications relating to that, but I'm in a position where I am not willing to call Mr. Johnson as a witness despite his desire to testify." In response to the court's question, Johnson indicated defense counsel had accurately described the situation and defense counsel indicated he would "[n]ot voluntarily" call Johnson as a witness.

The court, misunderstanding the situation, told Johnson that his attorney had decided it was not in Johnson's "best interest to testify" and confirmed Johnson wanted to testify. The following exchange then occurred:

> "[DEFENSE COUNSEL]: Judge, this is not a trial tactic issue. This is an ethical conflict. If it were just a trial tactic, you know, in other words, a decision of what's the best choice, I always defer to the client's wishes in circumstances like this.
>
> "THE COURT: What exactly are you trying to tell me . . . that you won't examine him if he takes the stand?
>
> "[DEFENSE COUNSEL]: I think under the—based upon the information I have, I would be ethically barred from calling him as a witness under the law as I have come to know it and very specifically researched it regarding this particular issue.
>
> "THE COURT: Okay. [¶] It's always very difficult for a trial judge based on my experience at least to sit in on these. It is like having both your hands tied behind your back because you have to make a decision. If your call based on what you know is that you have an ethical problem that will compel you not to call him and that that's over his objection, then I'll note it for the record. He will not be called—
>
> "[DEFENSE COUNSEL]: That's fine.
>
> "THE COURT:—Based on that. And we'll go forward. And you have in essence done everything you are required to do as an attorney by placing it on the record. And at this point in time I'm going to have to

> abide by it because you're the one that's making the call on the ethical issue.
>
> "[DEFENSE COUNSEL]: Yes. I just want to be clear that this isn't a judgment situation that falls in the realm of a trial tactic. It's more than that.
>
> "THE COURT: All right. [¶] I will note, then, that you believe that there are ethical reasons, strong ethical reasons, apparently, because otherwise we wouldn't be sitting in here right now,—
>
> "[DEFENSE COUNSEL]: Correct.
>
> "THE COURT:—That cause you to come to the conclusion that you cannot under any circumstances call the client. And I will note that. And I will note that it's over his objection, and that he desires to testify."

Johnson did not testify.

. . . . There has been much scholarly discussion of what an attorney should do when faced with a client who intends to commit perjury. Solutions range from the attorney providing full cooperation to his client in presenting the testimony to the attorney refusing to permit his client to testify. Intermediate solutions include persuading the client to not testify falsely, disclosing the perjurious intent to the court, making a motion to withdraw, or allowing the defendant to testify in a "free narrative" fashion. We examine these various options.

1. Full Cooperation with Presenting Defendant's Testimony even when Defendant Intends to Commit Perjury

Professor Freedman argues an attorney should fully cooperate with putting on his client's testimony even when the client intends to commit perjury. . . . Professor Freedman argues the importance of client confidentiality and, as well, the attorney's duty to provide effective representation by gathering all necessary information are more important than an attorney's duty to be candid with the court. Therefore, Professor Freedman argues defense counsel must sometimes permit his client to commit perjury and be prepared to argue the client's perjurious testimony to the jury.

No court has endorsed this view. Freedman's approach has also been much criticized by the legal commentators because it conflicts with legal ethics rules prohibiting an attorney from knowingly participating in presenting perjured testimony as well as rules requiring an attorney to disclose a client's intention to commit a crime. (See, e.g., Collett, *Understanding Freedman's Ethics* (1991) 33 Ariz. L.Rev. 455; Lefstein, *Client Perjury in Criminal Cases: Still in Search of an Answer* (1988) 1 Geo. J. Legal Ethics 521, 524–525.) One commentator has stated, "Freedman's approach may seem practical. However, in practice, a lawyer's use of this approach may likely end in disciplinary action." (Liskov, *Criminal Defendant Perjury: A Lawyer's Choice Between Ethics, the Constitution and the Truth* (1994) 28 New Eng. L.Rev. 881, 905.)

2. Persuading the Client not to Commit Perjury

All the legal commentators agree that when faced with a client who indicates he will commit perjury, an attorney should first attempt to persuade the client to testify truthfully. The United States Supreme Court has held an attorney acted consistently with professional rules of ethics and did not deny the defendant the right to effective assistance of counsel by persuading the defendant not to commit perjury. (*Nix v. Whiteside, supra,* 475 U.S. 157, 169 ["at a minimum the attorney's first duty when confronted with a proposal for perjurious testimony is to attempt to dissuade the client from the unlawful course of conduct"].)

The persuasion solution, when it succeeds, is the ideal solution since it involves neither the presentation of perjured testimony nor disclosure of client confidences. Yet, it does not answer the question of what should be done when the client insists on testifying falsely despite his attorney's best efforts to dissuade him.

3. Withdrawal From Representation

The Model Rules and Model Code provide an attorney should make a motion to withdraw from representation when the representation will result in a violation of law or rules of professional conduct. (Model Rules, rule 1.16(a)(1); Model Code, DR 2–110(B)(2); Cal. Rules of Prof. Conduct, rule 3–700(B)(2),(C)(1)(b) & (c).) In the California case of *People v. Brown* (1988) 203 Cal.App.3d 1335, 1339–1340, footnote 1, the court, in reliance on the California ethical rules for attorneys, stated that if an attorney is unable to dissuade his client from committing perjury, "the attorney must make a motion to withdraw so as to not give implied consent to the use of perjurious testimony." The court stated, "When faced with a criminal defendant who insists on testifying perjuriously, it is clearly appropriate under California law, even necessary, for counsel to present a request to withdraw to the court."

This approach, while it protects the attorney's interest in not presenting perjured testimony, does not solve the problem. The court may deny the motion to withdraw. Even if the motion to withdraw is granted, the problem remains. As the court stated in *People v. Gadson* (1993) 19 Cal.App.4th 1700, 1710, footnote 5:

> "[W]e note that permitting defense counsel to withdraw does not necessarily resolve the problem. That approach could trigger an endless cycle of defense continuances and motions to withdraw as the accused informs each new attorney of the intent to testify falsely. Or the accused may be less candid with his new attorney by keeping his

> perjurious intent to himself, thereby facilitating the presentation of false testimony. Lastly, there is the unfortunate possibility that the accused may find an unethical attorney who would knowingly present and argue the false testimony. Thus, defense counsel's withdrawal from the case would not really solve the problem created by the anticipated perjury but, in fact, could create even more problems."

One court has described the withdrawal solution as an "ostrich-like approach" which does little to resolve the problem.

4. *Disclosure to the Court*

Another alternative is that the attorney should disclose the perjury to the court. Initially, we note that some of the other proposed solutions involve some disclosure, i.e., implicit in solutions of making a motion to withdraw or having the defendant testify in a narrative manner is, at least, an implicit disclosure to the court that the attorney believes the defendant may commit perjury. Disclosure has been criticized because it compromises the attorney's ethical duty to keep client communications confidential and results in a significant conflict of interest between the attorney and his client if the attorney discloses to the court that the defendant has perjured himself. (See Silver, *Truth, Justice, and the American Way: The Case Against Client Perjury Rules, supra,* 47 Vand. L.Rev. 339, 415–418.) Additionally, until the defendant actually takes the stand and testifies falsely, there is always a chance the defendant will change his mind and testify truthfully. Finally, disclosure is only a partial solution. If the disclosure occurs before the defendant has taken the stand, the disclosure will require some additional action, i.e., a decision as to whether the defendant's statement is, in fact, false and a further decision whether the defendant will be permitted to testify and in what form and manner. Disclosure before the defendant testifies could result in a mini-trial on the perjury issue before the defendant has had the opportunity to take the stand and testify truthfully.

5. *The Narrative Approach*

Under the narrative approach, the attorney calls the defendant to the witness stand but does not engage in the usual question and answer exchange. Instead, the attorney permits the defendant to testify in a free narrative manner. In closing arguments, the attorney does not rely on any of the defendant's false testimony.

In the early 1970's, the American Bar Association adopted the narrative approach in its Project on Standards for Criminal Justice, Standards Relating to the Defense Function. Standard 7.7 provided:

"Testimony by the defendant.

"(a) If the defendant has admitted to his lawyer facts which establish guilt and the lawyer's independent investigation establishes that the admissions are true but the defendant insists on his right to trial, the lawyer must advise his client against taking the witness stand to testify falsely.

"(b) If, before trial, the defendant insists that he will take the stand to testify falsely, the lawyer must withdraw from the case, if that is feasible, seeking leave of the court if necessary.

"(c) If withdrawal from the case is not feasible or is not permitted by the court, or if the situation arises during the trial and the defendant insists upon testifying falsely in his own behalf, the lawyer may not lend his aid to the perjury. Before the defendant takes the stand in these circumstances, the lawyer should make a record of the fact that the defendant is taking the stand against the advice of counsel in some appropriate manner without revealing the fact to the court. The lawyer must confine his examination to identifying the witness as the defendant and permitting him to make his statement to the trier or the triers of the facts; the lawyer may not engage in direct examination of the defendant as a witness in the conventional manner and may not later argue the defendant's known false version of facts to the jury as worthy of belief and he may not receive or rely upon the false testimony in his closing argument." (See *People v. Guzman* (1988) 45 Cal.3d 915, 944, fn. 8.)

This standard, adopting the free narrative approach "was not included in the 1980 second edition of the ABA Standards for Criminal Justice (hereafter ABA Standards). The editorial note to that edition explained, 'the question of what should be done in situations dealt with by the standard has been deferred until the ABA Commission on Evaluation of Professional Standards reports its final recommendations.' In the 1983 Model Rules of Professional Conduct, standard 7.7 was rejected by rule 3.3 (lawyer has duty to disclose falsity of evidence, even if disclosure compromises client confidences.)" (*People v. Guzman, supra,* 45 Cal.3d 915, 944, fn. 8.)

The narrative approach has been criticized on the basis the attorney participates in committing a fraud on the court. (See *Stephenson v. State* (1993) 206 Ga.App. 273, 275, fn. 1 [appellant's "suggestion he should have been permitted to testify in narrative form would constitute the attorney's participation in fraud, and thus is no answer"].) The narrative approach has also been criticized as communicating to the jury that the defendant is committing perjury. One court has stated, "This procedure could hardly have failed to convey to the jury the impression that the defendant's counsel attached little significance or credibility to the testimony of the witness, or that the defendant and his counsel were at odds. Prejudice to the defendant's case by this trial tactic was inevitable." (*State v. Robinson* (1976) 290 N.C. 56, 67.). . . .

6. *Refusing to Permit the Defendant to Testify*

The opposite extreme from Professor Freedman's solution of full cooperation by the attorney in presenting the defendant's testimony is a refusal to permit the defendant to testify at all. This solution is justified by the theory that an attorney has an ethical obligation not to participate in the presentation of perjured testimony and the defendant has no right to commit perjury.

Preclusion of the testimony as a solution has been criticized because it essentially substitutes defense counsel for the jury as the judge of witness credibility; it puts the determination of whether the defendant is telling the truth or a lie into the hands of defense counsel. (See Rifkin, *The Criminal Defendant's Right to Testify: The Right to Be Seen But Not Heard* (1989) 21 Colum. Hum. Rts. L.Rev. 253, 272.) Further, under this approach, a determination is made that the defendant will commit perjury before he has even taken the witness stand. As we noted before, until the defendant is actually on the stand, there is always the possibility the defendant will change his mind and testify truthfully. (See, e.g., *Nix v. Whiteside, supra,* 475 U.S. 157 [defendant told his attorney he would testify falsely, but once on the stand, he testified truthfully].) Further, a determination of whether the defendant will commit perjury may result in a mini-trial, with the attorney essentially "testifying" against the defendant. Finally, this approach, while safeguarding the attorney's ethical obligations not to participate in presenting perjured testimony, results in a complete denial of the defendant's right to testify. . . .

8. *The Narrative Approach Represents the Best Accommodation of the Competing Interests*

None of the approaches to a client's stated intention to commit perjury is perfect. Of the various approaches, we believe the narrative approach represents the best accommodation of the competing interests of the defendant's right to testify and the attorney's obligation not to participate in the presentation of perjured testimony since it allows the defendant to tell the jury, in his own words, his version of what occurred, a right which has been described as fundamental, and allows the attorney to play a passive role.

In contrast, the two extremes—fully cooperating with the defendant's testimony and refusing to present the defendant's testimony—involve no accommodation of the conflicting interests; the first gives no consideration to the attorney's ethical obligations, the second gives none to the defendant's right to testify. The other intermediate solutions—persuasion, withdrawal and disclosure—often result in no solution, i.e., the defendant is not persuaded, the withdrawal leads to an endless chain of withdrawals and disclosure compromises client confidentiality and typically requires further action.

We disagree with those commentators who have found the narrative approach necessarily communicates to the jury that defense counsel believes the defendant is lying. As was pointed out in *Gadson,* the jury may surmise the "defendant desired to testify unhampered by the traditional question and answer format." (*People v. Guzman, supra,* 45 Cal.3d 915, 946.) Because the defendant in a criminal trial is not situated the same as other witnesses, it would not be illogical for a jury to assume that special rules apply to his testimony, including a right to testify in a narrative fashion. We do not believe the possibility of a negative inference the defendant is lying should preclude the use of the narrative approach since the alternative would be worse, i.e., the attorney's active participation in presenting the perjured testimony or exclusion of the defendant's testimony, neither of which strikes a balance between the competing interests involved.

The danger that the defendant may testify falsely is mitigated by the fact that the defendant is subject to impeachment and can be cross-examined just like any other witness. The jury is no less capable of assessing the defendant's credibility than it is of any other witness. As the Supreme Court stated in [*Rock v. Arkansas,* 483 U.S. 44, 52 (1987):] "Like the truthfulness of other witnesses, the defendant's veracity, which was the concern behind the original common-law rule, can be tested adequately by cross-examination." Further, to preclude the defendant's testimony entirely based on a possibility that defendant may lie, deprives the jury of making that assessment and may deprive the jury of hearing other, nonperjurious evidence to which the defendant would have testified about had he been given the opportunity. In utilizing the narrative approach, the jury has the benefit of hearing the defendant's version.

The narrative approach also avoids having a pre-perjury hearing, a mini-trial on whether the defendant might commit perjury if called to the stand; a hearing which could result in the attorney testifying against the client and which would require the court to be able to see into the future and determine that an individual who has stated only an intention to testify falsely (at least as according to his attorney) will actually testify falsely once on the witness stand.

We further note that not only has the narrative approach received approval in California but it has also been approved by several other jurisdictions. . . . We conclude the narrative approach best accommodates the competing interests of the defendant's constitutional right to testify and the attorney's ethical obligations.

9. The Trial Court's Solution

The trial court here followed the solution of excluding the defendant's testimony on the basis counsel had an "ethical conflict" with calling Johnson as a witness because, presumably, Johnson would commit perjury.

The trial court's approach, i.e., of precluding Johnson's testimony based only on his attorney's assertion of an "ethical conflict," attempted an impossible task, i.e., to determine, as a matter of fact, that Johnson would perjure himself once he took the stand. This is an impossible task since there is always the possibility a defendant will bc persuaded by counsel's arguments and testify truthfully. Further, the defendant's allegedly false testimony may not be a matter of "perjury" but of having remembered additional details upon further reflection; the change in the defendant's intended story may be the result of an effort to be more truthful.

Moreover, the trial court's approach substitutes the defendant's attorney for the jury as the trier of fact and determiner of witness credibility. . . The trial court's approach precluded the jury from hearing additional evidence, i.e., Johnson's version of the events. While Johnson's version may have been false (at least in part), it is the jury's function to determine the credibility of witnesses. Like other witnesses, Johnson's veracity could have been tested through cross-examination. . . .

Finally, we note that in California, no statutes, judicial decisions or ethical rules require preclusion of a defendant's testimony when the attorney believes or "knows" a client will commit perjury. California case law has approved of the narrative approach, which avoids the problems of prior factual determinations by defense counsel (and/or the court) that the defendant will commit perjury, allows a defendant to exercise his constitutional right to testify, permits defense counsel to play a passive role and places the factfinding and credibility determinations with the jury as should be the case. . . .

We conclude the trial court erred in denying Johnson his constitutional right to testify. The trial court should have followed the narrative approach, which has been approved by the courts in California and which would have best accommodated the conflicting interests of Johnson and his defense counsel. . . .

We conclude that while the trial court erred in precluding Johnson from testifying, based on the record we have before us on appeal, the error was harmless beyond a reasonable doubt.

What Do You Know II

In *Commonwealth v. Mitchell,* 438 Mass. 535, 545–46 (2003), the court noted that courts have adopted various standards to determine whether counsel "knows" a client plans perjury. These include:

> "good cause to believe the defendant's proposed testimony would be deliberately untruthful," *State v. Hischke,* 639 N.W.2d 6, 10 (Iowa 2002); "compelling support," *Sanborn v. State,* 474 So.2d 309, 313 n. 2 (Fla.Dist.Ct.App.1985); "knowledge beyond a reasonable doubt," *Shockley v. State,* 565 A.2d 1373, 1379 (Del.1989); a "firm factual basis," *United States ex rel. Wilcox v. Johnson,* 555 F.2d 115, 122 (3d Cir.1977); a "good-faith determination," *People v. Bartee,* 208 Ill.App.3d 105, 108, *cert. denied,* 502 U.S. 1014 (1991); and "actual knowledge," *United States v. Del Carpio–Cotrina,* 733 F.Supp. 95, 99 (S.D.Fla.1990) (applying "actual knowledge" standard to require firm factual basis).

The court rejected the "beyond a reasonable doubt" standard on the ground that the standard "is virtually impossible to satisfy unless the lawyer had a direct confession from his client or personally witnessed the event in question." The *Mitchell* court adopted a test under which counsel "knows" of intended client perjury if counsel acts "in good faith based on objective circumstances firmly rooted in fact."

In contrast to *Mitchell*, in *State v. McDowell*, 272 Wis.2d 488 (2004), the Wisconsin Supreme Court held that "an attorney may not substitute narrative questioning for the traditional question and answer format unless counsel knows that the client intends to testify falsely. Absent the most extraordinary circumstances, such knowledge must be based on the client's expressed admission of intent to testify untruthfully. While we recognize that the defendant's admission need not be phrased in 'magic words,' it must be unambiguous and directly made to the attorney." Similarly, comment 8 to Rule 3.3 states that lawyers "should resolve doubts about the veracity of testimony or other evidence in favor of the client" but not "ignore an obvious falsehood."

In *People v. Bolton*, 166 Cal.App.4th 343 (2008), the defendant, Bolton, was accused of beating a man on a trolley and beating and stabbing a man who came to help the first victim. There were several witnesses to these events. As trial approached Bolton told his lawyer, Cline, that he had acted in self-defense because one of the victims had wielded a razor. Bolton had not mentioned this to Cline before and no witness or other evidence corroborated this claim.

Cline concluded that Bolton planned to perjure himself and asked to be relieved from the case on the ground that he had a conflict of interest with Bolton. Cline was relieved and Bolton then chose to represent himself at trial rather than wait longer for a trial date. Bolton was convicted and appealed on the ground that his waiver of the right to counsel was coerced by decision to excuse Cline.

The court of appeal agreed. It held that,

> [w]hile Cline may have doubted Bolton's claim that one of the victim's had a razor blade, Cline did not *know* that this was false . . . even if Cline suspected that Bolton might testify falsely, requesting to be relieved as Bolton's counsel under these circumstances was not the appropriate method of dealing with the ethical concerns Cline may have had. "Although attorneys may not present evidence they know to be false or assist in perpetrating known frauds on the court, they may ethically present evidence that they suspect, but do not personally know, is false. Criminal defense attorneys sometimes have to present evidence that is incredible and that, not being naive, they might personally disbelieve. Presenting incredible evidence may raise difficult tactical decisions—if counsel finds evidence incredible, the fact finder may also—but, as long as counsel has no specific undisclosed factual knowledge of its falsity, it does not raise an ethical problem." (*People v. Riel* (2000) 22 Cal.4th 1153, 1217 (*Riel*).)

The court went on to reaffirm *Johnson* and held that Cline should have allowed Bolton to testify in the narrative.

PROBLEM 16–11

The defendant in *McDowell* was convicted of several counts of sexual assault at gunpoint. Evidence at trial showed that, with an accomplice who pleaded guilty, the defendant followed the victim off a bus and pushed her into an alley. As a result of the assault, a mixture of genetic material from the victim and the defendant was left at the crime scene. The police preserved a sample of this mixture, and DNA testing linked it to the defendant.

At trial, the defendant denied assaulting the victim. He testified that the previous night he had engaged in sexual conduct with his girlfriend at the same location in the alley, and that this conduct explained the presence of his genetic material at the scene. Suppose you represented McDowell and that he told you that he planned to relate this account in his testimony. Would you "know" he intended to perjure himself? Which of the standards mentioned above support which answer?

PROBLEM 16–12

Suppose you represent a client accused of sexually assaulting a woman after a party. The woman was drinking and taking drugs at the party at which your client was present. She went home with her boyfriend, but they quarreled. He left, leaving open the door to her home. Distraught and somewhat dizzy, the woman went to her bedroom and lay down on the bed. She heard a noise at the door. Thinking it was her boyfriend returning to apologize, she called out that she is in her bedroom. Your client enters the house and rapes the woman.

You know from your client that he did in fact rape the woman. May you use the true facts that (i) the woman was drinking and taking drugs at the party; (ii) went home with a man not her husband; and (iii) called your client back to her bedroom to argue either that she mistakenly identified your client as the rapist or (more likely given forensic evidence) that she consented to have sex with your client? *See* Eleanor W. Myers & Edward D. Ohlbaum, *Discrediting the Truthful Witness: Demonstrating the Reality of Adversary Advocacy*, 69 FORD. L. REV. 1059 (2000).

4. THE OBLIGATION TO CORRECT

Comment 10 to Rule 3.3 states that when you learn you have offered false evidence you should talk to the client confidentially, urge that the client withdraw or correct the false testimony, and advise the client of your duty of candor to the court and your corresponding obligation to remedy the false testimony. If none of that gains the client's cooperation, you are to "make such disclosure to the tribunal as is reasonably necessary to remedy the situation," even if doing so requires disclosures otherwise prohibited by Rule 1.6. This guidance is clear enough but leaves open some potentially important questions. For example, how quickly must you act? Consider the following example of that problem.

IDAHO STATE BAR V. WARRICK

137 Idaho 86 (2002)

WALTERS, JUSTICE.

This is an attorney disciplinary case. Steven Warrick appeals from a decision rendered by the Professional Conduct Board of the Idaho State Bar ("ISB") finding that Warrick violated Idaho Rule of Professional Conduct ("I.R.P.C") 4.4(a) concerning expressions of bias and I.R.P.C. 3.3(a)(4), relating to presentation of false evidence. We uphold the Board's findings. We impose on Warrick a sanction of thirty days suspension from the practice of law. We further order that Warrick pass the Multistate Professional Responsibility Examination as a condition for reinstatement to active practice. Finally, we award costs to the ISB for this proceeding. . . .

Steven Warrick was admitted to the practice of law in Idaho in 1983. He was elected as the Elmore County Prosecutor in 1996 and served until April 1, 1998. As such, Warrick was in charge of prosecuting Ronald E. Calfee, a.k.a. Ted Hulsey Hungate ("Calfee") for one count of felony trafficking of methamphetamine, a case from which both counts of Warrick's alleged misconduct stem.

On February 3, 1998, a jury trial for Calfee was vacated at the request of Calfee's attorney, Mr. Purviance, on the ground that the State had failed to timely disclose a witness, Scott Spaulding, whom the State intended to call during the trial. The hearing to vacate Calfee's trial followed disclosure by a deputy prosecutor that Spaulding had entered into a plea agreement in exchange for his testimony against Calfee. . . .

On March 3, 1998, Calfee's trial began before a jury with District Judge Michael R. McLaughlin presiding. Warrick called Spaulding as his second witness. After Warrick asked a few introductory questions, Spaulding's testimony in front of the jury proceeded as follows:

> Q. Now, just as a preliminary matter, you are currently incarcerated, sir?
>
> A. Yes, sir, I am.
>
> Q. And what is—what have you been charged with?
>
> A. I've been charged with multiple felonies leading to four counts of Delivery, one count of having something to do with child endangerment, and then Possession of a Controlled Substance, I believe.
>
> Q. Okay. And why is it that you've chosen to testify in this matter?
>
> A. Because I'm wishing to kind of like turn my life around and get away from all of this, and I feel this is a good place for me to start.
>
> Q. Are you receiving any sort of break or any sort of break in terms of your own prosecution because of this?
>
> A. Very little, from what I understand.
>
> On cross-examination by defense counsel, Spaulding testified as follows:
>
> Q. And what sort of deal have you worked out with the State to testify here today?
>
> A. At this point, nothing.
>
> Q. Okay. The State hasn't offered you any sort of break in your sentencing or anything like that to testify?
>
> A. No, sir, nothing will be guaranteed me. I came forward on my own free will.

The prosecutor, Warrick, conducted re-direct examination but did not inquire further about the plea agreement and then excused Spaulding as a witness.

Later that afternoon, Spaulding's arraignment was held before Judge McLaughlin. Spaulding pled guilty to four of nine felony counts and five were dismissed at the recommendation of the deputy prosecutor. Judge McLaughlin inquired as to when the plea bargain had been presented to and accepted by Spaulding. He was advised by the deputy prosecutor that the plea agreement had been negotiated a month previously. Judge McLaughlin then placed the State on notice that Spaulding's testimony given to the jury earlier that day at Calfee's trial was contrary to what was being presented at Spaulding's arraignment. Mr. Purviance, Calfee's defense counsel, was also present at Spaulding's arraignment and, based upon what transpired at the hearing, immediately prepared and filed that afternoon a motion to dismiss the charges against Calfee . . .

When Warrick found out that the motion to dismiss had been filed and that Spaulding had entered guilty pleas pursuant to the plea agreement, Warrick met with Spaulding that evening to discuss testimony for Calfee's trial the next morning. Warrick planned to re-call Spaulding as a witness and to disclose the terms of the plea agreement that had been omitted from Spaulding's earlier testimony during Calfee's jury trial.

The next morning, the second day of Calfee's trial, the district court heard Calfee's motion to dismiss. Warrick disclosed that he was prepared to have Spaulding retake the stand and testify as to the terms of the plea agreement. However, the district court granted the motion to dismiss and ended Calfee's trial without further testimony. . . .

As a result of the incidents in Elmore County, complaints against Warrick were filed with the Idaho State Bar. The ISB proceeded with a formal disciplinary action. . . . Count II of the complaint alleged Warrick violated I.R.P.C. 3.3(a)(4), 3.8(d), 8.4(c) and 8.4(d) for failing to take reasonable remedial measures when his witness, Spaulding, gave false testimony in the criminal matter that Warrick was prosecuting against Ronald Calfee. . . . [Warrick and the ISB each moved for summary judgment. The Board found that factual issues precluded summary judgment on count II.]

Warrick contends that he complied with I.R.P.C. 3.3(a)(4) because he did not knowingly offer false testimony when Spaulding was called as a witness in Calfee's trial. Warrick argues that once he became aware of the false testimony, he proceeded to undertake reasonable steps to correct the situation, and he intended to call Spaulding the next morning of the trial to remedy Spaulding's testimony. Further, Warrick asserts that the duty to take remedial measures lasts throughout the duration of a trial.

ISB argues that it did not charge Warrick with intentionally offering false testimony. Rather, ISB asserts that it charged Warrick with allowing false testimony to be presented without taking any measures to correct the testimony at the time the testimony was presented. ISB contends that the rule contemplates that the lawyer take remedial measures at the time he comes to know of the falsity, not the next day or before the end of trial. The rule, in pertinent part, is as follows:

> Rule 3.3—Candor Toward the Tribunal
>
> (a) A lawyer shall not knowingly:
>
> . . .
>
> (4) offer evidence that the lawyer knows to be false. If a lawyer has offered material evidence and comes to know of its falsity, the lawyer shall take reasonable remedial measures.
>
> (b) The duties stated in paragraph (a) continue to the conclusion of the proceeding, and apply even if compliance requires disclosure of information otherwise protected by Rule 1.6.

The Board found Warrick knew that a plea bargain had been offered to Spaulding whereby five of nine felony counts would be dismissed, in return for his testimony against Calfee. The Board further found that "during the presentation of Spaulding's testimony at the trial of Calfee, Steven Warrick failed to correct Spaulding's denial of the plea agreement which he knew was false." Warrick disputes that he was aware of the falsity of Spaulding's testimony at the time the evidence was presented. He submits that he was not paying attention to the testimony given and was focusing on the next set of questions he was going to ask Spaulding. Warrick further represents that had he realized Spaulding had testified falsely, he would have used leading questions to elicit the information.

Warrick asserts that he did not know of the falsity of Spaulding's testimony until a fellow prosecutor alerted him after Spaulding's arraignment before Judge McLaughlin in the afternoon following the close of the first day of Calfee's trial, when the circumstances of the plea bargain were disclosed, and the district court put the State on notice that false testimony had been presented in Calfee's trial. Warrick's arguments, however, are unavailing. The Board found that he knew Spaulding's testimony was false at the time it was presented, and the Board's findings are supported by the record.

Warrick contends that once he became aware of the false testimony given by Spaulding, he took reasonable remedial measures to correct the testimony. Warrick visited Spaulding in the jail following his arraignment, and planned to call Spaulding to the witness stand the next morning. Warrick argues that he was prepared to correct Spaulding's testimony on the second day of trial, however, a mistrial was granted before the remedial testimony could be presented.

Again, Warrick's arguments are misplaced because they ignore the factual finding by the Board concerning the timing when Warrick knew Spaulding's testimony was false. He knew it was false when the testimony was presented, and at that time he did not take any action to correct the testimony. Waiting until after the district judge and defense counsel learned the testimony was false was not reasonable.

This Court holds that Warrick did not take reasonable remedial measures to correct Spaulding's testimony. Warrick thereby violated I.R.P.C. 3.3(a)(4).

As a sanction covering both violations [including the Rule 4.4 violation, *see* chapter 12], the Court holds that Warrick should be suspended from practicing law in Idaho for a period of thirty days. This Court further concludes that Warrick must also take and pass the Multistate Professional Responsibility Examination prior to being reinstated to actively practice law in the state of Idaho.

CASE QUESTIONS

1. To avoid sanctions, when should Warrick have acted?
2. What should he have done?

Model Rule 3.3(a)(3)'s requirement that you remedy false testimony applies to pre-trial perjury as well as trial testimony. The rule also trumps the disciplinary rule requiring that you preserve client confidences. *E.g. In re Disciplinary Action against John E. Mack*, 519 N.W.2d 900 (1994) (illustrating both points). The court's opinion provides an important caution against waiting too long to remediate perjury, which may happen when an attorney (likely a senior attorney) says, in substance, "well take care of that at trial." There may never be a trial and, even if there is, an opponent may prove the perjury first, at which point no amount of protesting is likely to persuade a court that counsel would in fact have taken action when the time came. As the court put it in this case, had the client "not broken down on cross-examination during the trial, her lie probably would never have been revealed. Hence, Mack's silence was tantamount to acquiescence to the deception."

Both Warrick and Mack violated Rule 3.3 by failing to take remedial action soon enough. Warrick should not have let the hearing at which the perjured testimony was offered end without correcting the perjury. Mack should have corrected the perjury no later than on direct examination and, in fact, before trial. In each case, allowing the testimony to enter the record allowed someone else to reveal the perjury and, once that had happened, nothing Warring or Mack did counted as remedying perjury within the meaning of Rule 3.3. The courts and disciplinary officials quite reasonably suspected that waiting so long implied that the lawyers would have let the perjured testimony stand if they thought they could get away with it.

PROBLEM 16–13

The language of Rule 3.3 states that lawyers shall not make or fail to correct false statements of fact, and shall not "offer" false evidence. What if your client lies at a deposition and your opponent offers the evidence at trial? What if your client lies on cross-examination?

PROBLEM 16–14

Suppose you learn an expert witness retained by your opponent lied at his deposition. May you stay quiet, allow him to lie again on direct examination at trial, and then surprise the opposition by revealing the perjury on cross-examination? *See Flynn v. Edmonds*, 236 Ill.App.3d 770 (1992) (Illinois Rules).

PROBLEM 16–15

Why shouldn't counsel be able to help a client testify falsely? What is wrong with that? If the answer is that counsel should strive for truth rather than falsity, should defense attorneys be allowed to use only those arguments and tactics that are reasonably likely to find out the truth?

PROBLEM 16–16

Thinking dynamically, what does Rule 3.3 imply for your initial meetings with a client? How might you structure a conversation to both meet your need for information and avoid the formal strictures of the rule?

5. CLIENT PERJURY AND THE *STRICKLAND* STANDARD

Suppose a client wants to perjure himself and his criminal defense lawyer (1) tells him not to (and that perjury itself is illegal); and (2) tells him that counsel has a duty to inform the tribunal of perjured testimony. The client testifies truthfully and is convicted. On appeal, he argues that his lawyer's acts violated the standard of care followed by ordinarily competent criminal defense attorneys and that there was a reasonable probability that, but for counsel's actions, the defendant would have had a better result at trial. You will recognize these as the two elements of an ineffective assistance of counsel claim under *Strickland v. Washington*, 466 U.S. 668 (1984). Will the client's arguments succeed?

No. The Court answered this question in *Nix v. Whiteside*, 475 U.S. 157 (1986). Whiteside was convicted of second-degree murder for stabbing Calvin Love to death; the context was a drug deal in Love's apartment. Whiteside told his appointed lawyer, Gary Robinson, that he thought Love was reaching under his pillow (Love was stabbed in bed) to get a gun. At first Whiteside told Robinson he had not seen a gun but genuinely believed that Love had one. Later, however, Whiteside told Robinson that he felt he had no chance unless he testified that he saw a gun in Love's hand. No gun was found at the scene, and no witness saw a gun, though Love's relatives removed his things from the apartment soon after the murder.

Robinson told Love that he could assert a valid self-defense claim even if Love had no gun. Shortly before trial, however, Love told his lawyers that he had seen "something metallic" in Love's hand. When pressed, he said: "If I don't say I saw a gun, I'm dead." Robinson cautioned Whiteside that it would be perjury to offer this testimony, and reiterated that it was not necessary to claim self-defense. He also told Whiteside that

> " '[W]e could not allow him to [testify falsely] because that would be perjury, and as officers of the court we would be suborning perjury if we allowed him to do it; . . . I advised him that if he did do that it would be my duty to advise the Court of what he was doing and that I felt he was committing perjury; also, that I probably would be allowed to attempt to impeach that particular testimony.' "
>
> Robinson also indicated he would seek to withdraw from the representation if Whiteside insisted on committing perjury."

Whiteside testified that he "knew" Love had a gun and believed Love was reaching for it when Whiteside stabbed him. After he was convicted and exhausted his state appeals, Whiteside petitioned for a writ of habeas corpus, arguing that Robinson's refusal to allow him to testify about the metallic object denied him the effective assistance of counsel. The Eighth Circuit accepted for purposes of argument that this testimony would have been perjury but reversed the conviction. It reasoned that even a client intending to perjure himself has a right to counsel, and Robinson's statement that he would reveal the intended perjury to the court violated standards of effective representation with regard to confidentiality. It further reasoned that Robinson had a conflict between his own ethical duties and Whiteside's interests, thus satisfying the prejudice requirement under the more lenient conflict of interest standard.

The Supreme Court reversed. Excerpts from the opinions follow:

* * *

In *Strickland,* we recognized counsel's duty of loyalty and his "overarching duty to advocate the defendant's cause." *Ibid.* Plainly, that duty is limited to legitimate, lawful conduct compatible with the very nature of a trial as a search for truth. Although counsel must take all reasonable lawful means to attain the objectives of the client, counsel is precluded from taking steps or in any way assisting the client in presenting false evidence or otherwise violating the law.. . . .

It is universally agreed that at a minimum the attorney's first duty when confronted with a proposal for perjurious testimony is to attempt to dissuade the client from the unlawful course of conduct. . . .

The commentary thus also suggests that an attorney's revelation of his client's perjury to the court is a professionally responsible and acceptable response to the conduct of a client who has actually given perjured testimony. Similarly, the Model Rules and the commentary, as well as the Code of Professional Responsibility adopted in Iowa, expressly permit withdrawal from representation as an appropriate response of an attorney when the client threatens to commit perjury. Withdrawal of counsel when this situation arises at trial gives rise to many difficult questions including possible mistrial and claims of double jeopardy. . . . [16]

Considering Robinson's representation of respondent in light of these accepted norms of professional conduct, we discern no failure to adhere to reasonable professional standards that would in any sense make out a deprivation of the Sixth Amendment right to counsel. Whether Robinson's conduct is seen as a successful attempt to dissuade his client from committing the crime of perjury, or whether seen as a "threat" to withdraw from representation and disclose the illegal scheme, Robinson's representation of Whiteside falls well within accepted standards of professional conduct and the range of reasonable professional conduct acceptable under *Strickland*. . . .

The Court of Appeals' holding that Robinson's "action deprived [Whiteside] of due process and effective assistance of counsel" is not supported by the record since Robinson's action, at most, deprived Whiteside of his contemplated perjury. Nothing counsel did in any way undermined Whiteside's claim that he believed the victim was reaching for a gun. . . .

---

[16] FN6. In the evolution of the contemporary standards promulgated by the American Bar Association, an early draft reflects a compromise suggesting that when the disclosure of intended perjury is made during the course of trial, when withdrawal of counsel would raise difficult questions of a mistrial holding, counsel had the option to let the defendant take the stand but decline to affirmatively assist the presentation of perjury by traditional direct examination. Instead, counsel would stand mute while the defendant undertook to present the false version in narrative form in his own words unaided by any direct examination. This conduct was thought to be a signal at least to the presiding judge that the attorney considered the testimony to be false and was seeking to disassociate himself from that course. Additionally, counsel would not be permitted to discuss the known false testimony in closing arguments. See ABA Standards for Criminal Justice, Proposed Standard 4–7.7 (2d ed. 1980). Most courts treating the subject rejected this approach and insisted on a more rigorous standard, see, *e.g., United States v. Curtis,* 742 F.2d 1070 (CA7 1984); *McKissick v. United States,* 379 F.2d 754 (CA5 1967); *Dodd v. Florida Bar,* 118 So.2d 17, 19 (Fla.1960). The Eighth Circuit in this case and the Ninth Circuit have expressed approval of the "free narrative" standards. *Whiteside v. Scurr,* 744 F.2d 1323, 1331 (CA8 1984); *Lowery v. Cardwell,* 575 F.2d 727 (CA9 1978).

The Rule finally promulgated in the current Model Rules of Professional Conduct rejects any participation or passive role whatever by counsel in allowing perjury to be presented without challenge.

Paradoxically, even while accepting the conclusion of the Iowa trial court that Whiteside's proposed testimony would have been a criminal act, the Court of Appeals held that Robinson's efforts to persuade Whiteside not to commit that crime were improper, *first,* as forcing an impermissible choice between the right to counsel and the right to testify; and, *second,* as compromising client confidences because of Robinson's threat to disclose the contemplated perjury.

Whatever the scope of a constitutional right to testify, it is elementary that such a right does not extend to testifying *falsely*. . . . Robinson's admonitions to his client can in no sense be said to have forced respondent into an *impermissible* choice between his right to counsel and his right to testify as he proposed for there was no *permissible* choice to testify falsely. For defense counsel to take steps to persuade a criminal defendant to testify truthfully, or to withdraw, deprives the defendant of neither his right to counsel nor the right to testify truthfully. . . .

Since there has been no breach of any recognized professional duty, it follows that there can be no deprivation of the right to assistance of counsel under the *Strickland* standard.

We hold that, as a matter of law, counsel's conduct complained of here cannot establish the prejudice required for relief under the second strand of the *Strickland* inquiry. . . . Whether he was persuaded or compelled to desist from perjury, Whiteside has no valid claim that confidence in the result of his trial has been diminished by his desisting from the contemplated perjury. Even if we were to assume that the jury might have believed his perjury, it does not follow that Whiteside was prejudiced.

In his attempt to evade the prejudice requirement of *Strickland,* Whiteside relies on cases involving conflicting loyalties of counsel. In *Cuyler v. Sullivan,* 446 U.S. 335 (1980), we held that a defendant could obtain relief without pointing to a specific prejudicial default on the part of his counsel, provided it is established that the attorney was "actively represent[ing] conflicting interests."

Here, there was indeed a "conflict," but of a quite different kind; it was one imposed on the attorney by the client's proposal to commit the crime of fabricating testimony without which, as he put it, "I'm dead." This is not remotely the kind of conflict of interests dealt with in *Cuyler v. Sullivan.* Even in that case we did not suggest that all multiple representations necessarily resulted in an active conflict rendering the representation constitutionally infirm. If a "conflict" between a client's proposal and counsel's ethical obligation gives rise to a presumption that counsel's assistance was prejudicially ineffective, every guilty criminal's conviction would be suspect if the defendant had sought to obtain an acquittal by illegal means. Can anyone doubt what practices and problems would be spawned by such a rule and what volumes of litigation it would generate?

Whiteside's attorney treated Whiteside's proposed perjury in accord with professional standards, and since Whiteside's truthful testimony could not have prejudiced the result of his trial, the Court of Appeals was in error to direct the issuance of a writ of habeas corpus and must be reversed.

Reversed.

Justice Blackmun, with whom Justice Brennan, Justice Marshall, and Justice Stevens join, concurring in the judgment.

How a defense attorney ought to act when faced with a client who intends to commit perjury at trial has long been a controversial issue. But I do not believe that a federal habeas corpus case challenging a state criminal conviction is an appropriate vehicle for attempting to resolve this thorny problem. When a defendant argues that he was denied effective assistance of counsel because his lawyer dissuaded him from committing perjury, the only question properly presented to this Court is whether the lawyer's actions deprived the defendant of the fair trial which the Sixth Amendment is meant to guarantee. Since I believe that the respondent in this case suffered no injury justifying federal habeas relief, I concur in the Court's judgment. . . .

In light of respondent's failure to show any cognizable prejudice, I see no need to "grade counsel's performance." *Strickland v. Washington,* 466 U.S., at 697. The only federal issue in this case is whether Robinson's behavior deprived Whiteside of the effective assistance of counsel; it is not whether Robinson's behavior conformed to any particular code of legal ethics.

Whether an attorney's response to what he sees as a client's plan to commit perjury violates a defendant's Sixth Amendment rights may depend on many factors: how certain the attorney is that the proposed testimony is false, the stage of the proceedings at which the attorney discovers the plan, or the ways in which the attorney may be able to dissuade his client, to name just three. The complex interaction of factors, which is likely to vary from case to case, makes inappropriate a blanket rule that defense attorneys must reveal, or threaten to reveal, a client's anticipated perjury to the court. Except in the rarest of cases, attorneys who adopt "the role of the judge or jury to determine the facts," *United States ex rel. Wilcox v. Johnson,* 555 F.2d 115, 122 (CA3 1977), pose a danger of depriving their clients of the zealous and loyal advocacy required by the Sixth Amendment.

I therefore am troubled by the Court's implicit adoption of a set of standards of professional responsibility for attorneys in state criminal proceedings. . . . It is for the States to decide how attorneys should conduct themselves in state criminal proceedings, and this Court's responsibility extends only to ensuring that the restrictions a State enacts do not infringe a defendant's federal constitutional rights. Thus, I would follow the suggestion made in the joint brief *amici curiae* filed by 37 States at the certiorari stage that we allow the States to maintain their "differing approaches" to a complex ethical question. The signal merit of asking first whether a defendant has shown any adverse prejudicial effect before inquiring into his attorney's performance is that it avoids unnecessary federal interference in a State's regulation of its bar. Because I conclude that the respondent in this case failed to show such an effect, I join the Court's judgment that he is not entitled to federal habeas relief.

Justice Stevens, concurring in the judgment.

Justice Holmes taught us that a word is but the skin of a living thought. A "fact" may also have a life of its own. From the perspective of an appellate judge, after a case has been tried and the evidence has been sifted by another judge, a particular fact may be as clear and certain as a piece of crystal or a small diamond. A trial lawyer, however, must often deal with mixtures of sand and clay. Even a pebble that seems clear enough at first glance may take on a different hue in a handful of gravel.

As we view this case, it appears perfectly clear that respondent intended to commit perjury, that his lawyer knew it, and that the lawyer had a duty—both to the court and to his client, for perjured testimony can ruin an otherwise meritorious case—to take extreme measures to prevent the perjury from occurring. The lawyer was successful and, from our unanimous and remote perspective, it is now pellucidly clear that the client suffered no "legally cognizable prejudice."

Nevertheless, beneath the surface of this case there are areas of uncertainty that cannot be resolved today. A lawyer's certainty that a change in his client's recollection is a harbinger of intended perjury—as well as judicial review of such apparent certainty—should be tempered by the realization that, after reflection, the most honest witness may recall (or sincerely believe he recalls) details that he previously overlooked. Similarly, the post-trial review of a lawyer's pretrial threat to expose perjury that had not yet been committed—and, indeed, may have been prevented by the threat—is by no means the same as review of the way in which such a threat may actually have been carried out. Thus, one can be convinced—as I am—that this lawyer's actions were a proper way to provide his client with effective representation without confronting the much more difficult questions of what a lawyer must, should, or may do after his client has given testimony that the lawyer does not believe. The answer to such questions may well be colored by the particular circumstances attending the actual event and its aftermath.

Because Justice Blackmun has preserved such questions for another day, and because I do not understand him to imply any adverse criticism of this lawyer's representation of his client, I join his opinion concurring in the judgment.

United States v. Williams, 698 F.3d 374 (7th Cir. 2012), presents a fascinating variation on this issue. Dennis Ryan represented Corvet Williams, who was accused of armed bank robbery. Williams was in prison. He sent Ryan an envelope marked "legal mail" (so that it would not be opened by prison officials). Inside the envelope was a sealed letter addressed to a cousin of Williams and a note asking Ryan to forward the letter to the cousin. Suspicious, Ryan opened the letter, which asked the cousin to provide a false alibi for Williams. Ryan moved to withdraw from the case, gave the letter to the government, and agreed to testify against Williams at trial. Williams was convicted and contended on appeal that he received ineffective assistance of counsel because of Ryan's actions. (He made no complaint against the lawyer who replaced Ryan.)

The Seventh Circuit rejected this claim. It noted that Williams' letter constituted the crime of attempt to suborn perjury and held that Ryan's disclosure was permissible under the ethics rule in force at the time he acted (derived from the ABA Model Code, rather than the subsequent Model Rules). The court was not persuaded that Ryan should have attempted to dissuade Williams from suborning perjury before disclosing Williams' attempt. Writing for the majority, Judge Posner reasoned:

> Had Williams's lawyer merely refused to forward the letter, Williams might have found a different means of conveying his unlawful request to his family (maybe orally in jail to a visiting family)—perhaps with instructions to find someone other than the cousin to be the false alibi witness, someone the lawyer had never heard of and therefore would have no basis for refusing to call as a witness. Facing a possible sentence of more than 50 years for the bank robberies and having already attempted to suborn perjury, Williams was unlikely to hearken to an ethics lecture by his lawyer. . . This was not a case in which a client tells the lawyer that he would like to give testimony that the lawyer knows is a lie, and the lawyer tells him he must not do so and is confident the client will obey. Williams took a substantial step toward procuring a false witness and having embarked on that course had other means of reaching his destination even if the lawyer prevented the cousin from testifying. In such a case a lawyer is allowed to exercise discretion concerning whether to withdraw from representing the defendant and report the defendant's crime of attempting to suborn perjury.

Judge Hamilton dissented, reasoning that

> [T]here is a clear professional consensus on two central points. First, before a lawyer discloses the client's confidences, the lawyer has an obligation, where practicable, to try to convince the client to change course. If the persuasion is not successful and the lawyer seeks to

withdraw, the lawyer may or may not have to disclose the reasons for doing so. If the lawyer decides or is required to disclose the client's confidences, the second point of consensus is that the lawyer has an obligation to do so in a way that minimizes harm to the client. Lawyer Ryan failed to adhere to both of these standards and denied Williams the effective assistance of counsel. . . Recall that the standard for a lawyer's disclosure of client confidences is *necessity*. That's true under every relevant version of Rules 1.6(b) and 3.3.(b). Disclosure here could not have been *necessary* unless and until Ryan tried and failed to persuade Williams to change course. . . At a minimum, then, in this case Ryan should have told Williams that he had read the letter, advised against perjury, warned Williams that he would disclose the information to the court if necessary, and asked Williams about his intentions. Only if he was not satisfied with Williams's answer should he have asked the court for leave to withdraw. If he provided the court an explanation at all, it should have been filed under seal so the prosecutor would not see it. The duties of loyalty and confidence required at least this degree of effort to protect his client, even from his own criminal stupidity.

PROBLEM 16–17

Which opinion in *Williams* do you find more persuasive? Why?

The Rashomon Problem In Legal Ethics

United States v. Williams may be read as illustrating a general problem relevant to legal ethics: What you see depends a great deal on where you stand on issues implicated by your observations. Judge Posner is best known for his facility with economic issues rather than criminal law. It is fair to read his opinion as working from the premise that the point of a criminal proceeding is to determine whether they accused did in fact commit a crime (or, in some possible cases, whether a crime was committed).

From this perspective the point of the proceeding is not to reward the best advocate or provide lawyers a forum to realize their conception of state accountability to law, so that a defendant who attempts to undermine the accuracy of the process deserves harsh treatment and a lawyer who blows the whistle on the attempt deserves no condemnation. Judge Posner gives the back of his hand to the notion that the lawyer might have talked Williams out of suborning perjury; he treats as naive romanticism the notion that lawyers can trump rational, self-interested behavior by clients.

This perspective may be jarring to one accustomed to thinking of a defense attorney as the legal protector of a defendant and to thinking of a fair trial as a fair fight rather than merely as one that gets the right person. (Note that the *Strickland* case law tends to vacillate between these conceptions of a fair trial.) From this perspective things Judge Posner seems to dismiss as romantic indulgences seem central to the defense lawyer's role. The result is significant clash on premises, not just conclusions.

There are many different practice communities and things accepted as common or perhaps fundamental in one community may appear odd or perverse from a different perspective. It follows that any action you take may be viewed from very different normative perspectives and will appear different from each of those perspectives, yet you nevertheless must act if you are to serve your clients and pay your bills. The trick is to acknowledge that fact, and take it into account when necessary, without succumbing to paralysis.

The Main Points to Recall From Chapter 16 Are:

- You may not introduce testimony you know to be perjured. You must introduce criminal testimony you only suspect to be perjured, but may decline to introduce such testimony in a civil case.
- If you have unknowingly introduced perjured testimony and learn that fact later you must take reasonable steps to remedy the introduction of such testimony.
- You may not lie about the facts or law to a tribunal, or fail to cite controlling authority you know is adverse to your position.
- You may not use litigation to blackmail or extort others, or seek an advantage collateral to the claims asserted.

CHAPTER 17

PROBLEMS FOR BUSINESS LAWYERS

■ ■ ■

Law school employs the case method and much of law school focuses on the resolution of disputes through litigation. Comparatively little emphasis is placed on problems facing transactional lawyers, who use contract law, negotiating skills, and knowledge of particular regulatory environments to guide their clients through a variety of business deals. Such lawyers often have to deal with conflict of interest issues, both between clients and, if they do business with clients, between the client's interest and their own. They tend not to face problems such as preserving evidence or contacting unrepresented parties, and they rarely if ever encounter problems of improper argument or candor to a tribunal (unless they do so as witnesses).

Transactional lawyers also face some problems litigators rarely encounter, and this chapter surveys some of those problems. The materials are arranged chronologically, covering formation of an entity, litigation, and insolvency. The main point of the chapter is that the entity client principal is clear in theory but may be hard to follow in practice. That is especially true at the beginning and end of a company's life.

With respect to formation, transactional lawyers often deal with promoters who are putting ideas together with capital. Such lawyers work to create an entity and, if they succeed, their work is deemed to have been on behalf of the entity all the time. Things are more complicated if the entity is never formed. With respect to litigation, an exception to the attorney-client privilege recognized in many states allows plaintiffs in a derivative action to obtain privileged communications if they can show their claims are colorable (i.e., pass some not-very-well-defined threshold of merit). With respect to corporations in financial distress, entity lawyers must be sensitive to the interests of creditors, who may have standing to assert derivative claims for breach of duties owed to insolvent entities.

A. ENTITY FORMATION

Model Rule of Professional Conduct 1.13
Restatement of the Law Governing Lawyers § 96

JESSE V. DANFORTH

169 Wis.2d 229 (1992)

DAY, JUSTICE.

This is a review of a published decision of the court of appeals that reversed a non-final order of the Circuit Court for Milwaukee County, William J. Haese, Judge, which denied defendants Drs. Danforth's and Ullrich's motions to disqualify DeWitt, Porter, Huggett, Schumacher & Morgan, S.C. (DeWitt) as plaintiffs' counsel.

The issue in this case is whether a conflict of interest exists such that DeWitt should be disqualified from representing plaintiffs in their medical malpractice action against defendants. Because we find no conflict of interest to exist, we hold that the DeWitt firm should not be disqualified from representing plaintiffs in their action against the defendants. We therefore reverse the court of appeals and remand the cause to the circuit court for reinstatement of the DeWitt firm as plaintiffs' counsel.

Defendants Drs. Danforth and Ullrich are involved in several entities that own and operate sophisticated and expensive diagnostic tools, as well as entities that provide medical services. The relationship between these entities is complex.

Neurodiagnostic Associates is a division of Neurosurgical Specialists, S.C. Both are defendants in this case. Neurodiagnostic Associates is a partnership formed in 1975 to own and operate a computerized axial tomography scanning machine (CAT). The CAT scanner was subsequently sold to Dr. Ullrich who, in turn, leased it to Neurodiagnostic Associates. Drs. Danforth and Ullrich are both partners in Neurodiagnostic Associates.

In 1985, a group of twenty-three physicians, including Drs. Danforth and Ullrich, retained Attorney Douglas Flygt (Flygt) of DeWitt to assist them in creating a corporate entity for the purpose of purchasing and operating a magnetic resonance imaging (MRI) machine. An MRI scanner is currently the most advanced radioimaging technology and is an improvement on the previously available CAT scanner.

Flygt incorporated MRI Associates of Greater Milwaukee (MRIGM) in January, 1986 and continues as its corporate counsel. The twenty-three physicians, including Drs. Danforth and Ullrich, became the shareholders of MRIGM and Dr. Danforth became its president. Dr. Danforth was, and is, the main contact of DeWitt with MRIGM. In 1987, MRIGM formed a service corporation and elected subchapter S treatment under the Internal Revenue Code which permits a qualified small business corporation and its shareholders to elect to be taxed as a partnership while retaining the benefits of a corporation.

MRIGM is a general partner in Milwaukee Magnetic Resonance Consortium, which owns and operates a free-standing MRI facility in Milwaukee, and a partner in MRI Physicians of Greater Milwaukee, which provides the professional services at Milwaukee Magnetic Resonance Consortium. Neither MRIGM, Milwaukee Magnetic Consortium, nor MRI Physicians of Greater Milwaukee are parties to this action.

In May 1988, plaintiffs retained Attorney Eric Farnsworth (Farnsworth), of DeWitt, to represent them in a medical malpractice action against defendants. After consulting with the Jesse family, Farnsworth conducted an internal conflicts check that apparently did not list Drs. Danforth or Ullrich as clients. Farnsworth filed an initial summons and complaint as well as several amended summons and complaints.

The complaints allege, *inter alia,* that defendants were negligent for failing to obtain a tomography of sufficient quality or resolution to accurately serve as a diagnostic tool. The CAT scanner employed for plaintiff Jesse was allegedly the one owned by Dr. Ullrich which he leased to Neurodiagnostic Associates. Plaintiffs allege that Neurodiagnostic Associates made the CAT scanner available in the course of plaintiff's treatment and charged a fee to plaintiff Jesse. Plaintiffs further allege that a portion of that fee was shared with, or refunded to, defendants as a financial incentive for them to utilize the machine.

Drs. Danforth and Ullrich moved for disqualification of the DeWitt firm alleging a conflict of interest. On May 21, 1990, Judge Haese, ruling from the bench, denied the motions for disqualification and awarded DeWitt statutory costs. A written order denying the motions was subsequently issued. Drs. Danforth and Ullrich appealed, and on July 16, 1991, the court of appeals issued its decision reversing the circuit court's order. We granted petitioners' petition for review and now reverse the court of appeals.

We begin with SCR 20:1.7, the conflict of interest rule. Subsection (a) states: "A lawyer shall not represent a client if the representation of that client will be directly adverse to another, unless. . . . " Thus, the question is, who did or does DeWitt represent, *i.e.,* who were and are DeWitt's clients?

It is undisputed that DeWitt, through Farnsworth, represents Jean Jesse in this case. What remains disputed is whether Drs. Danforth or Ullrich were ever or are currently clients of DeWitt.

Defendants argue that Drs. Danforth and Ullrich are clients of the DeWitt firm due to Flygt's pre-incorporation representation of the twenty-three physicians and due to other advice provided to Drs. Danforth and Ullrich by Flygt. Defendants argue that, under SCR 20:1.7, DeWitt's representation of the plaintiffs is "directly adverse" to DeWitt's representation of defendants Drs. Danforth and Ullrich and therefore a conflict of interest exists disqualifying the DeWitt firm from representing plaintiffs.

Defendants argue that one must look to the facts of each particular case to determine whether an attorney-client relationship exists. Defendants cite to and quote affidavits and documents, discussed later in this opinion, which, to them, show that Drs. Danforth and Ullrich were DeWitt's clients.

Plaintiffs argue that DeWitt never represented Drs. Danforth or Ullrich. They readily concede that DeWitt, through Flygt, originally incorporated MRIGM and that Flygt remains corporate counsel to MRIGM. However, plaintiffs assert that DeWitt's representation of MRIGM does not translate into representation of its shareholders.

Plaintiffs argue, under the "entity rule," as expressed by SCR 20:1.13, that where a firm represents a corporate organization, the organization, not the shareholders, is the lawyer's client. Therefore, plaintiffs argue that DeWitt's representation of MRIGM does not equate with representation of Drs. Danforth or Ullrich. Plaintiffs conclude that because DeWitt never represented Drs. Danforth or Ullrich, there is no conflict of interest.

We conclude that the entity rule does extend to Drs. Danforth and Ullrich such that DeWitt's pre-incorporation involvement with Drs. Danforth and Ullrich is properly characterized as representation of MRIGM, not Drs. Danforth or Ullrich, *i.e.,* DeWitt's client was and is MRIGM, not Drs. Danforth or Ullrich.

The entity rule contemplates that where a lawyer represents a corporation, the client is the corporation, not the corporation's constituents. First, the title of the section is demonstrative, it states, "*Organization* as Client." (Emphasis added). Second, subsection (a) states, "A lawyer employed or retained by an organization *represents the organization* acting through its duly authorized constituents." (Emphasis added). Third, subsection (d) states, "In dealing with an organization's . . . constituents, a lawyer shall explain the identity of the client when it is apparent that the organization's interests are adverse to those of the constituents with whom the lawyer is dealing." This clearly implies it is the organization, not the constituent that is the lawyer's client. Fourth, subsection (e) begins, "A lawyer representing an organization may also represent any of its . . . constituents. . . . " The use of the phrase "may also represent" implies that the lawyer does not automatically represent the constituent when he or she represents the corporate entity. Fifth, the Comment to SCR 20:1.13 states in part:

> When one of the constituents of an organizational client communicates with the organization's lawyer in that person's organizational capacity, the communication is protected by Rule 1.6 [Confidentiality

> of Information]. Thus, by way of example, if an organizational client requests its lawyer to investigate allegations of wrongdoing, interviews made in the course of that investigation between the lawyer and the client's employees or other constituents are covered by Rule 1.6. *This does not mean, however, that constituents of an organizational client are the clients of the lawyer.*

SCR 20:1.13 (emphasis added).

Thus, the clear purpose of the entity rule was to enhance the corporate lawyer's ability to represent the best interests of the corporation without automatically having the additional and potentially conflicting burden of representing the corporation's constituents.

If a person who retains a lawyer for the purpose of organizing an entity is considered the client, however, then any subsequent representation of the corporate entity by the very lawyer who incorporated the entity would automatically result in dual representation. This automatic dual representation, however, is the very situation the entity rule was designed to protect corporate lawyers against.

We thus provide the following guideline: where (1) a person retains a lawyer for the purpose of organizing an entity and (2) the lawyer's involvement with that person is directly related to that incorporation and (3) such entity is eventually incorporated, the entity rule applies retroactively such that the lawyer's pre-incorporation involvement with the person is deemed to be representation of the entity, not the person.

In essence, the retroactive application of the entity rule simply gives the person who retained the lawyer the status of being a corporate constituent during the period before actual incorporation, as long as actual incorporation eventually occurred.

This standard also applies to privileged communications under SCR 20:1.6. Thus, where the above standard is met, communications between the retroactive constituent and the corporation are protected under SCR 20:1.6. And, it is the corporate entity, not the retroactive constituent, that holds the privilege. This tracks the Comment to SCR 20:1.13 which states in part: "When one of the constituents of an organizational client communicates with the organization's lawyer in that person's organizational capacity, the communication is protected by Rule 1.6." *See also Bobbitt v. Victorian House, Inc.,* 545 F.Supp. 1124 (N.D.Ill.1982).

However, where the person who retained the lawyer provides information to the lawyer not directly related to the purpose of organizing an entity, then it is the person, not the corporation which holds the privilege for that communication.

Applying the above standard to the case at hand, we observe that the evidence cited and quoted by the defendants demonstrates that the above standard is met and that DeWitt represented MRIGM, not Drs. Danforth or Ullrich. . . .

Moreover, that MRIGM was eventually incorporated is undisputed.

In addition, with respect to Flygt's advice concerning the structure of the entity, the fact that a particular corporate structure may benefit the shareholders or the fact that there was communication between Flygt and the shareholders concerning such structuring does not mean that Drs. Danforth and Ullrich were the clients of the law firm. Again, the very purpose of the entity rule is to preclude such automatic dual representation.

We are in complete agreement with the circuit court's finding that the services rendered by Flygt were of a corporate nature. The circuit court stated in part:

> At first blush it's difficult for the court to see any conflict except an identity of names. You've got a corporation here consisting of something in excess of 20 doctors. *The services previously rendered were of a corporate nature, advice, counsel given to a number of the doctors that were involved with this corporation and the present lawsuit involves a question of personal malpractice on the part of a person who happens to be a shareholder and member of that firm [corporation].* (Emphasis added).

Drs. Danforth and Ullrich also contend that they provided certain confidential information to attorney Flygt that should disqualify DeWitt under SCR 20:1.6, the confidential information rule. Defendants point to questionnaires Flygt provided to the physicians involved in the MRI project which inquire, in part, as to the physicians' personal finances and their involvement in pending litigation.

Because MRIGM, not the physician shareholders, was and is the client of DeWitt, and because the communications between Drs. Danforth and Ullrich were directly related to the purpose of organizing MRIGM, we conclude that Drs. Danforth or Ullrich cannot claim the privilege of confidentiality.

Dr. Ullrich asserts that there is also a conflict of interest between DeWitt's undisputed representation of MRIGM and DeWitt's undisputed representation of the plaintiffs. We disagree. For a conflict to exist, the representation of one client must be "directly adverse" to the representation of another client. Defendant Ullrich asserts that DeWitt's representation of plaintiff Jesse is directly adverse to DeWitt's representation of MRIGM by arguing that Drs. Danforth and Ullrich could lose their licenses to practice medicine if plaintiff Jesse prevails and MRIGM would face the loss of two of its shareholders and its president. Defendant Ullrich argues that, in light of plaintiffs' "financial incentive" allegations concerning the use of the CAT scanner, prosecution of this case could "mar" MRIGM's reputation and result in an adverse financial impact. Defendant Ullrich argues that DeWitt possesses information that most persons would consider confidential and, if DeWitt is allowed to continue as plaintiff Jesse's counsel, it may be difficult for MRIGM to secure additional shareholders who fear disclosure of such information.

Such possibilities fall short of "direct" adversity. While "directly adverse" and "indirectly adverse" are somewhat nebulous and factually dependent terms, the possible ramifications of DeWitt's representation of plaintiff Jesse are simply insufficient to be characterized as "directly adverse" to DeWitt's representation of MRIGM.

Motions to disqualify are reviewed under the abuse of discretion standard. . . . Our review of the record persuades us that the circuit court did not abuse its discretion. Based on the substantial difference in representing a corporate entity and representing one in an action against some of the shareholders of that entity, and based upon the finding that the services rendered by DeWitt to MRIGM were of a corporate nature, the circuit court's decision was firmly grounded on a reasonable basis. Furthermore, the circuit court's legal conclusion that no conflict of interest existed was correct.

We conclude that the circuit court did not abuse its discretion in denying Drs. Danforth's and Ullrich's motions for disqualification. We therefore reverse the court of appeals and remand the cause to the circuit court to reinstate DeWitt as legal counsel for the plaintiffs.

The decision of the court of appeals is reversed and the cause is remanded to the circuit court for further proceedings not inconsistent with this opinion.

Manion v. Nagin, 394 F.3d 1062, 1064 (8th Cir. 2005), endorsed the rule of *Jesse* but held the plaintiff promoter had alleged an individual attorney-client relationship with entity counsel because the promoter had sought counsel's advice on how the promoter could retain control of the corporation once it was formed as well as advice regarding the promoter's employment contract with the entity. *See also* Arizona Ethics Op. 02–06 ("A lawyer may form a business entity for various individuals and be counsel only for the yet-to-be-formed entity, if appropriate disclosures and consents occur. Alternatively, a lawyer may represent all of the incorporators, collectively, with appropriate disclosures.")

Contracting Around Ethical Default Rules

Jesse holds that if a firm is formed then it will be treated as having been counsel's client all along. The firm itself holds the rights of a client even as to work performed to bring the firm into existence. But what if the parties in a particular case would prefer joint representation, or prefer to have counsel represent only the promoters? The answer is that lawyers and clients can modify the rule in *Jesse* by explicit agreement, subject to the constraints of conflict of interest rules. The decision in *Jesse* can therefore be seen as an ethical "default rule"—a rule that applies unless the parties agree otherwise.

How might this work? Under the court's approach, a promoter would know that counsel would owe her no duties with regard to entity-relevant information once the entity was formed. If a promoter were concerned about the risk that information she disclosed might come back to haunt her, she could contract with formation counsel for joint representation. In that event, counsel would owe her duties throughout the formation period, and she would retroactively become a joint client (but still a client) when the entity was formed. She would have no attorney-client privilege as against the entity, but she would have such a privilege against third parties, such as Jesse, and formation counsel would owe her, individually, a duty of confidentiality. Because counsel would have agreed to represent her individually, these rights would not be divested by the creation of the entity. Problem solved.

Solving this problem could create new problems, of course. The most prominent is the risk of conflicts of interest between a promoter and an entity, or among promoters where there is more than one. In forming an entity promoters will have both complementary and conflicting interests. Creating an entity is presumably a positive-sum game but with respect to any given issue the game may be zero-sum. Only one promoter can be CEO, for example, and stock that does not go to A could go to B.[1] If each promoter sought to reverse the rule in *Jesse* by obtaining individual as well as entity representation, the promoters collectively could create a complex web of conflicts and potential conflicts, which would be costly to navigate. Of course, this problem could be solved if formation counsel informed each promoter of conflicts and potential conflicts, and obtained the informed consent of each promoter to joint representation notwithstanding these conflicts. The conflict problem created by contracting could be solved by contracting.

---

[1] For that reason, some scholars an ethics lawyers advise against joint representation in the formation of a business. Hiring one lawyer per promoter increases transaction costs of formation, however, and if the complementary aspects of the business are strong enough then rational investors should be able to agree on a bargain that benefits all of them. These facts cut strongly against a ban on joint representation in entity formation.

Now suppose the *Jesse* court had gone the other way, and held that formation counsel owes duties to promoters during the pre-formation period. The court would have to specify whether counsel represented some notional "lead" promoters or all promoters, which raises the question whether the court would also imply consent by the promoters to waive any conflicts. Such a rule would be more complex than the one it did adopt, but suppose that problem can be worked out (remember that the court's rule has problems, too). What would happen then?

If formation counsel did not want to be stuck with the obligations of individual representation, she could work around such a rule in a couple of ways. With respect to the sort of conflict at issue in *Jesse*, she could obtain conflict waivers from each promoter, written to allow her to represent future clients who might oppose a promoter.[2] With respect to conflicts among promoters (suppose the Court's rule was ambiguous on that point), she could obtain waivers of confidentiality (in addition to privilege, which is waived among joint clients by default), and of conflicts and potential conflicts of interest, which would at least reduce the risk that conflicts among promoters might force her to withdraw. If promoters can lower costs by using one formation attorney, and the conflicts problem would otherwise prohibit them from doing so, they would have an incentive to sign such waivers. Problem solved again.

Alternatively, if the *Jesse* Court had agreed with Danforth and Ullrich, formation counsel could simply draft a retainer agreement limiting the scope of representation to the promoters' joint interests and disavowing any obligation with respect to the individual interests of any single promoter.[3] If one promoter came up with an individual problem, counsel would have no responsibility for that problem. She would deal with the constituent simply on the basis of implementing with respect to formation whatever decision the constituent reached with regard to the constituent's personal interests.[4] This approach would limit the transaction costs of the joint endeavor and allocate the cost of individual issues to the constituent for whom those issues are relevant. (It also would clean up the sort of ambiguous dual representation the Court created when it said entity counsel would owe promoters a duty of confidentiality with respect to personal information.) Problem solved a third time.

As the Coase Theorem would predict, it seems that it does not matter which rule a court adopts so long as a jurisdiction allows parties to con-

---

[2] Technically, if the default rule were that creation of the entity terminated the attorney-client relationship with the promoters, then the conflict in *Jesse* would be (allegedly) between a current client and a former client. Conflicts in such cases are a problem only if the two matters are substantially related, which the matters in *Jesse* may or may not have been. Prudent entity counsel would obtain waivers with respect to even unrelated matters, however.

[3] Model Rule 1.2(c).

[4] Just as partnership counsel might deal only with partnership matters and leave the individual partners to seek counsel for their individual issues.

tract regarding the scope of representation, waivers of confidentiality, and conflicts. There is still some room for preferring one rule to another, however. Transaction costs in this context are likely to be low but they are not likely to be zero. Waivers of conflicts and confidentiality, and limitations on the scope of representation will cost something. One would therefore still favor the cheapest rule, following the general principle that rules governing entity counsel should lower the sum of agency and other transaction costs.

B. CONFIDENTIALITY AND MISCONDUCT BY ENTITY CONSTITUENTS

As noted in chapter 4.A.6, the duty of confidentiality follows the rule that counsel for an entity represents the entity and not its constituents. It follows that if an employee, officer, or director engages in misconduct that harms or threatens to harm the entity, lawyers must put the entity's interests ahead of those of any of the entity's constituents. That can be a hard rule to follow. The person committing the misconduct might be the lawyer's client contact or someone powerful enough to fight any recommendations a lawyer might make and, perhaps, to win the fight.

Model Rule 1.13(b) and (c) provides the ground rules for such situations. Under these provisions, if you know a constituent is (i) breaching a duty to the entity or breaking the law in a way attributable to the entity; (ii) the conduct is related to your representation; and (iii) threatens substantial harm to the entity; then (iv) you must act in the best interests of the entity and not the constituent. Such action may include (v) taking the matter to entity officials with enough power to take action to protect the entity including, if warranted, the board (reporting up); or (vi) if necessary to protect the entity in the event the highest authority with power to act for it won't act, such action also may include disclosure of confidential information whether or not permitted by Rule 1.6 (reporting out). (Reporting out is not authorized if you are retained to investigate or defend the conduct, however.) Not all states follow these rules. California, for example, does not authorize attorneys to report out if a client persists in misconduct; the duty of confidentiality trumps in such circumstances. Cal. R. Prof'l Conduct 3–600(B).

The Model Rules structure is paralleled by special rules pertaining to lawyers who practice before the Securities and Exchange Commission. Under Section 307 of the Sarbanes–Oxley Act (SOX), the SEC was required to adopt minimum standards of conduct for attorneys practicing before the SEC. This requirement extended to adopting certain specified rules, including one "requiring an attorney to report evidence of a material violation of securities law or breach of fiduciary duty or similar violation."

The SEC's SOX rules are set forth in 17 CFR § 205. The rules apply to attorneys who practice before the commission, which 17 CFR 205.2(a) defines to include (i) transacting business with the SEC, including any form of communication; (ii) representing an issuer in an SEC proceeding; (iii) with respect to a document a lawyer has notice will be filed with the commission, providing advice on the securities laws or commission rules; or (iv) advising an issuer as to whether information must be included with respect to any communication to be submitted to the SEC or incorporated into a submitted document.

The gist of the SOX rules requires a lawyer to report "up the corporate ladder" evidence of misconduct the lawyer discovers if a reasonable investor would consider the evidence important to an investment decision. The rules allow a lawyer voluntarily to report misconduct to the SEC but do not require such reporting.

More particularly, the SOX rules require an attorney practicing before the SEC to report to an issuer's chief legal officer (CLO), or to both that person and the CEO, evidence the lawyer discovers of "a material violation by the issuer or by any officer, director, employee, or agent of the issuer." 17 C.F.R. 205.3(b)(1). "Material violation" includes "a material violation of an applicable United States federal or state securities law, a material breach of fiduciary duty arising under United States federal or state law, or a similar material violation of any United States federal or state law." *Id.* § 205.2(i). (Note that this duty does not extend to violations of foreign laws.)

The SEC defined "evidence of a material violation" awkwardly: "Evidence of a material violation means credible evidence, based upon which it would be unreasonable, under the circumstances, for a prudent and competent attorney not to conclude that it is reasonably likely that a material violation has occurred, is ongoing, or is about to occur." 17 C.F.R. § 205.2(e). The SEC did not define the word "material" but referred to the accepted definition under the securities laws, under which a fact is material if a reasonable person would consider it important in making a decision (i.e., would consider the fact to have altered significantly the total mix of information available to the person). *E.g., Basic, Inc. v. Levinson*, 485 U.S. 224, 231–36 (1988); *TSC Indus. v. Northway, Inc.,* 426 U.S. 438 (1976). The SEC defined breach of fiduciary duty as follows (brackets inserted by the author): "Breach of fiduciary duty refers to any breach of [1] fiduciary or [2] similar duty [3] to the issuer recognized under [4] an applicable federal or state statute or [5] at common law, including but not limited to misfeasance, nonfeasance, abdication of duty, abuse of trust, and approval of unlawful transactions." 17 C.F.R. § 205.2(d)

The reporting obligations differ for supervisory attorneys and for subordinate attorneys. The rules for subordinate attorneys will be most relevant to most law students. The SOX rules define a subordinate attorney as one who practices before the SEC "under the supervision or direction of another attorney" unless the "other attorney" is the CLO of the issuer. A subordinate attorney may comply with the reporting obligation of 17 C.F.R. § 205.3(b) by reporting to his or her supervisory attorney. *Id.* § 205.5(c). Because a lawyer working for the CLO is not a subordinate attorney as defined, he or she cannot satisfy his or her reporting obligation just by reporting to the CLO. Such a lawyer may report to the CLO, of course, but if the CLO does not take action further reporting may be required.

After a subordinate attorney reports misconduct the supervisory attorney to whom she reports is supposed to report the misconduct to the CLO or CEO. The CLO is then supposed to inquire into the facts of the report in a manner reasonably appropriate under the circumstances. If the CLO determines no violation has occurred he or she is supposed to inform the reporting attorney of this determination and of the basis for it. If the CLO determines a violation has occurred, is about to occur, or is continuing, he or she most respond appropriately and inform the reporting attorney of this determination and response. If the CLO does neither of these things in a reasonable time, the reporting attorney must, and a subordinate attorney may, make a further report to the issuers audit committee, any committee comprised solely of outside directors, or the full board. (These rules vary somewhat if the issuer has formed a Qualified Legal Compliance Committee.)

In addition, the Dodd–Frank Wall Street Reform and Consumer Protection Act includes whistleblower incentive provisions pertaining to the Commodities Futures Trading Commission and the Securities Exchange Commission. These provisions require the commissions to award to "any person" voluntarily reporting to the respective commissions information showing violations of law of which the commissions previously were unaware at least 10% (and not more than 30%) of fines collected by the commission based on the report. The incentives apply only if the respective commission prevails in a judicial or administrative action yielding $1 million or more in sanctions. The provision does not require the internal reporting required by the SOX rules. The "any person" language is most naturally read to include lawyers, so this provision may affect lawyers' decisions regarding confidentiality.

C. PRIVILEGE IN DERIVATIVE ACTIONS

A derivative action is a suit brought on behalf of equity holders alleging and seeking to recover for harm to an entity. Such suits typically name officers and directors as defendants, alleging they have breached a duty owed to the entity or caused the entity to engage in unlawful conduct making it liable for damages or penalties. Because equity holders typically do not have management power (at least not as shareholders) but do have a residual interest in the entity, such suits create tension between the principle that equity holders do not manage and the principle that managers owe duties to the entity.

Corporate law rules such as the demand provision and the doctrine of demand excuse attempt to balance these conflicting principles. Some jurisdictions strike a balance with respect to the attorney-client privilege as well. The tension with respect to the privilege is that asserting it is typically a management decision but the entity holds the privilege, and managers may not be faithful to the entity's interests if their own conduct is at issue. The following case presents an influential way of striking a balance between the two interests.

GARNER V. WOLFINBARGER

430 F.2d 1093 (5th Cir. 1970)

GODBOLD, CIRCUIT JUDGE:

This case presents the important question of the availability to a corporation of the privilege against disclosure of communications between it and its attorney, when access to the communications is sought by stockholders of the corporation in litigation brought by them against the corporation charging the corporation and its officers with acts injurious to their interests as stockholders. Also we are asked to review the correctness of an order of the District Court transferring the case to another district.

The District Court in an order reported at 280 F.Supp. 1018 (N.D.Ala.1968), held the privilege was not available as against the stockholders as plaintiffs. . . .

Stockholders of First American Life Insurance Company of Alabama (FAL) brought, in the Northern District of Alabama, a class action alleging violations of the Securities Act of 1933, the Securities Exchange Act of 1934, SEC Rule 10(b)(5), the Investment Company Act of 1940, the Alabama Securities Act and common law fraud, seeking to recover the purchase price which they and others similarly situated paid for their stock in FAL. The defendants are FAL and various of its directors, officers and controlling persons. The plaintiffs also claim that FAL was itself damaged by alleged fraud in the purchase and sale of securities, and they assert against various individual defendants a derivative action on behalf of the corporation.

FAL filed a cross-claim against all other defendants, asserting in its own behalf the rights the plaintiff shareholders had claimed in the derivative aspect of their complaint.

R. Richard Schweitzer served as attorney for the corporation in connection with the issuance of the FAL stock here involved. After the transactions sued upon were complete he became its president. On deposition Schweitzer was asked numerous questions concerning advice given by him to the corporation about various aspects of the issuance and sale of the stock and related matters. Other questions went into the content of discussions at meetings attended by him and company officials and information furnished to him by the corporation. All questions related to times at which Schweitzer acted solely as attorney, before he became an officer of the company and before the filing of suit. Objections were made by counsel for the corporation and by Schweitzer himself that the attorney-client privilege barred his revealing both communications to him by the corporation and the advice which he gave to the corporation.

The plaintiffs had served a subpoena duces tecum on Schweitzer to bring various documents to the taking of his deposition. Both he and the corporation claimed the privilege with respect to some of the documents. The District Court treated the subpoena as though it were a motion to produce under Rule 34.

The District Judge held that the privilege is not available to the corporation as against these plaintiff stockholders. . . .

B. Background and choice of law

Turning to the merits, there is no contention by plaintiffs that FAL is outside the ambit of the attorney-client privilege because a corporation is not a client. Their argument is that the privilege is not available to FAL in the circumstances of this case against the demands of the corporate stockholders for access to the communications. The corporation says that its right to assert the privilege is absolute and of special importance where disclosure is sought in a suit brought by the shareholders against the corporation. The American Bar Association appears as amicus curiae and supports the view of an absolute privilege.

The privilege does not arise from the position of the corporation as a party but its status as a client. However, in this instance plaintiffs deny the availability to the corporation of the otherwise existent privilege because of the role of the corporation as a party defending against claims of its stockholders.

We do not consider the privilege to be so inflexibly absolute as contended by the corporation, nor to be so totally unavailable against the stockholders as thought by the District Court. We conclude that the correct rule is between these two extreme positions. . . .

C. The availability of the privilege

The privilege must be placed in perspective. The beginning point is the fundamental principle that the public has the right to every man's evidence, and exemptions from the general duty to give testimony that one is capable of giving are distinctly exceptional. 8 Wigmore, Evidence, § 2192 at 70. An exception is justified if—and only if—policy requires it be recognized when measured against the fundamental responsibility of every person to give testimony. Id., § 2285 at 527

The policy of the privilege has been plainly grounded since the latter part of the 1700s on subjective considerations. In order to promote freedom of consultation of legal advisers by clients, the apprehension of compelled disclosure by the legal advisers must be removed; hence the law must prohibit such disclosure except on the client's consent. Such is the modern theory. Id., § 2291 at 545.

The problem before us concerns . . . a balancing of interests between injury resulting from disclosure and the benefit gained in the correct disposal of litigation. We consider it in a particularized context: where the client asserting the privilege is an entity which in the performance of its functions acts wholly or partly in the interests of others, and those others, or some of them, seek access to the subject matter of the communications.

It is urged that disclosure is injurious to both the corporation and the attorney. Corporate management must manage. It has the duty to do so and requires the tools to do so. Part of the managerial task is to seek legal counsel when desirable, and, obviously, management prefers that it confer with counsel without the risk of having the communications revealed at the instance of one or more dissatisfied stockholders. The managerial preference is a rational one, because it is difficult to envision the management of any sizeable corporation pleasing all of its stockholders all of the time, and management desires protection from those who might second-guess or even harass in matters purely of judgment.

But in assessing management assertions of injury to the corporation it must be borne in mind that management does not manage for itself and that the beneficiaries of its action are the stockholders. Conceptualistic phrases describing the corporation as an entity separate from its stockholders are not useful tools of analysis. They serve only to obscure the fact that management has duties which run to the benefit ultimately of the stockholders. For example, it is difficult to rationally defend the assertion of the privilege if all, or substantially all, stockholders desire to inquire into the attorney's communications with corporate representatives who have only nominal ownership interests, or even none at all. There may be reasonable differences over the manner of characterizing in legal terminology the duties of management, and over the extent to which corporate management is less of a fiduciary than the common law trustee.

There may be many situations in which the corporate entity or its management, or both, have interests adverse to those of some or all stockholders. But when all is said and done management is not managing for itself.

The representative and the represented have a mutuality of interest in the representative's freely seeking advice when needed and putting it to use when received. This is not to say that management does not have allowable judgment in putting advice to use. But management judgment must stand on its merits, not behind an ironclad veil of secrecy which under all circumstances preserves it from being questioned by those for whom it is, at least in part, exercised.

The District Court relied upon two English cases. . . . Both cases treat the relationship between shareholder and company as analogous to that between beneficiaries and trustees, a basis which the defendants in the present case say has no viability for American corporations. Though not binding precedents, these English cases are persuasive recognition that there are obligations, however characterized, that run from corporation to shareholder and must be given recognition in determining the applicability of the privilege.

Apart from the conceptualism that surrounds the management-stockholder relationship, the ABA alternatively contends . . . that the benefits of disclosure are outweighed by the harm done to both client and attorney. In support of this policy argument, the ABA relies heavily upon In re Prudence Bonds Corp., 76 F.Supp. 643 (E.D.N.Y.1948), which held that a trustee for bondholders in an action for an accounting brought by the bondholders would not be required to produce opinions of counsel rendered to the trustee over a period of eighteen years. That case in turn distinguished the English cases cited above, speculating that the unavailability of the privilege might ultimately harm both attorneys and bondholders.

The ABA urges that the privilege is most necessary where the corporation has sought advice about a prospective transaction, where counsel in good faith has stated his opinion that it is not lawful, but the corporation has proceeded in total or partial disregard of counsel's advice. The ABA urges that the cause of justice requires that counsel be free to state his opinion as fully and forthrightly as possible without fear of later disclosure to persons who might attack the transaction, and that without the cloak of the privilege counsel may be "required by the threat of future discovery to hedge or soften their opinions."

The ABA brief does not always distinguish clearly between the separate interests of the corporate client and of the attorney in freedom from disclosure, nor is it possible always to do so. The privilege's exemptions from the broad duty to divulge are designed not only to protect the individual client who may assert the privilege but also to promote free and open communication between clients and attorneys in all matters. All these interests should properly be taken into account in any decision on the privilege. However, we reject the idea that the prospective decision of the client on whether to abide by advice or disregard it, or the guarantee of a veil of secrecy, either establishes or narrows the attorney's obligation in the giving of advice. And to grant to corporate management plenary assurance of secrecy for opinions received is to encourage it to disregard with impunity the advice sought.

Two traditional exceptions are also persuasive in negativing any absolute privilege in a corporation in the circumstances of this case. These are the exceptions for communications in contemplation of a crime or fraud, and for communications to a joint attorney.

Communications made by a client to his attorney during or before the commission of a crime or fraud for the purpose of being guided or assisted in its commission are not privileged. The stockholders claim to have been the victims of improprieties in the issuance and sale of FAL's stock. The questions, and the documents sought, concerned those alleged improprieties, with particular regard to whether the attorney advised the corporation that proposals it had in mind were not legal and that statements to be put in its prospectus were misleading.

The plaintiffs say that some of the matter claimed to be privileged concerned prospective criminal transactions, including issuance by FAL of a misleading prospectus, the circulation of which it is said was a criminal offense under federal securities law, and the granting of options (allegedly as bribes) for securing state registrations of FAL's stock and of its broker-dealer and salesmen. In considering the interplay of interest of management, of stockholders, and of the lawsuit, it must be recognized that management has an obligation to the corporation, to the stockholders and to the public to do what is lawful. But we do not consider unavailability of the privilege to be confined to the narrow ground of prospective criminal transactions. The differences between prospective crime and prospective action of questionable legality, or prospective fraud, are differences of degree, not of principle.[5]

A second exception is also instructive. In many situations in which the same attorney acts for two or more parties having a common interest, neither party may exercise the privilege in a subsequent controversy with the other. This is true even where the attorney acts jointly for two or more persons having no formalized business arrangement between them. 8 Wigmore, § 2312 at 603; *Grand Trunk W. R.R. v. H. W. Nelson Co.,* 116

[5] FN20. The crime-fraud exception is particularly instructive because it covers advice concerning prospective action. We recognize the much stronger policy justifications behind the confidentiality of communications with one who is already a wrongdoer and seeks legal advice appropriate to his plight as opposed to one who seeks advice concerning proposed future conduct and, having later acted, seeks to maintain the secrecy. See 8 Wigmore, § 2298 at 573. FAL does not recognize the unavailability of the privilege even as to communications about transactions wholly prospective (except, possibly, where relating to commission of a proposed crime).

F.2d 823, 835 (6th Cir. 1941). The exception applies to partners, *Billias v. Panageotou,* 193 Wash. 523 (1938); makers of mutual wills, *Wilson v. Gordon,* 73 S.C. 155 (1905), and joint trustors, *Boyle v. Kempkin,* 243 Wis. 86, 93 (1943); insured and insurer in an automobile death action, *Hoffman v. Labutzke,* 233 Wis. 365, 377 (1940); and many others.

In *Pattie Lea, Inc. v. District Court,* 161 Colo. 493 (1967) (en banc), a case strikingly similar to this one, the Supreme Court of Colorado held that the statutory privilege for communications between a certified public accountant and his corporate client did not protect the corporation from being required to disclose to its own stockholders in a good faith derivative suit brought by them against the corporation communications from the corporation to the CPA. The Colorado court relied upon the analogy of the joint attorney exception and pointed out that employment of certified public accountants by the corporation was for the benefit of all the stockholders.

In summary, we say this. The attorney-client privilege still has viability for the corporate client. The corporation is not barred from asserting it merely because those demanding information enjoy the status of stockholders. But where the corporation is in suit against its stockholders on charges of acting inimically to stockholder interests, protection of those interests as well as those of the corporation and of the public require that the availability of the privilege be subject to the right of the stockholders to show cause why it should not be invoked in the particular instance.[6]

D. Good cause

There are many indicia that may contribute to a decision of presence or absence of good cause, among them the number of shareholders and the percentage of stock they represent; the bona fides of the shareholders; the nature of the shareholders' claim and whether it is obviously colorable; the apparent necessity or desirability of the shareholders having the information and the availability of it from other sources; whether, if the shareholders' claim is of wrongful action by the corporation, it is of action criminal, or illegal but not criminal, or of doubtful legality; whether the communication related to past or to prospective actions; whether the communication is of advice concerning the litigation itself; the extent to which the communication is identified versus the extent to which the shareholders are blindly fishing; the risk of revelation of trade secrets or other information in whose confidentiality the corporation has an interest for independent reasons. The court can freely use in camera inspection or

[6] FN21. This approach is neither new nor world-shaking. At common law the stockholder has the right to see corporate books and records but it is not unlimited. His demand must be germane to his interest as stockholder, and the interests of the corporation and other shareholders may control to deny inspection. 5 Fletcher, Corporations, § 2218 at 799 (1967). The existent Alabama statute, which follows the Model Business Corporation Act, allows shareholder examination of books and records of account, minutes and record of stockholders, upon written demand and "for any proper purpose." Tit. 10, § 21(46), Code of Ala. (Supp.1969).

oral examination and freely avail itself of protective orders, a familiar device to preserve confidentiality in trade secret and other cases where the impact of revelation may be as great as in revealing a communication with counsel.

The order relating to availability of the attorney-client privilege is Vacated. The cause is Remanded for further proceedings not inconsistent with this opinion.

Garner is widely followed, but some states reject it. In *National Football League Props., Inc. v. Superior Court*, 65 Cal.App.4th 100, 108 (1998), for example the court refused to follow *Garner*, citing a provision of the California Evidence Code (Section 911) that precludes courts from creating exceptions to the attorney-client privilege.

D. CONFLICTS OF INTEREST IN DERIVATIVE ACTIONS AND SIMILAR LITIGATION

As noted above, derivative suits often assert claims nominally on behalf of an entity and against officers and directors who are alleged to have harmed the entity. In reality, officers and directors remain in control of the entity while the litigation proceeds. Their power includes choosing lawyers to defend the suit. (The entity generally will pay defense costs for officers and directors unless and until they are found liable for acts that cannot be indemnified.) The general rule is that because the entity is the nominal plaintiff the same lawyer cannot represent both the entity and the officers or directors alleged to have harmed it. The following materials survey this rule and the rule in similar situations.

GONG V. RFG OIL, INC.

166 Cal.App.4th 209 (2008)

MCINTYRE, J.

Jeffrey Gong appeals an order denying his motion to disqualify Dan Lawton and the Lawton Law Firm (together, Lawton) as counsel for defendants David Gong and RFG Oil, Inc. (RFG). Jeffrey asserts that an actual conflict of interest exists between David and RFG and that Lawton must be disqualified from representing RFG, but can remain as counsel for David. We agree and reverse and remand with directions.

FACTUAL AND PROCEDURAL BACKGROUND

RFG, a California corporation and franchisee of the Valvoline Instant Oil Change Stores, is owned by Jeffrey (holding 49 percent of the corporate stock) and David (holding 51 percent of the corporate stock). Jeffrey and David also function as the board of directors for RFG, with David acting as the majority of the board. The brothers executed a buy-sell agreement that provided, in part, that if one party left the business, the other party could purchase his shares at "book value." In 2001, David suffered a major spinal cord injury that required a three-month hospital stay and a lengthy rehabilitation process. Due to David's injury, Jeffrey assumed all management duties for RFG. In 2003, David reassumed his duties based on Jeffrey's alleged mismanagement of the company.

In late 2005, the brothers had a falling out and RFG terminated Jeffrey and forced him to resign his position as a corporate officer. Jeffrey then sued David and RFG for involuntary dissolution of RFG, declaratory relief regarding the proper interpretation of the buy-sell agreement, breach of fiduciary duty, and wrongful discharge. Jeffrey later added a cause of action for specific performance of the buy-sell agreement.

The trial court severed Jeffrey's claim for declaratory relief, tried the matter and issued a statement of decision determining that the buy-sell agreement required that David purchase Jeffrey's shares at "fair market value." Until then, the law firm of Luce Forward, Hamilton and Scripps (Luce) represented both David and RFG. After the trial, Jeffrey challenged Luce's continuing ability to represent both David and RFG, claiming that RFG now had a significant role in the dispute between the two brothers because the buy-sell agreement required RFG to pay for an appraiser, selected by David. As one of RFG's two directors, Jeffrey wanted to be sure that the counsel advising RFG on this point was neutral and not acting primarily in David's interest. Jeffrey also asserted that David dissuaded a potential third party from purchasing RFG and that Luce's duties to David prevented it from providing RFG neutral guidance.

Luce indicated that RFG would retain new counsel and Lawton later substituted in as counsel for RFG. When David also sought to retain new counsel, Jeffrey reiterated his concern that a single firm could not jointly represent David and RFG. Despite this concern, Lawton substituted in as counsel for David and RFG cross-claimed against Jeffrey for cancellation of Jeffrey's shares and other forms of relief based on Jeffrey's alleged fraud and breaches of fiduciary duty. Jeffrey immediately filed a disqualification motion. Lawton opposed the motion, arguing that there were no grounds for disqualification and the motion was untimely because Jeffrey did not object to joint representation by Luce at the outset of the litigation.

The trial court tentatively granted the motion, finding it was not untimely and that Lawton's joint representation would preclude it from providing unbiased counsel to RFG. After hearing oral argument, the trial court denied the motion, finding that Jeffrey had unreasonably delayed in seeking disqualification and that no conflict of interest existed. Jeffrey filed a petition for writ of mandate and notice of appeal seeking review of the trial court's decision. We treated the writ petition as a petition for writ of supersedeas requesting that the trial court proceedings be stayed until further order of this court and granted the stay.

DISCUSSION

I. *Standard of Review and Legal Principles*

. . . .

When the duty of loyalty applies, courts have found the conflict to require "*per se,* or automatic disqualification, in all but a few instances." (*Metro–Goldwyn–Mayer, Inc. v. Tracinda Corp.* (1995) 36 Cal.App.4th 1832, 1840.) "The strict proscription against dual representation of clients with adverse interests thus derives from a concern with protecting the integrity of the attorney-client relationship rather than from concerns with the risk of specific acts of disloyalty or diminution of the quality of the attorney's representation." (*Forrest v. Baeza* (1997) 58 Cal.App.4th 65, 74.)

For example, in a derivative suit, the organization named as a defendant is actually a plaintiff and case law forbids dual representation in a derivative suit alleging fraud by the principals, because the principals and the organization have adverse, conflicting interests. A potential conflict, however, does not warrant automatic disqualification of joint counsel. [citations omitted]

II. *Analysis*

Jeffrey asserts that the trial court erred in denying disqualification because Lawton is simultaneously representing David and FGF, two clients with conflicting interests. We agree.

As a threshold matter, an attorney representing a corporation "may also represent any of its directors, officers, employees, members, shareholders, or other constituents, subject to the provisions of rule 3–310." (Rule 3–600, subd. (E).) Although Jeffrey acknowledges this rule, he asserts that joint representation of David and RFG by Lawton is improper because the two clients are not 100 percent aligned on all issues in the litigation. To resolve this issue, we review the pleadings to determine whether the interests of David and RFG potentially or actually conflict. (Rule 3–310(C).)

Turning to Jeffrey's operative complaint, he seeks the involuntary dissolution of RFG and declaratory relief and specific performance of the buy-sell agreement against David and RFG. He also seeks damages from RFG for wrongful termination and from David for alleged breaches of fiduciary duties. David and RFG assert they are not adverse to each other on any of these claims because they have a common interest in defeating all claims. Although this argument has superficial appeal, we are not persuaded.

Jeffrey alleged that David has wrongfully conducted the affairs of RFG to further David's interests at his expense. He also alleged that David purchased real property in David's own name, but used corporate funds to discharge the promissory note and directed Jeffrey to prepare tax returns for RFG containing misinformation. Abuse of authority and waste of corporate property by a corporate director or officer are grounds upon which a court may order a corporation dissolved, a remedy Jeffrey seeks. (Corp.Code, § 1800, subd. (b)(4).) Although Jeffrey has not yet filed a derivative claim seeking damages on behalf of the corporation (which David and RFG admit would require Lawton's disqualification), Jeffrey's complaint alleges damage to RFG through David's personal use of corporate funds and the dissolution claim threatens its corporate existence.

As corporate counsel to RFG, Lawton's professional obligations are to the corporate entity and not to its officers, directors, or shareholders in their representative or individual capacities. (Rule 3–600(A.)) Here, however, RFG is a closely held corporation that can only speak through David. Additionally, RFG is not a passive litigant in this action as it has filed (through Lawton and David) a cross-complaint seeking damages against Jeffrey for, among other things, fraud and breaches of fiduciary duty. RFG also seeks to cancel Jeffrey's shares based on the alleged breach of a promise to share responsibility with David for meeting its need for cash. The cross-complaint raises a concern that David is using RFG as a pawn in his dispute with Jeffrey, possibly to RFG's detriment. Under these circumstances, Lawton cannot satisfy its undivided duty of loyalty to both David and RFG. Because an actual conflict exists between David and RFG, David's purported waiver of the conflict is ineffective. (*Forrest v. Baeza, supra,* 58 Cal.App.4th at p. 76.)

Accordingly, we conclude that the trial court abused its discretion when it denied the disqualification motion because Jeffrey's allegations and the dissolution cause of action show that the interests of David and RFG diverge. Separate counsel for RFG can exercise its professional judgment in the best interest of RFG without the constraint of simultaneously promoting and protecting David's interests in the litigation, thereby preserving the duty of loyalty and the public trust in the administration of justice and the integrity of the bar, the primary rationale behind the dual representation prohibition. . . .

RFG is a closely held corporation with David as the majority shareholder. Lawton has been working for RFG through David and any personal loyalties will be with David. Additionally, any confidential information Lawton learned from RFG during the time period it jointly represented RFG and David will be the same confidential information it received from David. Stated differently, if David were forced to retain new counsel, that new counsel would be privy to the same information that Lawton received from David and RFG.

In this situation, where the functioning of a corporation is so intertwined with the individual defendant that any distinction between them is fictional, it makes no sense to require Lawton's complete removal from this case based on its prior representation of RFG. (*Forrest v. Baeza, supra,* 58 Cal.App.4th at pp. 81–82.) Jeffrey agrees and does not object to Lawton remaining as counsel for David.

Requiring RFG to retain new counsel—without previous connections to it, David or Jeffrey—preserves the duty of loyalty and the public trust in the administration of justice. Ideally, David and Jeffrey, acting in their capacity as board members, will be able to agree on counsel for RFG. This decision does not call into question Lawton's good faith; rather, it recognizes a conflict presented by these unique circumstances.

DISPOSITION

The order denying Lawton's disqualification is reversed and the matter is remanded with directions for the trial court to enter an order consistent with the views expressed in this opinion. Jeffrey Gong is entitled to costs on appeal.

E. PRIMARY AND SECONDARY LIABILITY WHEN THE CLIENT IS AN ENTITY

Reynolds v. Schrock, 341 Or. 338, 142 P.3d 1062 (2006), which you read in chapter 8, holds that a lawyer may not be held jointly liable with a client for the client's breach of fiduciary duty unless the third party shows that the lawyer was acting outside the scope of the lawyer-client relationship. *Reynolds* distinguishes *Granewich v. Harding*, 329 Or. 47 (1999), in which majority shareholders were alleged to have breached the fiduciary obligation they owed, as shareholders, to a minority shareholder. The defendant attorney and his firm were alleged to have aided in this unlawful scheme (acting, as *Reynolds* says, outside the normal scope of attorney conduct and with knowledge of the breach), and the Oregon Supreme Court found these allegations sufficient to allow the case to proceed on that basis.

As is common, the majority shareholders in *Granewich* were also officers of the company; what if they were alleged to have breached duties they owed to the company, in their capacity as officers, rather than to a minority shareholder, in their capacity as shareholders? Could entity counsel be liable in such a case?

Possibly. The basic theory is similar to the reasoning in *Granewich* but is cast as a primary liability argument asserting malpractice or breach of fiduciary duty. Under this theory, if an officer or director involved the entity in unlawful conduct, such as by using the entity as a vehicle to defraud a third party, then the officer would harm the entity by making it liable for such conduct. If entity counsel assisted in the relevant scheme, he or she not only would have aided a breach of the officer or director's duty to the entity but also would have failed to act in the best interests of the client—the entity—as well. If new managers took over the entity, they could cause the entity to sue counsel for malpractice for failing to protect the entity from the entity's own officials. This claim would be for breach of counsel's own duty of care, not for aiding in the breach of the officer's duties.

Does this theory work? The case law is mixed. The theory finds some support in *Chem–Age Industries, Inc. v. Glover*, 652 N.W.2d 756 (S.D. 2002), in which the court dealt with a claim by two people who invested in a corporation established by an alleged scam artist named Dahl. The investors lost their money and sued both Dahl and Glover, the lawyer he had hired to set up the company. The investors' claims against Glover included causes of action for aiding and abetting Dahl in defrauding them and a claim for malpractice for allowing Dahl to misappropriate company assets, thus harming the entity.

The trial court granted summary judgment in favor of Glover, and the appellate court reversed. The Supreme Court reversed summary judgment on the aiding and abetting count for the same reasons explained in *Granewich*. As to malpractice, the Court reasoned that

> If it is shown that he represented the corporation, then it follows that Glover had a duty to the client corporation. Plaintiffs contend that Glover, along with Dahl, improperly arranged for the sale of corporate assets and that those assets were converted to personal use by Dahl. Consequently, plaintiffs assert that the company suffered losses. . . . plaintiffs have alleged sufficient facts to take this case beyond the reach of summary judgment. We reverse the circuit court's decision to the contrary and remand for trial.

This argument seems straightforward, but how can an entity sue for harm caused by entity constituents such as officers and directors? The knowledge and intention of such agents is often attributed to an entity, so one could argue that the entity should not be able to sue counsel for something the entity (through the misbehaving constituent) did to itself. Shouldn't subsequent managers or bankruptcy trustees be estopped from asserting claims against entity counsel? One answer to these questions is that in *Chem–Age* the officers were alleged to have done things that did not benefit the entity in any way—they allegedly converted corporate assets to their own use.

Some courts would limit liability for assisting corporate officials in harming a corporation to cases in which, as in *Chem–Age*, the officials' alleged conduct unequivocally harmed rather than benefitted the corporation; to cases, in other words, where corporate officials steal from a corporation rather than for it. The following case so holds, and surveys the range of arguments on this question.

KIRSCHNER V. KPMG LLP

15 N.Y.3d 446 (2010).

READ, J.

In these two appeals, plaintiffs ask us, in effect, to reinterpret New York law so as to broaden the remedies available to creditors or shareholders of a corporation whose management engaged in financial fraud that was allegedly either assisted or not detected at all or soon enough by the corporation's outside professional advisers, such as auditors, investment bankers, financial advisers and lawyers. For the reasons that follow, we decline to alter our precedent relating to in pari delicto, and imputation and the adverse interest exception, as we would have to do to bring about the expansion of third-party liability sought by plaintiffs here.

I.

Kirschner

This lawsuit was triggered by the collapse of Refco, once a leading provider of brokerage and clearing services in the derivatives, currency and futures markets. After a leveraged buy-out in August 2004, Refco became a public company in August 2005 by way of an initial public offering. In October 2005, Refco disclosed that its president and chief executive officer had orchestrated a succession of loans, apparently beginning as far back as 1998, which hid hundreds of millions of dollars of the company's uncollectible debt from the public and regulators. These maneuvers created a falsely positive picture of Refco's financial condition. In short order, this revelation caused Refco's stock to plummet and RCM, Refco's brokerage arm, to experience a "run" on customer accounts, forcing Refco to file for bankruptcy protection.

In December 2006, the United States Bankruptcy Court for the Southern District of New York confirmed Refco's Chapter 11 bankruptcy plan, which became effective soon thereafter. . . . The plan also established a Litigation Trust, which authorized plaintiff Marc S. Kirschner, as Litigation Trustee, to pursue claims and causes of action possessed by Refco prior to its bankruptcy filing. The Litigation Trust's beneficiaries are the holders of allowed general unsecured claims against Refco. Any recoveries are to be allocated, after repayment of up to $25 million drawn from certain Refco assets to administer the Trust, on the basis of the beneficiaries' allowed claims under the confirmed plan.

In August 2007, the Litigation Trustee filed a complaint in Illinois state court asserting fraud, breach of fiduciary duty and malpractice against Refco's President and CEO and other owners and senior managers (collectively, "the Refco insiders"); investment banks that served as underwriters for the LBO and/or the IPO; Refco's law firm; two accounting firms that had provided services to Refco; and several customers that participated in the allegedly deceptive loans. According to the Trustee, these defendants all aided and abetted the Refco insiders in carrying out the fraud, or were negligent in neglecting to discover it. . . .

Defendants subsequently moved to dismiss the Litigation Trustee's claims pursuant to Rules 12(b)(1) and 12(b)(6) of the Federal Rules of Civil Procedure, and the District Court granted the motion on April 14, 2009. Because the Trustee acknowledged that the Refco insiders masterminded Refco's fraud, the Judge identified as the threshold issue whether the claims were subject to dismissal by virtue of the Second Circuit's *Wagoner* rule (*see Shearson Lehman Hutton v. Wagoner,* 944 F.2d 114, 118 [2d Cir.1991] [bankruptcy trustee does not possess standing to seek recovery from third parties alleged to have joined with the debtor corporation in defrauding creditors]).[7] Further, since "[a]ll parties agree[d] that if the *Wagoner* rule applie[d], the Litigation Trustee lack[ed] standing to assert any of Refco's claims against the defendants," the Judge observed that "the parties' dispute focus[ed] solely on whether the narrow exception to the *Wagoner* rule—the 'adverse interest' exception—applie[d]".

Citing Second Circuit cases handed down after our decision in *Center v. Hampton Affiliates* (66 N.Y.2d 782 [1985]), the District Court noted that, in order for the adverse interest exception to apply, "the [corporate officer] must have totally abandoned [the corporation's] interests and be acting entirely for his own or another's purposes . . . because where an officer acts entirely in his own interests and adversely to the interests of the corporation, that misconduct cannot be imputed to the corporation" Further, "[i]n determining whether an agent's actions were indeed adverse to the corporation, courts have identified the relevant issue [as being the] short term benefit or detriment to the corporation, not any detriment to the corporation resulting from the unmasking of the fraud"

---

[7] FN3. Although the District Court broadly characterized the *Wagoner* rule as "an application of the substantive law of New York", this rule derives in significant part from federal bankruptcy law, and is a prudential limitation on standing under federal law (*see Baena v. KPMG LLP,* 453 F.3d 1, 5 [1st Cir.2006]). Thus, the *Wagoner* rule is not part of New York law except as it reflects the in pari delicto principle, and in New York, in pari delicto is an affirmative defense, not a matter of standing. Even so—and although the Litigation Trustee may be understood to imply otherwise—in pari delicto may be resolved on the pleadings in a State court action in an appropriate case (*see e.g. Donovan v. Rothman,* 302 A.D.2d 238, 239 [1st Dept 2003] [affirming dismissal of contract claim on ground of in pari delicto]).

The District Court concluded that "[t]his line of precedent foreclose[d] the Litigation Trustee's claims" because the complaint was "saturated by allegations that Refco received substantial benefits from the [Refco] insiders' alleged wrongdoing" Thus, under the Trustee's own allegations the Refco insiders stole *for* Refco, not *from* it—i.e., "the burden of the [Refco] insiders' fraud was not borne by Refco or its then-current shareholders who were themselves the [Refco] insiders—but rather by outside parties, including Refco's customers, creditors, and third parties who acquired shares through the IPO". . . .

Plaintiffs appealed to the Second Circuit Court of Appeals. After presenting a comprehensive account of the Litigation Trustee's factual allegations and the District Court's decision, the court remarked that the parties seemingly did not dispute several propositions in the lower court's decision, which "appear[ed] to correctly reflect New York law concerning the adverse interest exception;" specifically, that the adverse interest exception was "a narrow one and that the guilty manager must have totally abandoned his corporation's interests for [the exception] to apply"; and that "whether the agent's actions were adverse to the corporation turns on the short term benefit or detriment to the corporation, not any detriment to the corporation resulting from the unmasking of the fraud" (*id.* [quoting the District Court's opinion (internal quotation marks omitted)]). Nonetheless, the court observed, "[a]s [the District Court Judge] applied these propositions to the Trustee's allegations, . . . he interpreted New York law in ways that [brought] the parties into sharp dispute concerning certain aspects of the adverse interest exception"; namely, "the state of mind of the [Refco] insiders and the harm to their corporation".

The Second Circuit . . . sought our guidance as to the scope of New York's adverse interest exception. Accordingly, on December 23, 2009 the Second Circuit certified eight questions, inviting us to "focus [our] attention on questions (2) and (3)", which are "whether the adverse interest exception is satisfied by showing that the insiders intended to benefit themselves by their misconduct"; and "whether the exception is available only where the insiders' misconduct has harmed the corporation," respectively.

Teachers' Retirement System of Louisiana and City of New Orleans Employees' Retirement System

This lawsuit is a derivative action brought on behalf of American International Group, Inc. (AIG) by the Teachers' Retirement System of Louisiana and the City of New Orleans Employees' Retirement System (derivative plaintiffs). According to the complaint, senior officers of AIG set up a fraudulent scheme to misstate AIG's financial performance in order to deceive investors into believing that the company was more prosperous and secure than it really was. The complaint further accuses these officers of causing the corporation to avoid taxes by falsely claiming that workers' compensation policies were other types of insurance, and of engaging in "covered calls" to recognize investment gains without paying capital gains taxes. It is also claimed that AIG conspired with other companies to rig markets to subvert supposedly competitive auctions, and that the senior officers exploited their familiarity with improper financial machinations by selling the company's "expertise" in balance sheet manipulation. Specifically, AIG is alleged to have sold to other companies insurance policies that did not involve the actual transfer of insurable risk, with the improper purpose of helping those companies report better financial results; and to have created special purpose entities for other companies without observing the required accounting rules for the similarly improper purpose of helping those companies hide impaired assets. These financial tricks eventually came to light, resulting in serious harm to AIG. Stockholder equity was reduced by $3.5 billion, and AIG was saddled with litigation and regulatory proceedings requiring it to pay over $1.6 billion in fines and other costs.

Derivative plaintiffs do not allege that defendant Pricewaterhouse-Coopers LLP (PwC) conspired with AIG or its agents to commit accounting fraud. Rather, they contend that, as AIG's independent auditor, PwC did not perform its auditing responsibilities in accordance with professional standards of conduct, and so failed to detect or report the fraud perpetrated by AIG's senior officers. Had it done so, derivative plaintiffs argue, the fraudulent accounting schemes at AIG would have been timely discovered and rectified.

PwC moved to dismiss the action. On February 10, 2009, the Delaware Court of Chancery granted the motion, concluding that New York law applied to the claims and that, under New York law, the claims were barred (*In re Am. Intl. Group, Inc.,* 965 A.2d 763 [Del Ch 2009]). Consistent with the way in which the District Court handled the same issues two months later in *Kirschner,* the Vice Chancellor decided that, under New York's law of agency, the wrongdoing of AIG's senior officers was imputed to AIG and that, based on the allegations in the complaint, AIG's senior officers did not totally abandon AIG's interests such that the adverse interest exception to imputation would apply. Once the wrongdoing was imputed to AIG, the Court of Chancery decided that AIG's claims against PwC were barred by New York's in pari delicto doctrine and the *Wagoner* rule governing standing.

Derivative plaintiffs appealed. Determining that the appeal's resolution depended on significant and unsettled questions of New York law, on March 3, 2010, the Delaware Supreme Court issued a decision certifying the following question to us:

> "Would the doctrine of in pari delicto bar a derivative claim under New York law where a corporation sues its outside auditor for professional malpractice or negligence based on the auditor's failure

to detect fraud committed by the corporation; and, the outside auditor did not knowingly participate in the corporation's fraud, but instead, failed to satisfy professional standards in its audits of the corporation's financial statements?" (*In re Am. Intl. Group, Inc.,* 998 A.2d 280 [Del 2010]).

II.

In pari delicto

The doctrine of in pari delicto[8] mandates that the courts will not intercede to resolve a dispute between two wrongdoers. This principle has been wrought in the inmost texture of our common law for at least two centuries (*see e.g. Woodworth v. Janes,* 2 Johns Cas 417, 423 [N.Y. 1801] [parties in equal fault have no rights in equity]; *Sebring v. Rathbun,* 1 Johns Cas 331, 332 [NY 1800] [where both parties are equally culpable, courts will not "interpose in favor of either"]). The doctrine survives because it serves important public policy purposes. First, denying judicial relief to an admitted wrongdoer deters illegality. Second, in pari delicto avoids entangling courts in disputes between wrongdoers. As Judge Desmond so eloquently put it more than 60 years ago, "[N]o court should be required to serve as paymaster of the wages of crime, or referee between thieves. Therefore, the law will not extend its aid to either of the parties or listen to their complaints against each other, but will leave them where their own acts have placed them" (*Stone v. Freeman,* 298 N.Y. 268, 271 [1948] [internal quotation marks omitted]).

The justice of the in pari delicto rule is most obvious where a willful wrongdoer is suing someone who is alleged to be merely negligent. A criminal who is injured committing a crime cannot sue the police officer or security guard who failed to stop him; the arsonist who is singed cannot sue the fire department. But, as the cases we have cited show, the principle also applies where both parties acted willfully. . . .

Imputation

Traditional agency principles play an important role in an in pari delicto analysis. Of particular importance is a fundamental principle that has informed the law of agency and corporations for centuries; namely, the acts of agents, and the knowledge they acquire while acting within the scope of their authority are presumptively imputed to their principals (*see Henry v. Allen,* 151 N.Y. 1, 9 [1896] [imputation is "general rule"]; *see also Craigie v. Hadley,* 99 N.Y. 131 [1885]; *accord Center,* 66 N.Y.2d at 784). Corporations are not natural persons. "[O]f necessity, [they] must act solely through the instrumentality of their officers or other duly au-

[8] FN4. The doctrine's full name is in pari delicto potior est conditio defendentis, meaning "in a case of equal or mutual fault, the position of the [defending party] is the better one" (*Baena,* 453 F.3d at 6 n. 5 [internal quotation marks omitted]).

thorized agents" (*Lee v. Pittsburgh Coal & Min. Co.,* 56 How Prac 373 [Super Ct 1877], *affd* 75 N.Y. 601 [1878]). A corporation must, therefore, be responsible for the acts of its authorized agents even if particular acts were unauthorized (*see Ruggles v. American Cent. Ins. Co. of St. Louis,* 114 N.Y. 415, 421 [1889]). "The risk of loss from the unauthorized acts of a dishonest agent falls on the principal that selected the agent" (*see Andre Romanelli, Inc. v. Citibank, N.A.,* 60 A.D.3d 428, 429 [1st Dept 2009]). After all, the principal is generally better suited than a third party to control the agent's conduct, which at least in part explains why the common law has traditionally placed the risk on the principal.

Agency law presumes imputation even where the agent acts less than admirably, exhibits poor business judgment, or commits fraud (*see e.g. Price v. Keyes,* 62 N.Y. 378, 384–385 [1875] [critical issue is whether agent was acting in furtherance of his duties, regardless of his "selfish motive"]). As we explained long ago, a corporation "is represented by its officers and agents, and their fraud in the course of the corporate dealings [ ] is in law the fraud of the corporation" (*Craigie,* 99 N.Y. at 134; *accord Reynolds v. Snow,* 10 A.D.2d 101, 109 [1st Dept 1960], *affd* 8 N.Y.2d 899 [1960]). Like a natural person, a corporation must bear the consequences when it commits fraud (*see e.g. Wight v. BankAmerica Corp.,* 219 F.3d 79, 86–87 [2d Cir. 2000] [under "fundamental principle[s] of agency," managers' misconduct within the scope of their employment is imputed and "bars a trustee from suing to recover for a wrong that he himself essentially took part in"]).

When corporate officers carry out the everyday activities central to any company's operation and well-being—such as issuing financial statements, accessing capital markets, handling customer accounts, moving assets between corporate entities, and entering into contracts—their conduct falls within the scope of their corporate authority (*see e.g. Baena,* 453 F.3d at 7 ["The approval and oversight of [financial] statements is an ordinary function of management that is done on the company's behalf, which is typically enough to attribute management's actions to the company itself"]). And where conduct falls within the scope of the agents' authority, everything they know or do is imputed to their principals.

Next, the presumption that agents communicate information to their principals does not depend on a case-by-case assessment of whether this is likely to happen. Instead, it is a legal presumption that governs in every case, except where the corporation is actually the agent's intended victim (*see Center,* 66 N.Y.2d at 784 ["when an agent is engaged in a scheme to defraud his principal . . . he cannot be presumed to have disclosed that which would expose and defeat his fraudulent purpose"]). Where the agent is defrauding someone else on the corporation's behalf, the presumption of full communication remains in full force and effect (*see* 3 Thompson and Thompson, *Commentaries on the Law of Corporations*

§ 1778, at 347 [3d ed. 1927] ["However applicable the dictum that an agent about to commit a fraud will not announce his intention may be in the case of fraud by an agent upon his own principal, it has no application when the agent, acting in behalf of his principal, or ostensibly so, commits a fraud upon a third person"]).

In sum, we have held for over a century that all corporate acts—including fraudulent ones—are subject to the presumption of imputation (*Craigie,* 99 N.Y. at 134). And, as with in pari delicto, there are strong considerations of public policy underlying this precedent: imputation fosters an incentive for a principal to select honest agents and delegate duties with care.

Adverse Interest Exception to Imputation

We articulated the adverse interest exception in *Center* as follows:

"To come within the exception, the agent must have *totally abandoned* his principal's interests and be acting *entirely* for his own or another's purposes. It cannot be invoked merely because he has a conflict of interest or because he is not acting primarily for his principal" (*Center,* 66 N.Y. at 784–785 [emphasis added]). This rule avoids ambiguity where there is a benefit to both the insider and the corporation, and reserves this most narrow of exceptions for those cases—outright theft or looting or embezzlement—where the insider's misconduct benefits only himself or a third party; i.e., where the fraud is committed *against* a corporation rather than on its behalf.

The rationale for the adverse interest exception illustrates its narrow scope. As already discussed, the presumption that an agent will communicate all material information to the principal operates except in the narrow circumstance where the corporation is actually the victim of a scheme undertaken by the agent to benefit himself or a third party personally, which is therefore entirely opposed (i.e., "adverse") to the corporation's own interests (*see Center,* 66 N.Y.2d at 784). Where the agent is perpetrating a fraud that will benefit his principal, this rationale does not make sense.

A fraud that by its nature will benefit the corporation is not "adverse" to the corporation's interests, even if it was actually motivated by the agent's desire for personal gain (*Price,* 62 N.Y. at 384). Thus, "[s]hould the 'agent act[ ] both for himself and for the principal,' . . . application of the exception would be precluded" . . .

New York law thus articulates the adverse interest exception in a way that is consistent with fundamental principles of agency. To allow a corporation to avoid the consequences of corporate acts simply because an employee performed them with his personal profit in mind would enable the corporation to disclaim, at its convenience, virtually every act its officers undertake. "[C]orporate officers, even in the most upright enterprises, can always be said, in some meaningful sense, to act for their own interests" (*Grede v. McGladrey & Pullen LLP,* 421 B.R. 879, 886 [ND Ill 2008]). A corporate insider's personal interests—as an officer, employee, or shareholder of the company—are often deliberately aligned with the corporation's interests by way of, for example, stock options or bonuses, the value of which depends upon the corporation's financial performance.

Again, because the exception requires adversity, it cannot apply unless the scheme that benefitted the insider operated at the corporation's expense. The crucial distinction is between conduct that defrauds the corporation and conduct that defrauds others for the corporation's benefit. "Fraud on behalf of a corporation is not the same thing as fraud against it" (*Cenco Inc. v. Seidman & Seidman,* 686 F.2d 449, 456 [7th Cir.1982]), and when insiders defraud third parties *for* the corporation, the adverse interest exception is not pertinent. . . . So long as the corporate wrongdoer's fraudulent conduct enables the business to survive—to attract investors and customers and raise funds for corporate purposes—this test is not met (*Baena,* 453 F.3d at 7 ["A fraud by top management to overstate earnings, and so facilitate stock sales or acquisitions, is not in the long-term interest of the company; but, like price-fixing, it profits the company in the first instance"]).

The Litigation Trustee suggests that, to the extent that the adverse interest exception requires harm, "bankruptcy is harm enough" and that, whenever the corporation is bankrupt, "it is fair to assume at the pleading stage" that the adverse interest exception applies. But the mere fact that a corporation is forced to file for bankruptcy does not determine whether its agents' conduct was, at the time it was committed, adverse to the company (*see e.g., Barnes v. Hirsch,* 212 N.Y.S. 536 [1st Dept 1925] [trustee's claim dismissed where it sought to recover for agents' fraud "practiced on these customers" of debtor rather than debtor itself], *affd,* 242 N.Y. 555 [1926]). Even where the insiders' fraud can be said to have caused the company's ultimate bankruptcy, it does not follow that the insiders "totally abandoned" the company. As we have held when considering whether an agent's acts were a fraud on the principal prompted by "selfish" motives, it "is immaterial that it has turned out that it would have been better" for the agent to have acted differently (*Price,* 62 N.Y. at 385; *see also* Restatement [Third] of Agency § 5.04, Comment c ["the fact that an action taken by an agent has unfavorable results for the principal does not establish that the agent acted adversely"]). . . .

Consistent with these principles, any harm from the discovery of the fraud—rather than from the fraud itself—does not bear on whether the adverse interest exception applies. The disclosure of corporate fraud nearly always injures the corporation. If that harm could be taken into account, a corporation would be able to invoke the adverse interest exception and disclaim virtually every corporate fraud—even a fraud undertaken for the corporation's benefit—as soon as it was discovered and no longer helping the company.

Finally, to focus on harm from the exposure of the fraud would be a step away from the requirement of adversity. Generally, a fraud will suit the interests of both a company and its insiders for as long as it remains a secret (sometimes a considerable number of years, as was the case with Refco), and leads to negative consequences for both when disclosed.

III.

The Litigation Trustee and the derivative plaintiffs encourage us to broaden the adverse interest exception or revise New York precedents relating to in pari delicto or imputation for reasons of public policy—specifically, as they put it, to recompense the innocent and make outside professionals (especially accountants) responsible for their negligence and misconduct in cases of corporate fraud. Although they do not stress the point, their proposals to revise imputation rules are limited to in pari delicto cases. No one disputes that traditional imputation principles, including a narrowly confined adverse interest exception, should remain unchanged—indeed, are essential—in other contexts. For example, in a suit against Refco or AIG by an innocent victim of the frauds, no one would suggest that the wrongful acts of the corporate insiders could not be attributed to their principals. Instead, the Litigation Trustee and the derivative plaintiffs advance various ways for us to reformulate New York law where in pari delicto is in issue. All their proposals push the adverse interest exception up to if not beyond the point of extinction. We next explore these proposals and consider whether our precedent remains anchored in sound public policy and workable.

Subjective Intent and Illusory Benefits

First, the Litigation Trustee advocates that we "adopt the rule of [*In re CBI Holding Co.,* 529 F.3d 432, 448 (2d Cir.2008)], under which the insiders' intent is the touchstone and a short term, illusory benefit to the company does not defeat the adverse interest exception." The derivative plaintiffs similarly argue that analysis of the adverse interest exception should focus on the agent's overall intent. . . .

To recast the adverse interest exception in this fashion, as the District Court pointed out, would "explode" the exception, turning it into a "nearly impermeable rule barring imputation" in every case. This is so because fraudsters are presumably not, as a general rule, motivated by charitable impulses, and a company victimized by fraud is always likely to suffer long-term harm once the fraud becomes known. The Trustee's proposed rule would limit imputation to fraudsters so inept they gain no personal benefit and unexposed frauds, which is another way of saying the adverse interest exception would become a dead letter because it would encompass every corporate fraud prompting litigation.

The NCP and AHERF Rules

Alternatively, the Litigation Trustee urges us to take the approach to in pari delicto and imputation adopted by the New Jersey Supreme Court in 2006 (*NCP Litig. Trust v. KPMG LLP,* 187 NJ 353 [NJ 2006]) (supported by the derivative plaintiffs as well), or the Pennsylvania Supreme Court earlier this year (*Official Comm. of Unsecured Creditors of Allegheny Health Educ. and Research Found. v. PricewaterhouseCoopers LLP,* 989 A.2d 313 [Pa 2010] [AHERF]). Our sister states fashioned carve-outs from traditional agency law in cases of corporate fraud so as to deny the in pari delicto defense to negligent or otherwise culpable outside auditors (New Jersey) and collusive outside professionals (Pennsylvania). Thus, the adverse interest exception, while not abolished, is again rendered beside the point.

In the *NCP* case . . . the New Jersey Supreme Court held that "when an auditor is negligent within the scope of its engagement, the imputation doctrine does not prevent corporate shareholders from seeking to recover". These corporate shareholders must be "innocent," though: an auditor may still assert the "imputation defense" against those shareholders who engaged in the fraud; or who, by way of their role in the company, should have been aware of the fraud; or who owned large blocks of stock and therefore arguably possessed some ability to oversee the company's operations. Thus, the New Jersey rule calls for the relative faults of the company/shareholders and auditors to be sorted out by the fact finder as matters of comparative negligence and apportionment.

The *AHERF* case involved [a claim that an auditor colluded with management to misstate corporate finances. The district court granted summary judgment in favor of the auditor on *in pari delicto* grounds. On appeal] the Third Circuit Court of Appeals certified questions to the Pennsylvania Supreme Court seeking clarification of "the appropriate test under Pennsylvania law for deciding whether imputation [was] appropriate when the party invoking that doctrine [was] not conceded to be an innocent third party, but an alleged co-conspirator in the agent's fraud".

The Pennsylvania Supreme Court first rejected the approach taken by New Jersey, concluding that "the best course . . . for Pennsylvania common law [was] to continue to recognize the availability of the in pari delicto defense . . . , via the necessary imputation, in the negligent-auditor context" where the plaintiff's culpability was equal to or greater than the defendant's. But as to the issue of auditor collusion presented by the Third Circuit's certification, the court took a different view, holding that imputation (and therefore the in pari delicto defense) was unavailable where an auditor had not proceeded in material good faith. In light of the Pennsylvania Supreme Court's clarifying opinion, the Third Circuit subsequently held that when a third party, such as an auditor, colludes with agents to defraud their principal, "Pennsylvania law requires an inquiry into whether the third party dealt with the principal in good faith," and remanded to the district court to conduct such an inquiry (*AHERF Creditors' Com. v. PricewaterhouseCoopers,* 607 F.3d 346, 348 [3d Cir.2010]).

The *NCP* and *AHERF* decisions were both animated by considerations of equity—the notion that although the plaintiffs stood in the shoes of the principal malefactors, any recovery they achieved from the defendant accounting firms—which were alleged to have been either negligent or complicit—would, in fact, only benefit innocent shareholders or unsecured creditors and so should not be barred by in pari delicto. The Pennsylvania Supreme Court reflected this sentiment when it said that it would be "ill-advised, if not perverse" "[to] apply[ ] imputation as against AHERF" because that "would result in the corporation being charged with knowledge as against a third party whose agents actively and intentionally prevented those in AHERF's governing structure who were nonparticipants in the fraud from acquiring such knowledge" (*AHERF,* 989 A.2d at 336).

Comparative Negligence

Finally, the Litigation Trustee suggests that any in pari delicto defense "should not be a total bar to recovery, but at most a basis for apportionment of fault and damages as between the defendant and the company's successor trustee" under CPLR 1411. The derivative plaintiffs go even further, claiming that in pari delicto was abolished when the Legislature enacted CPLR 1411 in 1975. As PwC points out, though, there is no reason to suppose that the *statute* did away with common law defenses based on intentional conduct, such as in pari delicto, although we could presumably reinterpret New York common law in this area to provide for comparative fault, as New Jersey has done. The effect again would be to marginalize the adverse interest exception. And, of course, comparative fault contradicts the public policy purposes at the heart of in pari delicto-deterrence and the unseemliness of the judiciary "serv[ing] as paymaster of the wages of crime" (*Stone,* 298 N.Y. at 271).

Public Policy

This case reduces down to whether, and under what circumstances, we choose to reinterpret New York common law to permit corporations to shift responsibility for their own agents' misconduct to third parties. The Litigation Trustee and the derivative plaintiffs, with whom the dissent agrees, ask us to do this as a matter of public policy in order to compensate the innocent and deter third-party professional (and, in particular, auditor) misconduct and negligence.

On the first point, the Litigation Trustee and the derivative plaintiffs urge us to consider that, although they both stand in the shoes of corporate malefactors, any recovery they achieve will, in fact, benefit blameless unsecured creditors (in the Refco case) and shareholders (in the AIG case) at the expense of defendants who allegedly assisted the fraud or were negligent. They ask us to broaden the adverse interest exception and create exceptions to imputation along the lines adopted by the courts in *NCP* and *AHERF,* and endorsed by the dissent, in the interests of fairness. We are not persuaded, however, that the equities are quite so obvious. In particular, why should the interests of innocent stakeholders of corporate fraudsters trump those of innocent stakeholders of the outside professionals who are the defendants in these cases? The costs of litigation and any settlements or judgments would have to be borne, in the first instance, by the defendants' blameless stakeholders; in the second instance, by the public (*see Securities and Exchange Commn. v. Tambone,* 597 F.3d 436, 452–453 [1st Cir. 2010] [Boudin, J., concurring] ["No one sophisticated about markets believes that multiplying liability is free of cost. And the cost, initially borne by those who raise capital or provide audit or other services to companies, gets passed along to the public"]).

In a sense, plaintiffs' proposals may be viewed as creating a double standard whereby the innocent stakeholders of the corporation's outside professionals are held responsible for the sins of their errant agents while the innocent stakeholders of the corporation itself are not charged with knowledge of their wrongdoing agents. And, of course, the corporation's agents would almost invariably play the dominant role in the fraud and therefore would be more culpable than the outside professional's agents who allegedly aided and abetted the insiders or did not detect the fraud at all or soon enough. The owners and creditors of KPMG and PwC may be said to be at least as "innocent" as Refco's unsecured creditors and AIG's stockholders.

We are also not convinced that altering our precedent to expand remedies for these or similarly situated plaintiffs would produce a meaningful additional deterrent to professional misconduct or malpractice. The derivative plaintiffs caution against dealing accounting firms a "get-out-of-jail-free" card. But as any former partner at Arthur Andersen LLP—once one of the "Big Five" accounting firms—could attest, an outside professional (and especially an auditor) whose corporate client experiences a rapid or disastrous decline in fortune precipitated by insider fraud does not skate away unscathed. In short, outside professionals—underwriters, law firms and especially accounting firms—already are at risk for large settlements and judgments in the litigation that inevitably follows the collapse of an Enron, or a Worldcom or a Refco or an AIG-type scandal. Indeed, in the Refco securities fraud litigation, the IPO's underwriters, including the three underwriter-defendants in this action, have agreed to settlements totaling $53 million (www.refcosecuritieslitigation.com). In the AIG securities fraud litigation, PwC settled with shareholder-plaintiffs last year for $97.5 million (www.refcosecuritieslitigationpwc.com). It is not evident that expanding the adverse interest exception or loosening imputation principles under New York law would result in any greater disincentive for professional malfeasance or negligence than already exists. Yet the approach advocated by the Litigation Trustee and the derivative plaintiffs would allow the creditors and shareholders of the company that employs miscreant agents to enjoy the benefit of their misconduct without suffering the harm.

The principles of in pari delicto and imputation, with its narrow adverse interest exception, which are embedded in New York law, remain sound. The speculative public policy benefits advanced by the Litigation Trustee and the derivative plaintiffs to vindicate the changes they seek do not, in our view, outweigh the important public policies that undergird our precedents in this area or the importance of maintaining the "stability and fair measure of certainty which are prime requisites in any body of law" (Loughran, *Some Reflections on the Role of Judicial Precedent,* 22 Fordham L Rev 1, 3 [1953]). We are simply not presented here with the rare case where, in the words of former Chief Judge Loughran, "the justification and need" for departure from carefully developed legal principles are "clear and cogent" (*id.*). Finally, to the extent our law had become ambiguous, today's decision should remove any lingering confusion. . . .

JUDGES GRAFFEO, SMITH and JONES concur.

JUDGE CIPARICK dissents in an opinion in which CHIEF JUDGE LIPPMAN and JUDGE PIGOTT concur.

CIPARICK, J. (dissenting):

The majority opinion effectively precludes litigation by derivative corporate plaintiffs or litigation trustees to recover against negligent or complicit outside actors—even where the outside actor, hired to perform essential gatekeeping and monitoring functions, actively colludes with corrupt corporate insiders. In my view, the agency law principles upon which the majority rests its conclusions ignore complex assumptions and public policy that compel different conclusions than those reached by the majority. Accordingly, I respectfully dissent. . . .

[T]he concept of in pari delicto is not a rigid concept, incapable of shaping itself to the particulars of an individual case. Before the in pari delicto doctrine can be applied to circumstances such as those presented here, the actions of the corrupt insider/agents must be found to be attributable to the corporate entity/principal. . . .

An agent's actions and knowledge cannot be imputed to the principal, however, if the "agent is engaged in a scheme to defraud his principal, either for his own benefit or that of a third person" (*Center,* 66 N.Y.2d at 784). In such circumstances, "the presumption that knowledge held by the agent was disclosed to the principal fails because he cannot be presumed to have disclosed that which would expose and defeat his fraudulent purpose" (*id.*). This adverse interest exception can apply in circumstances where a corrupt corporate insider acts for its own benefit, rather than for the benefit of its principal. . . .

It is axiomatic that the adverse interest exception requires a showing of harm to the principal, but the premise that even an illusory benefit to a principal can serve to defeat the adverse interest exception to imputation misses the point. As the Second Circuit noted in *CBI Holding,* a "corporation is not a biological entity for which it can be presumed that any act which extends its existence is beneficial to it" (529 F.3d at 453, citing *Bloor v. Dansker,* 523 F.Supp. 533, 541 [SD N.Y.1980]). Indeed, "prolonging a corporation's existence in the face of ever increasing insolvency may be 'doing no more than keeping the enterprise perched at the brink of disaster' " (*id.,* quoting *Mirror Group Newspapers v. Maxwell Newspapers, Inc.,* 164 B.R. 858, 869 [Bankr SD N.Y.1994]). As was borne out here, in the case of Refco, insider fraud that merely gives the corporation life longer than it would naturally have is not a true benefit to the corporation but can be considered a harm. The majority's assertion that any corporate insider fraud that "enables the business to survive" defeats the adverse interest exception would, as alleged here, condone the actions of the defendants.

Moreover, in the corporate context where the fraud committed by corrupt insiders is either enabled by, joined in, or goes unnoticed by outside "gatekeeper" professionals, the use of these simple agency principles in such a manner has been rightfully criticized (*see NCP Litigation Trust v. KPMG LLP,* 187 N.J. 353, 366 [2006], quoting Morris, *Clarifying the Imputation Doctrine: Charging Audit Clients with Responsibility for Unauthorized Audit Interference,* 2001 Colum Bus L Rev 339, 353 [2001]). One commentator has observed that the results seemingly required by imputation and in pari delicto are "severe and unmodulated by concern for the specifics of individual cases" (Demott, *When is a Principal Charged with an Agent's Knowledge,* 13 Duke J Comp & Intl L 291, 319 [2003]). Indeed, these simplistic agency principles as applied by the majority serve to effectively immunize auditors and other outside professionals from liability wherever any corporate insider engages in fraud.

Important policy concerns militate against the strict application of these agency principles. There can be little doubt that the role played by auditors and other gatekeepers serves the public as well as the corporations that contract for such services. Investors rely heavily on information prepared by or approved by auditors, accountants, and other gatekeeper professionals. Corporate financial statements, examined by ostensibly independent auditors, "are one of the primary sources of information available to guide the decisions of the investing public" (*United States v.*

Arthur Young & Co., 465 U.S. 805, 810–811 [1984]). It is, therefore, in the public's best interest to maximize diligence and thwart malfeasance on the part of gatekeeper professionals (*see generally* Coffee, Jr., *Gatekeeper Failure,* 84 Boston U L Rev at 345–346 ["public policy must seek to minimize the perverse incentives that induce the gatekeeper not to investigate too closely"]; Shapiro, *Who Pays the Auditor Calls the Tune?: Auditing Regulations and Clients' Incentives,* 35 Seton Hall L Rev 1029, 1034 [2005] [the purpose of audits is to "provide some independent assurance that those entrusted with resources are made accountable to those who have provided the resources"]).

Moreover, it is unclear how immunizing gatekeeper professionals, as the majority has effectively done, actually incentivizes corporate principals to better monitor insider agents. Indeed, it seems that strict imputation rules merely invite gatekeeper professionals "to neglect their duty to ferret out fraud by corporate insiders because even if they are negligent, there will be no damages assessed against them for their malfeasance" (Pritchard, *O'Melveny Meyers v. FDIC: Imputation of Fraud and Optimal Monitoring,* 4 Sup Ct Econ Rev 179, 192 [1995]). . . .

In conclusion, I do not quarrel with the majority's statements of the applicable principles of agency law. Rather, my departure is from the majority's rigid application of those principles to cases by litigation trustees and derivative plaintiffs against gatekeeper professionals for enabling corporate insider fraud by colluding in or failing to detect such fraud. I agree with the litigation trustee and the derivative plaintiffs that no equitable basis exists for holding that litigation trustees or derivative plaintiffs are in pari delicto with culpable outside professionals. Indeed, in my view, the weight of the equities favors allowing suits such as these to go forward to deter active wrongdoing or negligence by auditors and similar professionals (*see generally FDIC v. O'Melveny & Myers,* 512 U.S. 79, 90 [1994] [Stevens, J., concurring]). Moreover, I am persuaded by the sound rationales employed by our sister state courts in the *AHERF* case and the *NCP Litigation Trust* case that a more reasonable approach is to recognize a carve-out or exception to the in pari delicto doctrine for cases involving corporate insider fraud enabled by complicit or negligent outside gatekeeper professionals.

CASE QUESTIONS

1. What agency law rules apply to this case?
2. What does the *in pari dilecto* doctrine hold in this context?
3. What rationale for the doctrine does the court identify?

4. What are the elements of the "adverse interest" exception to the doctrine?
5. What does the *CBI* case hold? Why does the court not adopt that holding?
6. What does the *NCP* case hold? Why does the court not adopt that holding?
7. What does the *AHERF* case hold? Why does the court not adopt that holding?
8. How does the court treat the trustee's comparative negligence argument?

FDIC v. O'Melveny & Myers, 969 F.2d 744 (9th Cir. 1992), interpreted California law to provide an arguably broader scope of liability for lawyers in certain cases. The FDIC became the receiver of a failed bank and sued O'Melveny, the bank's former counsel, for malpractice in connection with the bank's sale of securities. The firm wrote large portions of a private placement memorandum (PPM), which the parties agreed (in hindsight) was materially misleading. The FDIC alleged that the firm had a duty to the bank to ensure that the PPM was not materially misleading, even if the bank's officials at the time were insisting that the document be written a certain way. The basic notion was that the bank officials breached their duties to the bank by engaging in securities fraud for which the bank could be held liable, and the firm breached its duties to the bank by helping them.

The firm claimed it owed no duty to ferret out the bank officers' own fraud and that the officers' fraud was imputed to the bank (and thus the FDIC as receiver), which therefore was estopped from suing O'Melveny for that fraud. The court rejected this argument. Here are some excerpts from the opinion:

O'Melveny's position is that a lawyer owes no duty to uncover a client's fraud nor to advise the client and the world of that fraud. The Firm points out that California has recently reiterated its traditionally narrow construction of attorney malpractice exposure under California law. *See Kimmel v. Goland,* 51 Cal.3d 202, 213–14 n. 10 (1990); *Skarbrevik v. Cohen, England & Whitfield,* 231 Cal.App.3d 692, 701–707 (1991). There are two problems with O'Melveny's approach. The first is the implication that if the client happens to be committing a fraud, of which the attorney may or may not be aware, the presence of the fraud cancels the attorney's duty to use due care. No California cases advise us of an exception to the general rule that a lawyer has to act competently to avoid public harm when he learns that his is a dishonest client. The *Skarbrevik* and *Kimmel* cases merely decline to expand this duty of attorneys; they do not create any exceptions to it.

The second problem with O'Melveny's approach is its sharp differentiation between a "duty to investors," which it concedes, and a "duty to the client," which it denies. Given a broad duty to protect the client, this distinction is a false one. Part and parcel of effectively protecting a client, and thus discharging the attorney's duty of care, is to protect the client from the liability which may flow from promulgating a false or misleading offering to investors. An important duty of securities counsel is to make a "reasonable, independent investigation to detect and correct false or misleading materials." *Felts v. National Account Sys. Assoc., Inc.,* 469 F.Supp. 54, 67 (N.D.Miss.1978). This is what is meant by a due diligence investigation. *Koehler v. Pulvers,* 614 F.Supp. 829, 845 (S.D.Cal.1985) (due diligence required lawyer's independent investigation of information supplied by issuer for incorporation into offering materials). The Firm had a duty to guide the thrift as to its obligations and to protect it against liability. In its high specialty field, O'Melveny owed a duty of due care not only to the investors, but also to its client, ADSB. . . .

"Generally the knowledge of a corporate officer within the scope of his employment is the knowledge of the corporation. . . . [, however,] the knowledge acquired by the agent who is acting adversely to his principal will not be attributed to the principal." [citations omitted]. . . . there can be no attribution, and therefore no estoppel, when the insiders, rather than the corporation, benefit from the wrongdoing. . . . Furthermore, we note that O'Melveny cannot invoke an estoppel defense unless it is innocent itself.

The Supreme Court reversed this opinion, *O'Melveny & Myers v. FDIC*, 512 U.S. 79 (1994), on the ground that the Ninth Circuit might have applied federal rather than state law. On remand, the Ninth Circuit affirmed its original ruling. The court had originally looked to federal law regarding the firm's estoppel defense. On remand, it reached the same result under California law. *FDIC v. O'Melveny & Myers*, 61 F.3d 17 (9th Cir. 1995). The court later limited the reach of its holding, by stressing the unique demands of securities law, in *Loyd v. Paine Webber, Inc.*, 208 F.3d 755, 760 (9th Cir. 2000) (stating that *O'Melveny* did not hold "that, as a general matter, an attorney who represents corporate clients has an automatic duty to independently investigate whether its clients are engaging in fraudulent conduct.").

F. THE INSOLVENT OR NEARLY INSOLVENT ENTITY

WILLNER'S FUEL DISTRIBUTORS, INC. V. NOREEN

882 P.2d 399 (Alaska 1994)

RABINOWITZ, JUSTICE.

I. *FACTS AND PROCEEDINGS*

Thomas A. Rosson, Jr., formed a solely owned corporation, Rosson & Company, Inc. (Rosson, Inc.) in 1983. Rosson, Inc. was involuntarily dissolved on November 27, 1985 by the State of Alaska.

In 1986, attorney Robert S. Noreen (Noreen) filed a voluntary bankruptcy petition for Rosson, Inc. and for Thomas Rosson individually in the United States Bankruptcy Court for the District of Alaska. Willner's Fuel Distributors, Inc. (Willner's) was listed as one of the twenty largest unsecured creditors of Rosson, Inc. Willner's also was listed on the schedule of debts of Thomas Rosson individually. Both petitions were dismissed by orders dated April 9, 1988. No discharges were issued.

On April 8, 1988, Thomas Rosson and Rosson, Inc. sued the Fairbanks North Star Borough, R & M Engineering Consultants, and Glacier State Telephone Company (collectively referred to as "Borough") for breach of contract and negligence, and additionally sued the Fairbanks North Star Borough individually for business interference. The alleged breaches arose out of conduct following the August 20, 1984 award of a road contract, apparently to Rosson, Inc. Noreen was the attorney of record for both Thomas Rosson and Rosson, Inc. in this action. Noreen claims that "at some point during this time frame" Thomas Rosson told him that Rosson, Inc. had been involuntarily dissolved in 1985.

On May 9, 1988, Willner's filed suit against Thomas Rosson and Rosson, Inc. for $20,212.17. Noreen entered an appearance for Thomas Rosson individually, but did not enter an appearance for the corporation in the suit brought by Willner's. After filing its suit, Willner's learned that Rosson, Inc. had been involuntarily dissolved in 1985. On February 2, 1989, Willner's applied for default against Rosson, Inc.

At some time in March, the suit by Thomas Rosson and Rosson, Inc. against the Borough was settled for $100,000.00. Noreen explains that "Thomas Rosson settled the lawsuit against the Fairbanks North Star Borough for $100,000.00 both in his individual capacity and as the past president or assignee of interests in the dissolved corporation Rosson & Company, Inc." Noreen asserts that "[t]his settlement was concluded and settlement checks were received by attorney Noreen no later than March

26, 1989." The checks were made payable jointly to Thomas Rosson and Robert Noreen. Rosson, Inc. was not a payee.

The chronology of events on March 28, 1989 is disputed. On that date, Noreen and the attorney for Willner's signed and filed a stipulation that the lawsuit against Thomas Rosson individually would be dismissed without prejudice. According to Noreen, at sometime "in the morning" of March 28 Thomas Rosson accompanied Noreen to National Bank of Alaska (NBA), where Noreen deposited the settlement monies from the suit by Thomas Rosson and Rosson, Inc. against the Borough into his trust account. Noreen directed the NBA teller to transfer $80,000.00 from the trust account to Thomas Rosson, by cashier's check. Noreen explains that he then wrote a check to himself from the settlement proceeds for his fee of $20,000.00, and deposited the check into his business account. At the time of the two transactions, Noreen asserts, he had no knowledge that Willner's was procuring a default judgment, writ of execution, or levy against Rosson, Inc.

Also on March 28, a default judgment in the amount of $25,257.44 was entered against Rosson, Inc. in the suit by Willner's against Thomas Rosson and Rosson, Inc., because Rosson, Inc. had "failed to plead in or otherwise defend this action." Noreen states that he was presented with a levy on his trust account to satisfy this default judgment "in the afternoon of March 28, 1989." According to Noreen, the settlement proceeds had already been distributed "to his client Thomas Rosson individually and as sole corporate representative of Rosson Inc., pursuant to client demand" by this time. In a response to the levy, Noreen stated that he had no funds of Rosson, Inc. under his control.

On January 24, 1991, Willner's filed a complaint against Noreen and Thomas Rosson, alleging that Noreen had violated AS 09.40.040 in his response to the levy and had wrongfully disbursed the funds of an insolvent dissolved corporation. Willner's sought both the money award of Rosson, Inc.'s debt to Willner's and other damages. Willner's then filed a motion for summary judgment concerning Noreen's alleged violation of AS 09.40.040 based on his alleged false statements made in response to a court levy. Noreen filed a motion for judgment on the pleadings or, in the alternative, for summary judgment, contending *inter alia* that he owed Willner's no fiduciary duty. Noreen also moved for summary judgment regarding the AS 09.40.040 claim.

Thereafter, the superior court entered a memorandum decision and order denying the summary judgment motion by Willner's on the AS 09.40.040 claim and granting judgment to Noreen on this claim. Additionally, the superior court granted Noreen's summary judgment motion on the tort claims that Willner's raised. The superior court concluded that "[a]s a matter of law, Noreen did not violate any statutory or common law duty to Willner's."

The remaining claims of Willner's against Thomas Rosson were scheduled for a default judgment trial. Subsequently, the superior court issued an order stating that the judgment against Willner's on the claims against Noreen would not become effective until either the claims by Willner's against Thomas Rosson were resolved or until further order of the court. Thereafter, the superior court entered findings of fact and conclusions of law, and a final default judgment, against Thomas Rosson in favor of Willner's. This appeal followed.

II. *DISCUSSION*

B. *Noreen's Summary Judgment Motion as to the Breach of Fiduciary Duty Claims*

Willner's contends that Noreen owed and breached a fiduciary duty to corporate creditors. Willner's argues that once Rosson, Inc. was dissolved and became insolvent, Thomas Rosson, in his capacity as director, owed Willner's a fiduciary duty to preserve corporate assets, because those assets had become an informal trust fund for the benefit of Rosson, Inc.'s creditors. Willner's urges this court to fashion a similar fiduciary duty, running from Noreen in his capacity as corporate counsel to the creditors of the dissolved, insolvent corporation.

Thomas Rosson's liability to Willner's is not directly at issue in this appeal. Nonetheless, a determination whether Thomas Rosson owed a fiduciary duty to creditors bears on the existence of a similar duty on Noreen's part. Though it did not explain its reasons for holding Thomas Rosson liable under Alaska law to Willner's, the superior court properly could have proceeded under either of two theories.

First, under the "trust fund" theory, directors of an insolvent corporation may be personally liable to creditors for a breach of fiduciary duty resulting from an improper distribution of assets:

> An insolvent corporation is civilly dead in the sense that its property may be administered in equity as a trust fund for the benefit of creditors. The fact which creates the trust is the insolvency, and when that fact is established, the trust arises, and the legality of the acts thereafter performed will be decided by very different principles than in the case of solvency. . . .
>
> The courts . . . have held officers and directors of corporations to be at one time agents or mandataries, and at another time, trustees, and have defined their liability accordingly; and they have been held as trustees where they took such advantage of their position of trust as public policy could not tolerate.
>
> . . . .

> . . . Clearly, it [is] not meant that directors of a corporation are trustees, in a strict and technical sense, in all of their relations with the corporation, its stockholders and creditors; but, as clearly, it [is] implied that they should be treated as such when they have unlawfully profited through breach of duty, and at the expense of the corporation. . . .

Second, the superior court, viewing Rosson, Inc. as a dissolved corporation, could have held Thomas Rosson liable for a post-dissolution asset distribution in violation of former AS 10.05.216(c). Though this provision makes directors personally liable "to the *corporation* for the value of the assets distributed," former AS 10.05.216(c) (emphasis added), several courts construing similar statutory language apply the trust fund theory to allow creditors as a class to sue. *See Ficor, Inc. v. McHugh,* 639 P.2d 385, 393 (Colo.1982) (allowing statutory remedy to all creditors as a group); *cf. Kidde Indus., Inc. v. Weaver Corp.,* 593 A.2d 563, 566 (Del.Ch.1991) (Chandler, V.C.) (applying trust fund theory to allow creditors an action under a statute subjecting nonresident directors to personal jurisdiction based upon the directors' fiduciary duty to creditors). *Contra Nachazel v. Mira Corp., Mfg.,* 466 N.W.2d 248, 255–56 (Iowa 1991) (applying plain meaning analysis to statutory language, and holding that creditors had no cause of action against corporate officers and directors). We agree with the courts in *Ficor* and *Weaver,* and therefore hold that Thomas Rosson, in his capacity as director of Rosson, Inc., owed Willner's and the other creditors of the corporation a fiduciary duty to preserve its assets, in particular the proceeds from the Borough settlement, for their benefit.

As for Noreen's liability, we note that Noreen represented two clients: Thomas Rosson, a natural person, and Rosson, Inc., a dissolved corporation. The interests of these two clients with respect to the net proceeds of their claim, $80,000, were not identical. The corporation's interest was in maximizing its share of the proceeds and in disbursing the proceeds to its creditors in accordance with the priorities established by law. Thomas Rosson's interest was in maximizing his individual claim to the proceeds. A lawyer who represents clients with conflicting interests is in a sensitive position and may be liable for breach of the lawyer's fiduciary responsibilities to either client. Just as creditors may sue directors on behalf of a dissolved corporation, creditors may maintain similar actions against the attorney of the dissolved corporation for breach of the attorney's fiduciary obligations. . . . This case can be viewed as such an action. So viewed, there are questions of fact concerning whether Noreen breached his fiduciary duty to Rosson, Inc.

The corporate assets at issue here were placed in Noreen's attorney's trust account, and thus were in his custody and control. Requiring an insolvent or dissolved corporation's attorney to protect assets in his or her custody from a director's improper distribution would not impose an unwarranted burden on the legal profession. In fact, an attorney often has an ethical duty to protect third-party claims to funds in his or her custody from a client's wrongful interference. *See* Alaska Rules of Professional Conduct 1.15 cmt.

By way of summation, we hold that if an attorney represents both a dissolved or insolvent corporation and a director or officer of that firm, and if the attorney controls corporate assets, then the attorney must protect the financial rights of creditors to these assets, where he or she knows or should know that the director or officer intends to interfere with creditors' claims through an improper distribution of these assets. To do otherwise would sanction a class of wrongs without a remedy. Accordingly, as a matter of law, we hold that Noreen was not entitled to summary judgment.[9]

III. *CONCLUSION*

The superior court erred in granting summary judgment to Noreen on Willner's AS 09.40.040 motion, as there were genuine questions of material fact as to the relative timing of the service of the levy and the NBA transactions, and the possession of the funds at the time of the levy. The superior court also erred in holding that Noreen owed no duty to a creditor of the dissolved, insolvent corporation. We hold that such a duty may exist, that genuine issues of fact exist as to Noreen's violation of this duty, and accordingly that Noreen was not entitled to summary judgment as a matter of law.

Willner's Fuel is an extreme case, in which an entity actually had been dissolved by the state. What if an entity stays in business but is on

---

[9] FN13. Though it was one of many unsecured creditors to Rosson, Inc., Willner's is suing Noreen on behalf of itself alone, and is suing for the full amount of the debt owed it, plus interest. Had the proceeds from the Borough settlement remained with the corporation, they would have been allocated among all the creditors, with senior and secured creditors having priority over junior and unsecured creditors such as Willner's. Many jurisdictions that hold directors and officers of an insolvent or dissolved corporation liable to creditors for an improper asset distribution nonetheless disallow actions by single creditors or require single creditors to sue on behalf of all creditors. . . .

Had Noreen not disbursed the proceeds from the Borough settlement to Rosson, instead retaining the funds in his attorney's trust account, he could have been vulnerable to claims upon the funds not only from Willner's but also from Rosson, Inc.'s other creditors. In such a situation, Noreen, as stakeholder for the proceeds, could deposit them in the superior court registry and file a claim for interpleader, requiring the joinder of all of Rosson, Inc.'s creditors, in order to avoid multiple liability and vexatious litigation. *See, e.g., Johnston v. All State Roofing & Paving Co., Inc.,* 557 P.2d 770, 773 (Alaska 1976); Alaska R.Civ.P. 22.

If upon remand it is determined that Noreen is liable for wrongfully disbursing the proceeds for the Borough settlement to Thomas Rosson, then any recovery against Noreen should be deposited into the superior court registry, and Willner's should notify all other creditors of the availability of these funds for allocation. Allowing Willner's to recover on its own behalf is not permissible, because doing so would prejudice other creditors.

the brink of insolvency? *In re JTS Corporation*, 305 B.R. 529 (2003), dealt with such a case. JTS was a computer disk drive manufacturer that suffered when demand fell. It engaged in several transactions later challenged by its bankruptcy trustee. One of these was the sale of corporate property to a director. The sale provided cash JTS needed, but the properties were sold at their book value of around $10 million rather than their market value of around $16 million (though JTS did retain an option to re-purchase the properties within a year). The trustee alleged that this sale reduced the corporation's assets by $6 million.

In connection with this and other claims, the bankruptcy judge followed a line of corporate law doctrine which holds that the directors of an insolvent firm owe fiduciary duties to creditors. The court distinguished the "trust fund doctrine," which the *Willner's* court had mentioned as a possible source of liability in that case, from what it called an exception, triggered by insolvency, to the general rule that corporate directors owe no fiduciary obligations to creditors.[10] The court reasoned that "the fact of insolvency shifts the risk of loss from the stockholders to the creditors. While stockholders no longer risk further loss, creditors become at risk when decisions of the directors affect the corporation's ability to repay debt. This new fiduciary relationship is certainly one of loyalty, trust and confidence, but it does not involve holding the insolvent corporation's assets in trust for distribution to creditors or holding directors strictly liable for actions that deplete corporate assets."

The trustee accused JTS's counsel, Cooley, Godward, of breaching its fiduciary duty to JTS. The trustee alleged that Cooley knew the properties had been appraised at $15–16 million but failed to inform JTS's directors that "the property was being sold for less than fair market value, a fact that could have adverse legal consequences for the company." Cooley sought summary judgment on the claim, arguing that it merely documented a transaction JTS already had decided to close, and that it owed no duty to JTS beyond performing competently the tasks it had been assigned.

The bankruptcy judge rejected Cooley's argument. The court held that Pope, the Cooley attorney responsible for the matter

> was aware from the beginning that JTS, a struggling company, was about to sell its eight parcels of property for approximately $5–6 million less than their appraised value. Even if she had not been retained specifically to investigate the fair market value of the proper-

[10] The court thought the trust fund doctrine implied that corporate assets had to be managed as the *res* of a trust, for the benefit of claimants in order of the priority of their claims on dissolution. That might make sense for a firm such as Rosson & Company, which had been dissolved and for which the only task remaining was the distribution of assets, but it would be too strict a rule to govern the operations of a firm that continued to do business. The court's point is well-taken. It would make little sense to impose such strict limits on management that managers might be deterred from pursuing even sensible ventures that might turn a firm around.

> ties, the potential harm to JTS from such a deal should have been reasonably apparent. While Pope may have believed it was outside the scope of her representation to solve the problem, that does not relieve her of the duty to inform her client of the possible need for further legal advice. . . .
>
> Pope contends that she had no obligation to disclose the appraised value of the properties because Pope learned that information from JTS's chief financial officer. But, Pope's duty was not to simply advise JTS of the properties' value. Her obligation was to advise that, in light of that value, the transaction could have adverse legal consequences for JTS. Construed in the trustee's favor, it is reasonable to conclude from the evidence that JTS would have acted differently if it had been cautioned that a sale at less than fair market value might breach duties JTS owed to its creditors

The court's reasoning links Cooley's liability to the insolvency exception, which, the court held, created duties running from the entity to its creditors. The first step of the analysis holds that counsel may not simply follow orders and perform only the tasks assigned by entity management. Instead, counsel has a duty to advise the entity "on matters that they were hired to provide advice about, as well as any other legal issues outside their representation, 'which are reasonably apparent.' " It therefore did not matter that JTS management wanted to proceed with the sale, nor that JTS management was aware that the properties had been appraised at a price higher than the sale price (though the repurchase option seems not to have been figured into this calculation). In other words, that management knew the facts did not relieve entity counsel of its obligation to warn management of the legal implications of those facts.

Because JTS at least arguably owed duties to its creditors, its management could only approve the transaction if it satisfied those duties. Management could not rely on standard corporate tools, such as ratification of interested transactions, to comply with its obligations. The court held that a reasonable jury could conclude that, if Cooley had advised JTS that the transaction had to satisfy fiduciary obligations to *creditors*, management either would have structured the deal to discharge those obligations or (more likely, under the circumstances) not have approved the deal at all.

The result in *JTS* arguably would be no different if the corporation had been solvent. The transaction allegedly sold corporate property for less than fair value and sold it to a director to boot. But preferential asset sales look even worse when a corporation is insolvent, and the insolvency provided part of the context in which the court considered the allegations against the law firm.

In recent years courts have clarified the duties corporate officers and directors owe when a corporation is insolvent or nearly so. Most significantly in *North Am. Catholic Educ. Programming Foundation, Inc. v. Gheewalla*, 930 A.2d 92, 101 (Del.Supr. 2007), the Delaware Supreme Court held that even when a corporation "is navigating in the zone of insolvency, the focus for Delaware directors does not change: directors must continue to discharge their fiduciary duties to the corporation and its shareholders by exercising their business judgment in the best interests of the corporation for the benefit of its shareholder owners." In contrast, when a corporation actually is insolvent, creditors are the constituent group most likely to be harmed by breaches of fiduciary duties owed to the corporation, and creditors of an insolvent corporation therefore have standing to assert derivative claims on the corporation's behalf. *Id.* at 102. The court held creditors of an insolvent corporation have no direct cause of action for breach of fiduciary duty. *Id. See also Berg & Berg Enterprises, LLC v. Boyle*, 178 Cal.App.4th 1020, 1041 (Cal. Ct. App. 2009) ("under the current state of California law, there is no broad, paramount fiduciary duty of due care or loyalty that directors of an insolvent corporation owe the corporation's creditors solely because of a state of insolvency"; finding duty limited to a prohibition on self-dealing, preferential treatment of creditors, or diversion, dissipation, or undue risking of assets).

Main Points to Recall From Chapter 17 Are:

- When you represent an entity, you represent the entity as such, not the persons who run it or work for it.
- This rule extends backward from the time of entity formation; you represent founders in their capacity as founders, not as individuals, and the duties you owe them become entity assets upon formation.
- When constituents take actions that harm the entity, you must act for the entity's best interests and may not assist the constituents in harming the entity (your client).
- Such actions may include reporting violations up within the corporation to a level proportionate to the violation, including to senior management or the board if necessary.
- Such actions also may include disclosure reasonably necessary to prevent harm to the entity, regardless whether such disclosure is allowed by Rule 1.6.
- Not all jurisdictions (notably, not California) authorize such disclosure.

- Lawyers practicing before the SEC are subject to special reporting obligations imposed by rules promulgated pursuant to the Sarbanes–Oxley Act.
- Plaintiffs in derivative actions may pierce the entity attorney-client privilege upon showing cause why such piercing is justified.
- Creditors of insolvent entities may bring derivative claims on behalf of the entity, and lawyers advising insolvent entities should take creditor standing into account when advising the entity.

CHAPTER 18

ISSUES CONFRONTING GOVERNMENT LAWYERS

■ ■ ■

The preceding materials concerning duties of care, loyalty, and confidentiality presume that the lawyer's client is a private party. What if the lawyer works for the government? The duties generally point in the same direction. Government lawyers can no more serve their own interests, act incompetently, or misuse information than can lawyers for private clients. (Recall Daniel Bibb, for example, the prosecutor in the Introduction who "threw" a case in which he thought the defendants innocent; he was a government lawyer.)

But government lawyers do face some unique issues and some issues that are more complex in the government context than when the client is a private party. Perhaps the most basic issue—who is the client—is less settled in some government contexts than in most private contexts. We therefore begin with that issue.

A. WHOM DO GOVERNMENT LAWYERS REPRESENT?

Governments are complex. A lawyer working for the Antitrust Division of the Department of Justice works (i) for a supervisor; (ii) in a division; (iii) of a department; (iv) in the executive branch; of (v) the United States Government; which is elected by and represents (vi) the people of the United States and their interests.

Which of these six choices is the lawyer's client? Any selection among these choices presents problems. As a practical matter, the broadest and narrowest conceptions of the government lawyer's client can be ruled out: The government lawyer represents neither "the public" at large nor only individual government employees in their individual capacities (though joint representation is possible and common at the local government level). Which of the remaining choices provides the most useful answer depends on why the question is being asked and on the context that caused it to be asked. The following materials survey the options from the broadest to narrowest conceptions.

1. THE PUBLIC, OR THE PUBLIC INTEREST

It is sometimes argued that government lawyers represent the public generally, or the public interest.[1] Under this approach, the government lawyer serves as the government's conscience. For example, in discussing the OLC memoranda concerning the Bush administration's responses to the terrorist attacks of September 11, 2001, Professors Richard Bilder and Detlav Vagts argue that government lawyers' duties extend to "the U.S. government as a whole, and indeed the American public and its collective interests and values."[2]

Most scholars reject the notion that government lawyers represent the public or the public interest on the ground that these concepts are so diffuse and ill defined that they provide no meaningful constraint on a lawyer's discretion, nor any way of determining whether a duty has been discharged.[3] If the public or the public interest count as clients, a shrewd lawyer could always do just what he or she wanted and pick out some group whose interests that conduct served. Conversely, a shrewd critic could always pick out some group whose interests were not served and accuse the lawyer of misconduct on that ground. Both results are unhelpful to practical analysis but any middle ground between them would be intolerably subjective.

Allowing government lawyers such leeway to follow their individual consciences also presses against principles of representative democracy, at least in cases where a lawyer attempts to thwart otherwise lawful policies on the ground that they disserve the public interest. Separation of powers issues also might be raised, if a lawyer disputed or refused to help implement judicial decisions on public interest grounds.

These arguments do not show that government lawyers are identical to private lawyers in all respects. Sometimes the underlying law establishes for government lawyers duties that differ from those of private lawyers. For example, federal law requires federal government lawyers to report to the Attorney General evidence of certain illegal conduct they encounter in their work.[4]

---

1 *See Charles Fahy, Special Ethical Problems of Counsel for the Government,* 33 FED. B.J. 331, 332 (1974) (lecture delivered at Columbia Law School, April 11, 1950).

2 Richard B. Bilder & Detlev F. Vagts, *Speaking Law to Power: Lawyers and Torture,* 98 AM. J. INT'L L. 689, 692–94 (2004).

3 *E.g.* Roger C. Crampton, *The Lawyer As Whistleblower: Confidentiality and the Government Lawyer,* 5 Geo. J. Legal Ethics 291, 298–300.

4 28 U.S.C. § 535(b), provides that "[a]ny information . . . witnessed, discovered, or received in a department or agency of the executive branch of the Government relating to violations of Federal criminal law involving Government officers and employees shall be expeditiously reported to the Attorney General by the head of the department or agency, or the witness, discoverer, or recipient, as appropriate" unless certain exceptions apply. *See also In re Bruce R. Lindsey,* 158 F.3d 1263 (D.C. Cir. 1998); Model Rule 1.13 cmt 9 ("in a matter involving the conduct of government officials, a government lawyer may have authority under applicable law to question such conduct more extensively than that of a lawyer for a private organization in simi-

2. THE GOVERNMENT AS A WHOLE

Bilder and Vagts argued the duties of OLC lawyers extend to the "U.S. Government as a whole," and this concept can be extended to other levels of government, such as the State of California or the City of San Diego. In many cases this will be a satisfactory definition of the government lawyer's client. If a citizen sues a city police department alleging the use of excessive force, for example, a lawyer defending the case likely could treat the city as her client without running into any problems.

But not all cases pit private parties against some level of government. Sometimes different branches of government are at odds with each other, as when Congress subpoenas an executive branch official to testify regarding some aspect of the official's work. And some government agencies, such as the Securities and Exchange Commission, are "independent" agencies, which means they are notionally part of the executive branch but not part of any executive department (one headed by a cabinet officer). When different government branches disagree, or when one or more branches disagree with an independent agency, it is not helpful to say the lawyer for one of the disputing parties represents "the government." (As we see in the case below, the ability to make decisions independently is an important element in analyzing problems that may turn on identifying the government lawyer's client.) Most definitions of government clients therefore tend toward a more specific level.

3. THE GOVERNMENT AGENCY OR DEPARTMENT EMPLOYING THE LAWYER

There is considerable support for the view that the government lawyer's client is the agency that employs that lawyer. As Professor Roger Crampton puts the point:

> The simple rule of thumb that "the employing agency should in normal circumstances be considered the client of the government lawyer" offers useful guidance to government attorneys . . . For most day-to-day purposes, a government lawyer properly may consider the employing agency as the client. Responsible officials of that agency hire the lawyer, provide instructions and supervision, and make decisions concerning change or termination of employment.[5]

The view of the employing agency as client is probably the most workable place to start answering most questions, but it cannot answer all questions. For example, the law noted above requiring federal government lawyers to report misconduct to the attorney general applies to

---

lar circumstances. Thus, when the client is a governmental organization, a different balance may be appropriate between maintaining confidentiality and assuring that the wrongful act is prevented or rectified, for public business is involved").

[5] *Id.* at 300–301.

lawyers who work outside the Department of Justice (and who thus do not work directly for the attorney general). On this topic, therefore, one might say a lawyer represents an agency of the federal government and owes duties of care, loyalty, and confidentiality to that agency, but subject to a duty to disclose to the attorney general evidence falling within the parameters of the statute.

As a practical matter, the conception of the client as the agency or department that employs a lawyer encompasses choices (ii) through (iv) listed above. The department is choice (iii). As to choice (ii), divisions within an agency or department are likely administrative units formed to carry out the work of the department efficiently, and therefore are unlikely to have interests of their own, or at least any interests they could assert as against the head of a department. In other words, if two units of the Justice Department disagree on whether to prosecute a crime then the head of the department (or his or her designee) will decide what to do; neither division has independent authority. The same is true for agencies such as the SEC.

The analysis is slightly different for choice (iv), a branch of government. This is the obvious choice for some lawyers, for example those such as the White House Counsel, who are employed directly by the executive. It is less obviously the choice for other lawyers. Our Antitrust Division attorney, for example, works for the Department of Justice but the president likely retains ultimate authority to decide what the department shall do. In extreme cases the president can fire the attorney general and replace him or her with a new official who will execute the president's policy. In that sense, the justice department is not wholly independent; even the Antitrust Division lawyer works for the executive branch. But as a practical matter, for most day-to-day problems, conflicts between the president and the attorney general are unlikely. It better tracks reality to say that the antitrust lawyer works for the Justice Department, bearing in mind that circumstances may arise in which that department is itself controlled directly by the executive.

4. THE LAWYER'S IMMEDIATE SUPERVISOR

The narrowest possible client is also the least likely. Though it is conceivable that a government lawyer might represent his or her superior jointly with his or her department, it is unrealistic and legally untenable to suppose that a government lawyer represents *only* his or her superior. Model Rule 1.13(a) provides that a lawyer employed by an organization (as a government lawyer by definition is) represents the organization as such. Under Model Rule 1.13(g) the lawyer might also represent a constituent in certain circumstances, but absent some highly unusual and unlikely circumstance a government lawyer will not represent only an employee in his or her personal capacity.

The following case provides a concrete illustration of these general principles.

CIVIL SERVICE COMMISSION V. SUPERIOR COURT

163 Cal.App.3d 70 (1984)

WIENER, ACTING P. J.

The difficult and sensitive question in this case is whether ethical considerations require disqualifying the county counsel as attorney for the County of San Diego (County) in the pending litigation between the County and the Civil Service Commission of the County of San Diego (Commission). The Commission seeks a writ of mandate after it unsuccessfully moved to disqualify the county counsel. We will grant the writ.

Factual and Procedural Background

Preliminarily we observe the functions of government make it necessary for some public agencies within a governmental body to be accorded a considerable degree of independence vis-a-vis that body. The Commission is such an agency. It is charged with administering the County's personnel system, in the context of which it is empowered to investigate complaints filed by county employees regarding personnel actions taken by various county agencies, and to make rulings based on those investigations. Needless to say, an adverse Commission ruling is not always warmly embraced by the affected county agency.

The present case arises out of two such complaints—one filed by Ardelia McClure and one filed by William Chapman—and the consequent investigations. Both employees held positions with the County's department of social services (Department) and complained of assignment and classification actions taken by the Department to implement budget cutbacks. As is true with respect to nearly all Commission actions, Commission members and staff working on the McClure and Chapman investigations freely consulted with the office of county counsel for advice on legal matters. These consultations included discussions with County Counsel Lloyd Harmon and Deputy County Counsel Ralph Shadwell. At the time of the investigations, Shadwell was also the principal legal counsel for the department of social services, whose actions the Commission was investigating. The topics of discussion included the extent of the Commission's authority to remedy any perceived violation of the County's personnel regulations. The Commission kept county counsel apprised of the status of the investigation and the Commission deliberations with respect to the appropriate remedy.

Based on its investigations, the Commission ordered reinstatement of the affected employees, who had been demoted or laid off, and ordered backpay compensation. Disagreeing with the two rulings, the County filed suit in October 1983 against the Commission seeking judicial review of the Commission's action. . . .

The County is and has been represented in the underlying mandate proceeding by the office of county counsel. The Commission has obtained independent counsel. Based on county counsel's prior advisory role to the Commission on these matters, the Commission unsuccessfully moved to disqualify county counsel on the grounds of a conflict of interest. The court concluded the issues presented by the underlying writ proceeding were of a legal rather than factual nature—generally concerning the Commission's power to act—and that there was no showing that county counsel received any confidential information in the context of its prior representation of the Commission which could be used to the Commission's disadvantage in the present proceeding. . . .

I

We are thus faced with the question whether a public attorney who has advised a quasi-independent public agency with respect to a given matter may, consistent with his professional and ethical obligations, later represent other governmental entities suing the quasi-independent agency over the same matter. Our task is guided by two recent cases which reach different conclusions on questions of a public attorney's possible conflict of interest. Each party here relies on one of the cases and attempts to distinguish the other.

The County relies on *Ward v. Superior Court* (1977) 70 Cal.App.3d 23 in which Los Angeles County Assessor Phillip Watson sued Baxter Ward, Chairman of the Los Angeles County Board of Supervisors, and certain county employees for violation of his constitutional rights and defamation. The Los Angeles County Counsel represented Ward and the employees. Because county counsel's office had previously represented Watson and the assessor's office in numerous unrelated matters arising out of Watson's official duties, he moved to disqualify county counsel on the grounds of a conflict of interest. The *Ward* court rebuffed Watson's attempt on two separate bases. It first noted that county counsel had "only one client, namely, the County of Los Angeles." It therefore concluded that no independent attorney-client relationship had been established with Watson or the assessor's office. As a second ground, the court focused on Watson's claim that county counsel had obtained confidential information about him in the context of the prior representations. Because the prior representations of Watson and the assessor's office were substantively unrelated to the *Watson v. Ward* action, Watson necessarily contended that information concerning the operation of the assessor's office obtained by county counsel in the prior representations would be relevant to issues in the present case. The court responded by pointing out that whatever information was disclosed to county counsel, it could hardly be considered confidential in that the assessor's office was directly responsible to the board of supervisors, which was entitled to full disclosure from the assessor regarding all material facts. It concluded, therefore, that county counsel could not have obtained confidential information which could be used against Watson.

The County reads *Ward* for the broad proposition that there can never be a separate attorney-client relationship between county counsel and a County official or constituent county agency because county counsel has a single client, namely, the County. With only one client, a fortiori there can be no conflict of interest.

The Commission disagrees with the County's broad reading of *Ward*, relying heavily on *People* ex rel. *Deukmejian v. Brown* (1981) 29 Cal.3d 150. In *Deukmejian*, the Governor and various state agencies were sued by the Pacific Legal Foundation (PLF) and the Public Employees Service Association based on allegations that a major new piece of public employee collective bargaining legislation was unconstitutional. After the PLF suit was filed, deputies from the Attorney General's office met with members of the State Personnel Board, one of the respondent state agencies in the lawsuit, pursuant to the Attorney General's statutory mandate to serve as counsel for state agencies. At the meeting, the deputies outlined four options available to the board in responding to the suit and advised the board of the Attorney General's recommendation that it join in challenging the constitutionality of the statute. The board declined to follow the Attorney General's recommendation. Approximately one week later, he filed an independent action against, inter alia, the State Personnel Board asserting that the collective bargaining statute was unconstitutional.

The Governor successfully moved to disqualify the Attorney General. The *Deukmejian* court held there was "no constitutional, statutory, or ethical authority" allowing the Attorney General to "represent clients one day, give them legal advice with regard to pending litigation, withdraw, and then sue the same clients the next day on a purported cause of action arising out of the identical controversy." Of particular interest is the manner in which the *Deukmejian* court deals with *Ward*. Although Justice Richardson's dissent places considerable reliance on both prongs of the *Ward* holding, the majority finds it distinguishable because the assessor brought his action "not as a public official" but rather " 'individually and as a taxpayer.' "

As we shall explain, we believe *Deukmejian* controls the result in this case. *Ward*, to the extent it is not inconsistent with *Deukmejian*, does not compel a contrary result.

II

Before an attorney may be disqualified from representing a party in litigation because his representation of that party is adverse to the interest of a current or former client, it must first be established that the party seeking the attorney's disqualification was or is "represented" by the attorney in a manner giving rise to an attorney-client relationship. . . . Relying on *Ward*, the County here contends there was never an attorney-client relationship between the Commission and county counsel separate and distinct from county counsel's fundamental relationship with the County. We are unable to accept this contention for several reasons.

First, the identical situation existed in *Deukmejian* where the Attorney General was the statutorily authorized counsel for all state agencies, including the State Personnel Board. Relying on *Ward* the dissent in *Deukmejian* argued "the usual attorney-client relationship does not prevail. . . . " The majority apparently rejected this position, however, and consistently discussed and referred to the Attorney General as "counsel to the *board*. . . . " We think it significant the *Deukmejian* majority distinguished *Ward* on the grounds the allegedly former client was not bringing the lawsuit in his official capacity. Here, as in *Deukmejian*, the challenged counsel is suing a public agency in its official capacity.

We also believe there is a critical distinction between this case and *Ward* which would warrant a different result even in the absence of *Deukmejian.* We have previously referred to the Commission as a "quasi-independent" county agency. In contrast to most county agencies, which are directly supervised by the board of supervisors, the Commission's unique review function demands an independence which is specifically provided for in section 904.1 of the San Diego County Charter (as amended Dec. 17, 1982). . . . Thus, in the usual situation, we would expect that a conflict between or among county agencies would be resolved by the board of supervisors. Here, however, the conflict between the department of social services and the Commission cannot be resolved in the usual manner, because the County charter gives the Commission authority independent of the County's normal hierarchical structure. The board of supervisors has been forced to sue the Commission in an attempt to overturn its rulings.

We are able to accept the general proposition that a public attorney's advising of a constituent public agency does not give rise to an attorney-client relationship separate and distinct from the attorney's relationship to the overall governmental entity of which the agency is a part. Nonetheless we believe an exception must be recognized when the agency lawfully functions independently of the overall entity. Where an attorney advises or represents a public agency with respect to a matter as to which the agency possesses independent authority, such that a dispute over the matter may result in litigation between the agency and the overall entity, a distinct attorney-client relationship with the agency is created.

III

Notwithstanding the existence of an attorney-client relationship, the County argues that the Commission has failed to show county counsel obtained confidential information in the context of its prior representation of the Commission which it could now use on behalf of the County. Impliedly, the County contends that such a showing is necessary to support a disqualification order. While we believe there may be a distinct and independent reason for disqualifying the county counsel based on his ongoing professional relationship with the Commission, we address the County's argument solely as if it were presented in a "prior representation" case. . . . . [6]

On the facts of the present case, of course, there is no question but that a "substantial relationship" is present. County counsel advised the Commission on precisely the same matter as to which the County is now suing the Commission. The County's argument that county counsel obtained no confidential information from the Commission is thus irrelevant. . . . .

It strikes us that this situation is not dissimilar from the case where an attorney undertakes to advise two clients on a single matter or transaction. The attorney may be either an intermediary, actively attempting to accommodate the clients' competing interest, or merely an advisor, explaining to the clients their legal options. In either case, if the matter later results in litigation, the attorney is precluded from representing either client. . . .

Here, county counsel was advising both the Commission and the affected county agencies at the time of the McClure and Chapman investigations. In fact, the same attorney was assigned to advise both the Commission and the department of social services. To the extent that county counsel is ever permitted to place himself in such a position in the first

[6] FN1. Our statement that there may be an independent basis to disqualify the county counsel is grounded on the general rule that an attorney may simply not undertake to represent an interest adverse to those of a current client without the client's approval. . . . This record establishes the relationship between county counsel and the Commission is an ongoing one with respect to matters other than the one at issue here. The principle precluding representing an interest adverse to those of a current client is based not on any concern with the confidential relationship between attorney and client but rather on the need to assure the attorney's undivided loyalty and commitment to the client. . . .

Our reluctance to rely solely or primarily on this "ongoing representation" analysis is admittedly tied to its absence from the *Deukmejian* opinion. Confronted with a similar situation—the Attorney General had ongoing attorney-client relationships with the respondent state agencies on matters unrelated to State Employer–Employee Relations Act—the Supreme Court analyzed the situation as a case of representation of interests adverse to those of a former client.

place, it is clear if the situation escalates to litigation, he cannot remain as counsel for one of his clients in opposition to the other. . . . [7]

While we have determined that county counsel must be disqualified from representing the County in this case, we wish to indicate the limits of our holding. First, it should again be emphasized that a conflict of this nature only arises in the case of and to the extent that a county agency is independent of the County such that litigation between them may ensue. Second, disqualification of county counsel is not necessarily mandated in future cases involving quasi-independent agencies. We have noted that a fundamental conflict arises whenever county counsel is asked to represent both the Commission and the County. Moreover, it is clear from the course of this case that county counsel, with good reason, views his primary responsibility as being to the board of supervisors. If the Commission is afforded access to independent legal advice, however, there is no reason county counsel may not continue to vigorously represent the County even when such representation results in litigation against the Commission. We need not and do not decide whether the Commission, appropriately informed and advised in a given case, could validly waive the conflict at the advisory stage. . . .

CASE QUESTIONS

1. What does the *Ward* case hold?
2. What does the *Deukmejian* case hold?
3. Which of these controls this case?
4. What general rule does the court acknowledge?
5. What exception applies here?

B. GOVERNMENT LAWYER AS ADVISER

Like lawyers in private practice, government lawyers frequently advise government employees as well as litigate cases. In providing advice government lawyers may differ from private lawyers with respect to either or both of two issues.

The first issue concerns independence. Under Model Rule 2.1 lawyers are required to provide candid advice; some scholars argue government lawyers have additional obligations of independence, and may not simply provide opinions seeking to support the actions a client representative

[7] FN7. Because of the variety of situations and the organizational differences of the public entities we hesitate to define solutions for the difficult problem which is best deferred to the thoughtful judgment of public counsel on a case by case basis.

wishes to take or has taken. As we saw in chapter 8, up to a point private lawyers may, and commonly do, provide such opinions. The argument for a special obligation of independence is usually grounded in one of the arguments discussed above, regarding the identity of the government client's lawyer.

A second possible difference pertains to liability. Because they count as state actors, lawyers are sometimes named as defendants in either or both of two kinds of claims. These generally are known as "Section 1983" claims and "*Bivens* actions."

42 U.S.C. § 1983 provides in part that "[e]very person who, under color of any statute, ordinance, regulation, custom, or usage, of any State or Territory or the District of Columbia, subjects, or causes to be subjected, any citizen of the United States or other person within the jurisdiction thereof to the deprivation of any rights, privileges, or immunities secured by the Constitution and laws, shall be liable to the party injured in an action at law, suit in equity, or other proper proceeding for redress. . . . " 42 U.S.C § 1985(3) provides a similar cause of action against persons who conspire to deprive anyone of the privileges and immunities to which they are entitled under law. These actions apply to officials acting under state law or within the District of Columbia; they do not extend to officials acting under federal law.

Bivens v. Six Unknown Named Agents of the Federal Bureau of Narcotics, 403 U.S. 388 (1971), created a federal common law cause of action analogous to § 1983 actions but which may be alleged against federal officials accused of violating constitutional rights. *Bivens* actions, as they are called, allow plaintiffs to sue government officials acting under color of federal law for money damages.

An important doctrinal difference distinguishes the two types of claims. Section 1983 actions are based on a statute dating to the reconstruction era following the Civil War, in which federal law expanded and state power contracted. Section 1983 actions raise questions of federalism. *Bivens* actions, in contrast, are claims authorized by one branch of government, the judiciary, which commonly are asserted against the other two, most often the executive. They therefore raise separation of powers concerns, and in cases since *Bivens* the Supreme Court has been cautious not to expand the scope of the cause of action.[8]

Government lawyers are sometimes sued under these provisions. One such suit was brought against John Yoo, whose OLC memoranda were discussed in chapter 8, by Jose Padilla, a United States citizen who was detained as an enemy combatant and ultimately convicted of conspiracy

[8] *Bivens* involved a claim based on unlawful search; "[i]n the 38 years since *Bivens,* the Supreme Court has extended it twice only: in the context of an employment discrimination claim in violation of the Due Process Clause . . . and in the context of an Eighth Amendment violation by prison officials. . . . " *Arar v. Ashcroft*, 585 F.3d 559, 571 (2d Cir. 2009).

to harm persons in foreign countries and of providing support to a terrorist group. A district court denied Yoo's motion to dismiss the case, and an appeal from that ruling was pending when this book was written.

The following case illustrates these principles and provides an example of when government lawyers may be found liable for advice that violates a plaintiff's legal writes. In considering this opinion, note the absence of the sort of (tort law) privilege analysis found in *Reynolds v. Shrock*, in chapter 8.C. *Bivens* actions are subject to both absolute and qualified immunity defenses, which are discussed following the case.

LIPPOLDT V. COLE

468 F.3d 1204 (10th Cir. 2006)

BRISCOE, CIRCUIT JUDGE.

This suit concerns the City's response to the Summer of Mercy Renewal, plaintiffs' planned anti-abortion protests in July 2001, which commemorated the ten-year anniversary of similar protests in 1991. Plaintiffs Donna Lippoldt, OSA, and Philip Benham challenge the City's denial of their parade permits and the municipal court's bond order. OSA is an unincorporated association consisting of a group of volunteers who oppose abortion. Benham is OSA's Director, and Lippoldt volunteers for OSA–Wichita. The named defendants include the City, as well as Stephen Cole, Deputy Chief of Police for the City, and Elizabeth Harlenske, an Assistant City Attorney.

As part of the Summer of Mercy Renewal, on July 6, 2001, Lippoldt applied for eleven parade permits on OSA's behalf. Lippoldt requested permits for two parades per day from July 17, 2001, through July 21, 2001, with a proposed route that included Bleckley Street and East Kellogg Drive, where Dr. George Tiller's abortion clinic is located.[9] Lippoldt requested an additional parade permit for a parade in the downtown area.

Under the City's parade ordinance, the City Treasurer "shall issue" a parade permit, unless one of six enumerated exceptions applies. Wichita City Code § 3.13.050 (emphasis added). The parties agree that none of the exceptions listed in Section 3.13.050 provide grounds for denying plaintiffs' parade permits.

Deputy Chief of Police Cole reviewed plaintiffs' parade applications. Cole explained, "it was my belief that the situation that we were dealing with out there warranted a denial, and I asked the law department for an opinion on that and for assistance." Assistant City Attorney Harlenske

---

[9] Dr. Tiller is an abortion provider, and his Wichita clinic has long been a target for anti-abortion protests.

researched the law regarding applications for parade permits and drafted a letter denying plaintiffs' applications. After the City Attorney revised it, Harlenske read the final version of the letter aloud to the police chief over the phone. With the police chief's approval, Cole signed the denial letter in his name on behalf of the police chief. Cole did not suggest any alternative to plaintiffs for accommodating the parades for a shorter period of time at the Bleckley street location because "that location was not an acceptable location."

On July 10, 2001, one day before the City issued its decision on the plaintiffs' parade applications, the police chief signed a temporary regulation closing Bleckley Street to all vehicles, except those of residents or people conducting business in the area. The City closed Bleckley Street as part of a plan known as Operation Safe Protest, which the City had developed specifically in anticipation of the Summer of Mercy Renewal.

On July 11, 2001, the City issued one parade permit to OSA for a downtown parade, but denied OSA's ten applications for parade permits near Dr. Tiller's clinic. Defendants denied plaintiffs' parade applications for two reasons: (1) Bleckley Street was closed; and (2) the parades would interfere with local businesses in violation of Wichita City Code § 5.66.0557. Defendants claimed that once Bleckley Street was closed, it was no longer a street that fell within the parade ordinance. As to interference with businesses, Harlenske acknowledged that the parade ordinance did not allow the City to deny a parade permit merely because the planned parade would interfere with business. *See* Wichita City Code § 3.13.050. Deputy Chief Cole has approved other parades, knowing that the parades would interfere with local businesses. . . .

On July 13, 2001, plaintiffs filed suit against the City, Deputy Chief Cole, and Assistant City Attorney Harlenske pursuant to 42 U.S.C. §§ 1983 and 1985, alleging violations of the First and Fourteenth Amendments of the United States Constitution and state constitutional claims. In their complaint, plaintiffs requested declaratory relief, compensatory damages, injunctive relief, and attorney fees.

On July 16, 2001, the district court granted plaintiffs' request for a temporary restraining order so that plaintiffs could hold parades during the Summer of Mercy Renewal. Plaintiffs held parades from July 17, 2001, through July 21, 2001, in downtown and along the Bleckley Street route past Dr. Tiller's clinic.

After the parades were held, the parties pursued discovery and filed various motions. On May 28, 2003, the district court granted in part and denied in part defendants' motion for summary judgment. . . . Thereafter, the district court held a bench trial on May 28–29, 2003, to resolve plaintiffs' remaining claims. Ultimately, the district court concluded that defendants had no basis for denying plaintiffs' parade applications under the City's parade ordinance. The district court also concluded that defendants Harlenske and Cole violated plaintiffs' constitutional rights, but it denied plaintiffs' requests for compensatory damages and a permanent injunction. The district court awarded nominal damages to plaintiffs in the amount of $1.00. . . .

Defendants argue that the district court erred by concluding that Harlenske and Cole caused plaintiffs' deprivation of their First Amendment rights. We disagree.

Section 1983 requires plaintiffs to show causation, imposing liability on a defendant who "subjects, or causes to be subjected, any citizen . . . to the deprivation of any rights. . . . " 42 U.S.C. § 1983. We have explained Section 1983's causation requirement: "[A] defendant may not be held liable under § 1983 unless he or she subjected a citizen to the deprivation, or caused a citizen to be subjected to the deprivation." *Tonkovich v. Kan. Bd. of Regents,* 159 F.3d 504, 518 (10th Cir.1998). "A plaintiff must allege factual causation—i.e. 'but for' causation—in order to state a claim under § 1983." *Scott v. Hern,* 216 F.3d 897, 911 (10th Cir.2000). Where multiple "forces are actively operating," as in this case, plaintiffs may demonstrate that each defendant is a concurrent cause by showing that his or her conduct was a "substantial factor in bringing [the injury] about." *Northington v. Marin,* 102 F.3d 1564, 1568–69 (10th Cir.1996) (internal quotation marks omitted). In a case of concurrent causation, the burden of proof shifts to the defendants in that "a tortfeasor who cannot prove the extent to which the harm resulted from other concurrent causes is liable for the whole harm" because multiple tortfeasors are jointly and severally liable. *Id.* at 1568. Defendants argue that neither Cole nor Harlenske caused the deprivation because they were "subordinate to the causative actors" who actually made the decision to deny the parade permits.[10]

We address Harlenske's conduct first. Defendants argue that the causal connection between Harlenske's conduct and the ultimate denial is "too tenuous, and too heavily interrupted by the acts and decisions of others." We disagree. The record supports the district court's conclusion that Harlenske's conduct caused the violation of plaintiffs' First Amendment rights. Her conduct was a direct cause of the denial of the parade permits, and violation of plaintiffs' First Amendment rights was foreseeable. Harlenske drafted the letter denying the parade permits. After the plaintiffs filed their parade applications, she researched the law on parade applications and learned that the government must have clear guidelines to restrict parades. Despite discovering that denying the parade permits for the reasons offered by the City was most likely unconstitutional, Harlenske advised Cole to sign the denial letter. We agree with the dis-

[10] Defendants have not appealed the district court's determination that they acted unconstitutionally in denying the parade permits. Further, the defendants do not raise qualified immunity as an issue on appeal.

trict court that Harlenske's conduct was a substantial factor in denying the parade permits and violating plaintiffs' First Amendment rights. . . .

CASE QUESTIONS

1. What actions made the lawyer liable?
2. What standard of causation did the court apply?
3. Why was it met?

As noted above, two immunity defenses are relevant to Section 1983 claims and *Bivens* claims. Prosecutors are entitled to absolute immunity for decisions taken in their role as advocates for the government; typically this category of decisions includes the decision to indict and prosecution of the indictment in court rather than administrative or investigative decisions. *Hartman v. Moore*, 547 U.S. 250, 261–62 (2006) ("A *Bivens* (or § 1983) action for retaliatory prosecution will not be brought against the prosecutor, who is absolutely immune from liability for the decision to prosecute"); *Kalina v. Fletcher*, 522 U.S. 118, 129 (1997) ("critical question" in determining immunity was whether prosecutor "was acting as a complaining witness rather than a lawyer when she executed the certification '[u]nder penalty of perjury.' ").

Other officials, and prosecutors exercising discretion outside their core prosecutorial function of indictment and prosecution (advising on search and seizure procedures, for example) are entitled to qualified immunity. "[G]overnment officials performing discretionary functions generally are granted a qualified immunity and are 'shielded from liability for civil damages insofar as their conduct does not violate clearly established statutory or constitutional rights of which a reasonable person would have known.' " *Wilson v. Layne*, 526 U.S. 603, 609 (1999) (citation omitted). For purposes of these doctrines, a right is clearly established if the "contours of the right" are "sufficiently clear that a reasonable official would understand that what he is doing violates that right. This is not to say that an official action is protected by qualified immunity unless the very action in question has previously been held unlawful, but it is to say that in the light of pre-existing law the unlawfulness must be apparent." *Id.* at 615.

C. GOVERNMENT LAWYERS AND ATTORNEY CLIENT PRIVILEGE

Restatement (Third) of the Law Governing Lawyers § 74

IN RE WITNESS BEFORE SPECIAL GRAND JURY 2000–2

288 F.3d 289 (7th Cir. 2002)

DIANE P. WOOD, CIRCUIT JUDGE.

The central question on this appeal is whether a state government lawyer may refuse, on the basis of the attorney-client privilege, to disclose communications with a state officeholder when faced with a grand jury subpoena. The district court found that in the context of a federal criminal investigation, no such government attorney-client privilege existed. We agree with this determination, and therefore affirm.

I

Roger Bickel was employed by the state of Illinois as Chief Legal Counsel to the Secretary of State's office during the first four years of former Secretary (now Governor) George Ryan's administration. Bickel provided legal counsel and advice to Ryan and other Secretary of State officials as they carried out their public duties. Bickel has also served as a personal lawyer to Ryan, his wife, and Ryan's campaign committee, Citizens for Ryan, since at least 1989.

For the past three years, federal prosecutors have been investigating a "licenses for bribes" scandal in the Illinois Secretary of State's office, dubbed "Operation Safe Road." The alleged (and in some instances admitted) corruption extends to the improper issuance of commercial drivers' licenses, specialty license plates, leases, and other contracts; the improper use of campaign funds for the personal benefit of Secretary of State employees; and obstruction of justice in connection with internal office investigations. Because of his role in advising then-Secretary Ryan, federal prosecutors sought to discuss these matters with Bickel. Initially, they tried scheduling a voluntary interview with him for this purpose, but Ryan objected to the meeting and advised both Bickel and the federal prosecutors that he had not waived and would not waive the attorney-client privilege with respect to any of his prior conversations with Bickel.

After several avenues for resolving the problem proved unsuccessful, the federal prosecutors served a subpoena from the grand jury that commanded Bickel to appear and testify before that body about all conversations he had with Ryan in his official capacity as General Counsel. They also obtained a motion to compel Bickel to testify about those matters.

Finally, the United States secured a letter from Illinois' current Secretary of State, Jesse White, in which the latter purported to waive the Office's attorney-client privilege as to all of Bickel's official conversations with "all personnel and officials of the Secretary of State, regardless of their particular position or office." Ryan continued to oppose all efforts to obtain allegedly privileged information from Bickel.

On September 7, 2001, the district court granted the United States' motion to compel, finding that no attorney-client privilege attached to the communications at issue, and, alternatively, that if a privilege did attach. White had effectively waived it. . . .

II

. . . . One of the oldest and most widely recognized privileges is the attorney-client privilege, which protects confidential communications made between clients and their attorneys for the purpose of securing legal advice. *Swidler & Berlin v. United States,* 524 U.S. 399, 403 (1998). It is well established that a client may be either an individual or a corporation. But here, we have a special case: the client is neither a private individual nor a private corporation. It is instead the State of Illinois itself, represented through one of its agencies. There is surprisingly little case law on whether a government agency may also be a client for purposes of this privilege, but both parties here concede that, at least in the civil and regulatory context, the government is entitled to the same attorney-client privilege as any other client. See *Green v. IRS,* 556 F.Supp. 79, 85 (N.D.Ind.1982) (privilege "unquestionably" applies to conversations between government lawyers and administrative personnel), *aff'd,* 734 F.2d 18 (7th Cir.1984); *Restatement (Third) of Law Governing Lawyers* § 74 (2000) ("[T]he attorney-client privilege extends to a communication of a governmental organization."). We therefore proceed on that basis.

In the case of private parties, the privilege functions identically in both civil and criminal proceedings. *Swidler,* 524 U.S. at 408–09 (finding "no case authority for the proposition that the privilege applies differently in criminal and civil cases"). The United States, however, contends that the privilege between a government attorney and her official client does not extend to criminal proceedings, such as a grand jury investigation. It is supported in that position by decisions of two courts of appeals (both with thoughtful dissents) arising from Independent Counsel investigations of President Clinton. See *In re Lindsey,* 158 F.3d 1263 (D.C.Cir.1998); *In re Grand Jury Subpoena Duces Tecum,* 112 F.3d 910 (8th Cir.1997). Ryan argues that those cases were wrongly decided, at least insofar as they might apply here to support a distinction between governmental clients and private clients.

The first question we face is whether recognizing a privilege in this case would be an expansion of the current scope of the attorney-client privilege, or if a refusal to recognize the privilege would amount to a contraction of an existing privilege. Although this may seem like two sides of the same coin, it is not: the Supreme Court has instructed us, in developing a federal common law of privileges, to avoid either derogating existing privileges or extending privileges to new, uncharted waters absent compelling considerations. *Jaffee v. Redmond,* 518 U.S. 1 (1996). Unfortunately, there is no clear-cut answer to this question because, outside of former Secretary Ryan and the Clinton administration, only one government body, the Detroit City Council, has ever attempted to claim such a privilege in the criminal context. *In re Grand Jury Subpoena,* 886 F.2d 135 (6th Cir.1989). Thus, one could argue either that, since historically the privilege has never been claimed, recognizing it would be an extension, or that, since no court has ever recognized a civil-criminal distinction to the privilege, creating one here would constitute an exception.

While *Swidler* rejected a civil-criminal distinction for the privilege as to individuals, other courts have recognized that the governmental context is different, even after that decision, and have limited the privilege for governmental agencies in the criminal context. See *Lindsey,* 158 F.3d at 1272. This position is supported by the leading treatise. 24 Charles Alan Wright & Kenneth W. Graham, Jr., *Federal Practice and Procedure* § 5475, at 125–27. Furthermore, the pedigree of the privilege recognized in *Swidler* was far more impressive than the governmental privilege for which Ryan argues here. *Swidler* focused on whether the privilege survived the death of the individual client, a proposition that the common law had assumed for over a century. *Swidler,* 524 U.S. at 404 citing *Russell v. Jackson,* 68 Eng. Rep. 558 (V.C.1851). The government attorney-client privilege has no such deep historical roots. We therefore reject Ryan's contention that *Swidler* compels us to find an absolute privilege in the criminal context just because we acknowledge a government attorney-client privilege in the civil context. Even the dissenting judges in the Clinton cases were unwilling to go so far as this. . . . Our decision here instead must rest on whether the policy reasons for recognizing an attorney-client privilege in other contexts apply equally when the United States seeks information from a government lawyer.

Ryan argues that they do. His main contention is that the attorney-client privilege has been created "to encourage full and frank communication between attorneys and their clients and thereby promote broader public interests in the observance of law and the administration of justice." [*Upjohn Co. v. United States,* 449 U.S. 383, 389 (1981). If government officials know that conversations with attorneys in their offices are not privileged, they will avoid the candid discussion of sensitive legal matters. *Lindsey,* 158 F.3d at 1286–87 (Tatel, J., dissenting). This could lead to more legal violations and corruption in public office. *Duces Tecum,* 112 F.3d at 930–32 (Kopf, J., dissenting). Alternatively, uninformed public officials afraid to obtain legal advice will be unable effectively to carry out their policy objectives, hampering the implementation of government programs. Indeed, absent a privilege, citizens might be unwilling to serve in public office at all.

While we recognize the need for full and frank communication between government officials, we are more persuaded by the serious arguments against extending the attorney-client privilege to protect communications between government lawyers and the public officials they serve when criminal proceedings are at issue.

First, government lawyers have responsibilities and obligations different from those facing members of the private bar. While the latter are appropriately concerned first and foremost with protecting their clients—even those engaged in wrongdoing—from criminal charges and public exposure, government lawyers have a higher, competing duty to act in the public interest. *Lindsey,* 158 F.3d at 1273; Comment to ABA Model Rule 1.13 (noting that government lawyers may have higher duty to rectify wrongful official acts despite general rule of confidentiality). They take an oath, separate from their bar oath, to uphold the United States Constitution and the laws of this nation (and usually the laws of the state they serve when, as was the case with Bickel, they are state employees). Their compensation comes not from a client whose interests they are sworn to protect from the power of the state, but from the state itself and the public fisc.[11] It would be both unseemly and a misuse of public assets to permit a public official to use a taxpayer-provided attorney to conceal from the taxpayers themselves otherwise admissible evidence of financial wrongdoing, official misconduct, or abuse of power. Compare [*United States v. Nixon,* 418 U.S. 683, 713 (1974) (qualified executive privilege applies in the face of a criminal investigation). Therefore, when another government lawyer requires information as part of a criminal investigation, the public lawyer is obligated not to protect his governmental client but to ensure its compliance with the law.

This discussion necessarily points out another crucial difference between a government lawyer's clients and the clients of other lawyers. Individuals and corporations are both subject to criminal liability for their transgressions. Individuals will not talk and corporations will have no incentive to conduct or cooperate in internal investigations if they know that any information disclosed may be turned over to authorities. *Swidler,* 524 U.S. at 407. A state agency, however, cannot be held criminally liable by either the state itself or the federal government. See *United States v. Price,* 383 U.S. 787, 810 (1966). There is thus no need to offer

[11] FN2. Of course, a state may provide an officeholder with an individual taxpayer-provided attorney to represent her in, for example, a *Bivens* action or an independent counsel investigation and could perhaps even specify by statute that the first duty of an agency's general counsel ran always to the head of the agency as individual rather than officer. Here, however, there is no indication that Illinois has abrogated the traditional understanding that an organizational attorney's client is the organization.

the attorney-client privilege as an incentive to increase compliance with the laws. True, individual state employees can be held liable, and many have been found guilty of crimes in this very investigation. But the privilege with which we are concerned today runs to the office, not to the employees in that office. See Ill. Sup.Ct. R. 1.13 (2001) (making clear that an organizational lawyer's duty is to the organization, not the organization's individual officers). Just as a corporate attorney has no right or obligation to keep otherwise confidential information from shareholders. *Garner v. Wolfinbarger,* 430 F.2d 1093, 1101 (5th Cir.1970), so a government attorney should have no privilege to shield relevant information from the public citizens to whom she owes ultimate allegiance, as represented by the grand jury. [*Branzburg v. Hayes,*] 408 U.S. 655, 688 (1972) (noting grand jury's presumptive "right to every man's evidence").

In formulating privileges, this court cannot ignore the interests and responsibilities of the coordinate entities within our federal system, all of which are sworn to uphold the public interest and committed to the "general duty of public service." *Duces Tecum,* 112 F.3d at 920. Public officials are not the same as private citizens precisely because they exercise the power of the state. With this responsibility comes also the responsibility to act in the public interest. It follows that interpersonal relationships between an attorney for the state and a government official acting in an official capacity must be subordinated to the public interest in good and open government, leaving the government lawyer duty-bound to report internal criminal violations, not to shield them from public exposure. *Nixon,* 418 U.S. at 712–13 (recognizing executive interest in confidentiality may be lessened in face of criminal investigation); *Lindsey,* 158 F.3d at 1273 (noting public interest in "transparent and accountable government").

In the final analysis, reason and experience dictate that the lack of criminal liability for government agencies and the duty of public lawyers to uphold the law and foster an open and accountable government outweigh any need for a privilege in this context. An officeholder wary of becoming enmeshed in illegal acts may always consult with a private attorney, and there the privilege unquestionably would apply. While Ryan fears that our refusal to recognize a privilege will cause even the most trivial of matters to be taken to outside counsel, this strikes us as unduly alarmist. In fact, analogous rules apply in the corporate realm, where attorneys are repeatedly admonished to advise corporate officials that they are not personal clients of the attorney and may wish to retain other counsel. These rules do not appear to have stifled corporate discussion or proved impossible to administer, and we see no reason why a similar result cannot be countenanced here. . . .

III

The district court also determined that the current Secretary of State, Secretary White, was the holder of his Office's attorney-client privilege and had the power to waive that privilege as to conversations occurring before he took office. In light of our holding that none of the conversations between Bickel and Ryan made in their official capacities as General Counsel and Secretary of State are privileged in the face of a federal grand jury subpoena, we express no opinion on this determination. The judgment of the district court is AFFIRMED.

CASE QUESTIONS

1. Who or what did the court treat as the client in this case?
2. What was the client's position regarding privilege?
3. May government officials or agencies assert privilege in non-criminal cases?
4. What reasons did the court give for declining to recognize privilege as against a criminal subpoena?
5. The Supreme Court has instructed lower federal courts how to deal with privilege claims; what instruction has it given?

The Main Points to Recall From Chapter 18 Are:

- Government lawyers owe clients duties of care, loyalty, and confidentiality, as do private lawyers.
- Opinions vary regarding whom government lawyers represent; the best default view is the agency employing the lawyer.
- Subdivisions that are part of a larger government body (division or branch, for example) are probably not separate clients unless they have independent decision-making authority.
- Government lawyers may be held liable for violating civil or constitutional rights, subject to absolute immunity for prosecutorial advocacy and qualified immunity for other actions.
- Qualified immunity provides a defense against liability except where government lawyers act in violation of a clearly established statutory or constitutional right.
- Government lawyers are unlikely to be able to assert privilege in the face of criminal investigations and may have affirmative obligations to report wrongdoing that private lawyers may not have.

CHAPTER 19

JUDICIAL ETHICS

■ ■ ■

This chapter surveys the basic rules governing judges and provides examples of how those rules are applied. Four sources of rules are most relevant. From most general to most particular they are: General jurisprudential concepts, such as due process, the ABA Model Code of Judicial Conduct, which the ABA intends to apply to all judges, the Code of Conduct for United States Judges, which does apply to federal judges, and individual state codes of conduct, which apply only to state judges within a state.

The ABA Model Code is divided into Canons and Rules. The Canons state aspirations and goals, and provide interpretive context for the rules. The rules make those aspirations and goals concrete. Judges may be disciplined for violating the rules but not the canons. Like the Model Rules applicable to lawyers, the judicial rules are rules of reason; not every violation necessarily should lead to discipline. The judicial rules also leave some issues to judges' discretion, and no discipline may be imposed for choices within the scope of such discretion.

A. IMPARTIALITY AND INDEPENDENCE

In his novel *Burmese Days*, George Orwell writes of a magistrate whose "methods were simple":

> Even for the vastest bribe he would never sell the decision of a case, because he knew that a magistrate who gives wrong judgments is caught sooner or later. His practice, a much safer one, was to take bribes from both sides and then decide the case on strictly legal grounds. This won him a useful reputation for impartiality.

Orwell's joke makes a useful point: even such core concepts such as impartiality or disinterestedness can be thought of in various ways. Judicial ethics rules define these terms but their application varies depending on the context in which a judge works.

Most importantly, many state judges are elected while federal judges are appointed. Courts have reasoned that when citizens are allowed to choose judges candidates should be allowed to make at least some statements relevant to that choice. The ability to make statements implies a need for the resources needed to make them effectively. Judges who campaign and solicit money may look as much like politicians as judges, and the line between stating positions on legal issues (permitted) and promising results on such issues (not permitted) is not always clear.

And judges are people, too. They have opinions they may state, investments they may hold, clubs they may belong to, and so on, any of which might cause some people to suspect partiality in a given case. It is well and good to say that judges must have an open mind, but some things must stick there; otherwise it is a sieve, which is not helpful in deciding cases. It would be pointless and unrealistic to require judges to forget everything they know or believe every time they get a new case.

We begin with some core definitions. The ABA Model Code of Judicial Conduct defines "impartial" to mean "absence of bias or prejudice in favor of, or against, particular issues or classes of parties." The concept includes "maintenance of an open mind in considering issues." The Code defines "independence" to refer to "freedom from influence or controls other than those established by law." It defines "integrity" to refer to "probity, honesty, uprightness, and soundness of character." The code defines "impropriety" to mean "conduct that violates the law, court rules, or provisions of this Code" as well as conduct that "undermines a judge's independence, integrity, or impartiality."

Canon One of the Model Code requires judges to "uphold and promote" the "independence, integrity, and impartiality of the judiciary." Canon One also requires judges to avoid both impropriety and the appearance of impropriety. The "appearance of impropriety" standard is stricter than the rules governing lawyers; clients sometimes attempt to disqualify lawyers on the basis of an appearance of impropriety, but these attempts usually fail and are not supported by the rules.

The appearance of impropriety standard appears in Rule 1.2 as well, meaning a judge may be disciplined for conduct creating an appearance of impropriety. That rule requires a judge to act at all times in a manner that promotes public confidence in the independence, integrity, and impartiality of the judiciary. (Rule 1.1 requires judges to comply with the law, including the Code.) Comment five to this rule states that whether conduct creates an appearance of impropriety depends on "whether the conduct would create in reasonable minds a perception that the judge violated this Code or engaged in other conduct that reflects adversely on the judge's honesty, impartiality, temperament, or fitness to serve as a judge." Rule 1.3 prohibits judges from using, or allowing others to use, the prestige of the judicial office to advance personal or economic interests of the judge or others.

Canon Two of the Model Code requires judges to perform their work impartially, competently, and diligently. Rule 2.5 directly enforces these requirements and adds that judges must cooperate with each other in their work. Rule 2.1 requires that judicial work come before a judge's other activities; Rule 2.2 requires judges to uphold and apply to law and to do their work fairly and impartially. Comment one to Rule 2.2 requires that judges be "objective and open-minded," two definitions of impartiality found in *Republican Party of Minnesota v. White*, 536 U.S. 765 (2002), which we study below. Similarly, Rule 2.4 requires that judges not be swayed by public sentiment or fear of criticism, not permit social or other relationships to influence their conduct, and not convey or permit others to convey the idea that any person or group is in a position to influence the judge.

As noted above, these rules create tensions that are particularly acute for elected (and therefore state) judges. On the one hand, they must act impartially and uphold the independence, integrity, and impartiality of the judiciary. On the other, they must participate in, and often compete in, elections. Such competition may require them to seek financial and other support and, whether by their own initiative or in response to questions or challenges from others, to make statements that give supporters an idea of what they are supporting and voters an idea of what they are asked to vote for or against.

Our first two subsections explore these tensions. The first examines constitutional guarantees of judicial impartiality and independence, which the Supreme Court has found to be part of due process. The second examines the rights of candidates for judicial elections under the First Amendment's protection of the freedom of speech.

1. IMPARTIALITY AND INDEPENDENCE REQUIREMENTS OF DUE PROCESS

CAPERTON V. A.T. MASSEY COAL CO., INC.

129 S.Ct. 2252 (2009)

JUSTICE KENNEDY delivered the opinion of the Court.

In this case the Supreme Court of Appeals of West Virginia reversed a trial court judgment, which had entered a jury verdict of $50 million. Five justices heard the case, and the vote to reverse was 3 to 2. The question presented is whether the Due Process Clause of the Fourteenth Amendment was violated when one of the justices in the majority denied a recusal motion. The basis for the motion was that the justice had received campaign contributions in an extraordinary amount from, and through the efforts of, the board chairman and principal officer of the corporation found liable for the damages.

Under our precedents there are objective standards that require recusal when "the probability of actual bias on the part of the judge or decisionmaker is too high to be constitutionally tolerable." *Withrow v.*

Larkin, 421 U.S. 35, 47 (1975). Applying those precedents, we find that, in all the circumstances of this case, due process requires recusal.

I

In August 2002 a West Virginia jury returned a verdict that found respondents A.T. Massey Coal Co. and its affiliates (hereinafter Massey) liable for fraudulent misrepresentation, concealment, and tortious interference with existing contractual relations. The jury awarded petitioners Hugh Caperton, Harman Development Corp., Harman Mining Corp., and Sovereign Coal Sales (hereinafter Caperton) the sum of $50 million in compensatory and punitive damages.

In June 2004 the state trial court denied Massey's post-trial motions challenging the verdict and the damages award, finding that Massey "intentionally acted in utter disregard of [Caperton's] rights and ultimately destroyed [Caperton's] businesses because, after conducting cost-benefit analyses, [Massey] concluded it was in its financial interest to do so." In March 2005 the trial court denied Massey's motion for judgment as a matter of law.

Don Blankenship is Massey's chairman, chief executive officer, and president. After the verdict but before the appeal, West Virginia held its 2004 judicial elections. Knowing the Supreme Court of Appeals of West Virginia would consider the appeal in the case, Blankenship decided to support an attorney who sought to replace Justice McGraw. Justice McGraw was a candidate for reelection to that court. The attorney who sought to replace him was Brent Benjamin.

In addition to contributing the $1,000 statutory maximum to Benjamin's campaign committee, Blankenship donated almost $2.5 million to "And For The Sake Of The Kids," a political organization formed under 26 U.S.C. § 527. The § 527 organization opposed McGraw and supported Benjamin. Blankenship's donations accounted for more than two-thirds of the total funds it raised. This was not all. Blankenship spent, in addition, just over $500,000 on independent expenditures—for direct mailings and letters soliciting donations as well as television and newspaper advertisements—" 'to support . . . Brent Benjamin.' "

To provide some perspective, Blankenship's $3 million in contributions were more than the total amount spent by all other Benjamin supporters and three times the amount spent by Benjamin's own committee. Caperton contends that Blankenship spent $1 million more than the total amount spent by the campaign committees of both candidates combined.

Benjamin won. He received 382,036 votes (53.3%), and McGraw received 334,301 votes (46.7%).

In October 2005, before Massey filed its petition for appeal in West Virginia's highest court, Caperton moved to disqualify now-Justice Benjamin under the Due Process Clause and the West Virginia Code of Judicial Conduct, based on the conflict caused by Blankenship's campaign involvement. Justice Benjamin denied the motion in April 2006. He indicated that he "carefully considered the bases and accompanying exhibits proffered by the movants." But he found "no objective information . . . to show that this Justice has a bias for or against any litigant, that this Justice has prejudged the matters which comprise this litigation, or that this Justice will be anything but fair and impartial." In December 2006 Massey filed its petition for appeal to challenge the adverse jury verdict. The West Virginia Supreme Court of Appeals granted review.

In November 2007 that court reversed the $50 million verdict against Massey. The majority opinion, authored by then-Chief Justice Davis and joined by Justices Benjamin and Maynard, found that "Massey's conduct warranted the type of judgment rendered in this case." It reversed, nevertheless, based on two independent grounds—first, that a forum-selection clause contained in a contract to which Massey was not a party barred the suit in West Virginia, and, second, that res judicata barred the suit due to an out-of-state judgment to which Massey was not a party. Justice Starcher dissented, stating that the "majority's opinion is morally and legally wrong." Justice Albright also dissented, accusing the majority of "misapplying the law and introducing sweeping 'new law' into our jurisprudence that may well come back to haunt us."

Caperton sought rehearing, and the parties moved for disqualification of three of the five justices who decided the appeal. Photos had surfaced of Justice Maynard vacationing with Blankenship in the French Riviera while the case was pending. Justice Maynard granted Caperton's recusal motion. On the other side Justice Starcher granted Massey's recusal motion, apparently based on his public criticism of Blankenship's role in the 2004 elections. In his recusal memorandum Justice Starcher urged Justice Benjamin to recuse himself as well. He noted that "Blankenship's bestowal of his personal wealth, political tactics, and 'friendship' have created a cancer in the affairs of this Court." Justice Benjamin declined Justice Starcher's suggestion and denied Caperton's recusal motion.

The court granted rehearing. Justice Benjamin, now in the capacity of acting chief justice, selected Judges Cookman and Fox to replace the recused justices. Caperton moved a third time for disqualification, arguing that Justice Benjamin had failed to apply the correct standard under West Virginia law—*i.e.,* whether "a reasonable and prudent person, knowing these objective facts, would harbor doubts about Justice Benjamin's ability to be fair and impartial." Caperton also included the results of a public opinion poll, which indicated that over 67% of West Virginians doubted Justice Benjamin would be fair and impartial. Justice Benjamin again refused to withdraw, noting that the "push poll" was "neither credible nor sufficiently reliable to serve as the basis for an elected judge's disqualification."

In April 2008 a divided court again reversed the jury verdict, and again it was a 3–to–2 decision. Justice Davis filed a modified version of his prior opinion, repeating the two earlier holdings. She was joined by Justice Benjamin and Judge Fox. Justice Albright, joined by Judge Cookman, dissented. . . .

Four months later—a month after the petition for writ of certiorari was filed in this Court—Justice Benjamin filed a concurring opinion. He defended the merits of the majority opinion as well as his decision not to recuse. He rejected Caperton's challenge to his participation in the case under both the Due Process Clause and West Virginia law. Justice Benjamin reiterated that he had no " 'direct, personal, substantial, pecuniary interest' in this case.' " ___ W.Va., at ___, 679 S.E.2d, at ___, 2008 WL 918444; App. 677a (quoting [*Aetna Life Ins. Co. v. Lavoie,* 475 U.S. 813, 822]). Adopting "a standard merely of 'appearances,' " he concluded, "seems little more than an invitation to subject West Virginia's justice system to the vagaries of the day—a framework in which predictability and stability yield to supposition, innuendo, half-truths, and partisan manipulations."

We granted certiorari.

II

It is axiomatic that "[a] fair trial in a fair tribunal is a basic requirement of due process." [*In re Murchison,* 349 U.S. 133, 136 (1955)]. As the Court has recognized, however, "most matters relating to judicial disqualification [do] not rise to a constitutional level." *FTC v. Cement Institute,* 333 U.S. 683, 702 (1948). The early and leading case on the subject is *Tumey v. Ohio,* 273 U.S. 510 (1927). There, the Court stated that "matters of kinship, personal bias, state policy, remoteness of interest, would seem generally to be matters merely of legislative discretion."

The *Tumey* Court concluded that the Due Process Clause incorporated the common-law rule that a judge must recuse himself when he has "a direct, personal, substantial, pecuniary interest" in a case. This rule reflects the maxim that "[n]o man is allowed to be a judge in his own cause; because his interest would certainly bias his judgment, and, not improbably, corrupt his integrity." The Federalist No. 10, p. 59 (J. Cooke ed.1961) (J. Madison); see Frank, *Disqualification of Judges*, 56 Yale L.J. 605, 611–612 (1947) (same). Under this rule, "disqualification for bias or prejudice was not permitted"; those matters were left to statutes and judicial codes. *Lavoie, supra,* at 820; see also Part IV, *infra* (discussing judicial codes). Personal bias or prejudice "alone would not be sufficient basis for imposing a constitutional requirement under the Due Process Clause." *Lavoie, supra,* at 820.

As new problems have emerged that were not discussed at common law, however, the Court has identified additional instances which, as an objective matter, require recusal. These are circumstances "in which experience teaches that the probability of actual bias on the part of the judge or decisionmaker is too high to be constitutionally tolerable." [*Withrow v. Larkin,* 421 U.S. 35, 47 (1975)]. To place the present case in proper context, two instances where the Court has required recusal merit further discussion.

A

The first involved the emergence of local tribunals where a judge had a financial interest in the outcome of a case, although the interest was less than what would have been considered personal or direct at common law.

This was the problem addressed in [*Tumey v. Ohio,* 273 U.S. 510, 523 (1927)]. There, the mayor of a village had the authority to sit as a judge (with no jury) to try those accused of violating a state law prohibiting the possession of alcoholic beverages. Inherent in this structure were two potential conflicts. First, the mayor received a salary supplement for performing judicial duties, and the funds for that compensation derived from the fines assessed in a case. No fines were assessed upon acquittal. The mayor-judge thus received a salary supplement only if he convicted the defendant. Second, sums from the criminal fines were deposited to the village's general treasury fund for village improvements and repairs.

The Court held that the Due Process Clause required disqualification "both because of [the mayor-judge's] direct pecuniary interest in the outcome, and because of his official motive to convict and to graduate the fine to help the financial needs of the village." It so held despite observing that "[t]here are doubtless mayors who would not allow such a consideration as $12 costs in each case to affect their judgment in it." The Court articulated the controlling principle:

> "Every procedure which would offer a possible temptation to the average man as a judge to forget the burden of proof required to convict the defendant, or which might lead him not to hold the balance nice, clear and true between the State and the accused, denies the latter due process of law."

The Court was thus concerned with more than the traditional common-law prohibition on direct pecuniary interest. It was also concerned with a more general concept of interests that tempt adjudicators to disregard neutrality. . . .

The Court in *Lavoie* further clarified the reach of the Due Process Clause regarding a judge's financial interest in a case. There, a justice had cast the deciding vote on the Alabama Supreme Court to uphold a punitive damages award against an insurance company for bad-faith refusal to pay a claim. At the time of his vote, the justice was the lead plaintiff in a nearly identical lawsuit pending in Alabama's lower courts. His deciding vote, this Court surmised, "undoubtedly 'raised the stakes' " for the insurance defendant in the justice's suit.

The Court stressed that it was "not required to decide whether in fact [the justice] was influenced. The proper constitutional inquiry is "whether sitting on the case then before the Supreme Court of Alabama ' "would offer a possible temptation to the average . . . judge to . . . lead him not to hold the balance nice, clear and true." ' " The Court underscored that "what degree or kind of interest is sufficient to disqualify a judge from sitting 'cannot be defined with precision.' " In the Court's view, however, it was important that the test have an objective component.

The *Lavoie* Court proceeded to distinguish the state court justice's particular interest in the case, which required recusal, from interests that were not a constitutional concern. For instance, "while [the other] justices might conceivably have had a slight pecuniary interest" due to their potential membership in a class-action suit against their own insurance companies, that interest is " 'too remote and insubstantial to violate the constitutional constraints.' " 475 U.S., at 825–826 (quoting *Marshall v. Jerrico, Inc.,* 446 U.S. 238, 243 (1980)).

B

The second instance requiring recusal that was not discussed at common law emerged in the criminal contempt context, where a judge had no pecuniary interest in the case but was challenged because of a conflict arising from his participation in an earlier proceeding. This Court characterized that first proceeding (perhaps pejoratively) as a " 'one-man grand jury.' " *Murchison,* 349 U.S., at 133.

In that first proceeding, and as provided by state law, a judge examined witnesses to determine whether criminal charges should be brought. The judge called the two petitioners before him. One petitioner answered questions, but the judge found him untruthful and charged him with perjury. The second declined to answer on the ground that he did not have counsel with him, as state law seemed to permit. The judge charged him with contempt. The judge proceeded to try and convict both petitioners.

This Court set aside the convictions on grounds that the judge had a conflict of interest at the trial stage because of his earlier participation followed by his decision to charge them. The Due Process Clause required disqualification. The Court recited the general rule that "no man can be a judge in his own case," adding that "no man is permitted to try cases where he has an interest in the outcome." It noted that the disqualifying criteria "cannot be defined with precision. Circumstances and relationships must be considered." These circumstances and the prior relationship required recusal: "Having been a part of [the one-man grand jury] process a judge cannot be, in the very nature of things, wholly disinterested in the conviction or acquittal of those accused." That is because "[a]s a practical matter it is difficult if not impossible for a judge to free himself from the influence of what took place in his 'grand-jury' secret session."

The *Murchison* Court was careful to distinguish the circumstances and the relationship from those where the Constitution would not require recusal. It noted that the single-judge grand jury is "more a part of the accusatory process than an ordinary lay grand juror," and that "adjudication by a trial judge of a contempt committed in [a judge's] presence in open court cannot be likened to the proceedings here." The judge's prior relationship with the defendant, as well as the information acquired from the prior proceeding, was of critical import. Following *Murchison* the Court held in *Mayberry* v. *Pennsylvania*, 400 U. S. 455, 466 (1971), "that by reason ofthe Due Process Clause of the Fourteenth Amendment a defendant in criminal contempt proceedings should be given a public trial before a judge other than the one reviled by the contemnor.". . . .

III

Based on the principles described in these cases we turn to the issue before us. This problem arises in the context of judicial elections, a framework not presented in the precedents we have reviewed and discussed.

Caperton contends that Blankenship's pivotal role in getting Justice Benjamin elected created a constitutionally intolerable probability of actual bias. Though not a bribe or criminal influence, Justice Benjamin would nevertheless feel a debt of gratitude to Blankenship for his extraordinary efforts to get him elected. That temptation, Caperton claims, is as strong and inherent in human nature as was the conflict the Court confronted in *Tumey* and [*Ward v. Monroeville,* 409 U.S. 57 (1972)] when a mayor-judge (or the city) benefited financially from a defendant's conviction, as well as the conflict identified in *Murchison* and *Mayberry* when a judge was the object of a defendant's contempt.

Justice Benjamin was careful to address the recusal motions and explain his reasons why, on his view of the controlling standard, disqualification was not in order. In four separate opinions issued during the course of the appeal, he explained why no actual bias had been established. He found no basis for recusal because Caperton failed to provide "objective evidence" or "objective information," but merely "subjective belief" of bias. Nor could anyone "point to any actual conduct or activity on [his] part which could be termed 'improper.' " In other words, based on the facts presented by Caperton, Justice Benjamin conducted a probing search into his actual motives and inclinations; and he found none to be improper. We do not question his subjective findings of impartiality and propriety. Nor do we determine whether there was actual bias.

Following accepted principles of our legal tradition respecting the proper performance of judicial functions, judges often inquire into their subjective motives and purposes in the ordinary course of deciding a case. This does not mean the inquiry is a simple one. "The work of deciding cases goes on every day in hundreds of courts throughout the land. Any judge, one might suppose, would find it easy to describe the process which he had followed a thousand times and more. Nothing could be farther from the truth." B. Cardozo, The Nature of the Judicial Process 9 (1921). . . .

The difficulties of inquiring into actual bias, and the fact that the inquiry is often a private one, simply underscore the need for objective rules. Otherwise there may be no adequate protection against a judge who simply misreads or misapprehends the real motives at work in deciding the case. The judge's own inquiry into actual bias, then, is not one that the law can easily superintend or review, though actual bias, if disclosed, no doubt would be grounds for appropriate relief. In lieu of exclusive reliance on that personal inquiry, or on appellate review of the judge's determination respecting actual bias, the Due Process Clause has been implemented by objective standards that do not require proof of actual bias. In defining these standards the Court has asked whether, "under a realistic appraisal of psychological tendencies and human weakness," the interest "poses such a risk of actual bias or prejudgment that the practice must be forbidden if the guarantee of due process is to be adequately implemented." *Withrow,* 421 U.S., at 47.

We turn to the influence at issue in this case. Not every campaign contribution by a litigant or attorney creates a probability of bias that requires a judge's recusal, but this is an exceptional case. We conclude that there is a serious risk of actual bias-based on objective and reasonable perceptions—when a person with a personal stake in a particular case had a significant and disproportionate influence in placing the judge on the case by raising funds or directing the judge's election campaign when the case was pending or imminent. The inquiry centers on the contribution's relative size in comparison to the total amount of money contributed to the campaign, the total amount spent in the election, and the apparent effect such contribution had on the outcome of the election.

Applying this principle, we conclude that Blankenship's campaign efforts had a significant and disproportionate influence in placing Justice Benjamin on the case. Blankenship contributed some $3 million to unseat the incumbent and replace him with Benjamin. His contributions eclipsed the total amount spent by all other Benjamin supporters and exceeded by 300% the amount spent by Benjamin's campaign committee. Caperton claims Blankenship spent $1 million more than the total amount spent by the campaign committees of both candidates combined.

Massey responds that Blankenship's support, while significant, did not cause Benjamin's victory. In the end the people of West Virginia elected him, and they did so based on many reasons other than Blankenship's efforts. Massey points out that every major state newspaper, but one, endorsed Benjamin. It also contends that then-Justice McGraw cost himself the election by giving a speech during the campaign, a speech the opposition seized upon for its own advantage.

Justice Benjamin raised similar arguments. He asserted that "the outcome of the 2004 election was due primarily to [his own] campaign's message," as well as McGraw's "devastat[ing]" speech in which he "made a number of controversial claims which became a matter of statewide discussion in the media, on the internet, and elsewhere."

Whether Blankenship's campaign contributions were a necessary and sufficient cause of Benjamin's victory is not the proper inquiry. Much like determining whether a judge is actually biased, proving what ultimately drives the electorate to choose a particular candidate is a difficult endeavor, not likely to lend itself to a certain conclusion. This is particularly true where, as here, there is no procedure for judicial factfinding and the sole trier of fact is the one accused of bias.

Due process requires an objective inquiry into whether the contributor's influence on the election under all the circumstances "would offer a possible temptation to the average . . . judge to . . . lead him not to hold the balance nice, clear and true." *Tumey, supra,* at 532. In an election decided by fewer than 50,000 votes (382,036 to 334,301), Blankenship's campaign contributions—in comparison to the total amount contributed to the campaign, as well as the total amount spent in the election—had a significant and disproportionate influence on the electoral outcome. And the risk that Blankenship's influence engendered actual bias is sufficiently substantial that it "must be forbidden if the guarantee of due process is to be adequately implemented." *Withrow, supra,* at 47.

The temporal relationship between the campaign contributions, the justice's election, and the pendency of the case is also critical. It was reasonably foreseeable, when the campaign contributions were made, that the pending case would be before the newly elected justice. The $50 million adverse jury verdict had been entered before the election, and the Supreme Court of Appeals was the next step once the state trial court dealt with post-trial motions. So it became at once apparent that, absent recusal, Justice Benjamin would review a judgment that cost his biggest donor's company $50 million. Although there is no allegation of a *quid pro quo* agreement, the fact remains that Blankenship's extraordinary contributions were made at a time when he had a vested stake in the outcome. Just as no man is allowed to be a judge in his own cause, similar fears of bias can arise when—without the consent of the other parties—a man chooses the judge in his own cause. And applying this principle to the judicial election process, there was here a serious, objective risk of actual bias that required Justice Benjamin's recusal.

Justice Benjamin did undertake an extensive search for actual bias. But, as we have indicated, that is just one step in the judicial process; objective standards may also require recusal whether or not actual bias exists or can be proved. Due process "may sometimes bar trial by judges who have no actual bias and who would do their very best to weigh the scales of justice equally between contending parties." *Murchison,* 349 U.S., at 136. The failure to consider objective standards requiring recusal is not consistent with the imperatives of due process. We find that Blankenship's significant and disproportionate influence—coupled with the temporal relationship between the election and the pending case—" ' "offer a possible temptation to the average . . . judge to . . . lead him not to hold the balance nice, clear and true." ' " [citations omitted] On these extreme facts the probability of actual bias rises to an unconstitutional level.

IV

Our decision today addresses an extraordinary situation where the Constitution requires recusal. Massey and its *amici* predict that various adverse consequences will follow from recognizing a constitutional violation here—ranging from a flood of recusal motions to unnecessary interference with judicial elections. We disagree. The facts now before us are extreme by any measure. The parties point to no other instance involving judicial campaign contributions that presents a potential for bias comparable to the circumstances in this case.

It is true that extreme cases often test the bounds of established legal principles, and sometimes no administrable standard may be available to address the perceived wrong. But it is also true that extreme cases are more likely to cross constitutional limits, requiring this Court's intervention and formulation of objective standards. This is particularly true when due process is violated. . . .

[I]t is worth noting the effects, or lack thereof, of the Court's prior decisions. Even though the standards announced in those cases raised questions similar to those that might be asked after our decision today, the Court was not flooded with *Monroeville* or *Murchison* motions. That is perhaps due in part to the extreme facts those standards sought to address. Courts proved quite capable of applying the standards to less extreme situations.

One must also take into account the judicial reforms the States have implemented to eliminate even the appearance of partiality. Almost every State–West Virginia included—has adopted the American Bar Association's objective standard: "A judge shall avoid impropriety and the appearance of impropriety." ABA Annotated Model Code of Judicial Conduct, Canon 2 (2004); see Brief for American Bar Association as *Amicus Curiae* 14, and n. 29. The ABA Model Code's test for appearance of impropriety is "whether the conduct would create in reasonable minds a perception that the judge's ability to carry out judicial responsibilities with integrity, impartiality and competence is impaired." Canon 2A, Commentary; *see also* W. Va.Code of Judicial Conduct, Canon 2A, and Commentary (2009) (same).

The West Virginia Code of Judicial Conduct also requires a judge to "disqualify himself or herself in a proceeding in which the judge's impartiality might reasonably be questioned." Canon 3E(1); *see also* 28 U.S.C. § 455(a) ("Any justice, judge, or magistrate judge of the United States shall disqualify himself in any proceeding in which his impartiality might reasonably be questioned"). Under Canon 3E(1), " '[t]he question of disqualification focuses on whether an objective assessment of the judge's conduct produces a reasonable question about impartiality, not on the judge's subjective perception of the ability to act fairly.' " *State ex rel. Brown v. Dietrick,* 191 W.Va. 169, 174, n. 9 (1994); see also *Liteky v. United States,* 510 U.S. 540, 558 (1994) (KENNEDY, J., concurring in judgment) ("[U]nder [28 U.S.C.] § 455(a), a judge should be disqualified only if it appears that he or she harbors an aversion, hostility or disposition of a kind that a fair-minded person could not set aside when judging the dispute"). Indeed, some States require recusal based on campaign contributions similar to those in this case. See, *e.g.,* Ala.Code §§ 12–24–1, 12–24–2 (2006); Miss.Code of Judicial Conduct, Canon 3E(2) (2008).

These codes of conduct serve to maintain the integrity of the judiciary and the rule of law. The Conference of the Chief Justices has underscored that the codes are "[t]he principal safeguard against judicial campaign abuses" that threaten to imperil "public confidence in the fairness and integrity of the nation's elected judges." Brief for Conference of Chief Justices as *Amicus Curiae* 4, 11. This is a vital state interest:

"Courts, in our system, elaborate principles of law in the course of resolving disputes. The power and the prerogative of a court to perform this function rest, in the end, upon the respect accorded to its judgments. The citizen's respect for judgments depends in turn upon the issuing court's absolute probity. Judicial integrity is, in consequence, a state interest of the highest order." *Republican Party of Minn. v. White,* 536 U.S. 765, 793 (2002) (KENNEDY, J., concurring). It is for this reason that States may choose to "adopt recusal standards more rigorous than due process requires." *Id.,* at 794; *see also Bracy v. Gramley,* 520 U.S. 899, 904 (1997) (distinguishing the "constitutional floor" from the ceiling set "by common law, statute, or the professional standards of the bench and bar") "The Due Process Clause demarks only the outer boundaries of judicial disqualifications. Congress and the states, of course, remain free to impose more rigorous standards for judicial disqualification than those we find mandated here today." *Lavoie, supra,* at 828. Because the codes of judicial conduct provide more protection than due process requires, most disputes over disqualification will be resolved without resort to the Constitution. Application of the constitutional standard implicated in this case will thus be confined to rare instances.

The judgment of the Supreme Court of Appeals of West Virginia is reversed, and the case is remanded for further proceedings not inconsistent with this opinion.

It is so ordered.

CHIEF JUSTICE ROBERTS, with whom JUSTICE SCALIA, JUSTICE THOMAS, and JUSTICE ALITO join, dissenting.

I, of course, share the majority's sincere concerns about the need to maintain a fair, independent, and impartial judiciary—and one that appears to be such. But I fear that the Court's decision will undermine rather than promote these values.

Until today, we have recognized exactly two situations in which the Federal Due Process Clause requires disqualification of a judge: when the judge has a financial interest in the outcome of the case, and when the judge is trying a defendant for certain criminal contempts. Vaguer notions of bias or the appearance of bias were never a basis for disqualification, either at common law or under our constitutional precedents. Those issues were instead addressed by legislation or court rules.

Today, however, the Court enlists the Due Process Clause to overturn a judge's failure to recuse because of a "probability of bias." Unlike the established grounds for disqualification, a "probability of bias" cannot be defined in any limited way. The Court's new "rule" provides no guidance to judges and litigants about when recusal will be constitutionally required. This will inevitably lead to an increase in allegations that judges are biased, however groundless those charges may be. The end result will do far more to erode public confidence in judicial impartiality than an isolated failure to recuse in a particular case. . . .

In any given case, there are a number of factors that could give rise to a "probability" or "appearance" of bias: friendship with a party or lawyer, prior employment experience, membership in clubs or associations, prior speeches and writings, religious affiliation, and countless other considerations. We have never held that the Due Process Clause requires recusal for any of these reasons, even though they could be viewed as presenting a "probability of bias." Many state *statutes* require recusal based on a probability or appearance of bias, but "that alone would not be sufficient basis for imposing a *constitutional* requirement under the Due Process Clause." *Lavoie, supra,* at 820 (emphasis added). States are, of course, free to adopt broader recusal rules than the Constitution requires—and every State has—but these developments are not continuously incorporated into the Due Process Clause. . . .

In departing from this clear line between when recusal is constitutionally required and when it is not, the majority repeatedly emphasizes the need for an "objective" standard. The majority's analysis is "objective" in that it does not inquire into Justice Benjamin's motives or decisionmaking process. But the standard the majority articulates—"probability of bias"—fails to provide clear, workable guidance for future cases. At the most basic level, it is unclear whether the new probability of bias standard is somehow limited to financial support in judicial elections, or applies to judicial recusal questions more generally.

But there are other fundamental questions as well. With little help from the majority, courts will now have to determine:

1. How much money is too much money? What level of contribution or expenditure gives rise to a "probability of bias"?

2. How do we determine whether a given expenditure is "disproportionate"? Disproportionate *to what* ?

3. Are independent, non-coordinated expenditures treated the same as direct contributions to a candidate's campaign? What about contributions to independent outside groups supporting a candidate? . . .

These are only a few uncertainties that quickly come to mind. Judges and litigants will surely encounter others when they are forced to, or wish to, apply the majority's decision in different circumstances. Today's opinion requires state and federal judges simultaneously to act as political scientists (why did candidate X win the election?), economists (was the financial support disproportionate?), and psychologists (is there likely to be a debt of gratitude?).

The Court's inability to formulate a "judicially discernible and manageable standard" strongly counsels against the recognition of a novel constitutional right. The need to consider these and countless other questions helps explain why the common law and this Court's constitutional jurisprudence have never required disqualification on such vague grounds as "probability" or "appearance" of bias.

To its credit, the Court seems to recognize that the inherently boundless nature of its new rule poses a problem. But the majority's only answer is that the present case is an "extreme" one, so there is no need to worry about other cases. . . . But this is just so much whistling past the graveyard. Claims that have little chance of success are nonetheless frequently filed. The success rate for certiorari petitions before this Court is approximately 1.1%, and yet the previous Term some 8,241 were filed.

Every one of the "*Caperton* motions" or appeals or § 1983 actions will claim that the judge is biased, or probably biased, bringing the judge and the judicial system into disrepute. And all future litigants will assert that their case is *really* the most extreme thus far.

Extreme cases often test the bounds of established legal principles. There is a cost to yielding to the desire to correct the extreme case, rather than adhering to the legal principle. That cost has been demonstrated so often that it is captured in a legal aphorism: "Hard cases make bad law." . . . . I believe we will come to regret this decision as well, when courts are forced to deal with a wide variety of *Caperton* motions, each claiming the title of "most extreme" or "most disproportionate."

And why is the Court so convinced that this is an extreme case? It is true that Don Blankenship spent a large amount of money in connection with this election. But this point cannot be emphasized strongly enough: Other than a $1,000 direct contribution from Blankenship, *Justice Benjamin and his campaign had no control over how this money was spent.* Campaigns go to great lengths to develop precise messages and strategies. An insensitive or ham-handed ad campaign by an independent third party might distort the campaign's message or cause a backlash against the candidate, even though the candidate was not responsible for the ads. . . . The majority repeatedly characterizes Blankenship's spending as "contributions" or "campaign contributions," but it is more accurate to refer to them as "independent expenditures." Blankenship only "contributed" $1,000 to the Benjamin campaign.

Moreover, Blankenship's independent expenditures do not appear "grossly disproportionate" compared to other such expenditures in this very election. "And for the Sake of the Kids"—an independent group that received approximately two-thirds of its funding from Blankenship—spent $3,623,500 in connection with the election. But large independent expenditures were also made in support of Justice Benjamin's opponent. "Consumers for Justice"—an independent group that received large contributions from the plaintiffs' bar—spent approximately $2 million in this race. And Blankenship has made large expenditures in connection with several previous West Virginia elections, which undercuts any notion that his involvement in this election was "intended to influence the outcome" of particular pending litigation.

It is also far from clear that Blankenship's expenditures affected the outcome of this election. Justice Benjamin won by a comfortable 7–point margin (53.3% to 46.7%). Many observers believed that Justice Benjamin's opponent doomed his candidacy by giving a well-publicized speech that made several curious allegations; this speech was described in the local media as "deeply disturbing" and worse. Justice Benjamin's opponent also refused to give interviews or participate in debates. All but one of the major West Virginia newspapers endorsed Justice Benjamin. Justice Benjamin just might have won because the voters of West Virginia thought he would be a better judge than his opponent. Unlike the majority, I cannot say with any degree of certainty that Blankenship "cho[se] the judge in his own cause." I would give the voters of West Virginia more credit than that.

It is an old cliché, but sometimes the cure is worse than the disease. I am sure there are cases where a "probability of bias" should lead the prudent judge to step aside, but the judge fails to do so. Maybe this is one of them. But I believe that opening the door to recusal claims under the Due Process Clause, for an amorphous "probability of bias," will itself bring our judicial system into undeserved disrepute, and diminish the confidence of the American people in the fairness and integrity of their courts. I hope I am wrong.

I respectfully dissent.

JUSTICE SCALIA, dissenting.

The principal purpose of this Court's exercise of its certiorari jurisdiction is to clarify the law. See this Court's Rule 10. As THE CHIEF JUSTICE's dissent makes painfully clear, the principal consequence of today's decision is to create vast uncertainty with respect to a point of law that can be raised in all litigated cases in (at least) those 39 States that elect their judges. . . . The Court today continues its quixotic quest to right all wrongs and repair all imperfections through the Constitution. Alas, the quest cannot succeed—which is why some wrongs and imperfections have been called nonjusticiable. In the best of all possible worlds, should judges sometimes recuse even where the clear commands of our prior due process law do not require it? Undoubtedly. The relevant question, however, is whether we do more good than harm by seeking to correct this imperfection through expansion of our constitutional mandate in a manner ungoverned by any discernable rule. The answer is obvious.

CASE QUESTIONS

1. In what contexts before *Caperton* had the Court found due process violations based on judicial interests?
2. What standard did the Court adopt for assessing due process claims in this context?
3. Do campaign contributions need to be decisive in the election for a due process violation to be found?
4. What remedy does the Constitution require in this context?
5. How does the majority assess the probability of bias? How does the dissent assess it?

In July 2012 two ABA committees proposed an amendment to Rule 2.11 of the Model Code of Judicial Conduct. The proposal would require disqualification when a judge knows a party, the party's lawyer, or the lawyer's firm has contributed to "other organizations that contributed to or supported the judge's election or retention campaign" an amount greater than a sum to be specified by jurisdiction. If adopted, this language would provide at least the ABA's recommended answer to the third question Chief Justice Roberts posed in his *Caperton* dissent.

2. FREEDOM OF SPEECH IN JUDICIAL ELECTIONS

REPUBLICAN PARTY OF MINNESOTA V. WHITE

536 U.S. 765 (2002)

JUSTICE SCALIA delivered the opinion of the Court.

The question presented in this case is whether the First Amendment permits the Minnesota Supreme Court to prohibit candidates for judicial election in that State from announcing their views on disputed legal and political issues.

I

Since Minnesota's admission to the Union in 1858, the State's Constitution has provided for the selection of all state judges by popular election. Minn. Const., Art. VI, § 7. Since 1912, those elections have been nonpartisan. Act of June 19, ch. 2, 1912 Minn. Laws Special Sess., pp. 4–6. Since 1974, they have been subject to a legal restriction which states that a "candidate for a judicial office, including an incumbent judge," shall not "announce his or her views on disputed legal or political issues." Minn.Code of Judicial Conduct, Canon 5(A)(3)(d)(i) (2000). This prohibition, promulgated by the Minnesota Supreme Court and based on Canon 7(B) of the 1972 American Bar Association (ABA) Model Code of Judicial Conduct, is known as the "announce clause." Incumbent judges who violate it are subject to discipline, including removal, censure, civil penalties, and suspension without pay. Minn. Rules of Board on Judicial Standards 4(a)(6), 11(d) (2002). Lawyers who run for judicial office also must comply with the announce clause. Minn. Rule of Professional Conduct 8.2(b) (2002) ("A lawyer who is a candidate for judicial office shall comply with the applicable provisions of the Code of Judicial Conduct"). Those who violate it are subject to, *inter alia,* disbarment, suspension, and probation. Rule 8.4(a); Minn. Rules on Lawyers Professional Responsibility 8–14, 15(a) (2002).

In 1996, one of the petitioners, Gregory Wersal, ran for associate justice of the Minnesota Supreme Court. In the course of the campaign, he distributed literature criticizing several Minnesota Supreme Court decisions on issues such as crime, welfare, and abortion. A complaint against Wersal challenging, among other things, the propriety of this literature was filed with the Office of Lawyers Professional Responsibility, the agency which, under the direction of the Minnesota Lawyers Professional Responsibility Board, investigates and prosecutes ethical violations of lawyer candidates for judicial office. The Lawyers Board dismissed the complaint; with regard to the charges that his campaign materials violated the announce clause, it expressed doubt whether the clause could constitutionally be enforced. Nonetheless, fearing that further ethical complaints would jeopardize his ability to practice law, Wersal withdrew from the election. In 1998, Wersal ran again for the same office. Early in that race, he sought an advisory opinion from the Lawyers Board with regard to whether it planned to enforce the announce clause. The Lawyers Board responded equivocally, stating that, although it had significant doubts about the constitutionality of the provision, it was unable to answer his question because he had not submitted a list of the announcements he wished to make.

Shortly thereafter, Wersal filed this lawsuit in Federal District Court against respondents, seeking, *inter alia,* a declaration that the announce clause violates the First Amendment and an injunction against its enforcement. Wersal alleged that he was forced to refrain from announcing his views on disputed issues during the 1998 campaign, to the point where he declined response to questions put to him by the press and public, out of concern that he might run afoul of the announce clause. Other plaintiffs in the suit, including the Minnesota Republican Party, alleged that, because the clause kept Wersal from announcing his views, they were unable to learn those views and support or oppose his candidacy accordingly. The parties filed cross-motions for summary judgment, and the District Court found in favor of respondents, holding that the announce clause did not violate the First Amendment. 63 F.Supp.2d 967 (D.Minn.1999). Over a dissent by Judge Beam, the United States Court of Appeals for the Eighth Circuit affirmed. *Republican Party of Minn. v. Kelly,* 247 F.3d 854 (2001). We granted certiorari. 534 U.S. 1054 (2001).

II

Before considering the constitutionality of the announce clause, we must be clear about its meaning. Its text says that a candidate for judicial office shall not "announce his or her views on disputed legal or political issues." Minn.Code of Judicial Conduct, Canon 5(A)(3)(d)(i) (2002).

We know that "announc[ing] . . . views" on an issue covers much more than *promising* to decide an issue a particular way. The prohibition extends to the candidate's mere statement of his current position, even if he does not bind himself to maintain that position after election. All the parties agree this is the case, because the Minnesota Code contains a so-called "pledges or promises" clause, which *separately* prohibits judicial candidates from making "pledges or promises of conduct in office other than the faithful and impartial performance of the duties of the office," *ibid.*—a prohibition that is not challenged here and on which we express no view.

There are, however, some limitations that the Minnesota Supreme Court has placed upon the scope of the announce clause that are not (to put it politely) immediately apparent from its text. The statements that formed the basis of the complaint against Wersal in 1996 included criticism of past decisions of the Minnesota Supreme Court. One piece of campaign literature stated that "[t]he Minnesota Supreme Court has issued decisions which are marked by their disregard for the Legislature and a lack of common sense." It went on to criticize a decision excluding from evidence confessions by criminal defendants that were not tape-recorded, asking "[s]hould we conclude that because the Supreme Court does not trust police, it allows confessed criminals to go free?" It criticized a decision striking down a state law restricting welfare benefits, asserting that "[i]t's the Legislature which should set our spending policies." And it criticized a decision requiring public financing of abortions for poor women as "unprecedented" and a "pro-abortion stance." Although one would think that all of these statements touched on disputed legal or political issues, they did not (or at least do not now) fall within the scope of the announce clause. The Judicial Board issued an opinion stating that judicial candidates may criticize past decisions, and the Lawyers Board refused to discipline Wersal for the foregoing statements because, in part, it thought they did not violate the announce clause. The Eighth Circuit relied on the Judicial Board's opinion in upholding the announce clause, 247 F.3d, at 882, and the Minnesota Supreme Court recently embraced the Eighth Circuit's interpretation, *In re Code of Judicial Conduct,* 639 N.W.2d 55 (Minn.2002).

There are yet further limitations upon the apparent plain meaning of the announce clause: In light of the constitutional concerns, the District Court construed the clause to reach only disputed issues that are likely to come before the candidate if he is elected judge. 63 F.Supp.2d, at 986. The Eighth Circuit accepted this limiting interpretation by the District Court, and in addition construed the clause to allow general discussions of case law and judicial philosophy. 247 F.3d, at 881–882. The Supreme Court of Minnesota adopted these interpretations as well when it ordered enforcement of the announce clause in accordance with the Eighth Circuit's opinion.

It seems to us, however, that—like the text of the announce clause itself—these limitations upon the text of the announce clause are not all that they appear to be. First, respondents acknowledged at oral argument that statements critical of past judicial decisions are *not* permissible if the candidate also states that he is against *stare decisis.* Thus, candidates must choose between stating their views critical of past decisions and stating their views in opposition to *stare decisis.* Or, to look at it more concretely, they may state their view that prior decisions were erroneous only if they do not assert that they, if elected, have any power to eliminate erroneous decisions.

Second, limiting the scope of the clause to issues likely to come before a court is not much of a limitation at all. One would hardly expect the "disputed legal or political issues" raised in the course of a state judicial election to include such matters as whether the Federal Government should end the embargo of Cuba. Quite obviously, they will be those legal or political disputes that are the proper (or by past decisions have been made the improper) business of the state courts. And within that relevant category, "[t]here is almost no legal or political issue that is unlikely to come before a judge of an American court, state or federal, of general jurisdiction." *Buckley v. Illinois Judicial Inquiry Bd.,* 997 F.2d 224, 229 (C.A.7 1993).

Third, construing the clause to allow "general" discussions of case law and judicial philosophy turns out to be of little help in an election campaign. At oral argument, respondents gave, as an example of this exception, that a candidate is free to assert that he is a " 'strict constructionist.' " But that, like most other philosophical generalities, has little meaningful content for the electorate unless it is exemplified by application to a particular issue of construction likely to come before a court—for example, whether a particular statute runs afoul of any provision of the Constitution. Respondents conceded that the announce clause would prohibit the candidate from exemplifying his philosophy in this fashion. Without such application to real-life issues, all candidates can claim to be "strict constructionists" with equal (and unhelpful) plausibility.

In any event, it is clear that the announce clause prohibits a judicial candidate from stating his views on any specific nonfanciful legal question within the province of the court for which he is running, except in the context of discussing past decisions—and in the latter context as well, if he expresses the view that he is not bound by *stare decisis.*

Respondents contend that this still leaves plenty of topics for discussion on the campaign trail. These include a candidate's "character," "education," "work habits," and "how [he] would handle administrative duties if elected." Indeed, the Judicial Board has printed a list of preapproved questions which judicial candidates are allowed to answer. These include how the candidate feels about cameras in the courtroom, how he would go about reducing the caseload, how the costs of judicial administration can be reduced, and how he proposes to ensure that minorities and women are treated more fairly by the court system. Minnesota State Bar Association Judicial Elections Task Force Report & Recommendations, App. C (June 19, 1997), reprinted at App. 97–103. Whether this list of preapproved subjects, and other topics not prohibited by the announce clause, adequately fulfill the First Amendment's guarantee of freedom of speech is the question to which we now turn.

III

As the Court of Appeals recognized, the announce clause both prohibits speech on the basis of its content and burdens a category of speech that is "at the core of our First Amendment freedoms"—speech about the qualifications of candidates for public office. The Court of Appeals concluded that the proper test to be applied to determine the constitutionality of such a restriction is what our cases have called strict scrutiny, the parties do not dispute that this is correct. Under the strict-scrutiny test, respondents have the burden to prove that the announce clause is (1) narrowly tailored, to serve (2) a compelling state interest. *E.g., Eu v. San Francisco County Democratic Central Comm.,* 489 U.S. 214, 222 (1989). In order for respondents to show that the announce clause is narrowly tailored, they must demonstrate that it does not "unnecessarily circumscrib[e] protected expression." *Brown v. Hartlage,* 456 U.S. 45, 54 (1982).

The Court of Appeals concluded that respondents had established two interests as sufficiently compelling to justify the announce clause: preserving the impartiality of the state judiciary and preserving the appearance of the impartiality of the state judiciary. Respondents reassert these two interests before us, arguing that the first is compelling because it protects the due process rights of litigants, and that the second is compelling because it preserves public confidence in the judiciary. Respondents are rather vague, however, about what they mean by "impartiality." Indeed, although the term is used throughout the Eighth Circuit's opinion, the briefs, the Minnesota Code of Judicial Conduct, and the ABA Codes of Judicial Conduct, none of these sources bothers to define it. Clarity on this point is essential before we can decide whether impartiality is indeed a compelling state interest, and, if so, whether the announce clause is narrowly tailored to achieve it.

A

One meaning of "impartiality" in the judicial context—and of course its root meaning—is the lack of bias for or against either *party* to the proceeding. Impartiality in this sense assures equal application of the law. That is, it guarantees a party that the judge who hears his case will apply the law to him in the same way he applies it to any other party. This is the traditional sense in which the term is used. See Webster's New International Dictionary 1247 (2d ed.1950) (defining "impartial" as "[n]ot partial; esp., not favoring one more than another; treating all alike; unbiased; equitable; fair; just"). It is also the sense in which it is used in the cases cited by respondents and *amici* for the proposition that an impartial judge is essential to due process. *Tumey v. Ohio,* 273 U.S. 510, 523, 531–534 (1927) (judge violated due process by sitting in a case in which it would be in his financial interest to find against one of the parties); *Aetna Life Ins. Co. v. Lavoie,* 475 U.S. 813, 822–825 (1986) (same); *Ward v. Monroeville,* 409 U.S. 57, 58–62 (1972) (same); *Johnson v. Mississippi,* 403 U.S. 212, 215–216 (1971) *(per curiam)* (judge violated due process by sitting in a case in which one of the parties was a previously successful litigant against him); *Bracy v. Gramley,* 520 U.S. 899, 905 (1997) (would violate due process if a judge was disposed to rule against defendants who did not bribe him in order to cover up the fact that he regularly ruled in favor of defendants who did bribe him); *In re Murchison,* 349 U.S. 133, 137–139 (1955) (judge violated due process by sitting in the criminal trial of defendant whom he had indicted).

We think it plain that the announce clause is not narrowly tailored to serve impartiality (or the appearance of impartiality) in this sense. Indeed, the clause is barely tailored to serve that interest *at all,* inasmuch as it does not restrict speech for or against particular *parties,* but rather speech for or against particular *issues.* To be sure, when a case arises that turns on a legal issue on which the judge (as a candidate) had taken a particular stand, the party taking the opposite stand is likely to lose. But not because of any bias against that party, or favoritism toward the other party. *Any* party taking that position is just as likely to lose. The judge is applying the law (as he sees it) evenhandedly.[1]

B

It is perhaps possible to use the term "impartiality" in the judicial context (though this is certainly not a common usage) to mean lack of preconception in favor of or against a particular *legal view.* This sort of impartiality would be concerned, not with guaranteeing litigants equal application of the law, but rather with guaranteeing them an equal chance to persuade the court on the legal points in their case. Impartiality in this sense may well be an interest served by the announce clause, but it is not a *compelling* state interest, as strict scrutiny requires. A judge's lack of predisposition regarding the relevant legal issues in a case has never been thought a necessary component of equal justice, and with good rea-

[1] FN7. Justice STEVENS asserts that the announce clause "serves the State's interest in maintaining both the appearance of this form of impartiality and its actuality." We do not disagree. Some of the speech prohibited by the announce clause may well exhibit a bias against parties—including Justice STEVENS's example of an election speech stressing the candidate's unbroken record of affirming convictions for rape, *ibid.* That is why we are careful to say that the announce clause is "*barely* tailored to serve that interest," (emphasis added). The question under our strict scrutiny test, however, is not whether the announce clause serves this interest *at all,* but whether it is *narrowly tailored* to serve this interest. It is not.

son. For one thing, it is virtually impossible to find a judge who does not have preconceptions about the law. As then-Justice REHNQUIST observed of our own Court: "Since most Justices come to this bench no earlier than their middle years, it would be unusual if they had not by that time formulated at least some tentative notions that would influence them in their interpretation of the sweeping clauses of the Constitution and their interaction with one another. It would be not merely unusual, but extraordinary, if they had not at least given opinions as to constitutional issues in their previous legal careers." *Laird v. Tatum,* 409 U.S. 824, 835 (1972) (memorandum opinion).

Indeed, even if it were possible to select judges who did not have preconceived views on legal issues, it would hardly be desirable to do so. "Proof that a Justice's mind at the time he joined the Court was a complete *tabula rasa* in the area of constitutional adjudication would be evidence of lack of qualification, not lack of bias." *Ibid.* The Minnesota Constitution positively forbids the selection to courts of general jurisdiction of judges who are impartial in the sense of having no views on the law. Minn. Const., Art. VI, § 5 ("Judges of the supreme court, the court of appeals and the district court shall be learned in the law"). And since avoiding judicial preconceptions on legal issues is neither possible nor desirable, pretending otherwise by attempting to preserve the "appearance" of that type of impartiality can hardly be a compelling state interest either.

C

A third possible meaning of "impartiality" (again not a common one) might be described as open-mindedness. This quality in a judge demands, not that he have no preconceptions on legal issues, but that he be willing to consider views that oppose his preconceptions, and remain open to persuasion, when the issues arise in a pending case. This sort of impartiality seeks to guarantee each litigant, not an *equal* chance to win the legal points in the case, but at least *some* chance of doing so. It may well be that impartiality in this sense, and the appearance of it, are desirable in the judiciary, but we need not pursue that inquiry, since we do not believe the Minnesota Supreme Court adopted the announce clause for that purpose.

Respondents argue that the announce clause serves the interest in open-mindedness, or at least in the appearance of open-mindedness, because it relieves a judge from pressure to rule a certain way in order to maintain consistency with statements the judge has previously made. The problem is, however, that statements in election campaigns are such an infinitesimal portion of the public commitments to legal positions that judges (or judges-to-be) undertake, that this object of the prohibition is implausible. Before they arrive on the bench (whether by election or otherwise) judges have often committed themselves on legal issues that they must later rule upon. See, *e.g., Laird, supra,* at 831–833 (describing Justice Black's participation in several cases construing and deciding the constitutionality of the Fair Labor Standards Act, even though as a Senator he had been one of its principal authors; and Chief Justice Hughes's authorship of the opinion overruling *Adkins v. Children's Hospital of D.C.,* 261 U.S. 525 (1923), a case he had criticized in a book written before his appointment to the Court). More common still is a judge's confronting a legal issue on which he has expressed an opinion while on the bench. Most frequently, of course, that prior expression will have occurred in ruling on an earlier case. But judges often state their views on disputed legal issues outside the context of adjudication—in classes that they conduct, and in books and speeches. Like the ABA Codes of Judicial Conduct, the Minnesota Code not only permits but encourages this. See Minn.Code of Judicial Conduct, Canon 4(B) (2002) ("A judge may write, lecture, teach, speak and participate in other extra-judicial activities concerning the law . . . "); Minn.Code of Judicial Conduct, Canon 4(B), Comment. (2002) ("To the extent that time permits, a judge is encouraged to do so . . . "). That is quite incompatible with the notion that the need for open-mindedness (or for the appearance of open-mindedness) lies behind the prohibition at issue here.

The short of the matter is this: In Minnesota, a candidate for judicial office may not say "I think it is constitutional for the legislature to prohibit same-sex marriages." He may say the very same thing, however, up until the very day before he declares himself a candidate, and may say it repeatedly (until litigation is pending) after he is elected. As a means of pursuing the objective of open-mindedness that respondents now articulate, the announce clause is so woefully underinclusive as to render belief in that purpose a challenge to the credulous. . . .

Justice STEVENS asserts that statements made in an election campaign pose a special threat to open-mindedness because the candidate, when elected judge, will have a *particular* reluctance to contradict them. That might be plausible, perhaps, with regard to campaign *promises.* A candidate who says "If elected, I will vote to uphold the legislature's power to prohibit same-sex marriages" will positively be breaking his word if he does not do so (although one would be naive not to recognize that campaign promises are—by long democratic tradition—the least binding form of human commitment). But, as noted earlier, the Minnesota Supreme Court has adopted a separate prohibition on campaign "pledges or promises," which is not challenged here.

The proposition that judges feel significantly greater compulsion, or appear to feel significantly greater compulsion, to maintain consistency with *nonpromissory* statements made during a judicial campaign than with such statements made before or after the campaign is not self-evidently true. It seems to us quite likely, in fact, that in many cases the opposite is true. We doubt, for example, that a mere statement of position enunciated during the pendency of an election will be regarded by a judge as more binding—or as more likely to subject him to popular disfavor if reconsidered—than a carefully considered holding that the judge set forth in an earlier opinion denying some individual's claim to justice. In any event, it suffices to say that respondents have not carried the burden imposed by our strict-scrutiny test to establish this proposition (that campaign statements are uniquely destructive of open-mindedness) on which the validity of the announce clause rests. See, *e.g., Landmark Communications, Inc. v. Virginia,* 435 U.S. 829, 841 (1978) (rejecting speech restriction subject to strict scrutiny where the State "offered little more than assertion and conjecture to support its claim that without criminal sanctions the objectives of the statutory scheme would be seriously undermined"); *United States v. Playboy Entertainment Group, Inc.,* 529 U.S. 803, 816–825 (2000) (same).[2]

Moreover, the notion that the special context of electioneering justifies an *abridgment* of the right to speak out on disputed issues sets our First Amendment jurisprudence on its head. "[D]ebate on the qualifications of candidates" is "at the core of our electoral process and of the First Amendment freedoms," not at the edges. *Eu,* 489 U.S., at 222–223 (internal quotation marks omitted). "The role that elected officials play in our society makes it all the more imperative that they be allowed freely to express themselves on matters of current public importance." *Wood v. Georgia,* 370 U.S. 375, 395 (1962). "It is simply not the function of government to select which issues are worth discussing or debating in the course of a political campaign." *Brown,* 456 U.S., at 60 (internal quotation marks omitted). We have never allowed the government to prohibit candidates from communicating relevant information to voters during an election.

Justice GINSBURG would do so—and much of her dissent confirms rather than refutes our conclusion that the purpose behind the announce clause is not open-mindedness in the judiciary, but the undermining of judicial elections. She contends that the announce clause must be constitutional because due process would be denied if an elected judge sat in a case involving an issue on which he had previously announced his view. She reaches this conclusion because, she says, such a judge would have a "direct, personal, substantial, and pecuniary interest" in ruling consistently with his previously announced view, in order to reduce the risk that

[2] FN8. We do not agree with Justice STEVENS's broad assertion that "to the extent that [statements on legal issues] seek to enhance the popularity of the candidate by indicating how he would rule in specific cases if elected, they evidence *a lack of fitness for office.*" (emphasis added). Of course *all* statements on real-world legal issues "indicate" how the speaker would rule "in specific cases." And if making such statements *(of honestly held views)* with the hope of enhancing one's chances with the electorate displayed a lack of fitness for office, so would similarly motivated honest statements of judicial candidates made with the hope of enhancing their chances of confirmation by the Senate, or indeed of appointment by the President. Since such statements are made, we think, in every confirmation hearing, Justice STEVENS must contemplate a federal bench filled with the unfit.

he will be "voted off the bench and thereby lose [his] salary and emoluments," (internal quotation marks and alterations omitted). But elected judges—regardless of whether they have announced any views beforehand—*always* face the pressure of an electorate who might disagree with their rulings and therefore vote them off the bench. Surely the judge who frees Timothy McVeigh places his job much more at risk than the judge who (horror of horrors!) reconsiders his previously announced view on a disputed legal issue. So if, as Justice GINSBURG claims, it violates due process for a judge to sit in a case in which ruling one way rather than another increases his prospects for reelection, then—quite simply—the practice of electing judges is itself a violation of due process. It is not difficult to understand how one with these views would approve the election-nullifying effect of the announce clause.[3] They are not, however, the views reflected in the Due Process Clause of the Fourteenth Amendment, which has coexisted with the election of judges ever since it was adopted.

Justice GINSBURG devotes the rest of her dissent to attacking arguments we do not make. For example, despite the number of pages she dedicates to disproving this proposition, we neither assert nor imply that the First Amendment requires campaigns for judicial office to sound the same as those for legislative office. What we do assert, and what Justice GINSBURG ignores, is that, *even if* the First Amendment allows greater regulation of judicial election campaigns than legislative election campaigns, the announce clause still fails strict scrutiny because it is woefully underinclusive, prohibiting announcements by judges (and would-be judges) only at certain times and in certain forms. We rely on the cases involving speech during elections, only to make the obvious point that this underinclusiveness cannot be explained by resort to the notion that the First Amendment provides less protection during an election campaign than at other times.[4]

But in any case, Justice GINSBURG greatly exaggerates the difference between judicial and legislative elections. She asserts that "the rationale underlying unconstrained speech in elections for political office—that representative government depends on the public's ability to choose

[3] FN9. Justice GINSBURG argues that the announce clause is not election nullifying because Wersal criticized past decisions of the Minnesota Supreme Court in his campaign literature and the Lawyers Board decided not to discipline him for doing so. As we have explained, however, had Wersal additionally stated during his campaign that he did not feel bound to follow those erroneous decisions, he would not have been so lucky. This predicament hardly reflects "the robust communication of ideas and views from judicial candidate to voter."

[4] FN11. Nor do we assert that candidates for judicial office should be *compelled* to announce their views on disputed legal issues. Thus, Justice GINSBURG's repeated invocation of instances in which nominees to this Court declined to announce such views during Senate confirmation hearings is pointless. That the practice of *voluntarily* demurring does not establish the legitimacy of *legal compulsion* to demur is amply demonstrated by the unredacted text of the sentence she quotes in part from *Laird v. Tatum,* 409 U.S. 824, 836, n. 5 (1972): "*In terms of propriety, rather than disqualification*, I would distinguish quite sharply between a public statement made prior to nomination for the bench, on the one hand, and a public statement made by a nominee to the bench." (Emphasis added.)

agents who will act at its behest—does not carry over to campaigns for the bench." This complete separation of the judiciary from the enterprise of "representative government" might have some truth in those countries where judges neither make law themselves nor set aside the laws enacted by the legislature. It is not a true picture of the American system. Not only do state-court judges possess the power to "make" common law, but they have the immense power to shape the States' constitutions as well. See, *e.g., Baker v. State,* 170 Vt. 194, 744 A.2d 864 (1999). Which is precisely why the election of state judges became popular.

IV

To sustain the announce clause, the Eighth Circuit relied heavily on the fact that a pervasive practice of prohibiting judicial candidates from discussing disputed legal and political issues developed during the last half of the 20th century. It is true that a "universal and long-established" tradition of prohibiting certain conduct creates "a strong presumption" that the prohibition is constitutional: "Principles of liberty fundamental enough to have been embodied within constitutional guarantees are not readily erased from the Nation's consciousness." *McIntyre v. Ohio Elections Comm'n,* 514 U.S. 334, 375–377 (1995) (SCALIA, J., dissenting). The practice of prohibiting speech by judicial candidates on disputed issues, however, is neither long nor universal.

At the time of the founding, only Vermont (before it became a State) selected any of its judges by election. Starting with Georgia in 1812, States began to provide for judicial election, a development rapidly accelerated by Jacksonian democracy. By the time of the Civil War, the great majority of States elected their judges. E. Haynes, Selection and Tenure of Judges 99–135 (1944); Berkson, Judicial Selection in the United States: A Special Report, 64 Judicature 176 (1980). We know of no restrictions upon statements that could be made by judicial candidates (including judges) throughout the 19th and the first quarter of the 20th century. Indeed, judicial elections were generally partisan during this period, the movement toward nonpartisan judicial elections not even beginning until the 1870's. *Id.,* at 176–177; M. Comisky & P. Patterson, The Judiciary–Selection, Compensation, Ethics, and Discipline 4, 7 (1987). Thus, not only were judicial candidates (including judges) discussing disputed legal and political issues on the campaign trail, but they were touting party affiliations and angling for party nominations all the while.

The first code regulating judicial conduct was adopted by the ABA in 1924. 48 ABA Reports 74 (1923) (report of Chief Justice Taft); P. McFadden, Electing Justice: The Law and Ethics of Judicial Election Campaigns 86 (1990). It contained a provision akin to the announce clause: "A candidate for judicial position . . . should not announce in advance his conclusions of law on disputed issues to secure class support. . . . " ABA Canon of Judicial Ethics 30 (1924). The States were slow to adopt the canons, however. "By the end of World War II, the canons . . . were binding by the bar associations or supreme courts of only eleven states." J. MacKenzie, The Appearance of Justice 191 (1974).

Even today, although a majority of States have adopted either the announce clause or its 1990 ABA successor, adoption is not unanimous. Of the 31 States that select some or all of their appellate and general-jurisdiction judges by election, see American Judicature Society, Judicial Selection in the States: Appellate and General Jurisdiction Courts (Apr.2002), 4 have adopted no candidate-speech restriction comparable to the announce clause, and 1 prohibits only the discussion of "pending litigation." This practice, relatively new to judicial elections and still not universally adopted, does not compare well with the traditions deemed worthy of our attention in prior cases. *E.g., Burson v. Freeman,* 504 U.S. 191, 205–206 (1992) (crediting tradition of prohibiting speech around polling places that began with the very adoption of the secret ballot in the late 19th century, and in which every State participated); (SCALIA, J., concurring in judgment) (same); *McIntyre, supra,* at 375–377 (SCALIA, J., dissenting) (crediting tradition of prohibiting anonymous election literature, which again began in 1890 and was universally adopted).

* * *

There is an obvious tension between the article of Minnesota's popularly approved Constitution which provides that judges shall be elected, and the Minnesota Supreme Court's announce clause which places most subjects of interest to the voters off limits. (The candidate-speech restrictions of all the other States that have them are also the product of judicial fiat.) The disparity is perhaps unsurprising, since the ABA, which originated the announce clause, has long been an opponent of judicial elections. . . . That opposition may be well taken (it certainly had the support of the Founders of the Federal Government), but the First Amendment does not permit it to achieve its goal by leaving the principle of elections in place while preventing candidates from discussing what the elections are about. "[T]he greater power to dispense with elections altogether does not include the lesser power to conduct elections under conditions of state-imposed voter ignorance. If the State chooses to tap the energy and the legitimizing power of the democratic process, it must accord the participants in that process . . . the First Amendment rights that attach to their roles." *Renne v. Geary,* 501 U.S. 312, 349 (1991) (Marshall, J., dissenting); accord, *Meyer v. Grant,* 486 U.S. 414, 424–425 (1988) (rejecting argument that the greater power to end voter initiatives includes the lesser power to prohibit paid petition-circulators).

The Minnesota Supreme Court's canon of judicial conduct prohibiting candidates for judicial election from announcing their views on disputed legal and political issues violates the First Amendment. Accordingly, we reverse the grant of summary judgment to respondents and remand the case for proceedings consistent with this opinion.

It is so ordered.

JUSTICE O'CONNOR, concurring.

I join the opinion of the Court but write separately to express my concerns about judicial elections generally. Respondents claim that "[t]he Announce Clause is necessary . . . to protect the State's compelling governmental interes[t] in an actual and perceived . . . impartial judiciary." I am concerned that, even aside from what judicial candidates may say while campaigning, the very practice of electing judges undermines this interest.

We of course want judges to be impartial, in the sense of being free from any personal stake in the outcome of the cases to which they are assigned. But if judges are subject to regular elections they are likely to feel that they have at least some personal stake in the outcome of every publicized case. Elected judges cannot help being aware that if the public is not satisfied with the outcome of a particular case, it could hurt their reelection prospects. . . . Even if judges were able to suppress their awareness of the potential electoral consequences of their decisions and refrain from acting on it, the public's confidence in the judiciary could be undermined simply by the possibility that judges would be unable to do so.

Moreover, contested elections generally entail campaigning. And campaigning for a judicial post today can require substantial funds. Unless the pool of judicial candidates is limited to those wealthy enough to independently fund their campaigns, a limitation unrelated to judicial skill, the cost of campaigning requires judicial candidates to engage in fundraising. Yet relying on campaign donations may leave judges feeling indebted to certain parties or interest groups. Even if judges were able to refrain from favoring donors, the mere possibility that judges' decisions may be motivated by the desire to repay campaign contributors is likely to undermine the public's confidence in the judiciary. . . .

Minnesota has chosen to select its judges through contested popular elections instead of through an appointment system or a combined appointment and retention election system. . . . In doing so the State has voluntarily taken on the risks to judicial bias described above. As a result, the State's claim that it needs to significantly restrict judges' speech in order to protect judicial impartiality is particularly troubling. If the State has a problem with judicial impartiality, it is largely one the State brought upon itself by continuing the practice of popularly electing judges.

JUSTICE STEVENS, with whom JUSTICE SOUTER, JUSTICE GINSBURG, and JUSTICE BREYER join, dissenting.

. . . . The limits of the Court's holding are evident: Even if the Minnesota Lawyers Professional Responsibility Board (Board) may not sanction a judicial candidate for announcing his views on issues likely to come before him, it may surely advise the electorate that such announcements demonstrate the speaker's unfitness for judicial office. If the solution to harmful speech must be more speech, so be it. The Court's reasoning, however, will unfortunately endure beyond the next election cycle. By obscuring the fundamental distinction between campaigns for the judiciary and the political branches, and by failing to recognize the difference between statements made in articles or opinions and those made on the campaign trail, the Court defies any sensible notion of the judicial office and the importance of impartiality in that context.

The Court's disposition rests on two seriously flawed premises—an inaccurate appraisal of the importance of judicial independence and impartiality, and an assumption that judicial candidates should have the same freedom " 'to express themselves on matters of current public importance' " as do all other elected officials. Elected judges, no less than appointed judges, occupy an office of trust that is fundamentally different from that occupied by policymaking officials. Although the fact that they must stand for election makes their job more difficult than that of the tenured judge, that fact does not lessen their duty to respect essential attributes of the judicial office that have been embedded in Anglo–American law for centuries.

There is a critical difference between the work of the judge and the work of other public officials. In a democracy, issues of policy are properly decided by majority vote; it is the business of legislators and executives to be popular. But in litigation, issues of law or fact should not be determined by popular vote; it is the business of judges to be indifferent to unpopularity. Sir Matthew Hale pointedly described this essential attribute of the judicial office in words which have retained their integrity for centuries:

> " '11. That popular or court applause or distaste have no influence in anything I do, in point of distribution of justice.
>
> " '12. Not to be solicitous what men will say or think, so long as I keep myself exactly according to the rule of justice.' "[5]

Consistent with that fundamental attribute of the office, countless judges in countless cases routinely make rulings that are unpopular and surely disliked by at least 50 percent of the litigants who appear before them. It is equally common for them to enforce rules that they think unwise, or that are contrary to their personal predilections. For this reason, opinions that a lawyer may have expressed before becoming a judge, or a

[5] FN1. 2 J. Campbell, Lives of the Chief Justices of England 208 (1873) (quoting Hale's Rules For His Judicial Guidance, Things Necessary to be Continually Had in Remembrance).

judicial candidate, do not disqualify anyone for judicial service because every good judge is fully aware of the distinction between the law and a personal point of view. It is equally clear, however, that such expressions after a lawyer has been nominated to judicial office shed little, if any, light on his capacity for judicial service. Indeed, to the extent that such statements seek to enhance the popularity of the candidate by indicating how he would rule in specific cases if elected, they evidence a lack of fitness for the office.

Of course, any judge who faces reelection may believe that he retains his office only so long as his decisions are popular. Nevertheless, the elected judge, like the lifetime appointee, does not serve a constituency while holding that office. He has a duty to uphold the law and to follow the dictates of the Constitution. If he is not a judge on the highest court in the State, he has an obligation to follow the precedent of that court, not his personal views or public opinion polls.[6] He may make common law, but judged on the merits of individual cases, not as a mandate from the voters.

By recognizing a conflict between the demands of electoral politics and the distinct characteristics of the judiciary, we do not have to put States to an all or nothing choice of abandoning judicial elections or having elections in which anything goes. As a practical matter, we cannot know for sure whether an elected judge's decisions are based on his interpretation of the law or political expediency. In the absence of reliable evidence one way or the other, a State may reasonably presume that elected judges are motivated by the highest aspirations of their office. But we do know that a judicial candidate, who announces his views in the context of a campaign, is effectively telling the electorate: "Vote for me because I believe X, and I will judge cases accordingly." Once elected, he may feel free to disregard his campaign statements, but that does not change the fact that the judge announced his position on an issue likely to come before him *as a reason to vote for him.* Minnesota has a compelling interest in sanctioning such statements.

A candidate for judicial office who goes beyond the expression of "general observation about the law . . . in order to obtain favorable consideration" of his candidacy, *Laird v. Tatum,* 409 U.S. 824, 836, n. 5 (1972) (memorandum of REHNQUIST, J., on motion for recusal), demonstrates either a lack of impartiality or a lack of understanding of the importance of maintaining public confidence in the impartiality of the judi-

---

[6] FN2. The Court largely ignores the fact that judicial elections are not limited to races for the highest court in the State. Even if announcing one's views in the context of a campaign for the State Supreme Court might be permissible, the same statements are surely less appropriate when one is running for an intermediate or trial court judgeship. Such statements not only display a misunderstanding of the judicial role, but also mislead the voters by giving them the false impression that a candidate for the trial court will be able to and should decide cases based on his personal views rather than precedent. . . .

ciary. It is only by failing to recognize the distinction, clearly stated by then-Justice REHNQUIST, between statements made during a campaign or confirmation hearing and those made before announcing one's candidacy, that the Court is able to conclude: "[S]ince avoiding judicial preconceptions on legal issues is neither possible nor desirable, pretending otherwise by attempting to preserve the 'appearance' of that type of impartiality can hardly be a compelling state interest either."

Even when "impartiality" is defined in its narrowest sense to embrace only "the lack of bias for or against either *party* to the proceeding," the announce clause serves that interest. Expressions that stress a candidate's unbroken record of affirming convictions for rape, for example, imply a bias in favor of a particular litigant (the prosecutor) and against a class of litigants (defendants in rape cases). Contrary to the Court's reasoning in its first attempt to define impartiality, an interpretation of the announce clause that prohibits such statements serves the State's interest in maintaining both the appearance of this form of impartiality and its actuality. . . .

The Court boldly asserts that respondents have failed to carry their burden of demonstrating "that campaign statements are uniquely destructive of open-mindedness." But the very purpose of most statements prohibited by the announce clause is to convey the message that the candidate's mind is not open on a particular issue. The lawyer who writes an article advocating harsher penalties for polluters surely does not commit to that position to the same degree as the candidate who says "vote for me because I believe all polluters deserve harsher penalties." At the very least, such statements obscure the appearance of open-mindedness. More importantly, like the reasoning in the Court's opinion, they create the false impression that the standards for the election of political candidates apply equally to candidates for judicial office. . . .

JUSTICE GINSBURG, with whom JUSTICE STEVENS, JUSTICE SOUTER, and JUSTICE BREYER join, dissenting.

. . . . Through its own Constitution, Minnesota, in common with most other States, has decided to allow its citizens to choose judges directly in periodic elections. But Minnesota has not thereby opted to install a corps of political actors on the bench; rather, it has endeavored to preserve the integrity of its judiciary by other means. Recognizing that the influence of political parties is incompatible with the judge's role, for example, Minnesota has designated all judicial elections nonpartisan. See *Peterson v. Stafford,* 490 N.W.2d 418, 425 (Minn.1992). And it has adopted a provision, here called the Announce Clause, designed to prevent candidates for judicial office from "publicly making known how they would decide issues likely to come before them as judges." *Republican Party of Minn. v. Kelly,* 247 F.3d 854, 881–882 (C.A.8 2001). . . .

I would differentiate elections for political offices, in which the First Amendment holds full sway, from elections designed to select those whose office it is to administer justice without respect to persons. Minnesota's choice to elect its judges, I am persuaded, does not preclude the State from installing an election process geared to the judicial office. . . .

[T]he rationale underlying unconstrained speech in elections for political office—that representative government depends on the public's ability to choose agents who will act at its behest—does not carry over to campaigns for the bench. As to persons aiming to occupy the seat of judgment, the Court's unrelenting reliance on decisions involving contests for legislative and executive posts is manifestly out of place. . . . In view of the magisterial role judges must fill in a system of justice, a role that removes them from the partisan fray, States may limit judicial campaign speech by measures impermissible in elections for political office. See *Buckley v. Illinois Judicial Inquiry Bd.*, 997 F.2d 224, 228 (C.A.7 1993) ("Mode of appointment is only one factor that enables distinctions to be made among different kinds of public official. Judges remain different from legislators and executive officials, even when all are elected, in ways that bear on the strength of the state's interest in restricting their freedom of speech.").

The Court sees in this conclusion, and in the Announce Clause that embraces it, "an obvious tension,": The Minnesota electorate is permitted to select its judges by popular vote, but is not provided information on "subjects of interest to the voters,"—in particular, the voters are not told how the candidate would decide controversial cases or issues if elected. This supposed tension, however, rests on the false premise that by departing from the federal model with respect to who *chooses* judges, Minnesota necessarily departed from the federal position on the *criteria* relevant to the exercise of that choice. . . .

Minnesota did not choose a judicial selection system with all the trappings of legislative and executive races. While providing for public participation, it tailored judicial selection to fit the character of third branch office holding. See *id.*, at 425 (Minnesota's system "keep[s] the ultimate choice with the voters while, at the same time, recognizing the unique independent nature of the judicial function."). The balance the State sought to achieve—allowing the people to elect judges, but safeguarding the process so that the integrity of the judiciary would not be compromised—should encounter no First Amendment shoal. . . .

Coupled with the Announce Clause in Minnesota's Code of Judicial Conduct is a provision that prohibits candidates from "mak[ing] pledges or promises of conduct in office other than the faithful and impartial performance of the duties of the office." Minn. Code of Judicial Conduct, Canon 5(A)(3)(d)(i) (2002). Although the Court is correct that this "pledges or promises" provision is not directly at issue in this case, the Court errs in overlooking the interdependence of that prohibition and the one before us. In my view, the constitutionality of the Announce Clause cannot be resolved without an examination of that interaction in light of the interests the pledges or promises provision serves.

All parties to this case agree that, whatever the validity of the Announce Clause, the State may constitutionally prohibit judicial candidates from pledging or promising certain results. The reasons for this agreement are apparent. Pledges or promises of conduct in office, however commonplace in races for the political branches, are inconsistent "with the judge's obligation to decide cases in accordance with his or her role." This judicial obligation to avoid prejudgment corresponds to the litigant's right, protected by the Due Process Clause of the Fourteenth Amendment, to "an impartial and disinterested tribunal in both civil and criminal cases," *Marshall v. Jerrico, Inc.,* 446 U.S. 238, 242 (1980). The proscription against pledges or promises thus represents an accommodation of "constitutionally protected interests [that] lie on both sides of the legal equation." *Nixon v. Shrink Missouri Government PAC,* 528 U.S. 377, 400 (2000) (BREYER, J., concurring). Balanced against the candidate's interest in free expression is the litigant's "powerful and independent constitutional interest in fair adjudicative procedure." *Marshall,* 446 U.S., at 243; see *Buckley,* 997 F.2d, at 227 ("Two principles are in conflict and must, to the extent possible, be reconciled. . . . The roots of both principles lie deep in our constitutional heritage."). . . .

When a judicial candidate promises to rule a certain way on an issue that may later reach the courts, the potential for due process violations is grave and manifest. If successful in her bid for office, the judicial candidate will become a judge, and in that capacity she will be under pressure to resist the pleas of litigants who advance positions contrary to her pledges on the campaign trail. If the judge fails to honor her campaign promises, she will not only face abandonment by supporters of her professed views; she will also "ris[k] being assailed as a dissembler," willing to say one thing to win an election and to do the opposite once in office. . . .

Given this grave danger to litigants from judicial campaign promises, States are justified in barring expression of such commitments, for they typify the "situatio[n] . . . in which experience teaches that the probability of actual bias on the part of the judge . . . is too high to be constitutionally tolerable." *Withrow v. Larkin,* 421 U.S. 35, 47 (1975). By removing this source of "possible temptation" for a judge to rule on the basis of self-interest, *Tumey,* 273 U.S., at 532, the pledges or promises prohibition furthers the State's "compellin[g] interest in maintaining a judiciary fully capable of performing" its appointed task, *Gregory v. Ashcroft,* 501 U.S. 452, 472 (1991): "judging [each] particular controversy fairly on the basis of its own circumstances," *United States v. Morgan,* 313 U.S. 409, 421 (1941). . . .

In addition to protecting litigants' due process rights, the parties in this case further agree, the pledges or promises clause advances another compelling state interest: preserving the public's confidence in the integrity and impartiality of its judiciary. . . .

The constitutionality of the pledges or promises clause is thus amply supported; the provision not only advances due process of law for litigants in Minnesota courts, it also reinforces the authority of the Minnesota judiciary by promoting public confidence in the State's judges. The Announce Clause, however, is equally vital to achieving these compelling ends, for without it, the pledges or promises provision would be feeble, an arid form, a matter of no real importance. . . .

Uncoupled from the Announce Clause, the ban on pledges or promises is easily circumvented. By prefacing a campaign commitment with the caveat, "although I cannot promise anything," or by simply avoiding the language of promises or pledges altogether, a candidate could declare with impunity how she would decide specific issues. Semantic sanitizing of the candidate's commitment would not, however, diminish its pernicious effects on actual and perceived judicial impartiality. To use the Court's example, a candidate who campaigns by saying, "If elected, I will vote to uphold the legislature's power to prohibit same-sex marriages," will feel scarcely more pressure to honor that statement than the candidate who stands behind a podium and tells a throng of cheering supporters: "I think it is constitutional for the legislature to prohibit same-sex marriages." Made during a campaign, both statements contemplate a *quid pro quo* between candidate and voter. Both effectively "bind [the candidate] to maintain that position after election." And both convey the impression of a candidate prejudging an issue to win votes. Contrary to the Court's assertion, the "nonpromissory" statement averts none of the dangers posed by the "promissory" one. (emphasis deleted).

By targeting statements that do not technically constitute pledges or promises but nevertheless "publicly mak[e] known how [the candidate] would decide" legal issues, the Announce Clause prevents this end run around the letter and spirit of its companion provision. No less than the pledges or promises clause itself, the Announce / Clause is an indispensable part of Minnesota's effort to maintain the health of its judiciary, and is therefore constitutional for the same reasons. . . .

This Court has recognized in the past, as Justice O'CONNOR does today, a "fundamental tension between the ideal character of the judicial office and the real world of electoral politics," *Chisom,* 501 U.S., at 400. We have no warrant to resolve that tension, however, by forcing States to choose one pole or the other. Judges are not politicians, and the First Amendment does not require that they be treated as politicians simply because they are chosen by popular vote. Nor does the First Amendment command States that wish to promote the integrity of their judges in fact and appearance to abandon systems of judicial selection that the people, in the exercise of their sovereign prerogatives, have devised. . . .

CASE QUESTIONS

1. What types of statements are regulated by the provisions at issue in this case?
2. What standard of review did the majority apply?
3. What interests did the state assert to justify its regulation?
4. In what sense was the regulation overinclusive? In what sense was it underinclusive/
5. What standard did the dissents apply?

Cases following *Republican Party of Minnesota v. White* have not extended free speech protection to all statements a judge might make, either in an official or a personal capacity. For example, nothing in the Court's opinion calls into question the limitation in Rule 2.8(c), which forbids judges from commending or criticizing jurors for a verdict except in an order or opinion. Rule 2.10(A) forbids public statements that might reasonably be expected to affect the result of a proceeding or impair the fairness of a pending or impending proceeding.[7] And Rule 2.10(B) forbids judges from making pledges or commitments regarding cases, controversies or issues that are likely to come before a court and which are inconsistent with impartial judging.[8]

Similarly, the *White* majority was careful to note that prohibitions on promising or committing to rule a certain way were not at issue. Several provisions of the Code prohibit such commitments. Rule 2.10(B) forbids judges from making pledges, promises, or commitments that are inconsistent with the impartial performance of their duties. Rule 4.1(A)(13) forbids judges and judicial candidates from making, in connection with "cases, controversies, or issues that are likely to come before the court," pledges promises or commitments inconsistent with impartial judging.

Justice Ginsburg's dissenting opinion in *White* argued that such prohibitions are constitutional. In *Bauer v. Shepard*, 620 F.3d 704 (7th Cir.

---

[7] Under the Code, an "impending" proceeding is one that is "imminent or expected to occur in the near future."

[8] Subject to Rule 2.10(A), a judge may respond to allegations regarding the judge's conduct in a matter.

2010), Judge Easterbrook agreed. At issue were Indiana rules 2.10(B) and 4.1(A)(13), which are the same as the corresponding Model Code rules. Here are some excerpts from that opinion:

[The case arose because] Indiana Right to Life, Inc., sends questionnaires to candidates for election or retention, asking recipients to state, among other things, whether they agree with *Roe v. Wade,* 410 U.S. 113 (1973), which held many forms of abortion legislation unconstitutional, and whether they subscribe to propositions such as: "I believe that the unborn child is biologically human and alive and that the right to life of human beings should be respected at every stage of their biological development." (The district court's opinion includes excerpts that convey the gist of all nine questions.) Most recipients have either ignored this questionnaire or told Indiana Right to Life that they fear giving answers could jeopardize their judicial careers because of provisions in the state's Code of Judicial Conduct.

Indiana Right to Life filed suit seeking to have these provisions held invalid, but its suit was dismissed for want of standing, because no person actually or potentially covered by the Code was a plaintiff. *Indiana Right to Life, Inc. v. Shepard,* 507 F.3d 545 (7th Cir.2007). Indiana Right to Life then recruited a candidate for judicial office (Torrey Bauer) and a sitting judge (David Certo) as plaintiffs to join it in this new suit. The candidate and the judge both say that they refrain from speaking about abortion, and other controversial topics, because they fear the prospect of sanctions under the Code. Bauer answered the group's 2008 questionnaire but says that he will keep silent in the future because of the risk this would pose to his judicial career should he be elected. He expresses concern that his 2008 answers may come back to haunt him should he be elected. Certo has not answered the group's questionnaire in any year. He, too, says that the Code has led to silence.

While this suit was pending in the district court, Indiana substantially amended its Code of Judicial Conduct, in light of changes to a model code published by the American Bar Association. The revised Code, which took effect on January 1, 2009, is the focus of this appeal. . . .

Rules 2.10(B) and 4.1(A)(13) are the "commits clauses":

> [Rule 2.10(B)] A judge shall not, in connection with cases, controversies, or issues that are likely to come before the court, make pledges, promises, or commitments that are inconsistent with the impartial* performance of the adjudicative duties of judicial office.
>
> [Rule 4.1(A)] Except as permitted by law,* or by Rules 4.1(B), 4.1(C), 4.2, 4.3, and 4.4, a judge or a judicial candidate* shall not: . . . (13) in connection with cases, controversies, or issues that are likely to

come before the court, make pledges, promises, or commitments that are inconsistent with the impartial* performance of the adjudicative duties of judicial office.

The Code defines "impartial" as "absence of bias or prejudice in favor of, or against, particular parties or classes of parties, as well as maintenance of an open mind in considering issues that may come before a judge." Plaintiffs Bauer and Certo say that these rules have discouraged them from answering Indiana Right to Life's questionnaire, and the group relates that most judges who have replied have said the same thing; only a handful of judges and judicial candidates in Indiana have stated their positions on all of the nine questions.

Some, perhaps many, of the state's judges and judicial candidates may be using the commits clauses as a pretext to keep out of a political minefield. For no matter what a person says in response to Indiana Right to Life's questionnaire, some readers are going to be unhappy and will vote against the candidate as a result. It is hard to see how judges and candidates could have a substantial fear of adverse consequences under the *current* version of Indiana's Code. None of the nine questions calls for a "commitment" or "promise" on any issue. A judge who answers yes to the first proposition ("I believe that the unborn child is biologically human and alive and that the right to life of human beings should be respected at every stage of their biological development") has not committed to defying *Roe v. Wade* and its sequels. The proposition concerns morals, not conduct in office. Statements of views on moral and legal subjects do not imply that the speaker will act in accord with his preferences rather than the law. Every judge enforces laws and applies judicial decisions for which he would not have voted.

Similarly, a judge who states that he thinks *Roe v. Wade* wrongly decided has not committed to disregard that decision. Justices White and Rehnquist dissented in *Roe* itself, explaining at length why they thought the majority mistaken. But this did not commit them to any particular outcome in a future dispute about abortion. Many a judge dissents in one case but later follows the majority decision on the basis of *stare decisis*—and occasionally a judge who has written a decision, and thus commits to its correctness, writes a decision overruling his earlier opinion after concluding that he erred. See, e.g., *United States v. Scott,* 437 U.S. 82 (1978) (Rehnquist, J.), overruling *United States v. Jenkins,* 420 U.S. 358 (1975) (Rehnquist, J.). A judge whose mind is open to new evidence and arguments is not "committed" to any outcome in tomorrow's litigation.

White I holds that judges and judicial candidates are entitled to announce their views on legal and political subjects that will come before them as judges. 536 U.S. at 788. That's all Indiana Right to Life's questionnaire asks them to do. Defendants observe that some judges do answer the questionnaire, and that, even under the pre–2009 version of the

Code, none has been charged by the Commission with misconduct. Most judges and judicial candidates have views on issues such as those the questionnaire poses, and are entitled to have them. Making these views known does not call their impartiality into question. "[S]ince avoiding judicial preconceptions on legal issues is neither possible nor desirable, pretending otherwise by attempting to preserve the 'appearance' of that type of impartiality can hardly be a compelling state interest". *Id.* at 778.

Still, given the posture of this case—the suit was dismissed on the pleadings—we must assume that plaintiffs Bauer and Certo are in fear of sanctions under the Code if they answer the questions. This fear may be exaggerated, but if it is real (as we must assume it is), and not irrational (it isn't), it stifles speech. So we must decide whether there is anything wrong with the commits clauses. Plaintiffs say that they are unconstitutional because overbroad and vague.

Plaintiffs treat as "overbroad" any law forbidding any speech that is constitutionally protected. It is not clear to us that any speech covered by the commits clauses is constitutionally protected, as *White I* understands the first amendment. How could it be permissible to "make pledges, promises, or commitments that are inconsistent with the impartial performance of the adjudicative duties of judicial office"? The rule's own category (promises "inconsistent with the impartial performance of" judicial duties) identifies the sorts of speech that *White I* thought might be curtailed. A commits clause "secures a basic objective of the judiciary, one so basic that due process requires it: that litigants have a right to air their disputes before judges who have not committed to rule against them before the opening brief is read." *Carey,* 614 F.3d at 207. Judges must decide on the basis of the law and the case's facts, not on "express . . . commitments that they may have made to their campaign supporters or to others." *Buckley,* 997 F.2d at 227.

Although the Court held in *White I* that judges may state their views on contestable and controversial subjects—such as whether the exclusionary rule is wise policy, or whether mandatory minimum sentences should be repealed—it did not hold that judges may make commitments or promises about behavior in office. Imagine a judge or judicial candidate who said: "I will issue a search warrant every time the police ask me to." That speaker is promising to defy the judicial oath of office. Or imagine the statement: "I will always rule in favor of the litigant whose income is lower, so that wealth can be redistributed according to the principles of communism." (More plausibly, a candidate might say that he will award damages against drug companies, whether or not the drug has been negligently designed or tested, because they charge "too much" for their products.) Again that person is promising to disobey the law and disregard the litigants' entitlements. Nothing in *White I* deals with statements of this flavor, or any other promise to act on the bench as a partisan of a political agenda.

But it is unnecessary to decide whether *some* protected speech might come within the scope of the commits clauses. For when the Supreme Court speaks of overbreadth, it does not mean a statute or rule that catches the occasional protected tidbit. All rules are overbroad in that sense. "Overbreadth" in the Supreme Court's jurisprudence has to do with *substantial* amounts of protected speech. A law is unconstitutionally overbroad when "a substantial number of its applications are unconstitutional, judged in relation to the statute's plainly legitimate sweep." *Washington State Grange v. Washington State Republican Party,* 552 U.S. 442, 449 n. 6 (2008) (internal quotation marks omitted). See also, e.g., *United States v. Stevens,* 130 S.Ct. 1577 (2010). Plaintiffs do not seriously contend that the commits clauses are overbroad in *that* sense.

Under Indiana's language, judges and candidates can tell the electorate not only their general stance ("tough on crime" or "tough on drug companies") but also their legal conclusions ("I would have joined Justice White's dissent in *Roe*" or "the death penalty should be treated as cruel and unusual punishment" or "I am a textualist and will not resort to legislative history" or "I will follow *stare decisis*" or "I am a progressive who will use a living-constitution approach"). Judges who have announced these views, on or off the bench, sit every day without being thought to have abandoned impartiality. Indeed, judges who have announced legal views in exceptional detail, by writing a treatise about some subject (Weinstein on Evidence, or Martin on Bankruptcy) have not made an improper "commitment," even though a litigant can look up in the treatise exactly how the judge is apt to resolve many disputes. A judge who promises to ignore the facts and the law to pursue his (or his constituents') ideas about wise policy is problematic in a way that a judge who has announced considered views on legal subjects is not. The commits clauses condemn the former and allow the latter. That's because they are limited to commitments that are inconsistent with impartial adjudication and thus differ considerably from the rule at issue in *Carey*, where the sixth circuit expressed concern that limiting *all* commitments on "issues" would prevent a judicial candidate from declaring support for the rule of law or adherence to *stare decisis. Carey,* 614 F.3d at 201–03.

As plaintiffs see things, however, the phrase "inconsistent with the impartial performance of the adjudicative duties of judicial office" saves the commits clauses from a first amendment challenge by making them so vague that they violate the due process clauses. For what promises *are* "inconsistent with the impartial performance of the adjudicative duties of judicial office"? Neither the commits clauses nor the Code's definitions pin the meaning down. We have given a few examples, such as a promise to issue search warrants without bothering to read the affidavits, but the principle is clear only in these extremes. A candidate who says that he will never let a prisoner off on a "technicality" could be promising to ignore the fourth amendment (if in his view the rule against unreasonable searches and seizures is a "technicality") but could mean instead only that he plans to enforce the harmless-error and plain-error doctrines, see Fed.R.Crim.P. 52; Ind. R.App. P. 66(A), under which errors that don't impair a defendant's substantial rights do not justify setting aside a jury's verdict.

Context may help to disambiguate a statement, but there is an irreducible risk that a promise may be misunderstood—or that the Commission and the Supreme Court of Indiana may treat as "inconsistent with the impartial performance of the adjudicative duties of judicial office" even the sort of statements that are squarely protected by *White*. We think that statements such as "judges have been too ready to find antitrust problems with mergers" or "mandatory minimum sentences are unjust, and I will read those statutes narrowly" or "drunk drivers are a menace and should be dealt with severely" or "abortion should be freely available, and I will grant a minor's application for bypass of parental consent when a statute gives me that discretion" are outside the scope of the commits clauses. But will the Commission and the state judiciary agree?

The best way to find out is to wait and see. The Commission issues advisory opinions that reduce uncertainty, and when the Commission brings a proceeding the state judiciary will issue an opinion that makes the rule more concrete. Plaintiffs want us to deem the law vague by identifying situations in which state officials *might* take an untenably broad reading of the commits clauses, and then predicting that they *will* do so. It is far preferable, however, and more respectful of our judicial colleagues in Indiana, to assume that they will act sensibly and resolve the open questions in a way that honors candidates' rights under the first amendment.

When do non-literal promises (those that do not say "I promise" or some equivalent) violate rules such as 2.10(B) or 4.1(A)(13) or require disqualification under 2.11(A)(5)? *In re Watson*, 100 N.Y.2d 290 (2003), provides one example of such a case. There the New York Court of Appeal affirmed a finding that a City Court judge violated that state's prohibition on promises or commitments in a judicial campaign (the provision not at issue in *Republican Party of Minnesota*). The Court dealt with the issue of non-literal promises as follows:

"In 1999, petitioner took a leave of absence from his employment as an assistant district attorney in the Niagara County District Attorney's office to run as a candidate for a Lockport City Court judgeship. Petitioner had two opponents in the primary, both incumbent City Court judges. Beginning in April 1999 and continuing until the primary election in September of that year, petitioner made a series of campaign statements that one of his opponents found objectionable. A few days before the primary, the opponent lodged a complaint with the Commission on Judicial Conduct alleging that petitioner's campaign statements violated the Rules Governing Judicial Conduct. Petitioner defeated his opponents in the primary and won the general election, taking office as City Court judge in January 2000. . . .

The exhibits to the complaint included a letter petitioner forwarded to law enforcement personnel who resided in the City of Lockport asking them to elect him and "put a real prosecutor on the bench." Petitioner asserted in the correspondence that "[w]e are in desperate need of a Judge who will work with the police, not against them. We need a judge who will assist our law enforcement officers as they aggressively work towards cleaning up our city streets." The complaint also referenced three "letters to the editor" petitioner authored that were published in the Lockport Union–Sun & Journal in which he decried what he viewed as an increase in drug crime in the city. He contended that "Lockport is attracting criminals from Rochester, Niagara Falls and Buffalo to come into our city to peddle their drugs and commit their crimes." Petitioner stated that, as a prosecutor, he had "sent a message that this type of conduct will not be tolerated in Niagara County" and he urged the voters to elect him "so that the City of Lockport can begin to send this same message."

In newspaper advertisements, petitioner cited an increase in arrest statistics for various categories of crime, claiming that "arrests tell the story" and stating that he had "proven experience in the war against crime." Petitioner correlated the increase in arrests with the time period the incumbents were in office, indicating that if elected he would take action they had failed to take to deter crime. These statements echoed sentiments he expressed in the correspondence published in the local newspaper. For instance, in one letter, petitioner wrote: "[m]y opponents have been in office together for the last several years. Arrests have skyrocketed in Lockport recently, even though crime is down countywide, statewide and nationally."

Petitioner was quoted making similar statements in newspaper articles about the race. On one occasion when petitioner and his opponents were asked to respond in writing to questions posed by a reporter, petitioner cited drugs and crime as the main problem in the city and remarked that "the court must remain impartial and evenhanded, but the city must establish a reputation for zero tolerance" and "deter criminals before they come into the city." He posited that the caseload in City Court was large because "criminals from surrounding communities are flocking into Lockport. Once we gain a reputation for being tough, you'd be surprised how many will go elsewhere, making the caseload much more manageable." In another newspaper account, petitioner told a reporter that the city "must no longer put up with drug dealers and other violent criminals from Rochester, Buffalo and Niagara Falls, who feel that it is acceptable for them to come into the City of Lockport and commit crimes." He stated: "We need a city court judge who will work together with our local police department to help return Lockport to the city it once was" and suggested that a judge could use bail and sentencing to "make it very unattractive for a person to be committing a crime in the City of Lockport."

In his answer to the Commission complaint and during his testimony at the hearing before a Referee, petitioner admitted that he had written the letters and advertisements and made the statements attributed to him in the newspaper articles. He explained that his intention was to emphasize his experience and qualifications as a prosecutor and his concern over the increase in crime in the City of Lockport. . . .

Among other restrictions, a judicial candidate is prohibited from "mak[ing] pledges or promises of conduct in office other than the faithful and impartial performance of the duties of the office" (22 NYCRR 100.5[A][4][d][i]). Needless to say, statements that merely express a viewpoint do not amount to promises of future conduct. On the other hand, candidates need not preface campaign statements with the phrase "I promise" before their remarks may reasonably be interpreted by the public as a pledge to act or rule in a particular way if elected. A candidate's statements must be reviewed in their totality and in the context of the campaign as a whole to determine whether the candidate has unequivocally articulated a pledge or promise of future conduct or decisionmaking that compromises the faithful and impartial performance of judicial duties.

We find that petitioner's comments in this case, when viewed in light of his comprehensive campaign theme, violate the pledges or promises prohibition in section 100.5(A)(4)(d)(i). Petitioner explicitly and repeatedly indicated that he intended to "work with" and "assist" police and other law enforcement personnel if elected to judicial office. These statements were not related to administrative concerns, such as holding court in the evening or on weekends, but were directly associated with helping the police carry out their law enforcement functions. Petitioner buttressed his statements with arrest statistics, indicating that if elected he would take action the incumbents had failed to take to deter crime.

Petitioner's statements not only expressed a bias in favor of the police and against those accused of crimes, but also amounted to a pledge to engage in conduct antithetical to the judicial role because judges do not "assist" other branches of government—they are charged to apply the law impartially to every party appearing in court. Petitioner also singled out for biased treatment a particular class of defendants—those charged with drug offenses who reside outside the City of Lockport—claiming that, if elected, he would use bail and sentencing to deter these individuals from operating in Lockport.

Petitioner's statements were not isolated or spontaneous remarks but were repeated throughout his campaign, both in campaign materials he generated and in his written statements to the media. When viewed as a whole, petitioner's campaign effectively promised that, if elected, he would aid law enforcement rather than apply the law neutrally and impartially in criminal cases. . . .

We note that the Supreme Court did not decide what level of review was applicable to the First Amendment claim in *White* but applied strict scrutiny because the parties agreed on that standard (*id.* at 774–775). We need not decide the question in this case either because, even assuming strict scrutiny analysis is appropriate, the pledges or promises prohibition set forth in the New York rules meets that exacting standard. . . . "

---

3. PROHIBITIONS ON POLITICAL ACTIVITY

Caperton and *Republican Party of Minnesota* illustrate the reality of life in states that elect judges: Judges must engage to some degree in politics and must balance their political activities with the obligations of the judicial office they seek or (for those standing for re-election) hold. And the point is not limited to elected judges. Appointment may be a political process, though not an explicitly electoral process.

Canon 4 of the Model Code and rules implementing it try to strike a balance between the imperatives of disinterested and independent judging, on the one hand, and the advantage if not necessity of political activity to become and remain a judge, on the other.[9] The Canon provides that a judge or candidate for judicial office may not engage in political or campaign activity at odds with the independence, integrity, or impartiality of the judiciary.

The rules implementing this Canon are extensive and have been the subject of several recent constitutional challenges. Rule 4.1 states a general prohibition on 13 types of activities, which are subject to exceptions stated in Rules 4.2–4–4. Many of the limitations in these rules refer to a "political organization," a term the Code defines to include a party or other group sponsored by or affiliated with a party or candidate and princi-

---

[9] The Canon also applies to appointed judges, and Rule 4.3 provides that a candidate for appointment may communicate with the appointing authority or screening committee and may seek endorsements from any person or organization *other than* a partisan political organization.

pally designed to support election or appointment of judges; the term does not include campaign committees under Rule 4.4.

Rule 4.1 applies to all judges, appointed or elected. Some conduct generally prohibited by Rule 4.1 is permissible when a judge is also a judicial candidate; in other words, judges (and challengers) may do some things as candidates they may not do as judges. Rule 4.2 states certain exceptions to Rule 4.1 for judicial candidates, whether incumbents or challengers. Rule 4.2(A) states general provisions that apply to candidates, such as the rule that they must act at all times in a manner consistent with the independence, integrity, and impartiality of judges, must comply with the law, and must review and approve the content of campaign materials the candidate (or his or her committee) uses. Rule 4.2(B) states more particular provisions, which correspond with general limitations in Rule 4.1.

This somewhat unusual structure attempts to prevent judges from using the prestige of the judicial office for political purposes while allowing judicial candidates to run campaigns. The relevant provisions along with citations to cases resolving constitutional challenges to them are set forth in the following table:[10]

Rule	Judges may not	But candidates may	Rulings on constitutional challenges
4.1(A)(1)	Act as a leader or hold office in a political organization.	None	Held constitutional (not facially overbroad): *Bauer v. Shepard*, 620 F.3d 704 (7th Cir. 2010).
			Antecedent provision held unconstitutional: *Republican Party of Minnesota v. White,* 416 F.3d 738 (8th Cir. 2005).
4.1(A)(2)	Make speeches on behalf of a political organization	None	Held constitutional (not facially overbroad): *Bauer v. Shepard*, 620 F.3d 704 (7th Cir. 2010).
			Antecedent provision held unconstitutional: *Republican Party of Minnesota v. White,* 416 F.3d 738 (8th Cir. 2005).
4.1(A)(3)	Publicly endorse or oppose a candidate for any office	Endorse or oppose candidates for the office for which a candidate is running (Rule	Held constitutional (with respect to partisan endorsements) *Siefert v. Alexander,* 608 F.3d 974 (7th Cir.2010)

[10] The table does not include Rule 4.4, regarding campaign committees. A candidate for judicial office may establish a campaign committee to manage and conduct a campaign. Rules 4.2(B)(1), 4.4(A), 4.4(B)(3). The committee may solicit and accept campaign contributions from any given person or entity up to an amount left to the discretion of individual states. Rule 4.4(B)(1). The committee may not, however, solicit contributions too early, with the precise timing left to the discretion of the states. Rule 4.4(B)(2).

		4.2(B)(3))	Held unconstitutional: *Wersal v. Sexton,* 613 F.3d 821 (8th Cir.2010)
4.1(A)(4)	Solicit funds for or contribute to (either by cash or services) a political organization or can-	Make contributions to political organizations (but not solicit for them) subject to limita-	Held constitutional: *Siefert v. Alexander,* 608 F.3d 974 (7th Cir.2010); *Bauer v. Shepard,* 620 F.3d 704 (7th Cir. 2010).
	didate	tions on timing and amount (Rule 4.2(B)(6))	Held unconstitutional: *Carey v. Wolnitzek,* 614 F.3d 189 (6th Cir.2010); *Wersal v. Sexton,* 613 F.3d 821 (8th Cir.2010); *Weaver v. Bonner,* 309 F.3d 1312 (11th Cir. 2002).
4.1(A)(5)	Attend or buy tickets to events (such as dinners) sponsored by a political organization or candidate	Attend such events and/or buy tickets to them (Rule 4.2(B)(4))	
4.1(A)(6)	Publicly state they are the candidate of a political organization	So state, in a partisan judicial election only (Rule 4.2(c))	Held unconstitutional: *Carey v. Wolnitzek,* 614 F.3d 189 (6th Cir. 2010)
4.1(A)(7)	Seek, accept, or use endorsements from a political organization	Do so (Rule 4.2(B)(5)) except partisan endorsements may be used only in partisan judicial elections (Rule 4.2(c))	
4.1(A)(8)	Personally solicit or accept contributions other than through a campaign committee authorized by Rule 4.4		Held unconstitutional: *Wersal v. Sexton,* 613 F.3d 821 (8th Cir.2010)
4.1(A)(9)	Use or permit the use of contributions for the private benefit of any person		
4.1(A)(10)	Use court personnel or resources for campaign activities		
4.1(A)(11)	Knowingly or recklessly make any false or misleading statement		
4.1(A)(12)	Make any statement that reasonably could be expected to affect the result or fairness of a pending or impending matter in any court		
4.1(A)(13)	Make pledges, promises or commitments on matters likely to come before the court that		Held constitutional (not facially overbroad): *Bauer v. Shepard,* 620 F.3d 704 (7th Cir. 2010).
	are inconsistent with impartial judging		Remanded (with regard to commitments on issues): *Carey v. Wolnitzek,* 614 F.3d 189 (6th Cir. 2010)

4. RECUSAL

Recusal is the legal term for the requirement that judges not hear certain cases. The requirements apply regardless whether a party moves to disqualify the judge, meaning judges have an obligation to adhere to them on their own. Conversely, Rule 2.7 of the Model Code makes clear that if the Code or other law does not require recusal then the judge must hear and decide any matter to which he or she is assigned.

For federal judges, 28 U.S.C. § 455 is the primary recusal statute. It provides:

> (a) Any justice, judge, or magistrate judge of the United States shall disqualify himself in any proceeding in which his impartiality might reasonably be questioned.
>
> (b) He shall also disqualify himself in the following circumstances:
>
>> (1) Where he has a personal bias or prejudice concerning a party, or personal knowledge of disputed evidentiary facts concerning the proceeding;
>>
>> (2) Where in private practice he served as lawyer in the matter in controversy, or a lawyer with whom he previously practiced law served during such association as a lawyer concerning the matter, or the judge or such lawyer has been a material witness concerning it;
>>
>> (3) Where he has served in governmental employment and in such capacity participated as counsel, adviser or material witness concerning the proceeding or expressed an opinion concerning the merits of the particular case in controversy;
>>
>> (4) He knows that he, individually or as a fiduciary, or his spouse or minor child residing in his household, has a financial interest in the subject matter in controversy or in a party to the proceeding, or any other interest that could be substantially affected by the outcome of the proceeding;
>>
>> (5) He or his spouse, or a person within the third degree of relationship to either of them, or the spouse of such a person: (i) Is a party to the proceeding, or an officer, director, or trustee of a party; (ii) Is acting as a lawyer in the proceeding; (iii) Is known by the judge to have an interest that could be substantially affected by the outcome of the proceeding; (iv) Is to the judge's knowledge likely to be a material witness in the proceeding.[11]

[11] The statute also provides:

(d) For the purposes of this section the following words or phrases shall have the meaning indicated: (1) "proceeding" includes pretrial, trial, appellate review, or other stages of litigation; (2) the degree of relationship is calculated according to the civil law system; (3) "fiduciary" includes such relationships as executor, administrator, trustee, and guardian; (4) "financial interest"

The statute also provides that a judge may not accept a waiver from the parties for the grounds of disqualification specified in subsection (b) but may accept a waiver of disqualification specified in subsection (a) if the grounds are fully disclosed on the record. Finally, it provides that if after a judge has devoted substantial time to a matter it is discovered that a judge (or family member) has a financial interest in a party (other than an interest that might be affected by the decision in the case) then disqualification is not required if the judge divests himself or herself of the interest that provides the grounds for the disqualification.

In *Liljeberg v. Health Services Acquisition Corp.*, 486 U.S. 847 (1988), the Court held "[t]he very purpose of § 455(a) is to promote confidence in the judiciary by avoiding even the appearance of impropriety whenever possible." The Court therefore interpreted the statute to require disqualification where a judge's impartiality reasonably might be questioned even if the judge did not know the facts giving rise to such questions. "Scienter is not an element of a violation of § 455(a). The judge's lack of knowledge of a disqualifying circumstance may bear on the question of remedy, but it does not eliminate the risk that 'his impartiality might reasonably be questioned' by other persons."

The Model Code details recusal provisions in Rule 2.11. Many of its provisions largely track the federal statute. Some deviations are minor: Rule 2.11(A)(2) adds domestic partners to the list of persons count as familial interests, for example. Rule 2.11(A)(3) requires recusal where a judge knows that the judge or a member of his or her family residing in the same household has an "economic interest" in the subject of the case or a party to it. (The judge's disqualifying interest may be personal or as a fiduciary.) The Model Code defines economic interest to exclude *de minimis* interests; in this respect it differs from the corresponding federal rule, 28 U.S.C. § 455(d)(4), which extends to "ownership of a legal or equitable interest, however small." The Model Code definition also excludes interests in mutual or other common investment funds, accounts in a credit union or mutual savings association, securities held by charitable organization of which a judge is director or advisor, or in which the judge participates, or an interest in an issuer of government securities.

Rule 2.11(A)(5) requires recusal where a judge, while sitting or as a candidate, made a public statement other than in court proceedings or

---

means ownership of a legal or equitable interest, however small, or a relationship as director, adviser, or other active participant in the affairs of a party, except that: (i) Ownership in a mutual or common investment fund that holds securities is not a "financial interest" in such securities unless the judge participates in the management of the fund; (ii) An office in an educational, religious, charitable, fraternal, or civic organization is not a "financial interest" in securities held by the organization; (iii) The proprietary interest of a policyholder in a mutual insurance company, of a depositor in a mutual savings association, or a similar proprietary interest, is a "financial interest" in the organization only if the outcome of the proceeding could substantially affect the value of the interest; (iv) Ownership of government securities is a "financial interest" in the issuer only if the outcome of the proceeding could substantially affect the value of the securities.

opinions, that "commits or appears to commit the judge to reach a particular result or rule a particular way" in the proceeding in which recusal is required or sought. (Recusal is defined and discussed in the next subsection.) Rule 2.11(A)(4) requires recusal where a judge knows or learns by motion that a party, the party's lawyer or the lawyer's firm, has contributed (in the aggregate) amounts of money to be specified by states during a time period specified by the state.[12] (One purpose of the anti-solicitation provision of Rule 4.2 and the campaign committee structure established by Rules 4.2 and 4.4 is to keep judges from learning who contributes to their campaign.)

Rule 2.5(A)(5)'s recusal requirement limits the ability of a judicial candidate to make good on a campaign promise or commitment by requiring that the candidate not sit on cases implicating the commitment if they are elected. *Bauer v. Shepard,* 620 F.3d 704 (7th Cir. 2010), rejected a constitutional challenge to the recusal rule:

> "The recusal clause does not present a constitutional issue at all.
>
> The recusal clause applies to a judge in his role as public employee, not his role as candidate. It specifies how a public employee will perform official duties (or, rather, which public employee will be assigned to which duties). *Garcetti v. Ceballos,* 547 U.S. 410 (2006), holds that speech as part of a public employee's duties is categorically outside the scope of the first amendment. The state, as employer, may control how its employees perform their work, even when that work includes speech (as a judge's job does). Rule 2.11(A)(5) represents a decision by the State of Indiana to assign to each lawsuit a judge who has not made any statement "that commits or appears to commit the judge to reach a particular result or rule in a particular way in the proceeding or controversy." That decision is unexceptionable.
>
> No public employee is entitled to do any particular task; a state may select the employee who can best do the job. *Gregory v. Ashcroft,* 501 U.S. 452 (1991), tells us that this means that a state may choose to assign appeals to younger judges (the Court held that the Age Discrimination in Employment Act does not apply to an elected judiciary). Likewise a state may decide to assign each case to a judge whose impartiality is not in question. All Rule 2.11(A)(5) does is allocate cases among judges, just as 28 U.S.C. § 455(a) does for federal judges. States are entitled to protect litigants by assigning impartial judges before the fact, as well as by removing partial judges afterward. As we put it in *Siefert,* 608 F.3d at 985, "[i]t is small comfort

[12] Comment 4 to Rule 2.11 provides a judge need not remove himself or herself from a matter just because a relative of the judge works for the same firm as a lawyer in a proceeding, though in some cases disqualification might be required under Rule 2.11(a), which requires recusal where a judge's impartiality might reasonably be questioned.

for a litigant who takes her case to state court to know that while her trial was unfair, the judge would eventually lose an election."

Recusal cases sometimes present questions of bias against parties. The following case illustrates how the federal statute deals with such questions.

LITEKY V. UNITED STATES

510 U.S. 540 (1994)

JUSTICE SCALIA delivered the opinion of the Court.

Section 455(a) of Title 28 of the United States Code requires a federal judge to "disqualify himself in any proceeding in which his impartiality might reasonably be questioned." This case presents the question whether required recusal under this provision is subject to the limitation that has come to be known as the "extrajudicial source" doctrine.

I

In the 1991 trial at issue here, petitioners were charged with willful destruction of property of the United States in violation of 18 U.S.C. § 1361. The indictment alleged that they had committed acts of vandalism, including the spilling of human blood on walls and various objects, at the Fort Benning Military Reservation. Before trial petitioners moved to disqualify the District Judge pursuant to 28 U.S.C. § 455(a). The motion relied on events that had occurred during and immediately after an earlier trial, involving petitioner Bourgeois, before the same District Judge.

In the 1983 bench trial, Bourgeois, a Catholic priest of the Maryknoll order, had been tried and convicted of various misdemeanors committed during a protest action, also on the federal enclave of Fort Benning. Petitioners claimed that recusal was required in the present case because the judge had displayed "impatience, disregard for the defense and animosity" toward Bourgeois, Bourgeois' codefendants, and their beliefs. The alleged evidence of that included the following words and acts by the judge: stating at the outset of the trial that its purpose was to try a criminal case and not to provide a political forum; observing after Bourgeois' opening statement (which described the purpose of his protest) that the statement ought to have been directed toward the anticipated evidentiary showing; limiting defense counsel's cross-examination; questioning witnesses; periodically cautioning defense counsel to confine his questions to issues material to trial; similarly admonishing witnesses to keep answers responsive to actual questions directed to material issues; admonishing Bourgeois that closing argument was not a time for "making a speech" in a "political forum"; and giving Bourgeois what petitioners considered to be an excessive sentence. The final asserted ground for disqualification—and the one that counsel for petitioners described at oral argument as the most serious—was the judge's interruption of the closing argument of one of Bourgeois' codefendants, instructing him to cease the introduction of new facts, and to restrict himself to discussion of evidence already presented.

The District Judge denied petitioners' disqualification motion, stating that matters arising from judicial proceedings were not a proper basis for recusal. At the outset of the trial, Bourgeois' counsel informed the judge that he intended to focus his defense on the political motivation for petitioners' actions, which was to protest United States Government involvement in El Salvador. The judge said that he would allow petitioners to state their political purposes in opening argument and to testify about them as well, but that he would not allow long speeches or discussions concerning Government policy. When, in the course of opening argument, Bourgeois' counsel began to explain the circumstances surrounding certain events in El Salvador, the prosecutor objected, and the judge stated that he would not allow discussion about events in El Salvador. He then instructed defense counsel to limit his remarks to what he expected the evidence to show. At the close of the prosecution's case, Bourgeois renewed his disqualification motion, adding as grounds for it the District Judge's "admonishing [him] in front of the jury" regarding the opening statement, and the District Judge's unspecified "admonishing [of] others," in particular Bourgeois' two *pro se* codefendants. The motion was again denied. Petitioners were convicted of the offense charged.

Petitioners appealed, claiming that the District Judge violated 28 U.S.C. § 455(a) in refusing to recuse himself. The Eleventh Circuit affirmed the convictions, agreeing with the District Court that "matters arising out of the course of judicial proceedings are not a proper basis for recusal." 973 F.2d 910 (1992). We granted certiorari. 508 U.S. 939 (1993).

II

Required judicial recusal for bias did not exist in England at the time of Blackstone. 3 W. Blackstone, Commentaries 361. Since 1792, federal statutes have compelled district judges to recuse themselves when they have an interest in the suit, or have been counsel to a party. See Act of May 8, 1792, ch. 36, § 11, 1 Stat. 278. In 1821, the basis of recusal was expanded to include all judicial relationship or connection with a party that would in the judge's opinion make it improper to sit. Act of Mar. 3, 1821, ch. 51, 3 Stat. 643. Not until 1911, however, was a provision enacted requiring district-judge recusal for bias *in general*. In its current form, codified at 28 U.S.C. § 144, that provision reads as follows:

> "Whenever a party to any proceeding in a district court makes and files a timely and sufficient affidavit that the judge before whom the matter is pending has a personal bias or prejudice either against him

or in favor of any adverse party, such judge shall proceed no further therein, but another judge shall be assigned to hear such proceeding.

"The affidavit shall state the facts and the reasons for the belief that bias or prejudice exists, and shall be filed not less than ten days before the beginning of the term at which the proceeding is to be heard, or good cause shall be shown for failure to file it within such time. A party may file only one such affidavit in any case. It shall be accompanied by a certificate of counsel of record stating that it is made in good faith."

Under § 144 and its predecessor, there came to be generally applied in the courts of appeals a doctrine, more standard in its formulation than clear in its application, requiring—to take its classic formulation found in an oft-cited opinion by Justice Douglas for this Court—that "[t]he alleged bias and prejudice to be disqualifying [under § 144] must stem from an extrajudicial source." *United States v. Grinnell Corp.,* 384 U.S. 563, 583 (1966). We say that the doctrine was less than entirely clear in its application for several reasons. First, *Grinnell* (the only opinion of ours to recite the doctrine) clearly meant by "extrajudicial source" a source outside the judicial proceeding at hand—which would include as extrajudicial sources earlier judicial proceedings conducted by the same judge (as are at issue here).[13] Yet many, perhaps most, Courts of Appeals considered knowledge (and the resulting attitudes) that a judge properly acquired in an earlier proceeding *not* to be "extrajudicial." Secondly, the doctrine was often quoted as justifying the refusal to consider trial *rulings* as the basis for § 144 recusal. But trial *rulings* have a judicial *expression* rather than a judicial *source.* They may well be based upon extrajudicial knowledge or motives. Cf. *In re International Business Machines Corp.,* 618 F.2d 923, 928, n. 6 (CA2 1980). And finally, even in cases in which the "source" of the bias or prejudice was clearly the proceedings themselves (for example, testimony introduced or an event occurring at trial which produced unsuppressible judicial animosity), the supposed doctrine would not necessarily be applied.

Whatever the precise contours of the "extrajudicial source" doctrine (a subject to which we will revert shortly), it is the contention of petitioners that the doctrine has no application to § 455(a). Most Courts of Appeals to consider the matter have rejected this contention. Some, however, have agreed with it. To understand the arguments pro and con it is

---

[13] FN1. That is clear when the language from *Grinnell* excerpted above is expanded to include its entire context: "The alleged bias and prejudice to be disqualifying must stem from an extrajudicial source and result in an opinion on the merits on some basis other than what the judge learned from his participation in the case. *Berger v. United States,* 255 U.S. 22, 31. Any adverse attitudes that [the district judge in the present case] evinced toward the defendants were based on his study of the depositions and briefs which the parties had requested him to make." 384 U.S., at 583. The cited case, *Berger,* had found recusal required on the basis of judicial remarks made in an earlier proceeding.

necessary to appreciate the major changes in prior law effected by the revision of § 455 in 1974.

Before 1974, § 455 was nothing more than the then-current version of the 1821 prohibition against a judge's presiding who has an interest in the case or a relationship to a party. . . . The 1974 revision made massive changes, so that § 455 now reads as follows [Eds note: current version of statute quoted above]. . . .

Almost all of the revision (paragraphs (b)(2) through (b)(5)) merely rendered objective and spelled out in detail the "interest" and "relationship" grounds of recusal that had previously been covered by § 455. But the other two paragraphs of the revision brought into § 455 elements of general "bias and prejudice" recusal that had previously been addressed only by § 144. Specifically, paragraph (b)(1) entirely duplicated the grounds of recusal set forth in § 144 ("bias or prejudice"), but (1) made them applicable to *all* justices, judges, and magistrates (and not just district judges), and (2) placed the obligation to identify the existence of those grounds upon the judge himself, rather than requiring recusal only in response to a party affidavit.

Subsection (a), the provision at issue here, was an entirely new "catchall" recusal provision, covering both "interest or relationship" and "bias or prejudice" grounds, *see Liljeberg v. Health Services Acquisition Corp.,* 486 U.S. 847 (1988)—but requiring them *all* to be evaluated on an *objective* basis, so that what matters is not the reality of bias or prejudice but its appearance. Quite simply and quite universally, recusal was required whenever "impartiality might reasonably be questioned."

What effect these changes had upon the "extrajudicial source" doctrine—whether they in effect render it obsolete, of continuing relevance only to § 144, which seems to be properly invocable only when § 455(a) can be invoked anyway—depends upon what the basis for that doctrine was. Petitioners suggest that it consisted of the limitation of § 144 to "*personal* bias or prejudice," bias or prejudice officially acquired being different from "personal" bias or prejudice. And, petitioners point out, while § 455(b)(1) retains the phrase "personal bias or prejudice," § 455(a) proscribes all partiality, not merely the "personal" sort.

It is true that a number of Courts of Appeals have relied upon the word "personal" in restricting § 144 to extrajudicial sources. And several cases have cited the absence of that word as a reason for excluding that restriction from § 455(a). It seems to us, however, that that mistakes the basis for the "extrajudicial source" doctrine. Petitioners' suggestion that we relied upon the word "personal" in our *Grinnell* opinion is simply in error. The only reason *Grinnell* gave for its "extrajudicial source" holding was citation of our opinion almost half a century earlier in *Berger v. United States,* 255 U.S. 22 (1921). But that case, and the case which it in turn cited, *Ex parte American Steel Barrel Co.,* 230 U.S. 35 (1913), relied not upon the word "personal" in § 144, but upon its provision requiring the recusal affidavit to be filed 10 days before the beginning of the court term. That requirement was the reason we found it obvious in *Berger* that the affidavit "must be based upon facts antedating the trial, not those occurring during the trial," 255 U.S., at 34; and the reason we said in *American Steel Barrel* that the recusal statute "was never intended to enable a discontented litigant to oust a judge because of adverse rulings made, . . . but to prevent his future action in the pending cause," 230 U.S., at 44.

In our view, the proper (though unexpressed) rationale for *Grinnell,* and the basis of the modern "extrajudicial source" doctrine, is not the statutory term "personal"—for several reasons. First and foremost, that explanation is simply not the semantic success it pretends to be. Bias and prejudice seem to us not divided into the "personal" kind, which is offensive, and the official kind, which is perfectly all right. As generally used, these are pejorative terms, describing dispositions that are *never* appropriate. It is common to speak of "personal bias" or "personal prejudice" without meaning the adjective to do anything except emphasize the idiosyncratic nature of bias and prejudice, and certainly without implying that there is some other "nonpersonal," benign category of those mental states. In a similar vein, one speaks of an individual's "personal preference," without implying that he could also have a "nonpersonal preference." Secondly, interpreting the term "personal" to create a complete dichotomy between court-acquired and extrinsically acquired bias produces results so intolerable as to be absurd. Imagine, for example, a lengthy trial in which the presiding judge for the first time learns of an obscure religious sect, and acquires a passionate hatred for all its adherents. This would be "official" rather than "personal" bias, and would provide no basis for the judge's recusing himself.

It seems to us that the origin of the "extrajudicial source" doctrine, and the key to understanding its flexible scope (or the so-called "exceptions" to it), is simply the pejorative connotation of the words "bias or prejudice." Not *all* unfavorable disposition towards an individual (or his case) is properly described by those terms. One would not say, for example, that world opinion is biased or prejudiced against Adolf Hitler. The words connote a favorable or unfavorable disposition or opinion that is somehow *wrongful* or *inappropriate,* either because it is undeserved, or because it rests upon knowledge that the subject ought not to possess (for example, a criminal juror who has been biased or prejudiced by receipt of inadmissible evidence concerning the defendant's prior criminal activities), or because it is excessive in degree (for example, a criminal juror who is so inflamed by properly admitted evidence of a defendant's prior criminal activities that he will vote guilty regardless of the facts). The "extrajudicial source" doctrine is one application of this pejorativeness requirement to the terms "bias" and "prejudice" as they are used in §§ 144 and 455(b)(1) with specific reference to the work of judges.

The judge who presides at a trial may, upon completion of the evidence, be exceedingly ill disposed towards the defendant, who has been shown to be a thoroughly reprehensible person. But the judge is not thereby recusable for bias or prejudice, since his knowledge and the opinion it produced were properly and necessarily acquired in the course of the proceedings, and are indeed sometimes (as in a bench trial) necessary to completion of the judge's task. As Judge Jerome Frank pithily put it: "Impartiality is not gullibility. Disinterestedness does not mean child-like innocence. If the judge did not form judgments of the actors in those court-house dramas called trials, he could never render decisions." *In re J.P. Linahan, Inc.*, 138 F.2d 650, 654 (CA2 1943). Also not subject to deprecatory characterization as "bias" or "prejudice" are opinions held by judges as a result of what they learned in earlier proceedings. It has long been regarded as normal and proper for a judge to sit in the same case upon its remand, and to sit in successive trials involving the same defendant.

It is wrong in theory, though it may not be too far off the mark as a practical matter, to suggest, as many opinions have, that "extrajudicial source" is the *only* basis for establishing disqualifying bias or prejudice. It is the only *common* basis, but not the exclusive one, since it is not the *exclusive* reason a predisposition can be wrongful or inappropriate. A favorable or unfavorable predisposition can also deserve to be characterized as "bias" or "prejudice" because, even though it springs from the facts adduced or the events occurring at trial, it is so extreme as to display clear inability to render fair judgment. (That explains what some courts have called the "pervasive bias" exception to the "extrajudicial source" doctrine.)

With this understanding of the "extrajudicial source" limitation in §§ 144 and 455(b)(1), we turn to the question whether it appears in § 455(a) as well. Petitioners' argument for the negative based upon the mere absence of the word "personal" is, for the reasons described above, not persuasive. Petitioners also rely upon the categorical nature of § 455's language: Recusal is required *whenever* there exists a genuine question concerning a judge's impartiality, and not merely when the question arises from an extrajudicial source. A similar "plain-language" argument could be made, however, with regard to §§ 144 and 455(b)(1): They apply *whenever* bias or prejudice exists, and not merely when it derives from an extrajudicial source. As we have described, the latter argument is invalid because the pejorative connotation of the terms "bias" and "prejudice" demands that they be applied only to judicial predispositions that go beyond what is normal and acceptable. We think there is an equivalent pejorative connotation, with equivalent consequences, to the term "partiality." See American Heritage Dictionary 1319 (3d ed. 1992) ("partiality" defined as "[f]avorable prejudice or bias"). A prospective juror in an insurance-claim case may be stricken as partial if he always votes for insurance companies; but not if he always votes for the party whom the terms of the contract support. "Partiality" does not refer to all favoritism, but only to such as is, for some reason, wrongful or inappropriate. Impartiality is not gullibility. Moreover, even if the pejorative connotation of "partiality" were not enough to import the "extrajudicial source" doctrine into § 455(a), the "reasonableness" limitation (recusal is required only if the judge's impartiality "might *reasonably* be questioned") would have the same effect. To demand the sort of "child-like innocence" that elimination of the "extrajudicial source" limitation would require is not reasonable.

Declining to find in the language of § 455(a) a limitation which (petitioners acknowledge) *is* contained in the language of § 455(b)(1) would cause the statute, in a significant sense, to contradict itself. As we have described, § 455(a) expands the protection of § 455(b), but duplicates some of its protection as well—not only with regard to bias and prejudice but also with regard to interest and relationship. Within the area of overlap, it is unreasonable to interpret § 455(a) (unless the language *requires* it) as implicitly eliminating a limitation explicitly set forth in § 455(b). It would obviously be wrong, for example, to hold that "impartiality could reasonably be questioned" simply because one of the parties is in the fourth degree of relationship to the judge. Section 455(b)(5), which addresses the matter of relationship specifically, ends the disability at the *third* degree of relationship, and that should obviously govern for purposes of § 455(a) as well. Similarly, § 455(b)(1), which addresses the matter of personal bias and prejudice specifically, contains the "extrajudicial source" limitation—and *that* limitation (since nothing in the text contradicts it) should govern for purposes of § 455(a) as well.2

Petitioners suggest that applying the "extrajudicial source" limitation to § 455(a) will cause disqualification of a trial judge to be more easily obtainable upon remand of a case by an appellate court than upon direct motion. We do not see why that necessarily follows; and if it does, why it is necessarily bad. Federal appellate courts' ability to assign a case to a different judge on remand rests not on the recusal statutes alone, but on the appellate courts' statutory power to "require such further proceedings to be had as may be just under the circumstances," 28 U.S.C. § 2106. That may permit a different standard, and there may be pragmatic reasons for a different standard. We do not say so—but merely say that the standards applied on remand are irrelevant to the question before us here.

For all these reasons, we think that the "extrajudicial source" doctrine, as we have described it, applies to § 455(a). As we have described it, however, there is not much doctrine to the doctrine. The fact that an opinion held by a judge derives from a source outside judicial proceedings is not a *necessary* condition for "bias or prejudice" recusal, since predispositions developed during the course of a trial will sometimes (albeit rarely) suffice. Nor is it a *sufficient* condition for "bias or prejudice" recusal, since *some* opinions acquired outside the context of judicial proceedings (for example, the judge's view of the law acquired in scholarly reading) will *not* suffice. Since neither the presence of an extrajudicial source necessarily establishes bias, nor the absence of an extrajudicial source necessarily precludes bias, it would be better to speak of the existence of a significant (and often determinative) "extrajudicial source" *factor,* than of an "extrajudicial source" *doctrine,* in recusal jurisprudence.

The facts of the present case do not require us to describe the consequences of that factor in complete detail. It is enough for present purposes to say the following: First, judicial rulings alone almost never constitute a valid basis for a bias or partiality motion. See *United States v. Grinnell Corp.,* 384 U.S., at 583. In and of themselves (*i.e.,* apart from surrounding comments or accompanying opinion), they cannot possibly show reliance upon an extrajudicial source; and can only in the rarest circumstances evidence the degree of favoritism or antagonism required (as discussed below) when no extrajudicial source is involved. Almost invariably, they are proper grounds for appeal, not for recusal.

Second, opinions formed by the judge on the basis of facts introduced or events occurring in the course of the current proceedings, or of prior proceedings, do not constitute a basis for a bias or partiality motion unless they display a deep-seated favoritism or antagonism that would make fair judgment impossible. Thus, judicial remarks during the course of a trial that are critical or disapproving of, or even hostile to, counsel, the parties, or their cases, ordinarily do not support a bias or partiality challenge. They *may* do so if they reveal an opinion that derives from an extrajudicial source; and they *will* do so if they reveal such a high degree of favoritism or antagonism as to make fair judgment impossible. An example of the latter (and perhaps of the former as well) is the statement that was alleged to have been made by the District Judge in *Berger v. United States,* 255 U.S. 22 (1921), a World War I espionage case against German–American defendants: "One must have a very judicial mind, indeed, not [to be] prejudiced against the German Americans" because their "hearts are reeking with disloyalty." (internal quotation marks omitted). *Not* establishing bias or partiality, however, are expressions of impatience, dissatisfaction, annoyance, and even anger, that are within the bounds of what imperfect men and women, even after having been confirmed as federal judges, sometimes display. A judge's ordinary efforts at courtroom administration—even a stern and short-tempered judge's ordinary efforts at courtroom administration—remain immune.

III

Applying the principles we have discussed to the facts of the present case is not difficult. None of the grounds petitioners assert required disqualification. As we have described, petitioners' first recusal motion was based on rulings made, and statements uttered, by the District Judge during and after the 1983 trial; and petitioner Bourgeois' second recusal motion was founded on the judge's admonishment of Bourgeois' counsel and codefendants. In their briefs here, petitioners have referred to additional manifestations of alleged bias in the District Judge's conduct of the trial below, including the questions he put to certain witnesses, his alleged "anti-defendant tone," his cutting off of testimony said to be relevant to defendants' state of mind, and his post-trial refusal to allow petitioners to appeal *in forma pauperis.*

All of these grounds are inadequate under the principles we have described above: They consist of judicial rulings, routine trial administration efforts, and ordinary admonishments (whether or not legally supportable) to counsel and to witnesses. All occurred in the course of judicial proceedings, *and* neither (1) relied upon knowledge acquired outside such proceedings nor (2) displayed deep-seated and unequivocal antagonism that would render fair judgment impossible.

The judgment of the Court of Appeals is

Affirmed.

CASE QUESTIONS

1. What motion was at issue in this case?
2. What is the "extrajudicial source" rule?
3. Does it apply to motions under 28 U.S.C. § 455?
4. What makes bias wrongful or inappropriate?

---

5. EXPRESSIONS OF BIAS

Model Code Rule 2.3 requires judges to do their work free from bias or prejudice. In particular, Rule 2.3(b) provides that "in the performance of judicial duties" judges may not "by words or conduct" manifest bias or prejudice or engage in harassment on the basis of several characteristics including, without limitation, race, sex, gender, religion, national origin, ethnicity, disability, age, sexual orientation, marital status, socioeconomic status, or political affiliation. Rule 2.3(c) instructs judges to require lawyers appearing before them not to manifest bias or prejudice or to engage in harassment of parties, witnesses, lawyers, or others based on these same characteristics (again without limitation). Rule 2.3(d) allows judges to refer to such characteristics where relevant to a case.

Liteky indicated that the term bias implies an inappropriate disposition toward a person. Inappropriate need not mean malicious, however, and a judge may violate Rule 2.3 even though the judge subjectively may perceive his or her bias as sympathetic toward a party. The following case illustrates this point.

MEJIA V. UNITED STATES

916 A.2d 900 (D.C. 2007)

NEBEKER, SENIOR JUDGE:

This is an appeal from a misdemeanor sexual abuse conviction. After a bench trial, appellant was found guilty of one count of misdemeanor sexual abuse pursuant to D.C.Code § 22–3006. According to the government's evidence, J.C. was staying with her aunt and uncle in 2001 while her grandmother was in El Salvador. At that time, J.C. was nine-years-old. She was on the couch coloring when appellant, her uncle, climbed on top of her and tried to remove her clothing. After she screamed, appellant got off of her and went into the kitchen. J.C. tried to call her grandfather from her cousin's room, but no one was home. She testified that she took the phone off its hook in the kitchen and, because the cord was long, ran the cord under the door to her cousin's room to make the call.

During cross examination on April 20, 2004, appellant's trial counsel introduced a short phone cord in an attempt to show that J.C. could not have taken the phone into her cousin's room as she claimed. Also during cross examination, J.C. acknowledged that on April 12, 2004, prior to providing her direct testimony, she told the prosecutor that she had fabricated the allegations. The prosecutor then warned J.C. she could get into trouble for telling a lie and played a tape of J.C.'s earlier conversation with a detective. J.C. then testified for the government. On redirect, J.C. testified that she had recanted because she loved her cousins, she did not want anything bad to happen to appellant, and her grandmother told her that appellant could be sent to El Salvador. J.C. continued to assert under oath, however, that sexual abuse did occur.

On April 23, 2004, the trial court found appellant guilty of the 2001 incident.[14] The judge credited J.C.'s version of events because (1) J.C. harbored no animus toward appellant, (2) J.C.'s testimony was consistent, and (3) the phone cord introduced by appellant as the one J.C. used in 2001 looked "like a brand new cord . . . , much unlike the phone itself."

---

[14] FN1. J.C. also testified that appellant was driving her home in 2003 when he pulled the car over, stated "this is our chance, let's take advantage of it," tried to kiss her and put his hand on her shoulder. J.C. got out of the car, ran to her house and told her grandmother about both incidents. On redirect, she stated that appellant also put his hand on the inside of her knee. The trial judge found appellant not guilty with regard to the 2003 incident. The trial judge stated that she did not have "an abiding conviction with regard to the issue of the touching of the leg. And since touching an arm is not sexual contact, I thought that there was enough discrepancy . . . for me not to be comfortable concluding that that did occur."

After rendering a verdict and articulating the above reasons for the verdict, the trial court told the parties that she was "prepared to go to sentencing" and asked for a pretrial services report. A discussion ensued regarding when to schedule the sentencing hearing, and the judge remarked that she thought the verdict would disrupt the family dynamics. The trial judge then made the following comments:

> And I think that it is just unconscionable to me that this little child would have to bear that level of pressure for conduct by an adult that was inappropriate at best and criminal as I have found. . . . [A]nd in thinking about this as I thought about this yesterday and last night and thought about this this morning, . . . there are perhaps, . . . some cultural issues that I'm not really clear about. I know that in countries like El Salvador and even, . . . in frankly places in the surrounding jurisdiction, there are very young girls who are 12 and 13, 14 and 15 who are married of black descent. And I'm not clear whether or not there is, I don't know, and maybe that's something that counsel can, can help me with that there is a, I'm certainly not suggesting that it's cultural in general, that all people feel this way. But I have not been real clear about the issue of sexualizing young girls at a very early age. And whether or not any of that is happening and whether or not that's part and parcel of, of what was going on here. I don't know when Mr. Mejia came to this country. I don't know how long he had been there, what his status is. Obviously I do appreciate that by virtue of this, because I heard it on the witness stand, there may be some immigration implications that are adverse to him and to his family. But I mean, you know, she is, I mean she's . . . a beautiful but little girl. So I am prepared to hear it if you wish to do it now. Otherwise, we'd need to just defer sentencing for a time specific, and then I can hear it then.

Based on these statements, appellant asks that we reverse his conviction and remand his case for a retrial before a different judge. Such statements, it is argued, evidence an appearance of bias against appellant and thereby violated the Code of Judicial Conduct of the District of Columbia Courts. Canon 3(B)(5) of the Code of Judicial Conduct provides that "[a] judge shall perform judicial duties without bias or prejudice. A judge shall not, in the performance of judicial duties, by words or conduct manifest bias or prejudice, including but not limited to bias or prejudice based upon . . . national origin. . . . " In addition Canon 3(E)(1), which replaced Canon 3(C)(1) of the 1972 Code, provides that "[a] judge shall disqualify himself or herself in a proceeding in which the judge's impartiality might reasonably be questioned, including but not limited to instances where . . . (a) the judge has a personal bias or prejudice concerning a party . . . or personal knowledge of disputed evidentiary facts concerning the proceeding. . . . " The goal of Canon 3(E)(1) is "to prevent even the appearance of impropriety." *Scott v. United States,* 559 A.2d 745, 750 (D.C.1989) (referring to Canon 3(C)(1) of the 1972 Code).

We must view what was said in the complete context of the trial. We may not do so by making a subjective determination. *Id.* at 748–49 ("The necessity for recusal in a case is premised on an objective standard."). We must, rather, decide whether an objective person, informed of the trial proceedings, could reasonably conclude an appearance of bias existed, although in the context of the record, we are inclined to believe that she was seeking the views of counsel at sentencing on the question she broached. Though we do not draw any conclusion that the judge had an actual bias which influenced the verdict, or that the musings were not well intentioned, we hold that on this record, an appearance of bias to an informed, objective observer might exist, and the integrity of the judicial process compromised. Therefore, the judgment of conviction is reversed and the case remanded for a new trial if the prosecution so determines, in which event we are confident the case will be assigned to another judge without a directive from this court.

Reversed and remanded.

Rule 2.3 is directed toward judges acting as judges, but at least one case has found a violation of the antecedent provision to Rule 2.3 based on a candidate's campaign conduct. In *Mississippi Comm'n on Judicial Performance v. Osborne*, 11 So.3d 107, 109 (Miss. 2009), the Court found a violation of Mississippi Canon of Judicial Ethics 3(B)(5) (from which Rule 2.3 was taken) based on the following:

> "¶ 3. On September 13, 2006, while campaigning for reelection as a county court judge for Leflore County, Judge Solomon C. Osborne spoke before the Greenwood Voters League, a predominantly African–American political organization. Portions of his speech appeared the next day in the local newspaper, *The Greenwood Commonwealth.* In an article entitled: "Osborne: Blacks not where we should be. County judge says progress has been made, more is needed," the newspaper quoted Judge Osborne as stating:
>
> > White folks don't praise you unless you're a damn fool. Unless they think they can use you. If you have your own mind and know what you're doing, they don't want you around."

Prohibitions on expressions of bias are limited by the First Amendment's protection of the freedom of speech, however, as another Mississippi case shows. In *Mississippi Comm'n on Judicial Performance v. Wilkerson,* 876 So.2d 1006, 1008 (Miss. 2004), the Court found constitutional protection based on the following facts and reasoning:

¶ 2. After reading an article about certain states which have chosen to extend to homosexual partners the same right to sue previously reserved for spouses and family members, George County Justice Court Judge Connie Glen Wilkerson felt compelled to make known his disagreement with those states, and his views on homosexuality in general. The judge sent a letter to the editor of his local weekly newspaper, *The George County Times,* which he signed "Connie Glenn Wilkerson" and stamped "Bro. Connie G. Wilkerson." The letter provided his home address and telephone number, and provided no reference to his official capacity as a judge.

¶ 3. Declaring that his views were based on his Christian beliefs, and upon Biblical principles, the judge opined that homosexuals belong in mental institutions. The letter was published on March 28, 2002.

¶ 4. On April 9, 2002, a reporter from a radio network called the judge at home to discuss the letter. The judge contends that the reporter encouraged him to repeat his views on the legislation and homosexuality and that the conversation was aired without his permission.

¶ 5. In the interview he referred to homosexuality as an "illness" which merited treatment, rather than punishment. He faults the radio network for airing the recorded statements which the radio station "unfairly interspersed" with comments from known homosexual activists. . . .

¶ 7. The sole issue before us is whether the judge's right to send the letter and make the statements are protected by the First Amendment to the United States Constitution.

¶ 8. To be sure, we affirm our reverence for the judicial oath of office and the Canons which govern judicial conduct. This certainly includes Canon 4A(1), which requires judges to "conduct all extrajudicial activities so that they do not cast doubt on the judge's capacity to act impartially as a judge."

¶ 9. Today's decision does not void, amend or diminish any of the Canons found in our Code of Judicial Conduct, nor does it bring into question the validity of any of our firmly held beliefs regarding a judge's obligation to foster respect for, and bring honor to, the judiciary and to the legal profession, generally.

¶ 10. Nevertheless, because we are convinced that the statements made by the judge in this case constitute religious and political/public issue speech specially protected by the First Amendment and because we are further persuaded that in some cases (including the case sub judice), forced concealment of views on political/public issues serves to further no compelling governmental, public or judicial interest, we are compelled to reject the recommendation of the

Commission and hold that—under the particular facts of this case—sanctions are constitutionally impermissible.

---

6. EXTRA–JUDICIAL CONDUCT

Several provisions of the Model Code regulate judges' conduct off the bench. Canon Three provides that in their non-judicial activities judges shall act to minimize conflicts with their judicial obligations. Rule 3.1 permits extrajudicial activities not prohibited by law so long as they do not interfere with a judge's work, lead to frequent disqualification, undermine (in the eyes of a reasonable person) a judge's independence, integrity, or impartiality, coerce another person (as judged by a reasonable person standard) or make use of court resources (except for incidental uses that involve the law).

Rule 3.6 forbid judges from being members in any organization that "practices invidious discrimination" on the basis of race, sex, gender, religion, national origin, ethnicity, or sexual orientation. The test for discrimination by an organization is whether an excluded applicant would be eligible for membership if he or she did not possess one of the identified characteristics. Judges also should not use the benefits or facilities of such an organization, but isolated uses that would not support a reasonable belief that the judge endorses the organization do not violate this rule. Judges cannot schedule events at such facilities, in other words, but can attend events others schedule and over which the judge has no control.

Rule 3.14 allows judges to accept reimbursements and fee waivers from outside sources for activities otherwise permitted by the Code. This rule (or equivalents in adopted rules) is relevant to a controversy over whether judges may attend educational seminars sponsored by groups with a distinct ideological perspective. Comment 3 to the rule notes that a judge "must assure himself or herself that acceptance of reimbursement or fee waivers would not appear to a reasonable person to undermine the judge's independence, integrity, or impartiality." It lists as factors to consider in making this decision whether the sponsor is a bar association or school, whether funding comes from many sources rather than a few, whether the content of the seminar relates to pending or impending matters, or those likely to come before a judge.

The most recent exchanges in the controversy were prompted by a report entitled *Nothing For Free: How Private Judicial Seminars Are Undermining Environmental Protections and Breaking the Public's Trust* issued by the Community Rights Council (CRC), a nonprofit public-interest law firm. As summarized in Congressional testimony by Douglas Kendall, executive director of the CRC, the report found:

> Corporations and foundations that have a legal agenda in the courts are advancing this agenda by paying for free trips for federal judges to resorts and dude ranches. Once there, judges attend lectures making the case for curbing government regulation in favor of a free-market approach to matters like protecting the environment. . . . that judicial education is being paid for by entities that have an interest in or are parties to federal litigation creates an appearance of improper influence and undermines public trust and confidence in the judiciary . . . between 1992 and 1998 more than 230 federal judges—more than a quarter of the federal judiciary—traveled to resorts at the expense of private interests with a stake in federal litigation.[15]

The introduction to the report was written by the Hon. Abner J. Mikva, a former congressman, judge on the court of Appeals for the District of Columbia Circuit, and former White House counsel to President Clinton. Judge Mikva "emphasized the 'perception' problem that occurs when judges are wined, dined, and golfed at these seminars sponsored by groups that have an interest in the outcome of litigation." In a later article he offered two specific examples:

> A book is given to the judges who attend seminars sponsored by FREE (Foundation for Research on Economics and the Environment), the most successful of the privately funded seminars. It is the *Federal Judges' Desk Reference to Environmental Economics*. I hope that it is not in fact used as a desk reference because it is hardly a balanced work on the subjects of either the environment or economics. . . . there are other views on takings problems in addition to those of Professor Richard Epstein and that Milton Friedman's views are not the only position that one can take on the economics of environmental laws. . . .
>
> The Law and Economics Center (LEC) at George Mason University Law School is the prime case in point. LEC is the granddaddy in the seminar business. Founded by Henry Manne . . . it set out some years ago to educate federal judges about law and economics, Chicago style. LEC boasts that over one-third of the federal judges have participated in its seminars. (In one famous example, an attendee at one of the LEC seminars wrote that, as a result of his better understanding of the problems of predatory pricing, he had set aside a $15 million antitrust verdict.). . . .

Abner Mikva, *Judges, Junkets, and Seminars*, 28 LITIGATION 3 (2002).

Judge Mikva's article prompted a response by the Hon. A. Raymond Randolph, of the Court of Appeals for the District of Columbia Circuit:

[15] Douglas Kendall, Testimony before the House Committee on the Judiciary, Subcommittee on Courts, the Internet, and Intellectual Property, Oversight Hearing on Operation of Federal Judicial Misconduct and Recusal Statutes, November 29, 2001.

> FREE . . . is a private non-profit organization. It receives no money from corporations to reimburse judges for attending its seminars (which are now co-sponsored by Montana State University). The seminar money comes from so-called dead-man foundations not involved in federal litigation. So what is Judge Mikva talking about when he writes of judges being reimbursed for expenses at FREE's seminars "by groups having an interest in litigation"? Pay close attention to the words "interest in litigation." You probably thought FREE's seminar contributors were parties in federal court cases. If so, you were misled.
>
> [Judge Mikva] is visualizing foundations that contribute not only to FREE but also to public interest law firms, against whom Kendall occasionally litigates property and environmental cases. . . . Here is the chain: (1) the foundation providing funds to FREE for seminars has some control over the point of view conveyed there; (2) the viewpoint conveyed represents a litigating position of the foundation because (3) the foundation provides funds to public interest law firms representing third parties, and the foundation has some control over the law firms' position in court; and (4) judges attending the seminar know not only that the foundation has contributed funds to FREE and to a public interest law firm appearing in their court, but also that the foundation controls the positions of both. Since when do foundations have litigating positions in cases they are not litigating? When did foundations begin instructing attorneys how to represent their clients, and who are these attorneys so we can report them to the bar's ethics counsel?

A. Raymond Randolph, *Private Judicial Seminars: A Reply to Abner Mikva*, 28 LITIGATION 3 (2002).

After the CRC issued its report, but before the exchange between Judges Mikva and Randolph, the Court of Appeals for the Second Circuit ruled on a disqualification motion premised on the conclusions of the report:

IN RE AGUINDA

241 F.3d 194 (2001)

WINTER, CIRCUIT JUDGE.

Petitioners seek a writ of mandamus directing Judge Rakoff to recuse himself in the underlying action. That action involves claims by plaintiffs, who are citizens of Ecuador and Peru, that the defendant—here respondent—Texaco, Inc., polluted rain forests and rivers in those two countries, causing environmental damage and personal injuries. . . .

The issue now before us arises from Judge Rakoff's attendance at an expense-paid seminar on environmental issues during the period between his dismissal of the case and our remand. Petitioners argue that because Texaco contributed general funding to the organization that sponsored the seminar and a former Texaco chief executive officer was a speaker at the seminar, an appearance of partiality warranting disqualification was created. Judge Rakoff denied petitioners' motion essentially on the grounds that Texaco provided only minor general funding to the seminar's sponsor, nonprofit foundations funded the seminar itself, and neither the former Texaco CEO nor any other presenter at the seminar discussed any issues material to the merits of the underlying case.

We hold that Judge Rakoff did not abuse his discretion in denying petitioners' motion. Given Texaco's indirect and minor funding role and the lack of a showing that any aspect of the seminar touched upon an issue material to the disposition of a claim or defense in the present litigation, we deny the petition.

BACKGROUND

The present petition is based almost entirely on a July 2000 publication, offered as part of petitioners' recusal motion in the district court, by an organization named the Community Rights Counsel ("CRC"). The publication was entitled *Nothing for Free: How Private Judicial Seminars Are Undermining Environmental Protections and Breaking the Public's Trust* [hereinafter *CRC Report*]. Its highly critical focus was on three organizations that offer "privately funded" seminars for judges: the Law and Economics Center ("LEC"), which is affiliated with George Mason University; the Foundation for Research on Economics and the Environment ("FREE"); and the Liberty Fund, which is affiliated with the Manhattan Institute's Center for Legal Policy. FREE is the particular target of the CRC Report.

The CRC Report claims that "the marketplace of privately funded judicial education is overwhelmingly dominated by pro-market, anti-regulatory seminars offering a single and unchallenged line of reasoning" and that the " 'Big Three' [LEC, FREE, and Liberty Fund] . . . share a remarkably similar, and in some respects extreme, conservative/libertarian ideology." It further alleges that these seminars are offered in luxurious settings and funded by corporate donors who hope to obtain favorable judicial decisions as a result of judges attending these seminars. The CRC Report has attracted much attention from the media.

Turning specifically to the present matter, petitioners assert that Judge Rakoff must recuse himself because he attended an expense-paid seminar sponsored by FREE from September 15 through September 20, 1998, at a ranch in Montana. They note that Texaco provides funding to FREE and that a former chief executive officer of Texaco was a speaker at the seminar. The seminar was entitled, "Real and Alleged Environmental Crises–A Seminar for Federal Judges." Petitioners state that the topics of the seminar were "directly related to the issues bound to arise in the course of [their] litigation." . . . It was the seventh session, entitled "The Environment: Some Thoughts from the Corner Office," at which Alfred C. DeCrane, Jr., the retired chairman and chief executive officer of Texaco, spoke. Petitioners argue that Judge Rakoff's attendance at the seminar (after he had dismissed the case but before the remand) created an appearance of partiality and that, therefore, he is disqualified from presiding on the remand proceedings.

In denying the motion for disqualification, Judge Rakoff noted that Texaco did contribute to FREE but that the contributions comprised a "minor" portion of FREE's general funding.[16] He also noted that the seminar itself was funded by two nonprofit organizations that are strangers to this litigation.[17] Finally, the judge stated that none of the discussions in the formal sessions or in informal conversations related to legal issues arising in the litigation. Petitioners concede a lack of knowledge of the actual contents of the various discussions.

DISCUSSION

We review a denial of a recusal motion for abuse of discretion. . . .

The United States Judicial Conference Committee on Codes of Conduct has issued guidelines that specifically address whether a judge's expense-paid attendance at a seminar constitutes an improper gift. The guidelines are contained in Advisory Opinion No. 67, first issued in 1980 and revised and reissued in 1998. It states in pertinent part:

> Payment of tuition and expenses involved in attendance at non-government sponsored seminars constitutes a gift. . . .
>
> The education of judges in various academic disciplines serves the public interest. That a lecture or seminar may emphasize a particu-

---

[16] FN3. The record contains a tax document indicating that Texaco's contributions to FREE in 1998 and 1999 ranged from 3% to 6% of total reportable contributions. What other income FREE has, whether by gift, interest, or other source, is unknown. Whether FREE has other assets is also unknown.

[17] FN4. Petitioners argue that FREE's literature stating that the seminar was supported by the two nonprofit organizations does not exclude the possibility that FREE also used general funds to pay for the seminar. However, the plain implication of FREE's literature is otherwise, and, because petitioners bear the burden of establishing the grounds for issuing a writ of mandamus, their failure to show the use of general funds precludes such a finding. In addressing this argument we offer no view on whether Texaco's provision of minor general funding would alter the outcome if general funding were used to finance the seminar.

Judge Rakoff also stated that he did not know that FREE had received funds from Texaco prior to petitioners' motion. His lack of knowledge, however, is irrelevant in light of *Liljeberg v. Health Services Acquisition Corp.*, 486 U.S. 847 (1988), in which the Supreme Court held that "[s]cienter is not an element of a violation of § 455(a)," which requires disqualification "in any proceeding in which [the judge's] impartiality might reasonably be questioned," 28 U.S.C. § 455(a). Rather, the Court held, "advancement of the purpose of the provision—to promote public confidence in the integrity of the judicial process—does not depend upon whether or not the judge actually knew of facts creating an appearance of impropriety, so long as the public might reasonably believe that he or she knew." 486 U.S. at 859–60 (citations omitted).

> lar viewpoint or school of thought does not in itself preclude a judge from attending. Judges are continually exposed to competing views and arguments and are trained to weigh them.
>
> It would be improper to participate in such a seminar if the sponsor, or source of funding, is involved in litigation, or likely to be so involved, and the topics covered in the seminar are likely to be in some manner related to the subject matter of such litigation.

Administrative Office of U.S. Courts, *Codes of Conduct for Judges and Judicial Employees, in Guide to Judiciary Policies and Procedures* [hereinafter *Codes of Conduct*] IV–151 (1999). Application of these various guideposts is not mechanical but requires an exercise of reasoned judgment. They must be applied in an adversarial context in which counsel will seek to steer cases to judges deemed favorable to their cause—in the lexicon of the profession, "judge-shopping." As a result, the grounds asserted in a recusal motion must be scrutinized with care, and judges should not recuse themselves solely because a party claims an appearance of partiality. . . .

Section 455(a) requires a showing that would cause "an objective, disinterested observer fully informed of the underlying facts [to] entertain significant doubt that justice would be done absent recusal." *United States v. Lovaglia,* 954 F.2d 811, 815 (2d Cir.1992). "Where a case, by contrast, involves remote, contingent, indirect or speculative interests, disqualification is not required." *Id.* Moreover, where the standards governing disqualification have not been met, disqualification is not optional; rather, it is prohibited. As we have stated, "[a] judge is as much obliged not to recuse himself when it is not called for as he is obliged to when it is." *In re Drexel Burnham Lambert, Inc.,* 861 F.2d 1307, 1312 (2d Cir. 1988).

Finally, with regard to the appearance of partiality, the appearance must have an objective basis beyond the fact that claims of partiality have been well publicized. . . .

In addressing the merits, we write at some length even though the outcome is not in doubt. The principle set forth by petitioners is fairly sweeping and calls for a discussion commensurate with its breadth. Moreover, the issues raised by petitioners are serious and have implications regarding public confidence in the judiciary. It is, therefore, important that judges have some general guidance as to when attendance at meetings, seminars, or other presentations may be problematic. Judges should not forgo important educational opportunities where no impropriety can be perceived. However, judges' participation in such events in certain circumstances is ill-advised, and we add some cautionary notes in that regard.

Petitioners' showing is rather more limited than they claim. They have established that Judge Rakoff attended a seminar that was funded by nonprofit organizations that are not parties to the underlying litigation. The seminar was sponsored by an organization, FREE, that receives a small portion of its general funding from Texaco, and a former CEO of Texaco spoke at the seminar. Petitioners state that the seminar had, or might have appeared to a reasonable person to have had, a pro-development, anti-environmental-protection slant with which many would disagree. They have not, however, identified any legal issue material to the disposition of a claim or defense in the underlying litigation that was discussed, either favorably or unfavorably to their cause, at the seminar. Nor have they shown that the judge had any informal conversation bearing on such an issue. To the contrary, the judge has stated that neither the seminar discussions nor informal conversations had any such bearing.[18]

We turn now to the application of the legal guideposts described above to petitioners' showing. We conclude that the district judge did not abuse his discretion in denying the motion for disqualification.

With regard to Texaco's provision of a minor portion of FREE's general funding, no reasonable observer would believe that such funding would influence a seminar-attending judge's decision in litigation involving Texaco. Rather, such an observer would regard the donation to FREE as far too remote to create a plausible suspicion of improper influence. *See Lovaglia,* 954 F.2d at 815.

Judges are provided meals and often lodging by, *inter alia,* bar associations and law schools that are funded by donors who appear before the judges as parties or as counsel to parties. At bar association dinners, tables to which judges are assigned (by the association) as paid guests may be funded by particular law firms. Many law schools establish centers or projects to focus academic work on certain areas of the law and fund them through—often large—donations from—often small numbers of—alumni and others professionally active in the particular areas. Such centers or projects often conduct seminars, symposia, or workshops to which judges are invited and that provide meals and often lodging.

Academic institutions may also conduct programs to train judges whose expenses are paid. For example, the University of Virginia and New York University routinely sponsor seminars for judges that may cover topics involving issues that are involved in litigation. *See* NYU Law, *NYU Hosts Workshop For Federal Judges,* The Law School Magazine, Au-

[18] FN6. The judge did note, however, that, also while the prior appeal was pending in this court, he had attended an expense-paid seminar sponsored by the Aspen Institute in Wye River, Maryland. As described by the judge, this seminar concerned "international human rights law [and] consisted of speakers who, for the most part, espoused a view of public international law broadly similar to plaintiffs' position here."

tumn 2000, at 88 (describing "Workshop on Employment Law for Federal Judges"); Rector & Visitors of the University of Virginia, *University of Virginia School of Law: Programs & Centers* (2000), at http://www.law.virginia.edu (describing "Graduate Program for Judges"). Such institutions nevertheless raise private funding from persons or entities that are parties to litigation or counsel to parties.

No reasonable person would believe that expense-paid attendance at such events would cause a judge to be partial, or to appear so, in litigation involving a minor donor—whether a party or counsel to a party—to a bar association, law school, or program administering a particular seminar. Were we to take a different view, judges would as a practical matter either have to recuse themselves in a vast number of matters or decline invitations to numerous events of an entirely innocent nature that are of importance to the judiciary, the profession, and legal education. We therefore conclude that Section 455(a) did not require Judge Rakoff's recusal solely because of Texaco's donation of minor general funding to FREE. For similar reasons, we also conclude that it did not constitute a gift by Texaco to Judge Rakoff within the meaning of Section 303(a) of the Ethics Reform Act.

Indeed, in fairness to petitioners, we do not understand them to claim seriously that Texaco's provision of some minor funding to FREE by itself mandates recusal. We dispose of such a claim only out of an abundance of caution. The claim they do press seriously arises from the appearance they believe is created by the combination of: (i) Texaco's provision of minor general funding to an organization that (ii) sponsored a seminar for judges funded by non-parties that (iii) presented an "unbalanced" view on general environmental policy issues. However, we conclude that these circumstances also do not warrant recusal.

Although views differ on the merits and fairness of FREE's environmental seminars, we accept for purposes of the present analysis the allegation that the FREE seminar attended by Judge Rakoff was "unbalanced." Indeed, we have little choice. A determination that a presentation on policy issues is unbalanced must be based on establishing a set of parameters defining "balance" that in turn requires a weighing of the intellectual significance of differing positions on controversial issues. This weighing involves judgments resembling content regulation that are not appropriate for courts. A determination that a presentation is balanced depends so heavily on each individual's view as to whether his or her position on the issue is prominently featured that a search for a consensus as to what is a balanced presentation of a particular issue is almost chimerical. If the subject is controversial, some will inevitably say that a presentation on it is unbalanced. A court addressing a recusal motion should, therefore, accept a claim of lack of balance at least for purposes of determining whether an appearance of impropriety has been created.

Nevertheless, so long as: (i) a presentation does not relate to legal issues material to the disposition of a claim or defense in an action before a judge who attended the presentation, (ii) the funding by a party of a seminar's sponsor is too remote or minor to appear to a reasonable person to have an influence on the judge, and (iii) the nature of a party's funding of a sponsoring organization does not create an appearance of either control or impropriety, as discussed *infra,* no reasonable observer would believe that judges are subject to what amounts to brainwashing of a kind that would affect the outcome of such litigation. Even if a judge were persuaded by the FREE seminar that our environmental laws are on balance harmful in many respects, the presumption is that a judge will put personal beliefs aside and rule according to the laws as enacted, as required by his or her oath. Indeed, persons who have held elective office often become judges, and they are not recused from administering laws in whose enactment, in their prior capacity, they participated. *See, e.g., Laird,* 409 U.S. at 831–32 (noting past Supreme Court justices who sat on cases involving legislation they drafted or issues they decided as political figures); *United States v. Alabama,* 828 F.2d 1532, 1543–44 (11th Cir.1987) (per curiam) (holding judge's background as civil rights lawyer and state legislator did not mandate disqualification of judge ordering desegregation, but that other factors did); *Shaw v. Martin,* 733 F.2d 304, 316 (4th Cir.1984) ("One who has voted as a legislator in favor of a statute permitting the death penalty in a proper case cannot thereafter be presumed disqualified to hear capital cases as a judge or predisposed to give a death sentence in any particular case.").

Moreover, petitioners' view would commit courts addressing recusal motions to the unraveling of every contact a judge has had with a general subject matter and the weighing of the likelihood that the contact influenced his or her views on the subject. For example, the district judge in the present matter also attended a seminar whose speakers espoused a view of public international law that was in a general way close to that of petitioners, a contact that was arguably more closely related to claims and defenses in the underlying case than the FREE seminar. See *supra* Note 6. Moreover, federal judges routinely receive free copies of books, journals, magazines, and other publications that discuss disputed policy issues without any imputation until now that, if they read some of the unsolicited materials, they are thereafter recused on any matter connected with those issues. Even if possible, therefore, assessing the impact of any single presentation on the thinking of a judge is neither necessary nor useful.

Finally, as the Judicial Conference Advisory Opinion notes, the acquisition of general information is vital to judges, *see Codes of Conduct,* at IV–151, and we see little reason to adopt a rule with no beneficial effect that would deter judges from seeking to educate themselves in various disciplines. This is particularly the case in an age in which specialized knowledge is important to the exercise of the judicial function. . . . Moreover, the Committee on Codes of Conduct has specifically stated, in its Advisory Opinion No. 67, that the "education of judges in various academic disciplines serves the public interest. That a lecture or seminar may emphasize a particular viewpoint or school of thought does not in itself preclude a judge from attending. Judges are continually exposed to competing views and arguments and are trained to weigh them." *Codes of Conduct,* at IV–151; *see also United States v. Bonds,* 18 F.3d 1327, 1328–29 (6th Cir.1994) (denying recusal motion where circuit judge attended University of California conference on forensic use of DNA where government expert defended his own trial testimony that resulted in convictions on appeal).

A holding that an appearance of partiality was created in the present circumstances would as a practical matter mean that attendance by a judge at any presentation on a debated issue might lead to recusal, at least where a party or counsel to a party has provided any financial support, no matter how minor or remote. A vast array of educational opportunities for judges would thereby be indiscriminately foreclosed, or recusals would become routine. Moreover . . . the universe of seminars and other presentations available to judges extends far beyond the three organizations that are the focus of the CRC Report . . . and the subjects treated range widely over, *inter alia,* various social and hard sciences, technological issues, and statistical analyses. . . .

We add several cautionary notes, however. In particular, we caution judges that recusal may be required after accepting meals or lodging from organizations that may receive a significant portion of their general funding from litigants or counsel to them—whether or not in connection with an unbalanced presentation. The extent of funding is, of course, again a matter of judgment, but accepting something of value from an organization whose existence is arguably dependent upon a party to litigation or counsel to a party might well cause a reasonable observer to lift the proverbial eyebrow.

Moreover, where a presentation concerns issues material to the disposition of litigation or involves parties, witnesses, or counsel in particular actions, the recusal calculus will differ, albeit again without an applicable mechanical standard. Presentations at bar association meetings or law schools may well relate to particularized issues, and recusal should be considered seriously, but on a case-by-case basis. Judges should be wary of attending presentations involving litigation that is before them or likely to come before them without at the very least assuring themselves that parties or counsel to the litigation are not funding or controlling the presentation. *See In re Sch. Asbestos Litig.,* 977 F.2d 764, 781–85 (3d Cir.1992) (issuing writ of mandamus directing recusal where district judge approved *ex parte* request by plaintiffs to use money from settlement fund to pay indirectly for conference about crucial scientific issue in that litigation, where plaintiffs' proposed expert witnesses presented their views, and where judge also attended conference with many expenses paid). Where parties or counsel to them fund or control such a presentation, the appearance created bears too great a resemblance to an *ex parte* contact.

Another distinction is of importance where a claim of an appearance of partiality is made. A recusal-causing appearance must be based on the facts of the presentation involved and not on the amount of publicity partisans on the particular issues can muster. . . . Having said that, however, recusal may be required where judges attend presentations—expense-paid or not—and there is reason to believe that the sponsor solicits funds by suggesting to donors that the outcome of litigation in which donors are involved may be affected. In such a case, the appearance of partiality is created by the sponsor itself, unlike the present case in which the appearance is based solely on publicity generated by critics rather than underlying facts.

CONCLUSION

Because a reasonable person would not doubt the judge's impartiality in this case, we hold that neither Section 455(a) nor any other rule requires or permits his disqualification. We therefore deny the petition.

CASE QUESTIONS

1. What relief did the petitioners seek?
2. Why did the petitioners claim recusal was required?
3. Why did Judge Rakoff deny the motion?
4. What is the standard of review for such denials?
5. What standard did the Second Circuit apply in denying the petition?
6. What reason did it give for its conclusion?

B. JOB PERFORMANCE

In addition to general requirements that judges act impartially and independently, the Model Code provides some more specific instructions on how judges should do their jobs. Canon Two provides that judges should do their work competently and diligently as well as impartially. Rule 2.6 requires that judges afford every person with a legal interest in a proceeding the right to be heard (personally or through counsel) to the extent the law requires. The Rule also provides that judges may encourage but not coerce settlement. Rule 2.7 requires judges to hear and decide matters to which they are assigned unless they are disqualified (recall the Second Circuit's comment in *Aguinda* that if disqualification is not required it is prohibited). Rule 2.8 requires judges to maintain proper decorum and demeanor in court, as the judge in the case below did not.[19] Rule 2.1 requires judges to put their judicial work ahead of personal or extrajudicial activities. You might think there would be few violations of such a rule, but a recent case from California shows that violations are possible.

STATE OF CALIFORNIA

BEFORE THE COMMISSION ON JUDICIAL PERFORMANCE

INQUIRY CONCERNING JUDGE DEANN M. SALCIDO,	DECISION AND ORDER IMPOSING PUBLIC CENSURE PURSUANT TO STIPULATION
No. 189	(Commission Rule 127)

Count One

On January 26, 2009, Judge Salcido had the husband of her courtroom bailiff videotape her on the bench presiding over a variety of matters for approximately one hour. She did so to promote herself for a role in a potential television entertainment program featuring a judge. She provided the January 26 tape to an entertainment lawyer, who showed it to a production coordinator for existing television shows featuring judges (hereafter "the producer").

Judge Salcido thereafter was informed by the entertainment attorney that the producer would be interested in filming her conducting proceedings in the courtroom. On May 1, 2009, she allowed the producer to film proceedings in her courtroom for the entire day. The purpose of the filming was to promote herself for a role in a potential television entertainment program featuring a judge.

No request was made pursuant to California Rules of Court, rule 1.150, to record any portion of proceedings on January 26, 2009, or on May 1, 2009, nor would an order granting such a request have been properly issued as the filming was for the judge's personal purposes. The judge did not provide advance notice of the filming to the litigants or counsel whose cases were heard during filming on January 26,2009; advance notice of the filming was provided to some of the litigants or counsel whose cases were heard on May 1, 2009.

In an email message dated March 5, 2009, sent by the judge to the entertainment lawyer, the judge suggested that filming in her courtroom be scheduled for April 24. She told him that she has "been setting my

---

[19] Rule 2.8(c) forbids judges from criticizing jurors for a verdict other than in an order or opinion.

more interesting defendants and those with substance abuse issues for Friday April 24th." On March 9, 2009, following his suggestion that filming occur on May 1, Judge Salcido sent an email message in which she told him that "I will line up my most interesting cases for the afternoon of [Friday] May 1st." These statements give the appearance that the judge was scheduling cases based on their possible appeal in a videotape to be used to promote herself for a television program. It also creates an appearance of impropriety for the judge to represent that she would manipulate her calendar for non-judicial purposes.

The conduct described above violated canons 1 (a judge shall uphold the integrity of the judiciary), 2 (a judge shall avoid impropriety and the appearance of impropriety), 2A (a judge shall respect and comply with the law and shall act at all times in a manner that promotes public confidence in the integrity and impartiality of the judiciary), 2B(2) (improper use of the prestige of judicial office) and 3A (a judge's duties shall take precedence over all other activities). . . .

Count Two

On May 1, 2009, while proceedings in her courtroom were being filmed, Judge Salcido made the following improper remarks:

1. Around 10:43 a.m., she asked defendant Faustino Valdez, who was entering a change of plea to a charge involving marijuana, "You were born in 1980?" After he responded "yes," she remarked, "You look older than me. That's what smoking will do to you."

2. Around 10:53 a.m., defendant Juan Molina pled guilty to engaging in lewd conduct in public. The judge asked counsel for information about the case and was informed that the defendant had urinated in public and then turned around, exposing himself. After noting the number of days the defendant spent in custody, she joked, "Wow. Seventy-two days in custody giving new meaning to the term zip it." After ordering the defendant to stay away from a certain location, she joked, "Because I think they'll recognize you in more ways than one." She later joked, "again, new meaning to the term zip it."

3. Around 11:07 a.m., after placing Rodolf Rodriguez on probation, Judge Salcido made the following remark: "What that means is don't come before the court on another case . . . 'cause you will definitely be screwed and we don't offer Vaseline for that."

The judge used the term "screwed" on other instances on May I. Around 10:22 a.m., after defense counsel stated that defendant John Hedley had not been given written proof of attendance at AA meetings, she stated, "Then he would be screwed." Around 2:48 p.m., she remarked to defendant Shell, who had not appeared in court as ordered, "you basically screwed yourself by not coming in.". . . .

8. Around 3:21 p.m., defendant Daniel Lopez appeared in custody and admitted a probation violation. Judge Salcido gave him the option of an immediate 60day jail sentence or reenrolling in a program, but facing a longer jail sentence if he failed to complete that program. After the defendant said that he wanted to reenroll in the program and his counsel requested a moment to confer with his client, the judge remarked to the courtroom audience,

> "You guys know he doesn't want to do that don't you? Yeah. Does he need to call the lifeline? Try to tell him. Let's make a deal. I think he needs to call the lifeline. Yeah. Want to poll the audience? What should he do? Take the deal, take the deal, take the deal. The audience says, of course, the audience isn't going into custody. Really easy for you to tell him to take the deal because you're going to go home tonight and sleep on your pillows."

The judge and the courtroom audience repeatedly laughed at these comments. Counsel then said that defendant Lopez was not choosing the custody option because he was the only person available to take care of his 75–year–old mother, who was in poor health. The judge remarked, "Then God help her.". . . .

9. Around 3:29 p.m., the judge was told that defendant Jason Chavez, who had appeared before her earlier in the day, had tested positive for marijuana. The judge remarked to the courtroom, "He's not too clean?" to which the audience responded with a loud "woo." She said "THC," and the audience again said "woo." The judge then asked the audience, "Can I get a woo, woo, woo?" The audience responded as requested, and the judge and others in the courtroom laughed. The judge remarked, "See why my sons are screwed? I can just look at someone and I can tell." As she recalled the matter she remarked, in reference to the defendant and quoting him, ' "It's been years, Your Honor.' " The judge then told the defendant that it was her job to judge credibility, and remarked, "Did you take me for a fool?" After the defendant responded, "No, Your Honor," she asked, "Did you think I don't know what I'm doing?" After the defendant said he was going to try to do what is right, Judge Salcido said to the audience, "Here's that word again, it's pretty famous," and over the defendant's attempts to explain, had the courtroom audience repeat the slogan "Do or do not, there is no try." When calling the next case, she said, in apparent reference to this case, "If I had a dollar for everybody who told me they were clean I wouldn't need to work anymore.". . . .

The conduct described above under Count Two demonstrated a pattern of misconduct and violated canons 1 (a judge shall uphold the integrity of the judiciary), 2 (a judge shall avoid impropriety and the appearance of impropriety), 2A (a judge shall promote public confidence in the integrity and impartiality of the judiciary), 3B(3) (a judge shall require order and decorum in proceedings), and 3B(4) (a judge shall be patient, dignified, and courteous). It constitutes prejudicial misconduct . . . . .

III. DISCIPLINE

Article VI, section 18, subsection (d) of the California Constitution provides that the commission may "censure a judge . . . for action . . . that constitutes willful misconduct in office, . . . or conduct prejudicial to the administration of justice that brings the judicial office into disrepute." Judge Salcido concedes that her conduct as stipulated in the first two counts was prejudicial to the administration of justice that brings the judicial office into disrepute (prejudicial misconduct) and that her conduct as stipulated in the third count constitutes, at minimum, prejudicial misconduct. The purpose of a commission disciplinary proceeding is "the protection of the public, the enforcement of rigorous standards of judicial conduct, and the maintenance of public confidence in the integrity of the judicial system." *(Broadman* v. *Commission on Judicial Performance* 18 Cal.4th 1079, 1112 (1998), citing *Adams* v. *Commission on Judicial Performance* 10 Cal.4th 866, 912 (1995).) The commission concludes that this purpose is best served by the discipline proposed in the Stipulation: a public censure with an agreement that Judge Salcido will resign and will not at any time seek or hold judicial office in California or seek or accept judicial assignment from any California state court.

Judge Salcido admits that she engaged in thirty-nine separate instances of prejudicial misconduct. "The number of wrongful acts is relevant to determining whether they were merely isolated occurrences or, instead, part of a course of conduct establishing 'lack of temperament and ability to perform judicial functions in an even-handed manner.' [Citation.]" (*Wenger v. Commission on Judicial Performance*, 29 Cal.3d 615, 653 (1981); *Inquiry Concerning Judge Bruce Van Voorhis*, 48 Cal.4th CJP Supp. 257, 296 (2003).) The numerous incidents of misconduct as described in the stipulated facts cannot be characterized as isolated occurrences. Rather, they establish a pattern of misconduct which demonstrates a temperament ill-suited for judicial office.

In many instances, Judge Salcido's misconduct made a mockery of the judicial system. She used her court proceedings as an audition for her own television entertainment program, giving the unseemly appearance of playing to the cameras and the audience. While the cameras were rolling, the proceedings took on the atmosphere of a game show. Defendants were asked if they wanted to use "a life line," and "which door" they wanted to walk out. Another defendant was told "we're doing double or nothing now," and asked if he was prepared to "double down." The judge repeatedly solicited audience participation and even polled the audience: "Can I get a woo, woo?"; "Does he need to call the lifeline?"; asking the audience to repeat the slogan, "Do or do not, there is no try."; "What should he do? Take the deal, take the deal, take the deal." In response, the audience laughed and "wooed" without admonishment from the court. Judge Salcido failed to appreciate that "a courtroom is not the Improv and the presider's role model is not Judge Judy." *(Haluck v. Ricoh Electronics, Inc.* (2007) 151 Cal.App.4th 994, 1008.) The judge's showmanship behavior together with her statement to the producer that she would line up her more interesting cases for the day of the filming created the appearance that she was more interested in promoting herself for a role in a television show than in delivering justice to those who appeared before her.

It is self-evident that crude comments and sexually suggestive jokes from a judge have no place in a courtroom. Yet, Judge Salcido made manifestly inappropriate remarks of a lewd nature in an open courtroom as the proceedings were being filmed. For instance, she ordered a defendant charged with exposing himself in public to stay away from a certain location because "they'll recognize you in more ways than one." When a defendant smiled, she remarked to him that "they might like your smile in jail." In a particularly offensive instance, she told a defendant that he would be "screwed" If he violated his probation and "we don't offer Vaseline for that." We have previously condemned joking or making a casual comment about the possibility of an inmate having to endure same gender rape while incarcerated, which "may be perceived as not only an indifference to and acceptance of a tragic reality in our criminal justice system, but as a perhaps unintended admission of its inevitability under present conditions." *(Public Admonishment of Judge Susanne* S. *Shaw* (2000), p. 15.)

Even when not auditioning for her own television show, Judge Salcido engaged in conduct that was seriously at odds with her duty under the canons to be patient, dignified and courteous to litigants, attorneys, and those with whom she deals in an official capacity and to maintain decorum in the proceedings. (Code of Judicial Ethics, canons 3B(3), (4).) In open court, the judge ridiculed and belittled litigants, referred to court clerical staff as "cucumbers" who "aren't even potatoes because potatoes have eyes" or "corn because corn have ears," ridiculed a deputy district attorney, and made several disparaging remarks about an assistant public defender, often in the presence of his potential client. When a defendant accidentally called her "sir," Judge Salcido demonstrated a disturbing lack of decorum by raising her leg above the bench, holding her leg by the ankle, and stating, "Do these look like the boots of a sir?"

We appreciate that each judge has his or her own style, and that "a modest injection of humor at the appropriate time" can have a place in the courtroom. (Rothman, Cal. Judicial Conduct Handbook, (3d ed. 2007) § 3.42, p. 140.) "However, the cultivation of a particular judicial personality may not be used as an excuse for unethical conduct. . . . regardless of the judge's style, she or he must respect the litigants and attorneys who appear in her or his court." *(Public Admonishment of Judge Susanne* S.

Shaw (2000), p. 14.) Judicial humor should never be used in a courtroom, as it was by Judge Salcido, to ridicule, embarrass or disparage others, or in a manner that diminishes the dignity of the judicial process. Judge Salcido's brand of "humor," as exemplified by the stipulated facts is, without question, unbefitting a judge. . . .

Rule 2.9 governs *ex parte* communications, the subject of the problem that begins this book. The default position is that all parties to a matter should be included in all communications with the court if at all possible. Rule 2.9(A)(1) allows *ex parte* communications for scheduling purposes or for emergency purpose so long as a judge reasonably believes the communication will not advantage any party and so long as other parties are given notice and an opportunity to respond as soon as possible. Rule 2.9(A)(5) permits *ex parte* communications when authorized by law. Rule 2.9(A)(2) allows judges to obtain advice from disinterested experts so long as the judge notifies the parties in advance and allows them an opportunity to object and respond to both the notice and the advice. Rule 2.9(B) requires judges receiving inadvertent *ex parte* communications to notify the parties of the substance of the communication and provide them an opportunity to respond. Finally, but importantly, Rule 2.9(C) forbids judges from investigating facts independently and requires judges to decide cases only on evidence presented and facts properly subject to judicial notice.

Rule 2.15(A) requires that a judge report violations of the Code by other judges if those violations raise substantial questions regarding the violator's honesty, trustworthiness, or other aspects of fitness to be a judge. Rule 2.15(B) provides the same for lawyers. Finally, Rule 3.10 forbids judges from practicing law and advising family members informally (but judges may not appear for family members). Rule 3.11 allows judges to manage personal or family investments but forbids them from serving as an officer, director or similar official of any business entity other than a family business. Rule 3.12 allows judges to be paid for extrajudicial activities permitted by the Code.

C. MISUSE OF OFFICE AND ITS PRESTIGE

Rule 3.2 forbids judges from appearing voluntarily at public hearings or from consulting with executive or legislative bodies except in matters concerning the law, legal system, or administration of justice or in connection with matters on which the judge gained knowledge from his or her judicial work.[20] Rule 3.3 forbids judges from testifying as a character witness or otherwise vouching for a person in a legal proceeding unless

---

[20] The rule also allows judges to act *pro se* or as a fiduciary.

the judge is properly subpoenaed. (Comment one provides that except in unusual circumstances judges should discourage parties from subpoenaing the judge.) Rule 3.5 forbids judges from using or disclosing nonpublic information a judge acquires in his or her work.

Misuse of the judicial office may involve judges asserting their judicial status for personal benefit. In *Matter of Yaccarino*, 101 N.J. 342 (1985), for example, a judge's daughter was arrested after she physically assaulted an officer who impounded her dog for not having a license. The judge was disciplined in part because he contacted several law enforcement officials, identifying himself as a judge, and demanded that his daughter's arrest be investigated and the arresting officer be fired. Similarly, the judge disciplined in *In re Richardson*, 760 So.2d 932, 933 (Fla. 2000), mentioned his status as a judge upon arriving at the police station after his arrest for soliciting a prostitute (actually an undercover officer, of course; the judge was later acquitted).

Misuse need not be so heavy-handed to result in discipline, however. The judge disciplined in *In re Murphy*, 452 Mass. 796, 802 (2008), sent a letter to a newspaper he had successfully sued for libel, stating in part that the newspaper should settle because it would not win on appeal; the court found that "[f]or a sitting judge to state with repeated emphasis that he knows with complete certainty what will happen in a case is a misuse of the power and prestige of judicial office; the judge's use of an official court stationery envelope to mail the message exacerbated the misuse." In *In re Inquiry of Broadbelt*, 146 N.J. 501, 515 (1996), the court found that by appearing regularly on a television show a judge lent the prestige of his office to the show. Misuse need not even trade on a judge's status as a judge rather than as a supervisor of court staff. The judge in *In re Alford*, 977 So.2d 811, 831 (La. 2008), was disciplined in part because she used her judicial staff for personal work and to help her mother.

Nor is personal or familial benefit required for discipline, which may be imposed for such mundane acts as "fixing" (meaning dismissing based upon *ex parte* contact and without hearing) traffic tickets of others, *Mississippi Com'n on Judicial Performance v. Boykin*, 763 So.2d 872 (2000), or for conveying the impression (or allowing it to be conveyed) that another person was in a special position to influence a judge regarding parole. *In re Hughes*, 874 So.2d 746, 763 (La. 2004). Helping friends of friends get out of jail, either by demand or order, is a basis for discipline as well. *In re Maxwell*, 994 So.2d 974, 976 (Fla. 2008)(judge reprimanded for ordering pretrial release for sister of judge's former law associate based on ex parte communication from that associate); *In re Maloney,* 916 So.2d 786 (Fla.2005)(judge demanded release of driver of car in which judge's son was riding when driver was arrested for DUI).

The Main Points to Recall From Chapter 19 Are:

1. Judges must avoid both impropriety and the appearance of impropriety.
2. Judges must judge impartially.
3. Impartial means at least that the judge is disinterested with regard to the parties; it may also mean a judge is open-minded. At least for free speech purposes it does not mean a judge is disinterested with respect to issues or views on legal topics.
4. At a certain point defined by contextual factors, the risk of biased judging becomes impermissible under the due process clause.
5. Judges may express their views on legal issues; they may not promise to decide issues a certain way and must recuse themselves from cases implicated by their promise if they have done so.
6. The Model Code allows judges to do some things as candidates they may not do as judges; constitutional challenges are pending regarding some of these restrictions.
7. Subject to free speech protections, judges may not express invidious bias or support organizations that do so.
8. Judges must recuse themselves from cases in which their impartiality could reasonably be questioned.
9. Judges must put their judicial work first and not leverage the prestige of the judicial office for non-judicial ends.

INDEX

References are to Pages

D

E

O

P

R

S

T

U

W